Beginning Active Server Pages 3.0

Chris Ullman
David Buser
Jon Duckett
Brian Francis
John Kauffman
Juan T. Llibre
David Sussman

wrox
Programmer to Programmer

Beginning Active Server Pages 3.0

Published by
Wiley Publishing, Inc.
10475 Crosspoint Boulevard
Indianapolis, IN 46256
www.wiley.com

Copyright © 2003 by Wiley Publishing, Inc., Indianapolis, Indiana

Published simultaneously in Canada

Library of Congress Card Number: 2003107054

ISBN: 0-7645-4363-6

Manufactured in the United States of America

10 9 8 7 6 5 4 3 2 1

1B/QW/QW/QT/IN

Trademark Acknowledgements

Credits

Authors
Chris Ullman
David Buser
Jon Duckett
Brian Francis
John Kauffman
Juan T. Llibre
David Sussman

Technical Reviewers
Juan T. Llibre
John Kauffman
Brian Francis
Robert Chang
Steve Danielson
Andy Enfield
Marco Gregorni
Scott Haley
Mark Harrison
Ajoy Krishnamoorthy
Dave Navarro Snr
Pieter Reint Siegers Kort
John Timney

Technical Editors
Ian Nutt
Chris Goode
Tony Davis
Lisa Stephenson

Managing Editor
Chris Hindley

Development Editor
Sarah Bowers

Project Manager
Chandima Nethisinghe

Design/Layout
Tom Bartlett
Mark Burdett
Jonathan Jones
John McNulty
William Fallon

Figures
William Fallon
Jonathan Jones

Cover
Chris Morris

Index
Alessandro Ansa

About the Authors

Chris Ullman

Chris Ullman is a Computer Science graduate who came to Wrox five years ago, when 14.4 modems were the hottest Internet technology and Netscape Navigator 2.0 was a groundbreaking innovation. Since then he's applied his knowledge of HTML, ASP, Visual Basic, SQL, Linux, and Java to developing, editing and authoring books. When not trying to coax better performance out of his ageing P233 or trying to persuade Wrox's managing editors that writing three chapters in one day isn't really feasible, he can be found either playing keyboards in psychedelic band, The Bee men, tutoring his not fully house-broken cats in the delights of using a litter tray, or hoping against hope that this is the year his favorite soccer team, Birmingham City, can manage to end their exile from the Premier League.

Thanks to Ian, Chris G, Tony and Lisa for keeping my nonsenses to a minimum, thanks to Sarah, Chris H and Chandy for policing the authors and reviewers and making sure everything was delivered on time, and most importantly thanks to my wife Kate, for putting up with late nights and bad-tempered mornings.

David Buser

David Buser is President, CFO, and Janitor of BuserNet Consulting, LLC, in Herndon, Virginia. His first job out of college was in a titanium refinery, writing client/server applications using Access and SQL Server. This eventually led to a career in Internet development and ASP. Currently, his work is focused on teaching technical courses, writing for Wrox, developing e-commerce websites, and managing his server farm. See http://www.buser.net/david/ for more details. * In memory of my grandfather Thomas T. Buser, Sr., who taught me that real men do dishes.

Jon Duckett

Having graduated from Brunel University, London, with a degree in Psychology, Jon took a change of direction, coming back to his home town to work for Wrox in their Birmingham (UK) offices.

Brian Francis

Brian Francis is the Technical Evangelist for NCR's Retail Self Service Solutions. From his office in Duluth, Georgia, Brian is responsible for enlightening NCR and their customers in the technologies and tools used for Self Service Applications. Brian also uses the tools he evangelizes in developing solutions for NCR's customers. He has worked extensively with Wrox Press as a technical reviewer and has also co-authored on a number of projects.

John Kauffman

John's early research focussed on the molecular biology of the cocoa plant and chocolate production. Subsequently he moved to East Africa and managed an assistance program. In 1990 he moved to Taiwan and then mainland China where John provided software training services to multi-national corporations and the diplomatic community in Beijing, Hong Kong, Shanghai and Sichuan. John now divides his freelance consulting time evenly between teaching, writing and programming, primarily in the areas of Visual Basic, Word macros, Access and Access Programming, and ASP. John is available for contract training in Asia, Europe and North America by contacting `Training@Kauffmans.org`.

John deeply thanks his father, John, who taught him to make a list of knowns and unknowns before starting to find a solution to an algebraic problem. He equally thanks his mother, Ruth, who for many years suffered John's pilferage of her kitchen glassware for use in his early chemistry experiments.

Juan T. Llibre

Juan is a Microsoft MVP (Most Valuable Professional) for Internet development. His university degree is in Mass Communications and, as he puts it, "The Internet is the ultimate mass communications vehicle. It's just great to be able to talk to the whole world while taking in the sun at a tropical beach on the north coast of the Dominican Republic."

Currently he's developing Internet applications for the Caribbean Common Market and the Dominican Republic's Central Bank. He's also researching Multilingual Web Development with a view towards making the World Wide Web intelligible to, well, the whole wide world.

David Sussman

David has spent most of his professional life as a developer, starting with Unix and C, in the days when the Internet was only used for Usenet newsgroups. He then switched to Microsoft development languages, and spent several years moaning about the lack of pointers in Visual Basic. He lives in a quiet, rural village in Oxfordshire. He spends his spare time convincing himself that he'll get off his backside and get fit. He never does.

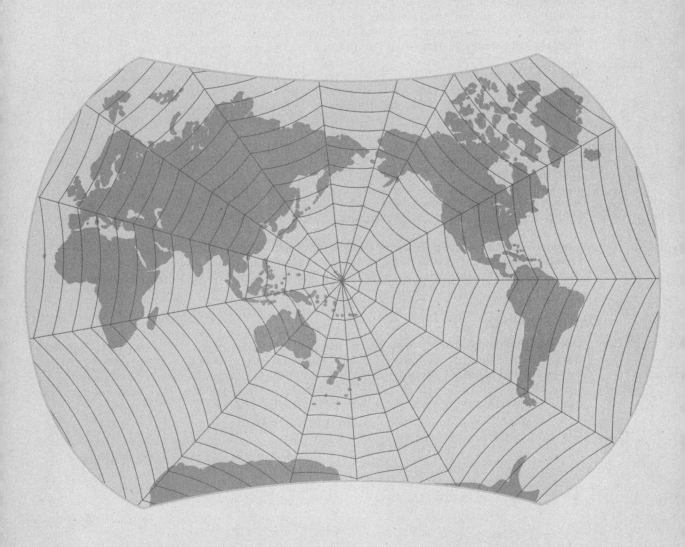

Table of Contents

Chapter 2: Server-Side Scripting and Client-Side Scripting 57

Chapter 4: Variables 127

Chapter 5: ASP Control Structures   169

Chapter 8: Applications, Sessions and Cookies 289

Chapter 9: Error Handling

Chapter 11: Active Server Pages Components   423

Chapter 12: ASP and Data Store Access   461

Chapter 15: Writing an Application   633

Chapter 18: An Introduction to XML   819

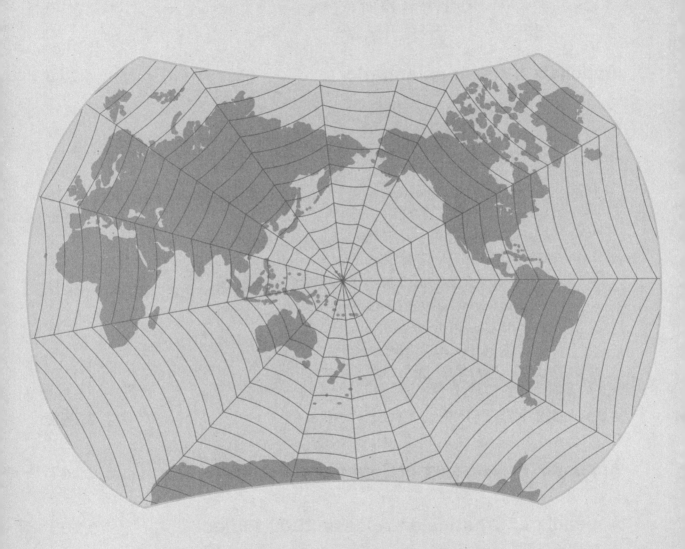

Introduction

This book is about **Active Server Pages 3.0**, as included with **Windows 2000**. Active Server Pages (ASP) is a powerful server-based technology from Microsoft, designed to create dynamic and interactive HTML pages for your World Wide Web site, or corporate intranet.

This book teaches ASP and script-based programming from the ground up. It will answer the fundamental questions:

- ❑ What exactly is ASP?
- ❑ How do I get up and running with ASP?
- ❑ How does it work?
- ❑ How can I use it to produce dynamic, interactive web applications?

We'll answer these questions in a thorough and comprehensive way, with plenty of complete working examples. So even if you're absolutely new to this technology, you will gain a deep understanding of what ASP is really about and how you can harness it to build powerful web applications.

The introduction of ASP was a milestone in the development of dynamic, interactive and scalable web applications and it has matured a great deal since its inception. ASP is now considered an integral part of working with Windows on the Internet. So, as well as giving a thorough grounding in the fundamentals of ASP, this book will cover all of the new developments and will show you how ASP integrates with the latest versions of exciting new technologies such ADO, COM+ and XML.

This book will help you to learn how to use ASP effectively to handle and transfer the information that you need for your web page. The aim of this book is to get you producing compelling, practical web applications with intelligent, dynamic pages.

Who is this Book For?

This is a Wrox *Beginning...* series book, so we will aim to teach you everything you need to know from scratch. If you already have some knowledge and experience of ASP, or some Visual Basic programming experience, then you might be more comfortable starting at a faster pace with our title *Professional Active Server Pages 3.0* (Wrox, ISBN-186002-61-0) instead. (That title also acts as a natural sequel to *Beginning Active Server Pages 3.0*.)

We appreciate that most, if not all, of the web page authors and developers who take up Active Server Pages will be reasonably familiar with ordinary HTML; therefore, we won't spend any time teaching you HTML. If you don't know HTML, then we suggest that you take a little time to get yourself familiar with HTML before attempting to learn about Active Server Pages. There are plenty of good HTML tutorials on the market.

There are two kinds of beginners for whom this is the ideal book:

- ❏ You're a **beginner to programming** and you've chosen ASP as the place to start. Great choice! Active Server Pages is easy, it's fun and it's also powerful. This book will hold your hand throughout.

- ❏ You can program in another language but you're a **beginner to web programming**. Again, great choice! Come in from the cold world of Visual Basic or whatever language you use, and enjoy. This book will teach you how ASP does things in terms you'll understand.

Most of all, you don't need to know anything more than the basic ins and outs of how to put your own web page together. If you've never written a single line of any programming language, then you have to nothing fear – this is the book for you. *The bottom line is that this book will teach you how to write ASP programs.*

What Does This Book Cover?

Conceptually, this book breaks down into seven sections, which cover a whole range of ASP-related topics. Hopefully we've done this in a logical and orderly fashion that will allow you to fully understand how ASP works, what it can do for you and how it integrates with surrounding technologies.

Chapters 1 and 2 lay the foundation for everything that follows in the book. You'll find out how to set yourself up to use ASP 3.0, and then we'll dive into the fundamentals of ASP and web pages. Once we've covered the ASP basics, we move on to consider web servers – how they interpret ASP and how they communicate with web browsers. You won't be doing too much programming in these initial chapters – we focus on providing the background information that is vital to you obtaining a through understanding of what ASP is about.

Chapters 3–5 build on the basic concepts learned in the first two chapters; these three chapters represent our first serious look at ASP code. We start with simple, practical examples in which we create dynamic web pages using ASP. We'll find out how to pass information from a browser to ASP, and back from ASP to the browser. We then take a look behind the scenes to find out how these examples work. In the process, we'll see how ASP stores data, and look at the control structures that allow us to perform more complex tasks with ASP.

Chapter 6–11 are all about objects. We start with a general introduction to objects and the properties, methods and events that allow us to retrieve information from them and get them to perform tasks for us. After introducing all of the objects in the **ASP object model** and covering their basic functionality, we delve deeper into specific objects. We start with the `Response` and `Request` objects, which allow us to encapsulate information and pass it between the browser and server. The we move on to discuss the flexibility added to this process by the `Application` object, the `Session` object and cookies – which allow us to organise our Active Server Pages into a powerful web-based application. Chapter 9 covers useful **error handling** and **debugging** techniques, with particular reference to the `ASPError` object, which is new to ASP 3.0 and greatly improves the error-handling process. In Chapter 10 we tackle **Scripting Objects** – a set of objects normally available in client-side VBScript as well as ASP. These allow us to store, view, manipulate and retrieve information from text files on the server. In Chapter 11 we enter the world of components – pre-packaged software objects that provide webmasters with complex and re-usable functionality for their ASP applications. We see how we can create instances of these components in ASP, using the `Server` object, and look at the functionality provided by several such components.

Chapters 12–14 are essentially about **ActiveX Data Objects (ADO)**, how we can incorporate these objects in our ASP pages, and how we use them to access all sorts of data from various types of data stores. We start with a general discussion of data access issues, and then investigate one particular type of data store – the **database**. We'll find out how to form a connection between the ASP page and the database, and how we retrieve and store the information contained within. Finally, we cover some objects that are new to ADO 2.5, and which allow us access to a vast array of different types of data.

Chapter 15 is a big one! It puts into practice everything we have learned in the first fourteen chapters. We spend the whole of this chapter building a working ASP application for advertising and selling items on the web.

Chapters 16 and 17 take us back into the realm of components. You will find out about the Windows Script Components, which allow us to create COM objects from script and use them with our ASP applications. We consider the use of these components in multi-user applications, and introduce the concept of **transactions**. You'll meet a new and exciting technology called **COM+**, which provides an excellent framework for managing scalable, transactional ASP applications.

Chapter 18 introduces **Extensible Markup Language (XML)** – a self-describing markup language that has revolutionized the way in which we can transfer data and share it between applications. Chapter 18 gives you a whirlwind introduction to this technology and shows you how you can use XML with your ASP applications.

The **Appendices** provide useful reference material covering such areas as the ASP and ADO objects & models, the VBScript language and commonly-used terminology.

What Do I Need To Use This Book?

Basically, what you need is a copy of Active Server Pages 3.0 and a web server for your platform! But let's take a slightly more scientific approach than that, by looking at the requirements in more detail:

❑ In order to complete all of the examples in this book (and in particular those demonstrating the latest developments in ASP 3.0), you will need a machine with **Windows 2000** installed. Internet Information Server and all of the associated services that you will need for this book are included with Windows 2000 Professional (which replaces Windows NT Workstation).

If you are using Windows 2000 Professional, you should aim for a machine with at least a 233MHz processor. You can get away with 64MB of RAM, though 128MB is ideal.

❑ You will need a **web server** that supports ASP 3.0. The Windows 2000 operating system comes with Internet Information Server 5.0 (IIS 5.0) but you need to make sure that it is actually installed on your machine. We will show you how to do this in Chapter 1.

❑ You will need a **web browser** in order to view your pages. Predominantly, we used Internet Explorer 5.0 (IE5), but *any* browser will do.

There are also some non-Microsoft platforms that you can use – we will cover these options in Chapter 1. However, the book concentrates on ASP 3.0 running on Internet Information Services version 5 and Windows 2000 Professional.

ASP Development Tools

We're not going to provide any tutoring on how to use any of the development tools so it's best to use whichever you're most comfortable with. Probably the most obvious development tool for working with ASP is Microsoft's own **Visual Studio** package; or just **Visual InterDev** (one of the components of Visual Studio) on its own. Visual InterDev, especially in the latest version, provides a whole range of editing, debugging and code building tools. There are also many 'wizards' that are designed to help you get the job done more quickly.

If you are a hardened keyboard hacker, and you don't like anything to get in the way of writing code your way, you might prefer to use a simple text editor to create ASP pages instead. You can even build them using a pure HTML page creation tool (such as Microsoft FrontPage), and then insert your ASP script afterwards. The old favorite ASP tool, Windows **Notepad**, will do quite nicely.

Conventions

We have used a number of different styles of text and layout in the book to help differentiate between the different kinds of information. Here are examples of the styles we use and an explanation of what they mean:

Try It Outs – How Do They Work?

1. Each step has a number.

2. Follow the steps through, and get the example running.

3. Then read 'How It Works' to find out what's going on.

   Advice, hints and background information comes in an indented, italicized font like this.

> **Important bits of information that you really shouldn't ignore come in boxes like this!**

Bulleted lists appear indented, with each new bullet marked as follows:

❑ **Important Words** are in a bold type font.

❑ Words that appear on the screen in menus like the File or Window menu are in a similar font to what you see on screen.

❑ Keys that you press on the keyboard, like *Ctrl* and *Enter*, are in italics.

Active Server Pages code has two fonts. If it's a word that we're talking about in the text, for example, when discussing the **For...Next** loop, it's in a bold font. If it's a block of code that you can type in as a program and run, then it's also in a gray box:

```
Private Sub cmdQuit_Click()
    End
End Sub
```

Sometimes you'll see code in a mixture of styles, like this:

```
Private Sub cmdQuit_Click()
    End
End Sub
```

In this case, we want you to consider the code with the gray background. The code with a white background is code we've already looked at, and that we don't wish to examine further.

Also you'll see that most of the code in *Beginning Active Server Pages 3.0* is either HTML tags, server-side script (ASP) or client-side script. In spite of it being recommended in the HTML 4.0 standard that tags should be specified in lower case, for ease of reading we have chosen to display HTML tags in upper case throughout the book and all script in lower case. Server-side script is usually surrounded by <% and %> marks. So an example might look like this:

```
<BODY>
<H1>This is some HTML </H1>
<SCRIPT LANGUAGE=VBScript>
obj1 = "This is some VBScript."
<% obj2 = "This is some ASP." %>
</SCRIPT>
</BODY>
```

These formats are designed to make sure that you know what it is you're looking at. I hope they make life easier.

Customer Support

We've tried to make this book as accurate and enjoyable as possible, but what really matters is what the book actually does for you. Please let us know your views, either by returning the reply card in the back of the book, or by contacting us via e-mail at feedback@wrox.com.

Downloading the Source Code

As you work through the examples in this book, you might decide that you prefer to type all the code in by hand. Many readers prefer this because it's a good way to get familiar with the coding techniques that are being used.

Whether you want to type the code in or not, we have made all the source code for this book available at our web site, at the following address:

http://www.wrox.com

If you're one of those readers who likes to type in the code, you can use our files to check the results you should be getting – they should be your first stop if you think you might have typed in an error. If you're one of those readers who doesn't like typing, then downloading the source code from our web site is a must!

Either way, it'll help you with updates and debugging.

Exercises

At the Wrox website you will also find additional exercises for each chapter (along with the solutions). It is highly recommended that you work through these examples. This book will give you the knowledge you need – but it is only through practice that you will hone your skills and get a true feel for what ASP can help you achieve.

Errata

We've made every effort to make sure that there are no errors in the text or the code. However, to err is human and as such we recognize the need to keep you informed of any mistakes as they're spotted and corrected. Errata sheets are available for all our books at `http://www.wrox.com`. If you find an error that hasn't already been reported, please let us know.

Our web site acts as a focus for other information and support, including the code from all our books, sample chapters, previews of forthcoming titles, and articles and opinion on related topics.

p2p.wrox.com

This book introduces a totally comprehensive and unique support system. Wrox now has a commitment to supporting you not just while you read the book, but once you start developing applications as well. We provide you with a forum where you can put your questions to the authors, reviewers and fellow industry professionals. You have the choice of how to receive this information; you can either enroll onto one of several mailing lists, or you can just browse the online forums and newsgroups for an answer.

Go to `http://p2p.wrox.com`. You'll find three different lists, each tailored to a specific support issue:

- **BegASP_Errata**
  You find something wrong with this book, or you just think something has been badly or misleading explained then leave your message here. You'll still receive our customary quick reply, but you'll also have the advantage that every author will be able to see your problem at once and help deal with it.

- **Code Clinic**
  You've read a Wrox ASP book, and you're sat at home or work developing your own application, it doesn't work in the way you think it should. Post your code here for advice and support from our authors and from people in the same position as yourself.

- **How to?**
  Something you think the book should have talked about, something you'd just like to know more about, a completely baffling problem with no solution, then this is your forum. If you're developing an application at work then chances are there's someone out there who's already done the same as you, and has a solution to your problem here.

Enroll now; it's all part of our free support system. For more instructions on how to enroll, please see the Appendix M at the back of this book.

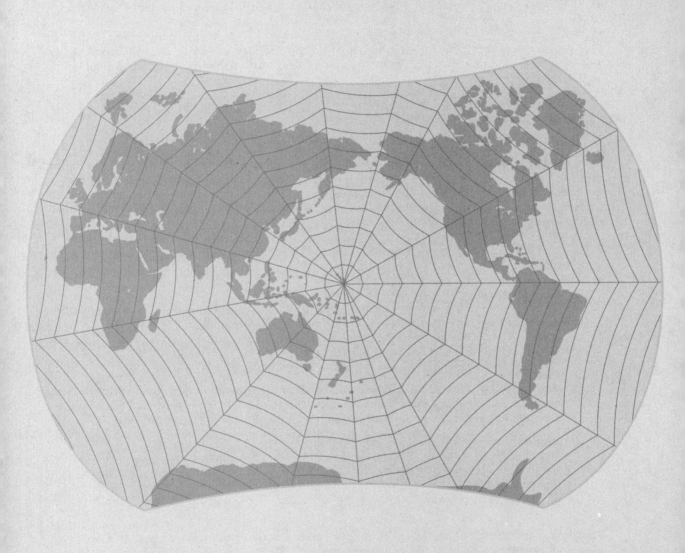

1

Getting Started With ASP

Active Server Pages (ASP) is a great tool for creating dynamic web pages. ASP is a Microsoft technology, and it works by allowing us the functionality of a programming language; we write programming code that will generate the HTML for the web page dynamically. So, whenever a user browses to our web site and requests one of our ASP pages, the ASP code is processed at that time by a special piece of software – the **web server**. This processing generates the HTML, which is then passed to the browser and used to create the page itself, on the user's screen.

The power of ASP lies in two facts: first, the HTML is not created until the user wants to see the web page, and second, it doesn't care what web browser is being used. ASP isn't the first technology to offer these features, but it's undoubtedly one of the most powerful and widely used in industry; and crucially, it's one of the fastest. Active Server Pages is different from many Microsoft technologies in the following respect: while ASP must be executed on a computer that supports it, we can view ASP-driven web pages from *any* computer, and with *any* modern browser. This has enabled developers to enhance their web pages with interactive features, and even to solve common business problems – to such an extent that pages with the .asp suffix are fast becoming as common as those with the .htm suffix.

ASP is potentially one of the most important innovations to emerge on the Web – for developers and users of the Internet and intranets alike.

So what can we do with ASP? Well, arguably the most important advantage that ASP brings is its ability to create pages that are sensitive to factors such as time and place, and the user's identity and previous choices and actions. In other words, we can use ASP to customize our web pages to the specific needs of each individual user. It means that the text, images, tables, forms, and even the layout of the page can be selected automatically at the time the user requests the page – and to suit that user's requirement.

ASP is relatively simple to learn. All you need is a little experience with HTML and a scripting language (this book teaches and uses the VBScript scripting language) – and you can start to build ASP functionality into your existing HTML pages. In short, ASP is a great way to bring the best features of programming to your web pages.

ASP was officially announced to the world by Microsoft on July 16, 1996, codenamed *Denali*. A beta version was released in November 1996, and **ASP version 1.0** was shipped on December 12, 1996. It gained much wider recognition when it was bundled with version 3.0 of Microsoft's **Internet Information Server** (IIS) web server suite in March 1997; and it has been gaining steadily in popularity since then.

Microsoft have continued to work on the development of ASP. In 1998, they released new versions of their web server software, Internet Information Server 4.0 (IIS 4.0) and Personal Web Server 4.0 (PWS 4.0): both of these supported the new **ASP version 2.0**. ASP 2.0 offered considerable enhancements over ASP 1.0, including an enriched model for managing communications between browser and web server.

With the release of Windows 2000, we have a further updated version Internet Information Server (version 5.0) and a new version of **Active Server Pages (version 3.0)**. Moreover, IIS 5.0 is more naturally integrated with the Windows 2000 operating system, resulting in a more streamlined overall package.

In this first chapter, we'll be looking at:

❑ What ASP is, and what ASP code looks like

❑ Pure HTML pages, and pages which use ASP to generate HTML – and the differences between them

❑ What a web server is

❑ An overview of how to install and set up ASP

❑ How to create your first ASP page

❑ Common errors that might prevent the page from working in the way you intended

❑ Which editors you can use to create and test your ASP pages

We'll start by understanding what we mean when we talk about a dynamic web page, and how dynamic web pages are different from static web pages. Then, we'll use that as a springboard into understanding ASP.

What is a Dynamic Web Page?

If you surf around the Internet today, you'll see that there are lots of static web pages out there. What do we mean by a **static** web page? Essentially, it's a page whose content consists of some HTML that was typed directly into a text editor and saved as an `.htm` or `.html` file. Thus, the author of the page has already completely determined the *exact* content of the page, in HTML, at some time before any user visits the page.

Static web pages are often quite easy to spot; sometimes you can pick them out by just looking at the content of the page. The content (i.e. text, images, hyperlinks, etc) and appearance of a static web page is *always* the same – regardless of *who* visits the page, or *when* they visit, or *how* they arrive at the page, or any other factors.

For example, suppose we create a page called `Welcome.htm` for our website, by writing some simple HTML like this:

```
<HTML>
<HEAD><TITLE>A Welcome Message</TITLE></HEAD>
<BODY>
  <H1>Welcome</H1>
  Welcome to our humble website. Please feel free to view our
  <A HREF="contents.htm">list of contents</A>.
  <BR><BR>
  If you have any difficulties, you can
  <A HREF="mailto:webmaster@wrox.com">send email to the webmaster</A>.
</BODY>
</HTML>
```

Whenever any client comes to our site to view this page, it will look like this. The content of the page was determined *before* the request was made – at the time the webmaster saved the `.htm` file to disk.

Static Pages vs Dynamic Pages

OK, so let's think for a moment about how a static, pure-HTML page finds its way onto a client browser:

1. A web author writes page composed of pure HTML, and saves it within an `.htm` file

2. Sometime later, a user types a page request into their browser, and the request is passed from the browser to the web server

3. The web server locates the `.htm` page

4. The web server sends the HTML stream back across the network to the browser

5. The browser processes the HTML and displays the page

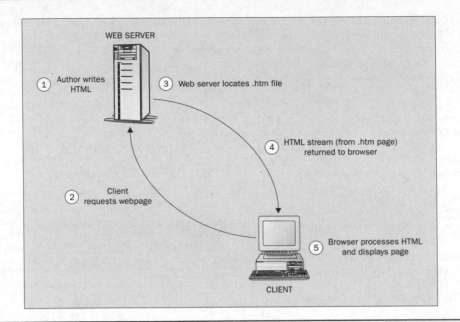

> We use the term web server to refer to the software that manages web pages and makes them available to 'client' computers – via a local network or via the Internet. In the case of the Internet, the web server and browser are usually on two different machines, possibly many miles apart.
>
> However, in a more local situation we might set up a machine that runs the web server software, and then use a browser on the *same* machine to look at its web pages. We'll talk more about web servers later in this chapter, and throughout the book.

Static, pure-HTML files like `Welcome.htm` file make perfectly serviceable web pages. We can even spruce up the presentation and usability of such pages by adding more HTML to create frames and tables. However, there's only so much we can achieve by writing pure HTML, precisely because their content is completely determined *before* the page is ever requested.

The Limitations of Static Web Pages

For example, suppose we want to enhance our Welcome page – so that it displays the current time or a special message that is personalized for each user. These are simple ambitions, but they are impossible to achieve using HTML alone. If you're not convinced, try writing a piece of HTML for a web page that displays the current time, like this:

As you type in the HTML, you'll soon realize the problem – you know that the user will request the page sometime, but you don't know *what the time will be* when they do so! Hard-coding the time into your HTML will result in a page that always claims that the time is the same (and will almost always display the wrong time).

In other words, you're trying to write pure HTML for a web page that displays the time – but you can't be sure of the *exact* time that the web page should display until the time the page is requested. It can't be done using HTML alone.

Since we can't create our page by saving our hard-coded HTML into a file *before* the page is requested, then what we need is a way to generate the HTML *after* the page is requested.

Dynamic Web Pages

In other words, we need to replace the hard-coded HTML source with a set of **instructions**, which will be used to generate HTML for the page at the time the user requests the page. In other words, the page is generated **dynamically** on request. So our set of five steps now becomes six:

1. A web author writes a set of instructions for creating HTML, and saves these instructions within a file

2. Sometime later, a user types a page request into their browser, and the request is passed from the browser to the web server

3. The web server locates the file of instructions

4. The web server follows the instructions in order to create a stream of HTML

5. The web server sends the newly-created HTML stream back across the network to the browser

6. The browser processes the HTML and displays the page

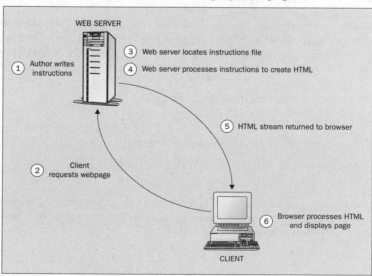

So the process of serving a dynamic web page is only slightly different from the process of serving a static web page – there's just one extra step involved (Step 4). But the difference is crucial – the HTML that defines the web page is not generated until *after* the web page has been requested. For example, we can use this technique to write a set of instructions for creating a page that displays the current time:

```
<HTML>
<HEAD><TITLE>The Punctual Web Server</TITLE></HEAD>
<BODY>
  <H1>Welcome</H1>
  In Webserverland, the time is exactly
  <INSTRUCTION: write HTML to display the current time>
</BODY>
</HTML>
```

In this case, we can compose most of the page using pure HTML. It's just that we can't hard-code the current time; instead, we can write a special code (which would replace the highlighted line here) that instructs the web server to generate that bit of HTML during Step 4, at the time the page is requested.

We'll return to this example later in the chapter, and we'll see how to write the highlighted instruction using ASP.

> *We could extend the notion of dynamic pages even further, by adding another step (between Steps 5 and 6 above) – in which we include more instructions that are carried out by the browser (not by the server). For the purpose of this chapter, we will not consider this type of 'dynamic page' – but we will return to it in Chapter 2.*

Using Dynamic Web Pages

So the idea is to have an extra step, which allows us to generate HTML at runtime. Of course, this extra step doesn't only allow web authors to write web pages that tell the time! We can use it to achieve a huge number of things that are impossible with pure HTML. We can capture all sorts of information that isn't known at the time the instructions are written – for example:

- ❑ The user's identity and personal preferences
- ❑ The type of browser they're using
- ❑ Other information provided by the user's request
- ❑ Information contained in databases, text files, XML files, etc

Our HTML-generation instructions can be written in such a way that they *use* this newly-captured information to create up-to-the-minute, personalized, interactive web pages, that serve fresh information every time they are requested.

You'll find that sites that contain ASP code are more dynamic – they're quite often tailored to the individual user, can reflect the fact that a user has visited the site before, can be customized easily to view preferred topics, and in general offer the user a more interactive and personalized experience. You can see this in pages on some of the larger, more commercial sites, such as those produced by Microsoft, ABC News, Dell, Compaq, Gateway 2000, ESPN SportsZone and the official NASCAR, NBA, NFL and WNBA sites. Many of these pages are easily identifiable as Active Server Pages, since they are suffixed by .asp (although some have ASP-driven code masquerading behind .htm pages). All of these sites have fairly guessable addresses – http://www.microsoft.com, http://www.abcnews.com, and so on – take a look!

Dynamic Web Pages and ASP

So far, we've analyzed the difference between static and dynamic web pages, but we've barely mentioned the subject of this book – Active Server Pages. So, without further ado, here's a quick and simple definition:

> **Active Server Pages is a technology that allows for the programmatic construction of HTML pages just before they are delivered to the browser.**

In other words, with ASP we can write a set of instructions that can be used to generate HTML just after the web page has been requested by a client, and just before it is delivered.

ASP is the perfect tool for any HTML writer to add to their toolkit, because (as we saw in the previous section, and will demonstrate throughout the book) it gives us the power and flexibility to generate fresher HTML, and ultimately to produce more spectacular, interactive, personalized, up-to-date web pages.

How can we describe ASP? It's not a language (in the sense that Pascal and C++ are languages) – although it does make use of existing scripting languages such as VBScript or JavaScript. Moreover, it's not really an application (in the sense that FrontPage and Word are applications) either. Instead, we describe ASP using a rather more ambiguous term, **technology**. ASP is a technology for building dynamic and interactive web pages.

What does ASP Code Look Like?

When a web author writes an ASP page, it is likely to be composed of a combination of three types of syntax – some parts ASP, some parts HTML tags, and some parts pure text. We save all these constituent parts of the ASP page in a file with an .asp extension.

The notion of mixing different types of logic (fragments of text, some HTML tags and some ASP code) within a single block of code is one that can be very useful in ASP – however, it can be one of the main stumbling blocks for ASP beginners. So, let's take a look at this breakdown with an example, to show that it's really not as tricky as it sounds.

The following table summarizes these three ingredients, their purpose and their appearance:

Type	Purpose	Interpreter	Hallmarks
Text	Hard-coded information to be shown to the user	Viewer's browser on their PC shows the text	Simple ASCII text
HTML tags	Instructions to the browser about how to format text and display images	Viewer's browser on their PC interprets the tags to format the text	Each tag within < > delimiters Most HTML tags come in pairs (an open tag and a close tag), e.g. <TABLE>, </TABLE>
ASP statements	Instructions to the web server running ASP about how to create portions of the page to be sent out	Web site host's web server software with ASP extensions performs the instructions of the ASP code	Each ASP section contained within <% %> delimiters ASP statements contain the structures of more 'traditional' programming languages, such as Visual Basic and Java, as they have features such as variables, decision trees, cyclical repetitions etc.

Let's take a look at a simple ASP page. At the moment, we don't need to be too concerned with exactly what it does – we'll learn all about that in good time. The main point here is that it's not too hard to distinguish the different elements of the ASP page. Anything that falls between the <% and %> markers is **ASP script**, and will be processed on the web server by the **ASP script engine**, after the ASP page is requested and just before it is delivered to the browser. The script code is shown on a gray background, and the HTML and text are on a white background:

```
<HTML>
<HEAD>
<TITLE>The Polite Web Server</TITLE>
</HEAD>
<BODY BGCOLOR="wheat">
<H1>Welcome</H1>
<FONT SIZE="3">
<B>This is the Polite Web Server, at <% = Time %> on <% = Date %></B></FONT><BR>
<BR>
<% If Hour(Now) < 8 Then  %>
  Do you know what time it is? I was still in bed!
<% Else
    Randomize
    intChoice = Int(Rnd * 4)
```

```
Select Case intChoice

        Case 0 %> So, where do you want me to go today?
    <% Case 1 %> Well, look who's back visiting us again!
    <% Case 2 %> Hi there, and welcome to our site.
    <% Case 3 %> It's raining here - would you like to play virtual checkers?
  <% End Select
  End If %> <BR>
<HR>
</BODY>
</HTML>
```

*Note that ASP code is known as **script**. We'll be looking at the notion of scripts and script engines in more detail in the next chapter.*

We've highlighted the script code that is executed by the server to make it easier to distinguish the ASP code from the plain HTML. The web server searches out the <% ... %> markers, and executes the code contained within to generate a pure HTML stream – which it sends back to the browser. Then, the browser can process the HTML and display the web page:

Thus, the content of the resulting web page depends on the HTML that is generated by the ASP code. In this particular example, the effect of the script code is to generate HTML for the time and date that the page is requested, and then to make a decision (based on the situation) on what text will be sent to the browser as part of the HTML stream. Juxtaposing bits of ASP, HTML and text in this way is an effective way of getting the result we want.

ASP Code is Browser-Independent

There's one more lesson to learn from what we've seen so far. Because ASP code is executed on the web server, and generates pure HTML, the client machine doesn't need to provide any kind of ASP support at all. In fact, the web browser handles `.htm` pages and `.asp` pages in exactly the same way – because from the browser's point of view, the process involves sending a page request to a web server and receiving a stream of pure HTML:

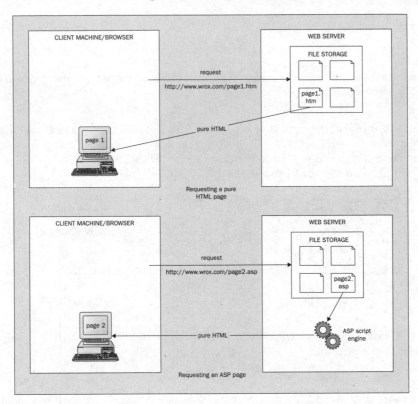

As the diagram shows, the browser is blissfully ignorant of any ASP processing that might be happening on the server – it only ever gets to see pure HTML. So, your dynamic `.asp` pages are just as viewable in Internet Explorer, Netscape Navigator, and other browsers as their static `.htm` counterparts!

Advantages of Using a Server-side Technology

So, we've already stressed that ASP is processed on the web server to generate HTML, while HTML is processed solely on the browser. So what is the advantage of performing actions on the web server first?

The main advantages are that it:

❑ Allows you to run programs in programming languages that aren't supported by your browser

❑ Enables you to program dynamic web applications *browser-independently*, without recourse to client-side programming features such as Java applets, Dynamic HTML, ActiveX controls, all of which are browser specific

❑ Can provide the client (browser) with data that does not reside at the client

❑ Often makes for quicker loading times than with client-side dynamic web technologies such as Java applets or ActiveX controls, because in the end, you're actually only downloading a page of HTML

❑ Provides improved security measures, since you can write code which can never be viewed from the browser

That's not to say ASP pages are perfect. For example, they increase the workload on the server, so if your web site becomes popular you may need to invest in more hardware – but this is true of any server-side technology, and ultimately many web developers decide that the benefits of server-side functionality outweigh any disadvantages.

What Do I Need to Run ASP?

So far, we've established what ASP and HTML offers us over and above pure HTML, a little about how it works, and some advantages of using it. But what software do we need in order to work with ASP?

To answer this we need to consider the role that we'll be playing in this book – namely that of the web author or webmaster. In this role, we'll be writing web pages, we'll be publishing them on a web server, and we'll be testing them to see what they look like and whether they work.

❑ In order to write pages, we'll need a **text editor** or other web development tool. Notepad works fine for this purpose, but there are plenty of other editors on the market. We'll discuss some of these options in more detail later in the chapter.

❑ In order to publish the pages, we'll need a **web server** that supports Active Server Pages. This book describes using ASP 3.0, which comes with a web server called Internet Information Server 5.0 (IIS 5.0), which in turn installs as part of the Windows 2000 operating system. IIS 5.0 supports ASP version 3.0. There are other web servers which also support various versions of ASP, and again we'll discuss some options shortly – but remember that if you're not running Windows 2000 and IIS 5.0 then you'll probably find one or two differences in the way some of the code works.

❑ In order to view and test the pages, we'll need a **web browser**! As we mentioned before, ASP is processed on the web server, not on the browser – this means that *any* browser should suffice.

Of course, when you're browsing pages on the Internet or your local intranet, the browser and web server software are generally hosted on two *different* physical machines – we refer to these machines as the **client** and the **server**. In fact, we even illustrated it this way in the diagrams that we've seen so far in this chapter. But it's quite possible to host browser, server and text editor all on the *same* machine – indeed, it's a technique often used by web developers as they write, test, rewrite and tweak their ASP pages. In this case, the single machine acts as both web client and web server.

Of course, if you're hosting your web server on one machine, and your browser on another machine, you'll need a network so that they can talk to one another. If you're doing it all on one machine, the network won't be necessary.

Using Windows 2000 with this Book

There are a number of different versions of Windows 2000 planned for release, and each version has slightly different installation routines and different tools. However, Internet Explorer 5.0 is built into all versions of Windows 2000 – so if you're planning to *view* pages with a machine that has the Windows 2000 operating system, you already have a browser.

Moreover (and as we mentioned a moment ago), Microsoft is distributing Windows 2000 with its own web server software, **Internet Information Server 5.0 (IIS 5.0)**, which supports ASP 3.0. So if you're planning to use a Windows 2000 machine as your web server, then your web server software is already available to you. You just need to check that IIS 5.0 has been *installed* onto your machine – we'll run through the check and the installation procedure shortly.

> The ideal set-up for this book is a single machine running the Windows 2000 operating system, with IIS 5.0 and a web browser installed and running on that machine. At the very least, you'll need a web server that supports ASP.

Using other Operating Systems with this Book

If you're planning to use a machine that's running a system *other* than Windows 2000 as your web server, don't worry – you can still build, publish and test ASP pages, but you'll need to download or purchase an ASP-supporting web server.

If you're in this position, you should note that many web servers *don't* come with ASP built-in – indeed, some web servers are not capable of supporting ASP at all. So you need to be careful when choosing your web server. Let's have a closer look at this.

Web Servers on Older Versions of Windows

If you're installing Windows NT Server 4.0 to serve web pages, then Microsoft's IIS 2.0 web server is an option available as part of the installation, and IIS 3.0 is available as part of Service Pack 3. A preferable alternative is to install **IIS 4.0**, which is available for free as part of Microsoft's **Windows NT 4.0 Option Pack**. At the time of writing, you can download the Option Pack from Microsoft's web site, at http://www.microsoft.com/ntserver/nts/downloads/recommended/NT4OptPk/default.asp. Note that IIS 4.0 supports ASP 2.0.

If you're using running Windows NT Workstation 4.0, Windows 95, or Windows 98, then you can use Microsoft's **Personal Web Server** (**PWS**) as your web server software. Again, PWS supports ASP 2.0 and is currently available from the NT 4.0 Option Pack. It's worth noting that while PWS on Windows 95 and 98 was an individual product, PWS on Windows NT Workstation was in fact IIS 4.0 under a different name.

We can't guarantee the continued availability of PWS on Microsoft's site in the future. However, it's worth noting that a number of ASP-related FTP sites – such as http://www.crackedrabbit.com/aspfirststeps – are also currently making PWS available, so take a look online for a copy.

> For his book Beginning Active Server Pages Databases *(Wrox, ISBN 1-861002-72-6)*, *John Kauffman created a comprehensive set of instructions on the installation and setup of PWS. We've reproduced those notes here in Appendix E.*

Web Servers on Other Operating Systems

There are many web servers available. Some (such as Netscape's web server) are available commercially; others (such as the Apache web server) are available for free. Some of these web servers may support ASP, and others won't. In this section we'll take a brief look at a couple of web servers from third party vendors.

When Microsoft released ASP 1.0, it was as an **extension** that could be installed onto an existing Microsoft web server. This 'extension' was just a piece of software that was written to run on a server operating system, and could be installed by the system administrator. But this extension could only be used in conjunction with Microsoft web servers. Since then, other companies have worked to provide ASP support for other web servers, and on platforms other than Windows. Chili!Soft and Halcyon Software are two such companies.

Chili!Soft

At the time of writing, you can download a developer edition of **Chili!Soft ASP** from http://www.chilisoft.com – this gives a 30-day trial edition of the product together with details of how to register for a permanent five-user session license. Once installed, Chili!Soft ASP enables you to run ASP on web servers from Apache, Lotus, Netscape, O'Reilly and Microsoft, running on Microsoft, Sun, and IBM systems. Chili!Soft version 3.0 is now available. For more details of this product, check the Chili!Soft web site.

Halcyon Software

Halcyon Software provides a product called **Instant ASP**, which runs as a Java servlet on your web server to provide ASP support. There is a free 'developer version' of Instant ASP available from Halcyon's web site, at http://www.halcyonsoft.com – the full version retailed at $495 at the time of writing. The developer version is an almost full-featured edition, with just a few unsupported functions (as listed in the **Release Notes** on their web page) and limited by the number of users that the server can support at any one time.

Because Instant ASP is a Java servlet, it also requires the Java Development Kit (JDK) to be installed on your web server. The JDK can be downloaded separately and for free, from Sun Microsystems' web site at http://www.sun.com.

Using these ASP Extensions

Once your web server has the ASP support software loaded and running, you can use it to host and interpret pages containing ASP code. Once again, it's worth noting that it isn't possible to run ASP on all web servers, even with ASP extension software installed – so check with these providers to confirm that their products will provide support for your web server.

Installing Internet Information Services 5.0

Now it's time to get your web server up and functioning. Since this book is geared towards users of Windows 2000, we'll walk through the steps for locating IIS 5.0, and (if necessary) installing it. If your web server machine has an older Microsoft system or another operating system, you'll need to consult the relevant documentation. Appendix E will be of interest to users of Windows 95/98/NT Workstation.

Let's press on with Windows 2000 and IIS 5.0. You might not have to do much in this initial stage, if you discover that you're already running IIS 5.0. We'll look at how to check that right now.

Try It Out – Locating IIS 5.0 on my Web Server Machine

1. Go to the control panel (Start | Settings | Control Panel) and select the Add/Remove Programs icon. The following dialog will appear, display a list of your currently installed programs:

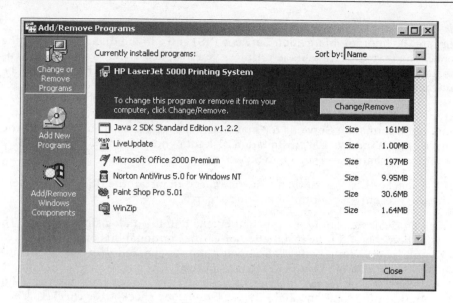

2. Select the Add/Remove Windows Components icon on the left side of the dialog, to get to the screen that allows you to install new windows components.

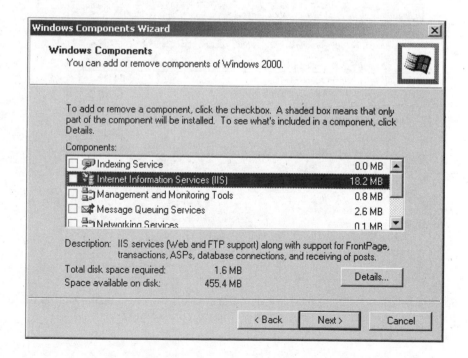

3. Locate the Internet Information Services (IIS) entry in the dialog, and note the checkbox that appears to its left. Unless you installed Windows 2000 via a custom install and specifically requested IIS, it's most likely that the checkbox will be unchecked (as shown above).

4.a If the checkbox is *cleared*, then place a check the checkbox and click on Next to load Internet Information Services 5.0 and Active Server Pages. You might be prompted to place your Windows 2000 installation disk into your CD-ROM drive. It will take a few minutes to complete. Then go to Step 5.

4.b If the checkbox is *checked* then you won't need to install the IIS 5.0 component – it's already present on your machine. Go to Step 5.

5. Click on the Details button – this will take you to the dialog shown below. There are a few options here, for the installation of various optional bits of functionality. For example, if the World Wide Web Server option is checked then our IIS installation will be able to serve and manage web pages and applications. If you're planning to use FrontPage 2000 or Visual InterDev to write your web page code, then you'll need to ensure that the FrontPage 2000 Server Extensions checkbox is checked. The Internet Information Server Snap-In is very desirable, as you'll see later in the chapter – so ensure that is checked too.

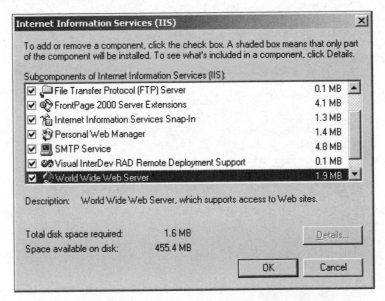

For the purpose of this installation, make sure all the checkboxes in this dialog are checked; then click on OK to return to the previous dialog.

There's one other component that we'll need to install, for use later in this book – it's the Script Debugger. If you scroll to the foot of the **Windows Components Wizard** dialog that we showed above, you'll find a checkbox for **Script Debugger**. If it isn't already checked, check it now and click on **Next** to complete the installation. Otherwise, if both IIS 5.0 and the script debugger are already present, then click on **Cancel** to abort the process.

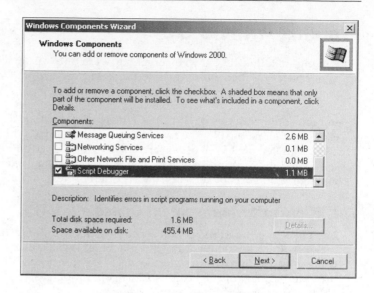

How It Works

Web Services start up automatically as soon as your installation is complete, and thereafter whenever you boot up Windows – so you don't need to run any further startup programs, or click on any short-cuts as you would to start up Word or Excel.

IIS installs most of its bits and pieces on your hard drive, under the `\WinNT\system32\inetsrv` directory; however, more interesting to us at the moment is the `\InetPub` directory that is also created at this time. This directory contains subdirectories that will provide the home for the web page files that we create.

If you expand the `InetPub` directory, you'll find that it contains several subdirectories:

- ❑ `\iissamples\homepage` contains some example ASP pages.
- ❑ `\iissamples\sdk` contains as set of subdirectories that hold ASP scripts which demonstrate the various ASP objects and components.
- ❑ `\scripts` is an empty directory, which is a useful place to store any ASP scripts you might create.
- ❑ `\webpub` is also empty. This is a 'special' virtual directory, used for publishing files via the **Publish** wizard. Note that this directory only exists if you are using Windows 2000 Professional Edition.
- ❑ `\wwwroot` is the top of the tree for your web site (or web sites). This should be your default web directory. It also contains a number of subdirectories, which contain various bits and pieces of IIS. This directory is generally used to contain subdirectories which hold the pages that make up our web site – although, in fact, there's no reason why you can't store your pages elsewhere. We'll be discussing the relationship between physical and virtual directories later in this chapter.
- ❑ `\ftproot`, `\mailroot` and `\nntproot` should form the top of the tree for any sites that use FTP, mail or news services, if installed.

Working with IIS 5.0

Having installed IIS 5.0 web server software onto our machine, we'll need some means of administrating its contents and settings. In this section, we'll meet the user interface that is provided by IIS 5.0.

In fact, some versions of IIS 5.0 provide two user interfaces, which come from PWS and the earlier versions of IIS – the two Microsoft web servers that existed in the time before Windows 2000. The **Personal Web Manager** was distributed with PWS, and is still supported by IIS 5.0 in *some* versions of Windows 2000. The **Microsoft Management Console** is a generic way of managing all sorts of services, and is often preferred. Let's take a quick look at both of them.

The Microsoft Management Console (MMC)

The beauty of the MMC is that it provides a central interface for administrating all sorts of services that are installed on your machine. We can use it to administrate IIS – but in fact, when we use it to administrate other services, the interface will look roughly the same. The MMC is provided as part of the Windows 2000 operating system – in fact, the MMC also comes with older Windows server operating systems.

IIS Administration using the MMC

The MMC itself is just a shell – on its own, it doesn't do much at all. If we want to use it to administer a service, we have to add a **snap-in** for that service. The good news is that IIS 5.0 has its own snap-in – the idea is that we snap the snap-in into the empty MMC shell, and it's this that allows us to administrate IIS. Let's take a look at it.

Try It Out – IIS Administration using the MMC

1. From the Start menu, select Run; in the resulting dialog, type MMC and press OK. What appears is a rather empty-looking MMC shell, like this.

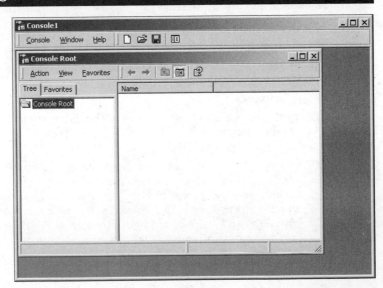

2. Before we snap in the IIS snap-in, we need to locate it. The IIS 5.0 snap-in is encapsulated in a file called `iis.msc`, which should be contained in your `\WinNT\system32\inetsrv` directory. Have a look for it now; and if it's not there, open your Windows Explorer and use the Search facility (at **View | Explorer Bar | Search**) and make a note of its location.

3. Now return to the MMC shell, select the **Console** menu, and choose **Open**.... You'll be presented with a dialog that allows you to browse the files on your machine. Use this to navigate to the `iis.msc` file that you located a moment ago – then click on **Open**. This will open the IIS snap-in within the MMC shell – a site that looks something like this should greet you:

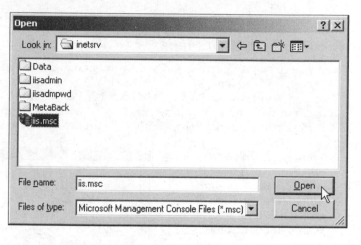

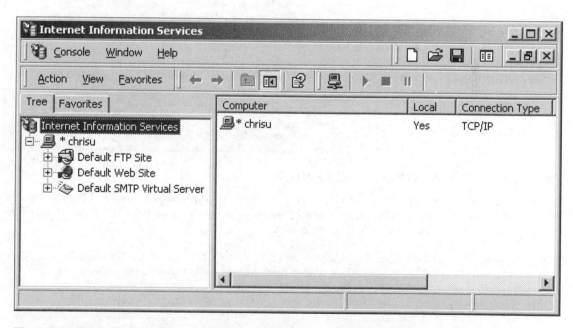

Having opened the IIS snap-in within the MMC, you can perform all of your web management tasks from this window. The properties of the web site are accessible via the **Default Web Site** node. We'll be using the MMC more a little later in the chapter. Before that, we'll take a look at the Personal Web Manager.

> *To avoid the inconvenience of stepping through this process each time you need to administrate IIS, you could choose to create a shortcut. To do this, use Windows Explorer to navigate to the iis.msc file. Then right-click on iis.msc, and select Create Shortcut – this creates a new shortcut (called Shortcut to iis.msc) in the same folder. Finally, drag the new shortcut from the Explorer window onto the desktop. You can rename the shortcut if you like.*

The Personal Web Manager (PWM)

If you're running Windows 2000 Professional, then there's another user interface to IIS – the Personal Web Manager (PWM). The PWM was the interface of PWS, Microsoft's web server for use on Windows 95/98 and Windows NT Workstation. It seems Microsoft has assumed that any users of these older Windows systems who decide to upgrade will choose to Windows 2000 *Professional* edition – because PWM is not available on other editions of Windows 2000.

You can get to it by opening the Control Panel, selecting the Administrative Tools icon and selecting Personal Web Manager. It looks like this.

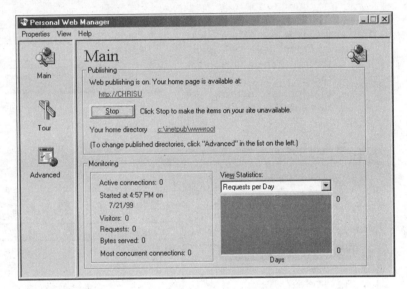

Which IIS User Interface Should I Use?

Depending on which version of Windows you're using, you might not have a choice. If you're using an older version of Windows, or one of the 'higher-end' versions of Windows 2000, then your choice will probably be restricted to one.

What if you do have an option? The MMC-based admin tool for IIS – the IIS snap-in – provides a richer interface than the PWM, and provides services not only for web pages, but also for FTP sites (enabling the transfer of files from one site to another), NNTP (newsgroup) services and video and audio services. The MMC is designed to integrate seamlessly with many of Microsoft's other products, including the database facilities of SQL Server, the management facilities of Site Server, and the emailing and messaging abilities of Exchange. For this reason, we'll be using the MMC-based interface in this book.

Testing your Web Server

The next thing to do is test the web server to see if it is working correctly, and serving pages as it should be. We've already noted that the web services should start as soon as IIS has been installed, and will restart every time you start your machine. In this section, we'll test that out.

In order to test the web server, we'll start up a browser and try to view some web pages that we know are already placed on the web server. In order to do that, we'll need to type a **universal resource locator** (or **URL**) into the browser's Address box, as we often do when browsing on the Internet. The URL is an `http://...` web-page address which indicates which web server to connect to, and the page we want to view.

What URL do we use in order to browse to our web server? If your web server and web browser are connected by a local area network, or if you're using a single machine for both web server and browser, then it should be enough to specify the name of the web server machine in the URL.

Identifiying your Web Server's Name

By default, IIS will take the name of your web server from the name of the computer. You can find this in the machine's network settings. On your web server machine, select Start | Settings | Network and Dial-up Connections, and from the Advanced menu select Network Identification. The Network Identification tab will display your machine name under the description Full computer name:

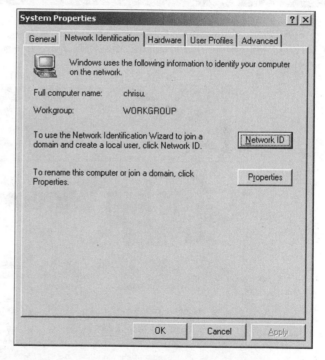

My machine has the name chrisu, and (as can see here and in the earlier screenshot of the MMC dialog) my web server has adopted the same name. Browsing to pages on this machine across a local area network (or, indeed, from the same machine), I can use a URL that begins http://chrisu/....

> *There are a couple of alternatives if you're using the same machine as both web server and browser. Try http://127.0.0.1/... – here, 127.0.0.1 is the loopback address that causes requests to be sent to a web server on the local machine. Or try http://localhost/... – 'localhost' is an alias for the 127.0.0.1 address – you may need to check the LAN settings (in your browser's options) to ensure that local browsing is not through a proxy server. We will discuss this in more detail a bit further into this chapter.*

Throughout this book, in the examples that require a web server name, we'll show the expression `my_server_name` whenever you need to insert your own web server's name. When you see this, you'll need to substitute your own server's name for `my_server_name`, rather than typing this expression in literally.

Browsing to a Page on your Web Server

Now you know the name of your web server, and that web services are running, you can view the ASP pages hosted on your web server by browsing to them with your web browser. Let's test out this theory by viewing our default home page.

Try It Out – Testing the Web Service

To verify that web services are working, start up your browser and type http://`my_server_name`/localstart.asp into the address box. (My server is named chrisu, so I typed in http://chrisu/localstart.asp.) Now press *Enter*; and (if all is well) you should get to see a page like this one:

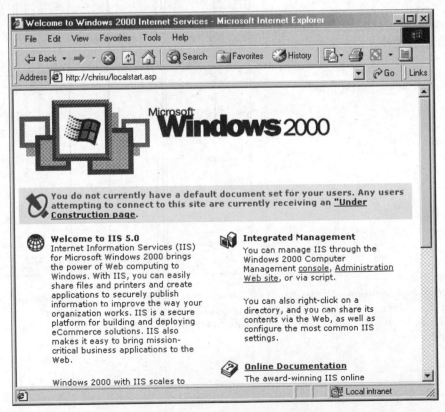

What do you do if this doesn't work?

If you don't get this page, then take a look at the following steps as we try to resolve the problem. If it's not working correctly, then most likely you'll be greeted with this screen.

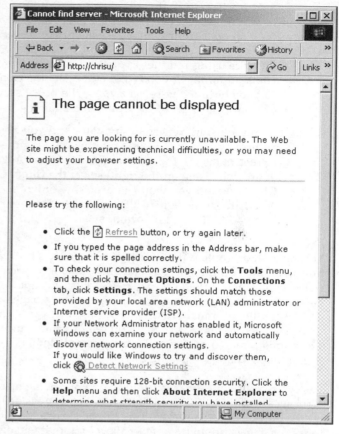

If you get this page then it means that your Web services are not switched on. To switch on Web services, you'll first need to start the IIS admin snap-in that we described earlier in the chapter (to reprise: select Start | Run, type MMC and hit OK; then select Open from the MMC's Console menu and locate the iis.msc file from the dialog; alternatively, just use the shortcut that you created there).

Now, click on the + of the root node in the left pane of the snap-in, to reveal the Default sites. Then right-click on Default Web Site, and select Start:

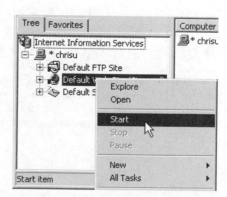

If it's still not working then here are a few more suggestions, which are based on particular aspects of your PC's setup. If you're running on a network and using a proxy server, there's a possibility that this can prevent your browser from accessing your web server. Most browsers will give you an opportunity to bypass the proxy server:

❑ If you're using Internet Explorer, you need to go to View | Internet Options (IE4) or Tools | Internet Options (IE5) and select the Connections tab. In IE5 press the LAN settings button and select Bypass the proxy server for local addresses. In IE4, this section forms part of the Connections dialog.

❑ If you're using Netscape Navigator and you are having problems then need to turn off all proxies and make sure you are accessing the Internet directly. To do this, select Edit | Preferences; in the resulting dialog select Advanced | Proxies from the Category box on the left. Then on the right, select the Direct Connection to Internet option, and hit OK. Although you won't be browsing online to the Internet, it'll allow Netscape Navigator to recognize all variations of accessing local ASP pages – such as http://127.0.0.1, http://localhost, etc.

You may hit a problem if your machine name is similar to that of some web site out there on the Internet – for example, if your machine name is jimmyd but there also happens to be a public web site out there called http://www.jimmyd.com. When you type http://jimmyd into your browser's address box, expecting to view a page on your local web server, you unexpectedly get transported to http://www.jimmyd.com instead. If this is happening to you, then you need to make sure that you're not using a proxy server in your browser settings – again, this can be disabled using the Internet Options | Connection dialog or the Edit | Preferences dialog.

Lastly, if your web server is running on your home machine with a modem, and you get an error message informing you that your web page is offline, this could in fact be a misperception on the part of the web server. This can be corrected by changing the way that your browser looks for pages. To do this, select View | Internet Options (IE4) or Tools | Internet Options (IE5), choose the Connections tab and select Never dial a connection.

Of course, you might encounter problems that aren't answered above. In this case, the chances are that it's related to your own particular system setup. We can't possibly cover all the different possible configurations here; but if you can't track down the problem, you may find some help at one of the web sites and newsgroups listed later in this chapter.

Managing Directories on your Web Server

These days, many browsers are sufficiently advanced that you can use them to locate and examine files and pages that exist on your computer's hard disk. So, for example, you can start up your browser, type in the physical location of a web page (or other file) such as C:\My Documents\mywebpage.html, and the browser will display it. However, this isn't real web publishing at all:

❑ First, web pages are transported using a protocol called HTTP – the HyperText Transfer Protocol. Note that the `http://` at the beginning of URL indicates that the request is being sent by HTTP. Requesting `C:\My Documents\mywebpage.html` in your browser doesn't use HTTP, and this means that the file is not delivered and handled in the way a web page should be. We'll discuss this in greater detail when we tackle HTTP at the start of Chapter 2.

❑ Second, consider the addressing situation. The string `C:\My Documents\mywebpage.html` tells us that the page exists in the `\My Documents` directory of the `C:` drive of the hard disk *of the machine on which the browser is running*. In a network situation, with two or more computers, this simply doesn't give enough information about the web server.

However, when a user browses (via HTTP) to a web page on some web server, the web server will need to work out where the file for that page is located on the server's hard disk. In fact, there's an important relationship between the information given in the URL, and the physical location (within the web server's file system) of the `.htm` or `.asp` file that contains the source for the page.

Virtual Directories

So how does this relationship work? In fact, it can work by creating a second directory structure on the web server machine, which reflects the structure of your web site. It sounds like it could be complicated, but it doesn't have to be. In fact, in this book it's going to be very simple.

The first directory structure is what we see when we open Windows Explorer on the web server – these directories are known as **physical directories**. For example, the folder `C:\My Documents` is a physical directory.

The second directory structure is the one that reflects the structure of the web site. This consists of a hierarchy of **virtual directories**. We use the web server to create virtual directories, and to set the relationship between the virtual directories and the real (physical) directories.

When you try to visualize a virtual directory, it's probably best not to think of it as a directory at all. Instead, just think of it as a nickname or alias for a physical directory that exists on the web server machine. The idea is that, when a user browses to a web page that is contained in the physical directory on the server, they don't use the name of the *physical* directory to get there: instead, they use the physical directory's nickname.

To see how this might be useful, consider a website that publishes news about many different sporting events. In order to organize his web files carefully, the webmaster has built a physical directory structure on his hard disk, which looks like this:

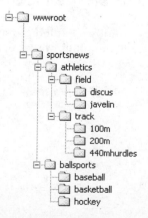

Now suppose you visit this web site to get the latest news on the Javelin event in the Olympics. If the URL for this web page were based on the physical directory structure, then the URL for this page would be something like this:

```
http://www.oursportsite.com/sportsnews/athletics/field/javelin/default.asp
```

That's OK for the webmaster, who understands his directory structure; but it's a fairly unmemorable web address! So, to make it easier for the *user*, the webmaster can assign a *virtual* directory name or *alias* to this directory – it acts just like a nickname for the directory. Here, let's suppose we've assigned the virtual name `javelinnews` to the `c:\inetpub\...\javelin\` directory. Then the URL for the latest Javelin news is:

```
http://www.oursportsite.com/javelinnews/default.asp
```

By creating virtual directory names for all the directories (such as `baseballnews`, `100mnews`, `200nnews`, etc) it's easy for the user to type in the URL and go directly to the page they want:

```
http://www.oursportsite.com/baseballnews/default.asp
http://www.oursportsite.com/100mnews/default.asp
http://www.oursportsite.com/200mnews/default.asp
```

Not only does this save the user from long, unwieldy URLs – it also serves as a good security measure, because it hides the physical directory structure from all the web site visitors. Moreover, it allows the webmaster's web site structure to remain independent of the directory structure on his hard drive – so he can move files on his disk between different physical folders, drives, or even servers, without having to change the structure of his web pages.

Let's have a crack at setting up our own virtual directories and permissions (please note that these permissions are set automatically, if you use Visual Interdev or FrontPage to create a new site).

Try It Out – Creating a Virtual Directory and Setting Up Permissions

Let's take a quick look now at how you can create your own virtual directory. We'll use this directory to store the examples that we'll be creating in this book. We don't want to over-complicate this example by creating lots of directories, so we'll demonstrate by creating a single physical directory on the web server's hard disk, and using the IIS admin tool to create a virtual directory and make the relationship between the two.

1. Start Windows Explorer and create a new physical directory named **BegASPFiles**, under the \Inetpub\wwwroot directory created by IIS on your hard drive.

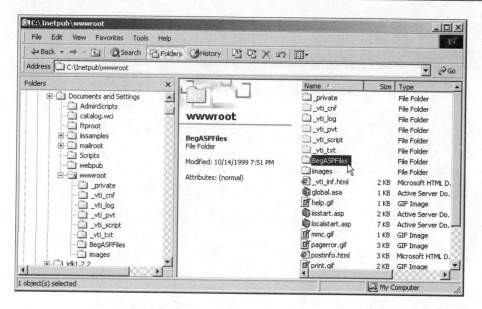

2. Next, start up the IIS admin tool (using the MMC, as we described earlier). Right-click on **Default Web Site**, and from the menu that appears select **New | Virtual Directory**. This starts the **Virtual Directory Creation Wizard**, which handles the creation of virtual directories for you and the setting up of permissions as well. You'll see the splash screen first, which looks like this. Click on **Next**.

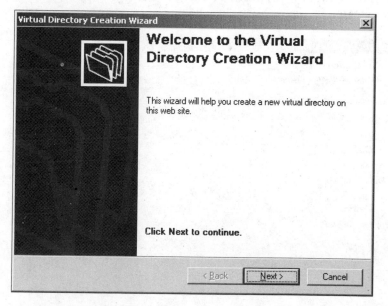

3. Type BegASP in the Alias text box; then click Next.

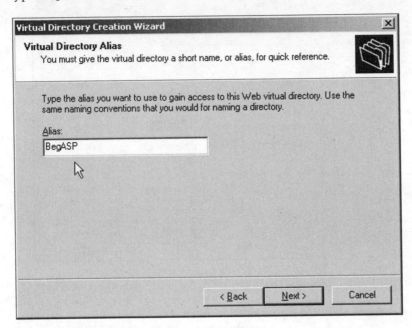

4. Click on the Browse... button and select the directory \Inetpub\wwwroot\BegASPFiles
that you created in Step 1. Then click Next.

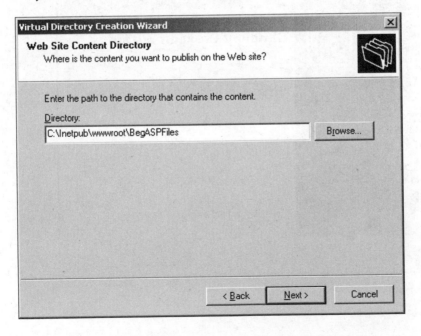

5. Make sure that the Read and Run scripts checkboxes are checked, and that the Execute checkbox is empty. Click on Next, and in the subsequent page click on Finish.

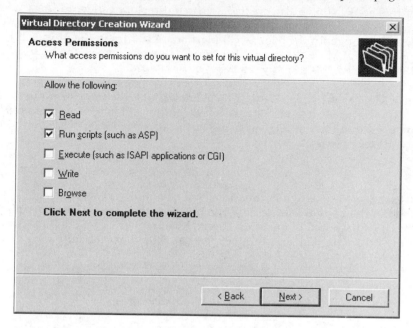

6. The BegASP virtual directory will appear on the tree in the IIS admin window.

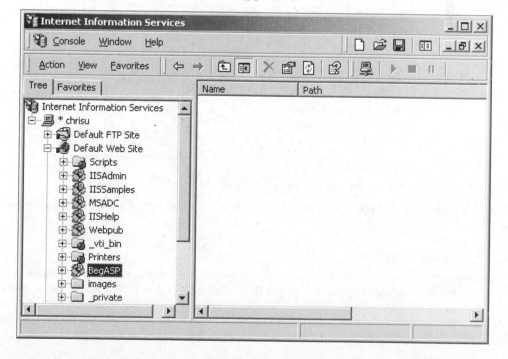

How It Works

You've just created a physical directory called `BegASPFiles`, in which we can store all of the examples for this book. You've also created a virtual directory called `BegASP`, which you created as an alias for the physical `BegASPFiles` directory. When we create examples later in this chapter, and throughout the book, we'll place the ASP files in the physical `C:\Inetpub\wwwroot\BegASPFiles` directory; and when we use the browser to test the pages, we'll use the URL `http://my_server_name/BegASP/....`

Note that the URL uses the alias `/BegASP` – IIS knows that this stands for the directory path `C:\Inetpub\wwwroot\BegASPFiles`. When executing ASP pages, you can reduce the amount of typing you need to do in the URL, by using *virtual* directory names in your URL in place of the physical directory names.

Permissions

As we've just seen, we can assign permissions to a new directory as we create it, by using the options offered in the Virtual Directory Wizard. Alternatively, we can set permissions at any time, from the IIS admin tool in the MMC. To do this, right-click on the **BegASP** virtual directory in the IIS admin tool, and select **Properties**. You'll get the following dialog:

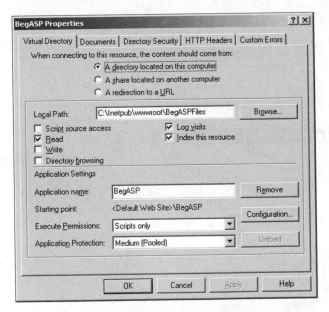

It's quite a complicated dialog, and it contains a lot of options – not all of which we wish to go into now.

Creating an Application

If you look at the above screenshot, you will notice that we have created an application called `BegASP` – the same as our virtual directory. If the box next to the Application name label is blank, you need to hit the **Create** button, which is on the right of the box. After the application is created, this button becomes **Remove**. This will enable us to use `Global.asa` in our scripts – we will discuss `Global.asa` in Chapter 8.

Access Permissions

The four check boxes on the left are of interest to us, as they govern the types of access for the given directory and dictate the permissions allowed on the files contained within that directory. Let's have a look at what each of these options means:

❑ **Scripts source access** This permission enables users to access the source code of a script. It's only possible to allow this permission if the **Read** or **Write** permission has already been assigned. But we generally don't want our users to be able to view our ASP source code, so we would usually leave this checkbox unchecked for any directory that contains ASP scripts. By default, all directories created during setup have **Scripts Source Access** permission disabled.

❑ **Read** This permission enables browsers to read or download files stored in a home directory or a virtual directory. If the browser requests a file from a directory that *doesn't* have the **Read** permission enabled, then the web server will simply return an error message (such as the one shown below). Generally, directories containing information that you want to publish (such as HTML files, for example) should have the **Read** permission enabled.

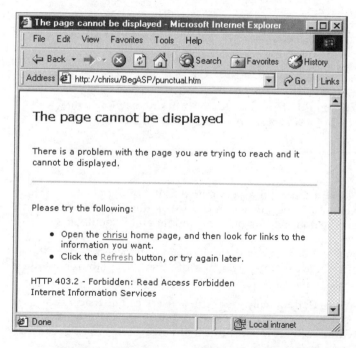

Note that when the folder has Read permission turned off, HTML files within the folder cannot be read; but ASP scripts within the folder can still be run.

❑ **Write** If the write permission on a virtual directory is enabled, then users will be able to create or modify files within the directory, and change the properties of these files.

❑ **Directory Browsing** If you want to allow people to view the contents of the directory (that is, to see a list of all the files that are contained in that directory), then you can allow this by checking the Directory Browsing option. Also, if someone tries to browse the contents of a directory that has Directory Browsing enabled but Read disabled, then they may receive the following message:

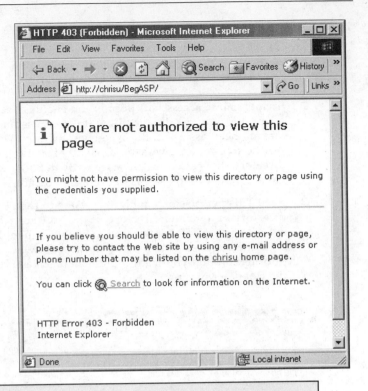

> For security reasons, we'd recommend disabling this option unless your users specifically need the **Directory browsing** option – such as when FTPing files from your web site.

Execute Permissions

There's a text box near the foot of the Properties dialog, labeled Execute permissions – this specifies what level of program execution is permitted on pages contained in this directory. There are three possible values here – None, Scripts only, or Scripts and Executables:

❑ Setting Execute permissions to None means that users can only access static files, such as image files and HTML files. Any script-based files of other executables contained in this directory are inaccessible to users.

❑ Setting Execute permissions to Scripts Only means that users can also access any script-based pages, such as ASP pages. So if the user requests an ASP page that's contained in this directory, the web server will allow the ASP script to be executed, and for the resulting HTML to be sent to the browser.

❑ Setting Execute permissions to Scripts and Executables means that users can execute any type of file type that's contained in the directory. It's generally a good idea to avoid using this setting, in order to prohibit users from executing potentially damaging applications on your web server.

For any directory containing ASP files that you're publishing, the appropriate setting for the Execute permissions is Scripts Only.

Writing Our First ASP Example

OK, if the web server and underlying web services are up and running, then it's time to demonstrate ASP in action. Do you remember the Punctual Web Server code that we talked about earlier in the chapter – in which we wanted to write a web page that displays the current time? We'll return to that example now. As you'll see, it's just a simple web page using HTML and a little bit of ASP script – but it's enough to check that the ASP is working OK.

The Punctual Web Server Example

You can follow these instructions to set up the web page; then we'll explain what's happening and look at some pitfalls.

Try It Out – The Punctual Web Server

1. Open a new text file using the Notepad text editor that comes with your machine. (We'll discuss other code editors later in the chapter, but Notepad will suffice for now.) Then type the following code in:

```
<HTML>
<HEAD><TITLE>The Punctual Web Server</TITLE></HEAD>
<BODY>
   <H1>Welcome</H1>
   In Webserverland, the time is exactly <% = Time %>
</BODY>
</HTML>
```

> The main advantage of typing the code in by hand is that it's a good way to become familiar with the syntax and techniques used in the code. The main disadvantages are that it's time-consuming, and it's possible to introduce typing errors. So, for your convenience, the source code for this example – and all the examples in the book – is available (for free!) in a downloadable file from the Wrox Press website, at http://www.wrox.com.

2. Now, save this code as a file – call the file punctual.asp, and ensure that you save it into the C:\inetpub\wwwroot\BegASPFiles directory that we created earlier in the chapter.

When you save the file, you should double-check that your new file has the correct suffix. It should be .asp – it's your opportunity to tell the web server that the page contains ASP script. Be aware that the text editor may consider .txt to be the default! So in the Save or Save As... dialog, make sure you change the Save as Type to read All Files, or All Files (*.*).

3. Now start up your browser, and navigate to
`http://my_server_name/BegASP/punctual.asp`:

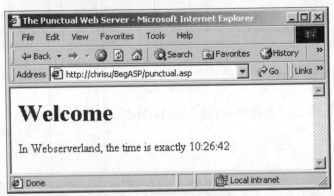

4. Click on the Refresh button: the displayed time will change. In effect, the browser is showing a new and different instance of the same web page.

5. Now on your browser, select View | Source (or View | Page Source, or similar, depending on which browser you're using) from the browser menu to see the HTML source that was sent from the web server to the browser. The result is shown below. You can see that there is no ASP script to be seen – the `<% = Time %>` ASP script has been processed by the web server and used to generate pure HTML, which is hard-coded into the HTML source that's sent to the browser.

Here, you can see the HTML that was sent to the browser when I Refreshed the page at 10.31:00am.

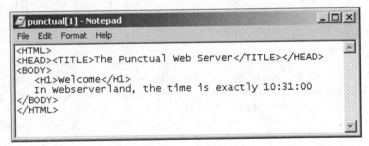

6. As we mentioned before, you can expect this to work in any browser – because the ASP is processed on the web server. If you have another browser available, try it out.

Easy wasn't it? (If you didn't get it to work first time, then don't rush off to email technical support just yet – have a little look at the next section, *Common Pitfalls and Errors with ASP*, first.) Now let's take a look at the ASP that makes this application tick.

How It Works

Of course, there is only one block of ASP in the whole program. It's enclosed by the `<%` and `%>` tags, on this line:

```
In Webserverland, the time is exactly <% = Time %>
```

This line tells the web server to go off and run the VBScript `Time` function *on the web server*. The VBScript `Time` function returns the current time *at the web server*. If the web server and browser are on different machines, then the time returned by the web server might not be the same as the time kept by the machine you're using to browse. For example, if this page is hosted on a machine in Los Angeles, then you can expect the page to show the local time in Los Angeles – even if you're browsing to the page from a machine in Cairo.

The `Time` function isn't unique to ASP: indeed, it's just a VBScript function, that's being run on the server.

This example isn't wildly interactive or dynamic, but it illustrates that we can ask the web server to go off and do something for us, and return the answer *within the context* of an HTML page. Of course, by using this technique with things like HTML forms and other tools, we'll be able to build a more informative, interactive interface with the user.

Common Errors and Pitfalls with ASP

If you had difficulty with the example above, then perhaps you fell into one of the simple traps that commonly snare new ASP programmers, and that can be easily rectified. In this section we'll look at a few common errors and reasons why your script might not run; if you did have problems, maybe this section will help you to identify the problem.

Program Not Found, or the Result of the ASP isn't being Displayed, or the Browser tries to Download the File

You'll have this problem if you try to view the page as a local file on your hard drive, like this:

```
C:\InetPub\wwwroot\BegASP\punctual.asp
```

You'll also get this problem if you click on the file in Windows Explorer. If you have Microsoft FrontPage or Visual InterDev installed, then it will start up and attempt to help you to edit the code. Otherwise, your browser may display a warning message:

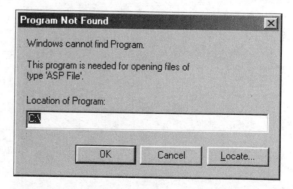

Older browsers may try to download the file:

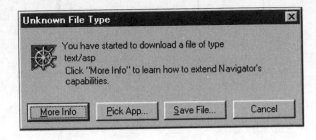

The Problem

That's because you're trying to access the page in a way that doesn't cause the ASP page to be requested *from the web server*. Because you're not requesting the page through the web server, the ASP doesn't get processed – and that's why you don't get the expected results of the ASP.

To call the web page through the web server and have the ASP processed, you need to reference the web server in the URL. Depending on whether you're browsing to the server across a local network, or across the Internet, the URL should look something like one of these:

```
http://chrisu/BegASP/punctual.asp
http://www.distantserver.com/BegASP/punctual.asp
```

Page Cannot be Displayed: HTTP Error 403

If you get the 403 error message, then it's probably because don't have permission to execute the ASP script contained within the page:

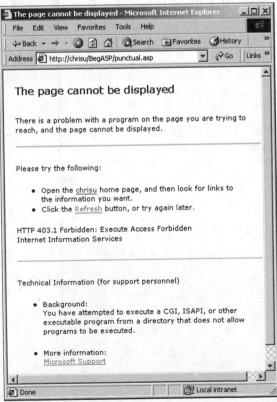

As you'll recall, the permissions are controlled by the properties of the virtual directory that contains the ASP page. To change these properties, you'll need to start up the IIS admin snap-in in the MMC, as we described earlier in the chapter. Find the BegASP virtual directory in the left pane, right-click on it and select Properties. This will bring up the BegASP Properties dialog that we met earlier in the chapter:

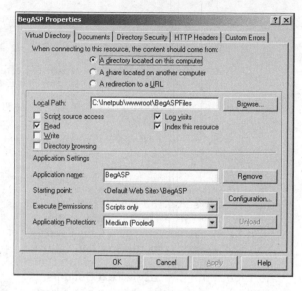

Here, you'll need to check that the value shown in the Execute Permissions box is Scripts only.

Page Cannot Be Found: HTTP Error 404

If you get this error message then it means that the browser has managed to connect to the web server successfully, but that the web server can't locate the page you've asked for. This could be because you've mistyped the URL at the browser prompt. In this case, you'll see a message like this:

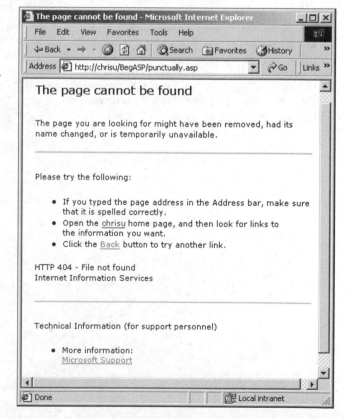

If you get this page, then you might suspect one of the following errors:

- ❑ A simple typing error in the URL, e.g. `http://chrisu/BegASP/punctually.asp`

- ❑ Including a directory separator (/) after the file name, e.g. `http://chrisu/BegASP/punctual.asp/`

- ❑ Using the directory path in the URL, rather than using the alias, e.g. `http://chrisu/Inetpub/wwwroot/BegASP/punctual.asp`

- ❑ Saving the page as `.html` or `.htm`, rather than as an `.asp`, e.g. `http://chrisu/BegASP/punctual.htm`

Of course, it may be that you've typed in the URL correctly, and you're *still* experiencing this error. In this case, the most likely cause is that you have used Notepad to save your file and that (when you saved the file) it used its default **Save As Type** setting, which is **Text Documents** (*.txt). This automatically appends a `.txt` suffix to the end of your file name. In this case, you will unwittingly have finished up with a file called `punctual.asp.txt`.

To check if that is what happened, go to Windows Explorer, and view the (physical) folder that contains the file. Go to the **Tools** menu and select **Folder Options...** Now, in the **View** tab, ensure that the **Hide file extensions for known file types** is unchecked, as shown here.

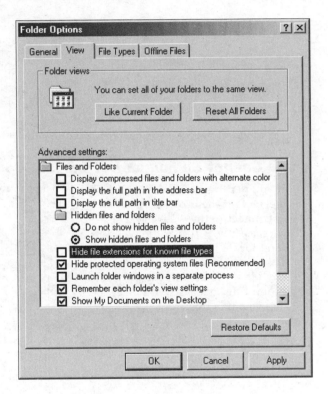

Now click **OK** and return to view your file in Windows Explorer. You may well see something like the following.

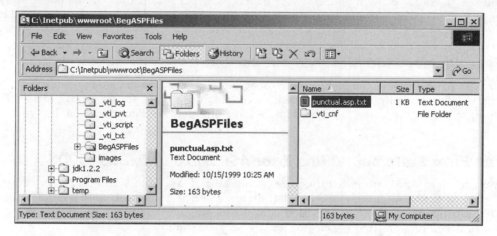

As you can see, Notepad has been less-than-honest in its dealings with you: when you thought that you had saved your file as `punctual.asp`, it had inconveniently saved it as `punctual.asp.txt`. Not surprisingly, your web server won't be able to find your file if it's been renamed accidentally. To correct the filename, right click on the filename in the right pane above, select **Rename** from the drop-down menu that appears and remove the .txt at the end.

Web Page Unavailable While Offline

Very occasionally, you'll come across the following message box:

This happens because you've tried to request a page and you haven't currently got an active connection to the Internet. This is a misperception by the server (unless your web server isn't the same machine as the one you're working on) – it is trying to get onto the Internet to get your page when there is no connection, and it's failing to realize that the page you've requested is present on your local machine. One way of retrieving the page is to hit the **Connect** button in the dialog; but that's not the most satisfactory of solutions (since you might incur call charges). Alternatively, you need to adjust the settings on your browser. In IE5, select the **File** menu and uncheck the **Work Offline** option.

This could also be caused if you're working on a network and using a proxy server to access the Internet. In this case, you need to bypass the proxy server or disable it for this page, as we described in the section *Browsing to a Page on your Web Server*, earlier in the chapter. Alternatively, if you're using a modem and you don't need to connect, you can correct this misperception by changing the way that IE looks for pages. To do this, select the **Tools | Connections** option and select **Never dial a connection**.

I Just Get a Blank Page

If you see an empty page in your browser then it probably means that you managed to save your `punctual.asp` without entering any code into it, or that you didn't remember to refresh the browser.

The Page Displays the Message but not the Time

If the web page displays the message In Webserverland, the time is exactly – but doesn't display the time – then you might have mistyped the code. For example, you may have missed the = symbol, by typing `<% Time %>`, or you might have misspelt the Time function, by typing `<%= Tme %>`.

I Get an Error Statement Citing Error ASP 0116 or 0x80004005

If you get a message stating that the page cannot be displayed, and citing an error code such as ASP 0116 or 0x80004005 then it means that there's an error in the ASP code itself. Usually, there's additional information provided with the message. For example, you'd get this error message if you had omitted the closing `%>` tag on your code.

I Have a Different Problem

If your problem isn't covered by this description, it's worth testing some of the sample ASP pages that are supplied with IIS and found in the `InetPub/IISSamples` directory. `IISSamples` is a virtual directory (just like the `BegASP` virtual directory that we have created), and it can be accessed in the same way, by typing the directory name after the server name – e.g. `http://chrisu/IISSamples`. These should help you to check that IIS has actually installed properly. You can always uninstall and reinstall if necessary.

You can get support from http://p2p.wrox.com, which is our web site dedicated to support issues in this book. Alternatively, there are plenty of other web sites which are dedicated to the ASP cause. Here are just a few:

http://www.15seconds.com
http://www.activeserverpages.com
http://www.asptoday.com
http://www.asp101.com
http://asptracker.com

There are lots of solutions, discussions and tips on these pages, plus click-throughs to other related pages. Moreover, you can try the newsgroup:

microsoft.public.inetserver.iis.activeserverpages

So, by now you should have successfully downloaded, set up and installed IIS, created your first application in ASP, and been able to get it up and running. Let's look at some of the more popular editors with which you can create and edit ASP scripts.

Creating and Editing ASP Scripts

There are a number of different text editors and other applications with which you can create and edit ASP pages. Ultimately, they're all just glorified text editors editing ASCII text files – and it's worth remembering that you can use *any* editor to edit pages, even if they were created in another editor.

Here, we'll have a quick look at four of the most common code editors. Three of them (Visual InterDev, FrontPage and Allaire's Homesite) are available commercially, while the fourth (Notepad) comes free with Windows.

Microsoft Visual InterDev 6.0

Visual InterDev (VI) comes as part of Microsoft's suite of professional programming tools, known as Visual Studio. VI is a tool for designing dynamic web applications. It is, in effect, just a development environment and a collection of useful tools and utilities.

VI 6.0 is the tool that Microsoft is promoting as their favored ASP editing tool. One simple but very useful feature of VI 6.0 is that it highlights ASP <% and %> tags in yellow, and the ASP script itself is highlighted using blue for legal keywords – so they stand out from the HTML. Unfortunately, this book isn't printed in color, so unless you try it out, you'll have to take our word for it. But here's a screenshot of a VI 6.0 session in action anyway:

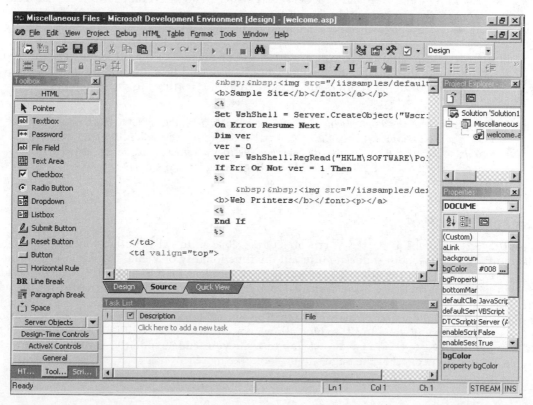

As you can see, there are three tabs in the main window here, which correspond to three possible views of your web page:

❑ The Design view, on the left of the three, is a WYSIWYG (What You See Is What You Get) interface. This allows you to put together a web page in much the same way as you might do when creating a document in Microsoft Word – you can insert pictures, links and sounds without having to write a single line of HTML.

❑ The middle tab is Source. If you go to this view, you'll see all of the HTML generated by any work that you've done in the Design view. You can also use the Source view to write and save your own code.

❑ You can use the Quick View tab, on the right of the three, to preview HTML pages in advance.

If you're using the Source view to write your own ASP code, you should note that the Design and the Quick View tabs aren't able to process the ASP. Both are limited to viewing HTML only. However, if the ASP file in the Source view is contained within what VI calls a **project**, there's an ASP-friendly alternative – you can select View | View in Browser to see what your processed ASP will look like.

In addition, Visual Interdev boasts strong links with SQL Server, which makes it very easy to set up databases combining ASP and SQL Server. It also provides several useful web-based tools for doing things like checking links, highlighting the broken ones on your site, and allowing you to drag-and-drop pages from one location to another.

Visual Interdev does have a couple of drawbacks – it's the most difficult to master of the editors discussed here, and also the most expensive. But having said that, it's undoubtedly the most powerful of these editors as it offers many more tools and features to the developer.

> *VI 6.0 has some of the most advanced features currently available; if you're intending to work in a web-development shop then it's worth learning to use Visual InterDev. We're not going to cover it in this book – its coverage justifies an entire book on its own. There's plenty of literature on VI 6.0 – you could try* Beginning Visual InterDev 6 *(Wrox, ISBN 1-861002-94-7).*

Microsoft FrontPage

FrontPage 2000 comes as part of Microsoft's Office 2000 suite – it's another tool for creating and designing web pages, but it doesn't offer all the functionality of Visual InterDev. It is ultimately a weaker but easier application to use, and it costs a lot less than Visual InterDev. If you don't mind the fact that there are fewer features, then it's a simpler, cheaper alternative for the novice.

Again, it offers three views of the web page. The Normal tab gives a WYSIWYG page creation view (like the Design view in VI), which allows you to write pages without having to code the HTML explicitly. The HTML tab allows you to write your code explicitly, and the Preview tab gives a quick view of what the page should look like in a browser.

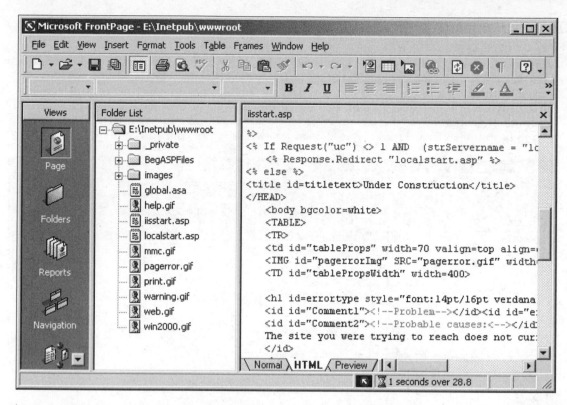

This screenshot is taken from FrontPage 2000, but you can also use Front Page 97 or 98 to edit ASP pages. Note, however, that the further back the release, the less the support there is for ASP and the more pitfalls you may run into.

Again, the Normal and Preview tabs are unable to process any ASP scripts in your page. In order to view the results of ASP scripts in FrontPage 2000, you need to create something that FrontPage calls a **web**, and place your `.asp` pages within the web; then you can select File | View in Browser to see what your processed ASP will look like.

Another quirk of FrontPage is that it likes to 'improve' your HTML and ASP, by rearranging it. FrontPage 2000 now has a Preserve existing HTML option on the Tools | Page Options | HTML Source dialog, but older versions will still 'autoedit' your HTML for you. Beware – this window dressing can change your code and even affect the intended function of the code.

Allaire's Homesite

One of the best non-Microsoft web page editors is **Allaire's Homesite**. The evaluation copy of version 4.0.1 is currently available from their web site at http://www.allaire.com. The evaluation copy allows you run the program 50 times or for 30 days –whichever elapses sooner. It has special features that allow you to edit and preview ASP scripts on a web server (i.e. actually physically run the ASPs). In fact, of the four editors that we discuss here, Homesite is the only one of the four that offers this capability. It also features an easy-to-use interface, which allows you to keep track of your files and folders at the same time as your file contents:

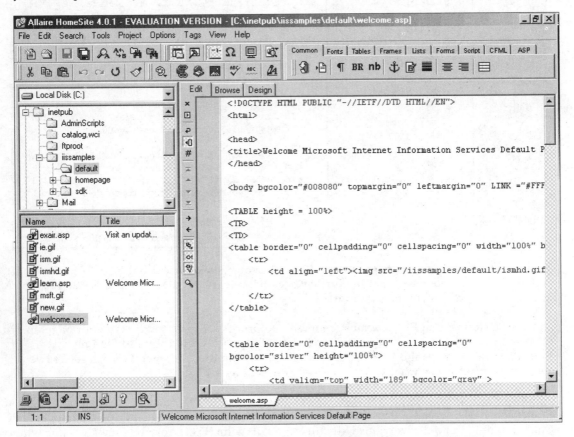

Homesite, like both Visual Interdev and FrontPage 2000, color-codes your ASP script to make it easy to identify. In short, Homesite is a very powerful editor, and well worth a look.

There are other editors, such as Sausage Software's HotDog, SoftQuad's HotMetal Pro and Adobe's PageMill. They all feature varying degrees of ASP support, and are all useful tools with which to create ASP scripts.

Notepad

Notepad is a time-honored text editor. No matter how much Microsoft promotes Visual InterDev, there will always be people who will use Notepad as their editor of choice. The fact that it's been free with every incarnation of Windows certainly helps sustain its popularity.

Of course, it doesn't highlight the ASP in any way, but also it doesn't generate any extra code. It doesn't feature many additional functions; but it's because it's so simple that it's still a very popular choice. In Windows 2000, Notepad offers a GoTo feature (under the Edit menu), which allows you to move around your documents using line numbers.

It doesn't really matter which editor you use in this book - it won't affect how you run the examples. We'll avoid any attempt to provide a tutorial on how to use any of these editorial tools – since this is really beyond the scope of the book.

Shielding ASP Source Code from the Browser

We'll highlight one more point before we wrap up this chapter. You've probably noticed that, when browsing the web, you can view HTML code directly using your browser. (For example, if you're browsing with IE5 then you can do this by choosing View | Source from the toolbar; if you're browsing with Netscape Navigator, then choose View | Page Source.) When you do this, remember that you're viewing the document *client-side* – the HTML has already been downloaded from the web server to the client, and you're now viewing that HTML source.

By contrast, you may also have noticed that your browser software doesn't enable the browser to view the *source ASP code* that generated this HTML. Instead, if you want to view the ASP code then you must view it on the *server*, by using a web page editor such as Visual InterDev or Notepad on the server.

If you're using different machines for your web server and your client, then this distinction will be fairly easy to grasp. But if you're using the same machine to perform both roles (which is a reasonable thing to do, especially in a learning or development scenario) then you may need to consider this distinction a little more carefully.

The fact that the browser doesn't allow the end-user to view the ASP source has a rather important and valuable consequence. Consider the following scenarios, as a couple of examples:

❑ You're writing an ASP page that uses a database query to get some data (which you want to display in the page). As we'll see in Chapter 12, you will need to code in connection details in order to access the database – and these connection details may contain sensitive information such as a username and password

❑ You're writing an ASP page that uses an algorithm to calculate an insurance quote. However, you don't want customers to know how the calculation works, so you need to keep the algorithm secret

If you code these things using ASP, then it means that your code isn't available for end-users to view through their browser. In other words, writing your pages with ASP is much more secure than writing them in pure HTML. Coding in ASP enables us to ensure that things like sensitive database queries and proprietary formulas are kept away from prying eyes.

Summary

In this chapter we've learned about the difference between static and dynamic web pages, and we've talked about some of the different ways in which you can add dynamic behavior to your web pages. This book focuses on ASP as a technology for writing dynamic web pages, so we have looked at some of the main advantages that ASP-generated HTML offers over pure hard-coded HTML, and why you might want to use ASP to enhance your web pages. There are other technologies on the Web that also rely on server-side processing, but we haven't considered them here.

We have looked at the things you'll need to run ASP, and where you can find them. We've covered how to set up IIS 5.0, and how to set up a directory in which to place the examples that we'll meet in the remainder of this book.

We created our first ASP page, and viewed it; we looked at some of the common pitfalls that you might encounter when checking that your ASP example is correctly set up. In order to provide a *general* overview of why you'd want use ASP, we've avoided detailed explanation of ASP code, and how to write the ASP scripts within your .asp files. We'll move onto that in forthcoming chapters.

Here's a reminder of some things we learned in this chapter, which are worth remembering at all times:

❑ You can use any text editor to create an ASP page

❑ ASP code is processed on the web server, and then the subsequent HTML code it creates is sent back to the browser

❑ You can use any modern browser to view an ASP page

In the next chapter we'll take a closer look at the differences between running your programs on the server and running them on the client; and we'll investigate why we might choose one of these in preference to the other.

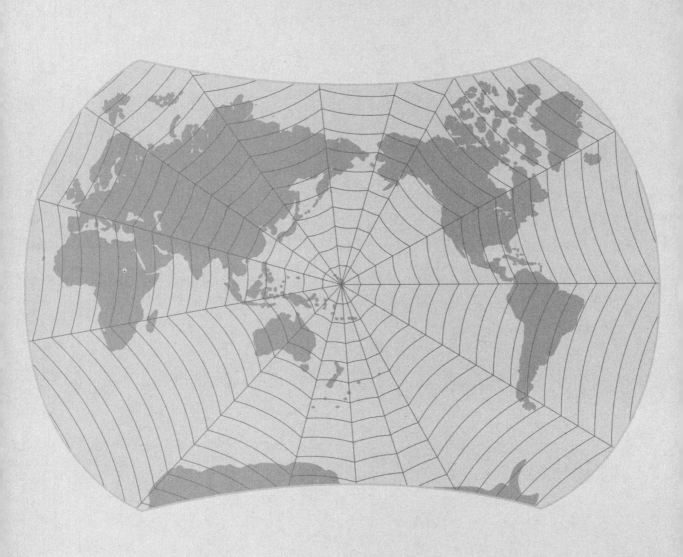

Server-Side Scripting and Client-Side Scripting

In the first chapter we introduced Active Server Pages, and we demonstrated how you'd go about setting up your web server and getting Active Server Pages working. We learned that ASP web pages are a mixture of plain text, HTML code and ASP script. We also learned that ASP pages are stored as `.asp` files on the server – when a user requests an ASP page, the ASP script contained in the `.asp` file is processed on the server before the resulting HTML is sent to the browser.

What we haven't done is discuss the workings of ASP in any detail, or how web servers interpret ASP. In this chapter, we aim to reinforce your understanding of the workings of ASP, by describing three different models. First, we'll look at how information is transmitted between the browser and web server; second, we'll examine how the web server handles web page requests; and third, we'll see how the ASP script engine on your web server actually handles lines of ASP script code.

We'll also look at the two ways at which script can be handled, either on the web server or the browser; and we will explain why ASP script can only be handled on the server. Once we've looked at how ASP works, we'll look in greater depth at ASP itself and break it up into its individual objects. So we'll be explaining the following:

❑   How do web servers work? What do they do?

❑   What is a web application?

❑   What is a request? What is a response? And how do they relate to the roles of the browser and web server?

❑   What's the difference between server-side scripting and client-side scripting?

❑   What is the ASP object model?

❑   What other methods, apart from ASP, can be used to generate dynamic web pages?

This is the second and last of our foundation chapters. We'll be writing some ASP pages in this chapter, but they'll be mainly for illustrative purposes – we'll avoid in-depth discussions of syntax and programming technique until we've laid down the concepts of ASP programming. We'll begin to work on ASP syntax and techniques in Chapter 3.

How the Web Server Works

In the first chapter we introduced the notion of a **web server** – a piece of software running on a computer that distributes web pages to users on demand, and provides an area in which to store and organize the pages of a web site. The machine that runs the web server software could be a remote machine sitting at the other side of your network, or even on the other side of the world, or it could be your very own home machine. We also introduced the idea that the user's browser was the **client** in this relationship, and we saw how ASP fits into this 'client–server' relationship.

These days, the term *client–server* is probably overused; but in fact, when used to describe the workings of the web, it's almost perfect. In a nutshell, the **client–server relationship** describes the distribution of tasks between a *server* (which stores, processes and distributes data, like an ATM or cashpoint machine) and the *clients* that access the server (like customers queuing to get their money out), in order to achieve universal access for the network on which they are connected.

The client–server scenario is also commonly known as a **two-tier system**. More generally, application architecture has talked in terms of *n*-tier systems, where *n* refers to the number of layers in the system. In the client–server scenario, there are two layers. In Chapter 12, we'll introduce a third layer – the database layer – and we'll start to think in terms of three-tier examples. But for now, let us expand on the two-tier or client–server system, as it relates to web pages.

How the Web Server and Browser Communicate

It probably won't surprise you to learn that, when we discussed the communication between web server and browser in Chapter 1, we gave an over-simplified picture of what really happens. In particular, we side-stepped any explanation of the physical processes involved in the transfer of information across the Internet. In this section, we return to discuss that topic in more depth. We won't digress into a full-scale history of the Internet and the World Wide Web – it's covered in many other places. Instead, we'll look at the physical workings of the Internet and intranet networks.

Internet Protocols and Railway Systems

The Internet is a network of interconnected nodes, in the same way that the subway system of a large city is a network of interconnected railway stations. The subway system is designed to carry *people* from one place to another; by comparison, the Internet is designed to carry *information* from one place to another.

While a subway system is built on a basis of steel (and other materials), the Internet uses a suite of networking protocols (known as **TCP/IP**) to transfer information around the Internet. A **networking protocol** is simply a method of describing information packets so they can be sent down your telephone-, cable-, or T1-line from node to node, until it reaches its intended destination.

One advantage of the TCP/IP protocol is that it can reroute information very quickly if a particular node or route is broken or is just plain slow. The perfectly-designed railway system would work in much the same way – taking passengers efficiently by a different route whenever one of the stations or tracks was closed down for repair.

When the user tells the browser to go fetch a web page, the browser parcels up this instruction using a protocol called the **Transmission Control Protocol** (or **TCP**). TCP is a transport protocol, which provides a reliable transmission format for the instruction. It ensures that the entire message is correctly packaged up for transmission (and also that it is correctly unpacked and put back together after it reaches its destination).

Before the parcels of data are sent out across the network, they need to be addressed. So a second protocol called **Hypertext Transfer Protocol** (or **HTTP**) puts an address label on it. HTTP is the protocol used by the World Wide Web in the transfer of information from one machine to another – when you see a URL prefixed with `http://`, you know that the internet protocol being used is HTTP.

> *Internet protocols (such as HTTP and FTP) control addressing and delivery, while transport protocols (such as TCP) ensure that each message is broken down, transported and reassembled correctly.*
>
> *So if the Internet is like a railway system, then a web page request is like a non-stop train journey from A to B. Here, TCP is like the seating system that breaks down a group of passengers and freight into different sections of the train; while HTTP or FTP is like the intended destination instruction that is given to the train driver before the train departs.*

The message passed from the browser to the web server is known as an **HTTP request**. When the web server receives this request, it checks its stores to find the appropriate page. If the web server finds the page, it parcels up the HTML contained within (using TCP), addresses these parcels to the browser (using HTTP), and sends them back across the network. If the web server cannot find the requested page, it issues a page containing an error message (in this case, the dreaded Error 404: Page Not Found) – and it parcels up and dispatches that page to the browser. The message sent from the web server to the browser is known as the **HTTP response**.

Here's an illustration of the process as we understand it so far.

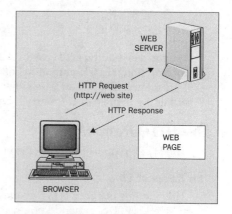

Going Deeper into HTTP

There's still quite a lot of technical detail missing here, so let's dig further down and look more closely at exactly how HTTP works. When a request for a web page is sent to the server, this request contains more than just the desired URL. There is a lot of extra information that is sent as part of the request. This is also true of the response – the server sends extra information back to the browser. It's these different types of information that we'll look at in this next section.

A lot of the information that is passed within the HTTP message is generated automatically, and the user doesn't have to deal with it directly, so you don't need to worry about transmitting such information yourself. While you don't have to worry about creating this information yourself, you should be aware that this extra information is being passed between machines as part of the HTTP request and HTTP response – because the ASP that we write can allow us to have a direct effect on the exact content of this information.

Every HTTP message assumes the same format (whether it's a client request or a server response). We can break this format down into three sections: the **request/response line**, the **HTTP header** and the **HTTP body**. The content of these three sections is dependent on whether the message is an HTTP request or HTTP response – so we'll take these two cases separately.

Let's just pause and illustrate our understanding of the process now:

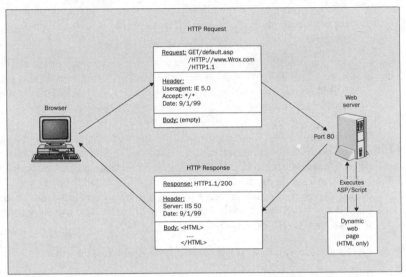

We can see that the HTTP request and HTTP response have broadly similar structures and that there is information that is common to both, which is sent as part of the HTTP header. There are other pieces of information that can only be known to either the browser or the server, and that are also sent as part of either the request or response. It makes sense to examine their constituent parts in greater detail.

The HTTP Request

The HTTP request is sent by the browser to the web server and it contains the following.

The Request Line

The first line of every HTTP request is the **request line**, which itself contains three pieces of information: first, an HTTP command known as a **method**; second, the URL of the file that the client is requesting; third, the version number of HTTP. So, an example request line might look like this:

```
GET /testpage.htm HTTP/1.1
```

The method is used to tell the server the amount of information the browser requires, and how much information is being sent. Here are three of the most common methods that might appear in this field:

Method	Description
GET	This is a request for information residing at a particular URL. The majority of HTTP requests made on the Internet are GET requests. The information required by the request can be anything from an HTML or ASP page to the output of a VBScript, JavaScript or PerlScript program or some other executable. You can send some limited data to the browser, in the form of an attachment to the URL.
HEAD	This is the same as the GET method except that it indicates a request for the HTTP header only and no data.
POST	This request indicates that data will be sent to the server as part of the HTTP body. This data is then transferred to a data-handling program on the web server. For example, we'll use this setting in Chapter 7 to pass information, which will then be used on the server as part of the ASP-handling process.

There are a number of other methods supported by HTTP – including PUT, DELETE, TRACE, CONNECT, OPTIONS. As a rule, you'll find that these are less common; they are beyond the scope of this discussion.If you want to know more about these, take a look at RFC 2068, which you'll find at http://www.cis.ohio-state.edu/htbin/rfc/rfc2068.html.

The HTTP Header

The next bit of information sent is the **header**. This contains details of what document types the client will accept back from the server; the type of browser that has requested the page; and the date and general configuration information. The HTTP request's header contains information that falls into three different types:

❑ **General**: contains information about either the client or server, but not specific to one or the other

❑ **Entity**: contains information about the data being sent between the client and server

❑ **Request**: contains information about the client configuration and different types of acceptable documents

An example header might look like this:

```
ACCEPT:*/*
ACCEPT_LANGUAGE:en-us
CONNECTION:Keep-Alive
HOST:webdev.wrox.co.uk
REFERER:http://webdev.wrox.co.uk/books/SampleList.asp?bookcode=3382
USER_AGENT:Mozilla/4.0 (compatible; MSIE 5.01; Windows NT 5.0)
```

As you can see, the header is composed of a number of lines; each line contains the description of a piece of header information, and then its value.

There are a lot of headers, and most of them are optional, so HTTP has to indicate when it has finished transmitting the header information. To do this, a blank line is used. A list of HTTP headers can be found in Appendix I.

The HTTP Body

If the POST method was used in the HTTP request line, then the HTTP request **body** will contain any data that is being sent to the server – for example data that the user typed into an HTML form. (We'll see examples of this later in the book). Otherwise, the HTTP request body will be empty.

The HTTP Response

The HTTP response is sent by the server back to the client browser, and contains the following.

The Response Line

The **response line** contains only two bits of information: first, the HTTP version number; and second, an HTTP request code that reports the success or failure of the request. An example response line might look like this:

```
HTTP/1.0 200 OK
```

This example returns the HTTP status code 200, which represents the message 'OK'. This denotes the success of the request, and that the response contains the required page or data from the server. You may recall that we mentioned the status code 404 a few pages ago – if the response line contains a 404 then the web server failed to find the requested page. Error code values are three-digit numbers, where the first digit indicates the class of the response. There are five classes of response:

Code class	Description
100-199	These codes are informational – they indicate that the request is currently being processed
200-299	These codes denote success – that the web server received and carried out the request successfully
300-399	These codes indicate that the request hasn't been performed, because the information required has now been moved
400-499	These codes denote a client error – that the request was either incomplete, incorrect or impossible
500-599	These codes denote a server error – that the request appeared to be valid, but that the server failed to carry it out

You'll find a full listing of these error codes in Appendix G.

The HTTP Header

The HTTP response **header** is similar to the request header, which we discussed above. In the HTTP response, the header information again falls into three types:

- ❑ **General**: contains information about either the client or server, but not specific to one or the other
- ❑ **Entity**: contains information about the data being sent between the client and the server
- ❑ **Response**: Information about the server sending the response and how it can deal with the response

Once again, the header consists of a number of lines, and uses a blank line to indicate that the header information is complete. Here's a sample of what a header might look like:

```
HTTP/1.1 200 OK                                  the status line
Date: Mon, 1st Nov 1999, 16:12:23 GMT            the general header
Server: Microsoft-IIS/4.0                        the response header
Last-modified: Fri, 29th Oct 1999, 12:08:03 GMT  the entity header
```

The first line we've already discussed, the second is self-explanatory. The third line indicates the type of software the web server is running, and as we are requesting a file somewhere on the web server, the last bit of information refers to the last time the page we are requesting was modified.

The header can contain much more information than this, or different information, depending on what exactly is requested. If you want to know more about the different types of information contained in the three parts of the header, you'll find them listed in RFC 2068 (Sections 4.5, 7.1 and 7.2).

The HTTP Body

If the request was successful, then the HTTP response **body** contains the HTML code (together with any script that is to be executed by the browser), ready for the browser's interpretation.

How Scripting Languages Work

So now we've got a better understanding of how a browser sends a web page request, and how the web server sends the page back to the browser. If you cast your mind back to the 6-step process for delivering a web page, you'll recognize that these correspond to Steps 2 and 5. Let's remind ourselves of those six steps again:

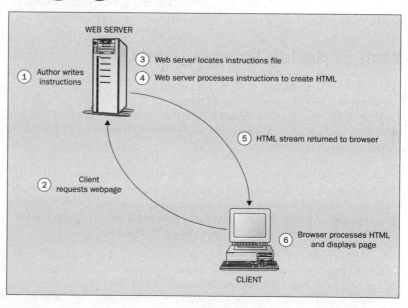

In between, as we saw in Chapter 1, the web server needs to locate the page that was requested (Step 3); and, if it's an ASP page, then the web server will need to process the ASP, in order to generate the HTML that is returned to the browser (Step 4).

Well, we've studied many of the necessary aspects surrounding ASP, but our understanding of the ASP processing itself is still rather sketchy. Up to now, for simplification, we've discussed it rather as though the ASP script engine were like a sausage machine – the web server feeds in the raw ASP code 'meat' at one end, and out of the other end comes a neatly packaged product. It's time to demystify this process.

The first attempts to add depth to the capability provided by the HTML language involved creating a mixture of pure HTML code and programming commands. As we saw in Chapter 1, it's this that allows us to write instructions about how the page is to be created – effectively, we can write code (in the form of the programming commands), that will describe how the HTML should be put together at the time the page is requested.

In order to distinguish these nuggets of programming capability embedded within our HTML, we refer to them as **scripts**. However, HTML isn't a programming language, and so it's necessary to write these commands in other languages. We use the term **scripting language** to describe the languages in which these scripts are written.

HTML allows us to include scripts at (almost) any point in our HTML code – it does this by providing us with legal ways of inserting scripts, which we'll come to shortly. Subsequently, when the page has been requested and its HTML is being generated, each script within the page is sent to a **script host** (an application that communicates with different scripting engines). The script host in turn instructs the appropriate **script engine** to interpret the script.

Scripting languages form the basis of ASP. We use scripts to write the instructions that allow pages to be created dynamically. We also use scripts to access the various bits and pieces that ASP provides; these bits and pieces are known as **objects**, and we will look at them shortly.

Which Scripting Language to Use

There are quite a number of scripting languages. Arguably the two most popular at the moment (and certainly the two of interest to us in this book) are **VBScript** and **JavaScript**. JavaScript was the first client-side scripting language (we'll talk about the difference between client-side and server-side scripting shortly). The VBScript scripting language was developed by Microsoft – it's based on their Visual Basic programming language.

Each script that we write must be interpreted at the time it is requested. For this purpose, each scripting language has a script interpreter – the **script engine**. So a script or program written in VBScript must be sent to a VBScript script engine, and a script or program written in JavaScript must be sent to a JavaScript script engine. Microsoft's IIS 5.0 web server comes with script engines for both VBScript and JScript. (JScript is Microsoft's implementation of JavaScript.)

> Note that JavaScript shouldn't be confused with Java. In fact, JavaScript was originally to have been named LiveScript; at that time, Netscape had intended to market the language completely separately from Java. However, following the popularity of Java, Netscape teamed up with Sun during the development of LiveScript, changed its name to JavaScript, and borrowed several structures from Java's syntax. Hence, the JavaScript scripting language shares some superficial resemblances with its namesake.

Server-Side Scripting and Client-Side Scripting

What difference does the introduction of scripts make to the way the page is processed? For the most part, our model of the browser making a connection to the web server, sending a request, receiving a response and then interpreting the received HTML to construct a web page still holds true.

The only difference comes when, in the act of preparing a page to be sent to the browser, the server comes across a script. The first thing that the server must do is identify which machine is responsible for processing the script. This is an important point because, when we write a script, we can choose whether it is to be processed by the server or by the browser. Let's make this difference more precise:

- ❏ A script that is interpreted by the *web server* is called a **server-side script**. A server-side script is an instruction set that is processed by the server, and which generates HTML. The resulting HTML is sent as part of the HTTP response to the browser.

- ❏ A script that is interpreted by the *browser* is called a **client-side script**. A client-side script is also an instruction set, but it is *not* processed by the web server. Instead, it is sent to the browser (as part of the HTTP response) and is processed by the browser; the result is then displayed by the browser on the monitor.

So we can complete the picture that we began in Chapter 1, by adding one more step to take care of the client-side scripts:

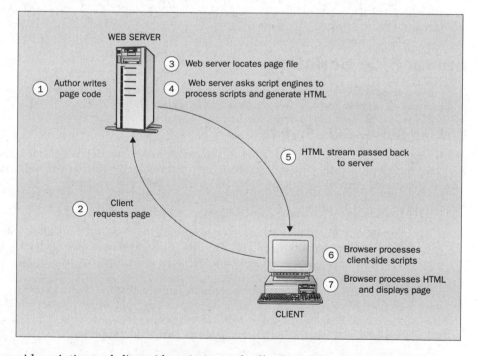

As we'll see, server-side scripting and client-side scripting each offer their own advantages. We'll have a look at client-side scripts later in the chapter, in order to put ASP (and other server-side scripting techniques) into context. First, let's take a look at some more ASP and other server-side scripts.

Identifying a Script

We've just been talking about how the web server identifies on which machine a script must be processed. But how do we identify a script, when it is embedded in a small or large amount of pure HTML? In fact, we already partially answered this question in Chapter 1 – because ASP (which is destined to be processed on the web server) will be enclosed in special <% ... %> tags, like this:

```
In Webserverland, the time is exactly <%= Time %>
```

Here, everything contained within the <% and the %> is assumed to be ASP, and is sent to the ASP script host for processing.

But there are other kinds of scripts, which are not ASP code, but which still need to be distinguished from the HTML and text in which they are embedded. For this reason, HTML provides a special tag – the <SCRIPT> tag:

```
<SCRIPT LANGUAGE=VBSCRIPT RUNAT=SERVER>
  Response.Write Time
</SCRIPT>
```

Anything that lies between an opening <SCRIPT> tag and a closing </SCRIPT> tag is dispatched for processing to the appropriate script engine, according to the instructions given by the SCRIPT tag's attributes. We'll use this to identify both client- and server-side scripts, as you'll see in the examples that follow.

Server-Side Scripting

As you've probably gathered by now, ASP is server-side scripting. However, it's not true to say that all server-side scripting is ASP – as we'll see in this section.

Writing Server-Side Scripts

If we're going to place any kind of server-side script within our web page source files, then we need to label the scripts – so that the server can identify them as server-side scripts and hence arrange for them to be interpreted correctly. There are two ways to label server-side scripts:

- ❑ Use the <% ... %> server script delimiters, which denote ASP code
- ❑ Use the HTML <SCRIPT> tag, specifying the RUNAT=SERVER attribute within the tag. If a tag like this is found within an .asp file, then it is treated as ASP. If such a tag is found within an .htm file, then it is treated as a non-ASP *client*-side script.

We must highlight an important difference here: namely, that the choice of .htm or .asp for the suffix of your web page file is not trivial – it really does have a bearing on how your code is processed. If you have any ASP at all, you can label it using either of the techniques used above. However, in order to ensure that it's processed as ASP, then it *must* be included as part of an .asp file.

Within an .htm file, it's only possible to use the <SCRIPT> ... </SCRIPT> tags – script contained within these tags will be interpreted as non-ASP scripts. If you try to include any ASP script within these tags, or if you write <% ... %> tags into an .htm file, then the script will not be executed and your web page won't look the way you intended.

Some Samples Using the HTML <SCRIPT> Tag

So, with all that under our belt, let's look at a sample using RUNAT=SERVER first:

```
...
<SCRIPT LANGUAGE=VBSCRIPT RUNAT=SERVER>
  ... VBScript code goes here
</SCRIPT>
...
```

In this first snippet, the <SCRIPT> tag specifies the scripting language that's been used for this script, and also indicates the target script host – the web server. The default (when using the <SCRIPT> tag) is for the script to be executed on the browser, so if you're writing a server-side script then you must specify this. By specifying the attribute of RUNAT as SERVER, we're making sure that it's processed on the server.

> *Bear in mind that this will be treated as ASP if and only if it is contained within an .asp file. That's especially useful later, when we come to write server-side scripts which use the ASP objects. We'll focus in-depth on the ASP objects from Chapter 7.*

The next sample looks rather similar:

```
...
<SCRIPT LANGUAGE=JSCRIPT RUNAT=SERVER>
  ... JScript code goes here
</SCRIPT>
...
```

The processes involved are similar to those we explained for the first sample. Notice that the script tag identifies the scripting language in which the enclosed scripts are written. You can use JScript and VBScript within the same page if you like, as long as each piece of script is contained within its own tags.

A <SCRIPT> section can be placed almost anywhere in the page. You'll often find scripts at the end of the HTML document, because that makes the code easier to read.

A Sample Using the ASP <% ... %> Tags

The second method doesn't involve the <SCRIPT> tag at all, but uses the <% and %> tags in place of them. These are generally more popular – they are a lot less cumbersome, they make the code easier to read, and they make it easier to distinguish between server and client side script:

```
...
<%
  ... ASP code goes here
%>
...
```

If you remembered that the <SCRIPT> tag allowed us to specify the scripting language, you might be wondering how you can specify the LANGUAGE attribute within the <% and %> tags. Well, it's done using a special notation, which applies to all of the script on a page:

```
<% @LANGUAGE = VBSCRIPT %>
```

67

However, ASP takes VBScript to be the default scripting language, so you'll rarely see this line. In fact, because this book chooses VBScript rather than other scripting languages, we won't need to specify the @LANGUAGE line in our ASP code.

An Example

Now we've looked at all the possible permutations and combinations for inserting scripts, it's time to try out an example.

Try It Out – Inserting a Server-Side (ASP) Script

For our first scripting example, we'll spare you the usual Hello World. Instead, we will use script instructions to 'write' the current date to an HTML document.

1. Using your preferred HTML editor, start a new document. Type the following code into it:

```
<HTML>
<HEAD>
<TITLE>Writing the Current Date to the Page with ASP Script</TITLE>
</HEAD>

<BODY BGCOLOR=WHITE>
<H2>Date Confirmation</H2>
<P>Today's date is
<SCRIPT LANGUAGE=VBSCRIPT RUNAT=SERVER>
Response.Write Date
</SCRIPT>
, and this is the first example in Chapter 2.
</BODY>
</HTML>
```

2. Save the file as `DateConf1.asp` in your `Inetpub\wwwroot\BegASP` directory.

3. Open your browser, and type the address http://*my_server_name*/BegASP/DateConf1.asp into the address line (don't forget to specify the name of your own server machine in this URL):

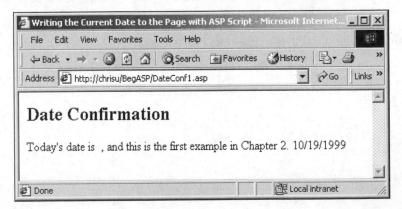

As you can see it works – sort of. The page contains all the right content, but not necessarily in the right order! The date comes *after* the period! There's a reason for this, which we'll explain in a moment.

4. Now create a new file, called `DateConf2.asp`. Place the following code into this new file (note that this code is similar to the code in `DateConf1.asp`, except for the lines that have been highlighted):

```
<HTML>
<HEAD>
<TITLE>Writing the Current Date to the Page with ASP Script</TITLE>
</HEAD>

<BODY BGCOLOR=WHITE>
<H2>Date Confirmation</H2>
<P>Today's date is
<%Response.Write Date %>
, and this is the second example in Chapter 2.
</BODY>
</HTML>
```

5. Save `DateConf2.asp` and view this example in your browser by typing in the URL http://*my_server_name*/BegASP/DateConf2.asp. You should get a similar result, however this time it'll be correctly formatted (subject to the odd floating space):

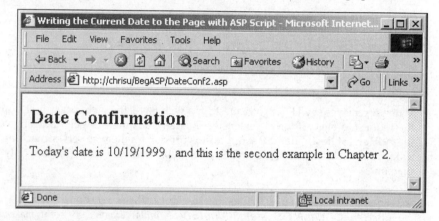

Well, what's that all about then?

How It Works

The first thing to notice is that both of these examples use the `.asp` suffix – so that the ASP script engine processes the server-side code.

In the body of the web page, we have a combination of some pure HTML, some plain text, and a little server-side script. In the first case, we specified the following script (the highlighted lines) that we wish to be processed on the server before the page is sent to the browser:

```
<P>Today's date is
<SCRIPT LANGUAGE=VBSCRIPT RUNAT=SERVER>
Response.Write Date
</SCRIPT>
, and this is the first example in Chapter 2.
```

As we explained earlier, the line `Response.Write Date` causes the date to be calculated and written to the HTML stream. But why did the date appear at the end of the page, rather than when it should have appeared after "Today's date is"?

The reason is this. When the web server finds a `<SCRIPT RUNAT=SERVER>` tag, it arranges for the script to be processed but it appends the resulting HTML at the *end* of the HTML stream. In other words, it takes no notice of the position of the `<SCRIPT>` tag relative to other elements of the page.

By contrast, the 'in-line' script command works perfectly when we use the ASP tags to denote it:

```
<P>Today's date is
<%Response.Write Date %>
, and this is the second example in Chapter 2.
```

There's an important lesson to be learned here. Namely, that all script tags do not have the same prevalence – some script tags are processed before others, depending on how we've identified them in the source.

We'll return to the issue of the **order of execution** later in this chapter.

How does IIS Handle Scripts in ASP Pages?

In the light of what we've just seen, let's look again at the process involved when a user requests an ASP page.

When it receives (by HTTP) a request for a web page, the web server first examines the file extension of the requested page. If the file extension is `.asp`, then the web server arranges for the ASP to be handled by the ASP script host. The ASP script host is present on the web server machine in the form of the file `asp.dll`, which is run by the web server itself. In fact the `asp.dll` can only be located on the web server machine.

> You can find the file `asp.dll` on the hard drive of your web server machine – try looking in the directory *C:\WinNT\System32\InetSrv* or similar. If you can't see it, make sure you've turned the **Show Hidden Files** option on in Windows Explorer. Be careful that you don't alter or delete the file!

The `asp.dll` file ensures that all the ASP code is interpreted. In fact, `asp.dll` is an Internet Services Application Programming Interface (ISAPI) extension to IIS, and is compiled as a Windows dynamic link library (DLL). Though this sounds daunting, it simply means that you can access your web server's functions directly, via the `asp.dll`, just by writing ASP code into your pages.

Now, `asp.dll` is a **script host**, so it farms out any scripts it finds to the appropriate script engines. It sends VBScript scripts to the VBScript engine, and it sends JScript scripts to the JScript engine. It's the responsibility of each script engine to interpret these scripts, and return a string of HTML to the script host. Then, the script host pulls all this together and returns it to the IIS web server, which in turn dispatches it to the browser – contained within the HTTP response.

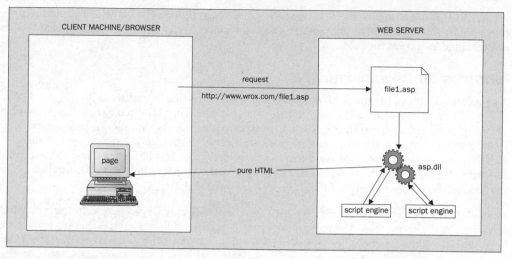

That's what happens if the user requested an `.asp` page. It's worth noting again that, if the file extension of the page is *not* `.asp`, then the web server will *not* use the ASP script host. Instead, the web server *itself* acts as the script host. So in this case, the web server takes responsibility for finding any server-side scripts, and sending them to the appropriate script engines (or to the browser) for interpretation.

Caching

Just to make your life a little bit harder, a process known as **caching** can further confuse the results that you get back from the web server. You may well be familiar with the process of caching on the browser. A **cache** is temporary storage area on your hard drive that is used by the browser to store web pages and graphics. This means that, if you browse a page that you've browsed before, the browser has the option of reading the pages from the local cache instead of connecting across the Internet to the web server.

Web servers also have caches and to save time when returning ASPs, they can cache the HTML results of previously-processed ASP scripts for immediate return. This can sometimes result in you receiving the output of a previously-processed ASP, even though you've updated it since. For example, if you amend a page and then view it in your browser, it can sometimes show old results. However, if you then try it again (perhaps by refreshing the browser) it will eventually deliver the new set of results. We touch upon caching again in Chapter 7, as one of the ASP objects makes use of it, but this is just a hint to make sure that when you run the examples you're seeing the same as our screenshots indicate.

Now, to put the notion of server-side scripting into context, let's look at what we mean by client-side scripting.

Client-Side Scripts

Client-side scripting is not directly related to ASP at all – it involves writing scripts that will be processed by the *browser*. When a web page source contains a client-side script, it does not attempt to process the script; instead, it simply downloads the script to the browser as part of the HTTP response, and assumes that the browser will know how to deal with it.

When the browser receives the HTTP response, it needs to process the HTML contained within, which describes how it is to display the page. The browser must also take care of the client-side scripts that were downloaded as part of the page.

Advantages and Disadvantages

As you might expect, the main advantage of client-side scripting over pure HTML is that it allows the developer to create more functional, interactive web pages. There are two clear advantages of client-side scripting over server-side scripting. First, the response times are often quicker, because the script is interpreted on the browser machine – so there is no network involved. This is a big advantage for repeated calculations because there's no round-trip to ask the server to calculate things. Second, executing script on the browser means that there's less script to be executed on the web server; reducing the web server's workload can be advantageous if lots of people use your web site.

However, when weighing up the choice between client-side and server-side scripting, you must also consider the disadvantages. The main disadvantage of client-side scripting is that we can't depend on the browser having the functionality to support the scripts we write. If you have two different client machines that host two different browsers, and you view a page that contains a client-side script on each, then you can reasonably expect the results to be quite different.

In other words, client-side scripting is **browser specific** – because some browsers do not have the capability to interpret certain scripting languages. For example:

❑ Recent versions of Internet Explorer come with script engines for both VBScript and for JScript – although older versions of the browser come by default with older versions of the scripting engines.

❑ Netscape Navigator browsers come with a JavaScript script engine only - there is no support for VBScript. So, at best, any client-side VBScript in your page does not look quite as intended – and at worst, it'll cause an error message.

It is possible to allow Netscape browsers to view the results of client-side VBScript – but it requires a manually-installed third party add-in on the client machine.

You'll find that JScript (or JavaScript) tends to be the language of choice on the web, as far as client-side coding is concerned. This has been further reinforced by the adoption of JavaScript as a standard, maintained by ECMA (European Computer Manufacturer's Standards) and known as ECMAScript – which sets a bottom line that both JScript and JavaScript can adhere to.

Another potential disadvantage of client-side scripting is that the code in your client-side scripts is completely visible to the user. Remember how we used the View | Source option in Internet Explorer, or the View | Page Source option on Netscape Navigator, to view the HTML source for the web page? Well, it also displays the code for any client-side scripts that were downloaded from the web server. So, if you want to keep your client-side script code a secret then you'll have to use complex encryption techniques – otherwise client-side scripting is not an option!

Writing Client-Side Scripts

As we now know, the HTTP response that is sent to the browser includes some pure HTML and some non-HTML code (that is, client-side script). In order to display the page, the browser first sends the client-side script to the appropriate script host on the client machine for interpretation; and it processes all of the HTML code itself.

So the browser, like the web server before it, needs to be able to look at the source and make a distinction between the pure HTML and the client script code. Once again, it is the HTML <SCRIPT> tags that allow this. If the browser detects a pair of <SCRIPT> and </SCRIPT> tags in the source, it assumes that anything that lies in between is script.

In order to illustrate this, we need a few samples. The following few snippets are fragments of HTML source files. Here's the first sample:

```
...
<SCRIPT LANGUAGE=VBSCRIPT>
   ... VBScript code goes here
</SCRIPT>
...
```

This code looks much like the samples we saw when we were discussing server-side scripts. There's one significant difference – we haven't specified the RUNAT attribute. Unless we specify otherwise, any scripts contained within the HTML <SCRIPT> ... </SCRIPT> tags are assumed to be client-side scripts; so in fact, this code fragment is equivalent to the following:

```
...
<SCRIPT LANGUAGE=VBSCRIPT RUNAT=CLIENT>
   ... VBScript code goes here
</SCRIPT>
...
```

Note that if you were to include code like this in a page, it must be saved as a .htm or .html page, and must not have the suffix .asp (because the RUNAT=CLIENT expression will cause an error). To run a script on the client side, you can completely omit the RUNAT attribute. For example, if we wanted to write a client-side script using JavaScript, we could use the following:

```
...
<SCRIPT LANGUAGE=JAVASCRIPT>
   ... JavaScript code goes here
</SCRIPT>
...
```

Again, you can write a page that contains both JavaScript scripts and VBScript scripts – you need to use a new <SCRIPT> tag for each new script. And again, each <SCRIPT> section can be placed almost anywhere in the page. In client-side scripting, some authors prefer to place most of their scripts at the end of the HTML document, so that the rest of the page can be loaded and rendered by the browser *before* the interpreter loads and runs the code. In this way, the whole of the page can be loaded first – instead of having to wait while alternate chunks of HTML and script are processed. Of course, if we were using 'in-line' scripts to write something into a particular position in the page, then we'd need to place the <SCRIPT> section at the appropriate position in relation to the surrounding HTML:

```
...
The local time in Browserland is exactly
<SCRIPT LANGUAGE=VBSCRIPT> Document.Write Time</SCRIPT>
<P>
...
```

In this snippet, the browser must execute the `Time` function (which is a VBScript function) and pass the result to the `Write` method of something called the `Document` object. The `Write` method writes the information into the page at the point where it's called, so the result is something like this (don't worry about typing this example in – we'll give you a full working one very shortly):

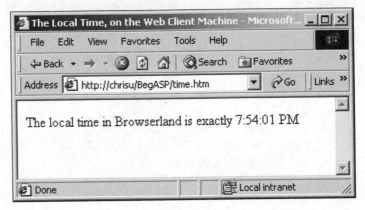

Don't worry – you're not expected to know about methods and objects just yet! In particular, the `Document` object is not of great importance to us in this book – all you need to know is that it is part of the browser (it's not an ASP object) and that it allows client-side scripts to write information on the web page.

Before we move on, you might like to compare the code above with the equivalent line in the Punctual Web Server example, from Chapter 1, in which we used the ASP <% ... %> tags to create a server-side script, and displayed the time as calculated by the web server:

```
In Webserverland, the time is exactly <% = Time %>
```

Comment Tags

As we've mentioned, successful execution of a snippet of script is dependent on whether your browser supports the requisite scripting language. What happens if you're using an older version of Navigator or Internet Explorer to browse a web page that contains script? The script will simply be displayed as text on the web page, which is all very messy and not at all what you'd want to happen.

So, the traditional way to prevent the code from being displayed as part of the page is to enclose the contents of the <SCRIPT> section within a pair of **comment tags**. If the user's browser is not script enabled, then it will ignore any code contained within comment tags; while browsers that *do* support scripting will still be able to interpret and execute the script. (If, for example, we have a browser that only supports JavaScript, then the comments will allow any VBScript to be ignored.) Here's how we'd add comment tags to the above code fragment:

```
...
The local time in Browserland is exactly
<SCRIPT LANGUAGE=VBSCRIPT>
<!-- hide from older browsers
Document.Write Time
-->
</SCRIPT>
...
```

In order to 'comment out' a JavaScript script, the comment tags used are slightly different (and you should be careful not to confuse them!). Here's an example:

```
The local time in Browserland is exactly
<SCRIPT LANGUAGE=JAVASCRIPT>
<!--
d = new Date();
document.write(d);
//-->
</SCRIPT>
```

Notice the positioning of the comment tags < ! - - ... - -> or < ! - - ... //- ->, and in particular, that we've placed the comment tags and the script code on different lines. Placing the tags on the same line as the script code can result in some browsers being unable to interpret the enclosed script. If the opening and closing tags both appear on the same line then the whole of that line acts as a comment; if the tags appear on two separate lines, the lines containing the opening and closing tags, and the lines contained within, are all considered as comment lines.

Of course, many browsers will be able to deal with script like this – indeed support for a scripting language is pretty much a prerequisite in many of the latest versions. But if you are writing client-side scripts, consider safety first – it doesn't hurt to use comments to 'hide' client-side scripting from any older browsers that might attempt to load your page.

A Client-Side Script using VBScript

OK, now we've talked enough about client-side scripts to try out a simple example.

Try It Out – A Client-Side Script Using VBScript

For our first client-side scripting example, we'll take the example that we created in server-side script and turn the script into a client-side script, which 'writes' the current date to an HTML document.

1. Use your editor to create a new file, and type in the following (note that this is quite similar to `DateConf2.asp` – the differences are highlighted):

```
<HTML>
<HEAD>
<TITLE>Writing the Current Date to a Document with Client-side VBScript</TITLE>
</HEAD>

<BODY BGCOLOR=WHITE>
<H2>Date Confirmation</H2>
<P>Today's date is
<SCRIPT LANGUAGE=VBSCRIPT>
<!--
Document.Write Date
-->
</SCRIPT>
, and this is the third example in Chapter 2.
</BODY>
</HTML>
```

2. Save the file as `DateConf3.htm`, in your `\Inetpub\wwwroot\BegASP` directory. Note that we're saving it as an `.htm` file, not as an `.asp` file. That's because there isn't any ASP in this example.

3. Open Internet Explorer, and type the address http://*my_server_name*/BegASP/DateConf3.htm into the address line:

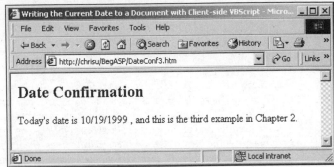

The HTML output shows a single sentence, containing the current date. The date is generated by the VBScript code, which is executed on the client, and is formatted in the default date format used by the client computer.

How It Works

The first thing to highlight is that we've saved this file with the suffix `.htm`. We *could* have saved it as an `.asp` file –and if we had, then the ASP script engine (on the web server, remember) would be called into action at the time the page is requested. However, there's no ASP code in this page so the ASP script engine would have been redundant.

In older versions of the IIS web server, just adding an `.asp` extension would actually have been enough to *impede* the performance of the page, because the web server would automatically send the page for processing. However, IIS 5.0 is intelligent enough to check your page for ASP code before sending it to the ASP script host; and if there's no ASP code then it won't send it for processing. There is still a small performance price to be paid for getting the page checked by the server for ASP code first anyway. But the point is this: when there's no ASP code in the page, an `.htm` or `.html` extension is normally sufficient.

In this case, the page consists of only text, some HTML and a client-side script – all of which are interpreted by the browser. When the browser comes across a `<SCRIPT>` tag, it knows that it needs to send the code to the appropriate script engine. In this example, we've specified the `LANGUAGE` attribute in the `<SCRIPT>` tag, for clarity:

```
<SCRIPT LANGUAGE=VBSCRIPT>
...
</SCRIPT>
```

This attribute indicates that the script contained within is written in VBScript and must be interpreted by a VBScript script engine.

The next part of the program is the VBScript itself:

```
Document.Write Date
```

This causes the browser's VBScript script engine to execute the built-in VBScript Date function, which returns a value containing the current date; and tells an entity known as the Document object to use its Write method to display this date value as part of the page.

Incidentally, the mysterious Document object is (quite literally) a representation of the HTML document or web page that is being currently displayed in the browser. However, as we said before, the Document object isn't part of ASP: it's something that is created by the browser, and is held only on the client side. You can use the Document object in Dynamic HTML to get information about the document, to analyze and modify the HTML elements and text in the document; and to process events.

We'll discuss the concept of objects more fully at the beginning of Chapter 6. We won't be looking at browser objects like Document in any detail, since they aren't part of ASP.

Let's see what happens if we try to run this example on a browser that doesn't support VBScript. Here's what the page looks like on Netscape Communicator 4.6.

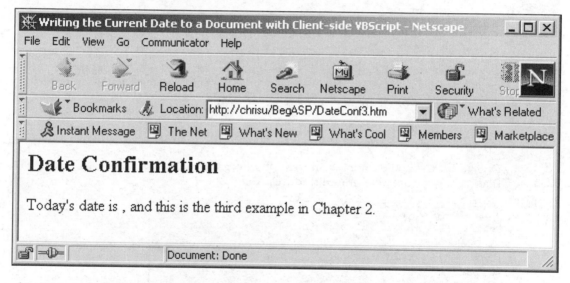

As you can see, the browser has detected the comment tags and recognized that it can't deal with the VBScript – so it's left it out. Note also that there's no error message, so the page appears to load smoothly. If your VBScript script only performs tasks that are non-essential to the overall page (things like dynamic graphics, for example) then it ensures that the user still has a smooth ride. But if, as in this case, the VBScript performs an essential task, then we still don't get the output that we want.

A Client-Side Script using JavaScript

That's all we need to know about VBScript scripts for now. Next, we'll have a look at how to insert a JavaScript script into our code.

Try It Out – Client-Side Script Using JavaScript

We'll reconstitute the date confirmation program once more, this time replacing the client-side VBScript with client-side JavaScript.

1. Use your HTML editor to create one more new file, and add the following code. It's similar to `DateConf3.htm`, and the differences have been highlighted below:

```
<HTML>
<HEAD>
<TITLE>Writing the Current Date to a Document with Client-side JavaScript</TITLE>
</HEAD>

<BODY BGCOLOR=WHITE>
<H2>Date Confirmation</H2>
<P>Today's date is
<SCRIPT LANGUAGE=JAVASCRIPT RUNAT=CLIENT>
<!--
d = new Date();
document.write (d);
//-->
</SCRIPT>
, and this is the fourth example in Chapter 2.
</BODY>
</HTML>
```

In this example, take extra care to ensure that you use the correct case when typing in this example. JavaScript is case sensitive, so – for example – it will treat date *and* Date *differently.* Date *is a built-in JavaScript object; however, if you try to use* date *then JavaScript will not recognize it, and will throw errors at you.*

2. Save the file as `DateConf4.htm`.

3. Open a browser, and type the address http://my_server_name/ BegASP/DateConf4.htm into the address line:

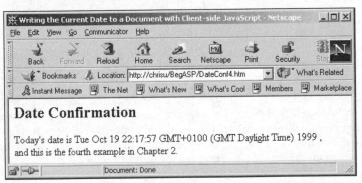

How It Works

It works in much the same way as the client-side VBScript example that we saw a moment ago. Here's the JavaScript:

```
d = new Date();
document.write (d);
```

This all looks rather frightening, doesn't it? The first line in this short two-line program basically creates the built-in JavaScript object, `Date`, which is found on the client-side, in the browser, and generates the current date. The program reads this date into something known as a **variable** (we're not going to explain variables here, but they are covered in detail in Chapter 4). The second line displays the contents of the variable.

Choosing Between VBScript and JavaScript

JavaScript can be more difficult than VBScript for the novice programmer to master – and it's often even more confusing to try to learn two languages at once! This, in itself, is a good enough reason for selecting VBScript as the language of choice for the remainder of this book. Of course, this book is oriented towards server-side scripting with ASP – and, conveniently, VBScript is the default scripting language on the IIS web server.

On the *client* side, the more widely-supported scripting language is JavaScript. It's worth noting that client-side script can help to ease your web server's load. We'll see an example of this in the **Wrox Classifieds** ASP application that we'll build in Chapter 15 – which employs a couple of useful little client-side scripts to perform data-checking functions on the browser, and hence reduce the number of times the browser needs to communicate with the web server.

So ultimately, you may wish to learn about JavaScript too. However, VBScript is a great way to get into scripting, and so it is the language that we'll be learning throughout the course of this book.

If you do want to know more about JavaScript, you may be interested in Beginning JavaScript *(Wrox, ISBN 1-861004-06-0).*

The Order of Execution

Now we've spent time understanding server-side and client-side scripts, and the role of the script hosts and script engines, we can write a series of examples which will allow us to explore the mysterious 'order of execution' a little further.

Try It Out – Testing the Order of Execution

For the first of these examples, we'll create a script that writes a series of ten lines of text to the browser. However, some of these lines will be written using pure HTML; some will be written using ASP (as indicated by the `<% ... %>` tags); and some will be written using server-side VBScript (as indicated by the `<SCRIPT LANGUAGE=VBSCRIPT RUNAT=SERVER>` tag).

1. Open your HTML editor, create a new file, and type the following code:

```
<HTML>
<HEAD>
<TITLE>Testing the Order of Execution</TITLE>
</HEAD>

<BODY BGCOLOR=WHITE>
Line 1: First HTML line<BR>
<% Response.Write "Line 2: First ASP line<BR>" %>
Line 3: Second HTML line<BR>
<SCRIPT LANGUAGE=VBSCRIPT RUNAT=SERVER>
  Response.Write "Line 4: First server-side VBScript line<BR>"
</SCRIPT>
Line 5: Third HTML line<BR>
<% Response.Write "Line 6: Second ASP line<BR>"%>
Line 7: Fourth HTML line<BR>
<SCRIPT LANGUAGE=VBSCRIPT RUNAT=SERVER>
  Response.Write "Line 8: Second server-side VBScript line<BR>"
</SCRIPT>
Line 9: Fifth HTML line<BR>
<% Response.Write "Line 10: Third ASP line<BR>"%>
</BODY>
</HTML>
```

As you can see, some of these lines will be interpreted by the ASP script host, and some directly by the server-side VBScript script engine. We've numbered these ten lines of text, and each one indicates the method that we've used to write the line.

2. Save the file as `ExecOrder1.asp` in your `\Inetpub\wwwroot\BegASPFiles` directory. Since this page contains ASP code, we *must* save the file using an `.asp` extension.

3. Go back to your browser and type the address http://*my_server_name*/ BegASP/ExecOrder1.asp into the address line. Don't forget to specify the name of your web server. If you follow these instructions you should get something that looks like this:

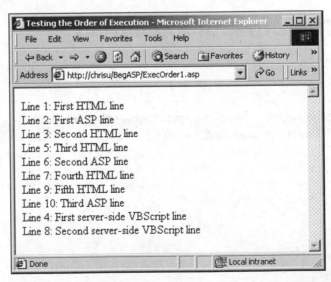

This is perhaps not exactly what you expected – after all, we did write lines 1 to 10 in the right order in the code! But we can use this result to determine which parts of the code are being interpreted in which order.

How It Works

As we noted at the start of the example, we've used three different methods to write different bits of the page's content:

❑   Pure HTML – for example, `Line 1: First HTML line<BR>`

❑   ASP code – for example, `<% Response.Write "Line 2: First ASP line<BR>"%>`

❑   Server-side script in a `<SCRIPT>` tag – for example,

```
<SCRIPT LANGUAGE=VBSCRIPT RUNAT=SERVER>
    Response.Write "Line 4: First server-side VBScript line<BR>"
</SCRIPT>
```

The unexpected order of the lines as they are displayed on the browser is due to the order in which the server processes the different elements of the code. The first of these methods doesn't require any processing on the part of the web server – it's pure HTML. The second and third parts both use the ASP command `Response.Write`, which allows to us to write things into the HTML stream that will be sent back to the browser. That's not the important issue in this example – in fact, we'll discuss `Response.Write` in depth in a later chapter. What's more important here are the *differences* between these two methods, and how they relate to the web server's order of execution.

To appreciate what the web server has done, let's take a look at the HTML source for the page. To do this in an IE browser, select View | Source from the browser's menu. In Netscape browsers, select View | Page Source. Here's what I get:

```
<HTML>
<HEAD>
<TITLE>Testing the Order of Execution</TITLE>
</HEAD>

<BODY BGCOLOR=WHITE>
Line 1: First HTML line<BR>
Line 2: First ASP line<BR>
Line 3: Second HTML line<BR>

Line 5: Third HTML line<BR>
Line 6: Second ASP line<BR>
Line 7: Fourth HTML line<BR>

Line 9: Fifth HTML line<BR>
Line 10: Third ASP line<BR>
</BODY>

</HTML>
Line 4: First server-side VBScript line<BR>Line 8: Second server-side VBScript
line<BR>
```

There are two important lessons we can get from this. First, note that lines 1, 2, 3, 5, 6, 7, 9, 10 appear in the HTML stream in the same order that we coded them originally. These are the lines that we wrote in pure HTML, and in <% ... %>-delimited ASP. This tells us that we can mix our pure HTML and our <% ... %>-delimited ASP in the original code as much as we like – and the web server will ensure that the order in which we code these things will be preserved.

In other words, we can write a mixture of bits of pure HTML and bits of 'in-line' ASP code, and the web server won't mess with that order. That's an important point – and one that we'll use to our advantage many times during this book.

There's a second lesson to learn here. It's pretty clear that, in the HTML source, lines 4 and 8 are missing from their original order – instead, they are appended at the *end* of the HTML source. Essentially, this is because the web server runs through the original code twice when it's generating the HTML to be sent to the browser. The first time, it *ignores* any script of the form <SCRIPT LANGUAGE=VBSCRIPT RUNAT=SERVER>, but handles other things (like pure HTML and ASP code); the second time it revisits those scripts, interprets them in order, and appends the resulting HTML onto the end of the existing HTML.

So, how is the order of execution affected if we try adding some JScript scripts? Let's try it out by making a small change to the example above.

Try It Out – Test the Order of Execution Using JScript

1. Copy the file `ExecOrder1.asp` to a new file; call that file `ExecOrder2.asp` and make the following changes to it:

```
<HTML>
<HEAD>
<TITLE>Testing the Order of Execution</TITLE>
</HEAD>

<BODY BGCOLOR=WHITE>
Line 1: First HTML line<BR>
<% Response.Write "Line 2: First ASP line<BR>" %>
Line 3: Second HTML line<BR>
<SCRIPT LANGUAGE=VBSCRIPT RUNAT=SERVER>
  Response.Write "Line 4: First server-side VBScript line<BR>"
</SCRIPT>
Line 5: Third HTML line<BR>
<% Response.Write "Line 6: Second ASP line<BR>"%>
Line 7: Fourth HTML line<BR>
<SCRIPT LANGUAGE=JSCRIPT RUNAT=SERVER>
  Response.Write ("Line 8: First server-side JScript line<BR>");
</SCRIPT>
Line 9: Fifth HTML line<BR>
<% Response.Write "Line 10: Third ASP line<BR>"%>
</BODY>
</HTML>
```

As you can see, it's quite similar to the previous example. All we've done is replace one of the server-side VBScript scripts with a server-side JScript script.

2. Save the `ExecOrder2.asp` file, and view it on your browser. The result, even more surprisingly, is this:

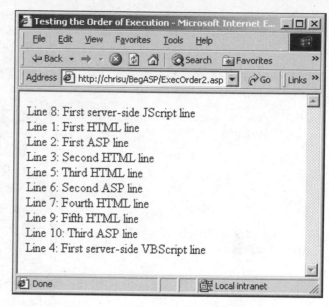

As you can see, the web server renders the JScript script first. Then it renders the HTML code and any code contained within `<% ... %>` delimiters, again ensuring that the code is processed 'in-line'; and the script contained within the `<SCRIPT LANGUAGE=VBSCRIPT RUNAT=SERVER>` tags is rendered last.

3. Now make the following changes to `ExecOrder2.asp`, and save the these changes as `ExecOrder3.asp`:

```
<%@ Language = JScript%>
<HTML>
<HEAD>
<TITLE>Testing the Order of Execution</TITLE>
</HEAD>

<BODY BGCOLOR=WHITE>
Line 1: First HTML line<BR>
<% Response.Write ("Line 2: First ASP line<BR>"); %>
Line 3: Second HTML line<BR>
<SCRIPT LANGUAGE=VBSCRIPT RUNAT=SERVER>
  Response.Write "Line 4: First server-side VBScript line<BR>"
</SCRIPT>
Line 5: Third HTML line<BR>
<% Response.Write ("Line 6: Second ASP line<BR>"); %>
Line 7: Fourth HTML line<BR>
<SCRIPT LANGUAGE=JSCRIPT RUNAT=SERVER>
  Response.Write ("Line 8: First server-side JScript line<BR>");
</SCRIPT>
Line 9: Fifth HTML line<BR>
<% Response.Write ("Line 10: Third ASP line<BR>"); %>
</BODY>
</HTML>
```

In this version, we've specified the ASP scripting language to be JScript (rather than the default, VBScript), and amended the syntax of the <% ... %>-delimited lines accordingly.

We won't be choosing JScript for our ASP scripts again in this book – but it's worthy of a mention. For the remainder of the book (after this example) we'll stick to using VBScript, the default scripting language for ASP.

4. Now view `ExecOrder3.asp` in your browser:

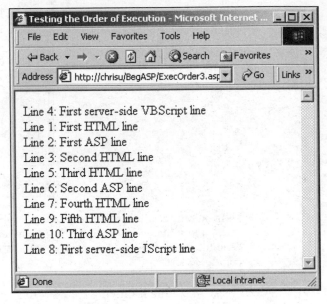

As a result of specifying JScript as the scripting language for ASP, lines 4 and 8 have been processed in a different order.

How It Works

ASP does not guarantee the order of execution of script written in different script blocks <SCRIPT RUNAT=SERVER>. At present it seems that the web server *first* processes scripts written in the language *other* than your ASP default language; and processes scripts written in your ASP default language at the end. In between, script written within <% ... %> delimiters are always processed in-line – relative to their position in the surrounding HTML.

If you write a script within a <SCRIPT RUNAT=SERVER> script block, it will be processed either at the beginning or at the end – it won't get processed in-line. Therefore, such script blocks are generally reserved for writing structures called **procedures** and **functions** – pieces of code that are separate from the main code for the page, and which are "called" into the page. We'll meet these later in the book.

In general, we'll be specifying server-side script using the <% ... %> delimiters – so these scripts are processed through the ASP script host, and are processed in-line.

What does ASP do for us?

Having looked at how the web server handles ASP, we've now studied its physical workings in as much detail as we will need for the purposes of this book. We've ascertained that ASP is actually an ISAPI DLL loaded onto your web server that allows server-side scripting. But this doesn't tell you about what ASP does, or how it manages the interaction between server and browser. Now let's take a look at all the different pieces that ASP provides us with and start considering what they may be used for.

ASP Objects and Components

ASP provides a compendium of objects and components, which manage interaction between the web server and the browser. For now, you can think of an **object** as being a neatly-packaged box, which contains a set of related functions and pieces of information, and you can think of a **component** as being a package of related objects. (Often, objects are grouped together into a single component so that they can be marketed as an application.) We'll take a more thorough look at objects in Chapter 6, and we'll build some components of our own in Chapter 16.

The ASP 'objects' can be manipulated by scripting languages. Take a look at the following diagram:

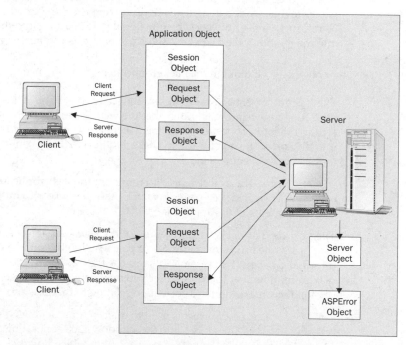

ASP functionality is divided up into seven **intrinsic objects**, each of which manages its own part of the interaction between the web client and web server. When we write ASP code, we use six of these objects – as you'll see over the course of the book, they are fundamental elements of our code, because they're what we use to program ASP actions. The seventh, the ASPError object, is used by IIS to handle errors and generate appropriate information about them. The components, by contrast, are self-contained pieces of functionality that are written specifically for ASP – each is a special add-on tool that allows the ASP author to achieve particular tasks, using ASP capability.

Let's take a quick tour through all of the different objects and components that come as part of ASP.

The ASP Intrinsic Objects

There are seven **ASP intrinsic objects**, which each deal with a specific aspect of interactivity: they are called `Request`, `Response`, `Server`, `Application`, `Session`, `ASPError` and `ObjectContext`. We'll look at each of these objects in much more detail over the Chapters 7–9 and 17, but for now we'll just explain them very briefly – because we'll begin to get used to using them as we progress through general scripting techniques in Chapters 3–5.

The `Request` and `Response` objects are, in a sense, the most self-explanatory. They represent the movement of information from client-to-server, and from server-to-client:

❑ The `Request` object is used to deal with a request that a user makes – that is, when they ask the browser to see a particular web page or web application. The 'request' might be made in the form of input from an HTML form, or just by typing in a URL.

❑ The `Response` object is used to deal with the server's response back to the browser. We've already seen an example of this, when we used the syntax `Response.Write "Hello!"`. When we write this, we're asking the web server to write the characters **Hello!** into the HTML that is to be returned to the browser. The functionality for writing into the HTML output is encapsulated into the method called `Write` – which, logically, is contained within the `Response` object.

The other objects work more in the background to further enhance the functionality available in ASP:

❑ The `Server` object is used represent the web server itself. Thus, it provides several commonly-used functions relating to things that the web server might do – such as creating new objects and setting timeout properties for scripts. There are also methods for translating character strings into the correct format for use in URLs and in HTML, by converting non-legal characters into the correct legal equivalent.

❑ The `Application` object is used to represent the web application (roughly speaking, a collection of related web pages hosted by the web server). Thus, we can use it to manage things like the contents of the application.

❑ The `Session` object is used to represent the user's session (essentially, the 'experience' that the user has while browsing a number of pages within the same web application), and to store information about that session. We can use the `Session` object to manage things like the maximum time that the web server will wait between user 'requests', before terminating the session (and releasing the information relating to that session).

❑ The `ObjectContext` object is used to manage transactions. It started out solely as part of ASP, but now has been integrated into the Windows 2000 operating system as a whole (along with Microsoft Transaction Server – a package with which it was closely related). It encompasses all of the other ASP objects, and you can reference each of them through `ObjectContext`. We'll talk about transactions and the `ObjectContext` object in Chapter 17.

❑ The `ASPError` object contains details of any errors generated by an ASP script or by the `asp.dll` itself.

We'll meet all of these objects formally, and learn how to use them, later in the book.

Active Server Components

Active Server components are components or DLLs that come freely with ASP (as opposed to components that are vended by third parties). They have a wide range of purposes, as you can see by the descriptions below. There are ten common components provided by Microsoft with IIS 5.0 (although different versions of the installation can add or remove components), and many more are available from third parties. We'll be looking at the most important ones in Chapter 11. For now, here's a brief summary of the components and what they do:

- ❑ The **Ad Rotator component** does exactly what you might expect – it's a rotator for the ads that appear on your page. More specifically, we use this component by supplying it with a list of images; it will arrange for one of the images to be displayed on the page each time the page is requested. It selects the images randomly, but takes account of a weighting factor, which reflects what proportion of the total number of requests should see that image. It also allows you to associate each image with a separate hyperlink, which takes the user straight to a related connected site by clicking.

- ❑ The **Browser Capabilities component** references a file called browscap.ini, which details every version of every Microsoft and Netscape browser ever created. It uses this information to determine whether or not the browser currently used supports frames, tables, and so on.

- ❑ The **Content Linking component** uses a text file to manage (and provide links for) a sequential set of web pages. It allows the administrator to provide extra information about each page in the sequence, and keeps the links in an orderly list so that they can be easily maintained. For example, it can be used to guide a visitor through a sequence of pages in a predetermined order.

- ❑ The **Content Rotator component** is a slimmed-down version of the Ad Rotator component, which just displays text.

- ❑ The **Counters component** creates an object that persists for the lifetime of an application and can be used to store, increment or retrieve a value. Counters are manually set, unlike page counters for example, which are set automatically, and persist until deleted.

- ❑ The **Logging Utility component** allows your applications to be able to read from your IIS log files which monitor who has been connecting to your site.

- ❑ The **MyInfo component** is used to store personal information about the server administrator.

- ❑ The **Page Counter component** provides a page counter, which increments by one each time a page is accessed. This is an automatic process, rather than a user-defined one.

- ❑ The **Permission Checker component** can be used to monitor whether a certain user has been given permission to read or execute a file.

- ❑ The **Tools component** provides a set of properties that are loosely grouped under the catch-all heading of 'miscellaneous utilities'. Includes checks to see if a certain file exists or if a certain user is the site owner.

The Microsoft Data Access Components – MDAC

In addition to the components listed above, there is a special group of components that come as part of the operating system, along with ASP, and are known as the **Microsoft Database Access Components** (**MDAC**). This in turn contains a group of objects that are known collectively as the **ActiveX Data Objects** (ADO). It also contains several components that are essential to the viewing of all sorts of data (databases, text files, spreadsheets etc) on all sorts of different platforms.

ADO enables data access, and allows data to be viewed, manipulated and updated via web pages (and, indeed, in other ways too). At the time of writing, the latest version is ADO 2.5 – which comes as part of MDAC 2.5. We look at data access via MDAC and ADO in detail in Chapters 12, 13 and 14.

The ASP Scripting Objects

Finally, there are three objects called `Dictionary`, `FileSystemObject` and `TextStream`, which are provided in a separate library file, and known as **Microsoft Scripting Runtime**:

❑ The `Dictionary` object is essentially a 2-column array, in which we might store a name/value or name/description pair on each row of the array.

❑ The `FileSystemObject` object is a tool for manipulating drives, folders and files on the web server.

❑ The `TextStream` object allows us to read the contents of a file as plain text.

We'll see more about these objects and some potential uses for them, in Chapter 10.

The Alternatives To ASP

Having explained what ASP is, you might be left with one or two nagging questions. For example: "What other technologies could do the same job as ASP?" Or, "If Microsoft provides ASP, then what are the non-Microsoft alternatives?"

Throughout these first two chapters we've avoided the temptation of describing ASP as something 'new', or as your 'only alternative', quite simply because neither of these statements would be true. ASP is only one of several technologies that can be used to create more dynamic and interactive web pages. Now that you have an idea of how ASP works, you'll be better able to understand how it stands in relation to other technologies and its contemporary competitors.

Microsoft is behind much of the drive towards the next generation of web technologies. However, Microsoft isn't the only organization pulling in the direction of interactive web sites: many of its competitors are also chipping away at the boundaries of interactive web capability.

Interactive web sites can be built with a combination of languages and technologies – you can use any one of these alone, or any number of them together, and they're all interdependent (in the sense that you don't have to learn one technology before you can learn another). Some exist on the client side while others (like ASP) work on the web server.

Client-Side Alternatives

There are four major client-side technologies, which can be used to augment your web pages. The technologies are a mish-mash of cross- and single-browser solutions that have persisted through the years. We'll look at them in roughly chronological order (the exception being that, although Java existed before JavaScript, they were implemented at the same time in Netscape Navigator 2.0).

Client-Side Scripting Languages

Scripting has been present in Internet Explorer since version 3, and in Netscape Navigator/Communicator since version 2. Internet Explorer versions 3, 4 and 5 support both JScript (Microsoft's implementation of JavaScript) and VBScript, while Communicator 4.5 (and probably 5 as well) supports only JavaScript. VBScript may be added to Navigator with the aid of a proprietary add-in, available (at a price) from http://www.ncompasslabs.com.

Scripting languages provide dynamic capabilities; for example, we can write a routine that is executed each time the user clicks on a particular button on the page. The main disadvantage, as we mentioned earlier, is that client-side scripts are dependent on the browser's implementation of the language, so not all browsers support all scripting languages; and even when they do, there are often marked differences between each browsers implementation and usage of different features.

Java

Java is a cross-platform language for developing applications. When Java first hit the Web in the mid-1990s, it created a tremendous stir. The idea is to use Java code in the form of **applets**, which are essentially Java components that can be easily inserted into web pages with the aid of the <APPLET> tag.

Java enjoys better functionality than scripting languages, offering better capabilities in areas such as graphic functions and file-handling. Java is able to provide these powerful features without compromising security because Java applets run in what is known as a **sandbox** – which prevents malicious programs downloaded from the web from doing damage to your system. Java also boasts strong database support through JDBC (Java Database Connectivity).

Microsoft and Netscape browsers both have built-in Java support, and there are several standard <OBJECT> and non-standard <APPLET> tags which are used to add Java applets to a web page. These tags tell the browser to download a Java file from a server and execute it with the Java Virtual Machine built into the browser. Of course, this extra step in the web page building phase means that Java applets can take a little while to download, and they can take even longer to process once on the browser. So while smaller Java applets (that provide features such as drop-down menus and animations) are very popular on the Web, larger ones are still not as widespread as scripted pages.

Although the popularity of Java today isn't quite what some people expected, it makes an ideal teaching tool for people wishing to break out into more complex languages; and its versatility makes it well-suited for programming web applications.

ActiveX Controls

An **ActiveX control** is a self-contained program (or component), written in a language such as C++ or Visual Basic. When added to a web page, an ActiveX control provides a specific piece of client-side functionality, such as a bar chart and graph, timer, client authentication, or database access. ActiveX controls are added to HTML pages via the <OBJECT> tag, which is now part of the HTML standard. ActiveX controls can be executed by the browser when they are embedded in a web page.

There is a catch. ActiveX controls were developed by Microsoft, and despite being compatible with the HTML standard, they are not supported on any Netscape browser prior to version 5 (which, at time of writing, was still in beta) without an ActiveX plug-in. Without this, they will only function on Internet Explorer, although there are plug-ins available if you want ActiveX functionality with Netscape browsers. Consequently, they still can't really be considered a cross-platform way of making your pages dynamic.

*ActiveX technology is also applicable to server-side functionality, in the form of **ActiveX** components.*

Dynamic HTML

Dynamic HTML (or DHTML) is really nothing more than a buzzword – it was introduced by both Microsoft and Netscape with their version 4 browsers, to advertise additional scripting features such as the ability to animate pages and graphics without a page refresh, and to position text precisely by using (x, y)-type coordinates. At the time, scripting was seeing a lower uptake than either company would have liked, so this move was intended to create a greater appeal to the masses, by dubbing it 'DHTML' and cashing in on HTML's familiarity and simplicity.

At the end of the day, the main innovation introduced in Dynamic HTML was the ability to manipulate any feature on a web page directly using client-side scripting. This was made available via the **Document Object Model**, but even together with the extra integration with style sheets, you're still creating your web page from client-side script and HTML. The main downside of DHTML was the fact that Microsoft and Netscape chose to implement these features in methods that were incompatible with one another. The advent of the version 5 browsers sees much tighter links with the standards, and hopefully a more cross-browser technology.

Server-Side Alternatives

There are also several more direct competitors to ASP. We're going to look at what we consider to be four important technologies, in chronological order starting with the oldest. They don't necessarily all perform the same tasks as ASP, but they all allow the user to achieve the same end-result – that of dynamic web applications. If ASP is not an ideal solution to your problems, then you might want to consider these following technologies, taking into account the following questions:

❑ Are they supported on the platform you use?

❑ Are they difficult to learn?

❑ Do they have extra capabilities, such as being able to parse XML?

We're not going to favor one option over another, but give a quick overview of what each one does.

CGI

The **Common Gateway Interface** (**CGI**) is a mechanism for creating scripts on the server, which can then be used to create dynamic web applications. It has been around for quite a bit longer than ASP, and right now the majority of dynamically-created pages on the web are created using CGI and a scripting language. However, it's incorrect to assume that CGI does the same job as ASP. Rather, CGI allows the user to invoke another program (such as a Perl script) on the web server to create the dynamic web page, and the role of CGI is to pass the user-supplied data to the this program for processing. However, it does provide the same end-result – a dynamic web application.

However, CGI has some severe shortcomings. The major one is that it adds an extra level to our browser–server model of interaction: namely, it's necessary to run a CGI program to create the dynamic page, before the page is processed on the server. Also, the format in which CGI receives and transmits data means that this data is not easily manipulated by many programming languages, so you have to use a programming language that has good facilities for manipulating text and communicating with other software. The most able programming languages that can work on any operating system for doing this are C, C++ and Perl. While they can adequately do the job for you, they're some of the more complex languages to learn. Visual Basic doesn't offer sufficiently adequate text-handling facilities, and is therefore rarely used with CGI.

ColdFusion

ColdFusion (http://www.allaire.com/products/ColdFusion) also enables servers to access data as the server builds an HTML page. Like ASP, ColdFusion pages are readable by any browser. ColdFusion also utilizes a proprietary set of tags, which are processed by the ColdFusion Server software. This server software can run on multiple platforms, including Microsoft IIS, Netscape Enterprise Server and Unix/Apache. The major difference is that while ASP solutions are built primarily with VBScript and objects, ColdFusion utilizes the tags, which encapsulate functionality. ColdFusion lacks some of the internal ASP objects; however it sports its own set of solutions to common problems, including access to ADO functionality.

Java Server Pages

JavaServer Pages (**JSP**) is a new technology that allows you to combine markup (HTML or XML) with Java code to dynamically generate web-pages. The JSP specification is implemented by several web servers, and plug-ins are available that allow you to use JSP with IIS 4.0. One of the main advantages of JSP is the portability of code between different servers. JavaServer Pages isn't directly related ASP, but it does boast the ability to embed Java code into your web pages using server-side tags, in the same way that ASP script can be embedded into web pages. More details can be found in the JSP FAQ at http://www.esperanto.org.nz/jsp/jspfaq.html.

PHP

Personal Home Pages (PHP) is a new server-side scripting language for creating dynamic web pages. When a visitor opens the page, the server processes the PHP commands and then sends the results to the visitor's browser, just as with ASP or ColdFusion. Unlike ASP or ColdFusion, PHP is open-source and cross-platform. PHP runs on Windows NT and many Unix versions, and it can be built as an Apache module and as a binary that can run as a CGI. When built as an Apache module, PHP is especially speedy. A downside is that you have to download PHP separately and go through a series of quite complex steps to install it and get it working on your machine. Also PHP's session management was non-existent until PHP 4, and still inferior to ASP's even now.

In addition to manipulating the content of your pages, PHP, like IIS, can also send HTTP headers. You can set cookies, manage authentication, and redirect users. It offers good connectivity to many databases (and ODBC), and integration with various external libraries that let you do everything from generating PDF documents to parsing XML.

PHP, like ASP, can also go right into your Web pages. You can start a block of PHP code with `<?php` and end it with `?>`. (You can also configure PHP to use ASP-style `<% ... %>` tags or even `<SCRIPT LANGUAGE="php"></SCRIPT>`.) The PHP engine processes everything between those tags. PHP's language syntax is similar to C and Perl. This might prove a barrier to people with no prior programming experience, but if you have a background in either language then you might want to take a look. PHP also has some rudimentary object-oriented features, providing a helpful way to organize and encapsulate your code.

Although PHP runs fastest embedded in Apache, there are instructions on the PHP Web site for set up with Microsoft IIS and Netscape Enterprise Server. If you want to try PHP, you can download it at `http://www.php3.net`. You'll also find a manual that documents all of PHP's functions and features.

Summary

So now, we hope you have a strong idea of the differences between the client and the server, client-side scripting and server-side scripting, and JavaScript, VBScript and ASP. We also hope you have a good idea about why you'd want to use ASP, and the other kinds of options available for dynamic web pages. We haven't actually showed you how to program in any way – that comes in the chapters that follow – but it's important, before you start programming, to be able to appreciate the differences between programming on the server side with ASP, and programming on the client side.

Briefly, we have learned that the browser and web server have the relationship of 'client and server'. The browser submits a URL to the web server, in the form of a request, using HTTP. The web server fetches the web page that matches the request: if there is any ASP script present, the web server will identify and process the ASP, generating the HTML that will define the content of the page. This new web page is returned to the server as HTML, which the browser then processes in order to create the page display that we see on the screen.

We learned that the most widely-accepted language among web browsers (i.e. on the client side) is JavaScript, while the default language for server-side scripting with ASP is VBScript. We will be using VBScript for our ASP code throughout the rest of the book: it's a less complex language than JavaScript, it's more widely used for ASP, and it is impractical to learn two languages at once.

We also learned that there is an 'order of execution'. The execution sequence of the program depends on the method used to insert the script, and the scripting language used: by using different methods we can produce different results on the screen display. And we prepared ourselves for upcoming chapters by giving the briefest of introductions to the ASP object model; and we and looked at the alternatives to ASP.

We've already programmed a few example pages, but we've avoided the details of their syntax and structure until the necessary foundations were laid. In the next chapter we'll start working on a few of the basic programming techniques we'll need in ASP, and get you to a point where you can start writing your own pages.

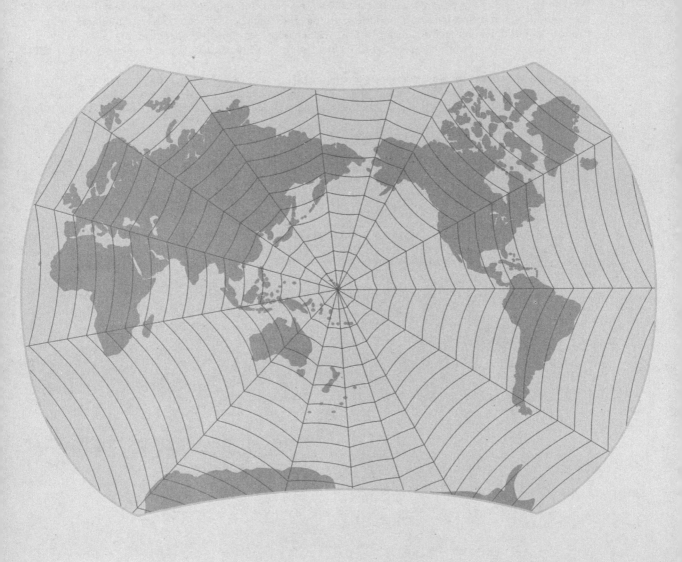

Basic ASP Techniques

When I first started to study Chinese my tutor, Lao Wang, gave me a Chinese–English dictionary, a Chinese grammar book and a primer. But he placed all of these books in a basket and said that they were not to be used until the next week. In the first week he instructed me just to listen and memorize some phrases. Before beginning a rigorous and orderly study he wanted me to learn how to repeat a few phrases. "Excuse me, where is a restaurant?" "Please sir, may I have some rice?" "How much does this cost?" That week, I had to accept on faith the content, sentence structure, pronunciation and grammar. But by Friday I could at least walk into a Chinese restaurant, order a bowl of rice and pay for it. Those first few phrases, without theory or explanation, gave me enough grammar and vocabulary to get by.

We will take the same approach in this book. After this chapter you will get an in-depth study of the syntax and techniques of ASP, but to start, we want to give you three basic techniques. Here we won't explain the theory, exceptions or intricacies; those will come later. But at the end of this chapter you will be able to:

❑ Create a web page that asks the user a question and returns the answer to another ASP page

❑ Instruct ASP to retain the information supplied by the user

❑ Use ASP code to write a line of text back to the user

So without further ado, let's get started.

Getting Information From the User

In the first chapter of this book, we discussed what ASP can do, and in the second chapter we looked at how to indicate to the web server exactly which sections of your HTML page are ASP code. Our first example in Chapter 1 just demonstrated how ASP works on your server. The simple text and HTML tags plus ASP code that you wrote, with the help of ASP on the server, generated an appropriate page, which returned the current time on the server. Two visitors requesting the page at different times on the same day will actually get two different pages back.

Now let's consider some real situations in the business world:

❏ We would like to ask the user which product they are interested in and then have ASP generate a page specific to that interest.

❏ We want to ask a visitor if they are a member of the organization. If they are, then they get a page that displays the organization's calendar. If not, they get a form, which they can complete and submit in order to join the club.

❏ We have a page that uses advanced HTML techniques (such as formatting), which do not show up well in some browsers. We would like to establish which browser this visitor is using, and then send out a page of information formatted appropriately for that browser.

❏ We want to give the visitor a tour of pages displaying this week's featured items. The user will proceed through the site by clicking on **Next** buttons. However, we want to update our pages weekly, so we need ASP to check our current list of pages featuring items and insert hyperlinks for those pages into the **Next** buttons at the moment the page goes to the user.

In each of these cases, we want to do some action beyond simply serving a page. We'll either need to make a decision about what page to serve, or we'll need to create a customized page for that particular request.

In order to make our decision we need to get some information from the user. In the first case, we need to know what product the user wants to see. In the second case we need to know if the user is a member or not. In the programming world this kind of information is considered as **input**. ASP needs input from the user in order to make its decisions.

Suppose that our web site has a 'page 1', which asks the user whether they want 'retail information' or 'wholesale information'. Once the user has selected from these options, how do we get that information from 'page 1' into the ASP of the second page? The simplest technique is to use a feature of HTML called the **form**. An HTML form performs four tasks:

❏ <FORM> tags can ask the user for information and provide a text box or check box into which the user can type or select the answer

❏ The form has a button, for submitting information back to the server

❏ The submission has instructions to open a new page (usually an ASP page)

❏ The submission also carries the information that the user typed into the fields which is to be used by the ASP code of the new page

We use forms to provide a means for users to input data to the server – the information that we need in order to make decisions in ASP.

If you are unfamiliar with forms and their methods for submitting information, then please refer to Appendix F for a comprehensive tutorial on forms.

Using a Form to Obtain Information from the User

Here is the first set of tags needed to set up the structure of a form (we will add the spaces for input in the next example). You begin and end the form section of the page with the <FORM> and </FORM> tags. Here's an example:

```
<P>Please fill in the following form:</P>
<FORM ACTION="Calendar.asp" METHOD=POST>
...
</FORM>
```

The opening <FORM> tag here has two attributes. The first, ACTION, gives the name of the ASP file that should be opened next, and which will use the information that we gather in the form. (Actually, it doesn't have to be an ASP file; but in this book, it usually will be.) The second attribute, METHOD, determines which of two ways (POST or GET) that the browser will use to send the information to the server. This directly corresponds to the method sent in the HTTP request to the server that we talked about in the previous chapter. In this chapter, we will always use POST; we will see the difference between POST and GET in Chapter 7, when we discuss both in more detail.

The ACTION attribute of the <FORM> tag tells the browser what page is going to be opened when the submit button is pressed. After the user has submitted the data, the browser automatically requests this file. The name of the file should be in double quotes, although it doesn't have to be. Most browsers can parse the name without the quotes but including them ensures compatibility with all browsers.

The Submit and Reset Input Tags

Within the <FORM> tags, you generally need to include three sets of <INPUT> tags. Two of them are the **submit** and **reset** buttons. Their tags are similar:

```
<P>Please fill in the following form:</P>
<FORM ACTION="Calendar.asp" METHOD=POST>
  <P><INPUT TYPE="SUBMIT" VALUE="Submit"></P>
  <P><INPUT TYPE="RESET" VALUE="Reset"></P>
</FORM>
```

The code above will produce the following page on the browser:

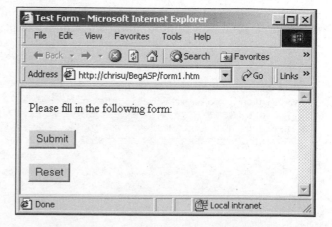

The Submit and Reset button tags have two attributes in this example. The first attribute, TYPE, tells the browser what kind of button to create. The second, VALUE, specifies the message that is to be displayed on the button. Note that both of these attributes should be enclosed in quotes. The TYPE attribute can be set to SUBMIT or RESET or even BUTTON; those are keywords to the browser so you should not try to rename them.

The VALUE will appear to the user on the face of the button, and thus it can be anything you like, as long as you type it in quotes. For example, consider the following form:

```
<FORM ACTION="Calendar.asp" METHOD=POST>
  <P><INPUT TYPE="SUBMIT" VALUE="Click here to submit this information."></P>
  <P><INPUT TYPE="RESET" VALUE="Whoa, man. I need to start over."></P>
</FORM>
```

This code produces a web page that behaves exactly as before, but that now looks something like this:

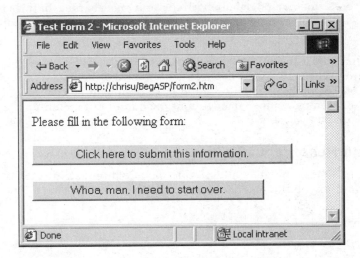

The Information Input Tags

OK, that's enough to give us the framework of a form: but now we need the item of real interest – a place for the user to input data. The input spaces on a form are called fields and are created with the <INPUT> tag. Now we need to get the field set up wherein the user will actually enter information. One such field is a text box, as we've added here in the code in the shaded lines:

```
<FORM ACTION="Calendar.asp" METHOD=POST>
  <P>Please type your name in the space below</P>
  <P><INPUT TYPE="TEXT" NAME="LastName"></P>
  <P><INPUT TYPE="SUBMIT" VALUE="Click here to submit this information."></P>
  <P><INPUT TYPE="RESET" VALUE="Whoa, man. I need to start over."></P>
</FORM>
```

This new line changes the browser page to the following:

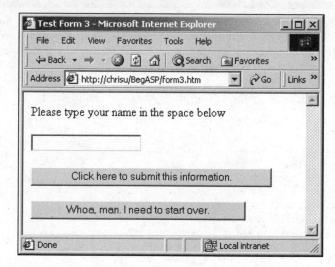

The new input line has two attributes, TYPE and NAME. In this case, we have specified TYPE="TEXT", which instructs the browser to give us a text box into which the user can type some input.

The second attribute, NAME, is the more important: every input field must have a NAME. The data (entered by the user) will be joined to the name of its field; these two attributes will be passed together to the ASP page specified by the <FORM> tag's ACTION attribute.

For example, suppose we have a page containing a form, and that the form has three fields that ask the user for his first name, middle name and last name as follows (of course, the form also has two fields presenting the Submit and Reset buttons):

```
<P><INPUT TYPE="TEXT" NAME="FirstName"></P>
<P><INPUT TYPE="TEXT" NAME="MiddleName"></P>
<P><INPUT TYPE="TEXT" NAME="LastName"></P>
<P><INPUT TYPE="SUBMIT"></P>
<P><INPUT TYPE="RESET"></P>
```

When the user clicks on the Submit button, a second page (usually with an .asp suffix) will be called: this new page will receive the three pieces of information from these three fields, in a format such as FirstName="Alexander", MiddleName="The" and LastName="Great". If the INPUT tag didn't contain a NAME attribute, then in the new page there would be no way to know which piece of information was from which field.

We can now put this together into a few practice forms. You won't be able to do anything with the information that you gather just yet, but it's important just to get the forms working first.

Try It Out – Form to Get Department Affiliation

Your boss wants to register employees for an upcoming 'spring retreat'. Each department will meet on a different weekend, so the organizers need to get each employee's department affiliation when the employee first visits the web site. In this example, we'll make a form page which asks for the user's department affiliation.

1. Open your preferred page editor and type in the following code for the form page:

```
<HTML>
<HEAD>
<TITLE>Spring Retreat - Get Department Form</TITLE>
</HEAD>

<BODY>
<IMG SRC="tulip1.jpg" WIDTH="221" HEIGHT="120">
<H1>Spring Retreat Logistics</H1>
<H2>Each department will meet at a different time and place.<BR>
Please provide the name of your department<BR></H2>
<FORM ACTION="SpringRetreatNotice.asp" METHOD=POST>
  Please type your department here:
  <P><INPUT TYPE="TEXT" NAME="Department"></P>
  <P><INPUT TYPE="RESET" VALUE="Reset data"></P>
  <P><INPUT TYPE="SUBMIT" VALUE="Click here to send this information."></P>
</FORM>
</BODY>
</HTML>
```

> *This page contains a reference to* `tulip1.jpg`. *You can download this file and any other images used in this chapter from the Wrox web site at* `http://www.wrox.com`. *Alternatively, you can substitute your own image – you'll need to adjust the WIDTH and HEIGHT attributes!*

2. Save this page as `SpringRetreatDepartForm.asp`, into your `\inetpub\wwwroot\BegASPFiles` directory.

3. Create a new page, which should contain the following code:

```
<HTML>
<HEAD>
<TITLE>Spring Retreat Notice</TITLE>
</HEAD>

<BODY>
<H1>Spring Retreat</H1>
<H2>Thank you for registering your department.</H2>
</BODY>
</HTML>
```

4. Save this as `SpringRetreatNotice.asp`, in the same directory.

5. Open your browser and run the page `SpringRetreat DepartForm.asp`, which will produce the following:

6. Type in the name of the department (for argument's sake, type Sales) and click on the Click here to send this information button. The following page should be displayed:

In this chapter all of the files have the extension `.asp`. The form files that do not have ASP code are not required to have the `.asp` extension: they would work fine with `.htm` or `.html`. However, as your site grows in complexity and you expand your repertoire of ASP skills, you will want to include ASP code on almost every page. Naming all of your files with the `.asp` extension from the start overcomes the problems of changing the extension to `.asp` at the time you add code.

How It Works

The first few lines of `SpringRetreatDepartForm.asp` are the standard lines of the header. The first line of the body creates the image and then we have five lines that format and display some opening text. The action starts with the opening `<FORM>` tag:

```
<FORM ACTION="SpringRetreatNotice.asp" METHOD=POST>
```

Within that tag we have two attributes. `ACTION` tells the browser which page to call when the user clicks on the **Submit** button. The `METHOD` tag tells the browser how to send the data the user types to the server.

> *At this point in your study, always use the* POST *method.*

Within the `<FORM>` and `</FORM>` tags we have one text line and three input lines:

```
Please type your department here:
<P><INPUT TYPE="TEXT" NAME="Department"></P>
<P><INPUT TYPE="RESET" VALUE="Reset data"></P>
<P><INPUT TYPE="SUBMIT" VALUE="Click here to send this information."></P>
```

Let's have a quick look at these four lines. The first line simply displays text so that the user knows what to type in the field. The second line actually creates the box in which the user will type. Note the two attributes: `TYPE="TEXT"` tells the browser this should be a text box, as opposed to a check box or options buttons. `NAME="Department"` gives the identifier, *Department*, that is attached to the data that the user will type.

> Never leave the **NAME** attribute out of an `<INPUT TYPE="TEXT">` tag; without it, the data can never be used by ASP.

The other two input lines provide the standard **Submit** and **Reset** buttons. In this case we have used the `VALUE` attributes to change the words on the buttons from the default values, so that the buttons contain text that is a bit more customized for our situation.

Then we close the form section with the `</FORM>` tag:

```
</FORM>
```

When the user sees this page, they can enter information in the box. If the user isn't happy with what they've entered, they can click on **Reset data** and enter different information in the text box.

What happens when the user clicks on the **Click here to send this information** button? First, the browser takes the information that was typed into the text box (this might be "Sales", if that's what you wrote in the text box) and assigns it to the input box name to make `Department="Sales"`. Then, the browser sends this to the server, along with a request for the page called `SpringRetreatNotice.asp`. When the server finds the `.asp` page, it will run it through the ASP DLL and it will have the information that the user typed into `SpringRetreatDepartForm.asp` available to it. In the next few pages we will learn how to use that information. The server then sends the `SpringRetreatNotice.asp` page back to the browser.

At this point, we have not used the information from the visitor; however, we have demonstrated how the `<FORM ACTION="page.asp">` is activated by the Submit button to send a request to the server for the next page. Now, let's create a form that gets several items of information from the user.

Try It Out – Forms: Get Jacket Information

For the upcoming corporate retreat, your Department of Employee Spiritual Growth plans to provide a jacket, with the company logo, to each employee. You have been asked to create a page for employees to visit and register information for ordering their jacket. You need to know their preferences in size (Small, Medium, Large or Extra Large), gender (Male or Female) and color (Argent or Azure).

1. You're probably getting used to the procedure by now: open up your preferred web page editor and type in the following code:

```
<HTML>
<HEAD>
<TITLE>Form for Spring Retreat Jacket</TITLE>
</HEAD>

<BODY>
<H1>Company Spring Retreat<BR>
Jacket Order Form</H1>
<H3>Please fill in this form and click on Save My Preferences</H3>
<FORM ACTION="SpringRetreatJacketConfirmation.asp" METHOD=POST>
  <P>Please type your gender</P>
  <P>("male" or "female"):
  <INPUT TYPE="TEXT" NAME="gender"></P>
  <P>Please type your preference of size</P>
  <P>"S"   "M"   "L"   "XL":
  <INPUT TYPE="TEXT" NAME="size"></P>
  <P>Please type your preference of color</P>
  <P>"Argent" or "Azure":
  <INPUT TYPE="TEXT" NAME="color"></P>
  <P><INPUT TYPE="RESET" VALUE="Start Over on This Page">
  <INPUT TYPE="SUBMIT" VALUE="Save my Preferences"></P>
</FORM>
</BODY>
</HTML>
```

2. Save the page as `SpringRetreatJacketForm.asp`, into your `\inetpub\wwwroot\BegASPFiles` directory. This is the page that will ask for the jacket information.

3. Keep your editor open and type in a new page:

```
<HTML>
<HEAD>
<TITLE>Spring Retreat Jacket Confirmation</TITLE>
</HEAD>
```

```
<BODY>
<H1>Company Spring Retreat<BR>
Jacket Order</H1>
<BR>
<H1>Confirmation</H1>
</BODY>
</HTML>
```

4. Save this as `SpringRetreatJacketConfirmation.asp`, in the same directory. This is a confirmation page to which the form information will be transferred.

5. Now start up your browser and run the page `SpringRetreatJacketForm.asp`, which will produce the following:

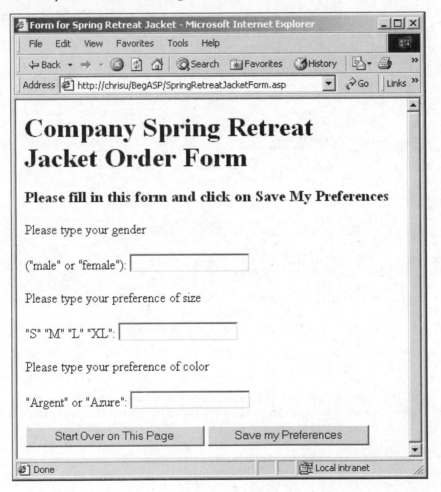

6. Enter some details, and click on the **Save my Preferences** button to send the information to the server. The browser then automatically opens up the page called `SpringRetreatJacketConfirmation.asp`:

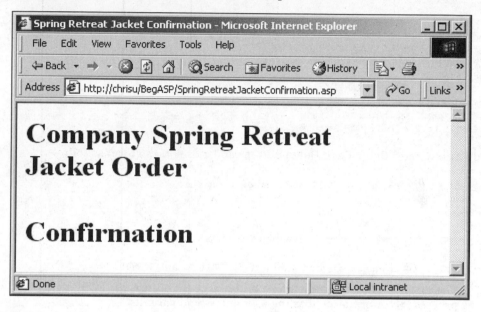

How It Works

This code is similar to the last except that we are now working with three fields of data instead of one. The first few lines are the page header. Within the body we first present three lines of simple HTML text giving the user some instructions for the page.

```
<HTML>
<HEAD>
<TITLE>Form for Spring Retreat Jacket</TITLE>
</HEAD>

<BODY>
<H1>Company Spring Retreat<BR>
Jacket Order Form</H1>
<H3>Please fill in this form and click on Save My Preferences</H3>
```

Then we begin the important part with the `<FORM>`. The `<FORM>` tag must contain at least the attribute to tell the browser what page to call when the **Submit** button is pressed. In this case that is the `ACTION=SpringRetreatJacketConfirmation.asp`. At this point in our study, we are only concerned with using the `METHOD=POST` attribute:

```
<FORM ACTION="SpringRetreatJacketConfirmation.asp" METHOD=POST>
```

105

In this next section, the code alternates between lines of plain HTML text and input fields (of type TEXT). The HTML text in this case is asking the user for information, and for each question asked there is a related input field – "gender", "size", and "color":

```
<P>Please type your gender</P>
<P>("male" or "female"):
<INPUT TYPE="TEXT" NAME="gender"></P>
<P>Please type your preference of size</P>
<P>"S"  "M"  "L"  "XL":
<INPUT TYPE="TEXT" NAME="size"></P>
<P>Please type your preference of color</P>
<P>"Argent" or "Azure":
<INPUT TYPE="TEXT" NAME="color"></P>
```

As always, we add Submit and Reset buttons and close off the form as follows:

```
<P><INPUT TYPE="RESET" VALUE="Start Over on This Page">
<INPUT TYPE="SUBMIT" VALUE="Save my Preferences"></P>
</FORM>
```

There are a few points to remember when working with forms

❑ The <FORM> tag needs two attributes: ACTION= and METHOD=

❑ The ACTION attribute is the name of the page (in our case, an ASP page) that will process the information that the user enters and submits

❑ For now, always use METHOD=POST

❑ Every input needs a name

❑ Every form must have a submit button and should have a reset button

❑ Don't forget to close off your forms, with the closing </FORM> tag

Using the Information Obtained From the User

Forms do a fine job of gathering information from the user and passing it to ASP, along with a request for a new ASP page. But how can the new ASP page use that information? We need to place that information in a holding tank and then have a way to use it in our ASP code.

In this section, we're going to show how ASP holds the incoming information at two levels. First, any information from the form is passed to the new ASP page and is automatically captured and held by ASP in its Request object. Second, we can write code in our script to harvest the information from the Request object, and put it into a script **variable**. In any programming language, variables can be used to store, test and manipulate information.

Chapter 4 explains in detail the subtleties of variable types and duration, and Chapter 7 will talk about the Request object in depth. But for now we'll look at the quick and dirty technique – a brief overview of variables.

Capturing and Storing the Information

Do you recall that, in the first Try-it-Out using forms, we asked the user for their department using a text box named `Department`? Well, here it is again on the third line below:

```
<FORM ACTION="SpringRetreatNotice.asp" METHOD=POST>
  Please type your department here:
  <P><INPUT TYPE="TEXT" NAME="Department"></P>
  <P><INPUT TYPE="RESET" VALUE="Reset data"></P>
  <P><INPUT TYPE="SUBMIT" VALUE="Click here to send this information."></P>
</FORM>
```

When the user types their name and clicks on the **Submit** button the browser sends *two* pieces of information to the server. The first is a request that the server should get the file named `SpringRetreatNotice.asp`. The second is the list of the data that the user typed in to the field – in this case, the word **Sales** was typed into the field named `Department`.

Within `SpringRetreatNotice.asp`, we can then do as follows:

```
<%
Dim strDepartment
strDepartment = Request.Form("Department")
%>
```

So what does this do? Well, the first line tells the server to begin a section of ASP code. The second line **dimensions** (or **declares**) a variable called `strDepartment`. Then in the third line we set the contents of `strDepartment` to a value that ASP is holding in the `Request` object – the piece of information that the user entered into the form and submitted to this page. Once that information is saved within a variable, we can use it any way needed in our ASP code until the page requested has finished processing. We will see this used in our next Try-it-Out.

Getting the Syntax Right

The key here is to get the syntax correct. You must start with a line that creates the variable using the keyword `Dim` (which means 'dimension'). For now, keep your variable names very simple by only using letters, no numbers or symbols. Variable names can never contain spaces. To make it easier for you in this chapter, we begin all variables with the letters `str` (which is an abbreviation for 'string') since we are working with text.

Once the variable has been created with the `Dim` keyword, it can be filled with some information. The line that populates the variable must begin with the name of the variable. The variable name is followed by a space and the equals sign (=) and then another space. On the right of the equals sign, we must use the exact words `Request.Form` then open parenthesis, a double quote and the name of the input field from the page. Finish the line with another double quote and close the parenthesis. The right hand side of this "equation" instructs our ASP processor to look in the `Form` collection of the `Request` object; and from within that collection, to give us the data that has been assigned the name `Department`.

> *Don't worry about understanding the details behind the Request object and its Form collection just now – we'll be looking at both in Chapter 7.*

Working with Lots of Pieces of Information

You can create more than one variable at once using the `Dim` keyword, and separating the variable names with commas, like this:

```
Dim strLastName, strMiddleName, strFirstName
```

> *These variables are all of type **Variant**. We'll discuss what variants are in detail in Chapter 4. For now, suffice it to say that a variant can hold any type of data – whether it be a string of text, or an integer, or whatever.*

In our second Try-it-Out for forms, the request for information on the jackets, we would use the following code in the action page:

```
<%
  Dim strGender, strSize, strColor
  strGender = Request.Form("Gender")
  strSize = Request.Form("Size")
  strColor = Request.Form("Color")
%>
```

The variables `strGender`, `strSize` and `strColor` would be created (on the second line above) and then filled with the data from the `Form` collection of the `Request` object, which holds the data typed in by the user into those fields.

Common Errors

We will be using this technique in our next few Try-It-Outs, but before we use this, let's just take a quick look at some common sources of errors. The most common errors are in typos. If variable assignments don't work you should check:

❑ Exact spelling of the name that you gave to the input tag. It is also a good habit to stick to using the same case throughout, because some scripting languages (like JavaScript) are case sensitive – so a Rose is different from a rose is different from a ROSE (contrary to the wisdom of William Shakespeare!)

❑ Exact typing of the objects, methods and properties: `Request.Form`

❑ Keep your variable names very simple for starters: all letters, no symbols. Never use spaces in variable names

❑ The field name must be in double quotes, and that within parentheses

❑ Be sure to put the variable name first (to the left of the equals sign) and the source of data second (to the right of the equals sign)

❑ The assignment of the variable must be within ASP code delimiters (between `<%` and `%>`)

❑ Be sure that in your form page you added the attribute `METHOD=POST` in the `<FORM>` tag

Let us learn one more idea before we do the next Try-It-Out.

Output to the User

If we want to display text on a page, there are two techniques available to us. The first technique is simply to type the text we want into a section of the HTML code, *outside* of the ASP <% ... %> delimiters. For example, if we wanted the words **Autumn Sweaters** to appear on our page, we could use the following construction:

```
<HTML>
...
Autumn Sweaters
...
</HTML>
```

The second technique is to instruct ASP to display the text on the screen – and to do that we use the Response.Write syntax. The Response.Write command instructs ASP's Response object to write the requested text to the browser. For example, if we want the words **Autumn Sweaters** to appear as before, but this time from within a section of ASP code, we could use the following construction:

```
<HTML>
...
<%
Response.Write "Autumn Sweaters"
%>
...
</HTML>
```

You can, of course, use the first technique on a page that contains ASP code, provided you make sure that you do not enter the text within an ASP code section, or within <SCRIPT> blocks. If we had accidentally forgotten that we were working within the ASP delimiters (the <% and %> tags) and not included the keywords Response.Write and the quotes, we would receive an error. That's because ASP would have tried to find a command with the name Autumn with a parameter Sweaters – since no command exists with this name, the user who requested the page would have an error page sent back to them.

On the other hand, if we had typed in Response.Write "Autumn Sweaters" from outside of the ASP code block, we would have a page with the text **Response.Write "Autumn Sweaters"** appearing on it.

To summarize, these techniques are correctly use in the following ways:

Region of code on page:	Type in	Result in Browser
HTML	Autumn Sweaters	Autumn Sweaters
ASP	<% Response.Write "Autumn Sweaters" %>	Autumn Sweaters

And if you use them like this, you won't get the results you were looking for:

Region of code on page:	Type in	Result in Browser
HTML	Response.Write "Autumn Sweaters"	Response.Write "Autumn Sweaters"
ASP	Autumn Sweaters	Error

So we can see that Response.Write is great for writing text into the page. But there's more: we can also use Response.Write to write HTML tags into the page. For example, to have ASP add a horizontal line to the page, we can use Response.Write to put the <HR> tag into the HTML page as follows:

```
<%
  Response.Write "<HR>"
%>
```

Outputting the Values of Variables

ASP also works well for putting the contents of a variable into a page's source HTML. Let's say we have asked the user in a form for the name of his item of interest. We could write the name of that item onto the page by using the following code:

```
<%
  Dim strItem
  strItem = Request.Form("ItemChoice")
  Response.Write strItem
%>
```

The first line indicates the start of the ASP code. Then we create a variable called strItem. The third line takes the data that the user typed into the form field called ItemChoice, and it copies that data into the variable called strItem. This line makes the user's input available for ASP. The fourth line writes the contents of strItem onto the HTML page and then the fifth line closes off the ASP section of code.

It's important not to underestimate the power of what we have just done! With this simple technique, the text that is written on this page can potentially be different for each different user. With static HTML, we can only send the *exact* same page to every visitor; but with ASP techniques like this we can customize our pages to reflect the exact needs of each user.

> Note that Response.Write uses a slightly different syntax for variables and for text or tags. When using Response.Write for variables, the variable name should *not* be in quotes; when using Response.Write for text and tags, the text and tags *should* be in quotes.

Mixing Lines of HTML and ASP Output

As we said at the beginning of this section, there are two ways to write output to the browser – the pure HTML technique and the ASP `Response.Write` technique – and we can use these two techniques interchangeably within the code of our ASP pages. For example:

```
<P>Next week's featured item:
<%
  Dim strItem
  strItem = Request.Form("ItemChoice")
  Response.Write strItem
%>
</P>
```

In the above example the first line consists of straight text and HTML tags, just as if you had never heard of ASP. The second line starts an ASP block, which writes some more text. (Inside the block we first create the `strItem` variable; then we populate our new variable with the user's information; then we direct ASP to write the contents of `strItem` onto the HTML page.) So if the user had typed the phrase **Autumn Sweaters** into the `ItemChoice` field and submitted that value, the result of the above code would be a page in the browser as shown below.

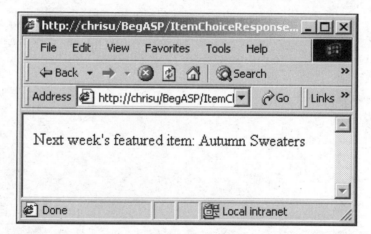

This intermingling of HTML and ASP-written text applies to the tags as well. If we wanted to make some of the words in our display bold (using the `<B>` and `</B>` tags), we could insert the tag from HTML like this:

```
<P>Next week's featured item: <B>
<%
  Dim strItem
  strItem = Request.Form("ItemChoice")
  Response.Write strItem
%>
</B></P>
```

In the above example the paragraph starts with some tags and text, including an opening `<B>` tag, before the ASP code begins. ASP writes the contents of the `strItem` variable in bold type. Then ASP finishes and the HTML page adds the closing `</B>` tag. Once the ASP has calculated the value of `strItem` (assuming the user typed in the value **Autumn Sweaters**), the result is the same as if you had just written straight HTML as follows:

```
<P>Next week's featured item: <B>Autumn Sweaters</B></P>
```

Alternatively, we could have written those `<B>` and `</B>` tags to the page from within the ASP code, like this:

```
<P>Next week's featured item:
<%
  Dim strItem
  strItem = Request.Form("ItemChoice")
  Response.Write "<B>"
  Response.Write strItem
  Response.Write "</B>"
%>
</P>
```

This time, we've removed the `<B>` and `</B>` tags from the pure-HTML lines. Instead, we've got three `Response.Write` statements, to write three different things to the browser. The ASP `Response.Write` command doesn't care if it is writing text, tags or a mixture. You can put text plus one or more tags in a single `Response.Write` (although this wouldn't look too pleasing to the eye):

```
<P>Next week's featured item:
<%
  Dim strItem
  strItem = Request.Form("ItemChoice")
  Response.Write "<B>"
  Response.Write strItem
  Response.Write "</B>. <I>Suits you, Sir!</I>"
%>
</P>
```

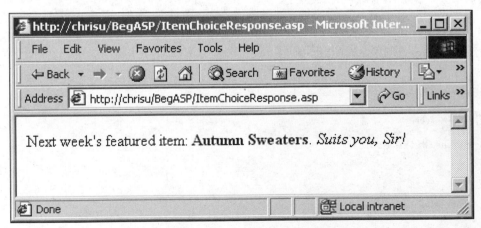

Of course, the power that ASP's `Response.Write` brings to our pages is that it allows us to write the values of variables and functions to the page. The exact display shown in the page happens because the user typed the string **Autumn Sweaters** into a form, and submitted that value; and it was then captured by the new page's `Request.Form` collection and used to write the new page. We simply can't do that using plain HTML.

If the user had typed in **Fleecy Trousers**, then the resulting page above would have been different:

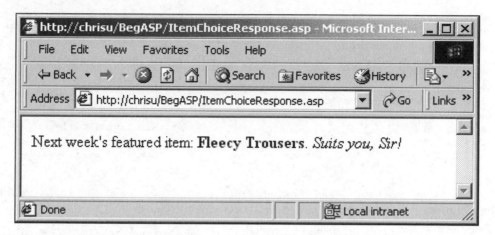

OK, this page isn't *much* different to the previous one – but imagine what we can do once we've got a few variables together, and made some decisions dynamically based on the values of those variables. We'll soon have some exciting, complex, dynamic pages that will get the users coming back for more.

A Shortcut for Response.Write

Now let us finish with a shortcut. We're likely to use the `Response.Write` many times in order to write the values of all our variables to the page – so for that very reason, ASP provides a special shorthand form of `Response.Write`. We can use the syntax `<%=strName%>` you can write the contents of the variable `strName` onto the page.

For example, suppose a customer is using a web site to buy a rectangular piece of carpet, and they have submitted values for the length and width of the piece of carpet they want to buy. In the page that handles these values, we might handle the inputted data like this:

```
<%
  intLength = Request.Form("CarpetLength")
  intWidth = Request.Form("CarpetWidth")
%>
Your piece of carpet will have length
<% Response.Write intLength %>
and width
<% Response.Write intWidth %>
```

The two `Response.Write` calls are rather clumsy, but we can rewrite this code using the shortcut instead, which makes the code much easier to read:

```
<%
  intLength = Request.Form("CarpetLength")
  intWidth = Request.Form("CarpetWidth")
%>
Your piece of carpet will have length <%=intLength %> and width <%=intWidth %>
```

Note that you can only use this shortcut to abbreviate a `Response.Write`, and it doesn't work if you mix it with other ASP commands in the same ASP code block. For example, in the following sample the highlighted lines will fail:

```
<%
  intLength = Request.Form("CarpetLength")
  intWidth = Request.Form("CarpetWidth")
  Response.Write "Your piece of carpet will have length "
  =intLength                                  ' this line is illegal
  Response.Write " and width "
  =intWidth                                   ' this line is illegal
%>
```

So, in this section we have talked about how to direct ASP to write characters to the HTML page before it goes out to the user. Here are the take-home points:

❑ These characters can be of three types: text, HTML tags, or the contents of a variable

❑ The command to write characters to the HTML page from within ASP code is `Response.Write`

❑ The syntax for text is: `Response.Write "text goes here"`

❑ The syntax for variables is: `Response.Write strName`

❑ We also covered a shortcut to put the contents of a variable into a line of HTML text using the equals sign, straight after the opening ASP delimiter: `<%=strName%>`

Let's now improve the confirmation page that we return after asking the user for their department in our example.

Try It Out – Registration of Department Reply

In our form `SpringRetreatDepartForm.asp`, the `<FORM>` tag has the attribute `ACTION="SpringRetreatNotice.asp"`. But the reply wasn't very informative: it just said Thank you for registering your department. It didn't even tell the user whether they had successfully registered the correct department name.

So let's amend this second page to show text that not only confirms the visitor's registration, but also confirms which department they have registered. Keep in mind that it won't be until later in the book that you will learn how to actually make a registration in a database. But for now, we will just focus on returning a message to the user.

1. This solution needs you to change and add the highlighted lines to
`SpringRetreatNotice.asp`.

```
<HTML>
<HEAD>
<TITLE>Spring Retreat Notice</TITLE>
</HEAD>

<BODY>
<H1>Spring Retreat</H1>
<H2>Thank you for registering as a member of the
<%
  Dim strDepartment
  strDepartment = Request.Form("Department")
  Response.Write strDepartment
%>
department.</H2>
</BODY>
</HTML>
```

2. Save the page with the same name as previously.

3. Now, open `SpringRetreatDepartForm.asp` in the browser; fill in the text box and
click the button marked Click here to send this information. This will cause our revised
version of `SpringRetreatNotice.asp` to appear on the browser. If you typed the
word Sales into the input field and submitted that, then you'll see the following
confirmation page:

How It Works

This code starts with the same initial information as we used in the first Try-It-Out for forms.

```
<HTML>
<HEAD>
<TITLE>Spring Retreat Notice</TITLE>
</HEAD>

<BODY>
<H1>Spring Retreat</H1>
<H2>Thank you for registering as a member of the
```

But at this point we kick in ASP with a `<%`, and our first ASP statement creates a variable named `strDepartment`. ASP populates this variable with the data sent from the browser and labeled as `Department` – which, in the case of the screenshot above, is the word `Sales`. The third ASP statement writes the contents of the variable `strDepartment` onto the page. Then the ASP code section is closed:

```
<%
  Dim strDepartment
  strDepartment = Request.Form("Department")
  Response.Write strDepartment
%>
```

In order to make the page look neater, we've add one line of simple HTML text to finish off the sentence. Then we close up the body and the page:

```
department.</H2>
</BODY>
</HTML>
```

OK, now our `SpringRetreatNotice.asp` page is a bit more useful – because it tells the user some useful information, based on what action they took in the first page.

What about our jacket registration form? That page sends three fields of data to the server. Now, since we now know how to put that information into variables, let's produce a more functional confirmation page that reads this information back to the user.

Try It Out – Jacket Order Confirmation

1. Open the form `SpringRetreatJacketConfirmation.asp` once again, and replace all of the code between the `<BODY>` tags with the following:

```
<BODY>
<%
  Dim strGender, strSize, strColor
  strGender = Request.Form("Gender")
  strSize = Request.Form("Size")
  strColor = Request.Form("Color")
%>
```

```
<H1>Company Spring Retreat</H1>
<H3>Jacket Order: Confirmation</H3>
For you, we will order a jacket in
<%Response.Write strColor%>
and size
<%Response.Write strSize%>
for a
<%Response.Write strGender%>
employee.
</BODY>
```

2. Save your changes to that file. Open `SpringRetreatJacketForm.asp` in a browser, fill in the details **male**, **L** and **Argent** into the relevant boxes and click on **Save my Preferences** to submit this to the server. Then you will see the following:

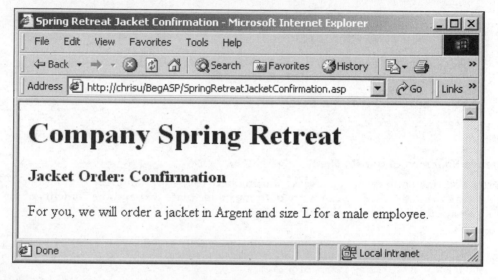

How It Works

We know how the HTML form works, so let's just look at how our revised `SpringRetreatJacketForm.asp` code handles the submitted data.

The first few lines of the page's body contain a block of ASP logic. First, we create the three variables, and assign to these variables the values that were entered by the user in the previous page:

```
<BODY>
<%
  Dim strGender, strSize, strColor
  strGender = Request.Form("Gender")
  strSize = Request.Form("Size")
  strColor = Request.Form("Color")
%>
```

Then we shift out of ASP and into HTML, to put some text on the page:

```
<H1>Company Spring Retreat</H1>
<H3>Jacket Order: Confirmation</H3>
For you, we will order a jacket in
```

The next line instructs ASP to write the contents of the variable named `strColor` on the HTML page. ASP respects the position of this command within the surrounding HTML and text, and writes the contents of `strColor` to just the right place in the page:

```
<%Response.Write strColor%>
```

Now we shift out of ASP again, to write a little more pure text. Then we shift back into ASP, to write the user's input for `Size` into just the right point in the page:

```
and size
<%Response.Write strSize%>
```

Then some more pure text, one last variable value (in an ASP block) and one more line of pure text to finish of the output:

```
for a
<%Response.Write strGender%>
employee.
```

Alternative Solutions to Our Problem

Here's a second solution that uses less shifting between HTML and ASP, but more `Response.Write` calls. We can write both the boiler-plate text and the contents of the variables using `Response.Write` as follows:

```
<BODY>
<%
  Dim strGender, strSize, strColor
  strGender = Request.Form("gender")
  strSize = Request.Form("Size")
  strColor = Request.Form("Color")
  Response.Write "<H1>Company Spring Retreat</H1>"
  Response.Write "<H3>Jacket Order: Confirmation</H3>"
  Response.Write "For you, we will order a jacket in "
  Response.Write strColor
  Response.Write " and size "
  Response.Write strSize
  Response.Write " for a "
  Response.Write strGender
  Response.Write " employee."
%>
</BODY>
```

There's less shifting into and out of ASP here – the whole body section is ASP code. Each block of ASP code, enclosed in a pair of <% ... %> delimiters, requires another call to the ASP DLL. This means that the more times you use <% ... %>, the longer your code will take to execute. Holding all our code within a single block of ASP can give you a noticeable run-time speed increase over using many blocks of ASP. There are more Response.Write statements, which can make the code look a little bulky, but the performance issue is am important one to consider.

> *We could reduce the number of Response.Write calls in the above sample by using a technique called **string concatenation**. This involves fixing two or more smaller strings together to make one big string. After concatenating all the small strings into one big string, we'd just call Response.Write once – to write the big string to the browser. There's more about string concatenation in Chapter 4.*

A third solution is easier to read, but uses more ASP blocks. In this case, we'll use the Response.Write shortcut when writing the output to the browser:

```
<BODY>
<%
  Dim strGender, strSize, strColor
  strGender = Request.Form("gender")
  strSize = Request.Form("Size")
  strColor = Request.Form("Color")
%>
<H1>Company Spring Retreat</H1>
<H3>Jacket Order: Confirmation</H3>
For you, we will order a jacket in <%=strColor%> and size <%=strSize%> for a
<%=strGender%> employee.
</BODY>
```

All three of these solutions produce the result on the browser. I recommend the second of the three solutions, because it is the fastest to execute – it requires fewer trips to the ASP DLL.

A Simple Business Example

Before we head on to the in-depth discussions in the rest of the book, I suggest you give these first techniques a few tries. Here is a simple business situation with which we can exercise our new techniques. The solution requires two files: the first contains an HTML form and the second is an ASP page that responds to the information submitted in the form, utilizing the data entered to return a customized page to the user. Once you are comfortable with the ASP projects in this chapter, you will be able to incorporate the scores of improvements that the rest of this book presents.

Try It Out – Sign-In Sheet Example

You travel to various offices around the world, presenting seminars to your colleagues on the new products that your company is about to introduce. Paris in April, Tokyo in September; it is a very glamorous job. But you do have some paperwork. At each seminar you need to make a sign-in sheet with the company logo, date, and so on; and a number of horizontal lines that each of the delegates of your seminar must sign to prove that they attended the seminar.

You want to make up a template of the sign-in sheet on your web site. The idea is that, wherever you are in the world, you can browse to your web server back home, type in the location and date of the seminar, and then have the web server create a sign-in sheet on the browser (with the location and date information written in). Then you can just print the page from the browser and have a beautiful sign-in sheet.

For this example, pick any piece of clipart for your company logo.

1. You've guessed it...crank up your trusty web page editor and type in the following:

```
<HTML>
<HEAD>
<TITLE>'Where Am I' form for Sign-in Sheets</TITLE>
</HEAD>
<BODY>
<H1>Sign-in Sheet template for my 'New Products' Seminars</H1>
<BR>
Just fill in the following details:
<FORM ACTION="SignInSheet.asp" METHOD=Post>
  <P>City:<INPUT TYPE="TEXT" Name="City"></P>
  <P>Date:<INPUT TYPE="TEXT" Name="Date"></P>
  <P><INPUT TYPE="SUBMIT" VALUE="Click here to submit the information"></P>
  <P><INPUT TYPE="RESET" VALUE="Click here to start over"></P>
</FORM>
</BODY>
</HTML>
```

2. Save this file as `WhereAmI.asp`, into your `\inetpub\wwwroot\BegASPFiles` directory.

3. Close this page down and start another new one; type the following into it:

```
<HTML>
<HEAD>
<TITLE>Sign In Sheet for New Products Seminar</TITLE>
</HEAD>
<BODY>
<H1>On-Line Clothiers <IMG SRC="Bizrun.jpg" WIDTH="105" HEIGHT="111"></H1>
<H1>Welcome to the New Products Seminar</H1>
<%
  Dim strCity, strDate
  strDate = Request.Form("Date")
  strCity = Request.Form("City")
  Response.Write "Held in "
  Response.Write strCity
  Response.Write " on "
  Response.Write strDate
%>
<P ALIGN="left">please sign in by printing your name</P>
<HR>
 <HR>
 <HR>
 <HR>
</BODY>
</HTML>
```

4. Save this file as `SignInSheet.asp`, in the same directory.

5. Open the `WhereAmI.asp` page in your browser, type in a city and a date and click on the Submit button:

6. If you submitted the name Beijing, and the date December 16, 1999, then you'd see
the following:

How It Works

The solution is contained in two pages. The first is a page that doesn't use ASP but does contain
a form with input fields for the user to submit data. That submission calls an ASP page,
`SignInSheet.asp`, in which the submitted data is available to be written at appropriate points
in the page.

The form page (code for the body shown below) is not dissimilar to things we've seen in the
other exercises in this chapter. The `<FORM>` tag must always have the action attribute – in this
case pointing to the page named `SignInSheet.asp`. There are two input fields in this form,
with the names `City` and `Date`, each reflecting the type of information expected and each very
important in allowing us to distinguish the different pieces of information in
`SignInSheet.asp`:

```
<H1>Sign-in Sheet template for my 'New Products' Seminars</H1>
<BR>
Just fill in the following details:
<FORM ACTION="SignInSheet.asp" METHOD=POST
  <P>City:<INPUT TYPE="TEXT" VALUE="Name of City" Name="City"></P>
  <P>Date:<INPUT TYPE="TEXT" VALUE="Date of Seminar" Name="Date"></P>
  <P><INPUT TYPE="SUBMIT" VALUE="Click here to submit the information"></P>
  <P><INPUT TYPE="RESET" VALUE="Click here to start over"></P>
</FORM>
```

Let us look at the form tags more closely, to review a few ideas. The open form tag `<FORM>` must have the attribute of `ACTION="filename.asp"`. The value for that attribute should be the ASP file that will be opened when the form is submitted – in this case it's `SignInSheet.asp`.

Then form itself contains four fields. The first two are both input tags of type `TEXT` – they are the places where the user types in the city and date. It is important to name each of these fields, using the `NAME` attribute, so we can identify them within the page that is called by the `ACTION`. The last two fields are the simple and standard **Submit** and **Reset** buttons. Remember that when the user clicks on the **Submit** button, the browser will gather the data typed into the input fields, give them the appropriate identifying labels (from the `NAME` attributes of the corresponding `<INPUT>` tags), and then send the data and label to the web server with a request to open the page indicated by the `ACTION` attribute of the `<FORM>` tag.

`SignInSheet.asp` contains the ASP that handles this input, and it's where the action happens. The objective of this page is to take the sign-in sheet template that we've designed, and add in the city and date details for this *particular* seminar (as the user entered in the first page). When the web server has done that, and has sent the result to the browser, we can print out the page from the browser and hand it round the lecture room during the seminar.

After the normal `<HEAD>` material, the `<BODY>` begins. Two heading level 1 lines splash the company name and logo across the top of the page, followed by a **Welcome...** line:

```
<BODY>
<H1>On-Line Clothiers <IMG SRC="Bizrun.jpg" WIDTH="105" HEIGHT="111"></H1>
<H1>Welcome to the New Products Seminar</H1>
```

In the next line we use `<%` to shift gears into ASP. The first line of script creates two a variables, named `strCity` and `strDate`:

```
<%
  Dim strCity, strDate
```

We use these two variables to hold the values that the user submitted to this page, via the form:

```
  strDate = Request.Form("Date")
  strCity = Request.Form("City")
```

So we haven't done any `Response.Write`-ing yet, but we *have* taken the time to prepare for it – by setting up all our variables in advance. This makes our code nice and tidy.

Now we use a sequence of `Response.Write` lines to write the location and date information to the page. There are four `Response.Write` lines in total, alternately writing a little plain text and then a variable value:

```
  Response.Write "Held in "
  Response.Write strCity
  Response.Write " on "
  Response.Write strDate
%>
```

The closing `%>` delimiter marks the end of the ASP. Then we write some more text and HTML to the page, to generate a few lines for the delegates to write on:

```
<P ALIGN="left">please sign in by printing your name</P>
<HR>
 <HR>
 <HR>
 <HR>
</BODY>
</HTML>
```

An Alternative Version of The Code

If you'd wanted to use the shortcut for `Response.Write`, then the code in `SignInSheet.asp` would have contained a block of code like this:

```
<%
  Dim strCity, strDate
  strCity = Request.Form("City")
  strDate = Request.Form("Date")
%>
Held in <%=strCity%> on <%= strDate%>
```

Once again, note that the `<%= ... %>` shortcut is a very useful syntax, when you need to use ASP to drop variable values into HTML output like this. Remember that each `<% ... %>` or `<%= ... %>` pair means another trip to the ASP DLL, which means that your ASP page will take a little longer to execute. If you only use it occasionally then it can be a boost to your code's readability, with no significant loss in performance. But if you use it very many times, then you will start to notice slower delivery times for your web pages.

This finishes our basic ASP examples. You might not have understood all of the working behind the code, but you should at least have an idea of how to send information in a form and display it on a separate page.

Summary

In this chapter, we first covered HTML forms and then we practiced making forms. We focused on the importance of the <FORM> tag's ACTION attribute, and the <INPUT> tag's NAME attribute. Once the user has submitted the form (by clicking the special SUBMIT button in the form), the browser submits the user's information to the web server, along with a request for a new web page (specified by the ACTION attribute).

In the new web page, we can access the submitted information using the Request.Form("*field_name*") syntax. One of the things we can do with that syntax is use it top assign the assocated value to a local variable in the page, like this:

```
strName = Request.Form("field_name")
```

Finally, we talked about using the Response.Write "*Text*" syntax to get ASP code to write text onto an HTML page that's being sent out to the browser.

And we looked at the powerful technique of writing the contents of a *variable* onto the page, using the syntax Response.Write strName or simply <%=strName%>. This is a crucially important technique in ASP, which we will use to dynamically add content to our pages many times in this book.

We haven't included much detail about the theory, logic or exceptions to these ASP techniques – all that will come in the remaining chapters. But at least now you have some basic tools that allow you to:

❑ Create an ASP page

❑ Get some information from the user

❑ Retrieve the submitted information, and store it in a variable

❑ Write the submitted information back to the browser within a subsequent ASP page

Now, as my professor of Chinese told me, you are ready to begin your study.

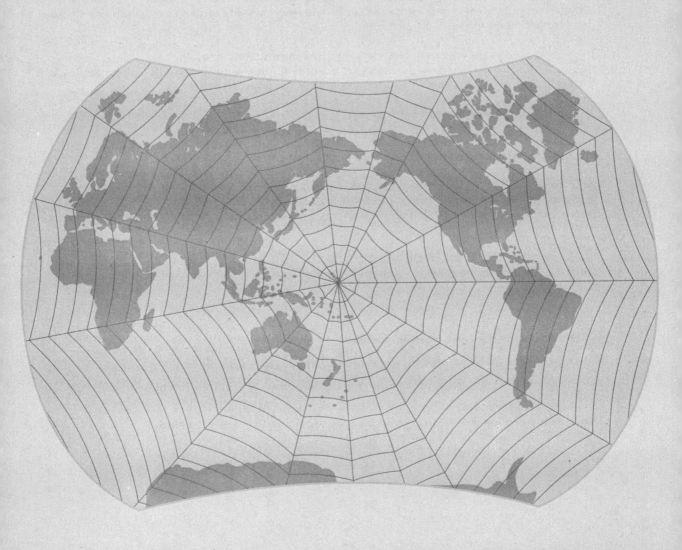

Variables

One of the most important concepts in any programming language is the ability to store information. Suppose a user is required to input their name: where do you store this information, so that it can be used later? How do you store other types of data, such as numerical data and dates? In addition, what if several users have all provided similar pieces of data – how does the computer know how to match up the information provided to the user who provided it? This can all be done using **variables**.

Your programming language gives you the power to create variables, to assign values to them, to test the contents, and to reuse them in your program. They will enable you to perform mathematical functions, calculate new dates, disassemble text, count the length of sentences, and so on. Variables are fundamental to programming – they'll form the foundations of nearly every business solution you'll come to program.

In this chapter we'll look at:

❑   What a variable is

❑   What a variant is

❑   How to declare a variable

❑   Different subtypes in VBScript

❑   How to perform calculations with variables

❑   What 'scope' is

❑   What an array is, and how it can be used to store information about several related data items

We'll start by establishing what a variable is.

What is a Variable?

A **variable** is a section of memory that is allocated a name by the programmer. These sections of memory can be used to store pieces of information that will be used in the program. Think of variables as you might think of boxes. They're simply containers for information that you wish to store. For example, here are three variables – they contain a string of text, a numerical value, and a date respectively:

```
Dim CapitalCityOfUK
Dim NumberOfStates
Dim IndependenceDay

CapitalCityOfUK = "London"
NumberOfStates = 50
IndependenceDay = #7/4/1863#
```

Any variable is empty until you put information into it (although the memory space is reserved while the script runs). You can then look at the information inside the variable, get the information out, or replace the information with new data. In fact, variables are essential for storing data in any computer language; in this book, we'll discuss variables in the context of VBScript and ASP.

Creating a Variable

In the above code example, two things are happening. Firstly, three variables are created and secondly they are given values to store. We'll discuss more about the latter a bit further on in this chapter, but for now, let's concentrate on the first three lines of this example:

```
Dim CapitalCityOfUK
Dim NumberOfStates
Dim IndependenceDay
```

We are instructing VBScript to create three empty variables called `CapitalCityOfUK`, `NumberOfStates` and `IndependenceDay`. You can create any variable in a similar manner, using the `Dim` keyword followed by the name of the variable. There is, however, a quicker way to declare many variables at once, for example:

```
Dim CapitalCityUK, NumberOfStates, IndependenceDay
```

This does exactly the same thing as the three lines above – it creates three separate variables as before, which are empty and ready to accept data.

We'll discuss creating (or declaring) variables again later in this chapter.

Data Types in VBScript, or One Type For All

In most programming languages, it is common to specify a data type for a variable, so that your system knows what type of variable it's dealing with. However, in VBScript this is not the case. In VBScript, all of the variables with seemingly different data types are actually only one type. This is because VBScript determines the data type for you. The variable type that VBScript uses to store the information in is the **variant**. A variant is a special type of variable, which can store a value of any type. This means that you don't have to specify a data type for a variant when you declare it as you do in most other programming languages. (In fact, you can't specify a data type in VBScript – you'll get an error.) At the moment that the variable is read, VBScript will self/itself assign a particular type, based on the data and on the context.

This does have a couple of downsides, there is a performance hit, and sometimes VBScript serves up a different type for the data than you want. However, you can normally go far by just using the variant and letting it automatically assign a type – it usually works. Hence, you could declare a variable like this:

```
Dim LengthOfAPieceOfString
```

Then you could assign an **integer** value to it:

```
LengthOfAPieceOfString = 5
```

Later on, you might decide that you want to replace this value with a **string** value:

```
LengthOfAPieceOfString = "Not very long"
```

This means that we need a mechanism for keeping track of the type of data that is being stored in each variant. VBScript assigns a **subtype** to the variant that reminds the variant of the type of data being stored. A subtype can be any of the following.

Numeric Subtypes

You can assign almost any number to a variable. We can assign whole numbers, fractions, and even negative floating pointing numbers:

```
IntegerNumber1 = 76
DecimalNumber2 = 2.5356
FloatingPointNumber3 = -1.4E06
```

> *Basically, we use floating point numbers to represent very small or very large decimals such as 0.00000123 or 1.14E-6 or 1.87x10 $^{-6}$.*

In VBScript, there are five different numeric subtypes, which are outlined below.

Integer

Integers are simply whole numbers. Examples of integers are 3, 12, and -5127. The integer data type can handle whole numbers within the range -32,768 to 32,767. For numbers that are outside this range then the long type is used, which we'll see shortly.

Byte

Bytes are integers within the range 0 to 255. They're used for very basic arithmetic. It's a useful type, because the method in which data is made available means that a variable can be easily stored by the computer within a single byte, which is the computer's basic storage unit. As VBScript uses variants, VBScript requires an extra byte on top of this, but the principle of bytes taking up very little memory space remains the same.

Long

The long type is very similar to the integer type, but supports a much larger range. A long variable can contain a value in the range -2,147,483,648 to 2,147,483,647.

Single

The single type can hold single precision floating point numbers, within the range -3.402823E38 to -1.401298E-45 (for negative values), and 1.401298E-45 to 3.402823E38 (for positive values).

Double

The double type holds double precision floating point numbers. This means that it will support a much larger range than the single type. In reality, this range is -1.79769313486232E308 to -4.94065645841247E-324 (for negative values), and 4.94065645841247E-324 to 1.79769313486232E308 (for positive values).

Currency

The currency subtype accepts numbers with up to four decimal places. It can support a range of -922,337,203,685,477.5808 to 922,337,203,685,477.5807.

String Subtype

Variants with the string subtype hold textual information or words. The string subtype will identify everything you store in it as text, even if you supply it as a mixture of text and numerical data, numerical data alone or even date information. For example, the following code creates a variant called CarType, with the value "Buick", a variant called CarEngineSize, with the value "2.0", and a variant called DatePurchased, with the value "July 4, 1999":

```
CarType = "Buick"
CarEngineSize = "2.0"
DatePurchased = " July 4, 1999"
```

String values are usually put in between double quotation marks, so that they can be differentiated from numerical values. Note that you can't perform mathematical functions on strings, even if the content of the strings involved are purely numerical. Hence, if you try to add the two strings "12" and "14" together, as shown in the following example, you won't get the result "26" that you might have anticipated:

```
Number1 = "12"
Number2 = "14"
Number3 = Number2 + Number1      'Will produce "1412"
```

This is because while the string subtype itself seemingly accepts different types of data, it is only holding textual representations of these types, such as Integer or Date. Therefore, while it might appear to you that Number1 contains a number, the presence of quotation marks indicates that this is to be treated as text.

We'll cover the process of joining, or concatenating, strings later in this chapter. VBScript also provides a number of special functions with which you can manipulate strings. These functions allow you to measure the length of a string, truncate a string at the beginning or end, return certain characters from a given string, or even convert a string into its numerical equivalent. We'll look at string manipulation functions later in this chapter. A basic rule of thumb is that strings are normally used for storing words or textual information – numeric information is normally stored in the appropriate numeric subtype. The exceptions to this rule are numbers such as telephone numbers and social security numbers, which are usually better stored as strings.

Date Subtype

VBScript also supports a subtype, date, that can be used to hold dates and times. Variants of this subtype use a predefined format. The same subtype is used to record both date and time. For example, we can use the variant DateTime to store a given date:

```
DateTime = #12/10/2001#
```

A date must be surrounded by the # symbol (and not the " symbol): if it isn't surrounded by any symbols, it will be evaluated as a numeric expression. (If it were surrounded by "" then it would be interpreted as a string.) Later in the same program, we could use the same variant to store a given time:

```
DateTime = #11.03#
```

The predefined format of the date type prevents 'regular' numerical arithmetic from being carried out on variants of subtype date. Once the computer is aware of their special format, it's possible to carry out simple numerical arithmetic on them. For example, if you subtracted July 20, 2001 from July 24, 2001, you'd get the answer 4.

Boolean Subtype

Boolean variants can be set to one of two values, namely TRUE or FALSE. In VBScript, if you convert these values to the integer type then they convert to the values −1 and 0 respectively. They can be used to record the state of the variable, in that if a variable isn't TRUE then it must be FALSE. They can be set when a user performs a certain action, i.e. runs a certain form, and they can then be used to determine a certain course of action:

```
blnVariant = FALSE
If blnVariant = FALSE Then do this
...
Else do that
...
```

Note that TRUE or FALSE should not be in quotes.

Special Subtypes

We should briefly outline some other subtypes here.

Empty

Empty variants are variables that have yet to be assigned a value (known as uninitialized variables). Note that you shouldn't confuse these variables with variables that have been assigned the value 0 (zero)! This is because 0 is a valid value (which also implies that the variable is likely to be a numeric type or a Boolean FALSE), while an empty variable has no value at all (because no value has yet been assigned to it).

NULL

NULL is an unusual subtype that is used in conjunction with databases, when we talk about fields that contain no data. NULL does not mean 0, or empty, it means that there is no data, nothing. The concept of NULL is a big stumbling block for the experienced programmer and novices alike.

There is also a set of things that NULLs are most commonly confused with. These are things that most definitely are not NULL:

❑ Zero

❑ A blank string

❑ A blank space

❑ A string of length zero

None of these values are "nothing" – they are all "something". Since NULL has no data type or value, it is only a NULL if it is nothing, contains no data, and no data type.

Object

The Object subtype refers to objects, which are block of codes, which can carry out jobs such as accessing a database or keeping track of advertisements. Since objects are more complex than simple data they are treated in a special way. We won't worry about this just yet, as we'll be taking a closer look at them in Chapter 6.

Error

The Error subtype is very rarely used and for that reason we're not going to cover it. Occasionally you'll come across a component or function that uses it, but we don't recommend using it in any circumstances, as there are no conversion functions that allow you to create or convert a variant with the Error subtype.

Determining Subtypes with TypeName()

So, if VBScript treats all these different subtypes as basically the same type, how can we find out which variant is of which subtype? Sometimes it is useful for you, as the programmer, to know the subtype of a variant, and we can find this out by using the VBScript function TypeName(). If you feed a variant into the TypeName() function, as follows:

```
LengthOfAPieceOfString = 5
WhatTypeOfVar = TypeName(LengthOfAPieceOfString)
```

Then depending on what you placed in `LengthOfAPieceOfString` then one of the following text descriptions of variant types is returned:

Empty

Null

Integer

Long Integer

Single

Double

Currency

Date

String

Object

Error

Boolean

Variant

Byte

Array

If some of these variant sub types are unfamiliar to you, don't worry: we'll be looking at arrays later in this chapter, objects in Chapter 6 and Data Access objects in Chapters 12 to 14.

We placed the number five in this example, so integer is returned. We'll now take a quick look at how you can use `TypeName()` to return the subtype that VBScript is storing for a particular variant.

Try It Out – Using TypeName to return a Variant Subtype

1. Start up your favorite ASP editor and type in the following:

```
<HTML>
<HEAD>
<TITLE>Using TypeName</TITLE>
</HEAD>
<BODY>

<%
  Dim dblPi, varWhatIsPi, datToday, whatIsDate, strText, whatIsText
  dblPi = 3.142
```

```
  varWhatIsPi = TypeName(dblPi)

  datToday = Date
  whatIsDate = TypeName(datToday)

  strText = "Hello World"
  whatIsText = TypeName(strText)

  Dim emp
  emptyVar = TypeName(emp)
%>

<P><B> dblPi returns <%= varWhatIsPi %></P>
<P>datToday returns <%= whatIsDate %></P>
<P>strText returns <%= whatIsText %></P>
<P>emp returns <%= emptyVar %></B></P>

</BODY>
</HTML>
```

2. Save it as `TypeName.asp`

Run this in your preferred browser.

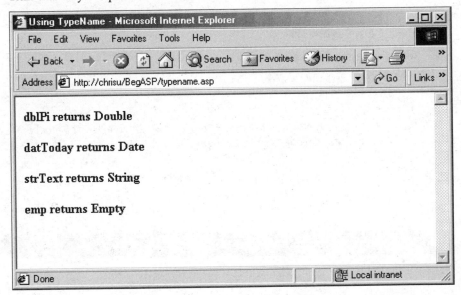

How It Works

This example is very simple. We dimension four variables and assign them values with different subtypes, and four corresponding variables to record the subtypes of the variables. We start by declaring all of the variables we're going to use and then we allocate the value of *pi*, 3.142, to the variable dblPi. Then we create a variable varWhatIsPi, which contains the TypeName value (of type string) of the dblPi variable:

```
<%
  Dim dblPi, varWhatIsPi, datToday, whatIsDate, strText, whatIsText
  dblPi = 3.142
  varWhatIsPi = TypeName(dblPi)
```

We then assign a variable datToday with today's date (provided by the VBScript Date function), and then assign TypeName(datToday) to the variable whatIsDate:

```
  datToday = Date
  whatIsDate = TypeName(datToday)
```

We assign a string value to the variable strText, and then assign TypeName(strText) to the variable whatIsText:

```
  strText = "Hello World"
  whatIsText = TypeName(strText)
```

We then declare a variable emp, but we don't actually assign it a value:

```
  Dim emp
  emptyVar = TypeName(emp) %>
```

Finally we return the four TypeName values in the ASP:

```
<P><B>dblPi returns <%= varWhatIsPi %></P>
<P>datToday returns <%= whatIsDate %></P>
<P>strText returns <%= whatIsText %></P>
<P>emp returns <%= emptyVar %></B></P>
```

When passed to the function TypeName, dblPi returns **double**, datToday returns **date**, strText returns **string** and emp returns **empty**. This confirms the fact that when you allocate data to a variable, VBScript also assigns a subtype to the variant. The subtype of the variant can be determined by using the VBScript TypeName function.

Naming Variables

As we go, we'll look at the different types of variables, how to assign values to them, and how to use them in expressions. We'll also talk about the kinds of names that you should give to your variables. For example, while the variable names above reflect their contents in a relatively self-explanatory way, the meanings of the variables in the following expressions are less obvious:

```
a = 1*x+73
varBoolean = true
```

They're not particularly helpful, are they? It's really up to the programmer to find a suitable name for his variable when he creates it. Ideally, you should find a name that is meaningful to a developer who subsequently reads your code. At the same time, excessively long variable names are unwieldy and easy to mistype, so you should avoid these too. If the variable names are chosen well, then the thinking behind the apparent gobbledygook in expressions like those above will become clearer. It's a good idea to make variable names descriptive even if this means making them longer. Here's some quick tips:

❑ `DateStart` and `DateEnd` are better then `StartDate` and `EndDate`, as these two related functions will then come next to each other in a search

❑ Variables like `Date`, `Price`, `Name` and `Number` are confusing because there are usually more than one of these, like `NameFirst`, `NameLast`, `NameSpouse`, `PriceBuy`, or `PriceSell`

❑ Avoid confusing abbreviations

❑ Never use the same variable name for two different variables, no matter how sure you are that there will not be a conflict

❑ Within a procedure or function you may want to start names with a code letter like p_ or f_

❑ Create name with multiple words, the first letter of each word in uppercase

In most languages, the name of a variable can be almost anything you choose, but there are usually a few restrictions:

❑ There's usually a practical limit to the length of your variable names. In VBScript, the limit is 255 characters – this should be more than ample for most people!

❑ There are usually restrictions on which characters you can use in your variable names. In VBScript there are restrictions, such as all variable names must begin with a letter, and variable names must not contain an embedded period/full-stop. In fact you're better off avoiding symbols altogether, other than dashes and underscores, to keep your code readable and to guarantee it will work as intended.

❑ Case-sensitivity is another important issue. VBScript is case-insensitive, which means that you can use upper- and lower-case characters to refer to exactly the same variable. For example, VBScript will interpret `counter` and `COUNTER` as one and the same. On the other hand, JScript/JavaScript is case sensitive and would interpret `counter` and `COUNTER` as two entirely different entities.

Naming Conventions

If we have many variants in a program, we need a way to keep track of which variants contain which subtype. The fact that we can convert variants from one type to another makes this 'tracking' even more important. The sensible answer is to use a good naming convention. By doing so, you can tell at a glance whether you're using an integer, a string, or date and can manipulate it in a consistent way.

Naming conventions aren't compulsory, can't be enforced and generally it's up to the programmer as to which convention to apply, but the most common one, known as Hungarian notation, is to use the first three letters of a variant's name to distinguish the sub type. The fourth letter of the variant is then typed in upper case, to indicate that this is where the actual variant name starts.

Here's the suggested naming convention: we'll be using it in our applications throughout the rest of the book:

Data Type	Prefix	Example
Boolean	bln	blnMember
Byte	byt	bytByte
Date / Time	dat	datToday
Double	dbl	dblDouble
Error	err	errError
Integer	int	intSalary
Long	lng	lngLong
Object	obj	objConn
Single	sng	sngSingle
String	str	strTextBox

Declaring Variables

We've got descriptions of the subtypes, and examples of how variables are used, but we missed an important step: how to declare a variable. Variables should be declared *before* they are used within a program, although when dealing with loops, there are exceptions as we shall see. A variable declaration is made with the keyword Dim, which is short for 'dimension'. This rather odd-looking incantation tells the VBScript that you're setting up a new variable. What this does is set aside the name and space for the variable in memory. Until the variable is assigned a value, it contains nothing (bear in mind zero is a value, so it won't contain zero or even a blank space).

For example, the first line here declares a variable with the name CarType; the second line assigns a string value to that variable:

```
Dim CarType
CarType = "Buick"
```

Declaring a variable in this way is known as **explicit** declaration, because we are explicitly telling the computer what the name of our variable is, before we use it.

Many programming languages require you declare your variables explicitly, before you can use them. This isn't strictly necessary in VBScript: indeed, you can just as easily assign a value to a variable without having first declared it. This process is known as **implicit** declaration of variables. As an example of implicit declaration, we can create another variable, CarType2, and assign the value to it, without using the Dim command:

```
CarType2 = "Pontiac"
```

It's generally good practice to explicitly declare a variable before you use it. This will allow you to keep track of all of the variables in VBScript that you've created. In fact, many programmers declare all the variables they intend to use at the beginning of the code. It should help you to avoid creating unnecessary variables, as you won't be creating them on the off chance that you might need them later in the program. Further, you can use explicit declaration together with the keywords Option Explicit to help debug your programs.

Using Option Explicit

Option Explicit is very simple. All you need to do is add this line to the beginning of your ASP scripts: then, every variable in the program must be explicitly declared in the code before it's used. If an implicitly declared variable is used, then Option Explicit generates an error highlighting the particular omission.

Here's an example of how Option Explicit is useful in keeping errors down. Consider the following program:

```
Option Explicit
Dim intHeight, intWidth, intTotal
intHeight = 150
intWidth = 140
intTotal = (intHeight * (intWidth +40))/(intHeigth+intWidth)
```

In such a short code fragment, you can probably spot pretty quickly that we've misspelled intHeight in the second usage on the last line. However, imagine that this fragment of code is buried in a list of 100 variables, about 50 lines into the page. Would you be able to spot it so quickly then?

With the Option Explicit line, this error would be detected immediately, when the script is run, as an illegal implicit declaration. Without Option Explicit, the implicit declaration is entirely legal, so your page would execute without an error. ASP will execute the page thinking that in fact you wanted to create a intHeigth as a second variable, completely different to intHeight. In fact, the only clue to the error is the value assigned to intTotal, which is calculated with the value of intHeigth (i.e. 0) instead of intHeight (i.e. 150). Indeed, if you didn't know what value to expect for intTotal, then you might not even notice the mistake at all!

When you place `Option Explicit` in a script, you must make sure it is the first line and not as follows:

```
Dim intHeight, intWidth, intTotal
Option Explicit
intHeight = 150
intWidth = 140
intTotal = (intHeight * (intWidth +40))/(intHeigth+intWidth)
```

The position of `Option Explicit` in this script will actually cause a syntax error. Moreover, on the server-side, in ASP, `Option Explicit` must come even before the first line of HTML:

```
<%Option Explicit%>
<HTML>
...
```

When you think about it, where else could it go? Scripts are run from top to bottom. If you want it to check for `Dim` statements, you had better tell it to do that before it starts reading the script. In ASP, the ASP is processed before the HTML, so it has to come before the HTML.

Arithmetic and Comparison Operators

Of course, variables aren't much use unless you can manipulate them in some way. In the descriptions above, we have already seen one or two examples of basic data manipulation, but in this section, we'll introduce the concepts more formally.

Assignment Operator

The familiar 'equal' sign (=) is probably the most common operator in computing. You've already seen it used several times to **assign** values to our variables. The variable **name** goes on the left; the variable **value** goes on the right:

```
Number1 = 2
```

VBScript doesn't enforce spaces either side of the 'equal' sign, but you may prefer to include some to make your code easier to read.

Mathematical Peculiarities

You can also use the assignment operator to increase (or decrease) the value of variables using the following, mathematically unsound, formula:

```
Number1 = 2
Number1 = Number1 + 1
```

Mathematicians will be scratching their heads, wondering how `Number1` can be equal to `Number1` plus 1: it's similar to saying 2 = 2 +1, which is impossible. The answer is, of course, that it can't. In this example, the equals sign takes on the role of an **assignment operator**, as it is assigning a new value to `Number1`. It's a way of saying whatever the old value of `Number1` is, take that and add it to 1 and this value comprises the new value of `Number1`.

Comparison Operators

The comparison operators are used slightly differently. The comparison operators available in VBScript are:

Equality	=	Inequality	<>
Less than	<	Greater than	>
Less than or equal to	<=	Greater than or equal to	>=

We've just seen the 'equal' sign (=) in its guise as the assignment operator. In this case, the 'equal' sign is used as the equality operator, to test for equality:

```
If Number1 = 2 Then
```

This statement says, "If the value inside `Number1` is already equal to 2 then (perform a certain operation)". It depends upon the context in which the equals sign is used. If it's used on its own, then it assigns one value to a variable, if it's used as part of an `If ... Then` statement, then it's being used as a comparison operator. You can also use these operators to compare the values of two operands – such as variables or expressions. The result of the comparison is a Boolean value – that is, either TRUE or FALSE.

We'll be looking at exactly how the `If ... Then` structure works in the next chapter.

Arithmetic Calculations

The arithmetic operations available in VBScript are:

Addition	+	Exponentiation	^
Subtraction	–	Negation	–
Multiplication	*	Modulus	MOD or \
Division	/		

Here is a very simple example: we'll assign values to the variables `Number1` and `Number2` before adding them together, and assigning the result to a third variable, `Number3`:

```
Number1 = 14
Number2 = 12
Number3 = Number1 + Number2
```

Because of this, `Number3` will contain the value 26.

You can also use brackets (parentheses) to influence the order in which a calculation is performed. For example, in the following code we divide the variable `Number2` by 6 and add the result to the variable `Number1`:

> *Quick reminder, normal mathematical procedure is start inside the innermost parentheses and from left to right performing exponentiation. Next go left to right performing multipication and division and then finally go left to right performing addition and subtraction. Then repeat the above steps again for next outer set of parenthesis, unti you've calculated the expression.*

```
Number1 = 14
Number2 = 18
Number3 = Number1 + (Number2/6)
```

First, the computer evaluates the contents of the brackets, following normal mathematical procedure: `Number2` divided by 6 yields the result 3. This is added to the value of `Number1`, and the result of this – 17 – is assigned to the variable `Number3`.

The most common mistake is to assign values using quotes or hashes:

```
Number1 = "14"
Number2 = 18
Number3 = Number1 + Number2
```

Even if this didn't generate an error, it certainly wouldn't hold the value 32. Let's have a go at a quick example that performs a simple calculation.

Try It Out – Using Variables to Perform a Simple Calculation

OK, we've seen lots of theory, so now it's time to try out an example. We're going to perform a simple calculation of tax. To do this we need to declare three variables: one for the earnings, one for the tax percentage, and one for the total. We're going to deduct the earnings by whatever percentage the tax rate is set at and display the final income in an ASP page.

1. Type the following program into your ASP editor:

```
<%Option Explicit%>
<HTML>
<HEAD>
<TITLE>Declaring Variables</TITLE>
</HEAD>
<BODY>
<%
  Dim intEarn, intTax, intTotal
  intEarn = 150
  intTax = 20
  intTotal = intEarn - ((intEarn/100)*intTax)
%>

<B><P>Your total earnings after tax are $<% = intTotal %> </P></B>
</BODY>
</HTML>
```

2. Save it as `taxcalc.asp` in your `inetpub\wwwroot\BegASPFiles` folder.

3. Now start your browser and run `taxcalc.asp`.

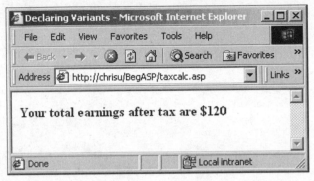

Please note that all of the Try-It-Outs in this chapter are available on our web site at `http://www.wrox.com`. You can either execute the examples directly or download them from here, whichever you prefer.

How It Works

There are only six lines of ASP code in this program. The first, of course, is our `Option Explicit` statement. The next declares three variables, `intEarn` for the earnings, `intTax` for the tax rate and `intTotal` for our final amount:

```
Dim intEarn, intTax, intTotal
```

In the next line, we set the value of the earnings to 150, and the tax rate to 20:

```
intEarn = 150
intTax = 20
```

The `intTotal` variable is where the calculation is performed. To gain our percentage, we first have to calculate what 20% of the earnings are: this is done by dividing the earnings by 100 and multiplying the result by the tax rate. Brackets are used to indicate the order of calculation within this expression:

```
intTotal = intEarn - ((intEarn/100)*intTax)
```

Finally, we return the value of `intTotal`, embedded in normal HTML code:

```
<B><P>Your total earnings after tax are $<% = intTotal %> </B></P>
```

You could calculate tax deductions for any percentage rate and any earnings, by altering the values of variables `intEarn` and `intTax`.

Logical Operators

There's also a set of logical operators you can use in your code:

AND

OR

NOT

Actually there are more than three logical operators, but they're only required in specialist situations, so we won't be using them in this book. The logical operators are used in the same way as comparison operators and also return a Boolean value:

```
If intNumber1 = 1 AND intNumber2 = 2 Then
```

They are used to determine a particular course of action. When using AND, both of these conditions have to be TRUE for the condition to be fulfilled. This differs from OR where only one out of the two conditions has to be TRUE for the condition to be fulfilled. If both conditions are true, the condition will also be true

```
If Number1 = 1 OR Number2 = 2 Then
```

The third logical operator NOT, simply implies the reverse of the condition. If Number1 isn't equal to 1 then the condition is fulfilled:

```
If NOT Number1=1 Then
```

There is a precedence for these logical operators in the way that they are calculated. This is:

❑   NOT

❑   AND

❑   OR

Take the following example:

```
If Number1=1 OR NOT Number2=1 AND NOT Number 3 =1 Then
```

Here the second part of the expression would be calculated first. You would check to see if Number2 wasn't equal to one and Number3 wasn't equal to one, before going back and checking to see if Number1 is equal to 1.

Concatenating Variables

It makes sense to add integers together, using expressions such as 2 + 3, or
Number1 + Number2 (as we showed above), but what happens if you wish to 'add' strings
together? It doesn't make much sense to add them in the arithmetic sense – "Beans" plus
"Rice" doesn't have a tangible meaning. However, VBScript allows us to 'add' strings together
in a different sense – using a process known as **concatenation**.

When two strings are concatenated, the second string is attached at the end of the first string,
creating a new string. In order to concatenate two strings we use the ampersand operator (&).
Let's run through a few examples. We can concatenate the strings "Helter" and "Skelter",
as follows:

```
strConcatenate = "Helter" & "Skelter"
```

Here, the result of the concatenation is the string "HelterSkelter", which will be assigned to
the variable strConcatenate, of type string. You should note that VBScript won't
automatically put in spaces or commas, though. You can also concatenate a number of strings
within the same expression. Here, we'll concatenate three strings, one of which is a space (which
is also a string since a space is a character):

```
strConcatenate = "Helter" & " " & "Skelter"
```

Now, strConcatenate will contain the string "Helter Skelter". You can concatenate as
many string variables as you like (within the maximum length of 255 characters in VBScript):

```
strFirst = "Never "
strLearline = strFirst & strFirst & strFirst & strFirst & strFirst
```

Then strLearLine will contain the line "Never Never Never Never Never ".

Comparing Variables with a String SubType

Although you can't add or subtract strings numerically, this doesn't account for the comparison
operators. These can be used to help compare and sort text into alphabetical order. So if you
wished to find out which came first in the alphabet aardvark or anteater, the following code
could be used:

```
strAnimal1 = "Aardvark"
strAnimal2 = "Anteater"
If strAnimal1 < strAnimal2 Then Response.Write "Aardvark"
If strAnimal2 < strAnimal1 Then Response.Write "Anteater"
```

It doesn't take a genius to figure out that the program will return Aardvark, however, if you
were comparing the contents of variables, which depend on input from users, then this can
alphabetically sort data for you without the need to refer to a database. We will look at sorting
in databases in detail in chapters 12 to 14.

Conversions

As we now know, when you assign a value to a variant, a subtype is also automatically assigned. Sometimes, however, the assigned subtype is not the one that you intend, and in such cases, a little force is required to explicitly convert the value into the type you actually wanted. VBScript provides plenty of functions to do this for you. In fact, it provides so many of these functions that you'll probably never use many of them. In a moment, we'll exercise the most common of these functions in an example. First, here's a complete list of them:

Function	Description
Abs	Returns the absolute value of number.
Asc, AscB, AscW	Returns the ANSI character code of the first letter in a string. AscB is used on byte data while AscW is used on 32-bit platforms that use UNICODE data (a format that falls outside the scope of this book).
Chr, ChrB, ChrW	This is the opposite of Asc, and returns the character of a specific character code. ChrB is used on byte data contained in a string while ChrW is used on 32-bit platforms that use UNICODE data.
CBool	Returns an expression that has been converted into a variant with the subtype Boolean.
CByte	Returns the variable that has been converted into a variant with the subtype Byte.
CCur	Returns the variable that has been converted into a variant with the subtype Currency.
CDate	Returns the variable that has been converted into a variant with the subtype Date.
CDbl	Returns the variable that has been converted into a variant with the subtype Double.
CInt	Returns the variable that has been converted into a variant with the subtype Integer and rounds it up to the nearest *whole* number. e.g. 0.5 converts to 0 while 1.5 converts to 2
CLng	Returns the variable that has been converted into a variant with the subtype Long.
CSng	Returns the variable that has been converted into a variant with the subtype Single.
CStr	Returns the variable that has been converted into a variant with the subtype String.
DateSerial	Returns the variable that has been converted into a variant with the subtype Date for given year, month, day. e.g. DateSerial (1999, 11, 1) would return 1st November 1999

Function	Description
DateValue	Returns a value representing a variant of subtype Date.
TimeSerial	Returns the variable that has been converted into a variant with the subtype Date for given hour, minute, second.
TimeValue	Returns a value representing a variant of subtype Date.
Hex	Returns a string containing the hexadecimal value of a number.
Oct	Returns a string containing the octal value of a number.
Fix	Returns the integer portion of a number using truncation. e.g. 7.2 becomes 7 as does 7.8
Int	Also returns the integer portion of a number using truncation. e.g. 7.2 becomes 7 as does 7.8.
Sgn	Returns the sign of a number, i.e. positive or negative.

If you assign a fraction or decimal value to an integer, normally the integer is rounded up or down to the next closest whole number. This process is known as an implicit conversion.

These functions all work in much the same way. As a demonstration, we'll have a look at how to use a couple of them now.

Try It Out – Converting a Variant

In this example we're going to take the value of *pi*=3.142, read it in as a string, convert to a single data type, convert it into an integer and then finally convert it back to a string. We're also going to display the value and subtype of each variant after the conversion.

1. Type the following program into your favorite editor:

```
<%Option Explicit%>
<HTML>
<HEAD>
<TITLE>Converting Variants</TITLE>
</HEAD>
<BODY>

<%
  Dim strPi, dblPi, intPi,strPi2
  Dim varWhatIsPi1, varWhatIsPi2, varWhatIsPi3, varWhatIsPi4

  strPi = "3.142"
  varWhatIsPi1 = TypeName(strPi)
  dblPi = CDbl(strPi)
  varWhatIsPi2 = TypeName(dblPi)
  intPi = CInt(dblPi)
  varWhatIsPi3 = TypeName(intPi)
  strPi2 = CStr(intPi)
  varWhatIsPi4 = TypeName(strPi2)
%>
```

```
<P><B>Pi is a <%= varWhatIsPi1 %> and Pi returns <%= strPi %> </B></P>
<P><B>Pi is a <%= varWhatIsPi2 %> and Pi returns <%= dblPi %> </B></P>
<P><B>Pi is a <%= varWhatIsPi3 %> and Pi returns <%= intPi %> </B></P>
<P><B>Pi is a <%= varWhatIsPi4 %> and Pi returns <%= strPi2 %> </B></P>
</BODY>
</HTML>
```

2. Save it as `convert.asp`.

3. Run the page on your preferred browser.

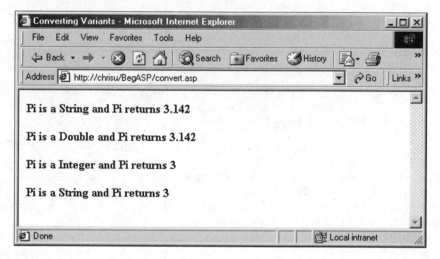

How It Works

This program explicitly declares all of the variants we will use and then assigns the variant `strPi` a value of "3.142", which is a string. It then reads the subtype of this variant into another variant, `varWhatIsPi1`:

```
<%
  Dim strPi, dblPi, intPi,strPi2
  Dim varWhatIsPi1, varWhatIsPi2, varWhatIsPi3, varWhatIsPi4
  strPi = "3.142"
  varWhatIsPi1 = TypeName(strPi)
```

Next, we declare three more variants; the value assigned to each is generated by converting the subtype of the preceding one. Hence, the value assigned to `dblPi` is the conversion of `strPi` from subtype string to subtype double. In addition, the `TypeName` of the variant `dblPi` is assigned to `varWhatIsPi2`:

```
  dblPi = CDbl(strPi)
  varWhatIsPi2 = TypeName(dblPi)
```

The value assigned to `intPi` is the conversion of `dblPi` from subtype double to subtype integer. The `TypeName` of `intPi` is assigned to `varWhatIsPi3`:

```
intPi = CInt(dblPi)
varWhatIsPi3 = TypeName(intPi)
```

Last, the value assigned to `strPi2` is the conversion of `intPi` back to subtype string. The `TypeName` of `intPi` is assigned to `varWhatIsPi4`:

```
strPi2 = CStr(intPi)
varWhatIsPi4 = TypeName(strPi2)
%>
```

The final lines simply display the subtype and value of each of these variants:

```
<P><B>Pi is a <%= varWhatIsPi1 %> and Pi returns <%= strPi %> </B></P>
<P><B>Pi is a <%= varWhatIsPi2 %> and Pi returns <%= dblPi %> </B></P>
<P><B>Pi is a <%= varWhatIsPi3 %> and Pi returns <%= intPi %> </B></P>
<P><B>Pi is a <%= varWhatIsPi4 %> and Pi returns <%= strPi2 %> </B></P>
```

Notice that because of the conversion from subtype double to subtype integer, the fractional part of the value of *pi* is lost. Further, when you convert back to subtype string, you don't regain the information! (This is because the final conversion is from type integer to subtype string: the value to be converted is 3, not 3.142.) It's easy to lose information in this way, so you should be sure to control your conversions carefully. Don't be put off, though: data conversions are a useful tool to have, and they're not difficult to use.

Constants

There will be occasions when you want a value assigned to a variable to remain constant throughout the execution of the code. A good example is statewide sales tax, this value will rarely, if ever, change, yet when calculating the total of a shopping basket, you'll probably need to refer to it several times. Even if the tax is changed, you'd still only need to refer to one value, and you'd only need to update one value. To represent the sales tax you can you use something other than a variable, namely a constant.

Constants are like variables except that, once they have been assigned a value, they don't change. Many programming languages provide an explicit facility for constants, by allowing the programmer to assign an initial value to the constant, and subsequently forbidding any alteration of that value. The main reason you'd assign a value to a constant is to prevent accidental alteration of that value.

VBScript supports constants with the `Const` keyword being used to define them. By convention, constants are named in upper case:

```
Const ABSOLUTEZERO = -273
```

If you tried then to assign another value to ABSOLUTEZERO, such as:

```
ABSOLUTEZERO = 0
```

The change would be rejected and an error message would be produced. Constants remain in force for the duration of the script, just like variables do, but no longer. While it isn't possible to amend their value once it has been set, it is possible to set them to something different in the page, when you run a page again. Constants make your code easier to read and maintain, as they require less updating and if you choose a self-explanatory name, then they make your code easily understandable.

VBScript Constants

VBScript also presents a list of its own type constants, with values that you can use but will be unable to change. These constants correspond to the list of subtypes that we looked at earlier:

Constant	Value
VbEmpty	0
VbNull	1
VbInteger	2
VbLong	3
VbSingle	4
VbDouble	5
VbCurrency	6
VbDate	7
VbString	8
VbObject	9
VbError	10
VbBoolean	11
VbVariant	12
VbDataObject	13
VbByte	17
VbArray	8192

You can use these constants in the same way that you use variants; each of them represents the particular constant value indicated, although you cannot alter their values in any way.

There are literally hundreds of constants, which we can't cover here, and commonly they are stored in a separate file and then included in a page when needed. We look at the concept of using included information in chapter 10.

Variable Scope

When we mentioned some of the restrictions on naming variables at the beginning of this chapter, we neglected to mention one rather odd requirement that you might have taken for granted. That requirement is the following: that when you name a variable, it should have a *unique* name.

The reasons for avoiding this in the early stages of this chapter are the complications that arise when a piece of code contains two variables of the same name, because under certain circumstances it *is* allowed. This doesn't mean, contrary to what we said earlier, that this is a practice you should be indulging in, because it still isn't. However, the idea that a variable need not have influence over the whole contents of a page, but rather only directly over the part of a page you want to use it for, is a powerful and confers performance enhancements. ASP only has to track it for a short amount of time, rather than the whole lifetime of a page, it uses less memory and when the procedure that uses the variable is over, then the memory is freed up.

It all depends on a rather glib sounding concept known as **scope**.

Local Variables

On the surface, it seems to defy logical explanation, but I promise you that there is logic here: let's look at it more closely. Consider two variables, both with the name strDifferent. We'll try to assign different values to these two variables:

```
strDifferent = "Hello I'm variable one"
strDifferent = "Hello I'm variable two"
```

If you returned the value of strDifferent, you'd find that is contains the string "Hello I'm variable two", thus overwriting the first value assigned to strDifferent. That's because we haven't created two variables at all; we simply created one variable, strDifferent, and then changed its value.

The exception to this rule is when we try using a similar structure in a **Subprocedure**. If you have a program that performs the same task repeatedly, it is sometimes more efficient to write the code that performs this task once, and access the same lines of code whenever the task is required. This is where Subprocedures come in. Subprocedures hold blocks of code that can be "called" from other parts of the program to run a specific set of actions whenever necessary. We'll discuss Subprocedures (and Functions, which are a similar concept) in detail in Chapter 5.

If you defined strDifferent twice *within two different procedures*, then you'd see a different result:

```
Sub Procedure_Number_1
  strDifferent = "Hello I'm variable one"
End Sub

Sub Procedure_Number_2
  strDifferent = "Hello I'm variable two"
End Sub
```

If you return the value of `strDifferent` in `Procedure_Number_1`, then you'd get `"Hello I'm variable one"`. If you return the value of `strDifferent` in `Procedure_Number_2`, you'd get `"Hello I'm variable two"`. However, if you *then* go back and run `Procedure_Number_1` again, you'd get `"Hello I'm variable one"` again. Hence, they are effectively two different variables, although they share the same name.

These variables are known as **local** variables (in the Microsoft documentation, they're called **procedure level** variables), because they are local to the procedure that created them. Outside the procedure, the local variable has no value: this is because the **lifetime** of the variable ends when the procedure ends. As these local variables are only in effect for a lifetime of a procedure, ASP doesn't have to worry about keeping track of them over the whole page. When a local variable is created, it only exists while the procedure that invokes it is running; once the program exits the procedure, the variable's lifetime is over, thus freeing memory and resources, increasing performance. Also you cannot create a variable twice within its scope.

Now, let's take a look at how to use two local variables. To demonstrate that they are local we will make them share the same name during our ASP program.

Try It Out – Creating Local Variables

1. Start your favorite editor and hammer out the following program:

```
<HTML>

<HEAD>
<TITLE>Scope</TITLE>
</HEAD>
<BODY bgcolor="white">

<%
  Sub Procedure_1
    strDifferent = "Hi I'm strDifferent in Procedure 1"
    Response.Write strdifferent
  End Sub

  Sub Procedure_2
    strDifferent = "Hi I'm strDifferent in Procedure 2"
    Response.Write strdifferent
  End Sub
%>

<P>Calling Procedure 1...<I><%Procedure_1()%></I></P>
<P>Calling Procedure 2...<I><%Procedure_2()%></I></P>
<P>Calling Procedure 1...<I><%Procedure_1()%></I></P>
</BODY>
</HTML>
```

2. Save the program as `local.asp`

3. Execute it in your browser of choice:

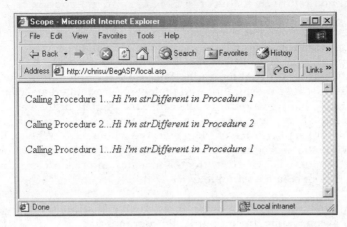

How It Works

This program contains two almost identical procedures:

```
<%
  Sub Procedure_1
    strDifferent = "Hi I'm strDifferent in Procedure 1"
    Response.Write strdifferent
  End Sub

  Sub Procedure_2
    strDifferent = "Hi I'm strDifferent in Procedure 2"
    Response.Write strdifferent
  End Sub
%>
```

However, each of the variables called `strDifferent` is defined within the confines of its respective procedure, and so doesn't exist outside the context of the procedure. If you asked the ASP program to print the value of `strDifferent` from *outside* either of these procedures, it would in fact return no value at all.

Script Level Variables

So, if variables created in procedures are local to the procedure that created them, how do you go about ensuring that the value of one variable persists from one procedure to the next, when you need it to? In other words, how do you extend the lifetimes of your variables? The answer comes in the form of **script level** variables, which are variables that are declared outside procedures.

The lifetime of a script level variable begins at the start of the script (or scripts in one page) and ends at the end of the script, and spans any procedures created within the script. In comparison, local variables contained within a procedure are destroyed when the procedure is exited, and hence the memory space is saved. It's a good idea to use local variables where possible, because it makes things easier to read and helps to avoid bugs in code and above all improves performance.

Now let's see how we can amend our previous program to include a script level variable:

Try It Out – Using Script Level Variables

We're going to simply add a new script level variable to this program and then display it from inside and outside the procedures.

1. Load up the previous program, `local.asp`, in your preferred ASP editor and add the following lines in the following locations:

```
<HTML>

<HEAD>
<TITLE>Using Script Level Variables</TITLE>
</HEAD>

<BODY BGCOLOR="white">
<%
  strGlobal = "I'm a persistent script-level variable"
  Response.Write strGlobal

  Sub Procedure_1
    strDifferent = "Hi I'm strDifferent in Procedure 1"
    Response.Write strdifferent
    Response.Write "<P>" & strGlobal & "</P>"
  End Sub

  Sub Procedure_2
    strDifferent = "Hi I'm strDifferent in Procedure 2"
    Response.Write strdifferent
    Response.Write "<P>" & strGlobal & "</P>"
  End Sub
%>

<P>Calling Procedure 1 ...<I><%Procedure_1()%></I></P>
<P>Calling Procedure 2 ...<I><%Procedure_2()%></I></P>
<P>Calling Procedure 1 ...<I><%Procedure_1()%></I></P>
</BODY>
</HTML>
```

2. Save it this time as `global.asp`

3. Open this page on your browser.

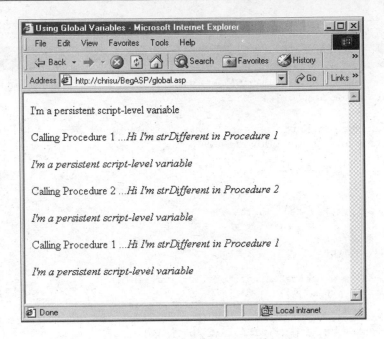

How It Works

We've not changed our original program much, other than adding new text the sole addition is a script level variable, strGlobal. This variable is assigned the text "I'm a persistent script-level variable" and is then called at various points in the program:

```
strGlobal = "I'm a persistent script-level variable"
```

We first display this string from outside both procedures; the second time, from within procedure 1; the third time from within procedure 2; and the final time from within procedure 1 again. Each time, the variable is displayed using the following code, so there's no trickery of any sort:

```
Response.Write "<P>" & strGlobal & "</P>"
```

The output shows how script level variables and local variables can be used side by side in any ASP program.

String Manipulation

Having outlined all of the different subtypes of variant available, let's take a look at some of the functions you have available to you, which allow you to operate on the information contained within. String manipulation is a completely new ball game that allows you to glean information from text. For example, if a user's full home address were stored in a string, how would you go about extracting just the house number and street name from the string, while removing all the other extraneous information? Have no fear: VBScript provides a set of functions, which allow you to chop, prune and order strings in any way you like. There are several functions provided; we'll only look at the major ones. These are:

- ❑ UCase and LCase
- ❑ Len
- ❑ Left
- ❑ Right
- ❑ Mid
- ❑ InStr
- ❑ LTrim, Rtrim and Trim

Note that if you are familiar with Visual Basic or VBA then you might be familiar with version of the functions LTrim, RTrim and Trim, which are LTrim\$, RTrim\$ and Trim\$. However these variations do not work in VBScript and therefore not in ASP either.

Changing the Case of a String

The two functions that allow you to alter the case of text are LCase and UCase. You can use them in the following way:

LCase(string) *or* UCase(string)

So if you applied LCase to "Hello" it would become "hello" and if you applied UCase to "Hello" then it would become "HELLO". If you applied either of these functions to a string that was already in the specified case then it wouldn't have any effect. These functions simply alter the case of text that is held in your variable, without actually altering the contents of the variable itself. You could use these functions as follows:

```
strText="HeLlO"
Response.Write UCase(strText)
Response.Write LCase(strText)
```

Returning the Length of a String

The Len function is used to return the length of a string – that is, the number of characters. You can use it in the following way:

```
Len(string)
```

This function only takes one argument, namely the string that you are measuring:

```
intHowLong = Len("HowLongIsAPieceOfString?")
```

In this example, there are 24 characters in this string, and so intHowLong is assigned the value 24. Any symbols, punctuation, and spaces within the string are valid characters, and therefore they are counted in the length of the string. You can also supply a variable name to the Len function; in this case, it will measure the contents of the named variable:

```
strText = "HowLongIsAPieceOfString?"
intHowLong = Len(strText)
```

In this example, the Len function would again return the value 24. Later on, we'll use this function in an example that loops through a string, character by character – the function is used to tell us when we've reached the end of the string.

Pruning the Beginning or End of a String

The Left and Right Functions can be used to extract a given number of characters from the beginning or end of a given string. They don't actually 'remove' the characters as such; instead, they act like the 'Copy' function of a word processor and copy the selected section into the new variable. Each of these functions takes two parameters:

```
Left(string, number_of_characters)
```

And

```
Right(string, number_of_characters)
```

The Left function's second parameter, *number_of_characters* specifies how many characters to extract from the beginning (left-hand side) of the string:

```
strLeftChars = Left("HowLongIsAPieceOfString?",3)
```

StrLeftChars would contain the string "How". Again, you can also supply a variable name to the Left function, which will extract the appropriate substring from the string contained by this variable. For example:

```
strText = "HowLongIsAPieceOfString?"
strLeftChars = Left(strText,7)
```

This would assign the string "HowLong" to the variable strLeftChars.

The Right function works in the same way, except that it extracts characters from the (right-hand) end of the string:

```
strRightChars = Right("HowLongIsAPieceOfString?",7)
```

Here, the variable strRightChars is assigned the string "String?". Again, this function supports the option of extracting characters from a string variant; and once again, symbols, spaces, and punctuation count as valid characters.

Removing the Middle of a String

Of course, that leaves the problem of extracting a section from the middle of a string. To do this, VBScript provides another function, Mid. The function Mid works along the same principles as Right and Left, but it takes an extra parameter:

```
Mid(string, where_in_the_string, number_of_characters_to_be_extracted)
```

Once again, the first parameter is the source string itself. The second parameter is the position of the first character in the substring that you want to extract, and the third is the number of characters in the substring. In our little example, we can isolate the word `"Piece"` by setting the second parameter to 11 (corresponding to the letter `"P"`) and the third parameter to 5 (indicating the number of characters in the desired substring). The following example extracts the word `"Piece"` from our original string, and assigns it to the variable `strMiddleChars`:

```
strText = "HowLongIsAPieceOfString?"
strMiddleChars = Mid(strText,11,5)
```

Finding a Particular Word

Of course, there will be times when you want to find a particular word within a string and the point where it occurs. The function that will do this for you is `InStr`. This function requires the string itself, and the text to be located as parameters:

```
InStr(string, text_to_be_located)
```

In our example, we can use it to isolate a particular word and return its position in a string.

```
strText = "HowLongIsAPieceOfString?"
intwhere = InStr(strText,"Long")
```

This example would return the number 4, as the word "Long" starts on the fourth character. However, `InStr` is also case-sensitive, so if you searched for "long" instead of "Long", you wouldn't find it at all. In this case `InStr` returns the value 0.

Giving it a Quick Trim

Finally, in this section, we'll have a look at the functions `Trim`, `LTrim`, and `RTrim`. These three related functions give us three different ways to remove extraneous space characters from a string. They're particularly useful when dealing with user input. Each function takes a single parameter – a string – and they are written as follows:

```
Trim(string)
LTrim(string)
RTrim(string)
```

The function `LTrim` removes spaces from the left-hand side of a string, while `RTrim` (you guessed it) removes spaces from the right-hand side of the string. The `Trim` function combines the two, by removing all of the spaces from the beginning and end of the string.

As an example, let's consider the following string, which has three spaces at each end:

```
strSpace="   feeling kinda spaced out   "
```

Then the code:

```
<%= Ltrim(strSpace) %>
```

Would return the string "feeling kinda spaced out   ". Meanwhile,

```
<%= Rtrim(strSpace) %>
```

Would return the string "   feeling kinda spaced out"; and of course,

```
<%= Trim(strSpace) %>
```

Would return the string "feeling kinda spaced out".

OK, we're ready to exercise nearly all of these functions in an example.

Try It Out – String Manipulation

This is quite a complex example. We're going to store a name, address, and date of birth in one line, in the form of a string. We are then going to identify and break out a name, address, and date of birth from our string separately Then we will return each item of information to the screen on a new line as each one is 'cut out' of our string. We'll do this by assigning our one line with the information to a variable, and then by detecting the occurrence of a 'bookmark' character in the sentence, we can identify which is the name, address and date of birth. This kind of code can be very useful if, for example, you were confronted with an address, and you might want to identify each part separately and store it individually.

1. Start your editor and type in the following code:

```
<HTML>
<HEAD>
<TITLE>String Manipulation Example</TITLE>
</HEAD>

<BODY >
<%
  Dim strText, intEndOfName, strName, strTemp, intEndofAddress, strAddress, strDOB
  strText ="Vervain Delaware;42 Chelworth Gardens;1st October 1901"
  intEndOfName = Instr(strText,";")
  strName = mid(strText, 1, intEndofName-1)
  strTemp = mid(strText, intEndofName+1, len(strText))

  intEndofAddress = Instr(strTemp,";")
  strAddress = mid(strTemp, 1, intEndofAddress-1)
  strDOB = mid(strTemp,intEndofAddress+1, len(strTemp))

  Response.Write "<BR>" & strName
  Response.Write "<BR>" & strAddress
  Response.Write "<BR>" & strDOB
%>
</BODY>
</HTML>
```

2. Save the file as string.asp.

3. Execute the file on your normal browser.

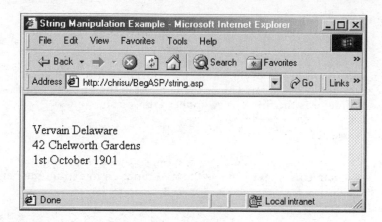

4. This program is very flexible, and will perform this operation on any sentence you feed in. So, go back to the source code and change the line that assigns a sentence to the variable `strText` to:

```
Dim strText, intEndOfName, strName, strTemp, intEndofAddress, strAddress, strDOB
strText ="Sherlock Holmes;221B Baker Street;6th January 1854"
intEndofName = Instr(strText,";")
```

5. Now run the program again.

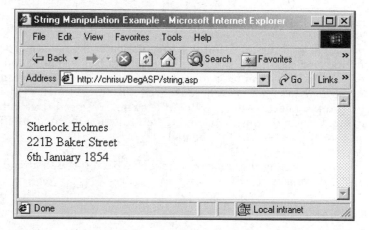

How It Works

Take a deep breath before we look at this one: there's a lot to absorb. The first line defines the seven variables we'll need:

```
Dim strText, intEndOfName, strName, strTemp, intEndofAddress, strAddress, strDOB
```

`strText` is used to store the whole line, while `strName`, `strAddress` and `strDOB` is used to store the name, address and date of birth separately. `intEndOfName` is used to store the position of the end of the name in our `strText`, and `intEndOfAddress` is used to store the end point of the address. `strTemp` is used to store a temporary version of our line that we can perform operations on.

Next, we store our sentence in our `strText` variable:

```
strText ="Vervain Delaware;42 Chelworth Gardens;1st October 1901"
```

We generate the position of the end of the name, by using the `Instr` function to find the first occurrence of the semi-colon character. This is then stored in the `intEndOfName` variable, since we know that this character is the first one to appear after our name:

```
intEndofName = Instr(strText,";")
```

Next, we know that we have encountered a semi-colon, so that everything that lies before it in `strText` is part of the name. Now we can use the `Mid` function to extract the name.

```
strName = mid(strText, 1, intEndofName-1)
```

In this line we need to supply the `Mid` function with three parameters to do this, the first being the text we are performing the operation on, the second being the character at which we start our extraction, the third being the position of the character *before* the semi-colon (the one which is 1 character before it, or `intEndofName-1`). Obviously, we don't want to include the semi-colon, so we have to go back to the position one before it in the text. We then store the result of the `Mid` function in `strName`.

Next we populate a temporary variable, called `strTemp`, which contains everything in our data line that comes after the name and semi-colon:

```
strTemp = mid(strText, intEndofName+1, len(strText))
```

To do this we again use the `Mid` function, but this time the parameters we supply are different. The first is our data line once again; the second is the position of the semi-colon in our line, plus one (indicating the first character to appear *after* the semicolon). The third parameter is the one that will look a little strange to you. This is because we're nesting a function inside a function. If you remember, the third parameter is the length of the string. We need to calculate the position of the end of our string. We can do this by using the `Len` function to calculate the length of the string `strText` and return it as the third parameter.

After that we're basically repeating the same process we've been through already. We use `Instr` to search for the next semi-colon:

```
intEndofAddress = Instr(strTemp,";")
```

Hopefully, you can see the purpose of extracting the name from the first part of our string. This is because when we use `InStr` again to find a semi-colon, we want the second occurrence of a semi-colon. As `Instr` only returns the position of the first semi-colon, we need to have removed the first occurrence. Next we can go on with the process of extracting the address:

```
strAddress = mid(strTemp, 1, intEndofAddress-1)
```

The same principle applies as with the name. Lastly, whatever we're left with must be the date of birth. So we use the Mid function to copy the last part of the string, starting one character after the position of our second semi-colon:

```
strDOB = mid(strTemp,intEndOfAddress+1, len(strTemp))
```

Once these three variables are stored then we can display the contents of our variables:

```
Response.Write "<BR>" & strName
Response.Write "<BR>" & strAddress
Response.Write "<BR>" & strDOB
```

The program continues, displaying each separate item of information in turn on the screen, until we reach the end of the line. Of course this is slightly artificial – if we wanted to store more than three items of information, then our program wouldn't be able to cope. To achieve this kind of flexibility, we need to make use of loops and branching structures. We look at these in the next chapter.

String manipulation functions are among some of the most useful features of VBScript. In order to apply them properly, they can take a little thought. However, they can be put to some very practical uses, such as identifying items of information within an address or a form, and being able to save only the pieces that we want while discarding the rest.

Arrays

Variables are fine for storing individual items of data. However, they're not so good if you wish to store many items of similar information. In this case, you'll need to use an array. Arrays are used to store a series of related data items, which are related by an index number at the end. You could use them to store the names of the Marx brothers, for instance:

```
strMarx(0) = "Groucho"
strMarx(1) = "Harpo"
strMarx(2) = "Chico"
strMarx(3) = "Zeppo"
strMarx(4) = "Gummo"
strMarx(5) = "Karl""
```

However, you don't have to store something in each item of the array, and you don't even have to store it sequentially:

```
strHouse(1) = "Mr Jones"
strHouse(3) = "Mr Goldstein"
strHouse(4) = "Mrs Soprano"
```

Arrays are particularly useful if you want to manipulate a whole set of data items as though they were all one item. For example, if you want to adjust the pay rates for a set of five employees, then the difficult way is the following:

```
intExtraPay = 10
intEmployeePay(0) = intEmployeePay(0) + intExtraPay
intEmployeePay(1) = intEmployeePay(1) + intExtraPay
intEmployeePay(2) = intEmployeePay(2) + intExtraPay
intEmployeePay(3) = intEmployeePay(3) + intExtraPay
intEmployeePay(4) = intEmployeePay(4) + intExtraPay
```

The following much simpler code utilizes your array structure, and has exactly the same effect:

```
intExtraPay = 10
For intLoop = 0 to 4
  intEmployeePay ( intLoop) = intEmployeePay(intLoop) + intExtraPay
Next
```

Arrays are much more versatile than plain regular variables when dealing with sets of data.

We will be discussing For ... Next *loops in the next chapter.*

Declaring Arrays

Arrays are declared in the same way as variables, using the Dim keyword. However, an array declaration needs a parameter at the end, which is used to specify the size of the array. We could set up an array to have 50 entries for each of the states in the US, with the following statement:

```
Dim StatesInUS(49)
```

The index number 49 isn't a mistake. It is just that arrays count from zero upwards in VBScript, rather than from one. So in this case the 50 states are indexed by the 50 different parameter values 0, 1, …, 49. This type of array is known as a **fixed-size array**, because you fix the maximum number of items that the array can contain. If you don't know the number of items there are to be in your array, or don't wish to specify, you can create a **dynamic array** instead:

```
Dim BritishAthleticsWorldChampionshipWinners()
```

You can then go back and specify how many items there should be at a later point, using the keyword Redim, which is short for re-dimension, although there is a performance penalty for using Redim, so try to find the number if possible first.

```
Redim BritishAthleticsWorldChampionshipWinners(0)
```

There was only one (sniff)…

Redeclaring Arrays

Sometimes there are situations when you've already specified the number of items in a dynamic array, but then you have to amend that amount. If, for example, you'd estimated the number of items but then found that you'd needed a larger array than first envisaged, you could use the Redim keyword once again, to set up the array with the new amount:

```
Dim amoeba()
Redim amoeba(1)
amoeba(0) = "Geronimo"
amoeba(1) = "Geronimee"
'amoebas divide...
Redim amoeba(3)
```

However, you'd lose the information already held in the existing array, so you'd have to reenter the information. Fortunately, help is at hand, in the form of another keyword, Preserve, which can be used together with Redim, to ensure that the existing contents of your array are not irretrievably lost:

```
Redim Preserve amoeba(3)
amoeba(2) = "Geronimo Mk II"
amoeba(3) = "Geronimee Mk II"
```

Now we're ready to a look a small example utilizing some of these concepts.

Try It Out – Setting Up An Array

In this example, we're going to set up a dynamic array, add some contents, and then display the contents. Then we're going to resize the array, add an extra item, and redisplay it just to prove that we haven't destroyed the original contents

1. Give your ASP editor a poke in the ribs to wake it up, and then type in the following:

```
<HTML>
<HEAD>
<TITLE>Using Arrays</TITLE>
</HEAD>
<BODY>

<P>Here are the Marx Brothers: </P>
<%
  Dim strMarx()
  Redim strMarx(4)
  strMarx(0) = "Groucho"
  strMarx(1) = "Harpo"
  strMarx(2) = "Chico"
  strMarx(3) = "Zeppo"
  strMarx(4) = "Gummo"
  Response.Write "<P><B>"

  For intCounter = 0 to 4
    Response.Write strMarx(intCounter) & "... "
  Next
```

```
  Response.Write "</B></P>"
  Response.Write "<P>Whoops! Nearly forgot the bearded leftish one... </P>"
  Redim Preserve strMarx(5)
  strMarx(5) = "Karl"
  Response.Write "<P><B>"

  For intCounter = 0 to 5
    Response.Write strMarx(intCounter) & "... "
  Next
%>

</B></P>
</BODY>
</HTML>
```

2. Save it as `array.asp` and close it down

3. Get your browser up and ready and run this program on it:

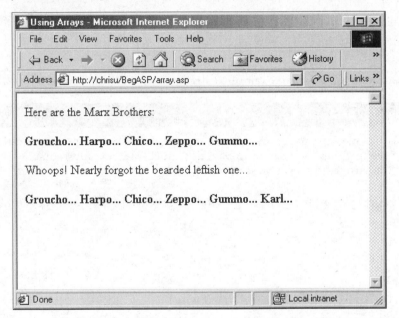

How It Works

This program starts by setting up a dynamic array `strMarx`, and then declaring that it contains five items (in a zero-based array – hence the count from 0 to 4):

```
<%
  Dim strMarx()
  Redim strMarx(4)
```

We then populate our array with five values, the names of the Marx Brothers:

```
strMarx(0) = "Groucho"
strMarx(1) = "Harpo"
strMarx(2) = "Chico"
strMarx(3) = "Zeppo"
strMarx(4) = "Gummo"
```

To display the contents of our array, rather printing out each one individually, we have to use a special construct known as a **loop**. We're going to look at loops in detail in the next chapter. For the time all you need to know is that it is an automatically incrementing counter that sets the value of intCounter to 0, in the first instance and runs the Response.Write line. Then the *key* aspect of the loop is once it reaches the word Next, it goes back to the beginning of the loop and runs the lines in between For and Next again, but this time setting intCounter to 1. It continues this repetition until the value of intCounter reaches the end of the range assigned in the For statement:

```
For intCounter = 0 to 4
```

In this way the loop increments the variable intCounter to go through each item in our array. The loop goes through five values, 0, 1, 2, 3 and 4 and substitutes the value in intCounter on each pass of the loop:

```
    Response.Write strMarx(intCounter) & "... "
Next
```

The first item in the array, strMarx(0), contains the string "Groucho", and this is displayed on the screen. The next statement tells the loop to go back and add another 1 to the value of intCounter. This time strMarx(1) is displayed, which contains the string "Harpo", that we assigned earlier. It's repeated for strMarx(2) and strMarx(3), and on the final iteration of the loop, the value of 4 is assigned to intCounter which enables the contents of the variable strMarx(4) to be displayed.

However, the program doesn't end there. Next, we display some more HTML, before going back into ASP and resizing the array so that it may hold six items. The keyword Preserve ensures that none of the original items are lost:

```
Response.Write "<P>Whoops! Nearly forgot the bearded leftish one... </P>"
Redim Preserve strMarx(5)
```

We set up a value for the new item in our dynamic array:

```
strMarx(5) = "Karl"
```

Then we go around the loop again, outputting the contents of the array, except that this time the loop is iterated six times, not five:

```
For intCounter = 0 to 5
  Response.Write strMarx(intCounter) & "... "
Next
```

If we were to omit the keyword Preserve when resizing the dynamic array, we would lose the names of the five original Marx brothers, so the array would be empty again before adding their political namesake. Try running the program again without the word Preserve, just to see.

Multi-Dimensional Arrays

If you need to keep information of a two-dimensional nature, then you can do it by declaring a two-dimensional array. For instance, if you wanted to store a set of related information separately such as a first and last name, a normal array would probably be unsuitable. Instead, you achieve it by adding another parameter to your array declaration. Thus:

```
Dim str2Darray(3,3)
```

Would set up a two-dimensional array of size 4 by 4, which could hold a total of 16 values. You can assign values to a multi-dimensional array by referencing each element of the array through its two-value index. For example, you could use such an array to store first and last names and phone number:

```
str2Darray(0,0) = "John"
str2Darray(1,0) = "Doe"
str2Darray(2,0) = "111-111-1111"
str2Darray(0,1) = "Jane"
str2Darray(1,1) = "Doe"
str2Darray(2,1) = "222-222-2222"
```

The first dimension stores the information that is related to one person, such as first, last name and phone number, while the second dimension holds data of the same type for different people, such as a set of phone numbers. In fact, VBScript is not limited to arrays of one or two dimensions; you can declare an array with up to 60 dimensions, should you so require. However using anything more than three dimensions is impractical and you'd be better off pursuing other solutions such as databases if you require more than three. This takes us as far as we need to go with arrays and variables, we'll be using them throughout the rest of this book, so take care to understand them.

Summary

In this chapter, we have considered how we can go about storing the data collected by the computer, both from the user and from its own calculations. We looked at what a variable is and how VBScript treats each of the different subtypes of data as just one type, the variant. We looked at how you would go about declaring variables, and how the Option Explicit commands can be used to lessen the chance of making a typing mistake in the variable name. We then looked at various functions that VBScript provides to manipulate variables.

We looked at why certain variables are only effective within certain scopes. We also considered why some variables keep their value throughout the whole script, while others keep their values only within the procedures that created them.

Finally, we looked at how you could store a series of related data items with an array, and referring to the elements of the array using an index. We looked at how you can size and populate arrays, and we finished off by looking briefly, at how you could make them multi-dimensional.

In the next chapter, we'll expand on a number of very useful programming tools, the control structures

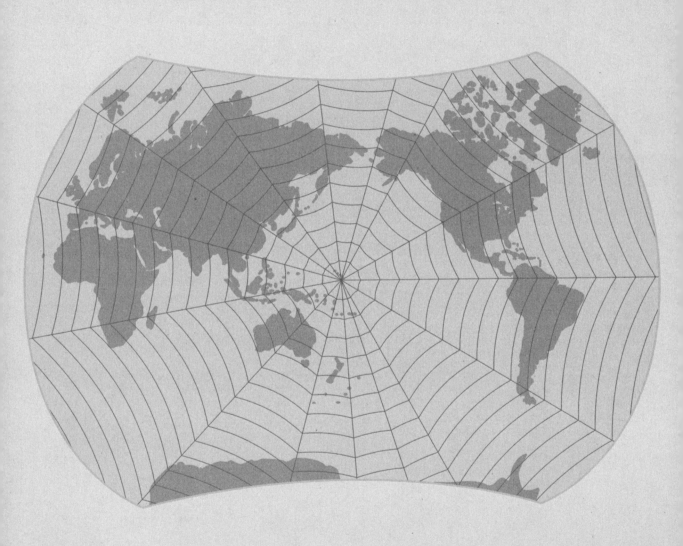

ASP Control Structures

In the first several chapters of this book, you have been writing simple Active Server Pages using VBScript code. Up until now your code has been read and executed in a very simple order: line 1 first, then line 2, then line 3 and so on until the last line, or occasionally we've repeated a small section of code several times. But in the real world, scripting languages can operate in a more complicated way than that: given certain conditions, they can skip or repeat lines – or groups of lines. This chapter will teach you ways to change the order in which the lines of your code are executed.

This chapter covers the three ways that you can use VBScript with your ASP scripts to sequence the execution of your lines of code. Respectively, these are:

- ❏ Deciding which of two or more sections of code to run.

- ❏ Repeating a section of code as many times as needed.

- ❏ Jumping out of the code sequence and executing sections of code in another part of your script.

  Note that this chapter refers to using VBScript with ASP, and hence some of the syntax shown in the following examples is specific to VBScript. If you were to try and use, for example, JavaScript, the structure of the examples would have to be changed appropriately. If you want to know more about JavaScript, you may be interested in Beginning JavaScript (Wrox, ISBN 1-861004-06-0)

Before we look at these processes in detail, let's step back and think in more general terms for a moment.

An Example in Plain English

Before we begin to look at ASP code let's think about these ideas in simple English for a business situation that you can easily picture in your mind. Let's consider the type of instructions a mechanic might be given by their boss. The code you have written so far is similar to the mechanic's boss telling them to:

- ❏ Take truck number one to the fuel pump.
- ❏ Fill up the tank with gasoline.
- ❏ Bring the truck back to its parking spot.

Although these instructions are very clear and easy to follow in order of line one, line two, line three, they do not cover some possible problems. What if the truck is already full of gasoline? What if the truck needs oil? What about providing service for the other trucks?

In order to get the job done the boss needs to provide a more complex set of instructions, for example:

1. Check if truck number one needs gasoline.

2. If truck number one needs gasoline, then take it to the fuel pump and fill it.

3. If the truck does not need gasoline then skip the filling and go to the next step.

4. Check if truck number one needs oil.

5. If truck number one needs oil, then get out the truck's manual and follow the instructions for adding oil. After you are done adding oil come back and finish these instructions.

6. If the truck does not need oil then skip the oil step and go to the next step.

7. When truck one is full of gas and full of oil, bring it back to its parking spot.

8. When you are done with truck one, repeat the above steps for the rest of the trucks.

The second set of orders will work better for three reasons. First, it covers a range of possibilities such as the gasoline and/or oil not needing refilling. Second, it takes advantage of existing instructions – the truck manual's pages for how to add oil. Third, it gives sufficient instructions to get the job done on the whole fleet of trucks.

This simple example illustrates the three types of constructs that you will use as an ASP programmer:

❑   **Branching statements** such as lines 2 and 3: If the truck needs gasoline then fill it up, but if it does not need gasoline then skip the filling up step.

❑   **Jumping statements** such as line 5: if you need oil, then stop executing these instructions and instead follow the instructions for adding oil. When you have finished following those adding oil instructions, then come back and continue with these instructions.

❑   **Looping statements** such as line 8: when you are done with truck one, go back and repeat these same steps for truck two, then truck three and so on until all of the trucks have been serviced.

Two Kinds of Statements

Note that all of the lines of your code can be divided into two types:

❑   **Action statements** carry out a task, such as showing the price of an item on a web page.

❑   **Control statements** have the task of *directing* the execution of the action statements. In other words, they decide how often and in which order, action statements are carried out.

In our Motorpool example, instructions such as "Fill the tank with gasoline" and "Add the oil" are **action** statements. The rest are **control** statements, such as "If the truck needs gasoline then..." or "Repeat the above steps for the next truck."

This idea of controlling which lines of code execute in what order, and how often, has several names. Some people refer to these techniques as **flow control** or **execution order**, and the sets of code that we use to control the flow of execution are called, logically enough, **Control Structures**.

Definitions

There are several new terms introduced in this chapter. Be particularly careful since some of these are interchangeable: for example, most programmers consider the terms **line**, **code**, **command** and **statement** to mean just about the same thing – that is, *one* line of programming instruction. Normally, however, **code** refers to one or more instructions.

In general use, the following terms can often be used interchangeably.

- ❑ **Flow**: The order of execution of statements. The flow may be designed to repeat or skip some statements
- ❑ **Execution**: the process of carrying out the instruction in a statement

And remember, there are two types of statements:

- ❑ **Action statements:** Statements that perform an activity, such as the creation of a part of a page, a change to a variable, a redirection to another page, or changing a setting on the server.
- ❑ **Control statements:** Statements that give instructions on which statements to execute, and in what order.

These statements can be organized into larger groups:

- ❑ **Code structures:** Several lines of code that work together to achieve a task. For example, five lines of code may work to put data into a table.
- ❑ **Control structures:** Since controlling flow frequently requires several control statements, we call a set of statements that govern the order of execution a control structure.

Types of Control Statements

When programming ASP or any other computer language, we have three types of structures (groups of control statements) to control the order in which the lines of code are executed. These are: **branching structures**, **looping controls**, and **jumping controls**. We'll now look at each of these in more detail.

Branching Structures

Branching controls perform some type of test. Based on the test results, a set of code will be executed and other sets of code will be skipped. From our Motorpool example, this is like testing if the gasoline tank is full. If it is not full then we perform the steps to fill it. If the tank *is* full then we skip the filling steps and move on to the next lines of code.

There are two types of branching structures.

❑ If...Then...Else – generally used to select one of several sets of lines to execute based on a condition to be met. A simple example would be in a page announcing a meeting: we could have one of two different meeting room numbers shown depending on whether the addressee was in the Sales or R&D department. If Then is also the tool of choice for complicated comparisons, such as expressions using the terms *and, or, not*.

❑ Select Case – generally used to select one set of lines to execute from *many* possibilities. For example, in a page announcing a meeting we could have the room number of one of five different meeting rooms shown, depending on whether the addressee was in the Sales, R&D, Distribution, Personnel, or Accounting department.

Looping Controls

Looping controls allow the same block of code to be run a number of times. Instead of skipping code – which is what the branching technique does – we *repeat* code. In the example of the mechanic, the idea of completing all the steps for the first truck, and then going back and repeating those same steps for the rest of the trucks demonstrates looping. In our clothing example we may want to generate a page with each item ordered listed on a line. The construction of those lines (print the description, print the quantity, print the price, put in a line break) would be looped to produce one line for each item ordered.

❑ For Next is used to repeat line(s) when, at the beginning of the repetition, we know exactly how many times we wish to repeat the line(s), or we can use a test (such as the sizeof function) to determine the amount of repetition we want. For example, if we know there are five trucks needing a wash, we could repeat five times the set of steps involved in successfully cleaning each truck.

❑ Do While is used to repeat line(s) when we *don't* know at design time how many times we wish to repeat our line(s). We build into the loop some type of test of condition, which is checked after each loop. The loop will repeat as long as the condition is true.

Jumping Controls

Jumping controls allow the programmer to pause the execution of the current code and jump to *another* named block of code. For example, we may have written a block of code called ShowOrder that produces lines that show the customer the goods that they ordered. Whenever we want VBScript to show those lines we don't have to re-write or copy all of that code. Instead we just have VBScript jump out of our current code, execute ShowOrder and then come back and continue executing our original bit of code. There are two types of jumping controls:

❏ Subprocedures can be called with the `Call` keyword, or alternatively you can just provide the name of the subprocedure, which will run the statements in the subprocedure, and then return control to the main procedure.

❏ Functions can be used to execute some statements and return an answer to the main body of code. They can also be preceded by the keyword `Call`.

Examples of Control Structures

With these three classes of controls – branching, jumping and looping – we can solve virtually any programming objective in ASP. In the table below we've listed several situations we might want to program for, and suggested which class of controls will help us achieve them.

Situation	Solution	Why?
I want ASP to show page A or page B.	Branching	We want to perform only one of two possible events.
I want ASP to list each member of the club. The data about each member is held in essentially the same manner, with a name, photo, address and other contact information.	Looping	We will be performing the same set of code (that retrieves a member's name) many times (once for each member, until we list all members).
I want to build a table.	Looping	We will perform the same code (make a row for a table) again and again until we have built all of the rows needed.
I need to calculate prices in several places on each page. The prices will be set according to input from a user form.	Call using a function	We will pause building the page, execute code to calculate the price of an item, then return to building the page. Since we will calculate many prices it is best to write the formula once and have it called when needed.
I need to show the user which of several meetings they should attend. The meeting displayed is based on which department they belong to.	Branching	We want to write to the page only *one* out of several possible meeting locations.
After every item that I describe in a catalog page, I want to put in a few lines of information about 'How to Order'.	Call using a subprocedure	We want to pause the main code and perform several lines of *another* set of code that describes 'How to Order'. Then we want to resume the main code. Since the 'How to Order' set of code will be performed at various times across the page, it is best to write it once and call that one piece of code as needed.

Let's recap on what we've discussed so far. There are three kinds of statements that control the flow of our code's execution:

- **Branching statements** that perform a test and then execute *some* lines of code but not others
- **Looping statements** that execute a set of code again and again
- **Jumping statements** that pause the execution of the current code, jump over to another set of code, and then return

Now let's have a closer look at branching statements, and what we can do with them.

Branching Statements

ASP offers two techniques for branching. If...Then is used when there are only a few choices of outcome. Bear in mind that the more lines you use in If...Then, the more difficult your code can become to follow. Select...Case is used when there are a lot of outcomes.

For example, if you are asking the user "Do you want a confirmation by telephone?" the outcome is either Yes (True) or No (False), so you would perform the branch using If...Then. But if you ask the user "Do you want confirmation by telephone or Fax or FedEx or E-mail or Voicemail or Telepathy?" given the amount of outcomes, then it is probably better to use Select...Case. We will start with If...Then.

If...Then Control Structure

The If...Then statement has four parts:

- An **expression**: that is, a test that gives a true or false answer
- An "**if true**" section of code
- An "**if false**" section of code
- An **ending** statement

The first part is the **expression**, which can be a combination of keywords, operators, variables, and constants that yield a result as a string, number, or object. We came across them first in the last chapter. It must answer either true or false. If the test answers true, then the lines of code in the "if true" section are executed. If the test answers false, then the lines of code in the "if false" section are executed. After the 'true' or 'false' section is executed the execution jumps down to the ending statement and continues with the next line of code. There is never a situation where both the true *and* the false sections would be used in a given case.

There are four ways of building If...Then statements. To select the proper syntax you must answer two questions:

- ❏ Do I want to do anything if the test is false?
- ❏ Do I want to execute more than one statement if the test is true?

The first and most simple way is used if you only have one statement to perform in the case of a 'true' test. You want to execute no statements at all if the test is false. For example, If varFaxConfirm = "Yes", then you want to print the fax number. If the expression evaluates to 'no' then you don't want to do anything. In this most simple case, you can use the one-line syntax:

```
<%
If varFaxConfirm = "Yes" then Response.Write "Please enter your fax number."
%>
```

The next, more complex level, is where you want to perform more than one statement in the case of truth, but still nothing if the test is false. For example, if varFaxConfirm = "Yes", then ask for the fax number and jump over to the fax entry page. In this case we must write the If...Then with two changes from case one above: the statements must go on their own lines, not the same as the simple If...Then example above. And, since there is now more than one line for the If...Then code, we must use a closing line of End If:

```
<%
  If varFaxConfirm = "Yes" Then
    Response.Write ("Please click below and provide your fax number.")
    Response.Write "<A HREF=http://www.On-LineClothier.com/FaxForm>Click here</A>"
  End If
%>
```

The third level is where you want to perform more than one statement in the case of 'true', and also one or more lines of code if the test is false. For example, if varFaxConfirm = "Yes" then ask for the fax number and jump over to the fax entry page. If varFaxConfirm is anything other than "Yes" then show a line that says that a fax will not be sent. In this situation we must write the If...Then with a line called Else to separate the code that is run in the true case from the code that will run in the false case.

```
<%
  If varFaxConfirm = "Yes" then
    Response.Write "Please enter your fax number."
  Else
    Response.Write "No fax confirmation will be sent."
  End If
%>
```

There is a fourth level, which we don't recommend using unless you have a specific set of constraints. It allows you to continually nest statements using ElseIf. To use ElseIf, you need to separate each new case with the keyword ElseIf (one word), closing the condition as normally with End If. For example, it can be structured a bit like this:

```
<%
  If varConfirm = "Fax" then
    Response.Write "Please enter your fax number."
  ElseIf varConfirm = "Email" then
    Response.Write "Please enter your email address"
  ElseIf varConfirm = "Voicemail" then
    Response.Write "Please enter your voice mail number"
  Else
    Response.Write "No confirmation will be sent."
  End If
%>
```

Here we test the data to see if it meets condition 1; if it doesn't, we test it to see if it meets condition 2; if it doesn't, we test it to see if it meets condition 3, and so on. When our data meets one of the criteria, or the criteria isn't met, the branch is decided and we arrive at a suitable outcome.

There is an alternative structure that provides a simpler solution to this same problem, and we'll be looking at this shortly.

Summary of Four kinds of If...Then Control Structures

Situation	Syntax	Example	Notes for use
If test is true do one statement otherwise do nothing	If test **Then** statement	If strAge < 18 Then Response.Write "You must be 18 or older to order by credit card."	If you want nothing to happen in the False case *And* You only want *one* statement to run in the true case

If the test is true
 	
do two or more statements
 	
If the test is false do nothing
	If test **Then**
	
	True code line 1
	True code line 2
	
	End If
		If strAge <18 Then
		
		Response.Write "You must be 18 or older to order by credit card."
		Display graphic
		
		End If	

Situation	Syntax	Example	Notes for use
If the test is true	If test **Then**	If strAge <18 Then	
do one or more statements	True code line 1 True code line 2	Response.Write "You are eligible for the student rate of $49."	
If the test is false	**Else**	Else	
do a different set of one or more statements	False code line 1 False code line 2	Response.Write "The fee for this service is $59."	
	End If	End If	
If the first test is true do one or more statements	If test **Then**	If strAge <18 Then	
	True code line 1 True code line 2	Response.Write "You are eligible for the student rate of $49."	
else if the second test is true	**ElseIf**	ElseIf strAge> 65 Then	
do a different set of one or more statements	True code line 1 True code line 2	Response.Write "You are eligible for the senior rate of $49."	
else if the *n*th test is true	**ElseIf** True code line 1 True code line 2	ElseIf strAge>18 And strAge<65 Then Response.Write "The fee for this service is $59."	
do a different set of one or more statements	**End If**	End If	

> **When using the one-line form of If...Then you do NOT use End If.**
> **When using any multi-line form of If...Then you MUST use End If**

So let's now look at an example where you're responsible for notifying your colleagues of the date and location for the Corporate Spring Retreats that we introduced in Chapter 3.

Try It Out – If...Then

1. There will be four meetings: two on March 15th running in Malibu, California and Myerstown, Pennsylvania, and two on April 16th in the same two cities. Your goal is to design a form that gathers user preferences for month and location, and then provide a response that confirms the date and city. We'll start by creating the form to gather user information. Open your web page editor and type in the following:

```
<HTML>
<HEAD>
<TITLE>Spring Retreat Form</TITLE>
</HEAD>

<BODY>
<H1>Corporate Retreat Registration</H1>
<H3>To get the logistics information for your meeting please answer these two
questions.</H3>
<FORM ACTION="IfThenOneResponse.asp" METHOD="post">
Please type your preference in month, either March or April:<BR>
<INPUT TYPE="text" NAME="MonthPref"><P>
Please type your preference in location, either East or West:<BR>
<INPUT TYPE="text" NAME="Location">
<BR>
<BR>
<INPUT TYPE="submit">
<INPUT TYPE="reset">
</FORM>
</BODY>
</HTML>
```

2. Save this page as `IfThenOneForm.asp`.

3. Close that page down. Next, we'll create the response page:

```
<HTML>
<HEAD>
<TITLE>Spring Retreat Response</TITLE>
</HEAD>
<BODY>
<%
  varMonthPref = Request.Form("MonthPref")
  varLocation = Request.Form("Location")

  Response.Write "<H1>Corporate Retreat Registration <BR>Your Details</H1>"

  If varMonthPref="March" Then
    Response.Write "Your meeting will be held on March 15th "
  Else
    Response.Write "Your meeting will be held on April 16th "
  End If
```

```
    If varLocation="East" Then
      Response.Write "in Myerstown, Pennsylvania"
    Else
      Response.Write "in Malibu, California"
    End If
%>
</BODY>
</HTML>
```

4. Save this as `IfThenOneResponse.asp` in your `BegASPFiles` directory.

5. Open up the page `IfThenOneForm.asp` in your web browser:

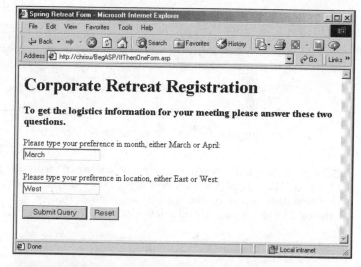

6. If you type in March and West and submit your query, you'd come up with the following:

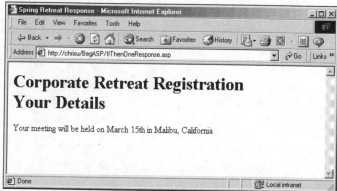

How It Works

The form simply follows the guidelines of Chapter 3.

```
<FORM ACTION="IfThenOneResponse.asp" METHOD="post">
Please type your preference in month, either March or April:<BR>
<INPUT TYPE="text" name="MonthPref"><P>
Please type your preference in location, either East or West:<BR>
<INPUT TYPE="text" name="Location">
<BR><BR><INPUT TYPE="submit"> <INPUT TYPE="reset">
</FORM>
```

The important points to remember in the code are:

- The ACTION attribute of the <FORM> tag must equal the URL of the page the server will return when the submit button is pressed

- You must use METHOD=Post in the <FORM> tag

- Always include INPUTs of TYPE "submit" and "reset"

- Each input must have a name, in this case MonthPref and Location

The response page is where we use the control structure If...Then. The page starts with the basic <HEAD> tags, then immediately starts the ASP VBScript code. The first job is to pass the information typed by the user into variables named varMonthPref and varLocation using the technique covered in the last chapter.

```
<%
  varMonthPref = Request.Form("MonthPref")
  varLocation = Request.Form("Location")
```

Then we use Response.Write to get some text on the page.

```
Response.Write "<H1>Corporate Retreat Registration <BR>Your Details</H1>"
```

The first control structure checks the contents of varMonthPref to see if it contains the word "March". Since that is a proper expression, it can be answered with a true or false. If it is true then two things happen:

- The *true* section of code is executed to put " ...March 15th" onto the HTML page

- VBScript skips the *false* line of code ("...April 16th") and jumps down to after the End If

If the expression is false (if the value entered isn't "March" we assume it to be "April") then VBScript will do the following:

- Skip the true section of code ("...March 15th")

❏ Perform the false section of code ("...April 16th") and continue on down through the End If

```
If varMonthPref="March" Then
  Response.Write "Your meeting will be held on March 15th "
Else
  Response.Write "Your meeting will be held on April 16th "
End If
```

The second If...Then works the same way. If it is *true* that varLocation is "East" then VBScript executes the writing of the city – Myerstown, Pennsylvania – and then jumps down to the line after End If. If VarLocation="East" is *false* we assume that the user typed "West" and so we skip the Myerstown line and go to the Malibu line.

```
If varLocation="East" Then
  Response.Write "in Myerstown, Pennsylvania"
Else
  Response.Write "in Malibu, California"
End If
```

Common Errors of the If...Then Statement

There are several common errors that we can make when creating an If...Then statement:

❏ Devising a test that does not resolve to True or False

❏ Try to use more than one statement with the one-line version of the If...Then construct.

❏ Leave out the End If when using the block version of the If...Then construct

❏ Leave out the Else

❏ Code End If as EndIf

Basic Rules of If...Then

❏ You can only evaluate one expression (do one test) in an If...Then structure

❏ There are only two possible results from the expression: True or False

❏ You can only use one statement in the one-line version of If...Then

❏ You can have multiple tests in If...Then...Else if you utilize ElseIf.

❏ If there is more than one line of action statements then you *must* use the End If

❏ If you want action in the case of a false result then you must use an Else line

Select Case

One problem of If...Then is that it can start getting unwieldy after more than two possible outcomes. What happens if you want to show a different page to visitors from each of five departments? What happens if you want to do a calculation based on the user providing one of twelve salary grades? What happens if you have different procedures for confirming an order by telephone, fax or E-mail? Your code is going to start looking pretty messy with all of those ElseIfs. Select Case is the alternative control structure we mentioned earlier for handling branching and it caters much more neatly for these type of situations, by providing a better structure and extra readability: anytime you need to make a choice among several answers (more than just True and False) then use Select Case.

The syntax for Select Case has four parts:

❑ State which variable to test

❑ State a possible answer and what to do if that answer is correct

❑ Repeat for as many possible answers as you want to handle

❑ End the Select Case control structure

The first example, below, carries out one of three actions depending on what is contained in the variable varConfirmation.

```
<%
  Select Case varConfirmation
    Case "Fax"
      Response.Write  "<A HREF='FaxConfirmation.asp'>Fax</A>"
    Case "Telephone"
      Response.Write  "<A HREF='telephone.asp'>Telephone</A>"
    Case "EMail"
      Response.Write  "<A HREF='EMail.asp'>Email</A>"
  End Select
%>
```

VBScript will know from the first line that you want to compare answers to the contents of the variable varConfirmation. Next, VBScript will begin testing the contents of the variable against the values shown in the Case lines. When VBScript finds a match it will execute the following code up to the next Case line, and will then jump down to the first line after the End Select statement. You may have noticed in the last Try It Out that if the user typed "march" in lower case then the program failed: it displayed April on the Spring Retreat Response page. This was because we only coded for the possibility of the user typing "March", and printed April in all other cases. You can get by this by accounting for more possibilities, for example march, March, april, April. You can even include a "catch-all" case – for example, what if the user decided to type Saturday? VBScript allows you to write a special test called Case Else, which will run some code if all other conditions fail. For example:

```
<%
  Select Case varMonthPref
    Case "march"
      Response.Write "Your meeting will be held on March 15th "
    Case "March"
      Response.Write "Your meeting will be held on March 15th "
    Case "april"
      Response.Write "Your meeting will be held on April 16th "
    Case "April"
      Response.Write "Your meeting will be held on April 16th "
    Case Else
      Response.Write "your request for " & varMonthPref
      Response.Write " is not recognized."
      Response.Write "Please click the back button on your browser "
      Response.Write "and reset then refill the form again.<BR>"
  End Select
%>
```

In this example, the user who decided to type **Saturday** will receive our own custom error message, telling them to try again.

We can further refine this code by having VBScript test for more than one result on one case line. As an example, for both `"march"` and `"March"` we would do the same action (`Response.Write "...March 15th"`). This syntax is simple, just line up the possible answers separated by commas as demonstrated in the code below:

```
Select Case varMonthPref
  Case "march", "March", "mar", "Mar", "MAR"
    Response.Write "Your meeting will be held on March 15th "
  Case "april", "April", "apr", "Apr", "APR"
    Response.Write "Your meeting will be held on April 16th "
  Case Else
    Response.Write "your request for " & varMonthPref
    Response.Write " is not recognized."
    Response.Write "Please strike the back button on your browser "
    Response.Write "and reset then refill the form again.<BR>"
End Select
```

This will work fine, but what if you wanted to test for many different possible inputs? You could end up with having case statements to catch several kinds of input (mar, Mar, march, March, MARCH, etc). VBScript offers a completely different way to solve the case problem. If you change all input text to uppercase before testing, you can reduce the number of tests needed. The `Ucase ()` function will convert a string to all uppercase as follows:

```
Select Case Ucase(varMonthPref)
  Case "MARCH", "MAR"
    Response.Write "Your meeting will be held on March 15th "
  Case "APRIL", "APR"
    Response.Write "Your meeting will be held on April 16th "
  Case Else
    Response.Write "your request for " & varMonthPref
    Response.Write " is not recognized."
    Response.Write "Please strike the back button on your browser "
    Response.Write "and reset then refill the form again.<BR>"
End Select
```

So, we've managed to cut down the number of test statements that we need to worry about. However, in some situations, it may become very difficult to account for all the possible answers the user may try to type into the entry field. One alternative is to provide the user with a fixed set of options to choose from, and we can do just that with a special type of input box called a 'drop-down' or 'combo' box. These appear in input forms as follows:

```
<SELECT NAME="dropbox">
  <OPTION VALUE="Option1">One</OPTION>
  <OPTION VALUE="Option2">Two</OPTION>
  <OPTION VALUE="Option3">Three</OPTION>
  <OPTION VALUE="Option4">Four</OPTION>
</SELECT>
```

By including this on a simple form page, within the `<FORM>` and `</FORM>` tags, this would produce a box that looks like this:

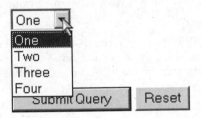

The NAME attribute of the select tag contains the name of the box – this name is used in the same way as we have seen with the text input boxes we've been using so far. What you may notice is that the text displayed can be different to the data that gets used on a result page. In this example, selecting **One** from the drop box will actually select the value `Option1`, so if we were using our `Select Case` structure, you could use the following in a result page:

```
varDropBox = Request.Form("dropbox")

Select Case varDropBox
  Case "Option1"
    Response.Write "You chose Option One"
  Case "Option2"
    Response.Write "You chose Option Two"
  Case Else
    Response.Write "You chose either Option Three or Option Four"
End Select
```

In this way, you can have a more detailed list of options for your users to choose from, but a simplified list of values that can be used with our `Select Case` statements

This next Try It Out will use a drop-down box to reply to two questions, and then we'll use `Select Case` to display appropriate results.

Try It Out – Select Case

We will modify the two pages we used in the If...Then example to use the Select Case structure

1. Open up IfThenOneForm.asp and change the following highlighted line:

```
<HTML>
<HEAD>
<TITLE>Spring Retreat Form</TITLE>
</HEAD>

<BODY>
<H1>Corporate Retreat Registration</H1>
<H3>To get the logistics information for your meeting please answer these two
questions.</H3>
<FORM ACTION="SelectCaseResponse.asp" METHOD="post">
  Which month would you prefer?<BR>
  <SELECT NAME="Month">
    <OPTION VALUE="Jan">January</OPTION>
    <OPTION VALUE="Mar">March</OPTION>
    <OPTION VALUE="May">May</OPTION>
    <OPTION VALUE="Jul">July</OPTION>
    <OPTION VALUE="Sep">September</OPTION>
    <OPTION VALUE="Nov">November</OPTION>
  </SELECT>
  <BR><BR>
  What is your preferred location?<BR>
  <SELECT NAME="Location">
    <OPTION VALUE="East">East</OPTION>
    <OPTION VALUE="West">West</OPTION>
  </SELECT>
<BR><BR>
<INPUT TYPE="submit">
<INPUT TYPE="reset">
</FORM>
</BODY>
</HTML>
```

2. Save this as SelectCaseForm.asp

3. Open up the page IfThenOneResponse.asp and change the following highlighted lines:

```
<HTML>
<HEAD>
<TITLE>Corporate Retreat Response</TITLE>
</HEAD>
<BODY>
<%
  varMonthPref = Request.Form("MonthPref")
  varLocation = Request.Form("location")
  Response.Write "<H1>Corporate Retreat Registration <BR> Your Details</H1>"
```

```
Select Case varMonthPref
   Case "Jan"
      Response.Write "Your meeting will be held on January 14th "
   Case "Mar"
      Response.Write "Your meeting will be held on March 15th "
   Case "May"
      Response.Write "Your meeting will be held on May 16th "
   Case "Jul"
      Response.Write "Your meeting will be held on July 17th "
   Case "Sep"
      Response.Write "Your meeting will be held on September 18th "
   Case "Nov"
      Response.Write "Your meeting will be held on November 19th "
End Select

If varLocation="East" then
   Response.Write "in Myerstown, Pennsylvania"
Else
   Response.Write "in Malibu, California"
   End If
%>
</BODY>
</HTML>
```

4. Save this as `SelectCaseResponse.asp`

5. Now if you open `SelectCaseForm.asp` in your browser, you'll find that the example prevents our user from typing in variations of the same month (march, MARCH, March etc.) or location, by supplying them with a list to choose from. After submitting the information, the user will see the corresponding result.

How It Works

The essential change is the replacement of an `If...Then` structure with a `Select Case` structure. When VBScript reads the `Select Case` it knows that ensuing tests will be against varMonthPref. The first possible answer it tries is "Jan" and if that *is* a match then it does the first `Response.Write` line, otherwise, it moves on to the next comparison which is for "Mar". If this does not produce a match, then VBScript will drop down to the next Case line and try "May" and so on.

> *Easy mistakes: Since this form and response are similar to the last Try It Out be careful not to accidentally call the wrong one up in you browser when testing. If you copied the last Try It Out response page and modified it here, be sure you changed the <FORM> ACTION attribute.*

Common Errors of the Select Case Structure

- ❑ Putting a comparison (= or < or >) on the first Select line. The first line says which variable to compare to, but it is NOT an expression.

- ❑ Putting more than one variable on the Select...Case line. For example, ASP will not accept: Select Case varNameFirst, varNameLast.

- ❑ Not making the possible answers mutually exclusive.

- ❑ Not including Case Else (Case Else is not required, but good programming practice as it can deal with unexpected user inputs).

- ❑ Each Case line should have a possible answer. That possible answer must be in quotes if it is text.

- ❑ Type Select Case or End Select as one word.

- ❑ Forgetting the End Select line

- ❑ Finishing the structure with End Case instead of End Select

- ❑ Trying to use "Where" or "Is" on a Case line (these comparison operators are only available in VB, and not VBScript).

- ❑ Using Select Case to check only two outcomes. For just two outcomes If...Then is faster.

Further Improving your Select Case Structures

Of course, things could get a little out of hand if say for example you were testing not just for a specific month, but for an available day in a given range of days in a specific month. You wouldn't want to type in the following:

```
Select Case (varDatePref)
  Case 1,2,3,4,5,6,7,8,9,10,11,12,13,14,15
    Response.Write "Your meeting will be held on March 15th "
  Case 16,17,18,19,20,21,22,23,24,25,26,27,28,29,30,31
    Response.Write "Your meeting will be held on March 30th "
  ...
End Select
```

Fortunately, one last trick of Select Case allows you to save your fingers. You can create Boolean expression in the Case part of the expression and depending on whether it evaluates to true or false when supplied with a value, it will choose one of the cases.

```
Select Case True
  Case varDatePref <= 15
    Response.Write "Your meeting will be held on March 15th "
  Case varDatePref >15
    Response.Write "Your meeting will be held on March 30th "
  ...
End Select
```

However, you must make sure that it is only possible for one of your expressions at any one time to evaluate to true.

Basic Rules of Select Case

❑   Use `Select...Case` for taking action for more than two possibilities.

❑   The first line states the variable to compare to, but does not define the comparison.

❑   ASP will execute the code after the first match.

❑   It is always best to use `Case Else` to cover unexpected circumstances

We've covered a lot of ground so far in looking at branching controls. Now we'll take a look at our next type of controls: **looping controls**.

Looping Controls

ASP has two types of looping structures: `Do While` and `For...Next`. When you require one of these structures, it's advisable that you decide which structure to use, depending on whether you know in advance how many loops you want to do. If you *can* determine the number of loops and have this number stored in a variable, then use `For...Next`. If you do *not* know ahead of time how many loops you want to do and will have to decide after each loop whether to continue, then I suggest using `Do While`.

For...Next

The `For...Next` structure has three parts. The first is a line that describes how many times to repeat the loop. Second come a set of lines with action statements that carry out the task you want repeated. Last is a line that indicates the end of the action statements and tells ASP to go back and repeat the action statements again.

Here is a simple case to get started: imagine that we have a sales rep. on the road that wants to print a sign-in sheet for attendees to seminars. The sales rep. would like to log in to the company's web site, get the sign-in sheet, and print it. In this first case we know that the seminars always have five attendees:

```
<%
  Response.Write "Sign-In sheet for Attendees"
  Response.Write "On-Line Clothing Store - Fashions of Spring<BR><BR>"
  For varCounter = 1 to 5
    Response.Write "Attendee Name _____   <BR><BR>"
    Response.Write "Attendee EMail _____   <BR><BR><HR><BR>"
  Next
%>
```

VBScript will execute the first two lines to display some introductory text for the sheet – this part is not inside the loop. On the third line, we begin the process of running the loop five times. In order to keep count we provide a variable called `varCounter` for VBScript to keep its count in. Here the variable is implicitly declared within the loop, and doesn't have to be declared prior to this. The lines that will be repeated five times are all of the lines in between (but not including) the `For...` line and the `Next` line. In this case, the two `Response.Write` statements create a line for an attendee to write their name and e-mail address.

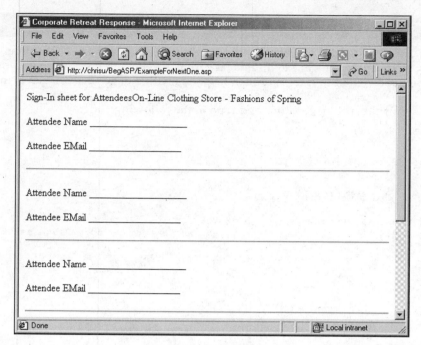

That simple first example assumed that we would always have five attendees. What if that number varies? We would like to have a first web page that asks for the number of attendees, and then use that number to determine how many lines to print. We can use the For Next (instead of Do While) because when we start the loop, the loop structure is fed the number of loops to execute.

If we assume that the text field called NumberAttendees contains the number of attendees input by the user, then the responding page (below) can grab the user's data from the field named NumberAttendees and stuff the data into the variable named varNumber. Then we can begin the For...Next loop. But this time we don't go up through exactly five cycles. Rather, we go through the number of cycles specified in the varNumber. Our sign-in sheet is now usable for any number of attendees:

```
<HTML>
<HEAD>
<TITLE>Example For Next Two Response</TITLE>
</HEAD>
<BODY>
<H2>Welcome to the Seminar<BR>Please Sign in below</H2><BR>
<%
  varNumber=Request.Form("NumberAttendees")
  For varLineCounter = 1 to varNumber
    Response.Write "Attendee Name _____  <BR><BR>"
    Response.Write "Attendee EMail _____  <BR><BR><HR><BR>"
  Next
%>
</BODY>
</HTML>
```

Now we're ready to try an example.

Try It Out – For...Next

Your boss asks you to turn in a sheet about once a week that lists the clients you have visited. Since you travel a lot you want to do this task from a web page form that asks you how many people you have visited in total, and then responds with a page that you can print and fill in.

1. Open your web page editor and type in the following code:

```
<HTML>
<HEAD>
<TITLE>For Next One Form</TITLE>
</HEAD>
<BODY>
<H2>Weekly Client Contacts</H2><BR>

<FORM ACTION=ForNextOneResponse.asp METHOD = post>
<P>Please enter the first day of the week in the form mm/dd/yy such as 09/20/98<BR>
<INPUT TYPE=text NAME="start">
<P>Please enter the last day of the week in the same form<BR>
<INPUT TYPE=text NAME="end"><BR>
<INPUT TYPE=submit>
<INPUT TYPE=reset>
</FORM>

</BODY>
</HTML>
```

2. Save this form as `ForNextOneForm.asp`

3. Close the form down and create a new file and this time type in the following code.

```
<HTML>
<HEAD>
<TITLE>ForNext One Response</TITLE>
</HEAD>

<BODY>
<H2>Weekly Client Contacts for George Washington</H2><BR>
<%
  varStart=Request.Form("start")
  varEnd=Request.Form("end")
  varStart = CDate(varStart)
  varEnd = CDate(varEnd)

  varNumberDays=(varEnd-varStart)

  For varLineCounter = 0 to varNumberDays
    Response.Write "Clients: _____"
    Response.Write "<BR ><BR><BR>"
  Next
%>
signed _____
George Washington
</BODY>
</HTML>
```

4. Save this page as `ForNextOneResponse.asp`

5. Open up the form page `ForNextOneForm.asp` in your web browser and fill in any two close dates:

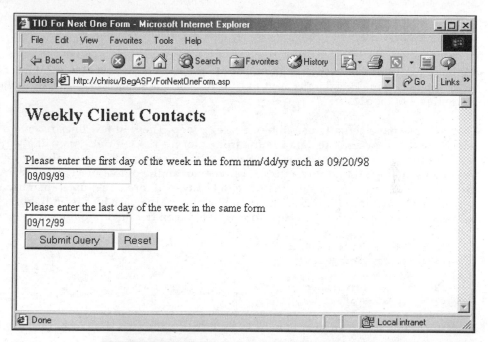

6. Click on Submit and you will see an entry on the Response page for each day:

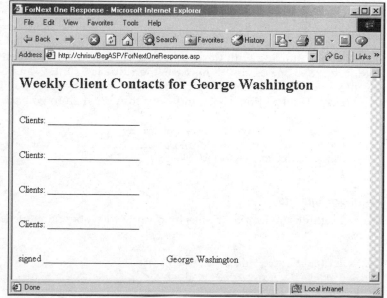

How It Works

The form page is nothing new to you, but we have started slimming the code down to fewer lines so that you get used to seeing some good coding practices.

> *Note that we have specified the* `Action= ForNextOneResponse.asp`*. If you are copying pages from earlier Try It Outs be sure you update this line.*

We have two pieces of user data going back to the server: the first and last dates of the week we're interested in. This data is used to stuff the variables that ASP will use to determine how many times to loop.

The response page actually uses the `For...Next` loop. The first few lines receive the first and last data from the browser. The data coming from a form's `text` input type will always be text, but we want to work with *dates*. So we convert the text by saying the new value of `varStart` will be equal to the result of doing a `CDate` conversion on the old value. This means ASP will read the contents of `varStart`, take that text and convert it into a real date, then use that real date to replace the text in `varStart`. The initial loading of the variables is on the first two lines below, and the conversion from text to true dates is on the final two lines:

```
varStart=Request.Form("start")
varEnd=Request.Form("end")

varStart = cdate(varStart)
varEnd = cdate(varEnd)
```

Then we calculate the number of days by subtracting the start date from the end date as below.

```
varNumberDays=(varEnd-varStart)
```

Then we can begin our loop. We need a counter, which we called `varLineCounter`, and we say "run the loop starting with the counter set at zero, and stop when the counter gets to the value held in `varNumberDays` (in this case, the value is 3 (0, 1, 2, and 3)). The lines of code to be executed on each cycle are simple: write the word `Clients`, a few underscores, and then some line breaks. The last line, `Next`, indicates to ASP when to go back and repeat the cycle.

```
For varLineCounter = 0 to varNumberDays
  Response.Write "Clients: _____"
  Response.Write "<BR><BR><BR>"
Next
```

A Few Improvements

We can tighten the first four lines by putting the conversion of text to dates in two commands as follows:

```
varStart=cdate(Request.Form("start"))
varEnd=cdate(Request.Form("end"))
```

A further improvement would be to number the days by actually printing the varLineCounter (taking note to increment the day by one):

```
For varLineCounter = 0 to varNumberDays
  Response.Write "Day " & varLineCounter+1
  Response.Write " Clients: _____"
  Response.Write "<BR><BR><BR>"
Next
```

More useful would be to print the actual date such as *09/12/99* at the beginning of the line. In the code below we add a line to the loop, which creates a new variable called varDateThisLine. Into that variable we stuff the result of a calculation which takes the start date and adds to it the number of the varLineCounter, that is, the number of the cycle we are on.

```
For varLineCounter = 0 to varNumberDays
  varDateThisLine =  varStart + varLineCounter
  Response.Write varDateThisLine
  Response.Write " Clients: _____"
  Response.Write "<BR><BR><BR>"
Next
```

Common Errors of the For...Next Structure

- ❏ Leave out a counter variable

- ❏ Forget the '=' symbol or the word "to" on the first line

- ❏ Leave out the statement Next

- ❏ Forget to put appropriate formatting (like a line break) within the repeated section

- ❏ Accidentally include a statement in the repeating section so that it is executed many times instead of only once. That line should have been above or below the For...Next structure

- ❏ Accidentally leave out a statement in the repeating section so that it is executed once instead of many times. That line should have been *within* the For...Next structure

Basic Rules of For...Next

- ❏ Line one must have: counter variable, equal sign, start number and end number.

- ❏ All lines within the For and Next will be repeated until the counter variable gets up to the end value

- ❏ You can use the counter variable within the loop

- ❏ Last line of control structure is Next

For Each...Next

A common cousin of the For...Next statement is For Each...Next, which works in a similar way to the For...Next statement, except that it's used for each element inside an array or a collection (We'll meet collections in Chapter 7. For now, you can think of a collection as being an ordered set of objects.) If you remember, in Chapter 4 we looked at arrays, and mentioned that they could be populated using a For...Next statement: well, For Each...Next makes that task even simpler. Here's an example bit of code:

```
<%
 Dim Item
 Dim strCities(1)                'Declare an array
 strCities(0) = "London"         'Populate it
 strCities(1) = "Paris"

 For Each Item In strCities
    Response.Write Item & "<BR>"    'List the contents of each item
 Next
%>
```

It looks almost identical to For...Next, doesn't it? The only difference is that you don't have to specify the number of items you want to loop through, VBScript will simply start with the first item in the array and repeat the loop until it reaches the last item in the array. In this case, each item in the array is listed on the screen, so, if there were one hundred cities in our array, each one would be displayed by this loop. The For Each...Next statement is also used to loop through the contents of collections of ASP objects. We'll look into this in more detail in the next four or five chapters. For the moment, we'll take a closer look at another looping control: the Do...While loop.

Do...While

We briefly mentioned the Do...While loop earlier in the chapter: you may remember that it's used to repeat a loop when we are not sure how many loops to perform. So on each loop it performs a test and continues looping as long as a *specified condition exists* (you can also use the construct Do...While NOT, i.e. loop while a specified condition *does not exist*). The Do...While loops and For...Next loops have two significant differences in syntax. First is the difference in key words: For...Next has only one word (For) in the opening statement and ends with the word Next. Do...While has *two* words in the opening statement (Do...While) and ends with the word Loop. The code between Do...While and Loop continues to run for as long as your specified condition exists.

Differences in Syntax Between For...Next and Do...While Loops

For...Next Key Words	Do...While Key Words
For...	Do While...
...	...
Lines of code to repeat	*Lines of code to repeat*
...	...
Next	Loop

The second difference is the nature of the test to end the looping. For...Next has a variable for counting, a start point, and an end point. Do...While has an **expression test**: at the beginning of each loop ASP checks the expression and if it is true then it runs the loop. If the expression is *false*, then the loop is not run and ASP jumps down in the code to the line after Loop.

For...Next technique to stop looping	Do...While technique to stop looping
For varCounter 1 to 5	Do While varEnough < varTooBig
	...
	(Here, one line of code would be incrementing varEnough during each cycle of the loop).

There is a serious trap that every beginning programmer falls into: if you start a loop and do not provide a means for it to stop then it will continue forever as an **infinite loop**.

> *Most servers will eventually cut off a given ASP page, since the server needs to attend to other visitors and tries to optimize its resources.*

The Do...While form of looping is perfect if we have to make a row in a table for each month of the year up to the present month. However, we don't know – at the time of writing our ASP code – in which month the user will be viewing the page. In May, the fifth month, we would like five rows. We can find the number of the current month (May = 5) using the code month(now()).

```
<HTML>
<HEAD>
<TITLE>Example Do While</TITLE>
</HEAD>
<BODY>
<H1>Year To Date: Monthly Sales Calls</H1><BR>

<%
  varMonthCount = 1
  varMonthNow = Month(now())

  Do While varMonthCount <= varMonthNow
    Response.Write "Number of clients met: _____  <BR>"
    varMonthCount = varMonthCount + 1
  Loop
%>

<BR>Signed _____ George Washington
</BODY>
</HTML>
```

The first line takes care of 'administrative' HTML matters, and then in the body of the code we have a line to write the opening title on the page. Next, the VBScript begins and we establish two variables: varMonthCount will track our progress in creating the rows (it starts with a value of zero since we have no rows printed so far). The second variable is varMonthNow, which we will use to hold the current month. This is obtained by running the month(now()) functions mentioned earlier.

Now we can begin the Do...While loop. The trick is to use the right expression to stop the loop. In this case we will test at the beginning of each loop whether the varMonthCount is still less than or equal to the current month. For example, if we run this in May, the first loop will be done if the varMonthCount is less than the MonthNow (which would be 5 for May). We then print some text from within the loop. The next line takes the old value of varMonthCount and replaces it with a new value exactly one increment higher. Now ASP loops back up and tests again. Since varMonthCount (which now = 2) is *still* less then MonthNow (which now = 5) the loop runs again: and this will happen five times. After the fifth loop varMonthCount will equal six and when ASP tests for the Do...While condition the answer is *false*. ASP immediately jumps down to the first line after the Loop statement and prints the signature line.

Try It Out – Do While...Loop

Your boss likes the sheet you made in the last Try It Out that lists the clients you met each day, but now your job will change. You will meet clients during the first half of the month, and then in the second half you will be at the office performing other duties. So, the 'meeting clients' sheet will cover from the first day of the month up to the day you return to the office. However, your boss's definition of the first half of the month is flexible. Sometimes you have twelve days of visits, sometimes twenty. You need a form that looks at today's date and gives you enough lines for enough days of client visits: that is, one line for each day from the beginning of the month until today, whichever day of the month that is.

1. Open up your web page editor and type in the following code.

```
<HTML>
<HEAD>
<TITLE>Do While</TITLE>
</HEAD>
<BODY>
<H1>Sales Calls for This Month</H1><BR>
<%
  varRowCount = 1
  varTodayDate = day(now())

  Do While varRowCount <= varTodayDate
    Response.Write "For _____ "
    Response.Write "number of clients met was _____<BR>"
    varRowCount = varRowCount + 1
  Loop
%>
</BODY>
</HTML>
```

2. Save this as `DoWhile.asp`

3. Open up your browser and run this page. When run on the 9th of September produces the following page.

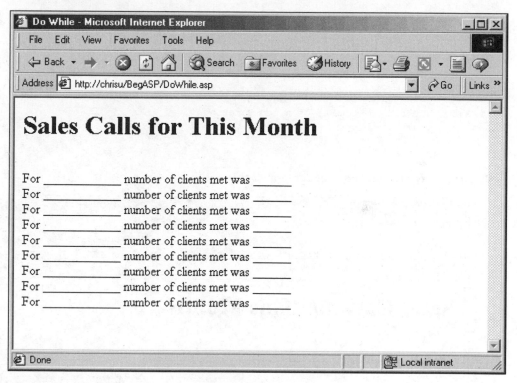

How It Works

This code starts by setting up two variables. The first is the counter, which we set at one. The second holds today's date which we get from the function day() applied to the function now(). The result of these functions is to provide the text "5" when this page is requested on the fifth day of the month.

Then the loop begins, with VBScript testing whether the varRowCount is still less than or equal to today's date. (We have to start varRowCount on one as the months always start on the first.) If that expression is true then VBScript goes through the cycle. There are two steps in the cycle: the first simply puts the text and HTML on the page. The second line takes the old value of varRowCount, adds one to it and uses that new number as a replacement for the old contents of varRowCount. We need to change some condition on each cycle of the loop so we can, at some point, return a 'false' value for the Do...While expression and end the loop.

Improvements

Since we are getting and using the actual date it would improve the product if we put the date on each line.

```
<%
  varRowCount = 1
  varTodayDate = day(now())
  varTodayMonth = MonthName(month(date()))

  Response.Write "<H2>Report for " & varTodayMonth & "</H2>"
  Do While varRowCount <= varTodayDate
    Response.Write "For " & varTodayMonth & " " & varRowCount
    Response.Write ": number of clients met was _____<BR>"
    varRowCount = varRowCount + 1
  Loop
%>
```

When requested on the ninth of September this will produce:

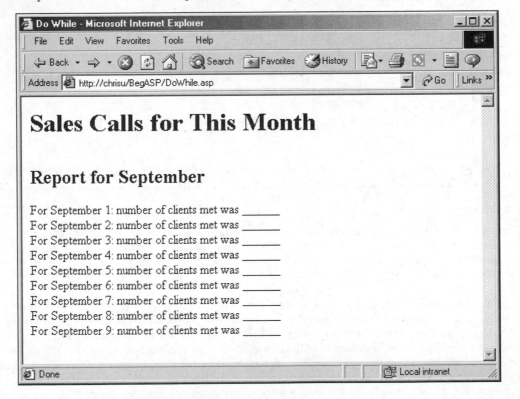

Common Errors of the Do...While Structure

- ❑ Using Next instead of Loop for the closing statement.
- ❑ Not having the variable of the expression change during the execution of each cycle. This results in the expression *never* becoming false and thus the loop never stops.

- ❑ Performing one too many or one too few cycles.

- ❑ Putting code that should be done once *inside* the loop by mistake.

- ❑ Putting code that should be repeated *outside* the code by mistake.

- ❑ Using < when a test condition should be <=, or > when it should be >=

- ❑ Creating an infinite loop that will never end, by testing for a condition that will never exist. If you replaced the less than operator with a greater than operator this would cause an infinite loop and your web page would hang.

Basic Rules of Do...While

- ❑ The opening statement uses the key words Do...While, followed by an expression.

- ❑ The expression, like all expressions, must resolve to true or false.

- ❑ There is usually a variable in the expression that will change with each cycle of the loop.

- ❑ The code to run in the loop is ended with the keyword Loop.

Do...Loop While

You're not restricted by having to place the condition at the beginning of your loop. If you wanted your condition at the end of the loop, then that is also possible. So, if you went back to the previous example, it could be amended as follows:

```
Do
   ...code here...
Loop While varRowCount <= varTodayDate
```

The difference here is that your block of code would be executed automatically, before we check our condition. So in this way, you can deduce that this loop would execute at least once, before exiting, while the first occurrence of the loop might never be executed at all.

Do Until Loop and Do Loop Until

Finally there's a subtle variation on the Do While Loop, which allows you to replace the keyword While with the keyword Until. The difference between them is one should be executed WHILE a condition is true, and the other should be executed UNTIL a condition is true. This variation is all that divides the two. So the previous example could also be written as:

```
Do Until varRowCount > varTodayDate
   ...code here...
Loop
```

Or even:

```
Do
   ...code here...
Loop Until varRowCount > varTodayDate
```

Notice that we've amended the condition, for looping slightly, so that we loop until the condition becomes true. The rules of when to use `While` and when to use `Until` are basically looking at your example and see which makes more sense to use.

We've spent a lot of time looking at the important **looping controls**. Next, we'll turn our attention to the equally important **jumping structures**.

Jumping Structures and the Art of Reusing Code

As you write more ASP code you'll find that you want to use the same code in more than one place. ASP allows you to write some code once, then run it as many times as needed to support the main body of code. These mini-programs are called **procedures** or **functions**. We will want ASP to jump away from execution of the main body of code, run through the commands of a procedure or function, before returning to execute the main body of code.

For example, you may have a few lines of code that insert some lines of text about how to contact the sales department. You would like to have this show up in various places on the page, but want to avoid having to rewrite the code separately each time. The solution is to put the lines of code into a procedure (sometimes called a `Sub Procedure` or a `Sub`). Then every place that you want that code to run you can invoke the subprocedure rather than rewrite the code.

A second example is to calculate the delivery date of a shipment. You may have to do this several times for different items on a page. In this case you want to start with information such as the ship date, and from that calculate the delivery date. There may be some branching in the procedure to accommodate the fact that there is no delivery on Sunday.

There are two types of procedures:

- ❑ **Subprocedures** carry out an action. For example, a `Sub` would be used to carry out the actions of putting text onto a page. A sub procedure does not return values, but can be used to set variables that are in scope.

- ❑ **Functions** carry out action statements and *return an answer* to your code. A function would be used to calculate a delivery date and return that answer to your main program.

Procedures

Procedures are easy to write – they have just three parts. First is the **name**, second is the **code** that the procedure should execute, and last is an **ending statement**. In addition you will have to direct your main body of code to *run* the procedure at the appropriate point.

In our first example we may want a procedure to put the contact information for the sales department on the web page. This can be done with the following code:

```
Response.Write "Price quotes for this product are available from "
Response.Write "Joe at 201/555-1212.<BR>"
```

In order to avoid writing this same code in many places throughout the page we can put it into a subprocedure:

```
Sub SalesContactInfo
  Response.Write "Price quotes for this product are available from "
  Response.Write "Joe at 201/555-1212.<BR>"
End Sub
```

This first line must start with the key word Sub, then a space and the name of the subroutine. The name should start with a letter and contain only letters and numbers – no spaces or symbols. The following lines hold the VBScript code to be performed in the subprocedure. The last line must be the command End Sub.

This subprocedure can then be called from your code whenever needed, by using the statement Call followed by the name of the procedure, as in the following example:

```
many lines about sweaters
Call SalesContactInfo
...
many lines about vests
Call SalesContactInfo
...
many lines about hats
Call SalesContactInfo
```

Although you can use the Call keyword to call the subprocedure, you could just as easily call the subprocedure without this keyword:

```
many lines about sweaters
SalesContactInfo
...
many lines about vests
SalesContactInfo
...
many lines about hats
SalesContactInfo
```

The subprocedure does not have to be in the same set of ASP code as the calling statement although it does have to be part of the same web page. The following two sets of code both work fine.

| Subprocedure in **separate** section of ASP from calling code | `<%`
`    Sub SalesContactInfo`
`    Response.Write "Call Joe at 201/555-1212."`
`    End Sub`
`%>`
`<H3>Sweaters For Autumn</H3>`
`Warmest, woolliest sweaters now in stock.`
`New colors for autumn including Orange/Black and an`
`Autumn Medley.`
`<%call SalesContactInfo%>` |

Table Continued on Following Page

| Subprocedure in **same** section of ASP as calling statement | <pre><%
   Sub SalesContactInfo
      Response.Write "Call Joe at 201/555-1212."
   End Sub
   Response.Write "<H3>Sweaters For Autumn</H3>"
   Response.Write "Warmest, woolliest sweaters "

   Response.Write "now in stock."
   Response.Write "New colors for autumn including
"
   Response.Write "Orange/Black and an Autumn
Medley."
   Call SalesContactInfo
%></pre> |

Parameters

You can improve your subprocedure by having more than one possible outcome. The result will depend on variables sent from your main code over into the subprocedure. You do this by sending parameters along with the subprocedure. A parameter or argument is in fact a piece of data, which is passed to the subprocedure. It is transferred by placing it in parentheses *after* the name of the subroutine.

```
Call SalesContactInfo(varParameter)
```

For example, let's say you have four sales specialists, each covering a different region, and you want to display the appropriate sales representative for a given user. Let us also assume that you have picked up from the user their region and stuffed it into varRegion by a simple form. You may have created a subprocedure that writes the name of the appropriate sales representative. The varRegion can be transferred from your main form over to the procedure by putting the name of the variable in parenthesis as an argument. The calling code would now look like:

```
<HTML>
<HEAD>
<TITLE>Example Procedures Two</TITLE>
</HEAD>
<BODY>
<%
  Dim varRegion
  varRegion = Request.Form("region")

  Sub SalesContactInfo(region)
    Response.Write "Price quotes for this product are available from "
    Select Case Region
      Case "North"
        Response.Write "Brian at 201/555-1212."
      Case "South"
        Response.Write "Rob at 719/555-1212."
      Case "East"
        Response.Write "Pat at 604/555-1212."
      Case "West"
        Response.Write "John at 312/555-1212."
    End Select
  End Sub
%>
```

```
<H2 align="center">On-Line Clothier<BR>
New Items for September, 1999</H2>
<H3>Sweaters</H3>
<P>New selections of warm and woolly Autumn Sweaters. Special line of
colors for fall festivities including Black/Orange and our new Autumn Medley.
<%call SalesContactInfo(varRegion)%>
<H3>Vests</H3>
<P>Get ready to dance around the MayPole in this season's brightest selection of
Flowered Vests. We're in-swing with the retro look featuring flowers from the 50's,
60's and 70's.
<%call SalesContactInfo(varRegion)%>
<H3>Ties</H3>
<P>No reason to look uncomfortable just because you're wearing a noose! We have a new
line of ElastoTies<EM>&#153;</EM> with lots of bungee in the middle to allow you to
<EM>Expand under Pressure</EM><SMALL>®</SMALL>.
<%call SalesContactInfo(varRegion)%>
</BODY>
</HTML>
```

If we called this code from a suitable form where we had declared that we were in the East for example, it would display the following:

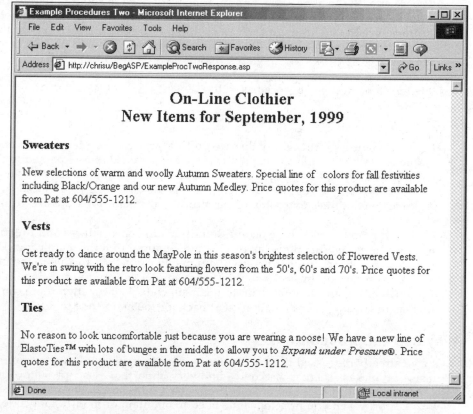

The above routine will put the appropriate `SalesRep` info into your code. There are three changes from our last example. The most obvious change is that inside the `Sub` where we used to have `Response.Write "Joe at..."`, we now have a `Select...Case` structure that determines which sales representative we should write onto the page.

Also notice two slight differences in the syntax. First is in the line that calls the `Sub`:

```
call SalesContactInfo(varRegion)
```

In order for the subprocedure to decide which sales rep to use it must know the regional location of the user. This information is passed over to the subroutine by enclosing it in parenthesis after the name of the subroutine.

Notice also that the subprocedure has a change in the first line. After the name of the subprocedure there are parenthesis that specify the data that is being sent over from the main body of code.

```
Sub SalesContactInfo(region)
```

You might be wondering why we're calling `SalesContactInfo` with the variable `varRegion`, yet when we get to the subprocedure, we're using the variable `region`. Is it an absentminded typo on the part of the author who has forgotten to adhere to a naming convention? The short answer is no. In the above line, `Sub` informs us that we're about to define a subprocedure; where `SalesContactInfo` is the name of the subprocedure, and region tells us that the subprocedure has an argument. We're calling this argument `region` only throughout the body of the subprocedure, as it describes what the subprocedure will do with the argument that's its been fed. E.g. `Select Case region`... In other words, it's a local variable.

Now let's look at the subprocedure call:

```
<%call SalesContactInfo(varRegion)%>
```

Here, we call the subprocedure that we defined above. When the subprocedure is called, there's a value contained within the variable `varRegion` – this value is passed to the subprocedure as an argument. Within the subprocedure, `region` adopts this value and allows the subprocedure to execute. When the subprocedure finishes its execution, `region` ceases to exist, but `varRegion` continues to exist; and we return to the main program execution.

A confusing point arises here on our definition of subprocedures and functions. Both subprocedures *and* functions can receive information from the main code. They can both take action on that information. But only the function can *return* a value to the main code. Notice that the subprocedure performs its action (For example, `Response.Write` a line on the page) without sending anything back up to the main code. In a function there can be some information (such as the result of a calculation) sent back for the main code to use.

Why use subprocedures?

We've already discussed the use of subprocedures as a way of saving you from re-typing code in several places. There is a second – and very important – use for Subprocedures: the clarification and readability of your programs. Code can easily run on for several screens in your editor. When you or a colleague need to maintain or modify that code, it can be difficult to see the organization of the whole page. Breaking your code into several blocks and making each of them a subprocedure can solve this. Then the beginning of your code calls each of these blocks. When a programmer looks at the beginning of the code they can immediately see the general idea of what is going on, and then jump to the appropriate subprocedure to perform the editing.

In the code below you can see how easy it would be to re-arrange the order of the subprocedures or to substitute a new model of sweaters. In this example, the first three lines after the <% call the three subprocedures that are coded in full further down into the code. You will find that these subprocedure blocks will not be executed unless they are called. Therefore, after the last Call (Call Tie98Autumn on line 11 of the following code) VBScript sees that the remainder of the page mostly contains subs; and so it skips over these, then it stops when it reaches the %> marker. (The browser will interpret the HTML tags that form the remainder of the page when the page is sent to it.) You can understand procedures better when you understand that they are only executed when (and if) called, *not* based on their position in the code.

```
<HTML>
<HEAD>
<TITLE>Example Procedures Three</TITLE>
</HEAD>
<BODY>
<H2 ALIGN="center">On-Line Clothier <BR>
New Items for September, 1998</H2>
<%
  Call Sweater98Autumn
  Call Vest98Autumn
  Call Tie98Autumn

  Sub Sweater98Autumn
   Response.Write"<P>New selections of warm and woolly Autumn " & _
                "Sweaters<SMALL>.</SMALL>"
   Response.Write "Special line of colors for fall festivities "
   Response.Write "including Black/Orange and our new Autumn Medley. "
  End Sub

  Sub Vest98Autumn
   Response.Write "<P>Get ready to dance around the MayPole in "
   Response.Write "this season's brightest selection of Flowered Vests. "
   Response.Write "We're in swing with the retro look featuring "
   Response.Write "flowers from the 50's, 60's and 70's. "
  End Sub

  Sub Tie98Autumn
   Response.Write"<P>No reason to be uncomfortable because you wear a noose! "
   Response.Write "We have a new line of ElastoTies<EM>&#153;</EM> "
   Response.Write "with lots of bungee in the middle to allow you to <EM>Expand "
   Response.Write "under Pressure</EM><SMALL>®</SMALL>."
  End Sub
%>
</BODY>
</HTML>
```

Procedures Summary

To review, procedures have a name and contain some lines of code. Whenever you did a Call of a procedure, its lines of code were run. Procedures are perfect for Response.Write or other actions, but what if you want to have some lines of code that give you back an answer? For example you may frequently calculate a 5% commission on a wholesale price. Or you may want to find out the due dates of library books Note that these questions require lines of code to generate an answer that you will use in the main body of your code. **Functions** fill this niche by accepting some information from your code, performing calculations or decisions, then returning an answer to your code.

Functions

Functions are written in a similar way to procedures, but with several special characteristics that handle the returning of information. There are five ideas to master for writing and using functions.

First, when you write a function you use `Function` (instead of `Sub`) on the first line and `End Function` (instead of `End Sub`) on the last line. The naming rules of functions are the same as for procedures: start with a letter, no spaces, and avoid symbols.

In the next few paragraphs we will build a function to calculate the due date of a library book (two weeks after the check-out date). The start and end of the function will look like this:

```
<%
Function FindDueDate()
  ...
  lines of code
  ...
End Function
%>
```

The function usually receives some information from your main code in the form of a parameter (subprocedures can also receive information from parameters in the same way, only they can't return the values directly). This information is passed to the variable that you have named in the parenthesis following the function's name. You do not have to declare this variable using `Dim` – it is available for use automatically. For example, in our `DueDate` function we would expect to receive the checkout date from the main body of the code – this would give the due date function the starting point for its calculations. So now our code looks like this:

```
<%
  Function FindDueDate(varCheckOutDate)
    ...
    lines of code, some of which can use the variable varCheckOutDate
    ...
  End Function
%>
```

Once the function has done its calculation, it has to report the result back to the VBScript engine. The VBScript engine processes whatever value is assigned to the name of the function. This is a little tricky for most beginners. Not only do you have available the variable which passed the data into the function (`varCheckOutDate`); there is also a variable (usable only within this function) that is automatically created with the name of the function, in this case `FindDueDate`. Whatever value is stuffed in that variable will be is sent back to the to the VBScript engine when the function is finished. For example:

```
<%
  Function FindDueDate(varCheckOutDate)
    FindDueDate = varCheckOutDate + 14
  End Function
%>
```

The fourth concept is easy: how to use a function. You can call a function by just typing the name of the function followed by double parenthesis (we'll discuss the contents of these parentheses in a moment). You can then assign a variable to the return value of the variable as we do below:

```
<%
  varOut = Date()
  varDueDate = FindDueDate(varOut)
  Response.Write "Your books are due on " & varDueDate
%>
```

varDueDate here contains the value returned by the calculations in our function. By assigning the value to this variable, we are running the function. The last idea is how to send the information from your main body of code to the function – in our case, the check out date of the book. We put whatever data we want to send to the function in the parenthesis. For example:

```
<%
  checkoutDate = date()
  varDueDate = FindDueDate(checkoutDate)
  Response.Write "Your books are due on " & varDueDate
%>
```

And so we get the final product; VBScript code that creates a function, and then some ASP code which outputs the values that the VBScript function returns to ASP.

```
<HTML>
<HEAD>
<TITLE>Sample Function Page</TITLE>
</HEAD>
<BODY>
<%
  Function FindDueDate(varCheckOutDate)
    FindDueDate = varCheckOutDate + 14
  End Function
%>
<H2>Thank you<BR>
for using the On-Line Library.</H2>
<%
  checkoutDate = date()
  varDueDate = FindDueDate(checkoutDate)
  Response.Write "Your books are checked OUT on " & checkoutdate
  Response.Write "<BR>Your books are due on " & varDueDate
%>

</BODY>
</HTML>
```

Common Errors when Writing Functions

❑ Forgetting that functions, except in special circumstances, can only return one answer.

❑ When using a function you must pass it the data it *expects* to receive. Sending a date when the function expects a price would hinder the function in carrying out its job

❑ The answer that the function will provide the main code must be assigned to a variable that is named the same as the function name.

So now we're ready to look at an example.

Try It Out – Function to Calculate Expenses

Your colleagues come to hear a seminar in your city that you provide once per month. They can attend for two, four or six days. They need a rough idea of how much they will be charged for travel, and per diem. Everyone gets $75 a day for food. Some people like to stay in the city (hotel is $175 per night) while others prefer to stay in the suburbs ($85 per night). If they stay in the city, it costs $85 for transport to and from the airport. If they stay in the suburbs, they rent a car for $45 per day. Your task is to design a form that asks for the visitor's preference (a hotel in the city or in a suburb) and then creates a response page that gives them an estimate of their trip cost if they stay for two, four or six days of the seminar.

1. Rouse your web page editor and type in the following:

```
<HTML>
<HEAD>
<TITLE>Function Form</TITLE>
</HEAD>
<BODY>
<H2>Cost Calculator for<BR>
Attendance at Corporate Conference</H2>
Please provide the following information so we can estimate your
local costs while attending the conference

<FORM ACTION = "FunctionResponse.asp" METHOD = post>
  Please select your preference in location: <BR>

  <SELECT NAME="location">
    <OPTION VALUE="city">City</OPTION>
    <OPTION VALUE="suburb">Suburb</OPTION>
  </SELECT>

  <BR><BR>
  <INPUT TYPE = submit>
  <INPUT TYPE = reset>
</FORM>

</BODY>
</HTML>
```

2. Save it as `FunctionForm.asp` in your `BegASPFiles` directory.

3. Now, create a new web page with the following code:

```
<HTML>
<HEAD>
<TITLE>Function Response</TITLE>
</HEAD>
<BODY>
<%
  Function CityCost(NumberDays)
    varHotelTotal = NumberDays*175
    varMealsTotal = NumberDays*75
    varAirportTransport = 85
    CityCost = varHotelTotal+varMealsTotal+varAirportTransport
  End Function

  Function SuburbCost(NumberDays)
    varHotelTotal = NumberDays*85
    varCarTotal = NumberDays*45
    varMealsTotal = NumberDays*75
    SuburbCost = varHotelTotal+varMealsTotal + varCarTotal
  End Function

  varLocation=Request.Form("location")
%>
<H3>You have chosen the hotel in the <%=varlocation%>.<BR>
your estimated costs for this seminar will be:</H3>
<%
  Select Case (varLocation)
    Case "city"
      varCost = CityCost(2)
      Response.Write "The two day course will cost $" & varCost & "<br>"
      varCost = CityCost(4)
      Response.Write "The four day course will cost $" & varCost & "<br>"
      varCost = CityCost(6)
      Response.Write "The six day course will cost $" & varCost & "<br>"
    Case "suburb"
      varCost = SuburbCost(2)
      Response.Write "The two day course will cost $" & varCost & "<br>"
      varCost = SuburbCost(4)
      Response.Write "The four day course will cost $" & varCost & "<br>"
      varCost = SuburbCost(6)
      Response.Write "The six day course will cost $" & varCost & "<br>"
  End Select
%>
</BODY>
</HTML>
```

4. Save it as `FunctionResponse.asp` in the usual directory.

5. If you start up your web browser and run the `FunctionForm.asp` form page, you'll see the following.

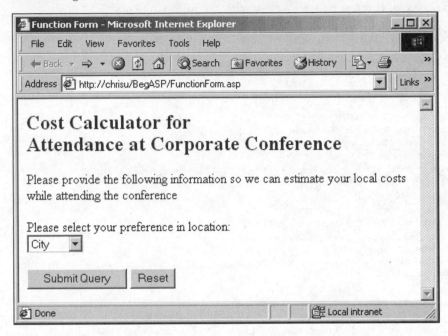

6. If you select City and press Submit Query, you'll see the following information.

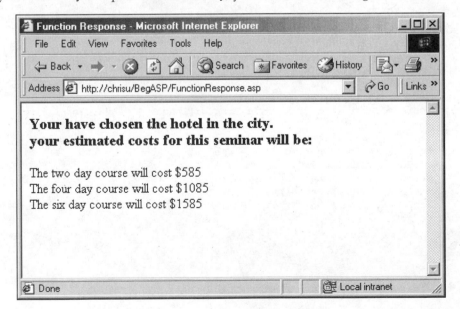

How It Works

The two functions that perform our calculations are relatively straightforward.

```
Function CityCost(NumberDays)
   varHotelTotal = NumberDays*175
   varMealsTotal = NumberDays*75
   varAirportTransport = 85
   CityCost = varHotelTotal+varMealsTotal+varAirportTransport
End Function
```

The first function `CityCost` assumes that the hotel costs 175 dollars a day. So it takes the number of days supplied by the user, multiplies them by 175 and the stores them in the variant `varHotelTotal`. It does the same for Meals assume that the meals cost 75 dollars a day. The cost of air transport is a one off and costed at 85 dollars. Then the variable `CityCost` is created, adding the three values generated previously altogether. This is the value returned by the function. The function that calculates the cost by suburb works in the same way, just applying different prices.

```
Function SuburbCost(NumberDays)
   varHotelTotal = NumberDays*85
   varCarTotal = NumberDays*45
   varMealsTotal = NumberDays*75
   SuburbCost = varHotelTotal+varMealsTotal+VarCarTotal
End Function
```

We then detect whether the hotel is in the city of the suburbs using the `Select Case` statement. For the City, we then call the `CityCost` function, and store the value returned by the `CityCost` function. We then execute the `CityCost` function for the 2, 4, and 6 day courses:

```
Select Case (varLocation)
  Case "city"
     varCost = CityCost(2)
     Response.Write "The two day course will cost $" & varCost & "<br>"
     varCost = CityCost(4)
     Response.Write "The four day course will cost $" & varCost & "<br>"
     varCost = CityCost(6)
     Response.Write "The six day course will cost $" & varCost & "<br>"
```

We do the same for the suburbs, displaying the result for the 2, 4, and 6 day courses.

```
  Case "suburb"
     varCost = SuburbCost(2)
     Response.Write "The two day course will cost $" & varCost & "<br>"
     varCost = SuburbCost(4)
     Response.Write "The four day course will cost $" & varCost & "<br>"
     varCost = SuburbCost(6)
     Response.Write "The six day course will cost $" & varCost & "<br>"
```

Improvement to our Functions

We can live without the intermediate variable in our functions. The longer way we used is shown below first:

```
Select Case varLocation
  Case "city"
    varCost = CityCost(2)
    Response.Write "The two day course will cost $" & varCost & "<BR>"
```

A faster technique is to directly write the function into the concatenation:

```
Select Case varLocation
  Case "city"
    Response.Write "The two day course will cost $" & CityCost(2) & "<br>"
```

Summary of Reusing Code

Remember that subroutines are used to meet one of two needs:

❑ Reusing sections of code

❑ Organizing your code into blocks

Remember that both subprocedures and functions receive data in order to perform calculations or perform one of several actions. The difference between a subprocedure and function is that a function returns a value back to the main code.

Summary

The real power of programming comes from the ability to control and direct the order of execution of statements. In this chapter we looked at three families of control structures:

❑ Branching, where only one of several possible sets of code is executed

❑ Looping, where a set of code is performed over and over

❑ Jumping, where VBScript pauses execution of the current script block, jumps over and executes a different script block, and then comes back to resume the execution of the original script block.

Each of these techniques has two ways of being implemented in ASP:

When **branching** between just two choices we use the If...Then statement that makes its decision based on an expression that evaluates to true or false. If we have more than one outcome then we use the Select Case structure.

When we write a **loop** we must consider how many cycles we want to run through. If we know the number of cycles before starting the loop we generally use the For...Next structure. If we *don't* know then we use the Do...While structure.

When writing **jumping** structures we must ask if we expect VBScript to return some kind of answer from the code that we jump to. If yes, then we write the other code as a *function*. If we expect the other code only to perform actions then it is written as a sub procedure.

With these tools we can now orchestrate the order in which our lines of code are executed. In some cases we may skip over lines while other times we may repeat code. Each of these control construction techniques will provide a supporting role in the use of the ASP objects and components that you will learn to use in the to use in the remainder of the book.

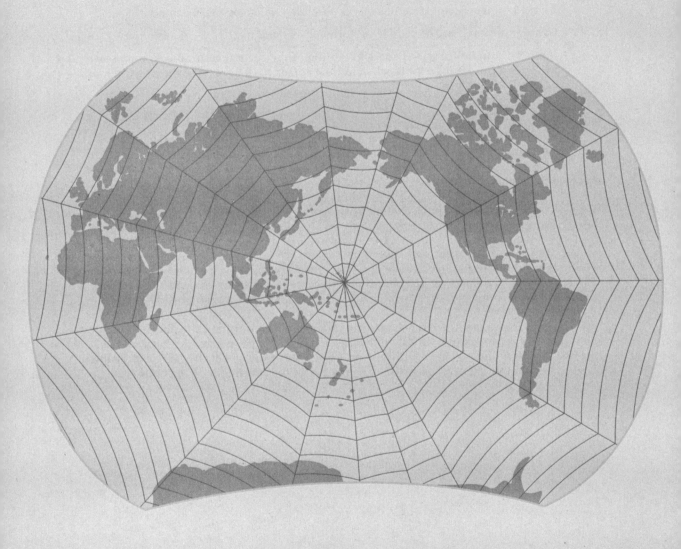

Objects, Properties, Methods and Events

In this chapter, we will be looking at objects. Some of you may have heard terms like "object oriented programming", "object models", and similar. In order for us to understand what these terms mean, we first need to look at the word found at the core of each of them: **object**.

In our study of objects, we will find that an object is a software representation of a real-world item, or object. Software objects feature properties (that describe the object), methods (that allow the object to do things for you), and events (code that is executed automatically when a certain situation – an event – occurs).

Once we have looked at what an object is, we'll then be able to look at how objects are useful to us in developing ASP applications. Developing web applications requires us to deal with both the client-side and server-side programming, and therefore we'll take a look at how objects can be used on both sides of the wire.

Before we get started, here is what we will cover in this chapter:

- ❑ What is an object?
- ❑ An introduction to properties, methods, and events
- ❑ How can we change the characteristics of an object?
- ❑ How do we know when the object tells us something?
- ❑ What is an object model?
- ❑ How do we use the object model in Active Server Pages?

We'll begin by taking a look at what an object is.

What is an Object?

In the real world, we already know what objects are. They're the things we look at, pick up, and use every day – things like our chairs, our telephones, and our computers. All these are solid, tangible entities.

However, if we want to describe a telephone to somebody in abstract terms, we can do this by talking about it in terms of its essential characteristics – what properties it has, what it can do, and how we can interact with it. All telephones have these characteristics, and we can use them to establish exactly how one telephone differs from the next.

So, for our telephone's physical properties, we could say that it has a microphone, a speaker, and a dialing pad. We could also say that it lets us do things, such as call someone and talk to them. Our telephone will also tell us when certain events are happening: for example, if a friend is trying to call you, your telephone will ring to let you know. This ringing will prompt you to take some action, like picking up the handset and talking to your friend. As an abstract object, our telephone has:

❑   Certain properties that define and describe it

❑   A set of things or methods that it lets us do

❑   The ability to prompt action when events occur

We can use these three attributes to describe physical objects and abstract concepts. In a few minutes we will describe how these real-world ideas are replicated in software objects, but for now let's go a little deeper into our real-world telephone. By learning about what objects are, we can then look at how to use them in a way known as **object-based programming**. In the object-based way of programming, the application is broken down into a set of objects. In doing this, you can build the application in a two stage process. Firstly, you create the objects you will need in your application and then you set up the relationships and interactions between objects. Later in this chapter, we will see how the objects of Active Server Pages relate and interact with each other and allow us to build our applications.

Our Telephone in Detail

 Here is our telephone. To look at this as an object, let's put down some information about it. We will be classifying the information into three categories:

❑   Things that describe the telephone

❑   Things that we can do with the phone

❑   Things that the telephone tells us and that we can react to

Let's look at each of these aspects in turn:

Describe the telephone	The telephone is gray
	The telephone is made of plastic
	The handset weighs 6.5 ounces
	The telephone has 12 keys
	The telephone number is (714) 555-1523
	The telephone is connected to the exchange
What can we do with it?	We can place an outgoing call
	We can answer an incoming call
	We can hang up the current call
	We can enter our calling card number
	We can disconnect it from the exchange
What can it tell us that we can react to?	Someone is trying to call us
	The person we are calling is busy
	Another person is calling while we are talking

How It Works

The three categories that we have created in the left-hand column can be applied to any object. In fact, the best way to describe an object is to break down its characteristics into these three categories, and put information about your object into these categories. Any information that you have about a particular object can be included in one of these categories.

If you have another telephone that features all these characteristics, except that its color is blue, then we can describe your telephone by changing that one part of the description above. Moreover, this technique works for any type of object, both real world and software.

Object Terms

So far, we have used verbose English terms to describe our three categories. In the world of objects, we need terms that concisely describe each of these three categories. These terms are **properties**, **methods** and **events**. In addition to these terms, we need to look at the term **instance** as it relates to objects. In this section, we'll look more carefully at what each of these mean in abstract terms.

Instances and Classes

When we are talking about a unique object, we can use the term **instance** to say that we are talking about a particular telephone object – *your* telephone for example – that has a specific set of properties and values. When we want to talk about another telephone, we use a different instance of the telephone object. In this way, both you and I can have instances of the telephone object. For example, my telephone (my *instance* of a telephone object) is gray and comes with special answer-phone facilities, your telephone (your *instance* of a telephone object) may be red, blue, green etc. These *instances* represent completely different physical objects. However, since they are both instances of the same object description or template, they share the same types of characteristics such as methods, properties (although the values can be different), and events. When a specific instance of an object is created from the template for the object, the object is said to have been **instantiated**. What actually happens is that a copy is made of all of the properties and events from the object description, but the methods (frequently a big chunk of code) remain in the original place and this section of code is used by all of the different instantiations of that one object.

So we've mentioned object descriptions or templates, but it's time to give them their proper name in ASP; **classes**. We mentioned that each object can have different instances. For instance, my telephone is small and white and has 12 buttons. Your telephone will probably be different to that, but they're both recognizable as telephones and they both provide the same function. They both conform to a set of rules for what a telephone does – they connect to the local telephone line, they both have a numeric keypad and somewhere to speak into. A class in ASP is like a set of design rules that an object must conform to. It would be no good if my telephone didn't have a handset, or a numeric keypad, even if it did plug into the telephone socket on the wall. In a class there should be a minimum set of functions that your object must be able to perform.

Properties

When talking about those characteristics that describe an object, we are talking about the **properties** of the object. Each property of the object describes a particular aspect of the object. The property is actually described as a **name/value pair**. This means that for every **named** property, there is a single unique **value** that describes that property for this instance of the object. If we go back to our telephone example, we can create a table that lists each of the property names and the value of each property.

Property Name	Property Value
Color	Grey
Material	Plastic
Weight	6.5 ounces
NumberOfKeys	12
TelephoneNumber	(714) 555-1523
Connected	Yes

We now have a set of properties that describe this instance. The properties of an object are used to represent a set of values associated with the object. A new instance of the object may have different property values, but it has the same property names.

Color	Grey	Blue
Material	Plastic	Thermoplastic
Weight	6.5 ounces	22 ounces
NumberOfKeys	12	12
TelephoneNumber	(714) 555-1523	(615) 555-8329
Connected	Yes	Yes

Even with different property values, these two telephones are instances of the same object template. Since we know that all telephone objects have a 'Color' property, we can determine the color of each of the phones by examining its 'Color' property value. We can use properties in two ways. We can read from them or we can also write to them. So if we wanted, we could have changed the cover of our telephone to a different color.

Now that we have a way of describing the telephone object, let's take a look at what we can do with it.

Methods

Another characteristic of objects is that they can perform functions for us. For example the PlaceCall method would perform several functions for you. It will connect you to the local exchange, the exchange will route your call, and then when it reaches the destination, it will make the destination phone ring. These built-in actions occur whenever you pick up the handset and dial a number. This is a capability that has been built in to the machine.

However not all objects have functions like this. A chair object allows you to sit in it, so you could say that it is functioning to support your body. Objects that perform tasks that are more 'functional' are said to have methods. The tasks that an object can perform are called **methods**.

A method is defined as an action that an object can take. The code in a method is executed when the method is called. This calling is done by a command you write in the script of your ASP page. Once we have created an instance of an object, we can tell it to perform a certain task by calling one of its methods.

Let's illustrate this using the telephone example. Our telephone object can carry out five methods. Each of these methods will cause the telephone object to perform an action. Here is a list of functions that the methods of the telephone object can perform:

Method Name	Description
PlaceCall	Place an outgoing call
Answer	Answer an incoming call
HangUp	Hang up the current call
SendCardNumber	Enter or send our calling card number
Disconnect	Disconnect the phone from the exchange

These methods are used when we want our telephone object to perform a certain function; all we need to do is tell it to execute the corresponding method.

Methods are actually blocks of code that are written by the designer of the object (Microsoft, for example). The reason methods exist is because lots of programmers want to do the same job, so it is worth it for the gurus at Microsoft to write the code to do that job, test it, optimize it, and get it in great shape, then bundle it up in the object. We, as programmers, can then use that code pre-made. Instead of re-inventing the wheel we spend our time on the unique parts of our project.

Parameters of Methods

You may have noticed that some of the methods can be executed directly, while others look like they will need additional information. To contrast these two ideas, consider the following examples:

❑ Suppose that our telephone receives an incoming call (in the next section, we'll see how we can tell that this is happening). All we need to do to answer the call is to use the 'Answer' method of our telephone object.

❑ Suppose that we want to place a call. Simply calling the PlaceCall method isn't enough in this case: we need to supply more information (for example, the telephone number!) in order to complete the action.

Let's look more closely at the second of these examples. The telephone object has a TelephoneNumber property, and this is used to identify our telephone's *own* telephone number (i.e. the number that other people use to call us). So, the TelephoneNumber property of our phone isn't going to help us to make outgoing telephone calls.

So, how do we tell the phone which number we want to call? It's possible, I guess, for the telephone object to have another property, called OutgoingTelephoneNumber, that would identify the desired number; but that would be too cumbersome, because every time we wanted to make a call we would have to:

❑ Set the OutgoingTelephoneNumber property value to the desired phone number

❑ Execute the 'Call' method of the telephone object to place the call

As you know, telephones just don't work that way. It would be much more elegant (and intuitive) to have some way of passing the outgoing phone number to the 'Call' method, so that we can place an outgoing call in a single step. This is done by passing a **parameter** to the 'Call' method. With this in place, we can place an outgoing call by simply executing the 'Call' method and telling it which number we want to call, like this:

❑ Execute the 'Call' method of the telephone object, passing the outgoing telephone number as a parameter. Parameters here are just the same as the arguments (parameters) we passed to functions and subroutines in the last chapter.

If we look again at the methods of the telephone object, we can identify those methods that require parameters, and what the values of those parameters mean to the object:

Method Name	Parameters
PlaceCall	Outgoing telephone number
Answer	*No Parameters*
HangUp	*No Parameters*
SendCardNumber	Calling card number, PIN
Disconnect	*No Parameters*

You can see that a method can have none, one, or more than one parameter. The `SendCardNumber` method actually requires two parameters. You are required to pass in both the calling card number and the personal identification number (PIN) in order for the method to execute properly. Information passed as parameters of the method for execution by the method, will only be executed if all parameters have been supplied.

Return Values

In addition to passing parameters to a method, the method can also return information to us. The value returned by a method is (rather conveniently) called a **return value**. If a method has a return value, then it will pass information back to us. This information could have a number of purposes. For example, the return value might be an indication of whether or not the method completed successfully. Alternatively, the method could also pass back the results of some processing that it did for us. It can even return another object as a result.

As the user of an object, we can decide whether we want to do anything with the return value. If the information is pertinent to what we are doing, then we can capture the return value and do something with it later. If we do not care what the return value is, we can just ignore it and continue with our work.

Just as the methods of the telephone object can have parameters, we can identify those methods that pass return values (and these can be passed as parameters to other methods), and what those values mean.

Method Name	Return Value
PlaceCall	True (if call completed successfully) False (if call failed)
Answer	No Return Value
HangUp	True (if telephone was hung up successfully) False (if not)
SendCardNumber	True (if card was accepted) False (if card was not accepted)
Disconnect	*No Return Value*

Events

We have now looked at two of the three characteristics of an object. The properties and methods of an object are ways that the user of the object can communicate with the object. Now, what if the object needs to communicate with the program that created it?

As an example, consider what happens when our telephone receives an incoming call. The fact is that it needs some way of telling us to answer the call. How will the telephone communicate this information to us?

Again, it's possible for the telephone object to have a property (called `IncomingCall`, perhaps) that was set to 'True' whenever an incoming call was present. However, there are two disadvantages to this. First, it would require the user of the telephone object to check this property on a regular basis. Second, the user would require a great deal of knowledge of the inner workings of the object, which isn't ideal.

What is needed is a way for the object to tell the user that something has happened. The mechanism for this is called an **event**. An object generates an event whenever something of interest happens. In our telephone example, when the telephone receives an incoming call it tells us so in the form of an event – we'll call it the `IncomingCall` event. (On most telephones, this particular event takes the form of the telephone ringing.)

The telephone object would generate an `IncomingCall` event every time an incoming call is received. In a physical phone, the ringing sound is the phone notifying you of the `IncomingCall` event. When the user receives this event, it can execute the 'Answer' method (pick up the handset), and begin the call. This frees the user from having to check regularly for incoming calls: the event is designed to notify the user just at the appropriate moment.

Just like methods, events can have parameters. These parameters can hold specific information about the event. For example, if our telephone supports *CallerID* – a feature that reveals the identity of the incoming caller – then the `IncomingCall` event could include a parameter that contains the telephone number of the incoming caller.

Here is a list of the events that our telephone object will generate, along with their associated parameters:

Event Name	Parameters
IncomingCall	Incoming CallerID information
LineBusy	*No Parameters*

There are a couple of useful pieces of terminology that are often used in this context. When an object generates an event, the object can be said to **fire** the event. When the object has fired the event, we say that the user must **handle** the event.

Synchronous vs Asynchronous

One of the advantages of working with objects and events is that it awakens us to the concept of asynchronous programming. First off, let's look at the definitions of synchronous and asynchronous.

These terms refer to how two separate actions are related to each other. If the first action must be completed before the second one begins, then these two actions are said to be **synchronous**. If the second action can begin at any time, no matter what the status of the first action, then these two actions are said to be **asynchronous**.

We've already discussed what it would be like if we our objects didn't support events. For example, to detect an incoming call, you would need to constantly check the value of some property to see whether an incoming call was waiting. While you're performing these frequent, regular checks, you would be unable to perform other tasks dependent on the outcome of that task. This is an example of synchronous activity. For example in the real world you might be waiting for a telephone call from a friend to let you know what time you should meet them. You can't go out until you've arranged a specific time. It's the same in programming. Your program could be waiting on a `WaitForAnIncomingCall` method in a `While ... Wend` loop, and it could be stuck there until the call was detected, refusing to return control to the main body of your program.

With events, we can have asynchronous activity. By having an event handler that is called when the object fires the 'IncomingCall' event, we can perform other tasks (for example, making an outgoing phone call) without having to devote any effort to monitoring the incoming call status. Our event handler code will be dormant until such a time as it detects the 'IncomingCall' event, and then sets about dealing with the incoming call.

This is not to say that all synchronous is bad and all asynchronous is good. You will see many instances in the real world where it makes sense to use a synchronous activity to perform a certain type of processing. Likewise, we will also see instances where an asynchronous activity is not an optimal way of dealing with an event.

Encapsulation

One great thing about objects is that you don't have to understand what's going on underneath the shell, to know how to operate them. With our telephone we don't need to know how our voice is projected from the phone, down the wires to the nearest exchange, and how from there it gets to our intended destination. This is all hidden from us. It's the same in ASP – you don't need to know how the object was programmed, for example, in C++ or VB (objects can be created in many languages), to be able to interact with it. The concept of a user of an object not being concerned with the inner workings of the object, is known as **encapsulation**. For example, when you use a telephone to answer an incoming call, all you need to do is pick up the handset. You don't need to know how the transistors are connected to each other inside the telephone. This is the equivalent of executing the `Answer` method. You do not need to know what's going on underneath – that's all encapsulated within the `Answer` method. This is an example of encapsulation.

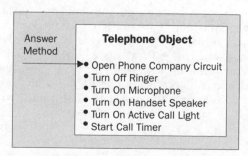

One advantage of encapsulating the workings of an object within a method is that the implementation of the method can be changed without having to adjust the client. For example, suppose the phone company decides to change the way that an incoming call is answered. Without encapsulation, all of the users of the telephone object would have to be adjusted to support this new way of answering the phone. Instead, by encapsulating these new steps within the Answer method, the actions of the client never need to be changed: with either system, all the client needs to do is execute the 'Answer' method. Not only does encapsulation make the telephone user's life easier; it allows the developer of the telephone object to change the implementation at any time.

Moving On to Programming

Now that we have a basic understanding of what an object is, we can move on to looking at how programming concepts have changed from traditional methods by using objects. When working with objects in software development, we will create objects that have properties, events and methods. We can use these three attributes to describe physical objects and abstract concepts. Either way, the programmatic object will allow us to interact with it through its properties, events and methods.

Programming with Objects

To begin our look at programming with objects, let's use our trusty telephone object again. Being a technophile and always needing to have the latest and greatest, you have even hooked up your telephone to your computer. Now you want to be able to do something with it. If we want the computer to interact with the telephone, we need a programmatic object that will allow us to control the physical telephone.

It is this **representation** of a physical object that gives programmatic objects their power. Representation is literally the process of taking our real world object and turning it into a software object. In our telephone object example the color of the phone is represented by a color property, the weight of the phone is represented by a weight property. The ability to pick up the receiver and dial a friend is modeled by the PlaceCall method. The real world telephone has a set of features or characteristics that can be broken down into properties, methods and events. Once we have identified these features it makes it easier, to represent them in our software object.

However, as described in the previous section, the concept of encapsulation means that the actual workings of the telephone object are hidden from us. When a phone rings, you don't need to know how the signal was transmitted to the exchange, you only need to interact with the interface (talk into the handset). This is what we're going to consider with our software object; the interfaces we use to communicate with it, rather than the software object itself. So when we use our computer to control our object, it's not going to use the inner workings of the objects, rather it's going to communicate with the object and control it using its interfaces (the methods and events).

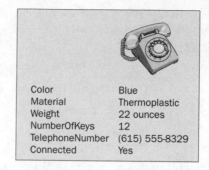

Color	Blue
Material	Thermoplastic
Weight	22 ounces
NumberOfKeys	12
TelephoneNumber	(615) 555-8329
Connected	Yes

This book will not cover how to create the software object itself (you will be able to download this from the Wrox website – details of this are in the Try It Out coming up): rather, we will take a look at the programmatic object, and then look at how we can use the object's properties, methods, and events.

The Software Telephone Object

So now we are shifting gears here from describing the real-world telephone as an object to describing a software `telephone` object. This is an example of representation. The properties of the telephone object are:

Property Name
Color
Material
Weight
NumberOfKeys
TelephoneNumber
Connected

As you can see, we have used the same names that we used when discussing the physical telephone object. The methods of the `telephone` object are the same as well. In this case, the methods that have parameters will have the same parameters as well:

Method Name	Parameters
PlaceCall	NumOutgoing
Answer	*No Parameters*
HangUp	*No Parameters*
SendCardNumber	NumCCN, NumPIN
Disconnect	*No Parameters*

Finally – as you will expect by now – events that the object will support are the same events that are supported by the physical telephone object:

Event Name	Parameters
IncomingCall	NumIncoming
LineBusy	*No Parameters*
CallWaiting	NumIncoming

Now that we have defined the interfaces of our `telephone` object, we can take a look at some code examples that will show you how to use these interfaces. For these examples, we will be using VBScript, which is the language that is being used throughout the book. Since there are three types of interfaces, we will look at three code samples – one for each type.

Setting Up the Telephone Object Example

We've supplied the `telephone` object on the Wrox web site. It comes as a DLL file, which has to be installed and registered before you can use it. The good news is that it is automatically installed and registered by running a self-contained exe file. Once you've run the file, you will have a `telephone` object, ready to include in the script of your ASP pages. Let's look at what needs to be done to install it.

Try It Out – Installing the Telephone DLL

1. Download the `MyTelephone.exe` file from the Wrox web site at `http://www.wrox.com`. You can also find full support with any problems encountered during the installation at this URL.

2. Once the file has been downloaded, you can run it to expand all of the files into a temporary directory.

3. Go to that temporary directory and run `setup.exe` to install the `MyTelephone` object. Click on OK on the first dialog to confirm installation, and then click the icon to proceed with installation.

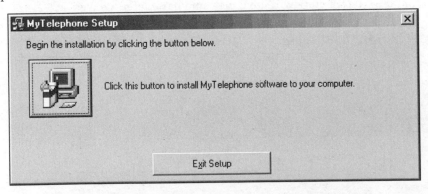

Troubleshooting Problems

The differences between each individual's computer, operating system and set up sometimes means that the software installs but may fail to register correctly. If you run any of the examples later in this chapter and encounter an error generated by a call to any of the methods, such as the `PlaceCall` method, then this will be the problem.

The problem is easy enough to rectify, all you need to do is manually register the DLL yourself. To do that, once you've run `setup.exe` you'll find that a file called `MyTelephone.dll` has been created. It's also a good idea to stop and restart the web application manager before you use the DLL in any examples. It can be placed in any directory - the only important thing is that the file be registered in that directory. To do that, there is a file (provided by the machine's operating system) called `REGSVR32.EXE`. If you run that file and pass the name of the `.dll` as a parameter (e.g. `regsvr32 MyTelephone.dll`), it will register the file in that location. The best way to do this is from the command prompt: copy the `.dll` file to the desired directory, go to that directory, and then run `regsvr32 MyTelephone.dll`. The OS should find `regsvr32.exe` since it is usually in the `WinNT/System32` folder, which is in the default path.

If it's still not working then check that the machine you are actually installing the file on is actually the web server, and not just the machine with your browser on, and then look at the web site `http://p2p.wrox.com` for support if you still have problems.

Altering the Properties of an Object

So, we have a `telephone` object, which defines the characteristics of any telephone. For a particular instance of the object – that is, a real physical telephone – values are associated to the properties that describe the characteristics of that one telephone.

A program that uses the instance can then retrieve the values associated to these properties. Alternatively, they can be used by a method or event to perform some action. The programmer working with the instance of the `telephone` object is responsible for setting the values of many properties; other properties will be set based on the results of methods being called.

Setting a Property

First, let's look at how to set a property. The four properties that we'll use here to describe our instance of the `telephone` object are:

- ❑ `Color`
- ❑ `Material`
- ❑ `Weight`
- ❑ `NumberOfKeys`

When the instance of our object is created, these values are left blank or set to default values. It is up to the program that creates the object to set the specific values that we want.

Try It Out – Setting Property Values

In this example, we will be configuring the properties of our object so that it represents this telephone:

Color	Blue
Material	Thermoplastic
Weight	22 ounces
NumberOfKeys	12
TelephoneNumber	(615) 555-8329
Connected	Yes

1. Using your editor of choice, enter the following source code:

```
<%
 Option Explicit
 Dim objTelephone
 Set objTelephone = Server.CreateObject("MyTelephone.Telephone")

 objTelephone.Color = "Blue"
 objTelephone.Material = "Thermoplastic"
 objTelephone.Weight = 22
 objTelephone.NumberOfKeys = 12

 Response.Write "Done"
 Set objTelephone = Nothing
%>
```

2. Save this file, with the name `SetProperties.asp`, to your `BegASPFiles` directory.

3. View the file in your web browser. If everything worked properly, then the browser will display the word **Done**.

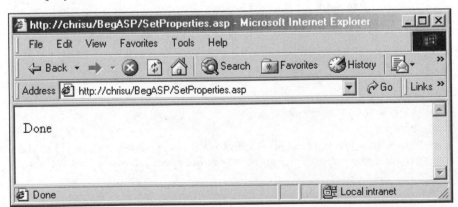

How It Works

The first step in obtaining a reference to an object is to allocate a variable to hold the reference. The variable is created using the `Dim` statement:

```
Dim objTelephone
```

You'll recall from Chapter 4 that the variables in VBScript are in fact variants.

The next step actually creates the object:

```
Set objTelephone = Server.CreateObject("MyTelephone.Telephone")
```

This is done using the `Server.CreateObject` method. This is the process of instantiation that we referred to earlier in the chapter, when we discussed the concept of instances. The `Server` object is one of the built-in ASP objects; objects are everywhere; here we are using an object to create an object. This method has one parameter – the name of the object you want to create. The method also has a return value – it's a reference to an instance of the object.

Since the value returned by the `CreateObject` method is a reference to an instance of the `Telephone` object, we must use the `Set` statement to assign its reference to our variable. The `Set` statement is a VBScript statement that lets us store object references in variables. Since the return value is a reference to the object, we have to use the `Set` method to store its value for later use. We will cover the `CreateObject` method in more detail in Chapter 11.

Now that we have our reference to the instance of the telephone object, we can go about setting the properties. To do this, we simply use the *object.property* notation and set it to the value that we desire:

```
objTelephone.Color = "Blue"
objTelephone.Material = "Thermoplastic"
objTelephone.Weight = 22
objTelephone.NumberOfKeys = 12
```

As you can see, the general syntax for this is:

object.property = value

Lastly we set the object to nothing to release the reference and free up memory:

```
Set objTelephone = nothing
```

This is general housekeeping you should perform every time you have finished with an object. Now that we have set some property values in our telephone object, we can look at how to retrieve these values.

Retrieving a Property

The last section showed how to set the values of properties of an object. Now that information is stored there, we can retrieve this information at a later time. In essence, we have an instance of an object that has some data stored in its properties. All we need to refer to this instance is the reference to the object's instance. All of the data that the object has stored inside of it comes along with the object.

Read-Only Properties

In addition to the data that we have explicitly stored in the object, there is information that the object uses to describe its state. In our `telephone` object, there is a property called `Connected` that describes whether or not a telephone is connected to the telephone exchange. In order to change the connection state of the phone, we would use a method. This method is read only for the user, so the user cannot change it themselves. The only way to change it is internally, as a result of using a method such as `PlaceCall`, which would change the property value of the `Connected` property from `False` to `True`.

You may wonder why we would not just change the property by hand? This is another example of encapsulation. There is more to disconnecting a phone than just changing a value of a property: the object needs to perform some actions, which the user of the object does not need to be concerned about. This functionality is encapsulated in a method, and the method is responsible for updating the value of the `Connected` property. This makes the `Connected` property a **read-only property**, which means that we cannot set its value, only retrieve it.

Try It Out – Retrieving Property Values

In this example, we will be retrieving the values of some of the properties of the object, and storing them in local variables.

1. Using NotePad or your editor of choice, adapt the program `SetProperties.asp`, from above, as follows:

```
<%
  Option Explicit
  Dim objTelephone
  Set objTelephone = Server.CreateObject("MyTelephone.Telephone")

  objTelephone.Color = "Blue"
  objTelephone.Material = "Thermoplastic"
  objTelephone.Weight = 22
  objTelephone.NumberOfKeys = 12

  Dim strColor
  Dim strMaterial
  Dim intNumKeys
  Dim intWeight
  Dim blnConnected
```

```
   strColor = objTelephone.Color
   strMaterial = objTelephone.Material
   intNumKeys = objTelephone.NumberOfKeys
   intWeight = objTelephone.Weight
   blnConnected = objTelephone.IsConnected

   Response.Write "objTelephone.Color = " & strColor & "<BR>"
   Response.Write "objTelephone.Material = " & strMaterial & "<BR>"
   Response.Write "objTelephone.NumberOfKeys = " & intNumKeys & "<BR>"
   Response.Write "objTelephone.Weight = " & intWeight & "<BR>"
   Response.Write "objTelephone.IsConnected = " & blnConnected & "<BR>"
   Set objTelephone = nothing
%>
```

2. Save this code in the file `RetrieveProperties.asp`, in the `BegASPFiles` directory.

3. View the page in your browser.

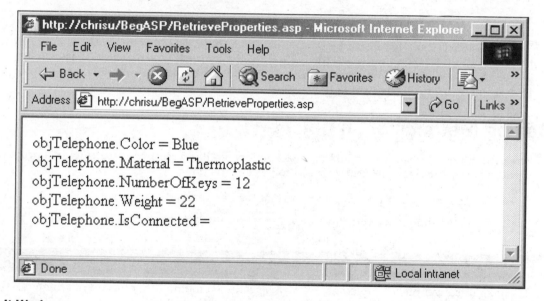

How It Works

First, we set the `Color`, `Material`, `NumberOfKeys` and `Weight` properties of our telephone, just as we did in the previous example. Next, we allocate some variables that will hold the values of the properties of our telephone object, using the `Dim` statement. We allocate one variable for each property that we are storing:

```
Dim strColor
Dim strMaterial
Dim intNumKeys
Dim intWeight
Dim blnConnected
```

Next, we set about retrieving the property values. To do this, we use the *object.property* notation again – this time to retrieve the property, and then we store the property in the appropriate variable. Here's the code that does this for the `Color` property:

```
strColor = objTelephone.Color
```

As you can see, the general syntax for this is:

myVariable = *object.property*

Then we output the results. Here's the line that does this for the `Color` property:

```
Response.Write "objTelephone.Color = " & strColor & "<BR>"
```

If the value of the property is a reference to an object, then you will need to use the `Set` statement to assign the property value to our local variable:

Set *myVariable* = *object.property*

We have now seen how to put information into the properties of an object and retrieve that information. You might also have noticed that the `IsConnected` property didn't return a value. That's because it can only be set by another method, the `Answer` method. As we haven't called the method, the value can't be assigned. Up until the moment that the method is called, it doesn't have a value. We'll be looking at how it can be changed next. So now let's get our object to do some work for us by calling its methods.

Calling Methods of an Object

The syntax for calling a method of an object is very similar to setting or retrieving a property value. There are two points that we need to be concerned about:

❑   If the method requires parameters, that they are passed correctly.

❑   If the method has a return value we must receive and capture it.

Try It Out – Calling a Basic Method

To make this example a simple one, we will be calling a method that has no parameters. Also, in this example, we are not interested in its return value. We will be using the same `objTelephone` instance of our `telephone` object that we have been using in the previous examples in this chapter.

1.   Using your editor of choice, enter the following source code:

```
<%
Option Explicit
Dim objTelephone
Dim blnIsConnected

Set objTelephone = Server.CreateObject("MyTelephone.Telephone")
```

```
      Response.Write "Answering the phone...<BR>"
      objTelephone.Answer()

      blnIsConnected = objTelephone.IsConnected
      Response.Write "The IsConnected property is " & blnIsConnected & "<P>"

      Response.Write "Hanging up the phone...<BR>"
      objTelephone.HangUp()
      Response.Write "The IsConnected property is " & objTelephone.IsConnected & "<P>"
      Set objTelephone = nothing
%>
```

2. Save this file, with the name `MethodsExample.asp`, to your `BegASPFiles` directory.

3. View the file in your web browser.

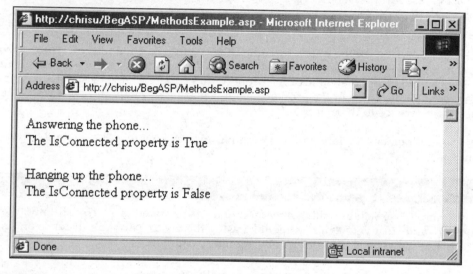

How It Works

In this example, we are using two of the methods that the `Telephone` object supports. We will also be checking one of the properties after calling the methods to see if they had any effect.

```
<%
  Option Explicit
  Dim objTelephone
  Dim blnIsConnected
  Set objTelephone = Server.CreateObject("MyTelephone.Telephone")
```

The first step, as we have done in the previous examples, is to create an instance of the `Telephone` object using the `Server.CreateObject` method. The reference that this method returns will be stored in a local variable. Remember that since we are storing a reference to an object, we have to use the `Set` statement.

```
  Response.Write "Answering the phone...<BR>"
  objTelephone.Answer()
```

The next step is to call the Answer method of the Telephone object. We will use the reference to the instance that we created to call the method. The preceding Response.Write line is being used to provide a visual indication that the method is being called.

```
blnIsConnected = objTelephone.IsConnected
Response.Write "The IsConnected property is " & blnIsConnected & "<P>"
```

Next, we will want to check the status of the IsConnected property. This property indicates if the phone is in use or not. Since we have just answered the phone, we would assume that this property would be set to True. We will store its value in a local variable, then use that local variable in a Response.Write method to display its value.

```
Response.Write "Hanging up the phone...<BR>"
objTelephone.HangUp()
Response.Write "The IsConnected property is " & objTelephone.IsConnected & "<P>"
Set objTelephone = nothing
%>
```

Finally, we will hang up the phone by calling the HangUp method of the Telephone object. Once that has completed, we will check the value of the IsConnected property again. This time, instead of storing the value of the property to a local variable before displaying it, we will directly display the value of the property. Both ways work exactly the same way. Then we can release the reference to the object.

Next, we will look at a variation of this example and see how to call a method that has a parameter.

Try It Out – Calling a Method with Parameters

In this example, we will be calling a method that has parameters – we're still not interested in the return value, just yet. Again, we will be using the objTelephone instance of our telephone object that we have been using in all the previous examples.

1. Using your editor of choice, enter the following code:

```
<%
Option Explicit
Dim objTelephone
Dim strPhoneNumber
Dim blnIsConnected

Set objTelephone = Server.CreateObject("MyTelephone.Telephone")

strPhoneNumber = "615-555-8329"
Response.Write "Calling " & strPhoneNumber & "...<P>"
objTelephone.PlaceCall(strPhoneNumber)

blnIsConnected = objTelephone.IsConnected
Response.Write "The IsConnected property is " & blnIsConnected & "<P>"
Set objTelephone = nothing
%>
```

2. Save this file, with the name `ParameterExample.asp`, to your `BegASPFiles` directory.

3. View the file in your web browser.

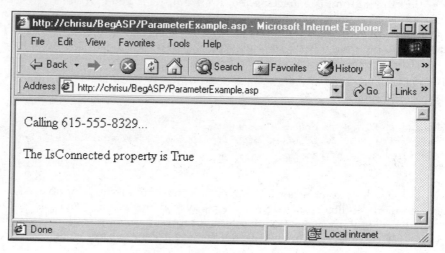

How It Works

Now we're telling the telephone to execute the `PlaceCall` method. As we know, the `PlaceCall` method doesn't work alone: we need to tell the telephone who to call! We do this by specifying the telephone number as a parameter to the `PlaceCall` method.

```
<%
  Option Explicit
  Dim objTelephone
  Dim strPhoneNumber
  Dim blnIsConnected

  Set objTelephone = Server.CreateObject("MyTelephone.Telephone")
```

First, as we have done in the previous examples, we will create an instance of the `Telephone` object. The reference to this instance is then stored in a local variable.

```
  strPhoneNumber = "615-555-8329"
  Response.Write "Calling " & strPhoneNumber & "...<P>"
  objTelephone.PlaceCall(strPhoneNumber)
```

The telephone number that we will be calling is stored as a string. In this example, the number is hard coded. We could have just as easily used a form to supply the value. We then will display a message indicating the number that will be called. We can then pass this value to the `PlaceCall` method. The parameter that we supply to the `PlaceCall` method is included within the method's parentheses. The contents of the parentheses are known as the **parameter list**. The entries in the parameter list could be variables or explicit values.

> One thing that you need to be careful with is the order of the parameters in the parameter list. If we were calling a method that requires multiple parameters, then the order of the parameters in the parameter list must *exactly* match the order that the method is expecting. So, for example, if you call the `SendCardNumber` method, then you must specify two parameters: the first must be the value of the `NumCCN` parameter, and the second must be the value of the `NumPIN` parameter and these parameters are separated by a single comma.

Finally, we check the value of the `IsConnected` property and display its value to the user and release the object reference.

```
blnIsConnected = objTelephone.IsConnected
Response.Write "The IsConnected property is " & blnIsConnected & "<P>"
Set objTelephone = nothing
%>
```

We have now seen how to program with the properties and methods of objects. In our examples, we have been using an object that represents a physical entity. The remainder of this chapter will be devoted to looking at a set of objects that represent an application environment in Active Server Pages. These objects comprise the Active Server Pages **object model**.

What is the Active Server Pages Object Model?

In this chapter, we have looked at how a physical object can be represented by a programmatic object. This programmatic object has all of the interfaces of the physical object, and it can be used as an interface between an application and the physical object itself. But what about objects that don't have a physical counterpart?

In the Active Server Pages programming model, there is a wide range of functionality that is accessible to the programmer. ASP helps us to track the state of a user, dynamically generate HTML output, and take data from forms to be inserted into a database. All of this functionality makes ASP a rather complex beast. Microsoft was tasked with finding the best compromise between offering a simple programming model and providing access to all of the power that ASP provides. To do this, the functionality was grouped into a set of objects. These objects were then related together into what is known as an **object model**.

An object model is a representation of a set of objects and their relationships to one another. These relationships can take the form of containment, where one object is embedded inside of another. Or, they can take the form of a parent–child relationship, where one object has a set of child objects associated with it.

We will not be examining the various methods for grouping objects together in this book. What is important to us is what the objects that make up Active Server Pages are, and how they are related to each other.

Object Model Structure

Seven objects make up the core of Active Server Pages. These are known as the **built-in objects**. The objects are:

- ❏ Server object
- ❏ Application object
- ❏ Session object
- ❏ Request object
- ❏ Response object
- ❏ ObjectContext object
- ❏ ASPError object

Each of these objects interacts with a different part of the ASP system. This chart shows how they are related to each other, and how they are related to the client and to the server.

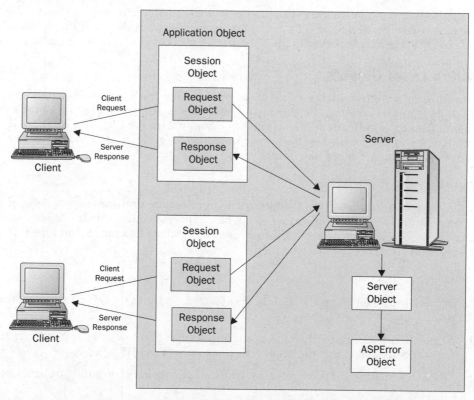

The following chapters in the book will go into each of these objects in greater detail. They will also provide a series of basic examples that will quickly show you how to use these objects to create ASP scripts. But for now, we will just take a quick look at what each object is for.

The Server Object

The `Server` object is an object that provides a home to a miscellaneous ragbag of properties and methods that can be used in almost every Active Server Page. While seemingly unrelated, these methods and properties are in fact abstractions of the properties and methods provided by the web server itself. This object will allow you to do things such as:

❑ Set the amount of time a script can run before an error occurs

❑ Take a user-supplied string and encode it into HTML format

❑ Convert a virtual path to a physical path on the server

❑ Take a user-supplied string and encode it into the proper format for a Uniform Resource Locator (URL) string

❑ Create an instance of an ActiveX component. You saw this earlier in the chapter with the `CreateObject` method of the `Server` object.

❑ Change the course of execution by jumping to another page using the `Transfer` and `Execute` properties.

These methods and properties are provided as utility functions for you to use in your pages. They are not directly used to affect the display of the page, but they still provide valuable support in creating Active Server Pages. Chapter 11 will cover this object in greater detail.

Application Level Objects

As the web is moving from just serving up pages to providing access to dynamic information from a wide range of systems, the sites that a user may access are beginning to look more like a traditional desktop application. We touched in Chapter 2 on the idea of a web application, and that all dynamically generated web sites are in fact web applications The application object represents your site and all of its visitors.

The Application Object

Since these pages are functioning together as an application, naturally the developer would want some control over the application as a whole. This is the responsibility of the `Application` object. This object will be covered in detail in Chapter 8, but let's just introduce a few things that it can do.

With this object, you can:

❑ Be notified when an application is first started, so that you can perform some startup processing.

❑ Be notified when an application is ending, so that you have the opportunity to perform functions to enable the application to close down cleanly.

❑ Store information that can be accessed by all clients accessing the application.

There is one instance of the `Application` object for each web application running on the web server. There may be many clients accessing the same application. They each can get a reference to the same `Application` object. Next, we will look at an object that is unique to each client of an application.

The Session Object

There is one `Application` object for each application on the web server. Every client accessing that application can get a reference to it. Each of these clients opens a **Session**, therefore, each of them has a reference to a unique `Session` object. This object will be covered in Chapter 8, but here is a little of what it can do. The `Session` object will allow you to:

❑ Be notified when a user session begins, so that you can take appropriate actions for a new client.

❑ Be notified when a client has ended their session. This can either be caused by a timeout or an explicit method called `Abandon`.

❑ Store information that can only be accessed by that particular client throughout the session.

The `Session` object is the most powerful object for continuity when using an application in Active Server Pages. One of the problems that have existed in creating web-based applications is that the connection between the client and the server is `stateless`. The web server itself has no mechanism for tying a request for a page by a client back to a previous request for a page by the same client. This means that each request that one client makes of a web server is treated independently from the rest. While this allows for a very efficient and fast web server, it makes writing applications nearly impossible.

Think of it this way. If you are writing an application using a standard web server, then every request to the server must carry along with it *everything* that you have done related to the application up to this point. Since the web server has no way of storing and retrieving that information, it is up to you to provide it *every time* you make a request of the server. Sounds pretty cumbersome? Well, with the `Session` object, Active Server Pages allows you to store and retrieve information about the client accessing your application. Nevertheless, this is just to whet your appetite. Stay tuned for Chapter 8 when the `Session` object will be explored in detail.

Page Scoped Objects

As we traverse our way through the object model, we now move from the Session level down to the individual page level. When working with pages of the application, we need to look at the basic function of a web server.

Basically, a web server operates by receiving a request from a client and then sending a response back to it. This request could be for an HTML page, or it could be the data from a Form submission that the user has made. To make our pages dynamic in ASP, we need to take the information that has been submitted and craft a customized response to send back to the client.

Active Server Pages provides two objects that allow you to interact at the page scope. The information that is sent from the client to the server is held, or encapsulated, in the `Request` object. The information that the server prepares to send back to client is encapsulated in the `Response` object. These two objects are good examples of objects that have physical manifestations, like our telephone. They are modeled on the HTTP request and response.

The Request Object

When a web browser or other client application asks for a page from a web server, this is called **making a request**. Along with the actual page that the client wants, it can send a great deal of information to the server as well. The Request object is responsible for packaging up that information to make it easily accessible to the ASP application.

The client asks the server to create an html page, by requesting an .asp script. When the server sees this request, it interprets this type of page as an Active Server Page. All of the information that the client is sending along with the request is then packaged into the Request object. This information is then accessible to the actual ASP script that is used to construct the page.

The information is categorized into five sets of information. Since each set of information can include multiple individual pieces of information, each set is stored as a **collection**. In a collection, each piece of information is stored as a name-value pair. We talked about name-value pairs earlier when we introduced object properties.

The collections in the Request object will be explained in detail in Chapter 7, but we will quickly introduce them here. The collections hold information about:

❑   The values that are provided in the URL that are sent by the client. In the URL, the client can include name-value pairs of information after the file name. This information is stored in the collection called QueryString.

❑   If the client is sending a Form request, then the values of the form elements are stored in another collection – the Form collection.

❑   The web server itself has a great deal of information about the request, response and general information about the server itself. These are called the **HTTP Server Variables**. This information is made available as a collection as well.

❑   If the client is sending any cookies along with the request, these are included in their own collection.

❑   In addition, if the client is sending any security certificates to the server, then these are included in their own collection.

By using the information that is included with the request, along with the script code in the Active Server Pages script file, the server can dynamically generate a page for the client to display. In order for the client to display the information, the server needs a mechanism to relay the data back to the client. This is the job of the Response object.

The Response Object

The primary feature of Active Server Pages is the ability to dynamically create web pages. The basic task needed to execute this feature is the ability to tell the client what information to display. There are a number of different ways to shape what the client will display. The Response object exists to provide an efficient interface to control the output to the client.

The Response object provides the ASP script with a set of interfaces that allow the script to control what information is being sent back to the client. The details of the Response object will be covered in Chapter 7. For now, we will just touch on some of the functions that the Response object provides.

With the `Response` object, the ASP script can:

❑ Insert information into the page being sent back to the client.

❑ Send instructions to the browser to create cookies on the client.

❑ Send the client to another page via a redirection.

❑ Control whether the page is sent as it is created, or whether it is completely built and then sent at one time.

❑ Control the various properties of the page, such as the HTML headers or the type of content.

These interfaces give the designer of the script the ultimate flexibility to decide how the information is presented back to the client.

The ObjectContext Object

The `ObjectContext` object helps you to develop applications out of components. It does this by allowing you to handle transactions from within an ASP page. A transaction is a single unit of work, that must either succeed in its entirety or if it fails, must be undone completely – returning the system to the state it was before the transaction was started.

When using applications made of out of components, its common to use transactions. If, for example, an action handled by a particular component fails, then you'd want details of the failure, and be able to take an alternative course of action. If a user tried to change details of their bank account and then bombed out mid-track, it would be logical to want track back to what the bank account details were previously, before trying to change the details again or continuing on alternative course.

The second type of application that uses transactions would be one that features data processing. If someone makes an alteration to a database via a web page, and somebody else makes another alteration at the same time, you need to be able to accept one alteration, while canceling, or postponing, the other. The management of these types of transactions was handled in IIS 4.0 and PWS 4.0 by a piece of software known as Microsoft Transaction Server (MTS). However, with IIS5 and Windows 2000, the functionality of MTS is now integrated directly into part of the Windows 2000 operating system known as COM +.

The `ObjectContext` object allows access to MTS in order to start or terminate a transaction. We don't want to go into how it does that now, that's a topic for later in this book, but this hopefully gives you an overview of this useful object.

The ASPError Object

The `ASPError` object contains details of any errors generated by an ASP script or by the `asp.dll` itself. Previously, there was no facility in ASP for storing details of errors that occurred. The `ASPError` object, with help from the `Server.GetLastError` method, allows more complex customized handling of error messages. It directs the user to a standard error page, or to a user-created page depending on the option selected in MMC.

Using the Object Model as a Road Map

While being able to create a page dynamically is a nice feature, the real power of Active Server Pages comes from its ability to create web-based applications. These applications allow the user to perform tasks that go beyond simply requesting pages. The logic and structure to create these applications are laid out in the object model.

We can use the object model as a road map that lays out:

❑ Where information should be stored in our applications

❑ How information specific to a single user can be tracked

❑ How to set up client pages to send the appropriate information to the server for it to dynamically build a page

❑ How to dynamically build a page, using all of the features that ASP provides, and then send that page back to the client

In the next few chapters, we will be walking through this landscape in detail and building up the expertise needed to put together an application using Active Server Pages.

Summary

In this chapter, we have introduced the concept of objects. For our purposes, an object is a programmatic tool that enables us to access a physical item, or a set of associated data. An object is described by its interfaces. These interfaces are broken into three categories:

❑ Properties – a property's value holds data that describes an attribute of the object.

❑ Methods are used to have the object perform some task for us.

❑ Events let the object notify us that something has happened and can also be raised to make something happen and can contain code that we write that can be executed.

In learning how to develop with objects, we have seen how to:

❑ Set and retrieve information from the object's properties

❑ Call the methods of an object

With the concepts of objects well in hand, we introduced the Active Server Pages object model. These seven objects encapsulate the functionality offered by the ASP server:

- ❑ The `Server` object provides basic functionality across the web server.

- ❑ The `Application` and `Session` objects provide the application functionality that is not present in a basic web server.

- ❑ The `Request` and `Response` objects are used to interpret the information sent by the client and then construct the HTML page that will be sent back in response.

- ❑ The `ObjectContext` object, is used to control transactions within a web page.

- ❑ The `Error` object handles any ASP-generated errors

By understanding the relationships of these objects to one another, we can start to build true applications by using the power of Active Server Pages. The next few chapters will begin to show us how.

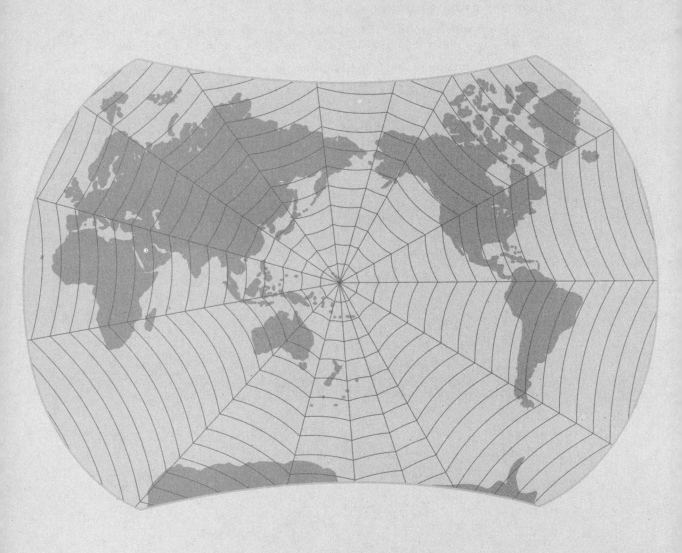

The Request and Response Objects

We'll now delve into the Active Server Pages object model. This chapter will consider two almost indivisible objects, Request and Response. These two objects handle communications between the browser and the web server. They are central to the Active Server Pages object model, and are vital for controlling how the user sends information to the server – via forms, for example, and how they get details back, such as a message saying "Thank you Mr. Ullman, your details have been submitted correctly".

Using the Request object, your ASP script can obtain information from the server about what the user wants: this information can then be manipulated within ASP. The Request object allows ASP to deal with all of the information that is sent to it from the client. This information can include form data, querystring data, browser data, client certificate data, authentication data, content length, request method, URL, and even cookies. With access to all of this information, we can now use the scripting power of ASP to create a customized or personalized page for the user. Once that page is created we need a way to get the page *back* to the user's browser; to do this, we use the Response object. While the Request object deals with everything sent from the client to the web server, the Response object will allow us to deal with everything sent from the web server back to the client.

The topics we'll look at in this chapter are:

- ❑ Using the Request object to send information to the server

- ❑ Sending information back to the client using the Response object

- ❑ The QueryString collection

- ❑ The Form collection

- ❑ The ServerVariables collection

- ❑ The ClientCertificate collection

- ❑ Request object properties and methods

- ❑ Controlling how information is returned

- ❑ Controlling what the browser does

- ❑ Additional information that can be sent

Handling Browser/Server communications

While the Request and Response objects deal with separate parts of the interaction between browser and server, we've decided to talk about them jointly, because when you make a request, the only way you can actually know if the request has succeeded is to use the Response object to return the requisite information. Similarly, it's pretty hard to talk about the Response object without mentioning the Request object, because it's common to use the result of a client's request to generate a response on the web server. However, you shouldn't assume that they're similar: while these objects often require each other to be able to return information to the user, the actual properties and methods of each object are completely different.

Let's do a very quick retread over what happens when a web browser or another client application asks for a page from a web server. This is known as making a **request**. In order to make a request from the server, the client must supply the specific page using an address (usually a URL); in addition, the client can send a whole host of other information to the server. The Request object is responsible for packaging all this information, and making it easily accessible to the ASP application. When the client asks the server to provide a page with an .asp suffix, this suffix tells the server to process any server-side scripting as part of an ASP Page. All of the information that the client sends along with the request is then packaged into the Request object. This information is then accessible to the ASP script that is used to dynamically construct the page that the user has requested.

Sending Information to the Server

The information supplied by the client is categorized, in the ASP model, into groups of items called **collections**. In a collection, each piece of information is stored as a **name/value pair**. We talked about name/value pairs in the previous chapter, when we introduced object properties. In ASP, a collection is simply a set of these name/value pairs, specific to the Request object. More particularly, a collection lists added items, each of which has a unique value that describes the property.

```
name=chris
luckynumber=23
date=1/1/99
```

If there are three fields in a form then the form collection will contain three name/value pairs. For each, the name comes from the <INPUT> tag's NAME attribute and the Value comes from what the user typed in the corresponding text box, or selected from the list box (or if no typing or selection, the default VALUE attribute). This information is all included in the request.

By using the information included with the request, along with the scripting logic in the ASP page, the server can dynamically generate a page for the client to display. In order for the client to display the information, the server needs a mechanism to relay the data back to the client. This is the job of the Response object. Let's see how you'd go about returning information to the client using the Response object.

Sending Information back to the Client

The primary function of the Response object is to send information to the client. Usually, this is a direct result of the client making a request of the server. It is the responsibility of the server-side script to come up with a response that will be understood by the client. Once this valid response information has been created, the Response object can be used to transmit the information.

There are two main ways that you can use the Response object to send text back to the client, which can be displayed on your web page. Both should be fairly familiar to you now – they are in fact two faces of the same beast. One way is by using the Write method of the Response object and the other way is a shortcut notation of Response.Write.

The Write Method

The Write method will be the most-used method of the Response object. The Write method is used to display text on your ASP page. It's a simple enough method, but when using it, there is a lot going on behind the scenes that we'll look at later in this chapter. For now we're going to take a simple overview, as it is very straightforward to use.

The Write method of the Response object allows you to display information on your web page. This information can be the contents of a server-side variable, the return value from a function, or a string constant. No matter what the information, the syntax of the method is consistent:

```
Response.Write value
```

The contents of value can contain any valid information that can be output in an HTML file. In other words, it is up to the developer to make sure that whatever data is contained in value can be properly displayed on a client browser. We'll be seeing many examples throughout this chapter, demonstrating how to use Response.Write.

Using Shortcuts

You can use a special 'shortcut' version of Response.Write to send information to the client. You can use shortcuts for outputting information to the client using a special form of the standard script delimiters. When adding ASP script to a HTML page, you use the <%....%> to indicate what is script and what is HTML. The shortcut method allows you to use a modified version of the script delimiter, <%= ... %> as a shortcut reference to Response.Write. For example, to use the shortcut method to write the contents of the variable value as we did above, you would write:

```
<%= value %>
```

This would result in exactly the same information being written to the HTML output stream as we would get with this statement:

```
<% Response.Write value %>
```

Now, the question is, "When should I use which method?"

When to Use each Method

We have just seen two ways to output information to the client. There are some very simple rules that you can follow to help choose which of the two methods you should use.

The **shortcut method** is best used when you have a block of HTML code into which you want to insert a single piece of dynamic code. As you can see in these two examples that do the same thing, the shortcut method really reduces the amount of code that you have to write:

```
<BODY>
The time is now:
<%
Response.Write Now
%>
</BODY>
```

Now, if you were to rewrite this using the shortcut method, you can see the savings in code that you would gain:

```
<BODY>
The time is now: <%= Now %><P>
</BODY>
```

However, the shortcut method is not always the most efficient method in terms of performance. If you have a big block of ASP script code and want to output information to the client, then using the Response.Write method directly would be the way to go. The performance of a page will drop if you use the shortcut method because of jumping into and out of script, creating the resultant HTML bit by bit, rather than continuously in one script block. In a larger scale situation, your users will notice a drop in speed. In many situations, using the full notation also improves the readability of your code, which will make it easier to remember what you were doing when you look at the page two months later.

Here are a few quick notes about what you can and can't do with Response.Write

❑ You *can't* have more then one line in the shortcut. The following is not acceptable

```
<%= "Hello world"
  ="Hello world%>
```

❑ You *can* concatenate two strings in a Response.Write

```
strOne = "Hello"
strTwo = "World"
Response.Write strOne & strTwo
```

❑ You *can* calculate the result of a mathematical expression

```
intInteger1 = 26
intInteger2 = 456
Response.Write intInteger2/intInteger1
```

❑   You *can* have a value which is from a `Request` object

```
Response.Write (Request.QueryString("Query1"))
```

Now let's take a look at an example.

Try It Out – Using Response.Write and the Shortcut method

In this example, we will be looking at the two ways that you can send dynamic information back to the client by using the two methods of the `Response` object.

1.   Using your editor of choice, create the `OutputTest.asp` file with the following source code:

```
<HTML>
<HEAD>
<TITLE>Testing the Write Method</TITLE>
</HEAD>
<BODY>
Here is some plain HTML being added to the HTML output stream<BR><BR>
<%
  Response.Write "Here is a string being output using Response.Write<BR><BR>"
%>
<%= "Here is a string being output using the shortcut method<BR><BR>" %>
<HR>Now let's try some dynamic text<BR><BR>
<%
  Response.Write "With Response.Write, the time is now: "
  Response.Write Now
  Response.Write "<BR><BR>"
%>
With the shortcut method, the time is now: <%= Now %><BR>
</BODY>
</HTML>
```

2.   Save the file to your usual `BegASP` directory.

3.   View the page in your web browser.

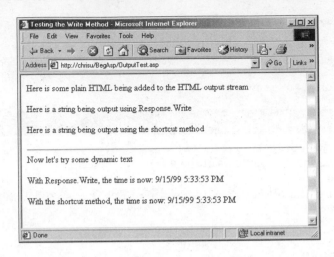

How It Works

The use of these two methods is fairly self-explanatory. Basically, whatever information you pass as the parameter to the method will be sent back to the client for display. This information can be a string constant, a variable, or the value of a built-in function. Anything goes, as long as the output is something that the browser will understand.

You can also see in this example that while you can use both `Response.Write` in full *and* the shortcut method to output information to the client, the context in which you output the information should determine what method you would use. Given a choice like this, most developers will choose the method that is the easiest to read and that also requires the fewest keystrokes. None of us likes typing, but it goes along with the job!

The Request Object

Now that we have taken a quick overview of the `Response` and `Request` objects, we can now delve into each in detail. We'll start by looking at the different ways for sending information from the page on the browser to the server. We've already noted that the `Request` object stores items that have been sent in a series of **collections**. These collections store information in pairs containing an identifying name and the corresponding value. Let's delve deeper.

Request Object Collections

The `Request` object has five collections. We'll explain these in detail later in this chapter, but we will quickly introduce them here:

❑ `QueryString`: When sending a request, the client can include name/value pairs of information within the URL, after the file name. This collection stores any values provided in the URL. For example, this is sent when the `METHOD` attribute of a `FORM` is set to `GET` and the `ACTION` attribute is set to the URL we wish to transfer to.

❑ Form: If the client sends a Form request, and sets the METHOD attribute to POST then the values of the form elements are stored in this collection.

❑ ServerVariables: The web server itself holds a great deal of information about the request, contained in **HTTP server variables**. This information is made available as a collection.

❑ Cookies: If the client is accepting cookies from the server, it sends the information to the server and the server stores it in the Cookies collection. While being able to create and access cookies with the Request and Response objects is a major feature, we will ignore this collection in this chapter as it has a more logical home in the next chapter on applications, sessions, and keeping track of users.

❑ ClientCertificate: A client certificate is a digital certificate exchanged between client and server to verify the identity of the user attempting to contact the server. If the client sends any security certificates to the server, then they are stored in this collection.

Let's now take a look at each of the collections (minus Cookies) in the Request object.

The QueryString Collection

A **querystring** is information that is passed to the server, in the form of a name/value pair. It could contain the client's username, an e-mail address, or personal information. A querystring is appended to a URL with a question mark, '?'. A typical querystring might look like this:

```
?username=DaddyKool
```

A querystring's name/value pair is composed of two strings: the name and the value. These two strings are separated by an equal sign, '='. If the request generates more than one querystring name/value pair, then subsequent name/value pairs are separated from each other by an ampersand, '&':

```
?username=DaddyKool&email=DaddyKool@kool.com
```

When this information is appended to a URL, it looks something like this:

```
http://chrisu/BegASP/demo.asp?username=DaddyKool&email=DaddyKool@kool.com
```

ASP retrieves the values of the variables that are given in the HTTP query string and stores them in the QueryString collection. The QueryString collection returns exactly the same information as the Query_String variable in the same format. So,
<%=Request.Querystring%> returns:

username=DaddyKool&email=DaddyKool@kool.com

and

<%= Request.ServerVariables ("QUERY_STRING")%> also returns:

username=DaddyKool&email= DaddyKool@kool.com.

How are Querystrings Generated?

There are three main situations in which a querystring can be generated.

The first is by clicking on a hyperlink generated with an anchor tag, <A>, which already has an in-built querystring:

```
<A HREF="somepage.ext?name=value">a querystring example</A>
```

This hyperlink, when clicked, generates a querystring variable named "name", with the value "value".

The second situation is when a form is sent to the server by the GET method. Take a look at the following code:

```
<FORM NAME=logging ACTION="RequestQuery.asp" METHOD ="GET">
Type your first name:   <INPUT TYPE="TEXT" NAME="FIRST"> <BR>
Type your last name:   <INPUT TYPE="TEXT" NAME="LAST"> <BR>
<INPUT TYPE="SUBMIT" VALUE="Login">
```

When the browser displays an ASP page containing this code, it might look something like this:

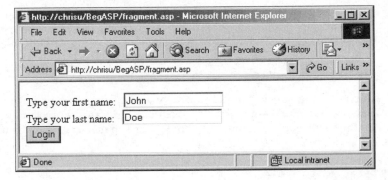

When the user enters his username and password, and clicks on the Login button, two querystring name/value pairs are generated. They correspond to the names of the form's input textboxes and their respective VALUE attribute values. In other words, a name/value pair is generated for every named INPUT element Hence, the URL requested by these actions might look like this:

```
http://chrisu/BegASP/RequestQuery.asp?first=john&last=doe
```

> *It's important to note that the POST form method won't allow you to retrieve querystring name/value pairs, because this stores information in a different collection. We'll look into the POST form method shortly.*
>
> *The main difference between POST and GET is that POST sends the information as part of the request body, while GET sends information by appending it to the Uniform Resource Locator, (URL).*

The final method is, very simply, via a user-typed HTTP address:

When the *Enter* key is pressed, two name/value pairs are generated, namely `first=john` and `last=doe`.

Retrieving a QueryString using the Response Object!

You can retrieve the contents of a querystring and place it in a variable as follows:

```
strUserInput = Request.QueryString
```

You can display the contents of a querystring in several different ways. In its simplest form, you could display it with just the following statement:

```
<%= Request.QueryString%>
```

We've already discovered that the equal sign was just a shorthand notation for `Response.Write`. So equally you could write the above as:

```
<% Response.Write(Request.QueryString) %>
```

We'll use the equal sign shorthand for the time being, as it distracts less from the querystring code. Either of the above lines will return *all* of the querystring name/value pairs. Thus, if the name/value pair was equal to `username=DaddyKool&pass=ChangeMe` then this command would return

`"username=DaddyKool&pass=ChangeMe"`.

In fact, it's more common to use the following:

```
<%= Request.QueryString("property_name")%>
```

This will return a specific value, corresponding to the *property_name*, providing it holds a single value. Thus, you can retrieve information for the string variable name using the following code:

```
<%= Request.QueryString("username")%>
```

In the example above, the result `"DaddyKool"` is returned.

Retrieving the contents of several name/value pairs

What happens though if you have several name/value with different names on the page, each generated by a different form element (e.g. one from a textbox, one from a check box etc)? Perhaps the best way is to employ the `For Each` notation that we looked at briefly in Chapter 4. You can reference each item separately using the following loop:

```
For Each Item in Request.QueryString
  Response.Write "Item - " & Request.QueryString(Item)
Next
```

As this goes through the loop, it displays the values for each name/value pair in the QueryString collection, for example:

Item – DaddyKool
Item – ChangeMe

Counting the number of name/value pairs

If another value is subsequently assigned to name, then (unlike variables) the original value persists, and the second value is appended to the name/value pair. For example, by assigning the value "Junior" to the name variable, the name/value pair passed as the querystring appended to the URL would be extended to "name=DaddyKool&name=Junior". Where more than one value exists for the same name, the values are returned by Request.QueryString separated by commas, thus: "DaddyKool,Junior".

In such a situation, you might need more than just a name/value pair to keep track of your data. Help is at hand in the form of the Count property, which is used to track the number of querystring name/value pairs. Let's see an example of this:

```
<%= Request.QueryString("name").Count %>
```

This line of code will return the number of querystring name/value pairs that have the name "name". So if the name/value pair was name=DaddyKool, then this code would return the value 1. If the name/value pair was name=DaddyKool,Junior then the code would return 2; and so on.

> Note that there is also a global count which returns the number of query strings held in total:
>
> Request.QueryString.Count

How can we use this to get hold of one specific value from a set of values? The answer is to use an **index**. An index enables you to retrieve one of multiple values for a given property name, and can be any integer value in the range 1 to Request.QueryString("*property_name*").Count.

To use an index for the property name would require code with the following format:

```
<%= Request.QueryString("name")(index_val)%>
```

Of course, *index_val* is an integer value between 1 and the value held in Count (this is different from a conventional array which starts from 0.) If the value of *index_val* doesn't correspond to a valid index value (that is, *index_val* doesn't fall between 1 and Count), then ASP returns an error similar to the following:

Request object error 'ASP 0105 : 80004005'
Index out of range
/directory/somefile.asp, line xxx
An array index is out of range

Let's now build an example using concepts we have looked at so far.

In this example, we'll request a holiday destination or several destinations from the user. We'll then place these values in a querystring and display the values, along with some complementary information, on a separate web page.

1. Open your HTML editor, create a new file, and type in the following:

```
<HTML>
<HEAD>
<TITLE></TITLE>
</HEAD>
<BODY>
<H3>Holiday Form</H3>
Please select one or more destinations that you would like brochures for:
<FORM ACTION="ResponseQueryString.asp" METHOD=GET>
<SELECT SIZE=3 NAME="HolidayLocation" MULTIPLE>
   <OPTION>Madrid</OPTION>
   <OPTION>Rome</OPTION>
   <OPTION>Paris</OPTION>
   <OPTION>Berlin</OPTION>
   <OPTION>Moscow</OPTION>
   <OPTION>Birmingham</OPTION>
</SELECT>
<INPUT TYPE="SUBMIT">
</FORM>
</BODY>
</HTML>
```

2. Save the file as `RequestQueryString.htm` in your `BegASPFiles` directory.

3. Now enter the following code into your editor:

```
<%Option Explicit%>
<HTML>
<HEAD>
<TITLE></TITLE>
</HEAD>
<BODY>
<H3>Holiday Response Form</H3>
<%
  If Request.QueryString("HolidayLocation").Count=0 then
    Response.Write "We won't send you any details "
  Else
    Response.Write "We will send you details on "
    Response.Write Request.QueryString("HolidayLocation")
  End If
%>
 as requested.
</BODY>
</HTML>
```

4. Save this as `ResponseQueryString.asp`

5. Start your browser and open the file `RequestQueryString.htm`. The resulting HTML output for this script is:

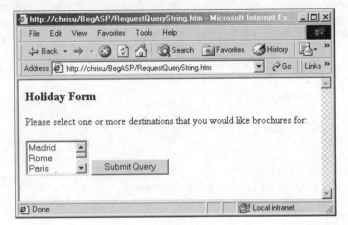

6. Now select one or more destinations (Hold down the *Ctrl* button while clicking to select more than one) and click on the **Submit** button. The result is:

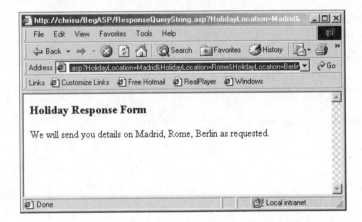

The full URL displayed on this example is:

```
http://My_Server_Name/BegASP/ResponseQueryString.asp?

HolidayLocation=Madrid&
HolidayLocation=Rome&HolidayLocation=Berlin
```

How It Works

We'll now look at how the ASP code works, and what is contained in the querystring. In the first page RequestQueryString.htm we set the ACTION attribute to the page we wish to transfer control to, and we set the METHOD attribute to GET. By setting the METHOD to GET we ensured that our information is transferred by query string:

```
<FORM ACTION="ResponseQueryString.asp" METHOD=GET>
<SELECT SIZE=3 NAME="HolidayLocation" MULTIPLE>
  <OPTION>Madrid</OPTION>
  <OPTION>Rome</OPTION>
  <OPTION>Paris</OPTION>
  <OPTION>Berlin</OPTION>
  <OPTION>Moscow</OPTION>
  <OPTION>Birmingham</OPTION>
</SELECT>
<INPUT TYPE="SUBMIT">
</FORM>
```

The rest of the code is straightforward. If you're unfamiliar with how forms transmit information via list boxes, radio buttons or the like, we suggest that you look at Appendix F where there is a detailed tutorial on the subject. One thing to note is that we name the list box HolidayLocation in the code for the form, this is important as we reference it in the next page.

In ResponseQuerySting.asp we set up a simple conditional structure, which first checks the count property of locations, to see if any locations have been selected:

```
<%
  If Request.QueryString("HolidayLocation").Count=0 then
```

Notice that we reference our querystring using the name assigned to the <SELECT> element created in the previous form, here. If the count is zero then we display the appropriate details:

```
    Response.Write " won't send you any details."
```

Otherwise, we get the server to display the contents of the HolidayLocation query string:

```
  Else
    Response.Write "We will send you details on "
    Response.Write Request.QueryString("HolidayLocation")
  End If
%>
 as requested.
```

In the example above, this will hold the values "Madrid, Rome, Berlin" – this of course will be different if you entered different places.

Amending Our Program

The property name stores several values associated with one name. In the above example we have three values stored with one name. However, what happens if you want to be able to access each value separately? After all, it stands to reason that if you're requesting brochures on three separate destinations, they might have to be dealt with separately.

This is where index values come in. We can use an index to query the name property: these queries allow us access to each of the values within name separately. Therefore, you could access the first element with the line:

```
<%= Request.QueryString("HolidayLocation")(1)%>
```

Here, Request.QueryString("HolidayLocation")(1) holds the value "Madrid". The second value can be accessed using:

```
<%= Request.QueryString("HolidayLocation")(2)%>
```

where Request.QueryString("HolidayLocation")(2) holds the value "Rome". You could then store each one in a separate variable:

```
strHolidayChoice1 = Request.QueryString("HolidayLocation")(1)
```

However, if you were using a long list of locations, this wouldn't be practical. So one proposed amendment to our program would be to loop through the QueryString collection, using the index property. As previously noted though if you access an invalid index value, you'll generate an error. The way to avoid this is to then loop only as far as the maximum number of items in the querystring. We can use the Count property to do this. If you were to replace the following code in our last example like this:

```
Dim intLoop
If Request.QueryString("HolidayLocation").Count=0 then
   Response.Write "We won't send you any details "
Else
   For IntLoop = 1 To Request.QueryString("HolidayLocation").Count
   Response.Write "<BR>We will send you details on "
   Response.Write (Request.QueryString("HolidayLocation")(IntLoop))
   Next
End If
```

This will separate out each value in the querystring as follows:

We will send you details on Madrid
We will send you details on Rome
We will send you details on Berlin as requested

Alternately, if you didn't want to separate out each value, you could access the whole value contained within the querystring:

```
<%= Request.QueryString%>
```

This holds the complete `QueryString` collection, which is shown on the resulting output:

```
"HolidayLocation=Madrid&HolidayLocation=Rome&HolidayLocation=Berlin"
```

Now that we've covered every facet of the `QueryString` collection, we'll move on to a related collection, `Form`.

The Form Collection

The `Form` collection holds the values of form elements sent to the HTTP request body via the `POST` method. In other words, when you fill in the text boxes on a form and pressed the Submit button, all of the values you have typed in can be stored in the `Form` collection.

Of course, text boxes aren't the only method of passing information on forms. In fact there are many different elements that you can use within a form to send information, such as:

- ❑ Text Boxes
- ❑ Checkboxes
- ❑ Option buttons
- ❑ Lists and their variations
- ❑ Hidden fields
- ❑ Text Area

If you're unsure of how any of these work within a form in HTML, we suggest you go to Appendix F, which provides a comprehensive tutorial on all of these features in forms and how the `Form` collection can be used to extricate information from them.

Assuming you are familiar with these form elements, then we'll only be looking at one example here of how you can retrieve information from the `Form` collection, as the method of retrieval is almost identical to that used with the `QueryString` collection. While there are several differences between `GET` and `POST` forms in terms of sending data, the only difference between them in using the data once it is in the `Request` object is the name of the collection itself. All other aspects are the same.

Again, this collection can be used together with the `Count` property, which enables the calculation of the number of values in a given name/value pair; also, the `Form` collection can use an index to access the individual values within a set of multiple values.

Items in the `Form` collection are also, like the `QueryString` collection, composed of name/value pairs. To construct items in a `Form` collection we follow a similar procedure to that used when creating items in the `QueryString` collection – that is, with two strings separated by an equal sign, "`=`". The first string is the form element's name, and the second string is the element's value. Again, multiple form name/value pairs in the form collection are separated by an ampersand, "`&`".

The main difference between a `QueryString` collection and a `Form` collection is that while the `QueryString` collection gets appended to a URL (with a question mark), the `Form` collection is sent as part of the HTTP request body and hence will not show up in the URL window in the browser. Note, also, that there's only one way to generate a form collection – by submitting the form using the `POST` method.

The best way to understand the `Form` collection is to dive in and take a look at another example.

Try It Out – Using Request.Form

In this example, we're going to do exactly the same thing as we did in the `QueryString` example – except that we'll be storing our values in the `Form` collection.

1. Open your HTML editor, open `RequestQueryString.htm`, and amend the following line:

```
Please select one or more destinations that you would like brochures for:
<FORM ACTION="ResponseForm.asp" METHOD=POST>
<SELECT SIZE=3 NAME="HolidayLocation" MULTIPLE>
```

2. Save the file as `RequestForm.htm` in your `BegASPFiles` directory.

3. Open the file `ResponseQueryString.asp` and amend the following lines:

```
<%
If Request.Form("HolidayLocation").Count=0 then
  Response.Write "We won't send you any details "
Else
  Response.Write "We will send you details on "
  Response.Write Request.Form("HolidayLocation")
End If
%>
```

Note: This assumes that you didn't make the amendments as suggested to our previous example.

4. Save this amended file as `ResponseForm.asp`.

5. Start your browser and type in the following URL into the address line:
`http://my_server_name/BegASP/RequestForm.htm`

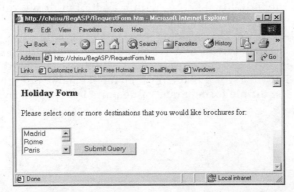

6. As in the first example, select some appropriate destinations then click the **Submit** button. The result is:

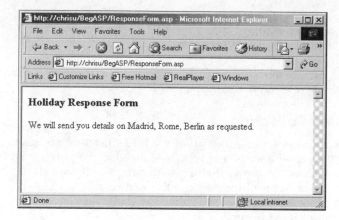

How It Works

The program looks the same, and it runs in the same way; it even returns the same answers. So, what's different? The answer is, very little. All we've done is changed every occurrence of `Request.QueryString` to read `Request.Form`:

```
<%
  If Request.Form("HolidayLocation").Count=0 then
    Response.Write "We won't send you any details "
  Else
    Response.Write "We will send you details on "
    Response.Write Request.Form("HolidayLocation")
  End If
%>
```

The only noticeable difference in the whole program is that the information is no longer passed to the server as part of the URL. Behind the scenes, you might also notice that you don't get a querystring attached to the URL.

Amending The Program

Again, we can separate out the values from the name/value pairs in the form collection, by using the index values:

```
Dim intLoop
If Request.Form("HolidayLocation").Count=0 then
  Response.Write "We won't send you any details "
Else
  For IntLoop = 1 To Request.Form("HolidayLocation").Count
    Response.Write "<BR>We will send you details on "
    Response.Write (Request.Form("HolidayLocation")(IntLoop))
  Next
End If
```

As expected (just like in the querystring example), that code displays the contents of HolidayLocation on separate lines:

We will send you details on Madrid
We will send you details on Rome
We will send you details on Berlin as requested

For explanations on how to extract information from different form elements and how to use it in the Form collection, we refer you to Appendix F.

The ServerVariables Collection

The ServerVariables collection holds all of the **HTTP headers** and also additional items of information about the server and the request. We looked at the function of HTTP headers in chapter 2. They are sent by the browser along with a request for a web page, and contain extra information, about the contents of the request. Every time an ASP page is executed the web server creates a set of server variables to accompany that page. These server variables can be interrogated and manipulated using ASP.

It's probably best to start with a list of all the ServerVariables available, but rather than list them all in the book, you'll learn more by physically retrieving the contents of the ServerVariables collection in an example.

Try It Out – Retrieving the Request.ServerVariables Collection

In this example, we'll list all of the variables contained in the ServerVariables collection in a two column table. The left-hand column lists the variables' names and the right-hand column their values.

1. Open your HTML editor, create a new file, and key in the following:

```
<%
Option Explicit
Dim Key
%>

<HTML>
<HEAD>
<TITLE>The HTTP Server Variables Collection</TITLE>
</HEAD>

<BODY BGCOLOR=white>
<CENTER>
<H2>The HTTP Server Variables Collection</H2>
</CENTER>

<TABLE BORDER=1>
<TR>
  <TD><B>Variable Name</B></TD>
  <TD><B>Value</B></TD>
</TR>
```

```
<%
  For Each Key in Request.ServerVariables
    Response.Write "<TR><TD>" & Key & "</TD><TD>"

    If Request.ServerVariables(key) = "" Then
      Response.Write " "
    Else
      Response.Write Request.ServerVariables(key)
    End If

    Response.Write "</TD></TR>"
  Next
%>


</TABLE>
</BODY>
</HTML>
```

2. Save the file as `ServVars.asp` in your `BegASP` directory.

3. Start your browser and open the file:
   `http://my_server_name/BegASP/ServVars.asp`

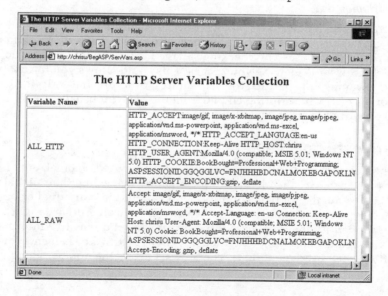

How It Works

The `ServerVariables` collection holds all HTTP header variables as well as lots of general information variables. For the querystring values to show, a form must be submitted, and the form's method must be `GET`.

To retrieve individual variables in the collection, the syntax is:

```
<%= Request.ServerVariables("variablename") %>
```

You must know the specific name of the variable you want to see. You can get the names from the table above or from Appendix I.

In our example, to retrieve every `ServerVariable` within the collection, we use a `For Each...Next` loop to iterate through each of the items in the collection.

```
<% For Each key in Request.ServerVariables
```

In this case, the variable `key` is used to store each different Server Variable name in the collection – so for the first iteration, the value in `key` is `ALL_HTTP`, in the second iteration it's `ALL_RAW`, and so on. For each unique value of `key` this loop will execute the following lines:

```
If Request.ServerVariables(key) = "" Then
  Response.Write " "
Else
  Response.Write Request.ServerVariables(key)
End If
```

If the variable `key` is empty then this displays a space, otherwise the formatting will be messed up; otherwise, it displays the value stored within the Server Variable contained by `key`.

What do Server Variables do?

`ServerVariables` are informative. `SERVER_SOFTWARE`, for example, tells you the name of the Server's software. For IIS 4.0 or PWS 4.0, it returns "Microsoft-IIS/4.0". You can use them to trigger a certain set of actions, so by checking say the `HTTP_USER_AGENT` value, you can determine which browser is viewing your pages. This could allows you to **customize** the page's content to take advantage of specific browser features, or to prevent scripting errors if a browser supports a different scripting engine from the one you usually script for. Consult the whole list in Appendix I for more details.

The ClientCertificate Collection

When the client makes contact with a web server over a secured channel, either end can gain high levels of assurance over the identity of the other by inspecting their **digital certificate**. A certificate contains a number of items of information about the individual or organization, and this is generated by a trusted third party known as a **Certificate Authority** (CA). The certificate allows a server to identify the user, so that the server can send sensitive information to a certified user via secure transmission methods. A client certificate is an encrypted number that is stored in a file on the user's computer. The browser sends the number along with a request for an ASP page.

In order to do that, the **secure sockets layer** (SSL) protocol must be used. SSL is a variation of the HTTP protocol that has much higher levels of security. The latest version of the SSL protocol is SSL3.0/PCT1. The acronym PCT stands for **Private Communication Technology**.

Using SSL/PCT allows server and client authentication, encryption, and the use of data integrity methods. **Authentication** ensures that the data is being sent from an 'approved' client to the correct server. **Encryption** ensures that the data can only be read by the server it is intended for or read by the client it is intended for. **Data Integrity** ensures that the information sent arrives unaltered, exactly as it was sent. When the SSL protocol is used, URLs are prefixed by `https://` (instead of `http://`). You will also need to connect to the server through a different port.

Before you can use the `ClientCertificate` collection, you must configure the web server (In IIS 5, from the Default **Properties** dialog, and select the **Directory Security** tab) so it can request client certificates, otherwise the `ClientCertificate` collection will be empty.

> *MS Certificate Server (CS) will not run on PWS/Win95 or Win98 because Windows95/98 cannot provide a secure environment. CS will run on Win 2000, NT 4.0 Server or Workstation. Coverage of this subject is beyond the scope of this book, but you can find more details in Professional ASP 3.0 – ISBN –1-861002-61-0, from Wrox Press.*

Once the web server is enabled and configured, only SSL-enabled clients will be able to communicate with the SSL-enabled WWW folders.

Two constants need to be declared when working with the `ClientCertificate` collection:

```
Const ceCertPresent = 1
Const ceUnrecognizedIssuer = 2
```

As with all `Request` object collections, you can iterate through the `ClientCertificate` collection's values:

```
<%
  For Each key in Request.ClientCertificate
    Response.Write( key & ": " & Request.ClientCertificate(key) & "<BR>")
  Next
%>
```

To retrieve an individual value, use the following syntax:

```
Request.ClientCertificate(key[SubField])
```

Here, *key* specifies the name of the certification field to retrieve. A client certificate may have these fields:

Key	Meaning
Certificate	A string containing the binary stream of the entire certificate content in ASN.1 format (a list of numbers separated by a period, e.g. (168.77.243.12)

Table Continued on Following Page

265

Key	Meaning
Flags	A set of flags that provide additional client certificate information. CeCertPresent - A client certificate is present.
	CeUnrecognizedIssuer - The last certification in this chain is from an unknown issuer.
Issuer	A string that contains a list of subfield values containing information about the issuer of the certificate. If this value is specified without a SubField, the ClientCertificate collection returns a comma-separated list of subfields. For example, C=US, O=Verisign, etc.
SerialNumber	A string that contains the certification serial number as an ASCII representation of hexadecimal bytes separated by hyphens (-). For example, 04-67-F3-02.
Subject	A string that contains a list of subfield values which contain information about the subject of the certificate. If this value is specified without a SubField, the ClientCertificate collection returns a comma-separated list of subfields. For example, C=US, W=Wrox, and so on.
ValidFrom	A date specifying when the certificate becomes valid. This date follows VBScript format and varies with international settings. For example, in the U.S., it could be: 6/31/98 11:59:59 PM.
ValidUntil	A date specifying when the certificate expires.

SubField is an optional parameter you can use to a retrieve an individual field in either the Subject or Issuer keys, or both. This parameter is added to the Key parameter as a suffix. For example, IssuerC, SubjectCN, SubjectS, SubjectL, etc.

This table lists some SubField values:

Value	Meaning
C	The name of the country of origin.
CN	The common name of the user. (This subfield is only used with the Subject key.)
GN	A given name.
I	A set of initials.
L	A locality.
O	The company or organization name.
OU	The name of the organizational unit.
S	A state or province.
T	The title of the person or organization.

The following script examples display all the fields of a client certificate:

```
Issuing organization: <%= Request.ClientCertificate("IssuerO")%><br>
Subject Name: <%= Request.ClientCertificate("SubjectCN")%><br>
Valid from: <%= Request.ClientCertificate("ValidFrom")%><br>
Valid until: <%= Request.ClientCertificate("ValidUntil")%><br>
Serial Number: <%= Request.ClientCertificate("SerialNumber")%><br>
Issuer: <%= Request.ClientCertificate("Issuer")%><br>
Subject: <%= Request.ClientCertificate("Subject")%><br>
<% TheCompleteCertificate = Request.ClientCertificate("Certificate") %>

Certificate Raw Data: <%= TheCompleteCertificate %><BR>
Certificate Length: <%= len(TheCompleteCertificate)%><BR>
Certificate Hex Data:
<%
For x = 1 to 100
  Response.Write Hex(Asc(Mid(TheCompleteCertificate,x,1))) & " "
Next
%>
```

Further discussion of this collection is beyond the scope of this book. For further information on the ClientCertificate collection, we suggest you consult Professional Active Server Pages 3.0 (ISBN –1-861002-61-0), available from Wrox Press.

Request Object Collection Shorthand

One nifty shortcut when using the Request object collections is to use the whole Request object as a collection. In addition to providing collection for QueryString, Form, Cookies, etc., the Request object can also combine all of these collections together. This allows you to access a piece of information without knowing exactly where it came from. It comes in very handy when processing forms, since you are not dependent on the method (GET or POST) used to submit the form. For example:

```
Request("myListBox")
```

The information could be from a querystring, form, or cookie etc. One thing to be careful with is to understand the order in which ASP organizes the information in the Request collection. This becomes important if you have a querystring variable with the same name as a form field or cookie. ASP will search through the collections in the following order:

- ❑ QueryString
- ❑ Form
- ❑ Cookies
- ❑ ClientCertificate
- ❑ ServerVariables

So, for example if you have a querystring with the same name as a form field, the value in the `Request` collection will be the value from the querystring. Therefore, it is good to develop the habit of never using the same name for a cookie and a Form Field Name. Just prefacing your cookie names with a "c" will do the trick.

Properties and Methods of the Request Object

The `Request` object also has a single property and a single method: we'll look at these briefly now. Their uses are interlinked and while being quite arcane, there might just be times when they're invaluable. If you're uploading a file or image from your browser to a web server, then they might just be what you need.

The TotalBytes Property

The `TotalBytes` property holds the total number of bytes the client sent in the body of the HTTP Request:

```
This Request's size is : <%= Request.TotalBytes%>  Bytes.
```

You might be tempted to say, so what, when am I going to use such a property? Well then, read on.

The BinaryRead Method

The `TotalBytes` property's real use becomes apparent when used with the `BinaryRead` method. The `BinaryRead` method retrieves data sent to the server from the client as part of a `POST` request sent by a form and stores it in a **Safe Array** of bytes. (A Safe Array is an array that contains information about the number of dimensions and the bounds of its dimensions.) This would be useful when the information contained within the form is something other than text.

Unlike the `Form` or `QueryString` collections, this method allows you to take the raw data from the form and parcel it up in a safe array of bytes. The problem is a safe array of bytes isn't exactly the most useful or user-friendly format and if you try to display the information directly using `Response.Write`, you will generate an error. If you wish to use the whole block then you need to know when the whole block of data has been transmitted in its entirety, and this is where the `TotalBytes` property comes in. The `TotalBytes` property is passed to the `BinaryRead` method as a parameter to indicate when to finish reading the data it has received, as follows:

```
<%
  Dim bread, bytecnt
  bytecnt = Request.TotalBytes
  bread = Request.BinaryRead(bytecnt)
```

You can then use a special VBScript function, `MidB` to 'unwrap' the information from the individual bytes of the array.

```
  For i = 1 to bytecnt
    Response.Write MidB( data, i, 1 )
  Next
%>
```

Then the information from the form can be used. The point is that we cannot mix and match binary read with standard form manipulation. So bearing this in mind, let's take a look at a quick example. In this example, we'll pass a first name, last name and password over and use the binary method to unwrap it. This is pretty much what we've already done with the `Querystring` and `Form` collections, and if you were using plain text, then you'd use one of these two collections ahead of this method. However when transferring something other than pure text (zipped file for example?), then the following method will come in useful.

Try It Out – Using the BinaryRead Method and TotalBytes Property

1. Open your HTML editor, create a new file, and type in the following:

```
<HTML>
<HEAD>
<TITLE>Request BinaryRead</TITLE>
</HEAD>

<BODY BGCOLOR="white">

<FORM NAME=BinaryRead ACTION="BinaryResponse.asp" METHOD="POST">
Type your first name:  <INPUT TYPE="TEXT" NAME="firstname">
<BR>
Type your last name:  <INPUT TYPE="TEXT" NAME="lastname">
<BR>
Type your password:  <INPUT TYPE="TEXT" NAME="password">
<BR>
<INPUT TYPE="SUBMIT" VALUE="Login">
</FORM>
</BODY>
</HTML>
```

2. Save it as `BinaryForm.asp` and close it and the type in the following:

```
<HTML>
<BODY>
<%
  intByteCnt = Request.TotalBytes
  intBread = Request.BinaryRead(intByteCnt)
  For intLoop = 1 to intByteCnt
    Response.Write MidB( intBread, intLoop, 1 )
  Next
%>
</BODY>
</HTML>
```

3. Save this as `BinaryResponse.asp` and open up `BinaryForm.asp` in your browser.

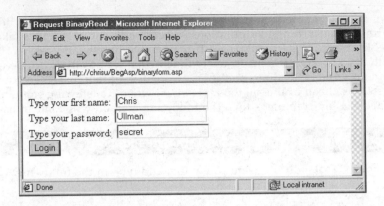

4.   Click on Login to submit the contents:

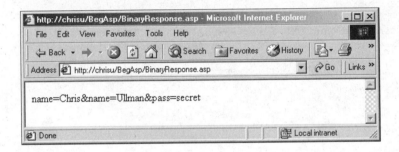

How It Works

Ok, we could have returned the contents of the Request.Form collection in this example and saved us all some code. The point however is to demonstrate that if you wished to use the form to upload some other file format apart from raw text, such as a graphics file, you could use BinaryRead to unload it at the other end.

In BinaryForm.asp we used the POST method to send the Form:

```
<FORM NAME=BinaryRead ACTION="BinaryResponse.asp" METHOD="POST">
```

However, when we got back the information we needed slightly more code to unwrap it. We started determining the total number of bytes in the file and assigned it to the variable intByteCnt:

```
intByteCnt = Request.TotalBytes
```

We then used the BinaryRead method, passing the Total Bytes count as a parameter:

```
intBread = Request.BinaryRead(intByteCnt)
```

Then we were able to loop through our data, one byte at a time, using the MidB function described previously. In this way, we were actually displaying one character at a time on the screen:

```
For intLoop = 1 to intByteCnt
   Response.Write MidB( intBread, intLoop, 1 )
Next
```

An important thing to note is that once you have called BinaryRead, you cannot query the other Request collections directly and vice versa, you cannot call binary read after calling the Request collection – the data is effectively transformed to a binary format.

The Response Object

As we have briefly mentioned earlier in the book, the Response object is used to send the server's output to the client. In this sense, the Response object is the counterpart to the Request object: the Request object gathers information mainly from the client (but also from the server), and the Response object sends, or resends, the information to the client by writing to the outgoing page. Whereas the Request object is rich in information and scarce in properties and methods, the Response object has only one collection but gives us many properties and methods with which to build pages.

With the Response object, the ASP script can:

❑ Send information back to the client

❑ Control *when* to send information back to the client

❑ Tell the browser how long – or until when – to cache the contents of the page

❑ Tell the browser to go fetch another page

❑ Perform other functions with the information that's being sent back to the browser

❑ Instruct browser to create a cookie (which we'll consider in the next chapter)

These features allow you to use ASP scripts to flexibly control how information is presented to the client. We've already dealt with how you can send information back to the client using Response.Write (or its shortcut); otherwise sending information to the server would have been a seemingly pointless process, as you wouldn't have been able to get any information back. What you might not know is that you can specify when you wish to send that information back.

Controlling How Information is Returned

Before we can look at how to control the return of information, we need to look at how information is normally returned. At the beginning of this chapter, we hinted that there was more going behind the scenes when we used the Response.Write method, and indeed there is. We need to discuss exactly what happens now. When this method is called, the Response object will take the information that the user has requested and add it to the **HTML output stream**.

HTML Output Stream

Let's step back a bit and take a look at what the HTML output stream is. It's a dynamically created queue of information that is waiting to be sent back to the browser. If you go back to our initial definition of what ASP is supposed to do, then you know that its primary job is to create an HTML page that can be displayed by a client. Although an ASP script can do much more than static HTML, whatever we want to put on the client's screen has to be displayed through the creation of an HTML page. ASP dynamically builds HTML pages to be displayed on the client's browser.

When an ASP script begins, it also creates an empty HTML output stream ready for the HTMLpage to be created in. So the stream can be thought of as a holding bin, where the web server builds a dynamic HTML page, and then the stream is sent down to the client. This temporary storage space where the stream is held is known as a **buffer**. The first method that ASP scripts use to add information to the output stream is using the Response object to set the HTTP headers. We will cover that later in the chapter. First, let's talk about the HTML output stream in general terms.

At the simplest level, the HTML output stream is always built in the same way: the stream is created with the first bit of data sent, and when new information is added to it, it can only be added to the *end*. It's like a simple queuing mechanism. If you got to the local bank, and join the queue, the people who got in before you are served before you. The HTML output stream is also a queue, one that is waiting to be sent to the client. Therefore, it has to be created in order, with required tags being sent in order to the browser.

This means that when we send the HTTP headers to the buffer, the HTTP header information has to be written to the buffer first. Once the headers have been sent to the buffer, we can start to send the contents of the HTML page to the buffer. The easiest way to do this is with native HTML in the ASP script file. Any HTML that is not created by the code within the <%...%> tags will be added to the HTML output stream. The diagram here illustrates this:

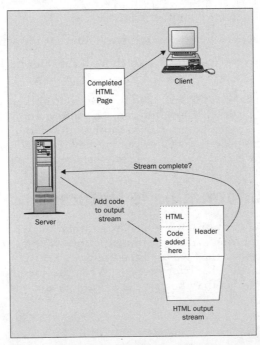

So the buffer is the place where the ASP uses the ASP script to generate a dynamic HTML page. As we just mentioned, the buffer starts out as empty when the script begins. As the script is run, information that is destined for the client is placed in the buffer, along with static HTML. The order in which information is placed in the stream is the same order that it will be sent to the browser. Once all of the ASP scripts have been processed, then the contents of the buffer is sent to the browser in one fell swoop.

This is fine for most pages, but what if your ASP script is going to take a long time to process? For example, maybe you are trying to access information from a remote system. Since the HTML output stream will not be sent to the client until the script has completed, the browser will just appear to be spinning its wheels waiting for the server to respond. In this case, we may want to send some information to the client, to let the user know that the script is processing. Then once the processing has completed, we can send all of the information back to the client.

To do this, we will be manually controlling the way that ASP **buffers** the HTML output stream. There are one property and three methods that will allow us to control when the output stream is sent to the client. These are: `Buffer`, `Flush`, `Clear`, and `End`. We'll look at each in turn.

Buffer

The `Buffer` property of the `Response` object is used to tell ASP that we will be manually controlling when the HTML output stream is sent back to the browser. Buffering is, by default, turned **on**. To turn it off, we would need to set the value of the property to `False`:

```
Response.Buffer = false
```

`Response.Buffer` has to be inserted after the language declaration (if one is used), but before any HTML is written (that is, before any output is generated):

```
<%@ LANGUAGE="scriptinglanguage"
Response.buffer = false %>
<HTML>
...
```

The `Buffer` property cannot be set after the server has sent output to the client. For this reason, the call to `Response.Buffer` should be the first line of your asp script (not the first line of the file though).

Flush

The `Flush` method sends any previously buffered output to the client immediately, but continues processing the script. This can be useful for displaying partial results before your script finishes processing so that your user does not get impatient while waiting for the full result of a long query.

To call this method, simply use:

```
<% Response.Flush %>
```

`Flush` causes a run-time error if the `Response.Buffer` property has not been set to `true`.

Clear

The `Response.Clear` method erases any already-buffered HTML. However, it only erases the response body and does not erase HTTP response headers. It will only erase information that has been added to the HTML output stream since the last call to `Response.Flush`. If you have not called `Response.Flush`, then it will erase all of the information that has been added since the beginning of the page, except the headers.

To call this method, simply use:

```
<% Response.Clear %>
```

`Clear` will cause a run-time error if `Response.Buffer` has not been set to `true`.

End

The `End` method causes the server to stop processing the script and send the buffered output. Any further script instructions are not processed, nor is any remaining HTML sent. Calling `Response.End` flushes the buffer, if `Response.Buffer` has been set to `true`.

To call this method, simply use:

```
<% Response.End %>
```

Try It Out – Controlling the Output Buffer

In this example, we will look at how you can use the buffer control in an ASP script to control when – and if – information is sent back to the browser.

1. Using NotePad or your editor of choice, create the `BufferOutput.asp` file with the following source code.

```
<% Response.Buffer = true %>
<HTML>
<HEAD>
<TITLE>Testing the Response Buffer</TITLE>
</HEAD>

<BODY>
Let's send some text to the HTML output stream.<P>
It is waiting to be sent - Let's send it.<P>
<% Response.Flush %>
Now we want to send this to client<P>
Oops, we just changed our minds - let's clear it<P>
<% Response.Clear %>
<%
  Response.Write "We can control the output of Response.Write method too<P>"
  Response.Flush
%>
I think we are finished - let's end it.<P>
<% Response.End %>
```

```
Wait a minute - I wanted to say this, but it is too late!
</BODY>
</HTML>
```

2. Save the `BufferOutput.asp` file in your `BegASP` directory.

3. View the page in your web browser - you should see something like this:

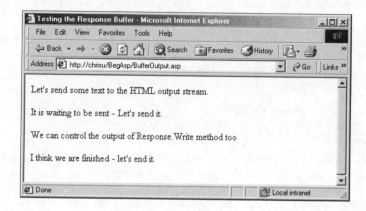

4. View the source of the ASP file so that you can see exactly where the `Response.End` was called, as no further HTML was sent either.

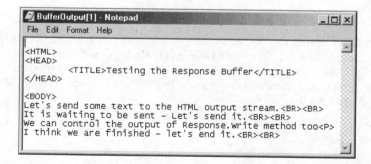

How It Works

The first step in taking control over how the HTML output stream is sent back to the browser is to turn buffering on:

```
<% Response.Buffer = true %>
<HTML>
```

By setting the `Buffer` property of the `Response` object to `true`, we are telling ASP that we will be controlling when information should be sent to the browser. This statement needs to be before any statements that may cause information to be written to the HTML output stream:

```
Let's send some text to the HTML output stream.<P>
It is waiting to be sent - Let's send it.<P>
<% Response.Flush %>
```

Now we want to output some HTML text to the browser. We are doing this by inserting our HTML code at a point in our code that is after the start of the ASP code and before the end of the ASP code. To do this we have to make sure we close and reopen our <% ... %> script delimiters appropriately. Even though we are not using one of the Response object's methods to send information back to the client, this HTML is still being written to the HTML output stream.

Once we have written some text, we want to send it immediately to the browser. This is done by calling Response.Flush. When ASP encounters this statement, it will immediately send whatever information is in the HTML output stream to the client, before clearing that information from the stream.

```
Now we want to send this to client<P>
Oops, we just changed our minds - let's clear it<P>
<% Response.Clear %>
```

Next, we want to output some more text to the browser. But this time, after adding the text to the HTML output stream, we decide that we really didn't want that text after all. There is no way to selectively remove it from the output stream, but we can erase everything that is already in the stream. To do this, we will call the Clear method of the Response object. If you look at what the browser is displaying, or even the source HTML for what the browser is displaying, you won't find these two lines of text there.

```
<%
   Response.Write "We can control the output of Response.Write method too<P>"
   Response.Flush
%>
```

All of the information that is sent to the HTML output stream, whether from a method of the Response object, such as Write, or from native HTML, is under our control when we have enabled buffering. In this step, we are adding information to the output stream by using the Response.Write method. After outputting the line of text, we will send it to the client by again using the Flush method.

```
I think we are finished - let's end it.<P>
<% Response.End %>
Wait a minute - I wanted to say this, but it is too late!
</BODY>
</HTML>
```

We then want to send some final information to the browser. Once we have added it to the output stream, we call the End method of the Response object. This tells ASP that we have sent all of the information that we want to the client. Its job is to send the remaining contents of the HTML output stream to the browser, then stop processing any more script.

If you look at the source HTML for the page that ASP generated, you will see that the last line of code is the line just before the call to Response.End. None of the other information that was in the ASP script, and neither the terminating </BODY> and </HTML> tags, have been sent to the client. So, in this case, calling End really does mean the end.

Using the Response Object to Control what the Browser does

In addition to sending HTML code back to the client, the Response object can be used to control some of the things that the browser itself does.

❏ If you want the browser to cache the page that you are creating until a certain date, or for a certain length of time, you can use the Response object to pass the browser this information.

❏ If the browser requested a certain page, but you really think that it should be displaying another page, you can use the Response object to tell the browser to go get another page. This could be used if you have moved a page in your site, but still want people with links to the original page to be able to get to the information. This technique is now becoming outdated with the introduction of the Transfer and Execute methods for the Server object in ASP 3.0 (which we'll look at shortly), although there are feasible occasions when you might still wish to use it.

The use of these methods is a bit more complex than just sending information back to the browser. They provide us with increased flexibility, and are worth discussing a little further here.

Content Expiration and Caching

As you are surfing the web using your web browser, you are downloading pages and images and other types of content to your computer so that the browser can display them. Since most people tend to visit the same sites regularly, browsers have been developed with a **cache** that exists on the client's computer. A cache is a temporary storage area, like a buffer, but while a buffer is effectively a queuing mechanism onto which information is placed in order, a cache retains no order and is used to retain information for a lot longer. You can see the cache for Internet Explorer on Windows 98/2000 in C:\Windows\Temporary Internet Files (Netscape uses a different area, along the lines of C:\Program Files\Netscape\Users\Default\Cache).

The browser will fill this cache up with the information that is downloaded from various web sites. Later, if the user returns to a site they had already been to, the browser can check to see if the page that the user is requesting is in its cache. If it is, then the page can be displayed immediately, rather than having to wait for it to download from the server. Web site developers can use this cache to their advantage as well. HTML pages are not the only items that are cached. All JPG and GIF images are also cached. Knowing this, web site developers can reuse graphics in their site, so that the only time they have to be downloaded is for the first page that uses them.

When the browser is asked to display a page that it already has in cache, it will check that cached page to see if it has expired. A web page developer can set the expiration date of a page so that they can ensure that the person viewing the page is always seeing the latest content, but not forcing them to download the page every time.

As an ASP developer, we have a bit of a dilemma. Our pages are dynamically created, so they are, in effect, different pages every time. Even if the underlying data that generated the page hasn't changed, a new page is always freshly created to send to the browser. There are many cases where the page will only change on a periodic basis. We would like the clients viewing the page to be able to take advantage of the caching that their browser offers. There are two properties of the `Response` object that we can use to control the expiration of the page that is generated. These properties are `Expires` and `ExpiresAbsolute`

Expires

The `Expires` property specifies the number of minutes before a page cached on a browser expires. If the user returns to the same page before the specified number of minutes have elapsed, the cached version is displayed.

To set this property, you would use:

```
<% Response.Expires = minutes %>
```

In this example, `minutes` represent the number of minutes before this page will expire. Setting `minutes` to 0 causes the page to be refreshed with each access. Setting the page to −1442 might be better if you're expecting users from anywhere in the world to browse the page, since all time zones are covered this way (60 min/hr times 24 hours plus two to cover rounding at both ends.)

ExpiresAbsolute

The `ExpiresAbsolute` property sets the date and/or time at which a page cached on a browser expires. If the user returns to the page before the specified date and/or time, the cached version is displayed. If no time is set, the page expires at midnight of that day. If a time *is* set, the page expires at the specified time on the day that the script is set to expire.

To set this property, you would use:

```
<% Response.ExpiresAbsolute = #DateTime# %>
```

The value of `DateTime` must be a valid date or time combination. The value must be enclosed within the # signs. If you set this value to a date in the past, this is the same as setting the `Expires` property to 0. Again, if you're expecting users from anywhere in the world, it's best to set this value to two days into the past to cover all times zones.

Note that both of these properties set HTTP response headers to achieve their task. Therefore, they both need setting before any text is output to the client.

Redirection

When a client requests a specific ASP page from the server, the script for that page is processed. As that page is being processed, we may determine that there is a different ASP page that the browser should actually be displaying. For example, we could have a page that validates a user's login. Based on the results of that validation, the user could be shown a guest page or a registered user's page.

We could have the code to create both pages within the same script, but that would make for a very complicated script file. It would also make it more difficult for another developer to look at the page at a later time, and understand what we were doing. It would be much easier if we could check the user's login and, based on what the results were, send the user to a completely different page.

The old way of doing this was using the `Redirect` method of the `Response` object. This method would tell the browser that it needed to go and fetch a different page. This page could be on the same site, or it could be on a completely different web site. There are now two newer, more flexible methods of the `Server` object, `Server.Transfer` and `Server.Execute`, which can also do the same task. We'll look at these in the next section. However, the `Redirect` method isn't totally obsolete, and one important difference is that you can't send a querystring in the `Server.Transfer` or `Server.Execute` methods, as you can with the `Redirect` method. This is because the `Redirect` method tells the browser to send another request, something the `Server` object methods can't do.

Another difference is that while `Transfer` and `Execute` hide the fact that you've been moved to another page, the `Redirect` method displays the new page address in its URL. Also, you may be have to debug or update a page that contains this method, so it helps to understand it. Consequently, we will consider all three methods, as there maybe times when you want redirection to be transparent.

To call the `Redirect` method, you would use:

```
<% Response.Redirect = destinationPage %>
```

The value of `DestinationPage` would need to be a string value, and hold a valid URL that the browser would then be told to retrieve. The destination page should be formatted just as a hyperlink would. If the URL is on the same site, then a relative reference can be used. If it is on a different site, then you need to include a full `http://` reference.

There are a few things that you need to be careful with when using the `Redirect` method. A browser is told to fetch a different page through the use of an HTTP header. The problem lies in the fact that we cannot modify the HTTP status and add a header to the response after the body has gone. So, if the ASP script has output the HTTP headers, or has added any information to the HTML output stream, then calling the `Redirect` method will cause an error.

Earlier in this chapter, we learned how to control the contents of the HTML output stream by using the `Buffer` property. Setting this property to TRUE goes hand in hand with using the `Redirect` method. By buffering the HTML output, we can call `Redirect` almost anywhere, as long as we clear out the buffer by calling the `Clear` method before redirecting the browser.

> Remember, if you are going to use the `Redirect` method, be sure to set the `Buffer` property to True at the beginning of the page.

Try It Out – Redirecting the Browser

In this example, we will show how you can create a page that processes some information from the `Request` object and makes a decision on which page (page number 1 or page number 2) the browser should display. Once it has made that decision, it will use the `Redirect` method to tell the browser to load that page.

1. Using your favored editor, create the `PageChoice.html` file with the following source code and save it in your `BegASP` directory:

```
<HTML>
<HEAD>
<TITLE>Redirection Example</TITLE>
</HEAD>
<BODY>

<H2>Choose which page you wish to display</H2>
<FORM ACTION="choosePage.asp" METHOD="POST">
<INPUT TYPE="Radio" NAME="PageChoice" VALUE="Page1" CHECKED>Page Number 1<BR>
<INPUT TYPE="Radio" NAME="PageChoice" VALUE="Page2">Page Number 2<P>
<INPUT TYPE="Submit" VALUE="Choose Page">   <INPUT TYPE="RESET">
</FORM>

</BODY>
</HTML>
```

2. Create another file and save it as `choosePage.asp` in the `BegASP` directory. This file should contain the following code:

```
<%
  Option Explicit
  Dim strChoice

  strChoice = Request.Form("PageChoice")

  If strChoice = "Page1" Then
    Response.Redirect "page1.html"
  Else
    Response.Redirect "page2.html"
  End If
%>
```

Remember that for this to work, Buffer needs to be set to True. We're not setting it true explicitly here, because it is already set to true by default.

3. Next, create and save a file called `Page1.html` with the following source code:

```
<HTML>
<HEAD>
```

```
<TITLE>Page 1</TITLE>
</HEAD>
<BODY>

<H1>This is Page Number 1</H1>

</BODY>
</HTML>
```

4. Create the `Page2.html` file with the following source code.

```
<HTML>
<HEAD>
<TITLE>Page 2</TITLE>
</HEAD>
<BODY>

<H1>This is Page Number 2</H1>

</BODY>
</HTML>
```

5. Make sure all these files are stored in you `BegASPFiles` directory

6. View the `PageChoice.html` file via your web browser:

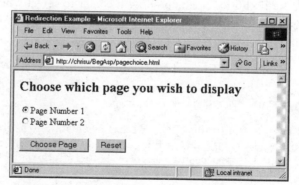

7. Select **Page Number 1** and press the **Choose Page** button. This should produce:

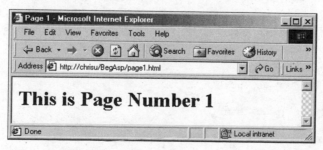

8. Go back to the `PageChoice.html` page and choose the other option.

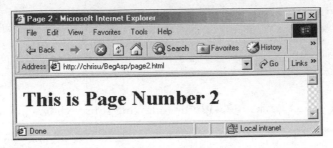

How It Works

The first page that we are creating is a straightforward static HTML page. The job of this page is to present a standard HTML form that will allow the user to select which page they wish to display.

```
<FORM ACTION="ChoosePage.asp" METHOD="POST">
<INPUT TYPE="Radio" NAME="PageChoice" VALUE="Page1" CHECKED>Page Number 1<BR>
<INPUT TYPE="Radio" NAME="PageChoice" VALUE="Page2">Page Number 2<P>
<INPUT TYPE="Submit" VALUE="Choose Page">  <INPUT TYPE="RESET">
</FORM>
```

The form displays two Radio buttons, which allow the user to select which page to display. The results of the form are going to be sent to the `choosePage.asp` file for processing.

```
<%
  Option Explicit
  Dim strChoice

  strChoice = Request.Form("PageChoice")
```

The first thing we want to do is add the `Option Explicit` statement to help ensure that we build up the good habit of always declaring the variables that we will be using in advance. The next thing we want to do, when processing the form, is to grab the selection that the user made in the previous page.

Once we have declared the variable to hold the user's selection, we will retrieve it from the `Form` collection of the `Request` object. In our HTML form, we had two radio buttons with the same name, `PageChoice`, but with different values. Depending on which button the user selected before submitting the form, the value for that button will be added to the `Form` collection.

```
  If strChoice = "Page1" Then
    Response.Redirect "page1.html"
  Else
    Response.Redirect "page2.html"
  End If
%>
```

We can then compare the value that was passed from the form with the *possible* values. Based on that comparison, we can choose to send the browser to either page1.html or to page2.html. You will notice that there are no Response.Write statements, or any HTML text outside of the <% ... %> block. This ASP file is designed to produce no output to send to the browser: it is simply designed to evaluate some data that is passed to it, and based on that evaluation, to send the browser that is making the request to another page. In this case, both of the possible destination pages are static HTML files. They could have just as easily been ASP scripts, or even pages on a completely different web server. If that were the case, then we would need to use the complete URL as the parameter to the Redirect method. For example:

```
Response.Redirect "http://www.wrox.co.uk"
```

The critical thing to remember from this example is that when you are using the Redirect method, make sure that you are not sending any information to the HTML output stream. If you are, then make sure that you turn buffering on, and clear the output stream before calling redirect.

Amending our Program

Of course, radio buttons aren't the only way to send information; you could as easily use a drop down list box for example to display the same selection of options. (These are covered in Appendix F.) In this case, all you would need to is open up PageChoice.html and make the following adjustments.

```
<H2>Choose which page you wish to display</H2>
<FORM ACTION="choosePage.asp" METHOD="POST">
<SELECT NAME="PageChoice">
<OPTION VALUE="Page1">Page 1
<OPTION VALUE="Page2">Page 2
</SELECT>
<BR>
<BR>
<INPUT TYPE="Submit" VALUE="Choose Page">   <INPUT TYPE="RESET">
</FORM>
```

None of the other programs need altering, as choosepage.asp simply works on a value passed from an 'entity' called PageChoice, whether it's a radio button or a drop down list box. The same principles apply for different types of list box or check box.

Using the Server Object to Control what the browser does

As we've already intimated, Response.Redirect is now pretty much outdated with the introduction of two new methods of the Server object. We described the Server object in chapter 6 as being pretty much a miscellaneous grab-bag of methods and properties that loosely relate to the web server and that don't really fit in elsewhere. Whereas before you had to rely on the Response object to redirect you, providing you hadn't sent any text to the client, the redirection is now all done at a meta-Server level.

As with all redirection in any .asp file, if the executed .asp file attempts to modify HTTP headers after it sends a response to the client, it will generate an error. So, let's take a look at the two methods together. We're going to study them side by side because, apart from one small difference, they're effectively the same.

Server.Execute and Server.Transfer

The `Execute` method transfers execution across to a second page, executes that in its entirety and then returns control to the original page. It works as follows:

```
Server.Execute(Destination page)
```

The `Transfer` method transfers execution across to a second page, and executes that in its entirety, but does not return to the original page.

```
Server.Transfer(Destination page)
```

In both cases, the value of `DestinationPage` could be a string value, or hold a valid URL that the browser would then be told to retrieve. The destination page should be formatted just like a hyperlink would. If the URL is on the same site, then a relative reference can be used. If it is on a different site, then you need to include a full `http://` reference.

One thing to note about both of these methods is that for all intents and purposes you are working on the same page as before. So in other words, the URL in the browser won't change, any objects you created in the previous page will still work, in fact the scope of the session (something we'll look at in the next chapter) will also be maintained.

Let's now take a look at an example which demonstrates the use of both methods. We'll use the methods to include the contents of the pages we created earlier, page one and page two.

Try It Out – Using Server.Transfer and Server.Execute

1. Open your HTML editor, and create a new file with the following source code, and save it in your `BegASP` directory:

```
<HTML>
<HEAD>
<TITLE>Transfer and Execute Example</TITLE>
</HEAD>
<BODY>

<%
  Response.Write "We're here on the original page<HR>"
  Server.Execute "page1.html"
  Response.Write "<HR>We're back again on the original page<HR>"
  Server.Transfer "page2.html"
  Response.Write "<HR>We're back again on the original page"
%>
</BODY>
</HTML>
```

2. Save this as `ExecuteTransfer.asp` and display it on your browser:

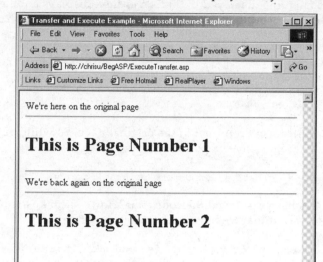

Note that you will have to have worked through the previous example where you created two pages, `page1.html` and `page2.html` for this to work.

How It Works

The code is brutally straightforward. We start with `Response.Write` and finish with a horizontal line to indicate we're about to execute the first redirection:

```
Response.Write "We're here on the original page<HR>"
```

We do the first redirection, using `Execute`, which lets the Server know that we want to come back to this point once the next page has finished:

```
Server.Execute "page1.html"
```

What we are actually doing is executing the contents of this page (even though this page is only HTML, it would execute any ASP script contained within):

```
<HTML>
<HEAD>
<TITLE>Page 1</TITLE>
</HEAD>
<BODY>

<H1>This is Page Number 1</H1>

</BODY>
</HTML>
```

Once we have displayed this page, control is returned back to `ExecuteTransfer.asp`, at the point we left. So the next line displayed in this screenshot, displays another horizontal line, and a message indicating we are back on the original page.

```
Response.Write "<HR>We're back again on the original page<HR>"
```

Next, we redirect to our second page.

```
Server.Transfer "page2.html"
```

This time however, control isn't returned to the original page. So while `page2.html` is executed in this example, the final line is never executed:

```
Response.Write "<HR>We're back again on the original page"
```

Once `page2.html` has been displayed the code ends. However, take a look at the browser's URL line – there's not a hint that we have even left our original page.

So, hopefully you can see that `Server.Transfer` and `Server.Execute` offer you a greater degree of flexibility when redirecting to other pages, and that when you use them, you adhere to the same rules that govern sending text to the client on the output stream with the `Response.Redirect` method.

Other Information the Response Object Can Send

The `Response` object gives you very fine control over the information that is returned to the client. In most cases, you will only need the broad-brush strokes that methods like `Write` and `Redirect` provide you. However, for limitless flexibility, there are other functions that the `Response` object provides you with.

Some of these functions include:

❑   Changing the content type of the response so that not only HTML can be sent back to the client.

❑   Detecting if the client making the request is still connected to the server. This allows you to abandon any processing if the browser has moved on to another page.

❑   Adding additional information to the log file entry that is made in the web server's log file.

These functions are defined in Appendix A. They are really beyond the scope of this book, but you can find more information about them in *Professional Active Server Pages 3.0, ISBN 1-861002-61-0*, from Wrox Press.

Summary

The Request object is a conduit for information between the client and the server: it encapsulates the information that the user sends, and packages it for storage and use on the server. The Response object has a critical role in handling ASP's transmission of data from the server back to the client. In this chapter, we started with an overview of the interaction, and considered the Write method of the Response object. Then we looked at the attributes of the Request object in some detail. It contains five **collections** that store information about the user's request. Briefly, they were:

- ❑ QueryString – this contains the values that are provided in the URL that is sent by the client.

- ❑ Form – this contains the values sent by the client in a form request.

- ❑ ServerVariables – this contains information about the request and about the server, stored in the form of server variables.

- ❑ Cookies – this stores details of any cookies sent with the request, we look at this in the next chapter

- ❑ ClientCertificate – this stores details of any security certificates included with the request

We also looked at the TotalBytes property and the BinaryRead method of the Request object. We then turned our attention to the Response object and considered:

- ❑ How to use the buffering methods to control when that information is sent back to the client

- ❑ How the Expires and ExpiresAbsolute properties can tell the browser how long or until when to cache the contents of the page

- ❑ How the Redirect method can be used to tell the browser to go fetch another page

- ❑ How we can use Server.Transfer and Server.Execute as alternatives to Response.Redirect

- ❑ And some of the other functions that can affect the information being sent back to the browser

In the next chapter we'll move on to look at two objects that help the server organize Active Server Pages and track the interaction between the server and the clients: the Application and Session objects.

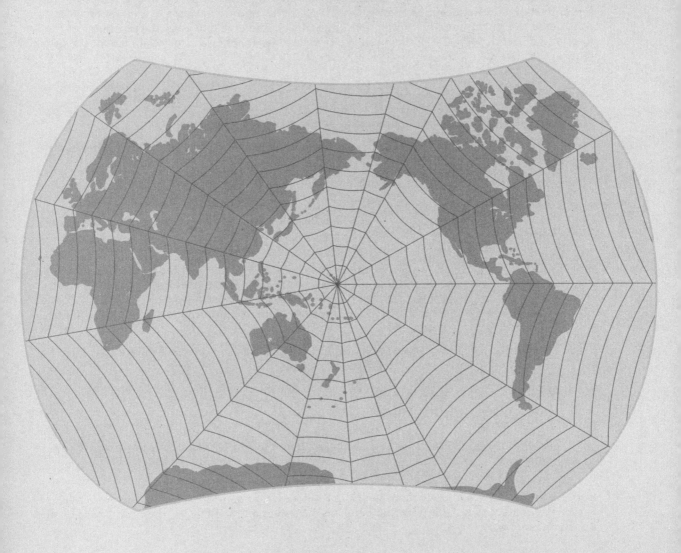

Applications, Sessions and Cookies

In our travels through the world of Active Server Pages, we have been dealing with how information can be sent from the client to the server, and how the server can dynamically create a page that is returned to the client. In all of these interactions, the request and the response existed by themselves. There has been no mechanism introduced that allows you to tie two pages, or a set of pages, together.

Until recently, existing web technologies meant that if you wanted to pass information from one page to another, you were restricting yourself to using cookies in JavaScript, hidden form fields or querystring parameters. Active Server Pages has extra tools to help pass information between pages: the Application and Session objects. It also provides collections and methods that make cookies far easier to use.

In this chapter, we will look at these objects and the power and flexibility they add to ASP. We'll also look at how cookies have survived the onslaught of time and are still as valid as they ever were. You will hopefully be able to see the concept of web applications in practice, and how these objects transform our sites into true applications rather than just a bundle of loosely linked web pages. Specifically, we will be examining:

❑ Why you can't use HTTP to track an individual user on your web site from start to finish

❑ How to use cookies to store information at the client's computer and what cookies should be used for.

❑ The Application object, which allows us to tie together all of the pages of a single web site into a consistent web application.

❑ The Session object, which allows us to treat a user's interaction with the web site within a specified period of time, as a set of saved variables, rather than just a disconnected series of page requests.

Let's start by taking a look at what you might expect from a web application.

Web Applications

As the web is evolving from simply serving up pages, to providing access to dynamic information from a wide range of systems, the sites that a user may access begin to look more like a traditional application, such as one written in Visual Basic or Powerbuilder. In ASP, each virtual directory on the server, which we first saw in Chapter 1, may also be an application as well (depending on whether you've specifically created it as an application). All of the pages in that directory, whether static or dynamically generated, are part of that application.

Now with most applications, for example an e-commerce shop front for automobile spare parts, you'd ideally have a profile of each user. In fact it almost goes without saying you'd want to be able to track each individual user as you'd want to put together a bill of the items they've purchased to date, what their address and credit card details are and so on. In fact there's a range of questions that you'd probably want to know such as:

❑ How many people are coming to our site?

❑ Who are they?

❑ Where are they coming from?

❑ How long are they staying on our site?

❑ Where do they go as they move through the site?

It might come as a bit of a surprise that the HTTP protocol on its own makes no provisions for doing any of this, as it cannot distinguish between users.

Tracking Users

If you are using a traditional desktop application, like Microsoft Word for example, you start up the application and open a file to edit. You can continue to make changes to the file until you save and close it. Each change you make is recorded into the file, whether you are adding new text or deleting existing text. The time period during which you are editing this file can be thought of as a session.

There is a connection between you – the user – and the file. All of your edits go to that file (that is, unless you switch to a different file). You do not have to tell Microsoft Word each time that you make a change which file you are editing, because the application maintains information about your current editing session.

Things are different on the web. In contrast to the way that traditional applications work, on the web the relationship between the client and the server is said to be **stateless**. In a stateless environment, the server does not track a client from request to request. HTTP is a client driven protocol, the client tells the server what it wants, and has to get an answer in the same connection. It's like writing a letter, then sending it; if you forget to put something in that letter, then that's too bad – you'll have to mail another letter with that separate request in.

The web server that runs the HTTP service basically sits there and waits for a request to come in. Typically a client will connect and make a request – the web server will then process the request and send back an answer to the client. The web server cannot determine whether this client has made any previous connections before, or has a past history. So, if you want to keep track of a user, then HTTP on its own is not suitable for the task, since it's not capable of storing this kind of information. Each request that comes in from a client is treated as if the server knows nothing about the client. There is no memory of *previous connections* between the client and server.

For serving up standard web pages, this is an ideal situation. Using HTTP, a web server can handle a large number of simultaneous requests for pages. It can also handle them quickly, the advantage of HTTP being that because the server never has to maintain a history for each request, the server can just concern itself with providing pages as fast as possible. It also does not have to worry about what a client did previously before it sends a page. Unfortunately, this can make writing applications very difficult.

Let's consider an example where a user logs on to an e-commerce site that sells books. The user starts on the home page of the site, and then gets asked to log in. Once they've logged on, they're directed to a customized home page that will hopefully show a range of books of particular interest to that user, such as new books by their favorite authors etc. They'll want to be able to browse a catalog of items, and from that catalog be able to select items to buy, and place in the shopping basket. This would make a total of at least five separate pages that the user would be navigating through. It would be ideal to maintain some kind of state for the entire time the user is logged in. The diagram below illustrates this:

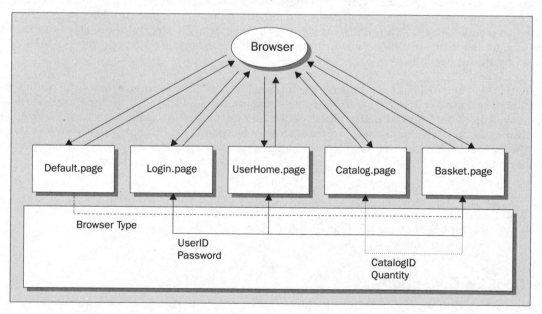

Firstly, you'd want only the user to be able see information about their own choices and own shopping basket. So you'd need to track a user id and password over several of the pages. Also when the user selects an item from the catalog, you'd need to be able to add it to the shopping basket, along with the quantity of the item selected. Then from the shopping basket you'd want to be able to return and continue browsing the catalog, possibly making further selections and adding to your shopping baskets, as you jumped between the two pages. Finally, it would be nice if the whole site was customized to your particular browser wouldn't it?

So, for both the user and for the people who wrote the application, the one request per connection can be more than a little frustrating. The good news is that ASP introduces several aids to the developer for tracking users. However the first one outdates ASP itself, and is known as a **cookie**. Cookies are used to solve the problem of web sites using an anonymous protocol system.

Using Cookies

A web site might have had a thousand visitors, but for all the web site coordinator could know, every visit might have been made by the same visitor! Cookies were introduced as a method of identifying and marking each different visitor to a web site.

Cookies are text files written by the client browser, containing information sent by a server, which reside on the user's computer. They store information about the user, and are used by a particular server (or server within the same sub-domain) *that the user has visited previously* to personalize web pages, and determine where a user has been before within the same domain. They can then be used to keep users up to date with relevant information. Each web server, when a user accesses it, can *send* a cookie, which the user must *accept* if the server is to read the cookie on the user's machine during future visits. If the user doesn't accept the cookie, it can't be read by the server in future.

There are all sorts of cookie myths on the Internet. Mostly they revolve around the notion that a smart programmer can get unauthorized information from a user, violating the user's " right to privacy". Let's set the record straight. A cookie can **only** store information, which the user sends **voluntarily** or selects on a page and that can only happen if the "accept cookies" option in the browser is turned on by the user. No one can get your e-mail address or your home address if you don't voluntarily send the information by filling and submitting a form.

> *Individual cookies on Netscape are limited to 4kb of data. On IE5 the theoretical size is unlimited. The maximum number of cookies is also browser specific and once this limit is reached, the oldest cookie will be deleted to make room for the newest one. So make sure you use cookies judiciously.*

The Cookies Collection

We mentioned in the last chapter that the `Request` object had a `Cookies` collection – it's now time to talk about this collection. The `Cookies` collection holds information from all the cookies set by any one application. That is, when a client establishes a session with the server the *values* that the server reads from the client's cache of cookies are held in the `Cookies` collection. This means that they are available for easy access by the server.

Unlike the `Form` and `Querystring` collections, the `Cookies` collection does not have a `Count` property but, like the `Form` collection, it can hold multiple values for the same cookie name. When this happens, the cookie is said to have **keys**, and each key holds a separate value.

Domains and servers can **only** read cookies that they themselves have set. If server X writes a cookie, then server Y **cannot** read it. If domain `http://Myapp` sets a cookie, then domain `http://MyApp2` cannot read the cookies set by `MyApp`, and vice versa, unless the second domain is a sub domain of the first. When demanded by the server, the cookie that comes with the request is read-only. You can set the value for a cookie using the `Response` object, which you will learn about later in this chapter.

The general syntax for retrieving cookies is:

```
Request.Cookies("cookie")[("key")].attribute
```

So display the contents of a cookie in your web page you could use:

```
Response.Write Request.Cookies("cookie")
```

Creating Cookies with the Response Object

As well as reading information supplied by a client's cookies, the server needs to be able to *write* information to cookies on the client's machine. ASP uses the `Response` object's features to set cookies' values.

Until ASP was released, the most common way to set cookies was using CGI or in client-side JavaScript. The syntax for doing this with JavaScript is fairly complex – even daunting – if you're not over-familiar with JavaScript. ASP (with VBScript) provides a one-line instruction method to set and retrieve cookies.

The syntax for writing cookies in ASP is:

```
<% Response.Cookies("cookie") = value %>
```

If *value* is a string, it must be enclosed in quotes.

If you use this method to set a cookie, the following HTTP header is generated:

```
Set-Cookie:YOURCOOKIENAME=somevalue
```

You can see that the `Response.Cookies` method is simply a way of sending the Set-Cookie HTTP header without resorting to complicated code. Therefore you should use `Response.Cookies` before you write any data in the response body.

Using Keys

If you add a *key* value, then you can access this cookie like a collection. This means that one cookie can have multiple values stored with it.

```
<% Response.Cookies("cookie")("key") = value %>
```

If a cookie is used to store more than one value we have to specify which of these multiple values we want to set. To do this, we refer to it via its *key* value. The key value is similar to a variable name. The general syntax for writing cookies with keys is:

```
Response.Cookies("thesameCookieName")("somekey") = "SomeValue"
Response.Cookies("thesameCookieName")("anotherkey") = "AnotherValue"
```

> *If you issue another cookie with the same name but without specifying the key, you will overwrite **all** cookie values for that cookie's name.*

The HasKeys Property

ASP uses the HasKeys property to determine whether or not a cookie holds multiple values. To check if a cookie holds multiple values, we interrogate the HasKeys property:

```
Request.Cookies("theCookie").HasKeys
```

If the cookie theCookie has keys, this statement returns True, otherwise it returns False. To iterate through the individual values for cookies with keys, use this model script:

```
For Each Cookie in Request.Cookies
  If Request.Cookies(Cookie).HasKeys Then
    For Each CookieKey in Request.Cookies(Cookie)
      Response.Write(Cookie) & " ."
      Response.Write(CookieKey) & " ="
      Response.Write(Request.Cookies(Cookie)(CookieKey))
    Next
  Else
    Response.Write(Cookie) & " ="
    Response.Write(Request.Cookies(Cookie)) & " <BR>"
  End If
Next
```

Making your Cookie Persist

A cookie set with the basic syntax will persist for as long as the browser is open, or until the session expires. As soon as the browser is closed, the cookie's value will disappear.

To make a cookie persist, i.e., for the cookie to be written to the client browser's hard disk (the "cookie jar"), you have to set an expiration date for the cookie. The general syntax for doing this is:

```
Response.Cookies("Cook").Expires = "July 4, 2001"
```

A Better Way to Set a Cookie's Expiration Date

Though setting the cookie's expiration date as " July 4, 2001" works, a better way to set the expiration date is to use *relative* date values. This is also better when the client and server are in different time zones. Since Date is a built-in VBScript function, you could set the expiration date as Date + X, where X stands for the number of days you want the cookie to "live":

```
Response.Cookies("Cook").Expires = Date + 1
```

This will set the expiration date to 1 day from today.

Deleting a Cookie

To delete a cookie, set its `Expires` property to any date prior to today. The easiest way to do this is to use relative date values, as shown in this example:

```
Response.Cookies("Cook").Expires = Date - 1
```

Again, this technique could fail due to different time settings on server and client, so maybe something like `Date - 1000` would be more secure.

Try It Out – Using Cookies in ASP

There are many sites on the web that will ask you to register in order to get some level of enhanced access. Once you have registered, you are given a user name and password. The next time you visit the site, you are asked to enter these before being granted access. Some sites will give you the option of saving your username and password as a cookie, so that you will automatically be logged in next time you visit. In this example, we will look at how to do this.

Open your favorite HTML editor, and create the following file:

```
<HTML>
<HEAD>
<TITLE>Cookie Test - Login</TITLE>
</HEAD>
<BODY>

Please enter your e-mail address and password to login to the system.
<FORM ACTION = "CheckLogin.asp"  METHOD="POST" >
E-Mail Address: <INPUT TYPE = "Text"  NAME = "Email"  SIZE = "40"><BR>
Password: <INPUT TYPE = "Password"  NAME = "Password"  SIZE = "10"><P>
<INPUT TYPE = "Checkbox"  NAME = "SaveLogin"> Save Login as a Cookie?<P>
<INPUT TYPE = "Submit"  VALUE = "Login">    
<INPUT TYPE = "RESET">
</FORM>

</BODY>
</HTML>
```

The Password type of input box hides values that are typed in by displaying asterisks instead of the actual character that was typed. You will probably be familiar with this from when you login to Windows when you start up your machine. You can find more details about password boxes in Appendix F.

Save the file as `login.asp` in a virtual directory of your web server.

Create another new file, and enter the following:

```
<%
  Dim bLoginSaved
  If Request.Form("SaveLogin") = "on"  Then
```

```
      Response.Cookies("SavedLogin")("EMail") = Request.Form("email")
      Response.Cookies("SavedLogin")("pw") = Request.Form("password")
      Response.Cookies("SavedLogin").Expires = Date + 30
      bLoginSaved = True
    Else
      bLoginSaved = False
    End If
%>
<HTML>
<HEAD>
<TITLE>Cookie Test - Check Login</TITLE>
</HEAD>
<BODY>
<%
  If bLoginSaved Then
    Response.Write "Saving Login information to a cookie<HR>"
  End If
%>
Thank you for logging into the system.<P>
E-Mail address confirmation: <%= Request.Form("email")%>
</BODY>
</HTML>
```

Save the file as checkLogin.asp in the same directory.

Load the login.asp page into your browser.

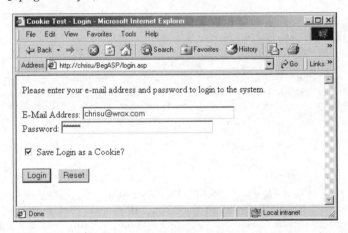

Enter an e-mail address and password. You should also check the Save Login as a Cookie button to save your login. The press the Login button. Note: we will not be validating the e-mail and password against anything, so feel free to enter whatever you want.

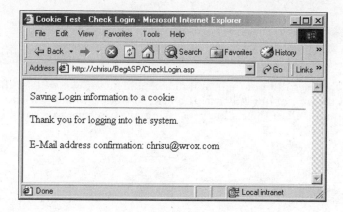

How It Works

In this example, we are using two ASP files. The first one will display the login screen for the user. They are asked to enter their e-mail address and password. They can also click on a checkbox that will have their login information saved as a cookie.

If you look at the code for `login.asp`, you will see no Active Server Pages code. So you may be wondering why this file is an `.asp` and not an `.htm`. In the next example, we will be adding some server-side script to this file, so we thought ahead and gave it the `.asp` name. Once the form is submitted, the `checkLogin.asp` page will handle the results.

```
<%
  Dim bLoginSaved
  If Request.Form("SaveLogin") = "on" Then
```

When the form information is passed to the `checkLogin.asp` page, the first thing that we want to do is see if the user has requested that their login information be saved in a cookie. We are declaring a variable called `bLoginSaved`. This boolean variable will be set to true if the user wants a cookie set. It will be false if they do not. This will allow us to display a notification later in the page.

```
  Response.Cookies("SavedLogin")("EMail") = Request.Form("email")
  Response.Cookies("SavedLogin")("pw") = Request.Form("password")
  Response.Cookies("SavedLogin").Expires = Date + 30
  bLoginSaved = True
```

The name of the cookie we are creating is `SavedLogin`. It will contain two keys of information. These keys will hold the e-mail address and password of the user. The values for these keys will come from the `Form` collection of the `Request` object. The information that the user entered in the fields on the `login.asp` page will be stored in this collection.

We will be setting this cookie to expire 30 days from today. As you saw earlier, you can use the VBScript `Date` function to determine the current date, and then add the desired lifetime of the cookie in days to that value. The last step is to set the flag that we declared earlier to true. This is to indicate that a cookie has been set for the user. If the user hasn't set this checkbox, then they didn't want the cookie saving so we set the Boolean variable to false to ensure we don't save the information as a cookie.

```
    Else
      bLoginSaved = False
    End If
%>
```

In the case where the user did not request that a cookie be set, we will set the flag to false. We have now reached the end of our ASP script block, so we terminate it with the %> statement. Now that we have done all of the cookie processing, we can turn to what the user sees.

```
<BODY>
<%
  If bLoginSaved Then
    Response.Write "Saving Login information to a cookie<HR>"
  End If
%>
Thank you for logging into the system.<P>
```

First, we want to inform the user that a cookie was saved to their machine. Since we set a boolean flag earlier in the page, we can check its value. If it is set to true, then we will display a message for the user. If not, then we will just go on displaying the rest of the page.

```
E-Mail address confirmation: <%= Request.Form("email")%>
</BODY>
</HTML>
```

Finally, we want to display the user's e-mail address that was just entered. This is done primarily as a validation that the correct information was entered. To display the e-mail address, we will retrieve it from the Form collection of the Request object.

Now that we have seen how to set the cookies, let's take a look at another example that will show how we can use the cookies in our login page.

Try It Out – Using Cookies in ASP Part 2

In this example, we will modify the two ASP scripts from the previous example so that the login page will check for the existence of a cookie. The login check page will inform the user if their login was entered via a cookie, or by direct input.

1. Using your favorite HTML editor, open the login.asp file and make the following changes.

```
<%
  If Request.Cookies("SavedLogin").HasKeys then
    Response.Redirect ("CheckLogin.asp?cookie=1")
  End If
%>
<HTML>
<HEAD>
<TITLE>Cookie Test - Login</TITLE>
</HEAD>
<BODY>
```

Please enter your e-mail address and password to login to the system.

```
<FORM ACTION = "CheckLogin.asp"  METHOD="POST">
E-Mail Address: <INPUT TYPE = "Text"  NAME = "Email"  SIZE = "40"><BR>
Password: <INPUT TYPE = "Password"  NAME = "Password"  SIZE = "40"><P>
<INPUT TYPE = "Checkbox"  NAME = "SaveLogin"> Save Login as a Cookie?<P>
<INPUT TYPE = "Submit"  VALUE = "Login">  
<INPUT TYPE = "RESET">
</FORM>

</BODY>
</HTML>
```

2.   Close and save the file.

3.   Open the `checkLogin.asp` file and make the following changes.

```
<%
  Dim strEmail
  If Request.QueryString("cookie") = 1 Then
    strEMail = Request.Cookies("SavedLogin")("Email")
  Else
    strEMail = Request.Form("email")
  End If

  Dim bLoginSaved
  If Request.Form("SaveLogin") = "on"  Then
    Response.Cookies("SavedLogin")("EMail") = Request.Form("email")
    Response.Cookies("SavedLogin")("pw") = Request.Form("password")
    Response.Cookies("SavedLogin").Expires = Date + 30
    bLoginSaved = True
  Else
    bLoginSaved = False
  End If
%>
<HTML>
<HEAD>
<TITLE>Cookie Test - Check Login</TITLE>
</HEAD>
<BODY>
<%
  If bLoginSaved Then
    Response.Write "Saving Login information to a cookie<HR>"
  End If
%>
Thank you for logging into the system.<P>
<%
  If Request.QueryString("cookie") = 1 Then
    Response.Write "Login submitted via cookie<P>"
  End If
%>
E-Mail address confirmation: <%= strEMail%>
</BODY>
</HTML>
```

4. Now when you view the login.asp page in your browser, it automatically detects once you've logged in previously and takes you to CheckLogin.asp and displays an appropriate message:

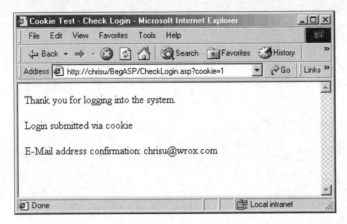

How It Works

In this example, we have made changes to both the login.asp file and the checkLogin.asp file. The changes to login.asp will be used to detect if a cookie has been set to save the login information.

```
<%
  If Request.Cookies("SavedLogin").HasKeys Then
    Response.Redirect "CheckLogin.asp?cookie=1"
  End If
%>
```

This section of ASP code that has been added to the top of the login.asp page will check to see if a cookie has been set. If you recall from the previous example, the cookie that is set actually contains two keys: one for the e-mail and one for the password. We can determine if the correct cookie has been set by checking to see if the cookie named SavedLogin has keys. This is why we named the file login.asp earlier.

If the correct cookie has been set, then we will use the Redirect method of the Response object to send the browser to the CheckLogin.asp page. We use the Redirect method rather than the Server.Transfer method, as we want to transmit a query string as well, and as we mentioned in the previous chapter, Server.Transfer is unable to do this. To notify this page that the request is due to the result of a cookie being read, we will set a query string parameter. We will then be able to check for this value when we are processing the checkLogin.asp page.

```
<%
  Dim strEmail
  If Request.QueryString("cookie") = 1 Then
    strEMail = Request.Cookies("SavedLogin")("Email")
  Else
    strEMail = Request.Form("email")
  End If
```

In the `CheckLogin.asp` page, we will first add some code that will determine if the page was requested by the redirection from the `login.asp` page. We set a query string parameter called `cookie` when we redirected the browser to this page. By checking to see if its value is set to 1, we will know if this page was called due to a cookie login.

There are two possible places that the user's email address can come from. If they have selected to save their logon information in a cookie, then their email address can be retrieved from that cookie. If they have entered their email address directly, then we can recover it from the `Form` collection of the `Request` object. In either case, we want to save its value into a local variable. This will allow us to use it later in the page, without having to check which method it was supplied by again.

```
<%
  If Request.QueryString("cookie") = 1 Then
    Response.Write "Login submitted via cookie<P>"
  End If
%>
E-Mail address confirmation: <%= strEMail%>
```

We want to display an indication to the user that their login information was supplied via a cookie. The query string parameter `cookie` being set to 1 indicates this. If this is the case, then we will display a message. We also need to change the `Response.Write` shortcut that displays the email address that the user logged on with. Earlier in the page, we stored the value in the `strEmail` local variable. We will now display the contents of that variable here.

All that would be left to do is add the proper user authentication code, and you can have a workable user login system for your web site. Later in the book, we will take a look at how to insert and retrieve information from databases. You can then tie this method of user login with the databases and have yourself a very robust authentication system.

However, tracking users with ASP doesn't just end with cookies, it also incorporates two objects that provide a more advanced method of dealing with the tracking of a visitor through the site, the `Application` and `Session` objects.

The Application Object

To understand what the `Application` object is, and what it can do, keep in mind that an application is defined as all the files contained in a virtual directory that has been explicitly configured to be the root of the application, and all of its subdirectories. So, with this object, you can:

❑ Be notified when an application is first *started*, so that you can perform some startup processing.

❑ Be notified when an application is *ending*, so that you have the opportunity to perform function so that the application closes down cleanly.

❑ *Store information* that can be accessed by all clients accessing the application.

There is one instance of the `Application` object for each application running on the web server, but there may be many clients accessing the same application. They can each get a reference to the same `Application` object.

An IIS Server can host any number of applications, and each application has its own `Application` object. This object stores variables and objects for **application-scope** usage. Application-scope means that variables (and objects) can be accessed from any ASP page that is part of the application. The `Application` object also holds information about the sessions active within a particular Application.

The diagram that follows shows the relationship between applications, `Application` objects and `Session` objects, although the containment of the `Session` in `Application` is only at logical level and not specified in any way by the object model.

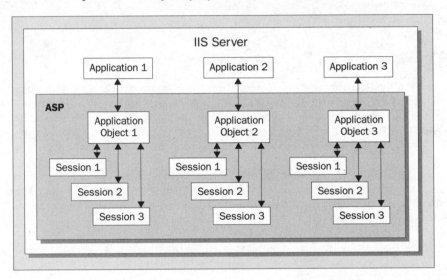

In the diagram, the **applications** at the top refer to the collections of web pages and objects defined on the server as virtual directories. The **Application objects** are the ASP objects that control access to the Application. The **Sessions** represent individual client sessions with the application – we'll discuss sessions in detail later. For the moment, remember that the first time a client asks for an `.asp` page belonging to a given application, from your server, a session is established for that client. Any number of sessions can be hosted by any one application, limited only by the memory resources of your server. .

Application Variables

One of the features of an application is that you can store information that is available to all clients that are accessing the application. This information is stored in what is known as an **application-scope** variable.

To initialize variables in the `Application` object, you store the information about them in a special ASP file named `global.asa`. Each application can have only one `global.asa`, and it's placed in the application's root. To make sure `global.asa` is read by ASP, it isn't enough just to make sure that it is stored in a virtual directory, you have to explicitly have created the application virtual directory it is stored in using the **Properties** Dialog in MMC, as we did in Chapter 1. If you've created one, then the button will read **Remove**.

Otherwise you will need to click on **Create** to create the application.

We will cover the items that can be placed in `global.asa` later in this chapter, but we will introduce what we need here to get us started on application-level variables.

Try It Out – Your First global.asa

In this example, we will create a very basic `global.asa` file so that we can declare some application-level variables. Later in this section, we will access these variables from an ASP page in our application.

1. Create a new file, and write the following:

```
<SCRIPT LANGUAGE="VBScript"  RUNAT="Server">

Sub Application_OnStart
  Application("myAppVariable") = " "
  Application("anotherAppVariable") = 0
End Sub

</SCRIPT>
```

303

2. Save the file as `global.asa` in your `BegASPFiles` directory.

*If you are using FrontPage 98 or another application that doesn't recognize .asa as a
'valid' file extension, then you can change this yourself by going to Windows Explorer's
View | Folder Options | File tab and typing in the following settings:*

Description - ASA File

Extension - ASA

Content type - <leave blank>

Opens with - Notepad (or your choice here)

What It Does

In our first `global.asa` file, we are declaring some application-level variables that we will use
later in our examples. The first thing that you will notice about this file is that there are no
`<%...%>` blocks. As you have seen before, these `<%` and `%>` tags are used to indicate ASP script
within a file. In the `global.asa` file, we will be using the following syntax instead (which can
also be used in ASP files):

```
<SCRIPT LANGUAGE="VBScript"  RUNAT="Server">
```

The procedures that are part of `global.asa` are defined within a script block. The language
that we are using for scripts is VBScript. Since these scripts will be run at the server, as opposed
to the client, we have included the `RUNAT` parameter, and passed it a value of `Server`. If you
include script that is not enclosed by `<SCRIPT>` tags, the server returns an error, as it won't be
marked up for server-side execution.

```
Sub Application_OnStart
  Application("myAppVariable") = " "
  Application("anotherAppVariable") = 0
End Sub
```

We've used one event (there are a possible four, which we'll discuss shortly) in our
`global.asa` file and this is `Application_OnStart`. This event will be fired only once when
the first visitor hits the page. So, an application is started the first time one of its pages is
accessed by a user. The `Application_OnStart` event occurs before the first new session is
created, that is, before the `Session_OnStart` event.

Inside of this event handler, we are initializing two application-level variables. Application-
level variables are actually elements of the `Application` object. We set and retrieve their
values in the same way that we set and retrieve the values in a collection.

In this example, we have created two application-level variables:

- ❑ `myAppVariable`
- ❑ `anotherAppVariable`

The `myAppVariable` variable has been initialized to an empty string. The `anotherAppVariable` variable has been initialized to a string containing 0. Once that is complete, the event handler has finished, and we can complete the `global.asa` file with a closing `</SCRIPT>` tag.

Application Object Collections

The Application object has two Collections:

❑ The `Contents` collection contains all variables that have been added to the application via through a script command. You can use this list to obtain a list of items that have been given application scope. You can also remove them with the addition of two new methods within ASP 3.0

❑ The `StaticObjects` collection contains the names of all objects added via the `<OBJECT>` tag in `global.asa`, with application scope, that is with `SCOPE=APPLICATION`. Objects that are added to `global.asa` can either be application-scoped objects or session-scoped objects, but session-scoped object belong to the `Session.StaticObjects` collection.

The Contents Collection

You use the `Contents` collection to get a list of items with application scope or to set a value for a particular Application-level variable.

The general syntax for retrieving a variable's value in the `Application.Contents` collection is:

```
Application.Contents("Key")
```

where *Key* specifies the name of the key to retrieve.

As `Contents` is the default collection, you could also use:

```
Application("Key" )
```

to specify it as well.

You can iterate through the `Contents` collection the same way you would for any collection, with a `For...Each` statement. An example of this is:

```
<%
  For Each Key in Application.Contents
    Response.Write (Key)
  Next
%>
```

Just as with a normal collection, you can retrieve the number of elements in the collection by using the `Count` property.

```
<%= Application.Contents.Count %>
```

The StaticObjects Collection

The `StaticObjects` collection contains all the objects that have been created using the `<OBJECT>` tag, and that fall within the `Application` object's scope. You can use the `StaticObjects` collection to determine the value of an `<OBJECT>`'s property. Alternatively you can iterate through the collection, and retrieve properties for all the objects stored. We will see how to create static objects when we take a deeper look at the `global.asa` file.

Application Object Methods

The Application object has two methods (and two further methods via the `Contents` collection):

- ❑   `Lock`
- ❑   `UnLock`

Lock Method

The `Lock` method prevents clients – other than the one currently accessing it – from modifying the variables stored in the `Application` object. This means you can't get one client changing the variables, taking a long time over it, and another one changing the same variables to a different set of values in the time between. This way data corruption can be avoided.

UnLock Method

This method removes the lock from variables stored in the `Application` object, freeing them up after `Application` object has been locked previously using the `Application.Lock` method.

The `Contents` collection itself has a further two methods:

- ❑   `Remove`
- ❑   `RemoveAll`

Remove Method

Removes an item from the `Contents` collection. For example, look at the following:

```
Application("FirstVariable") = "Cats"
Application("SecondVariable") = "Dogs"
Application.Contents.Remove("FirstVariable")
```

This would create two `Application` objects and then remove only the first.

RemoveAll Method

Removes all items from the Contents collection. For example, consider the following:

```
Application("FirstVariable") = "Cats"
Application("SecondVariable") = "Dogs"
Application.Contents.RemoveAll
```

This creates two Application objects and then removes the collection along with any other Application objects that might have been created prior to this.

Try It Out – Working with Application-Level Variables

In this example, we will take a look at an ASP script that will demonstrate how to interact with the application-level variables that were created in the global.asa file that we looked at earlier.

1. Create a new file, and enter the following:

```
<HTML>
<HEAD>
<TITLE>Application Variable Test</TITLE>
</HEAD>

<BODY>
Let's retrieve the values of the Application Variables:<P>
myAppVariable = <%= Application("myAppVariable")%><BR>
anotherAppVariable = <%= Application("anotherAppVariable")%><HR>

Now, let's set the variables:<HR>
<%
 Application.Lock
 Application("myAppVariable") = Now
 Application("anotherAppVariable") = CStr(CInt(Application("anotherAppVariable"))+1)
 Application.UnLock
%>
Variables set - <A HREF="appVarTest.asp">click here</A> to reload the page to view
</BODY>
</HTML>
```

2. Save the file as appVarTest.asp to the BegASPFiles directory.

3. View the file in your web browser. The first time you view the page the variables will be blank.

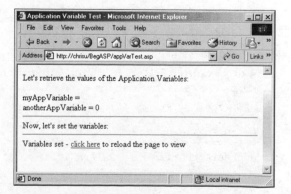

307

If on your browser `anotherAppVariable` *is also blank like* `myAppVariable`, *then your file isn't correctly locating global.asa. You need to make sure* `global.asa` *and* `appVarTest.asp` *are both in the* `BegAsp` *folder, and that this folder is set up as an application (mentioned in chapter 1).*

4. Click on Refresh or link at the bottom to view the contents.

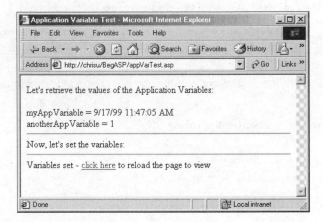

5. Open another copy of your browser and view the file again.

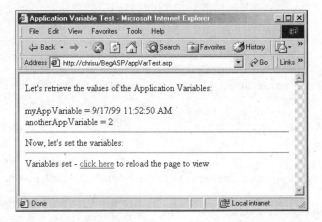

How It Works

In this example, we are using the application-level variables that were created in the `global.asa` example that we ran earlier.

```
<BODY>
Let's retrieve the values of the Application Variables:<P>
myAppVariable = <%= Application("myAppVariable") %><BR>
anotherAppVariable = <%= Application("anotherAppVariable") %><HR>
```

First, we will retrieve the values that are currently stored in the two application-level variables that we have declared. Since all we are doing is accessing the value stored in the variables, there is no need to call the Lock method.

```
Now, let's set the variables:<HR>
<%
 Application.Lock
 Application("myAppVariable") = Now
 Application("anotherAppVariable") = CStr(CInt(Application("anotherAppVariable"))+1)
 Application.Unlock
%>
```

The next step is to reset the values of the two application-level variables. In order to give this script exclusive control over the variables, we first need to call the Lock method of the Application object. This will give total control of all application-level variables to this script until the corresponding call to UnLock is made. Since there can be multiple users accessing a web site at the same time, and possibly accessing the same page, we need to take these precautions to ensure that the data is updated properly.

Now that we have exclusive control over the variables, we can update their values. The value of the myAppVariable variable is set to the current date and time. The value that is stored in anotherAppVariable is a string containing the number of times this page has been accessed. Here, we want to increment this count by one. We could rely on VBScript's automatic type conversion, but to make our code more readable by someone trying to learn what it is doing, we will explicitly convert the variable's type.

The first step is to convert the string value that is stored in the application-level variable to an integer value. This is done using the CInt function. Now that we have an integer value, we can add 1 to it to get the new count. Finally, to store the value back into the application-level variable, we will convert the new count back to a string using the CStr function.

With all of the changes successfully made, we will release our hold on the application-level variables by calling the UnLock method of the Application object.

Now that we have learnt some of the basics of the Application object, let's take a more in-depth look at the global.asa file.

Global.asa

Since we can now store objects and variables in an application-level scope, we need to have a file to store these declarations in. This file is global.asa. Each application can have only one global.asa, and it's placed in the virtual directory's root. In global.asa, you can include event handler scripts and declare objects that will have Session or Application scope. You can also store application-level variables and objects used by the application. The file has no display component, as it is not displayed to users.

Understanding the Structure of global.asa

If you are using VBScript, global.asa can contain only four event handling subroutines:

❑ Application_OnStart

❑ Application_OnEnd

❑ Session_OnStart

❑ Session_OnEnd

An example of the most basic global.asa file would be:

```
<SCRIPT LANGUAGE="VBScript"  RUNAT="Server" >

Sub Application_OnStart
'...your VBScript code here
End Sub

Sub Application_OnEnd
'...your VBScript code here
End Sub

Sub Session_OnStart
'...your VBScript code here
End Sub

Sub Session_OnEnd
'...your VBScript code here
End Sub
</SCRIPT>
```

Notice that we have to use the <SCRIPT> tag at the top of the page. Also as previously mentioned, there are no <%...%> blocks in the file, because in the global.asa file, all of the ASP script needs be enclosed in the <SCRIPT> block. Since these scripts will be running on the server rather than on the client's machine, we have to make sure that the RUNAT directive is included inside of the SCRIPT element, otherwise global.asa won't work correctly.

Application_OnStart

This event handler is run **once**, when the application starts. The application starts when the first visitor to the application calls the first .asp page. In this procedure, you should put any application initialization steps that need to be run before anyone can access the application. For example, you could store the database login information, which you will see in Chapters 12 to 14, in an application-level variable, so that all pages have easy access to it.

If you want to initialize an application-scoped variable in Application_OnStart, you'd use:

```
Sub Application_OnStart
  Application("YourVariable") = "SomeValue"
End Sub
```

Once this event handler is complete, Session_OnStart runs for the first session.

Application_OnEnd

An application ends immediately after the last active session within that application ends. This event handler runs when the application is unloaded. To unload the application manually, you can do this from the IIS MMC console by just opening the console, selecting the application you want to unload in the left hand pane, then right click on the application and select Properties. Under the Virtual Directory tab at the top, there is a button on the right hand side of the dialog box marked Unload. If you click this, the application will be unloaded. It may take a little time, but the way to tell when the application has finished unloading is to wait until the button is grayed out.

`Application_OnEnd` scripts are used for "cleaning up" settings after the Application stops. For example, you might want to insert code to delete unneeded database records or write information you want to keep to text files.

Declaring Objects in global.asa

You can declare application-scoped objects in `global.asa`. This will allow you to create one instance of an object and then use it on any page and in every session that accesses your web application. To declare an object in `global.asa`:

```
<OBJECT RUNAT=Server SCOPE=Scope ID=Application PROGID="progID">
</OBJECT>
```

Or if you are using the `CLASSID` of the object:

```
<OBJECT RUNAT=Server SCOPE=Scope ID=Application CLASSID="ClassID">
</OBJECT>
```

Important Note about Global.asa causing errors

`Global.asa` can be a real pain to novice and experienced developers alike. That is, it can cause errors in your script that are seemingly unconnected in anyway to `global.asa`. The problem is that only one `global.asa` can be read by ASP. Which `global.asa` is read will depend on which application was visited first. This won't be a problem if you have explicitly declared your application and provided you haven't nested your applications inside one another.

What kind of errors will you see? Well Object doesn't support this property or method: is one that should have you scrambling to find Windows Explorer, to check out whether you have declared your application or not, or whether you have nested one application inside of another. Think of it this way: if you declare an object in `global.asa` and for some reason, ASP doesn't process the `global.asa`, then any time you reference that object in your script, ASP will generate an error. Type Mismatch is another error caused for very similar reasons. If you declared a variable to hold an instance of an object in `global.asa`, and for some reason ASP is not reading the correct `global.asa`, then the ASP script could still be expecting you to read in a variable not an object.

If you think about it, this is perfectly reasonable, how can ASP know which `global.asa` to use if you nest applications or haven't declared your application, clairvoyance isn't one of things Microsoft have been able to program in yet. Only you know which `global.asa` should be read and therefore *you* have to make sure the applications are explicitly declared, and also not nested.

Extra Warnings on Declaring Objects in global.asa

You should be careful about creating components in application scope: some components are not designed to be given application scope, such as the `Dictionary` object. If you are not sure if an object can be used in application-scope, then you should err on the side of caution and find another place to store the object.

The use of objects in application or session scope is really an advanced topic that is beyond the scope of this book. There are advantages that can be gained by using them, but along with those advantages comes a host of possible problems. For a more detailed look at how to use objects in `global.asa`, take a look at Professional Active Server Pages 3.0, available from Wrox Press, *ISBN 1-861002-61-0*.

Next, we'll have a look at ASP's link between the Application and the client – the **Session**.

What is a Session?

In addition to providing support for applications across the web, Active Server Pages also supports sessions within an application. We have just looked at how applications are created and at some of the things that you can do with them. To begin our look at sessions, we first need to define what a session *is*.

ASP allows the developer to track a user from page to page in an application through the use of a **session**. A user's session begins when any user without a current session opens any `.asp` page within an ASP Application. The user's session will continue as they navigate from page to page in the site.

There are two ways that a session can be terminated. If the user stops interacting with the application, then the session will end after a certain period of time has elapsed. The default value for this time period is 20 minutes, which can be changed by setting the `Session.TimeOut` property. The `Session.Abandon` statement in an ASP page can also explicitly end the session.

The session can be used to store pieces of information that will be available to every page in the application and each user as private instances of those pieces of information. This can be used to track things like the contents of a user's shopping basket, or a flag indicating that this user has been properly authenticated with the system. In addition, just as there are event handlers in `global.asa` for the beginning and end of an application, you can also write an event handler that will be called when a session is started and when it is ended.

To interact with the session itself, you will be using the `Session` object.

The Session Object

There is one `Application` object for each application on the web server. Every client accessing that application can get a reference to it. Each client's unique interactions with the application is called a Session. For ASP to manage these processes, each client has a reference to a unique `Session` object.

The `Session` object will allow you to:

❑ Be notified when a user session begins, so that you can take appropriate actions for a new client.

❑ Be notified when a client has ended their session. This can either be caused by a timeout or an explicit method called `Abandon`.

❑ Store information that can be accessed by the client throughout the session

The `Session` object is a powerful object for developing web applications using Active Server Pages. With the session object, ASP can maintain an active session for a client, which lets your application keep track of each client and maintains all the variables that they have set and used.

Session Object Collections

Like the `Application` object, the `Session` object has two collections:

❑ `Contents` collection

❑ `StaticObjects` collection

Contents Collection

The `Contents` collection contains all the variables established for a session without using the `<OBJECT>` tag. The `Contents` collection is used to determine the value of a specific session item, or to iterate through the collection and retrieve a list of all items in the session.

```
Session.Contents("Key")
```

Where "*Key*" stands for a specific variable's name.

For example:

```
<%= Session.Contents("VisitorID")%>
```

For single session variables, because contents is the default collection, this is usually shortened to:

```
<%= Session("VisitorID")%>
```

Both code lines will produce the same result.

You can iterate through the `Session.Contents` collection with the following code:

```
<%
  For Each item in Session.Contents
    If IsObject(Session.Contents(item)) Then
      Response.write(item & " : Can't display object" & "<BR>")
    Else
      If IsArray(Session.Contents(item)) Then
        Response.write "Array: " & Session.Content(item)
        For each objArray in Session.Contents(item)
          Response.write "<LI>" & _
          Session.Contents(item)(objArray)& "<BR>"
      Next
          Response.write "</LI>"
      Else
          Response.write(item & " : " & Session.Contents(item) & "<BR>")
      End If
    End If
  Next
%>
```

This code will produce a list of all the `Session` variables' names and values. The `For Each` statement will iterate through each of the elements in the `Contents` collection. As you can store objects or arrays in the collection, we need to check for these specific occurrences and handle them. You can't display an object, so we need to just mention that a certain item is an object. You also need to iterate through an array and display each element. Finally you need to display the 'normal' items. Each of these elements will be a key into the collection. You can then display this key, as well as the element in the collection associated with that key. The `Next` statement will take you to the next key in the collection, or if you are at the end, it will take you to the next line in the script.

StaticObjects Collection

The Session `StaticObjects` collection contains all the objects created with the `<OBJECT>` tag within session scope. The `StaticObjects` collection is used to retrieve the value for an object's specific property, or to iterate through the collection and retrieve all properties for all objects.

Session Object Properties

The Session object has four properties

- ❑ `SessionID`
- ❑ `Timeout`
- ❑ `CodePage`
- ❑ `LCID`

SessionID Property

The SessionID property is a read-only property that returns the session identification number for each user. Each session has a unique identifier, generated by the application when the session is created. The session identification number is actually a cookie that is stored on the user's machine. It will expire only when the session times out. One rather large problem with the Session object is that it simply won't work if the user has cookies turned off. The session won't get started when the user browses the site and they won't get access to the Session object.

To retrieve the current user's SessionID, use:

```
<%= Session.SessionID %>
```

> Within the same server cycle, all SessionID's have unique values. If the Web server is stopped and restarted, some SessionID values may be the same as values generated before the server was stopped. For that reason, you should not use the SessionID property to generate primary key values for a database application. You could use it as a way of tracking all of the currently active users in an application-level variable such as an array.

Timeout Property

The Timeout property sets the timeout period assigned to the Session object for any application, in minutes. If the user does not request or refresh a page before the timeout period expires, the session ends.

You can set the Timeout value by:

```
<% Session.Timeout = 30 %>
```

This will cause the session to timeout in 30 minutes if there is no activity. If you want to retrieve the value of the Timeout property, you can use this:

```
<%= Session.Timeout %>
```

You should exercise caution when setting Timeout values. If you set Timeout to too short a duration, the server will terminate user sessions too quickly. If you rely on session variables to process user data and the user has not been able to complete the processing of an identification form, for example, the loss of session variables will cause all sorts of problems.

Setting Session Timeout to too long a duration also has its problems. All Session variables are stored in the server's memory. Since the server has no way to determine if the user is still viewing your sites' pages, you are probably going to have quite a few user sessions eating up server memory resources, if sessions last for too long a time. This is particularly critical if you store database query results in Session arrays. These results can hold a lot of data sometimes, and having multiple unused sessions still open with large amounts of data stored in them could slow down your server.

The best strategy is to analyze each application, by conducting average user browsing time tests, and then set the session timeout to a more appropriate value where needed. Generally though, the 20 minute timeout is a good compromise for most applications.

CodePage Property

The CodePage property determines the code page that will be used to display content. A code page is used to map between the characters that are displayed on the screen and an internal table. Unless you are developing sites that use non-Roman alphabets, such as Russian or Japanese, you will not have to worry about setting this property.

In order to be able to set the code page property you must have first enabled code page support with:

```
<%@ CODEPAGE = CodePage %>
```

Then, to set the code page to the Roman alphabet, use:

```
<% Session.CodePage=1252 %>
```

The LCID Property

A locale identifier determines time-zone and language rules for the system. The LCID property specifies the system's **location identifier,** which will be used to display content. LCID uniquely identifies one of the installed system-defined locales. If a location identifier has not been installed, it cannot be set.

To set the LCID to U.S. English, use:

```
<% Session.LCID = 1033 %>
```

This also happens to be the default value for the LCID property for servers installed in the US, meaning you don't need to explicitly set it. The various LCID values are usually defined in the documentation as hexadecimal values. You must convert these values to a decimal value to use when setting the LCID property.

Session Object Methods

The Session object has just one method, although the Contents collection also now boasts Remove and RemoveAll methods.

The Abandon Method

The Abandon method destroys all the objects stored in a Session object and releases the server resources they were occupying. If you do not call the Abandon method in a script, the server destroys the session objects when the session times out.

To call this method, you would use:

```
<% Session.Abandon %>
```

If you know that when a user finishes browsing a certain page they don't need any more session variables, you can call the Abandon method to release server memory resources associated with that session. Bear in mind that if you set certain useful session variable values, like UserName, all the values will be lost. On the other hand, if you are programming web games, which use server memory resources heavily, you might be better off explicitly ending the session and having the user visit the start page for another game.

A quirk of the abandon method is that it will not clear the session variables until the current page has been fully processed. If you have a page that displays the session variables, after the abandon method is called you will be still able to see the session variables.

One use of the Abandon method is during development when testing Session variables. If you create a page named abandon.asp, as described below, you can call a page when needed.

```
<%
  Session.Abandon
  Response.Redirect "default.asp"
%>
```

In this page, we first call the Abandon method of the Session object. This releases all of the session-level variables. Next, the Redirect method of the Response object is used to send the browser to the starting page of the application, creating a new session. In this example, that page is named default.asp.

The Session.Contents Collection's methods

Like the Application object, the Contents collection of the Session object has a further two methods:

❑ Remove

❑ RemoveAll

Remove Method

Removes an item from the Contents collection. Consider, for example, the following:

```
Session("FirstVariable") = "Fish"
Session("SecondVariable") = "Carrots"
Session.Contents.Remove("FirstVariable")
```

This would create two Session objects and then remove only the first.

RemoveAll Method

Removes all items from the Contents collection. So, for example, look at the following code:

```
Session("FirstVariable") = "Fish"
Session("SecondVariable") = "Carrots
Session.Contents.RemoveAll
```

This creates two Session objects and then removes both the collection, along with any other Session objects that might have been created prior to this.

Now we'll look at example of making variables persist across different ASP pages.

Try It Out – Passing Data from Page to Page

In this example, we will see how the `Session` object can be used to pass information from page to page within a particular user session. A good rule of thumb to remember is that session-level variables work by passing information between the pages of a single user's session. Application-level variables are used to store information that can be retrieved at any time by any user accessing the system.

1. Create a new file, and key in the following:

```
<HTML>
<HEAD>
<TITLE>Session Variable test</TITLE>
</HEAD>

<BODY>

<%
  Dim tAccessTime
  tAccessTime = Session("LastAccessTime")

  If tAccessTime = "" Then
    Response.Write ("This is the first time this page has been accessed!<P>")
  Else
    Response.Write ("This page was last accessed at " & tAccessTime & "<P>")
  End If
%>

<HR>Writing current access time to the Session object<BR><BR>
<% Session("LastAccessTime") = Now %>
<A HREF="sessVarTest.asp">Click here</A> to refresh the page.<BR><BR>
<A HREF="abandon.asp?dest=sessVarTest.asp">Click here</A> to abandon the
session.<BR><BR>

</BODY>
</HTML>
```

2. Save the file as `sessVarTest.asp` in your `BegASP` directory.

3. Create another new file, and enter the following:

```
<%
Session.Abandon
Response.Redirect Request("dest")
%>
```

4. Save the file as `abandon.asp` in your `BegASP` directory.

5. View the file `sessVarTest.asp` in your web browser.

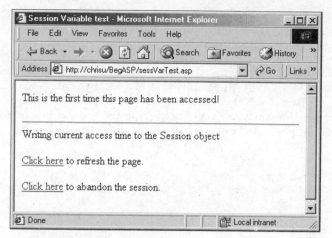

6. To create a new session click on **Refresh** and view the page again.

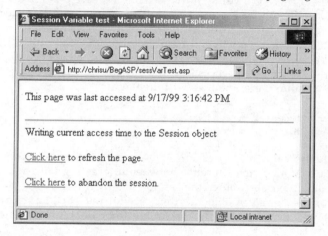

In Windows 2000 with ASP 3.0, all browsers (including Navigator etc) on the same machine now have the same session, the only way to create a new session is by refreshing the page. This wasn't the case previously with ASP 2.0, where if you opened new instances of the browser(not just a new window, using File/New/Window) by starting Internet Explorer from either a desktop shortcut or from the start menu, you would create a new session.

How It Works

In this example, we are using a session-level variable to store the date and time that this page was last accessed. If there is a value present, then it will be displayed for the user. If there is no value present, then the user will be shown a message telling them this.

```
<%
  Dim tAccessTime
  tAccessTime = Session("LastAccessTime")
```

This first thing that we will need to do when processing this page is to retrieve the value stored in the session-level variable. We will be storing it in a local variable, which we can use throughout this page. This is very efficient way of working with session-level variables. It's important to remember that since the act of retrieving the session-level variable tends to consume a good deal of processor time, it is better to store the data locally, and then work with the local variable.

```
  If tAccessTime = " " Then
     Response.Write ("This is the first time this page has been accessed!<P>")
  Else
     Response.Write ("This page was last accessed at "  & tAccessTime & "<P>")
  End If
```

Next, we check to see if there is a value in the variable that we just retrieved. If no value has been set, then the variable will be empty. This will be the case if the session has not been created before, if the session timed out, or if this is the first time a user has been to this page. This may seem a bit strange to some people who are familiar with other languages in which a variable must have a value before it can be accessed. But in ASP, you can check to see if a session-level variable exists simply by trying to access it. If the variable does not exist, then nothing will be returned. If there is a value there, then we will display it.

```
<HR>Writing current access time to the Session object<P>
<% Session("LastAccessTime") = Now %>
```

We will then update the value of the session-level variable called `LastAccessTime` with the current date and time. Notice the difference between interacting with a session-level variable, and an application-level variable. Since the session is only for one user, there are no `Lock` and `UnLock` methods for the `Session` object as there are for the `Application` object. To set a value in a session-level variable, nothing special has to be done beforehand.

```
<A HREF="sessVarTest.asp">Click here</A> to refresh the page.
<A HREF="abandon.asp?dest=sessVarTest.asp">Click here</A> to abandon the session.<P>
```

We then provide two hyperlinks to allow the user to navigate from this page. The first hyperlink will reload the current page. This will cause the value that was just stored in the session-level variable to be displayed, and a new time stored there. The second hyperlink will call the `abandon.asp` file, which will abandon the current session. The `abandon.asp` file needs to know where to send the browser once the session has been abandoned, and this page name is passed as the `dest` query string variable.

```
<%
  Session.Abandon
  Response.Redirect Request("dest")
%>
```

The abandon.asp file will perform two functions. First, it will explicitly end the current session by calling the Abandon method. This will free any session-level variables and reset their values. Next, the script will redirect the browser to the page that the user supplied. Notice that we have used the shortcut to retrieving the value of a query string variable, whereby we don't tell ASP which collection the information resides in. ASP will search each of the collections looking for the supplied key. When and if it finds it, it will return the value to the script. This is fine as long as you don't access a collection before the generic Request collection that has a variable with the same name, resulting in the wrong variable being read.

Sessions and global.asa

Earlier in this chapter, we saw how the global.asa file can be used to process the startup and the shutdown of web applications. The file can also be used to handle events fired by the startup and shutdown of user sessions within a specific web application. Just as there are two event handlers for the Application object, there are two for the Session object as well.

Session_OnStart

Session_OnStart is called every time a new user begins a session with the web site. If you want to initialize a session-scoped variable in Session_OnStart, you'd use:

```
Sub Session_OnStart
  Session("YourVariable") = "SomeValue"
End Sub
```

For example, let's say you want to track the number of visitors currently accessing your site. (This is different from a traditional counter which tracks total numbers of visitors.) To do this, you would have an application-level variable that tracked the current number of users that were currently accessing the site. This is the same number of sessions that are currently active. Every time that a new session was started, we would want to add one to that number, and that can be done in the Session_OnStart routine.

Session_OnEnd

Session_OnEnd is called whenever a session terminates. This can happen if the session times out, or if it is explicitly abandoned. This isn't the same as just closing a browser down, in which case the session has to time out, before it ends. In Session_OnEnd, you might want to transfer temporary session variables to databases, or set application-level variables to another value: for example, if you are tracking the number of users currently visiting a site in an application-level variable, then you would subtract one from this number every time Session_OnEnd was run.

```
Sub Session_OnEnd
  Application.lock
  Application("Active") = Application("Active") - 1
  Application.unlock
End Sub
```

Declaring Session Objects in global.asa

You can also declare session-scoped objects in `global.asa`:

```
<OBJECT RUNAT=Server SCOPE=SESSION ID=Session PROGID="progID">
</OBJECT>
```

```
<OBJECT RUNAT=Server SCOPE=SESSION ID=Session CLASSID="ClassID">
</OBJECT>
```

You can use either `ProgID` or `ClassID`, but not both.

As with application objects, session-level objects declared in `global.asa` are not created until the server processes a script that calls the object. Again, this saves resources by only creating objects that are actually used.

Try It Out – Visitor Tracking Using global.asa

In this example, we will take what we've learned and construct a `global.asa` file that will allow us to track the number of current visitors to the application, as well as the total that have visited since the application was started.

Unfortunately, since some of you might not have the facility to use multiple machines to track sessions, we're going to have to 'cheat' a little bit, to demonstrate the code working. We'll explain how the 'cheat' affects what we see, as we go along.

1. Create a new folder called Session, within the `c:\Inetpub\wwwroot` folder.

2. Start up MMC and right click on the Session folder and select the **Properties** option to bring up the Properties dialog.

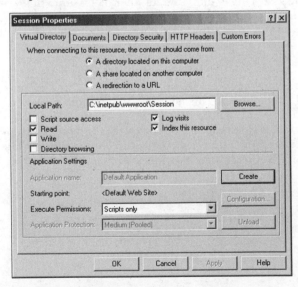

322

3. Click on the **Create** button to create a new application, and click on **OK** to close the dialog. (The folder must be turned into a application for this example to work.)

4. Create a new file, and key in the following:

```
<SCRIPT LANGUAGE=VBScript RUNAT=Server>
Sub Application_OnStart
  Application("visits") = 0
  Application("Active") = 0
End Sub

Sub Application_OnEnd

End Sub

Sub Session_OnStart
  Session.Timeout = 1
  Session("Start") = Now
  Application.lock
    Application("visits") = Application("visits") + 1
    intTotal_visitors = Application("visits")
  Application.unlock
  Session("VisitorID") = intTotal_visitors

  Application.lock
    Application("Active") = Application("Active") + 1
  Application.unlock
End Sub

Sub Session_OnEnd
  Application.lock
    Application("Active") = Application("Active") - 1
  Application.unlock
End Sub
</SCRIPT>
```

5. Save this file as `global.asa`. For this example, you need to store your `global.asa` file in a different directory. Store it in your **Session** folder, which should be found under **C:\InetPub\wwwroot\Session**.

If you are downloading the code for this chapter from the Wrox webisite, you will find that this file is called `global_session.asa`. *You will need to place it in the correct directory and rename it to* `global.asa` *in order for this example to work.*

6. Create a new file, and key the following:

```
<HTML>
<HEAD>
<TITLE>Retrieving Variables Set in Global.asa</TITLE>
</HEAD>
```

```
<BODY>
<P>
There have been <B><%= Session("VisitorID")%></B> total visits to this site.
<BR>You are one of <B> <%= Application("Active")%></B> active visitors.
<BR>Your session started at <%= Session("Start") %>

</BODY>
</HTML>
```

7. Save this file as `VisitorCount.asp`. You will need to save it in the **Session folder**, as it needs to be in the same folder as the `global.asa`.

8. View the file in your browser.

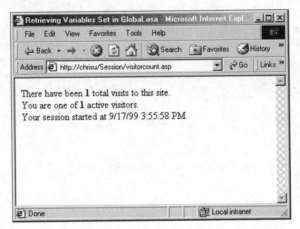

9. View the file in another browser or in another instance of your browser (if you simply open a new window, you will find that this won't work).

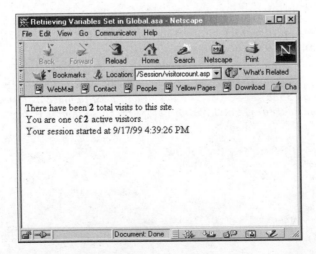

10. Close down the second browser immediately and press the Refresh on the first (time is of the essence as we'll explain shortly).

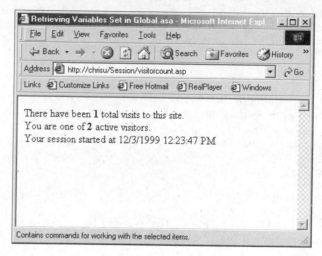

Note that the number of active visitors is two, even though we've just closed a session, we'll explain shortly. Also note that the number of total visits is still only one on this browser, even though two browsers have visited the site. This is because the number of total visits is actually set when the session is started, and not updated throughout. So when this browser viewed the site, it was the only browser to have viewed this site. Even though another browser has viewed this site, the total remains at one. So while strictly speaking our total number of visits is accurate for the beginning of the session, it doesn't adjust dynamically throughout the session.

11. Wait one whole minute and press the Refresh on the browser again

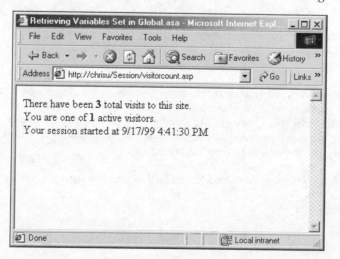

As explained earlier, we can't really mimic the action of several users browsing our site (unless you have a few spare PCs handy, or a lot of friends), so what we've done is set the value of the Session.Timeout to one minute in global.asa. When you close a browser your session doesn't automatically end, but the session will timeout after a minute, and be ended for you. Only then is the number of active users is reduced. So our count is accurate, but it takes a little while to update.

How It Works

In this application, we are using application-level variables to track the number of users that are currently looking at a site, as well as the total number that have accessed it.

```
<SCRIPT LANGUAGE=VBScript RUNAT=Server>
Sub Application_OnStart
  Application("visits") = 0
  Application("Active") = 0
End Sub
```

In the first event handler of the global.asa file, we will be working with the Application_OnStart method that is called whenever the application is started.

There are two variables that we will need to maintain throughout the life of the application. The visits variable will hold the total number of visits since the application was started. One thing to note is the Visits variable is initialized as zero. That means every time the application is unloaded, and restarted, this variable will be set to zero. If you don't want this to happen, each time you restart the application after unloading it, we suggest you remove the zero. The Active variable will hold the number of current user sessions in the application.

```
Sub Application_OnEnd

End Sub
```

We will not be doing any processing when the application is ended, so we are just adding this event handler as a placeholder.

```
Sub Session_OnStart
  Session.Timeout = 1
  Session("Start") = Now
```

When a session is started, we will perform some processing in the Session_OnStart event handler. To make our example work faster, we set the Timeout value of the Session object to 1 minute. In a real application, you would very rarely have your Timeout value set so low, but then again you would have people visiting your application using different machines, rather than having to rely on the one machine we are using.

We will also store the starting date and time for this session into a session-level variable.

```
Application.Lock
  Application("visits") = Application("visits") + 1
  intTotal_visitors = Application("visits")
Application.Unlock
Session("VisitorID") = intTotal_visitors
```

Next, we will need to find out the total number of visitors to the site since the application was started. This information is stored in an application-level variable. In order to change an application-level variable, we need to first Lock the Application object. We can then increment the value stored in the visits variable by one. This new value will represent the total number of visitors, including the one currently starting. The incremented value is stored back into the same application-level variable as it came from. Once we have made all the changes that we need to at this point, we will call Unlock to free up the Application object.

```
Application.Lock
  Application("Active") = Application("Active") + 1
Application.Unlock
```

Finally, we will update the current number of active users by one. This information is stored in another application-level variable.

```
Sub Session_OnEnd
  Application.Lock
    Application("Active") = Application("Active") - 1
  Application.Unlock
End Sub
```

When the user leaves the site and their session times out, this event handler will be called. The important thing that needs to happen in this file is for the number of active users to be decremented by one. Since this information is stored at the application-level, you will need to Lock the Application object when making the change, and the Unlock the object as quickly as possible.

```
There have been <B><%= Session("VisitorID")%></B> total visits to this site.
<BR>You are one of <b> <%= Application("Active")%></B> active visitors.
<BR>Your session started at <%= Session("Start") %>
```

In our test page, we will be displaying the total number of visits to this site since the application was started, at the time when the user's session is started. This is because we fix the total number of visits to the site, when we start the session in global.asa and we can't update it dynamically. We will also be showing the number of active visitors, as well as the time at which the current session began. Even though we are interacting with an application-level variable, we do not need to Lock and Unlock the Application object if we only want to *read* the data.

As you can see from the screen shots, once a session times out, the Session_OnEnd really is called. This can be seen by the change in number of active users as we look at each of the browser snapshots.

We've completed our discussions on how to preserve data from page to page using the Session object. Also, we have covered how to keep information from session to session in an application using the Application object.

Finally, we'll turn our attention back towards the mechanism that is now supposedly obsolete.

Cookies – The End of the Line?

Before the advent of Active Server Pages, cookies were the main way that data could be transferred between different pages on a site, as a user moved between them. As we saw earlier in this chapter, the Session object now gives us a very powerful mechanism that also allows you to do just that. So what is the role for cookies now? Well as we saw with the SessionID property, cookies still play a vital role behind the scenes in ASP. They serve as the mechanism that tells each page accessed by a user during a session, what session that request belongs to. ASP can take this cookie and retrieve all of the session information that is stored on the server. Without cookies, the Session object just wouldn't work.

Cookies also still play a role in storing information between sessions. While a session has a timeout value, of usually 20 minutes, after which all of its information is deleted, a cookie can persist for a much longer period of time. The reason sessions can't have very long time-outs is that every time a user comes to your site, the server would have to wait for the period specified by the timeout to determine whether the user had logged out or not. Remember that closing a browser doesn't end the session, rather it just begins the period for which a session is dormant, until it times out. The server would use up precious resources monitoring long dead sessions, and the more users who visit the site, the more resources would be stretched. For this reason, cookies also play a vital role in storing information during the times when the user is off visiting other sites, or is not even using their browser at all, and you won't see the back of them for a while yet.

Summary

The world of web-based applications is made possible by Active Server Pages and the Application and Session objects. These powerful objects allow you transform a web site from a series of linked pages to an actual application by creating a means to hold user information from page to page. In this chapter, we have looked at:

- ❑ How **cookies** can help us store information over a long period of time, and even after the user has left our site

- ❑ When and how to use cookies to store information at the client's computer

- ❑ How the Application object can be used to store information that can be accessed by all users accessing a web site

- ❑ What the global.asa file is used for, and how it helps us interact with the beginning and the end of sessions and applications

- ❑ The powerful Session object, which allows us to treat a user's interaction with the web site as a continuous action, rather than just a disconnected series of page requests

Now that we are on our way towards building web-based applications, we will need to look some good coding techniques and how we can go about debugging our code. That's the subject of our next chapter.

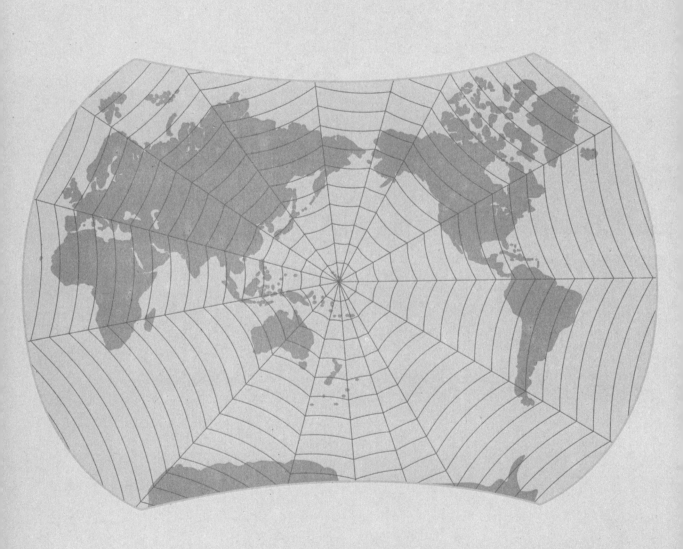

Error Handling

No matter how hard we try, it really is very difficult to write error-free software. We are inherently fallible. That's not to say it's impossible to write perfect software; it's just very hard, and takes effort, practice, diligence and lots of experience. Let's face facts; we all make mistakes occasionally!

So, given that we make these mistakes, how do we go about tracking them down? Most of the popular programming languages are supported by a rich set of development tools, and these tools usually include a debugger. However, it's a sad fact that web developers have all too often had to rely on the WYSINWYI or WYSIAAMEM approach to debugging – that's "What You See Is Not What You Intended" or "What You See Is An Arcane Microsoft Error Message".

In this chapter we are going to look at some good coding techniques, some debugging techniques and how we apply them to our ASP environment. You'll see how some additions to ASP 3.0 make life a lot easier than it used to be. In particular we will be looking at:

- ❑ How to start debugging your ASP code
- ❑ The difference between debugging client-side script and server-side script
- ❑ Different types of errors
- ❑ Good coding practices
- ❑ How to debug your script
- ❑ The Microsoft Script debugger
- ❑ How the `Server` object can help us debug
- ❑ The VBScript `Err` object and the `ASPError` object

Of course, none of these will make you a perfect programmer, but that's really a false goal anyway. The best that you can do is to understand your code, recognize where it might break, and be sure to handle possible error conditions. Making a mistake is acceptable, as long as you find out what the problem is quickly, and then learn from it.

Arrgh! I Goofed Again!

We've already said that it is acceptable to make mistakes. If you're a manager reading this, don't rip this chapter out before giving it to your programmers. The fact is that 'trial and error' is often a good way to learn a new technology – once you've crashed the server for the third time in 20 minutes, you will probably have worked out what it is you are doing wrong. OK, if you're writing monitoring software for a hospital intensive care unit, your quality goals might be a little stricter – but on your own, while learning, you will make mistakes. Guaranteed. You will learn from them; you won't make them again, and you'll go on to write books that tell people how to debug applications.

So what this chapter is really about is how to write code that, while not exactly bulletproof, is a lot more robust than it might otherwise be. When the worst does happen, we talk about how you track down those errors quickly and efficiently so that you can get to the root of the problem and fix it, or at least find sources of information when the error still mystifies you.

Isolating the Location of the Error

We're going to have a brief look at the ASP architecture again, because it's important to know where the error is occurring. This is partly revision from earlier chapters, but we're looking at it again here so you see its importance to debugging. Let's have a look at a request for an ASP page.

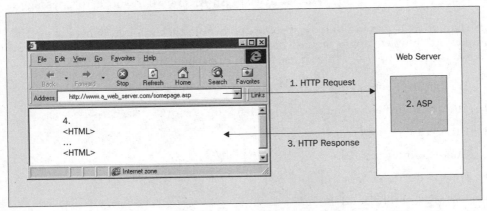

This shows a typical situation. In step 1, the user selects a URL for an ASP page and the request is forwarded to the web server. Step 2 shows ASP processing the ASP script code on the server. The processed HTML is then sent back to the client in step 3. And finally, in step 4 the web browser displays the HTML and executes any client-side script. Pretty obvious, but also very important as you must be aware of where certain actions are processed.

The thing to remember is the difference between server-side script and client-side script. Server-side script is enclosed in the following tags:

```
<%
' server-side script here
%>
```

Alternatively, server-side script can be denoted by using the standard script tag and the RUNAT property:

```
<SCRIPT LANGUAGE=VBScript RUNAT=Server>
    ' server-side script here
</SCRIPT>
```

Client-side script is enclosed in the standard script tag:

```
<SCRIPT LANGUAGE=VBScript>
    ' client-side script here
</SCRIPT>
```

You might already be used to this by now, but it's surprising how often you forget where the script code is being executed, especially if your ASP page has both server-side and client-side script.

Using Objects Correctly

Having decided where your script code is executing it's also important not to do the wrong thing in the wrong place, and knowing where you are means you won't try to use objects that aren't appropriate to your current location. Try using Guatemalan Quetzals to pay for souvenirs of your trip to France, and you'll get the idea.

What's all this leading to? Well, there are distinct sets of objects. Some are server-side objects, such as the Response object, and some are client-side, such as the Document object.

For example, consider this client-side script:

```
<HTML>
. . . ' some HTML tags

<SCRIPT LANGUAGE=VBScript>
Sub Window_onLoad()
  Response.Write "Hello"
End Sub
</SCRIPT>

</HTML>
```

Try running that and you'll get the following error:

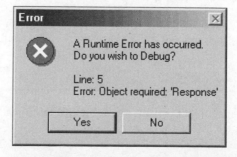

This is because the `Response` object is only available as part of ASP, that is, in server-side scripting. Thus this is a client-side error, not an ASP error.

Likewise, trying this code:

```
<HTML>
<BODY>
<A ID=FieldName>Some text</A>

<%
  Dim objField
  Set objField = Document.All("FieldName")
%>

</BODY>
</HTML>
```

will give the following error if you scroll down the page:

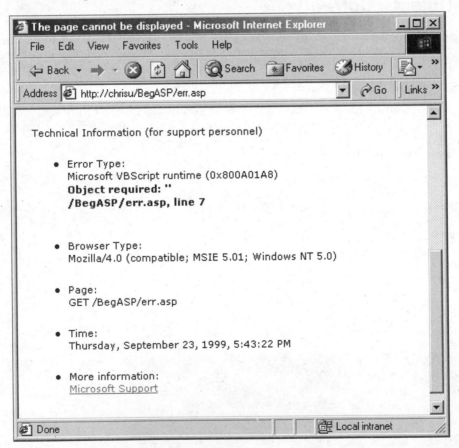

This is because the `Document` object is only available at the client, that is, in the web browser.

Also notice the difference between how the two error messages are displayed. The first example generated an error on the client, so it popped up an error dialog. The second example generated an error in ASP, so the error was returned as HTML code, which subsequently made up the web page. ASP, on its own, can't display error dialogs because it runs on the server – any dialog would appear on the screen of the web server, which isn't much good if you're five thousand miles away. As we're talking about ASP, we're not going to be paying much attention to client-side errors, but we will be looking at the difference between client and server debugging a little later.

Types of Error

So we've noted that errors can arise in two different places, but there are also several different types of error that may occur. This is important to realize, as some errors might not even generate an error message. Debugging is a lot easier if you know where to look and what you are looking for. There are lots of types and subtypes of errors, but in ASP you can very broadly classify them as one of the following three types: syntax error, logical error or ASP error.

Syntax Errors

Syntax errors are easily spotted, as they're the ones that cause your program to go belly up. Computers are very precise machines, and the applications that run on them are just as picky. You and I can muddle up words in our sentences and still expect somebody else to make general sense of them. For example, I could say "good morning" to you at one o'clock in the afternoon, and you'd still know what I meant. However your ASP programs can be thrown out by the mildest of typos.

```
<% Reponse.Write "Hello" %>
```

This would provoke an **Object Required** error, ASP failing completely to recognize that you merely missed an **s** out. Also if you fail to create a loop structure correctly, such as by missing a Next off the end of the structure:

```
<% For intLoop = 1 to 5
  Response.Write "Hello" %>
```

This would cause an error. Or if you fail to close a conditional structure with an End If, or requisite closing statement:

```
<%
If strChoice = "Yes" Then
  Response.Write = "Yes"
Else
  Response.Write = "No"
%>
```

This too will generate an error. In fact, ASP will also tell you very quickly about this. As you can imagine there are literally hundreds of different possible types of errors, so we can't go into them all here. Syntax errors are like abuses of the grammatical rules of language. If you wrote, "You was here on time", then your old English tutor would have put a big red line under it at school. Writing a program is almost like writing an English essay, yet you *have* to get everything correct – one spelling mistake and everything will come tumbling down around your ears. Ok, let's take a look at a few very common causes of syntax errors

Seven Things That Might Cause a Syntax Error

❑ **Typing Mistakes**: We've already mentioned it once, but let's say it again. Check your spelling.

❑ **Combining two keywords as one brand new keyword**: Sounds unlikely? I bet you've seen End If typed as EndIf more times than you care to remember.

❑ **Construct is not closed properly**: Most people take care to close loops and conditions, but it's still easy to be caught out when there are several combined. Look out for something like this:

```
For intLoop1 = 1 to 10
For intLoop2 = 2 to 20
For intLoop3 = 3 to 30
...Code here...
Next
Next
```

It is not always obvious if the loops are closed 10 pages of code later. However, indenting the code will certainly help.

❑ **Using the wrong method or property of an object**: I find that the Cookies collection is a classic source of this type of error. The following code will not work (I've tried it!):

```
Request.Cookies("Cookie").Expires = Date+1
```

❑ **Using a property as a method or a method as a property**: It seems obvious, but most experienced programmers have done this at least once:

```
Response.Write = "Hello" or
```

```
Response.Buffer True
```

❑ **Writing to a Read Only property**: there are certain properties that just return information. If you tried to assign a value to them, it would generate an error. Back in our Telephone object example, in Chapter 6, the IsConnected property was read only. The same goes for the TotalBytes property of the Request object. The following would not be allowed:

```
Request.TotalBytes = 200
```

❑ **Not creating an object properly**: If you don't use the keyword Set then the object won't get created. For example in Chapter 6

```
ObjTelephone = Server.CreateObject("MyTelephone.Telephone")
```

The one upside is that syntax errors are usually easy to spot, and if you do spot them then they are almost all very easy to correct, unlike the next type of error we will look at.

Logical Errors

I've seen these kinds of errors called everything under the sun from "algorithmic errors" to "why the heck isn't my program working, that can't possibly be the right answer ". Most often, you've checked your code, cleared up any typos and obvious coding errors, and yet the program's not returning data or is returning data that can't possibly be correct. That's usually because you've made a mistake in the programming logic. Let's consider some common types of logical error:

- ❑ Division By Zero Errors
- ❑ Type Mismatch Errors
- ❑ No Error message, but the output is wrong

Division by zero is where, for whatever reason, you end up dividing a number by zero. It's usually not an intentional mistake: you divide a variable by a positive number, but for some reason the variable is empty and so you inadvertently end up dividing your number by zero. Of course this is a mathematical impossibility and the computer will generate an error whenever this problem arises. However the problem might not always be apparent. Consider a form where you ask the user to enter a number of items for purchase, and you wish to give him/her a discount and calculate requisite taxation. The user accidentally forgets to enter this number in the box and submits it to your server. Your program multiplies the number of items by the price and ends up with zero. This result could then be used as basis for division, later in the calculation, and we end up with a division by zero error. However if the user had supplied a number other than zero then the program would have worked correctly.

Type mismatch errors occur, for example, when variants of one subtype (such as integers) are used to store the results of a calculation and then are added to information of another incompatible subtype (such as text). As variants are "variables for all seasons", they're normally very durable, so you can assign it a number one moment and text the next:

```
<%
varint = 1
Response.Write varInt
varint  = "Hello"
Response.Write varInt
%>
```

The implicit type conversion would make sure, that the first value is handled as a number and the second is handled as text. Thus, you'd get the response 1 followed by Hello. However, if you tried to add text to a variant storing a numerical value, then you'd generate an error:

```
<%
varInt = 1
Response.Write varInt
varInt = varInt + "Hello"
Response.Write varInt
%>
```

Another common occurrence of this type of error is where you attempt but fail to create an object and then try and use it as an object, while ASP still thinks you're using the variable designed to hold an instance of an object, as a variable. Later in this chapter we will look at a method that can help to reduce the frequency at which this type of error occurs.

I'd hazard that one of the most common types of logical error is where the programmer makes a mistake in his/her assumptions, and codes that error into the program. Consider the following pearl – whether it's unverifiable truth or merely urban myth is open to speculation, but it could have happened. In the 1950s/60s, on the U.S. nuclear defense system, a programmer calculated a number incorrectly – he or she managed to shift the decimal point one place to the left. Unfortunately, the number in question corresponded to a flight trajectory angle in the algorithm that detected whether a nuclear missile attack had been launched. Once in operation the program detected an object corresponding to its calculations, and displayed that it was 99.9% certain that it was an incoming missile. It turned out that the program had been triggered by the rising moon!

In the business world, such mistakes are probably less dramatic, but consider the following program to calculate the royalties that a best-selling novel writer might receive from his publishers:

```
<%
intSales = 10000                            'Sales for One Quarter
intRoyaltyRate = 0.1                        '1% Royalty Rate
intPrice = 40                               'Book Price
intRoyaltyReceived = intSales * intRoyaltyRate * intPrice
%>
```

All looks very plausible until you realize the mistake. The author is only meant to be getting 1% royalties, not 10%. The correct line should read:

```
intRoyaltyRate = 0.01                       '1% Royalty Rate
```

If you calculate the difference between the two totals, you'll find that the first is 40,000 dollars, while the corrected one is 4,000 dollars. This simple accounting mistake could be costing the publisher 36,000 dollars, if the author forgets to mention it.

Of course there are plenty of other types of logical errors, but hopefully these examples have given you an idea of the kind of thing you should be looking out for when you're checking and testing your code.

ASP Errors

Sometimes the operating system itself goes down. If you've used Windows 98/NT you'll be familiar with the "blue screen of death", where Windows itself generates an error and usually has to shut down. Sometimes these errors are caused by the user or programmer, and sometimes by bugs in the operating system. We explained in an earlier chapter that ASP was a DLL (Dynamic Link Library), and DLLs aren't immune to failure. If the ASP DLL fails it returns with an error code. Here's a list of them.

ASP Error Code	Error Message	Extra Information where applicable
0100	Out of Memory	
0101	Unexpected Error	
0102	Expected string name	
0103	Expecting numeric input	
0104	Operation not allowed	
0105	Index out of range	
0106	Type Mismatch	
0107	Stack Overflow	
0115	Unexpected Error	Trappable error occurred in external object. Script has to stop running.
0177	`Server.CreateObject` Failed	
0190	Unexpected Error	Trappable error occurred in external object.
0191	Unexpected Error	Trappable error occurred in `OnEndPage` method of external object
0192	Unexpected Error	Trappable error occurred in `OnStartPage` method of external object
0193	`OnStartPage` Failed	Error occurred in `OnStartPage` method of external object
0194	`OnEndPage` Failed	Error occurred in `OnEndPage` method of external object
0240	Script Engine Exception	
0241	`CreateObject` Exception	
0242	Query `OnStartPage` Interface Exception	

These errors are displayed on the user's own browser, as they are sent back in lieu of the expected page content. They can be recognized as ASP errors since 'ASP' always prefixes the error code, for example ASP 0100. Typically, ASP errors arise when there is a problem either with your web server or an external component. A failure to install a component correctly, or a problem with the component code, is a very common cause behind ASP errors. You should definitely suspect a problem of this nature if you experience either ASP 0115 or ASP 0177 errors. As for preventing them – well if it's somebody else's code that is broken then, unfortunately, there's not much you can do about them.

Good Coding Practice

So, you've spotted your error. Now what are you going to do about it? The first advice we're going to offer is almost blindingly obvious. Don't write code with errors in it in the first place! This may seem easier said than done, but if you stick to some well-worn practices, that programmers from Roman times onwards have used, then you can vastly reduce the chances of introducing errors into your page.

These techniques are, without exception, simple to understand, easy to execute and yet a lot of programmers don't use them! "Why not?" you might be wondering. Well, because your average programmer is a busy person, who doesn't like anything that distracts from the actual task of programming. The main objections are usually that a) these techniques are time-consuming, b) they require some degree of forward planning and organization and c) that they don't guarantee that your code will be error free. Programmers might not couch their objections in these terms, but that's what it boils down to. And remember, nothing can guarantee that your code will be error free and, as doctors maintain, prevention is better than cure...

Indent Your Code

While not necessary to ensure that your code works correctly, you can make your life so much easier by formatting and indenting your code as you write it. So for each loop structure or conditional structure, common convention is to indent the code with a tab or several spaces. So an example snippet of code might look like this:

```
If strText = "right" Then
  strNum = 7
  If strText2 = "right" Then
    StrNum2 = 8
  Else
    StrNum2 = 0
  End If
End If
```

In this case it makes it easier to see to which bit of code each End If refers. If an End If had been omitted, it would be much easier to spot with the code indented in this manner. When debugging, you would only need to glance at the code to spot, for example, code at the end of the structure that was still indented by several characters. You would know immediately that something had been left out.

Of course the flip side to this is that the excessive indentation can make your code more difficult to read. One line might start outside of your viewing area to the left and another line might finish outside it to the right. In other words, you can't read the ASP script all at once and find yourself constantly scrolling back and forth. To counteract this you always reduce the amount you indent code, to two or three characters per indent.

Comment Your Code

This one is very simple. If you write code, then you can't expect anyone else to understand it (even yourself a few weeks on) unless you comment it thoroughly. Use the single quotation mark to add a comment. Sensible places for comments are after variable or procedure declarations, to explain what each part does::

```
Dim strTextBox              'Text Box containing users name stored here
```

Comments are also useful after loops, to indicate what is being repeated, or after Else and End If to indicate what decision is being taken by that branch of the code:

```
If varQuestion = "Fax" Then  'If user selects fax then initiate fax confirmation
...code...
ElseIf varQuestion = "Email" 'If user selects email then initiate email confirmation
...more code...
Else                         'Don't send user confirmation
...yet more code...
End If                       'End of confirmation decision tree
```

Use Option Explicit

Back in Chapter 4 we mentioned this, and it really is worth using – especially if your typing is as bad as mine! If you remember, it just forces you to declare all of your variables before you use them, and it will force an error to be generated if you use a variable that hasn't been declared.

It's simple to use. For server-side script, just put the following line at the beginning of your ASP file, following the language and buffer tags:

```
<% Option Explicit %>
```

For client-side script you can add it at the beginning of the script:

```
<SCRIPT LANGUAGE=VBScript>
  Option Explicit
  . . .
</SCRIPT>
```

That's all there is to it, and it saves a lot of time hunting for those little typing mistakes. One thing to remember is that once you've completed your debugging and removed all of the typos, then you can remove Option Explicit; otherwise it may slow down your server.

Use Subprocedures

We introduced procedures in Chapter 5 and have already applied them to several of our examples. What you may not have realized is how useful they can be in optimizing your code. As you start writing more and more ASP code you'll find that you're using lots of similar routines in many of your pages, and possibly even several times in the same page. Instead of repeating this code you can put it into a sub procedure and then just call this procedure:

```
<%
  ' get the Form details

  Call ProcessFormDetails (strName, strEmail)

  ' some processing

  Call ProcessFormDetails(strName, strEmail)


Sub ProcessFormDetails (strN, strE)
  ' do some processing here
End Sub

%>
```

Now the processing of the form details is only done in one place, and if anything is wrong you only need to look for errors in one place. You can combine this with the trace statements too:

```
Sub ProcessFormDetails (strN, strE)
  Response.Write "Debug: ProcessFormDetails Started<BR>"

  ' do some processing here

  Response.Write "Debug: ProcessFormDetails Ended<BR>"
End Sub
```

This allows you to see when a sub procedure started and ended. You could even take this one step further and create some debugging and tracing routines:

```
Sub Trace (strString)

  Response.Write "Debug: " & strString & "<BR>"

End Sub
```

Your procedure to process the form details would now look like this:

```
Sub ProcessFormDetails (strN, strE)
  Trace "ProcessFormDetails Started"
```

```
    ' do some processing here

    Trace "ProcessFormDetails Ended"
End Sub
```

This makes it even easier to see what's going on.

Use Include Files

Using include files is just one step up from using procedures, as it allows you to make your procedures available to many ASP files. You'll see a really good example of this in the database chapters, where we have an include file that automatically creates an HTML table from data in a database. This file can be included in any ASP script and is run with only one command.

The one thing you have to watch out for, when using include files, is the possibility of changes affecting more than one ASP script. If you have taken out a set of routines and put them into an include file, and then made them available to other ASP developers in your organization, you must be careful not to suddenly change the functionality of those procedures. This could wreak havoc amongst other programs, so be careful when using this method in a shared development environment. To help safeguard against this, make sure you place comments in your include files that describe its purpose and intended output.

Convert Your Variants into the Requisite Subtypes

Earlier we talked about logical errors, one form of which is the type mismatch error. One way of avoiding type mismatches is to convert the value you're expecting from the user into the subtype needed for any calculations or manipulation *before* you perform any operations on the data. If you can't do this, then it's a fair guess that you're going to hit errors in your program. The VBScript conversion functions provide the ideal tools for performing conversions:

DataType to Convert to	Function
Boolean	CBool
Byte	CByte
Currency	CCur
Date	CDate
Double	CDbl
Integer	CInt
Long	CLng
Single	CSng
String	CStr

So, for example, to convert your user value to an integer you could do the following:

```
IntMyinteger = CInt(varUservalue)
```

The other functions are all used in the same way. Of course if you wish to convert a value, it's an idea to test the type of data you are converting; if the conversion is not possible then you will still end up generating an error. VBScript also presents some type check functions to help:

Function	Purpose of Check
IsArray	Checks to see if the expression is an array
IsDate	Checks to see if the expression is a date
IsEmpty	Checks to see if the variable has been initialized
IsNull	Checks to see if the variable contains valid data or a NULL (unknown) value
IsNumeric	Checks to see if the expression is a number
IsObject	Checks to see if the expression is an object

So, if you're expecting a variant containing data of a certain type, it might be a good idea to check for the type before converting. In our previous line of code, it would be wise to check and see whether the data contained is actually numeric, before trying to convert our data to integer format:

```
If IsNumeric(varUserValue) Then
    IntMyinteger = CInt(varUservalue)
  Else
    Response.Write "A number is required"
End If
```

Use a Variable Naming Convention (Consistently!)

In Chapter 4 we discussed the many benefits of using a good naming convention to help us keep track of which variables contain which subtype of data, especially when we have lots of variables in a program. We recommended a specific naming convention (go back and check it in Chapter 4, if you can't remember it). In this manner, you can tell at a glance whether you're using an integer, a string or date and can manipulate it in a consistent way. Our suggested convention was to use the first three letters of a variable's name to distinguish the subtype. The fourth letter of the variable was then typed in upper case, to indicate that this is where the actual variable name starts. For example:

```
blnBoolean      'where bln denotes Boolean in our convention, and Boolean is the
                'variable name
intInteger      'int denotes an integer in our convention, and Integer is the
                'variable name
```

One problem is that naming conventions are used inconsistently. Programmers often start out defining and naming all of their variables correctly – it is when a piece of a code has to be changed or updated that things often go awry. For example, a temporary variable (called something like test) is introduced and then, the next thing you know, that variable is being used to pass data as well. You might find variables that 'break' our suggested naming convention in this book – it's not deliberate, but this tip requires a lot of attention from the programmer and it is easy to miss something.

Try to Break your Code

When you test your code (you DO test it, don't you?) one thing to do is to supply your programs with rogue values (massive numbers, or letters instead of numbers and such like) to see how your program reacts. You may not have intended your program to be abused in such a way but, when it's out in the real world, these are exactly the type of values that may get put in to your program. If your program breaks under this sort of stress, then you'll have many perplexed and unhappy users.

A good strategy for doing this is to break down all the possible values into three types:

❑ **Expected values** – these are values in the range that you ask for. If you asked for numbers between 1 and 10, these would be 2 through to 9.

❑ **Boundary Condition values** – these are the values that lie at the boundaries of our range. If you asked for numbers between 1 and 10, then did you actually mean to include these values or not? Does your program deal with them correctly?

❑ **Out-of-Bounds values** – these are the values that fall anywhere outside the range. In our example, -5, 0 and 999 would all be out of bounds values. But, it doesn't stop there; this could equally apply to values of an unexpected type, such as a letter or date. For instance were you expecting one of these values: 0, -1, 0.9, -1E5, 10.1, 5.5, "dog", #5/9/58#, "true", "false", (empty), 4+4, 5/0, 9.9, 9.99, 9.999, 003, "three"? Will your program cope with all of these types?

Testing your code with the kind of values you'd expect your user to supply is an absolute must. If you ask a user to supply a number between 1 and 10, you must test your program using *each* and *every* number between one and ten. And while, realistically, you couldn't test every possible out of bounds value that could be input, you do need to hypothesize a large possible range of values and different types. If your program doesn't break when the user inputs 11, that's all very well and good, but does it still work when the user enters "three", which would be a perfectly "correct" answer to the question in some user's minds?

Creating Error Traps

In my Computer Science class it was a ritual routine that once we'd finished a large program, we'd pass it around other members of the class to see if they could break it. If someone did manage to break it they'd display the bug with great merriment to the rest of the class (OK, we were spotty teenagers then). On a more serious note, this is pretty much how everybody tests code. Microsoft, for instance has a team of people coding applications by day and then another team testing that same code at night.

In our case though, unlike Microsoft, a few simple lines of easily modifiable code usually made our little applications relatively weatherproof. Let's look at a trivial program that takes a number between 1 and 5 from the user and multiplies it by ten. The purpose of this exercise isn't the calculation, but actually ensuring we get what we want from the user.

Try It Out – Expecting the Unexpected

1. Open your trusty web page editor and type in the following:

```
<HTML>
<HEAD>
<TITLE>Userproof Page</TITLE>
</HEAD>
<BODY>
<FORM NAME="Form1" ACTION="check.asp" METHOD="POST">
Please enter a whole number from one to five (1-5)<BR>
<INPUT TYPE=TEXT NAME=TextBox1>
<BR>
<BR>
<INPUT TYPE=SUBMIT>
</FORM>
</BODY>
</HTML>
```

2. Save it as enter.asp, in the usual folder. Close it and then type in the following code:

```
<HTML>
<HEAD>
<TITLE>Check Page</TITLE>
</HEAD>
<BODY>
<% varTest = Request.Form("TextBox1")
  If IsNumeric(varTest) = False Then
    Response.Write "No Letters<BR>"
    Server.Transfer "enter.asp"
  End If
  If varTest<1 Then
    Response.Write "Too Small<BR>"
    Server.Transfer "enter.asp"
  End If
  If varTest>5 Then
    Response.Write "Too Large<BR>"
    Server.Transfer "enter.asp"
  End If
  If CDbl(varTest) <> CInt(VarTest)then
    Response.Write "No decimals<BR>"
    Server.Transfer "enter.asp"
  End If
  varTest = varTest * 10
  Response.Write "<BR>Your lucky number is " & varTest
%>
</BODY>
</HTML>
```

3. Save this as check.asp and close your editor.

4. Open up your browser and run enter.asp.

5. Enter a letter and submit it:

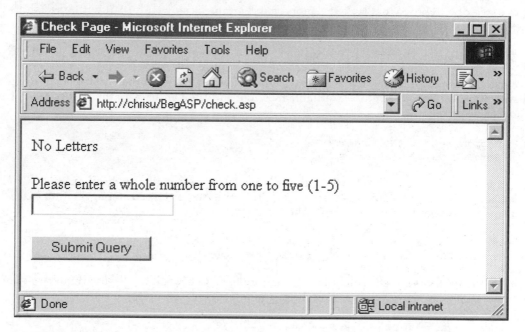

6. Try various other erroneous values. You will find that the only way you can get to this screen is by entering the numbers 1,2 3,4 or 5. For example we've entered 3:

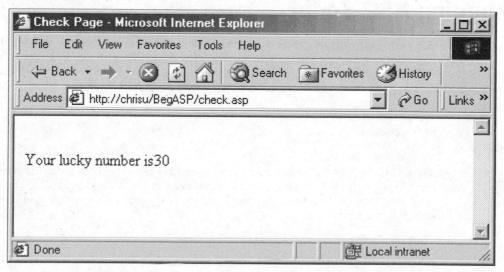

How It Works

We read the textbox on the form into a variable.

```
<% varTest = Request.Form("TextBox1")
```

As yet we don't know what type the subtype of variable is so we prefix it with var (short for variant). First, we test to see if a letter has been input:

```
If IsNumeric(varTest) = False Then
```

We use the VBScript function IsNumeric, which returns False if the variant is anything other than a number. Then we return a suitable message and transfer back to the first page and await another response:

```
Response.Write "No Letters<BR>"
Server.Transfer "enter.asp"
```

Then, in turn, we check to see if the variant is too large, too small or a decimal. If it fails any of these tests, we output a suitable message and return to the enter.asp page. Otherwise we multiply the variant by 10 and output the result:

```
varTest = varTest * 10
Response.Write "<BR>Your lucky number is " & varTest
```

The idea is that this code is reusable, as you only have to change the first variable assignation to whichever part of your form needs testing, and alter the values in the tests:

```
varTest = Request.Form("TextBox1")
```

Debugging ASP Script

Now you've done your best to waterproof your code, but errors always manage to seep through. So how do you go about removing the little blighters? One difficulty you might encounter when debugging is finding out exactly where the error is occurring. Remember the first ASP error we showed you? We tried to access the Document object from within ASP:

```
Microsoft VBScript runtime error '800a01a8'
Object required: 'Document'
/BegAsp/Debug.asp, line 5
```

That's pretty easy to follow, but we've already mentioned that not all errors generate messages. Even if your error does generate a message, it is not always the line that is at fault that generates the error message (as in a type mismatch error). Let's look at some tips you can use to make your errors easier to find.

Use Response.Write

This is one of the oldest methods of debugging, and involves putting in lots of trace statements that indicate where you are in a particular script. If you remember, `Response.Write` writes a line of text into the output stream, so this will be seen as text when the page is viewed. For example, consider the following ASP script that expects some details from a Form on the previous ASP page.

```
<%
  Dim strName
  Dim strEmail

  strName = Request.Form("Name")
  strEmail = Request.Form("Email")

  ' do some complex processing with the form details

  ' do more processing
%>
```

Let's suppose an error occurs in the 'complex processing', and you have little idea what it is doing. Changing the script can help track down the problem:

```
<%
  Dim strName
  Dim strEmail

  strName = Request.Form("Name")
  strEmail = Request.Form("Email")

  Response.Write "Debug: Name=" & strName & "<BR>"
  Response.Write "Debug: Email=" & strEmail & "<BR>"
  Response.Write "Debug: Now entering complex processing<BR>"

  ' do some complex processing with the form details

  Response.Write "Debug: Complex processing finished<BR>"

  ' do more processing

  Response.Write "<HR>More processing finished<BR>"
%>
```

Now when you run this script you'll see the name and email address displayed before the processing starts, and this can tell you whether or not they are correct. If the last message does not appear, then you know that the error occurred before it got to this line.

Although a very simple idea it's extremely valuable, and is a technique I still use to debug complex ASP pages.

> You can use another method of the `Response` object, namely `End` to stop execution before hitting a trouble spot. You can then walk that `Response.End` down through the code.

Conditional Tracing

Conditional tracing can be quite useful during the development of an ASP application, especially if it is quite large. The process of tracing is the process of running a program and returning information at each separate step of the program. This simply involves having a variable that tells you whether or not tracing is in action. So our tracing routine could look like this:

```
Sub Trace (strString)

  If blnTracing Then
    Response.Write "Debug: " & strString & "<BR>"
  End If

End Sub
```

You can now scatter `Trace` statements amongst your code, and you can simply turn tracing on or off by setting `blnTracing` to `True` or `False`.

You might think that these techniques are a bit cumbersome, but let's have a look at combining some of them into a set of tracing routines that can be included into any ASP script.

Try It Out – Doing a Trace

1. Open up your ASP editor and add the following code. This will be our HTML form.

```
<HTML>
<HEAD>
<TITLE>Tracing Form</TITLE>
</HEAD>
Enter your name and email address here:

<FORM NAME=Tracing ACTION="DoTracing.asp" METHOD="POST">
Name: <INPUT TYPE=TEXT NAME="Name"><BR>
Email: <INPUT TYPE=TEXT NAME="Email"><BR>
<INPUT TYPE=SUBMIT VALUE="Process">
<INPUT TYPE=RESET VALUE="Clear">
</FORM>

</HTML>
```

2. Save this file as `Tracing.html`, close it and create a new one. This will be the ASP file into which we have put the tracing statements.

3. Add the following code to this new file.

```
<% Option Explicit %>
<HTML>
<!-- #INCLUDE FILE="Trace.asp" -->
<HEAD>
```

```
<TITLE>Tracing Example</TITLE>
</HEAD>
<BODY>

Tracing is on for this bit<BR>
<%
  Dim strName
  Dim strEmail

  TraceStart

  Trace "Getting form details"

  strName = Request.Form("Name")
  strEmail = Request.Form("Email")

  ProcessFormDetails strName, strEmail

  TraceStop

  ProcessFormDetails strName, strEmail

Sub ProcessFormDetails (strName, strEmail)

  TraceProcedureStart "ProcessFormDetails"

  ' some form of processing goes here
  Response.Write "We are doing some processing here<BR>"

  Trace "Name=" & strName
  Trace "Email=" & strEmail

  TraceProcedureEnd "ProcessFormDetails"

End Sub
%>

</BODY>
</HTML>
```

4. Save this file as `DoTracing.asp`, and create a new one. This will be our include file.

An include file is a way to include the contents of one file within another. Thus we can define a routine or connection string etc. in one place and use it from other files. They will be discussed in more detail in Chapter 10.

Add the following code:

```
<%

Dim blnTracing

Sub TraceStart()

  blnTracing = True
  Trace "Tracing started"

End Sub

Sub TraceStop()

  Trace "Tracing stopped"
  blnTracing = False

End Sub

Sub Trace (strString)

  If blnTracing Then
    Response.Write "Debug: " & strString & "<BR>"
  End If

End Sub

Sub TraceProcedureStart (strProcedure)

  Trace strProcedure & " started"

End Sub

Sub TraceProcedureEnd (strProcedure)

  Trace strProcedure & " ended"

End Sub
%>
```

5. Save this file as `Trace.asp`, and close down your ASP editor.

6. Open the first file, `Tracing.html`, in your browser:

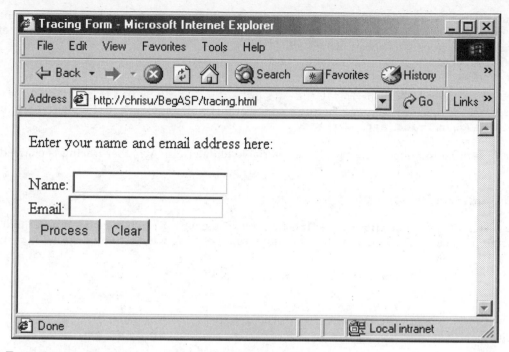

7. Enter some details and press the Process button.

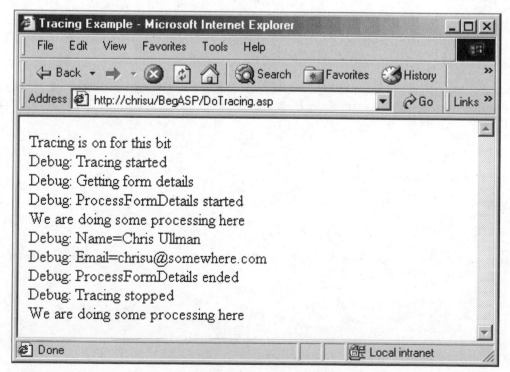

You can see that all of our trace lines start with Debug. You can also see that the processing procedure that outputs We are doing some processing here is run twice, but that the second time it is run tracing has been turned off.

How it Works

We don't need to look at the HTML file – it's just a standard file with a form on it, whose purpose is to call the ASP page. Before we look at this ASP page, let's first look at the actual tracing code in Trace.asp

The first thing to notice is that we have a variable to determine whether tracing is enabled or not.

```
Dim blnTracing
```

We then have two procedures to set this flag. We also have a trace message telling us that tracing has been turned on and off – this stops you worrying whether you have set it or not.

```
Sub TraceStart()

  blnTracing = True
  Trace "Tracing started"

End Sub

Sub TraceStop()

  Trace "Tracing stopped"
  blnTracing = False

End Sub
```

We then have the actual trace procedure. This accepts a single string as an argument, and it writes this to the output stream if the trace flag is True. This way you can still call the Trace statement even if tracing is disabled:

```
Sub Trace (strString)

  If blnTracing Then
    Response.Write "Debug: " & strString & "<BR>"
  End If

End Sub
```

Lastly we have two procedures that can be called at the start and end of procedures, just so you can see when procedures are called.

```
Sub TraceProcedureStart (strProcedure)

  Trace strProcedure & " started"

End Sub
```

```
Sub TraceProcedureEnd (strProcedure)

  Trace strProcedure & " ended"

End Sub
```

This gives you five procedures:

- ❑ `TraceStart` to turn on tracing.
- ❑ `TraceEnd` to turn off tracing.
- ❑ `TraceProcedureStart` to indicate the start of a procedure. The argument should be the procedure name.
- ❑ `TraceProcedureEnd` to indicate the end of a procedure. The argument should be the procedure name.
- ❑ `Trace` to indicate a trace message. The argument should be the string to be displayed.

Let's now see how they were used in the ASP script in `DoTracing.asp`. After declaring the script variables, the first thing to do is turn on tracing:

```
<%
  Dim strName
  Dim strEmail

  TraceStart
```

Now tracing is enabled, we write a message indicating that we are about to get the form details:

```
Trace "Getting form details"

strName = Request.Form("Name")
strEmail = Request.Form("Email")
```

Once we have the form details in variables we pass them to our processing routine:

```
ProcessFormDetails strName, strEmail
```

We then turn off tracing, and call our processing routine again:

```
TraceStop

ProcessFormDetails strName, strEmail
```

Now let's consider the actual processing routine. It doesn't actually do any processing in this case, but simply displays a string. The first thing we do is to trace the start of the procedure:

```
Sub ProcessFormDetails (strName, strEmail)

  TraceProcedureStart "ProcessFormDetails"
```

We then display our processing string, and display the name and email address using the `Trace` statement:

```
' some form of processing goes here
Response.Write "We are doing some processing here<BR>"

Trace "Name=" & strName
Trace "Email=" & strEmail
```

Lastly, we display the end of the procedure:

```
TraceProcedureEnd "ProcessFormDetails"

End Sub
%>
```

So all we have done is used a few simple routines to see exactly where in the ASP code we are. You can see that we can include tracing in routines, and then turn off tracing without worrying about it, because the tracing routine detects whether tracing is in action or not. In other words, you can turn on tracing to see what's happening and then turn it off with a single statement, without having to remove the tracing code.

So you can see that we have achieved our objectives here:

❑   We have reusable subroutines.

❑   We have those reusable routines in an include file, which can be used in other ASP scripts.

❑   We have conditional tracing so it can be turned on and off at will.

Although this include file won't stop you getting errors, it will allow you to start debugging them quicker. In large ASP projects you might like to include this file in all of your ASP scripts and place tracing statements throughout your code. Should you encounter problems you can simply turn tracing on. Once the ASP page is ready for the real world you can strip the tracing statements out so that execution isn't slowed down at all.

The Microsoft Script Debugger

There is also a ready-made tool that you can use to help you debug, namely the Microsoft Script Debugger. Why didn't you tell us about it earlier, I hear some of you cry exasperatedly? That's because you can still use the techniques I've just mentioned along with the Debugger. The Microsoft Script Debugger is a separate application to IIS 5.0 and comes with Windows 2000. We looked at its installation in Chapter 1. This debugger seems quite basic at first, but don't be fooled – it is actually quite powerful. Before you can debug ASP script code you need to mark your virtual directory as an **application** and enable the server-side debugging option within IIS.

Enabling Debugging in IIS

An application is a virtual directory, with a few more features. As well as allowing debugging, it also allows ASP to know the whereabouts of your Global.asa file. You can tell whether a virtual directory is an application or not by looking at the icon in the Management Console (to start this up, from the Start menu, select Run; in the resulting dialog, type MMC and press OK). Normal virtual directories, such as Scripts and Printers, are shown as a folder with a tiny blue world, whereas applications, such as IISSamples and Webpub, are shown as a little open box.

*In Chapter 1 we took our physical directory, BegASPFiles, and used the Virtual Directory Creation Wizard to create a virtual directory, BegASP. Our virtual directory appeared as a little open box. This is because the wizard automatically creates an application for us. To turn a normal folder into an application, without the wizard, right-click on the folder and select **Properties**; then on the **Directory** tab, click the **Create** button to turn the folder into an ASP application:*

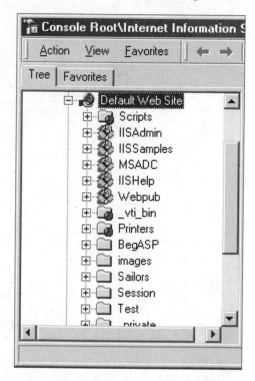

When you create an application it allows you to enter a name in the Name box, but more importantly, from the Properties Dialog in the Management Console, you can click on the Configuration button to access the application details, and then click on the App Debugging tab:

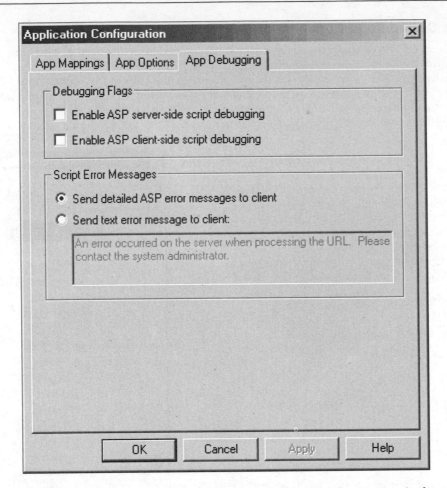

The **Debugging Flags** section is the one we are interested in. The first option is the most important as checking this allows the Script Debugger to be used for ASP script code. Make sure this is checked before you continue with the next example. We're not examining client-side debugging, so it doesn't matter whether this is checked or cleared.

Some important things to note are that when you have enabled script debugging for an application, error messages are not returned to the client as part of the page, but raised on the server where the debugger can intercept them. You should therefore only use the script debugger when you can work on the server itself, and remember you can only debug the server-side code. Also, having debugging enabled slows down the server so once you have finished debugging you should disable this option.

Using the Script Debugger

Before we start debugging, let's look at the various windows in the script debugger:

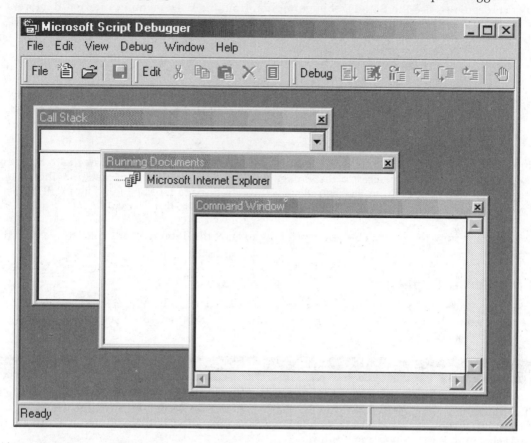

The **Call Stack** window displays a list of active procedure calls. The combo box at the top of this window displays the current threads, and is generally only used if you are debugging Java applets.

The **Running Documents** window displays a list of applications, along with their documents, that are hosting scripting (non-hosting scripting documents are not included).

The **Command Window** allows you to inspect and modify variables during the execution of the script code.

Starting the Debugger

So you've set the application up for debugging, and we've shown you what the debugger windows look like. Now, how do you actually start the debugger? The debugger is actually located on the server-side, but can be run in one of four ways:

❑ The first is the most obvious, by selecting it from the **Programs** menu under **Accessories**.

❑ You can also use the **Script Debugger** option from the **View** menu in Internet Explorer (if you have MS Visual InterDev 6.0 installed, this command will start it).

❑ You can force the debugger to start by placing a `Stop` statement (or `debugger` in JScript) in your script code. Note that this statement will have no effect if debugging isn't enabled.

❑ Lastly, you can respond to an error. Remember the ASP error shown earlier, where a dialog popped up and asked us whether we wanted to debug the current page? Selecting **Yes** will start the debugger.

It's important to remember that to debug server-side ASP script the debugger needs to be open on the web server. So if you access an ASP page with an error from a client machine, then the debugger dialog will appear on the web server. Your client page will be blank, and will suspend operation until the error dialog is cleared or the page reaches its timeout value.

Now you know how to set up debugging and how to start the debugger, it's time to see how it works.

Using the Script Debugger

The best way to learn how to debug scripts is to actually try it, so we'll jump straight in now. What we're going to do is create a script with some errors and then you'll see exactly how this works.

Try It Out – Debugging Scripts

During this Try It Out, don't worry if your browser displays a Timeout error message, stating it can't contact the server. It's lying. It can and has contacted the server, but we'll be using breakpoints, so the script may not complete before the time allocated for a timeout expires. You can just close the error dialog and continue.

1. Create a new asp file, calling it `Debug.asp`.

2. Add the following code. Note – copy this code exactly. There are deliberate errors in it, so don't correct them as you type it in.

```
<HTML>
<HEAD>
<TITLE>ASP Debugging with the Script Debugger</TITLE>
</HEAD>
<BODY>

<%
  strVar = Request.ServerVariables("HTTP_USER_AGEN") & "<P>"
  Response.Write "HTTP_USER_AGENT=" & strVsr
```

```
    ShowVariables

Sub ShowVariables

  For Each strVar In Request.ServerVariables
    Response.Write strVae & "<BR>"
  Next

End Sub
%>
</BODY>
</HTML>
```

3.   Run the file from your browser, and you should see this:

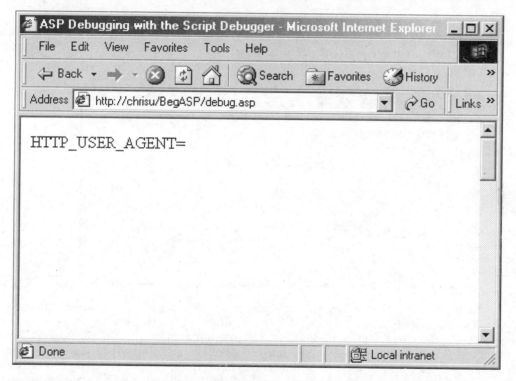

Now it doesn't work, but then you knew that already. So where are the errors, and how do you find them using the Script Debugger?

4.   Start the script debugger (on the server, if this is separate from the machine you're creating pages on), and from the **View** menu select **Running Documents**:

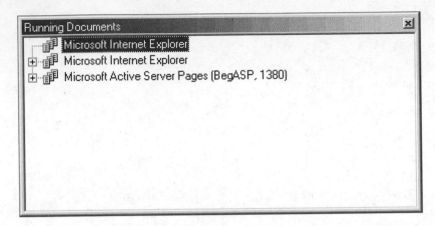

5. Expand both the Microsoft Internet Explorer and the Microsoft Active Server Pages levels, by clicking on the small plus signs. You might have to keep expanding these items if there are more under the ASP branch:

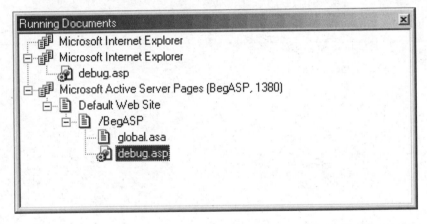

This shows that the script debugger is now attached to both IE and IIS, and it shows the current documents. Two copies of Debug.asp are shown, highlighting the two places where scripting can take place – at the client, shown under **Microsoft Internet Explorer**, and at the Server, shown under **Microsoft Active Server Pages**. It also shows a global.asa file, which was used in a previous example and previous chapter and has no bearing in this example. If you can see any other .asps, then this is because the sessions involved on these pages haven't timed out yet.

6. We are interested in ASP script so double click on the Debug.asp under **Microsoft Active Server Pages**. This will open the ASP page:

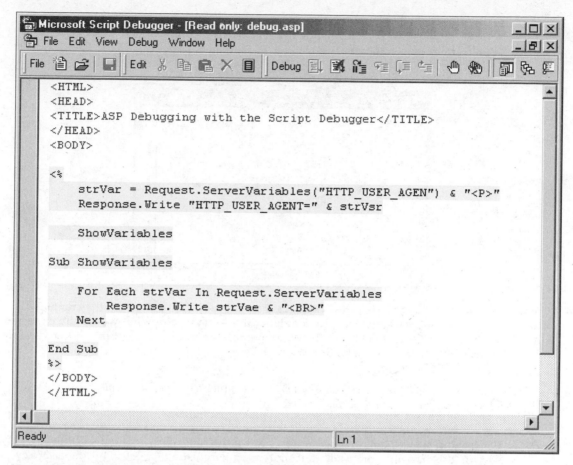

Notice that the title states that this is read only. This is because the Script Debugger only allows us to follow the script through and not actively change it. We can change variable contents though, as you'll see soon.

7. Place the cursor on the first `Response.Write` line and press *F9* to toggle a break point. Notice that the line is highlighted in red, with a large dot to show a breakpoint.

8. Switch back to your browser and press the **Refresh** button. You are either automatically switched into the Script Debugger, with the current highlighted line the one on which there is a breakpoint, or the corresponding application on your task bar will flash, and you will be switched to debugger when you click on it.

9. From your first run of this script you noticed that nothing was printed for `strVar`, but why? Well, you've probably spotted that the second time we use the variable we've spelt it incorrectly, putting `strVsr` instead of `strVar`. Because the script debugger only gives us read only access to the script we can't change the variable name, but we can check that `strVar` is correct.

10. From the View menu select Command Window.

11. Type ?strVar, pressing the enter key after you have typed this in:

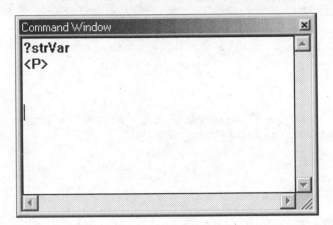

The question mark is how we tell the debugger that we want to print out (in the command window) the value of a variable. Now look at what the value is. Not what was really expected, but that's because we've also made another spelling mistake in the name of the server variable we wanted to look at – there's a T missing from the end.

> *You don't need to use the question mark to print out values when you are debugging Jscript – you can just type the variable name.*

12. Once again we can't modify the script, but we can modify the contents of the variable, so type this in – note there's no question mark here. Don't forget to hit the *Enter* key after you've typed it in:

```
strVar = Request.ServerVariables("HTTP_USER_AGENT")
```

This assigns strVar to the value of the server variable, using exactly the same syntax as if you were typing the script in. In fact, you type using the syntax of the current script language – in our case this is VBScript. Now examine strVar again:

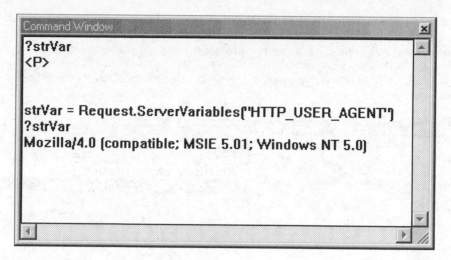

That's better – much more like we expected. You can also update strVsr, just so that the variable is returned to the browser, by typing:

```
strVsr = strVar
```

13. Now you've updated this variable, click back into the main script window and press F8 to step onto the next line.

14. Move the cursor to the second Response.Write line and press *F9* to set another breakpoint. Now press *F5* – this continues executing script until it finds another breakpoint, or it finishes the script.

15. As the script has stopped at the second breakpoint we are now in a function, so it's a good time to look at the call stack. From the View menu select Call Stack.

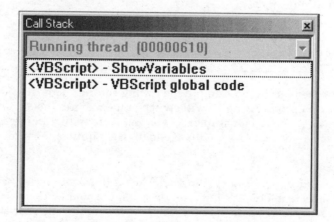

This shows where we are in the code, with the most recent procedure at the top. You can see we started in a set of global code, with no procedure, and then moved into the `ShowVariables` procedure. You can double-click on an item to get the main script window to show you exactly where you are in the code. For example, if `ShowVariables` was called several times, but you'd lost track of which time it was, you could double-click on the **VBScript global code** line to show which call it was:

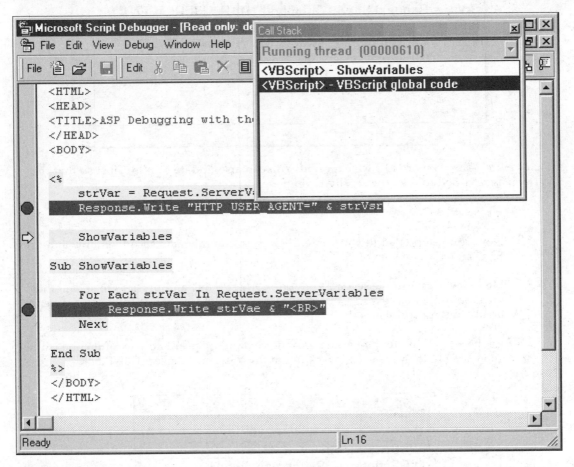

Notice the arrow in the margin, pointing to the calling routine. This doesn't change the currently executing line, so pressing *F8* will switch you back into the `ShowVariables` routine and continue executing, one line at a time. As you're in a loop that iterates through the whole of the `Server Variables` collection, you'll have to hit **Next** quite a few times to get to the end of it!

16. You'll also notice there is a spelling mistake on this `Response.Write` line, but because this is in a loop, it's not really practical to change this every time. At this stage you are best served by either continuing, even with the error, or stopping the script by selecting **Stop Debugging** from the **Debug** menu. These sort of spelling errors are much more easily caught by using `Option Explicit` to force all variable names to be declared, and any variable not declared generates a run-time error.

That's really all there is to using the Script Debugger. You can see that it's quite a simple tool, but very effective, allowing you almost everything you could expect from a more high-powered tool. If you make syntax errors in your script code, then the Script Debugger will be launched automatically, showing you the line with the problem.

Client-side versus Server-side Debugging

There's really no difference between client and server-side debugging. If you remember, in the Running Documents window, you have a chance to decide where you want your debugging to occur.

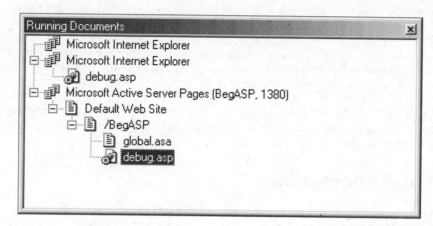

Remember that we double-clicked on the bottom instance of Debug.asp to open the main window, and then set break points in this window. But what happens if you do the same with the first instance of Debug.asp? Why not give it a try – you'll be rewarded with a window that might not make sense. Before you try you'll need to clear any breakpoints in the ASP script (*Ctrl-Shift-F9*) and then refresh your browser window.

```
<HTML>
<HEAD>
<TITLE>ASP Debugging with the Script Debugger</TITLE>
</HEAD>
<BODY>

HTTP_USER_AGENT=<BR><BR><BR><BR><BR><BR><BR><BR><BR>
</BODY>
</HTML>
```

This is the HTML page as returned by ASP. Remember when we are debugging the client-side, all of our ASP script has been executed, so all we see here is the HTML tags and any client-side script. Now this file doesn't have any client-side script, so it's not shown, but if it did have script you follow exactly the same methods as debugging server-side script.

The Server Object's Role in Debugging

One final aid is the ability to write your own custom-made ASP scripts to handle the occurrence of errors. The Server object provides some of the most used and, indeed, most useful properties and methods contained in any ASP page. However, unlike the rest of the objects in the ASP object model, it doesn't seem to have been designed for one specific purpose, but rather as a catch-all home for a miscellaneous and often unrelated set of properties and methods that run on the server. This shouldn't detract from the importance of these attributes of the Server object. Indeed, one method (CreateObject) is so important that we're taking a separate chapter out to talk about what you can do with it.

We're not going to discuss all of the properties and methods of the Server object here, but there is one method that has special relevance to debugging procedures and in the creation of custom made error pages.

The GetLastError Method

You can use this method to discover details about the last error that occurred. This method then returns an object in its own right, called ASPError. It is used like this:

```
Set objASPError = Server.GetLastError()
```

The objASPError variable now contains an ASPError object and you can query its different properties and methods. This is something new that has only been introduced with ASP 3.0, and we'll talk about it in more detail in a moment. But, what did developers use before this object?

The VBScript Err Object

Before ASP 3.0, the object that you could use to help debug programs in VBScript was the Err object. It is still present in ASP 3.0 and contains information about run-time errors, but it has only got five properties:

- ❑ Description is the descriptive text of the error
- ❑ Number is the error number
- ❑ Source identifies the object or application that originally generated the error
- ❑ HelpFile identifies the help file associated with the error
- ❑ HelpContext identifies the Context ID in the help file, for a particular error

And two methods:

❑ Raise, to raise an error of your own

❑ Clear, to clear the properties

And that's all there is to it. It isn't particularly detailed, but the advantage of it was that it's easy to use. You can suppress errors using the line On Error Resume Next, which tells the server to carry on reading the script, even if it comes across any more errors. This requires that you do your own error handling, and provide more detailed information, if you think it necessary.

This of course means a lot of extra work for ASP developers who have grown complacent from a lifetime of Visual Basic or Visual C++, and are used to all sorts of weird and wonderful tools for deconstructing and recompiling their code to get to the source of an error. So, you'll be glad to find out that ASP 3.0 finally adds the error-handling capability that developers have been crying out for, for a long time. It comes in the form of ASP's very own error object.

The VBScript Err object will still work, but a more comprehensive error object has been introduced with ASP 3.0 that works in a different way to the Err object.

The ASPError Object

To help debug your code, the ASPError object has a far more comprehensive set of properties than the humble VBScript Err object:

❑ ASPCode: Returns the ASP error code

❑ Number: Returns the COM error code

❑ Source: Returns the portion of code that caused the error

❑ Category: Returns whether the error was caused by the script, by the object or by ASP itself

❑ File: The name of the file in which the error occurred

❑ Line: The line number of the script on which the error occurred

❑ Column: The column position within the file where the error is located

❑ Description: A short description of the error

❑ ASPDescription: When ASP has raised the error, this returns a more detailed description of the error

In fact the ASPError object also does a lot of the dirty work for you. If you've generated an error in your scripts then you've probably already used it by now. You can use this tool more effectively if you understand what ASP is actually doing when an error is generated, so let's take a quick peek into this murky world and find out what actually goes on when you generate an error. Here's a very simple program with a very simple bug:

```
<%
  for intLoop = 1 to 5
  Response.Write intLoop
  Nxt                          'Error is on this line
%>
```

It's fairly obvious that we've missed out an 'e' in Next, but what does ASP do once it comes across the error? Of course, it displays a familiar **The Page Cannot be Displayed** message. However, if you scroll down to the foot of the screen, you'll find valuable extra information:

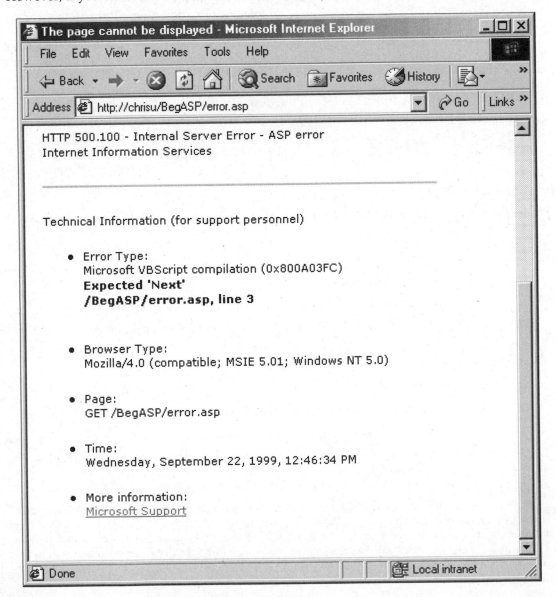

If you've used ASP 2.0 at all, then you'll know that you're now getting a lot more information than you used to. All this extra information is actually generated by the ASPError object. What happens when an error is generated? Well, ASP is told how to handle each type of error by the Custom Error dialog in IIS 5.0. For each type of error (denoted by the number of the error) that ASP encounters, you can use this dialog to instruct ASP to do one of three things. It can:

❑ Throw up the standard, unhelpful "There has been an error" message

❑ Redirect the user to a HTML file, which contains more details about that type of error

❑ Redirect the user to a URL, and then execute the ASP file (or whatever else is found there)

In the previous example, ASP actually performed the third of these options. You can check this for yourself, as follows. Start up the Internet Service Manager/MMC console and highlight the Default Web Site node in the left-hand box:

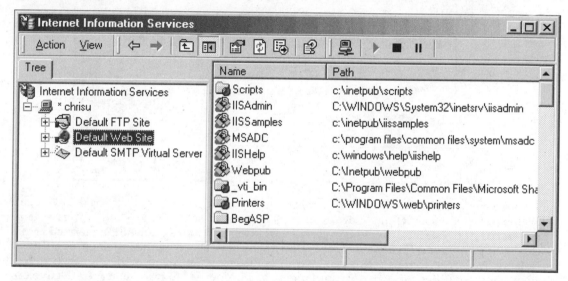

Go to the Action menu and select the Properties option then, when the dialog appears containing many tabs, select the Custom Error tab. From this dialog you can control what page ASP will display for each of the many possible different errors you may encounter. If you scroll down the dialog you'll see references to all the major errors, such as HTTP 404 (page not found) or HTTP 403 (access to the page is forbidden). If you check our previous example, you'll see that this was the type of error generated was HTTP 500.100. In general, any errors that are generated within the script on your page are going to fall under the header 500, which you will find is an Internal Server error (if you look it up in Appendix G)

An Internal Server error indicates that a program running on the server (not necessarily an ASP script, it could just as easily be CGI or another similar type of application) has encountered an error. The subdivision 100 is used to indicate, more specifically, that the ASP itself has generated an error. In which case the standard behavior set up in the Custom IIS error dialog is to transfer you to the URL indicated:

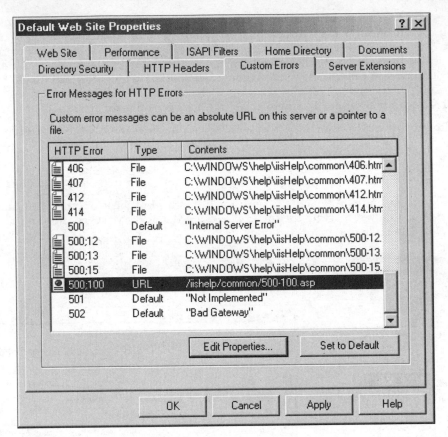

Of course, an Internal Server error isn't a particularly informative response for the average ASP developer. Usually, something more detailed is required. The page `500-100.asp` is a standard page stored in `C:\Windows\help\iishelp\common` and looks after ASP-generated errors. It deals with pretty much every eventuality that a script can throw up, using the properties available. However, there's nothing to stop you replacing these pages with your own web pages, which can then utilize the `Server.GetLastError` properties to provide more effective error notification.

Using Server.GetLastError

One upside/downside (depending on how you look at it!) is that you can't turn off error handling and use the `On Error Resume Next` statement to handle errors found in the `ASPError` object, as you could with VBScript `Err` object. Consider the following code:

```
<%
On Error Resume Next
Dim arrHello(3)
arrHello(5) = 6                          'this line has the error: index/array size
Set objASPError = Server.GetLastError()
Response.Write "<BR>VBScript Error: " & Err.Description
Response.Write "<BR>ASPError Object Error Number: " & objAspError.Number
%>
```

We've generated a quick error by trying to assign a value to an array outside its previously specified dimensions. The On Error Resume Next statement, as we mentioned earlier, would automatically tell ASP that, even if it did find any errors, it should just go on to the next line as though nothing untoward had happened. Under this scheme, you wouldn't generate an error by executing his code.

The idea was that you could then use the VBScript Err object to pick up any errors that had occurred. You could then return and deal with them separately, as indeed you *still can*. However, when you create an instance of the ASPError object, you have to go to the default page (500-100.asp or your own web page) to populate the ASPError object. If you use Server.GetLastError(), after On Error Resume Next, it won't pick up any errors and the ASPError object will be empty – just as if no error had occurred. So if we run our above program, this would be the result:

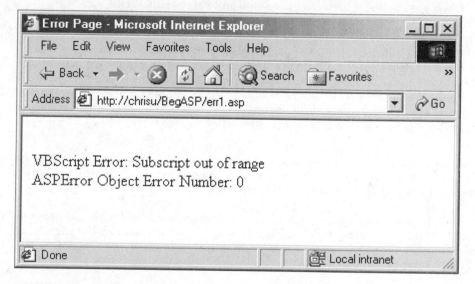

As you can see from the screenshot, we return the contents of the VBScript Err object's description method, which contains the message Subscript out of range, but the contents of the ASPError object's method is equal to zero, which is the code used to show that no error has occurred.

What is the long and short of this then? Well, if you want to create your own customized error handling web page you need to go to the Custom Error dialog and reroute it, with the methods described earlier, to your new URL (if its an ASP) or file (if its an HTML page). You can't just stick Server.GetLastError in your own page and expect it to pick up error information – you have to have been redirected to a page by the Custom Error dialog. Thus, if you do change error handling and redirect ASP to your own custom page, just remember that you are changing the error handling for *all* errors generated in ASP. So please take care!

Summary

You can clearly see that debugging and error handling in the world of ASP is not fraught with the problems that you might have thought. With a little careful planning and a simple set of rules to follow, it can be made even easier. Here are some of the simple rules that you should follow:

❑ Use `Option Explicit`. This saves huge amounts of time looking for typing mistakes. Remember to take it out of your scripts after the page has been successfully debugged otherwise it could degrade performance.

❑ Reuse code where possible, by use of sub routines and include files.

❑ Don't get confused between client-side and server-side script.

❑ Use sensible variable names. This helps prevent confusion as to what the variable is for.

❑ Comment your code. A lot of experienced programmers joke that if it was difficult to write, then it should be difficult to read. That's just an excuse for laziness. Try to provide code for others to read that you would like to read yourself. If you're worried about the slower processing of a commented page, then why not keep two versions: one version with comments for development and documentation and a second version without comments, for use in the production environment.

The script debugger provides a very useful tool, which can make locating and testing errors that much easier. Also, the addition of an `ASPError` object, in ASP 3.0, means that errors are reported in a more detailed and comprehensive way in ASP 3.0.

If you've done any programming before, you've probably realized that ASP programming is not that different from any other type of programming and that you need the same range of skills. You need to plan ahead and be prepared to think laterally when errors occur, as the problem isn't always where you think it is.

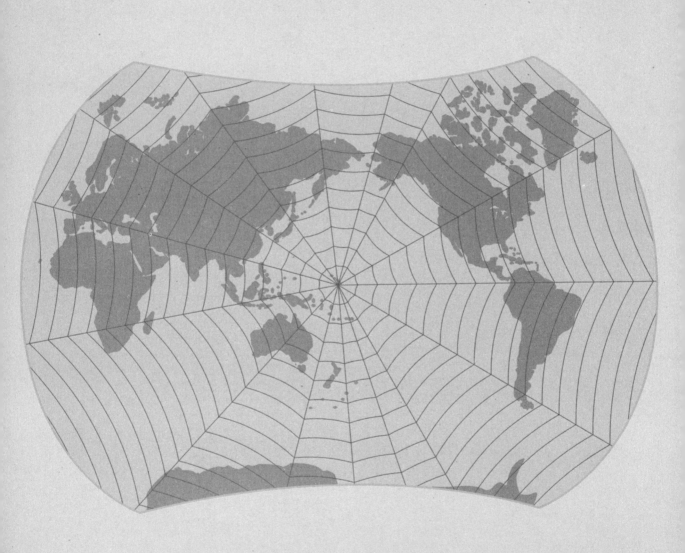

The Scripting Objects

In the last few chapters, we have been looking at some of the different objects that can be used with Active Server Pages. These objects, such as the `Application` and `Session` objects, are built-in to Active Server Pages. We have mentioned in previous chapters that there are also objects on the client-side that are built into the scripting language. As ASP utilizes scripting languages to access its own built-in objects, it stands to reason that you should, in ASP, be able to use the built in objects provided by VBScript, Jscript, or the different objects that come free with libraries distributed as part of IIS 5.0, and indeed you can.

These objects do not directly deal with the communication between the client and the web server, as the built-in objects do. These objects provide additional functionality to the scripting language itself. This is why they are known as the **scripting objects**. The scripting objects add some important features to ASP, such as the `Dictionary` object and the `RegExp` object. The `Dictionary` object allows you to store and index data about your application, in a manner similar to a dictionary, and the `RegExp` object allows you to search for multiple occurrences of a sequence of characters within a large volume of text.

In this chapter we'll look at:

- ❑ The `Dictionary` object
- ❑ The `FileSystemObject` object
- ❑ Collections of the `FileSystemObject` object
- ❑ Server-side includes
- ❑ The `TextStream` object
- ❑ The `RegExp` object

But first, let's look in more detail at what exactly the scripting objects are.

What are Scripting Objects?

Scripting Objects are, quite simply, objects that can be used in any form of script, both client and server-side. This contrasts with the ASP objects, which are only available on the server. There are two sets of scripting objects that can be used in both client and server side script. The first set is known as the **Scripting Runtime objects**. These are provided with IIS 5.0, among other products, and are a set of objects that provide functionality that was "missed out" from Visual Basic. These objects come as part of the **Scripting Runtime Objects library**, which is the file `scrrun.dll`. The second set of objects is the **VBScript objects**. These come as part of VBScript itself, or rather the file `vbscript.dll`. This file provides the scripting language support to both ASP and Internet Explorer. Collectively these two libraries of objects are known as the **Scripting Objects**.

> *Objects that form part of the Scripting Run Time library can also be accessed from other scripting languages, such as JScript. In this book, we are creating all of our examples in VBScript, so you will need to refer to the Microsoft documentation of JScript if you want to see how to use these objects with JScript. This documentation, along with the latest information on all Microsoft scripting technologies, can be found at* `http://msdn.microsoft.com/scripting`.

We're going to look at six scripting objects that a developer can use from within their scripts (there are over twice that amount). The first that we'll consider is the `Dictionary` object, which allows you to store information in a single data structure for easy retrieval. It is similar to an array, and it is also similar to a collection. The `FileSystemObject` object provides access from an Active Server Pages script to the hard disk file system of the server. This object will allow you to work with files, as well as directories and sub-directories.

The `TextStream` object allows you to deal with the contents of a file that you have got information about using the `FileSystemObject` object. You can read information from the file and write data *to* it. These are all Scripting Runtime objects.

The odd one out we'll look at is the `RegExp` object, which comes as part of the VBScript itself. Regular expressions are something that JScript has enjoyed support of for years, and they have been added to version 5.0 of VBScript. They can be used to search for and manipulate a sequence of characters in a large amount of data. We'll first look at how you'd create an instance of a scripting object in your pages.

Creating an Instance of a Scripting Object

When you want to use a Scripting object, the first step is to create an **instance** of an object using the VBScript method `CreateObject`.

> *You'll recall our discussion of the relationship between objects and instances from Chapter 6. Essentially, the class is the template of the object; and an instance is a particular copy of the object which is created in the shape of that template. This action is similar to cookies (the instance) coming out of a cookie cutter (the class).*

Creating an Instance of a Scripting Runtime Object

In ASP, we create an instance of an object in the `Set` statement with the `CreateObject` method and the location and name of the object. The location and name of the object goes together to create a unique identifier for the object known as a **ProgID**. So the ProgID for the `Dictionary` object is `Scripting.Dictionary`. Used in conjunction with the `CreateObject` method it would look like this:

```
CreateObject("Scripting.Dictionary")
```

Once we've created an instance, it must be assigned to a variable name (the above line wouldn't work on its own) – this allows you to refer to the instance later on in your code.

Although you can use any name, many programmers prefix the name of their object (and indeed our suggested naming convention does), by appending the letters `obj` before it. For example, if you were using an instance of the `Dictionary` object, then you might want to give it a variable name like `objDictionary` or `objDict`. A typical instantiation might look something like this:

```
Set objDictionary = CreateObject ("Scripting.Dictionary")
```

> **Instantiation** *is the name we give to the process of creating an instance of an object. For example, in this piece of code we have **instantiated** `objDictionary`, which is an instance of the `Dictionary` object.*

As you can see, we have used the `Set` statement, followed by the name that we have chosen for our instance. Once you've used the `Set` statement, and the `CreateObject` method in this way, the instance of the object will be ready to use. Subsequently, you use the instance by referring to it using the name you give within the `Set` statement.

Creating an instance of a VBScript object

When using objects from the VBScript library, as well as using the above method to create an object, you can also create an instance of the object by using the keyword `New`. However, the `New` keyword can only be used to create an instance of a VBScript class or built-in VBScript object, not a generic object (such as a scripting runtime one). So, you could do this for the `RegExp` (regular expression) object. It works in a similar way to the `CreateObject` method, although it doesn't require the ProgID, rather just the name of the object:

```
Set objRegExp = New RegExp
```

The difference is that `CreateObject` goes through COM for creation while `New` means the object goes to the VBScript runtime engine. At the moment you don't need to worry about why this happens, but you need to be aware that it is preferable for your object to be created by COM if you intend it to use it in either a secure application, or one that involves transactions.

Since dealing with data is very important to a lot of web applications, let's take a look at how the `Dictionary` object allows you to manipulate sets of data very easily.

The Dictionary Object

When you pick up a copy of Webster's dictionary, you have the ability to find out information about a particular word. In this case, the information is the definition of the word. All of the words are organized in a particular order. In a dictionary, this order is alphabetical. Associated with every word in the dictionary is its definition. This could also very easily be a synonym for the word, or a picture of what the word represents. The key concept is that for each word, there is a piece of information.

The `Dictionary` object can be thought of as a Webster's for your application. You can store information in it and attach a keyword to each piece of information. Later, when you want to retrieve the information, all you do is provide the dictionary with the keyword, and it will return the information you have stored there.

Try It Out – Simple Dictionary Example

To start becoming familiar with the `Dictionary` object, let's take a look at a very simple example that shows you how to store and retrieve information from a `Dictionary` object.

1. Use your editor of choice to create the `SimpleDictionary.asp` file with the following source code.

```
<%
  Dim objDictionary, strKey, strValue
  Set objDictionary = CreateObject("Scripting.Dictionary")
  objDictionary.Add "Apple", "Red"
  objDictionary.Add "Lemon", "Yellow"

  Response.Write "<P>All Data Stored in the Dictionary"
  Response.Write "<P>Let's retrieve"
  Response.Write "<HR>"
  Response.Write "<P>Retrieving Data..."
  strValue = objDictionary.Item("Apple")
  Response.Write "<P>Value stored with key of 'Apple' is " & strValue

  strKey = "Lemon"
  strValue = objDictionary.Item(strKey)
  Response.Write "<P>Value stored with key of '" & strKey & "' is " & strValue
%>
```

2. Save the file in your `BegASPFiles` folder.

3. View the page in your web browser.

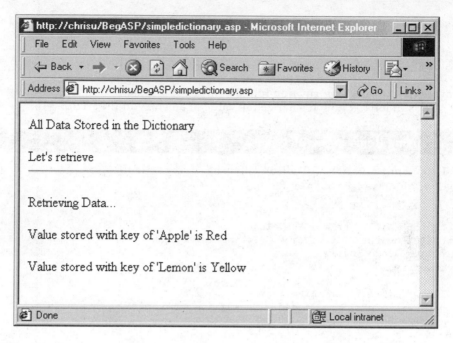

How It Works

Using the Dictionary object is actually quite easy. The first step is to create an instance of the Dictionary object. The ProgID is Scripting.Dictionary, so all we need to do is:

```
Set objNewDictionaryObj = CreateObject("Scripting.Dictionary")
```

Once we have created an instance of the Dictionary object, we are ready to add data to it. The data that is stored in the dictionary is stored as a name/value pair. The name part of the pair is known as the **key**. When you add an item to the dictionary, you will use the Add method. This method takes the key and the value associated with the key and adds it to the Dictionary.

```
objDictionary.Add key, value
```

You can either pass the explicit values of the key and value parameters, or you can pass variables that hold the data that you want for either parameter.

After we have stored items in the Dictionary object, the next logical step is to retrieve the information. To access information in a Dictionary, you need to supply the key. Given that key, the Dictionary object will return the value associated with it. This returned value can either be stored in a variable, or used immediately in another method. As with the Add method, you can either pass an explicit reference to the key's name, or you can pass a variable that contains the name of the key.

> *Since in VBScript all variables are treated as variants, you don't need to worry about what the data type of the data that is stored in the Dictionary object is: except in one case, that is. If you have stored a reference to an object as a value in your dictionary, you need to use the Set statement to assign the reference to another variable.*

To access the information for a specific key, you will use the Item method of the Dictionary object.

```
value = objDictionary.Item(key)
```

Now that we have loaded information into the Dictionary object and successfully retrieved it, the next step is to look at how to change the value of an entry in the Dictionary.

Try it Out – Changing Items in the Dictionary

1. Using your favorite ASP editor, enter the source code for ChangeValueDictionary.asp.

```
<%
  Dim objDictionary, strKey, strValue
  Set objDictionary = CreateObject("Scripting.Dictionary")
  objDictionary.Add "Apple", "Red"
  objDictionary.Add "Lemon", "Yellow"

  strValue = objDictionary.Item("Apple")
  Response.Write "<P>Value stored with key of 'Apple' is " & strValue

  strKey = "Lemon"
  strValue = objDictionary.Item(strKey)
  Response.Write "<P>Value stored with key of '" & strKey & "' is " & strValue
  Response.Write "<HR>"

  objDictionary.Item("Apple") = "Green"
  Response.Write "<P>Changed the value of Apple to Green"
  Response.Write "<HR>"
  Response.Write "<P>Value stored with key of 'Apple' is "
  Response.Write objDictionary.Item("Apple")
  Response.Write "<HR>"

  objDictionary.Key("Lemon") = "Banana"
  Response.Write "<P>Changed the key of Lemon to Banana"
  Response.Write "<HR>"
  Response.Write "<P>Value stored with key of 'Banana' is "
  Response.Write objDictionary.Item("Banana")
%>
```

2. Save the file in your BegASPFiles folder.

3. View the ChangeValueDictionary.asp file in your web browser.

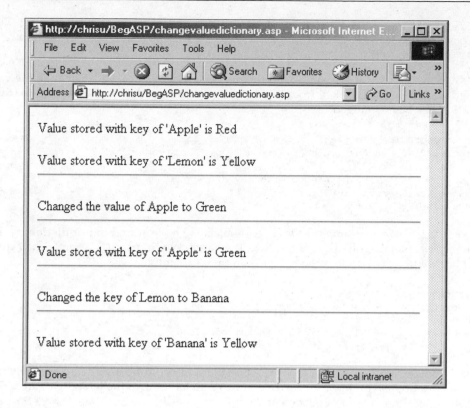

How It Works

In the first example, we manually stored information in the Dictionary object. In this example we do the same thing again. You might be tempted to think why not store this in a Session variable, and then this information would persist between pages? Unfortunately due to a fault in ASP this isn't possible, and if you try it, you will slow your server to a crawl. We'll point you to a workaround at the end of this section, but for now you'll have to accept that we need to populate the Dictionary object by hand, each time we use it.

The first part of the code is identical to our previous example:

```
Dim objDictionary, strKey, strValue
Set objDictionary = CreateObject("Scripting.Dictionary")
objDictionary.Add "Apple", "Red"
objDictionary.Add "Lemon", "Yellow"
```

We confirm once again that we've successfully stored our items and keys in the Dictionary object, by displaying them on the screen:

```
strValue = objDictionary.Item("Apple")
Response.Write "<P>Value stored with key of 'Apple' is " & strValue

strKey = "Lemon"
```

```
strValue = objDictionary.Item(strKey)
Response.Write "<P>Value stored with key of '" & strKey & "' is " & strValue
Response.Write "<HR>"
```

So far, so good, this is still the same as in the previous example. Next, we change the value contained within our `Apple` key from `red` to `green`. We display details showing that the information has been changed:

```
objDictionary.Item("Apple") = "Green"
Response.Write "<P>Changed the value of Apple to Green"
Response.Write "<HR>"
Response.Write "<P>Value stored with key of 'Apple' is "
Response.Write objDictionary.Item("Apple")
Response.Write "<HR>"
```

Our next step is to do the same for the second object we have stored in our dictionary, except this time we're changing the key, rather than the value. We change it in exactly the same way, except here we use the `key` method rather than the `item` method:

```
objDictionary.Key("Lemon") = "Banana"
Response.Write "<P>Changed the key of Lemon to Banana"
Response.Write "<HR>"
Response.Write "<P>Value stored with key of 'Banana' is "
Response.Write objDictionary.Item("Banana")
```

In the previous example, you saw that the `Item` method could be used to access the value. Now using this method, as you have seen above, it can also be used as the left side of an assignment statement to set the value for a particular key:

```
objDictionary.Item(keyValue) = newValue
```

We also changed the key itself. While this technically makes sense, from a real-world perspective it may not be a wise thing to do. If you are familiar with relational databases, then you know that each record in a table must have a unique key, and you cannot change the identity of that key. Changing the key itself in a `Dictionary` object is a very similar operation. A good word of advice is to be very sure you know why you are doing this when you decide to do it. The method we used to change the key itself was as follows:

```
objDictionary.Key (key) = newKey
```

These examples have shown you how to retrieve values from the `Dictionary` object by knowing the keys themselves. But what if you want to access information without knowing the keys? This next example will show you how to do this.

Try it Out – Retrieving Values When You Don't Know the Key

1. Using your favorite ASP editor, enter the source code for `GetAllValuesDictionary.asp`.

```
<%
  Dim objDictionary, strKey, strValue
  Set objDictionary = CreateObject("Scripting.Dictionary")
  objDictionary.Add "Apple", "Red"
  objDictionary.Add "Lemon", "Yellow"

  strValue = objDictionary.Item("Apple")
  Response.Write "<P>Value stored with key of 'Apple' is " & strValue

  strKey = "Lemon"
  strValue = objDictionary.Item(strKey)
  Response.Write "<P>Value stored with key of '" & strKey & "' is " & strValue
  Response.Write "<HR>"

  Response.Write "<P>Retrieve list of keys"

  For Each key in objDictionary
    Response.Write "<P>Key = " & key & "  --  Value = " & objDictionary.item(key)
  Next

  Response.Write "<HR>Retrieve list of values"
  For Each item in objDictionary
    Response.Write "<P>Value = " & objDictionary(item)
  Next
%>
```

2. Save the file in your `BegASPFiles` folder.

3. View the `GetAllValuesDictionary.asp` file in your web browser.

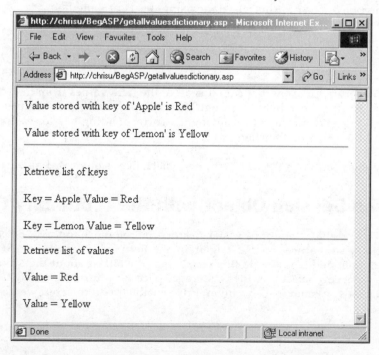

How It Works

In this example, we are looking for a way to retrieve all of the keys or items in the Dictionary object at once. There are many practical applications of this. For example, you could have multiple pages all dumping information into a Dictionary object. Another page could quickly access all of the information without having to know all of the keys that have been added.

There are two sets of information that can be retrieved from the Dictionary object:

- ❑ A list of all keys in the Dictionary
- ❑ A list of all values for the keys in the Dictionary

There are different uses for both of these sets of information. If you retrieve all of the keys from a Dictionary object, then you can use the Item method to retrieve each corresponding value. Unfortunately, if you retrieve all of the items in the Dictionary object, there is no way to tie each item back to its key.

Once again we started by manually populating the Dictionary object. The first way we retrieved information in bulk from the Dictionary object was with the Keys method. This method returns an array, where each element contains one key. Once we have this array, we can loop through the array and display each of the keys on the client.

```
For Each key in objDictionary. keys
   Response.Write "<P>Key = " & key & "  --  Value = " & objDictionary.item(key)
Next
```

The other type of information that we retrieved in bulk from the Dictionary object was all of the values in the Dictionary. This was done using the Items method.

```
For Each item in objDictionary. items
   Response.Write "<P>Value = " & item
Next
```

This method will return an array that contains all of the item values from the Dictionary object. With this array, we can iterate through it and display each of the values to the client. As we stated before, we have no way of retrieving the corresponding key for each item. So all we can do is display the value on the client.

Before we close this section on the Dictionary object, here's one word of warning.

Don't use the Session Object with the Dictionary Object

Earlier we mentioned that it might be easier to store the reference to the Dictionary object in a Session variable so that we can use it again in another page. Indeed the ASP team themselves recommended that you do this very thing. We talked about the Session object in Chapter 8. The Session object provides a storage space for information that can span multiple pages during a user's session. It seems inherently sensible to do this, but we don't recommend it.

This is a bit beyond the scope of this book, so we won't be covering this problem in too much detail. The basic problem is this: if you store a `Dictionary` object in a `Session` object, your web server will slow down in direct proportion to the amount of people accessing it. Worse still, if you store a `Dictionary` object in an `Application` object, you could crash the web server completely. This is due to a bug in the `Dictionary` object (when the `Dictionary` object was originally written, it was only intended to be used on the client side). There is a component available from Microsoft, which allows you to pass this kind of information between pages. It is the `Lookuptable` component and it is available from `http://msdn.microsoft.com/workshop/server/downloads/lkuptbl_eula.asp`. You can find more details about this error and how to avoid it at `http://msdn.microsoft.com/msdn-online/MSDNchronicles2.asp`.

We have now covered the various ways that the `Dictionary` object can be used. Next, we will take a look at a pair of objects that will allow you access to the file system and files of your web server. These objects will allow you to manipulate the files and directories on your server, as well as manipulate the contents of the individual files themselves.

The FileSystemObject Object

When our ASP server is handling requests from its clients, there are two types of pages it can return. As we have seen in this book, we can use the scripting power of ASP to dynamically create pages on-the-fly and send them back to the client. We can also serve static pages that are stored on the web server itself. But up until this point, we, as web application developers, had to know which files were stored in what place on what drive.

With the `FileSystemObject` object we now can use our code to access the file system of the web server itself. This will allow us to:

❑   Get and manipulate information about all of the drives in the server. These can be physical drives or mapped drives that the web server is connected to

❑   Get and manipulate information about all of the folders and sub-folders on a drive

❑   Get and manipulate information about all of the files inside of a folder

With this information, there is a very broad range of things that we can do with the file system. Aside from setting security information, basically anything that you can do with the file system using Windows Explorer or File Manager can be done using the `FileSystemObject` object

The FileSystemObject Object and its Object Model

In chapter 6, we talked about what an object model was. This is a group of related objects that are working together to provide access to a certain group of functions on the server. The FileSystemObject object has an object model associated with it as well. This object model follows this hierarchy:

- ❑ FileSystemObject object
    - ❑ Drives collection
    - ❑ Drive object
        - ❑ Folders collection
        - ❑ Folder object
            - ❑ Files collection
            - ❑ File object

Let's take a look at each of the objects in the object model and briefly describe what they are used for. Then, our examples will show different ways to use the FileSystemObject object in real-life web applications.

The Drive Object

Each of the Drive objects that form part of the Drives collection contains a wealth of information about a drive in the web server. This information includes:

- ❑ Free space available
- ❑ The Volume name of the drive
- ❑ An indication of whether or not the drive is ready
- ❑ The type of file system that exists on the drive
- ❑ The physical type of drive it is
- ❑ A reference to the root folder on the drive

Most of the information contained in the Drive object is read-only. You can't change the amount of free space that a drive has available using the Drive object. However, you can change the Volume name of a drive, if it can physically be changed.

The Drives Collection

This collection contains one Drive object for each of the drives on the system. This includes all of the local drives, both fixed and removable, as well as any currently connected network drives.

The Folder Object

A Folder object allows you to access all of the properties of a folder. These properties include the name of the folder, the collection of files within it, the size of the folder in bytes, and what its attributes are (such as whether it's read-only, hidden, compressed, a system file or a folder). In addition, if there are subfolders within this folder, then it will contain a reference to a collection of folder objects that represent its subfolders. With the folder object, you can also copy, delete, and move folders within the file system.

The Folders Collection

The Folders collection contains a set of Folder objects. This collection is a bit different than the others in that you will usually find a Folders collection as a property of a Folder object. If you think about how these objects map to the physical world, then it begins to make sense. With IIS we have wwwroot as our root folder, and then underneath we have BegASPFiles as a subfolder. The Folders collection also provides a way for you to add a folder object to it. This is like adding a sub-folder to an existing folder.

The File Object

The lowest-level object in the FileSystemObject object model is a File object. Each File object allows access to all of the properties of an individual file in the file system. These properties include the file name, the path to the file, a reference to the folder object where the file exists, and the size of the file. With a File object, you can also copy, delete, and move files in the file system. Another method allows you to open the file itself, and read it as a text stream. In the next part of this chapter, we will be looking at the TextStream object and how it can be used to manipulate the actual contents of a file.

The Files Collection

The Files collection contains all of the File objects within a folder. Each Files collection corresponds to a particular folder or sub-folder in the file system. By iterating through a Files collection, you can examine in turn each of the files within a particular folder.

Now, let's take a look at a few examples that show you the different ways that you can use the FileSystemObject object.

Try It Out – Display a Directory

When displaying content from a web page, we can either display static information that is retrieved from a file stored on the web server, or we can dynamically create information to be displayed. One thing that we may want to do is combine these two choices. We may want to be able to display a list of the files stored on the web server.

With IIS 5.0 we have the ability to enable directory browsing. This can be done from the **Properties** option of the **Action** menu of the MMC for the directory we wish to enable browsing for. In the following screenshot we would be enabling browsing for the BegASPFiles directory/application only:

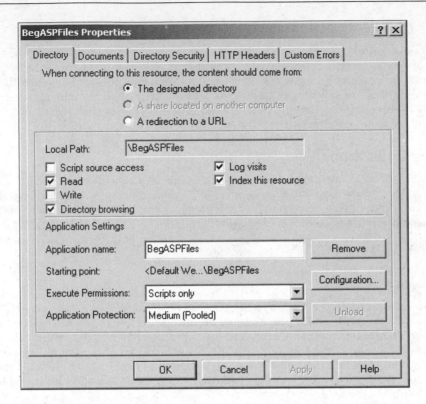

By checking the **Directory Browsing** checkbox, then the client is able to view the contents of the selected directory. However, this method has some drawbacks. If there is a default document, such as index.htm in this example, then there is no way to display the directory. Also, if the directory is displayed, then there is no way to control the fact that each file in the directory is also an active link. This has many implications, especially in the area of security. This setting will allow unauthorized individuals to see hidden files and URLs. This is why most commercial sites disable directory browsing.

This first example will show how to use the FileSystemObject object to display a listing of the files in the current directory.

1. Using your editor of choice, create the DisplayDirectory.asp file with the following source code.

```
<HTML>
<HEAD>
<TITLE>Chapter 10 Example - Display Directory</TITLE>
</HEAD>
<BODY>

<%
  Dim strPathInfo, strPhysicalPath
  strPathInfo = Request.ServerVariables("PATH_INFO")
```

```
      strPhysicalPath = Server.MapPath(strPathInfo)

  Dim objFSO, objFile, objFileItem, objFolder, objFolderContents
  Set objFSO = CreateObject("Scripting.FileSystemObject")

  Set objFile = objFSO.GetFile(strPhysicalPath)
  Set objFolder = objFile.ParentFolder
  Set objFolderContents = objFolder.Files
%>

<TABLE cellpadding=5>
<TR align=center>
  <TH align=left>File Name</TH>
  <TH>File Size</TH>
  <TH>Last Modified</TH>
</TR>

<%
  For Each objFileItem In objFolderContents
    Response.Write "<TR><TD align=left>"
    Response.Write objFileItem.Name
    Response.Write "</TD><TD align=right>"
    Response.Write objFileItem.Size
    Response.Write "</TD><TD align=right>"
    Response.Write objFileItem.DateLastModified
    Response.Write "</TD></TR>"
  Next
%>

</TABLE>
</BODY>
</HTML>
```

2. Save the file in your `BegASPFiles` folder.

3. View the page in your web browser.

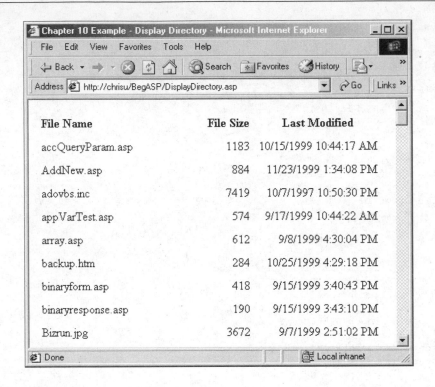

*When you're trying out this example, you might come across the error **Object doesn't support this property or method: 'GetFile'**. If so, it's because the Scripting Runtime Library (`scrrun.dll`) hasn't been installed properly. We recommend that you go back and reinstall the Scripting Runtime Library (available from `http://msdn.microsoft.com/scripting`).*

How It Works

After putting all of the requisite header stuff at the top of the page, the first thing that we need to do is determine the physical path to the current file. Our ASP page will display a list of the files in the directory that the file resides in. The URL that is used to display this file is a **virtual path**. This means that the path is defined by the web server's configuration. The virtual path does not necessarily correspond to the file's location in the drive's local directory tree. It's also very important to remember that, for the `FileScriptingObject` objects to work, they need the *physical* path and not the virtual path.

To get the physical path to the current file, we need to start with the virtual path to the file. This information can be found in the HTTP variable `PATH_INFO`. In our example program, this variable contains the following string:

```
/BegASPFiles/displayDirectory.asp
```

This should look familiar – it's the part of the URL that follows the name of the server. To retrieve this value, we will use the `Request` object's `ServerVariables` collection.

Now that we have this value, we need to translate it to the physical path. There is a `Server` object method that will allow you to do this. The `MapPath` method will take a virtual path and convert it to a physical path. After we convert our virtual path to a physical path, we have:

```
C:\InetPub\wwwroot\BegASPFiles\DisplayDirectory.asp
```

This is the data that we need to use with the `FileScriptingObject` objects. In this example, the virtual path looks very similar to the physical path. This is a just a coincidence in the way that this particular web server is configured. In other cases, only the file name could be similar.

To start working with the `FileSystemObject` object, we will need to create an instance of it using:

```
Set objFSO = CreateObject("Scripting.FileSystemObject")
```

We create the object and save its reference in the `objFSO` variable. Before we dive into how the code itself works, let's look at the strategy we will use to generate the directory.

We are starting with the physical path to the file. This file is in the directory that we want the contents for. So, we need to find a way to relate this file to the directory that it's in. Fortunately, one of the `FileSystemObject` objects provides this type of functionality.

To get started, we need to get a `File` object that corresponds to the file that we have the path for. If you remember, the `File` object allows you to get information about a particular file. The `FileSystemObject` object itself provides a method called `GetFile` that will take a physical path to a file and return a reference to a `File` object that represents that file.

Now that we are armed with a `File` object representing a file in the directory we are interested in, we can use a property of the `File` object to get a reference to the folder that it's in.

> *We have been using the words directory and folder interchangeably. For those of us who came from the DOS world, our files have always been arranged in directories. With the advent of Windows 95 and the addition of Windows Explorer, the folder term has become more prevalent. But they both still refer to the same thing.*

One of the properties of the `File` object is the `ParentFolder` property. Given a valid file object, this will return a reference to a `Folder` object that represents the folder that the file resides in. If you have a `File` object in the root folder, the `ParentFolder` property will be null (not known or missing). We have now reached our objective of having an object that represents the directory we are interested in.

Now it is time to look at the files that are in this directory. To do this, we will use the `Files` collection that is stored as a property of the `Folder` object. This collection is a set of `File` objects; one object for each file in the directory.

To display the files, we will be using a <TABLE> for formatting. There will be three columns in the table, we will display the file name, the size of the file in bytes, and the date and time the file was last modified. The easiest way to go through all of the items in a collection is to use the For Each loop statement.

```
For Each objFileItem in objFolderContents
```

This statement will set up a loop structure that will be called one time for each object in the objFolderContents collection. Each time through the loop, the reference to the current object will be available using the objFileItem variable. The information that we are interested in displaying is available in three properties of the File object:

❑ objFileItem.Name – returns the name of the file

❑ objFileItem.Size – returns the size of the file in bytes

❑ objFileItem.DateLastModified – returns the date and time of the last modification of the file

Each of these pieces of information will be stored in their own table cell. Before moving to the next item in the collection, we will need to end the current row in the table. Once we have reached the end of the collection, we can end the table, then finish the page and send it back to the client to be displayed.

The next example will enhance the directory viewer page that we have just completed. While displaying a list of files is nice, we may want to be able to interact with the files in the list. This will make the directory an interactive directory, similar to the directory provided by the web server, but with you – the developer – in control of the way the information is presented. If we enable the web server to allow directory browsing, then the contents of the directory we are working in would look like this:

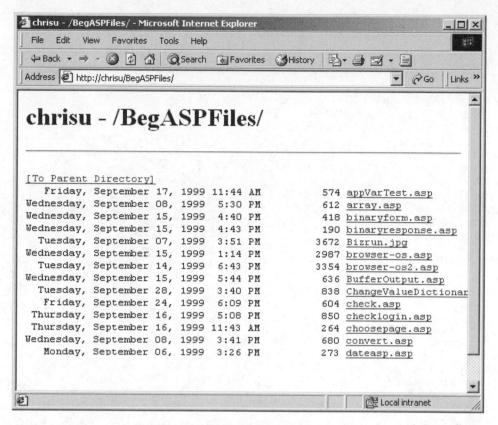

Since this page is generated by the server itself, there is no way that we can change how that page looks. So let's take a look at how to use the `FileSystemObject` objects to obtain the same information, and using the power of ASP, create a different presentation of the data.

Try It Out – Make the Directory Interactive

1. Copy the `DisplayDirectory.asp` file from the last example to a new file and name it `InteractiveDirectory.asp`.

2. Using your favorite editor, make the following additions and changes to the `InteractiveDirectory.asp` file:

```
<HTML>
<HEAD>
<TITLE>Chapter 10 Example - Display Directory</TITLE>
</HEAD>
<BODY>

<%
  Dim strPathInfo, strPhysicalPath
```

```
    strPathInfo = Request.ServerVariables("PATH_INFO")
    strPhysicalPath = Server.MapPath(strPathInfo)

    Dim objFSO, objFile, objFileItem, objFolder, objFolderContents
    Set objFSO = CreateObject("Scripting.FileSystemObject")

    Set objFile = objFSO.GetFile(strPhysicalPath)
    Set objFolder = objFile.ParentFolder
    Set objFolderContents = objFolder.Files
%>

<TABLE cellpadding=5>
<TR align=center>
  <TH align=left>File Name</TH>
  <TH>Type</TH>
  <TH>File Size</TH>
  <TH>Last Modified</TH>
</TR>

<%
  For Each objFileItem in objFolderContents
%>

    <TR>
      <TD align=left>
      <A HREF="<%= objFileItem.Name %>">
      <FONT FACE="Verdana" SIZE="3">
      <%= objFileItem.Name %></FONT>
      </A>
      </TD>
      <TD align=right>
      <FONT FACE="Tahoma" SIZE="2" COLOR="DarkGreen">
      <%= objFileItem.type %></FONT>
      </TD>
      <TD align=right>
      <FONT FACE="Tahoma" SIZE="2" COLOR="DarkGreen">
      <%= objFileItem.size %></FONT>
      </TD>
      <TD align=right>
      <FONT FACE="Tahoma" SIZE="2" COLOR="DarkGreen">
      <%= objFileItem.DateLastModified %></FONT>
      </TD>
    </TR>

<%
  Next
%>

</TABLE>
</BODY>
</HTML>
```

3. Save the file in your `BegASPFiles` folder.

4. View the page in your web browser.

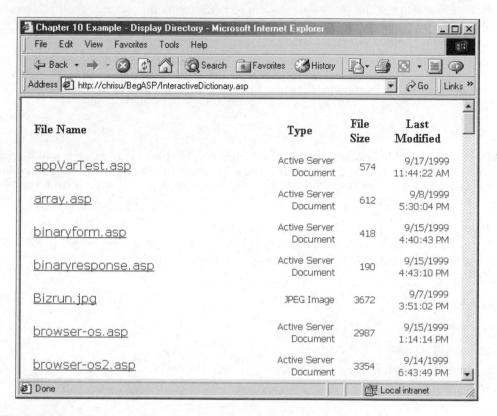

How It Works

We have made three major changes to the previous example to arrive at this new interactive directory display.

First, we have added some text formatting of the file information. There are two text styles that we will be using. One will be for the display of the file name itself in the directory listing. The other will be for the display of the other pieces of information about each file. To make the file names stand out, we have put the file names in a different font at a larger font size.

Note that while we set the color for the file data information, we did not set a color for the file name. This is because the file name will be an active link to the file. This means that the color of this text will be controlled by the settings in the user's browser. If we were to change the colors, then we run the risk of confusing the user as to which files they may have already visited.

Second, we added an `<A HREF>` tag to the name of the file itself. This is to replicate the functionality that is in the standard directory browsing display. All files in that display have a link associated with them. This will allow the user to click on the name of the file to navigate to it. To support this functionality in our page, we need to wrap the name of the file with a `<A HREF>` tag. The value of the `HREF` will need to be the same as the name of the file, so that when the user clicks on the link they will be taken to that file.

> *Even though the user may be able to navigate to any file in the directory, there may be files present that, when clicked on, will not return any valid information. Other files may actually include information that you don't want the user to be able to see. So while the ability to list files in a directory may be powerful, you need to exercise some care when using it.*

Finally, we have added another column to our directory display. This column will display the file type for each file. This is the same file type that would be displayed for the file when viewed using Windows Explorer. To display this information, we retrieve it from the `Type` property of the `File` object.

Displaying directories is a nice feature, but let's look at some of the other things we can do with the `FileSystemObject` objects. One thing that you see on a lot of web pages is some small text at the bottom of the page that identifies certain properties about the page. Some of these properties include:

❑   File Name

❑   Size

❑   Creation Date

❑   Last Modification Date

❑   Last Accessed Date

For a person viewing the page, this information can be helpful in determining the accuracy of the information on the page, or it can be useful for debugging purposes. Whatever it is used for, there should be an easy way to add it to each page. We'll now look at another method that can be used in ASP to further enhance our directory display example; the practice of including information already processed by the server.

Server-Side Includes

Server-side includes (SSIs) are a very useful way of making your site easier to manage, and for providing extra information. The 'including' is done *at the same time as* the Active Server Pages interpreter gets to see the page, so generally include files should be placed at the head of your ASP file. This means that information placed in the file, when included in the web page at the top, can be used throughout the script code. If you wanted to, it is possible to use code to decide *which* SSI `#include` directives we want to put into action, if you place them within an `If...Then` construct. There are five basic types of SSI we can use. We can:

❑   Include text files in our pages, as they are loaded

❑   Retrieve the size and last modification date of a file

❑   Define how variables and error messages are displayed

❑   Insert the values of HTTP variables in the page sent back to the browser

❑   Execute other programs or scripts, such as CGI and ISAPI applications

Only the first of these is directly applicable to Active Server Pages. SSIs are normally used in a separate file, which can be referenced and loaded from an ASP file.

Including Text Files in a Page with #include

One of the most useful techniques with SSI is to insert pre-built blocks of text into a page. As an example, we created a function for our calendar page that calculated the last day of any month. We can save this as a text file called, say, `GetLastDay.txt`. Then, anytime that we want to use the function, we just add an include statement to the page and call the function:

```
<!-- #include file="GetLastDay.txt" -->
...
intLastDayAugust = GetLastDay(datAugust)     'call our included function
...
```

> *Note that an SSI is a file, and as such it's common for the filename to have an extension such as `.asp`, `.txt` or `.inc`. Beware of the security implications of choosing your file extension. For example, if your SSI has an `.inc` extension, and a user manages to browse to it by typing a URL into their browser, then the contents of the SSI will not be parsed by the ASP engine. This means that the user will get to see the code that you wrote in your SSI. For this reason, it's always safer to use the `.asp` extension for your SSIs.*

One thing to watch out for is if you want to include script from another file, this file must contain complete script sections. In other words, it has to have opening and closing `<SCRIPT>` or `<%...%>` tags – we can't place part of the code section in an included file, and the rest in the main page. Theoretically, we could include half of, say, an `If...Then` construct in the file, and the rest in the main page, as long as each part was enclosed in `<%...%>` tags. This isn't likely to produce code that is easy to read or debug later, though!

Of course, the text we include doesn't have to be VBScript or JScript code. We can quite easily use it to include HTML or just plain text. If your site uses pages with standard footers for your copyright notice, or a standard `<STYLE>` tag to set up the text and page styles, these can equally well be stored as a separate file, and referenced with a `#include` statement.

Virtual and Physical File Addresses

The `#include` directive allows us to specify a file using either its **physical** or **virtual** path. For example, the file `MyFile.txt` could be in the directory `TextFiles`, contained underneath your current folder. If this directory also had an alias (virtual path) of `/Texts` set up, we could then reference it using either method:

```
<!-- #include file="TextFiles\MyFile.txt" --> 'physical path
<!-- #include virtual="/Texts/MyFile.txt"    -->          'virtual path
```

We can also, as you've already seen, use relative paths. If the file is in the same folder, we just use the file name. If it's in the `Projects` subdirectory, we can use:

```
<!-- #include file="Projects\MyFile.txt" -->              'physical path
```

In this example, we will actually be building an SSI that can be added to any Active Server Page.

Try It Out – Enhanced File Info Display

The SSI in this example will display information about the current file to the client.

1. Use NotePad to create the `FileDetails.asp` file with the following source code.

```
<%
  Dim strFDPathInfo, strFDPhysicalPath
  strFDPathInfo = Request.ServerVariables("PATH_INFO")
  strFDPhysicalPath = Server.MapPath (strFDPathInfo)

  Dim objFDFSO, objFDFile
  Set objFDFSO = CreateObject("Scripting.FileSystemObject")

  Set objFDFile = objFDFSO.GetFile(strFDPhysicalPath)
%>
<P>
<HR>
<DIV STYLE="font-size:11; font-family: Verdana; ">
File Name: <B><%= objFDFile.Name %></B><BR>
Server Path: <B><%= strFDPathInfo %></B><BR>
Physical Path: <B><%= objFDFile.Path %></B><BR>
File Size: <B><%= objFDFile.size %> bytes</B><BR>
Date Created: <B><%= objFDFile.DateCreated %></B><BR>
Date Last Modified: <B><%= objFDFile.DateLastModified %></B><BR>
Date Last Accessed: <B><%= objFDFile.DateLastAccessed %></B><BR>
</DIV>
```

2. Save the file in your `BegASPFiles` folder.

3. This example is of a sever-side include file. This means that we will need to add it to an existing ASP file. For this example, let's pick the `InteractiveDirectory.asp` file from the previous example. Open this file in your favorite editor and add this entry near the bottom.

```
<TD align=right>
<FONT FACE="Tahoma" SIZE="2" COLOR="DarkGreen">
<%= objFileItem.size %></FONT>
```

```
      </TD>
      <TD align=right>
      <FONT FACE="Tahoma" SIZE="2" COLOR="DarkGreen">
      <%= objFileItem.DateLastModified %></FONT>
      </TD>
    </TR>

<%
Next
%>

</TABLE>
<!-- #include file="FileDetails.asp" -->
</BODY>
</HTML>
```

4. View the page in your web browser.

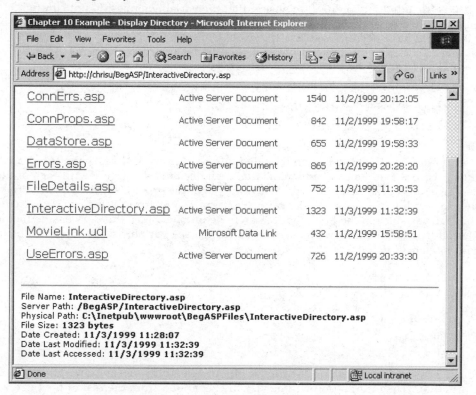

How It Works

This server-side include file has two primary functions. First, it needs to obtain a `File` object for the file that it is included in. Then, using that `File` object, we can display the information about the file itself.

If we were to just load this file directly from the server, then it would be displayed as text rather than being passed through the ASP engine. This would not be what we are looking for. The nice part about making it a server-side include file is that even though it is a separate file, when the server includes it into the other file, it acts as if it were part of that file. This means that when we get the File object that corresponds to the current file, we get the file that we are really interested in.

In the previous examples, we have shown how to get a File object that corresponds to the current file. In those examples, we went a step further and used that File object's ParentFolder property to get a reference to the current folder. In this server-side include file, we will stop once we get the reference to the File object.

One change that we have made from the earlier examples is that we are going to use different variable names. In the earlier examples, the variable names were both easy to read and corresponded closely to the data the variable contained. In a server-side include file, you need to be careful about the naming of any variables. Since this file is actually treated as part of the file that it is included in, you need to ensure that the variable names do not conflict. In our example, since we are leveraging code from the InteractiveDirectory.asp example, our variables would have been named

- ❑ strPathInfo
- ❑ strPhysicalPath
- ❑ objFSO
- ❑ objFile

If this server-side include file is then included into the InteractiveDirectory.asp file itself, then there would be two statements that each declared a variable with each of these names. This would cause a script error when the page was processed since these variables already exist within InteractiveDirectory.asp. To get around this, we have changed the names of the variables in the hope that they will be unique. Since this server-side include file provides additional file data, we have added a *FD* to each variable name. This results in variables named

- ❑ strFDPathInfo
- ❑ strFDPhysicalPath
- ❑ objFDFSO
- ❑ objFDFile

With our File object referencing the file we are interested in, we can now turn to the display of the information. The information will be visually separated from the rest of the page with a horizontal line generated by the <HR> tag. To set the formatting for all of the information, we have created a <DIV> section and set the text format properties for that container element. All of the information that is displayed is retrieved from a property of the File object except one. Since the FileSystemObject objects deal with files in their physical space, the File object has no information about the virtual path to the file as seen by the web server. Since we want to display that information on the client, we will need to retrieve that information from the HTTP Server Variables that are passed with each request to the server. The strFDPathInfo variable will contain the virtual path that points to the file we are currently viewing.

Up until now, we have been using the `FileSystemObject` objects to access information about the properties of folders and files in the physical file system. They also provide one other function with respect to files. With a valid `File` object, you can open the file itself as a text file and deal with the data contained inside it. To do this, you will interact with the file's data using the `TextStream` object.

The Text Stream Object

The `TextStream` object allows you access the contents of a file as a text file. This does not mean that the file has to have a `.txt` extension. Rather, its contents have to be in text readable form. Naturally, `.txt` files work fine. But you can also open `.html` files, `.asp` files, and even `.log` files. Once you have access to the text contents of a file, you can read information from it and write information to it.

There are three ways that you can get a `TextStream` object. With a valid `File` object, you can use the `OpenAsTextStream` method. This will return a `TextStream` object that you can then use to manipulate the contents of the file. If you know the physical file name of the file, and don't want to worry about creating a `File` object for it, then the `FileSystemObject` object's `OpenTextFile` method will open the file in the same way. Lastly, if you want to create a brand new file and add text to it, you can use the `CreateTextFile` method of the `FileSystemObject` object and pass it the name of the file you want to create. This method will return a `TextStream` object, which you can use to add text to the file.

Try It Out – ASP Source Code Viewer

Our first example will look at just accessing the information contained in a file. One of the best ways to learn how to program on the web is to look at other people's source code. You can learn many HTML tricks by looking at the source code of pages you like. But how can you use this same approach to learn the insides of ASP? With ASP, the source is interpreted on the server, and all the client sees is the completed HTML.

In this example, we will create an Active Server Pages script that will display the source of any of the ASP files on your server. The file name will be passed in as a URL parameter. We will also show how to link it to an existing ASP page.

1. Using your editor of choice, create the `DisplaySource.asp` file with the following source code:

```
<%
  Const ForReading = 1, ForWriting = 2, ForAppending = 8
  Const TristateUseDefault = -2, TristateTrue = -1, TristateFalse = 0
  Dim strPathInfo, strPhysicalPath
  strPathInfo = Request.QueryString("FileName")
  strPhysicalPath = Server.MapPath(strPathInfo)

  Dim objFSO, objFile
  Set objFSO = CreateObject("Scripting.FileSystemObject")
  Set objFile = objFSO.GetFile(strPhysicalPath)
%>
```

403

```
<HTML>
<HEAD>
<TITLE><%= objFile.Name %> Source Code</TITLE>
</HEAD>
<BODY>
Source code for <%= objFile.Name %><HR><P>
<FONT FACE=Courier SIZE=2>

<%
  Dim objFileTextStream
  Set objFileTextStream = objFile.OpenAsTextStream(ForReading, TristateUseDefault)

  Dim strLine
  Do While objFileTextStream.AtEndOfStream <> True
    strLine = Server.HTMLEncode(objFileTextStream.ReadLine)
    strLine = Replace (strLine, Chr(9), "    ")
    Response.Write strLine
    Response.Write "<BR>" + vbCrLf
  Loop
  objFileTextStream.Close
%>

</FONT>
<BR>
<BR>
<HR>
<A HREF="<%= strPathInfo %>">Return to Displayed File</A>
</BODY>
</HTML>
```

2. Save this file in your `BegASPFiles` folder.

3. To link to this file, add this source code to the `InteractiveDirectory.asp` file from a previous example:

```
</TABLE>
<!-- #include file="FileDetails.asp" -->
<HR>
<A HREF="DisplaySource.asp?FileName=
<%= Server.URLEncode(Request.ServerVariables("PATH_INFO")) %> ">
Click here to see ASP source</A>
</BODY>
</HTML>
```

4. View the page `InteractiveDirectory.asp` in your web browser.

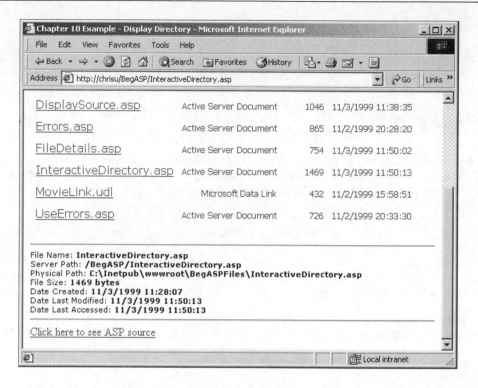

5. When you click on the hyperlink at the bottom of the page, you will then see this in your browser.

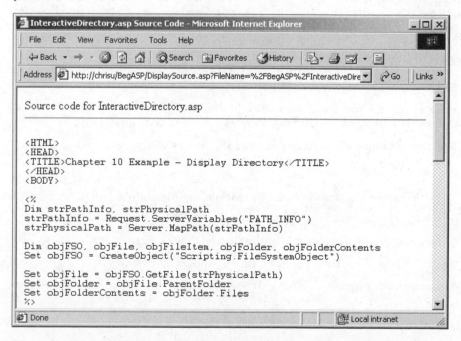

How It Works

For this application to work, we need to build on what we did in the previous examples. In order to create a TextStream object, we need to start with a valid File object for the file we are interested in. To get this, we will use the tried and tested method that we have used in the previous examples.

```
Dim objFSO, objFile
Set objFSO = CreateObject("Scripting.FileSystemObject")
```

The difference in this case is that the virtual path to the file we are interested in is passed in as a query string variable. So, to begin our steps to getting a File object, we need to use that passed in value to compute the physical file path, instead of using a server variable as we did in the other examples.

```
Set objFile = objFSO.GetFile(strPhysicalPath)
```

Once we have the valid File object, the next step is to open that file as a text file. To do this, we will use the OpenAsTextStream method of the File object. This method will return a reference to a TextStream object that contains the contents of the file.

```
Dim objFileTextStream
Set objFileTextStream = objFile.OpenAsTextStream(ForReading, TristateUseDefault)
```

The OpenAsTextStream method takes two parameters:

```
OpenAsTextStream(ForReading, TristateUseDefault)
```

The first parameter is used to determine the state the file is opened in. There are three possible states for opening the file. To make the code more readable, we have defined constants at the top of the source file for these three states.

The possible values are:

❏ ForReading – The file is read-only. You cannot write any information to this file.

❏ ForWriting – You are able to write to the file. If there is any data that was already in the file, it will be overwritten as soon as you open it in this mode.

❏ ForAppending – You are able to read the file, as well as add text to the end of it. You cannot change any of the text that was originally there.

The second parameter indicates in what file format the file should be opened. Possible values are:

❏ TristateTrue – This will open the file in UNICODE format.

❏ TristateFalse – This will open the file in ASCII format.

❏ TristateUseDefault – This will use the default setting for the web server.

To be safe, you should usually open the file in the default mode, unless you are absolutely sure that the contents are not of the default type.

Once the file is open, we can begin reading the information from the file. There are a number of ways information can be read from the file. It can be read all at once, using the `ReadAll` method. This will return all of the text in the file in one big chunk. While this is the easiest to implement, it isn't very effective for large files. Rather than reading the file all at once, it can be read in pieces. There are two different size chunks that can be read from a file. The `Read` method can be used to read a certain number of characters from the file into a string. This number of characters is determined by a parameter passed to the `Read` method. Alternatively, the file can be read one line at a time, as we have done in this example - using the `ReadLine` method:

```
Dim strLine
Do While objFileTextStream.AtEndOfStream <> True
   strLine = Server.HTMLEncode(objFileTextStream.ReadLine)
   strLine = Replace (strLine, Chr(9), "    ")
   Response.Write strLine
   Response.Write "<BR>" + vbCrLf
Loop
objFileTextStream.Close
```

This method will return all of the text starting at the current location in the file up to the first line break. When you have a file open for reading, the `TextStream` object maintains a pointer in the file indicating where you last read text. When you first open the file, this pointer is pointing at the beginning of the file. When you read text from the file using either the `Read` or `ReadLine` methods, the object moves this pointer to a point just after where you finished reading. In the case of the `ReadLine` method, the pointer will be pointing at the first character *after* the line break.

As you are reading the file piece by piece, you will need some indication as to when you have run out of file to read. The `TextStream` object provides a property that is very simple to access, which will tell you when you are at the end of the file. The `AtEndOfStream` property will return True when you have reached the end of the file.

As we want to read the file one line at a time, we use the `ReadLine` method. Since we want to read the entire file, we will need to call the `ReadLine` method over and over again until we have read the entire file. This can be easily done using a loop. The condition that we are checking every time we go through the loop is based on the `AtEndOfStream` property. As long as this property's value is not true, we still have more data to read, so we can grab the next chunk using the `ReadLine` method.

Once we have the line stored in a string, there is one more procedure that we need to perform on it. Since we will be displaying primarily the source code for Active Server Pages files, we need to take care of how special characters in the file are handled.

If we were to just spit the contents of the file back to the client using a `Response.Write` method, we will probably not get the desired results. Since a large part of an ASP source file is HTML, when this is sent back to the client, it will just display it as if it were regular HTML. This will not give us the display that we are interested in.

In order to display the HTML as source, we need to change the way the HTML tags are presented. When the client is displaying an HTML page, it is looking for HTML tags that are bounded by < >. When it finds one of these, it will use it as formatting instructions, and not as text to be displayed. In order for the browser to display the HTML source as text, we need to change the < > to a character that will look the same, but will be interpreted differently.

To do this, we need to look through the string and wherever we find a < or > we need to replace it with a < or > respectively. When the client sees this set of characters, it will display a <, but it will not treat what is inside as an HTML tag. This is exactly what we need for our source code viewer. Lucky for us, there is a very convenient Server object method called HTMLEncode. It does exactly what we need. Given a string, it will search for characters that would be interpreted as HTML by a browser, when we really want it to display as text.

The last bit of formatting that we need to do concerns the area of indented text. Many ASP source files use indented sections to make the code more readable. These indents are usually made using tab characters. Unfortunately, when a web client is told to display a tab character, it will just ignore it. We want our source code display to retain the formatting that the developer added. Again, we will be using the Replace method. This time we will be looking for a tab character. The tab character is one of those **non-printable characters**. This means that there is no visible character that represents it. But we need a tab character as input to the Replace method. VBScript also provides us with a Chr function. This function will convert a number into its equivalent ASCII character. After consulting our ASCII character chart, we know that the ASCII code for the Tab character is 9. So we will be using Chr(9) as our search sub-string in the Replace method. We will be replacing each of the tab characters with four non-breaking space characters. These are represented as   and when the client encounters one of these, it adds an explicit space character to the output.

Now that the whole line is properly formatted, we can output it to the client using the Response.Write method. Since the client will ignore any carriage returns in the text file, we need to add our own line break to the displayed source code. To do this, we add the <BR> tag to the end of the line. Having finished all of the processing on this line, we start our loop all over again with the next line. When we run out of lines to process, we close the TextStream and send the completed page back to the client.

In order to launch this page, we need to add a few lines of code to an existing ASP file. We will be using one of the examples from earlier in this chapter. At the bottom of the page, we will add a hyperlink that will request the DisplaySource.asp file. The name of the file that we are displaying the source for is passed as a URL parameter. Before we pass the file name as a query string variable, we need to make sure that all of the characters in the file name are valid URL characters. The easiest way to do this is to use the Server.URLEncode method. This method will replace any invalid characters in a URL string with their corresponding URL representations. This will ensure that the file name is properly passed to the DisplaySource.asp file, regardless of the characters in the file name. So now, when the user clicks on this link, the source code of the ASP file that generated the page will be displayed for the user.

This example has shown us how to read information from a text file on the server and display it on the client. Next, we will take a look at how to write information to a text file. There are many instances in web applications where you want more detail than is available in the standard server logs, yet you don't want to have a database to write the information to. This example will show how to create an application log file routine that can be packaged into a server-side include and dropped into any ASP file.

Try It Out – Application Log File

In this example, we will be creating a server-side include file that can be added to any of your Active Server Pages script files. This file will provide your script with a method that can be called to write information to a log file. All that your script will need to do is add this include file and then call the method to write the information to the file.

1. Using NotePad, create the `WriteLog.asp` file with the following source code:

```
<%
  Const ForAppending = 8

  Dim strLogFileName
  strLogFileName = "c:\AppLogFile.log"              'enter your preferred path here

  Dim objLogFileFSO
  set objLogFileFSO = CreateObject("Scripting.FileSystemObject")

  Dim objLogFileTS
  If objLogFileFSO.FileExists(strLogFileName) Then
    Set objLogFileTS = objLogFileFSO.OpenTextFile(strLogFileName, ForAppending)
  Else
    Set objLogFileTS = objLogFileFSO.CreateTextFile(strLogFileName)
  End If

  Sub WriteToLog (strNewEntry)
    Dim strLogEntry

    strLogEntry = FormatDateTime(Now) & " - "
    strLogEntry = strLogEntry & strNewEntry
    objLogFileTS.WriteLine strLogEntry
  End Sub

  Sub CloseLog()
    objLogFileTS.Close
  End Sub
%>
```

2. Save this file in your `BegASPFiles` folder.

3. Next, add the include statement to your ASP file. For this example, we will be using the `DisplayDirectory.asp` file that we looked at earlier.

```
  set objFolderContents = objFolder.Files
%>
<!-- #include file="WriteLog.asp" -->

<TABLE cellpadding=5>
```

4. We'll add another line to `DisplayDirectory.asp` which will call the `WriteToLog` method to write information to the log file.

```
      Response.Write objFileItem.DateLastModified
      Response.Write "</TD></TR>"
      WriteToLog "Directory Entry for " + objFileItem.Name
   Next
%>
```

5. At the end of `DisplayDirectory.asp`, add a call to the `CloseLog` method to close the log file.

```
      Response.Write objFileItem.DateLastModified
      Response.Write "</TD></TR>"
      WriteToLog "Directory Entry for " + objFileItem.Name
   Next
   CloseLog
%>
```

6. View the `DisplayDirectory.asp` file in your web browser. This will cause the server to generate the page, which will write the information to the log file. The contents of the log file, which will be called `AppLogFile.log`, can be found under the `C:\` folder on your web server's hard drive and can be viewed using any editor. In this example, we're using Notepad. The contents will look something like this:

How It Works

This server-side include file will need to perform two functions. First, it will need to get the `TextStream` object that represents our log file properly prepared to accept information written to it. Secondly, it will need to provide an easy mechanism for the file that includes it to write information to the log file.

In our example, we have defined the name of the log file. This could have just as easily been stored in a variable and retrieved by the include file. Once we have this file name, which is already a physical file name, we can then prepare the `TextStream` object to accept information written to it.

```
Dim objLogFileTS
If objLogFileFSO.FileExists(strLogFileName) Then
   Set objLogFileTS = objLogFileFSO.OpenTextFile(strLogFileName, ForAppending)
Else
   Set objLogFileTS = objLogFileFSO.CreateTextFile(strLogFileName)
End If
```

There are two states that we need to work with when preparing the `TextStream` object. The first state is when there is no log file present. In this case, we need to create the log file and then open it with write permissions enabled. To check to see if the file is present, we will be using the `FileExists` method of the `FileSystemObject` object. This method takes the name of a physical file and returns true if the file exists and false if it does not.

If this method returns True, then we know that our log file exists (although it could possibly be empty) and all we need to do is open it. To open it, we will use the `OpenTextFile` method of the `FileSystemObject` object. This method will return a `TextStream` object that represents the file. There are two parameters that we will pass to this method. The first is the name of the physical log file. This is stored in the `strLogFileName` variable. The second parameter is used to tell the `FileSystemObject` object what we want to do with this file once we have opened it.

There are two possible values for this parameter. If we just want to read information from the file, then we can set this parameter's value to `ForReading`. This value will cause the file to be opened as read-only, meaning we can only read information from the file. Since our task here is to create a file that we can write information to, we need to supply the other value for the parameter. The value of `ForAppending` means that we will be able to both write information to the end of the file. To define the actual value for this parameter, we have included a `Const` statement to set the value of `ForAppending` to 8.

If the `FileExists` method returns False, then we know that we have to create the log file so that we can write to it. This is done using the `CreateTextFile` method of the `FileSystemObject`. For this method, we will be supplying one parameter. We will pass in the physical name of the file that we want to create. This method will return a `TextStream` object that represents our new physical file. This `TextStream` object will be set up so that information can be written to the file.

The steps involved in opening or creating the file are the first steps in our server side include file. These steps need to be executed as soon as the server reads them from the source file. The other step in the log file is writing information to the log file itself. This needs to be able to be called from anywhere in the source file. In order to do this, we have created a **subroutine**.

```
Sub WriteToLog (strNewEntry)
  Dim strLogEntry

  strLogEntry = FormatDateTime(Now) & " - "
  strLogEntry = strLogEntry & strNewEntry
  objLogFileTS.WriteLine strLogEntry
End Sub
```

This subroutine is a feature of the server-side include file. It will accept one parameter and then perform some processing. The parameter will be the text information that is written to the log file. When the method receives this information, it will add a date and time stamp to the beginning of it, then writes the information to the log file. To write the information to the log file, we will be using the `WriteLine` method of the `TextStream` object. This method will add the text contained in its one parameter to the file associated with the instance of the `TextStream` object. It will also add a line break at the end of the text that it adds to the file.

Now that we have created our server-side include file, we need to add the logging functionality to another ASP file. For this example, we will be adding it to the `DisplayDirectory.asp` file that we looked at earlier in this chapter.

```
    set objFolderContents = objFolder.Files
%>
<!-- #include file="WriteLog.asp" -->
```

There are three steps to adding the logging capabilities to this file. First, we will need to include the `WriteLog.asp` file that we just created. This will be done using the `#include` directive in the `DisplayDirectory.asp` file. This statement needs to be included prior to any calls to the `WriteLog` method, so that the method can be properly defined before it is called.

```
    Response.Write objFileItem.DateLastModified
    Response.Write "</TD></TR>"
    WriteToLog "Directory Entry for " + objFileItem.Name
  Next
%>
```

The next step will be to call the `WriteLog` method whenever we want to add information to the log file. For this example, we will be writing the name of each file that is read in the current directory to the log file. When you view the log file in Notepad, you can see that the date and time that the entry was made has been added to the beginning of each entry in the log.

```
    Response.Write objFileItem.DateLastModified
    Response.Write "</TD></TR>"
    WriteToLog "Directory Entry for " + objFileItem.Name
  Next
  CloseLog
%>
```

The final step is to call the `CloseLog` subroutine, which will close the log file on the server.

While logging this type of information may not be very useful on a production basis, because the volume of information being written is just too large, and the problems involved with several sessions trying to write to the same log file at once. There are a number of occasions where a method like this can come in useful. This method can be used to output information to a log file as you are developing a page. If a problem occurs, it is very easy to go back to the log file to see what processing actually took place, and thereby determine what the error was.

The RegExp Object

The Regular Expression object, to give it its full name, is new in VBScript 5.0 and adds to the language something JavaScript developers have enjoyed for ages. But what is a regular expression, and why have VBScript developers been missing out on this important feature? Rather than describe what it is straightaway in rather abstract terms, I'm going to recount a short story of my juvenile delinquent days, which will help you visualize why regular expressions might be useful. Back to my Computer Science classes, when we were starry-eyed by the stories of hackers breaking into the Pentagon files with little more than a Commodore Vic20, we were convinced that we could break into anything too – well at least our colleagues' accounts, to check to see whether their coursework answers tallied with ours. Our coursework was stored on a UNIX system, and everybody kept theirs under a user account and password.

Now, one week we learned about the UNIX command GREP (it stands for Get Regular ExPression) and how it is used to look for a sequence of characters. Rumor quickly passed that if you got onto the system and forced it to make a dump of everything it had in its memory currently (known as a core dump), then you would come across the various user accounts logged on at the time together with the unencrypted passwords. As these core dumps would often amount to thousands of pages it just wasn't feasible to check every page of garbled information by hand, for these few nuggets, but the GREP command could be used to sift through the information. As everybody's account in our class started with the prefix dh1 followed by another two numbers, it was possible to set the GREP command to search for this pattern of letters along with another 2 characters after to locate the errant passwords. Not that we ever put them to use, of course.

So a regular expression is a sequence of characters, both known and unknown. You replace the unknown characters with wildcards. The regular expression forms what is known as a **search string**. The search string is what the object will attempt to locate within the data. The RegExp object provides a set of properties and methods for manipulating this search string.

RegExp Properties

The RegExp object has the following three properties:

- ❏ Global: used to indicate whether every occurrence of the search string should be matched, or just the first one VBScript comes across

- ❏ IgnoreCase: used to indicate whether or not the case should be taken into account when trying to match a search string

- ❏ Pattern: used to set (or return) the sequence being searched for

The first two properties mentioned both taken Boolean values and so they can only be set to true or false. Consider the following:

```
objRegExp.Pattern = "Hello Hello"
objRegExp.IgnoreCase = False
objRegExp.Global = True
```

In this example we are searching for the pattern "Hello Hello". Because we have set Global to True, we are saying that we want every occurrence of this sequence that is matched to be returned. By setting IgnoreCase to false then it will take account of the case of the text to be matched. So for example "hello hello" or "Hello hello" would both be ignored by the search.

The Pattern Property

However what gives RegExp its power is the fact that you don't have to know exactly what you're looking for. The Pattern property can take the form of a regular expression - a sequence of special characters and wildcards which specify which parts of the string are required for a match, and which parts we aren't interested in.

The regular expression is compared to the text we want to search character by character. If the RegExp object finds a match for the first character, it then looks to see if the following character matches the next character in the regular expression, and if so, it checks the next, and so on. The clever part is that we can tell the RegExp object to match one of a specific set of letters, or any letter, or a sequence of repeated letters. We do this using wildcards and special characters, and we'll take a look at those most commonly used now:

Character	Purpose
*	Matches zero or more occurrences of the preceding character. For example "be*" would match "b", "be", "bee", "beee" and so on.
?	Matches the preceding character zero or one times. For example "bottles?" would match both "bottle" and "bottles".
+	Matches preceding character one or more times. For example "to+" would match "to" and "too", but not t on its own
.	Matches any character. For example "ba." would match "bat", "bag" and "ban". It won't match anything that contains more or less characters.
(x | y)	Matches the x pattern OR the y pattern. "(bat|hit)" would match both "bat" and "hit", but nothing else.
{x}	Matches the preceding character exactly x times (obviously it can't be negative). So "e{3}" is the equivalent of the expression "eee".
[xyz]	Will match any of the enclosed characters, so "b[aeu]d" would match "bad", "bed" or "bud".
[^xyz]	Matches any of the character NOT contained in the set, so "[^sb]et" would match "get", but wouldn't match "set" or "bet".
[a-z]	Matches any character within the range specified. "[a-z]{3}", for example, will match any three letter word.

Character	Purpose
^	Matches the start of a line, for example "^a" would match any line beginning with the letter "a".
$	Matches the end of a line, for example "e$" would match any line ending with the letter "e".
\	This is used to allow us to match characters which otherwise have a special meaning in regular expressions, or which we can't type. for example, "*" is used to match an asterisk character, and "\t" matches a tab. "\\" is used to match a backslash character.

Let's take a string and look at whether some regular expressions will return a match.

```
The quick brown fox jumps over the lazy dog
```

First, remember that unless we specify the character "^" or "$", we'll get a match for our expression if it occurs anywhere within the string. So, the following regular expressions will all match:

```
quick
jumps
ver th
row
```

^The will match, since this word occurs at the start of the string, but ^lazy won't match.

Now, let's try something a bit more complicated.

The expression [a-z]+ can be used to match any word consisting of more than one letter (it matches one or more occurrences of a character between a and z). We could use that as follows:

```
The quick [a-z]+ fox jumps over the [a-z]+ dog
```

This will match our string, but it will also match different strings with different colored foxes and differently tempered dogs. Why? The RegExp object comes to the b in brown, and sees it is allowed, because it's in the range a to z. Likewise the r, the o, the w, and the n. When it comes across the next character, a space, it sees it is no longer allowed by the [a-z] expression, but that the next character is a space, so it carries on matching the literal characters we specified.

Here are some useful regular expression shorthands you might use:

Sequence	Purpose
.*	Matches zero or more characters. That's any character – including spaces, tabs and punctuation
[a-z]{x}	Matches an x letter word
[0-9]+	Matches a number consisting of one or more digits
[a-z]+@[a-z]+\.com	Matches any .com email address (assuming it doesn't contain any non alphabet characters)
[0-2]?[0-9]:[0-5][0-9]	Matches a time in 12 or 24 hour format

RegExp Methods

The RegExp object has three methods:

- ❑ Replace: replaces text found within the search
- ❑ Test: executes a search and returns a Boolean True or False value indicating whether the string was matched anywhere
- ❑ Execute: the method used to actually carry out the search, once the Pattern property has been specified. Execute is better than Test because it can return a number of matches rather than just the simple yes/no answer that Test returns indicating whether a match was found.

Replace is used where you supply the string you wish to search, followed by the new text you wish to insert. You must have previously defined the text to be replaced in the Pattern property. So if there had been computers available in medieval England, you might have found yourself charged with the following task:

```
objRegExp.Pattern = "Richard III"
objRegExp.Replace(strRoyalDocument, "Henry VII")
```

This acts just like a find and replace does in Word or the Replace function in VBScript does, the first string is the string to find, and the second is the one to replace. Simple!

The next method is only slightly more complex. Test takes one parameter – that of the original text or string being searched. If the Pattern property has already been set then it returns a True or False value. This value can then be used to clarify whether the search item was found or not, and then take appropriate action depending on the outcome:

```
strSearch = "abcdefghijklmnopqrstestuvwyz"
objRegExp.Pattern = "test"
blnFind = objRegExp.Test(strSearch)
If blnFind Then
```

```
   Response.Write "Pattern matched"
Else
   Response.Write "Pattern not matched"
End If
```

In this example, we'd just have one match of the pattern 'test'. Consider what might happen if we were searching for the letter 't' as our pattern instead. In which case there would be two matches. How would this be dealt with? The Execute method proves more complex than you might imagine. We've already hinted that you can return more than one match in a search, so what happens when you make more than one match in a search; how are details of them stored?

The Match Object

For each match made in the search string, a separate read-only Match object is created. Each Match object is stored in a Matches collection. The Match object itself has three properties. These are:

❑ FirstIndex: Returns a numerical value indicating where in the search string a match was found, as an offset from the first character. So a value of one would indicate that a match beginning at the second character.

❑ Length: The length of the match found within the search string

❑ Value: Returns the matching text or value found within the search string

So every time a match is made, you can use these properties to return the position and length of the match. If you go back to our previous example and wished to iterate through the Matches collection you could do the following:

```
set objRegExp = New RegExp
strSearch = "abcdefghijklmnopqrstestuvwyz"
objRegExp.Pattern = "t"
objRegExp.Global = True     'So search won't just return the first match only
Set Matches = objRegExp.Execute(strSearch)

For Each Match in Matches
  Response.Write "Text " & Match.Value &  " found at position " & Match.FirstIndex &
"<BR>"
Next
```

You would return the following answer:
Text t found at position 19
Text t found at position 22

This is a relatively trivial example, so now we've introduced all of the requisite properties and methods, let's look at a more detailed example.

Try It Out – Finding and Replacing a Name

Having asserted that the RegExp object has a method that allows you to find and replace text within a given search string let's actually use a more taxing example. A while ago, members of my office found that the funniest thing they could possibly do was to take famous quotes from a well-known film, and replace the key words with the word "pants". Much hilarity ensued, to the general bewilderment of most, but in honor of these great gaffes, we've got a great program that can do this for you automatically.

> *This example could also be done using the* Replace *function in VBScript, however we wish to demonstrate the* RegExp *objects power to return the position of a certain search string in a text. You can adapt the search string contained within the* Pattern *property with wildcards and whatever, to demonstrate that ultimately, it offers a lot more power.*

1. Download from the Wrox web site at `http://webdev.wrox.co.uk/books/3382`, the file `textfile.txt`. This file is a large custom-made text file, which contains a tiny snippet of said film's script.

2. Open up your trusty ASP editor and type in the following:

```
<!-- #include file="textfile.txt" -->
<HTML>
<HEAD>
<TITLE></TITLE>
</HEAD>
<BODY>

<%
  Set objRegExp = New RegExp
  objRegExp.Pattern = "Force"
  objRegExp.Global = True
  Set Matches = objRegExp.Execute(strSearch)

  For Each Match in Matches
    Response.Write "Text " & Match.Value & " was found at position "
    Response.Write Match.FirstIndex & "<BR>"
  Next

  strReplace = objRegExp.Replace(strSearch,"Pants")
  Response.Write "With the text replaced, the script now reads:<BR>"
  Response.Write (strReplace)
%>

</BODY>
</HTML>
```

3. Save it as `match.asp` and view it in the browser.

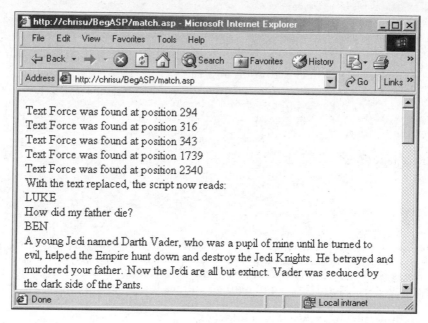

Text Force was found at position 294
Text Force was found at position 316
Text Force was found at position 343
Text Force was found at position 1739
Text Force was found at position 2340
With the text replaced, the script now reads:
LUKE
How did my father die?
BEN
A young Jedi named Darth Vader, who was a pupil of mine until he turned to evil, helped the Empire hunt down and destroy the Jedi Knights. He betrayed and murdered your father. Now the Jedi are all but extinct. Vader was seduced by the dark side of the Pants.

How It Works

We're not really doing anything more than we've done in the previous explanations. We start by creating an instance of the RegExp object

```
Set objRegExp = New RegExp
```

We set the Pattern property to equal "force" as that's the word we're going to replace with "pants". We also set the Global property to equal true, as we don't just want to replace one occurrence, but every occurrence.

```
objRegExp.Pattern = "Force"
objRegExp.Global = True
```

At the beginning of the ASP we've added the include file `textfile.txt` which contains our target text. However, cunningly, we've surrounded the text with the ASP declaration `strSearch =` so that our whole text is now kept in string format. So in the next line we can start our search in the Matches collection, using strSearch as our target search string:

```
Set Matches = objRegExp.Execute(strSearch)
```

We then create a loop to iterate through each occurrence of the `Match` object and display the text it contains and the position it was found at:

```
For Each Match in Matches
  Response.Write "Text " & Match.Value & " was found at position "
  Response.Write Match.FirstIndex &"<BR>"
Next
```

Finally we go back to our text and replace whatever is held in the Pattern property with the word "Pants" and display it using Response.Write.

```
strReplace = objRegExp.Replace(strSearch,"Pants")
Response.Write "With the text replaced, the script now reads:<BR>"
Response.Write (strReplace)
```

That's all there is to it.

Summary

In this chapter, we have looked at the Scripting Objects and how they can be used inside of Active Server Pages. We have considerd a set of objects which are normally available in client-side VBScript as well as ASP, via two libraries, the Scripting Runtime library and the VBScript library itself. They are useful as a set of helper routines for developing web applications.

The Scripting Runtime objects we looked at were:

- ❏ The Dictionary object, which lets you store and retrieve information in a flexible data structure. In a Dictionary, each piece of information that you store is associated with a key. At a later time, that information can be retrieved simply by producing the key.

- ❏ The FileSystemObject object, which provides access to the physical file system of the web server. With this object, you can view and manipulate the directories and files that make up the server's file system.

- ❏ The TextStream object, which gives you access to the contents of text files stored on the web server. This object allows you to read text from the file as well as write information to the file.

The VBScript objects we looked at were:

- ❏ The RegExp object is used to search and manipulate text files using what are known as regular expressions

- ❏ The Match object stores details of any matches encountered during our searches

By using these objects, you can extend the reach of your web applications beyond what exists inside of the six built-in ASP objects. They allow you to categorize and store information more efficiently, as well as manipulate the physical file system of the server itself.

In the next chapter, we will look at how we can extend ASP's functionality further by using a set of built-in components provided with ASP, and also how we'd go about installing ones available from third party sources.

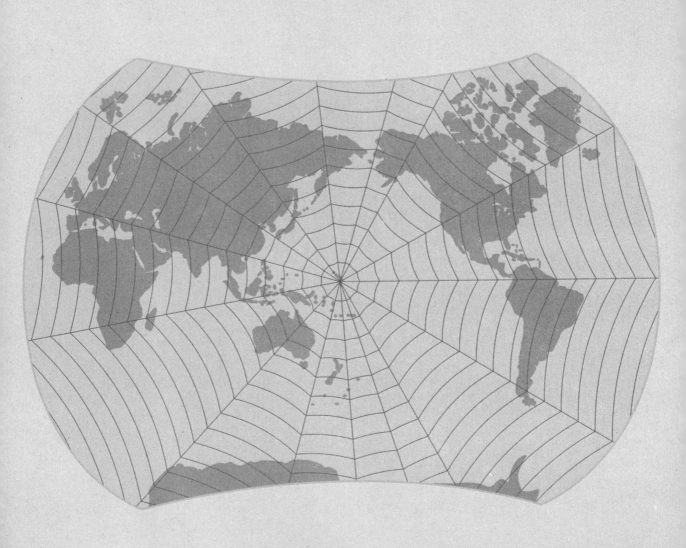

Active Server Pages Components

Most web site designers have similar basic goals for their site, including:

❑ A technique to navigate through their web site

❑ A way to manage advertisements on the site

❑ Molding pages to accommodate the capabilities of the visitor's browser

It would be inefficient for all web masters to spend time writing the code to achieve these common goals. Far better, then, for a single team of experts to develop, troubleshoot and optimize the code, then make it available for everyone. Microsoft has done just this with a set of tools that automate these common tasks, called **Installable Components for ASP**. In this chapter we will cover the general concept, then look at four components:

❑ The Server Object and how to use Server Components – the basics of the techniques.

❑ The Advertisement Rotator Component – A tool used to display advertisements on your site.

❑ The Content Linker – A tool to allow the website manager to link together a series of pages, for example to create a tour of the site or to step through the pages of a tutorial.

❑ The Browser Capabilities Component – a tool to determine what features, like tables, scripting and frames, your visitor's browser supports. With that knowledge you can build pages that take advantage of every feature available, but do not rely on unsupported functions.

The Server Object

The tools that Microsoft provides with ASP are organized into objects, as we covered in Chapter 6. To review; the software designer (in this case, Microsoft) creates an object which can hold and/or provide information (**properties**) and can carry out certain tasks (**methods**). ASP has seven objects: the Server, Application, Request, Response, Session, Error, and ObjectContext objects.

The Server object allows you to create **components,** which are pre-packaged software objects that Microsoft and others have created to provide commonly needed functions. As you move further into ASP, you will probably create your own components as well – this is introduced in chapter 16. Microsoft has provided about a dozen components that contain the ability to add powerful features to your site. We will look at three of these components in this chapter.

> *The rest of these Microsoft components are covered in the ASP 3 Programmer's Reference (Wrox Press – ISBN 1861003234).*

Many students ask why some capabilities are encapsulated in components, whereas others (like reading information from a querystring) are not. MS put a reflection of the information defined in the HTTP standards into the intrinsic ASP objects. These are the most basic and frequently used functions, such as reading from a request and writing to the nascent page. Then, the MS designers built additional goal-oriented features into components. With this split, the core functions are always loaded and quickly available, whereas less-universal tasks are loaded in memory only as needed. Furthermore, Microsoft tries to focus on developing the core of each software product and then allows other companies to build accessories to enhance that core. In ASP, this means that Microsoft includes a few rudimentary components, but encourages the development of additional components from third party vendors.

To summarize, the more basic and closely matched a function is to the HTTP standards, the more likely it is contained in one of the seven intrinsic ASP objects. The more specialized a function, the more likely it is to be available in a component; either from Microsoft, a third party, or custom developed from your own programming team.

Creating an Instance of a Component

When you want to use a Server component, the first step is to create an **instance** of a component using the `CreateObject` method of the `Server` object.

You'll recall our discussion of the relationship between objects and instances from Chapter 5. Essentially, the component (sometimes a *class* or *type*) is the template; and an instance is a particular copy that is created in the shape of that template. This action is similar to cookies coming out of a cookie cutter. The act of creating an object from a component is called instantiation.

In ASP, we first `Dim` a variable to hold a reference to the object. We then create an instance of the component with the `Server.CreateObject` method. This returns a reference to that object, which is assigned to our variable using the `Set` statement. The instance must be assigned to a variable name – this allows you to refer to the instance later on in your code. If we go by the naming convention outlines that we discussed previously, these are prefixed with `obj` before an abbreviation of the name of the component. For example, if you were using an instance of the Next Linker, then you might want to give it a variable name like `objNextLink` or `objNL`. Since the instance of your object is held in a variable, it should also be named in a similar manner. You may recall that we discussed naming conventions and rules in Chapter 4.

A typical instantiation would look like the following piece of code:

```
<%
  Dim objNL
  Set objNL = Server.CreateObject("MSWC.NextLink")
  ...
      'These lines can contain code that uses objNL
  ...
%>
```

We Dim the variable that will hold the instance of our object in the normal manner – avoiding characters other then the underscore, starting with a letter and preferably starting with the obj abbreviation to designate an object. Then we use the Set statement, followed by the name that we have chosen for our instance. On the right of the equal sign is the code that we use to create an instance of the Server object's NextLink component. To give you the proper vocabulary, we are instantiating from a ("Library.Class"), or ("Vendor.Component"). (Class can sometimes be called ObjectType.) All of the Microsoft components that ship with ASP are in the Library "MSWC", standing for the Microsoft Web Class. Components from third parties or from other Microsoft software will have other class names.

Many students ask how to find out more about a given component. You can view all of the properties and methods of a class by using the Object Browser that comes with Microsoft Visual Basic and also with the VBA editors in Word, Excel and Access. (Of course, it must be a machine with IIS installed.) The techniques for VB and VBA Editors are a bit different; so pick the appropriate paragraph below.

To use the Object Browser in VB, you open a new project and click through Menu:Project/References, scroll down to MSWC (after "Microsoft") and you will see the ASP components listed, for example MSWC Advertisement Rotator Object Library and MSWC Content Linking Object Library. Click the corresponding checkboxes (to the left) to include those of interest, then close the References dialog box. Now click through Menu:View/ObjectBrowser or strike F2.

To use the Object Browser in one of the VBA Editors you start the application (Word, Excel or Access), then strike Alt+F11 to open the VBA editor. Click through Menu:Tools/References, scroll down to MSWC (after "Microsoft") and you will see the ASP components listed, for example MSWC Advertisement Rotator Object Library and MSWC Content Linking Object Library. Click the corresponding checkboxes (to the left) to include those of interest, then close the References dialog box. Now you can open the object browser by Menu:View/ObjectBrowser or striking F2.

Once the Object Browser is open, drop down the Project/Library list in the top left corner. Click on the component of interest and you can see its methods and properties in the pane to the right. Properties have an icon with a hand pointing to a list, methods have a flying green box and Events have a lightening bolt. By single clicking on a feature on the right you can get a short description and syntax guide in the gray pane below.

Common Instantiation Errors

- ❏ Forgetting the keyword `Set`

- ❏ Forgetting the equal sign

- ❏ Leaving off the `obj` prefix and ending up with a name that is a keyword

- ❏ Subsequently using a different name for the object

- ❏ Using unallowable characters in the object name

- ❏ Wrong ProgID or ClassType

- ❏ Errors in that pesky syntax of quotes-within-parenthesis. Remember that after `Server.CreateObject` we have a pair of parenthesis. Within the parenthesis we have a pair of double quotes. Within those double quotes we have the Library and Class separated by a period.

Now, we'll look at the specific techniques of using three components: the Ad Rotator, Content Linking, and Browser Capability.

The Ad Rotator Component

To date, one of the most common sources of revenue on the World Wide Web has been the sale of advertising space. Although the Ad Rotator is not limited to Banner ads, in this book we will concentrate on this standard format of a .GIF file: 440 pixels wide by 60 pixels high. Since viewers will pay little attention to the same ad again and again, site designers want to rotate a collection of ads in the hope of giving each visit a fresh and inviting look. Furthermore, many sites charge advertisers by the number of hits or impressions (both mean the number of times an ad is shown to viewers) or the number of click-throughs that you track for invoicing. ASP includes a component, the **Ad Rotator**, which performs and manages the task of presenting ads in rotation as pages are requested.

The Ad Rotator component utilizes the following four files. The first two you make specifically to implement the Ad Rotator. The third is an existing page in your site, upon which you want to display ads. The fourth, the Targets, are provided by and hosted at the site of the advertiser.

File	Purpose	Type	File Name in the Try-It-Out
Scheduler	Hold information on the ads	DOS ASCII text	AdRotatorSchedule.txt
Redirector	React to user clicking on an ad, including statistics and redirection to advertiser's site	.ASP	AdRotatorRedirector.asp

File	Purpose	Type	File Name in the Try-It-Out
Display Page	Web page that will display ads along with the rest of the information on the page	.ASP	AdRotatorHomePage.asp
Targets	Pages on advertisers' site where users are sent when an ad is clicked	Any URL	Wrox Press homepage Wrox Conferences homepage ActivePath homepage

When a visitor requests the display page, the ad rotator will calculate which ad to show next, gather the information for that ad from the scheduler.txt and pass it to the display page. The ad will appear on the display page, along with the rest of the text and graphics of the page. If the visitor clicks on the ad then the redirector page is opened, with the URL for the ad's target page passed along in the querystring. Usually the redirector page contains no viewable HTML; rather it has code that updates click-through statistics and then immediately redirects the user to the advertiser's site.

The click-through statistics can be sent to a datastore or held in application or session level variables. Our exercise will use application variables created in global.asa and we will create a small page called AdRotatorViewHits.asp to check on the number of times visitors have clicked on each ad. So, we will also work with the following two files.

File	Purpose	Type	File Name in the Try-It-Out
global.asa	Holds application variables which hold count of clicks on ads	global.asa	global.asa
Hits Viewer	Used by webmaster (not visitors) to view number of click-throughs	.asp	AdRotatorViewHits.asp

Let's take a closer look at the structure of the **scheduler file** before we try out the ad rotator. The schedule keeps track of which ads should be displayed, how frequently to display them, the advertiser's URL where the user will be sent, and an alternate text to display. Create your scheduler file as a simple ASCII text file with two sections. The first section sets the general parameters for displaying all ads and ends with an asterisk. The second section sets specific parameters for each ad in the rotation.

In the first section, there are four general parameters that can be set to apply to all ads in the file. If you leave any of these parameters out, then ASP will provide the default shown in parenthesis.

- The name of the file that is used to redirect the user when he/she clicks on the ads, as listed in row one of the table below (No default)

- The width of the ad as it will appear on the page (460)

- The height of the ad as it will appear on the page (65)

- The width of the borders of the ad as it will appear on the page (1)

Remember that this section must end with a single line containing an asterisk, and nothing else on that line. In the following example schedule file, we will depart from the normal ad size to illustrate changes from the defaults.

```
Redirect AdRotatorRedirector.asp
Width 460
Height 65
Border 1
*
wroxconferences.gif
http://www.WroxConferences.com
WroxConferences - Held in America, Europe and Asia
20
activepath.gif
-
Activepath provides textbooks and teaching materials for software training
10
wroxpress.gif
http://www.wrox.com
Wrox Press, Programmer to Programmer
50
```

In the second section of the above file, we write four lines for each ad in the rotation. Since there is no marker dividing the entries, the parser counts off every four lines as a group. Therefore, use no more and no less then four lines per ad and do not revise the order of information. Note that we do not type double quotes around any of the parameters, in either of the two sections of the scheduler file. The four lines used for each ad represent the following:

- The name of the file that holds the ad graphic (for example, WroxConferences.gif).

- The URL of the hyperlink to be sent to the Redirector file if the user clicks on the ad. If no hyperlink is required – that is, the user's click causes no action – then we use a single hyphen (with no spaces) in place of an URL.

- Text description of the ad graphic for text-only browsers.

- The frequency with which the ad should be displayed.

Calculate the frequency of display for an ad by dividing its frequency parameter by the total of all the frequency parameters. So, in the sample below, the total of the frequencies is 20+10+50 = 80. The WroxConferences ad will run 20/80 or 25% of the time. (Remember that a number is not a *percentage* unless the total comes to 100.)

Common Errors in the Scheduler file include:

- ❑ Putting quotes around parameters in the scheduler file (as we mentioned earlier, this isn't necessary).

- ❑ Leaving out the asterisk after the section containing the four general parameters.

- ❑ More or less than four lines of information for each ad – you must have **exactly** four lines.

- ❑ Wrong order of information for an ad – the information must follow the order described above: Filename, URL, Description, and Frequency.

Try It Out – The Ad Rotator Component

We'll create a page that gives a tip for programming students. Each time the page is viewed, it will also display one of three ads.

1. Begin by downloading three sample ad files. In the real world, your advertisers would send these to you, but for this exercise, we will download `WroxConferences.gif`, `ActivePath.gif` and `WroxPress.gif` from the Wrox Press web site at `http://www.wrox.com/`, and save them into your `BegASPFiles` directory.

At the same time, you can also download all of the files that we will be creating in this chapter from the website.

2. Next, we set up the scheduler file. Either download `AdRotatorSchedule.txt` from the Wrox site or open up your editor of choice and type the following lines. Save this as `AdRotatorSchedule.txt` in your `BegASPFiles` directory.

```
Redirect AdRotatorRedirector.asp
Width 460
Height 65
Border 1
*
wroxconferences.gif
http://www.WroxConferences.com
WroxConferences - Held in America, Europe and Asia
20
activepath.gif
-
Activepath provides textbooks and teaching materials for software training
10
wroxpress.gif
http://www.wrox.com
Wrox Press, Programmer to Programmer
50
```

3. Now, we need a place to hold the number of clicks on each ad. In this exercise, we will do that in an application variable. Add the following shaded lines to your `global.asa`. More sophisticated editors will create a `global.asa` for you and you will just have to add the shaded lines below. If you do not already have an `.asa`, then type all of the lines below into a simple text file and name it `global.asa` in your `BegASPFiles` directory.

```
Sub Application_OnStart
  Application("iWroxPress") = 0
  Application("iWroxConf") = 0
End Sub
</SCRIPT>
```

4. Next, we create the file to handle a user's click on an ad. Open your editor, type the following code, and save as `AdRotatorRedirector.asp` in your `BegASPFiles` directory.

```
<%
  ' This page handles logging of clicks, then redirects

  strURL = Request.Querystring("url")

  Select Case lcase(strURL)
    Case "http://www.wrox.com"
      Application.Lock
      Application("iWroxPress") = Application("iWroxPress") + 1
      Application.Unlock
    Case "http://www.wroxconferences.com"
      Application.Lock
      Application("iWroxConf") = Application("iWroxConf") + 1
      Application.Unlock
  End Select

  Response.Redirect strURL
%>
```

5. Lastly, we can create a page that will display ads using the Ad Rotator Component and the above files. Clear your editor, type the following code, and save as `AdRotatorHomePage.asp`, again in the `BegASPFiles` directory.

```
<HTML>
<HEAD>
<TITLE>Ad_Rotator_Home_Page</TITLE>
</HEAD>
<BODY>

<H3>Ad rotator home page</H3>
Programmer's tip:<BR>
When writing a loop always double check which commands <BR>
should be inside the loop and which should be outside the loop.<BR><BR>
<%
  Dim objAR
  Set objAR = Server.Createobject("MSWC.AdRotator")
  Response.Write (objAR.GetAdvertisement("AdRotatorSchedule.txt"))
%>
</BODY>
</HTML>
```

6. That takes care of the pages for the visitor using the ad rotator. However, as webmasters, we would like to know how many clicks our ads have accumulated. We will now make a final page that displays the statistics. Clear your editor and type the following code and save this code as `AdRotatorViewHits.asp`, again in the `BegASPFiles` directory.

```
<HTML>
<HEAD>
<TITLE>Ad_Rotator_Hit_Viewer</TITLE>
</HEAD>
<BODY>
This page gives you feedback on number of click-throughs<BR>

<TABLE Border = 1>
  <TR>
    <TD>WroxPress</TD>
    <TD><%= Application("iWroxPress")%></TD>
  </TR>
  <TR>
    <TD>WroxConferences</TD>
    <TD><%= Application("iWroxConf")%></TD>
  </TR>
</TABLE>

</BODY>
</HTML>
```

7. We have now finished entering our code. However, before testing, close your browser and then stop your application to reset the application variables back to zero. Open up the MMC and select the Default Web Site. Click on the **Action** Menu, and then select **Stop** to stop your web server. Wait a few seconds and click **Start**, then close the MMC.

8. Test your Ad Rotator by using your browser to look at `http://my_server_name/AdRotatorHomePage.asp`. Try viewing the page a number of times by pressing the **Refresh/Reload** button. You should get the text information (Programmer's tip) every time, but a different ad appearing. Clicking on the ad should take you to the appropriate advertiser.

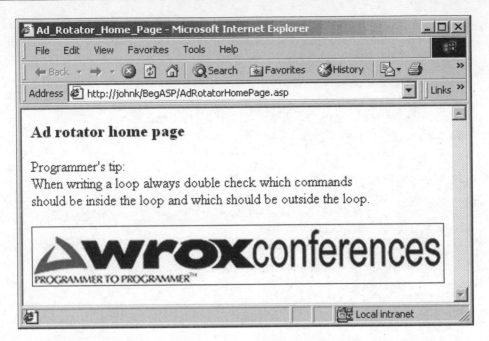

After several clicks on ads, use the browser to open `AdRotatorViewHits.asp` to see the click-through statistics.

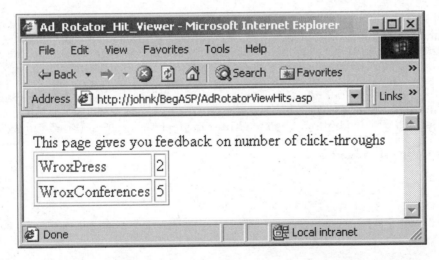

How It Works

We set up an ad rotation scheme featuring the ads of three companies in our `AdRotatorSchedule.txt`. First, we specify the name of the file to which is sent the advertiser's URL after a click. Then we slightly change the ad size and border width from the default. Then we end the first section with a line containing nothing more than an asterisk:

```
Redirect AdRotatorRedirector.asp
Width 460
Height 65
Border 2
*
```

Next, we code the details of the three ads, ensuring that this section contains exactly four rows for each ad. These rows contain the name of the ad image file, the hyperlink URL, a comment that the browser associates with the graphic, and the relative frequency with which the ad should be shown. Note that in this example, Active Path has asked us to show their ad but do not offer click-throughs, therefore their URL is replaced with a hyphen. The frequencies have been set based on selling eighths of the total volume of ad appearances. While Wrox Conferences bought two eighths (20 out of a total of 80), Active Path bought one eighth only:

```
wroxconferences.gif
http://www.wroxconferences.com
WroxConferences - Held in America, Europe and Asia
20
activepath.gif
-
Activepath provides textbooks and teaching materials for software training
10
wroxpress.gif
http://www.wrox.com
Wrox Press, Programmer to Programmer
50
```

In this exercise, we store the statistics on click-throughs in an application variable in the global.asa. Application and Session variables are covered in depth in Chapter 8. For now, we just need to create a variable for each ad within the Application_Open event. In this case, we set them equal to zero since there will be no click-throughs when the application is started:

```
<SCRIPT LANGUAGE=VBScript RUNAT=Server>
Sub Application_OnStart
  Application("iWroxPress") = 0
  Application("iWroxConf") = 0
End Sub
</SCRIPT>
```

The file to handle a user's click is, like Gaul, divided into three parts. Note that this page will perform some processing and then send the user on his way to one of the advertiser's sites. Therefore we do not need <HTML>, <HEADER> or any other tags for setting up a "real" page that the user would view. Firstly, we grab the data named "url" from the querystring and store it in a variable:

```
<%
  ' this page handles logging of clicks, then redirects

  strURL = Request.Querystring("url")
```

Then we figure out which URL we have got using a `Select Case`. Depending on the match, we update one or the other of the application variables. Just prior to changing the application variable we lock the application and just after the change we unlock it. Since there are no click-throughs from ActivePath (remember the hyphen in the `Schedule.txt`?) we do not need to include ActivePath in the `Select Case`:

```
Select Case lcase(strURL)
  Case "http://www.wrox.com"
    Application.lock
    Application("iWroxPress") = Application("iWroxPress") + 1
    Application.unlock
  Case "http://www.wroxconferences.com"
    Application.lock
    Application("iWroxConf") = Application("iWroxConf") + 1
    Application.unlock
End Select
```

Our last step is to send the visitor to the advertiser's site:

```
  Response.Redirect strURL
%>
</BODY>
</HTML>
```

The `AdRotatorHomePage.asp` starts with the usual headings, and then displays the Programmer's tip:

```
<HTML>
<HEAD>
<TITLE>Ad_Rotator_Home_Page</TITLE>
</HEAD>
<BODY>

<H3>Ad rotator home page</H3>
Programmer's tip:<BR>
When writing a loop always double check which commands <BR>
should be inside the loop and which should be outside the loop.<BR><BR>
```

The code that actually shows the ad is very concise. We `Dim` and `Set` an object of the `AdRotator` class. Then we run its `GetAdvertisement` method and put that result onto the page with a `Response.Write`:

```
<%
  Dim objAR
  Set objAR=Server.CreateObject("MSWC.AdRotator")
  Response.Write (objAR.Getadvertisement("AdRotatorSchedule.txt"))
%>
</BODY>
</HTML>
```

Viewing the statistics with the AdRotatorViewHits.asp again relies on the techniques of Application variables as covered in Chapter 8. We build a simple table and write the current value of the application variables:

```
<HTML>
<HEAD>
<TITLE>Ad_Rotator_Hit_Viewer</TITLE>
</HEAD>
<BODY>
This page gives you feedback on number of click-throughs<BR>
<TABLE Border = 1>
<TR>
  <TD>WroxPress</TD>
  <TD><%= Application("iWroxPress")%></TD>
</TR>
<TR>
  <TD>WroxConferences</TD>
  <TD><%= Application("iWroxConf")%></TD>
</TR>
</TABLE>
</BODY>
```

Common Errors

If you had trouble with this example, here's a checklist of things that you might have missed:

- ❏ Testing before all elements are in place; scheduler, ads and redirector

- ❏ Redirector file does not do a `Server.Execute` or `Server.Transfer` to actually get the user to the advertiser's site

- ❏ Files are scattered across different folders without paths

- ❏ Mismatches between variable names in `global.asa`, `AdRotatorRedirector.asp` and `AdRotatorViewHits.asp`

- ❏ Mismatch in file names between `Schedule.txt` and `Redirector.asp`

After reading the chapter on data access you may want to try making another `AdRotatorRedirector.asp`, this time keeping the click counts in a datastore rather then an application variable. At the simplest level you would set up a table named `Ads` with each record being an advertisement, and having fields called `ClickCounter` and `AdURL`. Then instead of the `Select Case` section you would use:

```
///// Store to database an increment
SQLtext = "UPDATE Ads"
SQLtext=SQLtext& " SET Ads.ClickCounter = Ads.ClickCounter+1"
SQLtext=SQLtext& " WHERE Ads.AdURL='" & strURL & "');"
```

We'll be talking more about using datastores with ASP in Chapter 12.

The Content Linking Component

A well-designed web site will provide the visitor with tools and guidance to navigate the site. ASP allows you to create one type of guidance tool by using the **Content Linker**, also called the NextLink component. You can create a list of pages in a specific order as a path through the site. Then on any given page in this path, the user can click on the Next or Previous buttons, and display the appropriate page in the path. The Content Linker even allows you to display a description of the next/previous pages. Additional features of the Content Linker allow you to program sophisticated jumps or loops. For example, the Content Linker would enable the following objectives:

- ❑ Tutorial
- ❑ Five-minute tour
- ❑ Review of new products (we'll use this as the example in this chapter)
- ❑ Multi-page forms

In this section of the chapter, we'll start with a very simple example, which you can have a go at yourself as we walk through the first Try-It-Out. Then we'll improve on the example in a step-by-step manner (with Try-It-Outs for you) until you have a very sophisticated set of navigation tools.

Structure of the Content Linking Component

The content linker has two parts:

- ❑ **The index file**. An ASCII text file that holds a list of .asp pages, in the order that they should be presented to the viewer. The index file can easily be changed to add new pages, revise the order of pages, or substitute newer pages for older pages.

- ❑ **The ASP pages**. Each .asp file contains two parts. The first part consists of the normal content of the page, such as the text and graphics. The second part is the ASP code that uses the Content Linker to give the user options for moving through the list of pages. These options are typically hyperlinks for the Next Page, Previous Page, First Page, and Last Page.

Although most people refer to this component as the Content Linking or Content Linker component, in IIS5 it is referred to as NextLink. For our purposes, the two terms will be used interchangeably.

Using Content Linking

Over the next few pages, we will build several examples of increasing complexity, but let's start here by looking at an example that doesn't even use ASP. Consider the HTML page shown below, which displays information about the first item on our tour of new products – hat model #501. We'll refer to this as CL-less-Hat501.htm, the CL for content linker. You can try making this page, but it is not required for the other exercises of this chapter.

```
<HTML>
<HEAD>
<TITLE>Hat with no content linking</TITLE>
</HEAD>
<BODY>
<P>Hat of the Week:</P>
<P>Featuring an expanding elastic rim</P>
<A HREF="CL-Sweater.asp">Click here for next item</A>
</BODY>
</HTML>
```

At the top of the page, the user will see text that describes this hat; at the bottom of the page, there is a hyperlink which, when clicked, takes the user to the next item on the tour of products (in this case, the page describing sweater #304). In this context, what we're really interested in is the site navigation technique. Here's the line that should jump to our attention:

```
<A HREF="CL-Sweater.asp">Click here for next item</A>
```

In this first case, the HREF to the next page is hard-coded: that is, it's typed in raw HTML. Note that the target of the HREF attribute must be in double quotes. Provided you've already created the target page CL_Sweater.asp, the user will have no problem with this.

However, when it is time for the web master to make changes to the order of the pages, he will have to dig through every page, find each of these Next hyperlinks, and write in the new HREF. It's a laborious task (believe me, I've done it); and it's also very confusing, since there is no stage at which the web master ever sees the whole list of pages on the tour. This problem can be neatly overcome by using the content linker which, in turn, uses the index file containing the full list of the tour.

A note on the files used in the Try It Outs for Content Linking

We will be creating a site with four pages of clothing products which we want the visitor to tour. Our focus in this section will be on the code to navigate from page to page. We will put all of the code for navigation into a file called "CL-Navigation.asp" which will be included as a footer in each product page. In this way we only have to make changes in one place and they will apply to all pages. At the end we will add a table of contents page. So the files in the next table will be created and modified. Note that each file name begins with CL- so that they stay together in an alphabetical listing of files in your BegASPFiles directory. There is no other purpose to the naming. Note that we will be making several improvements to the navigation footer file. I suggest you keep the old ones so that you can review the simpler versions of the code. You can name them CL-Navigation01, CL-Navigation02, etc., but your currently utilized file will always be the one named simply CL-Navigation.asp.

File	Purpose	Type	File Name in the Try-It-Out
Index File	Hold list of pages and order to visit	DOS ASCII text	`CL-NewProductsTour.txt`
Navigation code file	Page that holds the navigation code which is included as a footer in each page on the tour	`.ASP`	`CL-Navigation.asp`
Web pages	Pages on the tour which utilize the content linker	`.ASP`	`CL-Hat.asp` `CL-Sweater.asp` `CL-Tie.asp` `CL-Trouser.asp` `CL-vest.asp`
Table of Contents Page	A page with code to demonstrate building a TOC from a Content Linker Index	`.ASP`	`CL-TOC.asp`

Content Linker Index File

A good first step in creating a tour of our pages is to build the Index file. After creating an index file in this Try-it-Out we will create pages for sweaters, hats, trousers, etc. in the next Try-It-Outs. Eventually, each page will have 'next' and 'previous' buttons to guide the visitor through the tour.

Try It Out – Creating an Index File

We first need to construct the index file. We will be using this file in our examples, so it is important to create it exactly as shown below.

1. Start your text editor and create a file with one line for each URL that will be in the tour of pages. Save this file in your `BegASPFiles` folder, giving it the name `CL-NewProductsTour.txt`. Note that to make troubleshooting a little easier, I have put the pages in alphabetical order.

```
CL-hat.asp        This Week's Hat       Run for Sept 01-08 2001
CL-sweater.asp    This Week's Sweater   Run for Sept 01-15 2001
CL-tie.asp        This Week's Tie       Run for Sept 01-08 2001
CL-trouser.asp    This Week's Trousers  Run for Sept 01-23 2001
CL-vest.asp       This Week's Vest      Run for Sept 01-15 2001
```

It's important to format this file correctly, so separate the entries on each line with a Tab *– nothing else – and press* Enter *at the end of each line, to start the new line. Hence, each line should be typed as:* URL *Tab* Description *Tab* Comments *Enter. The URL does not need to be prefixed with* http:// *provided you intend to store the page in the same directory as the other pages. The order of the entries from top to bottom determines the order that the visitor will be guided through the site.*

How it Works

In the lines of the index file, we have created three columns separated by tabs:

- ❏ URL column
- ❏ Description column
- ❏ Comments column

The URLs are the files that are contained in our tour of pages: we must list them in the order in which we want them to appear in the tour. The contents of the **Description** column will be used later to give information to the user. The contents of the **Comments** column will only be seen by the site designers when they look at the index file. The **Comments** column is optional. You can add various comment lines such as a title for the file, comments or a revision date.

Common Errors with Index files

- ❏ Adding more than one tab between the columns
- ❏ Using spaces between columns rather than the required tab
- ❏ Forgetting to save the file to the BegASPFiles folder
- ❏ Forgetting to put the file extension (for example, .asp) on the file names in column one

ASP Pages that Use Content Linker to Hyperlink to the Next Page

Our first example will use the Content Linker simply to show us the next URL based on what ASP finds in the index file. This example uses the NewProductsTour.txt file from the last Try-It-Out.

Try It Out – A Simple Content Linker Example

This example uses the index file, CL-NewProductsTour.txt, CL-NavigationFooter, and five other ASP files that are the pages we want the visitor to walk through on her tour. This looks like a lot of code, but the five ASP files are similar enough that you can cut and paste.

1. We will start with the footer that will hold the navigation code. Open your editor of choice, type in the following and save in your `BegASPFiles` folder as `CL-Navigation.asp`. If you are downloading files from the Wrox website, the file below will be `CL-Navigaton01.asp`; rename it to `CL-Navigaton.asp`.

```
<%
  Response.Write "<HR>"
  Dim MyPageNext
  Dim objNL
  Set objNL = Server.Createobject("MSWC.NextLink")
  MyPageNext = objNL.GetNextURL("CL-NewProductsTour.txt")

  Response.Write "Next: <A HREF='" & MyPageNext & "'>Click here for next item </A>"
%>
```

2. Open your editor of choice, type in the following and save in your `BegASPFiles` folder as `CL-Hat.asp`.

```
<% Option Explicit %>
<HTML>
<HEAD>
<TITLE>Hat</TITLE>
</HEAD>
<BODY>
<P>Hat of the Week:</P>
<P>Featuring an expanding elastic rim</P>
<!--#include file="CL-Navigation.asp"--></BODY>
</HTML>
```

3. Now we need to make very similar pages for the next four items of clothing that we sell. To make life easier we will just change a few lines in the `CL-Hat.asp` page and use **SaveAs** to make that our Sweater page. After you have saved the above Hat file, use the editor to change it to the following and use **SaveAs** to store this file in the same directory as `CL-Sweater.asp`:

```
<% Option Explicit %>
<HTML>
<HEAD>
<TITLE>Sweater</TITLE>
</HEAD>
<BODY>
<P>Sweater of the Week:</P>
<P>Perfect for yachting in navy blue</P>
Just in from Pat's Sweaters</P>
<!--#include file="CL-Navigation.asp"--></BODY>
</HTML>
```

4. Once you have saved the sweater file, repeat the above step to create three more files as follows.

A file named `CL-Tie.asp`.

```
<TITLE>Tie</TITLE>
...
<P>Tie of the Week:</P>
<P>Power Yellow, for that bid presentation</P>
```

A file named `CL-Trouser.asp`.

```
<TITLE>Trouser</TITLE>
...
<P>Trousers of the Week:</P>
<P>With special pockets for PDAs</P>
```

A file named `CL-Vest.asp`.

```
<TITLE>Vest562</TITLE>
...
<P>Vest of the Week:</P>
<P>Flowered Vest for dancing around the MayPole</P>
```

5. Now, test your Hat page by opening your browser of choice and typing in the URL `http://my_server_name/BegASP/CL-Hat.asp`. Click on the **Next** hyperlink, to move forward through the tour.

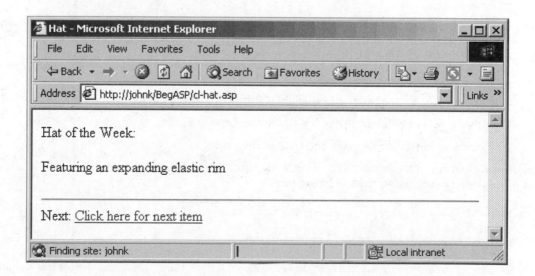

How It Works

Let's look at the file CL_Hat.asp first. In fact, it looks very similar to the HTML file CL-Hat-NoContentLinking.asp that we saw earlier in this chapter, when considering the benefits of using Content Linker. However, instead of the hard-coded <A HREF> we have inserted the CL-Navigation.asp file, which contains the code of interest:

```
<HTML>
<HEAD>
<TITLE>Hat</TITLE>
</HEAD>
<BODY>
<P>Hat of the Week:</P>
<P>Featuring an expanding elastic rim</P>
<!--#include file="CL-Navigation.asp"-->
</BODY>
</HTML>
```

Within CL-Navigation.asp we create a horizontal line so you can see where the navigation area begins, then Dim a variable and an object. We use the Set statement to create an instance of the NextLink component, named objNL:

```
<%
  Response.Write "<HR>"
  Dim MyPageNext
  Dim objNL
  Set objNL = Server.Createobject("MSWC.NextLink")
```

Then, we ask objNL to use a method called GetNextURL and leave VBScript:

```
  MyPageNext = objNL.GetNextURL("CL-NewProductsTour.txt")
%>
```

The GetNextURL method will perform five steps:

- ❑ Make a note of the URL of the current page
- ❑ Open the index file, NewProductsTour.txt
- ❑ Find the line of the index file that shows the URL of the current page
- ❑ Move down one line in the index file to the *next* line
- ❑ Return to your current page the URL of the *next* line

In our original file, CL-less-Hat501.htm the HREF names the hyperlink target directly as CL-Sweaters.asp, using the following line:

```
<A HREF="CL-Sweater.asp">Click here for next item</A>
```

Now, with our added ASP code, it's much smarter:

```
  Response.Write "Next: <A HREF='" & MyPageNext & "'>Click here for next item </A>"
```

This line is a little confusing, so let's step through it piece by piece. In our previous example, we explicitly named the target file in our link. In this example, the URL of the target file (the next page on our tour) is held in the variable `MyPageNext`. We are also still within our script block, so we start with our `Response.Write` statement, and then the first part of our HTML code. However, when using the `<A HREF='target'>` syntax, we need to enclose our target within quotes. This is where things get a little tricky. When using `Response.Write`, any text or HTML is enclosed in *double* quotes, so we have to use *single* quotes to enclose everything within the HREF. We use the & character to join items within the Response.Write statement. We have now recreated our HTML code using a slightly longer Response.Write statement. The result will be the same as if we had typed the URL directly, but there is a huge difference: if we want to change the URL we can do so in the Index file rather then on this page

If you view the source of the page, you will see the end result of our hard work - we have produced a standard HTML link:

```
cl-hat[2] - Notepad
File  Edit  Format  Help
<HTML>
<HEAD>
<TITLE>Hat</TITLE>
</HEAD>
<BODY>
<P>Hat of the Week:</P>
<P>Featuring an expanding elastic rim</P>
<HR>Next: <A HREF='CL-Sweater.asp'>Click here for next item </A>
</BODY>
</HTML>
```

Beginners to ASP are frequently confused about the variables and object here. First, we must supply two (later three) variable names. The first variable name identifies the instance of the `NextLink` object – in this case, we used `objNL`. The second name is for the variable which will hold the URL found by the `objNL.GetNextURL` method – here, I used `MyPageNext`. The third variable will appear later to hold the URL of the previous page. You should also note that although we get two pieces of data (next and previous URLs) we don't need to create two Content Linker objects here. We have only created a single Content Linker object, namely `objNL`, and then use two of its methods, namely `GetNextURL` and `GetPreviousURL`.

The other four files are the same as `CL-Hat.asp` in that they include the navigation page. The Content Linker will take care of inserting the appropriate `Next` URL for whatever page is using the Content Linker. Some folks get confused about which page we mean by 'current', 'next' and 'previous'. Recall that the ASP code is written within a page. That ASP code will be executed on the server in the process of the server building a page to send to the browser. The server considers the *current* page to be the one that it is now building. If your user clicks on next page then that sends an `<A HREF>` for the next page to the server, and as that page is being built, its URL becomes the *current* page for the ASP Content Linker methods finding the next and previous pages.

Adding Descriptions and Previous to Our Link

When we created the index file, we saw that it was organized into three columns of data with a row for each URL in the progression. The first column contains the name of the URL, the second column contains a description, and the third column held comments about the page.

We can adapt the previous example, so that the user can click on the description rather than Previous or Next. In fact, we will even embellish that description with some hard-coded text to give us a dynamic hyperlink label. Hence, when the user clicks on the hyperlink text, they know exactly what they are going to learn about in advance.

Furthermore, we can improve this tour to accommodate a viewer that might want to go back to a product page. With a bit of copying and syntax "changing" we can add a Previous Page hyperlink.

Try It Out – Using Content Linker with Descriptions and Previous

Since all of the navigation code is contained in one file we do not have to edit the product pages. We just modify CL-Navigation.asp.

I suggest that prior to these steps you save your old navigation file as CL-Navigation01.asp. That way, if you ever need to review it you have it in its simplest form. Remember that the product pages always include CL-Navigation.asp, so whichever version has that name will be the one in effect. If you are downloading files from the Wrox website, the file below will be CL-Navigator02.asp; rename it to CL-Navigation.asp.

1. With your editor of choice, open up CL-Navigation.asp, make the following changes, and save the file with the same name.

```
<%
  Response.Write "<HR>"
  Dim MyPageNext
  Dim MyPagePrevious
  Dim MyDescriptNext
  Dim MyDescriptPrevious
  Dim objNL
  Set objNL = Server.Createobject("MSWC.NextLink")
  MyPageNext = objNL.GetNextURL("CL-NewProductsTour.txt")
  MyPagePrevious = objNL.GetPreviousURL("CL-NewProductsTour.txt")
  MyDescriptNext = objNL.GetNextDescription("CL-NewProductsTour.txt")
  MyDescriptPrevious = objNL.GetPreviousDescription("CL-NewProductsTour.txt")

  Response.Write "Next: <A HREF='" & MyPageNext & "'>" &_
                 MyDescriptNext & "</A>   "
  Response.Write "Back: <A HREF='" & MyPagePrevious & "'>" &_
                 MyDescriptPrevious & "</A>"
%>
```

2. Open up your browser of choice. At the address line, type in the URL http://my_server_name/BegASP/CL-Hat.asp. Click on the hyperlinks to move back and forward through the tour.

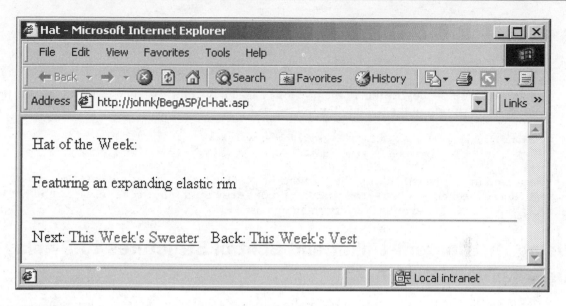

How It Works

In this example, we have added to the navigation file a few lines that utilize new methods – ones that can get the description of a page and can get the information for the previous page. Note that even though we have an additional method, we can still use the same instance of the NextLink object. In other words, there's no need for a second CreateObject statement. Here's the statement, for a given page, that calls the description of the next page in the tour:

```
MyDescriptNext = objNL.GetNextDescription("CL-NewProductsTour.txt")
```

The description is contained in the variable MyDescriptNext. Then we use this to make the hyperlink even more complex, as follows:

```
Response.Write "Next: <A HREF='" & MyPageNext & "'>" &_
              MyDescriptNext & "</A>   "
```

This looks similar to our previous link, but you should now notice that we use two variables within our link. We start by building up the statement as we did before, using single quotes to enclose the HREF and double quotes to enclose any HTML and text. We insert the target variable (which, if you remember, holds the URL of the next item in our index) between the two HTML blocks that end and begin with the single quote, enabling the variable to be used like a standard link. Instead of inserting the text saying "Click here for next item", this time we call up the description of the next item in the index with the MyDescriptNext variable. We then close off the tag and insert a couple of spaces. Again, try viewing the source to our page in your browser, to see the HTML.

> *Keep in mind that the URL of the HREF needs double quotes, but the hyperlinked text does not*

We then do exactly the same style of procedure to produce a link to the previous item in our index:

```
MyDescriptPrev = objNL.GetPreviousDescription("NewProductsTour.txt")
```

This line calls up the description of the previous page on the tour. We then use this variable to insert the description of the file into the link:

```
Response.Write "Back: <A HREF='" & MyPagePrevious & "'>" &_
               MyDescriptPrevious & "</A>"
```

The second improvement, adding the previous links is the exact same as the next link except that we use the methods GetPreviousURL and GetPreviousDescription. Be careful not to accidentally type GetPrevURL, a very common mistake.

Using the Content Linker and Control Structures to Display Only Appropriate Links

By now your hyperlinks for touring the on-line clothier are efficient for several reasons:

❑   The user is guided through the pages of the tour in the order of your design.

❑   The viewer gets a description of the next and previous pages, which assist his or her orientation.

However, there remain some rough edges. For example, the first page should not contain a "Previous link" and the last should not contain a "Next Link." So we need to improve the Navigation file so that it can sense if it is on the first page (don't print previous link) or on the last page (don't print Next link).

Try It Out – Using Appropriate Links

In this example, we will perform a test to see if a next link exists, *i.e.* if there is a line following the current line in the Index file. Only if there is a next link will we display the Next hyperlink on the page. We will also test for a previous line to determine whether to print the previous link.

Again, you may want to save the existing version of CL-Navigation.asp as CL-Navigation02.asp so you can review the exact syntax of the second content linker Try-It-Out. If you are downloading files from Wrox, the file below will be CL-Navigator03.asp, rename it to CL-Navigation.asp so that you don't need to change all of your links within each product page.

1.   Open the file CL_Navigation.asp and amend it to the following, then save.

```
<%
   Response.Write "<HR>"
   Dim MyPageNext
   Dim MyPagePreviousious
   Dim MyDescriptNext
   Dim MyDescriptPrev
   Dim MyListCount
   Dim MyListIndex
   Dim objNL
   Set objNL = Server.Createobject("MSWC.NextLink")
   MyPageNext = objNL.GetNextURL("CL-NewProductsTour.txt")
   MyPagePrevious = objNL.GetPreviousURL("CL-NewProductsTour.txt")
   MyDescriptNext = objNL.GetNextDescription("CL-NewProductsTour.txt")
   MyDescriptPrevious = objNL.GetPreviousDescription("CL-NewProductsTour.txt")
   MyListCount = objNL.GetListCount("CL-NewProductsTour.txt")
   MyListIndex = objNL.GetListIndex("CL-NewProductsTour.txt")

   If MyListIndex > 1 Then
      Response.Write "Back: <A HREF='" & MyPagePrevious & "'>" &_
                     MyDescriptPrevious & "</A> <BR>"
   End If

   If MyListIndex < MyListCount Then
      Response.Write "Next: <A HREF='" & MyPageNext & "'>" &_
                     MyDescriptNext & "</A> <BR>"
   End If
%>
```

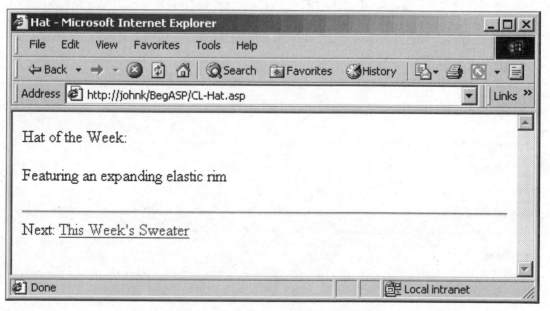

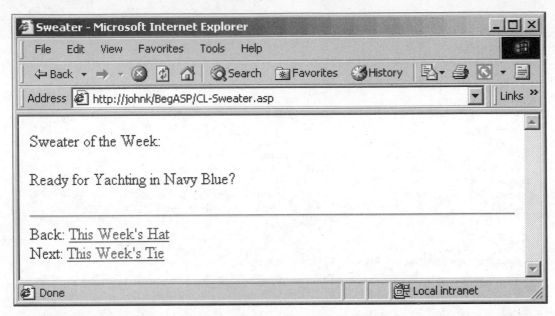

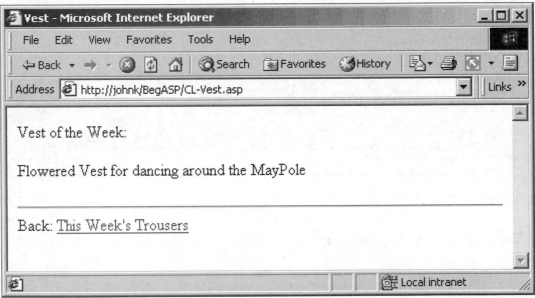

How It Works

The whole thing works because we are able to use our NextList object to obtain the following information from the index file:

❑ The number of URL lines in the index file

❑ The number of the URL that is currently shown

The first difference from previous CL-Navigation files is that we create two more variables:

```
Dim MyListCount
Dim MyListIndex
```

We fill the first using the method objNL.GetListCount which returns a number that ASP obtains by counting the lines in the Index file:

```
MyListCount = objNL.GetListCount("CL-NewProductsTour.txt")
```

Note that the Count will be the same for all of the pages.

Then, objNL.GetListIndex returns the number of the URL line for the current page:

```
MyListIndex = objNL.GetListIndex("CL-NewProductsTour.txt")
```

For example, in the file CL-Tie.asp, this line looks up CL-Tie.asp in the index file, CL-NewProductsTour.txt, and returns the value 3 (because CL-Tie.asp is the third on the list).

Armed with these values we can use logic to say that if we are not on the first page (that is, MyListIndex is greater than 1), then we should show a **Previous** hyperlink:

```
If MyListIndex > 1 Then
   Response.Write "Back: <A HREF='" & MyPagePrevious & "'>" &_
                  MyDescriptPrevious & "</A> <BR>"
End If
```

We can also say that, provided our current URL number is less than the total number of URLs (that is, MyListIndex is less then MyListCount), then we should show a **Next** hyperlink:

```
If MyListIndex < MyListCount Then
   Response.Write "Next: <A HREF='" & MyPageNext & "'>" &_
                  MyDescriptNext & "</A> <BR>"
End If
```

If the Webmaster changed the order of these pages in the index file the pages would automatically compensate their Next/Previous appearance and descriptions, all from the magic of the Content Linker.

Using the Content Linker with Home and End Hyperlinks

Most modern computer users are accustomed to the idea of having options for **Home** and **End** when in a series of steps. This probably comes from Microsoft Wizards, as much as from well-designed web pages. The Content Linker gives you two more methods, GetNthURL and GetNthDescription. In these methods, Nth is the programmer's way of implying that a page number is to be determined; for example the first page number is N=1. However, since our Webmaster frequently adds and removes pages from the index file, we will never be sure what the last page number will be. Therefore, we can ask ASP to count them at the moment it builds the page by using the method GetListCount. As you recall from the previous example, this is done by the following line:

```
MyListCount = objNL.GetListCount("CL-NewProductsTour.txt")
```

We can then get the number of the last page, since we recognize that N is equal to the current value of MyListCount. To use the GetNthURL method, we need to know how to tell the method the number that we want. This transfer of information is done by a second parameter after the name of the index file separated by a comma. For example, to get the URL of the first page we use:

```
MyFirstPage = objNL.GetNthURL("NewProductsTour.txt", 1)
```

And to get the URL of the last page we use our a variable as the second parameter:

```
MyEndPage = objNL.GetNthURL("NewProductsTour.txt", MyListCount)
```

Try It Out – Adding Home and End Links

1. Open your file CL-Navigation.asp (if you want, save the current version as CL-Navigaton03.asp). To this file, add the following highlighted lines. If you are downloading these files from the Wrox site, you can open CL-Navigation04.asp and rename this to CL-Navigation.asp when you run the example.

```
<%
  Response.Write "<HR>"
  Dim MyPageNext
  Dim MyPagePreviousious
  Dim MyDescriptNext
  Dim MyDescriptPrev
  Dim MyListCount
  Dim MyListIndex
  Dim MyFirstPage
  Dim MyLastPage

  Dim objNL
  Set objNL = Server.Createobject("MSWC.NextLink")
  MyPageNext = objNL.GetNextURL("CL-NewProductsTour.txt")
  MyPagePrevious = objNL.GetPreviousURL("CL-NewProductsTour.txt")
  MyDescriptNext = objNL.GetNextDescription("CL-NewProductsTour.txt")
  MyDescriptPrevious = objNL.GetPreviousDescription("CL-NewProductsTour.txt")
  MyListCount = objNL.GetListCount("CL-NewProductsTour.txt")
  MyListIndex = objNL.GetListIndex("CL-NewProductsTour.txt")
  MyFirstPage = objNL.GetNthURL("CL-NewProductsTour.txt",1)
  MyLastPage = objNL.GetNthURL("CL-NewProductsTour.txt",MyListCount)

  If MyListIndex > 1 Then
    Response.Write "<A HREF='" & MyFirstPage & "'>Home</A><BR>"
    Response.Write "Back: <A HREF='" & MyPagePrevious & "'>" &_
                   MyDescriptPrevious & "</A> <BR>"
  End If
```

```
    If MyListIndex < MyListCount Then
        Response.Write "Next: <A HREF='" & MyPageNext & "'>" &_
                    MyDescriptNext & "</A> <BR>"
        Response.Write "<A HREF='" & MyLastPage & "'>End</A><BR>"
    End If
%>
```

2. Open up your browser of choice. At the address line, type in the URL
`http://my_server_name/BegASPFiles/CL-Hat.asp`. Click on the hyperlinks, to
move back and forward through the tour.

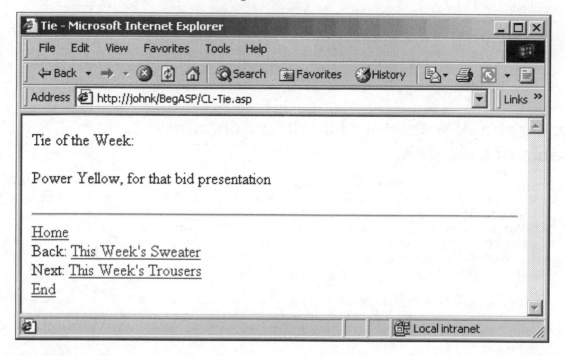

How It Works

The differences between this file and our previous version start with the addition of two more
variables:

```
Dim MyFirstPage
Dim MyLastPage
```

We fill the first variable with a URL returned by the GetNthURL method, where we specify to
use the first page:

```
MyFirstPage = objNL.GetNthURL("CL-NewProductsTour.txt",1)
```

The second variable is filled with the URL returned when we ask for the last page in the index
file. Since at design time we don't know how many pages are in the file, we specify the number
sitting in the variable MyListCount.

```
MyLastPage = objNL.GetNthURL("CL-NewProductsTour.txt",MyListCount)
```

Now we can include a Home link if we are not on the first page already.

```
If MyListIndex > 1 Then
   Response.Write "<A HREF='" & MyFirstPage & "'>Home</A><BR>"
   Response.Write "Back: <A HREF='" & MyPagePrevious & "'>" &_
                   MyDescriptPrevious & "</A> <BR>"
End If
```

And we add an End link only in the cases where we are not already on the last page.

```
If MyListIndex < MyListCount Then
   Response.Write "Next: <A HREF='" & MyPageNext & "'>" &_
                   MyDescriptNext & "</A> <BR>"
   Response.Write "<A HREF='" & MyLastPage & "'>End</A><BR>"
End If
```

Using the ASP Content Linker to Generate a Table of Contents

Now we have some very clever hyperlinks for jumping to the next and previous pages, as well as to the first and last pages. Best of all, during maintenance of the site we will never have to go into the actual pages holding those hyperlinks. All we have to do is open the index file in NotePad and reorder, delete or add pages. If you are writing ASP pages on contract, you can charge your clients more for writing such programmer-friendly code. In addition, if you write ASP as part of a salaried job, you can ask your boss for a raise. Before you do that, however, let's cover another trick so you can ask your boss for a double increase in salary grade.

As long as we have the index file made up, what else could we do with it? Well, we could use that information to make a hyperlinked table of contents for the tour of new products. We will create a loop that reads the first URL and description out of the index file and writes it as a hyperlink on the page, then puts in a
 (line break) tag, and then repeats these steps for each URL in the index file. Since we can easily find out how many URL lines exist in the IndexFile with the GetListCount, we will use the For...Next syntax here.

A Solution for a Table of Contents based on an Index File

We will create a separate table of contents page, so no need to make any changes to our existing .asp files or the index file.

Try It Out – A Basic Table of Contents Page

1. Open your editor, type in the following code and save in the BegASPfiles folder with the file name cl-TOC.asp.

```
<%Option Explicit%>
<HTML>
<HEAD>
```

```
<TITLE>Tour of Products TOC</TITLE>
</HEAD>
<BODY>
<P>Tour of New Products - Table of Contents</P>
<%
  Dim MyCurrentURL
  Dim MyCurrentDescription
  Dim MyListCount
  Dim objNL
  Dim URLCounter

  Set objNL=Server.CreateObject("MSWC.NextLink")
  MyListCount = objNL.GetListCount("CL-NewProductsTour.txt")

  For URLcounter = 1 To MyListCount
    MyCurrentURL = objNL.GetNthURL("CL-NewProductsTour.txt", URLcounter)
    MyCurrentDescription = objNL.GetNthDescription("CL-NewProductsTour.txt", URLcounter)
    Response.Write "<A HREF='" & MyCurrentURL & "'>" & MyCurrentDescription & "</A>"
    Response.Write "<BR>"
  Next
%>
</BODY>
</HTML>
```

2. Fire up your browser, and at the address line type the URL
`http://my_server_name/BegASPFiles/cl-TOC.asp`.

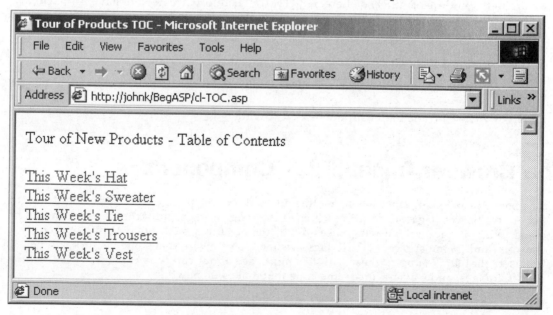

453

How It Works

First, we must set up an instance of the Content Linker:

```
Set objNL = Server.CreateObject("MSWC.NextLink")
MyLastCount = objNL.GetListCount("CL-NewProductsTour.txt")
```

The instance is called `objNL`. We then store the total number of URL lines in the index file, in the variable `MyLastCount`:

```
MyLastCount = objNL.GetListCount("CL-NewProductsTour.txt")
```

Now we are ready to loop. Our loop will iterate once for each of the values between 1 and `MyLastCount` inclusive:

```
For URLcounter = 1 To MyLastCount
```

Within each iteration of the loop, we give the value of `URLcounter` to the method `getNthURL` to acquire the URL and description corresponding to the value of `URLcounter`. That data is deposited in the two variables:

```
MyCurrentURL = objNL.GetNthURL("CL-NewProductsTour.txt", URLcounter)
MyCurrentDescription = objNL.GetNthDescription("CL-NewProductsTour.txt", URLcounter)
```

Then, we use `Response.Write` to create hyperlinks for each page in the tour. Remember that we are in the middle of ASP code here, not HTML. Therefore, we need to have ASP actually write out the four characters"
" to the page that HTML will send out to the browser. As you can see, we do that using the `Response.Write` method:

```
Response.Write "<A HREF='" & MyCurrentURL & "'>"
Response.Write MyCurrentDescription & "</A>"
Response.Write "<BR>"
```

Finally, we close off the loop with the `Next` keyword.

The Browser Capabilities Component

One of the problems we face when creating all kinds of web pages, not just dynamic ones that use Active Server Pages, is deciding which of the range of tags and techniques we should be using. While it's great to be able to use all the latest features, such as Java applets, ActiveX controls, and the most recent HTML tags, we need to be aware that some visitors will be using browsers that don't support these. All they might see of our carefully crafted pages is a jumble of text, images, and – even worse – the code that makes them work.

We mentioned in Chapter 7 that you could use a Server variable, HTTP_USER_AGENT, to help detect which type of browser is viewing your page. However, life can be made much easier with the Browser Capabilities component, which translates from the USER_AGENT, into a list of features that a browser supports. Each feature can be tested for True (supported) or False (not supported) before using the feature. You can create an instance of the Browser Capabilities component as follows:

```
Set objBCap = Server.CreateObject("MSWC.BrowserType")
```

You can then use it by testing for True/False for support of dozens of features, for example:

```
If objBCap.Tables = "True" Then
' code that uses tables
Else
' code that avoids tables
End If
```

Recall that If...Then checks if the expression is "True". In the above code we wrote out a test, but since the contents of objBCap will be either "True" or "False" we don't have to write an equation. We can just use:

```
If objBCap.Tables Then
' code that uses tables
Else
' code that avoids tables
End If
```

The Browscap.ini File

The Browscap.ini file is the translation file that contains a list of browsers and their capabilities. There is also a default section of the file, which is used when the browser details don't match any of the ones more fully specified in the file. A default Browscap.ini comes with W2000 and is normally found in C:\WINNT\System32\InetServ, but you will probably want to get a more up to date version. You can find one that is maintained by Juan Llibre at asptracker.com/browscap.zip. Normally there is no need for you to build a BrowsCap.ini; you just download and copy to your InetServ folder, but we will give you an overview of this file so you have an idea of how the BrowserType component will handle your code.

All of the entries in Browscap.ini are optional, however it's important that we always include the default section. If the browser in use doesn't match any in the Browscap.ini file, and no default browser settings have been specified, all the properties are set to "UNKNOWN".

```
; we can add comments anywhere, prefixed by a semicolon like this

[IE 5.0]
browser=IE
Version=5.0
majorver=5
minorver=0
frames=True
```

```
tables=True
cookies=True
backgroundsounds=True
vbscript=True
javascript=True
javaapplets=True
ActiveXControls=True
Win16=False
beta=False
AK=False
SK=False
AOL=False
crawler=False
MSN=False
CDF=True
DHTML=True
XML=True

[Default Browser Capability Settings]
browser=Default
Version=0.0
majorver=#0
...
```

The brackets of the [HTTPUserAgentHeader] line define the start of a section for a particular browser. Then each line defines a property that we want to inspect through the browser capabilities component, and its value for this particular browser. The properties list depends on the Browscap.ini, the above list for IE5 is about as complete as you will find. If can find what properties are available by opening your browscap.ini in any text editor and searching for the property of interest.

The Default section lists the properties and values that are used if the particular browser in use isn't listed in its own section, or if it is listed but not all the properties are supplied. In more sophisticated Browscap.ini files there are parent/child relationships so families of browsers can inherit characteristics.

Try It Out – Using the Browser Capabilities Component

Having grasped how the Browscap.ini file can translate a User_Agent into True/False/Unknown properties, it's time to actually see the Browser Capabilities component in use. This example checks to see whether or not the browser supports VBScript, and displays the appropriate message. This example can be modified to direct the user to different pages, depending on the response given by the browser.

1. Open up your favorite editor, type in the following code and save this page as BrowserCap.asp:

```
<% Option Explicit %>
<HTML>
<HEAD>
```

```
<TITLE> Browser Capabilities Component Example </TITLE>
</HEAD>
<BODY>
<%
  Dim objBCap,blnVBScriptOK
  Set objBCap = Server.CreateObject("MSWC.BrowserType")

  blnVBScriptOK = objBCap.VBScript  'save the value in a variable

  If blnVBScriptOK Then
    Response.Write "This browser supports VBScript"
  Else
    Response.Write "This browser doesn't support VBScript"
  End If
%>
</BODY>
</HTML>
```

2. Open up this page in Internet Explorer version 4.0 or higher:

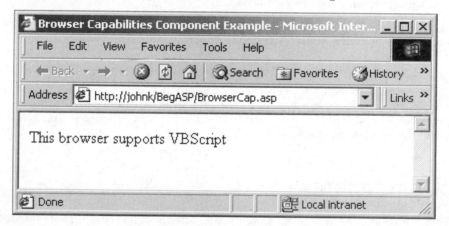

3. Now view the same page in Netscape version 4.0 or higher:

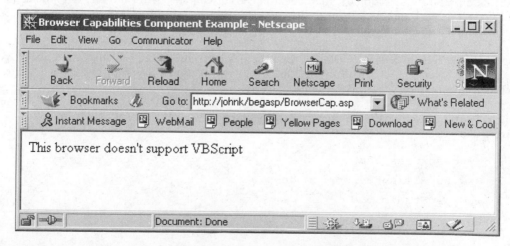

How It Works

We first set up two variables for the object itself and a Boolean variable that will hold true or false for the ability to support VBScripting:

```
Dim objBCap,blnVBScriptOK
```

The first is then used to hold the instance of a BrowserType object:

```
Set objBCap = Server.CreateObject("MSWC.BrowserType")
```

Then we get the true/false property for VBScript and place it into the second variable:

```
blnVBScriptOK = objBCap.VBScript   'save the value in a variable
```

If the VBScript property holds the value True in browscap.ini, then we can assume that this browser supports VBScript:

```
If blnVBScriptOK Then
    Response.Write "This browser supports VBScript"
```

Otherwise, we can assume the browser doesn't:

```
Else
    Response.Write "This browser doesn't support VBScript"
End If
```

That's all there is to it. Of course, we can use the properties to do other things. One of the favorite techniques is to load a different index page for a site, depending on what features the browser supports. If our site has a set of pages using frames, and a different set using only simple text, we can check the browser's ability to display frames when it first hits our site, and redirect it to the appropriate index page.

Other Components

There are three sources of additional components. Microsoft has components beyond those discussed in this chapter, and you can view them several ways. If you use Visual InterDev you can click on **Menu:View/Toolbox**, then click on **Server Objects**. Alternatively if you use VB you can create a project and click through **Project/References**/scroll to "MSWC..." and add them. They are then viewable in the object browser.

A second source is to create your own. This topic is introduced later in this book, and covered in depth in *Professional ASP 3.0* (ISBN 1861002610), Peter Wright's *Beginning VB6 Objects* and Rockford Lhotka's *Visual Basic 6 Business Objects*.

A third source is to investigate the third-party components that are for sale from such sources as:

- ❑ www.aspxtras.com
- ❑ www.aspalliance.com/components
- ❑ www.aspStudio.com

Summary

Web site developers that have preceded you have found that almost everyone shares a need for some types of code, such as rotating ads. Microsoft has written code to perform these tasks and made it available as Server Components. To use a component you must first create an instance of the component using `Server.CreateObject("MWSC.ComponentName")`. Then you can use that server with *myComponent.method* or *myComponent.property*.

The first component rotates advertisements on a page without making any changes directly on the page. The number and source of ads can be changed in a scheduler file. In that same file, we can also change the frequency of appearance for each ad.

To direct users through a set of pages on a site we can use the content linker component. Once we make a list of pages, we can get the URL and description of the next and previous pages from the content linker. A webmaster can easily change the order of pages, additions, and deletions in one text file.

We finished with an examination of the browser capabilities component which relies on a file which reads the browser type from the server variable, then sets a range of properties such as the ability to use <TABLE> tags to either true or false. These properties can be tested, and the user redirected to code which best fits his browser.

Keep in mind that many more components are available. Several sources review or sell these components. As your skills increase, you will begin to write your own components to meet the specific needs of your business.

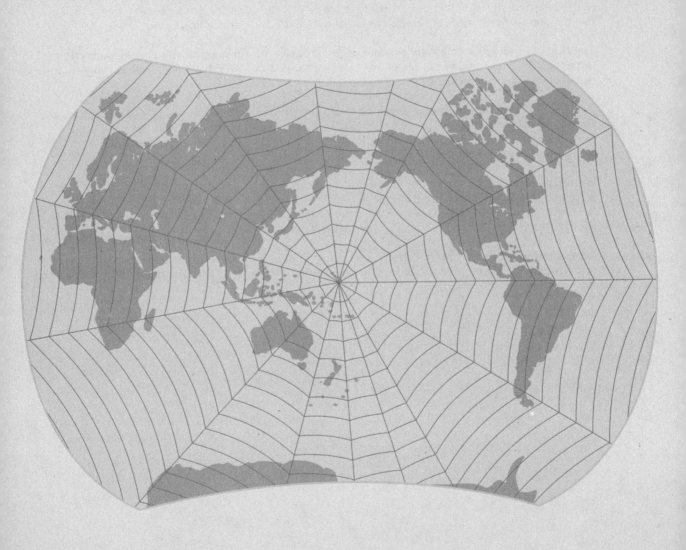

ASP and Data Store Access

We've reached an important juncture in this book. In the chapters up to and including Chapter 11, everything we've discussed and coded has involved data stored in local variables within the ASP page, or captured (for example, by an HTML form) and stored in one of the collections of the ASP Request method. These information storage techniques are excellent for the purposes of temporary data storage within an ASP page or application. But clearly, neither of these techniques is going to be suitable for storing large amounts of information, or for storing data indefinitely. Therefore, we need to look to other data storage methods.

Many companies use databases of one sort or another to store the data required in the creation of their web pages, and also to store data that is entered by the end-users and captured by the web pages. But it goes further than databases – there aren't many of us who store *all* of our data on databases. Most companies have data sources of many other formats, such as mail systems, legacy mainframes, spreadsheets and word-processed text files. Data stored in these formats might also benefit from being published on the web – and so we'd like to be able to extend database access techniques to these other forms of data.

Until recently, the idea of having a common method of data access – which could access the data held in all these diverse applications and formats – was a far off dream. Microsoft use the term **Universal Data Access** (UDA) to refer to their strategy for dealing with this problem. As part of its UDA strategy, Microsoft developed a technology known as OLE-DB, which has brought this dream much closer to reality.

Moreover, this dream affects ASP – because we can use OLE-DB in ASP, via a set of programming interfaces known as the **ActiveX Data Objects**, or **ADO**. Through the WWW, intranets and other browser-based applications, the humble Web browser is becoming one of the most widely-used interfaces between data and end-user.

The first 11 chapters of this book have demonstrated how to put active scripting into our ASP pages; in the next few chapters, we'll look at how we can use this scripting capability to access data stores and populate our pages dynamically with the most current, up-to-date information. This is the real significance of the word 'Active' when we talk about 'Active Server Pages'. In this chapter, we will begin our study of data access by concentrating on the data store and how to connect to one. So we are going to look at:

❑ What we mean by a data store

❑ What ODBC is

❑ What OLE-DB is

❑ How ADO fits in

❑ Exactly what a database connection is

❑ How to use the ADO `Connection` object

Databases: Are they a Thing of the Past?

I guess some of you are hoping that databases, along with their seemingly cryptic methods of holding your information in the rows and fields of various tables, are destined for the waste bin. Their archaic and rigid structures and their esoteric terminology can be very confusing to the novice. I mean: who *honestly* uses normalization in their day-to-day jobs?!

Databases aren't as bad as all that, once you start using them – and we won't be seeing the back of database technology for quite some time, if ever. If you've never been initiated into the world of databases, then let's do it now.

How Databases Store Data

Databases store information in **tables** and **records** so that, in theory at least, the information contained within is easily accessible to whoever needs it. For example, if you work for a large company, then they probably have a database that contains a table of employee data, with lots of employee **records** – and one of those records will contain information about yourself. My record in the Employees table of the 'Wrox Press Human Resources' database probably looks something like this:

Name	Address 1	Address 2	City	State	Zip	Phone
Chris Ullman	29 LaSalle Street	Suite B01	Chicago	Illinois	60603	392-893-8004

There's a **field** for my name, two fields for the first two lines of my address, a field for the city...and so on.

> In database-speak, a record is a collection of data containing information from each field, relating to a specific entry. For example an **Address Book** database takes the form of a table consisting of the columns (or fields) "Name", "Address", "Phone Number". Then each row of the table is referred to as a record.

Standardization of Data

How does the database ensure that each employee's record is stored in the same way? We don't want a situation where one employee's name is stored across two fields while another's name is stored in a single field; or where half the employees have their entire address packed into a single field.

Databases standardize the way that information is stored. If you are obliged to put your first and last name information into a single column – then everybody else who uses the database has to adhere to the same template as well. So in this case, each employee record contains a single Name field, in which the employee's full name is stored – no matter how many names they might have. Some employees might have an email address while others don't, but if you include an email field then you will have the option of entering an email address for *every* employee.

Keys

How is the database designed so that we can tell two different records apart? Principally, we could look at the data contained in each one. Ah, but what if there are two employees with the same name? How do we set about differentiating between the Chris Ullman who works on the fifth floor in the budgeting department, and the Chris Ullman who works in the basement writing technical books? You could look at the telephone numbers, which are likely to be different – but that's not guaranteed.

Instead, we use **keys**. A key is a unique identifier – each record in the database table has a key that is guaranteed to be unique from all the other keys in the key column:

Employee Key	Name	Address 1	Address 2	City	State	Zip	Phone
A100	Chris Ullman	29 LaSalle Street	Suite B01	Chicago	Illinois	60603	392-893-8004
A101	Chris Ullman	29 LaSalle Street	Suite 520	Chicago	Illinois	60603	392-893-8006

Key values can be numeric or alphanumeric so long as they're unique within the key column. If your database table has a key, then you can use it in other tables to link them back to other information stored in your database. For example, I can use the Employee Key values in the following Books table of the database to refer to the information contained back in the Employees table:

Book Key	Author Key	Book Title
LB01	A100	Instant HTML
LB02	A100	Beginning Active Server Pages 3.0
LB03	A101	Budgeting for Buffoons
LB04	A100	IE5 Dynamic HTML Programmer's Reference

Thus, the values in the Author Key field simply refer back to the values in the Employees table – thus identifying the author of each book uniquely and without ambiguity. From this table you should be able to deduce that the author of this chapter was also author of the best-selling titles *Instant HTML* and *IE5 Dynamic HTML Programmer's Reference*, and that it was the other Chris Ullman who wrote the less well-known *Budgeting for Buffoons*. You might also be wondering why there is a second key in the Books table – the Book Key field. This key belongs to the Books table, and is a unique identifier for the books in the table. Remember, an author might have written more than one book and we still need to be able to differentiate each book.

The reason we usually choose to store information in different but related tables like this – and not to store it in one great big table – is because it can help us to avoid logging the same information multiple times. The Book table here doesn't need to store all the personal details of the author of each book – instead, it stores a simple key value. It means that my details aren't repeated three times in the Books table – they're just stored once in the Employees table.

It also means that if my telephone number changes, the database administrator won't need to trawl through the Books table looking for the books that I wrote, in order to update that data multiple times. Instead, they can just go straight to my record in the Employees table, where they need to make exactly one update! So, keeping this kind of repeatable information separate means that you can simplify admin tasks dramatically, by ensuring that you only need to change it in one place. In fact, the process of carrying out this simple piece of common sense is the nuts-and-bolts of the **normalization** process! See how terminology can often obscure the most straightforward of tasks…

Universal Access for Databases

You've probably heard of the different kinds of database applications that are available. Perhaps your Accounts department upstairs are using Oracle to store the payroll information, while you've got Microsoft Access at home because it came as part of the Microsoft Office suite. Yet these two are totally different applications. They don't even have to run on the same operating system!

> We use the term 'database' to refer to exactly the sort of storage structure we discussed in the previous section: related tables, records, keys, and so on. When we need to refer to data storage in a broader sense, we use the term 'data store'.

So, is there a method that you can use to get information from a database onto your web pages – regardless of whether the database type is Microsoft Access on Windows 98, or Oracle on UNIX?

Up until very recently the best answer to this question was to use ODBC, but this technology restricted the user to certain types of data store (mainly databases). Fortunately a better, broader-based solution is now at hand in the form of OLE-DB, the data access technology of choice for this book. However, in order to fully understand OLE-DB you really need to see what preceded it. So let's start with ODBC and the idea of universal access to one type of data store: the database.

What is ODBC?

Open DataBase Connectivity, or **ODBC**, is a standard for accessing data. It was designed to allow the programmer to use a common set of routines to access the data stored in databases, regardless of the *type* of database in which the data was stored. This meant that once the programmer was connected to the database using ODBC, they could manipulate the data without worrying exactly where the data was stored, or which type of database was storing it. It provided interface transparency – so the programmer could access an Oracle database in the same way that they accessed a SQL Server database:

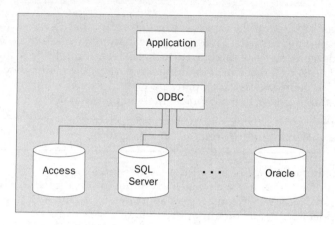

There's no common format for saving databases to file, so you can't save a database using one database application and then directly open the same file using a different database application (in the way that a word-processed file in the .txt format can be opened and read as plain text in NotePad, WordPad, Microsoft Word, or whatever).

Fortunately, all sorts of database applications store data using the structure we've already seen: tables, records, and keys. ODBC allows you to get at this data without worrying about the nuts and bolts of the hosting database application.

So, ODBC allows you to get at the basic information held in any database. This gives the programmer freedom to concentrate on the functionality of the application without worrying too much about the underlying data, or even how to access it.

Universal Data Access

So databases store information in a form that is accessible in a uniform way via ODBC. But what happens when you want to access data that's stored in one of the following formats:

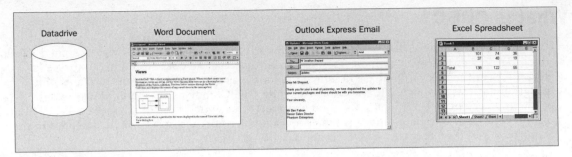

The point is that, aside from all the databases in the world, there's a wealth of *other* data out there that's stored in other formats. There's a generic property of all the receptacles shown above, including databases – they're all used to store data. It might be a spreadsheet containing your company finances, or a text file containing a report on the conference you visited last month, or an email system and its accompanying mail messages – but it's all data. We use the generic term **data store** to refer to a receptacle that contains data.

> *Any* persisted collection of information is a data store.

There's another common factor linking all these data stores: we might want to access the data contained within and use it in our web pages and other applications! In this book, we're particularly interested in how we can access data stores from our ASP pages, and use their data to influence the appearance and content of our dynamic web pages.

These next few chapters will cover the techniques required to do just that. In our introduction to data access from ASP pages, we *will* use a database as the data store – but the techniques can be used to get at many different types of data store. Therefore, we'll be using the term 'data store' from now on whenever we refer to a generic type of data source.

So the question is one of how to access the data contained within these data stores. There's a problem with using ODBC here: generally, the information contained within each of the other media doesn't fit neatly into a database-type format – and more often than not, ODBC can't help you get at that kind of data.

In other words, the notion of *database access* isn't enough to fulfil the dream of *universal data access* – we need a way of getting at the other forms of data too. So, how can we get at the contents of your data stores quickly and easily?

Microsoft's UDA strategy has yielded a technology that has the potential to access the data contained in any kind of data store. This technology is known as OLE-DB.

What is OLE-DB?

OLE-DB is the next step in the evolution of the anonymous data store. As well as being more generic than ODBC, Microsoft has done a great deal of work to ensure that OLE-DB is faster and easier to use than ODBC. Eventually it may well replace ODBC, although that won't be for a long time yet, if only for the reasons that you often have to rely on third parties writing new OLE-DB providers and then when they are available they are often more expensive than existing ODBC drivers. So, consequently, there's a lot more ODBC drivers out there still in use.

The following diagram begins to build up a picture of data access using OLE-DB:

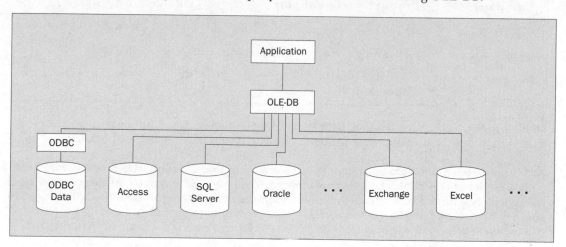

As you can see, the idea behind OLE-DB is very similar to the idea behind ODBC – but in fact it allows access to a much broader range of data stores. In fact, you'll notice that OLE-DB even supports database connections *through* ODBC – so that effectively your generic OLE-DB layer will allow you to connect to your legacy databases through your existing ODBC connections.

Data Providers and Data Consumers

OLE-DB introduces the notion of **data providers** and **data consumers**. The relationship between a data provider and a data consumer is fairly obvious: a data provider is something that *provides* data, and the data consumer is something that *uses* that data. In reality, you might have several data providers – one for each different type of data store.

At the time of writing, Microsoft itself has made available quite a number of OLE-DB providers for different types of data store, including data providers for their Access, SQL Server, Oracle, Exchange Server, Excel and Foxpro. If you're interested in other external OLE-DB providers here's a list of some of the companies currently in the market:

Company	Product name/support	URL
ASNA	Acceller8DB, DataGate/400	http://www.asna.com
IBM	AS/400	http://www.ibm.com
ISG	Oracle, Sybase, RDB, Informix, Inres, D_ISAM, C_ISAM, RMS, Adabas C, VSAM, DB2, IMS/DB	http://www.isgsoft.com
Merant (formally Intersolv and Micro Focus)	DataDirect (Connect OLE DB and SequeLink OLE DB), Lotus Notes, MAPI-based email, Microsoft Exchange	http://www.merant.com

Table Continued on Following Page

Company	Product name/support	URL
MetaWise	AS/400, VSAM	http://www.metawise.com
SAS	SAS datasets, SAS/SHARE server	http://www.sas.com
Sequiter	Codebase (FoxPro, dBase, Clipper)	http://www.sequiter.com

Don't worry if you're not familiar with some of these names. The point to take from all this is that, although this is a fairly new technology, it's got a lot of industry support.

As we said above, the data consumer is just something that uses the data that the data provider provides. So, in this book, the data consumers will be our ASP pages (or more specifically, the ADO objects within our ASP pages that will manipulate the data for display on the page). In another context, we might use the OLE-DB data providers to provide data for *other* data consumers, such as an application written in a language like Visual Basic or Visual C++.

ASP and OLE-DB

In fact, each OLE-DB data provider is a unit of code, written in a language such as C++ or Java, which uses **OLE-DB objects** to provide the instructions required to communicate and pass data between the data store and the data consumer. Once you know this, you may be tempted to ask: "Why don't we use the OLE-DB objects *directly* within our ASP pages, and cut out these OLE-DB providers?"

There's a good reason: the OLE-DB objects themselves are very low-level objects. Scripting languages like VBScript (and even languages like Visual Basic), are simply not sufficiently powerful to allow us to manipulate the OLE-DB objects (although, of course, languages such as C++ and Java are!). That's why we take advantage of the data provider/data consumer mechanism, to pass the data between the data store and the ASP page across a number of intermediate layers.

We've already discussed the data providers – but what of the data consumer? It comes in the form of a set of objects known as the **ActiveX Data Objects** (or **ADO**). ADO is an interface that allows our ASP pages to talk to OLE-DB. So, when we use ASP to talk to a data store, we're actually using ASP to talk to ADO, which in turn talks to OLE-DB, which in turn gets information from our data store.

ActiveX Data Objects (ADO)

You might like to think of the ActiveX Data Objects (ADO) as being the friendly face of OLE-DB. ADO is a set of objects that allow programmers to program their data access logic from languages like Visual Basic as well as scripting languages. ADO is a higher-level model than OLE-DB, which means that it simplifies some of the complexities of programming with OLE-DB. Thus, ADO is much easier to use than OLE-DB.

How does ADO fit into overall structure? The ADO layer sits neatly between the application itself and the OLE-DB layer. In our case, we'll refer to the ADO objects explicitly within the code of our ASP pages, instructing them to read records, update data, and carry out other tasks that relate to the data in our data stores:

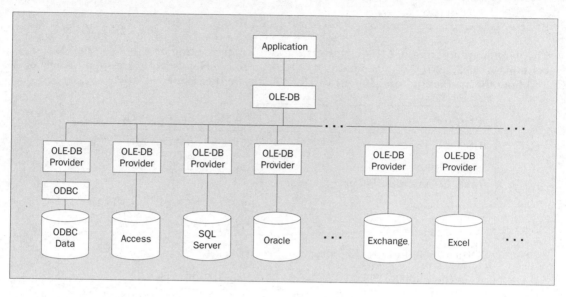

*In this sense, we can think of ADO as being an **application programming interface** – in our case, it's the interface between our ASP code and the OLE-DB providers. This will becvome more apparent when we see our first examples.*

If you've done any database programming in Access or Visual Basic then you'll have come across Data Access Objects (DAO) or Remote Data Objects (RDO). If so, that's OK – in fact, it'll stand you in good stead for ADO, because ADO is a superset of DAO and RDO and is much easier to understand. If not, that's OK too – we'll explain and demonstrate ADO over the course of the next few chapters, and we'll be using it in our ASP pages to access data stores.

ADO and ASP are Different Technologies!

Don't fall into the trap of assuming that ADO is part of ASP, or that it's designed specifically for use with ASP! It's true to say that ADO is the ideal tool to use for achieving data access from ASP pages, and that ADO is shipped as part of the IIS 5.0/ASP 3.0 package. But ADO is more generic than that. If you're planning to write other data-dependent applications, in languages such as Visual Basic, Java or Visual C++, there's nothing to stop you from using ADO in those applications too.

In fact, you can use ADO with any COM-compliant programming language.

So where does ADO come from? In fact, ADO is one of a suite of components, which are known collectively as the **Microsoft Data Access Components** (or **MDAC**). This set of components has enjoyed a release schedule that is separate to that of IIS/ASP. You can download the latest version of ADO from Microsoft's web site – at the time of writing, you'll find it at:

```
http://www.microsoft.com/data/download.htm.
```

The version numbering of MDAC reflects the version numbering of ADO – so that MDAC 2.1 contains ADO 2.1, MDAC 2.0 contains ADO 2.0, an so on. Here's a quick potted history of ADO, and how the availability of different versions relates to the history of ASP:

Product	...was released with...
IIS 3.0	ASP 1.0 and ADO 1.0
IIS 4.0, PWS 4.0 (aka. NT4 Option Pack)	ASP 2.0 and ADO 1.5
Windows 98	PWS 4.0, ASP 2.0 and ADO 1.5
Visual Studio 6.0	ADO 2.0
Office 2000, Internet Explorer 5.0	ADO 2.1
Windows 2000, IIS 5.0	ASP 3.0 and ADO 2.5

ADO has gradually evolved over these releases into the product we'll meet over the next few chapters. The latest release – ADO 2.5 – sees the addition of two brand new objects (Record and Stream), which are designed to give us extra capabilities for accessing data stores.

However, the main point to understand is that the object models of ASP and ADO are quite separate. It's important not to consider them as a single package – instead, they should be treated as separate but complementary technologies. ASP enables dynamic web sites, ADO allows you to use data stores as part of a dynamic web site.

The ADO Object Model

Before we start looking in detail at the various parts of data access, let's have a quick look at ADO's object model. This should help us to understand how it all links together as we come to meet the objects individually. We won't go into each object in detail here because we'll be covering them over the course of this chapter and the next two – but this will give a good overall picture:

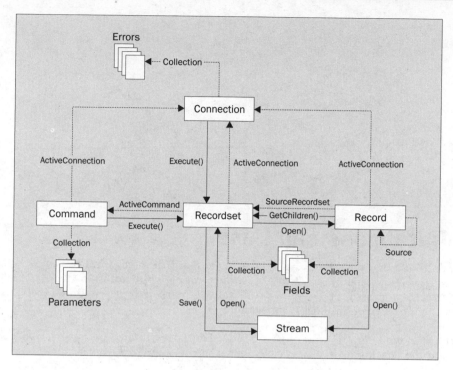

As you can see from the diagram, there are five main objects:

❑ Connection – the link between the program and the data store

❑ Command – allows you to run commands against the data store

❑ Recordset – contains all the data returned from a specific action on the data store

❑ Record – allows you to handle data kept in semi-structured storage (such as files in a directory structure) as though they were records in a database

❑ Stream – allows the manipulation of data held in web resources, such as HTML files

The five main objects enjoy a "flat" hierarchy – this means that we can create any ADO object we need in our ASP code, without the need to create a hierarchy of parent and grandparent objects. For example, we can use a Recordset object to make a direct request from the data store. In this case, there's no need to create an explicit Connection object in our code first – ADO does the necessary work under the hood.

The five main objects are shaded in the above diagram. There are four subsidiary objects – Property, Parameter, Field and Error (and their associated collections, Properties, Parameters, Fields and Errors). Only three of the four collections are shown. The Properties collection was deliberately left off, so that you can easily see the interaction between the main objects. The relationship between the Properties collection and the other objects is shown here:

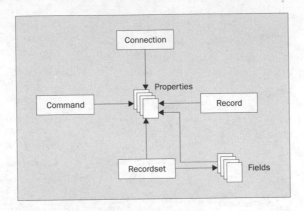

What Databases can I use?

We've mentioned that we'll be using databases for many of the examples in these chapters – and indeed, we'll do the same in the Wrox Classifieds sample application in Chapter 15. They're still the most straightforward type of data store that you're likely to use within a web page (and probably the most commonly used data source).

In this chapter, we're going to be working with two types of database application – Microsoft Access, and the cut down version of SQL Server, namely the MSDE:

❑ Access 2000 is available as part of the Office 2000 Professional or Premium editions – older versions of Access are available with older editions of the Office suite. Access is the desktop database for home users, and isn't intended for deployment when a large number of concurrent users will access data.

❑ SQL Server is Microsoft's leading Windows database and data-warehousing package. The MSDE (Microsoft Data Engine) is a SQL Server 7.0-compatible data server. MSDE ships with any version of Office 2000 that contains Access 2000 (Professional, Premium and Developer) – if you have any of these you'll find the appropriate files on your Office 2000 installation disks (as we'll explain in a moment).

> If you have a copy of Microsoft Visual Studio, then you can download MSDE free from the Microsoft web site at
> `http://msdn.microsoft.com/vstudio/msde/`. During the download process, you will be required to register your Visual Studio product and provide the Product ID – which can be found in the **About** box on your Visual Studio product's **Help** menu.

You won't need both types of database application for this book. We have made available sample databases for both, and the examples in Chapters 12–14 will work with both types of database, unless stated otherwise. If you are in a position to choose between the two, then we recommend that you use Access for these examples, purely on the grounds that it is both easier to use and simpler to set up.

However, if you're planning to graduate to anything that might be used within a corporate environment, then you might prefer to use MSDE – as the SQL Server compatible engine is much better suited to many-user applications. Just bear in mind that MSDE is the more complex system to install and use.

Don't worry if you are working with a different database application, such as Oracle. You will have to set up the actual database data and configure the connection correctly but after that the scripts outlined in the next few chapters should work without further changes.

If you're unfamiliar with MSDE, and you're intending to use it with this book, here are some tips on installation that will help you to get it up and running. We'll cover installation from the Office 2000 route first; then from the Visual Studio route.

Try It Out – Installing MSDE from the Office 2000 Disks

1. From **Disk 1** of your Office 2000 installation disks, browse to the folder `\SQL\x86\setup`. Locate and run the file `sqlsetup.exe`, and follow the setup instructions to complete the setup and installation.

2. Now jump to Step 3 of the *Installing MSDE from a Visual Studio Registration* 'Try It Out', below.

Try It Out – Installing MSDE from a Visual Studio Registration

1. Download the `msdex86_pkg.exe` from the Microsoft web site, using your Visual Studio Product ID (as outlined above). Then run `msdex86_pkg.exe` to unpack its contents onto your local hard drive – the dialog will suggest that the contents are placed into a new folder called `\MSDE_PKG`.

2. Now go to the **Start** menu, select **Run** and, very carefully, type the following into the dialog box:
C:\MSDE_PKG\MSDEx86.exe –a –s –f1 "C:\MSDE_PKG\unattend.iss"

3. When the installation process has finished, one of the following icons will appear on your task bar:

If it doesn't appear immediately, try restarting your machine.

A little red square denotes that the service is stopped; a green triangle denotes that the service is started. Double click on it and the following dialog will appear:

If the service is stopped, click the Start/Continue button to start it.

Getting the Data

Whichever database application you're using, you're going to need some data. For the examples that follow, we'll be using a Movies database, which contains information pertaining to a number of recent Hollywood releases. This database is available in the following two formats, both of which are available for download from the Wrox Press web site at `http://www.wrox.com`.

Microsoft Access (.mdb) Files

Microsoft Access databases come in an easily transportable `.mdb` format. The file containing the Movies database in Microsoft Access format is called `Movie2000.mdb`. Simply download this file from the Wrox web site, and save it in a folder on your local hard drive. In these examples, we've saved the file into our `C:\datastores` folder.

Microsoft SQL Server/MSDE (.mdf) Files

SQL Server is a back-end (Server) tool, and therefore these databases aren't designed to be so easily portable. However, if you follow the instructions in the examples in this chapter, you'll find that the SQL Server `.mdf` format (while larger than the Access `.mdb` format) can be moved around with the same ease.

If you're planning to use MSDE, and you've installed it using either of the 'Try It Out's above, then you're ready to set up the data file. Download the file `sqldb.zip` from the Wrox Press web site – this contains a single data file called `Movie2000.mdf`, which you should extract to `C:\MSSQL7\Data`.

If you want to use SQL Server then you need to import the `Movie2000` database. There are several ways to do this. One is to open the `.mdb` from Access 2000 and use the **Upsizing Wizard**. If you have Access 97, the upsizing tools are available for download from the following web site:

```
http://www.Microsoft.com/accessdev/prodinfo/AUT97dat.htm
```

The wizard is very easy to follow and will create the database on SQL Server. Another way is to use the **Import and Export Data** utility on SQL Server (effectively, the **Data Transformation Services** wizard).

Testing our Data Store

We're not going to waste any time explaining details, and some of the code you'll see won't be explained until the next chapter, but this short section of code shows how simple it is to get data from a data store.

Try It Out – Displaying Data from a Data Store

1. Using your favorite ASP editor, type the following lines of code, taking care to type in the correct file location for your own database setup in the middle:

```
<%Option Explicit%>
<HTML>
<HEAD>
<TITLE>Testing our connection</TITLE>
</HEAD>
<BODY>

<%
  Dim adOpenForwardOnly, adLockReadOnly, adCmdTable
  adOpenForwardOnly = 0
  adLockReadOnly = 1
  adCmdTable = 2

  Dim objConn, objRS
  Set objConn = Server.CreateObject("ADODB.Connection")
  Set objRS = Server.CreateObject("ADODB.Recordset")

  Dim strDatabaseType
  'Choose one of the following two lines, and comment out the other
  strDatabaseType = "Access"
  'strDatabaseType = "MSDE"

  'Now we use this selection to open the connection in the appropriate way
  If strDatabaseType = "Access" Then
    objConn.Open "Provider=Microsoft.Jet.OLEDB.4.0;" & _
              "Data Source=C:\datastores\Movie2000.mdb;" & _
              "Persist Security Info=False"
  Else
```

```
      objConn.Open "Provider=SQLOLEDB;Persist Security Info=False;" & _
              "User ID=sa;Initial Catalog=Movie;" & _
              "Initial File Name=C:\MSSQL7\Data\Movie2000.mdf"
  End If

  objRS.Open "Movies", objConn, adOpenForwardOnly, adLockReadOnly, adCmdTable

  While Not objRS.EOF
    Response.Write objRS("Title") & "<BR>"
    objRS.MoveNext
  Wend

  objRS.Close
  objConn.Close
  Set objRS = Nothing
  Set objConn = Nothing
%>

</BODY>
</HTML>
```

2. Save the code into a file with the name Connect.asp, in the \inetpub\wwwroot\BegASPFiles folder.

3. Now type the URL into your browser, to view the page:

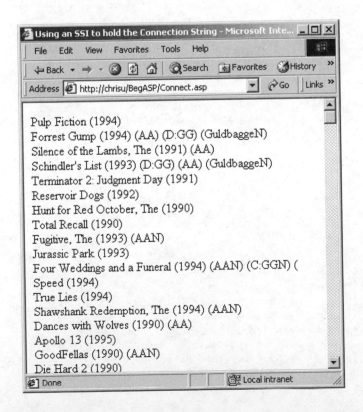

It's pretty easy, huh? Who told you ASP database programming was hard?!

How It Works

As we said at the top of this example, we won't study every detail of this example at this stage in the book. We'll see more about some of the features seen here later in this chapter, and in Chapters 13 and 14. But for now, there are a few points to get your teeth into.

Here's the first piece of code that's completely new to us:

```
Set objConn = Server.CreateObject("ADODB.Connection")
```

This line creates an ADO Connection object; we're going to refer to this object in our code by giving it the name objConn.

To build the connection to the data store via an OLE-DB provider, we must supply the relevant connection information – such as the name of the OLE-DB provider and the location of the data store– to the Open method of the Connection object. The Open method will use this information to open a connection.

> In this example, we've used a variable called strDatabaseType in the code, which you can use to specify the database type that you're using on your local system. Select one of the lines:

```
    strDatabaseType = "Access"
    strDatabaseType = "MSDE"
```

> Comment out the other. The code will use your selected value in the If...Then statement to select the appropriate connection details.

For the Access example database, we achieve this using the following code:

```
    objConn.Open "Provider=Microsoft.Jet.OLEDB.4.0;" & _
                 "Data Source=C:\datastores\Movie2000.mdb;" & _
                 "Persist Security Info=False"
```

Alternatively, if you're using an MSDE database application to supply the data then you can achieve the same using the following code:

```
    objConn.Open "Provider= SQLOLEDB;Persist Security Info=False;" & _
                 "User ID=sa;Initial Catalog=Movie;" & _
                 "Initial File Name=C:\MSSQL7\Data\Movie2000.mdf"
```

> This example will only work if you haven't already set a password for the sa account. In any corporate environment, or with data you wouldn't want to compromise, you should set a password, and provide it in the connection string.In order to simplify the examples in these three chapters, we have not done this.

Notice that MSDE requires more information than the Access database.

The output on the screen comes from using our `Connection` object to open a `Recordset` object (which will contain data retrieved from the `Movies` table of the data store), and then displaying that data as part of the web page:

```
objRS.Open "Movies", objConn, adOpenForwardOnly, adLockReadOnly, adCmdTable
While Not objRS.EOF
  Response.Write objRS("Title") & "<BR>"
  objRS.MoveNext
Wend
```

> *Don't worry about the recordset manipulation for now – we'll cover it in detail in Chapter 13.*

When we've finished with the connection, we can `Close` it and release it from memory (we do the same for the recordset):

```
objConn.Close
Set objConn = Nothing
```

At its very simplest, that's all there is to displaying data from a data store. As you can see, this program has just three steps:

- ❑ Making a connection to the data store
- ❑ Displaying the data
- ❑ Closing the connection

But, we don't need to create a 'connection' when we open up a document or spreadsheet using Word or Excel. So why do we even need to establish a 'connection' from the ASP page to the data store? Let's focus on the physical act of connecting your data store.

What is a Connection?

This might seem pretty obvious, but a **connection** is the thing that links the ADO objects (in your code) to the data store. We can understand it by comparing it to the way your telephone works. You can use the same telephone (at different times) to call your bank, or the local cinema, or the *Weatherline* service – and get information on your bank details, the current film releases, and your local weather. Each time, you're just creating a connection from your telephone to the service in question – and when you've finished you cut off the connection by terminating the phone call.

A database connection works in much the same way. At one end, replacing the telephone, we have the ADO objects – specifically the ADO `Connection` object. At the other end, replacing the bank teller or the Weather Office's recorded message, we have one or other data store. In between, we have a connection that ties them together for as long as they need to communicate.

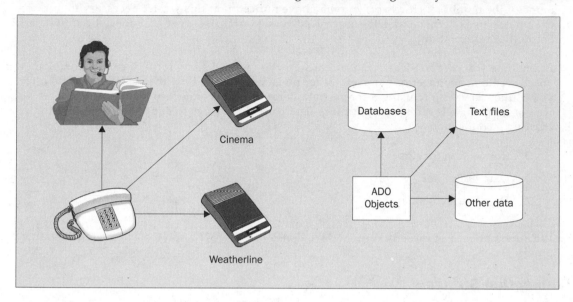

When the `Connection` object has finished communicating with one data store, you can disconnect (using the `Close` method as we did in the previous example). Then, if you like and as long as you don't remove the object from memory, you can use the *same* `Connection` object to connect to another data store (just as we can use the same telephone to call different services at different times).

Of course, if you had lots of telephones (and telephone lines) then you could call lots of different services at the same time (although you'd probably need to ask some of your office-mates to help with all the ensuing conversations!). You can do the same with `Connection` objects. You can have lots of `Connection` objects in your code, with each one connected to a different data store.

Describing the Connection

When we use our telephone to make a connection, we describe the connection we want by punching the telephone number into the telephone's keypad. It's a similar situation when we create a connection between a web page and a data store – we need to provide the `Connection` object with details of the connection we're trying to create. The difference is that a data connection requires a little *more* information – things like the type of data store, its location, what part of the data store, etc.

For example, an Access database is identified by the name and location of the .mdb file. SQL Server, on the other hand, is designed to handle more (and larger) databases, and there is often more than one machine running SQL Server – so in order to uniquely identify a database, it could be necessary to provide enough information to identify the data server as well as the name of the database. However, you may have noticed that this wasn't necessary in our example. This is because MSDE is a reduced version of SQL Server and doesn't require the same amount of information.

Every time you communicate with a data store, you'll need some form of connection. Sometimes you'll create the connection yourself; other times you might allow the system to create it for you. Either way, you're using a connection. Before we can connect to a data store, we need some way of knowing *what* it is and *where* it is. There are three ways to supply this information when creating a connection:

❑   Connection Strings

❑   Data Link Files

❑   Data Source Names

We'll look at each of these in turn, and we'll also consider why some of them are preferable to others.

Connection Strings

A **connection string** is a simple character string that lists all of the information needed to connect to a source of data. Of the three methods listed above, they're probably the most difficult to use because you have to write the strings yourself, instead of using some neat wizard. However, they give you the most power. We used connection strings to specify the connection details for the .mdb and .mdf data stores in the Connect.asp example above. A typical connection string will contain some or all of the following key pieces of information (dependent on the type of data store we are connecting to):

❑   Provider: the type of OLE-DB provider used in the connection.

❑   Driver: the type of ODBC driver, such as the ODBC Driver for Microsoft Access or ODBC Driver for Microsoft SQL Server (if you're using ODBC directly instead of OLE-DB)

❑   Initial File Name or Data Source: the physical database path and file name

❑   Initial Catalog: the name of the database

❑   User ID: the user name needed to connect to the database (sa is the default for the administrator user name)

❑   Password: the password of the user specified in the User ID field above

❑   Persist Security Info: a Boolean, set to True if you want Windows to remember your password for you

Writing a connection string is just a case of joining the various pieces of information together – separating consecutive pieces with semi-colons. Let's have a look at a few sample connection strings, to get a feel for how they are constructed to suit a particular set-up.

Some Sample Connection Strings

If we're connecting to an Access database then we might use a connection string like the following (this is the connection string from the `Connect.asp` example above):

```
"Provider=Microsoft.Jet.OLEDB.4.0;Data Source=C:\datastores\Movie2000.mdb;" & _
"Persist Security Info=False"
```

Microsoft Access uses the Microsoft Jet engine, so here the OLE-DB provider we've specified is for the Jet engine (rather than Access itself). We've also specified the location and name of the Access database, as the `Data Source`, and the `Persist Security Info` Boolean.

If we were accessing the same database using the ODBC driver for Access (instead of an OLE-DB provider), then we might use the following instead:

```
"Driver={Microsoft Access Driver (*.mdb)}; DBQ=C:\datastores\Movie2000.mdb"
```

This time we specify the ODBC driver (using `Driver`) and the database name and location (using `DBQ`).

For a SQL Server-type database, the information required in the connection string is different again. Here's the connection string we used to connect to the `Movie2000.mdf` data file in the `Connect.asp` example above:

```
"Provider= SQLOLEDB;Persist Security Info=False;" & _
"User ID=sa;Initial Catalog=Movie;" & _
"Initial File Name=C:\MSSQL7\Data\Movie2000.mdf"
```

This adds the `Initial Catalog` and the user ID to the required information as well.

If the Movies database were properly installed into a SQL Server (rather than being accessed via MSDE as we're doing here), then it would be different again. In that case, a connection string such as the following should do the trick:

```
"Provider= SQLOLEDB;Data Source=MyDataMachine;" & _
"Database=Movie;User ID=sa;Password="
```

You're probably starting to get the idea – the structure of the connection string is dependent on the type of data store you're trying to connect to.

Connection Strings and Include Files

If you're quick off the mark, and you're mind is racing ahead, then you might be thinking of a situation in which you have a number of related ASP pages on your web site, each of which uses connection strings to the same database – and how, if you changed the location of the database then it would be a maintenance nightmare to change the connection string details in every single ASP file. Fortunately, there's a really simple way around this, in the form of **server-side include (SSI) files**.

We've already come across the notion of SSIs – remember that an SSI is a way to include the contents of one file within another. When ASP sees the #INCLUDE command, it looks for the FILE argument, which specifies the SSI (the file to be included). Then it places the contents of the specified SSI into the first file, in place of the #INCLUDE command (see the example below). Thus, the contents of the SSI behave as though they were typed directly into the first file.

In the context of database access, we can use SSIs to store our connection string details. Using this technique, we can write the connection string into an SSI, and then include the SSI into each ASP page that needs it. Thus, the connection string is only defined in a single place.

> *We recommend that you avoid file extensions such as* .txt *and* .inc *when naming your SSI files. Instead, always use the file extension* .asp *for you SSIs, which (as we explained in Chapter 10) provides additional security for your SSI code.*

For example, we could create a new SSI file called DataStore.asp, with the following contents:

```
<%
strConnect = "Provider=Microsoft.Jet.OLEDB.4.0;" & _
             "Data Source=C:\datastores\Movie2000.mdb;" & _
             "Persist Security Info=False"
%>
```

Here, DataStore.asp is a single central file that contains your connection details. Now, we can include this into each ASP page that uses such a connection, by writing the following line into each ASP page:

```
<!-- #INCLUDE FILE="DataStore.asp" -->
```

If the connection details change (for example, if the location of the data store changes, or if we manage to acquire a more efficient OLE-DB data provider), we don't need to edit each-and-every affected ASP file: instead, we just change the contents of DataStore.asp.

So let's go back to our example, and rewrite it so that the connection string is stored in its own little SSI.

Try It Out – Using an SSI to store a Connection String

1. Open up Notepad or any other code editor, and type in the following connection string information. You'll recognize some of this code from the Connect.asp example, above. Again, ensure that the connection string reflects the location of the database on your machine:

```
<%
  Dim strDatabaseType

  'Choose one of the following two lines, and comment out the other
  strDatabaseType = "Access"
  'strDatabaseType = "MSDE"
```

```
'Now we use this selection to specify the connection string
If strDatabaseType = "Access" Then
  strConnect = "Provider=Microsoft.Jet.OLEDB.4.0;" & _
               "Data Source=C:\datastores\Movie2000.mdb;" & _
               "Persist Security Info=False"
Else
  strConnect = "Provider=SQLOLEDB;Persist Security Info=False;" & _
               "User ID=sa;Initial Catalog=Movie;" & _
               "Initial File Name=C:\MSSQL7\Data\Movie2000.mdf"
End If
%>
```

*Notice that we put the <% ... %> tags around this information, to make sure that it is
identified as a server-side script and executed on the server.*

2. Save this file as `DataStore.asp`, in your `C:\inetpub\wwwroot\BegASPFiles`
directory.

3. Copy the file `Connect.asp` to a new file, called `Connect2.asp`. Then open
`Connect2.asp` in your ASP editor, and amend the contents of that file as indicated
by the shaded lines:

```
<%
  Option Explicit
  Dim strConnect
%>
<!-- #include file="datastore.asp" -->
<HTML>
<HEAD>
<TITLE>Using an SSI to hold the Connection String</TITLE>
</HEAD>
<BODY>

<%
  Dim objConn, objRS
  Dim adOpenForwardOnly, adLockReadOnly, adCmdTable

  adOpenForwardOnly = 0
  adLockReadOnly = 1
  adCmdTable = 2

  Set objConn = Server.CreateObject("ADODB.Connection")
  Set objRS = Server.CreateObject("ADODB.Recordset")

  objConn.Open strConnect

  objRS.Open "Movies", objConn, adOpenForwardOnly, adLockReadOnly, adCmdTable

  While Not objRS.EOF
    Response.Write objRS("Title") & "<BR>"
    objRS.MoveNext
  Wend
```

483

```
        objRS.Close
        objConn.Close
        Set objRS = Nothing
        Set objConn = Nothing
    %>

    </BODY>
    </HTML>
```

4. Don't forget to save your changes to `Connect2.asp`.

5. Browse to the page `Connect2.asp` in your browser:

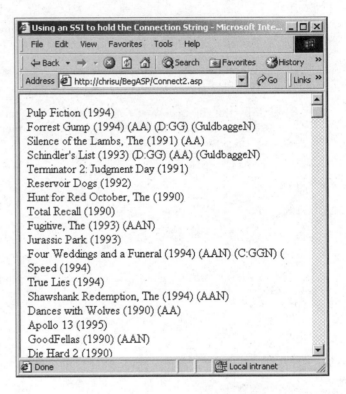

How It Works

In `Connect2.asp`, the cumbersome connection details have been replaced with a simple `#INCLUDE` command that inserts the connection string definition as required. Once we've performed that include, the `strConnect` variable is available for us to use with the `Connection` object's `Open` method (and anywhere else, if we want to).

The connection string is that which is defined in the SSI, `DataStore.asp`. If you ever need to update any of the information contained within the connection string, then you only have to do it once – within `DataStore.asp`.

Data Link Files

So we've seen how to create a connection string by hand – but what if you're unsure of what information to put in the string? There is a nifty little way to get Windows to create a string for you. Way back with the release of ADO 2.0 (which, admittedly, was only a couple of years ago), Microsoft introduced **data link files** – a method for connecting to your data store which avoided the need to type all of the code into a connection string by hand.

In Windows Explorer in Windows 98 or NT 4.0, you could create a data link file by selecting the New option from the File menu – and thus generate and store the necessary connection string information in a UDL (Universal Data Link) file. Since then, Microsoft has deemed the ready accessibility of this functionality as 'confusing' to novices, and has thus partially removed it from Windows 2000.

In other words, it's still there – but creating a UDL in Windows 2000 is just a little less convenient than it was in Windows 98 and NT 4.0. So how do you go about using it now? Let's see…

Try It Out – Creating a Data Link

As we discussed, with Windows 2000 Microsoft has removed the ability to create a data link from a Windows Explorer menu. However, with a little sly jiggery-pokery, we can still create one – it just takes a little more effort.

1. Start up Notepad, but don't add any code to the file. Select File | Save As…. In the dialog, change the Save As Type from Text Documents (*.txt) to All Files (so that Notepad doesn't try to save the file with a `.txt` extension). Then use the dialog to save the blank file as `MovieLink.udl` in your `C:\InetPub\wwwroot\BegASPFiles` folder:

2. In Windows Explorer, find `MovieLink.udl` and right-click on it. From the resulting menu, select the **Properties** option. This will present you with the **MovieLink.udl Properties** dialog.

3. Select the **Provider** tab and select the OLE-DB provider you wish to create a data link for (select **Microsoft Jet 4.0 OLE DB Provider** for an Access database, or **Microsoft OLE DB Provider for SQL Server** for MSDE):

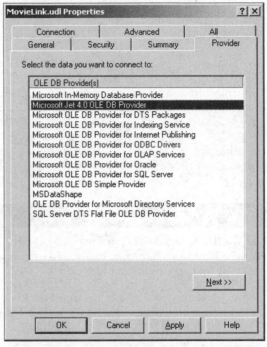

4. Now select the **Connections** tab. If you selected the Jet provider (for an Access database) in the previous screenshot, you'll get something that looks like this. Enter the full folder path to the `Movie2000.mdb` file, and check the **Blank password** check box, as shown here:

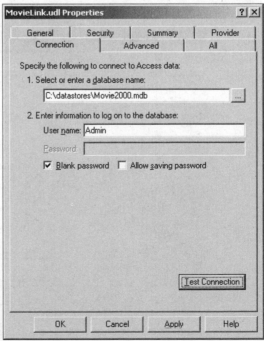

Alternatively, if you're using MSDE then the **Connections** tab will look like this. Here, you need to supply a server name (the name of the machine that is hosting the data), user ID and password, and specify that you're actually attaching a database file:

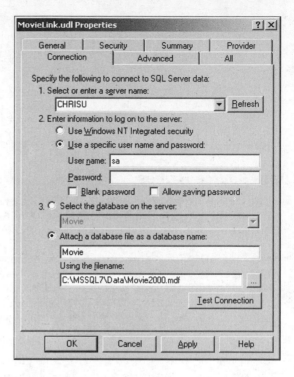

5. Click on **Apply** and then follow this with **OK** to dismiss the dialog.

6. Open up Notepad and view the `MovieLink.udl`. This is what it looks like if created in MSDE (I've used **Format | Word Wrap** for this screenshot, just so that you can see the entire contents of the string):

How It Works

There's two ways you can make this work. First, you could copy the connection string from the `.udl` file, and paste it into your ASP code, as shown here:

```
objConn.Open "Provider=SQLOLEDB.1;Persist Security Info=False;" & _
             "User ID=sa;" & _
             "Initial Catalog=Movie;Initial File Name=C:\MSSQL7\Data\Movie2000.mdf"
```

> *Note that in the above code fragment, I've broken the connection string at various points, using a string concatenation character, &, and a line continuation character, _, to make the code more legible.*

Alternatively, you could reference the data link file by its file name in your ASP code:

```
objConn.Open "File Name=C:\InetPub\wwwroot\BegASPFiles\MovieLink.udl"
```

Either way, it saves some of the dirty work.

Data Source Names

The **Data Source Name (DSN)** is another way to establish your connection string without typing it explicitly – again, it involves getting Windows to do most of the hard work for you. DSNs boast the advantage that they are very simple to use.

However, DSNs are now considered to be an outdated method of establishing a data connection. Unfortunately they use ODBC drivers – so you lose many of the advantages that come with using the OLE-DB providers, because DSNs don't support them. As we've remarked before, OLE-DB is the way that Microsoft are encouraging people to go – it is faster and more efficient, and you're going to have to get used to it anyway in the end.

However, at the moment, DSNs are still in everyday usage – many people still use this method of creating a connection in preference to either explicit connections strings or UDLs, simply because they're so simple to use. Therefore, you should be aware of how to create one.

Creating a DSN

You can use the ODBC Data Sources administrator to create a DSN automatically for you – you supply the information, and give it an identifier. Then you can use the identifier within your ASP code to access the DSN (and hence the data).

In Windows 2000, you'll find the ODBC administrator by selecting Start | Settings | Control Panel, then choosing Administrative Tools. There, double-click on the Data Sources (ODBC) icon. You'll be presented with the following dialog:

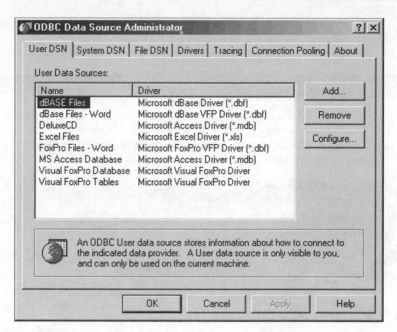

Yours may look slightly different from this, depending on which data sources are set up. The drivers shown above (and others, such as SQL Server, which isn't shown here) are supplied with a variety of Microsoft products, such as Microsoft Office.

The User DSN tab (above) shows all data sources for the user who is currently logged on. This allows you to have data sources that are only available for selected people who log onto the machine. This is no good for ASP, since ASP can only use System DSNs. So let's have a look at the System DSN tab:

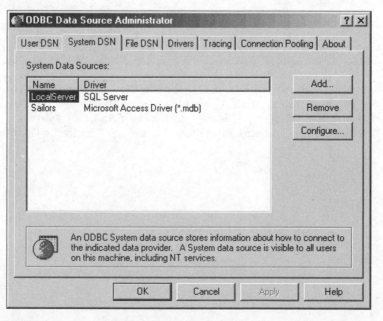

A data source that appears in this tab is available to anyone who logs onto the local machine – including ASP itself. The screenshot above shows the System DSN tab on my machine – as you can see, this machine already has one SQL Server data source and one Access data source.

Try It Out – Creating an Access Data Source Name

1. To create a new data source for an Access database, start from the System DSN tab of the Data Source administrator, and click the Add... button. This will give you a list of available drivers. The **driver** is the underlying code that handles the connection for you, but you don't need to know anything about it except its name:

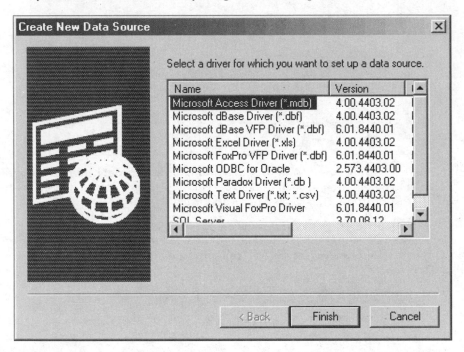

2. Select the Microsoft Access Driver (*.mdb) and then click the Finish button. This presents you with second dialog, in which you can name the data source and pick the .mdb file to use. So first, type Movie into the Data Source Name textbox (this will be your DSN identifier) and add an appropriate description in the Description textbox.

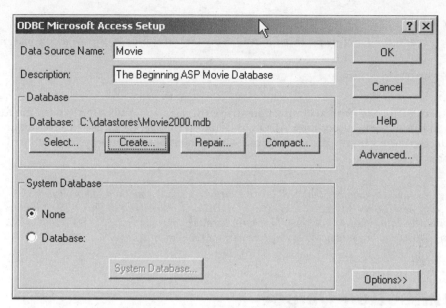

Now click the **Select...** button to get the **Select Database** dialog – use this to locate the Access database `Movie2000.mdb`. (You could click the **Create** button to create a new database.)

3. If you now click **OK** you'll see that your new data source has been added to the list.

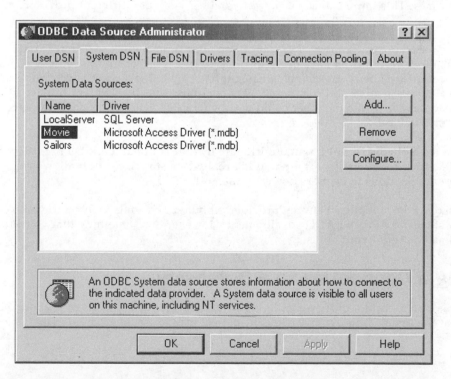

How It Works

Once you've created a DSN using this method, you can reference it within a connection string, like this:

```
objConn.Open "DSN=Movie"
```

Instead of providing the normal connection string information, you simply pass the identifier of your DSN to the `Open` method; then ADO will look up the DSN and use the connection information contained there. It's very simple – but remember it can only be used for ODBC driver connections.

> *Again, we should remember that DSNs are a largely outdated method of specifying connection details, mainly because they use ODBC drivers instead of OLE-DB providers to handle the data. We include them here only because you may come across DSNs when working with legacy systems. We won't be using DSNs in this book.*

The Connection Object

So now we know what a connection is, it's time to look at the ADO object of the same name. The `Connection` object is what ADO uses to store our information about the data store connection. In fact, it actually represents a unique session with the data store. As we mentioned earlier, this means that we can use a single `Connection` object to connect to different data stores at different times. This implies that a `Connection` object can use different providers at different times.

Moreover, we can use a number of `Connection` objects to connect to different data stores at the same time (and we can even have multiple `Connection` objects simultaneously connecting to the *same* data store!). So, for example, we might have an ASP page with two `Connection` objects, called `objConn1` and `objConn2`. One could use the OLE-DB Jet provider to connect to an Access database, while the other could use the OLE-DB SQL Server provider to connect to a SQL Server database.

This may seem obvious – but it's an unfortunate truth that not all OLE-DB providers support exactly the same functionality. This shouldn't really be a surprise – after all, we can expect some data store applications to be more powerful than others.

This difference in capability between providers shouldn't be a big problem to you – especially in the early stages of ASP and ADO development. However, it's something that you should be aware of as you build your skills.

Creating a Connection to a Database

We've spent an awful lot of time explaining what this connection business is about, so lets start looking at the real coding issues. This is the easiest way to create a `Connection` object in ASP:

```
Dim objConn
Set objConn = Server.CreateObject("ADODB.Connection")
```

This uses the `CreateObject` method of the `Server` object to create an instance of the `Connection` object – in much the same way, we've used the same method to create instances of other objects in earlier chapters. The programmatic identifier (or `ProgID`) for the ADO `Connection` object is `ADODB.Connection`. So that we can use the object within our code, we've given it a name – `objConn`.

Opening a Connection

So, the two lines above are enough to create a `Connection` object. However, we've done nothing with it yet. Just because we have created a `Connection` object, that doesn't mean that we're connected to the database! In order to actually establish the connection we use the `Open` method of the `objConn` `Connection` object. The syntax for using the `Open` method is:

```
objConn.Open ConnectionString, UserId, Password, Options
```

In fact, we used this in the examples we've seen so far in this chapter. For example:

```
objConn.Open strConnect
```

Here, we've only specified the first argument – the connection string – and the other arguments assumed default values. In fact, all four arguments are *optional* arguments – we don't have to specify any of them at the time we call the `Open` method. Instead of the above line, we could achieve the same effect by setting the connection string using a special property of the `Connection` object – its `ConnectionString` property. After that we call the `Open` method without any arguments, like this:

```
objConn.ConnectionString = strConnect
objConn.Open
```

Here's an example where we use the `Open` method directly, passing the user ID and password as well as the connection string:

```
objConn.Open strConnect, "ChrisU", ""
```

> *If you pass user ID/password details in the second and third arguments like this, but you also specify user ID/password details in your connection string then– according to the ADO documentation – the results are unpredictable. It is wise to avoid this kind of potential confilict of information by choosing one method of input only and sticking to it.*

The above examples assume that `strConnect` is the connection string, like the one we created in `DataStore.asp` earlier in this chapter. But of course, we could equally well write an *explicit* connection string as the first argument instead:

```
objConn.Open "Provider=SQLOLEDB;Persist Security Info=False;" & _
             "User ID=sa;" & _
             "Initial Catalog=Movie;Initial File Name=C:\MSSQL7\Data\Movie2000.mdf"
```

493

Closing the Connection

Once you have finished with a connection, you should `Close` it, in order to free associated system resources:

```
objConn.Close
```

This doesn't actually remove the object from memory; so you can `Open` it again if you need to. Once you've closed the connection, you can change the connection string and other properties, and use the same object to open a different connection.

Alternatively, if you've finished with the object you can remove it from memory, by setting the name of the object to `Nothing`:

```
Set objConn = Nothing.
```

The Properties Collection

You've seen one of the properties of the `Connection` object – the `ConnectionString` property – in the code fragments above. However, there's a whole lot of information behind the `Connection` object that we haven't met – and some of which we'll never need! But it's useful to know that the names and values of all the connection properties can be accessed from a single location – the `Connection` object's `Properties` collection. The `Properties` collection contains a `Property` object for each property that the connection supports.

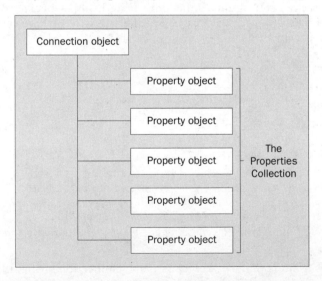

A **collection** is much like an array (we covered arrays in Chapter 4, and we met the collections of the ASP `Request` object in Chapter 7). You can look through the elements of the `Properties` collection in much the same way as we can look through the elements of the ASP `Request.Querystring` collection (or any of the other collections of the `Request` object). Let's try this out, and then we'll examine how it works.

We're going to establish a connection to the database; we won't pass any data across the connection, but instead we'll just examine the properties of the established connection.

1. Create a new file, and type in the following HTML and script. Don't forget that this file, like all the code in the book, can be obtained from the Wrox Press web site at http://www.wrox.com, so if your typing is like mine then you might prefer to download it instead of typing it in:

```
<%
  Option Explicit
  Dim strConnect
%>
<!-- #INCLUDE FILE="DataStore.asp" -->
<HTML>
<HEAD>
<TITLE>ADO Connection Properties</TITLE>
</HEAD>
<BODY>

<TABLE BORDER=1>
  <TR>
    <TD><B>Property</B></TD><TD><B>Value</B></TD>
  </TR>
  <%
    Dim objConn        ' Connection object
    Dim objProp        ' Property object

    ' create the connection object
    Set objConn = Server.CreateObject ("ADODB.Connection")

    ' and open it
    objConn.Open strConnect

    ' loop through the properties
    For Each objProp In objConn.Properties
      Response.Write "<TR>" & _
          "<TD>" & objProp.Name & "</TD>" & _
          "<TD>" & objProp.Value & " </TD>" & _
        "</TR>"
    Next

    ' now close and clean up
    objConn.Close
    Set objConn = Nothing
  %>
</TABLE>
</BODY>
</HTML>
```

2. Save this file into the `\inetpub\wwwroot\BegASPFiles` folder, calling it `ConnProps.asp`.

3. Ensure that the SSI file `DataStore.asp`, which we gave earlier in this chapter, is also in the same folder.

4. In your web browser, browse to `ConnProps.asp`:

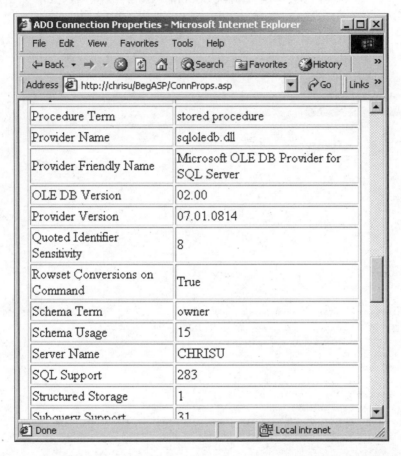

As you can see by scrolling down the page, there are a lot of properties in this collection! But there's no cause for alarm: you don't need to know about them all in order to continue and, in fact, you'll probably find that you'll rarely need to use most of them in your entire programming career. But it's useful to know that they're there.

How It Works

First of all we specify `Option Explicit` – as it is good practice for catching typographical errors in the code – and declare the `strConnect` variant ready for our connection string. Then we include the data store SSI – just as we did in `Connect2.asp` – to define the value of `strConnect`:

```
<%
  Option Explicit
  Dim strConnect
%>
<!-- #INCLUDE FILE="DataStore.asp" -->
```

Now we begin a table that will show the properties and their values:

```
<TABLE BORDER=1>
  <TR>
    <TD><B>Property</B></TD><TD><B>Value</B></TD>
  </TR>
```

Once the table header is created, we need to create the table body. For this, we loop through all of the properties using a `For Each ... Next` statement – each iteration through the loop will look at each property in turn and write a single row of the table. In preparation, we declare a couple of variants – one for the ADO `Connection` object, and one for the ADO `Property` object.

```
<%
  Dim objConn        ' Connection object
  Dim objProp        ' Property object
```

Now we create the `Connection` object, and open it.

```
  ' create the connection object
  Set objConn = Server.CreateObject ("ADODB.Connection")

  ' and open it
  objConn.Open strConnect
```

Once the connection is open we can start looping through the `Properties` collection. The `For Each ... Next` statement is perfect for iterating through collections, because the control variable (in this case `objProp`), which references each member of the collection in turn, can also be used inside the loop. Inside this loop, we write the property's `Name` and `Value` into cells in the table:

```
  ' loop through the properties
  For Each objProp In objConn.Properties
    Response.Write "<TR>" & _
        "<TD>" & objProp.Name & "</TD>" & _
        "<TD>" & objProp.Value & " </TD>" & _
      "</TR>"
  Next
```

We've included a non-break space here – the   bit. It's there to ensure that each cell in the table contains at least one character, even if the property value itself is empty. It's just a formatting trick to make the table look tidier.

And finally we can close the connection and clean up (and complete the table with a closing </TABLE> tag):

```
    ' now close and clean up
    objConn.Close
    Set objConn = Nothing
  %>
</TABLE>
```

That's all there is to it. You'll find this technique of looping through a collection quite useful, and you will see it again later.

You can use the Properties collection to find out what functionality is supported on a connection. For example MSDE allows you to have a maximum row size of 8060 characters, while Access only allows 4049. Admittedly, this is unlikely to be a problem, but you could check the Maximum Row Size property to find this out. To do this you don't need to loop through the whole collection – you can just access the element you need directly, like this:

```
Response.Write "Cols = " & objConn.Properties("Maximum Row Size")
```

This uses the same collection, but you are retrieving a Connection's property value using the property name.

The Errors Collection

The Connection object's Errors collection contains all errors that have been created in response to a single failure. You'll probably find that you use the Errors collection far more often than the Properties collection. The words **single failure** in this definition are quite important, because when an ADO operation generates an error, the Errors collection is cleared before the new error details are inserted. So, in other words, your code could contain two or more separate operations that failed, but the Errors collection might only contain one Error object, containing details of the error that occurred last. The previous ones will have been overwritten. In fact the only time multiple Error objects may be returned is if the same line of code generated the errors. Even then Access will only generate one, but you will find that MSDE/SQL Server generates more than one.

The Errors collection contains Error objects, in much the same way as the Properties collection contains Property objects. Each Error object contains several properties that you'll need when looking at errors:

Property	Description
Number	The number of the error
Description	The description for the error
Source	Identifies the object that raised the error
SQLState	Holds the SQL error code
NativeError	Holds the database-specific error code

Using these properties you'll be able to find out, in more detail, what error occurred so that this can be reported back to the user. Let's see how to do this.

1. Open up your editor, create a new file and add the following HTML and script:

```
<%
  Option Explicit
  Dim strConnect
%>
<!-- #INCLUDE FILE="DataStore.asp" -->
<HTML>
<HEAD>
<TITLE>ADO Errors</TITLE>
</HEAD>
<BODY>

<%
  On Error Resume Next

  Dim objConn         ' Connection object
  Dim objProp         ' Property object
  Dim objError        ' Error object

  ' create the connection object
  Set objConn = Server.CreateObject ("ADODB.Connection")

  ' and open it
  objConn.Open strConnect

  ' now we can execute some SQL
  objConn.Execute "SELECT MissingColumn FROM MissingTable"

  ' Errors means the count will be greater than 0
  If objConn.Errors.Count > 0 Then

    ' loop through the errors
    For Each objError in objConn.Errors
      Response.Write "<TABLE BORDER=1>" & _
          "<TD>Error Property</TD>" & _
          "<TD>Contents</TD>" & _
          "<TR><TD>Number</TD><TD>" & _
                  objError.Number & "</TD></TR>" & _
          "<TR><TD>NativeError</TD><TD>" & _
                  objError.NativeError & "</TD></TR>" & _
          "<TR><TD>SQLState</TD><TD>" & _
                  objError.SQLState & "</TD></TR>" & _
          "<TR><TD>Source</TD><TD>" & _
                  objError.Source & "</TD></TR>" & _
          "<TR><TD>Description</TD><TD>" & _
                  objError.Description & "</TD></TR>" & _
          "</TABLE><P>"
```

```
    Next
  Else
    ' no errors
    Response.Write "There were no errors."
  End If

  ' now close and clean up
  objConn.Close
  Set objConn = Nothing
%>
</BODY>
</HTML>
```

2. Save the code as `ConnErrs.asp`.

3. Ensure that the SSI file `DataStore.asp`, which we gave earlier in this chapter, is also in the same folder.

4. Type the URL into your browser, and view the page.

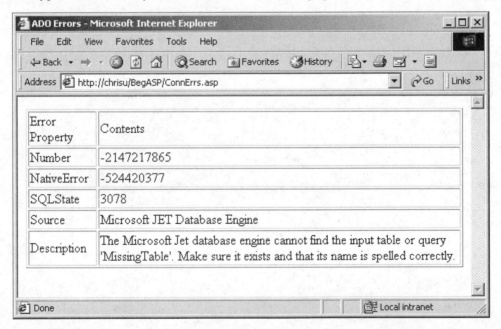

This is exactly what we expect to happen, because there's a deliberate error in the code. Whilst the SQL statement we executed is syntactically correct, it's requesting a non-existent column in a non-existent table.

How It Works

Once again we start with the include file, and give the `.asp` file a header:

```
<%
  Option Explicit
  Dim strConnect
%>
<!-- #INCLUDE FILE="DataStore.asp" -->
<HTML>
<HEAD>
<TITLE>ADO Errors</TITLE>
</HEAD>
```

To ensure that the ASP script is not terminated when an error occurs, we need to use the On Error statement. This is similar to one that you may have seen used in Visual Basic and VBA, but has less flexibility. All we can do is Resume Next, to continue processing at the next statement:

```
<BODY>
<%
  On Error Resume Next
```

Next we declare the variables. This time we declare a variable that will represent an Error object. Then we create the connection and open it:

```
  Dim objConn        ' Connection object
  Dim objProp        ' Property object
  Dim objError       ' Error object

  ' create the connection object
  Set objConn = Server.CreateObject ("ADODB.Connection")

  ' and open it
  objConn.Open strConnect
```

Then we can execute our SQL statement, which contains the deliberate error. We haven't covered the Execute statement yet – this will be part of the next chapter. For now, we'll just use it to force the error:

```
  ' now we can execute some SQL
  objConn.Execute "SELECT MissingColumn FROM MissingTable"
```

The Count property of the Errors collection tells us how many errors there have been. We can test this before going into our error display section of code:

```
  ' Errors means the count will be greater than 0
  If objConn.Errors.Count > 0 Then
```

If there are errors, we can start looping through the Errors collection, using the same technique as we used on the Properties collection. We build up an HTML table containing all of the error information that we need to see:

```
' loop through the errors
For Each objError in objConn.Errors
  Response.Write "<TABLE BORDER=1>" & _
        "<TD>Error Property</TD>" & _
        "<TD>Contents</TD>" & _
        "<TR><TD>Number</TD><TD>" & _
              objError.Number & "</TD></TR>" & _
        "<TR><TD>NativeError</TD><TD>" & _
              objError.NativeError & "</TD></TR>" & _
        "<TR><TD>SQLState</TD><TD>" & _
              objError.SQLState & "</TD></TR>" & _
        "<TR><TD>Source</TD><TD>" & _
              objError.Source & "</TD></TR>" & _
        "<TR><TD>Description</TD><TD>" & _
              objError.Description & "</TD></TR>" & _
        "</TABLE><P>"
Next
```

If there are no errors, we can display a message that says so:

```
Else
  ' no errors
  Response.Write "There were no errors."
End If
```

This won't happen, because we know that there's a deliberate error in there! But we include this for completeness.

Finally, we clean up and close the connection:

```
' now close and clean up
objConn.Close
Set objConn = Nothing
%>
</BODY>
</HTML>
```

A Generic Error Routine

You could turn this error display into a separate SSI file of its own, which could then be #included into any .asp file. It's a good practice to generalize and modularize code that you're likely to use repeatedly – this makes it easier to maintain and debug larger applications. Anything that makes your life easier has got to be worth a go!

1. Start up your editor, and type in the code for the following include file:

```asp
<%
Sub CheckForErrors (objConn)
  ' Errors means the count will be greater than 0
  If objConn.Errors.Count > 0 Then

    ' loop through the errors
    For Each objError in objConn.Errors
      Response.Write "<TABLE BORDER=1>" & _
          "<TR><TD>Error Property</TD>" & _
            "<TD>Contents</TD></TR>" & _
          "<TR><TD>Number</TD><TD>" & _
              objError.Number & "</TD></TR>" & _
          "<TR><TD>NativeError</TD><TD>" & _
              objError.NativeError & "</TD></TR>" & _
          "<TR><TD>SQLState</TD><TD>" & _
              objError.SQLState & "</TD></TR>" & _
          "<TR><TD>Source</TD><TD>" & _
              objError.Source & "</TD></TR>" & _
          "<TR><TD>Description</TD><TD>" & _
              objError.Description & "</TD></TR>" & _
          "</TABLE><P>"
    Next
  End If
End Sub
%>
```

2. Save the code, with the name Errors.asp, into the
\inetpub\wwwroot\BegASPFiles folder.

We're going to use this as an SSI in other ASP pages. Note that, once again, we're using the .asp suffix for the SSI's filename. This ensures that anyone stumbling on this file via a browser will only see the version parsed by the ASP engine – so our ASP source code is safe.

3. Ensure that the SSI file DataStore.asp, which we gave earlier in this chapter, is also in the same folder.

4. Now open up a new file, and type in the following code (it's the same as ConnErrs.asp, except at the shaded lines):

```asp
<%
  Option Explicit
  Dim strCOnnect
%>
<!-- #INCLUDE FILE="DataStore.asp" -->
<!-- #INCLUDE FILE="Errors.asp" -->
<HTML>
<HEAD>
```

```
<TITLE>ADO Errors, Part 2</TITLE>
</HEAD>
<BODY>
<%
  On Error Resume Next

  Dim objConn        ' Connection object
  Dim objProp        ' Property object
  Dim objError       ' Error object

  ' create the connection object
  Set objConn = Server.CreateObject ("ADODB.Connection")

  ' and open it
  objConn.Open strConnect

  ' now we can execute some SQL
  objConn.Execute "SELECT MissingColumn FROM MissingTable"

  ' now check for errors
  CheckForErrors (objConn)

  ' now close and clean up
  objConn.Close
  Set objConn = Nothing
%>
</BODY>
</HTML>
```

5. Save this in the same directory, with the name UseErrors.asp.

6. Call up the page UseErrors.asp from your browser. You'll see that this has the same result as before. Let's see how it works.

How It Works

Let's first look at Errors.asp. Here, we define a sub-procedure called CheckForErrors(), which has one argument – objConn. This will be used to hold the Connection object:

```
<%
Sub CheckForErrors (objConn)
```

Now we can check how many errors are in the collection:

```
  ' Errors means the count will be greater than 0
  If objConn.Errors.Count > 0 Then
```

If there are errors, create a table as before:

```
' loop through the errors
For Each objError in objConn.Errors
   ...
Next
```

That's all there is to it. Notice that the SSI file doesn't open the connection, and so it doesn't close the connection either: responsibility for this is taken by the calling ASP page.

The `UseErrors.asp` file is familiar too. The first thing you notice is that we include two files – `DataStore.asp` for the connection details, and `Error.asp` for the error routine.

```
<!-- #INCLUDE FILE="DataStore.asp" -->
<!-- #INCLUDE FILE="Errors.asp" -->
```

Much of the rest of the code is the same as that in `ConnErrs.asp`. The only other difference is at the point where we call the new error routine, passing in our open connection:

```
' now check for errors
CheckForErrors (objConn)
```

This gives us the same result as before. Easy, huh? Moreover, you now have a simple generic error routine that you can use from *any* `.asp` file to display information about your ADO errors. This saves having to write it each time, and makes it easier to update.

Summary

We've covered quite a lot of ground in this chapter, and although we haven't really done a lot of database-type things, it's been important to get some of this groundwork covered. Essentially, in this chapter we have studied connections between applications and data stores, and we've learned that:

❑ We use a connection to pass data between an application (such as an ASP page) and a data store, in the same way that two telephones communicate via a connection

❑ The data store can talk to an OLE-DB data provider, which in turn communicates with a data consumer

❑ In our case, the data consumer will be a set of interfaces called the ActiveX Data Objects (ADO). We use these objects in our ASP code

❑ The main ADO objects are called `Connection`, `Command`, `Recordset`, `Record` and `Stream`

❑ The ADO `Connection` object is an object that we use to represent the physical connection between the ASP page and the data store

Along the way, we met the old standard of ODBC – which was a standard for achieving access to databases. And we looked at what OLE-DB can do for us, and noted that we can think of ADO as just a high-level wrapper for OLE-DB.

Remember that ASP and ADO are quite separate technologies – they perform quite different tasks and can exist independently of one another. For the purpose of creating dynamic web pages, however, ASP and ADO provide very complimentary functionality.

Having laid a firm foundation on the subject of connections, it's time to put them to good use by manipulating some data. In the next chapter, we'll meet the ADO `Recordset` object and see how we can use it to organize the information that we retrieve from the data store, and the information that we send to the data store.

Using Recordsets

In the previous chapter we spent a lot of time looking at the connection to the data store. While it's fundamental to the process of passing data between our ASP pages and our data stores, it's not really very exciting – what we really want to see is lots of data in your ASP pages. For that, we need to build on what we've learned about ADO so far. So, in this chapter we will:

- ❑ Examine what recordsets are, and how we use them

- ❑ Explain the notion of a cursor, and meet the different types of cursor

- ❑ Understand the concept of 'locking' a data store

- ❑ Learn how to move back and forwards through the records of our recordset

- ❑ See how we can search the recordset for individual records

- ❑ Hide all the items in a recordset that don't meet a specific criterion

- ❑ Get more information about the recordset

In this chapter we'll really begin to get to the heart of using ADO for data access within our ASP pages. We'll be looking at how you can run queries and stored procedures, to both return and insert data. We'll also be looking at ways to build HTML tables automatically from a set of data.

Before we start, we should just highlight that data can pass between the data store and the ASP page, in *either* direction. To keep things fairly simple, the examples in this chapter will all involve *reading* data from the data store and using it within our ASP pages. In the next chapter, we'll look at how we can *write* data from the ASP page to the data store, and hence keep a permanent copy of data that is generated by the user, or by the ASP, or by scripting logic as part of the page.

The Recordset Object

Let's recall the players in the ADO 2.5 object model again:

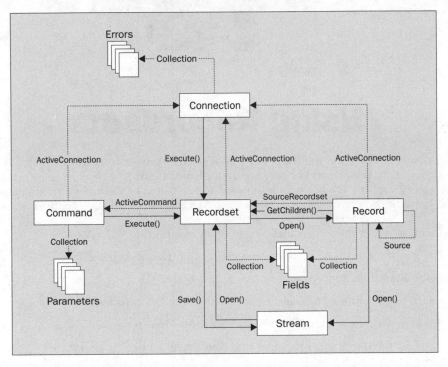

So far, of the main ADO objects, we've looked only at the Connection object and how it represents a real connection between the (ASP) application and the data store. Of course, if information is to pass between two places (such as an ASP page and a data store), then there needs to be a connection between them – and the ADO Connection object is a representation of that connection which we can use in our code.

But how do we manage the data, once we've got it from the data store into our page? Happily, it's organized into a fashion that reflects its original format in the data store, and that is relatively easy and intuitive to work with. In our code, we can manipulate the data through another of the main ADO objects – we can use a Recordset object.

As you can see, the Recordset object sits right in the middle of our ADO object diagram – which reflects the fact that it is probably the most heavily used ADO object in code. After all, it represents the data that we're working with – which is, in a sense, the *raison d'être* of ADO.

What is a Recordset?

In the previous chapter, we talked about the notion of an employee record being a collection of (one or more) values, for different types of data that all relate to a particular thing. We gave the example of the employee record:

Employee Key	Name	Address 1	Address 2	City	State	Zip	Phone
A100	Chris Ullman	29 LaSalle Street	Suite B01	Chicago	Illinois	60603	392-893-8004

This is just a single record. This record contains a number of pieces of data – one for each of the fields 'Employee Key', 'Name', 'Address 1', etc. Each piece of data is information about this employee, on the subject of that field.

Now imagine a whole collection of records just like this one. Each record pertains to one individual employee, and the information in that record is information about that employee. Moreover, each record has the same structure – that is, it represents values of the same fields ('Employee Key', 'Name', 'Address 1', etc.) in the same order:

Employee Key	Name	Address 1	Address 2	City	State	Zip	Phone
A192	Chris Masters	29 LaSalle Street	Suite 278	Chicago	Illinois	60603	392-893-8103
A203	David Minter	42 Downing Alley	Room 29	Oxford	Oxon	OX98 1QY	1865-000000
A229	John Morrissey	29 LaSalle Street	Suite 502	Chicago	Illinois	60603	392-893-8115

This is a set of records – or a **recordset**. This recordset has three records in it – one record each for the information of Messrs Masters, Minter and Morrissey. In order to define this recordset, we've chosen a particular set of fields (i.e. the 'classes' of information that we've selected in the top row of the table) and some criterion specifying which records we're interested in (e.g. here we wanted to know about employees whose surname begins with 'M', but none of our other employees).

In ADO, we represent a recordset – the data received when we query the database – by using its `Recordset` object. In fact, an ADO `Recordset` object is more than just a set of related data, like the table shown above – it has functionality to allow us to manipulate data, add, remove or hide records, search for data within the record, and so on. We'll meet much of this functionality during the course of this chapter.

Recordsets and Cursors

In addition, an ADO `Recordset` uses something called a **cursor**. A cursor is a 'pointer', which points to one of the records in the recordset, thus indicating our current position in the recordset.

> Every active `Recordset` object has a cursor, and at any given time, the cursor is pointing to exactly *one* of the records in the recordset.

What's the cursor for? Predominantly, it's there to help us to find our way around the records of a `Recordset` object. We can move the cursor so that it points to exactly the single record that we're interested in; and then we can use the names of the fields to single out individual 'cells' of information. There are various ways of moving the cursor around – for example, we can search the recordset for a particular record, or we can use special `Recordset` methods called `MoveFirst`, `MoveLast`, `MoveNext` and `MovePrevious` (which we'll meet later in the chapter).

For example, in order to find John Morrissey's telephone number we can instruct the cursor to move to Mr Morrissey's record (either by 'searching' for that record, or – in this case – using the `MoveLast` method). In the following table, the asterisk (*) on the left-hand side indicates the position of the cursor:

Employee Key	Name	Address 1	Address 2	City	State	Zip	Phone
A100	Chris Masters	29 LaSalle Street	Suite 278	Chicago	Illinois	60603	392-893-8103
A203	Alan Minter	42 Downing Alley	Room 29	Oxford	Oxon	OX98 1QY	1865-000000
*A229	John Morrissey	29 LaSalle Street	Suite 502	Chicago	Illinois	60603	392-893-8115

Then we can ask for the `Phone` field of the current record.

Creating a Recordset

That's all very well; now how do we go about creating a recordset? Well, ADO is quite flexible and consequently there's more than one way. If you want to create an explicit `Recordset` object in your code then you'll need to define a variable and then set it equal to a new `Recordset` object, like this:

```
Dim objRS
Set objRS = Server.CreateObject("ADODB.Recordset")
```

> *If this looks familiar to you it's because it's very similar to the syntax we used for creating an explicit `Connection` object in our code, in the previous chapter:*

```
Dim objConn
Set objConn = Server.CreateObject("ADODB.Connection")
```

Once again, the two shaded lines above are enough to create a `Recordset` object; but the object is not connected to a database and it doesn't yet contain any data! Let's see how to put some data into the `Recordset`; and then we'll exercise our knowledge in an example.

Recordsets and Connections

It's clear from the previous chapter that the connection is fundamental part of the practice of passing information between our ASP page and our data store. The connection is the route by which the information is transferred from one to the other. If there's no connection, then there's no way for the data to be transported.

So, when we're trying to get data from the data store into a `Recordset` object (or *vice versa*), we need to consider the connection too. However, the necessity for a connection *doesn't* imply that we need to create an explicit ADO `Connection` object in out code.

Using an Explicit Connection Object

The most obvious way to get some data from a data store is to explicitly create an ADO `Connection` object in our code, and then use the `Connection` object's properties when working with the `Recordset`:

```
Dim strConn, objConn, objRS
strConn = "Provider=Microsoft.Jet.OLEDB.4.0;Data Source=C:\Movie2000.mdb"

Set objConn = Server.CreateObject("ADODB.Connection")          ' Connection object
objConn.Open strConn

Set objRS = Server.CreateObject("ADODB.Recordset")             ' Recordset object
objRS.Open "Movies", objConn              ' use objConn to supply connection info
```

This is the technique we used in the `Connect.asp` example in Chapter 12. What's the advantage of doing it this way? Well, connecting to a data store is quite 'expensive' – it's a task that takes a relatively long time to complete. So if you need to use several recordsets in your code, or if you're going to use one recordset to make a number of queries, it is best to only connect to the data store once. In this case, create an explicit `Connection` object and use it whenever you need to use the data store connection.

Avoiding an Explicit Connection Object

So, several `Recordset` (or `Command`) objects can share an explicitly created `Connection` object. This is a good reason to do it this way. However, it's not always the most efficient or convenient way to work. Instead, we can make good use of one of the distinct advantages of ADO: namely, that the ADO objects enjoy a **flat hierarchy**, in which the interdependence of objects within our code is hidden in order to make our code simpler. In this example, we can open the `Recordset` object directly – we don't need to create an *explicit* `Connection` object:

```
Dim objRS, strConnect
strConnect = "Provider=Microsoft.Jet.OLEDB.4.0;Data Source=C:\Movie2000.mdb;"

Set objRS = Server.CreateObject("ADODB.Recordset")          ' Recordset object
objRS.Open "Movies", strConnect       ' use strConnect to supply connection info
```

What's happening here? Well, we've explicitly created a `Recordset` object in our code, and we've used its `Open` method to forge a connection between our code and the data store. This action is enough to create a physical connection, and to use `objRS` in the same way – yet there is no `Connection` object in sight!

In fact, there *is* an ADO `Connection` object – but ADO creates it under the covers, and (at the moment) we can't see it in our code. That's great – ADO creates the extra objects we need, so we don't need to worry about any kind of 'object hierarchy'. It keeps the logic simple and our code tidy.

If we *never* need to use the underlying `Connection` object in our code, this is perfect – it's a very tidy way of letting ADO deal with it for us. And if we decide that we *would* like to use it, we can give it a name in our code by referencing it via the `Recordset` object's `ActiveConnection` property:

```
Dim objRS, strConnect
strConnect = "Provider=Microsoft.Jet.OLEDB.4.0;Data Source=C:\Movie2000.mdb;"

Set objRS = Server.CreateObject("ADODB.Recordset")          ' Recordset object
objRS.Open tablename, strConnect        ' use strConnect to supply connection info
...
Dim objConn
objConn = objRS.ActiveConnection
```

Once we've done this, we can treat `objConn` just as if we had created it explicitly using the `Set` command.

> *This notion of a 'flat' hierarchy extends to the other ADO objects too. We can specify connection details directly to a `Recordset` object (cutting out the need for an explicit `Connection` object); equally, you'll find that it's possible to specify the details of a SQL command directly to a `Connection` or `Recordset` object (cutting out the need for an explicit `Command` object).*
>
> *This just gives us greater flexibility in our code. The interdependence between objects (like the relationship shown here between the `Connection` and `Recordset` objects) means that they can be handled explicitly in the code, if that's appropriate, or left for ADO to handle under the covers.*

So, let's use this to create a `Recordset` object and populate it with data from our **Movies** database – which we'll then show on screen. We've done it before, but this time we'll do it without an explicit `Connection` object in our code.

1. We'll use the connection details that you used in Chapter 12, so make sure you have the `DataStore.asp` SSI file, from Chapter 12, saved into your `\Inetpub\wwwroot\BegASP` directory. You'll also need the `Movies.mdb` or `Movies.mdf` data files set up, as described in Chapter 12.

2. Create a new file, called `Recordset.asp`, and put the following lines into it:

```
<%
  Option Explicit
  Dim strConnect
%>
<!-- #INCLUDE FILE="DataStore.asp" -->
<HTML>
<HEAD>
<TITLE>ADO Recordset Object</TITLE>
</HEAD>
<BODY>
<%
  Const adOpenForwardOnly = 0
  Const adLockReadOnly = 1
  Const adCmdTable = 2

  Dim objRS                                          ' recordset object
  Set objRS = Server.CreateObject ("ADODB.Recordset")    ' create recordset object
  objRS.Open "Movies", strConnect, _
            adOpenForwardOnly, adLockReadOnly, adCmdTable        ' now open it

  While Not objRS.EOF                                ' now loop through the records
    Response.Write objRS.Fields("Title") & ", "
    objRS.MoveNext
  Wend

  objRS.Close                   ' now close it
  Set objRS = Nothing           ' ...and clean up
%>
</BODY>
</HTML>
```

3. Save the `Recordset.asp` file into your `\inetpub\wwwroot\BegASPFiles` folder.

4. Load the page into your browser.

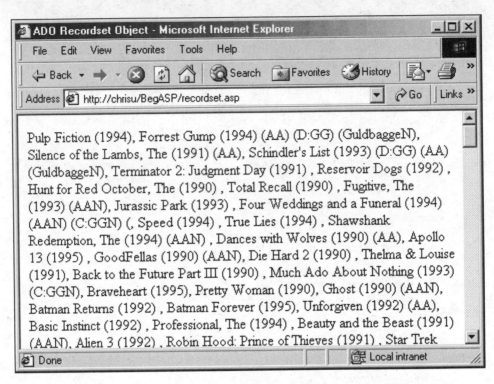

And *voila*—a list of all the titles of every name in the table. We did pretty much the same in the last chapter, with the help of the Connection object, but there are some important differences in the way it has been achieved here. Let's see how it works.

How It Works

The first few lines of code are familiar to us – we used them in most of the examples in Chapter 12. The Option Explicit command demands that we define all our variable names, and we follow that by including the DataStore.asp SSI that contains our connection string definition:

```
<%
  Option Explicit
  Dim strConnect
%>
<!-- #INCLUDE FILE="DataStore.asp" -->
<HTML>
<HEAD>
<TITLE>ADO Recordset Object</TITLE>
</HEAD>
<BODY>
```

Next, we define three constants, which we'll use in a moment with our `Recordset` object:

```
Const adOpenForwardOnly = 0
Const adLockReadOnly = 1
Const adCmdTable = 2
```

As you'll see shortly, we'll pass these constant values to the `Recordset` object when we open it – they tell the `Recordset` object about the type of recordset we want ADO to create for us. Don't worry about the different types of recordset available for now – all will be explained later in the chapter.

The next thing to do is declare our object variable, `objRS`:

```
Dim objRS                                             ' recordset object
```

Now we can create the `Recordset` object itself. We use the `Server.CreateObject` method for this task, and we specify the ADO `Recordset` object's `ProgID`, which is `ADODB.Recordset`:

```
Set objRS = Server.CreateObject ("ADODB.Recordset")    ' create recordset object
```

Once the object is created, we can open it. For that, we use the `Open` method of `objRS`:

```
objRS.Open "Movies", strConnect, _
          adOpenForwardOnly, adLockReadOnly, adCmdTable          ' now open it
```

The `Recordset` object's `Open` method has five parameters, and as you can see, we have specified a value for each of them here:

❑ The first parameter is the source of the data. In this case it's the `Movies` table from our database.

❑ The second parameter is the connection information. We need to tell the recordset that we want a connection to the `Movie2000.mdf` or `Movie2000.mdb` database. But we don't need to pass a `Connection` object – instead, we can just pass the connection string and ADO will set up the `Connection` object under the covers. So here, we've passed the connection string, `strConnect`

The last three parameters use the constants that we defined earlier on in the page:

❑ The third and fourth parameters tell ADO what *type* of recordset to use – they define two characteristics of the required recordset, called the **cursor type** and the **lock type**. We'll be looking at these recordset characteristics later in the chapter.

❑ The fifth parameter states that `Movies` is a database table.

The recordset is now open, and requested data has been copied from the database into our recordset. Now, we're in a position to examine the contents of the recordset – and to do that, we'll simply step through each record and write the contents of its Title field to the browser.

In order to step through the recordset, we use the cursor. Happily, when we open the recordset, ADO points the cursor at the first record. So in order to examine each record, we just need to create a loop in which we:

❑ Examine the current record (i.e. the record to which the cursor is currently pointing); then

❑ Move the cursor to the next record in the recordset

Starting at the first record, we'll just do that repeatedly until we run out of records. How do we know when we've run out of records? The Recordset object has a property called EOF ('end-of-file'), which is a Boolean value. It is True when the cursor runs past the last record in the recordset, and it's False otherwise. So, while we're stepping through the recordset, the value of EOF is False; if we step past the last record then EOF will be set to True. Hence, we repeat the loop while EOF is Not True.

So here's the whole of the loop we've just described:

```
While Not objRS.EOF                            ' now loop through the records
  Response.Write objRS.Fields("Title") & ", "
  objRS.MoveNext
Wend
```

Finally we close the recordset:

```
objRS.Close                  ' now close it
Set objRS = Nothing          ' ...and clean up
%>
```

That's all there is to it, and this is a process you'll become familiar with during this chapter.

Introducing the ADO Constants

When using ADO you'll find that there are predefined constants for a lot of the options. For example, in the Recordset.asp file above we used the following lines to define three constants:

```
Const adOpenForwardOnly = 0
Const adLockReadOnly = 1
Const adCmdTable = 2
```

These constants were then used later in the code, to define particular features of the recordset:

```
objRS.Open "Movies", strConnect, adOpenForwardOnly, adLockReadOnly, adCmdTable
```

Here, we use these constants as arguments to the Open method – they tell the Open method more about the type of Recordset object we want. The integer values of the constants are determined, and these values are interpreted by ADO – which goes away and forms a particular type of recordset. In this case, they specify that we want a recordset with a forward-only, read-only cursor and that we're asking for an entire table (don't worry about what *that* means just now – we'll learn more about it later in this chapter).

So, the above Open command is interpreted like this:

```
objRec.Open "Movies", strConnect, 0, 1, 2
```

Why Use ADO Constants?

In fact, we could have used either of the above versions of the Open statement in our code – the result would have been the same. So which one should we choose?

Well, ADO doesn't mind which one you use. However, consider what happens when a colleague comes to read the code we've written. Your colleague would find the second version rather more difficult to understand – the integers 0, 1, 2 don't have any intuitive meaning, so it's rather less obvious that we're trying to open a forward-only, read-only recordset with a query in the form of a table.

In other words, we use constants in ADO because they make our code easier to write and to read. That's why the ADO constants are given special names – to reflect the purpose of the integer values that they represent.

Using the ADO Type Library for Constants

So where did the names of these constants come from? Well, the authors of this book didn't invent them! There's a library of constant names and values created by Microsoft, and available for us to use in our code.

If you ever write applications using languages such as Visual Basic or Visual C++, you'll find that these constants are automatically available to you once you reference the **ADO type library**.

In order to save us from having to explicitly define these constants we can make use of the ADO type library in our ASP code. The ADO type library is contained in a file called msado15.dll, which you should be able to find on your web server machine. The default location for this file is C:\Program Files\Common Files\System\ado. To use the ADO type library, you need to use a line such as the following:

```
<!-- METADATA TYPE="typelib" FILE="C:\Program Files\Common Files\System
                          \ado\msado15.dll" -->
```

You can include this METADATA statement in each .asp file that uses ADO constants where it's required (as we'll do in this book). Alternatively, you can put it in the global.asa file, in which case the constants will be available to every Web page in the application.

Using the msado15.dll type library is the recommended way to make the ADO constants in your code. We'll be demonstrating this in the remaining examples in this book.

adovbs.inc

If you'd like to see the values of the constants contained in the ADO type library, you can view them in the file adovbs.inc. This file is also contained in the default directory (probably C:\Program Files\Common Files\System\ado). If you want to view them, make a *copy* of the adovbs.inc file (into another directory) and open up the copy in Notepad. For example, along with the definition for adOpenForwardOnly, you'll find the constants for the other values we could use in its place:

```
'---- CursorTypeEnum Values ----
Const adOpenForwardOnly = 0
Const adOpenKeyset = 1
Const adOpenDynamic = 2
Const adOpenStatic = 3
```

> Be careful not to change the contents of adovbs.inc! After all, this file is a global store for ADO constants.

Although it's no longer recommended, it's possible to use this file as a server-side include (SSI) file, to insert the ADO constant definitions into your .asp pages. To do this, you'd use a line such as this:

```
<!-- #INCLUDE FILE="C:\Program Files\Common Files\System\ado\adovbs.inc" -->
```

One disadvantage of this method is that it makes your ASP page larger – because it defines nearly 400 constants, most of which you usually won't need. That doesn't happen when we use msado15.dll – because it's a dynamic link library (DLL), so the constants are only defined as they're needed.

To summarize this short section: the ADO constants are there for use with all of the ADO objects, and make reading and writing ADO code much easier. In the remainder of the book, we'll use the ADO type library (msado15.dll) to define our ADO constants, via the METADATA statement shown above.

Now let's move back to the main subject of this chapter – the Recordset object.

Characteristics of the Recordset Object

Perhaps the best way to appreciate some of the important characteristics of a recordset is to consider the method that we use to *create* a recordset – the Open method. Perhaps the strangest-looking line in our last example – and certainly the longest – was the line that used the Open method to open our recordset:

```
objRS.Open "Movies", strConnect, adOpenForwardOnly, adLockReadOnly, adCmdTable
```

We looked briefly at the five parameters, but we didn't study them in detail. So let's start work on the demystification of the `Recordset` object by looking at the syntax of the `Open` method:

```
recordset.Open Source, ActiveConnection, CursorType, LockType, Options
```

Let's break down the parameters and examine each of them in more detail.

What is a Source?

The **source** is where the data comes from. In the example's we've seen so far, we've always used a table name. But the `Source` parameter could take the form of a SQL statement:

```
objRec.Open "SELECT * FROM Movies", ...
```

...or a stored procedure or query:

```
objRec.Open "sp_contact"
```

...or an ADO `Command` object:

```
objRS.Open "qryContact"
```

We'll be looking at stored procedures, queries and the `Command` object a little later.

The Recordset Object's Source Property

When you call the `Recordset` object's `Open` method, specifying the `Source` parameter, you fill the `Recordset`'s `Source` property indirectly.

In fact, you don't have to use the first parameter of the `Open` method to specify the source. Instead, you can set the `Source` property directly:

```
objRS.Source = "SELECT * FROM Movies"
objRS.Open
```

What is the Active Connection?

The **active connection** identifies the data store connection. In the `Recordset.asp` example above, we used a connection string to specify the connection we wanted:

```
objRS.Open "Movies", strConnect, adOpenForwardOnly, adLockReadOnly, adCmdTable
```

Instead, you could use a `Connection` object, like we did in the `Connect.asp` example in Chapter 12:

```
objConn.Open strConnect
objRS.Open "Movies", objConn, adOpenForwardOnly, adLockReadOnly, adCmdTable
```

We discussed this earlier in the chapter. Essentially, you'd use the first technique if you're only making a *single* query to the data store – because it saves us from creating an explicit `Connection` object in our code, and keeps the code more tidy.

By contrast, you'd use the second technique if you were making a number of queries to the same data store. You can create the connection once using the `Connection` object, and then use the open connection each time you need it:

```
objConn.Open strConnect
objRSTitles.Open "SELECT Title FROM Movies", objConn
objRSLinks.Open "SELECT * FROM MovieLinks", objConn
...
```

That's a useful technique, because creating a connection is a resource-expensive task.

The ActiveConnection Property

Alternatively, you can set the *ActiveConnection* using the Recordset object's `ActiveConnection` property. For example:

```
objRS.ActiveConnection = strConnect
```

or

```
Set objRS.ActiveConnection = objConn
```

Although the two lines above appear to achieve the same thing, we get the same subtle difference. In the first, a connection string is passed in, and this causes a new connection to be created. In the second, the existing `Connection` object (`objConn`) is used as the connection.

What is the Cursor Type?

As we've said, we can think of the recordset's cursor as a type of pointer. Every recordset has exactly one cursor, which (at any given time) points to exactly one of the records in the recordset.

We've also very gently hinted that there are different types of cursors. When we open the recordset, we can specify the cursor type – and this will affect the available functionality of the recordset that is returned to us. For example, if we select a forward-only cursor (as we've done in the examples so far), we'll get a recordset whose cursor is only able to move forwards through the records.

> *In addition to the cursor type, there are other factors that also affect the available functionality of the recordset – including the **lock type** and the **cursor location**. We'll be looking at what these things are, and what they mean, shortly.*

Recordset Characteristics

So before we consider the available values for the cursor type, let's consider some of the characteristics that we may want our recordset to display. This will help us decide what cursor type and lock type we'll need when we use the Open method in future.

There are four major characteristics that we are interested in:

Updateable vs Non-Updateable

Are you planning to open a recordset in order to *change* the data within it? If not, then it makes sense to use a **non-updateable** (or **read-only**) recordset to read the data. Using a non-updateable recordset means that the data provider can simply send the data to you and forget about it. You're telling it not to expect any changes – this means that it doesn't need to keep track of what you are doing. This can give performance benefits.

By contrast, if you're planning to change the data in your recordset, then you'll need your recordset to be **updateable**.

Scrollable vs Non-Scrollable

When you're moving the cursor through the records in your recordset, will you need to move backwards as well as forwards? If so, you'll need a **scrollable** recordset. The cursor of a scrollable recordset allows both backward and forward movement of the cursor.

If you're only going to need forward movement of the cursor – as in the Recordset.asp example earlier in this chapter – then a **non-scrollable** recordset will suffice. A non-scrollable recordset can also give performance benefits over a scrollable one, because the recordset doesn't have to keep track of the data once the cursor has moved passed it.

Keyset vs Non-Keyset

Most tables in a database have some kind of unique key – and this is the heart of a keyset recordset. Even those that don't have a visible (defined by us) unique key will have a unique key that the database maintains. When you request a **non-keyset** recordset you get *all* of the data back; while a **keyset** recordset just returns the unique keys, and only fetches the data itself at the time you request that record.

> *In fact, this is a generalization: in reality you'll probably find a set of records returned as well. The idea is that if all of the keys, plus data contained in the first few records, are returned then there is very little delay in getting the first set of data. If you move to a key that is not within the current block, then another block of data is fetched. The advantage of a keyset recordset is that the recordset only has to keep track of the keys, which are generally small, rather than a large amount of data.*

Dynamic vs Static

This characteristic determines the availability of particular records in the recordset, at a specific time. A **static** recordset contains only those records that were available when the recordset was created. The records are cached in local memory and the recordset will be unaware of any changes to data in the data store, made by other users. For example, another user could subsequently delete a record included in your static recordset when it was created, but this will not be reflected in your recordset.

In contrast, a **dynamic** recordset will accurately represent any changes made to the data, either by you or by another database user. You can think of a dynamic cursor as a "window" onto the data in the database. The rows are loaded into the recordset "as requested" (and not cached locally, as for a static cursor). This means that if new records are added, deleted, or changed by other users while you are accessing the database they will become visible when these records scroll into the part of the recordset you are viewing. The recordset changes dynamically, in demand to the records you are actually managing at the time.

So it all boils down to how you see the records and how you navigate through the records. Let's look at the ADO cursor types, and how they relate to the characteristics we've outlined here.

ADO Cursor Types

The updateability of your recordset isn't directly related to the cursor type – that's more the territory of the lock type (which we'll come to shortly). However, the other three characteristics are closely related to the list of possible cursor types we have to choose from. There are four in total, as follows:

❑ **Forward-only** (adOpenForwardOnly): this is the default type and gives you a non-scrollable recordset. This is often perfect in ASP code, because we can often find ourselves just stepping through a list of records in order to display each of them on the browser. In that case, we just need to start at the first record and move forwards through the recordset until we get to the end – we don't need to move backwards. It's also static, so changes to the underlying data are not represented.

❑ **Static** (adOpenStatic): this is similar to a forward-only recordset, except that it is scrollable, so you can move back to previous records as well as moving forwards.

❑ **Dynamic** (adOpenDynamic): the recordset is fully dynamic, and lets you see additions, amendments and deletions that are made by other users. It's fully scrollable so you can move around the recordset any way you like.

❑ **Keyset** (adOpenKeyset): this is similar to the dynamic recordset, but you can't see records that other users add, although you *can* see changes to existing records. Any records that other users delete become inaccessible.

All you have to bear in mind is what you actually want to *do* with your records. If you just want to step through them one at a time, then a forward-only cursor is the one you need. If you want to scroll backwards too, but still don't want to make any changes, then you need a static cursor. If you need to be able to see any changes you make to your recordset, then a dynamic or keyset cursor is required (otherwise you may need to Close and re-Open it).

The CursorType Property

If you flick back through the pages of this chapter to the Recordset.asp example, you'll see that we specified the cursor type in the third parameter of the Open method (here we created a recordset with a forward-only cursor):

```
objRS.Open "Movies", strConnect, adOpenForwardOnly, adLockReadOnly, adCmdTable
```

Alternatively, you can also the set the cursor type directly, using the `CursorType` property like this:

```
objRS.CursorType = adOpenForwardOnly
```

You can read the `CursorType` property at any time, but you can only set it before the recordset is assigned a live connection.

Cursor Location

The location of your cursor can also have an effect on how your recordset operates. By cursor location we don't mean the record that the cursor is currently pointing to – rather, we mean the body that's responsible for creating the cursor – the client or the server.

> **'Client' and 'server' here refer to the relationship between the data consumer that's using the data (in our case, ADO), and the data provider that's providing it (in our case, OLE-DB). Thus client=application; server=data provider.**

Particular functionality will be available depending on which you choose. If you want a dynamic cursor, you must choose server-side. If you choose a client-side cursor then it will be a static cursor.

Certain methods won't work on server-side cursors and you can't do things such as creating local indexes, which can only be done on the client. However, at least 90% of methods will function the same on both the client and server, but it is something to look out for.

What is Locking?

We're all familiar with locking. If you lock your front door then it prevents burglars from walking off with your TV and video recorder. If you lock your cellar door then it stops your teenage children drinking your much-valued 1961 *Chateaux Petrus*! The same applies to records in a data store – if you lock the records then it prevents other people from changing them.

The locking type is closely related to whether or not the recordset is updateable. If you're using your recordset to query a data store, then the recordset is a *copy* of the records that you requested in the data store. That means that there's one copy of the record in your recordset and another copy of the record in the data store. Then, updating a record is a two-stage process:

❑   First, you edit the copy of the record that's contained in your recordset

❑   Second, you update your changes to the copy of the record that's in the data store

Here's where the locking comes in: you can choose to lock the data store copy of the record while you're making your changes – and keep other users from touching them. There are four types of locking you can use:

❑ **Read-only** (`adLockReadOnly`): This gives you a non-updateable recordset. No locking is performed, since you can't change the data in a read-only recordset. This is the default.

❑ **Pessimistic** (`adLockPessimistic`): This gives you an updateable recordset, in which the lock type is very protective. In this case, the copy of the record that exists in the data store is locked as soon as you start editing it. This means that no one else can change the record until you release the lock, which is after you finished editing the record and have committed the update.

❑ **Optimistic** (`adLockOptimistic`): This also gives you an updateable recordset, but the lock type is a little more carefree. In this case, the copy of the records in the data store remains unlocked while you're editing your changes within the recordset. The data store records are *only* locked when you update your changes. So, if you choose this setting you're assuming that no one else will edit the record while you are editing it. If this does happen then the person who commits their update first will "win". The first person will successfully update the record. The second person's initial state will be checked and found to differ for the current state of the database and the change will be rejected.

❑ **Optimistic Batch** (`adLockBatchOptimistic`): Batch update mode allows you to modify several records, and then have them updated all-at-once, so this only locks each record as it is being updated.

The LockType Property

Recalling the `Recordset.asp` example once again, you can see that it was the `Open` method's fourth parameter that allowed us to set the lock type (this requested a read-only recordset, because we weren't planning to change any data):

```
objRS.Open "Movies", strConnect, adOpenForwardOnly, adLockReadOnly, adCmdTable
```

Again, we can also set the lock type by using the `Recordset` object's `LockType` property:

```
objRec.LockType = adLockReadOnly
```

> *Again, you can read the LockType property at any time, but you can only set it before the recordset is assigned a live connection.*

What are Options?

The last attribute in the list is known in the documentation as the *Options*. This rather unhelpful description does nothing to explain that this attribute is used to define what type of data source is being referred to. For example:

```
objRec.Open "Movies", strConnect, adOpenForwardOnly, adLockReadOnly, adCmdTable
```

The source here is a database table called `Movies` – and so we use the constant `adCmdTable` to *tell* ADO that `Movies` is a database table.

In other words, the `Options` parameter tells the recordset what form the data source will take. Are you using a database table, or a SQL query, or a stored procedure... or perhaps you're not sure? This parameter allows you to tell ADO how to evaluate the request, and hence enable it to make the most efficient use of its resources.

The most common options you can set are as follows:

❑ **Text command** (`adCmdText`) is used to indicate that `Source` parameter holds command text, for example, a SQL command.

❑ **Table name** (`adCmdTable`) is used to indicate that `Source` parameter holds the name of a table.

❑ **Stored procedure** (`adCmdStoredProc`) is used to indicate that `Source` parameter holds the name of a stored procedure or query.

❑ **Table** (`adCmdTableDirect`) is used to indicate that `Source` parameter holds the name of a table.

❑ **Saved Recordset** (`adCmdFile`) is used to indicate that `Source` parameter holds the file name of a saved recordset

❑ **URL** (`adCmdURLBind`) is used to indicate that `Source` parameter holds a URL.

The `Options` parameter doesn't map directly to a property of the `Recordset` object, in the way that the cursor type and lock type do. However, it does map onto the `CommandText` property of the `Command` object. We'll be looking at this in the next chapter.

Using the Recordset Object

So now we have a better understanding of some of the recordset's characteristics, we can get to grips with some of the exciting functionality that makes it really easy to manipulate data. In the remainder of this chapter, we'll see how many of the `Recordset` object's methods and properties work, and we'll see them in action in a series of examples. We'll start with `BOF` and `EOF`.

The BOF and EOF Properties

As we've already seen, we view the data contained in a record by first moving the recordset's cursor so that it's pointing at that record. But there are only a finite number of records in the recordset – we need some way of knowing when we've pushed the cursor past the last record, or past the first one.

There are two properties whose values provide that information – they're called `BOF` (beginning-of-file) and `EOF` (end-of-file). Both are Boolean values, so each holds a value `True` or `False` which reflects the current position of the cursor.

To understand, let's consider a recordset that contains four records. The following diagram shows the same recordset six times – the four boxes represent the four records and the gray rectangles represent the cursor stepping through the records of the recordset. Notice that, in addition to the four records in our recordset, there are two additional 'positions' (one at the beginning and one at the end). They aren't records – they're just imaginary 'markers' that represent the extremes of the recordset:

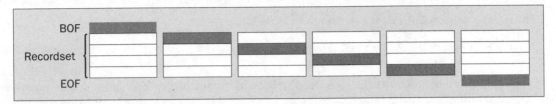

As we step through the recordset, we see that:

❑ When the cursor is pointing to a valid record (as in the middle four instances), then BOF and EOF are both False (because the cursor is neither at the beginning or the end of the recordset).

❑ If we move the cursor so far backwards through the recordset that we go past the first record (as in the left-most instance), then the cursor lands on the 'marker' preceding the first record. Then, the value of BOF changes to True

❑ Alternatively, if we move the cursor so far forwards through the recordset that we go past the last record (as in the right-most instance), then the cursor lands on the 'marker' after the last record. Then, the value of EOF changes to True

We've seen already that this can be very useful. We've already used the EOF property as the control that allows us to step through every record and to stop as soon as we move past the last one:

```
While Not objRS.EOF                          ' now loop through the records
    Response.Write objRS.Fields("Title") & ", "
    objRS.MoveNext
Wend
```

The BOF and EOF properties work just like this, provided there's at least one record in the recordset. If there are no records in the recordset, then the 'beginning' and 'end' markers coincide – and therefore the values BOF and EOF are simultaneously True. (Conversely, if you have a recordset in which BOF and EOF are simultaneously True, then the recordset has no records in it!)

Moving Through Records

In our first example, we saw how to step through a recordset using the MoveNext method. But what about other ways of moving? In fact, the Recordset object gives us four very easy-to-use methods that allow us to move the cursor backwards and forwards through its records:

❑ The `MovePrevious` and `MoveNext` methods allow us to move the cursor from the current record to the record immediately preceding or immediately after

❑ The `MoveFirst` and `MoveLast` methods move the cursor directly to the first or last record in the recordset

These methods don't require any arguments. For example, and as we've already seen, we call the `MoveNext` method, pure and simple, like this:

```
objRS.MoveNext
```

In addition, to these, there is a fifth method, called `Move`. The `Move` method allows us to make the cursor jump over a specified number of records from its current position (or some other specified position). It has two parameters, and its syntax is as follows:

```
objRecordset.Move NumRecords, Start
```

Here, *objRecordset* is the name of our `Recordset` object. The first parameter, *NumRecords*, specifies the size of the jump – that is, the number of records that we want to jump. The second parameter, *Start*, specifies the point that you wish the move to start from. For example, if we want the cursor to jump forward two places from the current record we'd use the following:

```
objRS.Move 2
```

Alternatively, if we wanted to jump back three records (and if our recordset doesn't have a 'forward-only cursor type!) then we could use this:

```
objRS.Move -3
```

Note that the *Start* parameter is optional. We'll be looking at some possible values for this parameter when we look at **bookmarks**, later in this chapter.

> Note also that the availability of these methods is dependent upon the recordset type. For example, it's impossible to use `MoveFirst` or `MovePrevious` on a 'forward-only' cursor, because it involves moving the cursor backwards! In the case of `MoveLast` to find the last record in a recordset you actually have to move one beyond the last record in the recordset, to discover that it is the last record. Bizarrely, some forward-only recordsets(such as those used by a SQL Server provider) do allow `MoveFirst` as they allow the query to be resubmitted to the server. It's best to be careful if you plan to do a lot of moving around the recordset.

> Later in the chapter we'll meet the `Find` method, which is another useful technique for moving the cursor around.

So let's try an example in which we'll exercise these methods. This example provides a departure from the recordsets that we've seen so far, in that it's the first one we've created that doesn't have a forward-only cursor.

Try It Out – Moving Through Records (Data store Viewer)

We'll create a recordset that contains film details taken from the `AllMovies` table of our database. Then we'll simply step through all the records in the recordset, displaying the values of each record's TitleID, Director and Title fields as we go.

We'll add a little extra option that allows the user to decide whether they want to step through the recordset forwards or backwards, and which record they want to start with. For example, if the user selects 14 and **Reverse**, we'll begin our list at the 14th film in the database, not the first; then we'll step through all the films in the recordset backwards, till we reach the first – then we'll jump to the very last film and step (backwards) through the rest.

In the course of the action, we'll exercise all of the five `Move...` methods we mentioned above, and the `BOF` and `EOF` properties too.

1. We're going to use the Movies database again, so make sure you've set it up using the `Movie2000.mdb` or `Movie2000.mdf` database file as described in Chapter 12.

2. We also need the connection string details, so ensure that the `DataStore.asp` file (from Chapter 12) is saved into the folder `\inetpub\wwwroot\BegASPFiles`.

3. Open up your editor, create a new file called `Moving.asp`, and enter the following into it:

```
<%
  Option Explicit
  Dim strConnect
%>
<!-- #include file="DataStore.asp" -->
<!-- METADATA TYPE="typelib"
            FILE="C:\Program Files\Common Files\System\ado\msado15.dll" -->
<HTML>
<HEAD>
<TITLE>Working your Way round a Recordset</TITLE>
</HEAD>
<BODY>

<%
  Dim intChosenRecord, strDirection, strOutputString, intCounter, intNoOfRecords
  If Request.Form("ChosenRec") <> "" Then
    intChosenRecord = Request.Form("ChosenRec")
    strDirection = Request.Form("Dir")
  Else
    intChosenRecord = 1
    strDirection = "Forward"
  End If

  Dim objRS
  Set objRS = Server.CreateObject("ADODB.Recordset")
  objRS.Open "AllMovies", strConnect, adOpenStatic, adLockReadOnly, adCmdTable
  intNoOfRecords = objRS.RecordCount
  objRS.Move intChosenRecord-1
```

```
      strOutputString = "<TABLE BORDER=1>" & _
                        "<TR><TD WIDTH=""30%""><B>Director</B></TD>" & _
                          "<TD><B>Film</B></TD></TR>"
   If strDirection = "Forward" Then
      While Not objRS.EOF
         strOutputString = strOutputString & "<TR>" & _
           "<TD> " & objRS("TitleID") & ": " & objRS("Director") & "</TD>" & _
           "<TD>"        & objRS("Title")   & "</TD>" & _
           "</TR>"
         objRS.MoveNext
      Wend
      objRS.MoveFirst
      For intCounter = 1 To intChosenRecord-1
         strOutputString = strOutputString & "<TR>" & _
           "<TD> " & objRS("TitleID") & ": " & objRS("Director") & "</TD>" & _
           "<TD>"        & objRS("Title")   & "</TD>" & _
           "</TR>"
         objRS.MoveNext
      Next
   Else
      While Not objRS.BOF
         strOutputString = strOutputString & "<TR>" & _
           "<TD> " & objRS("TitleID") & ": " & objRS("Director") & "</TD>" & _
           "<TD>"        & objRS("Title")   & "</TD>" & _
           "</TR>"
         objRS.MovePrevious
      Wend
      objRS.MoveLast
      For intCounter = intNoOfRecords To intChosenRecord+1 Step -1
         strOutputString = strOutputString & "<TR>" & _
           "<TD> " & objRS("TitleID") & ": " & objRS("Director") & "</TD>" & _
           "<TD>"        & objRS("Title")   & "</TD>" & _
           "</TR>"
         objRS.MovePrevious
      Next
   End If
   strOutputString = strOutputString & "</TABLE>"
   objRS.Close
   Set objRS = Nothing
   Response.Write strOutputString
%>

<BR><HR>
<FORM ACTION="Moving.asp" METHOD="POST">
  <H2>Format the list!</H2>
  Where do you want ths list to begin? Record
  <SELECT SIZE=1 NAME="ChosenRec">
  <%
    For intCounter=1 To intNoOfRecords
      Response.Write "<OPTION VALUE=" & intCounter & ">" & intCounter & "</OPTION>"
    Next
  %>
```

```
</SELECT><BR><BR>
Do you want the records to be listed
in <INPUT TYPE="RADIO" NAME="Dir" VALUE="Forward" CHECKED><B> forward</B></INPUT>
or <INPUT TYPE="RADIO" NAME="Dir" VALUE="Reverse"> <B>reverse</B></INPUT>
order (select one)?
<INPUT TYPE="SUBMIT" VALUE="View the list"></INPUT>
</FORM>
</BODY>
</HTML>
```

4. Save `Moving.asp` into the same folder: `\inetpub\wwwroot\BegASPFiles`.

5. Now view the page `Moving.asp` in your browser. You'll see a long table, listing all 330 records in order from 1 to 330 (you can see the last few rows of the table in the following screenshot). At the end, you'll see the form that allows us to choose where to start the listing, and in what order:

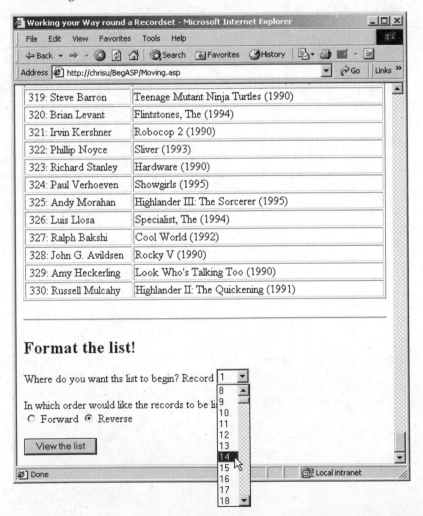

6. Select a record from the drop-down list and select either Forward or Reverse. Then click on View the List, which refreshes the page according to your options:

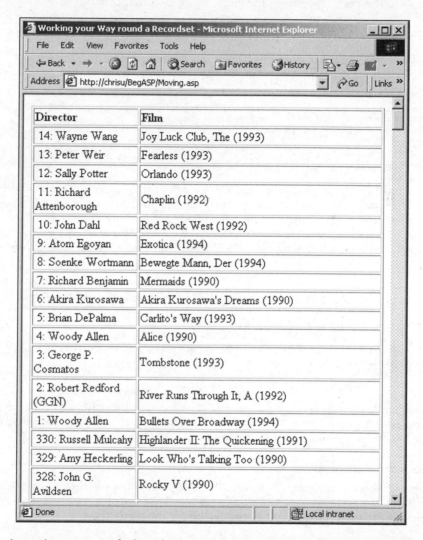

Try it a few times, just to get a feeling for how the example works. The numbers on the left of the table rows are the record numbers as they appear in the database and in the table – we've displayed them here so you can see how the cursor is moving around the recordset.

How It Works – the Form

This is quite a long example, but if you examine the code you'll see that it's not complicated. Let's start with the very last part of the code, by getting the form out of the way. The form is really very simple: it asks the user for two values. First, it asks for an integer which will specify which record appears first in our table, when we submit to refresh the page:

```
<FORM ACTION="Moving.asp" METHOD="POST">
  <H2>Format the list!</H2>
  Where do you want ths list to begin? Record
  <SELECT SIZE=1 NAME="ChosenRec">
  <%
    For intCounter=1 To intNoOfRecords
      Response.Write "<OPTION VALUE=" & intCounter & ">" & intCounter & "</OPTION>"
    Next
  %>
  </SELECT><BR><BR>
```

When we submit the form, this will create an entry in the `Request.Form` collection, called `ChosenRec`. Its value is taken from the value selected in the drop-down list. We've created the drop-down list using ASP – creating one line of the list for each integer between 1 and `intNoOfRecords`. The variable `intNoOfRecords` was populated earlier on in the page (when the recordset was open), by using the `Recordset` object's `RecordCount` property:

```
intNoOfRecords = objRS.RecordCount
```

Second, it asks whether we want the records listed in forward- or reverse-order:

```
Do you want the records to be listed
in <INPUT TYPE="RADIO" NAME="Dir" VALUE="Forward" CHECKED><B> forward</B></INPUT>
or <INPUT TYPE="RADIO" NAME="Dir" VALUE="Reverse"> <B>reverse</B></INPUT>
order (select one)?
<INPUT TYPE="SUBMIT" VALUE="View the list"></INPUT>
</FORM>
```

This creates another variable in the `Request.Form` collection, called `Dir`. If we select **Forward**, then the cursor will move forwards through the recordset; If we select **Reverse**, then the cursor will move backwards through the recordset.

How It Works – the Recordset

OK, assuming we've made those choices, what happens when we submit them? First, we `#INCLUDE` the `DataStore.asp` file that contains our connection string details, reference the ADO constant library `msado15.dll`, and we create the page head:

```
<%
  Option Explicit
  Dim strConnect
%>
<!-- #include file="DataStore.asp" -->
<!-- METADATA TYPE="typelib"
              FILE="C:\Program Files\Common Files\System\ado\msado15.dll" -->
<HTML>
<HEAD>
<TITLE>Working your Way round a Recordset</TITLE>
</HEAD>
```

Now we can set the variables that we'll need. The `intChosenRecord` and `strDirection` variables are used to contain the values passed into the page from the HTML form (and found in the `Request.Form` collection):

```
<BODY>
<%
  Dim intChosenRecord, strDirection, strOutputString, intCounter, intNoOfRecords
  If Request.Form("ChosenRec") <> "" Then
    intChosenRecord = Request.Form("ChosenRec")
    strDirection = Request.Form("Dir")
  Else
    intChosenRecord = 1
    strDirection = "Forward"
  End If
```

Note that the first time you call the page, you don't get a chance to fill in a form – so we set default values for the `intChosenRecord` and `strDirection` variables.

> *The default behavior, as you probably noticed the first time you called the page, is to start at the first record and iterate in a forward direction.*

Now we can create the `Recordset` object, and `Open` it:

```
  Dim objRS
  Set objRS = Server.CreateObject("ADODB.Recordset")
  objRS.Open "AllMovies", strConnect, adOpenStatic, adLockReadOnly, adCmdTable
```

Let's look more carefully that the five parameters we've chosen here. Since we studied them earlier in the chapter, they should now be a little less mysterious to you:

❑ The first parameter specifies the `AllMovies` table of the database

❑ The second parameter is the `strConnect` connection string which is specified in the `DataStore.asp` SSI, and which specifies the location of the database

❑ The third parameter specifies the value `adOpenStatic`, which requests a static cursor type. This will allow the forward and backward movement through the recordset that we need.

> *We could have selected adOpenDynamic or adOpenKeyset – but we're not interested in viewing changes made to records (either by ourselves or by other users of the database) so neither are necessary.*

❑ The fourth parameter specifies the value `adLockReadOnly`, which specifies that we can't use this recordset to make changes to the database. That's fine, because we're only using it to read data from the database

❑ The fifth parameter specifies the value `adCmdTable`, which tells ADO that the data source specified in the first parameter is a database table

Once the recordset is open and contains the necessary data, we can begin to write it all to the browser. We can build a table to display all the film details. In this example we built a string called `strOutputString`, over a sequence of statements, which contains all the HTML for the entire table. When we've finished writing the string, we `Response.Write` the whole thing in one go.

So here goes. The first thing to do is position the cursor on the record that will be the first to appear in the table:

```
objRS.Move intChosenRecord-1
```

Remember that the expression `intChosenRecord-1` is just an integer. For example, if `intChosenRecord` is 14, then this moves the cursor 13 places from the first record in the recordset to 14th record.

Now we write the body of the table into our string. The overall structure of this part is as follows:

```
strOutputString = "<TABLE BORDER=1>" & _
                  "<TR><TD WIDTH=""30%""><B>Director</B></TD>" & _
                    "<TD><B>Film<B></TD></TR>"
If strDirection = "Forward" Then                ' iterate forward through the RS
  ' write one table row for each record from the chosen record to the end
  ' jump to the beginning of the recordset
  ' write one line for each record from the beginning to the chosen record
Else                                            ' iterate backward through the RS
  ' write one table row for each record from the chosen record to the beginning
  ' jump to the end of the recordset
  ' write one line for each record from the end to the chosen record
End If
strOutputString = strOutputString & "</TABLE>"
```

Let's fill in the gaps here. If we're iterating forwards through the recordset, we do so using the `MoveNext` method. When we get to the end of the recordset, `objRS.EOF` becomes `True`. At this stage, we jump to the first record using the `MoveFirst` method and then iterate through the remaining records using `MoveNext` again:

```
While Not objRS.EOF
  strOutputString = strOutputString & "<TR>" & _
    "<TD> " & objRS("TitleID") & ": " & objRS("Director") & "</TD>" & _
    "<TD>"        & objRS("Title")   & "</TD>" & _
    "</TR>"
  objRS.MoveNext
Wend
objRS.MoveFirst
For intCounter = 1 To intChosenRecord-1
  strOutputString = strOutputString & "<TR>" & _
    "<TD> " & objRS("TitleID") & ": " & objRS("Director") & "</TD>" & _
    "<TD>"        & objRS("Title")   & "</TD>" & _
    "</TR>"
  objRS.MoveNext
Next
```

On the other hand, if we're iterating backwards through the recordset then we do things the other way around. Iterate from the chosen records, backwards towards the first record, using the `MovePrevious` method. When we get past the first record, `objRS.BOF` becomes `True`. Then, we jump to the last record using the `MoveLast` method and then iterate backwards through the remaining records using `MovePrevious` again:

```
While Not objRS.BOF
  strOutputString = strOutputString & "<TR>" & _
    "<TD> " & objRS("TitleID") & ": " & objRS("Director") & "</TD>" & _
    "<TD>"        & objRS("Title")   & "</TD>" & _
    "</TR>"
  objRS.MovePrevious
Wend
objRS.MoveLast
For intCounter = intNoOfRecords To intChosenRecord+1 Step -1
  strOutputString = strOutputString & "<TR>" & _
    "<TD> " & objRS("TitleID") & ": " & objRS("Director") & "</TD>" & _
    "<TD>"        & objRS("Title")   & "</TD>" & _
    "</TR>"
  objRS.MovePrevious
Next
```

And that's just about all there is to it. All that remains is to tidy up the recordset, since we don't need it anymore:

```
objRS.Close
Set objRS = Nothing
```

Then we can write the output string to the browser:

```
Response.Write strOutputString
```

And finally, we display the HTML form (which we covered at the beginning of this explanation).

Bookmarks

A **bookmark** is really quite intuitive – it's a way of marking a particular record in the recordset. In fact it uniquely identifies a record within the recordset so that you can make your cursor jump straight back to it, from any other place in the recordset.

A bookmark is stored as a `variant` value (although you'll probably never want to view the bookmark itself, as its value is really only meaningful to ADO). There are several important facts to note about bookmarks:

- ❑ It's possible to have two bookmarks that point at the same record but have different values. This means that you can't compare bookmarks directly.

- ❑ You can create two similar or identical recordsets from the same source, and set a bookmark on the same record of each recordset. But the bookmarks are *not* the same

- ❑ Some types of recordset don't support bookmarks. You can find out whether your recordset supports bookmarks by using the `Supports` method (the expression `objRS.Supports(adBookmark)` returns a Boolean value)

Using Bookmarks

The following section of code demonstrates how we might use bookmarks:

```
Dim varMyBookmark                    ' create a variant to hold the bookmark
... ' code to create the Recordset object
varMyBookmark = objRS.Bookmark       ' later, set a bookmark at the current record,
                                     ' and save it to varMyBookmark

... ' some processing of records
objRS.Bookmark = varMyBookmark       ' later still, move the cursor to the record
                                     ' specified in the varMyBookmark bookmark
```

First, this creates a variant called varMyBookmark. Later, we use the Bookmark property to set a bookmark at the current cursor position – the bookmark is stored in the varMyBookmark variant. Later still, we want to return the cursor to the bookmarked record – so we set the recordset's Bookmark property back to the value contained in varMyBookmark.

Bookmarks and the Move Method

We've already seen how we can use the Move method to move the cursor a specified number of places from its current position. But as we mentioned there, we can use the Move method along with a bookmark too. This allows us to move the cursor to any bookmarked record, and then move it from there by a specified number of records. For example, consider the following:

```
objRS.Move 3, varMyBookmark
```

This moves the cursor to the third record *after* the record bookmarked by varMyBookmark. Here, we're using the Move method's second parameter to specify the starting point for the move, and the first parameter to specify the offset. So, effectively this says " move the cursor forwards three places, using the record bookmarked by varMyBookmark as a starting position".

As we saw earlier, we can use the Move method without specifying the second parameter – in that case, the Move method adopts its default behavior of moving the cursor from its current position. There are some other special predefined bookmarks that you can use in the second parameter:

Value	Meaning
adBookmarkCurrent	Use the current record as the starting position (this is the default)
adBookmarkFirst	Use the first record as the starting position
adBookmarkLast	Use the last record as the starting position

Note that we don't need to create these bookmarks. These values are ADO constants, and are predefined in the ADO constant library msado15.dll.

For example, to move three records further on from the current position you would use this:

```
objRec.Move 3, adBookmarkCurrent
```

or this:

```
objRec.Move 3
```

So, to move to the fourth record in the recordset we'd use the following:

```
objRec.Move 3, adBookmarkFirst
```

To move to the penultimate record in the recordset we'd use this:

```
objRec.Move -1, adBookmarkLast
```

> *If you attempt to move beyond the beginning or end of a recordset then BOF or EOF is set accordingly.*

Finding Records

We've seen how we can move the cursor around the recordset using the Move, MoveNext, MoveLast, MovePrevious and MoveFirst methods. But what happens if we're stepping through a big recordset, with thousands of records, and the record we're looking for is right in the middle? Instead of iterating through using MoveNext or MovePrevious hundreds of times, wouldn't it be much easier if we could use a single instruction to take the cursor straight there?

That's exactly what the Recordset object's Find method can do for us. The Find method is a full table scan, so with large recordsets it can be rather slow – but it is functional. Its job is to move the cursor from its current position to a record that fits our description.

> *We'll see in the next chapter an even more effective way of retrieving information, using SQL.*

The syntax for the Find method is:

objRecordset.Find *Criteria*, *SkipRecords*, *SearchDirection*, *Start*

We'll see the Find method in action shortly, but first we should explain what the parameters are for. In fact, they're fairly straightforward:

❑ *Criteria* is a string that contains a set of comparisons, which describe the record that we're looking for

❑ *SkipRecords* is the offset from the start position where the search itself should start (see also *Start*, below). Default is 0

❑ *SearchDirection* can be set either to adSearchForward or adSearchbackward, to specify the search direction. Default is adSearchForward

❑ *Start* is a bookmark that specifies the start position of the search. Then the parameter *SkipRecords* specifies the offset from this position. Default is adBookmarkCurrent (to start the search at the current record)

So in essence, the Find method starts at the record denoted by *Start*; skips the number of records specified by *SkipRecords*; then it searches in the direction specified by *SearchDirection*, and moves the recordset's cursor to the first record it finds that matches the *Criteria*.

The first parameter, *Criteria*, is the most important one here, and if you've ever worked with **SQL (Structured Query Language)** then you'll be familiar with the way we use it. The general form of a criterion is shown below:

```
<recordset_field> <comparison_operator> <value>
```

Here, *recordset_field* is the name of the field that we want ADO to search against, *comparison_operator* is the type of search, and *value* is the value that we're looking for.

The *comparison_operator* can be one of the following:

❑   > to search for records greater than the value

❑   < for records less than the value

❑   = for records equal to the value

❑   LIKE for matching records

For example, if we want to search for a film whose title is Pulp Fiction, we could use the criterion Title = 'Pulp Fiction'. Thus, if we search the recordset objRS for this film, searching forwards from the current record, we could use a line like this:

```
objRS.Find "Title = 'Pulp Fiction'"
```

Notice that we've left out the last three arguments, since they are optional – this causes the default parameter values to be used. The default behavior is to start the search at the current record, and search forwards through the recordset.

In the example above, we're searching for a string, 'Pulp Fiction' (the comparison isn't case sensitive). In this case, we must enclose the search string in single quotation marks. You don't need to do this for fields whose data type is numeric:

```
objRS.Find "Price = 34.95"
```

And when searching for dates in an Access database, you should surround the date with # marks (single quotes for MSDE):

```
objRS.Find "Birthday = #10/23/98#"        ' Note that you need to use single quotes
                                          ' in places of hashes in MSDE
```

When searching for strings you can also use the SQL keyword LIKE to specify matching records. For example, the following will find the next film in the database whose title begins with the word Pulp:

```
objRS.Find "Title LIKE 'Pulp*'"
```

We're looking for any string that begins with the characters `Pulp`, and then continues with any number of any other characters at all. The * character indicates that we don't mind what comes after those first specified characters – the * is known as a wildcard. If you are using a database other than Access, MSDE (or full SQL Server) then the syntax may vary slightly. For example, Oracle uses a % character as the wildcard (but other than that the method should work in the manner described).

Successful and Unsuccessful Searches

How do we know whether the search was successful? Easy – we just check the position of the cursor:

- ❏ If the search is successful then the cursor is placed at the specified record.
- ❏ If you're searching forwards and no record is found, then EOF is set to True.
- ❏ If you're searching backwards and no record is found, then BOF is set to True.

Consequently, you must be aware of the fact that the position of the cursor will change – even if the search is unsuccessful. So you might want to use a bookmark to keep a note of the current record, like this:

```
varTempBkMk = objRs.Bookmark          ' original position
objRS.Find "Title LIKE 'Pulp*'"
If objRS.EOF Then
  Response.Write "No records found - " & _
                 "now moving the cursor back to its original position"
  objRS.Bookmark = varTempBkMk
End If
```

Try It Out – Finding Records

OK, let's have an example that demonstrates the Find method. We'll use a two-page example. In the first page, the user is asked to type in the name of a film director. In the second page, we'll use this information to find a film made by that director.

1. Once again, we're going to use the Movies database again, so make sure you've set it up using the Movie2000.mdb or Movie2000.mdf database file as described in Chapter 12.

2. And again, we'll need the connection string details, so ensure that the DataStore.asp file (from Chapter 12) is saved into the folder \inetpub\wwwroot\BegASPFiles.

3. Open your editor, create a new file called PromptForDirector.htm and enter the following code:

```
<HTML>
<HEAD>
<TITLE>Using the Find Method to find a Director's Films</TITLE>
</HEAD>
<BODY>
```

```
<H1>Who Directed What?</H1>
<FORM ACTION="FindDirector.asp" METHOD="POST" id=form1 name=form1>
  Type in the name of a film director: <BR>
  <INPUT TYPE="TEXT" NAME="director" SIZE=50><BR><BR>
  <INPUT TYPE="submit" NAME="send" VALUE="What films did this director direct?">
</FORM>
</BODY>
</HTML>
```

4. Save the code for `PromptForDirector.htm` in your `BegASPFiles` folder.

5. Now create a second new file, and call it `FindDirector.asp`. Type in the following:

```
<%
  Option Explicit
  Dim strConnect
%>
<!-- #include file="DataStore.asp" -->
<!-- METADATA TYPE="typelib"
            FILE="C:\Program Files\Common Files\System\ado\msado15.dll" -->
<HTML>
<HEAD>
<TITLE>Using the Find Method to find a Director's Films</TITLE>
</HEAD>
<BODY>

<%
  Dim strDirector, strCriteria
  strDirector = Request.Form("director")

  Dim objRS
  Set objRS = Server.CreateObject("ADODB.Recordset")
  objRS.Open "AllMovies", strConnect, adOpenStatic, adLockReadOnly, adCmdTable

  strCriteria = "Director='" & strDirector & "'"

  objRS.Find strCriteria         ' show the first relevant record
  If objRS.EOF Then
    Response.Write "The database does not contain any films by the director " & _
                  strDirector
  Else
    Response.Write "<H2>Directed by " & strDirector & ":</H2>" & _
        "<B>Title:</B> "   & objRS("Title")   & "<BR>" & _
        "<B>Summary:</B> " & objRS("Summary") & "<BR>" & _
        "<B>Genre:</B> "   & objRS("Genres")  & "<BR><BR><BR>"
  End If
  objRS.Close
  Set objRS = Nothing
%>
</BODY>
</HTML>
```

In this database there are no director names that contain apostrophes, such as O'Neill. If there was then this would cause an error in this script. To get around this, you would have to add a replace method to look for the single quotes and replace them with char(39) – the code for a single quote.

6. Save `FindDirector.asp` into the `BegASPFiles` folder. Now open `PromptForDirector.htm` in your browser, type in the name of a well-known film director from the 1990s, and hit the big gray button at the bottom:

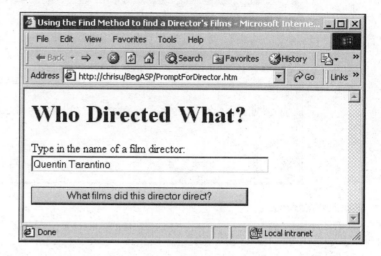

7. The page will search for the first appropriate record, and stop.

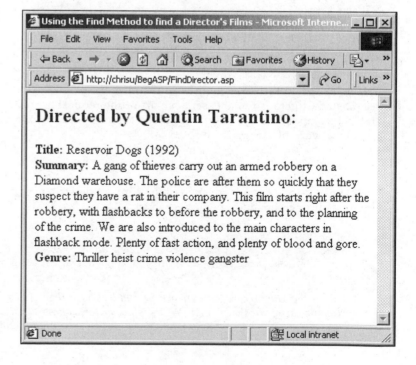

Alternatively, if the director isn't found in the database, then you'll get the appropriate message.

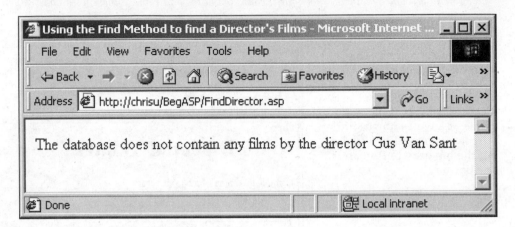

How It Works

The first page, PromptForDirector.htm, is a pure HTML page that contains a form. It collects the name of a director that the user types in:

```
<FORM ACTION="FindDirector.asp" METHOD="POST" id=form1 name=form1>
  Type in the name of a film director: <BR>
  <INPUT TYPE="TEXT" NAME="director" SIZE=50><BR><BR>
  <INPUT TYPE="submit" NAME="send" VALUE="What films did this director direct?">
</FORM>
```

We've specified the POST method in the form. So when the user clicks the submit button, the requested director's name is sent as part of the request for the FindDirector.asp page, where it finishes up in the director variable of the Request.Form collection. We capture this value in a local variable, strDirector:

```
strDirector = Request.Form("director")
```

In FindDirector.asp, we specify the connection string (within the SSI, DataStore.asp) and then use it to create and open a recordset:

```
Dim objRS
Set objRS = Server.CreateObject("ADODB.Recordset")
objRS.Open "AllMovies", strConnect, adOpenStatic, adLockReadOnly, adCmdTable
```

This is the same recordset, cursor type and lock type that we used in the Moving.asp example earlier in the chapter. We're using a static cursor, instead of a forward-only cursor, because some data providers don't support the Find method for recordsets with a forward-only cursor.

The next two lines are key lines:

```
strCriteria = "Director='" & strDirector & "'"
objRS.Find strCriteria          ' show the first relevant record
```

The purpose of the first line is to create the criteria that the `Find` method will use to search for a matching record. We're using a string, `strCriteria`, to store these criteria. After this line, the `strCriteria` variant should contain a string such as `Director='Quentin Tarantino'`.

The second line is the `Find` method call. For the search criteria, we specify the `strCriteria` string in the first parameter. We've left the remaining parameters blank. This means that the search will begin at the current record (which is the first record in the recordset, since we've only just opened it) and the search direction is forward.

Now we can examine the results of the search. By checking the value of the `EOF` property, we can establish whether the search was successful. If no matching records were found, then the `Find` method places the cursor at the end-of-recordset, so `EOF` is `True`:

```
If objRS.EOF Then
   Response.Write "The database does not contain any films by the director " & _
                  strDirector
```

Otherwise, the search was successful – which means that the `Find` method found a matching record, changed the cursor to point to that record and then stopped searching. We can use this to write the data in that record to the browser:

```
Else
   Response.Write "<H2>Directed by " & strDirector & ":</H2>" & _
        "<B>Title:</B> "   & objRS("Title")   & "<BR>" & _
        "<B>Summary:</B> " & objRS("Summary") & "<BR>" & _
        "<B>Genre:</B> "   & objRS("Genres")  & "<BR><BR><BR>"
End If
```

Then we just close up and tidy up the recordset:

```
objRS.Close
Set objRS = Nothing
```

And that's it. Note that the `Find` method is just a tool for pointing the cursor at a particular record. If you want to use the `Find` method to find lots of records, you have to call the `Find` method lots of times. For example, if you wanted to extend this example to find *two* relevant records, you'd need to call the `Find` method twice:

```
objRS.MoveNext
objRS.Find strCriteria
```

Or equivalently:

```
objRS.Find strCriteria, 1
```

The MoveNext is important. Having found the *first* successful record, you'd need to point the cursor *away* from it before searching for the *next* suitable record. That's because the default behavior of the Find method is to start searching at the *current* record (which you wouldn't want, because you would already have found the current record!). So, the sensible thing to do is move the cursor on one.

If you want to point the cursor at a record that satisfies a specific criterion, then the Find method is a good way to do it. But if you want to find *lots* of records that match the same criterion, then the Find method isn't always ideal. Instead, you can use your search criterion in conjunction with the Recordset object's Filter property, as we'll see next.

Filtering Records

Filtering involves identifying all the records in the recordset that meet a certain specified criterion. While you'd expect filtering to be quite similar to finding, ADO considers these two tasks to be very different. Accordingly, ADO implements these two concepts very differently:

❑ Finding a record involves searching the recordset until we find *one* record that matches what we're looking for – then pointing the cursor to that record. Therefore, Find is a *method*, whose job is to point the cursor at a specific record

❑ Filtering involves identifying *every* record that matches what we're looking for. Therefore, Filter is a *property*, which specifies exactly which records are visible to our code and which are invisible

That's right – by setting the Recordset object's Filter property, you can hide some of the records in the recordset and ensure that the only visible records are the records that satisfy the criterion.

For example, consider a recordset of movie data from the AllMovies table. By default, the Filter property is set to the ADO constant adFilterNone, which means that the filter is turned off – no records are filtered out, and all records in the recordset are visible. Now, we can implement a filter by setting the recordset's Filter property with our criterion. As an example, let's filter out all the records of films that *weren't* directed by Quentin Tarantino:

```
objRS.Filter = "Director = 'Quentin Tarantino'"
```

Now, the only visible records are those that *were* directed by Mr. Tarantino. Now, when you use methods like MoveNext and MovePrevious, you'll be moving between the records that aren't hidden by the filter.

Note that the other records in the objRS recordset *haven't been deleted* from the recordset – they're still there. It's just that they're hidden. You can reveal them again by removing the filter:

```
objRS.Filter = adFilterNone
```

The filter can also take the form of an array of bookmarks, or one of the following ADO constants:

Constant	Meaning
adFilterNone	Removes the current filter and restores all records to view.
adFilterPendingRecords	Shows only those records that have changed but whose changes have yet to be sent to the data store. This is only applicable in batch update mode (more on this in the next chapter).
adFilterAffectedRecords	Shows only records affected by the last Delete, Resync, UpdateBatch or CancelBatch call. (We'll discuss these calls in the next chapter.)
adFilterFetchedRecords	Shows the records from the last call to retrieve records from the data store.

Try It Out – Filtering Records

Let's have a look at an example. We're going to break down our list of films, categorizing them by the first letter of the film title. In order to do this, we're going to query the data store just once. Then, for each letter in the alphabet, we'll use the appropriate filter to hide all records except those whose film title begins with that letter. If we do that 26 times, we'll have covered every letter in the alphabet!

1. Once again, we're going to use the Movies database, so make sure you've set it up using the Movie2000.mdb or Movie2000.mdf database file as described in Chapter 12.

2. And again, we'll need the connection string details, so ensure that the DataStore.asp file (from Chapter 12) is saved into the folder \inetpub\wwwroot\BegASPFiles.

3. Create a new file, called `Filter.asp`, and add the following code to it:

```asp
<%
  Option Explicit
  Dim strConnect
%>
<!-- #include file="DataStore.asp" -->
<!-- METADATA TYPE="typelib"
              FILE="C:\Program Files\Common Files\System\ado\msado15.dll" -->
<HTML>
<HEAD>
<TITLE>Filtering the Recordset</TITLE>
</HEAD>
<BODY>
<%
  Dim objRS, intLetter, strChar, strCriteria
  Set objRS = Server.CreateObject("ADODB.Recordset")
  objRS.Open "AllMovies", strConnect, adOpenStatic, adLockReadOnly, adCmdTable

  For intLetter = 1 To 26
    strChar = Chr(intLetter+64)
    strCriteria = "Title LIKE '" & strChar & "*'"
    objRS.Filter = strCriteria
    If Not objRS.EOF Then
      Response.Write "<H2>" & strChar & "</H2>" & _
        "<TABLE BORDER=1><TR><TD><B>Film</B></TD><TD><B>Director</B></TD></TR>"
      While Not objRS.EOF
        Response.Write "<TR><TD>" & objRS("Title") & "</TD>" & _
                           "<TD>" & objRS("Director") & "</TD></TR>"
        objRS.MoveNext
      Wend
      Response.Write "</TABLE>"
    End If
  Next
  objRS.Close
  Set objRS = Nothing
%>
</BODY>
</HTML>
```

4. Save the `Filter.asp` file into the `\inetpub\wwwroot\BegASPFiles` folder. Now browse to that page, to see the categorization of films.

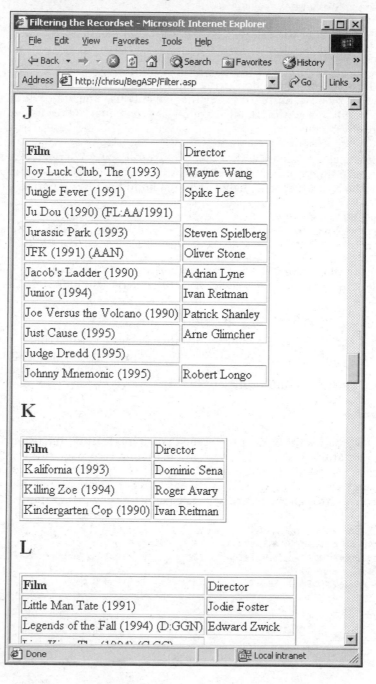

As you can see, we get a number of tables – but they're all populated from the same recordset! For each table, all we've done is hide the records that we don't want, and put the rest into the table. Let's have a look at how easy it is.

You can see that the filter has categorized the records in the recordset.

How It Works

We won't go through the connection string and recordset creation code again – you should be familiar with that by now. Suffice it to say that we only use one Recordset object in this example, and it only queries the database once. That one query gives us enough data to populate all of these tables.

All the interesting action occurs within the For ... Next loop. We're going to loop through the same procedure 26 times, once for each letter of the alphabet. We use a variant called strChar to hold one of the letters of the alphabet and then build the filter criterion from that letter:

```
For intLetter = 1 To 26
   strChar = Chr(intLetter+64)
   strCriteria = "Title LIKE '" & strChar & "*'"
```

Like the last example, we're using a variant called strCriteria to store the string containing our filter criteria. In this example, in each case the criteria will look something like this:

```
Title LIKE 'A*'
```

Note that, once again, we're using our wildcard character (*). This criterion will make visible all the records whose film titles begin with the letter A, and will hide all other records.

Now we apply the filter to the recordset:

```
   objRS.Filter = strCriteria
```

Now we can test the results of the filter. When you apply a filter, the recordset automatically points the cursor at the first visible record in the filtered recordset. If there are no visible records in the filtered recordset, then the EOF property will be True – in that case we don't display anything. Otherwise, we display the visible contents of the recordset, by using MoveNext to step through the records as we've done in previous examples:

```
   If Not objRS.EOF Then
      Response.Write "<H2>" & strChar & "</H2>" & _
        "<TABLE BORDER=1><TR><TD><B>Film<B></TD><TD>Director</TD></TR>"
      While Not objRS.EOF
         Response.Write "<TR><TD>" & objRS("Title") & "</TD>" & _
                        "<TD>" & objRS("Director") & "</TD></TR>"

         objRS.MoveNext
      Wend
      Response.Write "</TABLE>"
   End If
```

Having written the table, we move onto the next letter in the alphabet:

```
Next
```

Notice that we don't need to reset the filter before applying the next filter – we can just replace the old value of the `Filter` property with the new value.

The Fields Collection

In the examples we've seen so far, we've always requested the value of a particular field by naming that field explicitly. For example, When requesting the value of the film title and director fields in the example above, we used the expressions `objRS("Title")` and `objRS("Director")` like this:

```
Response.Write "<TR><TD>" & objRS("Title") & "</TD>" & _
               "<TD>" & objRS("Director") & "</TD></TR>"
```

But what if you want to use all the fields in a recordset, perhaps to build a table from the recordset? Well, we could refer to each field individually in the same way, but this becomes tedious after a while – especially if there are lots of fields in the recordset. For a start, the task of typing out these field names individually is labor-intensive; moreover, it makes for excessively long and potentially untidy code.

We all want an easy life. So, let's introduce the `Fields` collection, which can skim *hours* off our development time.

> *While using the Fields collection is fine, if we want to save coding time, you can't use aliases for the field names. If the field names are cryptic or written in shorthand notation, like many databases, then those exact names will be returned when the Fields collection is used.*

Each `Recordset` object has its own `Fields` collection, which contains an entry for each field in the current record. That means that you can iterate through each field in the fieldset without knowing what the names of the fields are. So, for example, we can use this to display the value of each field with just a few short lines. Alternatively, we can actually use the `Fields` collection to find out the names of the fields that are contained in our recordset.

Aha, now were talking. Let's use this to create a central reusable routine, which will generate an HTML table showing all the data contained in a recordset.

Try It Out – The Fields Collection

We're going to create a routine, called `RecToTable()`, which generates the HTML for a table containing all the data in a recordset. We'll store this routine in its own file, `RecToTable.asp` – then, we'll be able to use it within any ASP page that we write, simply by including `RecToTable.asp` as a server-side include (SSI). To demonstrate, we'll write a second page, called `StaffTable.asp`, which uses the `RecToTable()` routine to show the values of all the fields in all the records of an obscure little table called `Staff`.

1. We're going to use the `Movies` database and the `strConnect` connection string again, so you'll need to ensure they're set up as for previous examples in this chapter.

2. The first thing to do is write the `RecToTable()` routine. Create a new file called `RecToTable.asp`, and add the following code to it (don't worry about all the new stuff; we'll look at it after we've seen it working):

```
<%
  Function RecToTable (objRS)
    Dim strT                                ' table html string
    Dim fldF                                ' current field object
    strT = "<TABLE BORDER=1><TR ALIGN=CENTER>"   ' build the table header

    For Each fldF In objRS.Fields           ' each field as a table column name
      strT = strT & "<TD>" & fldF.Name & "</TD>"
    Next
    strT = strT & "</TR>"

    While Not objRS.EOF                      ' now build the rows
      strT = strT & "<TR ALIGN=CENTER>"
      For Each fldF In objRS.Fields          ' loop through the fields
        strT = strT & "<TD>" & fldF.Value & "</TD>"
      Next
      strT = strT & "</TR>"
      objRS.MoveNext
    Wend
    strT = strT & "</TABLE>"
    RecToTable = strT                        ' and finally return the table
  End Function
%>
```

3. Save the `RecToTable.asp` file in the `\inetpub\wwwroot\BegASPFiles` directory.

4. Now create another new file, called `StaffTable.asp`, and enter the following code into it:

```
<%
  Option Explicit
  Dim strConnect
%>
<!-- #include file="DataStore.asp" -->
<!-- METADATA TYPE="typelib"
            FILE="C:\Program Files\Common Files\System\ado\msado15.dll" -->
<!-- #INCLUDE FILE="RecToTable.asp" -->
<HTML>
<HEAD>
<TITLE>ADO Fields Collection</TITLE>
</HEAD>
<BODY>
<%
  Dim objRS
  Set objRS = Server.CreateObject ("ADODB.Recordset")
  objRS.Open "Staff", strConnect, adOpenStatic, adLockReadOnly, adCmdTable

  Response.Write RecToTable(objRS)     ' pass the recordset to the table function
  objRS.Close
  Set objRS = Nothing
%>
</BODY>
</HTML>
```

5. Save the `StaffTable.asp` file into the `\inetpub\wwwroot\BegASPFiles` directory.

6. Start up your browser, and view the page `StaffTable.asp`.

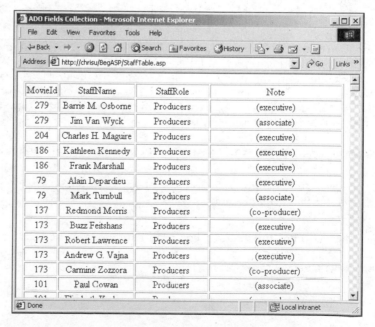

It's amazing, don't you think? Remember that this is actually produced by an SSI file, so you can include this in any ASP file where you need a table like this. Let's look at how it works.

How It Works

Let's look at `RecToTable.asp` first, since it's the one that does the work.

First we declare our function. The `RecToTable()` function will take a single argument, namely the recordset from which it will build the table. It needs to be a function because after it has generated a string containing all the HTML tags and text that make up the table, it will *return* that string to the calling routine:

```
<%
  Function RecToTable (objRS)
```

Next we declare a couple of variables. The first will hold the HTML tags that will make up the table, and the second will hold an ADO `Field` object:

```
    Dim strT                              ' table html string
    Dim fldF                              ' current field object
```

Now we can really start. We'll begin the HTML string by writing the `<TABLE>` tag, and the first `<TR>` tag for the table header:

```
    strT = "<TABLE BORDER=1><TR ALIGN=CENTER>"    ' build the table header
```

Now we need to build the header line:

```
    For Each fldF In objRS.Fields            ' each field as a table column name
      strT = strT & "<TD>" & fldF.Name & "</TD>"
    Next
```

Remember how, in Chapter 12, we used a `For Each … Next` loop to iterate through all the properties in the `Properties` collection? Well, this is the same. We are looping through the `Fields` collection, and using `For Each … Next` will set `fldF` to a different `Field` object each time we go round the loop. The expression `fldF.Name` refers to the name of the field. So this code creates one table cell for each field in the `Fields` collection, surrounding each field name with the table cell start and end tags, like so:

```
<TD>MovieID</TD><TD>StaffName</TD><TD>StaffRole</TD><TD>Note</TD>
```

In a moment we'll use the expression `fldF.Value` *to refer to the value contain in that field, for the current record.*

Once that loop has finished, we can terminate the table header:

```
    strT = strT & "</TR>"
```

Now we've finished the header line we can start on the rows of data. For each record, we need to iterate through each `Field` object in the `Fields` collection, capture the value of that field (using `fldF.Value`) and adding this value to the body of the HTML table. We're going to iterate through all the records in the recordset, and for each record we'll iterate through the `Fields` collection – so this involves a nested loop.

We can start looping through the records, using a `While ... Wend` loop as we've used before, checking for `EOF`:

```
    While Not objRS.EOF                          ' now build the rows
```

For each record, we need a row in the table, so we add the row tag to the output string:

```
        strT = strT & "<TR ALIGN=CENTER>"
```

Now we iterate through the fields, adding each field's value (for this record) as a cell in the table. This is where we use the `fldF.Value` expression that we mentioned above – the `Value` property of the `Field` object is what holds the value of this field for this record:

```
        For Each fldF In objRS.Fields             ' loop through the fields
          strT = strT & "<TD>" & fldF.Value & "</TD>"
        Next
```

That takes care of all the fields for one record, so we add the row terminator tag, and move onto the next record:

```
        strT = strT & "</TR>"
        objRS.MoveNext
    Wend
```

And when the `While ... Wend` loop has ended we can terminate the table and return the string-of-tags-and-text bag to our calling routine:

```
    strT = strT & "</TABLE>"
    RecToTable = strT                            ' and finally return the table
  End Function
%>
```

So this is actually quite simple. We just loop through the records, and for each record we loop through the fields. Now let's look at how we test this out in the calling routine, `StaffTable.asp`.

We have the usual #INCLUDE and METADATA commands, but this time we also have a new #INCLUDE directive for the `RecToTable.asp` SSI file that we've just created:

```
<!-- #INCLUDE FILE="RecToTable.asp" -->
```

The creation of the recordset is much the same as we've seen before:

```
Dim objRS
Set objRS = Server.CreateObject ("ADODB.Recordset")
objRS.Open "Staff", strConnect, adOpenStatic, adLockReadOnly, adCmdTable
```

The recordset, objRS that we've just created contains the data from the Staff table of the movies database. Now here's the new bit: we use Response.Write to write the contents of the generated string to the HTML stream:

```
Response.Write RecToTable(objRS)      ' pass the recordset to the table function
```

When we call RecToTable(), we pass the recordset objRS that we've just created as a parameter to the function. As we know, RecToTable() uses this recordset to generate a character string containing all the HTML for the table, and returns this character string on its completion. The returned character string is then sent straight to the HTML stream (and hence to the browser) via the Response.Write method.

Then we close the recordset and tidy up:

```
objRS.Close
Set objRS = Nothing
```

That's it. You can include RecToTable.asp in any file and use it to create a table.

> *The sample files (available for download from* http://www.wrox.com*) contain an extra file,* RecToTableFormat.asp*; this file is much the same the same as* RecToTable.asp*, but has the added bonus that it formats the values according to their types. So a currency value, for example, is formatted with the currency sign, etc.*

Arrays of Rows

We'll look at one more method of the Recordset object in this chapter. The GetRows method returns a multi-dimensional array, which contains the data of whatever fields you specify, from a specified number of records in the recordset. Its syntax is:

varArray = *objRecordset*.GetRows (*Rows, Start, Fields*)

All three parameters are optional. In its simplest form, you can use the GetRows method in a line like this:

```
varMyArray = objRS.GetRows
```

In this case, GetRows will adopt its default behavior – which is to returns an array containing all field values, for each record between the current record and the last record inclusive. When all of the rows are returned, then the cursor is set to point to the end of the recordset and EOF is set. Let's look at the three parameters:

- ❑ The *Rows* parameter allows us to restrict the number of records that will be returned in the array. You can specify an integer here, or you can use the constant adGetRowsRest to return all the rows including and subsequent to the current record. (Default is adGetRowsRest.)

- ❑ The *Start* parameter is a bookmark (or one of the adBookmark constants shown earlier), which allows us to specify which record to start on. (Default is adBookmarkCurrent.)

- ❑ The *Fields* parameter represents the fields whose values are to be placed in the array. *Fields* can be a single field name, or a single ordinal value (i.e. an integer reflecting the position of the field within the Fields collection). Alternatively, it can be an array of field names or an array of ordinal values. (Default is 'all fields'.)

The array that GetRows returns is sized automatically to fit the number of fields and records returned by the method.

Try It Out – The GetRows Method

OK, let's give it a try. We'll create a recordset of data, and then use it to generate an array of data (via the GetRows method). Then, just to prove that it works, we'll close the recordset and display the data using the array.

1. We're going to use the Movies database and the strConnect connection string again so you'll need to ensure they're set up as for previous examples in this chapter.

2. Start up your editor, and enter the following code for the file GetRows.asp:

```
<%
  Option Explicit
  Dim strConnect
%>
<!-- #include file="DataStore.asp" -->
<!-- METADATA TYPE="typelib"
             FILE="C:\Program Files\Common Files\System\ado\msado15.dll" -->
<HTML>
<HEAD>
<TITLE>ADO GetRows Method</TITLE>
</HEAD>
<BODY>

<%
  Dim objRS            ' recordset object
  Dim avarFields       ' array of fields
  Dim intRow           ' current row
  Dim intCol           ' current column
  Dim intLastRow       ' ordinal of last row in the array
  Dim intLastCol       ' ordinal of last column in the array

  ' create and open the recordset object
  Set objRS = Server.CreateObject ("ADODB.Recordset")
  objRS.Open "Movies", strConnect, adOpenKeyset, adLockReadOnly, adCmdTable
```

```
' get the data
avarFields = objRS.GetRows

' now close the recordset and clean up
objRS.Close
Set objRS = Nothing

' now use the array to display thre data
intLastCol = UBound(avarFields, 1)
intLastRow = UBound(avarFields, 2)
For intRow = 0 To intLastCol                 ' loop through the array
  For intCol = 0 To intLastRow
    Response.Write avarFields(intCol, intRow) & "  "
  Next
  Response.Write "<BR>"
Next
%>
</BODY>
</HTML>
```

3. Save the GetRows.asp file in the \inetpub\wwwroot\BegASPFiles folder.

4. View the page from your browser:

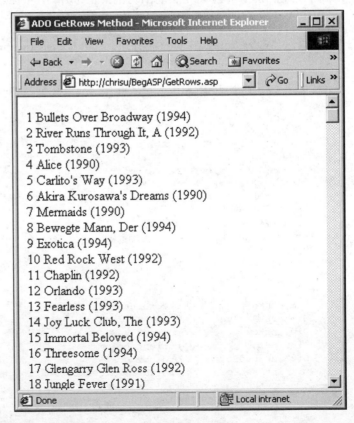

As you can see this just displays every field in every row of the Movies table.

How It Works

We'll skip past the (now familiar) header code, and the variable declarations. The recordset is created much as before:

```
Set objRS = Server.CreateObject ("ADODB.Recordset")
objRS.Open "Movies", strConnect, adOpenKeyset, adLockReadOnly, adCmdTable
```

Now we call the `GetRows` method. We're not passing in any arguments, so this will extract *all* records into our arrray:

```
avarFields = objRS.GetRows
```

Now we've captured the data in the array, we don't need the recordset anymore, so we can get rid of it:

```
objRS.Close
Set objRS = Nothing
```

Now we'll display the data, directly from the array. We use the VBScript function, `UBound()` to find out how many elements there are in each dimension of the array (the first dimension of the array is columns, the second is rows):

```
intLastCol = UBound(avarFields, 1)
intLastRow = UBound(avarFields, 2)
```

And then we can iterate through both dimensions in a nested loop, printing out the values:

```
For intRow = 0 To intLastCol              ' loop through the array
  For intCol = 0 To intLastRow
    Response.Write avarFields(intCol, intRow) & "  "
  Next
  Response.Write "<BR>"
Next
```

You might be wondering why we didn't use the `GetRows` method in `RecToTable()` to create the HTML table. There are two reasons for this:

❑ First, `RecToTable()` generated a table header with the names of the fields; the `GetRows` method can't help us with that, because the array that it generates doesn't contain the field names (it only contains the field values for each record)

❑ Second, the array takes up memory – since we already have the fields and values in the recordset, what's the point of copying them all to an array and then copying them out to the table? In the `RecToTable` example, we just created the table straight from the recordset

When are the best occasions to use the GetRows method? Well, it's probably not a good idea to use it for large recordsets, but for small ones, or even small sets of data from a large recordset, it's fine. You may find that you need to use this method when you end up with a recordset cursor that is not scrollable. For example, if you are using ADO and Oracle and execute a parameterized query from the Command object, the recordset cursor provided is read-only and totally non-scrollable. How, then, do you navigate backwards and forwards through the records? The answer is that you extract the rows into an array using GetRows and navigate through the array instead. Another occasion when you may want to use this method is with custom functions or routines that accept an array as a parameter, but couldn't cope with a recordset.

Summary

We've covered an awful lot of ground in this chapter – looking at the most important aspects of the ADO Recordset object in the process. We've understood the concepts of a record, a field and a recordset in their broader senses, and seen how ADO models the recordset using a Recordset object. We can create a Recordset object using the Server.CreateObject method. One way of populating the recordset with data is to use its Open method – to connect it directly to a data store and grab some data. We've also seen much of the functionality that comes with an ADO recordset:

- ❑ We use a cursor to find our way around the recordset. The cursor always points to one of the records in the recordset, and there are four different types of cursor. Some cursor types are more resource-hungry than others

- ❑ A Recordset object can have one of four lock type settings. Our choice of lock type is dependent on whether or not we intend to change the data in the data store, on whether we want to see existing changes, and on the existence of other people using the data store. Some lock types are more resource-hungry than others

- ❑ There are various methods that we can use to point the cursor at different records. For example, the Move, MoveFirst, MoveLast, MoveNext and MovePrevious methods allow us to move in forwards and backwards directions

- ❑ The Find method allows us to search for a particular record that fits our criterion. If the search is successful, it points the cursor at that record (and if it fails, it points the cursor at BOF or EOF)

- ❑ The Filter property allows us to hide all the records that don't specify a particular criterion

- ❑ The Fields collection contains one Field object for each field in the recordset. We can use a loop to iterate through it in the same way as we iterate through any other collection

- ❑ The GetRows method allows us to create an array containing data from the recordset

Along the way, we've seen that the ADO object model has an essentially flat hierarchy. We've also met the ADO constants, and seen that they can help us to create more readable code.

The Recordset is really at the heart of ADO, and as you use ASP more you'll probably discover you use it to do one main task – namely generating dynamic pages from a recordset. It's quite possible to create web sites that are almost entirely data bound, having only a few ASP pages – with all of the data generated from a data store using recordsets. Updating the site simply becomes a matter of updating the data store. In fact, much of the Wrox Press web site is generated in this way. Obviously you won't be limited to this task, but you'll find that they can take away a lot of the effort involved in site maintenance.

In the next chapter we look at more advanced data handling techniques. For example, you'll find out how we go about updating the data store, or getting back information from data stores other than databases, and this will conclude our whistle-stop tour of ADO.

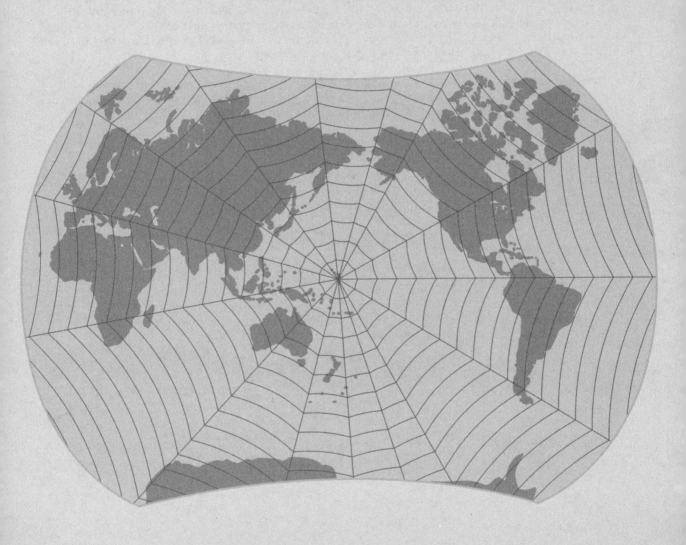

Advanced Data Handling Techniques

This chapter is the final one in our ADO trilogy. It brings together the remaining objects in the ADO object model and demonstrates finally how we can get our information back to our web pages from other sources, such as text files as well as our databases.

In all there are five standalone objects in ADO 2.5, yet we've spent the last two chapters discussing just two of them. That's because the `Recordset` and `Connection` objects are at the heart of all we do. However, if we want to do anything more than just ask simple questions of the data store, then we'll need the functionality offered by the other objects in ADO 2.5. We can't hope to do anything more than touch very briefly upon some much larger subject areas and point you in a direction where you'll be able to learn more, but this shouldn't detract from the fact that the subjects we will discuss in this chapter are fundamental to you using databases in web pages.

In this chapter we'll discuss:

- ❑ The `Command` object
- ❑ A quick introduction to SQL
- ❑ Stored procedures
- ❑ The `Parameters` collection
- ❑ Adding and updating your databases using the `Recordset` object and SQL
- ❑ Customized data access
- ❑ Semi-structured data and the `Record` and `Stream` objects

The Command Object

In the examples we've seen so far in Chapters 12 and 13, we've been using the ADO `Connection` and `Recordset` objects to make a connection between our ASP page and our data store, and then to retrieve data from the data store for use in the page. In those examples, every request for data was effectively given by executing a **command** against the data store.

When we use the phrase 'executing a command against the data store', we mean that we're instructing the data store that we want to perform some task with its data. So far, all our examples have used the same type of command – each time, we've been telling the data store that we wish to **select** certain data (and have that data returned to the page within a recordset). For example, when we specified the appropriate criteria within the parameters of the Recordset object's Open method, we were *selecting* which data we wanted to see within our recordset:

```
objRS.Open = "AllMovies", strConnect, adOpenforwardOnly, adLockReadOnly, adCmdTable
```

So, although we didn't mention it at the time, in Chapters 12 and 13 we *were* executing commands against the data store. There are other types of command too: for example, we might use a command to tell the data store to **insert** a new record, or to **update** the contents of a record, or to **delete** an existing record.

Although we can use the Connection and Recordset objects to execute such commands, ADO also provides an object called the Command object, which is specially designed for the purpose of specifying and running commands against the data store.

In terms of managing and executing commands, we can get much greater flexibility and functionality from the Command object, because it allows us to run much more complex queries – enabling us to make the most of things like **stored procedures** and **parameters**, as we'll see later. But before we leap into such lofty topics, we'll do two things:

❑ First, we'll warm to the Command object by having a look at how it's used in its simplest form

❑ Then, we'll have a look at how to use a query language called SQL to write commands

Using the Command Object

We can create a Command object by using the CreateObject method of the ASP Server object:

```
Set objCommand = Server.CreateObject("ADODB.Command")
```

This statement creates a new Command object called objCommand. This should look familiar; we've already used the same technique to create Connection and Recordset objects.

Executing a Command

In order to run a command, we use the Command object's Execute method. The Execute method has three parameters:

```
objCommand.Execute RecordsAffected, Parameters, Options
```

All three arguments are optional – if you omit any of them then the Execute method will adopt the default value for that parameter. Let's have a look at them:

❑ The *RecordsAffected* parameter is for action queries (those that insert, update or delete data and, thus, don't return a recordset). If you want to know the number of records that were affected by the command, then you can pass a variable name into this parameter – when the command is complete, the number of affected records will be placed into this parameter.

It's worth noting that this is the first ADO method we've met that is capable of returning information to you within one of its parameters.

❑ The *Parameters* parameter holds an array of parameters that are to be passed to the command. This means that we can write a generic command and use it lots of times. Each time we execute the command, we can make it specific by using the command's parameters to pass in the information specific to this one `Execute` call. Don't confuse this with the `Parameters` collection, which we'll be looking at in more detail later in the chapter when we look at stored procedures and queries. Also bear in mind that a parameter value that you provide in the *Parameters* parameter will override a value specified in the `Parameters` collection.

We write our generic commands using a query language called SQL. We'll meet SQL properly after the following example.

❑ The *Options* parameter is like the *Options* parameter in the `Recordset.Open` method. It specifies the type of command being run.

Specifying the Command

It's all very well that we can execute a command, but you might have noticed that there's nothing in the `Execute` method that specifies what command we want to run. Well spotted! For that, we need to add something to the `CommandText` property:

```
objCommand.CommandText = "Movies"
objCommand.Execute , , adCmdTable
```

In this case, we've specified the name of the database table, `Movies`, as the command text. (We'll see later that we can use SQL to create more complex queries than this.) Then we use the `Execute` method to execute the command. Notice that, in this code fragment, the first two arguments have been omitted; however, we've left the two commas in because we want to specify a value for the third parameter. The third parameter itself is used to specify the type of command being run – and so, since the command text is in the form of a table name, we've used the ADO constant `adCmdTable` to reflect that (this gives ADO the opportunity to optimize the way the command is executed).

Instead of the two lines above, we could achieve the same result by taking an extra line to set the command type, using the `CommandType` property, like this:

```
objCommand.CommandText = "Movies"
objCommand.CommandType = adCmdTable
objCommand.Execute
```

This time, we don't need to specify the command type as a parameter of the `Execute` method, because we'd already specified it by setting the `CommandType` property explicitly.

Specifying the Connection

There's also been no mention of the connection: so how does the command know which data store to use? Well, from what we've shown you so far it doesn't! So before we use the `Command` object's `Execute` method, we need to assign its `ActiveConnection` property too.

The `ActiveConnection` property can be a `Connection` object or a connection string. This example uses a connection string, which has been previously defined and stored in a variant called `strConnect`:

```
objCommand.ActiveConnection = strConnect
objCommand.CommandText = "Movies"
objCommand.CommandType = adCmdTable
objCommand.Execute
```

Capturing any Selected Data

In this case, the command is a 'select' type command – we're asking the data store to *select* all of the data in the `Movies` table and to return it to us in the form of a recordset. So in this case, the `Execute` method actually returns a physical ADO `Recordset` object!

If we want to use that recordset elsewhere in our program, we should give it a name so that we can reference it. We can do that by using the `Set` statement to assign the result of the `Execute` statement to a variant of our choice:

```
objCommand.ActiveConnection = strConnect
objCommand.CommandText = "Movies"
objCommand.CommandType = adCmdTable
Set objRS = objCommand.Execute
```

So, now we've arrived at a set of statements that make a lot of sense, given that the code is just returning the `Movies` table. Let's give it a go in an example page.

Try It Out – Running a Query with the Command Object

1. We're going to use the `Movies` database and the `strConnect` connection string, which we first set up in Chapter 12 and which we used all through Chapters 12 and 13. For this, you'll need to ensure that your `Movie2000.mdb` or `Movie2000.mdf` file is set up as described in Chapter 12; you'll also need the `DataStore.asp` SSI file placed in the `\inetpub\wwwroot\BegASPFiles` folder, as we explained in Chapter 12.

2. In your editor, create a new file, which we'll call Command.asp. Into this file, add the following code:

```
<%
  Option Explicit
  Dim strConnect
%>
<!-- #include file="DataStore.asp" -->
<!-- METADATA TYPE="typelib"
            FILE="C:\Program Files\Common Files\System\ado\msado15.dll" -->
```

```
<HTML>
<HEAD>
<TITLE>ADO Command Object</TITLE>
</HEAD>
<BODY>

<%
  Dim objCommand, objRS
  Set objCommand = Server.CreateObject("ADODB.Command") ' create the Command object

  ' fill in the command properties
  objCommand.ActiveConnection = strConnect
  objCommand.CommandText = "AllMovies"
  objCommand.CommandType = adCmdTable

  ' now execute the command, and capture the selected records in a recordset
  Set objRS = objCommand.Execute

  ' The Command object has done its job, so clean it up
  Set objCommand = Nothing

  ' now loop through the records
  While Not objRS.EOF
    Response.Write objRS("TitleID") & ": " & objRS("Title") & "<BR>"
    objRS.MoveNext
  Wend

  ' now close and clean up
  objRS.Close
  Set objRS = Nothing
%>
</BODY>
</HTML>
```

3. Save the Command.asp file into your BegASPFiles directory.

4. View the Command.asp page in your browser:

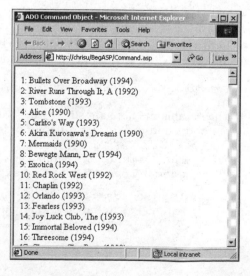

567

As you can see, we've just used the Command object to perform the same task of opening and populating the Recordset object – effectively, it has done the same job that we've done previously using the Recordset object's Open method. In fact, you can mix-and-match the Recordset's Open method with the functionality of the Command object, because the first parameter of the Open method (the *Source* parameter) is able to take a value in the form of an ADO Command object, like this:

```
objCommand.ActiveConnection = strConnect
objCommand.CommandText = "Movies"
objCommand.CommandType = adCmdTable
objRS.Open objCommand
```

This sort of flexibility among the ADO objects is another demonstration of the 'flat hierarchy' of the ADO object model. Using a Command object doesn't depend on having first created a Recordset, or a Connection object. By contrast, if you've got an existing Recordset object then you can use it to run a command (as we've done here) – so you're not forced into creating a new Recordset object if you don't want one. Using ADO objects is a mix'n'match scenario – and it's useful, because it means that you're not forced to create any more objects in your code than you actually intend to use.

While we're talking of the flexibility of the ADO objects, let's return briefly to the Connection object and see how that handles commands.

The Connection Object's Execute Method

When we looked at the Connection object, back in Chapter 12, we touched very briefly on its Execute method, but we deliberately left an explanation of that method until now – because, with a better understanding of recordsets and commands, we can now get a better appreciation of what it does.

The Connection object's Execute method is a little different in its syntax from the Command object's Execute method, even though the two methods have the same name. Don't get mixed up in this section! The full list of parameters for the Connection object's Execute method is:

objConn.Execute *CommandText*, *RecordsAffected*, *Options*

In fact, if the command is one that selects and returns records, we can use a variant to refer to the returned recordset (and thus use the recordset elsewhere in the code), like this:

Set *objRS* = *objConn*.Execute *CommandText*, *RecordsAffected*, *Options*

The parameters here are slightly different to the parameters of the *objCommand*.Execute method – and they're in a different order. Here:

❑ The *CommandText* parameter can contain the command text (so it corresponds to the Command object's CommandText property)

❑ The *RecordsAffected* and *Options* parameters work just like their namesake parameters in the Command object's Execute method

So in fact, we don't really need to revisit this, because the functionality provided is very similar to that we've already seen for the `Command` object. We've included it here to reinforce and demonstrate the flexibility of the 'flat hierarchy' of the ADO object model once again.

So far in this book, the only commands that we've used have been 'select' commands – in which we *select* particular records and/or fields from a table (or indeed, the whole table), and have the data store return those data in the form of a recordset. But the process of selecting fields and records is much more subtle and clever than we've shown so far. Moreover, as we hinted in the first paragraphs of this chapter, data access isn't only about *selecting* data from the data store – we want our commands to be able to do other things too.

In order to learn more about these different types of commands, we need to know a little of the basic language in which they are submitted – and that language is SQL.

The Structured Query Language (SQL)

We've been hinting at the usage of **Structured Query Language** (usually called **SQL**) over the last few pages, and right back into Chapter 13. SQL is the universal language used for programming databases, and we'll introduce SQL at this stage because it's at the heart of our ability to issue commands.

> *If you've ever used the Query By Example (QBE) grid in Microsoft Access, then you've already been using SQL (albeit behind the scenes). Every time you request information from an Access database using the QBE grid, the query is translated into SQL and the result is returned to you as a recordset.*

As we've already said, all SQL does is provide you with a format for retrieving the information you want from the database.

SQL seems to have a reputation as being a difficult language, but don't be put off by it – getting the hang of it is really quite simple. In fact, SQL is a **declarative** language. The term 'declarative' means that we use SQL to tell the computer what it is we want, and then we let the machine decide how best to achieve the correct result. We, as programmers, never need to see the details; all we see is the result.

> *By contrast, other languages (such as Visual Basic,COBOL,C++ or Java) are **procedural** languages. These languages are characterized by statements, which tell the computer exactly what to do in a structured step-by-step way.*

We've already seen something close to a SQL command. For example, we used something very like a SQL statement when we used the `Recordset` object's `Filter` method in Chapter 13:

```
objRS.Filter = "Director = 'Quentin Tarantino'"
```

Consider the logic behind this: it's asking the `Recordset` object to *select* every record whose `Director` field contains the exact string `Quentin Tarantino` (and to hide any other records). Even more appropriately, we could use a SQL query when we are requesting data from the data store in the first place:

```
objRS.Open = "SELECT TitleID, Title FROM AllMovies", strConnect
```

This statement tells the data store to *select* the values of the `TitleID` and `Title` fields for all the records in the `AllMovies` table, and to pump that data into a new `Recordset` object. In fact, this command uses two SQL keywords – `SELECT` and `FROM`. We'll see more of this SQL syntax as we progress through this chapter – but as you can see, it's not too difficult to read.

SELECT, INSERT, UPDATE and DELETE

There are four main different types of command that you can run against the database using the `Command` object:

❑   A `SELECT` command returns a recordset, populated with data from the data store

❑   An `INSERT` command adds records into your data store

❑   An `UPDATE` command updates portions of existing information within a record in the data store (i.e. not just the record in a recordset)

❑   A `DELETE` command removes records from the data store

As we said earlier, we've been performing `SELECT`-type commands in all of the ADO examples so far in this book. For example, in the `Command.asp` example above we used the following command to 'select' every single record and field from the `Movies` database table:

```
objCommand.CommandText = "AllMovies"
objCommand.CommandType = adCmdTable
Set objRS = objCommand.Execute
```

In fact, we can use a SQL `SELECT` statement to perform exactly the same thing:

```
objCommand.CommandText = "SELECT * FROM AllMovies"
objCommand.CommandType = adCmdText
Set objRS = objCommand.Execute
```

Note that the SQL `SELECT` command is the only one of these four commands that returns a recordset. The other commands are not concerned with fetching data from the data store – instead, they're all concerned with making *changes* to the data store, and as such they don't return any data. Collectively, the `INSERT`, `UPDATE` and `DELETE` commands are known as **action commands** or **action queries**.

In the course of this chapter, we'll see all four of these SQL commands in action. We'll deal with `SELECT` first, and see how it gives us more flexibility for selecting data – so we don't have to select entire tables all the time! Then we'll move on to `UPDATE`, and later in the chapter we'll look at how to use `INSERT` and `DELETE` to create and destroy records.

The SELECT Command

So, a very flexible way to request data from a database table is via SQL's `SELECT ... FROM ...` clause. As we've already seen, this clause is phrased in a logical way, that is very readable – we specify what data we want, and which table we want it from, and the results of this query are returned in the form of a table.

The act of requesting data from a data store in this way is often referred to as a **query***. Querying the database doesn't affect the structure or contents of the data store, or the order of the data within the data store. A query simply presents the data to the user in a certain way.*

A Simple SELECT Command

In its simplest form, the `SELECT` command will simply return an entire table, or specific columns and rows of a table. Such a query would take the following form:

`SELECT <field_name(s)> FROM <table_name>`

So, to extract the list of movie titles from the **Movies** table, we'd write a `SELECT` command that queries the database for the `Title` field of every record in the `AllMovies` database table, like this:

```
SELECT Title FROM AllMovies
```

We're not limited to querying the data store for one field at a time – we can ask for as many fields as we like (so long as each field we request is a field that belongs to the specified table!). Querying for more than one field is simple – we just list each field name, separated with commas. The following command queries the `Cast` table for a list of records of characters (held in the `CastRole` field), along with the actors who portrayed those characters (the `CastName` field):

```
SELECT CastRole, CastName FROM Cast
```

What if we want to query the database for the data contained in all of the fields in a table? Well, you can do it by using the wildcard `*` in your query, like this:

```
SELECT * FROM AllMovies
```

This returns the data in every field of record in the `AllMovies` table. The `*` symbol is effectively a shorthand which means 'all fields'.

Of course, the amount of time it takes to complete a query is related to the amount of data you ask for. So, if you ask for all fields then don't be surprised if your query takes a long time to complete! It's much better to write commands that only query those fields that you're actually going to *use*. Only ask for all fields if you really *do* need the data in all of those fields.

> When you're writing SQL `SELECT` commands, don't query the data store for more data than you need. It's a good practice that helps to keep your queries brief, your code tidy and your web server's resources free.

Conditional SELECT Commands

As we've seen, we can reduce the amount of data requested by querying for the required fields only. In fact, there's *another* way that we can reduce the size of our queries – by being specific about which database records we're interested in. For this, we can use a slightly more advanced version of the SQL statement, which has the following form:

```
SELECT <field_name(s)> FROM <table_name> WHERE <condition>
```

This is just an extension of the original SELECT ... FROM ... clause – we've appended a WHERE ... subclause at the end. And again, you'll see that it's very easy to read. The WHERE ... subclause allows us to specify what kind of records we're interested in. For example, if we wanted a list of all the films in the AllMovies table that were directed by Quentin Tarantino, we could specify that we're only interested in those specific records:

```
SELECT Title FROM AllMovies WHERE Director = 'Quentin Tarantino'
```

> *You might notice that the Director Name is surrounded by single quotes. This is because the name is a text string. You might be wondering why we don't use double quotes – after all when using variants, that's what we would do normally. You must consider that, here, the whole SQL statement will be appear in double quotes, which are used to denote where the SQL statement starts and ends. So, in place of double quotes in a SQL statement, we use single quotes instead.*

The <condition> part of this SQL command is actually something we've seen before. It works in the same way as the *Criteria* parameter of the Recordset object's Find method and Filter property:

```
strCriteria = "Director = 'Quentin Tarantino'"    ' set criteria
objRS.Find strCriteria                            ' apply criteria
```

More Complex Conditional SELECT Commands

Now let's go one stage further, and create a SQL command that will return a list containing the movies directed by Quentin Tarantino plus the movies directed by Francis Coppola:

```
SELECT Title FROM AllMovies WHERE Director = 'Francis Coppola'
                              OR Director = 'Quentin Tarantino'
```

Here, we've just extended the <condition> clause to take in the films of both directors. Let's actually see how you could run this last statement in an ASP script.

Try It Out – Running a SQL SELECT statement using the Command object

1. You guessed it – we're using the Movies2000 database and the strConnect connection string again! So you need Movie2000.mdb or Movie2000.mdf set up as described in Chapter 12; and the DataStore.asp SSI file placed in the \inetpub\wwwroot\BegASPFiles folder, as explained in Chapter 12.

2. Start your code editor, and create a new file (which we'll call `SQLSelect.asp`). Type in the following code:

```asp
<%
  Option Explicit
  Dim strConnect
%>
<!-- #include file="DataStore.asp" -->
<!-- METADATA TYPE="typelib"
              FILE="C:\Program Files\Common Files\System\ado\msado15.dll" -->
<HTML>
<HEAD>
<TITLE>Using SQL's SELECT Command and the ADO Command Object</TITLE>
</HEAD>
<BODY>

<%
  Dim objCommand, objRS
  Set objCommand = Server.CreateObject("ADODB.Command")

  objCommand.ActiveConnection = strConnect
  objCommand.CommandText = "SELECT Title, Director FROM AllMovies " & _
                     "WHERE Director LIKE 'Quentin Tarantino' " & _
                     "  OR Director LIKE 'Francis Coppola'"
  objCommand.CommandType = adCmdText

  Set objRS = objCommand.Execute
  Set objCommand = Nothing

  While Not objRS.EOF
    Response.Write objRS("Title") & " was directed by " & objRS("Director") & "<BR>"
    objRS.MoveNext
  Wend

  objRS.Close
  Set objRS = Nothing
%>
</BODY>
</HTML>
```

3. Save `SQLSelect.asp` into the `\inetpub\wwwroot\BegASPFiles` directory.

4. Navigate to the `SQLSelect.asp` page, in your browser:

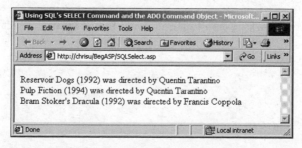

How It Works

We start by declaring variants for the Command and Recordset objects, and creating an instance of the Command object:

```
Dim objCommand, objRS
Set objCommand = Server.CreateObject("ADODB.Command")
```

Note that we don't need to create a Recordset object using Server.CreateObject – we'll get a real Recordset object shortly, when we use the Execute method.

Now we can set the Command object up ready to execute the command. This involves assigning values to the ActiveConnection, CommandText and CommandType properties:

```
objCommand.ActiveConnection = strConnect
objCommand.CommandText = "SELECT Title, Director FROM AllMovies " & _
                         "WHERE Director LIKE 'Quentin Tarantino' " & _
                         "  OR Director LIKE 'Francis Coppola'"
objCommand.CommandType = adCmdText
```

For the connection, we're using the strConnect connection string, defined in DataStore.asp. For the command text, we're using a more complex SQL command now – of the form SELECT...FROM...WHERE.... We want to retrieve a recordset containing the Title and Director fields of the AllMovies table; but we're only asking for those movies directed by Tarantino or Coppola, so we're using the WHERE clause to reflect that. The query is in the form of a text string, so the command type is adCmdText.

> *There's an interesting technicality regarding the WHERE clause here – note that we've used the LIKE keyword (an expression parser on character fields) in place of the equals sign (=). You can try the text-based condition Director = 'Quentin Tarantino' instead; but if you're using **SQL Server (with OLE-DB or ODBC providers)**, you'll find that it causes a syntax error. SQL Server doesn't allow you to use text, ntext or image data types in the WHERE clause except with the LIKE keyword. Not all providers are as fussy as this (Access isn't) – but it's something to be aware of. We'll use the LIKE keyword because it's more widely accepted.*

Now we run the command using the Execute method, and store the results in the Recordset object (here, note that we're using the Set statement because we're assigning an instance of an object to the objRS variable):

```
Set objRS = objCommand.Execute
```

Once we've got our recordset we don't need to keep the Command object any longer. So we'll get rid of it:

```
Set objCommand = Nothing
```

Lastly, we display the contents of our recordset, using the EOF property to control the While...Wend loop as we've seen in previous examples:

```
While Not objRS.EOF
   Response.Write objRS("Title") & " was directed by " & objRS("Director") & "<BR>"
   objRS.MoveNext
Wend
```

Selecting Information from More than One Table

So far, we've been writing queries that request data from just a single database table. However, you have probably noticed that our Movies2000 database comprises sixteen different tables – with names like Movies, Cast, ProductionCompanies, ReleaseDates. Each table contains different types of data (all relating to different aspects of the cinematic recordings listed within).

In fact, the AllMovies table is an amalgamation of some of the data contained in the other fifteen tables in the database. We included it for convenience, in order to simplify some of the preceding examples. In a real-life situation, amalgamated tables such as AllMovies are often discouraged.

By contrast, multi-table databases are common, and there are a number of reasons for designing databases in this way. The most obvious reason is that these tables contain many different types of data – a single table containing all these different types of data would have more than 20 different fields, which would be rather unmanageable, as you'll see if you try to view the entire contents of the AllMovies table in one go.

There are other reasons. Single-table data storage can appear disorganized, with apparently unrelated fields stored in adjacent columns. Also, they can be very inefficient – potentially, a single table database can end up with lots of repeated data. We first encountered these issues in the early sections of Chapter 12. Let's briefly consider how these issues relate to our Movies2000 database.

If you're a cinema expert, then you'll know that the film *Pulp Fiction* was directed by Quentin Tarantino, featured Amanda Plummer, John Travolta and Samuel L. Jackson (in the roles of Honey Bunny, Vincent Vega and Jules), and had a release certificate 'R' in the United States and '18' in the United Kingdom. If we stored this information within a single table in the database, we'd have a set of records like this:

Movie	Director	CastName	CastRole	USA Cert	UK Cert
Pulp Fiction	Quentin Tarantino	Amanda Plummer	Honey Bunny	R	18
Pulp Fiction	Quentin Tarantino	John Travolta	Vincent Vega	R	18
Pulp Fiction	Quentin Tarantino	Samuel L. Jackson	Jules	R	18

There are two problems with storing the data like this. First, there's a lot of unrelated data all contained in the same table – it just doesn't demonstrate good organization. Second (and possibly more importantly), there's a lot of repetition. Therefore, in Movies2000, we have dissected this data into four related tables like this:

MovieID	Title
67	Pulp Fiction

MovieID	Director
67	Quentin Tarantino

MovieID	CastName	CastRole
67	Amanda Plummer	Honey Bunny
67	John Travolta	Vincent Vega
67	Samuel L. Jacksona	Jules

MovieID	USA Cert	UK Cert
67	R	18

When you consider that there are 330 films in our database, and 22 different fields, you can see how a set of tables is easier to use and vastly more efficient than a single table. In this case, we just use each movie's unique identifier, as defined in the Movies table, to indicate to which movie the data relates. The unique identifier for *Pulp Fiction* is 67.

The consequence of this is that we need to be able to write a command that can query data from two or more database tables at the same time. Fortunately, SQL provides us with a number of ways of doing this – by way of a **table join**. SQL even provides a keyword, JOIN, just for the purpose.

In fact, there are many different types of join in SQL, but we are only going to cover one of them – an **inner join**. This allows us to write a command that queries two or more tables at the same time, returning the results of the query as a single recordset.

So, let's put aside the AllMovies table, which we've used in the past, and show how we can write an example that pairs up movies with their directors using *only* the much smaller Movies and Directors tables of our database.

Try It Out - Running a SQL SELECT statement that joins two tables

In order to do this, we'll write a new command that queries the two tables and returns a single recordset. We'll create a new example by simply adapting the code from SQLSelect.asp.

1. Create a copy of the file SQLSelect.asp – call the copy SQLSelectInnerJoin.asp.

2. Instead of selecting all the data from the AllMovies table, we'll select the text from a JOIN of smaller tables. So open up SQLSelectInnerJoin.asp, and change the following highlighted lines:

```
...
<%
  Dim objCommand, objRS
  Set objCommand = Server.CreateObject("ADODB.Command")

  objCommand.ActiveConnection = strConnect
  objCommand.CommandText = "SELECT Movies.Title, Director.DirectorName " & _
      "FROM Movies INNER JOIN Director ON Movies.MovieID= Director.MovieID " & _
      "WHERE (Director.DirectorName LIKE 'Quentin Tarantino'  " & _
      "  OR  Director.DirectorName LIKE 'Francis Coppola') "
  objCommand.CommandType = adCmdText

  Set objRS = objCommand.Execute
  Set objCommand = Nothing

  While Not objRS.EOF
    Response.Write objRS("Title") & " was directed by " & _
                  objRS("DirectorName") & "<BR>"
    objRS.MoveNext
  Wend
  objRS.Close
  Set objRS = Nothing
%>
...
```

3. Save these changes. Now use your browser to view the page:

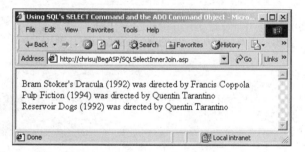

How It Works

By amending only one line in our script, we've completely changed the whole query. Let's have a look at that query line again:

```
objCommand.CommandText = "SELECT Movies.Title, Director.DirectorName " & _
    "FROM Movies INNER JOIN Director ON Movies.MovieID = Director.MovieID " & _
    "WHERE (Director.DirectorName LIKE 'Quentin Tarantino'  " & _
    "  OR  Director.DirectorName LIKE 'Francis Coppola') "
```

There's a lot in this command but when we break it up you'll see that it's quite simple to understand. The first thing to note is that the command still has the form SELECT...FROM...WHERE... – it's just that the table (in the FROM clause) is a little more complex. Let's look at the FROM clause first.

The FROM clause begins by saying that we'll create an INNER JOIN of the Movies and Director tables. Each record in that table is created by joining a record from the Movies table to a record of the Director table, where the MovieID field of the first is equal to the MovieID of the second:

```
... FROM Movies INNER JOIN Director ON Movies.MovieID = Director.MovieID ...
```

Here, we need to use the 'dot notation' to indicate the table to which each field belongs – so Movies.MovieID refers to the MovieID field of the Movies table. Here's what the inner join does:

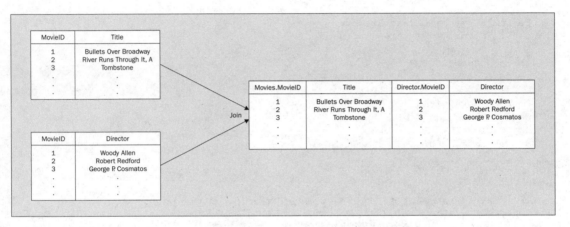

From the resulting table, we'll select the fields corresponding to the Title field of the Movies table and the DirectorName field of the Director table:

```
SELECT Movies.Title, Director.DirectorName ...
```

However, we don't want every record. We only want those records that correspond to the films of Tarantino and Coppola:

```
... WHERE (Director.DirectorName LIKE 'Quentin Tarantino'
    OR  Director.DirectorName LIKE 'Francis Coppola')
```

Having created the join, and indicated the required fields and conditions, the resulting data is put into a single recordset. Then it's just a case of using the default field names to access the values from the recordset. The default field names are taken from the field names of the database tables:

```
While Not objRS.EOF
   Response.Write objRS("Title") & " was directed by " & & _
                  objRS("DirectorName") & "<BR>"
   objRS.MoveNext
```

The UPDATE Command

Let's move on from the SELECT command, to consider the first of the three action commands that we listed earlier in this chapter. The UPDATE command allows you to update the data contained within the data store. This opens the door to a whole new concept for us – making *changes* to the data store itself. Before now, we have only been concerned with reading the data.

SQL's UPDATE statement is used as follows:

UPDATE <table> SET <field_name> <operator> <value>

For example, if you were so inclined you could go through the AllMovies table and change every Director's name to your own:

```
UPDATE AllMovies SET Director = 'Chris Ullman'
```

Of course, it wouldn't be very easy to undo a change like this, so we don't advise that you try it!

The above line can be quite brutal, because it makes the requested change to every single record. Fortunately, the UPDATE command also allows us to specify the exact condition under which records in the table will get changed. The format for this is:

UPDATE <table> SET <field_name> = <value> WHERE <condition>

So you could go ahead and try the following:

```
UPDATE AllMovies SET Director = 'Chris Ullman' WHERE Title LIKE 'Pulp Fiction'
```

OK, once again we've changed the value in the Director field of the AllMovies table, but this time only for any record whose title is Pulp Fiction. As it happens, there's only one record of this description in the AllMovies table – and the Director field of that one record is updated from Quentin Tarantino to Chris Ullman. As in the earlier examples, we've used the LIKE keyword in place of the equality operator (=), though it provides the same functionality.

When you perform an update, you'll probably want to know whether it succeeded and how many records it changed – and in the following example we'll demonstrate how to do that too (you might recall, from our discussions at the beginning of the chapter, that it's the RecordsAffected parameter of the Execute method that allows us to do this).

Try It Out – Running a SQL UPDATE statement

We'll perform two commands in this example. First, we'll find all the records corresponding to films directed by Quentin Tarantino (there are two in this database), and we're going to change the value of the Director field from Quentin Tarantino to some fictional value. The object of this exercise is just to demonstrate how to update records, and how to determine how many of the table's records have been affected.

Then, in order to restore the accuracy of the database, we'll change these values back from our fictional value to Quentin Tarantino.

1. We're going to use the `Movies2000` database and the `strConnect` connection string again, so you'll need the appropriate database files and SSI included (as we have for the other examples in this chapter).

2. Open up your favorite ASP editor, and create the following page (called `SQLUpdate.asp`):

```
<%
  Option Explicit
  Dim strConnect
%>
<!-- #include file="DataStore.asp" -->
<!-- METADATA TYPE="typelib"
             FILE="C:\Program Files\Common Files\System\ado\msado15.dll" -->
<HTML>
<HEAD>
<TITLE>Using SQL's UPDATE Command and the ADO Command Object</TITLE>
</HEAD>
<BODY>
<%
  Dim objComm, intNoOfRecords
  Set objComm = Server.CreateObject("ADODB.Command")

  Response.Write "<B>Harry the Ham directs Tarantino films? </B><BR>"
  objComm.ActiveConnection = strConnect
  objComm.CommandText="UPDATE AllMovies SET Director = 'Harry the Ham' " & _
                     "WHERE Director LIKE 'Quentin Tarantino'"
  objComm.CommandType=adCmdText
  objComm.Execute intNoOfRecords
  Response.Write "This UPDATE command has affected " & _
                  intNoOfRecords & " records<BR><BR>"

  Response.Write "<B>Tarantino returned to his rightful place as director:</B> <BR>"
  objComm.CommandText="UPDATE AllMovies SET Director = 'Quentin Tarantino' " & _
                     "WHERE Director LIKE 'Harry the Ham'"
  objComm.Execute intNoOfRecords
  Response.Write "This UPDATE command has affected " & _
                  intNoOfRecords & " records<BR><BR>"
  Set objComm = Nothing
%>
</BODY>
</HTML>
```

3. Save it as `SQLUpdate.asp` in the usual place – `\inetpub\wwwroot\BegASPFiles`.

4. Now view the page in your browser:

The results indicate that for the first command, two records were affected – and the two records for the two Tarantino films in the `AllMovies` table were updated, with the imposter Harry the Ham instated as director of these films. The second command locates the records that claim that Harry the Ham is director, and reinstates Quentin Tarantino as director. Okay, let's look through the code.

How It Works

We're using a command that does not return a `Recordset` object; in fact, we don't need a recordset at all in this example, so we don't create one. All the changes that we make are made directly, to records that exist the database.

However, we are aiming to return the number of records that have been updated, so we need to define a variable which will hold that total, called `intNoOfRecords`. We also create the `Command` object:

```
Dim objComm, intNoOfRecords
Set objComm = Server.CreateObject("ADODB.Command")
```

Next we set all the properties for the first of our commands. The `ActiveConnection` property takes the value of the connection string, `strConnect`. The `CommandText` property takes the value of the UPDATE command. And the `CommandType` property is `adCmdText`, to reflect the fact that the command is a SQL statement:

```
objComm.ActiveConnection = strConnect
objComm.CommandText="UPDATE AllMovies SET Director = 'Harry the Ham' " & _
                    "WHERE Director LIKE 'Quentin Tarantino'"
objComm.CommandType=adCmdText
```

The command text itself says that it will locate every record in the `AllMovies` table whose `Director` field holds the value `Quentin Tarantino`, and it will change that value to `Harry the Ham`.

Now we execute the command, and return the number of records affected within the variable `intNoOfRecords`:

```
objComm.Execute intNoOfRecords
```

To prove that `intNoOfRecords` really does hold the number of affected records, we'll use it in our report of the command's effect:

```
Response.Write "This UPDATE command has affected " & _
               intNoOfRecords & " records<BR><BR>"
```

This gives us a good way to double-check that the command performed the actions that we expected it to perform. In this case, we know that there are two Tarantino films in the `AllMovies` table, because we've seen them in an earlier example. So if this variable contains a value other than 2, we know that something has gone wrong. If the command has failed in any way, then `intNoOfRecords` won't hold a value. In this case, we've checked by printing the value out, but you might do something subtler, like this:

```
If intNoOfRecords = 2 Then
   Server.Execute Successful.asp
Else
   Server.Execute SomethingWentWrong.asp
End If
```

Next we set about changing those two records back. The `ActiveConnection` and `CommandType` properties are already set, so we only need to change the `CommandText` property before executing this second command:

```
objComm.CommandText="UPDATE AllMovies SET Director = 'Quentin Tarantino' " & _
                    "WHERE Director LIKE 'Harry the Ham'"
objComm.Execute intNoOfRecords
```

Again, we can display the number of affected records:

```
Response.Write "This UPDATE command has affected " & _
               intNoOfRecords & " records<BR><BR>"
```

Using Queries and Stored Procedures

We've seen some examples of SQL `SELECT` commands that return recordsets, and `UPDATE` commands that change the data stored in the database. It's great to have the freedom to write commands straight into our ASP code like that, because (now we are getting a grasp of SQL) it gives us real flexibility to make any queries and changes that our applications require.

But sometimes these queries are rather unwieldy, and sometimes we use them very often. So wouldn't it be nice if we could write a query, give it a name, store it in the database, and then just use the query's name in our ASP code? Well, yes it would – and this functionality is already available in the form of **stored procedures** (as they're known in SQL Server) and **queries** (as they're known in Access) – they're ready-to-run SQL statements.

> *Throughout this chapter, we'll refer to them as stored procedures.*

There are a few good reasons to use stored procedures:

- ❑ First and foremost, it's quicker to run a stored procedure because it's stored in a precompiled form on the database. This means that, unlike the SQL commands that we write in the ASP page, they don't need to be compiled before they can be executed.

- ❑ They make your code more readable (because they're effectively a shorthand).

- ❑ We can reuse the same stored procedures over and over, in many ASP pages.

We're not going to teach you how to write stored procedures in this book. That's really beyond the scope of this title and belongs in the realms of a book on your favorite database server. However, we will see what a simple stored procedure looks like, and we'll demonstrate how to use it within an ASP page.

Using Stored Procedures in ASP Pages

So, assuming we've written a stored procedure, how would we use it in an ASP page? Well, the code doesn't look much different to the samples you've already seen. For example, to run a stored procedure called `usp_NameAndState`, which returns a recordset, you could do this:

```
objCommand.ActiveConnection = strConnect
objCommand.CommandText = "usp_NameAndState"
objCommand.CommandType = adCmdStoredProc
Set objRS = objCommand.Execute
```

Notice that we've used a different `CommandType` value to reflect the fact that this command is in the form of a stored procedure, and not a table or a command string. Other than that, the command structure is just the same as we've seen previously. At this level, there's no difference between an Access query and a SQL Server stored procedure.

Using Parameters

You might think that using stored procedures give you less flexibility because you can't customize them as easily – but this is where the `Parameters` collection comes in. A **parameter** is the means by which we can pass a value into a stored procedure, or receive an output parameter from a stored procedure – in just the same way we pass parameters to functions. So, at design time we write a generic query in the form of a stored procedure; and then at runtime we can use its parameters to pass user-supplied information to and from it.

A Query in Microsoft Access

If you're using the `Movie2000.mdb` file with Microsoft Access, then you'll find that it contains a query already. It's called **qryFilmsByDirector**, and you can view it by opening the `Movie2000.mdb` file using Microsoft Access, selecting **Queries** from the list on the left of the following window, then **qryFilmsByDirector** from the list on the right, and then clicking the **Design** button:

This will present you with the following view. Note, in the **Criteria** field, the string [Director], which indicates that this query expects a parameter – and that the query will search for records whose `Director` field contains the value of that parameter.

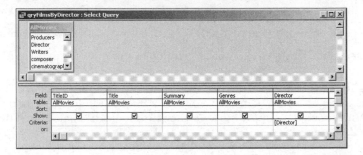

If you wish, you can view the parameters for the query (select **Parameters** from the **Query** menu) and from section; here you are able to specify a data type for the parameter name.

We'll test this out in an ASP page, in a moment; first, let's look at a stored procedure in MSDE.

A Stored Procedure in MSDE

When you're working with a SQL Server/MSDE database, the traditional method for creating a stored procedure is to write the necessary SQL statements yourself, adding the parameters to the declaration. Then you have to add it to your database. In SQL Server you can add a stored procedure to your database simply by selecting **New Stored Procedure** at the **Stored Procedures** icon for your database, entering the code and clicking **OK** (there is also an ISQL tool available). However, with MSDE you don't get this luxury. The good news is that it is possible to use Access as a front end for creating stored procedures with MSDE. If you don't know how to do this, then we suggest you consult Appendix L, which gives you a quick tutorial.

If we wanted to create a stored procedure equivalent to the Access query described above, we'd write a SQL command like this:

```
CREATE PROCEDURE usp_FilmsByDirector
    @Director VarChar(50)
AS
    SELECT    *
    FROM      AllMovies
    WHERE     Director = @Director
    ORDER BY Title
```

This SQL Server stored procedure has the same functionality as the Access query above, so we've given it a similar name: usp_FilmsByDirector. We've already created this stored procedure for you within the Access .mdb file and within the .mdf file for MSDE users. If you are using MSDE you will have to view the stored procedure using an ADP file, which is also available from the Wrox web site (ADP is an Access front-end for MSDE databases). Again, see Appendix L for more details on ADP.

Here the parameter is @Director (note that, in SQL Server-based data stores, parameters are preceded by the @ sign) and is a character string of length 50.

Passing in Parameter Values

If you're writing an ASP page that uses queries or stored procedures that expect parameter values, and your code doesn't provide those parameter values, then the data provider will generate an error message telling you exactly that. If you're querying an Access database for data via an Access query, and you forget to pass the required parameter values, then you'll get an error message like this from the OLE-DB provider for Jet databases:

Error Type:
Microsoft JET Database Engine (0x80040E10)
Parameter Required Director has no default value.
/BegASP/accQueryParam.asp, line 30

Alternatively, if you're querying for data via a SQL Server-based stored procedure, and your code doesn't pass required parameter values, then the OLE-DB provider for SQL Server will tell you something like this:

Error Type:
Microsoft OLE DB Provider for SQL Server (0x80040E10)
Procedure 'usp_FilmsByDirector' expects parameter '@Director', which was not supplied.
/BegASP/StoredProcParam.asp, line 26

In each case, the error message tells you quite clearly that it is expecting a parameter, and that you didn't supply one.

The Parameters Collection

So how *do* we pass parameters into a query that expects them? It's simple: we use the ADO Parameters collection. This is a collection of a number of ADO parameter objects – one for each of the parameters that you wish to pass into a query. The Parameter object has a number of properties that contain the parameter's name, data type, value (etc), and whether the parameter is used to supply data or to return it.

The Parameters collection is a collection of the ADO Command object (as you'll see if you flick back through to the beginning of Chapter 13, to remind yourself of the ADO object model diagram). In other words, the Parameters collection (and its Parameter objects) is only accessible through the Command object. Because parameter-based stored procedures require Parameter objects, this means that you can't use ADO to call parameter-based stored procedures *except* through the Command object. (By contrast, it's possible to call non-parameter-based stored procedures through the methods of the Connection or Recordset object.)

Let's demonstrate a simple parameter-based query. There are a couple of examples in the following pages that do this:

❏ In the first example, we'll write an ASP page that uses the `qryFilmsByDirector` Access query (which is built into `Movie2000.mdb` database file) to ask for data from the `Movie2000.mdb` database.

❏ In the second, we'll write an ASP page that uses the `usp_FilmsByDirector` stored procedure (which is built into `Movie2000.mdf`) to query the MSDE database for the same data.

They're not very different – we've presented the code separately but we'll explain them both together. Choose which of these two examples you want to go with (according to whether you're using Access or MSDE) and away we go.

Try It Out – The Parameters Collection and Access

The Access `Movie2000.mdb` already contains the query called `qryFilmsByDirector` that we outlined above, and we'll use it in this example to fetch some data; then we'll display it in our ASP page.

1. We'll need the Access database `Movie2000.mdb` for this example. We'll also need to check the code in our `DataStore.asp` SSI file, to ensure that the `strConnect` connection string contains the connection details for the Access database (not the MSDE database). You can do that by ensuring the appropriate line is commented out, in `DataStore.asp`:

```
...
  'Choose one of the following two lines, and comment out the other
  strDatabaseType = "Access"
  'strDatabaseType = "SQLServer"
...
```

2. In your trusty ASP editor, create a new file (which we'll call `AccQueryParam.asp`). Add the following code to this new file:

```
<%
  Option Explicit
  Dim strConnect
%>
<!-- #include file="DataStore.asp" -->
<!-- METADATA TYPE="typelib"
            FILE="C:\Program Files\Common Files\System\ado\msado15.dll" -->
<HTML>
<HEAD>
<TITLE>Access Parameter Query</TITLE>
</HEAD>
<BODY>
```

```
<%
  Dim objRS, objComm, objParam, strDirector
  Set objComm = Server.CreateObject("ADODB.Command")

  objComm.ActiveConnection = strConnect     ' fill in the command properties
  objComm.CommandText = "qryFilmsByDirector"
  objComm.CommandType = adCmdStoredProc

  ' now the parameters (actually, there's only one parameter here)
  Set objParam = _
    objComm.CreateParameter("Required Director", adVarChar, adParamInput, 50)
  objComm.Parameters.Append objParam

  strDirector = "Quentin Tarantino"           ' you can change this if you like
  objComm.Parameters("Required Director") = strDirector

  Set objRS = objComm.Execute      ' execute the command and generate the recordset

  Set objComm = Nothing        ' don't need the Command and Parameter objects
  Set objParam = Nothing        ' ... so we can clean them up

  Response.Write "<H2>Films by " & strDirector & ":</H2>"
  While Not objRS.EOF           ' now loop through the records
    Response.Write objRS("Title") & ", directed by " & objRS("Director") & "<BR>"
    objRS.MoveNext
  Wend

  objRS.Close        ' now close and clean up
  Set objRS = Nothing
%>
</BODY>
</HTML>
```

3. Save the AccQueryParam.asp file into the \inetpub\wwwroot\BegASPFiles folder. Then use your browser to view the page:

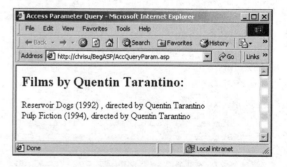

Notice that this shows only the films in which the Director field is equal to Quentin Tarantino – the query has picked out all the Tarantino films stored in the AllTitles table of the database. We'll explain the structure of the code in a moment. First, we'll try another one, this time using the MSDE.

Again, the SQL Server Movie2000.mdf already has a stored procedure, named usp_FilmsByDirector, installed. We'll use it here to query the database for some specific data, and then we'll display the retrieved data in the page.

1. This example uses the MSDE data source with the Movie2000.mdf database file; so check the code in our DataStore.asp SSI file to ensure that the strConnect connection string contains the connection details for the MSDE database (not the Access database). You can do that by ensuring the appropriate lines are commented out, in DataStore.asp:

```
...
'Choose one of the following two lines, and comment out the other
'strDatabaseType = "Access"
strDatabaseType = "SQLServer"
...
```

2. Now we'll create the main ASP file. In your editor, create a new file (which we'll call StoredProcParam.asp). This ASP page should contain the following code. In fact, it's almost the same as the Access-based AccQueryParam.asp example above, so I've highlighted the lines that are different:

```
<%
  Option Explicit
  Dim strConnect
%>
<!-- #include file="DataStore.asp" -->
<!-- METADATA TYPE="typelib"
            FILE="C:\Program Files\Common Files\System\ado\msado15.dll" -->
<HTML>
<HEAD>
<TITLE>Access Parameter Query</TITLE>
</HEAD>
<BODY>

<%
  Dim objRS, objComm, objParam, strDirector
  Set objComm = Server.CreateObject("ADODB.Command")

  objComm.ActiveConnection = strConnect     ' fill in the command properties
  objComm.CommandText = "usp_FilmsByDirector"
  objComm.CommandType = adCmdStoredProc

  ' now the parameters (actually, there's only one parameter here)
  Set objParam = _
     objComm.CreateParameter("@Director", adVarChar, adParamInput, 50)
  objComm.Parameters.Append objParam
```

```
    strDirector = "Quentin Tarantino"          ' you can change this if you like
    objComm.Parameters("@Director") = strDirector

    Set objRS = objComm.Execute     ' execute the command and generate the recordset

    Set objComm = Nothing          ' don't need the Command and Parameter objects
    Set objParam = Nothing         ' ... so we can clean them up

    Response.Write "<H2>Films by " & strDirector & ":</H2>"
    While Not objRS.EOF            ' now loop through the records
      Response.Write objRS("Title") & ", directed by " & objRS("Director") & "<BR>"
      objRS.MoveNext
    Wend

    objRS.Close          ' now close and clean up
    Set objRS = Nothing
%>
</BODY>
</HTML>
```

3. Save the `StoredProcParam.asp` file into the `\inetpub\wwwroot\BegASPFiles` directory and then view the page from your browser. The result should look like the previous screenshot.

You might like to try changing the value of the `strDirector` string from `Quentin Tarantino` to `Woody Allen`, just to prove that you can control the parameter value using the ASP logic – and more importantly, without amending the stored procedure itself.

How It Works

As we said before introducing the code, these two examples are very similar – the only difference being in the name of the precompiled query/stored procedure, and in the name of the parameter.

There's no change to the header, so we'll just skip that, and jump straight into the meat of the code. First, we declare the variants that we'll need – for the three ADO objects and a string to hold the parameter value. Then we set one of them, `objComm`, to point to an ADO `Command` object:

```
Dim objRS, objComm, objParam, strDirector
Set objComm = Server.CreateObject("ADODB.Command")
```

We don't need to set the other two ADO objects yet – that will come in a moment.

Now we can start to set up all the properties of our `Command` object. We start with the `ActiveConnection`, `CommandText` and `CommandType` properties (that we've met in previous examples). This is the code from the example that uses Access (the MSDE example uses extremely similar code:

589

```
objComm.ActiveConnection = strConnect     ' fill in the command properties
objComm.CommandText = "qryFilmsByDirector"
objComm.CommandType = adCmdStoredProc
```

The `ActiveConnection` is set equal to the connection string found in `strConnect`; the `CommandText` is set to the name of our Access query or stored procedure; and the `CommandType` is set to the ADO constant `adCmdStoredProc`, to indicate to ADO that we're using a stored procedure.

The next step is to create our parameter. For each parameter we need, we'll add an ADO `Parameter` object to the `Parameters` collection. This process has two stages: in the first stage we create a standalone `Parameter` object and define it by applying values to its properties; and in the second step we append our `Parameter` object to the `Parameters` collection.

Here's the first of these two stages. We use the `Command` object's `CreateParameter` method to create a standalone `Parameter` object, and we give it the name `objParam`:

```
Set objParam = _
    objComm.CreateParameter("Required Director", adVarChar, adParamInput, 50)
```

We've passed four values to the `CreateParameter` method – giving the parameter name (which is `Required Director` for Access and `@Director` for MSDE), its data type (`adVarChar` signifies a character string), the input/output type (`adParamInput` signifies that it's an input parameter – more on that later) and the maximum size of the value (50 characters in this case, though you can give a byte value).

> *We'll look at the `CreateParameter` method in more detail after we've completed this example.*

Now we've built the parameter, we can append it to the `Parameters` collection by using the `Command` object's `Append` method:

```
objComm.Parameters.Append objParam
```

Next, we'll give the input parameter a value. In this case we're passing a variable that contains a character string:

```
strDirector = "Quentin Tarantino"          ' you can change this if you like
objComm.Parameters("Required Director") = strDirector
```

We only need one parameter so we can now execute the query. To do that, we use the `Execute` method, as we've seen before. Because we're selecting data, the results of the query are returned to us in an ADO `Recordset` object. We'll use the variant `objRS` to point to that `Recordset` object:

```
Set objRS = objComm.Execute        ' execute the command and generate the recordset
```

Now we've got our recordset, the job of our `Command` and `Parameter` objects is complete. We don't need them again in this example, so we'll set the variants to `Nothing`:

```
Set objComm = Nothing          ' don't need the Command and Parameter objects
Set objParam = Nothing         ' ... so we can clean them up
```

Now we'll display the contents of our recordset in the page:

```
Response.Write "<H2>Films by " & strDirector & ":</H2>"
While Not objRS.EOF              ' now loop through the records
  Response.Write objRS("Title") & ", directed by " & objRS("Director") & "<BR>"
  objRS.MoveNext
Wend
```

Finally, we can clean up the `Recordset` object:

```
objRS.Close          ' now close and clean up
Set objRS = Nothing
```

Creating Parameters

Let's look at that `CreateParameter` method in more detail. The full syntax for the method is as follows:

Set *objRS* = *objComm*.`CreateParameter`(*Name*, *Type*, *Direction*, *Size*, *Value*)

There are five parameters to the `CreateParameter` method:

❑ The first, *Name*, can be used to specify the name of the parameter, as defined in the query or stored procedure

❑ The second, *Type*, can be used to define the data type of the parameter value. (For a full list of these constants, see the `DataTypeEnum` list in the ADO constants file, `adovbs.inc`)

❑ The third, *Direction*, can be used to specify whether the parameter is used to *send* data to the procedure, or *return* data from the procedure, or both

❑ The fourth, *Size*, can be used to specify the maximum of the parameter's value, in terms of the length of a character string or number of bytes. This is most useful for text parameters.

❑ The fifth, *Value*, can be used to specify the value of the parameter.

In fact, all five of these parameters are optional. In the examples above, we specified four of them but not the fifth – choosing instead to specify the parameter's value *after* we'd appended the `Parameter` object to the `Parameters` collection. There are many other ways to go about this. For example, you might choose to create the `Parameter` object without setting any of its properties, and then set the properties in several subsequent lines of code:

```
Set objParam = objComm.CreateParameter
objParam.Name = "@Director"
objParam.Type = adVarChar
objParam.Size = 50
objParam.Direction = adParamInput
objParam.Value = "Quentin Tarantino"
```

At the other extreme, you might choose to use the `Append` method first, to add an 'anonymous' `Parameter` object to the `Parameters` collection, which is then created and defined within the same statement using the `CreateParameter` method:

```
objComm.Parameters.Append objComm.CreateParameter("@Director", _
                                adVarChar, adInput, 50, "Quentin Tarantino")
```

Output Parameters

As well as returning data (which we've seen), SQL Server stored procedures are able to return values in the form of **output parameters**. For example, using the `Movie2000` database, suppose we wanted a count of all movies in the database that were made by a particular director.

One way of obtaining this value would be via a SQL stored procedure like this one:

```
CREATE PROCEDURE usp_NumberOfMovies
    @Director varchar(50)
AS
SELECT COUNT(*)
FROM    AllMovies
WHERE  Director LIKE @Director
```

When we run this stored procedure from our code, it will return a recordset containing just one column and one row (and hence one cell). The single cell in that recordset would contain the value we're after, which in this case is 2. We could call this by using the `Execute` method of the `Command` object, and passing in the name of the director in whom we are interested.

But there's another way – we can cut out the need to deal with a recordset, and use an output parameter instead. For this, we'd use a slightly different stored procedure, like this:

```
CREATE PROCEDURE usp_NumberOfMovies
    @Director  varchar(50),
    @Number    int OUTPUT
AS
SELECT @Number = COUNT(*)
FROM    AllMovies
WHERE  Director LIKE @Director
```

Here, the second parameter is an `OUTPUT` parameter, which means that during the course of the stored procedure we can assign a value to that parameter, and that value will be returned to the calling program when the procedure has finished executing. Our ASP code to call this stored procedure might look something like this:

```
Dim intNumber, objComm
Set objComm = Server.CreateObject ("ADODB.Command")
objComm.ActiveConnection = strConnect
objComm.CommandText = "usp_NumberOfMovies"
objComm.CommandType = adCmdStoredProc

objComm.Parameters.Append objComm.CreateParameter("@Director", adVarChar, _
                          adParamInput, 50, "Quentin Tarantino")
objComm.Parameters.Append objComm.CreateParameter("@Number", adInteger, adParamOutput)

objComm.Execute
intNumber = objComm.Parameters("@Number")
```

Here, we've used the `Append` and `CreateParameter` methods twice – once to append the input parameter `@Director` to the `Parameters` collection, and once to append the output parameter `@Number` to the collection. Note that the order of parameters in the collection is the same as the order of parameters in the stored procedure. In particular, for the second parameter we've specified that the *Direction* parameter should be `adParamOutput` (to match the fact that the second parameter of the stored procedure is an OUTPUT parameter).

You can also see that, in the ASP code, we haven't specified a value for the output parameter. However, after the command has been executed the output parameter will hold a value, and this value is returned from the stored procedure.

Return Values

In addition to returning output parameter values, a stored procedure can also return a **return value**. This is a special kind of parameter, which does pretty much the same job as an output parameter, but it allows us to assign a data type to the value that we have returned. If you tried this with the output parameter in the example above, then if you tried to assign a type other than `adInteger` (which is defined within the stored procedure) you'd create an error.

When a stored procedure returns such a value, then it is always the *first-named* parameter (i.e. the 'zero parameter' – parameter lists are zero-based) in the `Parameters` collection. When we append a return value parameter to the `Parameters` collection, we distinguish it by specifying a *Direction* of `adParamReturnValue`:

```
objComm.CreateParameter("Return", adVarChar, adParamReturnValue, 8)
```

This creates a return value parameter that is a character string of eight characters. Because the return value is the first in the `Parameters` collection, you must append it before appending any other `Parameter` objects.

> Let me emphasize once more that the order in which you append parameters to the `Command` object is very important. The order of parameters in the stored procedure must be the same as that in the `Parameters` collection, and a return value parameter (if there is one) must always be first.

Once the command has run you can access this parameter like any other:

```
strReturn = objComm.Parameters("Return")
```

or:

```
strReturn = objComm.Parameters(0)
```

Asking for the Parameters

If you don't want to go to the bother of adding parameters for a parameterized query, you can use the `Parameters` collection's `Refresh` method, to tell ADO to query the data provider for the parameter details. For example:

```
objComm.Parameters.Refresh
```

ADO then contacts the data provider and updates the `Parameter` objects in the `Parameters` collection for you. You can then access a parameter by ordinal number (or name), assign a value to it and execute the command. For example:

```
objComm.Parameters.Refresh
objComm.Parameters(1).Value = "Quentin Tarantino"
```

This allows you to avoid getting bogged down by the details of the parameters. In particular, if you're working with a single `Command` object and a number of different stored procedures, then the `Refresh` method is a quick-and-clean way to set up your `Parameters` collection with the appropriate parameters. You can do this just before each new stored procedure call. It's also extremely useful if you are having problems in setting the correct data types and sizes. If you find that you're getting a lot of errors because your parameter settings aren't right, try using a `Refresh` instead and then print out the data types and values from the properties of the resulting `Parameter` objects.

The `Refresh` method is a useful tool, but it does come at a price in terms of performance. Each time you call the `Refresh` method, ADO makes a trip to the data store to extract the parameter information. The more you use it in your code, the slower your code will run. Also, you should be aware that some data sources, such as SQL Server 6.5, don't support the `Refresh` method. As such, it's well worth considering in a development environment, but when you come to write the code for your public web site then it's probably worthwhile using the `CreateParameter` and `Append` methods to build your parameters.

Modifying Data

We've covered a myriad of ways of getting data out of data stores, and we've touched on just one technique for changing the data in a data store (via the `Command` object's `Execute` method, and a SQL `UPDATE` command). But as you've probably guessed by now, ADO gives us other ways to "change" the contents of a data store.

The act of changing the data in the data store can itself be broken up into three types of changes – **updating** existing data, **adding** new data, and **removing** existing data. These are the three activities we referred to earlier in the chapter as the **action commands**. We can perform all three of these activities using the `Command` object – using the `UPDATE`, `INSERT` and `DELETE` SQL commands, respectively. However, we can also perform them using the special properties of the `Recordset` object, or by passing the appropriate SQL command to the `Connection` object's `Execute` method.

We can't demonstrate all these possibilities in this book, so we're going to be selective. In this section, we'll see how to add and delete records from a recordset (and ultimately the data store) through the methods and properties of a `Recordset` object. Later, we'll perform similar tasks by writing some SQL commands and using them with the `Command` object.

Adding Data Using a Recordset

This is where the `AddNew` and `Update` methods come in. Let's jump straight in by running an example that adds a record to the `Movies` table of the `Movie2000` database.

Try It Out – Adding New Records

1. We'll use the `Movies` database and the `strConnect` connection string that we've used many times before in these ADO examples. Check that your `Movie2000.mdb` or `Movie2000.mdf` file is set up as described in Chapter 12, and that the `DataStore.asp` SSI file is situated in the `\inetpub\wwwroot\BegASPFiles` folder.

2. In your editor, create a new file (which we'll call `AddNew.asp`) and add the following code:

```
<%
  Option Explicit
  Dim strConnect
%>
<!-- #include file="DataStore.asp" -->
<!-- METADATA TYPE="typelib"
            FILE="C:\Program Files\Common Files\System\ado\msado15.dll" -->
<HTML>
<HEAD>
<TITLE>Adding a New Record</TITLE>
</HEAD>
<BODY>
<%
  Dim objRS, intIDForNewRecord
  Set objRS = Server.CreateObject ("ADODB.Recordset")
  objRS.Open "Movies", strConnect, adOpenStatic, adLockOptimistic, adCmdTable

  objRS.MoveLast
  intIDForNewRecord = objRS("MovieID") + 1
```

```
objRS.AddNew            ' add a new record
objRS("MovieID") = intIDForNewRecord
objRS("Title") = "Psycho"
objRS.Update
objRS.Close

objRS.Open "SELECT * FROM Movies WHERE MovieID=" & intIDForNewRecord, _
               strConnect, adOpenForwardOnly, adLockReadOnly, adCmdText
If objRS.EOF Then
  Response.Write "New record not found - something went wrong"
Else
  Response.Write "You've successfully added a new record:<BR> " & _
               "Movie title = '" & objRS("Title") & "'<BR>" & _
               "MovieID = "       & objRS("MovieID")
End If

objRS.Close        ' now close and clean up
Set objRS = Nothing
%>
</BODY>
</HTML>
```

3. Save the `AddNew.asp` file to the `\inetpub\wwwroot\BegASPFiles` and open your browser to view the page:

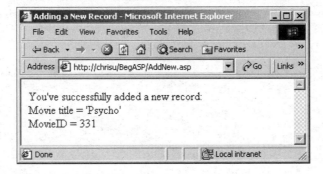

How It Works

As usual we start with a couple of variable declarations, and then create a `Recordset` object:

```
Dim objRS, intIDForNewRecord
Set objRS = Server.CreateObject ("ADODB.Recordset")
```

Then we open the recordset, so that it contains the data from the `Movies` table. Notice that this is a static recordset with optimistic locking. All our other recordsets have been read-only, but that won't do if we are intending to make changes to the data store:

```
objRS.Open "Movies", strConnect, adOpenStatic, adLockOptimistic, adCmdTable
```

With the recordset open, we're going to move directly to the last record in the recordset, make a note of its `MovieID` value, and add one to that value. We'll use this in a moment to create the new record:

```
objRS.MoveLast
intIDForNewRecord = objRS("MovieID") + 1
```

Now we can add the new data to the recordset. The `AddNew` method creates a new, empty record within the recordset:

```
objRS.AddNew          ' add a new record
```

This gives us a new record in the recordset, and so we can add some new data to its fields. And here's a clever bit: when the `AddNew` method has added the new record to the recordset, it *assumes* that we're going to do some work on it – so it *also* points the cursor at the new record. So, we're ready to add the new data straight away:

```
objRS("MovieID") = intIDForNewRecord
objRS("Title") = "Psycho"
```

For the `MovieID` field, we're using the value that we assigned to `intIDForNewRecord` that we calculated a moment ago. This is an integer value which is one more than the `MovieID` of the previous last record in the recordset. In this case, that should be enough to keep the `MovieID` fields of this table unique.

> In Access, MSDE, and other database software, it's possible to configure the fields that must contain unique values so that these values are automatically generated whenever a new field is created. For simplicity, we've avoided that here. In Chapter 15, the `Classified.mdb` database file uses autogenerated field values.

Now, at this stage, we've only added the data to the *recordset* – the data store hasn't seen this new record yet. In order to tell the data store of our changes, we must call the `Update` method:

```
objRS.Update
```

Now we'll prove that the new record really has entered the database. To do this, we'll `Close` the recordset to disconnect it from the database, then `Open` it again to reconnect (this time using a forward-only read-only cursor, and using a SQL command to select only the new record):

```
objRS.Close

objRS.Open "SELECT * FROM Movies WHERE MovieID=" & intIDForNewRecord, _
                strConnect, adOpenForwardOnly, adLockReadOnly, adCmdText
If objRS.EOF Then
  Response.Write "New record not found - something went wrong"
Else
  Response.Write "You've successfully added a new record:<BR> " & _
                "Movie title = '" & objRS("Title") & "'<BR>" & _
                "MovieID = "       & objRS("MovieID")
End If
```

The newly opened recordset contains fresh data from the database – so if it contains a record with the `MovieID` value equal to `intIDForNewRecord`, we can conclude that the earlier `Update` method successfully added our new record to the database. The browser output will confirm that for us. Finally, we can clean up the `Recordset` object:

```
objRS.Close          ' now close and clean up
Set objRS = Nothing
```

Updating Existing Data

Updating an existing database record involves almost the same process, except there's no new record to add so you don't need to issue an `AddNew` call. Once you've got a recordset containing the data that you want to change, you make the changes within the recordset (by maneuvering the cursor to the record in question, and applying the changes to the record) and then using the `Update` method to update those changes to the database itself:

For example, this amends the record in the recordset by changing the value of the `Genre` field to `Thriller`, and then updates the database with that change:

```
objRS("Genre").Value = "Thriller"
objRS.Update
```

It's also worth noting that if you make changes to your recordset and then call any of the `Move...` methods, the `Move...` method call will implicitly call the `Update` method and update the data store. So for example, the following two lines have the effect of changing the value in the `Genre` field, updating that change in the database and then moving the cursor to the first record in the recordset:

```
objRS("Genre").Value = "Thriller"
objRS.MoveFirst
```

There's one exception to this, which is when you're working in batch update mode.

Batch Updates

If you're working in **batch update** mode, it means that you can make multiple changes to multiple records in the recordset and then send *all* of those changes back to the data store *in one go*. In other words, ADO doesn't update the data store every time you move from one record to another – it just waits until you use the `UpdateBatch` method to update the entire batch of changes.

If you want to use batch update mode, you need to set the `LockType` property of the recordset to be `adLockBatchOptimistic`. For example, you can do this in the fourth parameter of the `Open` method when you open a recordset:

```
objRS.Open "Movies", strConnect, adOpenStatic, adLockBatchOptimistic, adCmdTable
```

Having made some changes to the recordset, you can choose to update the data store by calling the `UpdateBatch` method. The `UpdateBatch` method has one optional parameter, which (if you use it) can take one of the following ADO constant values:

❏ `adAffectCurrent`, which means that the update will note which record the cursor is currently pointing to, and will only write changes relating to that record

❏ `adAffectGroup`, which means that the update will write changes to records that match the current `Filter` property

❏ `adAffectAll`, which means that the update will write all pending changes (this is the default value)

So you could have some code like this:

```
objRS.Open "Genres", strConnect, adOpenStatic, adLockBatchOptimistic, asCmdTable

objRS("Genre").Value = "Horror"
objRS.MoveNext                      ' doesn't update
objRS("Genre").Value = "Comedy"
objRS.UpdateBatch adAffectAll       ' updates all changes since the previous update
```

Cancelling Changes

You'll notice that, when you make changes to a record in the recordset, those changes aren't updated on the data store immediately. In fact, they're not made until you call another method (such as `Update` or `MoveFirst`, for example). This means that, having made the changes on the recordset, you have a chance to undo those changes before they reach the recordset. In order to undo those changes, we use the `CancelUpdate` method:

```
If blnMakeTheChange = "True" Then
  objRS.Update
  Response.Write "Data store updated"
Else
  objRS.CancelUpdate
  Response.Write "Changes to recordset undone; changes to data store not made "
End If
```

The `CancelUpdate` method undoes all the changes made to the recordset since the last time the data store was updated.

If you're making changes in batch update mode, the get-out clause involves the `CancelBatch` method instead:

```
objRS.CancelBatch adAffectAll
```

Like `UpdateBatch`, the parameter is optional and can take any of the values `adAffectCurrent`, `adAffectGroup` or `adAffectAll`.

Deleting Records Using a Recordset

Next, we come to **deleting** records. You probably won't be surprised to learn that there is a `Delete` method for the recordset:

```
objRS.Delete
```

This statement deletes the record that the cursor is currently pointing to. The record is deleted immediately (unless you are in batch update mode – in which case the `Delete` requests remain pending until you call the `UpdateBatch` method). If you're deleting records in batch update mode, you can filter the recordset using `adFilterPendingRecords` to show only the records that have been deleted.

Let's look at an example in which we delete a record. I don't know how many times you ran the `AddNew.asp` example above, but every time you refreshed the page you will have added another record to the `Movies` table (each new record having a unique `MovieID` value and a `Title` of 'Psycho'). Whether you created one new record, or lots of them, we don't really want to include Psycho in our database so let's delete any records referring to Psycho now.

Try It Out – Deleting our previously added record

1. We'll assume by now that you've got your `Movie2000.mdb` or `Movie2000.mdf` database file set up, along with the `DataStore.asp` SSI file.

2. Open up a new file, which we'll call `Delete.asp`, and insert the following code:

```
<%
  Option Explicit
  Dim strConnect
%>
<!-- #include file="DataStore.asp" -->
<!-- METADATA TYPE="typelib"
            FILE="C:\Program Files\Common Files\System\ado\msado15.dll" -->
<HTML>
<HEAD>
<TITLE>Adding a New Record</TITLE>
</HEAD>
<BODY>
<%
  Dim objRS, intIDForNewRecord
  Set objRS = Server.CreateObject("ADODB.Recordset")

  objRS.Open "Movies", strConnect, adOpenDynamic, adLockOptimistic, adCmdTable

  objRS.Filter = "Title = 'Psycho'"
  Response.Write "We'll delete all of the following records:<BR> "
  While Not objRs.EOF
    Response.Write objRS("MovieID") & "<BR>"
    objRS.Delete
    objRS.MoveNext
    Wend
```

```
    objRS.Close

    Response.Write "<BR>Just to check:<BR>"
    objRS.Open "SELECT * FROM Movies WHERE Title LIKE 'Psycho'", _
               strConnect, adOpenForwardOnly, adLockReadOnly, adCmdText
    If objRS.EOF Then
      Response.Write "All records of Psycho have been removed from the database<BR> "
    Else
      Response.Write "Psycho still exists in the database, " & _
                 "at the record with MovieID=" & objRS("MovieID")
    End If
    objRS.Close        ' now close and clean up
    Set objRS = Nothing
%>
</BODY>
</HTML>
```

3. Save `Delete.asp` into the `\inetpub\wwwroot\BegASPFiles` folder, and open it up in your browser. In this screenshot, you can see that I was a bit enthusiastic when testing `AddNew.asp`, and I managed to create four records containing the film 'Psycho'. However, `Delete.asp` has deleted them all.

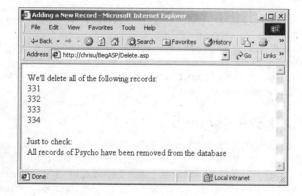

How It Works

We start by opening a recordset that contains all the records of the `Movies` table:

```
    objRS.Open "Movies", strConnect, adOpenDynamic, adLockOptimistic, adCmdTable
```

Now we apply a filter to hide all records except those whose title is 'Psycho':

```
    objRS.Filter = "Title = 'Psycho'"
```

Now we'll loop through the filtered records. We'll display the `MovieID` of each record, and then we'll delete it from the recordset:

```
    Response.Write "We'll delete all of the following records:<BR> "
    While Not objRs.EOF
      Response.Write objRS("MovieID") & "<BR>"
      objRS.Delete
      objRS.MoveNext
    Wend
```

We're not working in batch update mode (because the recordset was not opened using adOpenBatchOptimistic), so we don't need to call the UpdateBatch method – the deletions are passed to the database automatically.

Now, we'll check that it worked. We'll close the recordset and reopen it with fresh information from the database, asking for any records of Psycho in the database. There shouldn't be any such records, and therefore EOF should be true and we'll get the output message we want:

```
objRS.Close

Response.Write "<BR>Just to check:<BR>"
objRS.Open "SELECT * FROM Movies WHERE Title LIKE 'Psycho'", _
              strConnect, adOpenForwardOnly, adLockReadOnly, adCmdText
If objRS.EOF Then
   Response.Write "All records of Psycho have been removed from the database<BR> "
Else
   Response.Write "Something went wrong. Psycho still exists in the database, " & _
              "at the record with MovieID=" & objRS("MovieID")
End If
objRS.Close        ' now close and clean up
Set objRS = Nothing
```

Using SQL Commands to Insert and Delete Data

The Recordset object, being arguably the central object in ADO, is the one that features the special methods like AddNew, Update and Delete that enable us to insert and delete records easily. But as you'd expect, there's more than one way. In this section we'll demonstrate that we can use SQL commands to do the job too.

The INSERT and DELETE Commands

We've already seen the SQL SELECT and UPDATE commands in action, and now we'll look at two more: INSERT and DELETE. We'll demonstrate these together, since they obviously have complementary abilities. The INSERT and DELETE statements perform the same functions as the AddNew and Delete methods of the Recordset object that we've just discussed.

In SQL, the INSERT command takes the following structure:

INSERT INTO <table> (<fields>) VALUES (<values>)

Here, <fields> is a list consisting of none, some, or all of the fields on the table, and <values> is a list of the values that are to be assigned to those fields. Be careful to get the <fields> and their corresponding <values> in the same order! Here's an example:

```
INSERT INTO Movies (MovieId, Title) VALUES (331, 'Psycho')
```

Bear in mind that the MovieId field is intended to be a unique identifier (although in this database it is not actually defined as a primary key) in the Movies table so each value entered should be unique. We can only enter the value '331' here because we know for a fact that this value doesn't currently exist for this field. A much better way of maintaining a unique field, as you will see in Chapter 15, is to let the database generate the value.

If you omit a field, then a NULL (unknown) value will be inserted into that field. Beware that some fields are specifically unable to accept a NULL value (such as a primary key field) – and if you don't specify a value for such a field then your command will be rejected. The existence of 'non-NULL' fields within your database will depend on how your database was designed.

The SQL DELETE command is even easier to use. It takes the following format:

DELETE FROM (*<table>*) WHERE (*<condition>*)

You can only use DELETE to delete one or more *whole* records from the database. In particular, if you want to remove values from a number of the fields in a record then DELETE is the wrong thing to use – you need to assign specific 'empty' values to those fields instead.

We can use the DELETE command to delete multiple values at the same time, so be careful when specifying criteria. Make sure that your criteria are specific enough – otherwise you may find yourself deleting records that you really wanted to keep. If we were to DELETE the above record from the table we could use:

```
DELETE FROM AllMovies WHERE Title LIKE 'Psycho'
```

This would delete the record that we created with the INSERT command above (and it would also delete any other records in the AllMovies table whose Title value was equal to Psycho!). To give a brief demonstration, let's look at an example that inserts a record, displays it and then deletes it.

Try It Out – Running the SQL INSERT and DELETE statements

This example uses a single ADO Command object to execute three different SQL commands at different times: first an INSERT, then a SELECT (which returns a recordset), and finally a DELETE.

1. We're using the Movies database and the strConnect connection string again, so have the DataStore.asp SSI file and either Movie2000.mdb or Movie2000.mdf at the ready!

2. Start up your favorite ASP editor and create the following code (which we'll call SQLInsertDelete.asp):

```asp
<%
  Option Explicit
  Dim strConnect
%>
<!-- #include file="DataStore.asp" -->
<!-- METADATA TYPE="typelib"
              FILE="C:\Program Files\Common Files\System\ado\msado15.dll" -->
<HTML>
<HEAD>
<TITLE>Using SQL and the Command Object</TITLE>
</HEAD>
<BODY>
<%
  Dim objRS, objComm, intNoOfRecords
  Set objComm = Server.CreateObject("ADODB.Command")

  objComm.ActiveConnection = strConnect
  objComm.CommandText = "INSERT INTO Movies(MovieId, Title) VALUES (331, 'Psycho')"
  objComm.CommandType = adCmdText
  objComm.Execute intNoOfRecords
  Response.Write "The INSERT command has been executed; " & _
                 "Number of records inserted = " & intNoOfRecords & "<HR>"

  objComm.CommandText = "SELECT * FROM Movies WHERE Title LIKE 'Psycho'"
  Set objRS = objComm.Execute
  Response.Write "The SELECT command has been executed, " & _
                 "and has selected the following records: <BR>"
  While Not objRS.EOF
    Response.Write "MovieID = " & objRS("MovieID") & _
                   "; Title = " & objRS("Title") & "<BR>"
    objRS.MoveNext
  Wend

  objRS.Close
  Set objRS = Nothing

  objComm.CommandText = "DELETE FROM Movies WHERE Title LIKE 'Psycho'"
  objComm.Execute intNoOfRecords
  Response.Write "<HR>The DELETE command has been executed, " & _
                 "Number of records deleted = " & intNoOfRecords & "<BR>"

  Set objComm = Nothing
%>
</BODY>
</HTML>
```

3. Save `SQLInsertDelete.asp` into your `\inetpub\wwwroot\BegASPFiles` folder. Now view it in your browser.

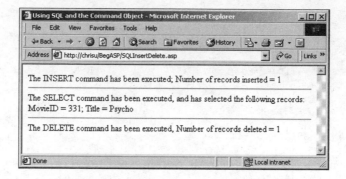

How It Works

We'll ignore the lines that set up the database, as they'll be very familiar by now. The first line of interest is where we set up the first of our three commands – the `INSERT` – which inserts an entry for Psycho into the `Movie2000` database:

```
objComm.ActiveConnection = strConnect
objComm.CommandText = "INSERT INTO Movies(MovieId, Title) VALUES (331, 'Psycho')"
objComm.CommandType = adCmdText
```

We also use the `CommandType` property to indicate that the command is a SQL statement. We then execute our `INSERT` command, and specify a variable to capture the value of the `RercordsAffected` parameter, which will inform us of how many records were affected by the action. We can use that captured information in our report of the command's execution:

```
objComm.Execute intNoOfRecords
Response.Write "The INSERT command has been executed; " & _
               "Number of records inserted = " & intNoOfRecords & "<HR>"
```

Now we set up the second command – the `SELECT` command, which will select only our new record from the data store:

```
objComm.CommandText = "SELECT * FROM Movies WHERE Title LIKE 'Psycho'"
```

Note that we don't need to set the `ActiveConnection` and `CommandType` properties – they will retain the values we set earlier on in the page.

The `SELECT` statement looks for any movies with the title 'Psycho' and displays all of the information in the associated record. We then execute the command. Of course, because it's a `SELECT` it returns a recordset, which we capture:

```
Set objRS = objComm.Execute
```

Now we'll quickly report the contents of the recordset, just to show that the new record really does exist in the data store:

```
        Response.Write "The SELECT command has been executed, " & _
                       "and has selected the following records: <BR>"
    While Not objRS.EOF
      Response.Write "MovieID = " & objRS("MovieID") & _
                     "; Title = " & objRS("Title") & "<BR>"
      objRS.MoveNext
    Wend

    objRS.Close
    Set objRS = Nothing
```

After we've written this report we've finished with the objRS recordset, so we remove it from memory.

Lastly, we re-assign the CommandText property to the third of out SQL commands – the DELETE command, which deletes every record whose title is 'Psycho'. Again, we don't need to re-assign the values of the ActiveConnection and CommandType properties. We execute the command and return the number of records affected to demonstrate the success of the operation:

```
    objComm.CommandText = "DELETE FROM Movies WHERE Title LIKE 'Psycho'"
    objComm.Execute intNoOfRecords
    Response.Write "<HR>The DELETE command has been executed, " & _
                   "Number of records deleted = " & intNoOfRecords & "<BR>"
```

Using the User's Choices to Customize the Page

You probably noticed that in some of the ADO examples you've seen over the last three chapters, the requests for data were hard-coded into the ASP code – and thus the user had no control over them. This isn't really a great technique for interactive web sites – we want to give the user a chance to decide for themselves what data they want!

One of the great things about the ASP/ADO combination is that we can use it to offer the user as little or as much control of the page's content as we like. In this example we'll write a page that displays data from the AllMovies table – but allows the user to decide exactly *what* data they want to see. When they've submitted their choices, we'll use them to build up a SQL SELECT statement, and thus create a table of their records.

The user interface in this example is blunt and direct. There's no subtlety about it – it just asks the user to select the name of a director (using a text box) and one or more field names (using a set of checkboxes). However, when you design your own pages, you don't *have* to be so rough-and-ready: you can design a more attractive, easy-to-use interface that still offers choices to the user. Underneath, you can submit those choices using much the same technique we see here.

Try It Out – A Customized Recordset

1. We're using the AllMovies table of the Movies database and the strConnect connection string again, so you'll need the DataStore.asp SSI file and either Movie2000.mdb or Movie2000.mdf as described in Chapter 12.

2. We'll also be using the `RecToTable.asp` SSI file from Chapter 13 (recall that this file contains a procedure called `RecToTable()`, which accepts a single parameter (an ADO `Recordset` object) and uses it's contents to generate an HTML table of data). So make sure that `RecToTable.asp` is also present in your `\inetpub\wwwroot\BegASPFiles` folder.

3. In your editor, create a new file (which we'll call `FindByDirector.asp`) and add the following code:

```
<%
  Option Explicit
  Dim strConnect
%>
<!-- #include file="DataStore.asp" -->
<!-- METADATA TYPE="typelib"
            FILE="C:\Program Files\Common Files\System\ado\msado15.dll" -->
<!-- #INCLUDE FILE="RecToTable.asp" -->
<HTML>
<HEAD>
<TITLE>Find Director</TITLE>
</HEAD>
<BODY>
<%
  Dim strSQL             ' SQL String
  Dim objRS, objField    ' ADO Recordset and Field objects
  Dim intCount           ' number of fields selected
  Dim vbQuote            ' quote character
  vbQuote = Chr(34)


  Response.Write "<H2>Find Movies by Director</H2>"

  ' Check whether the user has checked any boxes to select some fields.
  ' If so, we'll display a table of data
  If Request.Form("Field").Count > 0 Then
    ' Find out which fields are to be selected
    strSQL = ""
    For intCount = 1 to Request.Form("Field").Count
      strSQL = strSQL & Request.Form("Field")(intCount) & ", "
    Next

    ' Strip the trailing comma and space (added in the loop) from end of strSQL
    strSQL = Left(strSQL, Len(strSQL) - 2)

    ' Add the SELECT command and the FROM criteria
    strSQL = "SELECT " & strSQL & " FROM AllMovies"

    ' If user requested a particular director, add a WHERE clause
    ' (otherwise they'll get data for all directors)
    If Request.Form("Director") <> "" Then
      strSQL = strSQL & " WHERE Director LIKE '%" & Request.Form("Director") & "%'"
    End If
```

```
      ' Create the recordset
      Set objRS = Server.CreateObject ("ADODB.Recordset")
      objRS.Open strSQL, strConnect, adOpenForwardOnly, adLockReadOnly, adCmdText


      ' Write a table of the recordset
      Response.Write RecToTable (objRS)

      ' Clean up
      objRS.Close
      Set objRS = Nothing
  End If
%>

<FORM NAME=MovieInfo ACTION="FindByDirector.asp" METHOD="POST">
  Enter the Director to find:
  <INPUT TYPE="TEXT" NAME="Director"><BR><BR>

  Please select which fields you would like:<BR>
  <%
    ' Create a recordset on the AllMovies table
    Set objRS = Server.CreateObject ("ADODB.Recordset")
    objRS.Open "AllMovies", strConnect, _
                  adOpenForwardOnly, adLockReadOnly, adCmdTable

    ' Create a checkbox in the form for each field in the recordset
    For Each objField in objRS.Fields
      Response.Write "<INPUT TYPE=CHECKBOX NAME=" & vbQuote & "Field" & vbQuote & _
                " VALUE=" & vbQuote & objField.Name & vbQuote & ">" & _
                objField.Name
    Next
    objRS.Close    ' clean up
    Set objRS = Nothing
  %>
  <BR><INPUT TYPE=SUBMIT VALUE="Find"><INPUT TYPE=RESET VALUE="Clear">
</FORM>
</BODY>
</HTML>
```

4. Save this file as `FindByDirector.asp`. Now call up this page in your browser. Here's what it should look like; as you can see it shows the `<FORM>` part of the page, with a text box (for a director's name) and a set of checkboxes (one for each field in the `AllMovies` table). I've added the name of a famous director and checked a few checkboxes ready to submit.

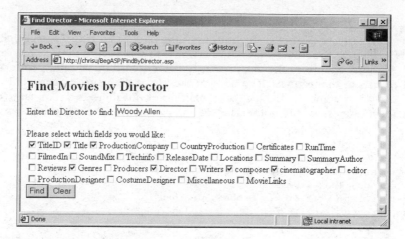

5. Type the name of a film director, and select a few checkboxes, and then click the Find button. You should get something like this:

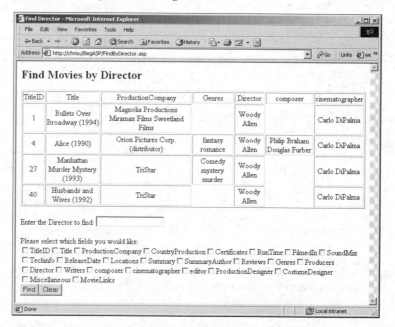

This shows the table of data requested by the user; here, you can see that I selected the director **Woody Allen** and six of the available fields, and the table shows all that data. (Below it, we've displayed the `<FORM>` again so that the user can submit another query).

Pretty cool eh? And pretty simple too. Let's examine it a little more closely.

How It Works

This page is clearly in two parts. At the bottom of the page is an HTML form that uses some ASP to prompt the user to tell us what data he wants to see. Before that, at the top of the page, is a block of ASP that examines the most recently submitted request, and produces a table that displays the results of that request. The table at the top of the page is generated within a big If...Then...End If statement, which checks whether or not there is a request to deal with (if there's no request, then we don't bother generating a table). So the outline of what we are doing is this:

```
Check the Request.Form collection to see whether the user selected any checkboxes
If <there is at least one checkbox selected> Then
   Check which checkboxes were selected, and build a SQL command string
   If <a particular director was requested> Then
     Append director details for SQL command string
   End If
   Use SQL command string to create a recordset
   Use recordset to display the table
End If
Write empty textbox to browser
Use recordset to write checkboxes to browser
Allow user to Submit request
```

Let's look at how we capture the user's request first – that's the second half of the page. The HTML form will submit data to a refreshed version of FindByDirector.asp, passing it to the Request.Form collection:

```
<FORM NAME=MovieInfo ACTION="FindByDirector.asp" METHOD="POST">
...
</FORM>
```

Inside the form, the data collection is in two parts. First, we want the name of a director, so we create a text box for this purpose:

```
Enter the Director to find:
<INPUT TYPE="TEXT" NAME="Director"><BR><BR>
```

Second, we want to know which fields the user wants to know about. For this, we create a checkbox for each field in the AllMovies table. One way to create this list is to query the AllMovies table directly from the database, and iterate through the Fields collection of the resulting recordset, making one checkbox for each field:

```
Please select which fields you would like:<BR>
<%
   ' Create a recordset on the AllMovies table
   Set objRS = Server.CreateObject ("ADODB.Recordset")
   objRS.Open "AllMovies", strConnect, _
                   adOpenForwardOnly, adLockReadOnly, adCmdTable
```

```
  ' Create a checkbox in the form for each field in the recordset
  For Each objField in objRS.Fields
    Response.Write "<INPUT TYPE=CHECKBOX NAME=" & vbQuote & "Field" & vbQuote & _
                   " VALUE=" & vbQuote & objField.Name & vbQuote & ">" & _
                   objField.Name
  Next
  objRS.Close    ' clean up
  Set objRS = Nothing
%>
```

As you can see, that involves creating a recordset, populating it with data from the database, using its `Fields` collection, and then cleaning up the `Recordset` object when we've finished. This will give us a set of checkboxes like this:

```
<INPUT TYPE=CHECKBOX NAME="Field" VALUE="TitleID">TitleID
<INPUT TYPE=CHECKBOX NAME="Field" VALUE="Title">Title
```

We mustn't forget to add a SUBMIT button to the form (and also a RESET button, for good measure):

```
<BR><INPUT TYPE=SUBMIT VALUE="Find"><INPUT TYPE=RESET VALUE="Clear">
```

The user types text into the text box, checks a few checkboxes and then clicks the **Find** button. That causes the page to be reloaded, with the requested data passed to the `Request.Form` collection.

That deals with the second part of the page. Now to the first part – the request handling and table display. Whenever the page is loaded (or reloaded), the first thing we need to know is whether we have a request to deal with. To do that, we'll check to see whether there are any values in `Request.Form("Field")`. If so, then it means the user clicked at least one checkbox; if not, it means that no checkboxes were checked (or that the page is being requested for the first time):

```
If Request.Form("Field").Count > 0 Then
```

Assuming this condition returns `True`, then we have a request to deal with, and so we execute the contents of the `If...Then...End If` block. Before we build the recordset, we'll need to analyze the request to find out what the user asked for – we'll use this to build a SQL `SELECT` command, which we'll store in a string called `strSQL`. First, iterate through the contents of `Request.Form("Field")`, and add the substring "*field_name,*" to the `strSQL` string for each field that was chosen:

```
  ' Find out which fields are to be selected
  strSQL = ""
  For intCount = 1 to Request.Form("Field").Count
    strSQL = strSQL & Request.Form("Field")(intCount) & ", "
  Next
```

Next, remove the final comma and space at the end of the string we just generated:

```
  strSQL = Left(strSQL, Len(strSQL) - 2)
```

Next, append SELECT at the beginning and FROM AllMovies at the end:

```
strSQL = "SELECT " & strSQL & " FROM AllMovies"
```

Now the string in strSQL is starting to look like a proper SELECT command! Next, we'll check whether the user asked for a particular director, and use that criterion as a WHERE clause:

```
If Request.Form("Director") <> "" Then
  strSQL = strSQL & " WHERE Director LIKE '%" & Request.Form("Director") & "%'"
End If
```

Now use the completed SQL command to query the database, and produce a recordset:

```
Set objRS = Server.CreateObject ("ADODB.Recordset")
objRS.Open strSQL, strConnect, adOpenForwardOnly, adLockReadOnly, adCmdText
```

Now we can display the contents of the recordset on screen. We'll use a shortcut here – by borrowing the RecToTable() routine that we wrote in Chapter 13. It is conveniently contained in the RecToTable.asp SSI file, which we included at the top of the page using a #INCLUDE directive. All we need to do is call the RecToTable() function, passing the name of our recordset as parameter:

```
Response.Write RecToTable(objRS)
```

The RecToTable() routine returns a string containing all the HTML for the table, so we just Response.Write it to the browser. Then we just clean up the recordset:

```
  objRS.Close
  Set objRS = Nothing
End If
```

Manipulating Data in your non-database Data Store

In Chapter 12, our first ADO chapter, we said that one of the main strengths of OLE-DB is its ability to retrieve information from *any* data store – not only from databases. However, for the examples so far in these chapters we've used a database as our data store. We haven't deliberately sidestepped the issue of using other types of data store, it's just that in order to extract data from other types of data store, it's helpful to first understand the principles of data retrieval from a database. It's also because the principle of data retrieval from other forms of data storage is much more complex than with databases.

The technology that is added in ADO 2.5 to enable you to make use of other forms of data store is still in its relative infancy and quite difficult to get working across servers on a network. However, it forms the cornerstone of a new Microsoft technology, namely **Distributed Author Versioning** or DAV for short. In fact, IIS 5.0 is referred to as a WebDAV server. WebDAV is actually a specification that uses extensions to the HTTP 1.1 protocol and, thus, can be used on any platform. WebDAV is of great interest because it enables someone browsing on the client to move files on the server, or change the contents of files on the server using these objects. It allows distributed authoring of documents on the Web. It can also equally apply to e-mails on a remote mail server or to any other form of data store for which there is an OLE-DB provider. As the technology is still evolving and not supported by many web servers, we won't be spending that much time on it. However, as an important part of future development, it merits some coverage.

The two new objects that enable WebDAV, and come with ADO 2.5 are:

❑ The `Record` object: this can be used to represent a record in a recordset, or it can represent a file or even a folder in a file system

❑ The `Stream` object: this can be used to represent the most basic denomination of data – that is, either binary data or just plain text

> *As we've said, ADO 2.5 is the version of ADO released with Windows 2000. If you're using another operating system then you'll be able to acquire ADO 2.5 as part of the MDAC 2.5 download from the Microsoft web site. Watch out for more up-to-date editions of ADO in the future!*

Detailed discussion of these two objects is really beyond the scope of this book. However, the following pages serve to introduce their purpose and usage.

> *If you'd like to know more about the ADO `Record` and `Stream` objects, the titles Professional ASP 3.0 (Wrox, ISBN 1-861002-61-0) and Professional ADO 2.5 (Wrox, ISBN 1-861002-75-0) provide progressively more detailed explanations.*

Semi-Structured Data

The main purpose of these two new objects is to facilitate the movement of data access techniques towards the new arena of **semi-structured data**. Up to now, we've been considering databases, which have a rigid structure of tables, rows, and fields. Data held within spreadsheets, mail servers (and so on) doesn't conform to the same rules. For example, consider the folders on the mail client that we use at Wrox Press. We store copies of each feedback message we receive in a folder system – the messages are categorized by subject area, and then by book title, and finally by chapter. The mail folder structure that reflects this categorization looks something like this:

In fact, this system of mail folders resembles nothing so much as the file and folder system you might see if you started Windows Explorer and browsed your own hard drive. The point is that the data contained in here certainly wouldn't fit neatly into a database – yet the data storage system still has a well-defined structure.

In this example, we replace the notion of a table row that represents a single record with a new idea, whereby each **node** in this folder structure is considered to represent a record. Thus, each folder (such as the ASP folder in the diagram above) is a record in its own right.

As you can see, the ASP folder contains several subfolders or subnodes – we can refer to these as **children**. As each node can have several children, these children will be grouped together into a recordset.

This is a potential source of confusion, so let's clear it up now:

❑ Every single node is a single record, and can be represented by a Record object.

❑ When we have a collection of subfolders, then they form a recordset – although each folder might not be the same as others, it will share common information such as name and date created. The common properties form the names of the fields in the recordset.

What we're saying is that the ASP folder is a record in its own right, but it is also a field name in the Web recordset. Let's now take a closer look at the ADO object used to represent these records and fields, namely the Record object.

The Record Object

So, we can use the Record object to represent a record in a recordset, or to represent a file or even a folder in a file system or an email message in an email folder structure. As not everyone will have access to an email server (and because it's simpler), we are going to be using the Record object to return information from a folder hierarchy. The Record object can be used to model tree-structured systems where each separate folder, or node, is an instance of a Record object in its own right. Creating an instance of the Record object is simple enough: you use the Server object's CreateObject method:

```
Set objRecord = Server.CreateObject("ADODB.Record")
```

In order to use a Record object, we have to populate it with the data that we want to work with – and once again, we can do that using the Open method of the Record object.

The Open Method

The Record object's Open method is a little different from the Recordset object's Open method – but both are related to the task of retrieving data from a data source. If you wanted to use the Record object to handle the files and folders on your web server, you could use the Open method, passing a URL on your web server, like this:

```
objRecord.Open "Delete.asp", "URL=http://chrisu/BegASP/"
```

The technology behind these objects is not always easy to set up. Security settings, for example, are very specific to your system setup. In order to open a URL on a different server, you will have to make sure that all of the relevant permissions are set.

This method takes two arguments: the first is the file or folder that we're looking for, and the second is the URL to which any actions will apply. In this case, the record will represent the file named `Delete.asp`, which it expects to find in the physical directory corresponding to the `BegASP/` virtual folder on my web server. Having opened the `Record` object on that folder or file, we can use it to access the different field names in the record. This information is stored within a `Fields` collection.

Rather than explain in laborious detail, it's easier to look at how you can access this information with a quick example.

Try It Out – Using The Record Object's Properties

We'll write an example that uses a `Record` object to view the properties of a physical directory, which corresponds to a virtual directory on our web server.

1. Open up your ASP editor to create a new page, which we'll call `Record.asp`. Type in the following:

```
<%Option Explicit %>
<HTML>
<HEAD>
<TITLE>Retrieving Semi-structured Data</TITLE>
</HEAD>
<BODY>
<%
  Dim objNodeRecord, objNodeField
  Set objNodeRecord = Server.CreateObject("ADODB.Record")
  objNodeRecord.Open "","URL=http://my_server_name/BegASP/"

  Response.Write "<H2>Properties of the folder:</H2>"
  Response.Write "<TABLE BORDER='1'>"
  For Each objNodeField in objNodeRecord.Fields
    Response.Write "<TR>" & _
           "<TD>" & objNodeField.Name & "</TD>" & _
           "<TD>" & objNodeField.Value & "</TD>" & _
        "</TR>"
  Next
  Response.Write "</TABLE>"
  objNodeRecord.Close
  Set objNodeRecord = Nothing
%>
</BODY>
</HTML>
```

2. Save `Record.asp` into your `\inetpub\wwwroot\BegASPFiles` directory, and then view it within your browser.

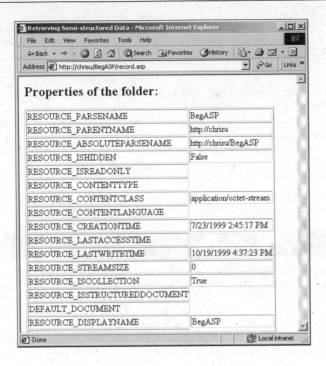

How It Works

We start by initialising two variables. One will be used to refer to an instance of the Record object, and the other will hold the different fields of the record. Then we create our instance of the Record object:

```
Dim objNodeRecord, objNodeField
Set objNodeRecord = Server.CreateObject("ADODB.Record")
```

Then we open the URL of our node that will be our record:

```
objNodeRecord.Open "","URL=http://my_server_name/BegASP/"
```

To display the contents of our record, we create a two-column table. The first column will contain the names of the fields of the record. The second column will contain the values of those fields for our record:

```
Response.Write "<H2>Properties of the folder:</H2>"
Response.Write "<TABLE BORDER='1'>"
For Each objNodeField in objNodeRecord.Fields
  Response.Write "<TR>" & _
          "<TD>" & objNodeField.Name & "</TD>" & _
          "<TD>" & objNodeField.Value & "</TD>" & _
      "</TR>"
Next
Response.Write "</TABLE>"
```

We iterate through fields of the record, using a For Each...Next loop, displaying the Name and Value properties of each Field object in the Record object's Fields collection. As you can see, the fields of this record represent properties of the folder such as its absolute name, and when the folder was created and last written to.

When we've finished, we can close and clean up:

```
objNodeRecord.Close
Set objNodeRecord = Nothing
```

Properties and Methods of the Record Object

As you've probably guessed from the previous example, we can use the Record object to manage our web server resources from a remote location. We've seen that we can write pages that allow us to manage database content remotely – it can be as simple as writing ASP/ADO pages that use SQL UPDATE, DELETE or INSERT commands. If you're using a Record object, there are three methods that we can use to move these records around:

- ❑ MoveRecord
- ❑ CopyRecord
- ❑ DeleteRecord

The functions of these three methods are all fairly obvious – and as they suggest, they manage the resources in a more 'physical' way. That makes sense when you think about it: dealing with database data is easier because all the data is stored within one database; but when you're dealing with something like an email folder system, the location of your record is likely to be related to the overall organization of the data store.

Let's take a look at these three methods.

The CopyRecord Method

The CopyRecord method takes two parameters – a source file or folder and a destination file or folder. It copies the former to the location specified in the latter. In this example it copies the File.txt file from my own BegASP virtual folder into the Examples virtual folder on the www.wrox.com web server:

```
objRecord.Open "File.txt", "URL=http://chrisu/BegASP/"
objRecord.CopyRecord "", "http://www.wrox.com/Examples"
```

Of course, you need write permissions on the www.wrox.com web server, otherwise it won't allow you to put the file on its server – or you need to pass a relevant UserID and password as parameters. One limitation of the CopyRecord method is that you can't use it to copy a file from a folder into one of its subfolders.

What happens when you try to make a copy of a file, only to find that there's already a file or folder with the same name as your specified destination? In that case, you can use the fifth parameter to the Open method to specify what behavior you prefer. This parameter will take one of the CopyRecordOptionsEnum constants, some of which are shown here:

❑ `adCopyOverWrite` allows the existing file to be overwritten with the new file

❑ `adCopyNonRecursive` allows you to copy only a folder, and none of the folder's subfolders

You specify this option with the `Open` method, like this:

```
objRecord.Open "File.txt", "URL=http://chrisu/BegASP/", , , adCopyOverWrite
```

Note that this is specified as the `Open` method's *fifth* parameter – here, we've left the third and fourth parameters empty. The missing third and fourth parameters would usually be used to specify UserId and password for remote access to the file on your server. So the full set of parameters is:

```
objRecord.Open Source, Destination, UserId, Password, Options
```

The MoveRecord Method

The `MoveRecord` works in a similar way to `CopyRecord`, but *moves* the file from the source to the destination rather than copying it. For example:

```
objRecord.Open = "File.txt", "URL=http://chrisu/BegASP/"
objRecord.MoveRecord "", "http://www.wrox.com/Examples"
```

Like `CopyRecord`, there's a limitation on this method – you cannot use it to move a record from a folder into one of it's own subfolders. And again, the `MoveRecord` method allows you to specify a UserID and password to the data source if appropriate:

```
objRecord.Open = "File.txt", "URL=http://chrisu/BegASP/", _
                "UserId=Chrisu", "Password=OpenSesame"
```

The fifth parameter allows you to select from a number of options. Valid values are:

❑ `adMoveOverWrite` allows you to overwrite an existing file of the same name

❑ `adMoveDontUpdateLinks` allows you to move the file without updating any hyperlinks to the file

For example:

```
objRecord.Open = "File.txt", "URL=http://chrisu/BegASP/", _
                "UserId=Chrisu", "Password=hello", adMoveOverWrite
```

The DeleteRecord Method

Rather obviously, the `DeleteRecord` method requires no destination. Therefore, it's quite a bit simpler:

```
objRecord.Open = "File.txt", "URL=http://chrisu/BegASP/"
objRecord.DeleteRecord
```

Try It Out – Using your web page to manipulate files on the web server

Now you have an idea of how to move the records around on the server, let's run through an example that allows you to copy, move or delete a record on your web server. To give you an idea of how it works, we'll create a simple text file called `MyFile.txt`, and a new web folder called `TestFolder`, and we'll write an example that allows us to move the file between the `TestFolder` and `BegASP` web folders, or delete it altogether. It takes a bit of preparation because we need `TestFolder` to be a proper virtual directory, but once we've done that the code is quite simple.

1. First we'll create the file – this will be the node that our `Record` object represents. Start Notepad, type in some random text, and save it in your `\inetpub\wwwroot\BegASPFiles` folder with the name `MyText.txt`.

2. Now we'll create a new folder. On your web server machine, start Windows Explorer; in the `\inetpub\wwwroot` folder create a new subfolder, called `TestFolder`. Now, the `\inetpub\wwwroot` folder should contain two child subfolders called `TestFolder` and `BegASPFiles`.

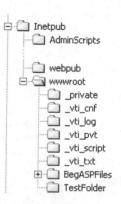

3. Now fire up the Microsoft Management Console (MMC) – select Start | Run and type MMC, and press OK; then select Console | Open and navigate to the snap-in file iis.msc (which you'll probably find in your `C:\WINNT\system32\inetsrv` folder – if not, do a search to find it on your machine). The IIS snap-in in the MMC should reveal the **TestFolder** file as being a regular file.

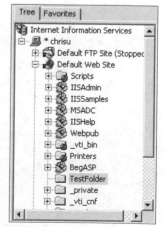

Right-click on **TestFolder** and select
Properties; then on the **Directory** tab, click
the **Create** button to turn **TestFolder** into an
ASP application:

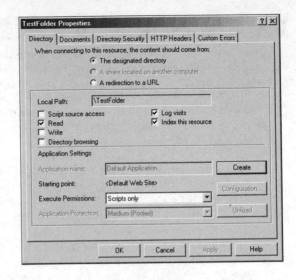

4. That's the preparations; now here's the code. Create the following new file, called
   `RecordMove.asp`, using your ASP editor:

```
<%Option Explicit %>
<!-- METADATA TYPE="typelib"
     FILE="c:\program files\common files\system\ado\msado15.dll" -->
<HTML>
<HEAD>
<TITLE>Retrieving Semi-Structured Data</TITLE>
</HEAD>
<BODY>
<%
  If Request.Form("Task")="" Then %>
    <FORM NAME=MovieInfo ACTION="RecordMove.asp" METHOD="POST">
      What do you want to do? <BR><BR>
      <INPUT TYPE="RADIO" NAME="Task" VALUE="Copy" CHECKED>
      Copy MyText.txt to a new file called MyText2.txt</INPUT><BR>
      <INPUT TYPE="RADIO" NAME="Task" VALUE="Move">
      Move MyText.txt to a new file called MyText2.txt</INPUT><BR>
      <INPUT TYPE="RADIO" NAME="Task" VALUE="Delete">
      Delete MyText.txt from the BegASP file</INPUT><BR>
      <INPUT TYPE=SUBMIT VALUE="Go">
    </FORM><%
  Else
    Dim objRecord
    Set objRecord = Server.CreateObject("ADODB.Record")
    objRecord.Open "MyText.txt", "URL=http://my_server_name /BegASP"
    If Request.Form("Task") = "Copy" Then
      objRecord.CopyRecord "", _
              "http://my_server_name/TestFolder/MyText2.txt",,,adCopyOverWrite
      Response.Write "MyText.txt file copied to a new file called MyText2.txt"
    ElseIf Request.Form("Task") = "Move" Then
```

```
            objRecord.MoveRecord "", _
                   "http://my_server_name/TestFolder/MyText2.txt",,,adMoveOverWrite
        Response.Write "MyText.txt file moved to a new file called MyText2.txt"
      ElseIf Request.Form("Task") = "Delete" Then
        objRecord.DeleteRecord
        Response.Write "MyText.txt has been deleted"
      End If
      objRecord.Close
      Set objRecord = Nothing
   End If
%>
</BODY>
</HTML>
```

5. Save `Recordmove.asp` into your `\inetpub\wwwroot\BegASPFiles` folder.

6. Open `Recordmove.asp` in your browser of choice. Because the `Request.Form` collection is empty, you'll see the following form:

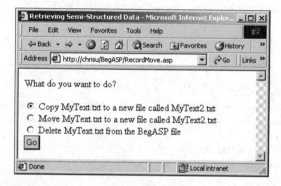

7. Select the first radio button, which will have the file copied to a new filename in the `TestFolder` directory. Then hit **Go**, an the page will reload – this time it will detect the value of `Request.Form ("Task")`, copy the file and then display a report. But don't just take the word of the ASP page. Instead, go to Windows Explorer and the check this for sure:

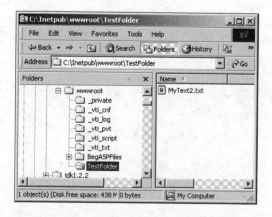

8. Use Windows Explorer to delete this occurrence of `MyText2.txt`, go back to Step 6 and try the other two options.

How It Works

The page is split into two. The first part is an HTML form that is just designed to find out which task you want to perform – copy, move or delete. There's nothing new here – the real action is in the second part of the form. We start by creating an instance of the `Record` object:

```
Dim objRecord
Set objRecord = Server.CreateObject("ADODB.Record")
```

We open our instance of the `Record` object, so that the record represents the `MyText.txt` file that lives in the `http://my_server_name/BegASP` virtual directory:

```
objRecord.Open "MyText.txt", "URL=http://my_server_name/BegASP"
```

Then we check the `Task` value that was passed as part of the HTTP request. If it's equal to `Copy` then we execute the `CopyRecord` method to copy our file from its current location to the new `TestFolder` directory, with the filename `MyText2.txt`. Then we display an appropriate message:

```
If Request.Form("Task") = "Copy" Then
  objRecord.CopyRecord "", _
           "http://my_server_name/TestFolder/MyText2.txt",,,adCopyOverWrite
  Response.Write "MyText.txt file copied to a new file called MyText2.txt"
```

Otherwise, if it's equal to `Move`, then we execute the `MoveRecord` method to move our file to its new location; then we display an appropriate message:

```
ElseIf Request.Form("Task") = "Move" Then
  objRecord.MoveRecord "", _
           "http://my_server_name/TestFolder/MyText2.txt",,,adMoveOverWrite
  Response.Write "MyText.txt file moved to a new file called MyText2.txt"
```

Otherwise, if it's equal to `Delete` then we delete the file altogether, and display a message:

```
ElseIf Request.Form("Task") = "Delete" Then
  objRecord.DeleteRecord
  Response.Write "MyText.txt has been deleted"
End If
```

Finally, we've finished with the `Record` object so we clean up:

```
objRecord.Close
Set objRecord = Nothing
```

The Stream Object

We can use the Record object in a file system or mail system to move and copy the files or mail messages and their containing files, but that still doesn't tell us how to access the data that's contained within them. And let's face it, that's what we really want to do – there's only so much satisfaction we can get from moving files around! To meet this demand, we use the ADO Stream object. The Stream object is used to represent the most basic denomination of data – binary data or just plain text. In this chapter, we'll only look at the latter case, as the former is quite a bit more complex.

In order to create an instance of the ADO Stream object, we use the Server object's CreateObject method. The ProgID for the ADO Stream object is ADODB.Stream:

```
Set objStream = Server.CreateObject("ADODB.Stream")
```

The Open Method

The Stream object, like the Record and Recordset objects, has its own Open method. Similarly, we use its Open method to open the object on a data source and hence access the stream of data contained within:

```
objStream.Open "http://chrisu/BegASP/ReadMe.txt", adModeRead, adOpenStreamFromURL
```

This example opens the Stream object on the stream of text contained in the file ReadMe.txt, which is contained in a virtual directory of my web server machine. It specifies values for three of the parameters:

❑ *Source*: this the URL of the file whose content we want to access

❑ *ModeofAccess*: the second is the mode of access (whether we're allowing read or write access). The example above specifies the value adModeRead, which allows read-only access to the contents of the file. A value of adModeReadWrite would allow read and write access to the source file

❑ *OpenOptions*: the third parameter specifies from where we're getting the data. The value adOpenStreamFromURL specifies that we're opening the stream using a URL as the source, while the value adOpenStreamFromRecord should be used when opening a stream using an existing Record object

We're not going to cover the full list of available parameter values here, because it's beyond the scope of this book. You can find more details in our title Professional Active Server Pages 3.0 *(Wrox, ISBN 1-861002-61-0).*

The Open method has two more optional parameters, which we can use to specify a UserID and password when accessing the web server remotely; so the full syntax for the Open method is:

```
objStream.Open Source, ModeOfAccess, OpenOptions, UserId, Password
```

Before we try an example, we'll quickly cover some of the Stream object's other methods and properties.

The ReadText Method

Once the `Stream` object has been opened on a file we can use its `ReadText` method to examine the contents of the file. Then, by sending the results of this method to `Response.Write`, we can display the contents of the file. However, you'll hit a problem if you try a line like the following:

```
Response.Write (objStream.ReadText)     ' ...may give unexpected redults!
```

If you try this you'll find that the output to the page takes the form of a sequence of question marks, and not the text that you might have expected. This is because the `Stream` object needs to know which character set it is supposed to be using. In order to give that information, we also need to use the `Charset` property.

The Charset Property

The default character set used by the `Stream` object is UNICODE, and that's what it will use unless we tell it specifically to use a different character set. In this case, we're using the traditional ASCII set. So in order to achieve the expected output, we need to set the `Charset` property of the `Stream` object to `ASCII`. Then, when we call the `ReadText` method, we should get some recognizable text:

```
objStream.Charset = "Ascii"
Response.Write (objStream.ReadText)
```

The WriteText Method

There is also a `WriteText` method, which allows you to write text *into* the source file of the `Stream` object. For example, we could declare and define a character string (like the `strText` string below), and then pass this string as a parameter to the `WriteText` method, ready for writing:

```
strText = "We'll write this text into the stream"
objStream.WriteText(strText)
```

Of course, we need to think about at what point in the stream we want the new string to be added. For that, we have the `Position` property.

The Position Property

The Position property, quite simply, is used to indicate the position within the stream that you wish to start writing. It's an integer value, which indicates the position in terms of the number of characters after the first character. For example:

```
objStream.Position = 0
```

This would set the pointer for writing to the beginning of the file.

The EOS Property and the SetEOS Method

If we want to set the position to the end of the file, but we don't know how long the file is then we can use the EOS (end-of-stream) property:

```
intNum = objStream.EOS
```

Alternatively, we can force the stream to end at a particular position by using the setEOS method, which updates the value of the EOS property by setting it to be the same as the current Position. For example:

```
objStream.Position = 0
objStream.SetEOS
```

This would set the end of stream property to 0. Beware – when you call SetEOS, you'll lose any data that lies between the position specified in the Position property and the old EOS. In particular, the above two lines will succeed in deleting the contents of the file.

We haven't covered all of the Stream object's methods and properties here, but we've covered enough to put it into practice. Let's look at an example that allows the user to change the contents of a text file. Here's what we'll do: we'll ask the user to provide the URL of a text file that needs backing up, and a location for the new backup file to be placed. We'll use a Record object to create the copy of the text file. Then we'll open a Stream object on the contents of the backed-up file, and we'll change the contents of the stream, adding a datestamp.

Try It Out – Creating a Backup

1. Open up your favourite ASP editor to create a new file (which we'll call PromptForURL.htm. Type in the following:

```
<HTML>
<HEAD>
<TITLE>Backup</TITLE>
</HEAD>
<BODY>
<FORM NAME=form1 METHOD=POST ACTION=CreateBackup.asp>
  Type the full URL of the file to be backed up here:<BR>
  <INPUT TYPE=TEXT SIZE=50 NAME=URLofFile><BR><BR>
  Type the full URL of the desired location for the backup file here:<BR>
  <INPUT TYPE=TEXT SIZE=50 NAME=URLofBackup><BR><BR>
  <INPUT TYPE=SUBMIT VALUE="Create Backup">
</FORM>
</BODY>
</HTML>
```

Save PromptForURL.htm into the \inetpub\wwwroot\BegASPFiles folder.

2. Now open another new file (this one will be called CreateBackup.asp) and type in the following:

```
<%Option Explicit %>
<!-- METADATA TYPE="typelib"
            FILE="c:\program files\common files\system\ado\msado15.dll" -->
<HTML>
<HEAD>
<TITLE>Writing the backup</TITLE>
</HEAD>
<BODY>
<%
  Dim objStream, objRecord, strURLofFile, strURLofBackup, strText, strDatestamp
  strURLofFile = Request.Form("URLofFile")
  strURLofBackup = Request.Form("URLofBackup")

  Set objRecord = Server.CreateObject("ADODB.Record")
  objRecord.Open "", "URL=" & strURLofFile
  objRecord.CopyRecord "", strURLofBackup, , , adCopyOverWrite
  objRecord.Close
  Set objRecord = Nothing

  strDatestamp = "'This backup file was created on " & Date & " "
  Set objStream = Server.CreateObject("ADODB.Stream")
  objStream.Open "URL=" & strURLofBackup, adModeReadWrite, 8'adOpenStreamFromURL
  objStream.Charset = "ascii"              ' select character set
  strText = objStream.ReadText             ' read stream into local variable

  objStream.Position = 0                   ' set current position
  objStream.SetEOS                         ' set EOS to be position 0
          ' now use strDatestamp and strText to rewrite contents of the stream
  objStream.WriteText (strDatestamp + vbcrlf  + vbcrlf + strText)

  Response.Write "Backup created."
  objStream.Close
  Set objStream = Nothing
%>
</BODY>
</HTML>
```

Save CreateBackup.asp into the same folder.

3.　Now start up your browser and browse to PromptForURL.htm. Type in the full URL of a text or HTML file on your server, and the location of a place where you'd like it to be backed up:

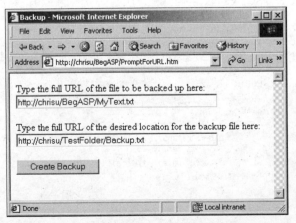

In order to keep the example simple, we haven't written any error handling – so be careful to enter a valid URL in each text box.

4. When you click the **Create Backup** button, the `CreateBackup.asp` page will create the backup and add the datestamp to the backed up copy; and you'll see a message in the browser, informing you that the backup has been created.

But the real proof of the pudding is in the eating, so use your Windows Explorer to open the backup file and view its contents

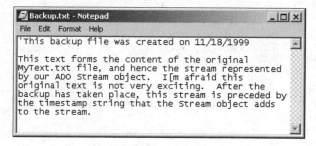

How It Works

The first page, `PromptForURL.htm`, just contains an HTML form that prompts the user for the URLs of the original file and the desired location for the backup copy:

```
<FORM NAME=form1 METHOD=POST ACTION=CreateBackup.asp>
   Type the full URL of the file to be backed up here:<BR>
   <INPUT TYPE=TEXT SIZE=50 NAME=URLofFile><BR><BR>
   Type the full URL of the desired location for the backup file here:<BR>
   <INPUT TYPE=TEXT SIZE=50 NAME=URLofBackup><BR><BR>
   <INPUT TYPE=SUBMIT VALUE="Create Backup">
</FORM>
```

These URLs are passed to the page `CreateBackup.asp`, where they are accessible via the `Request.Forms` collection (with the names `URLofFile` and `URLofBackup`). The first thing we do there is to save those values to local variables:

```
strURLofFile = Request.Form("URLofFile")
strURLofBackup = Request.Form("URLofBackup")
```

The rest of the page is concerned with two tasks: first, to create the backup copy (which we'll do using the `Record` object's `CopyRecord` method); second, to append the datestamp to the contents of the backup copy (which requires the `Stream` object's `ReadText` and `WriteText` methods).

So let's deal with the first task. We create a new ADO `Record` object, and open it using the first URL:

```
Set objRecord = Server.CreateObject("ADODB.Record")
objRecord.Open "", "URL=" & strURLofFile
```

Now we create the copy of the file. This is just like the code we saw in the `RecordMove.asp` example, earlier in the chapter. The first parameter of the `CopyRecord` method is blank, ensuring that we take the default (i.e. the record on which the `Record` object is opened); the second parameter is the URL of the destination of the backup copy. The option `adCopyOverWrite` is used to indicate that writing over an existing version of the destination file is allowed:

```
objRecord.CopyRecord "", strURLofBackup, , , adCopyOverWrite
```

This is enough to create a copy of the original file. Now the `Record` object has done its job, we can `Close` it and release its resources:

```
objRecord.Close
Set objRecord = Nothing
```

And that's the first task done; now to the second. We'll start by defining a character string containing the text of the datestamp:

```
strDatestamp = "'This backup file was created on " & Date & " "
```

The datestamp string contains the current date, which is generated when needed using the VBScript `Date` function.

Now we'll open the backup file for modification. To do this, we open an ADO `Stream` object on the backup file, so that the `Stream` object represents the character stream of that file:

```
Set objStream = Server.CreateObject("ADODB.Stream")
objStream.Open "URL=" & strURLofBackup, adModeReadWrite, adOpenStreamFromURL
```

We've specified three parameters here. The first parameter is a URL specifying the source of the stream. The second parameter gives us read and write permissions of the stream, and the third indicates that we're opening a stream from a URL.

> Note: in a prerelease version of `msado15.dll` for ADO2.5, the constant `adOpenStreamFromURL` was undefined. If you have difficulty with this, try adding the following line to your ASP before this point:
>
> ```
> Const adOpenStreamFromURL = 8
> ```
>
> This is enough to define the missing constant.

We need to specify the character set we're using, to prevent ADO from assuming that we are using UNICODE and generating an error. To specify the character set as ASCII we set the `Charset` property:

```
objStream.Charset = "ascii"                    ' select character set
```

Now we read the existing contents of the file into a variable called `strText`:

```
strText = objStream.ReadText              ' read stream into local variable
```

Now that we have the original contents of the file stored in a string variable, we can write new contents to the file. First, we set the current position to the beginning of the stream, and the EOS (end-of-stream) property to the same position (thus cleaning out the entire stream):

```
objStream.Position = 0                    ' set current position
objStream.SetEOS                          ' set EOS to be position 0
```

Then we write our new text into the file. The new content of the stream will consist of the datestamp first, followed by two carriage returns and then the whole of the original contents of the text file:

```
objStream.WriteText (strDatestamp + vbcrlf  + vbcrlf + strText)
```

Next we write to the browser to inform the user that the backup process has been completed.

```
Response.Write "Backup created."
```

Finally we tidy up our `Stream` object:

```
objStream.Close
Set objStream = Nothing
```

And that concludes our basic backup utility.

In this section we've tried to provide only a very brief introduction to ADO's two new objects – the `Record` and `Stream` objects. An in-depth discussion is beyond the scope of this book, but hopefully the techniques demonstrated here will go some way to illustrating the kind of functionality that is available from these objects, particularly in the remote administration of web sites, and will tempt you to investigate them further. For more information, try *Professional Active Server Pages 3.0* (Wrox, ISBN 1-861002-61-0) and *Professional ADO 2.5* (Wrox, ISBN 1-861002-75-0).

Summary

This chapter ends our whirlwind three-chapter tour of ADO. Having already established a foundation in using the `Connection` and `Recordset` objects, and in requesting data from databases, this chapter broadened our ADO horizons by looking at the remaining major objects in ADO:

❑ The `Command` object, which allows us to run SQL statements against a database

❑ The `Record` object, which allows us to represent non-database structures, as having records and fields

❑ The `Stream` object, which is used to represent binary data or plain text, held in a record

In addition to talking about these three objects, we introduced the notion of writing a SQL command that tells ADO exactly what we want from the data store. We identified two important types of SQL command:

❑ A SQL SELECT command can be used to request data from the data store. It gives us flexibility over what data we request because it means that each data query doesn't necessarily have to ask for an entire table – instead, we can be choosy over which fields and records we want to see.

❑ The SQL UPDATE, INSERT and DELETE commands are collectively known as **action commands**. They are different because (unlike SELECT) they are all used in the process of making *changes* to the database – changing records, adding new records and deleting records.

We looked at how we can use ASP logic to generate our SQL commands dynamically – allowing the user to choose and dictate, at runtime, the records and fields to be selected, amended, inserted or deleted. Using a SQL command is as simple as specifying the command string as a parameter of the Recordset object's Open method, or the Connection object's Execute method; or by assigning the command string to the Command object's CommandText property and then running the Command.Execute method.

We saw that there are also two very direct ways to execute commands on the database:

❑ Methods of the Recordset object, such as AddNew, Delete, Update and UpdateBatch

❑ Calling an Access query or a stored procedure – a precompiled command that is written and contained within the database (in this case, we can extend the capability by the use of parameters in our precompiled queries and stored procedures, which requires the use of the Parameters collection of the Command object)

Lastly, we touched briefly on the subject of manipulating data contained in sources other than databases. To do this we introduced the two new objects of ADO 2.5 – the Record and Stream objects. They allow you to manipulate the records and the contents of records. We ran through a few quick examples of how they might be put to use on some simple web administration tasks.

We'll be using ADO for our data access in the remaining chapters of this book. In the next chapter, we'll be showcasing ASP and ADO functionality in one big example – the **Wrox Classifieds** ASP application. Over the course of the chapter, we will see what it does, how to build it, and how it all works.

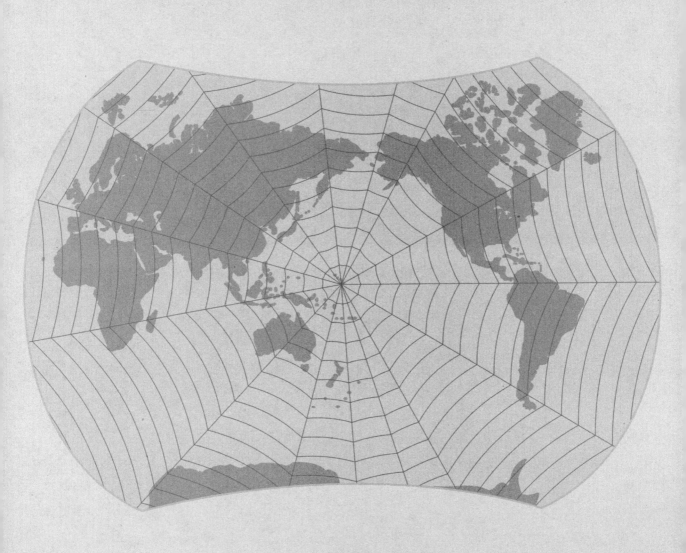

Writing an Application

In the first 14 chapters of this book, we've covered most aspects of ASP and had exposure and practice in using many on the techniques involved. Each chapter looked at a different part of the ASP technology, and demonstrated ideas using small, self-contained examples. In this chapter we'll set out to write a much larger application using Active Server Pages.

This application will make use of many of the different functions that we've already seen in this book. For example, we'll be using:

- Client-side scripting with JavaScript
- Server-side scripting with VBScript
- The ASP Request and Response objects, to communicate with the web client
- The ASP Session object, to manage a user session
- The ADO Connection, Command and Recordset objects, to manipulate information contained in a database

We'll build our application from the ground up, and as we do so we'll be able to see how these different aspects interact with each other in a 'real-life' environment. While this chapter won't explain every single line of code in detail, it *will* provide you with sufficient information to allow you to implement the application as-is, or modify it to suit your needs. You might also use it as a starting point or a guide to writing your own applications.

Introducing the Wrox Classifieds Application

The emergence of the Internet as a worldwide standard for communicating information has opened up a huge number of new business opportunities. One of these opportunities is the area known as **electronic commerce**. Essentially, the Internet is able to take the place of a traditional bricks-and-mortar store – playing the role of the vendor (or the retailer who sits between buyer and vendor). For very little overhead, people are now able to sell their products electronically. The Internet has enabled the buyer and the seller to be brought together in a virtual (rather than a physical) manner.

Let's consider a simple example of commerce between two people, involving the kind of classified advertisements that are traditionally to be found in almost any 'local' newspaper. In a listing of classified ads, an advertiser will place a small ad that lists items that he wishes to sell, and provides a means (usually a telephone number) by which prospective buyers can contact them.

Let's briefly examine the nature of a sale via a newspaper classified. During the course of the sale, the information flows in different directions at different stages. First, there is a downstream flow of information (from seller to buyer) – the listing in print on the newspaper. (Thus, the classified ad listing is just a way of bringing a buyer and seller together.) When a potential purchaser's interest has been raised, then that interest must be relayed upstream (from buyer to seller) – usually by telephone or in person. Finally, a meeting should result that uses face-to-face negotiation to finalize the sale – if the sale can be agreed.

By placing the entire system on the Internet, the upstream and downstream communications are accomplished using a single medium – a web browser. The sale becomes more of an auction, because many potential buyers, all with equal status, can bid for the same item. So it's fairer for all purchasers, and gets a better deal for the seller.

A Web-based Classifieds System

We'll implement a web-based classified ad system. Any user who us trying to buy an item can:

- ❑ View items for sale
- ❑ Bid on an item they wish to purchase

In addition, any user who is trying to sell an item can:

- ❑ Place a new item for sale
- ❑ Browse a list of the items that they're trying to sell, and examine the bids that have been made on each of those items
- ❑ Accept a bid on an item that they're selling

This system will also allow users to do straightforward administrative tasks like:

- ❑ Browse the listings to see what's for sale
- ❑ Register with the system (users can browse without registering; but they must register if they want to sell an item or bid for an item)
- ❑ Log on to the system
- ❑ Change their registration details

If our web site takes off, we'll have a large user-base – some will be buyers and some will be sellers (and hopefully some will do some buying and some selling via our system). In addition, some users will be unregistered 'window-shoppers' – these users will need to register when they spot something they want to bid for.

The Advantages over a Print-based Classifieds System

Our Internet-based classified ad system provides certain advantages to the seller over traditional printed classifieds:

❑ When a seller submits an item for sale, it's immediately viewable by potential buyers. There's no time delay while we all wait for the newspaper to be printed

❑ Responses from potential buyers are held by the system's data store – rather than being passed directly back to the seller. This means that the seller doesn't have to be available to respond 24 hours a day

❑ The seller can dynamically adjust the price – based on the amount of response an item receives

The Internet classified ad system also provides advantages for potential buyers:

❑ Shoppers can see the level of interest in an item before determining the price they are willing to pay

❑ When a shopper makes a bid, he is told whether the bid is the highest bid made on that item

❑ The global nature of the Internet means that the potential audience for each advert is global – it's not limited to the encatchment area of a printed newspaper

Building the Application

We'll build our application in stages. Each stage will build on the previous stages, and will add a new piece of functionality to the application. The sequence we'll follow in this chapter is:

❑ Database setup

❑ Home page construction

❑ User registration and login

❑ Adding items to the sale listings

❑ Browsing the listings and bidding for items

❑ Accepting a bid and completing the sale

To get us started, let's take a look at the ASP pages that will feature in our application. There are 14 pages altogether. Each of these pages serves a different function and contains the code for carrying or certain tasks. The pages are given names that reflect their functionality:

Page	Purpose
`Default.asp`	The home page. Provides links to the login, registration and browse pages.
`BrowseListings.asp`	Shows a table containing brief details of each item that is currently available for purchase. From this page, registered users will be also able to select a particular product for sale, and click-through to `Bid.asp` (and thus to bid on the object).
`Login.asp`	Enables a registered user to enter a username and password, and hence login to the system.
`CheckLogin.asp`	Contains ASP logic for checking the username and password (from the form in `Login.asp`) against details contained in the database. This page has no user interface.
`Register.asp`	Contains a form that enables new users to enter the necessary registration details. Also used to enable existing users to change their registration details.
`AddUser.asp`	Contains ASP logic for placing user details (from the form in `Register.asp`) into the database. This page has no user interface.
`MenuForRegisteredUsers.asp`	This is the first page that a user sees once he has logged in – it welcomes the registered user to the site, presenting a simple menu of options that the user can choose from. Sometimes it also performs a second function: if the user placed a bid on an item during a previous visit to this site, and if the vendor of that item has subsequently accepted the bid, then this page will alert the user to the fact that his bid was successful.
`ViewMySaleItems.asp`	Allows a registered user to view the details of all of the items that he has made available for sale. From this page, the user can click-through to `Item.asp` and edit these details. The 'highest bid' for each of these items is also displayed, and the user can accept a bid on an item via this page.
`Item.asp`	Allows a registered user to enter details of an item that he wishes to make available for sale. Also used (as a click-through from `ViewMySaleItems.asp`) to allow the user to edit the details.

Page	Purpose
`AddItem.asp`	Contains ASP logic for placing the details of a sale item (from the form in `Item.asp`) into the database. This page has no user interface.
`Bid.asp`	Allows a potential buyer to view the details of a sale item, and to enter a bid.
`AddBid.asp`	Contains ASP logic for placing the details of a bid (from the form in `Bid.asp`) into the database. This page has no user interface.
`SaleDetailsForSeller.asp`	When a user accepts a bid (on `ViewMySaleItems.asp`), this page updates the database accordingly, and displays the sale details to the seller.
`BuyerAcceptance.asp`	When a potential buyer's bid has been accepted, the buyer is alerted via `MenuForRegisteredUsers.asp`. At this stage, the buyer can click-through to `BuyerAcceptance.asp` and acknowledge the alert, and thus complete the sale.

When we consider any application of this size, we can gain a lot of understanding by representing the relationship between pages in a graphical way. As you work through the application, you may find the following diagram useful – it shows the routes that we'd expect our users to travel as they use the application:

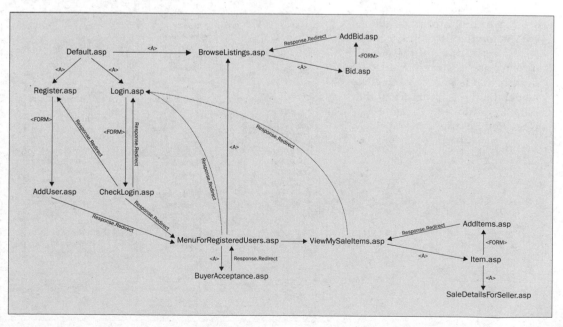

The click-throughs and redirections shown in this diagram illustrate the key stages of the sale process. As you'll see when we come to write the code, there are other click-throughs which are not shown in this diagram. These additional links give users the option of moving directly to pages like Login.asp, Register.asp *and* BrowseListings.asp *– thus allowing the user a controlled amount of extra freedom to move between the pages of the application.*

Setting up the Database

Like many web-based applications, the underlying structure of the Wrox Classifieds application is dependent on the ability to store and retrieve information. Therefore, we need to support some form of data storage.

We might store data in one or more forms – in temporary memory, in text files, in custom file formats, in relational databases, etc. For the purposes of this application, we'll be using a Microsoft Access relational database to store all of the application's data: Access is relatively easy to set up and deploy, and also leaves open the option of scaling the application to a full server-based database system such as SQL Server.

In this section we'll look at how to set up the database tables that will support the Internet classified ad system. You can also download the database file, Classified.mdb, along with the other files needed for this application, from http://www.wrox.com.

The Data Model

Whatever form we choose for storing the data, the *physical* storage of the information is complemented by a 'theoretical' or *logical* description of the way the information is stored. This logical description is known as the **data model**. Below is a picture of the data model for our Internet classified ad application.

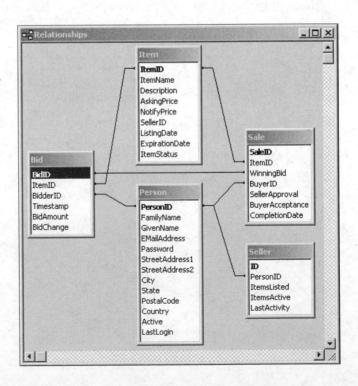

A data model consists of the tables that store the information, as well as the relationships that these tables have with each other. Let's look at the different data tables in our application and see what types of information are stored in each.

The Person Table

The Person table is used to store information about each user that is accessing the system. This information includes the user's name (their family name and their given name) and address, as well as their e-mail address. In our application, each individual user will be identified uniquely in the database via a unique numeric identification number, which is generated by Access and will be stored in the PersonID field. In order to log in to the system, users will identify themselves by giving their e-mail address and password – which are also stored in the Person table.

The structure of the Person table is:

Field Name	Data Type	Description
PersonID	Long	System-generated unique identifier
FamilyName	Text	User's family name *(required)*
GivenName	Text	User's given name *(required)*
EmailAddress	Text	User's e-mail address – used for login *(required)*
Password	Text	User-defined password – used for login *(required)*
StreetAddress1	Text	
StreetAddress2	Text	
City	Text	
State	Text	
PostalCode	Text	
Country	Text	
Active	Boolean	Flag indicating that the user is currently an active user
LastLogin	Date/Time	Date and time of the last time this user logged into the application

The Seller Table

The Seller table is used to store additional information about any registered user who is a seller – that is any user who makes an item available for sale. This information is primarily statistical, detailing the numbers of items that the seller currently has for sale, as well as the total number of items that they have *ever* listed. This table is associated directly with the Person table – each user defined in the Person table can have either zero or one seller record, indicating whether or not they are a seller.

The structure of the Seller table is:

Field Name	Data Type	Description
ID	Long	System-generated unique identifier
PersonID	Long	Foreign key (from the Person table), relating this record to the corresponding user in the Person table
ItemsListed	Long	Total number of items that this user has ever listed for sale
ItemsActive	Long	Number of items that are currently for sale
LastActivity	Date/Time	Date and time of the most recent time that this seller changed the items they have for sale

We noted above that there is an association between the Person and Seller tables. This association is defined using keys.

What is a Key?

When we're accessing the records of a database, we need to be able to do so with confidence that we're accessing exactly the *right* records. To help us do this, we use **keys**. A key is a field (or set of fields) that uniquely identifies a particular record in the table. For example, the PersonID field of the Person table is uniquely generated by the Person table (as we mentioned a moment ago), and so we can use it as a key for the Person table.

The way in which we set up the keys in our tables determines the uniqueness of records, and also allows us to link these records to records in other tables.

We can set up a relationship between two tables by using a **foreign key**. The idea is to include a foreign key as a field of one table – it gives us a way of referencing a unique record in another table. For example, the PersonID field of the Seller table refers us to the PersonID field of the Person table, which is a key and thus describes a unique individual. So the Seller table's PersonID is a foreign key for the Person table. This process links Seller records to the corresponding Person record. This process of having two seperate tables ensures that we don't have blank fields for people who only buy or browse the system.

The Item Table

Now that we have defined the users and the sellers in the application, we need a place to store the goods that are being sold. These are stored in the Item table. The Item table holds descriptive information about the item for sale, the pricing information, and some 'current status' information as well.

The structure of the Item table is:

Field Name	Data Type	Description
ItemID	Long	System-generated unique identifier
ItemName	Text	Descriptive name of the item
Description	Memo	Textual description of the item
AskingPrice	Currency	Price that the seller desires
NotifyPrice	Currency	Price level at which the seller should be notified
SellerID	Long	Foreign key (from the Person table) indicating the seller of the item
ListingDate	Date/Time	Date and time that the item was listed for sale
ExpirationDate	Date/Time	Date and time that the item will no longer be for sale
ItemStatus	Text	Current item status – can be blank, Pending, or Sold

The Bid Table

When a potential buyer finds an item that they'd like to buy, they can place a bid on that item. A bid is an intention to buy an item at a specified price. This bid price must be higher than any previous bid prices for the same item. Each new bid is saved to the Bid table. The bid history for each item is retained in the Bid table, so that the seller can review the interest in each item they're selling.

The structure of the Bid table is:

Field Name	Data Type	Description
BidID	Long	System-generated unique identifier
ItemID	Long	Foreign key (from the Item table), indicating the item being bid on
BidderID	Long	Foreign key (from the Person table) indicating the person bidding on the item

Table Continued on Following Page

Field Name	Data Type	Description
Timestamp	Date/Time	Date and time that the bid was submitted
BidAmount	Currency	Amount that the buyer is willing to pay for the item
BidChange	Currency	Difference between current bid and previous bid

The Sale Table

The seller of an item is able to review the various bids that have been made on that item. When the seller finds an acceptable bid, they can accept that bid. This will begin the actual sale process. The first part of the sale process involves recording information about the winning bid in the Sale table, and notifying the user who placed the winning bid. The sale is considered 'pending' (see the ItemStatus field of the Item table above) until the successful bidder acknowledges the purchase of the item.

The structure of the Sale table is:

Field Name	Data Type	Description
SaleID	Long	System-generated unique identifier
ItemID	Long	Foreign key (from the Item table) indicating the item being bid on
WinningBid	Currency	Final selling price of the item
BuyerID	Long	Foreign key (from the Person table) indicating the successful buyer of the item
SellerApproval	Boolean	Indicates that the seller has approved the sale
BuyerAcceptance	Boolean	Indicates that the buyer has accepted the sale
CompletionDate	Date/Time	Date and time that the sale was completed

Try It Out – Creating the Database

1. The first step is to create the database, using Microsoft Access (we've used Access2000, but you can use Access97). First, start up Access from your Start menu. To create the database, select File | New from the toolbar and select the Database icon. You'll be presented with the following dialog:

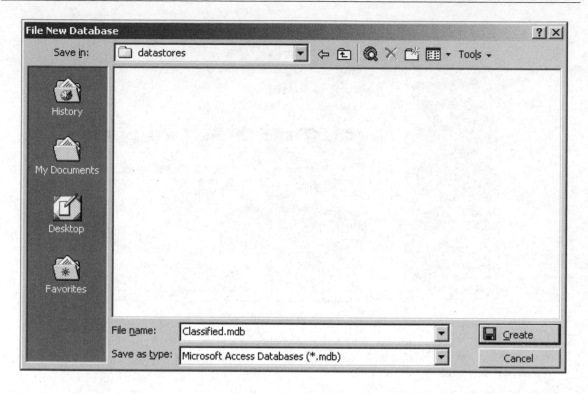

Note that if you are using Access97 to create this database then the appearance of these dialogs will be slightly different.

You should also note that this database is available for download from the Wrox site at www.wrox.com, in both Access97 and 2000 versions

Choose a location for your database: In this example, we've chosen the directory `E:\datastores`. Type in the name of your database: here, we've called it `Classified.mdb`. Then hit the **Create** button. Once you've created the empty `Classified.mdb` database, Access should present you with a new **Classified:Database** dialog.

2. Now that our empty database exists, we can start to build it up. We'll begin with the **Person** table. To create the new table, click on the **New** button on the **Classified:Database** dialog, and select **Design View** to create the new table. Then hit **OK**.

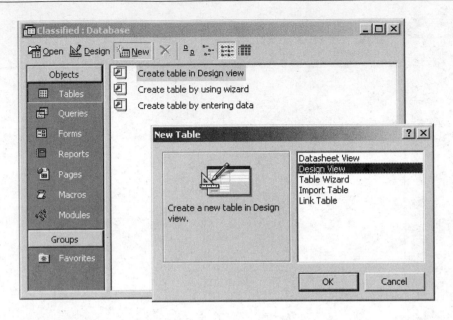

3. Now, we can begin setting up the fields in our database. Add the fields and set their data types so that it looks like this (don't worry about the *name* of the table just yet – we'll set it in a moment):

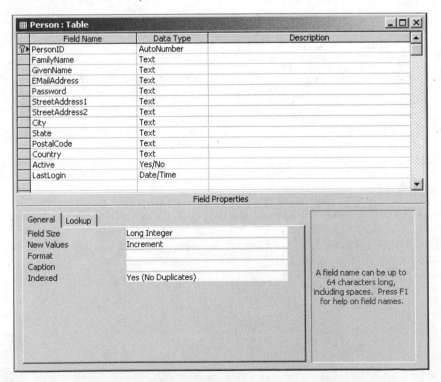

We've only completed the Field Name and Data Type columns here – this information is compulsory for each field. Completing the Description column is optional, but it's useful if you want to add your own notes about the fields.

4. In order to enforce the uniqueness of records within this table, we'll create a **primary key**. To do this, select the PersonID field with your cursor, and press the Primary Key icon in the toolbar:

This will ensure that, for every record in this table, the PersonID field contains a unique value.

5. The StreetAddress1, StreetAddress2, City, State, PostalCode and Country fields will be optional – that is, an end-user will be able to leave these fields blank when registering with our system. All the other fields in this table will need to be populated.

To arrange this configuration, we need to ensure that the six fields listed above will allow zero-length strings. To do this, select each of these fields in turn, then left-click on the Allow Zero Length field, and select Yes in the resulting dropdown menu.

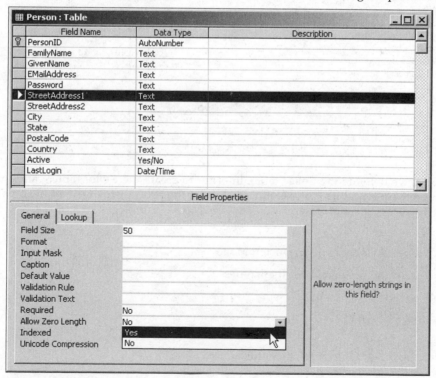

6. Finally, save the table by pressing the **Save** icon, 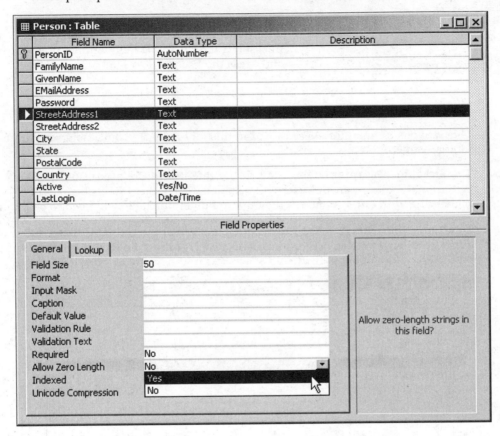, and naming the table **Person** when prompted to do so.

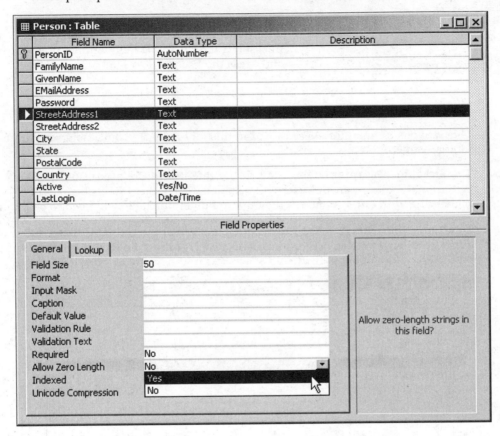

7. Next, we'll create the **Seller** table. In order to create the **Seller** table – and indeed all the remaining tables – we essentially repeat the procedure outlined in steps 2 through 6. To recap, these steps are:

    ❑   Create a new table in **Design Mode**

    ❑   Add the fields and set their types

    ❑   Set the primary key

    ❑   Save the table

    For the **Seller** table, add the fields shown here:

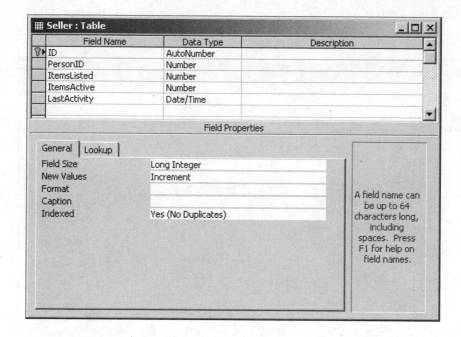

Set the ID field as the primary key, and save the table with the name Seller.

8. Next, create the Item table. For the Item table, add the fields as shown here:

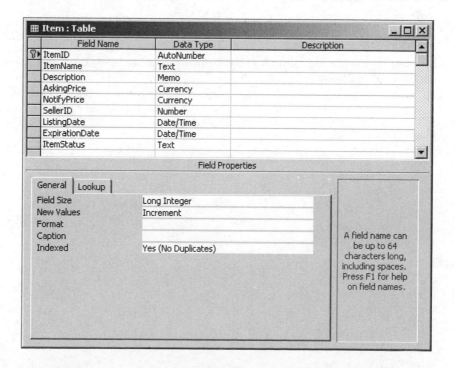

Set the ItemID field as the primary key and save the table as the Item table.

9. Create the Bid table. For the Bid table, add the fields as shown here:

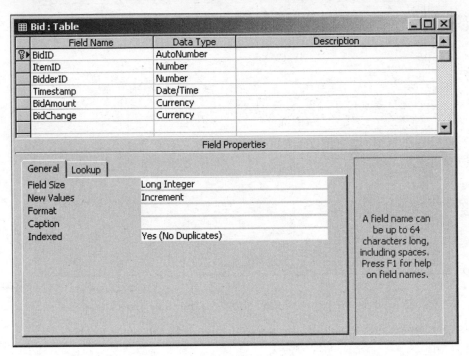

Set the BidID field as the primary key, and save the table using the name Bid.

10. While setting up the Bid table, highlight the Timestamp field; then, in the Default Value box, insert Now():

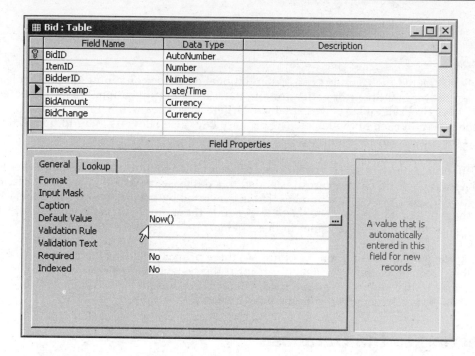

11. Finally, create the Sale table, with fields as shown here:

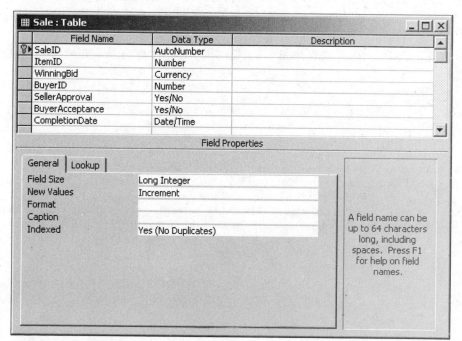

Set the SaleID field as the primary key, and save the table as the Sale table.

How It Works

Here, we've created the `Classified.mdb` relational database containing the five tables that we'll need to store all the information for our classified ads application. We have created primary keys for each table: as we explained earlier, these keys will help us to retain consistency within each of the tables. The primary keys also allow us to build up relationships between the tables, which mimic our data model.

Notice that the data type of the primary key of each table is AutoNumber. AutoNumber is a special data type. When a new record is added to a database, any field of type AutoNumber is automatically populated with a number that is generated by the database at the time. That means that we won't have to write script to generate these numbers; moreover, the database will prevent us from changing the values in these fields.

Note that the New Values option for of each of these primary fields is Increment (you can see this in the screenshots above). This indicates that the system will generate new values for the field incrementally. Moreover, such a field will contain a unique value for each record in the table – thus we easily generate a unique primary key for the table.

Connecting to the Database

When we come to write the code for our application, we'll need to refer to our database. We'll do so via the ActiveX Data Objects (ADO) – we'll be using the ADO `Connection`, `Command` and `Recordset` objects to handle the connection to the database, and we'll use the Microsoft Jet Provider for MS Access Databases to privide the `data`.

In order to specify the data connection, we'll be using the ADO Connection object, like this:

```
Dim objConn
Set objConn = Server.CreateObject("ADODB.Connection")
objConn.Open "Provider=Microsoft.Jet.OLEDB.4.0; " & _
             "Data Source= E:\datastores\classified.mdb"
...
```

This is a syntax that you've seen earlier in this book – we use `Server.CreateObject` to instantiate an ADO `Connection` object (called `objConn`), and then `Open` it, specifying the data provider that we want to use and the location of the database (I've specified `E:\datastores\classified.mdb` in this code fragment – your path may differ depending on where you saved your database). You'll see how this fits into the application later in the chapter.

Coding the Application

We've taken a look at the overall structure of our application's ASP pages, and we've built the database. The next step is to create the pages that make up the application. The first page that we will create is the starting point of the application – the home page.

The Home Page

The home page of the application is responsible for welcoming the user to the application, providing some information about what the application is for, and displaying the top-level menu selections for the user. We'll call it `Default.asp` – this means that the user can simply type in the URL of a virtual directory on our web server, and they'll automatically be directed to this page.

The application's home page will simply display a welcome message, plus some links to other pages that will enable the user to:

- ❑ Browse the items that are for sale

- ❑ Log into the system (if they are a *registered* user)

- ❑ Register with the system (if they are a *new* user)

Try It Out – Creating the Home Page

1. Using NotePad, or some other web page editor, create a new ASP file.

2. Enter the following code into your editor (if you want, you can download this file, and all of the other files in this example, from the Wrox web site at `http://www.wrox.com`):

```
<% Session.Abandon %>
<BASEFONT FACE="Comic Sans MS" COLOR="DarkBlue">
<HTML>
<HEAD>
<TITLE>Wrox Classifieds</TITLE>
</HEAD>

<BODY BGCOLOR="#FFFF80">
<CENTER><H1>Wrox Classifieds<BR>Main Menu</H1></CENTER>
<P>Thank you for visiting the Wrox Classifieds website.  We offer you the opportunity
to:
<UL>
  <LI>Browse for items on sale
  <LI>Bid for items on sale
  <LI>Sell your own items on these pages
</UL>
<P>Feel free to browse our listings - you don't need to register to do that.
If you find an item that you'd like to bid on, or if you'd like to sell something
through these pages, we will ask you to register with us.
```

```
<HR>
<TABLE BORDER=0 WIDTH=100%>
  <TR ALIGN=CENTER>
    <TD WIDTH=33%><A HREF="BrowseListings.asp">Browse the listings</A></TD>
    <TD WIDTH=33%><A HREF="Login.asp">Login</A></TD>
    <TD WIDTH=33%><A HREF="Register.asp">I'm a new user</A></TD>
  </TR>
</TABLE>
</BODY>
</HTML>
```

3. Save the file as `Default.asp`. Of course, all the `.asp` files in this application will need to be contained in a folder that is accessible to the web server, so that the ASP script within will be processed correctly. I saved the files in my `inetpub/wwwroot/BegASPFiles` folder.

4. View the page in your web browser:

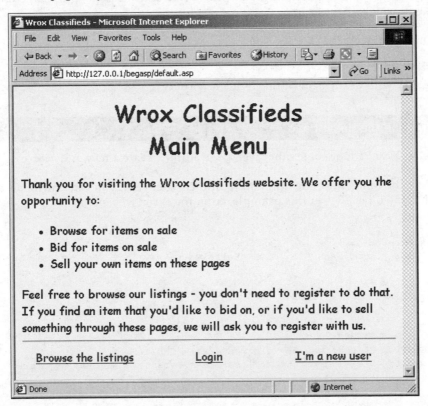

How It Works

As you can see from the code, `Default.asp` is a pretty straightforward web page. The function of this page is twofold: first, to present the user with information about what can be done at this site, and second, to give them the navigation controls needed to begin using the system.

When you look at the page, you'll notice that it is mostly straight HTML. There is only one piece of ASP script in it:

```
<% Session.Abandon %>
```

This is the first line of the file, so it's the first statement processed by ASP when a user makes their inaugural visit to the site.

We'll be using session-level variables throughout the application to store information about the current user's session. To be on the safe side, we'll want to reset all of these variables when the user first enters the site. This could prove useful if the application is called up from a public access terminal, where multiple users could be getting in to the site from the same browser. The `Abandon` method of the `Session` object will terminate any current user session, thus automatically resetting any session-level variables. This does mean that we expect the user to navigate the site using the supplied links. If they hit the back button on their browser and end up at the `default.asp` page, then their session will be terminated and they will have to log back on again.

We have placed the navigation controls at the bottom of the page. Each control is just a piece of hyperlinked text, which we use to make certain pages available to the users. At this stage, the only pages that we want to make available are `BrowseListings.asp`, `Login.asp` and `Register.asp`. We'll write these pages shortly.

User Registration and Login

So, our user arrives at the site and is presented with `Default.asp`, which offers three options:

❑ They can choose to browse the sale items list (by choosing the **Browse the listings** hyperlink).

❑ If they're a first-time user, they can register with the system (by selecting the **I'm a New User** hyperlink).

❑ If they've visited the site before, they can use their email/password combination to log on to the system (by selecting **Login** hyperlink).

We'll cover the browsing option later in the chapter; in this section, we'll focus in on registration and login.

Collecting Registration Details

In order to allow a new user to register for the first time, we'll need to collect the user's personal details, check their password, and enter all the information into the database. In order to manage this, we'll create two new pages:

❏ Register.asp will be responsible for collecting the data from the user

❏ AddUser.asp will take that data and add it to thedatabase, and then pass the user on to MenuForRegisteredUsers.asp

In fact, the process of collecting a new user's details and adding them to the database is not very different from the processes needed to allow an existing user to edit their registration details. Therefore, we'll design Register.asp and AddUser.asp so that they are able to handle both tasks.

We'll see this arrangement unfold as we take a look at the code, in the following pages. First, let's write Register.asp.

Try It Out – Collecting Registration Details with Register.asp

1. Create a new ASP file, containing the following code. You may notice a section of JavaScript at the beginning of this code – we'll discuss this in a moment. In the meantime, don't forget that JavaScript is case-sensitive:

```
<BASEFONT FACE="Comic Sans MS" COLOR="DarkBlue">
<HTML>
<HEAD>
<SCRIPT language="JavaScript">
<!--
  function VerifyData()
  {
    if (document.frmUser.Password.value != document.frmUser.VerifyPassword.value)
    {
      alert ("Your passwords do not match - please reenter");
      return false;
    }
    else
      return true;
  }
-->
</SCRIPT>

<TITLE>Wrox Classifieds - User Registration</TITLE>
</HEAD>
<BODY BGCOLOR="#FFFF80">
<CENTER>
<%
  If Request("Update") = "True" Then
    Response.Write "<H1>Wrox Classifieds<BR> Update User Registration</H1>"
  Else
    Response.Write "<H1>Wrox Classifieds<BR> New User Registration</H1>"
  End If
%>
</CENTER>
<P>
```

```
<%
  If Request("Update") = "True" Then
    Response.Write "Please change your registration information as listed below<P>"
  Else
    If Request("NotFound") = "True" Then
      Response.Write "<I>We were unable to locate your information. " & _
                     "Please take the time to register again.</I><P>"
    Else
      Response.Write "<CENTER>(If you're already registered with us, " & _
                     "then click the 'Login' link below.)</CENTER><P>"
    End If
    Response.Write "You only need to register with our system if you want to " & _
                   "bid on existing 'for-sale' items, or sell your own items " & _
                   "on these pages. <BR> " & _
                   "In order to use these services, please take a few minutes " & _
                   "to complete the form below. Once you have done that, " & _
                   "you will have full access to the system."
  End If
%>

<FORM ACTION="AddUser.asp" NAME="frmUser" METHOD="POST"
              onSubmit="return VerifyData()">
  <TABLE BORDER=0>
    <TR>
      <TD WIDTH=20% ROWSPAN=11> </TD>
      <TD>E-Mail Address:</TD>
      <TD><INPUT TYPE="Text" NAME="email" VALUE="<%= Session("EMailAddress")%>"
          SIZE="40"></TD>
    </TR>
    <TR>
      <TD>Given Name:</TD>
      <TD><INPUT TYPE="Text" NAME="GivenName" VALUE="<%= Session("GivenName")%>"
          SIZE="40"></TD>
    </TR>
    <TR>
      <TD>Family Name:</TD>
      <TD><INPUT TYPE="Text" NAME="FamilyName" VALUE="<%= Session("FamilyName")%>"
          SIZE="40"></TD>
    </TR>
    <TR>
      <TD>Address:</TD>
      <TD><INPUT TYPE="Text" NAME="Address1" VALUE="<%= Session("StreetAddress1")%>"
          SIZE="40"></TD>
    </TR>
    <TR>
      <TD></TD>
      <TD><INPUT TYPE="Text" NAME="Address2" VALUE="<%= Session("StreetAddress2")%>"
          SIZE="40"></TD>
    </TR>
    <TR>
      <TD>City:</TD>
      <TD><INPUT TYPE="Text" NAME="City" VALUE="<%= Session("City")%>"
          SIZE="40"></TD>
    </TR>
```

```
    <TR>
      <TD>State:</TD>
      <TD><INPUT TYPE="Text" NAME="State" VALUE="<%= Session("State")%>"
          SIZE="40"></TD>
    </TR>
    <TR>
      <TD>Postal Code:</TD>
      <TD><INPUT TYPE="Text" NAME="PostalCode" VALUE="<%= Session("PostalCode")%>"
          SIZE="40"></TD>
    </TR>
    <TR>
      <TD>Country:</TD>
      <TD><INPUT TYPE="Text" NAME="Country" VALUE="<%= Session("Country")%>"
          SIZE="40"></TD>
    </TR>
    <TR>
      <TD> <P>Password:</TD>
      <TD VALIGN=bottom><INPUT TYPE="Password" NAME="Password"
                          VALUE="<%= Session("Password") %>" SIZE="40"></TD>
    </TR>
    <TR>
      <TD>Verify Password:</TD>
      <TD><INPUT TYPE="Password" NAME="VerifyPassword" SIZE="40"></TD>
    </TR>
    <TR>
      <TD></TD>
      <TD ALIGN=CENTER COLSPAN=2><BR>
          <INPUT TYPE="Submit" VALUE="Submit Registration">
               <INPUT TYPE="RESET"></TD>
    </TR>
  </TABLE>
</FORM>

<HR>
<TABLE BORDER=0 WIDTH=100%>
  <TR ALIGN=CENTER>
    <TD WIDTH=33%><A HREF="BrowseListings.asp">Browse the listings</A></TD>
    <TD WIDTH=33%><A HREF="Login.asp">Login</A></TD>
    <TD WIDTH=33%>I'm a new user</TD>
  </TR>
</TABLE>

</BODY>
</HTML>
```

2. Save the file as `Register.asp`, in the same folder as you placed `Default.asp`.

3. From the home page, click on the I'm a new user hyperlink to view the registration page. Add some registration details, but don't press the Submit button – we haven't added the page to handle that yet.

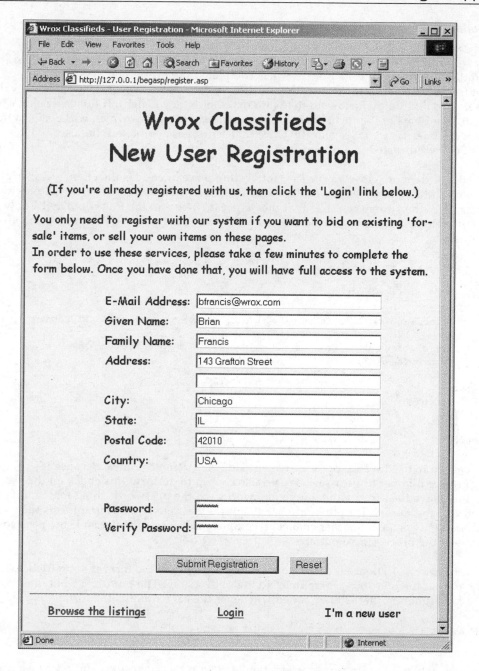

How It Works

There seems to be quite a lot of code here, but it's not too difficult. The main task of
Register.asp is to present the user with a form, which they will use to submit their
registration information. When the user has completed the form, they press the
Submit Registration button. At this stage, a client-side script is executed to parse the values of
the **Password** and **Verify Password** fields (to make sure they match). If this brief check is
successful, contents of the form are submitted to AddUser.asp – which will perform the
database updates, as we'll see shortly. Once that script has completed, the user will be
automatically redirected to another page.

Let's look a little more closely. The first interesting piece of code is the client-side script section,
which we've placed near the top of the page. To ensure that the user entered the password that
they intended, the system requires that they enter it twice – in the **Password** and **Verify
Password** fields on the form. So the purpose of the VerifyData() function is to compare these
two values:

```
<SCRIPT language="JavaScript">
  <!--
    function VerifyData()
    {
      if (document.frmUser.Password.value != document.frmUser.VerifyPassword.value)
      {
        alert ("Your passwords do not match - please reenter");
        return false;
      }
      else
        return true;
    }
  -->
</SCRIPT>
```

We've chosen to use JavaScript for our client-side validation routines, because it's compatible
with a greater number of browsers. We've also chosen to perform this check on the *client*-side,
rather than have the *server* validate the passwords – if the passwords don't match, this saves us
a round-trip to the server. In this case, we display a message box which informs the user of the
problem and gives them another chance to complete the password fields. If the passwords do
match, then the processing continues.

The VerifyData() client-side function is called at the time the form is submitted. We achieve
this by adding the onSubmit parameter to the <FORM> tag. The onSubmit parameter identifies
a client-side function that is to be called whenever the user submits the form:

```
<FORM ACTION="AddUser.asp" NAME="frmUser" METHOD="POST"
          onSubmit="return VerifyData()">
```

In this case, when the form is submitted, the VerifyData() executes and returns a result of
either true or false (according to whether or not the values of the **Password** and **Verify
Password** fields matched).

As we mentioned earlier, `Register.asp` is dual-purpose – as well as collecting registration details for *new* users, we can use it to allow *existing* users to modify their details. How do we differentiate between these two cases? We've used a querystring variable called `Update`. If the value of this variable is `True` then we know that we're dealing with a user who wants to update existing registration details. Otherwise, we're dealing with a new user. Thus, we can customize the display accordingly:

```
<%
  If Request("Update") = "True" then
    Response.Write "<H1>Wrox Classifieds<BR> Update User Registration</H1>"
  Else
    Response.Write "<H1>Wrox Classifieds<BR> New User Registration</H1>"
  End If
%>
```

> *If you flick forward a few pages, you'll find that pages such as `BrowseListings.asp` and `MenuForRegisteredUsers.asp` contain an* **Edit Registration Info** *hyperlink, which provides a click-through to* `Register.asp?Update="True"`.

In fact, we've customized the message even further. We've added a special message for any user who tries to log on using `Login.asp` (see later), but whose login details are not matched with data contained in the database. In this case, we need to ask the unrecognized user to re-register with the system. To do this, we redirect the user to `Register.asp?NotFound="True"` – and we use the querystring variable called `NotFound` to tailor the message accordingly:

```
<%
  If Request("Update") = "True" Then
    Response.Write "Please change your registration information as listed below<P>"
  Else
    If Request("NotFound") = "True" Then
      Response.Write "<I>We were unable to locate your information. " & _
                     "Please take the time to register again.</I><P>"
    Else
      Response.Write "<CENTER>(If you're already registered with us, " & _
                     "then click the 'Login' link below.)</CENTER><P>"
    End If
    ...
  End If
%>
```

The registration information itself is collected in an HTML form. If we're using the form to update existing information, then it would be good to display the existing information within the form (so the user can see their 'initial values'). In our application, each logged-on user's information is stored in session-level variables. Hence, it is a simple matter of retrieving the information for each of the fields from its corresponding session-level variable:

```
<FORM ACTION="AddUser.asp" NAME="frmUser" METHOD="POST"
              onSubmit="return VerifyData()">
  <TABLE BORDER=0>
    <TR>
```

```
        <TD WIDTH=20% ROWSPAN=11> </TD>
        <TD>E-Mail Address:</TD>
        <TD><INPUT TYPE="Text" NAME="email" VALUE="<%= Session("EMailAddress")%>"
            SIZE="40"></TD>
    </TR>
    <TR>
      <TD>Given Name:</TD>
      <TD><INPUT TYPE="Text" NAME="GivenName" VALUE="<%= Session("GivenName")%>"
            SIZE="40"></TD>
    </TR>
    . . .
```

In the case of a new user, the session-level variables will be 'undefined', and consequently will have no values – so they will just return blank strings.

> *This works because, if the session variable has not been assigned any other value, then it is assumed to contain an empty string.*

There's one exception to this – the **Verify Password** field. We want to force the user to type in their password at least once, in order to verify their identity. Hence, we *don't* associate a default value with the **VerifyPassword** verification field:

```
    . . .
      <TD> <P>Password:</TD>
      <TD VALIGN=bottom><INPUT TYPE="Password" NAME="Password"
                      VALUE="<%= Session("Password") %>" SIZE="40"></TD>
    </TR>
    <TR>
      <TD>Verify Password:</TD>
      <TD><INPUT TYPE="Password" NAME="VerifyPassword" SIZE="40"></TD>
    </TR>
    <TR>
      <TD></TD>
      <TD ALIGN=CENTER COLSPAN=2><BR>
          <INPUT TYPE="Submit" VALUE="Submit Registration">
                <INPUT TYPE="RESET"></TD>
    </TR>
  </TABLE>
</FORM>
```

When the user clicks on the **Submit Registration** button, and the form is accepted (that is, their password values match), processing is passed to the `AddUser.asp` file (as specified in the `ACTION` attribute of the `<FORM>` tag above). Let's look at `AddUser.asp` now.

Handling Registration Details

`AddUser.asp` is a bit different from most ASP script files, in that it doesn't have a user interface. Its sole purpose is to take the information submitted by the form in the `Register.asp` page, and to put those values into the database. Based on the results of these database functions, the browser is directed to another page, where the user continues with the application.

1. Create a new file in your editor and enter the following code:

```
<!--#include file="Clssfd.asp"-->
<%
 Dim rsUsers
 Set rsUsers = Server.CreateObject("ADODB.Recordset")
 rsUsers.Open "Person", objConn, adOpenForwardOnly, adLockOptimistic, adCmdTable

 If Session("PersonID") <> "" Then                         ' currently logged-on user
   rsUsers.Filter = "PersonID = '" & Session("PersonID") & "'"
 Else                                                        ' New session
   rsUsers.Filter = "EMailAddress = '" & Request.Form("email") & "'" & _
                    "AND Password = '" & Request.Form("password") & "'"
   If rsUsers.EOF Then                                      ' User not found
     rsUsers.AddNew                                         ' ...so add a new record
 '   Else
 '   Email address and password matched with DB records -
 '   In this case we'll allow this to update user's personal details
   End If
 End If

                                                            ' write personal details to record
 rsUsers("EMailAddress") = Request.Form("email")
 rsUsers("Password") = Request.Form("password")
 rsUsers("Surname") = Request.Form("Surname")
 rsUsers("FirstName") = Request.Form("FirstName")
 rsUsers("StreetAddress1") = Request.Form("Address1")
 rsUsers("StreetAddress2") = Request.Form("Address2")
 rsUsers("City") = Request.Form("City")
 rsUsers("State") = Request.Form("State")
 rsUsers("PostalCode") = Request.Form("PostalCode")
 rsUsers("Country") = Request.Form("Country")
 rsUsers("Active") = True
 rsUsers("LastLogin") = Now
 rsUsers.Update                                             ' update the database

 Dim strName, strValue                                      ' create session variables
 For each strField in rsUsers.Fields
   strName = strField.Name
   strValue = strField.value
   Session(strName) = strValue
 Next
 Session("blnValidUser") = True            ' declare that current user is validated
 Response.Redirect "MenuForRegisteredUsers.asp"
%>
```

2. Save this file as AddUser.asp.

3. Now we'll create the include file that was called from the file above. Create another file in your editor and enter the following code:

```
<!-- METADATA TYPE="typelib"
              FILE="E:\Program Files\Common Files\System\ado\msado15.dll" -->
<%
  Dim objConn
  Set objConn = Server.CreateObject("ADODB.Connection")
  objConn.Open "Provider=Microsoft.Jet.OLEDB.4.0; " & _
               "Data Source= E:\datastores\classified.mdb"

  If Session("blnValidUser") = True and Session("PersonID") = "" Then
    Dim rsPersonIDCheck
    Set rsPersonIDCheck = Server.CreateObject("ADODB.Recordset")
    Dim strSQL
    strSQL = "SELECT PersonID FROM Person " & _
             "WHERE EMailAddress = '" & Session("EMailAddress") & "';"
    rsPersonIDCheck.Open strSQL, objConn
    If rsPersonIDCheck.EOF Then
      Session("blnValidUser") = False
    Else
      Session("PersonID") = rsPersonIDCheck("PersonID")
    End If
    rsPersonIDCheck.Close
    Set rsPersonIDCheck = Nothing
  End If
%>
```

4. Save this file as `Clssfd.asp`, in the same folder as the other `.asp` files.

5. Note that `Clssfd.asp` uses the ADO type library that we have used previously. You'll need to check that the path of this file is correct for your machine.

6. We'll add just one more ASP page at this stage – so create one more new file and insert the following code:

```
<%
  If Session("PersonID") = "" Then
    Response.Redirect "Login.asp"
  End If
%>

<BASEFONT FACE="Comic Sans MS" COLOR="DarkBlue">
<HTML>
<HEAD>
<TITLE>Wrox Classifieds</TITLE>
</HEAD>

<BODY BGCOLOR="#FFFF80">
<CENTER><H1>Wrox Classifieds<BR>Registered Users' Menu</H1>
<H3>Welcome <%= Session("GivenName") %></H1>
</CENTER><P>
Thank you for visiting the Wrox Classifieds site. We offer you the opportunity to:
<UL>
  <LI>Browse for items on sale
```

```
  <LI>Bid for items on sale
  <LI>Sell your own items on these pages
</UL>
<HR>
<TABLE BORDER=0 WIDTH=100%>
  <TR ALIGN=CENTER>
    <TD WIDTH=33%><A HREF="BrowseListings.asp">Browse the listings</A></TD>
    <TD WIDTH=33%><A HREF="ViewMySaleItems.asp">List/Edit Sale Items</A></TD>
    <TD WIDTH=33%><A HREF="Register.asp?Update=True">Edit Registration Info</A></TD>
  </TR>
</TABLE>
</BODY>
</HTML>
```

7. Save this file as `MenuForRegisteredUsers.asp`, in the same folder as the other `.asp` files.

8. In `Register.asp`, type some registration details into the form and click the **Submit Registration** button. If your details are valid, this will handle your registration and take you to the `MenuForRegisteredUsers.asp` page:

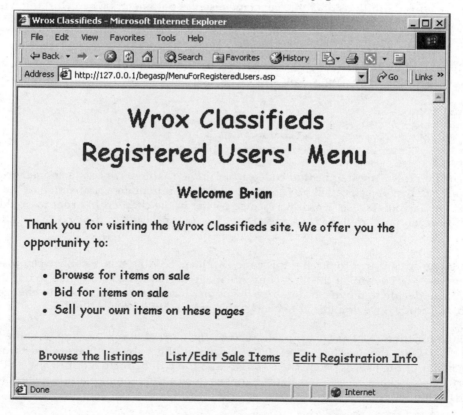

How It Works

AddUser.asp leaps into action when the user submits the form on Register.asp.
AddUser.asp captures the contents of the form (with in the Request object's Form collection)
and places this data into the database. The first line of the AddUser.asp file is a server-side
include (SSI) directive:

```
<!--#include file="Clssfd.asp"-->
```

This directive instructs the ASP script processor to load the file named Clssfd.asp, and
process its contents as if it were part of the AddUser.asp file. In this application, the
Clssfd.asp SSI is used to encapsulate all the data access connection information into a single
file.

The first line of Clssfd.asp contains a reference to the ADO type library that we encountered
in Chapter 12:

```
<!-- METADATA TYPE="typelib"
          FILE="E:\Program Files\Common Files\System\ado\msado15.dll" -->
```

This file contains definitions of all the constants used as parameters when working with the
ADODB objects. By using these predefined constants, instead of their numerical equivalents,
our code will be more readable.

The remainder of Clssfd.asp is used to perform two functions. The first declares a variable
that will hold the database connection and then creates and opens that connection:

```
Dim objConn
Set objConn = Server.CreateObject("ADODB.Connection")
objConn.Open "Provider=Microsoft.Jet.OLEDB.4.0; " & _
          "Data Source= E:\datastores\classified.mdb"
```

We touched on this little fragment of code earlier in the chapter. We create an instance of the
ADO Connection object, called objConn. Then we use it to open a connection to the
Classified.mdb database, which we created earlier in the chapter. In order to do this, we use
the Microsoft Jet data Provider for Access Databases (as specified in the Provider attribute
here).

There are two advantages to placing this code within an SSI like this. First, we can place the SSI
directive for Clssfd.asp at the top of any ASP page that needs a connection to our database.
Second, if we decide to move our database to another location, we only need to change the
Clssfd.asp code – we don't need to change the code in all the other files.

The second function of Clssfd.asp is to retrieve the current user's PersonID value from the
Person table. Once the user has successfully registered, this value will be needed throughout
the remainder of the user session. The Clssfd.asp file will be included into any ASP script
that performs database access, and it just happens to be a convenient place to ensure that we
have this value.

Here's how this works. We have a session variable called `blnValidUser` – if we're working with a logged-in user then the value of this variable is `True`. (You'll see `blnValidUser` cropping up elsewhere in the application too.) If we're working with a logged-in user but the `PersonID` session variable is blank, then we set about repopulating it from the database:

```
If Session("blnValidUser") = True and Session("PersonID") = "" Then
```

We do this simply by querying the **Person** table of the database for the information that we need. The results of the query will be returned as a recordset – so first we need to *create* the recordset:

```
Dim rsPersonIDCheck
Set rsPersonIDCheck = Server.CreateObject("ADODB.Recordset")
Dim strSQL
strSQL = "SELECT PersonID FROM Person " & _
        "WHERE EMailAddress = '" & Session("EMailAddress") & "';"
rsPersonIDCheck.Open strSQL, objConn
```

The SQL query here is written so that it retrieves only the **PersonID** field, rather than the entire record. The `WHERE` clause tells the SQL query the e-mail address of the user in question. Then the query goes in search of the user's `PersonID` value.

If there is no information in the database for the given e-mail address, then the current user is logged out by setting the session-level variable `blnValidUser` to `False`. Otherwise, the `PersonID` value is stored in a session-level variable called `PersonID`. Finally, we can close the `rsPersonIDCheck` recordset and release its resources:

```
If rsPersonIDCheck.EOF Then
  Session("blnValidUser") = False
Else
  Session("PersonID") = rsPersonIDCheck("PersonID")
End If
rsPersonIDCheck.Close
Set rsPersonIDCheck = Nothing
End If
```

And that's it for `Clssfd.asp` – so we can return to the execution of `AddUser.asp`. We've already used `objConn.Open` to open the database connection, and (if the user is already a valid user) we've ensured that the `Session("PersonID")` variable is populated. We're now in a position to add the necessary data to the database. To handle the interaction with the **Person** table, we'll use another recordset object called `rsUsers`:

```
Dim rsUsers
Set rsUsers = Server.CreateObject("ADODB.Recordset")
rsUsers.Open "Person", objConn, adOpenForwardOnly, adLockOptimistic, adCmdTable
```

The `rsUsers.Open` command will populate the recordset with the contents of the **Person** table. We've used the `adLockOptimistic` parameter to this method call, which will allow us to write information into the table.

Recall that `adOpenForwardOnly`, `adLockOptimistic` and `adCmdTable` are all constants, and are defined within the ADO type library (`msado15.dll`).

Now, if we're working with a new user then we'll need to add a new record to the recordset. On the other hand, if we're working with an existing user it wouldn't make sense to add a new record – instead we'll need to locate the existing record in the recordset. To handle all this, we check to see whether the `PersonID` session variable is populated, and then we filter the recordset according to the result:

```
If Session("PersonID") <> "" Then                       ' currently logged-on user
   rsUsers.Filter = "PersonID = '" & Session("PersonID") & "'"
Else                                                     ' New session
   rsUsers.Filter = "EMailAddress = '" & Request.Form("email") & "'" & _
                    "AND Password = '" & Request.Form("password") & "'"
   If rsUsers.EOF Then                                   ' User not found
      rsUsers.AddNew                                     ' ...so add a new record
'   Else
'      Email address and password matched with DB records -
'      In this case we'll allow this to update user's personal details
   End If
End If
```

Remember that the `PersonID` field is unique to the user. If the `Session("PersonID")` variable is populated then it will refer to a unique record in the **Person** table of the recordset – so we can be sure that the user is not overwriting another user's information.

By contrast, if `Session("PersonID")` is not populated, and the email/password combination doesn't match any record in the **Person** table, then we know we're dealing with a new user – and we add a new record to the recordset, using `AddNew`.

Having located the existing record or created a new one, it's time to retrieve the user's registration details from the `Request` object's `Form` collection, and copy them into the corresponding fields of the current record of the recordset:

```
rsUsers("EMailAddress") = Request.Form("email")
rsUsers("Password") = Request.Form("password")
rsUsers("FamilyName") = Request.Form("FamilyName")
rsUsers("GivenName") = Request.Form("GivenName")
...
rsUsers("LastLogin") = Now
```

If we're updating an existing record, then the new values will simply overwrite any existing data. Otherwise, the data is written to the new user's record. Once all of the information has been added, the data is written to the database by using the `Update` method of the recordset object.

```
rsUsers.Update
```

The next step is to write all of the information from the recordset into session-level variables. There is no single method that will automatically perform this copying process. We could have written a series of statements that copied each field from the recordset to the session-level variable, but that would have been pretty tedious. Instead, we utilize the `Fields` collection of the `Recordset` object, which contains all of the individual `Field` objects in the recordset:

```
Dim strName, strValue
For Each strField in rsUsers.Fields
  strName = strField.Name
  strValue = strField.value
  Session(strName) = strValue
Next
```

We use the `For Each` statement to iterate through each field in the collection. We retrieve the name and value of each `Field` object; then we can create a corresponding session-level variable that has the same name as the `Field` object, and assign it the same value.

Now, the user is successfully registered. Ideally, the user shouldn't need to go back and log in straight away – so we immediately grant them "logged-on" status. We set the `blnValidUser` session-level variable to `True`, and instruct the client browser to load the `MenuForRegisteredUsers.asp` page automatically. This will present a registered user's home page to our newly-registered user:

```
Session("blnValidUser") = True
Response.Redirect "MenuForRegisteredUsers.asp"
```

Let's take a quick look at `MenuForRegisteredUsers.asp`. This page provides a different set of navigational tools, and displays a personalized greeting to the user. Later in this chapter, we will add to the registered user's home page to provide additional information.

Since this page is for registered users only, the first thing we do on this page is check the value of `Session("PersonID")`, to confirm that the user really *is* properly registered. If they are not, then their browser is redirected to the login page, so that the user may log into the system:

```
<%
  If Session("PersonID") = "" Then
    Response.Redirect "Login.asp"
  End If
%>
```

To provide a personalized greeting to the user, we display their name in a welcome message. Since all of the user information is stored as session-level variables, there is no need to perform any database access to retrieve this information. It can simply be retrieved from the appropriate session-level variables:

```
<CENTER><H1>Wrox Classifieds<BR>Registered Users' Menu</H1>
<H3>Welcome <%= Session("GivenName") %></H1>
</CENTER><P>
```

Managing User Login

If you were a user who'd registered on a previous occasion, and you were coming to revisit the site, then you wouldn't expect to be asked to go through the registration process again. So, to allow previously-registered users to identify themselves, we will present a login page, `Login.asp`. We'll also need another page, `CheckLogin.asp`, which will check the details against the database and redirect the user accordingly. These two pages serve as an alternative route from `Default.asp` to `MenuForRegisteredUsers.asp`.

Try It Out – The Login Screen and Login Checker

1. Create a new ASP file and key in the following code:

```
<!DOCTYPE HTML PUBLIC "-//W3C//DTD HTML 3.2 Final//EN">
<BASEFONT FACE="Comic Sans MS" COLOR="DarkBlue">
<HTML>
<HEAD>
<TITLE>Wrox Classifieds - Login</TITLE>
</HEAD>

<BODY BGCOLOR="#FFFF80">
<CENTER><H1>Wrox Classifieds<BR>Login</H1></CENTER>
<P>
<%
<% If Request("Again") = "1" then if Request("BadPW") = "True" then %>
  Invalid Password<BR>
<% Else %>
     E-Mail Address not found. Try again<BR>
  <% End If %>
<% End If %>
Please enter your e-mail address and password to login to the system.
<FORM ACTION="CheckLogin.asp<% If Request("Again")="1" then %>?Again=1
                    <% End If %>" METHOD="POST">
  <TABLE BORDER=0>
    <TR>
      <TD>E-Mail Address:</TD>
      <TD><INPUT TYPE="Text" NAME="email"
          <% If Request("Again") = "1" then %>
            VALUE="<%= Session("EMailAddress") %>"
          <% End If %>
          SIZE="40"></TD>
    </TR>
    <TR>
      <TD>Password:</TD>
      <TD><INPUT TYPE="Password" NAME="Password" SIZE="40"></TD>
    </TR>
    <TR>

      <TD></TD>
      <TD align=center><INPUT TYPE="Submit" VALUE="Login">  
                    <INPUT TYPE="RESET"></TD>
    </TR>
  </TABLE>
</FORM>
```

```
<HR>
<TABLE BORDER=0 WIDTH=100%>
  <TR ALIGN=CENTER>
    <TD WIDTH=33%><A HREF="BrowseListings.asp">Browse the listings</A></TD>
    <TD WIDTH=33%>Login</TD>
    <TD WIDTH=33%><A HREF="Register.asp?NotFound=True">I'm a new user</A></TD>
  </TR>
</TABLE>

</BODY>
</HTML>
```

2. Save the file as Login.asp, in the same directory as your other ASP files.

3. Create another new ASP file using your editor and enter the following code:

```
<!--#include file="Clssfd.asp"-->
<%
  Dim strEMail, strPassword
  strEMail = Request("EMail")
  strPassword = Request("Password")

  Dim rsUsers
  set rsUsers = Server.CreateObject("ADODB.Recordset")
  strSQL = "SELECT * FROM Person WHERE EMailAddress = '" & strEMail & "';"
  rsUsers.Open strSQL, objConn

  If rsUsers.EOF Then                                    ' User not found
    Session("EMailAddress") = Request("EMail")
    If Request("SecondTry") = "True" then               ' User's had two goes
      Response.Redirect "register.asp?NotFound=True"        ' - must register
    Else                                          ' Username wrong; password wrong
      Response.Redirect "login.asp?SecondTry=True"          ' - allow another go
    End If
  Else                                      'One or more users found - check password
    While Not rsUsers.EOF
      If UCase(rsUsers("Password")) = UCase(strPassword) Then    ' password matched
        Dim strName, strValue
        For Each strField in rsUsers.Fields
          strName = strField.Name                      ' populate session variables
          strValue = strField.value
          Session(strName) = strValue
        Next
        Session("blnValidUser") = True
        Response.Redirect "MenuForRegisteredUsers.asp"       ' successful login
      Else
```

```
        rsUsers.MoveNext
    End If
  Wend
  Session("EMailAddress") = Request("EMail")          ' if we get this far then...
                                        ' ...password doesn't match any of DB entries


  If Request("SecondTry") = "True" then                ' User's had two goes
    Response.Redirect "register.asp"                    ' - must reregister
  Else                                      ' Username right; password wrong
    Response.Redirect "login.asp?SecondTry=True&WrongPW=True"
                                                        '- allow another go

  End If
End If
%>
```

4. Save the file as `CheckLogin.asp`, in the same directory as your other ASP files.

5. Now, you can start a fresh session at `Default.asp` – click on the Login hyperlink to view the login page, and enter your login information:

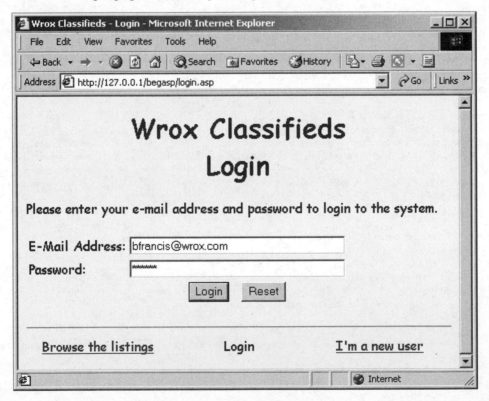

6. Now click on the Login button. This will check your login information against the information contained in the database and then take you to the registered user's home page, `MenuForRegisteredUsers.asp`.

How It Works

`Login.asp` allows a previously-registered user to log into the system without going though the entire registration process again. They just type their e-mail address and password into the form, and submit this data. With some web servers, the user registration can be accomplished with the web server itself. In our example, we will be performing the validation within our own ASP code.

Like `Register.asp`, there is more than one scenario in which `Login.asp` may be called, and again we can customize the exact appearance of the page to suit the occasion. In the code above, you'll see that `CheckLogin.asp` handles an unsuccessful login attempt by redirecting the user to `Login.asp`, specifying the querystring `SecondTry=True` (and possibly also `WrongPW=True`). We use these values in `Login.asp`, to tailor the message that the user sees, based on the results of any previous login attempt:

```
If Request("SecondTry") = "True" Then        ' User's second attempt at logging in
   If Request("WrongPW") = "True" Then                  ' Right email; wrong PW
     Response.Write "Invalid Password. Please try again: " & _
                 "if you get it wrong we'll ask you to re-register.<BR>"
   Else                                                 ' Wrong email
     Response.Write "E-Mail Address not found. Please try again: " & _
                 "if you get it wrong we'll ask you to re-register.<BR>"
   End If
End If
Response.Write "Please enter your e-mail address and password " & _
             "to login to the system."
```

Like `Register.asp`, we use an HTML form to collect the login information. If the user is *re-entering* login information, we can help them by displaying e-mail address that they entered on their first attempt:

```
<TR>
  <TD>E-Mail Address:</TD>
  <TD><INPUT TYPE="Text" NAME="email"
     <% If Request("SecondTry") = "True" then %>
       VALUE="<%= Session("EMailAddress") %>"
     <% End If %>
     SIZE="40"></TD>
</TR>
```

This helps the user to work out what they might have done wrong on their first attempt.

To submit the login information, the user presses the **Login** button. Then, the `CheckLogin.asp` script file performs the task of validating this information against the database.

`CheckLogin.asp` is like the `AddUser.asp` script file in that it has no user interface. Since it will perform database access, we include the `Clssfd.asp` SSI file. Then, to add to the legibility of the text and increase the performance of the script, we copy the user's e-mail address and password values from the `Request.Form` collection into a couple of locally-defined variables, `strEMail` and `strPassword`:

```
<!--#include file="Clssfd.asp"-->
<%
  Dim strEMail, strPassword
  strEMail = Request("EMail")
  strPassword = Request("Password")
```

In order to parse the user's login details, we need to query the **Person** table of the database. We place the results of the query into a recordset, and then compare the values of `strEMail` and `strPassword` with the values contained in the recordset. If there's a match, then the user is successfully identified. If not, we need to take alternative action.

So, first let's look at the database query. We create a new ADO `Recordset` object, define the SQL query and execute the query by opening the recordset against the database like this:

```
Dim rsUsers
set rsUsers = Server.CreateObject("ADODB.Recordset")
strSQL = "SELECT * FROM Person WHERE EMailAddress = '" & strEMail & "';"
rsUsers.Open strSQL, objConn
```

Here, the SQL statement queries the **Person** table for all records whose e-mail address matches the one supplied by the user. The results of this SQL query are stored in the `rsUsers` recordset.

Now we can start the check. First, did the SQL query return any records at all? If not, then the e-mail address given by the user doesn't match anything found in the database. In this case, we place the user's e-mail address into a session variable and redirect them to `Register.asp` (if it's their second attempt to register) or back to `Login.asp` (if it's their first attempt):

```
If rsUsers.EOF Then                                    ' User not found
  Session("EMailAddress") = Request("EMail")
  If Request("SecondTry") = "True" then                ' User's had two goes
    Response.Redirect "register.asp?NotFound=True"      ' - must register
  Else                                        ' Username wrong; password wrong
    Response.Redirect "login.asp?SecondTry=True"         ' - allow another go
  End If
  ...
```

The alternative is that the SQL query succeeds in populating the recordset with one or more records – which means that we have one or more records whose `EmailAddress` field matches that given by the user. In this case, we now need to compare passwords. In our application, passwords are not case sensitive. We force both the password from the database and the one submitted by the user to uppercase, before performing the comparison:

```
Else                                    'One or more users found - check password
  While Not rsUsers.EOF
    If UCase(rsUsers("Password")) = UCase(strPassword) Then     ' password matched
```

If the passwords do match, then we have a valid user. In this case, we copy the contents of the current record into a set of session variables, set the `blnValidUser` flag to `True` and redirect the client to `MenuForRegisteredUsers.asp` (in fact, this next fragment is very similar to code that we saw earlier, in `AddUser.asp`):

```
Dim strName, strValue
For Each strField in rsUsers.Fields
  strName = strField.Name                    ' populate session variables
  strValue = strField.value
  Session(strName) = strValue
Next
Session("blnValidUser") = True
Response.Redirect "MenuForRegisteredUsers.asp"        ' successful login
```

If the user's password and the password contained in the record are not the same, then we move to the next record in the recordset, and try the comparison again:

```
  Else
      rsUsers.MoveNext
  End If
Wend
```

If we get to the end of the recordset in this way, then we've got a successful email match but we can't match the passwords successfully. In this final case, we will again redirect the user either to Register.asp or to Login.asp:

```
Session("EMailAddress") = Request("EMail")         ' if we get this far then...
                              ' ...password doesn't match any of DB entries

If Request("SecondTry") = "True" then               ' User's had two goes
  Response.Redirect "register.asp"                  ' - must reregister
Else                                     ' Username right; password wrong
  Response.Redirect "login.asp?SecondTry=True&WrongPW=True"  '- allow another go
End If
End If
```

*Finally, note that we've used Response.Redirect here to redirect the user to a different page. As we've mentioned in previous chapters, ASP 3.0 offers two new methods for executing other pages – they are Server.Transfer and Server.Execute. Note that all three methods work quite differently. In this situation in particular, Response.Redirect is preferred to Server.Transfer – although the latter avoids a round-trip to the client, it doesn't support querystrings and it doesn't reflect the current page in the browser's **Address** window.*

We've now got a complete, albeit simplistic, user login and registration system for our application. The next step is to allow registered users to start managing the items that they have for sale.

Managing Items for Sale

Once a user is registered, they can start posting items for sale. When posting an item for sale, the user must provide some information about it. The information involved for each sale item is:

- ❑ A descriptive name of the item
- ❑ A long description of the item
- ❑ The desired price for the item
- ❑ The price at which the system should notify you
- ❑ The date after which the item will no longer be for sale

Some of this information will be displayed to potential buyers, and some is used internally in the system. And there's more to managing the 'for sale' items than just adding items to a list – we need a mechanism that allows the seller to edit the details or to remove an item from listings. We'll cover these interfaces in the following Try It Out's.

Viewing one's Own Sale Items

First, we'll write a page called `ViewMySaleItems.asp` – this page displays a list of the items that the current user has already made available for sale.

Try It Out – Displaying the Items that a User Has for Sale

1. Create a new ASP file; enter the following code into your editor:

```
<!--#include file="Clssfd.asp"-->
<%
  If Session("PersonID") = "" Then
    Response.Redirect "Login.asp"
  End if
%>

<BASEFONT FACE="Comic Sans MS" COLOR="DarkBlue">
<HTML>
<HEAD>
<TITLE>Wrox Classifieds</TITLE>
</HEAD>

<BODY BGCOLOR="#FFFF80">
<CENTER>
<H1>Wrox Classifieds<BR>Selling Items</H1>
<H3>Welcome <%= Session("GivenName") %></H3>
</CENTER>

<P>You currently have the following items for sale:</P>
<%
  Dim rsItems
  Set rsItems = Server.CreateObject("ADODB.Recordset")
  rsItems.Filter = "SellerID = " & Session("PersonID")
  rsItems.Open "Item", objConn, adOpenForwardOnly, adLockOptimistic, adCmdTable
```

```
If Not rsItems.EOF Then                          ' current user has items for sale
   Response.Write _
      "<TABLE BORDER=""1"" CELLSPACING=""3"" CELLPADDING=""3"">" & _
      "<TR>" & _
      "  <TH>Item ID<BR><FONT SIZE=""-1"">Click to <BR>Edit/Delete</FONT></TH>" & _
      "  <TH>Name</TH>" & _
      "  <TH>Asking Price</TH>" & _
      "  <TH>Listing Date</TH>" & _
      "  <TH>Current Bid</TH>" & _
      "  <TH>Bid Time</TH>" & _
      "</TR>"
   Do While Not rsItems.EOF
     Response.Write _
        "<TR ALIGN=CENTER>" & _
        "  <TD><A HREF=""item.asp?Action=Edit&Item=" & rsItems("ItemID") & """>" & _
                rsItems("ItemID") & "</A></TD>" & _
        "  <TD>" & rsItems("ItemName") & "</TD>" & _
        "  <TD>" & FormatCurrency(rsItems("AskingPrice")) & "</TD>" & _
        "  <TD>" & FormatDateTime(rsItems("ListingDate"),2) & "</TD>" & _
        "</TR>"
     rsItems.MoveNext
   Loop
   Response.Write "</TABLE>"
 Else                                             ' current user has no items for sale
   Response.Write "<CENTER><H2>No items currently for sale</H2></CENTER>"
 End If
 rsItems.close
%>
<HR>
<TABLE BORDER=0 WIDTH=100%>
  <TR ALIGN=CENTER>
    <TD WIDTH=33%><A HREF="BrowseListings.asp">Browse the listings</A></TD>
    <TD WIDTH=33%><A HREF="Item.asp?Action=AddNew">Add Sale Items</A></TD>
    <TD WIDTH=33%><A HREF="Register.asp?Update=True">Edit Registration Info</A></TD>
  </TR>
</TABLE>
</BODY>
</HTML>
```

2. Save the file as ViewMySaleItems.asp, in the folder that contains your other .asp files.

3. From the registered users' home page (MenuForRegisteredUsers.asp), click on the **List/Edit Sale Items** hyperlink to view the 'Items for Sale' page. It looks fairly dull at the moment because we haven't added any items to the sale listings, but it will look a bit livelier later in the chapter.

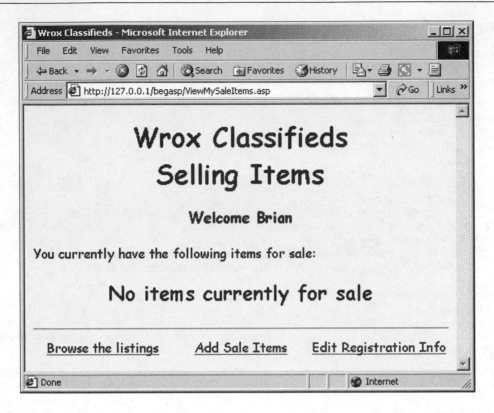

How It Works

`ViewMySaleItems.asp` is used to display the items that the logged-in user currently has for sale. In order to retrieve this information, we query the database's Item table for all records where the `SellerID` field is the same as the `PersonID` of the current user. Then we display this information in a table for the user to see.

Since this page performs database queries, we include the `Clssfd.asp` file (which, as we've already seen, contains the necessary code for connecting to the database). Since this should only be visible to registered users (who are also logged in), we check whether the user is logged in – and if not, we redirect them to the login page:

```
<!--#include file="Clssfd.asp"-->
<%
  If Session("PersonID") = "" Then
    Response.Redirect "Login.asp"
  End If
%>
```

We use a recordset to query the database for the list of items for sale; we populate the recordset with the entire contents of the Item table. However, we'll only need the records pertaining to the current user, so we'll apply a filter. The filter hides any record that doesn't match the criterion of the filter. In this case, we tell the recordset to hide those records whose SellerID value doesn't match the PersonID of the current user (this value is stored in a session-level variable). Then we use the EOF property to see if there are any records that match the filter:

```
Dim rsItems
Set rsItems = Server.CreateObject("ADODB.Recordset")
rsItems.Filter = "SellerID = " & Session("PersonID")
rsItems.Open "Item", objConn, adOpenForwardOnly, adLockOptimistic, adCmdTable
If Not rsItems.EOF Then                          ' current user has items for sale
```

If the recordset contains any records that match our filter, we display some of the data contained in those records in a table. The Do ... While statement loops through each of the rows in the recordset, and creates a new table row for each. When all the information for one record is formatted within a table row, we use the recordset's MoveNext method to move on to the next record. When we've gone through all the records, we can finish the table and close the recordset:

```
If Not rsItems.EOF Then                              ' current user has items for sale
   Response.Write _
      "<TABLE BORDER=""1"" CELLSPACING=""3"" CELLPADDING=""3"">" & _
      "<TR>" & _
      "  <TH>Item ID<BR><FONT SIZE=""-1"">Click to <BR>Edit/Delete</FONT></TH>" & _
      "  <TH>Name</TH>" & _
      "  <TH>Asking Price</TH>" & _
      "  <TH>Listing Date</TH>" & _
      "  <TH>Current Bid</TH>" & _
      "  <TH>Bid Time</TH>" & _
      "</TR>"
   Do While Not rsItems.EOF
      Response.Write _
         "<TR ALIGN=CENTER>" & _
         "  <TD><A HREF=""item.asp?Action=Edit&Item=" & rsItems("ItemID") & """>" & _
                   rsItems("ItemID") & "</A></TD>" & _
         "  <TD>" & rsItems("ItemName") & "</TD>" & _
         "  <TD>" & FormatCurrency(rsItems("AskingPrice")) & "</TD>" & _
         "  <TD>" & FormatDateTime(rsItems("ListingDate"),2) & "</TD>" & _
         "</TR>"
      rsItems.MoveNext
   Loop
   Response.Write "</TABLE>"
Else                                              ' current user has no items for sale
   Response.Write "<CENTER><H2>No items currently for sale</H2></CENTER>"
End If
rsItems.close
```

Note that the first column, which contains the ItemID, is a hyperlink: when clicked, it takes the user to a page called Item.asp, which displays details specific to that item (and allows the user to edit these details). Note that we use the FormatCurrency and FormatDateTime functions to format the values of the AskingPrice and ListingDate fields (FormatDateTime presents the date in its short format). Here's the code for all that:

We present a set of navigation controls across the bottom of the page. There's a new control on this page: it allows the user to add a new sale item:

```
<TABLE BORDER=0 WIDTH=100%>
  <TR ALIGN=CENTER>
    <TD WIDTH=33%><A HREF="BrowseListings.asp">Browse the listings</A></TD>
    <TD WIDTH=33%><A HREF="Item.asp?Action=AddNew">Add Sale Items</A></TD>
    <TD WIDTH=33%><A HREF="Register.asp?Update=True">Edit Registration Info</A></TD>
  </TR>
</TABLE>
```

Adding and Editing Sale Items

Now, we'll build `AddItem.asp` and `Item.asp`. These pages will allow the logged-in user to add a new item to the sale listings, and edit the details of his existing sale items.

Try It Out – Adding and Editing Items

1. Create a new ASP file, and add in the following code:

```
<!--#include file="Clssfd.asp"-->
<BASEFONT FACE="Comic Sans MS" COLOR="DarkBlue">
<HTML>
<HEAD>
<TITLE>Wrox Classifieds - Item for Sale</TITLE>
</HEAD>

<BODY BGCOLOR="#FFFF80">
<%
  Dim blnNew
    ' detect whether the user is adding a new item or editing an existing one
  Select Case Request.QueryString("Action")
    Case "AddNew"
      blnNew = True
    Case "Edit"
      blnNew = False
  End Select

  If blnNew Then
    Response.Write _
      "<CENTER><H1>Wrox Classifieds<BR>Add New Sale Item</H1></CENTER>" & _
      "<P>Please add the following information for the item you have for sale. "
  Else
    Response.Write _
      "<CENTER><H1>Wrox Classifieds<BR>Edit Sale Item</H1></CENTER>" & _
      "<P>Please edit the information for this item currently for sale. "
    Dim rsItem
    Set rsItem = Server.CreateObject("ADODB.Recordset")
    strSQL = "SELECT * FROM Item WHERE ItemID = " & Request.QueryString("Item") & ";"
    rsItem.Open strSQL, objConn, adOpenForwardOnly, adLockOptimistic, adCmdText
  End If
%>
```

```
<FORM ACTION="addItem.asp" METHOD="POST">
<%
  If blnNew Then %>
    <INPUT TYPE="Hidden" NAME="ItemID" VALUE=""> <%
  Else %>
    <INPUT TYPE="Hidden" NAME="ItemID" VALUE="<%= Request("Item") %>"> <%
  End If
%>
<TABLE BORDER=0>
  <TR>
    <TD WIDTH=20% ROWSPAN=11> </TD>
    <TD>Item Name:</TD>
    <TD><INPUT TYPE="Text" NAME="ItemName"
        VALUE="<% If Not blnNew Then Response.Write rsItem("ItemName") End If%>"
        SIZE="40" MAXLENGTH="75"></TD>
  </TR>
  <TR>
    <TD>Description:</TD>
    <TD><TEXTAREA NAME="Description" COLS="40" ROWS="3" WRAP="VIRTUAL">
      <% If Not blnNew Then Response.Write rsItem("Description") End If %>
      </TEXTAREA></TD>
  </TR>
  <TR>
    <TD>Asking Price:</TD>
    <TD><INPUT TYPE="Text" NAME="AskingPrice"
        VALUE="<% If Not blnNew Then Response.Write rsItem("AskingPrice") End If%>"
        SIZE="40"></TD>
  </TR>
  <TR>
    <TD>Notify Price:</TD>
    <TD><INPUT TYPE="Text" NAME="NotifyPrice"
        VALUE="<% If Not blnNew Then Response.Write rsItem("NotifyPrice") End If%>"
        SIZE="40"></TD>
  </TR>
  <TR>
    <TD>Sale Expiration Date:</TD>
    <TD><INPUT TYPE="Text" NAME="ExpirationDate"
        VALUE="<% If Not blnNew Then
                    Response.Write FormatDateTime(rsItem("ExpirationDate"),2)
                  End If %>"
        SIZE="40"></TD>
  </TR>
  <TR>
    <TD></TD>
    <TD ALIGN=CENTER COLSPAN=2><BR><%
      If Not blnNew Then %>
        <INPUT TYPE="Submit" NAME="Delete" VALUE="Delete Item"><%
      End If %>
        
      <INPUT TYPE="Submit"
        VALUE="<% If blnNew Then %>Add New Item<% Else %>Update Item<% End If %>">
        
```

```
        <INPUT TYPE="RESET"></TD>
    </TR>
</TABLE>
</FORM>

<HR>
<TABLE BORDER=0 WIDTH=100%>
    <TR ALIGN=CENTER>
      <TD WIDTH=33%><A HREF="BrowseListings.asp">Browse the listings</A></TD>
      <TD WIDTH=33%>Add Sale Items</TD>
      <TD WIDTH=33%><A HREF="Register.asp?Update=True">Edit Registration Info</A></TD>
    </TR>
</TABLE>
</BODY>
</HTML>
```

2. Save the file as `Item.asp`, in the same folder as your other `.asp` files.

3. Create another new file and enter the following code:

```
<!--#include file="Clssfd.asp"-->
<%
  Dim rsItem
  Dim blnNew
  Set rsItem = Server.CreateObject("ADODB.Recordset")
  rsItem.Open "Item", objConn, adOpenForwardOnly, adLockOptimistic, adCmdTable
  If Request.Form("Delete") <> "" Then              ' user wishes to delete an item
    rsItem.Filter = "ItemID = " & Request("ItemID")
    If Not rsItem.EOF Then rsItem.Delete
  Else                                              ' user wishes to edit/add an item
    If Request("ItemID") = "" Then
      blnNew = True
      rsItem.AddNew
    Else
      rsItem.Filter = "ItemID = " & Request("ItemID")
      blnNew = False
    End If
    rsItem("ItemName") = Request.Form("ItemName")
    rsItem("Description") = Request.Form("Description")
    rsItem("AskingPrice") = Request.Form("AskingPrice")
    rsItem("NotifyPrice") = Request.Form("NotifyPrice")
    rsItem("SellerID") = Session("PersonID")
    rsItem("ItemStatus") = "Active"
    If blnNew = True Then
      rsItem("ListingDate") = Now
    End If
    If Left(Request.Form("ExpirationDate"),1) = "+" Then
      Dim datDelta
      datDelta = _
        Mid(Request.Form("ExpirationDate"),2,len(Request.Form("ExpirationDate")))
      rsItem("ExpirationDate") = DateAdd("d", datDelta, Now)
    Else
      rsItem("ExpirationDate") = Request.Form("ExpirationDate")
    End If
```

```
    rsItem.Update

  If blnNew Then
    Dim rsSeller
    Set rsSeller = Server.CreateObject("ADODB.Recordset")
    rsSeller.Open "Seller", objConn, _
                  adOpenForwardOnly, adLockOptimistic, adCmdTable
    rsSeller.Filter = "PersonID = " & Session("PersonID")
    If rsSeller.EOF Then
      rsSeller.AddNew
      rsSeller("PersonID") = Session("PersonID")
      rsSeller("ItemsListed") = 0
      rsSeller("ItemsActive") = 0
    End If
    rsSeller("ItemsListed") = rsSeller("ItemsListed") + 1
    rsSeller("ItemsActive") = rsSeller("ItemsActive") + 1
    rsSeller("LastActivity") = Now
    rsSeller.Update
    rsSeller.Close
    Set rsSeller = Nothing
  End If
End If
rsItem.Close
Set rsItem = Nothing

Response.Redirect "ViewMySaleItems.asp"
%>
```

4. Save the file as `AddItem.asp`, in the same folder as your other `.asp` files.

5. Go back to your browser. From the 'Selling Items' page (`ViewMySaleItems.asp`), click on the **Add Sale Items** button, and insert sale details for some item that you wish to sell:

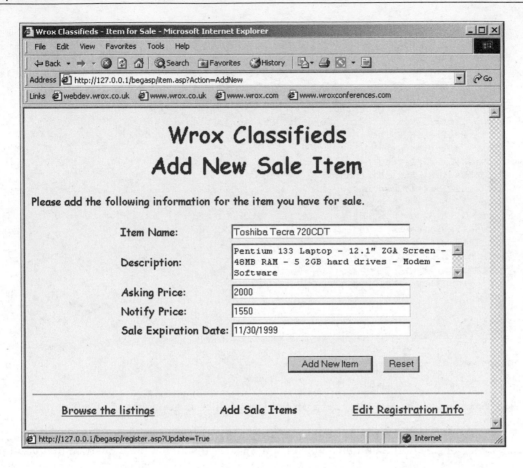

In the last field, be sure to enter the sale expiration date – not the current date!

6. Now click on the **Add New Item** button. This will return you to the 'Selling Items' page (`ViewMySaleItems.asp`). We promised that this page would become more exciting: it now sumarizes the items that the user has for sale:

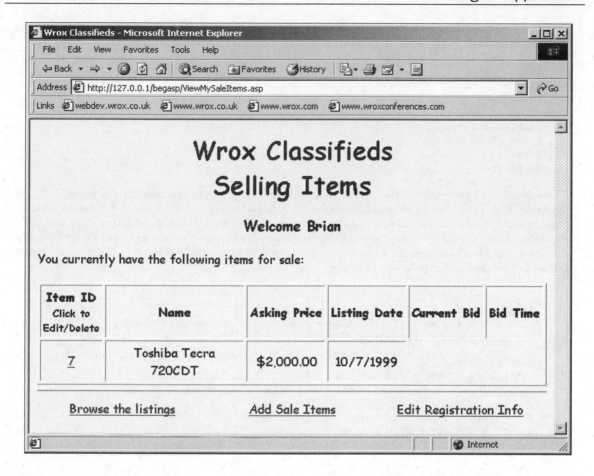

7. Click on the ItemID of an item that you wish to edit (there's only one here at the moment) – this takes you to the URL `Item.asp?Action=Edit`. Alternatively, you can click on the **Add Sale Items** hyperlink at the bottom to add more new entries, via the URL `Item.asp?Action=AddNew`.

How It Works

`Item.asp` is dual-purpose: it allows a user to add new sale items to the listings, and to edit the details of his existing sale items. In this application, every link to `Item.asp` also provides a querystring called `Action`, with a value of `Edit` or `AddNew` – this value will determine the function that the page will need to perform:

- ❑ If the user arrived at this page via `Item.asp?Action=AddNew`, then the page is being used to add a new sale item

- ❑ If the user arrived at this page via `Item.asp?Action=Edit`, then the user intends to edit the details of an *existing* sale item

We use a `Select Case` statement (at the top of `Item.asp`) to evaluate the value of the `Action` querystring, and assign a value to a Boolean flag called `blnNew` accordingly:

```
Dim blnNew
    ' detect whether the user is adding a new item or editing an existing one
Select Case Request.QueryString("Action")
  Case "AddNew"
    blnNew = True          ' user is adding a new item
  Case "Edit"
    blnNew = False         ' user is editing an existing item
End Select
```

We use `blnNew` throughout the rest of this page to determine the content of the page dynamically. First, we'll use it to determine the precise wording of the header information. In addition, in the case `blnNew=False` it's also a good idea to retrieve the *existing* data on that item from the database, so that we can display them for the user's convenience. To do this, we create a recordset, and use `If` to query records from the Item table whose `ItemID` value is the same as that of the item we want to edit:

```
If blnNew Then
  Response.Write _
    "<CENTER><H1>Wrox Classifieds<BR>Add New Sale Item</H1></CENTER>" & _
    "<P>Please add the following information for the item you have for sale. "
Else
  Response.Write _
    "<CENTER><H1>Wrox Classifieds<BR>Edit Sale Item</H1></CENTER>" & _
    "<P>Please edit the information for this item currently for sale. "
  Dim rsItem
  Set rsItem = Server.CreateObject("ADODB.Recordset")
  strSQL = "SELECT * FROM Item WHERE ItemID = " & Request("Item") & ";"
  rsItem.Open strSQL, objConn, adOpenForwardOnly, adLockOptimistic, adCmdText
End If
```

Now we can start to build the HTML form, which allows the user to modify the item's details. When the user submits the information, the data in the form will be processed by `AddItem.asp`. If the user is editing an *existing* item, then we'll need to pass the item's `ItemID` to `AddItem.asp` (which we do using a hidden FORM INPUT field). If the user is creating a *new* item, then the item's ID is still to be determined – so we pass a blank value to the `AddItem.asp` script.

```
<FORM ACTION="addItem.asp" METHOD="POST">
<%
  If blnNew Then %>
    <INPUT TYPE="Hidden" NAME="ItemID" VALUE=""> <%
  Else %>
    <INPUT TYPE="Hidden" NAME="ItemID" VALUE="<%= Request("Item") %>"> <%
  End If
%>
```

Note that we've coded the `<INPUT>` tag as straight HTML here, inside of the ASP page. This illustrates an important point, that we've seen elsewhere in the book: namely, that flow control statements like `Select Case...End Select` and `If...Then` can be used to control the flow of both ASP script and HTML to the page. The HTML code in the fragment above is only displayed when the user is adding a new item.

The remainder of the form is nicely formatted using an HTML table. In the case that an existing item's details are being edited (`blnNew="False"`), we need to display the existing item information in the appropriate fields. We do that within each field by checking the value of `blnNew`, and (if `Not blnNew`) we take the appropriate value from the recordset and display it in the form, using `INPUT` element's `VALUE` property. In the case of the `Description` field we've used a `TEXTAREA` element, so the existing data goes within the `<TEXTAREA></TEXTAREA>` tags:

```
<TABLE BORDER=0>
  <TR>
    <TD WIDTH=20% ROWSPAN=11> </TD>
    <TD>Item Name:</TD>
    <TD><INPUT TYPE="Text" NAME="ItemName"
        VALUE="<% If Not blnNew Then Response.Write rsItem("ItemName") End If%>"
        SIZE="40" MAXLENGTH="75"></TD>
  </TR>
  <TR>
    <TD>Description:</TD>
    <TD><TEXTAREA NAME="Description" COLS="40" ROWS="3" WRAP="VIRTUAL">
      <% If Not blnNew Then Response.Write rsItem("Description") End If %>
        </TEXTAREA></TD>
  </TR>
  ...
```

When the form is complete, the user can select one of three buttons:

```
    <TD ALIGN=CENTER COLSPAN=2><BR><%
    If Not blnNew Then %>
      <INPUT TYPE="Submit" NAME="Delete" VALUE="Delete Item"><%
    End If %>
      
    <INPUT TYPE="Submit"
      VALUE="<% If blnNew Then %>Add New Item<% Else %>Update Item<% End If %>">
      
    <INPUT TYPE="RESET"></TD>
  </TR>
</TABLE>
</FORM>
```

Here, the user can choose to:

❑ Delete the item from the database. This is only relevant when the user is editing an *existing* item, so this button is only displayed when the value of `blnNew` is False. In addition to having a `VALUE` parameter (which controls the button caption), the **Delete** button also has a `NAME` parameter. In a moment, we'll see how the `NAME` parameter is used within `AddItem.asp` to determine which of the buttons was clicked by the user.

❑ Submit the information on the form. Again, we use the value of blnNew to control the label on the Submit button dynamically.

❑ Reset the information in the form and start over.

That's it for the Item.asp code. In AddItem.asp, we interact with the Item table via a recordset that is populated with the contents of the table. We set the locking parameter to adLockOptimistic – this will allow us to change the information in the table.

```
Dim rsItem
Dim blnNew
Set rsItem = Server.CreateObject("ADODB.Recordset")
rsItem.Open "Item", objConn, adOpenForwardOnly, adLockOptimistic, adCmdTable
```

We break the logic in this page into two parts: **deleting** an item, and **adding/editing** an item. First, if the user wants to delete the selected item then they will have selected the Delete button on Item.asp. In this case, the contents of the button's NAME parameter are placed in the Delete element of the Request object's Form collection. Thus, we can check the value of Request.Form("Delete") – if it's not empty then we know the user wishes to delete this item:

```
If Request.Form("Delete") <> "" Then          ' user wishes to delete an item
  rsItem.Filter = "ItemID = " & Request("ItemID")
  If Not rsItem.EOF Then rsItem.Delete
```

To perform the deletion, we set the recordset's Filter property to search for the ItemID of the item in question. There should be exactly one record detected by the filter – just before we delete the record, we use EOF to ensure that there really *is* a record there to delete.

The second part to handle is that of adding/editing an item. Naturally, we break this into two subcases – **adding** and **editing**. We can determine which we're dealing with by checking the value supplied in the ItemID element of the Request object's QueryString collection:

```
Else                                          ' user wishes to edit/add an item
  If Request("ItemID") = "" Then
    blnNew = True
    rsItem.AddNew
  Else
    rsItem.Filter = "ItemID = " & Request("ItemID")
    blnNew = False
  End If
```

If the user is adding a new item, then we call the recordset's AddNew method to create a new record. If we are editing an existing item, then we set the Filter property to so that the recordset exposes only the item that we're interested in.

We've used a little programmer's shortcut here – by using the expression
`Request("ItemID")` *instead of* `Request.QueryString("ItemID")`. *We saw this originally in Chapter 7 – if we don't specify which of the Request object's collections we mean here, then the collections are searched in this order:* `QueryString`, `Form`, `Cookies`, `ClientCertificate`, `ServerVariables`. *If the same name appears in multiple collections, then the value returned will come from the first collection in which it is detected.*

Whether we're adding an item or editing one, we're now in a position to add the details to the fields of the record:

```
rsItem("ItemName") = Request.Form("ItemName")
rsItem("Description") = Request.Form("Description")
rsItem("AskingPrice") = Request.Form("AskingPrice")
rsItem("NotifyPrice") = Request.Form("NotifyPrice")
rsItem("SellerID") = Session("PersonID")
rsItem("ItemStatus") = "Active"
If blnNew = True Then
  rsItem("ListingDate") = Now
End If
If Left(Request.Form("ExpirationDate"),1) = "+" Then
  Dim datDelta
  datDelta = _
    Mid(Request.Form("ExpirationDate"),2,len(Request.Form("ExpirationDate")))
  rsItem("ExpirationDate") = DateAdd("d", datDelta, Now)
Else
  rsItem("ExpirationDate") = Request.Form("ExpirationDate")
End If
rsItem.Update
```

In the case of editing an existing record, we only need to update those fields that the user was able to edit. Therefore, we only populate the `ListingDate` field if we're adding a *new* record (and we use the value of `blnNew` again to detect that dynamically).

We'll allow our user interface to support a handy feature here: namely, the ability to enter the sale expiration date as a number of days. Thus, if the user wants to enter a sale period of three weeks, then they simply enter +21 – the system will figure out what the expiration date should be. We use the `DateAdd` method to add the number of days specified to the current date.

Once all of the changes have been made, the `Update` method of the recordset is called and the changes are written to the database.

If we're adding a new item for sale, then we also need to update the `Seller` table – which contains statistical information about an individual seller. To update this information, we create a new recordset, which we populate with the contents of the `Seller` table. We apply a `Filter` so that the recordset exposes only the record for the current user. We can use the `EOF` property to discover whether the recordset is exposing any records. If `EOF` is `True`, then the recordset is exposing no records. This means that we need to add a new record to the `Seller` table for this user. To do this, we call the `AddNew` method, and then update the information in the record. If we're adding a record to the **Seller** table, then we initialize the `ItemsListed` and `ItemsActive` fields to 0:

```
   If blnNew Then
     Dim rsSeller
     Set rsSeller = Server.CreateObject("ADODB.Recordset")
     rsSeller.Open "Seller", objConn, _
                   adOpenForwardOnly, adLockOptimistic, adCmdTable
     rsSeller.Filter = "PersonID = " & Session("PersonID")
     If rsSeller.EOF Then
       rsSeller.AddNew
       rsSeller("PersonID") = Session("PersonID")
       rsSeller("ItemsListed") = 0
       rsSeller("ItemsActive") = 0
     End If
     rsSeller("ItemsListed") = rsSeller("ItemsListed") + 1
     rsSeller("ItemsActive") = rsSeller("ItemsActive") + 1
     rsSeller("LastActivity") = Now
     rsSeller.Update
     rsSeller.Close
     Set rsSeller = Nothing
   End If
 End If
```

Since the user has just added a new item for sale, we add 1 to the values of the `ItemsListed` and `ItemsActive` fields. (This is the reason for initializing these values in the case of adding a new record: if the field contains a non-numeric value, and we try to add 1, an error would result.) Finally, we set the `LastActivity` field to today, then update and close the recordset.

Once all of the information has been updated in the database, we can close and release the `rsItem` recordset, and redirect the browser back to `ViewMySaleItems.asp`:

```
 rsItem.Close
 Set rsItem = Nothing
 Response.Redirect "ViewMySaleItems.asp"
%>
```

Of course, `ViewMySaleItems.asp` is generated dynamically – so it will immediately display the new or updated item information in its table.

Browsing and Bidding

OK, now any registered user can place items in the sale listings. The next step is to allow users to browse the listings and to bid for the items that are on sale there. For these tasks, we'll write three more new pages: `BrowseListings.asp`, `Bid.asp` and `AddBid.asp`.

Browsing the Listings

The next step is to allow users (whether registered or not) to *browse* all of the items our users have placed for sale. Our system provides a very simple interface for doing this – all of the items are presented in a list. This leaves the door open for later enhancement, such as providing other ways of viewing the items that are for sale.

1. Create a new text file and key up the following code:

```
<!--#include file="Clssfd.asp"-->
<BASEFONT FACE="Comic Sans MS" COLOR="DarkBlue">
<HTML>
<HEAD>
<TITLE>Wrox Classifieds</TITLE>
</HEAD>

<BODY BGCOLOR="#FFFF80">
<CENTER><H1>Wrox Classifieds<BR>Items for sale</H1>
<%
  If Session("PersonID") <> "" Then
    Response.Write "<H3>Welcome " & Session("GivenName") & "</H3>"
  End If
%>
</CENTER>
<P>Here's a list of all the items that our users have made available for purchase:
</P>
<%
  Dim rsItems
  strSQL = "SELECT * FROM Item " & _
          "WHERE ExpirationDate > #" & FormatDateTime(Now,2) & "# " & _
          "AND ItemStatus = 'Active';"
  Set rsItems = Server.CreateObject("ADODB.Recordset")
  rsItems.Open strSQL, objConn
  If Not rsItems.EOF Then
    Response.Write _
      "<TABLE BORDER=""1"" CELLSPACING=""3"" CELLPADDING=""3"">" & _
      "  <TR>" & _
      "    <TH>Item ID"
            If Session("PersonID") <> "" Then
              Response.Write "<BR><FONT SIZE=""-1"">Click to Bid</FONT>"
            End If
          Response.Write "</TH>" & _
      "    <TH>Name</TH>" & _
      "    <TH>Asking Price</TH>" & _
      "    <TH>Listing Date</TH>" & _
      "    <TH>Current Bid</TH>" & _
      "    <TH>Bid Time</TH>" & _
      "  </TR>"
    Do While Not rsItems.EOF
      Response.Write "<TR ALIGN=CENTER>"
      If Session("PersonID") <> "" Then
        Response.Write _
          "<TD><A HREF=""Bid.asp?Item=" & rsItems("ItemID") & """>" & _
          rsItems("ItemID") & "</A></TD>"
      Else
        Response.Write "<TD>" & rsItems("ItemID") & "</TD>"
      End If
```

```
      Response.Write _
         "<TD>" & rsItems("ItemName") & "</TD>" & _
         "<TD>" & FormatCurrency(rsItems("AskingPrice")) & "</TD>" & _
         "<TD>" & FormatDateTime(rsItems("ListingDate"),2) & "</TD>" & _
       "</TR>"
       rsItems.MoveNext
    Loop
    Response.Write "</TABLE>"
    rsItems.close
    Set rsItems = Nothing
  Else
    Response.Write "<CENTER><H2>No items currently for sale</H2></CENTER>"
  End If
%>
<P>
<HR>
<TABLE BORDER=0 WIDTH=100%>
  <TR ALIGN=CENTER>
    <% If Session("PersonID") <> "" Then %>
      <TD WIDTH=33%>Browse the listings</TD>
      <TD WIDTH=33%><A HREF="ViewMySaleItems.asp">List/Edit Sale Items</a></TD>
      <TD WIDTH=33%><A HREF="Register.asp?Update=True">
                    Edit Registration Info</A></TD>
    <% Else  %>
      <TD WIDTH=33%>Browse the listings</TD>
      <TD WIDTH=33%><A HREF="Login.asp">Login</A></TD>
      <TD WIDTH=33%><A HREF="Register.asp">I'm a new user</A></TD>
    <% End If %>
  </TR>
</TABLE>
</BODY>
</HTML>
```

2.   Save the file as `BrowseListings.asp`, in the same folder as your other ASP files.

3.   From the **Selling Items** page (`ViewMySaleItems.asp`), click on **Browse the listings**. Don't click to bid on anything yet; we haven't covered the pages for that yet. The following screenshot shows what David Sussman sees when he's logged on and browsing the listings:

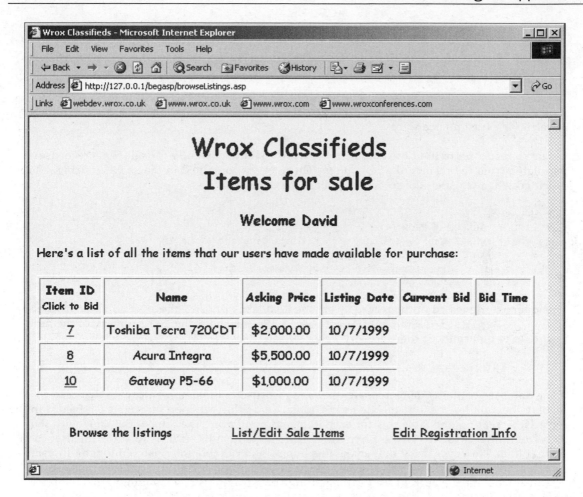

As you can see, I've added a couple of other users who are also selling items. Our Toshiba has some competition in the marketplace!

How It Works

The technique used to display these items is very similar to that used in the List/Edit Sale Items page. The main difference is that this page displays *all* items for sale by all users (while the List/Edit Sale Items page displays *only* those items being sold by the current user).

As we mentioned before, *any* users can view this page – whether they're registered with the system or not. If the user has already logged-in, then we'll give a visual indication that the system recognizes who they are. To do this, we'll check the value of the session-level `PersonID` variable – if it is populated then we know that we're dealing with a currently logged-in user, and in this case we can respond by displaying a special greeting on the page:

```
<%
  If Session("PersonID") <> "" Then
    Response.Write "<H3>Welcome " & Session("GivenName") & "</H3>"
  End If
%>
```

As we've already seen, all of the information about the user is stored in session-level variables, so retrieving it is quick and easy.

We use a recordset to hold the details of the items that are currently for sale. This recordset is populated from the results of a SQL query. The query is contained in the strSQL string, and is executed when we open the recordset against the database:

```
Dim rsItems
strSQL = "SELECT * FROM Item " & _
         "WHERE ExpirationDate > #" & FormatDateTime(Now,2) & "# " & _
         "AND ItemStatus = 'Active';"
Set rsItems = Server.CreateObject("ADODB.Recordset")
rsItems.Open strSQL, objConn
```

This query retrieves all of the records from the Item table whose ItemStatus value is Active, and whose ExpirationDate has not yet passed. We can check the EOF property of the new recordset to determine if there are any items for sale:

```
If Not rsItems.EOF Then
```

If the database contains items for sale, then the recordset will be non-empty. In this case we display the data for the 'for sale' items in a table. To do this, we loop through each record in the recordset, creating one table row for each item and populating the cells of the table with the data from the record. We create a hyperlink around the Item ID – this is to allow the user to bid on that item. However, we'll only make this hyperlink available to registered logged-in users – so again, we check against the value contained in the session-level PersonID variable to establish whether the current user is logged-in. Apart from this small subtlety, the display is very similar to the display used in the List/Edit Sale Items page:

```
Do While Not rsItems.EOF
  Response.Write "<TR ALIGN=CENTER>"
  If Session("PersonID") <> "" Then
    Response.Write _
      "<TD><A HREF=""Bid.asp?Item=" & rsItems("ItemID") & """>" & _
      rsItems("ItemID") & "</A></TD>"
  Else
    Response.Write "<TD>" & rsItems("ItemID") & "</TD>"
  End If
  Response.Write _
    "<TD>" & rsItems("ItemName") & "</TD>" & _
    "<TD>" & FormatCurrency(rsItems("AskingPrice")) & "</TD>" & _
    "<TD>" & FormatDateTime(rsItems("ListingDate"),2) & "</TD>" & _
  "</TR>"
  rsItems.MoveNext
Loop
```

If there are no items for sale, then the `rsItems` recordset will be empty. In this case, we just display a message to the user to indicate that there are no items currently for sale:

```
Else
    Response.Write "<CENTER><H2>No items currently for sale</H2></CENTER>"
End If
```

You may have noticed the **Current Bid** and **Bid Time** columns in the screenshot above. These will be used later on, to display any current bid information about each item. Our next task is to talk about how to bid for an item; after that, we'll return to this page and show you how to display the bid information.

Bidding for an Item

The user uses `BrowseListings.asp` to browse the list of items for sale, and selects an item that they'd like to purchase. When this happens, the user can place a bid on that item, by clicking on the hyperlinked **ItemID**. This will take them to a page called `Bid.asp`, where they can enter their bid.

Try It Out – Bidding for an Item

1. Create a new ASP file, and enter the following. Don't forget that the JavaScript is case-sensitive:

```
<!--#include file="Clssfd.asp"-->
<BASEFONT FACE="Comic Sans MS" COLOR="DarkBlue">
<HTML>
<HEAD>
<TITLE>Wrox Classifieds - Item Bid</TITLE>
</HEAD>

<BODY BGCOLOR="#FFFF80">
<%
  Dim rsItem, strItemName, strDescription
  Set rsItem = Server.CreateObject("ADODB.Recordset")
  strSQL = "SELECT * FROM Item WHERE ItemID =" & Request("Item")
  rsItem.Open strSQL, objConn
  strItemName = rsItem("ItemName")
  strDescription = rsItem("Description")
  rsItem.Close
  Set rsItem = Nothing

  Dim rsBids
  Set rsBids = Server.CreateObject("ADODB.Recordset")
  strSQL = "SELECT * FROM Bid WHERE ItemID =" & Request("Item") & _
           " ORDER BY TimeStamp DESC;"
  rsBids.Open strSQL, objConn
%>

<CENTER><H1>Wrox Classifieds<BR>Bidding for <%= strItemName %></H1></CENTER>
<P>
```

```
<%
  Dim varHighBid
  varHighBid = 0
  If rsBids.EOF Then
    Response.Write "So far, no bids have been placed on this item"
  Else
    Response.Write "Bid History (Highest bid first)" & _
      "<TABLE BORDER=""2"" CELLSPACING=""3"" CELLPADDING=""3"">" & _
      "  <TR>" & _
      "    <TH>Bidder ID</TH>" & _
      "    <TH>Timestamp</TH>" & _
      "    <TH>Amount Bid</TH>" & _
      "    <TH>Last Change</TH>" & _
      "  </TR>"
    Do While Not rsBids.EOF
      Response.Write _
      "  <TR>" & _
      "    <TD>" & rsBids("BidderID") & "</TD>" & _
      "    <TD>" & rsBids("Timestamp") & "</TD>" & _
      "    <TD ALIGN=RIGHT>" & FormatCurrency(rsBids("BidAmount")) & "</TD>" & _
      "    <TD ALIGN=RIGHT>" & FormatCurrency(rsBids("BidChange")) & "</TD>" & _
      "  </TR>"
      If varhighBid = 0 Then varHighBid = rsBids("BidAmount")
      rsBids.MoveNext
    Loop
    rsBids.Close
    Response.Write "</TABLE>"
  End If
%>
<FORM NAME="frmBid" ACTION="AddBid.asp" METHOD="POST"
                    onSubmit="return VerifyData()">
  <INPUT TYPE="Hidden" NAME="ItemID" VALUE="<%= Request("Item") %>">
  <P>
  <TABLE WIDTH="70%" BORDER="0" CELLPADDING=5>
    <TR>
      <TD WIDTH=20% ROWSPAN=11> </TD>
      <TD WIDTH=20%>Item:</TD>
      <TD><%= strItemName %></TD>
    </TR>
    <TR>
      <TD>Description:</TD>
      <TD><%= strDescription %></TD>
    </TR>
    <TR>
      <TD>Bid:</TD>
      <TD><INPUT TYPE="Text" NAME="Bid" SIZE="40"></TD>
    </TR>
    <TR>
      <TD></TD>
      <TD ALIGN=CENTER COLSPAN=2><BR>
          <INPUT TYPE="Submit" VALUE="Bid on Item">  
          <INPUT TYPE="RESET"></TD>
```

```
      </TR>
    </TABLE>
  </FORM>
  <HR>
  <TABLE BORDER=0 WIDTH=100%>
    <TR ALIGN=CENTER>
      <TD WIDTH=33%><A HREF="BrowseListings.asp">Browse the listings</A></TD>
      <TD WIDTH=33%>Add Sale Items</TD>
      <TD WIDTH=33%><A HREF="Register.asp?update=True">Edit Registration Info</A></TD>
    </TR>
  </TABLE>
  </BODY>

  <SCRIPT language="JavaScript">
  <!--
  function VerifyData()
  {
    if (document.frmBid.Bid.value <= <%= varHighBid %>)
    {
      alert ("You must bid higher than the previous bid of " +
            "<%= FormatCurrency(varHighBid) %>.");
      return false;
    }
    else
      return true;
  }
  -->
  </SCRIPT>

  </HTML>
```

2. Save the file as `Bid.asp`, in the same folder as your other ASP files.

3. Create another blank file in your editor and enter the following code:

```
<!--#include file="Clssfd.asp"-->
<%
  Dim objCmd, rsHighBid, srtSQL, varHighBid

  Set objCmd = Server.CreateObject("ADODB.Command")
  Set objCmd.ActiveConnection = objConn
  strSQL = "SELECT Max(BidAmount) AS MaxBidAmount FROM Bid " & _
          "WHERE ItemID = " & Request("ItemID") & ";"
  objCmd.CommandType = adCmdText
  objCmd.CommandText = strSQL
  Set rsHighBid = objCmd.Execute

  If IsNull( rsHighBid("MaxBidAmount") ) Then
    varHighBid = 0
  Else
    varHighBid = rsHighBid("MaxBidAmount")
  End If
  rsHighBid.Close
```

```
Set rsHighBid = Nothing

Dim rsBid
Set rsBid = Server.CreateObject("ADODB.Recordset")
rsBid.Open "Bid", objConn, adOpenForwardOnly, adLockOptimistic, adCmdTable
rsBid.AddNew
rsBid("ItemID") = Request.Form("ItemID")
rsBid("BidderID") = Session("PersonID")
rsBid("BidAmount") = CCur(Request.Form("Bid"))
rsBid("BidChange") = CCur(Request.Form("Bid")) - varHighBid

rsBid.Update
Response.Redirect "BrowseListings.asp"
%>
```

4. Save the file as `AddBid.asp`, in the same folder as your other ASP files.

5. From the Browse page (`BrowseListings.asp`), click on the ItemID of an item that you want to bid on:

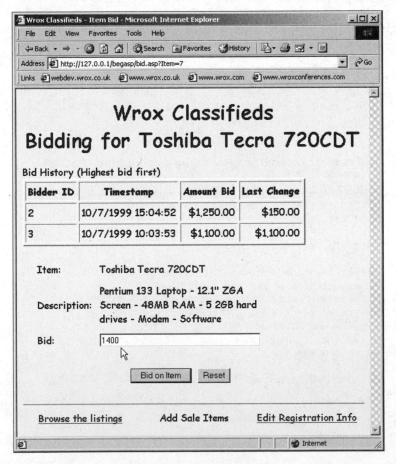

I've added a couple of 'previous bids' here, so you can see what they look like. The first time you make a bid, you'll receive the message "No bids currently placed" instead of the 'Bid History' table.

6. Insert your bid, and hit the **Bid on Item** button. This will process the bid and return you to `BrowseListings.asp`. There's still nothing in the **Current Bid** and **Bid Time** columns yet, but we'll fix that in a few pages time:

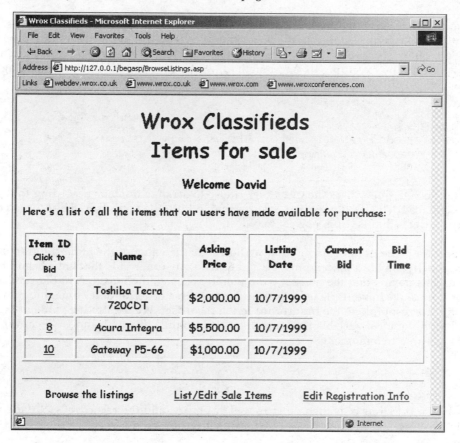

How It Works

`Bid.asp` is the page on which a user can place a bid. There are two parts to this page. First, we display a summary of all previous bids on that item; and second, we provide a form that allows the user to place a new bid.

The first step is to retrieve the descriptive information about the item. This information is stored in the **Item** table. We create a recordset called `rsItem`, and populate it using a SQL query to retrieve the data from the `Item` table. Then we copy the item's name and description in local variables for later use (and so that we can close and release the recordset):

```
Dim rsItem, strItemName, strDescription
Set rsItem = Server.CreateObject("ADODB.Recordset")
strSQL = "SELECT * FROM Item WHERE ItemID =" & Request("Item")
rsItem.Open strSQL, objConn
strItemName = rsItem("ItemName")
strDescription = rsItem("Description")
rsItem.Close
Set rsItem = Nothing
```

Next, we will turn our attention to building the list of previous bids for the item. The information about bids is stored in the Bid table. We create a new recordset called rsBids, and write a SQL query (contained in strSQL) to retrieve all of the bids for the current item. We populate rsBids by executing its Open method, which executes the strSQL query against the database:

```
Dim rsBids
Set rsBids = Server.CreateObject("ADODB.Recordset")
strSQL = "SELECT * FROM Bid WHERE ItemID =" & Request("Item") & _
         " ORDER BY TimeStamp DESC;"
rsBids.Open strSQL, objConn
```

Note that the SQL query uses the ORDER BY clause to arrange the bids according to the time that they were placed. The DESC modifier ensures that, within the recordset, the records are ordered in reverse order – that is, from newest to oldest.

One important piece of information that we'll need is the value of the highest bid to date. As we'll see shortly, any bid placed must be higher than any other bids that have been placed on that item. This means that the highest bid on an item is also the most recent bid on that item. Therefore, since we have retrieved our records in reverse order of date/time, the previous highest bid corresponds to the first record in the recordset. We'll store the value of this previous highest bid in the local variable varHighBid. We initialize this to 0, and we'll capture the highest bid value in a moment:

```
Dim varHighBid
varHighBid = 0
```

If there are no previous bids then rsBids will be empty, and the recordset's EOF file will immediately be True. In this case, we display an appropriate message:

```
If rsBids.EOF Then
  Response.Write "So far, no bids have been placed on this item"
```

Otherwise, we loop through all of the bids and display each bid on a new row of an HTML table. Notice that the value of varHighBid will only be 0 on the first iteration of the loop. We use that fact to copy the highest bid value into our varHighBid variable:

```
Else
  Response.Write "Bid History (Highest bid first)" & _
    "<TABLE BORDER=""2"" CELLSPACING=""3"" CELLPADDING=""3"">" & _
    "  <TR>" & _
```

```
           "      <TH>Bidder ID</TH>" & _
           "      <TH>Timestamp</TH>" & _
           "      <TH>Amount Bid</TH>" & _
           "      <TH>Last Change</TH>" & _
           "   </TR>"
     Do While Not rsBids.EOF
       Response.Write _
       "   <TR>" & _
       "      <TD>" & rsBids("BidderID") & "</TD>" & _
       "      <TD>" & rsBids("Timestamp") & "</TD>" & _
       "      <TD ALIGN=RIGHT>" & FormatCurrency(rsBids("BidAmount")) & "</TD>" & _
       "      <TD ALIGN=RIGHT>" & FormatCurrency(rsBids("BidChange")) & "</TD>" & _
       "   </TR>"
       If varhighBid = 0 Then varHighBid = rsBids("BidAmount")
       rsBids.MoveNext
     Loop
     rsBids.Close
     Response.Write "</TABLE>"
   End If
```

Notice that we've used the FormatCurrency function, which helps us to display the amount of each bid and the change since the last bid in a currency format.

Having displayed the bid history, we can display the form – this will allow the user to enter the amount that they wish to bid. This form will send its contents to the AddBid.asp script file for processing:

```
<FORM NAME="frmBid" ACTION="AddBid.asp" METHOD="POST"
                 onSubmit="return VerifyData()">
  <INPUT TYPE="Hidden" NAME="ItemID" VALUE="<%= Request("Item") %>">
```

The rest of the form is quite simple – there's nothing new there so we won't discuss it here. The last thing to note about Bid.asp is that we've included a little client-side validation script, to parse the value of the bid being submitted. This involves including an onSubmit parameter to the <FORM> tag, which tells the browser to execute the VerifyData() method when the form's submit button is pressed, but *before* the form is actually submitted to the web server.

The VerifyData() function executes client-side to ensure that the bid being submitted is higher than the previous highest bid. By running the function client-side, we can perform this check without making a round trip to the server:

```
<SCRIPT language="JavaScript">
<!--
function VerifyData()
{
  if (document.frmBid.Bid.value <= <%= varHighBid %>)
  {
    alert ("You must bid higher than the previous bid of " +
           "<%= FormatCurrency(varHighBid) %>.");
    return false;
  }
  else
```

```
        return true;
}
-->
</SCRIPT>
```

If the bid is verified as being higher than the previous highest bid, then the form will continue to be submitted. Otherwise, the form will not be submitted and we display an error message box for the user:

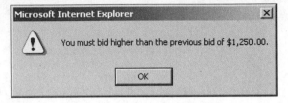

When the form is successfully submitted for processing, the processing is performed by the AddBid.asp script file. AddBid.asp is like some of the other files we've seen in this application, in that it has no user interface. It is simply responsible for adding the bid information to the database, and redirecting the user towards another page.

The first task in AddBid.asp is to determine the item's previous high bid. To do this, we first create an ADO Command object called objCmd – we will use it to execute a SQL statement against the database. We must set three properties of the Command object, before it can function properly:

❑   The ActiveConnection property should specify our database connection. Here, we reference objConn – the same ADO Connection object that we've used for a database connection throughout this application.

❑   We're going to use a SQL query to retrieve information, so we need to set the CommandType property to adCmdText. This tells the Command object that we will be passing a text command, rather than a table name, for it to process.

❑   The CommandText property should be assigned the SQL statement that we have created in the strSQL variable.

Here's the code for all that:

```
Set objCmd = Server.CreateObject("ADODB.Command")
Set objCmd.ActiveConnection = objConn
strSQL = "SELECT Max(BidAmount) AS MaxBidAmount FROM Bid " & _
         "WHERE ItemID = " & Request("ItemID") & ";"
objCmd.CommandType = adCmdText
objCmd.CommandText = strSQL
```

Then we call the Command object's Execute method. This executes the query against the database, and returns a recordset full of data. We assign the resulting recordset to a variable called rsHighBid:

```
Set rsHighBid = objCmd.Execute
```

We've used the Command object here to demonstrate that there's more than one way to populate a recordset! We could have avoided the Command object altogether, and populated the recordset by using its Open method – as we've done elsewhere in this application.

Before we go on, note that our SQL statement performs a calculation as it retrieves information from the Bid table. We're only interested in the time and value of the previous *highest* bid, so we use the Max() function inside of the SQL statement. This function will be performed on each record that matches the WHERE clause – of all those records, only the record with the highest BidAmount value will be returned.

We have also added an AS statement to the SQL query, which renames the results of the Max() functions within the recordset. This allows us to access the recordset's field as MaxBidAmount, instead of Max(BidAmount).

Since our SQL query asks for the *highest* bid value, there will always be a result returned. That means we can't use the EOF property to determine whether or not any information is present. Instead, we must check whether each value is Null. A Null value implies that there are no previous bids; and therefore the high bid is 0:

```
If IsNull( rsHighBid("MaxBidAmount") ) Then
   varHighBid = 0
Else
   varHighBid = rsHighBid("MaxBidAmount")
End If
```

Once we have retrieved the high bid information, we can close this recordset and release its resources:

```
rsHighBid.Close
Set rsHighBid = Nothing
```

Now, we can add the new bid to the Bid table. To do this, we create a recordset (called rsBid) and populate it with the contents of the Bid table. We open it using the adLockOptimistic parameter, so that we can write the new bid to the table:

```
Dim rsBid
Set rsBid = Server.CreateObject("ADODB.Recordset")
rsBid.Open "Bid", objConn, adOpenForwardOnly, adLockOptimistic, adCmdTable
```

Now we add a new record to the recordset and insert all the new bid details. The value of the BidChange field is calculated by subtracting the previous highest bid from the new bid. Once all of the data has been entered, the Update method is called to write the changes to the database:

```
rsBid.AddNew
rsBid("ItemID") = Request.Form("ItemID")
rsBid("BidderID") = Session("PersonID")
```

```
rsBid("BidAmount") = CCur(Request.Form("Bid"))
rsBid("BidChange") = CCur(Request.Form("Bid")) - varHighBid
rsBid.Update
```

Finally, we can close and release the recordset, and redirect the user back to the browse page:

```
rsBid.Close
Set rsBid = Nothing
Response.Redirect "BrowseListings.asp"
```

Updating the Listings to Show the Bid History

Now that we know how to retrieve bid information from the database, we can go back to some of the previous screens and add in the code to display the bid history.

Try It Out – Adding the Bid History Display

We will be adding bid history information to the BrowseListings.asp and Item.asp pages. We'll also need to add some additional code to the item deletion script in AddItem.asp.

1. Open the BrowseListings.asp file for editing.

2. Amend the BrowseListings.asp file as shown by the following highlighted fragments:

```
...
Response.Write _
  "<TABLE BORDER=""1"" CELLSPACING=""3"" CELLPADDING=""3"">" & _
  "  <TR>" & _
  "    <TH>Item ID"
          If Session("PersonID") <> "" Then
            Response.Write "<BR><FONT SIZE=""-1"">Click to Bid</FONT>"
          End If
        Response.Write "</TH>" & _
  "    <TH>Name</TH>" & _
  "    <TH>Asking Price</TH>" & _
  "    <TH>Listing Date</TH>" & _
  "    <TH>Current Bid</TH>" & _
  "    <TH>Bid Time</TH>" & _
  "  </TR>"
Dim objCmd, rsBid
Set objCmd = Server.CreateObject("ADODB.Command")
Set objCmd.ActiveConnection = objConn
strSQL = "SELECT Max(BidAmount) AS MaxBidAmount, " & _
              "Max(TimeStamp) AS LastBidTime FROM Bid"
objCmd.CommandType = adCmdText
Do While Not rsItems.EOF
  Response.Write "<TR ALIGN=CENTER>"
  If Session("PersonID") <> "" Then
    Response.Write _
      "<TD><A HREF=""Bid.asp?Item=" & rsItems("ItemID") & """>" & _
      rsItems("ItemID") & "</A></TD>"
  Else
```

```
        Response.Write "<TD>" & rsItems("ItemID") & "</TD>"
      End If
      Response.Write _
        "<TD>" & rsItems("ItemName") & "</TD>" & _
        "<TD>" & FormatCurrency(rsItems("AskingPrice")) & "</TD>" & _
        "<TD>" & FormatDateTime(rsItems("ListingDate"),2) & "</TD>"

      objCmd.CommandText = strSQL & " WHERE ItemID = " & rsItems("ItemID") & ";"
      Set rsBid = objCmd.Execute
      If IsNull( rsBid("MaxBidAmount") ) Then
        Response.Write _
          "<TD COLSPAN=2><FONT SIZE=""-1"">No bids placed</FONT></TD>"
      Else
        Response.Write _
          "<TD>" & FormatCurrency(rsBid("MaxBidAmount")) & "</TD>" & _
          "<TD>" & rsBid("LastBidTime")   & "</TD>"
        Dim strSQL2, rsHighBidder
        strSQL2 = "SELECT BidderID FROM Bid " & _
                  "WHERE ItemID = " & rsItems("ItemID") & _
                  " ORDER BY TimeStamp DESC"
        objCmd.CommandType = adCmdText
        objCmd.CommandText = strSQL2
        Set rsHighBidder = objCmd.Execute
        If rsHighBidder("BidderID") = Session("PersonID") Then
          Response.Write "<TD><FONT size=""-1"" COLOR=""Red"">" & _
                        "You are the current high bidder</FONT></TD>"
        End If
        rsHighBidder.Close
        Set rsHighBidder = Nothing
      End If
      rsBid.Close
      Set rsBid = Nothing
      Response.Write "</TR>"
      rsItems.MoveNext
    Loop
    Response.Write "</TABLE>"
    rsItems.close
    Set rsItems = Nothing
```

3. Save these changes to the BrowseListings.asp file. (Alternatively, replace BrowseListings.asp with the contents of the BrowseListings_v2.asp, which you'll find with the source code that accompanies this book at http://www.wrox.com.)

4. Click on the **Browse the listings** hyperlink to view the revised browse page:

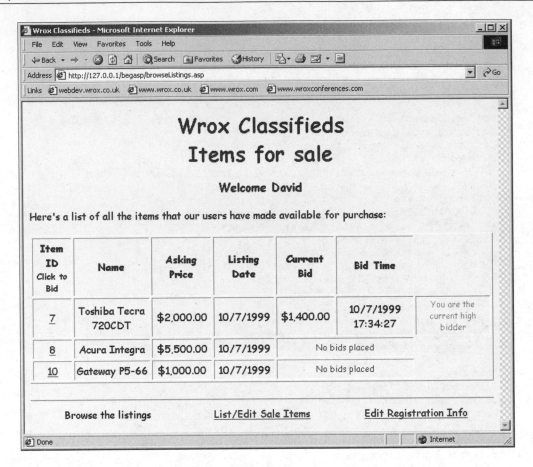

5. Next, open the `ViewMySaleItems.asp` file in your editor.

6. Make the following changes to the body of the `ViewMySaleItems.asp` file:

```
...
Response.Write _
  "<TABLE BORDER=""1"" CELLSPACING=""3"" CELLPADDING=""3"">" & _
  "<TR>" & _
  "  <TH>Item ID<BR><FONT SIZE=""-1"">Click to <BR>Edit/Delete</FONT></TH>" & _
  "  <TH>Name</TH>" & _
  "  <TH>Asking Price</TH>" & _
  "  <TH>Listing Date</TH>" & _
  "  <TH>Current Bid</TH>" & _
  "  <TH>Bid Time</TH>" & _
  "</TR>"
Dim objCmd, rsBid
Set objCmd = Server.CreateObject("ADODB.Command")
Set objCmd.ActiveConnection = objConn
```

```
        strSQL = "SELECT Max(BidAmount) AS MaxBidAmount, " & _
                      "Max(TimeStamp) AS LastBidTime FROM Bid"
        objCmd.CommandType = adCmdText
        Do While Not rsItems.EOF
          Response.Write _
            "<TR ALIGN=CENTER>" & _
            "  <TD><A HREF=""item.asp?Action=Edit&Item=" & rsItems("ItemID") & """>" & _
                     rsItems("ItemID") & "</A></TD>" & _
            "  <TD>" & rsItems("ItemName") & "</TD>" & _
            "  <TD>" & FormatCurrency(rsItems("AskingPrice")) & "</TD>" & _
            "  <TD>" & FormatDateTime(rsItems("ListingDate"),2) & "</TD>"
          objCmd.CommandText = strSQL & " WHERE ItemID = " & rsItems("ItemID") & ";"
          Set rsBid = objCmd.Execute
          If IsNull( rsBid("MaxBidAmount") ) Then
            Response.Write _
              "  <TD></TD><TD></TD>" & _
              "</TR>"
          Else
            Response.Write _
              "  <TD>" & FormatCurrency(rsBid("MaxBidAmount")) & "</TD>" & _
              "  <TD>" & rsBid("LastBidTime") & "</TD>" & _
              "</TR>"
          End If
          rsBid.Close
          Set rsBid = Nothing
          rsItems.MoveNext
        Loop
        Response.Write "</TABLE>"
      Else                                    ' current user has no items for sale
        Response.Write "<CENTER><H2>No items currently for sale</H2></CENTER>"
      End If
      rsItems.close
```

7. Save these changes to the `ViewMySaleItems.asp` file. (Alternatively, replace `ViewMySaleItems.asp` with the contents of `ViewMySaleItems_v2.asp` – again, this is available as part of the source code that accompanies this book, at `http://www.wrox.com`.)

8. Click on the List/Edit Sale Items hyperlink to view the changes to the page:

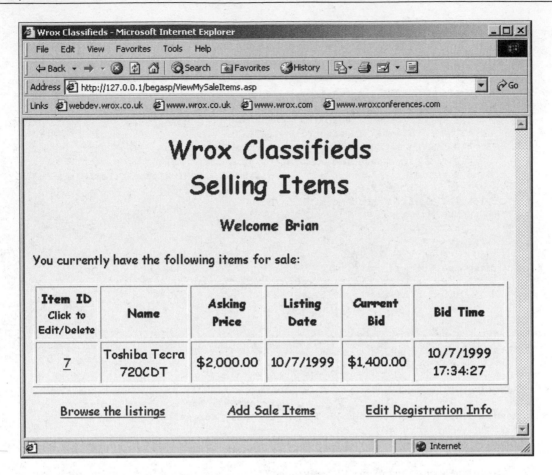

9. Now open the `AddItem.asp` file and add the following highlighted code:

```
If Request.Form("Delete") <> "" Then                    ' user wishes to delete an item
  rsItem.Filter = "ItemID = " & Request("ItemID")
  If Not rsItem.EOF Then rsItem.Delete
  Dim rsBids
  Set rsBids = Server.CreateObject("ADODB.Recordset")
  strSQL = "DELETE FROM Bid WHERE ItemID = " & Request("ItemID")
  rsBids.Open strSQL, objConn, adOpenForwardOnly, adLockOptimistic, adCmdText
  Set rsBids = Nothing
Else                                                    ' user wishes to edit/add an item
```

10. Save these changes to the `AddItem.asp` file. (Alternatively, replace `AddItem.asp` with the contents of `AddItem_v2.asp` – available at `http://www.wrox.com`.)

How It Works

Now that we know how to retrieve information about bids from the database, it is relatively simple to add that information wherever we display information about items.

In the **Browse the Listings** page (`BrowseListings.asp`), we can add two new pieces of information concerning bids – the time and value of the most recent bid. Further, if the current user is currently the highest bidder on an item, then we can provide a visual indicator of that status.

So, in `BrowseListings.asp` we first need to need to prepare our ADO `Command` object. We'll only need one `Command` object in this page, but we'll use it repeatedly – once for each item – to retrieve the last bid and timestamp for each item. The `SELECT` and `FROM` portions of the SQL statement will remain the same, so we store those in a variable called `strSQL`:

```
Dim objCmd, rsBid
set objCmd = Server.CreateObject("ADODB.Command")
set objCmd.ActiveConnection = objConn
strSQL = "SELECT Max(BidAmount) AS MaxBidAmount, " & _
                "Max(TimeStamp) AS LastBidTime FROM Bid"
objCmd.CommandType = adCmdText
```

In order to generate the HTML table, we loop through each item in the **Item** table (just as we did previously). But in our first version of this page we only displayed data relating to the item; in this new version, we'll also display the latest bid information. So for each item in the list, we do this by querying the **Bid** table using the `SELECT` and `FROM` clauses in `strSQL`, and appending a `WHERE` clause to specify the item that we're currently dealing with. We call the `Execute` method of the `Command` object, and populate the `rsBid` recordset:

```
objCmd.CommandText = strSQL & " WHERE ItemID = " & rsItems("ItemID") & ";"
Set rsBid = objCmd.Execute
```

We're retrieving computed information, rather than information from a record itself – so the `rsBid` recordset will always contain exactly one record. If the value of `MaxBidAmount` (within the recordset) is not null, then we know that we have a previous bid – so we can display the amount along with the timestamp for the user:

```
If IsNull( rsBid("MaxBidAmount") ) Then
  Response.Write _
    "<TD COLSPAN=2><FONT SIZE=""-1"">No bids placed</FONT></TD>"
Else
  Response.Write _
    "<TD>" & FormatCurrency(rsBid("MaxBidAmount")) & "</TD>" & _
    "<TD>" & rsBid("LastBidTime")  & "</TD>"
```

The final new part of `BrowseListings.asp` determines whether it's the current user that placed the current highest bid. Ideally, we'd use a single SQL query to retrieve both the high bid amount *and* the highest bid `PersonID` – but the use of the `Max()` function does not permit that. However, we do benefit from the reuse of the `Command` object – we can just create a new SQL query to retrieve the `BidderID` from the bid record containing the latest bid for this item. If this `BidderID` value matches the value currently stored in the session-level `PersonID` variable, then we know that the current user is also the high bidder – and so we can display a message stating so:

```
Dim strSQL2, rsHighBidder
strSQL2 = "SELECT BidderID FROM Bid " & _
          "WHERE ItemID = " & rsItems("ItemID") & _
          " ORDER BY TimeStamp DESC"
objCmd.CommandType = adCmdText
objCmd.CommandText = strSQL2
Set rsHighBidder = objCmd.Execute
If rsHighBidder("BidderID") = Session("PersonID") Then
  Response.Write "<TD><FONT size=""-1"" COLOR=""Red"">" & _
                 "You are the current high bidder</FONT></TD>"
End If
rsHighBidder.Close
Set rsHighBidder = Nothing
```

The changes to ViewMySaleItems.asp are very nearly the same as those that we've made to BrowseListings.asp. The only significant difference is that we don't need the additional column for the You are the current high bidder message.

Finally, we need to look at one part of the AddItem.asp script file. You'll recall that the purpose of this script is to add, edit, or delete items in the Item table of the database. When we delete an item, it's also a good idea to clean up all of the bids that are associated with that item. To do this, we create a new recordset object, called rsBids, which issues a SQL query. This SQL query is a bit different from those that we've seen before: instead of using a SELECT statement to retrieve information from a table, we use a DELETE statement:

```
Dim rsBids
Set rsBids = Server.CreateObject("ADODB.Recordset")
strSQL = "DELETE FROM Bid WHERE ItemID = " & Request("ItemID")
rsBids.Open strSQL, objConn, adOpenForwardOnly, adLockOptimistic, adCmdText
Set rsBids = Nothing
```

This will delete every record in the Bid table whose ItemID value matches the value of Request("ItemID"). When we use a DELETE SQL query to open a recordset, the deletion is carried out and then the recordset is automatically closed.

Completing a Sale

The last section of this chapter explains how we'll tie up a sale – by having the seller accept a bid, and then having the successful bidder acknowledge the acceptance and thus complete the sale.

Accepting a Bid

First, we'll look at how we can allow the seller to accept a bid. When this happens, the buyer is notified, and can accept (or reject) the deal at that point. When the deal is accepted by both parties, the information is logged to the database.

Try It Out – Accepting a Bid

1. Open the `Item.asp` file.

2. Add the following highlighted code, between the end `</TABLE>` and end `</FORM>` tags:

```
   ...
   </TR>
</TABLE>
<%
  If Request.QueryString("Action") = "Edit" Then
    Dim rsBids
    Set rsBids = Server.CreateObject("ADODB.Recordset")
    strSQL = "SELECT * FROM Bid WHERE ItemID =" & Request("Item") & _
             " ORDER BY TimeStamp DESC;"
    rsBids.Open strSQL, objConn
    If rsBids.EOF Then
      Response.Write "<HR><P>No bids currently placed"
    Else
      Response.Write "<HR><P>Bid History (Newest to Oldest)<P>" & _
        "<TABLE BORDER=""2"" CELLSPACING=""3"" CELLPADDING=""3"">" & _
        "  <TR>" & _
        "    <TH>Bidder ID</TH>" & _
        "    <TH>Timestamp</TH>" & _
        "    <TH>Amount Bid</TH>" & _
        "    <TH>Last Change</TH>" & _
        "  </TR>"
      Dim blnFirst
      blnFirst = True
      Do While Not rsBids.EOF
        Response.Write _
          "<TR>" & _
          "  <TD>" &  rsBids("BidderID") & "</TD>" & _
          "  <TD>" & rsBids("Timestamp") & "</TD>" & _
          "  <TD ALIGN=RIGHT>" &  FormatCurrency(rsBids("BidAmount")) & "</TD>" & _
          "  <TD ALIGN=RIGHT>" &  FormatCurrency(rsBids("BidChange")) & "</TD>"
        If blnFirst Then
          Response.Write _
          "<TD ALIGN=RIGHT><A HREF=""SaleDetailsForSeller.asp?Item=" & _
                     Request("Item") & "&BidID=" & rsBids("BidID") & """>" & _
                     "Click to sell to this bidder</A></TD>"
          blnFirst=False
        End If
        Response.Write "</TR>"
        rsBids.MoveNext
      Loop
      rsBids.Close
      Response.Write "</TABLE>"
    End If
  End If
%>
</FORM>
   ...
```

3. Don't forget to save your changes to this file, with the same filename. Alternatively, you'll find these changes contained in the file Item_v2.asp, in the source code files that accompany this book.

4. From the Selling Items page (ViewMySaleItems.asp), click on the ItemID of an item that has a current bid on it. That will take you to the updated Item.asp page. In this screenshot, we're looking at the details and bids that have been made on our Toshiba laptop:

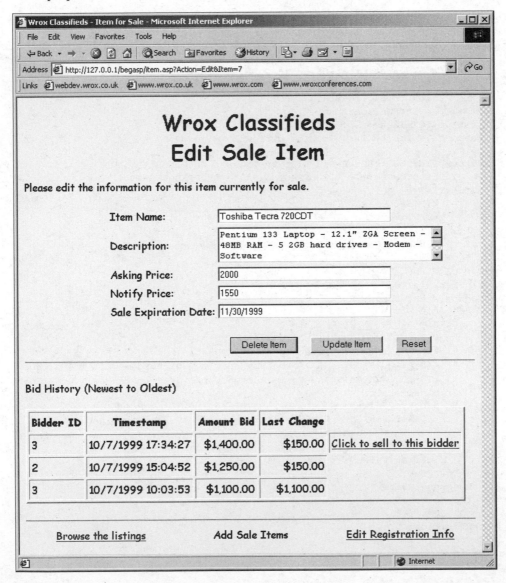

5. Now, create a new ASP file and enter the following code:

```
<!--#include file="Clssfd.asp"-->
<BASEFONT FACE="Comic Sans MS" COLOR="DarkBlue">
<HTML>
<HEAD>
<TITLE>Wrox Classifieds - Item Sale</TITLE>
</HEAD>

<BODY BGCOLOR="#FFFF80">
<CENTER><H1>Wrox Classifieds<BR>Item Sale</H1></CENTER>
<P>
<%
  Dim rsBid
  Set rsBid = Server.CreateObject("ADODB.Recordset")
  strSQL = "SELECT BidderID, FamilyName, GivenName, EMailAddress, " & _
           "BidAmount, ItemName, AskingPrice FROM Person " & _
           "INNER JOIN (Item INNER JOIN Bid ON Item.ItemID = Bid.ItemID) " & _
           "ON Person.PersonID = Bid.BidderID " & _
           "WHERE (((Bid.BidID)=" & Request.QueryString("BidID") & "));"
  rsBid.Open strSQL, objConn, adOpenForwardOnly, adLockOptimistic, adCmdText
%>
<TABLE BORDER=0>
  <TR>
    <TD WIDTH=20% ROWSPAN=11> </TD>
    <TD>Item Name:</TD>
    <TD><FONT COLOR="Blue"><%= rsBid("ItemName") %></TD>
  </TR>
  <TR>
    <TD>Asking Price:</TD>
    <TD><FONT COLOR="Blue"><%= FormatCurrency(rsBid("AskingPrice")) %></FONT></TD>
  </TR>
  <TR>
    <TD>Bid Amount:</TD>
    <TD><FONT COLOR="Blue"><%= FormatCurrency(rsBid("BidAmount")) %></TD>
  </TR>
  <TR>
    <TD>Bidder:</TD>
    <TD><FONT COLOR="Blue"><FONT COLOR="Blue">
        <%= rsBid("FamilyName") & ", " & rsBid("GivenName") %></TD>
  </TR>
  <TR>
    <TD>E-Mail:</TD>
    <TD><FONT COLOR="Blue"><%= rsBid("EMailAddress") %></TD>
  </TR>
</TABLE>

<%
  Dim objCmd
  Set objCmd = Server.CreateObject("ADODB.Command")
  strSQL = "UPDATE Item SET ItemStatus = 'Pending' " & _
           "WHERE (((Item.ItemID)=" & Request.QueryString("Item") & "));"
```

```
objCmd.CommandText = strSQL
objCmd.CommandType = adCmdText
Set objCmd.ActiveConnection = objConn
objCmd.Execute

strSQL = "INSERT INTO Sale (ItemID, BuyerID, WinningBid, SellerApproval) " & _
         "VALUES (" & Request.QueryString("Item") & ", " & _
         rsBid("BidderID") & ", " & rsBid("BidAmount") & ", Yes);"
objCmd.CommandText = strSQL
objCmd.Execute
Response.Write "<P>" & _
  "<CENTER>Sale Completed - The purchaser will now be notified</CENTER>"
%>
<HR><P>
<TABLE BORDER=0 WIDTH=100%>
  <TR ALIGN=CENTER>
    <TD WIDTH=33%><A HREF="BrowseListings.asp">Browse the listings</A></TD>
    <TD WIDTH=33%>Add Sale Items</TD>
    <TD WIDTH=33%><A HREF="Register.asp?Update=True">Edit Registration Info</A></TD>
  </TR>
</TABLE>
</BODY>
</HTML>
```

6. Save the file as `SaleDetailsForSeller.asp`, in the usual directory.

7. Click on the **Click to sell to this bidder** hyperlink to begin the sale process.

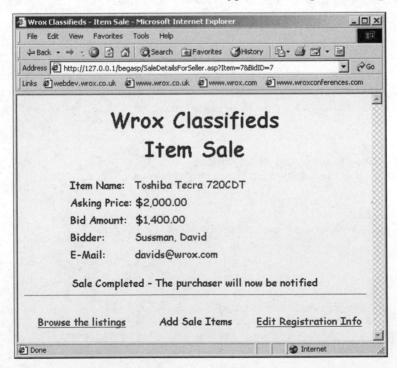

How It Works

To begin the sales process, we need to add the bid history to `Item.asp`. We do this in much the same way that we added the bid history to `BrowseListings.asp` and `ViewMySaleItems.asp`. The primary difference here is that we'll retrieve *all* the bids, not just the highest.

To retrieve the bids from the database, we use a SQL query to generate a recordset. This query will return all of the bids for the current item, ready-sorted into order from newest to oldest:

```
<%
  If Request.QueryString("Action") = "Edit" Then
    Dim rsBids
    Set rsBids = Server.CreateObject("ADODB.Recordset")
    strSQL = "SELECT * FROM Bid WHERE ItemID =" & Request("Item") & _
             " ORDER BY TimeStamp DESC;"
    rsBids.Open strSQL, objConn
```

We're going to display these bids in a table – with each row corresponding to one bid. Before we go through the list of bids, we will create a local variable called `blnFirst` and set it to `True`. This will be used to identify the first time through the loop:

```
    Dim blnFirst
    blnFirst = True
    Do While Not rsBids.EOF
```

Now we can generate the table rows:

```
      Response.Write _
        "<TR>" & _
        "  <TD>" &  rsBids("BidderID") & "</TD>" & _
        "  <TD>" & rsBids("Timestamp") & "</TD>" & _
        "  <TD ALIGN=RIGHT>" &  FormatCurrency(rsBids("BidAmount")) & "</TD>" & _
        "  <TD ALIGN=RIGHT>" &  FormatCurrency(rsBids("BidChange")) & "</TD>"
      If blnFirst Then
        Response.Write _
        "<TD ALIGN=RIGHT><A HREF=""SaleDetailsForSeller.asp?Item=" & _
                   Request("Item") & "&BidID=" & rsBids("BidID") & """>" & _
                   "Click to sell to this bidder</A></TD>"
        blnFirst=False
      End If
      Response.Write "</TR>"
      rsBids.MoveNext
    Loop
```

Because the SQL query specified `ORDER BY TimeStamp DESC`, and because we know each successive bid was higher than the last, we know that the first iteration through this loop corresponds to the highest bid. We make the assumption that, if the seller wishes to sell the item, then they'll want to sell it to the highest bidder. So, when the `blnFirst` value is `True` we display the **Click to sell to this bidder** hyperlink – by clicking on this link, the seller agrees to sell the item to the highest bidder. After we've displayed the hyperlink, we set `blnFirst` to `False` – so it only appears once on the page.

So what happens when the **Click to sell to this bidder** link is clicked? The link is an anchor tag that directs the user to `SaleDetailsForSeller.asp`. This page updates the database tables and displays information about the sale. The information displayed here comes from data contained in three different tables:

❑ The **Bid** table has the ID of the winning bidder and the amount that they bid.

❑ The **Item** table has the name of the item and its asking price.

❑ The **Person** table has the name and e-mail address of the bidder.

To retrieve all of this information at once, we will be creating a SQL statement known as a `JOIN`:

```
<%
  Dim rsBid
  Set rsBid = Server.CreateObject("ADODB.Recordset")
  strSQL = "SELECT BidderID, FamilyName, GivenName, EMailAddress, " & _
           "BidAmount, ItemName, AskingPrice FROM Person " & _
           "INNER JOIN (Item INNER JOIN Bid ON Item.ItemID = Bid.ItemID) " & _
           "ON Person.PersonID = Bid.BidderID " & _
           "WHERE (((Bid.BidID)=" & Request.QueryString("BidID") & "));"
  rsBid.Open strSQL, objConn, adOpenForwardOnly, adLockOptimistic, adCmdText
%>
```

At the beginning of this chapter, we discussed primary keys and foreign keys. Well, this is where they really come into their own. The **Bid** table contains foreign keys for both the **Item** table and the **Person** table. To create the join, we use the value of these foreign keys to pull information from the other tables.

To better examine how this SQL statement works, let's break it down into pieces. The first piece is the `WHERE` clause:

```
strSQL = "SELECT BidderID, FamilyName, GivenName, EMailAddress, " & _
         "BidAmount, ItemName, AskingPrice FROM Person " & _
         "INNER JOIN (Item INNER JOIN Bid ON Item.ItemID = Bid.ItemID) " & _
         "ON Person.PersonID = Bid.BidderID " & _
         "WHERE (((Bid.BidID)=" & Request.QueryString("BidID") & "));"
```

This will retrieve every record from the **Bid** table, whose `BidID` value is equal to the value passed into this page in the querystring. Since the `BidID` is a primary key of the **Bid** table, this `WHERE` clause can return at most one record.

Next, we will look at the `SELECT` portion of the SQL statement:

```
strSQL = "SELECT BidderID, FamilyName, GivenName, EMailAddress, " & _
         "BidAmount, ItemName, AskingPrice FROM Person " & _
         "INNER JOIN (Item INNER JOIN Bid ON Item.ItemID = Bid.ItemID) " & _
         "ON Person.PersonID = Bid.BidderID " & _
         "WHERE (((Bid.BidID)=" & Request.QueryString("BidID") & "));"
```

The SELECT statement is the same as other select statements except in one detail: namely, that the fields that we have named are coming from *different* tables. The BidderID and BidAmount fields are in the Bid table, while FamilyName, GivenName, and EMailAddress are from Person, and ItemName and AskingPrice are from Item.

It is in the FROM clause that the tables are tied together:

```
strSQL = "SELECT BidderID, FamilyName, GivenName, EMailAddress, " & _
         "BidAmount, ItemName, AskingPrice FROM Person " & _
         "INNER JOIN (Item INNER JOIN Bid ON Item.ItemID = Bid.ItemID) " & _
         "ON Person.PersonID = Bid.BidderID " & _
         "WHERE (((Bid.BidID)=" & Request.QueryString("BidID") & "));"
```

Starting from the inside, we have joined Item and Bid together using an INNER JOIN for those records where the value of ItemID in the Item table matches the value of ItemID in the Bid table (that is, on Item.ItemID = Bid.ItemID). An INNER JOIN means that we will retrieve only the records that match on both sides. Then, moving outward, we join the results of the first join with the Person table, where the PersonID in the Person table matches the BidderID in the Bid table (that is, on Person.PersonID = Bid.BidderID). All of these records will be combined together and returned as a single recordset, rsBid, which we use to display the appropriate information to the seller.

Once that's done, we can update the database tables to begin recording the sale. We use an ADO Command object called objCmd to interact with the database:

```
Dim objCmd
Set objCmd = Server.CreateObject("ADODB.Command")
```

This interaction will be in the form of SQL statements. We've already seen some SELECT and DELETE SQL statements in this chapter; now, we'll use a couple of new SQL commands. Here's the first:

```
strSQL = "UPDATE Item SET ItemStatus = 'Pending' " & _
         "WHERE (((Item.ItemID)=" & Request.QueryString("Item") & "));"
objCmd.CommandText = strSQL
objCmd.CommandType = adCmdText
Set objCmd.ActiveConnection = objConn
objCmd.Execute
```

The UPDATE SQL statement is used to change the value of fields in an existing record. In our example, we will be changing the value of the ItemStatus field to Pending, in the record that corresponds to the item being sold. In this case, we're updating only one record.

Using the SQL UPDATE statement is probably overkill – we could have just used a recordset. But, for updating multiple records at once, nothing can beat the UPDATE statement as it is much faster.

Here's the second new SQL statement:

```
strSQL = "INSERT INTO Sale (ItemID, BuyerID, WinningBid, SellerApproval) " & _
         "VALUES (" & Request.QueryString("Item") & ", " & _
           rsBid("BidderID") & ", " & rsBid("BidAmount") & ", Yes);"
objCmd.CommandText = strSQL
objCmd.Execute
```

The INSERT SQL statement is used to add new records to an existing table. This is very similar to opening a recordset and then using the AddNew method. Again, either method could be used in this case. We just wanted to look at something new. The INSERT statement has three separate parts:

❑ **The target table:** First, we have to identify that table into which we want to insert the record. In this example, we will be adding a record to the Sale table.

❑ **The target fields:** Second, we list the fields to which we will be adding data. By default, you add data to all the fields. In this case, we only want to add data to four fields, so we list them (enclosed in parentheses) after the name of the table.

❑ **The values to insert:** Finally, we identify the actual values that will be inserted into the specified fields. It's important to list these values in the order that corresponds to the list of fields that we've already specified.

When we use the Command object's Execute method to run the SQL statement, we create a new record in the Sale table, whose fields will be populated with the specified values.

Notifying the Bidder

Now that all of the database tables have been updated, there's just one last step: to notify the buyer that their bid has been accepted.

Try It Out – Notifying the Buyer

1. Open the MenuForRegisteredUsers.asp file.

2. Add the following highlighted line at the very beginning of MenuForRegisteredUsers.asp:

```
<!--#include file="Clssfd.asp"-->
<%
If Session("PersonID") = "" then
  Response.Redirect "Login.asp"
End If
%>
```

3. Also, add the following highlighted code to the body of MenuForRegisteredUsers.asp:

```
...
<UL>
  <LI>Browse for items on sale
  <LI>Bid for items on sale
  <LI>Sell your own items on these pages
</UL>
<%
  Dim rsPendingSales
  Set rsPendingSales = Server.CreateObject("ADODB.Recordset")
  strSQL = "SELECT SaleID, WinningBid, ItemName " & _
           "FROM Sale INNER JOIN Item ON Sale.ItemID = Item.ItemID " & _
           "WHERE BuyerID=" & Session("PersonID") & " AND BuyerAcceptance=FALSE;"
  rsPendingSales.Open strSQL, objConn
  If Not rsPendingSales.EOF Then
    Response.Write "You have placed the winning bid on these items:<P>" & _
      "<TABLE cellpadding=3  border=1>" & _
        "<TR>" & _
        "<TH>Item Name<BR><FONT SIZE=-1>Click to Complete Purchase</FONT></TH>" & _
        "<TH>Winning Bid</TH>" & _
        "</TR>"
    Do While Not rsPendingSales.EOF
      Response.Write _
        "<TR>" & _
        "  <TD ALIGN=CENTER><A HREF=""BuyerAcceptance.asp?SaleID=" & _
                  rsPendingSales("SaleID") & """>" & _
                  rsPendingSales("ItemName") & "</TD>" & _
        "  <TD ALIGN=RIGHT>" & _
                  FormatCurrency(rsPendingSales("WinningBid")) & "</TD>" & _
        "</TR>"
      rsPendingSales.MoveNext
    Loop
    Response.Write "</TABLE><P>"
  End If
%>
<HR>
...
```

4. Now save the changes that you've made to `MenuForRegisteredUsers.asp`. (Alternatively, use the code contained in `MenuForRegisteredUsers_v2.asp` – available as part of the source code that supports this chapter, at `http://www.wrox.com`.)

5. Now create a new ASP file, and type in the following code:

```
<!--#include file="Clssfd.asp"-->
<%
  Dim rsSale, strItemID
  Set rsSale = Server.CreateObject("ADODB.Recordset")
  rsSale.Open "Sale", objConn, adOpenForwardOnly, adLockOptimistic, adCmdTable
  rsSale.Filter = "SaleID = " & Request("SaleID")
  rsSale("BuyerAcceptance") = True
  rsSale("CompletionDate") = Now
```

```
strItemID = rsSale("ItemID")
rsSale.Update
rsSale.Close
Set rsSale = Nothing

Dim objCmd
Set objCmd = Server.CreateObject("ADODB.Command")
strSQL = "UPDATE Item SET ItemStatus = 'Sold' " & _
         "WHERE (((Item.ItemID)=" & strItemID & "));"
objCmd.CommandText = strSQL
objCmd.CommandType = adCmdText
Set objCmd.ActiveConnection = objConn
objCmd.Execute
Set objCmd = Nothing
Response.Redirect "MenuForRegisteredUsers.asp"
%>
```

6. Save the file as `BuyerAcceptance.asp`, in the usual directory.

7. View the **Registered User Home** page by logging into the system again – a successful login takes you to `MenuForRegisteredUsers.asp`. If you've had any bids accepted, then you'll be notified of it here.

In this screenshot, that's exactly what's happened. David's seller details page is a little different than before, because we just accepted his bid on the Toshiba:

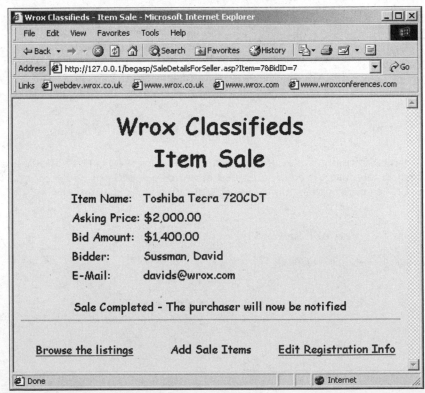

8. Click on the hyperlinked item name to acknowledge the bid acceptance. This will
update the database accordingly, and return you to
`MenuForRegisteredUsers.asp`.

How It Works

Any user who has placed a bid on an item will want to be informed if their bid is accepted by
the seller. We designed our application so that the **Registered Users** home page is displayed
when a user logs into the system – so this is an excellent opportunity to notify the user of any
successful bids that they made.

To do this, we've added some code to `MenuForRegisteredUsers.asp`, which checks the **Sale**
table for any pending sales associated with the current user. We create a recordset and populate
it by executing a SQL query which pulls information from both the **Sale** table and the **Item** table:

```
Dim rsPendingSales
Set rsPendingSales = Server.CreateObject("ADODB.Recordset")
strSQL = "SELECT SaleID, WinningBid, ItemName " & _
         "FROM Sale INNER JOIN Item ON Sale.ItemID = Item.ItemID " & _
         "WHERE BuyerID=" & Session("PersonID") & " AND BuyerAcceptance=FALSE;"
rsPendingSales.Open strSQL, objConn
```

Again, we've used a `JOIN` to pull information from the two tables – joining the **Sale** table to the
Item table using the `ItemID` field that exists in each table. We retrieve only those **Sale** records
whose `BuyerID` field matches the current user's `PersonID`, and whose `BuyerAcceptance`
field is `FALSE` (indicating that the bidder has not yet acknowledged the successful sale).

If there are any pending sales for this user to acknowledge, then the `rsPendingSales`
recordset will be non-empty – the cursor will be on the first record in the recordset and
therefore `EOF` will be false. Using this, we can display the details of each pending sale in the
rows of a table:

```
If Not rsPendingSales.EOF Then
  Response.Write "You have placed the winning bid on these items:<P>" & _
    "<TABLE cellpadding=3  border=1>" & _
      "<TR>" & _
      "<TH>Item Name<BR><FONT SIZE=-1>Click to Complete Purchase</FONT></TH>" & _
      "<TH>Winning Bid</TH>" & _
      "</TR>"
  Do While Not rsPendingSales.EOF
    Response.Write _
      "<TR>" & _
      "  <TD ALIGN=CENTER><A HREF=""BuyerAcceptance.asp?SaleID=" & _
                rsPendingSales("SaleID") & """>" & _
                rsPendingSales("ItemName") & "</TD>" & _
      "  <TD ALIGN=RIGHT>" & _
                FormatCurrency(rsPendingSales("WinningBid")) & "</TD>" & _
      "</TR>"
    rsPendingSales.MoveNext
  Loop
  Response.Write "</TABLE><P>"
End If
```

In the first column, the name of the item is displayed as a hyperlink. The user can click on the hyperlink to indicate that they approve the purchase of the item. This loads the `BuyerAcceptance.asp` script.

`BuyerAcceptance.asp` updates the information in the **Sale** table, to take account of the bidder's acknowledgement. Again, we use an ADO `Recordset` object. We're interested in one specific record of the **Sale** table, which we retrieve by setting a `Filter` on the recordset:

```
<!--#include file="Clssfd.asp"-->
<%
  Dim rsSale, strItemID
  Set rsSale = Server.CreateObject("ADODB.Recordset")
  rsSale.Open "Sale", objConn, adOpenForwardOnly, adLockOptimistic, adCmdTable
  rsSale.Filter = "SaleID = " & Request("SaleID")
```

This places the recordset's cursor at the record we want to change. Now we just set the `BuyerAcceptance` field to `True` and set the sale `CompletionDate` to the current date and time. Also, we take the `ItemID` associated with the sale and copy it into a temporary local variable, `strItemID`, because we'll need it to update the **Item** table. Once the fields are updated, we can write the changes to the database and then close the recordset:

```
  rsSale("BuyerAcceptance") = True
  rsSale("CompletionDate") = Now
  strItemID = rsSale("ItemID")
  rsSale.Update
  rsSale.Close
  Set rsSale = Nothing
```

The final step is to update the `ItemStatus` field in the **Item** table:

```
  Dim objCmd
  Set objCmd = Server.CreateObject("ADODB.Command")
  strSQL = "UPDATE Item SET ItemStatus = 'Sold' " & _
           "WHERE (((Item.ItemID)=" & strItemID & "));"
  objCmd.CommandText = strSQL
  objCmd.CommandType = adCmdText
  Set objCmd.ActiveConnection = objConn
  objCmd.Execute
  Set objCmd = Nothing
  Response.Redirect "MenuForRegisteredUsers.asp"
```

Here, we've adapted code that we first saw in `SaleDetailsForSeller.asp` (where it was used to change the `ItemStatus` value to `Pending`). Here, we need to make one further change – to update the `ItemStatus` value to `Sold`. To find the right record, we use the `ItemID` value we stored in the local `strItemID` variable a moment ago. Once we've made this change, we can send the user back to the **Registered Users** home page – which is generated dynamically, and will display the most up-to-date list of pending sales.

Adding to this Application

In this application, we've merely scratched the surface of what we could achieve with an online classified ad system. There are lots of ways in which you could extend and enhance the application, to provide better functionality. For example, you could:

- ❏ Add a Category field to the Item table. This would allow the seller to categorize their items better, and also opens possibilities for different ways of browsing, instead of presenting a one-dimensional list of items.

- ❏ Create a bid status window, which the seller could leave open on their desktop. Ideally, this would automatically refresh itself periodically, showing the current highest bids on items they have for sale.

- ❏ Add support for richer information about the items – such as pictures, links to other sites, and reviews from buyers.

- ❏ Extend the database to support multiple quantities of the same item being sold. For example, suppose you had 10 computers to sell – you could enter your batch of computers as a single item with a quantity of 10, rather than as 10 separate items.

As your web site grows in popularity and generates increasing traffic, you can begin to think about migrating to a Windows 2000 Server platform. This migration will allow you to:

- ❏ Upsize the database from Access to SQL Server. With SQL Server, you get the benefits of a true database server, along with the increased performance that it affords.

- ❏ Utilize the Collaborative Data Objects (CDO) support on 2000 Server to allow the server to automatically generate e-mail message that can be sent to users of the system.

- ❏ Take advantage of the enhanced scalability that comes with employing transactions through COM+, by creating custom components that perform the same application functionality with much greater performance.

In-depth coverage of these subjects is beyond the scope of this book. We'll take a look at some elementary components in the following chapters, and we cover these issues in the titles that you'll find on the back cover of this book.

Summary

In this chapter, we built a working application using Active Server Pages. The application used features such as:

- ❏ Client-side scripting, using JavaScript to validate passwords and proper bid amounts.
- ❏ Server-side scripting, using VBScript to present custom presentations to different users.
- ❏ ASP's Request and Response objects, to communicate with the web client and pass information back and forth.
- ❏ ASP's Session object, to manage a user session which tracks a user through the application and holds all of their pertinent information as they move from page to page.
- ❏ The ActiveX Data Objects (ADO), to manipulate the information in our database.

The intention of this example application was to demonstrate many of the techniques that we've seen so far in the book. In the remaining chapters, we'll take a look at a couple of technologies that are very relevant to ASP – namely, components and XML.

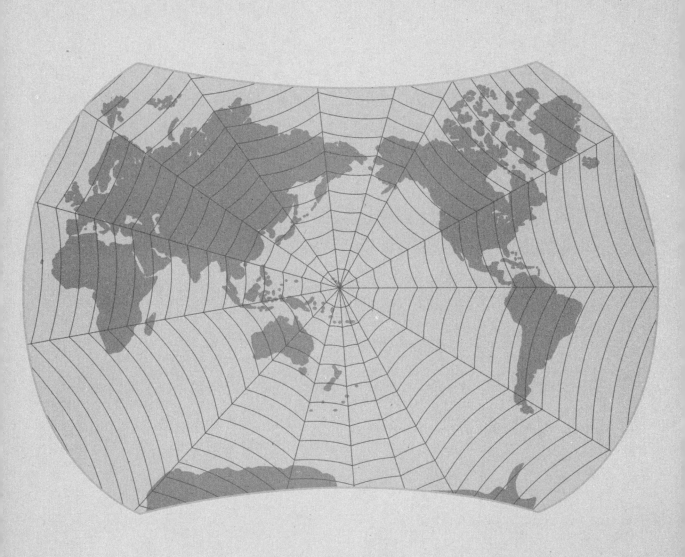

Building Script Components for ASP

We've already seen a number of components in this book, and we've seen some of the advantages that they can bring to our ASP applications. In Chapter 6, the `MyTelephone.dll` component encapsulated the functionality of a `Telephone` object – with methods like `PlaceCall` and `Answer`, and events like `CallWaiting`, which reflected the functionality and behavior of a real telephone.

In Chapter 11, we looked at the so-called 'Active Server components' – a particular group of components provided with IIS 5.0, that we can use in our ASP applications to perform a whole range of different tasks. One such is the Ad Rotator component – a component that decides which of a number of ads or images will appear at a particular point in your ASP page, using a weighted rotation system to do so. Another is the Browser Capabilities component, which provided the functionality required to peek at the user's setup and establish what type of browser is being used to view the page.

More generally, components come from all sorts of sources, and perform all sorts of tasks. And because of the advantages that components can bring to our applications, component design has become a hugely important part of application development today.

Many components are written in compiled languages, such as Visual Basic or C++, and there are good reasons for this (as we'll see later). However, this doesn't mean that we need to learn a new programming language in order to write a component. In this chapter we'll meet the **Windows Script Components (WSC)** tool – an accessible way to develop components and the ideal tool with which to begin learning the art of component design. We'll see how to write some simple components using WSC, and we'll be exercising these new components within ASP pages.

So, in this chapter, we will:

- ❑ Explain what a component is
- ❑ Discuss the benefits of components, and the fundamentals of how they work
- ❑ Talk about the pros and cons of writing components in script, or writing components in a compiled language
- ❑ Discuss the elements and syntax of WSCs, showing how XML is used as the framework of the script object
- ❑ Build some script-based components of our own, using the Windows Script Component Wizard
- ❑ Use our components within our own ASP pages

A Brief Introduction to Components

As you progress to building bigger and bigger web applications, you'll soon reach a point where your applications are sufficiently complex that it's not possible to solve the whole problem using one huge block of code. Instead, you need to consider a different approach:

- ❑ First, consider the best way of breaking your complex problem into smaller, more manageable chunks
- ❑ Second, solve each chunk by writing a piece of manageable 'standalone' code
- ❑ Third, bring together the solutions to each of those chunks to create an overall solution to your problem

In fact, we've already started to do this. If you've stepped through Chapter 15, then you'll know that the **Wrox Classifieds** application that we built there is divided into some 14 ASP pages that each performs some small part of the overall application. We've got pages that handle the registration, login, browsing, bidding and purchasing tasks that the user must accomplish when using the application.

In this book we have also had occasion to use procedures and functions. Recall that each function and procedure is just a block of code that is self-contained, and whose code is written in one place only. Once we've written the code once, we can call the function or procedure as many times as we need within our main code. And later, if you find that there's a bug in the function, you don't need to go through your entire application changing bits of code – instead, you just need to fix the bug in the one place.

What is a Component?

So these are two approaches that are very much encouraged in application programming of all kinds (not only web application programming). Breaking a large application down into smallish, logical, self-contained sections makes the whole thing much easier to understand, to write and to maintain. Using procedures and functions means that those pieces of code only need to be written once, and can be used often – again facilitating the design, writing and maintaining processes.

In fact, these approaches are well-recognized, but we can go further than that. In fact, in order to optimize the way that we implement our application in logically-dissected self-contained blocks, we can use **components**.

You can think of a component as being a small, self-contained nugget of code that provides a certain amount of related functionality and information – in the form of **methods**, **properties** and **events**. When we write an application, we might use a number of components – each component is designed to do a specific job, and the application utilizes the specific functionality of each component in a particular way, to achieve its goal.

Even better, there is an established technology available that allows us to build components in a way that allows them to talk to one another – that technology is **COM** (the Component Object Model). COM is a framework for creating and using components in such a way that their functionality is well-defined and unambiguous. Also, many programming languages are COM-compliant, which is good news for us. It means that COM-compliant languages and COM components can all work together, without language barriers, to solve large and complex problems.

> We won't spend much time in this book getting into the complexities of COM – it's beyond the scope of the book. There are many good books on COM; for an introduction, you might like to try Beginning Components for ASP (Wrox, ISBN 1-861002-88-2).

Examples of Components

Before we think about a programming example, let's draw an analogy with a real-life example. Consider the art of photography. Here are some of the different basic camera parts that you'd need to buy if you were choosing to take up photography as a hobby:

- ❑ You'd need a camera body, of course – that's the bit that you put the film into, and which has the button that takes the photograph

- ❑ You'd need a lens, which you attach to the camera body and which focuses the light from outside onto the film inside the camera's body

- ❑ You might want to put a filter on the end of the lens, to create a particular effect

- ❑ You might want a flash, for taking indoor photographs in poor light

OK, let's suppose that you've bought a basic photographer's kit that contains a camera body, a regular lens with zoom facility, a filter or two and a flash mechanism. Then a month later, you decide that you *really* want to start taking pictures of landscapes instead. Your regular lens with zoom facility isn't great for landscapes; what you really need is a wide-angle lens instead. But you don't go and buy a whole new camera – all you need to do is buy a new lens, detach the zoom lens and attach the wide-angle lens.

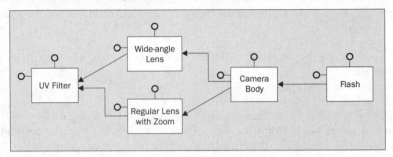

So each component here is a bit like a black box – it is responsible for a certain part of the overall job, and we use whichever components are appropriate for our purpose, by piecing them together in the way we need.

OK, that's photography, but what about programming? Well, working with components in our programming code is just like working with different photographic components when preparing to take photos. Each component is designed to provide a specific piece of functionality, or a set of related functionality, and we can piece any number of required components together in our application in order to do the job.

If fact, you may not have realized it but we have been using components all the way through this book! For example:

❑ We have been writing web applications using ASP, and for that we needed the ASP intrinsic objects (`Request`, `Response` etc). In fact, whenever we need one of these objects in our code, the object is created from a COM component – this component provides the compiled code that defines the object's properties, methods and events. The code for this component is contained in a dynamic link library (DLL) file called `asp.dll`; you'll be able to find this file somewhere on the hard disk of your machine. The `asp.dll` file is used by your web server when a user requests an ASP page; but if the user requests an HTML page then the `asp.dll` component isn't required.

❑ The ADO data access objects (`Connection`, `Recordset` etc) that we've used are also defined by a COM component, whose compiled code is contained in the file `msado15.dll`. When we're involved in data access with ADO, the system digs out `msado15.dll` and uses it to provide data access functionality.

❑ Even better, consider one of the very familiar applications that we use every day – perhaps something like Internet Explorer. Many applications like this are written using components. For example, when you start up Internet Explorer, the system runs the base executable file `Iexplore.exe`. But `Iexplore.exe` is very small – it's only around 60Kb. All the functionality associated with Internet Explorer is actually contained in the numerous components that are only called into action (by `Iexplore.exe`) when they're needed.

Why do we Use Components?

So hopefully you should be persuaded by now that it's a good idea to divide the functionality of a large application into smaller sections. But one question we haven't answered yet is why we might use components to do this job. What's wrong with simply dividing the work up among a number of ASP pages, or writing a number of functions within a server-side include file, and #INCLUDE-ing the SSI into each page?

Well, in some cases there's nothing wrong with those other solutions. But there are numerous advantages that component-based solutions have over script-based solutions, and in this section we'll examine some of these advantages.

Code Re-use and Distribution

As we've already said, two common reasons for using components are:

- ❑ Breaking up a complex application into manageable chunks
- ❑ Packaging up code that you are likely to need more than once

Cutting and pasting the same piece of script into different areas of your ASP pages can be problematic. If you've ever done this with your own code, you'll know how difficult it is to remember how you originally intended the code to work – you may have to work out what each line is doing in order to select precisely the correct amount of code. If you've ever done it with someone else's code, you'll know that it's even harder! Even if you're using a prewritten script function or procedure, you need to paste it into your code or include it via an SSI – you can get problems with naming clashes or simply with the process of cutting and pasting.

When you package code into a COM component, you are automatically providing a clear definition of precisely how to call up the functionality of that component. It's still a good idea to have some documentation for the component, but you won't need to do any clumsy cutting and pasting of code.

Easy Distribution

Because there's no cutting and pasting involved, components make for a very convenient code distribution technique. Your code is neatly packaged into a file such as a `.dll`, which can be easily passed to your colleagues and customers. They don't need to understand the code behind it to get it to work – you just tell them what tasks it can achieve and what information they'll need to pass to it.

For example, when we use the ADO objects in our code, we don't need to know anything about the underlying code that is contained in `msado15.dll`, and which defines how those objects work. All we have to do to is consult Microsoft's documentation, which explains how we employ their methods, properties and events in our code.

Binary Distribution and Re-Use

Moreover, we can *write* a COM component using one language, and then *use* the compiled component using any other language that understands COM. For example, the `MyTelephone.dll` component (from Chapter 6) was written in Visual Basic, but we can use `MyTelephone.dll` in Visual Basic, VBScript, JavaScript, Java, C++, ... in fact, in any COM-compliant programming language. That's because the compiled component (for example, the `.dll` file) is in a **binary format**, which is usable by any COM-compliant language.

Maintenance and Replacability

Suppose you've written an application that uses a number of components and some ASP pages to perform some large application, and you've sold it to a number of customers. Then, a report comes in that there is a bug in your application.

Ordinarily, this would send a chill down the spine of the average programmer. Of course, the first job is to track down the bug and fix it; but the real problem often lies in telling all your customers how to fix the bug. If the bug were in ASP script, then it would be difficult and messy to tell your customers how to fix the problem. But if the bug is in a *component*, then all you need to do is re-compile the debugged component, and distribute it in an executable `.exe` file that simply reinstalls the new component over the old one. For your customers, fixing the bug can be as simple as running the executable.

Performance Advantages

When you are executing some complicated code, then you want to reduce the time it takes to process. However, if your code is in the form of ASP or other script, then you can reasonably expect it to take a while. That's because scripting languages are *interpreted*. That is to say, each line of code needs to be converted into more elementary instructions (binary code) that the processor can understand, before that line can be executed. That happens every time that a script is run.

By contrast, components are usually already *compiled*, which means that they have already been converted into the binary format (we mentioned this a moment ago). This means that the component's methods can be executed straight away. The result is that components often execute much more quickly than plain scripts do. Set against that there is an overhead associated with calling up the component in the first place.

Hiding Sensitive Code

If you're distributing code, then you need to think about whether you want other people to see it. If they can see it, they can figure out how it works, and they can probably also tamper with it. If you're distributing script files, you're code is open to these kinds of threat.

If you get into writing components with languages such as Visual Basic or C++, then you compile the component before it can be used. By compiling the component you produce the binary representation that we mentioned a moment ago – not only does this execute efficiently but it protects your code from snoopers and code-changers.

Splitting Tasks Into Distinct Areas

If you have several developers or teams working on an application that is split up into discrete chunks, componentization makes it possible for each of the different groups to work on a different part of the application. Each task can be clearly defined, and you can specify the values that the different parts of the application need to share in order for the application to come together as a whole afterwards.

Commercially Available Components

There's an ever-growing number of components that are available commercially. This means that, when you're building your application, you don't necessarily have to create every single component that you need. If there's a component out there on the open market that's tried and tested, you can purchase that component and use it as part of your application.

The thing is to compare the cost of purchasing a ready-made, ready-tested component with the cost of developing, writing, testing and supporting a home-made component. Sometimes it pays to build-your-own; sometimes it pays to buy a ready-made component.

> *To get an idea of the number of components on the market today, check out some of the sites that specialize in selling components over the web. For example, try http://www.componentsource.com, http://www.serverobjects.com and http://www.greymatter.co.uk.*

Sometimes Script is Not Adequate

There are some programming tasks that we cannot achieve with scripting languages. For example, making calls through the Win32 API is just not possible using scripting languages such as VBScript and JScript. There *are* other languages that support this functionality, such as Perl – but this does not have a strong user base within the ASP community.

Instead we can create components in languages which offer us access to these abilities, such as Visual Basic and C++, which are use more widely amongst the ASP community. We can then write components that make this functionality available to an ASP.

How Components Work

When we refer to a component in code, the system needs to know where to look for that component. For example, consider what happens when we used the Ad Rotator component back in Chapter 11. In our ASP code, we used the `Server.CreateObject` method to create an instance of the Ad Rotator component, for use in our code:

```
Set objAR = Server.CreateObject("MSWC.AdRotator")
```

When the web server runs this code and finds this line of code, it knows that it needs to create an instance of the component specified by the parameter `MSWC.AdRotator`. At this stage, the web server doesn't know what component `MSWC.AdRotator` refers to – so it asks our machine's **registry**. The machine's registry is the place that stores information about all the components that have been registered on our machine – and it will tell the web server where to find the file that contains the executable code for the Ad Rotator component.

Let's take a quick look at the registry now. Select Start | Run; in the dialog box, type RegEdit and click OK – this will start the registry viewer. Let's move straight to the entry for the Ad Rotator component. In the left part of the registry viewer, navigate to the node HKEY_LOCAL_MACHINE\SOFTWARE\Classes\CLSID\ {1621F7C0-60AC-11CF-9427-444553540000}:

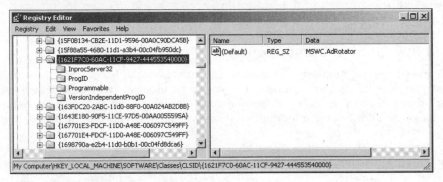

Here, you can see a number of important features:

❑ The long string of numbers and letters highlighted on the left of the screen is the **ClassID** (or **CLSID**). This string uniquely identifies the component from all other components – that is, the Ad Rotator component is the only component whose ClassID is 1621F7C0-60AC-11CF-9427-444553540000

❑ You'll recognize the name MSWC.AdRotator on the right-hand side of the screen as the name that we specified in the parameter of the Server.CreateObject method. This name is the component's **ProgID**; this is the name that the web server passed to the registry, in order to find out more information about the associated component.

The ProgID isn't guaranteed to be unique, but it is rather easier to use in our code.

If you highlight the InProcServer32 node in the registry viewer now, you'll see some more interesting information:

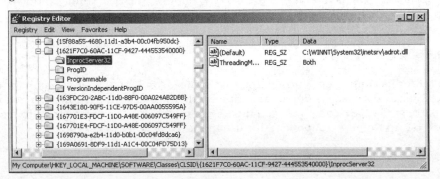

On the right, you can see the string C:\WINNT\System32\inetsrv\adrot.dll – this is the exact location of the .dll file that contains the executable code for the Ad Rotator component. Once the web server knows this, it can grab an instance of that component and proceed with executing the ASP page.

Writing Our Own Components

We've talked about how components work, and why we want to use components – and hopefully you're now fired up and keen to start writing components of your own! In this chapter, we're going to write some script-based components, each of which provides pieces of related functionality and information (in the form of methods and properties), and we'll write ASP pages that demonstrate our components in action.

The good news is that you don't need to learn a new language, such as Visual Basic or C++, in order to write components – because, as I hinted in the previous paragraph, the components in this chapter are **script-based components**. In order to do this, we will use a technology call **Windows Script Components** (**WSC**). A component written using WSC has a file extension .wsc.

Components written using WSC work in a similar way to pre-compiled components, but they're a lot easier to use. There is one important difference to note:

❑ A pre-compiled component is already compiled into binary format before it can be used (like the Ad Rotator component we discussed above).

❑ A WSC component is not pre-compiled, and therefore must be compiled at runtime before it can be used.

The fact that a WSC component must be compiled at runtime means that it's not as efficient as a pre-compiled component, and also that the code contained in the .wsc file isn't protected from prying eyes (because it's not in a binary format). But for our purposes, this is no problem – because WSC is still very easy to use and is a great way of learning the basics of componentization.

Using Windows Script Components

In order to build components using WSC, you'll need the **WSC wizard**. The wizard takes care of setting up the framework of the component. We'll use this in our examples in this chapter, but first you need to obtain the wizard from Microsoft's web site. At the time of writing, you'll find it at http://msdn.microsoft.com/scripting/. Go to the Windows Script Components page, and download the Microsoft Script Component Wizard – this comes in a single executable file called wz10en.exe.

Download this file to a location on your hard disk; when the download is complete, execute the file to install the wizard. When you've done that, you're ready to go!

The Basic WSC Elements

There are three basic elements to a WSC: the XML framework, the script itself, and a runtime DLL called scrobj.dll. Let's take a quick look at these three elements, and then we'll get our teeth into an example.

The Extensible Markup Language (XML) Framework

When we use the WSC wizard to create a component, it generates a `.wsc` file that contains a framework for the component. Then, we add our own script to this framework, which defines the functionality of the component.

As it happens, the framework is written in a language called **Extensible Markup Language** (**XML**), which we'll learn more about in Chapter 18. For now, it's enough to know that XML uses tags (similar to HTML tags) to label different parts of the code. In our WSC files, we'll meet five different tags that are used to label five different parts of the code:

XML Tags in a .wsc file	Description
`<component>` ... `</component>`	Contains the entire component definition
`<registration>` ... `</registration>`	Contains information that is used to register the component
`<public>` ... `</public>`	Contains the definitions of the properties, events, and methods of the component
`<script>` ... `</script>`	Contains the script logic that describes how the component works. Includes the script that defines how the methods, properties and events work
`<implements>` ... `</implements>`	Contains the definition of the component type

How do these tags work? The name of the tag describes the contents of the tag. For example, between the `<registration>` and `</registration>` XML tags, we expect to find information relating to the way the component is to be registered on the server machine. In this way, it works rather like, say, the HTML `<SCRIPT>` and `</SCRIPT>` tags.

The Component Implementation Script

As part of the design process, we have to decide what methods, properties and events our component should support. When we come to write the component, we need to provide the executable code that describes how these methods, properties and events will work.

In a WSC component, we write the component's logic using a scripting language (for example, VBScript, JScript, PerlScript, etc.). This script has a very specific place within the XML framework that we met a moment ago – we place it between the `<script>` and `</script>` tags. We'll see an example in a moment.

The Runtime DLL – scrobj.dll

Finally, WSC provides a file called `scrobj.dll`, which organizes the compilation of the `.wsc` file. Here's how `scrobj.dll` fits into the workings:

❑ In our ASP page, we request an instance of our WSC component, using a line like this:

```
Set objObject = Server.CreateObject("MyComponent.wsc")
```

❑ Our WSC component (`MyComponent.wsc` in this case) should already be registered in the registry. It works like the registry entry for the AdRotator component that we looked at earlier – it tells the system where to find the `MyComponent.wsc` code. However, this entry has an extra piece of information that tells the system where to find `scrobj.dll`

❑ The system uses `scrobj.dll` to compile the contents of `MyComponent.wsc`, after which it has executable component code

So you can see that a WSC component works slightly differently than a precompiled component. As we said before, the WSC component is compiled at runtime – after it is called but before it can be used. However, a WSC component (like any other component) still has its own entry in the registry.

Now, let's jump right in by building a simple component.

Try It Out – Write a Simple Script Component

For our first look at script components, we will create a component called `CarpetPricer`, which will contain all the functionality needed to calculate the price of a piece of carpet. Our component will be a very simple component, exposing just one method and one property:

Method name	Parameters	Purpose
`CalculatePrice`	`intLength, intWidth`	Calculates the price of a rectangle of carpet of the size specified by `intLength` and `intWidth`

Property name	Possible Values	Purpose
`CarpetType`	Draylon Axeminster Twistpile	Specifies the *type* of carpet that the customer wants to buy. In the component, each carpet type refers to a different price

You might imagine this component being used in a page that offers the customer (or the sales assistant, on behalf of the customer) to select from one of the available types of carpet, and also to specify the size of the room that they're buying carpet for. Then, when the user submits these values, the page passes these values to the component, which calculates the price of a piece of carpet based on the submitted values, and returns them to the ASP page for display on the browser.

Let's use the **Windows Script Component Wizard** to build the framework for our `CarpetPricer` component. When we've done that, we'll insert the executable script code within the `<script>` ... `</script>` tags. Finally, we'll register our new component, and we'll write an ASP page to test it.

1. Start up the Windows Script Component Wizard (from the Start menu, select **Programs** | **Microsoft Windows Script** | **Microsoft Script Component Wizard**). The first screen in the wizard looks like this:

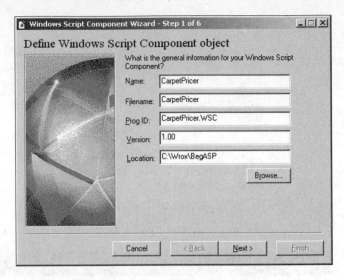

The text fields in this dialog will be blank, and you'll need to fill them in. As you fill in the **Name** field, you'll notice that the **Filename** and **Prog ID** fields are filled in automatically. We're going to call the component **CarpetPricer** – the `CarpetPricer.wsc` script file will be created automatically by the wizard.

You can specify the version number (we'll leave it as version 1, since this is our first attempt at writing this component). You can also specify a folder on your hard disk, where the resulting `.wsc` script file will be stored. I've selected **C:\Wrox\BegASP**, but you can choose any folder that is convenient for you. When you've filled in all the text boxes like this, click **Next**.

If you've specified a new folder in the Location field, you'll get a dialog warning you that the folder doesn't currently exist and asking you to confirm that you want it to be created. Just click Yes.

2. The second wizard dialog invites you to specify various characteristics for the component:

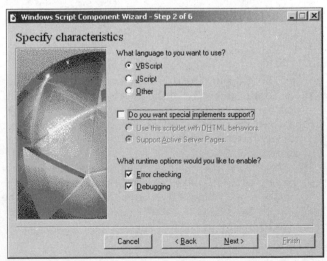

The first part asks us to choose the scripting language in which we will write the executeable code for the component. As you can see, the wizard gives us a choice of scripting languages. We're going to use VBScript for all our script-based components in this book – since that's the scripting language of choice for this book – so ensure **VBScript** is selected here.

The second block gives us options relating to the situations where we want to use the script component with DHTML behaviors, or if we want the component to support ASP. We aren't using DHTML behaviors (indeed, they're beyond the scope of this book). The 'support for ASP' option allows us to access the ASP intrinsic objects (Request, Response etc) within the executable script in the component. That's not necessary either in this particular component. Therefore, ensure that the checkbox is empty – as shown above.

Under the runtime options list, enable both **Error checking** and **Debugging** – they'll make it easier to find any errors that occur. Click **Next** again when you've made all these settings.

3. Now we can define the properties that our component will expose. In this case, there's just one property, which we'll call **CarpetType**. This will have a default value of **Draylon**. Note that we've specified specified that it should have **Read/Write** permission – thus, when we use the component in the ASP page we'll be able to change its value and write it to the page.

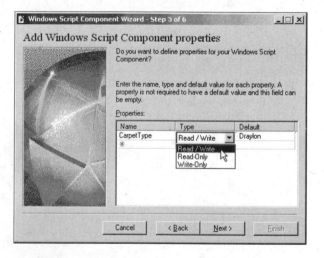

When you've done this, click **Next**.

4. The next dialog is similar to use – it's where we define the component's methods. Note that each method's 'definition' consists of the method's name and a list of parameters, and that the the parameters are listed in the order that we must specify then when we come to use the method in our code. We don't specify the executable code for the methods yet – that comes later.

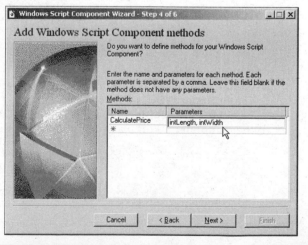

The CarpetPricer component will have just one method, called CalculatePrice. This method has two parameters: intLength and intWidth. When you've completed the two boxes as shown above, click Next.

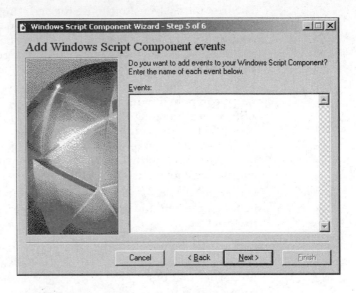

5. The next step allows us to create the events handlers that we want our component to support. The CarpetPricer component won't be implementing any events, so just leave the dialog box empty and click Next.

6. On the final page of the wizard, we see a display of the attributes of our new component:

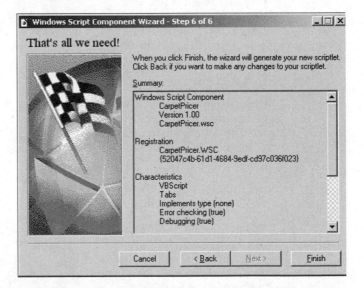

Notice that under the **Registration** heading, there are two items listed. The first, CarpetPricer.WSC, is the component's ProgID – you'll recall that this is the 'common name' for the component, and the name that we might when creating an instance of the component. For example, in ASP, we might use the line:

```
Set objCP = Server.CreateObject("CarpetPricer.wsc")
```

As we mentioned earlier in the chapter, the ProgID of the component is not necessarily unique – it's possible to create other components that have the same ProgID. However, the ClassID *is* an automatically-generated unique identifier for the component. As you can see, the wizard has generated a ClassID for our component, and it's listed here as the second item under the **Registration** heading. The ClassID for the component I've created here is **52047c4b-61d1-4684-9edf-cd97c036f023** – the ClassID for your component will be different of course, because all ClassIDs are unique.

Click **Finish** – the wizard will complete the task of generating the component. You should get a dialog box confirming the location of the new `.wsc` file.

7. The WSC wizard has generated the framework for the component, based on the instructions we gave in the steps of the wizard. However, we still haven't written the executable script code that will define how the methods work. We'll do that in this step.

Using Windows Explorer, go to the folder that you specified in Step 1 of the wizard (I specified **C:\Wrox\BegASP**) – there, you'll find the `CarpetPricer.wsc` file that we just created. Now start Notepad and use it to open the `CarpetPricer.wsc` file, so that you can see its code (we'll take a look at what it all means after we've built and tested the example). For now, we must make only one change to the existing code, and that is to add the functionality for the `CalculatePrice` method. To do that, locate the following code in the `CarpetPricer.wsc` file:

```
function CalculatePrice(intLength, intWidth)
  CalculatePrice = "Temporary Value"
end function
```

Remove the shaded line above, and replace it with the following shaded code:

```
function CalculatePrice(intLength, intWidth)
  Dim intPricePerSqFoot
  Select Case CarpetType
    Case "Axeminster"
      intPricePerSqFoot = 10
    Case "Draylon"
      intPricePerSqFoot = 15
    Case "Twistpile"
      intPricePerSqFoot = 18
  End Select
  CalculatePrice = intWidth * intLength * intPricePerSqFoot
end function
```

Now save and close the `CarpetPricer.wsc` file without changing its name.

8. Now we need to create an entry in the registry for our new component. To do this, right-click on the CarpetPricer.wsc file in your Windows Explorer window and select Register from the resulting menu:

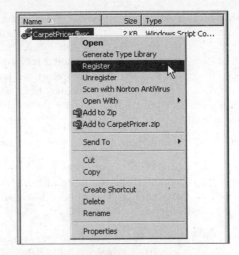

If the script component registers correctly, you'll get the following message box:

How It Works – The XML Framework

The first thing to notice relates to the message box that we get at the end of this process. The message is generated by RegSvr32.exe, which we first saw in Chapter 11 and is responsible for registration and unregistration of components on our machine. Here, it's telling us that DllRegisterServer and DllInstall in scrobj.dll succeeded (but note that it doesn't mention our CarpetPricer.wsc file). This makes sense, because the scrobj.dll file is the COM-compliant 'wrapper' that handles the calls to our script components.

Now let's take a look at the code in our CarpetPricer.wsc file. Part of the code (the XML framework) is generated by the WSC wizard, and part of the code (the implementation of the component) was written by us.

The first thing that the .wsc script does is declare the version of XML that it's using:

```
<?xml version="1.0"?>
```

All of the code for the component (including registration information, public methods and properties, and script) is enclosed in <component> ... </component> tags. There's also a <?component?> tag, which specifies that we selected the error checking and debugging options for this component:

```
<component>
<?component error="true" debug="true"?>
```

Next, the `<registration>` ... `</registration>` tags contain information that is used when the component is registered into the registry:

```
<registration
  description="CarpetPricer"
  progid="CarpetPricer.WSC"
  version="1.00"
  classid="{52047c4b-61d1-4684-9edf-cd97c036f023}"
>
</registration>
```

This is so that, when we come to use the component in our code, the machine will know where to look for it. In our code, we can specify the ProgID of the component like this:

```
Set objCP = Server.CreateObject("CarpetPricer.wsc")
```

When the code executes, the server consults its registry to find out the location and other details relating to the given ProgID, and then uses that information to access the component's functionality.

Next come the declarations of the public methods of the component. These are the names of the methods, properties and events that the component exposes to any application that's using it:

```
<public>
  <property name="CarpetType">
    <get/>
    <put/>
  </property>
  <method name="CalculatePrice">
    <PARAMETER name="intLength"/>
    <PARAMETER name="intWidth"/>
  </method>
</public>
```

In this example, the `CarpetPricer` component is exposing a property called `CarpetType`. It is also exposing a method called `CalculatePrice` (which takes two parameters, as we can see here). This tallies with the information we inserted when we used the WSC wizard to build the component.

What do we mean when we say that the component *exposes* only these methods and properties? It means that, regardless of the internal workings of the component, any application that uses this component can only access the values contained in the properties of this component, and it can only access the functionality of the methods of this component. It can't use the component for any other (hidden) properties or functionality that the component might use under the covers.

In this example, it means that the only methods and properties available to our ASP page are the `CarpetType` property and the `CalculatePrice` method.

The Component's Implementation

Finally, we come to the `<script> ... </script>` tags, which should look familiar – they contain the implementation of the component's methods and properties. In the `<script>` tag, we declare that we intend to use the VBScript language in the code that defines our methods and properties:

```
<script language="VBScript">
<![CDATA[
  VBScript code goes in here
]]>
</script>
```

> *Don't worry about the `<![CDATA[ ... ]]>` that the wizard puts here. It is simply there to tell the XML engine to ignore anything that lies between the `<![CDATA[` and the `]]>`. This makes sense if you think about it, because the code is VBScript, not XML!*

The VBScript itself is quite simple. First, it declares a variable called `CarpetType` that will hold the value of the component's `CarpetType` property:

```
dim CarpetType
CarpetType = "Draylon"
```

In the wizard, we set the default value of this property to "Draylon" – the second line above assigns the default value to the property at this stage. Next, come two functions called `get_CarpetType()` and `put_CarpetType()`:

```
function get_CarpetType()
  get_CarpetType = CarpetType
end function

function put_CarpetType(newValue)
  CarpetType = newValue
end function
```

These two functions are internal to the component, which means that we can't call them from outside the component (for example, we can't call these functions directly from the ASP page). What do they do? Well, `get_CarpetType()` is responsible for getting the current value of the `CarpetType` variable whenever it is requested; and `put_CarpetType()` is responsible for changing the value of the `CarpetType` variable whenever we assign a new value to the `CarpetType` property.

So, for example, suppose we need to get hold of the value of the `CarpetPricer` object's `CarpetType` property sometime, using a line of ASP like this:

```
strTempString = objCP.CarpetType
```

This causes the component to execute its `get_CarpetType()` function, which fetches the current value of its `CarpetType` varaiable and returns it to our ASP page. And if we try to assign a new value to the property, like this:

```
objCP.CarpetType = strTempString
```

This causes the component to execute its `put_CarpetType()` function, passing the newly-assigned value as a parameter – and it assigns that parameter value to its `CarpetType` variable.

Finally, we have the `CalculatePrice()` function, which contains our own implementation of the `CalculatePrice` method that the component exposes:

```
function CalculatePrice(intLength, intWidth)
  Dim intPricePerSqFoot
  Select Case CarpetType
    Case "Axeminster"
      intPricePerSqFoot = 10
    Case "Draylon"
      intPricePerSqFoot = 15
    Case "Twistpile"
      intPricePerSqFoot = 18
  End Select
  CalculatePrice = intwidth * intlength * intPricePerSqFoot
end function
```

This function checks the value of the component's `CarpetType` property, and sets the price-per-unit for that type of carpet. Then it multiplies that value by the area of carpet required to calculate the price of the required carpet, and returns the result.

In order to see our component in action, we'll write an ASP page.

Try It Out – Using the Script-Based Carpet Pricer Component in an ASP Page

We'll try it out by creating a little 'front-end' for the component – a simple ASP page that allows the user to select from a choice of different types of carpet, and then displays sample prices for different carpet sizes based on the user's selection. The ASP code for this is really quite straightforward.

Remember that you can obtain all this code from the Wrox Press web site, at http://www.wrox.com, if you don't want to type it all in.

1. Create a new file using your code editor, and enter the following code:

```
<HTML>
<HEAD>
<TITLE>Testing the CarpetPricer</TITLE>
<HEAD>
<BODY>
<H2>Carpet Sir?</H2>
<%
  If Request.ServerVariables("HTTP_METHOD") = "POST" Then
    Dim objCarpetPricer, strCarpetType
    strCarpetType = Request.Form("carpettype")

    Set objCarpetPricer = Server.CreateObject("CarpetPricer.wsc")
    objCarpetPricer.CarpetType = strCarpetType
```

```
      Response.Write "Last time, you selected to view prices of our range " & _
                  "of <B>" & strCarpetType & "</B> carpets. " & _
                  "Here is a sample range of prices:<BR><BR>"
      Response.Write "<TABLE BORDER=1><TR><TD></TD>" & _
                  "<TD COLSPAN=6 ALIGN=CENTER>Length</TD></TR>" & _
                  "<TR><TD ROWSPAN=7>Width</TD><TD></TD>" & _
                  "<TH>2</TH><TH>4</TH><TH>6</TH><TH>8</TH><TH>10</TH></TR>"
    For intWidth = 1 To 5
      Response.Write "<TR><TH>" & intWidth & "</TH>"
      For intLength = 2 To 10 Step 2
        Response.Write "<TD> $" & _
              objCarpetPricer.CalculatePrice(intLength, intWidth) & "</TD>"
      Next
      Response.Write "</TR>"
    Next
    Response.Write "</TABLE>" & _
        "<HR>Would you like to view sample prices " & _
        "for a different type of carpet?<BR><BR>"
        Set objCarpetPricer=Nothing
  End If
%>
<FORM ACTION="CarpetPricer.asp" METHOD="POST">
  Select carpet type:
  <SELECT NAME="carpettype">
    <OPTION>Draylon</OPTION>
    <OPTION>Axeminster</OPTION>
    <OPTION>Twistpile</OPTION>
  </SELECT>
  <INPUT TYPE="SUBMIT" VALUE="View Prices">
</FORM>
</BODY>
</HTML>
```

2. Save the file into your \inetpub\wwwroot\BegASPFiles directory, as CarpetPricer.asp.

3. Open your web browser, and browse to the page.

Select a carpet type from the drop-down list, and click the **View Prices** button. You should get a screen that looks something like this:

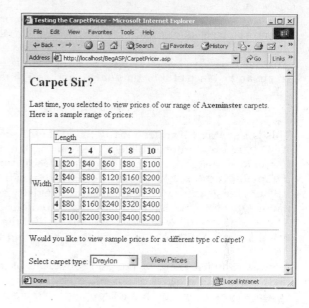

How It Works

This page is in two parts – the HTML form that captures the user's input, and the HTML table that displays the prices on the browser. Let's look at the form first – it simply asks the user to select one of three different carpet types:

```
<FORM ACTION="CarpetPricer.asp" METHOD="POST">
  Select carpet type:
  <SELECT NAME="carpettype">
    <OPTION>Draylon</OPTION>
    <OPTION>Axeminster</OPTION>
    <OPTION>Twistpile</OPTION>
  </SELECT>
  <INPUT TYPE="SUBMIT" VALUE="View Prices">
</FORM>
```

The name of the inputted data will be `carpettype`, and since the form uses the `POST` method to submit the selection, the data will be captured in the new page by the `Request.Form` collection.

Now let's look at the display part, which is much more exciting. The `If` statement at the top checks to see whether any data was posted to the page. If so, then we know that the user is submitting input about a carpet type, about which he wants to know sample prices and so we continue:

```
<%
  If Request.ServerVariables("HTTP_METHOD") = "POST" Then
    Dim objCarpetPricer, strCarpetType
    strCarpetType = Request.Form("carpettype")
```

The first thing we do is assign the submitted information (the `carpettype` value in the `Request` object's `Form` collection) to a local variable called `strCarpetType`.

Now we're ready to start using our `CarpetPricer` component. The first thing we must do is create an instance of the component, and assign the instance to a variant name in our code:

```
Set objCarpetPricer = Server.CreateObject("CarpetPricer.wsc")
```

This is a syntax we've seen many times before – for example, when creating an instance of an ADO `Connection` object. Here, we're using the ASP `Server` object's `CreateObject` method to create an instance of the component specified in the parameter. In this case, the specified parameter is `CarpetPricer.wsc` – which you'll recall is the ProgID of our component. The ASP engine goes away to our machine's registry and asks where it will find a component of that name. Of course, we have already registered our component, so the registry is able to tell the ASP engine exactly where it must look to find the necessary code for the instance (in this case, using a combination of the `scrobj.dll` file and the `CarpetPricer.wsc` file).

Now, we can use the methods and properties of this object in just the same way as we use the methods and properties of any other object. First, we'll assign our `objCarpetPricer` object's `CarpetType` property to the type selected by our user:

```
objCarpetPricer.CarpetType = strCarpetType
```

Now we can set about building the table of values. First, we display a message and set up the first part of the table:

```
Response.Write "Last time, you selected to view prices of our range " & _
               "of <B>" & strCarpetType & "</B> carpets. " & _
               "Here is a sample range of prices:<BR><BR>"
Response.Write "<TABLE BORDER=1><TR><TD></TD>" & _
               "<TD COLSPAN=6 ALIGN=CENTER>Length</TD></TR>" & _
               "<TR><TD ROWSPAN=7>Width</TD><TD></TD>" & _
               "<TH>2</TH><TH>4</TH><TH>6</TH><TH>8</TH><TH>10</TH></TR>"
```

Now, we write the rows of the table. The rows of the table are numbered 1 to 5 here, to represent the widths of different rooms, and the columns are numbered 2 to 10 to represent the lengths of different rooms. Then, for each of these room sizes we call our object's `CalculatePrice` method, specifying the width and length in the two parameters:

```
For intWidth = 1 To 5
  Response.Write "<TR><TH>" & intWidth & "</TH>"
  For intLength = 2 To 10 Step 2
    Response.Write "<TD> $" & _
            objCarpetPricer.CalculatePrice(intLength, intWidth) & "</TD>"
  Next
  Response.Write "</TR>"
Next
Response.Write "</TABLE>" & _
    "<HR>Would you like to view sample prices " & _
    "for a different type of carpet?<BR><BR>"
```

Right in the middle of this block of code, is a line where the ASP page calls the `CalaculatePrice` method of our `CarpetPricer` component. It's just like calling the method of any other object – something we've done many times already in this book. Easy, isn't it?

At the end, we've finished with our `CarpetPricer` object so we clean up, just as we would do with any other objects we were using:

```
    Set objCarpetPricer = Nothing
    End If
%>
```

Components and Data Access

We've already talked about data access in this book. We've talked about taking data from a data store at the time a page is requested, and using it with in the ASP page (either displaying it directly, or using the retrieved data in some other way to decide what content should appear on the page).

We've also talked about capturing information that the user types or selects in our pages in an HTML form, and other information passed from the browser during a web page request – and storing the captured data in a data store.

Overall, the use of data stores to provide and to store information relating to our ASP pages is a very important part of our dynamic web page creation strategy. And that's still true when we're using components to provide some of the logic in our pages.

In this section we're going to look at a particular example, involving a component that provides some of the logic for the application, and will also handle any of the data access requirements that relates to that logic. To do that, the code contained in the component will use both ASP and ADO techniques and objects.

Writing a Component that Accesses a Data Store

In Chapters 12–15 we saw plenty of ASP pages that used ADO functionality to access a database or other data store, either to fetch data for use in our ASP page or to write data from the page back to the data store. And in this chapter, we used the WSC wizard to write a simple component that contains the logic for calculating the price for a piece of carpet – and we used that example in an ASP page too.

Of course, we can use these two techniques together, and write highly functional pages that use data access and also take advantage of functionality encapsulated into our own home-made components.

So let's look at another example that uses both techniques. We'll write a little example that simulates some of the workings of a bank account. We'll have a database which contains the current details of all the existing accounts (including account numbers and account balances), and we'll use the WSC to write a component called `BankAccount.wsc` that represents the bank account itself. The component will expose two properties:

Property name	Type	Purpose
AccountID	String, Read/Write	Contains the ID of the account.
Balance	Currency, Read-Only	Read-only balance of the account.

> *We could add lots of other properties, such as `AccountType`, `AccountHolder`, `AccountHolderAddress` – but we'll avoid these properties here for the sake of simplicity.*

The component will also expose two methods:

Method name	Parameters	Purpose
AddMoney	CheckNumber, CheckAmt	Credits amount of check to target account, and places an entry in the check register.

> *Once again, recall what we mean when we say that the component **exposes** only these methods and properties. It means that, regardless of the internal workings of the component, any application that uses this component can only use the methods and properties listed in the tables above.*

We'll also write a couple of ASP pages that use this component, to allow the user (in this case, a bank teller at the local branch of the bank) to transfer cash from one account to another. The ASP page will act simply as the user interface, and the component will do most of the work of transferring money around. Therefore, when transferring the money it is the *component* (not the ASP page) that will need to be able to retrieve data from the data store, and to write data to the data store – so it is the component's code that will use the ADO objects that we see in this example. In other words, we have a very simple three-tiered structure for the process of making a cash transfer:

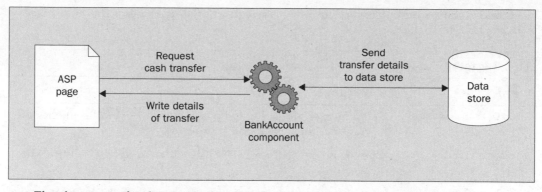

*There's a reason for choosing to demonstrate this technique using the 'cash transfer' scenario. As we'll see in the next chapter, there's more to the cash transfer than we meet in this example – we will need to make it more robust by exploiting a technique known as **transaction processing**. However, we'll work up to that; and ultimately, at the end of the next chapter, we'll pull together components and transactions to build a scalable robust version. First, in this example, we'll lay down some foundations by examining a less robust model.*

Setting up the Database

Once again, we've provided two types of database file with the source code for this example:

❑ Bank.mdb – an Access database file. If you're planning to use the simpler Access database, then all you need to do is place the Bank.mdb file somewhere on your hard disk (in this case, I placed it in my C:\datastores\ folder).

❑ Bank_Data.mdf – a database file for use with MSDE. If you're using MSDE, then place the Bank_Data.mdf file in your \MSSQL7\Data\ folder. MSDE will detect the file automatically when we need it.

Whichever you use, you'll find that there are two tables in the Bank database. The first is the Account table, which contains information relating to the ID and ownership of each account. It contains two fields:

The Account Table	
Field	Purpose
Account	The ID number of the account
HolderName	The name of the account holder

The second is the `Register` table. This table is a register of all the actions that take place on all the accounts in the bank.

The Register Table	
Field	**Purpose**
SeqID	An integer indicating the position in the overall sequence of all transfers, in chronological ordering
AccountID	A string of the form 1111-1111, which uniquely identifies the account
CheckNumber	A check number, entered by the user when the transfer request is made
TransDate	The date of the transfer
TransType	The type of action being made on the account – W for withdrawal or D for deposit
TransNote	An optional string containing notes about the transfer
Amount	The amount being transferred into or out of the account
PriorBalance	The balance immediately before the action
ResultingBalance	The balance immediately after the action

Note that the `Account` table itself doesn't have a `Balance` field. Instead, when we need to establish the account's current balance, we will search the `register` table for the most recent transfer relating to that account – and we'll take the current balance value from there.

We will also assume, for simplicity, that cash transfers in this system are between two accounts that are listed in the Account table of the database. There will be no cash transfers to or from accounts held at other banks!

Building the Script Component

Now that we have the background, let's create the component in script.

Try It Out – Building the BankAccount.wsc Component

1. First, we'll create the framework for our component. Start up the Windows Script Component Wizard, by selecting Start | Programs | Microsoft Windows Script | Windows Script Component Wizard.

In the first screen, type the name of the component into the Name field. The next two fields will be filled in automatically. Leave the version number as 1.0, and enter the folder name where you want your .wsc file to be saved:

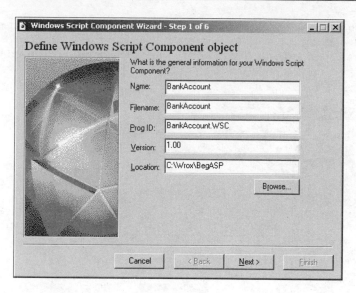

Click **Next** when you've done this.

2. In the second page, you'll recall that we have the opportunity to specify various characteristics of the component. Again, our scripting language of choice will be VBScript. This time, we'll also enable the **special implements support** option, and give ourselves the option of using ASP logic within the body of our code. This will allow us to use the ASP built-in objects (`Response`, `Request`, and so on) within the code that defines our methods. Also enable the **Error checking** and **Debugging** options, which will ease bug tracking if we get any problems:

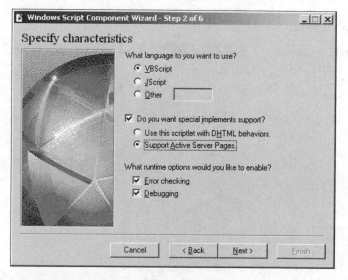

Again, click **Next** when you've done this.

3. As we mentioned above, our component will expose only two properties to the calling application – AccountID and Balance. We'll specify a default value of 0 for both of these properties, in order to reduce errors when the component is used by other developers:

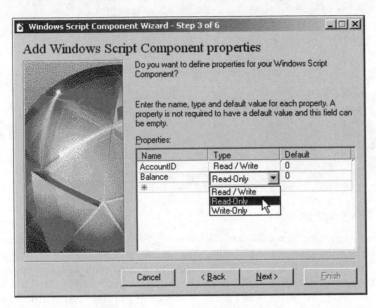

Note that we've made **Balance** a **Read-Only** property – the component will read this value directly from the database, and we want to prohibit the calling application from being able to write directly to this value. The only way the application can change the of the **Balance** property is via the method that we'll declare in the next screen. When you've completed this page, click **Next**.

4. Now we'll declare the single method that will be exposed by this component, and its parameters:

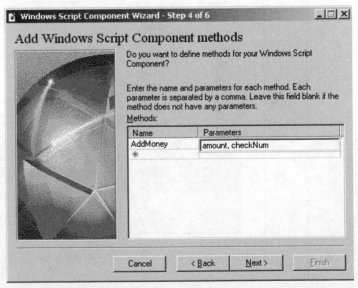

The `AddMoney` method takes two parameters – the amount involved in the cash transfer and, if there's a check involved in the transfer, the check number. Remember that the order of parameters specified here will be the same order of parameters that we'll need to use when we call the method from our ASP page.

5. When you've done this, click Next to take you to the Events page. This component won't have any events, so click Next again.

6. Now we get the final screen of the wizard, which summarizes the selections we've made:

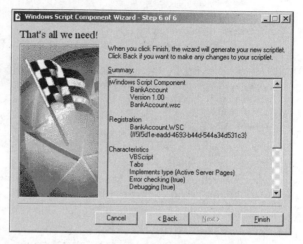

Click Finish to generate the `BankAccount.wsc` file – you'll get a dialog which confirms that the file was created successfully.

7. Now we just have to fill in the code for the functions. to do this, use Windows Explorer to locate the `BankAccount.wsc` on your machine, and double-click on its icon to view the code in Notepad. We'll add our functionality by inserting extra code to the code that exists between the <script> and </script> tags. In what follows, the affected lines are shaded.

First, add an extra line of code to declare three internal variables – `dcBank`, `rsBank` and `strSQL`:

```
dim AccountID
AccountID = 0
dim Balance
Balance = 0
Dim dcBank, rsBank, strSQL, strDataConn
```

Second, immediately after this, assign a connection string to the variable called `strDataConn` – this is the connection string that the component will use to connect to the data store. If you're using the Access database file `Bank.mdb`, then your connection string assignment should look something like this:

```
strDataConn = "Provider=Microsoft.Jet.OLEDB.4.0;" & _
              "Data Source=E:\datastores\Bank.mdb;" & _
              "Persist Security Info=False"
```

If you're using MSDE and the database file `Bank_Data.mdf`, then the connection string assignment should look something like this:

```
strDataConn = "Provider=SQLOLEDB;Persist Security Info=False;" & _
              "User ID=sa;Initial Catalog=Bank;" & _
              "Initial File Name=E:\MSSQL7\Data\Bank_Data.mdf"
```

Third, find the generated definition for the `get_Balance()` function, and change it so that it reads thus:

```
function get_Balance()
    Set rsBank = Server.CreateObject("ADODB.Recordset")
    strSQL = "SELECT ResultingBalance FROM Register " & _
             "WHERE AccountID='" & AccountID & "' ORDER BY SeqID DESC"
    rsBank.Open strSQL, strDataConn
    Balance = rsBank("ResultingBalance")
    get_Balance = Balance
    rsBank.Close
    Set rsBank = Nothing
end function
```

Fourth and last, find the generated definition for the `AddMoney()` method, and change it so that it reads thus:

```
function AddMoney(amount, checkNum)
  Dim curBalance, strWorD, strTransNote
  curBalance = get_Balance()
  If CDbl(curBalance) + CDbl(amount) < 0 Then
    Response.Write "<BR>ABORT: Insufficient balance in Source Account."
    AddMoney = "0"
  Else
    If amount < 0 Then
      strWorD = "W"
      strTransNote = "Cash withdrawal"
    Else
      strWorD = "D"
      strTransNote = "Cash credit"
    End If
    Set dcBank = Server.CreateObject("ADODB.Connection")
    dcBank.Open strDataConn
    ' move the money into or out of the account
    strSQL = "INSERT INTO Register(AccountID, CheckNumber, TransDate, " & _
                                  "TransType, TransNote, Amount, " & _
                                  "PriorBalance, ResultingBalance) " & _
             "VALUES ('" & AccountID & "', " & Cint(checkNum) & ", '" & _
                     Date & "', '" & strWorD & "', '" & strTransNote & "', " & _
                     amount & ", " & curBalance & ", " & curBalance + amount & ")"
    dcBank.Execute strSQL
    dcBank.Close
    Set dcBank = Nothing
    If amount < 0 Then
      Response.Write "<BR>COMPLETE: Withdrew $" & -amount & " successfully."
    Else
```

```
      Response.Write "<BR>COMPLETE: Credited $" & amount & " successfully."
    End If
    AddMoney = "1"
  End If
end function
```

8. Save your changes to the `BankAccount.wsc` file, without changing the filename.
Now register the component: in Windows Explorer, right-click on the
`BankAccount.wsc` icon and select **Register** from the menu. You will see a message box
confirming that the component registered successfully.

We'll write a set of ASP pages to test this in a moment – before that, let's just take a quick look
inside the component itself.

How It Works – The Script Component

There's one important thing to note before we look at anything else. Each instance of the
`BankAccount` object will represent one of the accounts in our bank system. The account will be
identifiable by its `AccountID`, which is contained in the `BankAccount` object's `AccountID`
property. In our ASP pages later, we'll need two instances of the `BankAccount` object in order
to make a transfer – one instance to represent the source account, and one instance to represent
the destination account.

We needn't concern ourselves with most of the code contained in the `BankAccount.wsc` file –
it is mostly XML code that is used in the component's registration and in the identification of
which methods and properties are exposed to users of the component. Of more interest to us is
the implementation of the properties and methods, and this is all contained within the
`<script> ... </script>` tags.

So let's start by looking at the structure of what's contained inside these tags:

```
<script language="VBScript">
  <![CDATA[

  dim AccountID
  AccountID = 0
  dim Balance
  Balance = 0
  Dim dcBank, rsBank, strSQL, strDataConn
  strDataConn = "Provider=Microsoft.Jet.OLEDB.4.0;" & _
                "Data Source=E:\datastores\Bank.mdb;" & _
                "Persist Security Info=False"

  function get_AccountID()
    get_AccountID = AccountID
  end function

  function put_AccountID(newValue)
    AccountID = newValue
  end function
```

```
function get_Balance()
   ' ... implementation of get_Balance() ...
end function

function AddMoney(amount, checkNum)
   ' ... implementation of AddMoney() ...
end function
]]>
</script>
```

I've missed out the function implementation code here – we'll come back to that in a moment. The first thing that's done in this block is to declare two variables called AccountID and Balance – these will hold the values of the BankAccount object's AccountID and Balance properties (which we declared in Step 3 of the wizard). You'll recall that we told the wizard to set the default values of these properties equal to 0 – so the value of 0 is assigned to each of these variables within the first few lines of the code above.

Next, we declare some more variables – dcBank, rsBank, strSQL, and strDataConn. These are all variables that we'll use during the course of the component's existence, so it makes sense for them to be declared here. In fact, strDataConn will contain the connection string that is used on various occasions by the component, so we also assign the appropriate value to strDataConn immediately.

Then there are definitions of four functions – get_AccountID(), put_AccountID(), get_Balance() and AddMoney(). Here's what they are for:

❑   Whenever we use the BankAccount object's AccountID property in our ASP code, the component calls get_AccountID(). This function goes and fetches the current value of the component's AccountID variable, and returns it to the calling application.

❑   When we write a new value to the BankAccount object's AccountID property in our ASP code, the component calls its put_AccountID(), passing the desired new value as the only parameter to the function. Then, the put_AccountID() function assigns the parameter value to the component's AccountID variable.

❑   Whenever we use the BankAccount object's Balance property in our ASP code, the component calls get_Balance(). This function works just like the get_AccountID() function described above: it fetches the current value of the component's Balance variable, and returns it to the calling application.

   Note that the component doesn't have a put_Balance() function. That's because the BankAccount component's Balance property is a read-only property (as we specified in Step 3 of the wizard).

❑   When we call the BankAccount object's AddMoney method in our ASP code, we want to update the database to reflect the change that's being made; so the component calls its AddMoney() function.

We've provided our own code for those last two functions, so let's take a look at that next.

The get_Balance() Function

The get_Balance() function simply queries the data store for the latest balance assigned to this particular account, and returns the value to the calling application. To do this, we use an ADO Recordset object. We've already declared the variable rsBank in the global declarations for the component, so the first thing we need to do is set rsBank to be a Recordset object:

```
function get_Balance()
  Set rsBank = Server.CreateObject("ADODB.Recordset")
```

Now, we'll write the SQL command that will be used to populate the Recordset object. We've already declared the variable strSQL in the global declarations for the object, so it is ready for us to assign a SQL string to it:

```
strSQL = "SELECT ResultingBalance FROM Register " & _
         "WHERE AccountID='" & AccountID & "' ORDER BY SeqID DESC"
```

Here, we're requesting all of the records in the Register table that correspond to cash transfers relating to this particular back account. We identify the account in question by using the component's AccountID variable (remember that an instance of the BankAccount object represents one particular bank account in our system, and is identified by its AccountID).

Now we open the recordset. Because we've requested the records to be ordered in descending order by SeqID, the first record in the recordset will be the record relating to the most recent transfer (and hence will contain the *current* balance for the account). Since the cursor is automatically placed on the first record in the recordset after opening, we can immediately assign the value of that record's ResultingBalance field to the component's Balance variable:

```
rsBank.Open strSQL, strDataConn
Balance = rsBank("ResultingBalance")
```

Now we can assign the return value of the function to the same value:

```
get_Balance = Balance
```

Finally, we don't need the Recordset object anymore, so we Close it and clean up:

```
rsBank.Close
Set rsBank = Nothing
end function
```

The AddMoney() Function

The AddMoney() function writes a new record to the Register table, each time we add an amount to (or subtract an amount from) the account's balance. It takes two parameters – the amount to be added and the check number.

> *Each cash transfer requires that we call the AddMoney method twice – once to deduct the amount from the source account, and once to add the money to the destination account.*
>
> *Also, remember that in the next chapter we'll identify why this transfer would be more robust if we also employed **transaction processing**; and we'll build an improved version that uses transactional processing to complete the transfer.*

After declaring a few necessary variables that are local to this function, we get hold of the current balance for this account by using the get_Balance() method:

```
function AddMoney(amount, checkNum)
  Dim curBalance, strWorD, strTransNote
  curBalance = get_Balance()
```

Remember that we can only call the get_Balance() function explicitly within the code for the component itself. Later on, in our ASP pages, we'll be able to request the value of an account's balance by using the BankAccount object's Balance property (which itself calls the get_Balance() function).

Next we quickly check to see whether the account's balance will go overdrawn after the transfer. If so, we don't want to make the transfer at all so we just write a message to the screen and set the return value for the function to 0:

```
If CDbl(curBalance) + CDbl(amount) < 0 Then
  Response.Write "<BR>ABORT: Insufficient balance in Source Account."
  AddMoney = "0"
```

Otherwise, we go ahead with the addition or subtraction of cash. First, we check the value of the amount parameter to determine whether we're adding or subtracting an amount:

```
Else
  If amount < 0 Then
    strWorD = "W"
    strTransNote = "Cash withdrawal"
  Else
    strWorD = "D"
    strTransNote = "Cash credit"
  End If
```

Now we use an ADO `Connection` object to add the new record to the `Register` table. First we `Open` the `Connection` object using the connection string specified in the component's `strDataConn` variable. Then we write the SQL `INSERT` command required to add the record, assigning the string to the `strSQL` variable. Then we use the `Connection` object's `Execute` method to execute the command and add the record:

```
Set dcBank = Server.CreateObject("ADODB.Connection")
dcBank.Open strDataConn
' move the money into or out of the account
strSQL = "INSERT INTO Register(AccountID, CheckNumber, TransDate, " & _
                        "TransType, TransNote, Amount, " & _
                        "PriorBalance, ResultingBalance) " & _
        "VALUES ('" & AccountID & "', " & checkNum & ", '" & _
                Date & "', '" & strWorD & "', '" & strTransNote & "', " & _
                amount & ", " & curBalance & ", " & curBalance + amount & ")"
dcBank.Execute strSQL
```

Note that the SQL command writes values to eight of the nine fields contained in the `Register` table. The remaining field, `SeqID`, is an 'autogenerating' field – which means that the database will generate a value for this field at the time the record is created.

Now we've finished with the ADO `Connection` object, so we tidy it up:

```
dcBank.Close
Set dcBank = Nothing
```

And finally we write a short message to the browser, and set the return value of the function to 1:

```
If amount < 0 Then
    Response.Write "<BR>COMPLETE: Withdrew $" & -amount & " successfully."
Else
    Response.Write "<BR>COMPLETE: Credited $" & amount & " successfully."
    End If
    AddMoney = "1"
  End If
end function
```

OK, let's build some pages that we can use to test this component.

Try It Out – Build the Front Page of our Bank Application

In order to test the `BankAccount.wsc` component, we'll build three ASP pages. The first page, `Bank.asp`, will allow the bank teller to select the appropriate details for the cash transfer: the debit account, the credit account, and amount to be transferred. The second page, `ExecuteTransfer.asp`, will use the component to process the information submitted by the user. A third page, `BankConn.asp`, is an SSI that contains the connection string details for accessing the data store.

So let's build these pages and test the component, and then we explain how it all works.

1. Create a new file (which we'll call `Bank.asp`), and enter the following code into it:

```
<!--#INCLUDE FILE="BankConn.asp"-->
<HTML>
<HEAD>
<%
  Dim dcBank, rsBank
  Set dcBank = Server.CreateObject("ADODB.Connection")
  Set rsBank = Server.CreateObject("ADODB.Recordset")

  dcBank.Open strConn
  rsBank.Open "SELECT * FROM Account", dcBank
  Dim strOptionString
  strOptionString = ""
  Do Until rsBank.EOF
     strOptionString = strOptionString & _
                "<OPTION VALUE='" & rsBank("AccountID") & "'>" & _
                rsBank("HolderName") & " [" & rsBank("AccountID") & "]" & _
                "</OPTION>"
     rsBank.MoveNext
  Loop
  rsBank.Close
  dcBank.Close
  Set rsBank = Nothing
  Set dcBank = Nothing
%>
<TITLE>A First Banking Example</TITLE>
</HEAD>
<BODY>
<H2>Elementary Banking for Very Small Banks</H2>
<H3>Cash Transfer Request - Please enter the following details:</H3>

<FORM ACTION="ExecuteTransfer.asp" METHOD="POST">
  Select source account:
  <SELECT NAME="SourceAccount"> <%= strOptionString %></SELECT><BR>
  Select destination account:
  <SELECT NAME="TargetAccount"> <%= strOptionString %></SELECT><BR>
  Enter check number: <INPUT TYPE="TEXT" NAME="CheckNum"><BR>
  Enter check amount: $<INPUT TYE="TEXT" NAME="AmtToTransfer"><BR><BR>
  <INPUT TYPE="SUBMIT" VALUE="Process This Check">
</FORM>
</BODY>
</HTML>
```

2. Save `Bank.asp` into your `\inetpub\wwwroot\BegASPFiles` directory.

3. Now start a new text file – this one is going to be called `ExecuteTransfer.asp`. Insert the following code:

```
<HTML>
<HEAD><TITLE>A First Banking Example</TITLE>
</HEAD>
<BODY>
<H2>Elementary Banking for Very Small Banks</H2>
<H3>This page will execute your Cash Transfer Request</H3>
<%
  Dim srcAccountID, destAccountID, intCheckNum, dblAmtToTransfer
  Dim srcBalance, destBalance
  Dim strAbortReason, blnSuccess

  intCheckNum = Request.Form("CheckNum")
  dblAmtToTransfer = Request.Form("AmtToTransfer")
  srcAccountID = Request.Form("SourceAccount")
  destAccountID = Request.Form("TargetAccount")

  If srcAccountID = destAccountID Then
    Response.Write "Can't transfer funds when " & _
                   "the source and destination account are the same"
  Else
    Set objSourceAcct = Server.CreateObject("BankAccount.WSC")
    Set objDestAcct = Server.CreateObject("BankAccount.WSC")
    objSourceAcct.AccountID = srcAccountID
    objDestAcct.AccountID = destAccountID

    Response.Write "<B>Prior Balances:</B><BR>" & _
       "Source Account ID: <B>" & objSourceAcct.AccountID & "</B> " & _
       "Balance: <B>$" & objSourceAcct.Balance & "</B><BR>" & _
       "Destination Account ID: <B>" & objDestAcct.AccountID & "</B> " & _
       "Balance: <B>$" & objDestAcct.Balance & "</B>" & _
       "<HR><BR>" & _
       "We are about to transfer <B>" & FormatCurrency(dblAmtToTransfer) & _
       "</B> from the source account to the destination account...<BR><HR>"

    blnSuccess = objSourceAcct.AddMoney (-dblAmtToTransfer, intCheckNum)
    If blnSuccess <> 0 Then
      objDestAcct.AddMoney dblAmtToTransfer, intCheckNum
      Response.Write "<BR><BR>Cash transfered!"
    End If

    Response.Write "<BR><BR>Cash transfered!<BR><BR>" & _
       "<B>Final Balances:</B><BR>" & _
       "Source Account ID: <B>" & objSourceAcct.AccountID & "</B> " & _
       "Balance: <B>$" & objSourceAcct.Balance & "</B><BR>" & _
       "Destination Account ID: <B>" & objDestAcct.AccountID & "</B> " & _
       "Balance: <B>$" & objDestAcct.Balance & "</B>" & _
       "<HR><BR>"
  End If
%>
</HTML>
```

4. Save ExecuteTransfer.asp into your \inetpub\wwwroot\BegASPFiles
directory. You probably noticed the the Bank.asp page needs some connection
details, which we'll provide in the form of an SSI file called BankConn.asp. So start
one more new text file, and insert the following code:

```
<%
  Dim strConn, strDatabaseType
  ' Use one of these lines, and comment out the other
  strDatabaseType = "Access"
  'strDatabaseType = "MSDE"

  ' Now use that to set the connection string
  If strDatabaseType = "Access" Then
     strConn = "Provider=Microsoft.Jet.OLEDB.4.0;" & _
               "Data Source=E:\datastores\Bank.mdb;" & _
               "Persist Security Info=False"
  Else
     strConn = "Provider=SQLOLEDB;Persist Security Info=False;" & _
               "User ID=sa;Initial Catalog=Movie;" & _
               "Initial File Name=C:\MSSQL7\Data\Bank_Data.mdf"
  End If
%>
```

5. Select the appropriate database type for your setup, by setting the value of
strDataBaseType equal to either "Access" or "MSDE", and then save
BankConn.asp into your \inetpub\wwwroot\BegASPFiles directory.

6. Now you can test the pages.
Using your browser, browse to
the Bank.asp page:

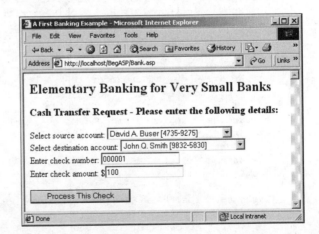

Select the source and destination accounts from the drop-down lists, type in a check number (it can be any arbitrary integer, but *not* an arbitrary string of characters) and the cash transfer value (as shown in the screenshot above). Then click the Process This Check button:

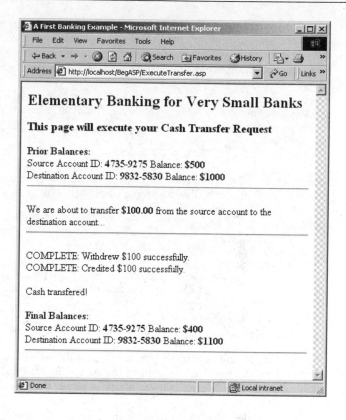

How It Works

Let's have a quick look at Bank.asp first – this page contains the HTML form that prompts the user to submit information for processing. The form is quite simple: on submission of the form, the submitted information will be passed to the ExecuteTransfer.asp page using the POST method:

```
<FORM ACTION="ExecuteTransfer.asp" METHOD="POST">
  Select source account:
  <SELECT NAME="SourceAccount"> <%= strOptionString %></SELECT><BR>
  Select destination account:
  <SELECT NAME="TargetAccount"> <%= strOptionString %></SELECT><BR>
  Enter check number: <INPUT TYPE="TEXT" NAME="CheckNum"><BR>
  Enter check amount: $<INPUT TYE="TEXT" NAME="AmtToTransfer"><BR><BR>
  <INPUT TYPE="SUBMIT" VALUE="Process This Check">
</FORM>
```

There are four fields – the source account, the destination (or target) account, the check number and the amount that is to be transferred.

In order to facilitate the user's choice of account ID (and to reduce the possibility of errors), the first two fields offer the user a choice of *only* those accounts that exist in our data store. So we use an ADO Recordset object to query the database for all of the account IDs that are contained there, and we use that information in the form.

To do this, we need to create the list of <OPTION> tags for the form dynamically, based on information contained in the data store – we'll use ADO and ASP to generate a string of HTML. We first create an ADO Connection and Recordset object, open the connection and execute a SQL command against the database to populate the Recordset object:

```
Set dcBank = Server.CreateObject("ADODB.Connection")
Set rsBank = Server.CreateObject("ADODB.Recordset")

dcBank.Open strConn
rsBank.Open "SELECT * FROM Account", dcBank
```

Now we declare the variable that will contain our string, and use the contents of the Recordset object build the string of HTML <OPTION> tags:

```
Dim strOptionString
strOptionString = ""
Do Until rsBank.EOF
   strOptionString = strOptionString & _
             "<OPTION VALUE='" & rsBank("AccountID") & "'>" & _
             rsBank("HolderName") & " [" & rsBank("AccountID") & "]" & _
             "</OPTION>"
   rsBank.MoveNext
Loop
```

Here, there is one record in the Account table for each account in our bank system. So we loop through all the records, obtaining the AccountID field and creating a string of HTML output around it. For each account, we'll add a string that looks something like this:

```
<OPTION VALUE='4839-1532'>Montague L. Donovan [4839-1532]"</OPTION>"
```

These consecutive strings of HTML will be used as output to the browser, later in the page. Having created our HTML string, we don't need the Recordset and Connection objects so we Close them and clean up:

```
rsBank.Close
dcBank.Close
Set rsBank = Nothing
Set dcBank = Nothing
```

And as we saw a moment ago, we use the strOptionString string within the form to create all the options in the drop-down listbox, like this:

```
Select source account:
<SELECT NAME="SourceAccount"> <%= strOptionString %></SELECT><BR>
Select destination account:
<SELECT NAME="TargetAccount"> <%= strOptionString %></SELECT><BR>
```

We're just using Response.Write to output the list of <OPTION> tags to the browser. In fact, there are two drop-down list-boxes, containing the same set of options, so we use the same string twice.

OK, now let's move on to the `ExecuteTransfer.asp` page. The first thing we do in this page is capture the information submitted by the user, which arrived at this page via the POST method and is therefore found in the `Request.Form` collection:

```
intCheckNum = Request.Form("CheckNum")
dblAmtToTransfer = Request.Form("AmtToTransfer")
srcAccountID = Request.Form("SourceAccount")
destAccountID = Request.Form("TargetAccount")
```

If the source and destination accounts are the same, we save ourselves the trouble of doing the transfer:

```
If srcAccountID = destAccountID Then
  Response.Write "Can't transfer funds when " & _
              "the source and destination account are the same"
```

Otherwise, we get on with the job of transferring the cash. The logic for transferring the cash is all contained within the methods of the `BankAccount` object, so we'll use that functionality here. First, we create two instances of the `BankAccount` object – one for the source account and one for the destination account. We identify them as such by setting the `AccountID` property of each instance:

```
Else
  Set objSourceAcct = Server.CreateObject("BankAccount.WSC")
  Set objDestAcct = Server.CreateObject("BankAccount.WSC")
  objSourceAcct.AccountID = srcAccountID
  objDestAcct.AccountID = destAccountID
```

Next, we write to the browser the balance details of each of these accounts in advance of the transfer:

```
Response.Write "<B>Prior Balances:</B><BR>" & _
    "Source Account ID: <B>" & objSourceAcct.AccountID & "</B> " & _
    "Balance: <B>$" & objSourceAcct.Balance & "</B><BR>" & _
    "Destination Account ID: <B>" & objDestAcct.AccountID & "</B> " & _
    "Balance: <B>$" & objDestAcct.Balance & "</B>" & _
    "<HR><BR>" & _
    "We are about to transfer <B>" & FormatCurrency(dblAmtToTransfer) & _
    "</B> from the source account to the destination account...<BR><HR>"
```

Then we perform the transfer itself. The transfer itself is a two-step process: first, we call the `AddMoney` method of the source account, passing the amount as a negative number (so that the amount is *deducted* from the account's balance). Second, we call the `AddMoney` method of the destination account, passing the amount as a positive number (so that the amount is *added* to the account's balance):

```
blnSuccess = objSourceAcct.AddMoney (-dblAmtToTransfer, intCheckNum)
If blnSuccess <> 0 Then
  objDestAcct.AddMoney dblAmtToTransfer, intCheckNum
  Response.Write "<BR><BR>Cash transfered!"
End If
```

Note that we check the success of the deduction before executing the credit part. If the transfer of cash will cause the source account to go overdrawn, then the first `AddMoney` method does *not* deduct the money (it does not allow the account's balance to go overdrawn), and it returns a 'success' report of 0 (denoting failure). We use that to ensure that the credit doesn't take place either.

Finally, we report the final balances of the two accounts:

```
    Response.Write "<BR><BR>Cash transfered!<BR><BR>" & _
        "<B>Final Balances:</B><BR>" & _
        "Source Account ID: <B>" & objSourceAcct.AccountID & "</B> " & _
        "Balance: <B>$" & objSourceAcct.Balance & "</B><BR>" & _
        "Destination Account ID: <B>" & objDestAcct.AccountID & "</B> " & _
        "Balance: <B>$" & objDestAcct.Balance & "</B>" & _
        "<HR><BR>"
  End If
%>
</HTML>
```

And that's it. In the next chapter, we'll explain how this example, functional as it is, could still cause problems in a multi-user situation or if there is a failure of some kind – and how we can use transactions to fix that.

Summary

This chapter has been all about components. We've learned that we can thing of a component as a self-contained nugget of code that provides a certain amount of related functionality and information – in the form of methods, properties and events. There are lots of advantages to writing and using components in our code:

❑ A component makes for easy code re-use, and allows us to distribute our code safely and simply among our colleagues and customers

❑ Components make for more easy maintainability of our applications

❑ Compiled components bring performance advantages, because the code doesn't need to be compiled before it is executed

❑ Compiled components are also more secure, because they exist in a binary format which is almost impossible for a human to read

❑ Components make it easy to dissect functionality into related parts, collecting related bits of functionality in the same component

We discussed two kinds of components in this chapter:

- ❑ Compiled components are components that are written in a language such as Visual Basic or C++. These components are compiled before they are registered. The compiled executable code is in a binary format, which makes it secure and efficient

- ❑ Script components are not compiled; they are written in a scripting language such as VBScript, JScript or PerlScript. We used the Windows Script Component wizard to create script components. A WSC component is a .wsc file that contains the logic for our components, in a scripting language. This component's script must be compiled before it is executed, which makes it less efficient and less secure, but more easy to use

We've seen two examples in which we encapsulated parts of our application logic into a component. Then we registered the component, and created an instance of the component from script using the Server.CreateObject method. Then, we were able to use the methods and properties of those components in just the same way as we have used the methods and properties of other objects, all the way through this book.

We've even seen how a WSC component can encapsulate ASP logic and data access logic.

We'll begin the next chapter with a look at transactions, and how they can make our applications more robust. Then we'll return to the notion of componentization, and bring components and transactions all together in our final example of that chapter.

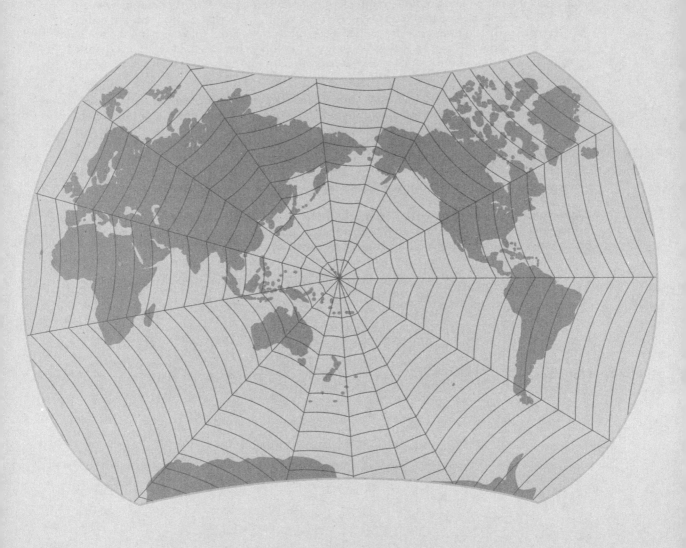

Introducing Transactions and COM+

In the previous chapter, we looked at components and how we can use them to encapsulate related pieces of our programming logic – and we thought about some of the reasons why that is a good thing to do. At the end of the chapter, we saw a very simple example – it used a simple component and an ASP page to manage a transfer of cash from one back account to another.

That example served us well in that it demonstrated how to build and use a simple component. However, in a large banking organization, that example wouldn't be a very robust one to use. There was nothing in particular wrong with the component, or with the ASP page – it's just that, for the purposes of simplicity, we didn't take account of a number of important things. For example:

❑ There might be hundreds (or even thousands) of cashiers accessing the data store at the same time. What if two cashiers were simultaneously trying to withdraw cash from the same account, but the account owner only has enough cash to support *one* of the checks?

❑ No system is totally immune to breakdowns and power failures. What happens if there's a breakdown in the system part-way through the cash transfer?

These are just a couple of scenarios in which our current banking system will fail. However, there is an established technique that we can exploit in order to deal with these potential disaster scenarios. That is, we implement the transfer as part of a **transaction**.

So in this chapter we'll begin by taking a step back from the components, and understanding what a transaction is – and we'll re-implement our banking system using pure ASP (without a component) and transactions. Then, we'll pull together the power of components and transactions, to implement the system a third time – and this will be the most powerful and robust of all.

As we step through this, we will be taking a look at:

❑ What a transaction is, and why we need transactions

❑ How we can make ASP work together with COM+ to implement transactional web applications

❑ Building a transactional web application that uses ASP and ADO

❑ How we can use COM+ and the Component Services tool to install components into COM+, and have COM+ manage the components and their related transactions for us

❑ Creating a COM+ Application with a transaction-aware component, that can be called from ASP

In a nutshell, COM+ provides a framework for managing transactions, components, and other aspects of application design – and it is built-in to the operating system and ready-to-use. COM+ really is a fantastic advance in creating robust and scalable applications.

We'll explore all these ideas during the course of the chapter. Let's get started with an introduction to transactions and transactional applications.

Understanding Transactions

So we've been commissioned by a large banking organization to write a web-based application that their cashiers will be able to use in their day-to-day dealings with customers.

Of course, our web-based Internet Bank application is likely to have a great deal of functionality in the end, but one of the first tasks we need to implement is the ability to transfer money from one account to another. Let's say that a customer walks into the bank with the intention of transferring $100 from his own account into his father's account. While the transfer appears to be a single flow of cash from one place to another, we've already seen that this movement of money is actually a *two*-step process:

❑ First, the money must be removed from the customer's account (the source account), which will reduce the balance in that account

❑ Second, the money must be added to the customer's father's account (the destination account), which will increase the balance in the destination account

So if the balances of these two accounts are, say, $1000.00 and $500.00 before the transfer, then the balances shall be $900.00 and $600.00 after the transfer. One important thing to note here is that the total amount of money in these two accounts is $1500.00 before the transfer, and it's still $1500.00 after the transfer.

Of course, it's important for *both* parts of this transfer to execute successfully, because a part-failure could cause problems with the bank's accounts:

❑ If the money were deducted from the customer's account but not credited to his father's account, then the balances would be $900.00 and $500.00, and the customer would want to know why his $100 had disappeared.

❑ On the other hand, if the deduction part failed but the credit part succeeded then the resulting balances would be $1000.00 and $600.00; thus causing an extra $100 to materialize out of nowhere! While the customer and his father might be pleased with this outcome, the bank manager is more likely to be unhappy.

Maintaining Application Integrity

A critical part of any application is to ensure that any operations it performs are performed correctly. If our application were required to execute a particular operation, but it only *partially* completed that operation, then the resulting state of the application could be incorrect. In this context, we use the term **state** to refer to the values contained in any data relating to the application – for example, data contained in the data store.

For example, in Internet Bank application that we considered a moment ago, the state of the application includes the balance values of each of the accounts in the bank's data store. Suppose we try to perform a cash transfer, but something goes wrong: during the course of the transfer the deduction part succeeds and then there is a power failure, so that the credit part fails. The result would be that the overall state of the application (the values in the account balances) would be incorrect. We might say that the application's state had 'lost its integrity'.

So what we need is a way of packaging these constituent parts of the transfer into a whole, and ensuring that either *all* of these parts execute fully or that *none* of them execute. What we need is a **transaction**.

What is a Transaction?

A **transaction** is an atomic unit of work that either fails as a whole or succeeds as a whole. It is particularly useful in scenarios like the cash transfer that we've just described, where the completion of a single task involves the successful execution of a number of related but separate actions – and that the failure of any one or more actions will cause an inconsistency or a similar problem.

So a transaction can be made up of multiple actions, and if each part of the transaction is successful then the transaction itself is successful. By contrast, if any one part of the transaction fails (or if more than one part of the transaction fails), then the entire transaction will be marked as failed. When a transaction is marked as 'failed', the system will automatically return everything back to the state that it was in before the transaction was started – by undoing all the changes that the system had made since the beginning of the transaction. The process of undoing changes is known as **rollback**.

For example, consider our cash transfer transaction, which involves two separate but related actions – one updates a database table to reflect a deduction in one account balance, and the other updates the database to reflect a credit to another account balance. If either the deduction or the credit parts of the transaction fail then all changes made by the transaction will be rolled back. The transaction will only complete successfully if all of the composite parts complete successfully. The following table demonstrates this:

	Credit part succeeds	Credit part fails
Deduction part succeeds	Outcome = **success**: all parts of the transaction have succeeded, so the changes made by the transaction are committed	Outcome = **rollback**: one part of the transaction has failed, so all changes made by the transaction are undone
Deduction part fails	Outcome = **rollback**: one part of the transaction has failed, so all changes made by the transaction are undone	Outcome = **rollback**: two parts of the transaction have failed, so all changes made by the transaction are undone

Voting for Success or Failure

How does the transaction decide whether it has succeeded or failed? As we said, we can divide the transaction up into different parts, each of which takes care of a different action. Then, we give each action the opportunity to **vote** on whether or not it has completed successfully and satisfactorily:

- ❑ If the action succeeds, then it can register a vote for 'completion'
- ❑ If the action fails, then it can register a vote for 'failure'

But there's an extra point to note here: as you might have expected, the voting system in a transaction requires a **unanimous consensus**. The transaction will only succeed if *all* of its constituent parts succeeded – a majority verdict is not enough to allow the transaction to succeed! If any part of the transaction registers a vote for 'failure', then the transaction as a whole must fail.

The ACID Properties

We've talked about the notion of a transaction guaranteeing that the application maintains a consistent state. But we can define a transaction more precisely than that. In fact, a transaction is an action or group of actions that demonstrates four very particular characteristics – **atomicity, consistency, isolation** and **durability** (collectively known by the acronym **ACID**). In order for a set of related actions to form a true transaction, they must exhibit all four characteristics. Let's have a look at them now.

Atomicity

A transaction is **atomic** – which refers to the 'one-ness' of the constituent parts of the transaction. The transaction atomicity guarantees that the constituent parts of the transaction are completed either all together or not at all. If the transaction makes updates to the system, then they too should be completed entirely (if the transaction is voted to be successful) or rolled back to their original state (if any part of the transaction registered a vote for failure). If the transaction breaks down in the middle, then the atomicity property will ensure that everything that occurred before the breakdown will be rolled back to its original state.

Let's consider how our cash transfer transaction is atomic. The transaction is in two parts – a deduction from account A followed by a credit to account B. So as we saw above, if there's a power failure after the money was deducted from account A, then the 'credit' part of the transaction will be deemed to have failed. Then, the system will roll the transaction back, returning the deducted amount to account A and hence returning the system to its original state.

Consistency

A transaction enforces **consistency** in the system state, by ensuring that the system is in a valid state at the end of any completed or failed transaction. If the transaction completes successfully then its consistency is a guarantee that all changes to the system will have been made properly, and the system is in a valid state. If the transaction fails then any changes already made will automatically be rolled back (and the original state will be resumed); and since the system was in a consistent state when the transaction was started, it will once again be in a consistent state.

Let's look again at the account transfer system: one measure of consistency in the system is to note that the total of the balances of all the accounts does not change – the bank does not have a license to create money, and we certainly don't want any money to disappear. If an error occurs in a cash transfer, all parts of the transaction are rolled back and the total of all balances remains the same as before. If the transaction completes, then an equal sum has been deducted from one account and added to another account: the total of all balance remains the same, and the system as a whole retains its consistency.

Isolation

A transaction is **isolated**, which means that the transaction runs in isolation from other transactions and processes that might be going on around it. Thus, at the time the transaction is running, it runs in the belief that it has exclusive use of the system – it thinks that it is the *only* action that the system is carrying out at that time.

This is important, because the state of the system may not be consistent during the execution of a transaction (the consistency property ensures that the system is consistent a the beginning and end of a transaction, but not necessarily *during* the transaction). If one transaction accesses inconsistent data that exists as a result of the fact that there's currently another transaction running, then we'll get problems. Isolation avoids this by prohibiting the possibility that two transactions may run concurrently.

Here's an example of how isolation might be useful in our banking application. Suppose that you had exactly $200 in your account, and that you'd written two checks, each for $100.00. Suppose also that these checks were being processed at exactly the same moment by two different bank tellers. If the checks were processed concurrently, then each bank teller would note the initial balance of $200, each would deduct $100 from that and each would return a final balance of $100. But in fact, the final balance should be $0. By enforcing isolation, the transactions would automatically be scheduled to run one-after-another, and this error would not occur.

Durability

A transaction is **durable** in that, once it has been successfully completed, all of the changes it made to the system are permanent. There are safeguards that will prevent the loss of information, even in the case of system failure. By logging the steps that the transaction performs, the state of the system can be recreated even if the hardware itself has failed. The concept of durability allows the developer to know that a completed transaction is a permanent part of the system, regardless of what happens to the system later on.

How does our cash transfer transaction demonstrate durability? By writing the results of the transaction to the bank's data store.

Writing Transactional Applications

By now you should be fairly convinced that there is a place for transactions in application design. But how do we build a transaction? There's a hard way and an easier way.

In the traditional programming model, the developer would need to anticipate all the different ways in which the operation could fail. Then, from any point of failure, the developer must write the code that will return the application to the state it was in *before* the operation was started. In other words, it would be the developer's responsibility to add the code to support a rollback of the operation from any point at which it might fail.

Does this sound like a daunting task? It should do! But there's another, much easier way to do this. We can have the operation take place within the environment of a **transaction processing system**. The job of such a system is to ensure that the entire transaction completes successfully or does nothing at all. If all of the tasks are completed successfully then the changes in the application are committed to the system, and the system can proceed to its next transaction or task. If any part of the operation does not complete successfully, then the system will rollback the changes made and put the application back into its original state.

The power of a transaction processing system is that the functionality required to perform these operations is embedded into the system itself. This means that we developers don't have to write the code to support all the different sorts of rollback that might be required. Instead, we just have to program a couple of simple method calls into each of our tasks – these methods are used to vote on whether or not the task was successful. The transaction processing system takes care of the rest!

In a moment we'll take a look at the SetComplete and SetAbort methods, which we use in our code to vote on the success or failure of each task.

Transactions and COM+

So how does COM+ come into play here? Put simply, **COM+** is a new technology that arrives with the release of Windows 2000. It is a natural amalgamation of a number of existing technologies – including COM and MTS – and some other bits and pieces of functionality.

> *Microsoft Transaction Server (MTS) is essentially an environment that provides plumbing for scalable, robust, transactional, secure components in our applications. MTS is supported by older versions of the Windows NT Server operating system, and is superceded in Windows 2000 by COM+.*

To say that COM+ is a way to manage transactional components is something of an understatement! But it is true to say that, among other things, we can use COM+ as a transaction processing system.

If we implement the system using COM+, and a resource manager (such as SQL Server), then the ACID properties of the transaction will be maintained automatically for us. COM+ counts the votes; if the votes indicate that all parts of the transaction were successful, then the money is successfully transferred. But if any of the votes indicate that a part of the transaction failed, then the transaction is aborted – COM+ will tell the resource manager to roll back any changes made to the data. As a developer, all we have to do is let COM+ know if our transaction was successful or not – COM+ will take care of the rest.

> *The role of the **resource manager** is to implement transactions over a specific data source – their responsibility is to maintain durable data, in a consistent state. We'll look more at resource managers shortly.*

Shortly, we'll re-model our cash transfer system using ASP pages and transactions; and later in the chapter we'll use a COM+ component, written in Visual Basic, which encapsulates all of our banking functionality and allows COM+ to manage the transaction without the need for transactional logic in the ASP page.

Before that, let's take a closer look at one of the primary uses for transactions – working with databases.

Transactions and Databases

There are many criteria that go into choosing a database. For example:

- ❑ Capacity – can the database support the amount of information we want to store?
- ❑ Scalability – can it support the number of simultaneous users we're expecting?
- ❑ Cost – how much does the database system cost?
- ❑ Administration – how hard or easy is it to administer the system?
- ❑ Compatibility– does the database work with our other systems?
- ❑ Performance – how many queries can the database engine execute in a given time?

When it comes to working with transactions, one of the most important of these criteria is the database's *compatibility*. As we stated earlier, COM+ provides us with the ability to automatically undo changes made to a system when a transaction fails and is rolled back. When COM+ rolls back the failed transaction, any database servers that participated in that transaction are told to undo the changes that they made to their databases. Of course, in order for this to happen then it's important that the database software is capable of reversing these changes for us.

It's not only important for the database software to be able to support rollback – it's also important for us (as developers) to *know* whether the database software is capable of supporting rollback. If we write an application whose transactions depend on database software that is not capable of rollback, then there's every chance that we will end up with errors in our data.

As we've already said, the idea of writing our own custom-built system for rolling back failed transactions is unfeasibly terrifying! So it's clear that we need to find a database that will do it for us.

In this section we will look at three different types of database software, reminding ourselves about them and exploring how they play in the COM+ and ASP world. We'll look at:

❑ Microsoft Access, or the Jet Database

❑ Microsoft SQL Server

❑ Microsoft Data Environment (MSDE)

> *It's worth noting at this stage that it's possible to use COM+ to manage transactional data stored in non-Microsoft databases, providing they are **XA-compliant**. In particular, COM+ is able to work with transaction state persisted in Oracle databases. However, we won't cover these other database engines any further in this book.*

Each of these databases allows access to data that is stored in a relational data format. As we've seen, we can retrieve information from these databases using standard SQL commands, through various different interfaces. When working with ASP, the most prevalent data access method is ADO. There are many differences between these three databases when looking at the criteria we mentioned earlier. The critical criteria for us to examine is the compatibility of the database with COM+.

Microsoft Access

The Microsoft Access database uses the Microsoft Jet database engine (which is why you may also see it referred to as the Jet database). This database includes the Access front-end to a relational database as well as the database itself. The Jet database tables for a single database are stored in a single data file, usually with the extension `.mdb`. The general way of accessing this database is through an ODBC driver or OLE DB provider, via ADO.

There are a couple of notable advantages to using the Jet database for ASP. First, like MSDE, it is free from any license fee. Second, it comes with its own front-end for quickly creating and modifying databases.

However, the Jet engine is not able to support more than 5–10 simultaneous users; moreover, there are problems inherent in relying on a single file to store all database information. But as far as COM+ is concerned, the bigger problem with the Jet database is that it does not support a resource manager interface – so it is incapable of managing durable data during a transaction.

> *There is a way round this – but it's the difficult route again! If you're using an Access database to maintain transactional data then you will need to access it via the **ODBC resource dispenser**. A resource dispenser also manages state, and is independent of any resource manager, but it does not give you automatic support for database transactions and rollbacks.*

> *This means that if your transaction were to not complete successfully, then any changes made to the database will not be automatically reversed. The database code in your application will need to detect that the transaction didn't complete, and will need to reverse the changes. In order to do this, the application must track the changes made to the database in the first place – and it's the developer's responsibility to write the code to achieve this.*

Microsoft SQL Server

Microsoft SQL Server is a relational database engine that is available for the Windows NT platform. It is a true database server system – as opposed to the file-based system used by the Jet database. This gives it vastly increased power, scalability, and robustness advantages over Jet. The two most common versions of SQL Server are SQL Server 6.5 and SQL Server 7.0.

When working with COM+, the biggest advantage of using SQL Server is that it supports access to its data via a resource manager. The resource manager will support the maintenance of durable data – which means that any changes made to the database system during a transaction will be automatically reversed if the transaction does not complete successfully. In other words, when a transaction fails, COM+ sends a message to SQL Server via the resource manager, telling it to undo the changes made during the course of the transaction.

This means that the application *doesn't* have to track database changes – COM+ and the resource manager will do it all for us.

Microsoft Data Engine

Microsoft released the Microsoft Data Engine (MSDE) early in 1999. This new data engine is designed to alleviate some of the problems that the Jet database was running up against when dealing with larger and more active web sites.

Previously, users of Microsoft data engines had a stark choice when scaling up from the Jet engine – the most obvious choice was SQL Server. This conversion path was relatively straightforward, but not 100% foolproof. So MSDE was intended to provide a kind of halfway house – based on SQL Server technology, but with the option of using Access as a 'front-end' user interface for easy management of the data bases involved.

Essentially, MSDE is SQL Server 7.0 without the scalability and management components. However, the database structures are identical, and both MSDE and SQL Server are true database systems. This helps to alleviate the problems of the file-base Jet system. Another advantage of MSDE is that it provides full SQL Server compatibility free of charge to developers using the Microsoft Visual Studio programs, as well as the ability to distribute applications developed using MSDE without any license fees.

From the point of view of COM+, MSDE is able to use the same resource manager that is employed when working with SQL Server – which means that MSDE gives us all the transaction rollback capabilities of SQL Server.

Transactional ASP Pages

Ever since the integration of IIS 4.0 and MTS, ASP developers have been able to place ASP scripts within a transaction. These **transactional ASP pages** can include calls to server components that will also participate within the same transaction. These transactions are just like all transactions – if any one part of the transaction fails, then the entire transaction will be rolled back. The advantage of transactional ASP scripts is that it makes it easy to tie multiple components together into one single transaction.

Normally, all of the processing for a single transaction can be done on a single ASP page. So if you want to write an ASP that uses a number of different components within a single component, you can do so by including all the logic and method calls for that transaction within a single transactional ASP page.

To declare an ASP page as transactional, you would use the @TRANSACTION directive. For example:

```
<%@TRANSACTION = Required %>
```

Here, we've set the value of the @TRANSACTION directive to Required. In fact, there are four possible values:

❑ Not_Supported – Tells COM+ that the page will not join a transaction, even if one already exists.

❑ Supported – Tells COM+ not to start a transaction, but that the ASP page will join one if it already exists.

❑ Required – Tells COM+ to start a new transaction if one does not exist, or to join an existing one.

❑ Requires_New – Tells COM+ to start a new transaction for the ASP page, even if one already exists.

These values have the same effect as the settings for the transaction participation states that can be set for a component, using the COM+ administration tool. We'll see this later in the chapter.

If you're including an ASP page in a transaction, then the @TRANSACTION directive must be on the first line of the ASP page. If you put anything in the page before the @TRANSACTION directive, then you'll get a script error when you try to run the page.

If an ASP page is transactional, but the transaction finishes without having cast any votes for 'failure' or 'success', then COM+ will assume that the transaction has succeeded – and it will arrange for the changes to be written to disk. Also, if any objects are used within a transactional ASP page, then they can (and usually do) use the same **context object** of the ASP page to participate in the transaction.

The ObjectContext Object

When coding a transactional ASP script, you may want to be able to affect the outcome of the transaction in which the ASP page is executing. You can do that by casting a vote on the outcome of the transaction. For this, we are provided with a special object called the ObjectContext object.

The ObjectContext object has been available since the release of IIS 4.0 and ASP 2.0. It provides the functionality for all of the transaction-handling routines that a developer may need. This is exactly the same object that the server components participating in the transaction will be accessing, and features the SetAbort and SetComplete methods:

❑ We use the SetAbort method to cast a 'transaction failure' vote, and hence to tell COM+ that we think the transaction should not be completed. COM+ will then arrange for all the changes made during the transaction to be rolled back.

❑ We use the SetComplete method to cast a 'transaction success' vote, and hence to tell COM+ that we cannot see any reason that the transaction should not be completed. If every component participating in the transaction calls the SetComplete method, and none of the components call the SetAbort method, then COM+ will know that the transaction has completed successfully and that all of the changes must be written to disk.

Note that when we write components for use in transactions, they too will use the SetAbort and SetComplete methods to cast their votes on how they feel the transaction should complete.

So let's have a look at a short step-by-step example of an ASP script that shows both the @TRANSACTION directive and the use of the ASP ObjectContext object:

```
<%@ TRANSACTION=Required%>
<HTML>
<%
  Dim objA, objB
  Set objA = Server.CreateObject("MyDll.MyClass")
  Set objB = Server.CreateObject("MyDll.MyClass")
  If Not objA.Go = 0 Then
    ObjectContext.SetAbort
  Elseif objB.Go = 0 Then
```

```
      ObjectContext.SetAbort
   Else
      ObjectContext.SetComplete
   End If
%>
</HTML>
```

This a deliberately simplified example just to show how SetComplete and SetAbort might be used:

❑ At the top, you can see the @TRANSACTION directive which indicates that the content of the page must be executed within a transaction – this means that COM+ will monitor the votes cast and will decide at the end whether the transaction is successful or not.

❑ Next, we declare two variables (objA and objB) and we use Server.CreateObject to create two instances of a fictional component called MyDll.MyClass

❑ Next, we call the Go method of the first object. If it returns the value 0, then we opt to vote for 'transaction failure'

❑ Next, we call the Go method of the second object. Similarly, we only vote for 'transaction failure' if the method returns the value 0

❑ If neither objA.Go not objB.Go returned the value 0, then we cast a vote for 'transaction success'

Whatever happens here, we actually only cast one vote in this example. The transaction finishes at the end of the ASP page's output – at that time, COM+ will analyze all the votes (in this case, there's one vote to check from the ASP page, plus any votes cast by the components during the execution of the Go method). Then COM+ will commit or roll back the transaction based on the votes.

Transaction Events

Within our ASP pages, we can listen to COM+ at the time it analyzes the votes and judges on whether the transaction should be committed or aborted – and it can react according to the decision that COM+ makes. In order to do this, we use two special transactional **event hanlders**, called OnTransactionCommit and OnTransactionAbort. When COM+ knows its decision, IIS listens to that decision and executes one of these two routines *just* before actually COM+ commits or aborts the transaction.

The OnTransactionCommit event handler is fired just before COM+ commits a transaction. If COM+ decides to abort the transaction then the OnTransactionAbort event handler will fire. Here's an example of what the code for these event handlers might look like:

```
<%@ TRANSACTION=Required%>
<%
   ... ASP content goes here.
   ... May call SetComplete or SetAbort any number of times during this ASP block.
   ... May also use components that contain calls to SetComplete and/or SetAbort.
```

```
'fires if the transaction commits
Sub OnTransactionCommit
  Response.Write "<HTML>"
  Response.Write "The transaction committed."
  Response.Write "</HTML>"
End Sub

'fires if the transaction aborts
Sub OnTransactionAbort
  Response.Write "<HTML>"
  Response.Write "The transaction aborted."
  Response.Write "</HTML>"
End Sub
%>
```

Like most transactional ASP pages, this page starts by declaring that it requires a transaction. Then the script performs some actions; when the page has finished, COM+ will determine the outcome of the transaction by checking whether any part of the transaction called the `SetAbort` method.

If the `SetAbort` was not called then the `OnTransactionCommit` event will fire, and the transaction will be committed. Otherwise the `OnTransactionAbort` will be called and the transaction will be rolled back.

OK, it's time to exercise all we've learned using an example. As we said at the beginning of this chapter, there are no home-made components in this chapter – we'll control the entire transaction using logic coded using ASP and VBScript. COM+ will manage the transaction behind the scenes, and decide on the success or failure of the transaction as a whole (by analyzing the votes that occur in the form of calls to the `SetComplete` and `SetAbort` methods).

Try it Out – A Transactional Active Server Page

In this example, we will create an HTML form page and a response ASP page that will let us move money from one bank account to another. This example will use transaction processing to ensure that the balances in the two accounts maintain their ACID properties if there is a problem.

As we explained above, our choice of database is important here – in particular, the example won't work using a Microsoft Access database because there is no resource manager. We'll explain how to complete this example using the MSDE (or SQL Server).

> *Remember that, if you wish, you can download all the code for these examples from the Wrox Press web site at* `http://www.wrox.com`.

1. First, we'll set up the two server-side include (SSI) files that are needed for this example. The first of these is `BankConnection.asp` – this will contain the connection string that's necessary when we use the ADO `Connection` and `Recordset` objects in this example. So, create a new file in your editor, and add the following code to it:

```
<%
  Dim strConn, strDatabaseType
  ' Use one of these lines, and comment out the other
  strDatabaseType = "MSDE"
' strDatabaseType = "SQLServer"

  ' Now use that to set the connection string
  If strDatabaseType = "MSDE" Then
    strConn = "Provider=SQLOLEDB;Persist Security Info=False;" & _
              "User ID=sa;Initial Catalog=Bank;" & _
              "Initial File Name=C:\MSSQL7\Data\Bank.mdf"
  Else
    strConn = "Provider=SQLOLEDB; Data Source= my_server_name; Database=Bank; " & _
              "User ID=sa; Password=;"
  End If
%>
```

Save this file into your \inetpub\wwwroot\BegASPFiles folder, with the name
BankConnection.asp.

2. If you're using MSDE then you'll need to place the file Bank.mdf into the
    C:\MSSQL7\Data\ folder, as specified above.

    On the other hand, if you're using SQL Server then you'll need to set up the **Bank**
    database. One way is to use SQL Server's **Import and Export Utility** to import the data
    from the Bank.mdb file into SQL Server (Bank.mdb is provided as part of the
    supporting source code for this book, at http://www.wrox.com), and you'll also need to
    insert your own data server name in place of *my_server_name* above.

    Whichever you're using, you'll need to be sure that you've selected the correct value
    for the string strDatabaseType, in the file BankConnection.asp.

    Note again that it's not possible to run this example using a Microsoft Access database,
    because it does not have support for transactions.

3. Now here's the second of our two SSIs – it's a file called BankFunctions.asp, which
    contains the code for the five predefined functions that we'll use in the body of our
    example (as you'll see shortly). So create a second new file in your editor, and add the
    following code to it:

```
<%
' Function isAccountValid checks that the user has provided valid account details
  Function isAccountValid(AccountID)
    Dim rsAcct
    strSQL = "SELECT AccountID FROM Account " & _
             "WHERE AccountID='" & AccountID & "';"
    Set rsAcct = dcBank.Execute (strSQL)
    If Not rsAcct.EOF Then
      isAccountValid = True
    Else
      isAccountValid = False
```

```
      End If
      rsAcct.Close
      Set rsAcct = Nothing
   End Function

' Function Balance requests balance details from the database
   Function Balance(AccountID)
      Dim rsBalance
      strSQL = "SELECT ResultingBalance FROM Register " & _
               "WHERE AccountID='" & AccountID & "' ORDER BY SeqID DESC;"
      Set rsBalance = dcBank.Execute (strSQL)
      Balance = rsBalance("ResultingBalance")
      rsBalance.Close
      Set rsBalance = Nothing
   End Function

' Function AddMoney transfers the cash from the source account balance
' to the destination account balance
   Function AddMoney(acctID, amount, CheckNum)
      ' positive amount for deposit, negative amount for withdrawl
      Dim strTransType
      If amount < 0 Then
        strTransType = "W"
      Else
        strTransType = "D"
      End If
      Dim curBalance
      curBalance = Balance(acctID)
      strSQL = "INSERT INTO Register " & _
                  "(AccountID, CheckNumber, Transdate, TransType, " & _
                  " Amount, PriorBalance, ResultingBalance) " & _
             "VALUES ('" & acctID & "'," & CheckNum & ",'" & Date & "','" & _
                     strTransType & "'," & amount & "," & curBalance & "," & _
                     CDbl(curBalance + amount) & ");"
      dcBank.Execute strSQL
   End Function

' Sub onTransactionCommit explains what to do when a transaction commits
   Sub onTransactionCommit()
      Response.Write "<HR><B>Resulting Balances:</B><BR>" & _
          "Source Account ID: <B>" & srcAccountID & "</B> " & _
          "Balance: <B>$" & srcBalance & "</B><BR>" & _
          "Destination Account ID: <B>" & destAccountID & "</B> " & _
          "Balance: <B>$" & destBalance & "</B>" & _
          "<HR>[ <A HREF='BankHome.asp'>Write Another Check</A> ] " & _
          "</BODY>" & _
          "</HTML>"
      If Not dcBank Is Nothing Then
        If dcBank.State = adStateOpen Then
          dcBank.Close
        End If
        Set dcBank = Nothing
      End If
```

```
  End Sub

' Sub onTransactionAbort explains what to do when a transaction is aborted
  Sub onTransactionAbort()
    Response.Write "<HR>" & _
      "Transaction Aborted<BR>" & _
      "Reason: " & strAbortReason & _
      "<HR>[ <A HREF='bankHome.asp'>Write Another Check</A> ]" & _
      "</BODY>" & _
      "</HTML>"
    If Not dcBank Is Nothing Then
      If dcBank.State = adStateOpen Then
        dcBank.Close
      End If
      Set dcBank = Nothing
    End If
  End Sub
%>
```

4.   Save `BankFunctions.asp` in your `BegASPFiles` directory.

5.   Now we'll create the file that allows the user to input values into this example. Using the editor of your choice, create a file called `BankHome.asp` and add the following code to it:

```
<!-- #INCLUDE FILE="BankConnection.asp" -->
<HTML>
<HEAD>
<TITLE>Rocks Banking for Programmers</TITLE>
</HEAD>
<BODY>
<%
 Dim dcBank, rsBank
  Set dcBank = Server.CreateObject("ADODB.Connection")
  Set rsBank = Server.CreateObject("ADODB.Recordset")

  dcBank.Open strConn
  rsBank.Open "SELECT * FROM Account", dcBank
  Dim strOptionString
  strOptionString = ""
  Do Until rsBank.EOF
    strOptionString = strOptionString & _
              "<OPTION VALUE='" & rsBank("AccountID") & "'>" & _
              rsBank("HolderName") & " [" & rsBank("AccountID") & "]" & _
              "</OPTION>"
    rsBank.MoveNext
  Loop
  rsBank.Close
  dcBank.Close
  Set rsBank = Nothing
  Set dcBank = Nothing
%>
```

```
<H2>Rocks Banking for Programmers</H2>
<H3>Cash Transfer Request - Please enter the following details:</H3>

<FORM ACTION="ExecuteTransaction.asp" METHOD="POST">
  Select source account:
  <SELECT NAME="SourceAccount"> <%= strOptionString %></SELECT><BR>
  Select destination account:
  <SELECT NAME="TargetAccount"> <%= strOptionString %></SELECT><BR>
  Enter check number: <INPUT TYPE="TEXT" NAME="CheckNum"><BR>
  Enter check amount: $<INPUT TYPE="TEXT" NAME="AmtToTransfer"><BR><BR>
  <INPUT TYPE="SUBMIT" VALUE="Process This Check">
</FORM>
</BODY>
</HTML>
```

6. Save `BankHome.asp` into your `BegASPFiles` directory.

7. Now we'll create the main file in our little application – this last page is called `ExecuteTransaction.asp`. Create one more new file in your editor and add the following code to that file:

```
<%@ TRANSACTION=REQUIRED %>
<!--#INCLUDE FILE="BankConnection.asp"-->
<!--#INCLUDE FILE="BankFunctions.asp"-->
<!-- METADATA TYPE="typelib"
            FILE="C:\Program Files\Common Files\System\ado\msado15.dll" -->
<HTML>
<HEAD><TITLE>Rocks Banking for Programmers</TITLE>
</HEAD>
<BODY>
<H2>Rocks Banking for Programmers</H2>
<H3>This page will execute your Cash Transfer Request, and report success or

failure</H3>
<%
  Dim dcBank, srcAccountID, destAccountID
  Dim strSQL, intCheckNum, dblAmtToTransfer
  Dim srcBalance, destBalance
  Dim strAbortReason

  intCheckNum = Request.Form("CheckNum")
  dblAmtToTransfer = Request.Form("AmtToTransfer")
  srcAccountID = Request.Form("SourceAccount")
  destAccountID = Request.Form("TargetAccount")

  If srcAccountID = destAccountID Then
    ObjectContext.SetAbort
    strAbortReason = "Can't transfer funds when " & _
                    "the source and destination account are the same"
    Response.End
  End If
```

```
Set dcBank = Server.CreateObject("ADODB.Connection")
dcBank.Open strConn

If Not isAccountValid(srcAccountID) Or Not isAccountValid(destAccountID) Then
  ObjectContext.SetAbort
  strAbortReason = "Invalid account numbers"
  Response.End
End If


srcBalance = Balance(srcAccountID)
destBalance = Balance(destAccountID)

Response.Write "<B>Prior Balances:</B><BR>" & _
  "Source Account ID: <B>"       & srcAccountID  & "</B> " & _
  "Balance: <B>$"                & srcBalance    & "</B><BR>" & _
  "Destination Account ID: <B>" & destAccountID & "</B> " & _
  "Balance: <B>$"                & destBalance   & "</B><HR><BR>" & _
  "We are about to transfer <B>" & FormatCurrency(dblAmtToTransfer) & _
  "</B> from the source account to the destination account...<BR>"

AddMoney srcAccountID, -dblAmtToTransfer, intCheckNum
AddMoney destAccountID, dblAmtToTransfer, intCheckNum

srcBalance = Balance(srcAccountID)
destBalance = Balance(destAccountID)

If srcBalance < 0 Or destBalance < 0 Then
  ' Account out of Balance - Roll Back
  ObjectContext.SetAbort
  strAbortReason = "Insufficient Funds in Source Account to Perform Transfer"
Else
  ' Accounts in Balance - Commit Transaction
  ObjectContext.SetComplete
End If
%>
```

Note that this page uses the five functions that we defined in BankFunctions.asp, earlier in this example.

8. Save ExecuteTransaction.asp into your BegASPFiles directory.

9. Using your browser, open the BankHome.asp page:

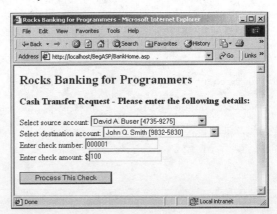

10. Select a source account and a destination account, and type in a check number and the amount that you want to transfer. (For this first effort, we'll transfer $100.00 from account 4735-9275 to account 9832-5830 – there should be enough in the source account to support this transfer without going overdrawn!) Then press the Process This Check button to begin the transfer. You should see a page like this:

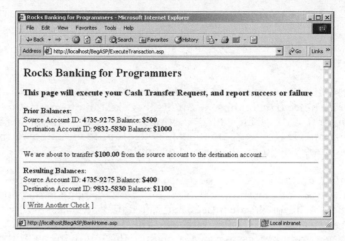

11. Note the balance that remains in the source account – we'll use that information to try a transaction that fails. To try a second transaction, press the Write Another Check link. This time, select the *same* source account (and any other destination account); and enter a check amount that is *greater* than the balance that currently remains in the source account. Then click the Process This Check button to begin the transaction:

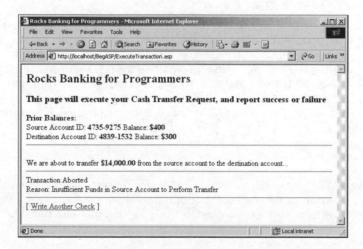

As expected, the transaction failed and was aborted – and this page tells us that. Conveniently, it also explains *why* the transaction failed.

Let's take a look at what's happening when a transaction fails – and also when one completes successfully.

How it Works

Our first page, `BankHome.asp`, is very similar to the form that we used in the final example of Chapter 16. We're using an HTML form in this page to handle the request:

```
<FORM ACTION="ExecuteTransaction.asp" METHOD="POST">
...
</FORM>
```

We're using the `ExecuteTransaction.asp` page to handle this request, so we specify that in the attributes for the `<FORM>`.

In order to facilitate the user's choice of account ID (and to reduce the possibility of errors), we will offer the user a choice of *only* those accounts that exist in our data store. The list of account IDs is contained in an HTML string called `strOptionString` – this string is used twice in the form to create a list of HTML `<OPTION>` tags for the drop-down listboxes in the form. We covered this technique in detail in the second example of Chapter 16.

But we want to move on to the most important new feature in this example, which is implemented in the `ExecuteTransaction.asp` page. This page is responsible for both the **database access** and the **business rule processing**. The database access will allow for reading and updating of the `Register` table, in the database. The business rules are the rules of the system – in this case, business rule processing means making the following validity checks on the cash transfer before the transfer itself actually takes place:

- ❑ First, that the balance on any account must *not* fall below 0

- ❑ Second, that the source and destination accounts chosen by the user are *different* accounts

If the user requests a cash transfer that fails to adhere to these two business rules, then the transfer will not take place – it will be aborted.

In order to achieve this, we will perform our database updates within the scope of a transaction. As we saw earlier, the `@TRANSACTION` directive will determine the transaction characteristics of the page. The value of `REQUIRED` will ensure that this page is executed within the context of a transaction, and that any objects used by this page will have a chance to participate in the transaction as well:

```
<%@ TRANSACTION=REQUIRED %>
```

Then we follow good programming practice, by declaring our variables before we use them. Four of these local variables will be used to hold the values passed to the page via the `Request.Form` collection, and we also assign those values straight away:

```
<%
   Dim dcBank, srcAccountID, destAccountID
   Dim strSQL, intCheckNum, dblAmtToTransfer
   Dim srcBalance, destBalance
   Dim strAbortReason
```

```
intCheckNum = Request.Form("CheckNum")
dblAmtToTransfer = Request.Form("AmtToTransfer")
srcAccountID = Request.Form("SourceAccount")
destAccountID = Request.Form("TargetAccount")
```

These four values are the identity numbers for the source and target accounts, the check number for the check being processed, and the cash amount that the user wishes to transfer. These are the values that the user entered and submitted via the HTML form in the `BankHome.asp` page.

Of course, this is a technique that we've seen elsewhere in the book. We'll be using each of these values more than once during the course of this ASP page, so it makes sense to assign the values to local variables. They make the code more readable; more importantly, they avoid the need for repeated trips to search the `Request.Form` collection for values, so they actually make our code more efficient!

Applying the Business Rules – Comparing Account Numbers

Now it's time to get to the meat of this example. In the next part of `ExecuteTransaction.asp`, we're going to start checking the details of the requested transfer to ensure that it meets the rules of the system – the **business rules**. If the transfer meets these rules, then we'll allow it to complete – otherwise, we will force any changes made in relation to that transfer to be rolled back.

So our first step is to compare the ID values of the source and target accounts, and confirm that they are indeed different accounts. This is basically to prevent spurious entries from clogging up the database – because we don't want to waste system resources executing redundant transfers and storing their details. So we use an `If ... Then ... End If` block to compare the account ID values, and to take action if they are the same:

```
If srcAccountID = destAccountID Then
   ObjectContext.SetAbort
   strAbortReason = "Can't transfer funds when " & _
                    "the source and destination account are the same"
   Response.End
End If
```

Here, if the accounts are the same, then the transfer shall not be allowed to continue. So the first thing we need to do is abort the transaction (using the `SetAbort` method). By calling the `SetAbort` method, we are registering a vote that states that the transaction should abort (i.e. that it should *not* complete).

Now, as we mentioned earlier, it only needs one 'abort' vote to abort the transaction – so if the account IDs were the same then we know that the transaction will be doomed to failure. But we also want to let the user know *why* the transaction has failed. To do this, we will write a descriptive error message, and store it in a string called `strAbortReason`. In this case, we tell the user that they can only transfer funds if they choose different accounts for the source and destination.

Having called `SetAbort` and written the abort reason, there are three ways that we could deal with the rest of the ASP script. Before we look at the method we've used here (the `Response.End` method), let's consider the other two options:

❑ Since we know that the transaction will be aborted in the end, we *could* let the rest of the script run to completion, and then rely on the rollback of the changes to the database to get back to the starting condition. But this just amounts to a lot of needless processing, because we'd just be making lots of changes in the knowledge that we were going to undo them again at the end. Let's avoid that.

❑ We could have built the entire page on a series of nested `If ... Then ... Else` statements, which would have avoided the unnecessary processing but would look clumsy and confusing, so let's avoid that too.

The solution that we *do* use in this example relies on two characteristics of ASP itself. First, as you can see in the code above, we use the `Response.End` to force the execution of the page to stop *as soon as* we reach the error condition. But don't forget that we still want to output the text of our `strAbortReason` string. We could do that after we've assigned the `strAbortReason` string and before we call `Response.End`, but this would again make for a good deal of cluttered code. So instead, we make use of a second ASP tool – by using one of the transactional events.

Here's what happens. Normally, when `Response.End` is called, the execution of the ASP script ends immediately. But in the occasion of a *transacted* ASP page, the `Response.End` causes the transactional event to be fired. This causes the contents of the event handler to be run, and *they* will form the last piece of code executed on the page. In this case, we've called `SetAbort` – so the `TransactionAbort` event will be raised and the contents of the `OnTransactionAbort()` event handler will run.

It is in this method that we can output the appropriate error message to the user. Here's our code for `OnTransactionAbort()`:

```
Sub onTransactionAbort()
  Response.Write "<HR>" & _
     "Transaction Aborted<BR>" & _
     "Reason: " & strAbortReason & _
     "<HR>[ <A HREF='bankHome.asp'>Write Another Check</A> ]" & _
     "</BODY>" & _
     "</HTML>"
  If Not dcBank Is Nothing Then
    If dcBank.State = adStateOpen Then
      dcBank.Close
    End If
    Set dcBank = Nothing
  End If
End Sub
```

As you can see, if the transaction aborts (for any reason) then we simply write a message to the user explaining what went wrong, and we close the HTML. Then, optionally (if we've been using the ADO `Connection` object `dcBank`), we also tidy up its resources.

Applying the Business Rules – Validating Account Numbers

The next thing we do is check that the account numbers selected by the user are valid – i.e. that they exist and represent valid account in our data store. To so this, we first establish a connection to the data store, and create a recordset:

```
Set dcBank = Server.CreateObject("ADODB.Connection")
dcBank.Open strConn
```

Now we make a quick check on the account numbers provided by the user, and if there is a problem with either of them then we abort the transaction:

```
If Not isAccountValid(srcAccountID) Or Not isAccountValid(destAccountID) Then
   ObjectContext.SetAbort
   strAbortReason = "Invalid account numbers"
   Response.End
End If
```

This is quite similar to the If ... Then ... End If structure we saw a moment ago: essentially, it says "if there's a problem with an account number, then vote to abort the transaction, declare the reason, and wrap up the page's execution". When Response.End is called, this fires the TransactionAbort event, and the OnTransactionAbort() event handler will fire (as we described above).

In order to validate the account number given, we're using a pre-written helper function called isAccountValid (whose code is contained in the SSI BankFunctions.asp). Here it is:

```
Function isAccountValid(AccountID)
   Dim rsAcct
   strSQL = "SELECT AccountID FROM Account " & _
            "WHERE AccountID='" & AccountID & "';"
   Set rsAcct = dcBank.Execute (strSQL)
   If Not rsAcct.EOF Then
     isAccountValid = True
   Else
     isAccountValid = False
   End If
   rsAcct.Close
   Set rsAcct = Nothing
End Function
```

This function takes a single parameter that represents the account ID that we want to examine. The function will query the database using a SQL query, which creates a recordset containing any record in the Account table whose AccountID field matches the value passed as a parameter. If the Recordset object returned by this query is empty (i.e. EOF is True), then we can conclude that the account doesn't exist – in this case the function will return False. If the Recordset object is not empty, then we can conclude that the value passed represents a valid account – and in this case the function will return True.

The Pre-Transfer Message

Now we return to the `ExecuteTransaction.asp` file. If the transaction reaches this point without aborting, then we know that the account numbers are valid and different. Then, we can use another helper function, `Balance()`, to fetch the balance values of these two accounts from the data store, and assign them to a couple of local variables, whose values we can then display to the user:

```
srcBalance = Balance(srcAccountID)
destBalance = Balance(destAccountID)

Response.Write "<B>Prior Balances:</B><BR>" & _
  "Source Account ID: <B>"        & srcAccountID  & "</B> " & _
  "Balance: <B>$"                 & srcBalance    & "</B><BR>" & _
  "Destination Account ID: <B>"   & destAccountID & "</B> " & _
  "Balance: <B>$"                 & destBalance   & "</B><HR><BR>" & _
  "We are about to transfer <B>"  & FormatCurrency(dblAmtToTransfer) & _
  "</B> from the source account to the destination account...<BR>"
```

Let's have a look at the `Balance()` helper function, whose code is contained in the `BankFunctions.asp` SSI file:

```
Function Balance(AccountID)
  Dim rsBalance
  strSQL = "SELECT ResultingBalance FROM Register " & _
           "WHERE AccountID='" & AccountID & "' ORDER BY SeqID DESC;"
  Set rsBalance = dcBank.Execute (strSQL)
  Balance = rsBalance("ResultingBalance")
  rsBalance.Close
  Set rsBalance = Nothing
End Function
```

This function accepts a single parameter – the account ID of one of our bank accounts – and returns the balance for that account. The balance of the account is determined by the latest entry for that account in the `Register` table. Don't forget that we've already validated the account number, using the `isAccountValid()` function; so we don't need to confirm the validity of the account number again here. Our query returns an ADO `Recordset` object, which contains all of the register entries sorted into reverse `SeqID` order. This means that the latest entry in the register (the one with the current balance) will be the first record in the recordset. We do that because the recordset's cursor is automatically placed onto the first record in the recordset – which is the record that we're interested in.

Making the Transfer

Returning to the `ExecuteTransaction.asp` page, once we've completed our pre-transfer message to the browser, it is time to make the transfer itself. As we've noted, the transfer of money from one account to another involves two discrete steps:

```
AddMoney srcAccountID, -dblAmtToTransfer, intCheckNum
AddMoney destAccountID, dblAmtToTransfer, intCheckNum
```

The first is to deduct the amount from the source account: this is done by calling the AddMoney() helper function, passing in the ID of the source account, the amount of the check as a negative number, and the check ID. The second step is to add the amount to the destination account: this is done by calling the AddMoney() function again, this time specifying the destination account's ID, the amount as a positive number, and the check ID again.

Let's take a look at the AddMoney() helper function. Its purpose is to perform an update to the Register table for a specified account. Whether we're deducting an amount from the account's balance, or adding an amount to an account's balance, the processes required are almost exactly the same – we're just adding a negative or positive number to the account's balance. So if we're making a deduction then we pass in the amount as a negative value; if we're making a credit then we pass in a positive value:

```
Function AddMoney(acctID, amount, CheckNum)
  ' positive amount for deposit, negative amount for withdrawl
  Dim strTransType
  If amount < 0 Then
    strTransType = "W"
  Else
    strTransType = "D"
  End If
  Dim curBalance
  curBalance = Balance(acctID)
  strSQL = "INSERT INTO Register " & _
           "(AccountID, CheckNumber, Transdate, TransType, " & _
           " Amount, PriorBalance, ResultingBalance) " & _
           "VALUES ('" & acctID & "'," & CheckNum & ",'" & Date & "','" & _
               strTransType & "'," & amount & "," & curBalance & "," & _
               CDbl(curBalance + amount) & ");"
  dcBank.Execute strSQL
End Function
```

The AddMoney function accepts three parameters – the ID of the account whose balance we want to change, the amount by which we want to change the balance, and the check number associated with the change. The first step of this function is to determine whether the function is dealing with a deduction or a credit (this is based on the sign of the amount). This information will be added to the new record that we create in the Register table. Next, we need to know the current balance in the account, so that we can compute the new balance after the transaction. To do this, we simply use the Balance() helper function to retrieve the value.

Once we know the starting balance, we can build a SQL command that will perform the task of updating the account's balance. We'll do this by using a SQL INSERT command to add a new record to the Register table. The values that will be inserted include the type of the transaction (withdrawal or deposit), a date/time stamp, the balance prior to the transaction, and the balance after the transaction. Once we have created the SQL command, we process it by passing it to the Execute method of our ADO Connection object.

There are two parts to the transaction – the deduction and the credit – so remember that we call the AddMoney() method twice during the execution of ExecuteTransaction.asp. When we call the AddMoney() function and pass a negative value in the amount parameter, the function actually deducts money from the specified account.

Checking for Overdrawn Accounts

Now we return to `ExecuteTransaction.asp` once again. Once the transfer is made, we update the values of the variables that hold the current account balances:

```
srcBalance = Balance(srcAccountID)
destBalance = Balance(destAccountID)
```

Now, the `AddMoney()` method (that we used to update the balances) is an unintelligent method. All it does is change the balance of an account as specified by the parameters – it doesn't check the validity of such changes. It is up to us to apply the business logic, to check that the resulting balance in each account is valid within our system. As it happens, the business rules that govern our system dictate that no account must go overdrawn – the balance of any account must be greater than or equal to zero at all times.

So the next thing to do is check that this is the case for the new balance values of both accounts. If either account balance has dipped below zero, then we will need to abort the transaction, roll back the changes we've made and report the reason for the failed transfer:

```
If srcBalance < 0 Or destBalance < 0 Then
   ' Account out of Balance - Roll Back
   ObjectContext.SetAbort
   strAbortReason = "Insufficient Funds in Source Account to Perform Transfer"
```

Isn't transaction processing great? In the case above, we have made changes to the database, and then determined that some business rule has been violated – so we use `SetAbort` to vote for 'transaction failure', and that's enough to ensure that the transaction will be **rolled back**.

> **All we need to do is register a vote for 'transaction failure', by calling the `SetAbort` method, and that will roll back the transaction and undo those changes from the database. Without transaction processing, we would have to write all kinds of code to track the changes made to the database, and then back those changes out if it was necessary.**

Well that's what happens if an account balance dips below zero. What happens if both account balances remain healthily above zero? In that case, the transaction has succeeded, and will be **committed**:

```
Else
   ' Accounts in Balance - Commit Transaction
   ObjectContext.SetComplete
End If
```

We vote for 'transaction completion' by calling the `SetComplete` method. This casts our vote to make the transaction permanent in the database.

Unless we called the `Response.End` method at any point, the execution of the page finishes at the end of the ASP page. It's at this point that the transaction ends too – so the system must count up all the votes and decide whether the transaction was successful or not. Remember, if there were any votes for 'transaction failure' then the transaction will fail, and the `TransactionAbort` error message will fire: the `onTransactionAbort()` event handler will be executed, and any changes that were made will be rolled back.

> Recall that the voting system for a transaction is not a 'first-past-the-post' system. The transaction will fail unless the votes are *unanimously* in favor of 'transaction success'. A majority verdict is not good enough!

If there were no votes for 'transaction failure', then the transaction is a success, and the changes that we made to the data store can be committed and made permanent and durable (the transaction processor will arrange all that – we don't have to worry about it). The `TransactionCommit` event will fire, and the `onTransactionCommit()` event handler will be executed to handle the event. We haven't seen `onTransactionCommit()` yet, so let's look at it now:

```
Sub onTransactionCommit()
  Response.Write "<HR><B>Resulting Balances:</B><BR>" & _
      "Source Account ID: <B>" & srcAccountID & "</B> " & _
      "Balance: <B>$" & srcBalance & "</B><BR>" & _
      "Destination Account ID: <B>" & destAccountID & "</B> " & _
      "Balance: <B>$" & destBalance & "</B>" & _
      "<HR>[ <A HREF='BankHome.asp'>Write Another Check</A> ] " & _
      "</BODY>" & _
      "</HTML>"
  If Not dcBank Is Nothing Then
    If dcBank.State = adStateOpen Then
      dcBank.Close
    End If
    Set dcBank = Nothing
  End If
End Sub
```

In an earlier step, after the transaction was processed, we queried the database for the balances of the accounts. This was stored in a local variable and then the value was checked to make sure it was valid (not negative). Since these are the ending balances in the accounts, we can use these values to display the final balances to the user in the event handler. We will also provide a link for the user to click on if they wish to process another transfer.

The last step will be to close the connection to the database, and then release the connection object. You may think that this is superfluous, in that when the page ends the reference to the connection will be deleted, and the connection will automatically be closed. But good programming practice dictates that we should explicitly close all database objects, and then release the references to those objects, rather than relying on the system to do it for us.

You can see from the two example scripts that were run that if the business rules said the processing was OK, then a confirmation message will be printed, and the data in the database will be changed. If there was a business logic error, as would have happened if we tried to write a check for more money than we have, then the error would be displayed for the user, and any changes to the database would have been rolled back.

COM+ Can't Roll Back your Script Code

Before we move on to look at transaction scope, there's one more point to note in this section. We've talked about how, in the event of an aborted transaction, COM+ tells your database's resource manager to organize the rollback of any changes that have been made during the course of the transaction. However, you should be aware that COM+ is *unable* to rollback changes made during the transaction *within the script itself* – for instance, if the ASP page made changes made to session or application variables, they will not be automatically rolled back by COM+ when the transaction aborts.

One way round this is to use the transactional event handlers – particularly onTransactionAbort() – to manually rollback any changes to your script variables that COM+ cannot perform automatically.

Transaction Scope

The **scope** of a transaction refers to all the actions that lie between the beginning of the transaction and the end of the transaction:

- ❑ Any actions that are executed as part of the transaction are contained within the transaction's scope. These actions should be rolled back if the transaction is aborted at any stage.

- ❑ Any actions that are not executed as part of the transaction are said to be outside the transaction's scope.

So when we're dealing with transacted ASP pages, what is the scope of the transaction? Well, in ASP we *start a* transaction by setting the @TRANSACTION directive to a value such as REQUIRED, using the following line:

```
<%@TRANSACTION=REQUIRED%>
```

This line must be placed at the beginning of the ASP page, so in ASP the scope of a transaction always coincides with the beginning of an ASP page.

The transaction ends when the page ends – either naturally, when the execution reaches the last line of code in the ASP page, or forcibly, when we call a method such as Response.End.

So in short, it's usual that in ASP a transaction begins at the beginning of a page, and it finishes at the end of a page. So the next question is: "Can our transaction scope encompass more than one page?"

Transaction Scope Across Multiple ASP Pages

As we first learned in Chapter 7, IIS 5.0 gives us two new methods in ASP 3.0 – the Server.Execute method and the Server.Transfer method – which allow us to call functionality from other ASP scripts into the current ASP script. For example, the following lines uses Server.Execute to force execution to jump from the currently-executing page to the beginning of a page called OtherPage.asp:

```
Server.Execute OtherPage.asp
```

When `OtherPage.asp` has finished executing, IIS will return to execute the remainder of the original page.

By contrast, if we use the following line then execution will jump from the current page to `OtherPage.asp`, and will *not* return to the original page on completion:

```
Server.Transfer OtherPage.asp
```

This has interesting consequences for our transactions. In particular, it's interesting to note what happens when we call one of these methods from an ASP page that has already started a transaction. For example, consider a page that contains the following code:

```
<%@TRANSACTION=Required%>
<%
   ... other ASP code ...
   Server.Execute OtherPage.asp
   ... more ASP code ...
%>
```

Clearly this page is transactional, so there is a transaction in process already at the time the `Server.Execute` method is called. As soon as that happens, execution moves from this page to the page called `OtherPage.asp`. If we want the contents of `OtherPage.asp` to form part of the existing transaction (i.e. to be contained within the existing transaction's scope) then we can, but we need to be a little careful about the `@TRANSACTION` directive at the top of `OtherPage.asp`.

As you may recall from earlier in the chapter, there are four possible values that we can assign to the `@TRANSACTION` directive – they are `Not_Supported`, `Supported`, `Required` or `Requires_New`. We can choose any one of these values for the `@TRANSACTION` directive at the top of `OtherPage.asp` – and our choice will dictate whether the contents of `OtherPage.asp` are contained within the scope of the existing transaction:

@TRANSACTION= … in OtherPage.asp	Behavior
Not_Supported	The contents of `OtherPage.asp` are *outside* the scope of the existing transaction
Supported	The contents of `OtherPage.asp` are *within* the scope of the existing transaction
Required	The contents of `OtherPage.asp` are *within* the scope of the existing transaction
Requires_New	COM+ will create a *second* transaction, nested within the existing transaction, just for the contents of `OtherPage.asp`

If you look back at our definitions of these four values, you'll see that they tie in with the behaviors that we've described here. Don't worry too much about nested transactions – they are a rather advanced topic, and we won't be reaching such advanced stages in this book.

If you find all this a little confusing, let's have an example that illustrates some of the issues involved here.

Try It Out – A Transaction with Multiple-page Scope

In this example, we'll create a couple of pages the bank teller can use to create a brand new account within our banking system. The bank teller will enter the name of the customer, and a new account number (unfortunately we haven't implemented that auto-generation method for account numbers yet, but we'll use a little 'business rule' logic to check the chosen account Id against the existing IDs in the database). The teller is also required to enter the initial balance for the new account.

In the page that manages these changes, we'll start a transaction, and then attempt to write the new Account ID and account owner's name to the `Account` table of our database. Then we'll use the `Server.Execute` method to invoke a second ASP page, which writes the initial balance to the `Register` table of the database. Along the way, we'll think about what @TRANSACTION directives are appropriate for these two pages.

1. We'll be using the Bank database that was used in the previous example in this chapter. Therefore, you'll need to ensure that your `Bank.mdf` file is contained within the `C:\MSSQL7\Data` folder (or, if you're using SQL Server, that your **Bank** database is set up on the SQL Server machine).

2. We'll also be using the connection string details contained in the `BankConnection.asp` page (which we provided with the previous example in this chapter). So, ensure that the `BankConnection.asp` file is still saved into your `BegASPFiles` folder.

3. Now we'll create the new code for this example. The first page is called `BankAddAccount.asp`. Open your code editor and add the following code:

```
<HTML>
<HEAD>
<TITLE>Rocks Banking for Programmers</TITLE>
</HEAD>
<BODY>
<H2>Rocks Banking for Programmers</H2>
<H3>Add a New Account - Please enter the following details:</H3>

<FORM ACTION="CreateAcct.asp" METHOD="POST">
  Enter a number for the new account:
    <INPUT TYPE="TEXT" NAME="AccountNo"><BR>
  Enter the name of the owner of the new account:
    <INPUT TYPE="TEXT" NAME="AccountName"><BR>
```

```
.Enter an initial balance: $<INPUT TYPE="TEXT" NAME="InitialBalance"><BR><BR>
  <INPUT TYPE="SUBMIT" VALUE="Create New Account">
</FORM>
</BODY>
</HTML>
```

4. Save this as `BankAddAccount.asp`, into your `BegASPFiles` folder.

5. Here's the first of our two transactional pages – it's called `CreateAcct.asp`. So create a second new file and add the following to it:

```
<%@ TRANSACTION=REQUIRED %>
<!--#INCLUDE FILE="BankConnection.asp"-->
<!-- METADATA TYPE="typelib"
              FILE="C:\Program Files\Common Files\System\ado\msado15.dll" -->
<HTML>
<HEAD><TITLE>Rocks Banking for Programmers</TITLE>
</HEAD>
<BODY>
<H2>Rocks Banking for Programmers</H2>
<H3>We'll try to create a new account for you, and report success or failure</H3>
<%
  Dim dcBank, rsBank, strSQL, strAbortReason
  Dim strAcctName

  Session("strAcctNo") = Request.Form("AccountNo")
  strAcctName = Request.Form("AccountName")
  Session("dblInitialBalance") = Request.Form("InitialBalance")

  If dblInitialBalance < 0 Then
    ObjectContext.SetAbort
    strAbortReason = "Can't create an account with a negative initial balance. " & _
                     "Please return and re-enter. "
  End If

  Set dcBank = Server.CreateObject("ADODB.Connection")
  Set rsBank = Server.CreateObject("ADODB.Recordset")
  dcBank.Open strConn

  strSQL = "SELECT AccountID FROM Account WHERE AccountID LIKE '" & _
           Session("strAcctNo") & "'"
  rsBank.Open strSQL, dcBank
  If Not rsBank.EOF Then
    ObjectContext.SetAbort
    strAbortReason = "You have used the number of an existing account. "
  End If
  rsBank.Close
  Set rsBank = Nothing

  strSQL = ""
  strSQL = "INSERT INTO Account (AccountID, HolderName)" & _
           "VALUES ('" & Session("strAcctNo") & "', '" & strAcctName & "');"
  dcBank.Execute strSQL
```

```
    If dblInitialBalance >=0 Then
      Server.Execute "SetBalance.asp"
    End If

  ' Sub onTransactionCommit explains what to do when a transaction commits
    Sub onTransactionCommit()
      Response.Write "<HR><B>You've created a new account!</B><BR>" & _
          "Account ID: <B>" & Session("strAcctNo") & "</B><BR> " & _
          "Account Owner: <B>" & strAcctName & "</B><BR> " & _
          "Initial Balance: <B>" & FormatCurrency(Session("dblInitialBalance")) & _
          "</B><BR>" & _
          "<HR>[ <A HREF='BankAddAccount.asp'>Create another new account</A> ] " & _
          "</BODY>" & _
          "</HTML>"
      If Not dcBank Is Nothing Then
        If dcBank.State = adStateOpen Then
          dcBank.Close
        End If
        Set dcBank = Nothing
      End If
    End Sub

  ' Sub onTransactionAbort explains what to do when a transaction is aborted
    Sub onTransactionAbort()
      Response.Write "<HR>" & _
        "Transaction Aborted<BR>" & _
        "Reason: " & strAbortReason & _
        "<HR>[ <A HREF='BankAddAccount.asp'>Create another new account</A> ] " & _
        "</BODY>" & _
        "</HTML>"
      If Not dcBank Is Nothing Then
        If dcBank.State = adStateOpen Then
          dcBank.Close
        End If
        Set dcBank = Nothing
      End If
    End Sub
%>
```

6. Save this as `CreateAcct.asp`, into your `BegASPFiles` folder.

7. Here's the second of our transactional ASP pages. It's called `SetBalance.asp`. So create one more new file and add the following code to it:

```
<%@TRANSACTION=Supported %>
<!--#INCLUDE FILE="BankConnection.asp"-->
<%
  Dim dcBank, strSQL
  Set dcBank = Server.CreateObject("ADODB.Connection")
  dcBank.Open strConn

  strSQL = "INSERT INTO Register " & _
            "(AccountID, CheckNumber, Transdate, TransType, " & _
```

```
            "TransNote, Amount, PriorBalance, ResultingBalance) " & _
        "VALUES ('" & Session("strAcctNo") & "', 0, '" & Date & _
            "', 'D', 'Initial Deposit', " & CDbl(Session("dblInitialBalance")) & -
            ", 0, " & Session("dblInitialBalance") & ");"
    dcBank.Execute strSQL

    dcBank.Close
    Set dcBank = Nothing
%>
```

8. Save this as `SetBalance.asp`, into your `BegASPFiles` folder.

9. Now fire up your browser, browse to the page `BankAddAccount.asp`, and add some details to the input boxes:

Then click the **Create New Account** button to submit the request and create the new account.

10. The resulting page will report the success (or otherwise!) of your request:

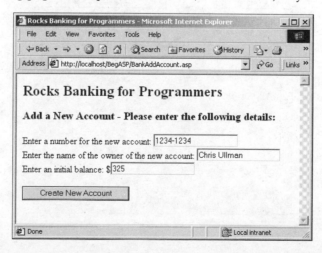

How It Works

The first page in this example, `BankAddAccount.asp`, should be simplicity itself by now! It just contains an HTML form, asking the user to input values for the new account ID, account name and initial balance:

```
<FORM ACTION="CreateAcct.asp" METHOD="POST">
  Enter a number for the new account:
    <INPUT TYPE="TEXT" NAME="AccountNo"><BR>
  Enter the name of the owner of the new account:
    <INPUT TYPE="TEXT" NAME="AccountName"><BR>
  Enter an initial balance: $<INPUT TYPE="TEXT" NAME="InitialBalance"><BR><BR>
  <INPUT TYPE="SUBMIT" VALUE="Create New Account">
</FORM>
```

As we've said before, the account ID needs to be unique, and usually we would write a small function to automatically generate the account IDs for this application. But in this case, we'll allow the cashier to choose the account ID. Later, as part of the transaction, we'll check the 'candidate' account ID against the other IDs in the database – if the chosen account ID is already being used by an existing account then we'll 'abort' the transaction.

Now, we have two pages that perform the job of creating the account:

❑   The first is `CreateAcct.asp`, which is called directly by the HTML form above. This performs a couple of validation checks, and then adds the account ID and account name to the `Account` table of the database

❑   The second is `SetBalance.asp`, which is executed via a `Server.Execute` call from `CreateAcct.asp`. Its job is to add the opening balance details to the `Register` table of the database.

In other words, `CreateAcct.asp` executes the code contained in `SetBalance.asp` (by calling `Server.Execute`), before completing the remainder of its own code. If you like you can think of `SetBalance.asp` as being 'embedded' within `CreateAcct.asp`. With that clear in our minds, let's think about the transactional status of these two pages.

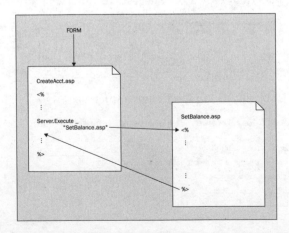

We've got a few validity checks to perform here, and we're updating both the Account and Register tables, so it would be ideal to put all these things into a transaction. Therefore, we set the following at the top of CreateAcct.asp:

```
<%@ TRANSACTION=Required %>
```

This tells COM+ that the page *must* run within a transaction – since there was no transaction running previously, a new transaction will start at this point.

As we've said, we don't only want the contents of CreateAcct.asp to be contained in the transaction scope – we also want the contents of the SetBalance.asp file to be contained within the scope of the same transaction. In order for this to work correctly, which value should we choose for the @TRANSACTION directive for SetBalance.asp?

If you look back to the previous pages, you'll see that we've actually used the following for the first line of SetBalance.asp:

```
<%@TRANSACTION=Supported %>
```

This means that this ASP page will take part in any existing transaction, but will not start a new one. That's fine for us – it means that the SetBalance.asp file will take part in the transaction that was started at the beginning of CreateAcct.asp.

> *It's important to get this right. For example, if we had chosen @TRANSACTION= Not_Supported, then the contents of SetBalance.asp would still execute when called, but they would exist outside the scope of our transaction. So, if there was something wrong with the submitted account ID and the transaction was aborted, SetBalance.asp would still execute – it would not be rolled back – resulting in us attempting to set an initial balance for a non-existant account.*

OK, now we know the best choices for the @TRANSACTION directives of these two pages, let's run through what else this example does.

In CreateAcct.asp, we capture the values submitted in the form, and save them as local variables:

```
strAcctNo = Request.Form("AccountNo")
strAcctName = Request.Form("AccountName")
dblInitialBalance = Request.Form("InitialBalance")
```

Then we perform a couple of validity checks. First, we check that the bank teller has entered a, initial account balance that is greater than or equal to zero. If not, we abort the transaction and create a strAbortReason string, containing the reason for the failed transaction.

```
If dblInitialBalance < 0 Then
  ObjectContext.SetAbort
  strAbortReason = "Can't create an account with a negative initial balance. " & _
                   "Please return and re-enter."
End If
```

The second validity check is the one we mentioned before – to confirm that the requested account ID is not one that already exists in the database:

```
Set dcBank = Server.CreateObject("ADODB.Connection")
Set rsBank = Server.CreateObject("ADODB.Recordset")
dcBank.Open strConn

strSQL = "SELECT AccountID FROM Account WHERE AccountID LIKE '" & _
Session("strAcctNo") & "'"
rsBank.Open strSQL, dcBank
If Not rsBank.EOF Then
  ObjectContext.SetAbort
  strAbortReason = "You have used the number of an existing account. "
End If
rsBank.Close
Set rsBank = Nothing
```

To do this, we Open a recordset using a SQL command that selects any account whose AccountID field is the same as the 'candidate' account ID. If EOF is True, then the recordset is empty and that's enough to prove that the bank teller has submitted a valid (unique) account ID. Otherwise, we abort the transaction.

At this point, we're ready to insert a new record into the Account table, containing the new account ID and name. For this, we just create a SQL INSERT command and execute it using the Connection object's Execute method:

```
strSQL = ""
strSQL = "INSERT INTO Account (AccountID, HolderName)" & _
         "VALUES ('" & Session("strAcctNo") & "', '" & strAcctName & "');"
dcBank.Execute strSQL
```

Now we can use the Server.Execute method to execute the contents of SetBalance.asp page, which takes care of setting the initial balance for the new account:

```
If dblInitialBalance >=0 Then
  Server.Execute "SetBalance.asp"
End If
```

As we've already discussed, SetBalance.asp has the @TRANSACTION=Supported directive, so that the entire page is contained within the scope of the existing transaction. This means that, if the transaction is aborted for any reason, then the changes made by SetBalance.asp will be rolled back along with the other state changes in this transaction.

The contents of the page are very simple. We use an ADO Connection object to open a connection to the database (we can't use the existing Connection object from CreateAcct.asp, because the object's scope does not span across the pages). Then we write a SQL INSERT command that inserts a new record into the Register table, containing the details of the initial balance of the account, and we execute it using the Connection object's Execute method:

```
<%
  Dim dcBank, strSQL
```

```
    Set dcBank = Server.CreateObject("ADODB.Connection")
    dcBank.Open strConn

    strSQL = "INSERT INTO Register " & _
             "(AccountID, CheckNumber, Transdate, TransType, " & _
             "TransNote, Amount, PriorBalance, ResultingBalance) " & _
          "VALUES ('" & Session("strAcctNo") & "', 0, '" & Date & _
             "', 'D', 'Initial Deposit', " & CDbl(Session("dblInitialBalance")) & _
             ", 0, " & _
             Session("dblInitialBalance") & ");"
    dcBank.Execute strSQL

    dcBank.Close
    Set dcBank = Nothing
%>
```

The SQL command looks fairly illegible here; but once you work out the ASP, string concatenation and line continuation characters it might look something like this:

```
"INSERT INTO Register (AccountID, CheckNumber, Transdate, TransType, TransNote,
                        Amount, PriorBalance, ResultingBalance)
 VALUES ('1234-1234', 0, '09/30/1999', 'D', 'Initial Deposit', 325.00, 0, 325.00);"
```

Now, back in CreateAcct.asp all that remains is to write the onTransactionComplete() and onTransactionAbort() routines. They are very similar to the event handlers that we saw in the previous example, so we will not cover them again here. Suffice it to say that, in this example, we use them simply to report success of failure to the user and to tidy up any remaining objects.

COM+ Components

We've already talked about how COM+ can manage and control our transactions, and how it can tell the resource manager to set about undoing database changes when a transaction is aborted – and we've even seen a couple of examples that use this facility.

But (as we've also mentioned), COM+ does a whole lot more than that. So in this final section, we'll take a quick look at some of the other facilities that Microsoft have built into COM+ – facilities which are now an integral part of the Windows 2000 operating system. As we'll see, COM+ is really an all-round management system for the components that we use in our applications.

Finally, we'll complete our short discussion on components and transactions by returning to our Internet Banking scenario once more. We'll rewrite the cash transaction problem one last time, drawing together the techniques of componentization and transactional processing, and using COM+ to manage both of these aspects.

> We don't intend to give a complete introduction to COM+ here – indeed, the expanse of COM+ as a subject easily justifies the many books that do and will exist on COM+. But we will meet Component Services, and see how Microsoft has given us a platform for our transactional and componentization ideas to fit naturally together.

COM+ and Component Services

We've mentioned in passing that in COM+, Microsoft have taken the transaction and component management capabilities of Microsoft Transaction Server (MTS) and integrated them with COM – along with 'some other bits and pieces of functionality'. So let's break it up a bit, and try to understand some of the different facilities that COM+ provides.

COM+ as a Transaction Manager

As we've seen, we can use COM+ as a **transaction manager** for our applications. As we saw earlier, this means (for example) that COM+ is able to listen to our transacted applications as each transaction is performed; it can analyze the votes cast and determine whether the transaction should be committed or aborted; and it can help us to manage the commit and rollback procedures within our durable data (in our data stores).

In the examples we've seen in this chapter so far, we've seen this in action – in each case we saw a simple ASP application that used COM+ to manage the transactions involved.

COM+ as a Component Manager

Moreover, COM+ can also manage the components themselves. So, how would we use COM+ as a **component manager**? Well, we can tell COM+ to create a deployment unit called a **COM+ Application** (or just an **Application**). Then, we install the necessary components into the COM+ Application. Then, when some other ordinary application (such as an ASP application) needs to use the objects of such a component, COM+ manages the instantiation of these objects for us.

So, if you like, these COM+ components belong to COM+ itself (by virtue of being installed into a COM+ Application) – and COM+ manages the way that they are farmed out to the applications that require them.

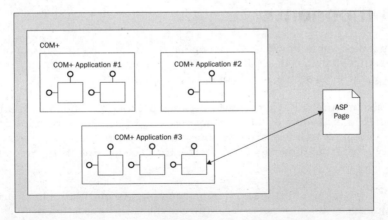

Further, if these components require transactional support, then COM+ is able to act as transaction manager to those components. We tell COM+ about the transactional needs of a component at the time we install the component into COM+ (we'll do exactly that in our example shortly). This means, for example, that we can call a transactional component from an ASP page, and we don't need to set the @TRANSACTION directive in our ASP page. Because the component is installed into a COM+ Application, COM+ will automatically act as the transaction manager for the component.

We haven't used this technique so far in this chapter. In a moment, we'll see an example that uses a transacted component, installed into a COM+ Application, to perform a cash transfer. We'll see that the ASP page that uses this component doesn't need to concern itself with transactions at all – the COM+ Application does it all for us.

COM+ as a Security Manager

COM+ also provides a number of security features for the components that are installed into the COM+ Applications. There are automatic security features, which can be added and configured using the Component Services administrative tool that we'll meet in a moment. Other security features can be integrated directly into the development of the component. COM+ also allows us to implement **role-based security** – this is the central feature of COM+ security. It allows us to set our security preferences for individual methods of a component, so that we can allow some methods to be accessible to all users, but allow other methods to be accessible to only certain privileged users.

COM+ Services

In addition to the 'integration' of COM and MTS, COM+ also brings a number of COM-related facilities, called **services**. A service is some facility that is provided by COM+, and which the installed component can choose to use when it is called. For example, if the component can generate COM+ events, then COM+ provides support for this by loading and initializing the appropriate set of libraries at runtime, when the component is called. These libraries are COM+ services.

We've skimmed over the main points of COM+ here. A detailed discussion of COM+ is beyond the scope of this book. One popular book that covers the basics of COM+ in more detail is Understanding COM+ *(Microsoft Press, ISBN 0-735606-66-8).*

The Component Services Snap-In

So how do we control and configure the COM+ Applications, COM+ Services and all the other things provided by COM+? The easy answer lies in the Microsoft Management Console (MMC). Microsoft have provided a snap-in, called **Component Services**, which snaps into the MMC shell and gives us easy access to all the different areas of COM+.

Let's have a look at the Component Services snap-in now. The easiest way to open this snap-in is from the Start menu There, select Programs | Administrative Tools | Component Services. This will automatically start up the MMC shell, with the Component Services snap-in (and a couple of other snap-ins) within:

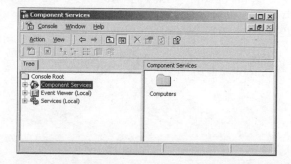

This is an easy-to-use interface that allows us to configure our COM+ components and other aspects of COM+. The pane on the left of this dialog works just like a folder structure in Windows Explorer. Expand the **Component Services** node a few levels, until you see something like this:

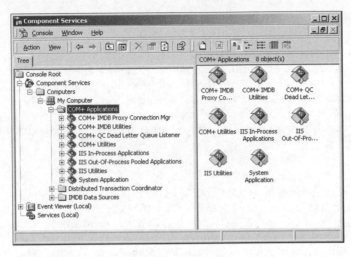

As you can see, there are a number of nodes under the **My Computer** node, and one of them is **COM+ Applications**. Under here, we can access for all the COM+ Applications that are installed into COM+ on this computer.

As we mentioned above, a COM+ Application is a set of COM components. Generally, the components within a particular COM+ Application perform related functions. By grouping a set of components together in this way (i.e. within a COM+ Application), we can perform administration and configuration on the entire group of components as a whole, if we wish.

You should find that a number of COM+ Applications already exist in your **Component Services** window – as they do here, on my machine. In the example below we'll be creating a new COM+ Application of our own, adding a component to it, configuring it and then using it in an ASP page.

An Example using a COM+ Application

Now, we'll complete this chapter by using the techniques of componentization and transactions all-in-one. Our example returns to the cash transfer problem in our Bank scenario. We'll take a ready-made component that encapsulates the cash transfer logic, the data access logic *and* the transaction logic, and we'll install it into a COM+ Application; then we'll use that component within a non-transactional ASP page.

Before we look at the example, let's just think briefly about the process that we would go through when creating components for installation into COM+. It is, essentially, a three-step process:

❑   Designing and building the components

❑   Creating the COM+ Application, and installing the components

❑   Configuring the COM+ Application to meet our requirements

You'll be able to see these three steps in the example that follows – except that we're going to take a short-cut for the first step by using a ready-written component.

Our Ready-Written BankAccount Component

We've done a little component design and creation, back in Chapter 16 – we used the Windows Script Component tool to build the script-based components CarpetPricer.wsc and BankAccount.wsc, and we used them within ASP pages. But for this example we'll use something a little more robust than a script-based component.

In fact, in this example we're going to use a component called WroxBank.Account, which is contained in the dynamic link library file WroxBank.dll. This component was written using Visual Basic 6.0, and compiled into the DLL (the DLL is the executable version of the component). Components written in languages such as Visual Basic, Java, and C++ are generally more robust than their script-based counterparts – they're more easy to transport, more efficient and considerably easier to install into a COM+ Application (which expects a file such as a .dll or and .exe).

We're not going to show you how to program this component in Visual Basic. If you'd like to know how it works, you can take a look at the WroxBank.vbp file that contains the source code for the component. If you like, you can use the source files provided to compile the .dll for yourself – you'll need a copy of the Visual Basic 6.0 development software. Alternatively, we've provided the compiled WroxBank.dll file too, so you don't need to compile it if you don't want to.

The source files and the .dll are available along with the other files for this chapter at http://www.wrox.com.

The WroxBank.Account component will support the ability to transfer funds from one account to another, through a single method called Transfer. The syntax for this method is as follows:

blnSuccess = objBank.Transfer(strDB, srcAcctID, destAcctID, amount)

Here, the *strDB* parameter expects a database connection string – we'll use this parameter to pass the connection string for the database that holds our bank account information. The *srcAcctID* and *destAcctID* parameters expect the account IDs of the two accounts involved in the transfer. The *amount* parameter represents the amount of money being transferred from the source to the destination. Note that the method will return a Boolean value, which indicates whether or not the transfer was successful.

OK, that's all we need to set up this example and get it running.

Try It Out – Creating a COM+ Application, Installing a Component and Using it in ASP

There are lots of steps in this example, but as you'll see it's not difficult to complete. First, we'll register the `WroxBank.dll` file on our machine. Then we'll use two wizards – the first will help us to create a COM+ Application, and the second will help us to install our component into the new COM+ Application. Then we'll configure the component within the COM+ Application (to tell COM+ that the component requires transaction support); and finally we'll test it using a simple ASP page.

1. We'll be using the Bank database that we've used in the other examples in this chapter. Therefore, you'll need to ensure that your `Bank.mdf` file is contained within the `C:\MSSQL7\Data` folder (or, if you're using SQL Server, that your **Bank** database is set up on the SQL Server machine).

2. Take a copy of the `WroxBank.dll` file, which you'll find with the other files for this chapter, and save it to a convenient folder on your hard disk. (Alternatively, use Visual Basic to compile `WroxBank.dll` for yourself, using Visual Basic 6.0.)

3. Now we need to register the component. To do this, select Start | Run. In the resulting dialog, type RegSvr32 *<path>*\WroxBank.dll. For example, if you saved `WroxBank.dll` into a folder called `C:\Wrox\BegASP` folder, then you should type something like this:

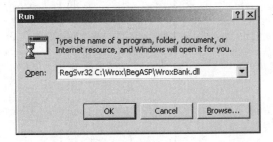

When you click on OK, the component should be added to your machine's registry. Then you'll receive the following confirmation of success:

Click **OK** again to continue. Now the component is ready to be installed into COM+.

4. The next step is to create a new COM+ Application, which can contain any components that we wish to group together. If you haven't already done so, open up the Component Services snap-in (by selecting Start | Programs | Administration Tools | Component Services). Expand the nodes on the left of the dialog until you can see the COM+ Applications node. Then highlight the COM+ Applications node, and from the Action menu select New | Application:

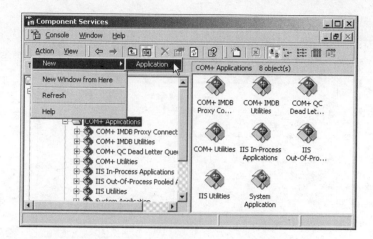

This will launch the **COM Application Installation Wizard**, which will walk us through the creation of our new COM+ Application.

5. The first screen in the wizard is just a splash-screen; just click **Next**. The second screen asks us whether our new COM+ Application is based on a pre-built Application, or should be a new one. We are creating a new application, so select **Create an empty application** (this will immediately take you to the next step of the wizard):

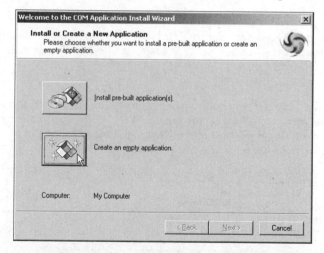

6. Now we need to enter the name of our new COM+ Application – type the name Bank into the text box. We also need to specify whether we want a **Server** or **Library** application. The default is **Server**, which means that our installed components and the ASP application that calls it would run in different pieces of processing space on our machine. That's fine for our application, so select **Server application** and click **Next**.

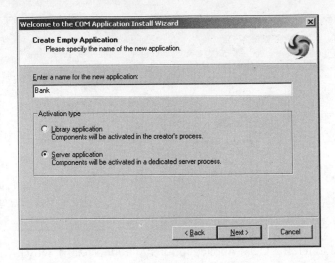

*If we'd opted for a **Library application**, then the components of the application would run in the same piece of processing space as the calling application. A Server application provides a slight performance penalty, because calls to the component must cross the boundary between pieces of processing space. However, they are a little safer because if one part of the application crashes then the other parts of the application are protected and will not crash.*

*Also, we can **Stop** and re-**Start** a Server COM+ Application without affecting the web server, which means that it's much easier to change and retest the component repeatedly if necessary.*

7. The next step is to determine the 'user identity' under which the application will execute. For our example, and for most of the COM+ applications that will be used with ASP, we will select **Interactive User**. This means that the incoming user's credentials will be used for the component:

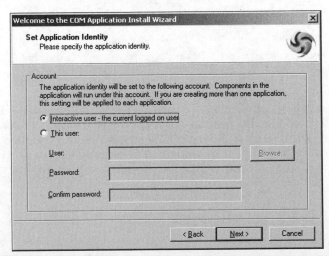

Then click **Next**. That's the last step of the wizard – the final page just informs you that the COM+ Application is created (so just click **Finish**). If you return to look at the **Component Services** snap-in, you'll see that there is a new node called **Bank**, under the **COM+ Applications** node.

8. Now we can install our components into the COM+ Application. Expand the tree a little further until you can see the **Components** node underneath it (the right-hand pane of the window displays any components installed in the application – at this stage it will be empty). Highlight the **Components** node, and from the **Action** menu select **New | Component**:

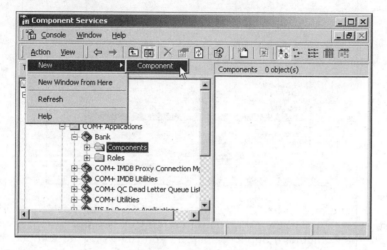

9. This will fire up the **Add Component Wizard** (again, the first screen is just a splash-screen, so click **Next**). This wizard helps us to install components and event classes into our COM+ Application. We're not concerned with COM+ events or new components – we're going to install our `WroxBank` component, which is already registered. Therefore, in the second screen select the second button:

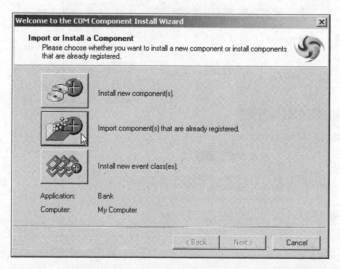

10. After a short wait, the next screen will display a list of all components that are registered on the system (and which aren't part of a COM+ Application). Place a check in the Details checkbox – this will allow us to view the filenames and CLSIDs of the components. Now scroll though the list until you find the WroxBank.Account component that we just installed. Click on the component to install it into our COM+ Application. Then click Next:

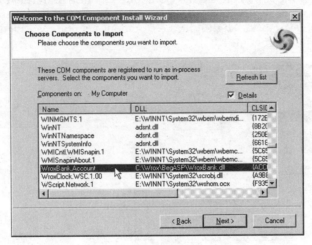

11. That's the end of the wizard. The final screen tells us that we've provided enough information to install the component into our COM+ Application. If you return once more to the Component Services snap-in, you'll see that our component has appeared under the Components node.

12. Now we can modify the properties of any components in the COM+ Application. To do this, highlight the WroxBank.Account node in the snap-in, and from the Action menu select Properties:

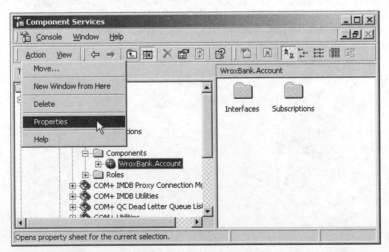

This will bring up the WroxBank.Account Properties dialog. All we need to do here is set the transaction properties of this component; so choose the Transactions tab. Since we want this component to *always* work inside of a transaction, we will set the Transaction Support radio button to Required. Then press OK to close this property page:

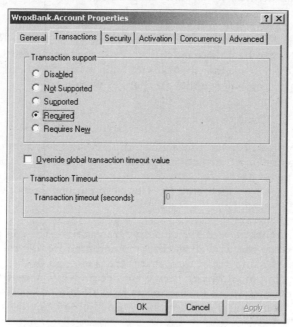

13. Now our component is ready to use, so we'll write an ASP page that will use it. Here's a very simple page to test it – you can build a more complex page in the style of earlier pages In this chapter if you like. Open up your favorite editor, create a new file (which we'll call ComponentBank.asp), and enter the following code:

```
<!-- #INCLUDE FILE="BankConnection.asp" -->
<%
  Dim objAcct, strDB
  Set objAcct = Server.CreateObject("WroxBank.Account")
  strDB = strConn

  Dim srcAcct, destAcct, amt, blnSuccess
  srcAcct = "9832-5830"
  destAcct = "4735-9275"
  amt = 225

  blnSuccess = objAcct.Transfer(strDB, srcAcct, destAcct, amt)
  Response.Write "<P>Transaction Success = " & blnSuccess & "</P>"
  Set objAcct = Nothing
%>
```

14. Save this file as `ComponentBank.asp`, into your `\inetpub\wwwroot\BegASPFiles` folder. Then use your browser to view the page, and observe the results. If the account IDs in the code were valid, the source account balance was large enough to support the transasction, and the other business rules were met, then the transfer should complete successfully.

15. Change the amt variable in the `ComponentBank.asp` file to a number greater than the balance in the source account; or change the account details to specify an invalid account ID. Now reload the page in your browser so that another transfer is attempted. You will see that the transaction is aborted – and if you observe the values in the database, you will see that no changes were made.

How It Works

Since the COM+ component has its transaction property set to **Required**, it will always be executed within the scope of a transaction. Note that our sample ASP page does not have a `@TRANSACTION` parameter at the top – this means that there is not an existing transaction when the page calls the component's methods. The **Required** parameter on the component will force a new transaction to be started.

So now within this component, we have an active transaction. The component performs interactions with the database, as well as checking and maintaining the business rules (such as validating the account IDs and confirming that there is enough in the source account to support the transfer without going overdrawn). If an error occurs while accessing the database, or if one of the bank system's business rules is violated as a result of a database operation, then COM+ will detect the failure and will arrange for the transaction to be aborted.

When the transaction is aborted, COM+ steps in and ensures that any changes made to the database are rolled back. This is just like what happened when we were controlling th transaction from the ASP page, in the earlier examples of this chapter– when the `@TRANSACTION` directive is set to `REQUIRED` and `SetAbort` is called.

So by simply writing transaction-aware components, and then configuring these components to require a transaction, we can take advantage of transaction processing without having to worry about them in our ASP pages.

This technique has great advantages in a development shop, where one team is responsible for component building, and another team is responsible for ASP script-writing. The component builders can have all of the transaction knowledge, and build that knowledge into the design and installation of their components. All the ASP developers have to do is write ASP pages that use these components, and all of the transaction handling is transparent to them.

Summary

COM+ provides the capability for managing transactions, components, and other aspects of application design. These capabilities are built into COM+ and exist as part of the Windows 2000 operating system. This means that we developers don't have to think too hard about these issues when we're designing and writing our ASP applications (or any other kind of application!).

What did we learn about COM+ and transactions in this chapter? We saw that:

- A transaction is a set of (usually related) tasks, which are executed either all-together or not-at-all

- The completion or failure of the transaction is decided by a 'voting system' – each part of the transaction can elect that the transaction should 'complete' or 'abort'. The transaction will complete *only* if there are no votes to abort, and if there are no system crashes

- The `ObjectContext` object provides us with the functionality for voting one the transaction's outcome – via its `SetComplete` and `SetAbort` methods

- There are two event handlers – `onTransactionComplete` and `onTransactionAbort` – which handle the `TransactionComplete` and `TransactionAbort` events that are fired when a transaction completes or aborts

- We can employ transactions directly in our ASP pages by using the `@TRANSACTION` directive in our pages. This tells COM+ to provide an `ObjectContext` object for the page, and to judge on the outcome of the transaction

- We can write components that encapsulate tasks that require a transaction. We can install these components into a COM+ Application, indicating the transactional requirements of the component. Then COM+ will manage the instances of the component, its transactional activity, and other aspects such as security

In fact, by allowing COM+ to manage our component instances and monitor our transactions, we achieve a more scalable system. How? Because COM+ uses a **pool** to hold component instances that aren't being used within a transaction, and to can manage these instances by handing them out when ever an application requires one. This means that fewer component instances are created overall, which means a lower burden on our server resources. This in turn means that our application will be more scalable, because our resources will be able to serve a greater number of users.

In the next chapter, we'll move away from COM+ and onto another exciting new technology – XML. We'll take a look at what XML is, and we how can use it within our ASP applications to deliver data to our users.

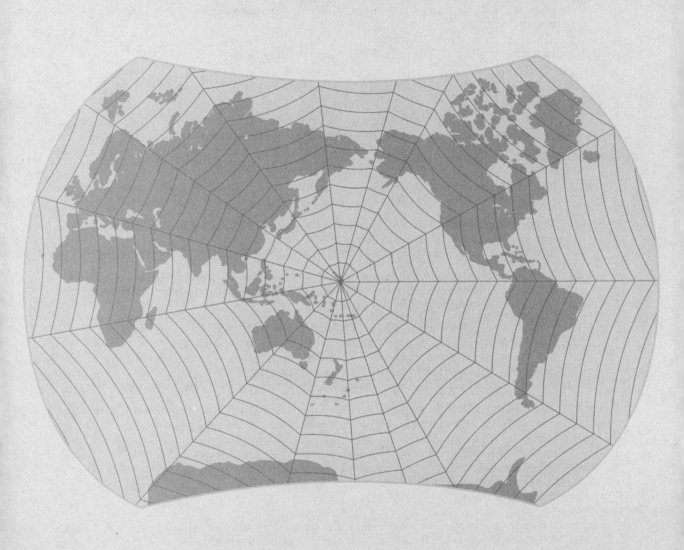

An Introduction to XML

Over the past couple of years, the acronym XML, which stands for **Extensible Markup Language**, has been cropping up with increasing frequency. As it has gained more coverage, the spin-doctors have been out in force, claiming that it will solve all manner of programming problems. While some of these claims have yet to be implemented, there are certainly some very strong reasons why you should be learning it, not least that it could just make your life a lot easier.

The first thing to make clear is that, assuming you are familiar with HTML, XML offers a new way of tagging (or marking up) your data that is so straight forward you will wonder why it is making such big waves. Yet, while HTML and XML may look very similar, they are in fact quite different.

In this chapter we will see what all the fuss is about. It will introduce XML and get you used to writing XML, styling XML for the Web, and how to access and manipulate data in an XML document. It will also cover some of the advantages to using XML in your web development, and how ASP helps harness the benefits of XML.

So in this chapter we will see:

- ❑ Some background to help us understand the importance of XML
- ❑ What XML is and how to write an XML document
- ❑ Some of the associated specifications surrounding XML
- ❑ How to style XML for display in a browser
- ❑ How to get details from an XML file using the Document Object Model
- ❑ How to create an XML document on the server
- ❑ How to create XML documents from a web page
- ❑ How to create XML from a relational database
- ❑ How to use IE5 to display and navigate through XML documents

Before we dive into using XML and showing you how it can be used, it would be helpful to have a quick look at markup languages in general, what markup is, and the history that has lead to XML.

What is a Markup Language?

While you may not realize it, we come across markup every day. Quite simply, markup refers to anything put on a document that adds special meaning or provides extra information. For example, highlighted or bolded text is a form of markup.

But unless others understand our markup it is of little use, so we need a set of rules encompassing the following points for it to be understood:

❑ To declare what constitutes markup

❑ To declare exactly what our markup means

A **markup language** is such a set of rules.

The Characteristics of Markup Languages

It is possible to classify markup as one of four types:

❑ **Stylistic Markup.** This indicates how the document is to be presented. When we use bolding or italics on a word processor it is stylistic markup. In HTML the <FONT>, <I>, <B>, and <U> tags are all stylistic markup.

❑ **Structural Markup.** This informs us how the document should be structured. The <Hn> (where n is a number), <P> and the <DIV> tags are examples of structural markup, which indicate a heading, paragraph and container section respectively.

❑ **Semantic Markup.** This tells us something about the content of the data, as such <TITLE> and <CODE> are examples of semantic markup in HTML.

❑ **Functional Markup.** This adds functionality to the data that is marked up, such as hyper links and pointers, sound files etc.

Markup languages define the markup rules that add meaning to the style, structure, and content of documents. They are the grammar and the syntax which specify how a language should be 'spoken'. A familiar example is HTML – which is a markup language that enables you to write a document for display on the Web.

Tags and Elements

Even those of us who are familiar with HTML still often get the meaning of tags and elements mixed up. Just to clarify, tags are the angled brackets (known as delimiters), and the text between them. Here are some examples of tags used in HTML:

<P> is a tag that marks the beginning of a new paragraph
<I> is a tag indicating that the following text should be rendered in italic type
</I> is a tag that indicates the end of a section of text to be rendered in italic type

Elements, however, refer to the tags *plus* their content. So the following is an example of an element:

```
<B>Here is some bold text</B>
```

In general terms, a tag is a label that tells a user-agent (such as a browser) to do something to whatever is encased in the tags.

> *A user-agent is anything that acts on your behalf. You are a user agent working for your boss, your computer is a user agent working for you, your browser is a user agent working for you and your computer, and so it goes on.*

Empty elements which don't have closing tags, such as the `<IMG>` element in HTML, have to be treated differently in XML to make up for them not having a closing tag – but don't worry about that for now, we will come back to them later.

The following diagram illustrates the parts of an element:

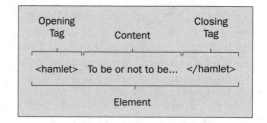

Attributes

Any tag can have an attribute as long as it is defined. They take the form of **name/value pairs** (also referred to as attribute/value pairs), in that the element can be given an attribute (with a name), and the attribute must carry a text value surrounded by quotation marks. They take the form:

```
<tagname attribute="value">
```

For example, in HTML 4.0 the `<BODY>` tag can take the following attributes:

```
CLASS ID      DIR       LANG      STYLE     TITLE
BACKGROUND    BGCOLOR   ALINK     LINK      VLINK    TEXT.
```

So, for example, in HTML BODY could take the following attributes:

```
<BODY BGCOLOR="#000000" ALINK="#999999" LINK="#990099" VLINK="#888888"
TEXT="#999999">
```

Examples of Markup Languages

Let's take a quick look at three markup languages, so that we can see where XML fits into the picture. We'll look at SGML, HTML and of course XML.

SGML

Standardized Generalized Markup Language (SGML) is a markup language that is used to create other markup languages. The most famous language written in SGML is HTML, which we all know and love for its use on the Web. HTML is known as an **application** of SGML. The problem with SGML is that it is very complicated – hence our interest in XML. XML is a simplified version of SGML, retaining much of SGML's functionality, yet designed for use on the web.

Back in 1986 SGML became an international standard (ISO 8879) for defining markup languages, before the Web was even conceived (in fact, SGML has been in existence since the late 1960's). Its purpose was to describe markup languages, by allowing the author to provide formal definitions for each of the elements and attributes in the language, thus allowing authors to create their own tags that related to their content. In effect, they could write their own markup language using SGML, which is exactly what happens when a new version of HTML is created. The World Wide Web Consortium (W3C) makes up the new tags, and it is up to browser manufacturers to implement them.

As a language SGML is very powerful, but with its power comes complexity, and many of the features are rarely used. It is very difficult to interpret an SGML document without the definition of the markup language, kept in a **Document Type Definition** (DTD). The DTD is where all the rules for the language are kept in SGML; after all you cannot make up your own markup language without specifying how it should be used. The DTD has to be sent with, or included in, the SGML document so that the custom created tags can be understood. In particular, it was adopted in industries where large amounts of documentation had to be marked up.

HTML

As we just saw, HTML was originally an SGML application. It describes how information is to be prepared for the World Wide Web. HTML is just a set of SGML rules and as such it also has a DTD. In fact there are several DTDs, ones for loose and tight structured HTML, ones for different versions, and so on. Being far simpler than SGML, and a fraction of its size, HTML is very easy to learn – a factor that quickly made it popular and widely adopted by all sorts of people.

It is common knowledge that Tim Berners-Lee created HTML in 1991 as a way of marking up technical papers so that they could easily be organized and transferred across **different platforms** for the scientific community. This is not meant to be a history lesson, but it is important to understand the concepts behind HTML if we are to appreciate the power of XML. The idea was to create a set of tags that could be transferred between computers so that others could render the document in a useful format. For example:

```
<H1> This is a primary heading</H1>
<H2>This is a secondary heading</H2>
<PRE>This is text whose formatting should be preserved</PRE>
<P>The text between these two tags is a paragraph</P>
```

Back then the scientific community had little concern over the aesthetic appearance of their documents. What mattered to them was that they could transfer their documents and that the meaning would be preserved. They weren't worried about the color of their fonts or the exact size of their primary heading!

HTML uses a protocol called HTTP (Hypertext Transfer Protocol) to transfer information across the Internet. It is one of a number of protocols used on the Internet, which are collectively knows as the Internet Protocol Suite.

What gives HTTP the edge over other protocols is the relative ease with which it can be used to retrieve another document. The combination of an easy-to-use protocol and a simple to learn language is an attractive proposition – and one that has ensured the rapid spread of systems implementing HTML and HTTP.

As HTML usage exploded and web browsers started to become readily available, non-scientific users soon started to create their own pages *en masse*. These non-scientific users became increasingly concerned with the aesthetic presentation of their material. Manufacturers of browsers, used to view web sites, were all too ready to offer different tags that would allow web page authors to display their documents with more creativity than was possible using plain ASCII text. Netscape were the first, adding the familiar <FONT> tag, which allowed users to change the actual text font as well as its size and weighting. This triggered a rapid expansion in the number of tags that browsers would support.

With the new tags, however, came new problems. Different browsers implemented the new tags inconsistently. Today we have sites that display signs saying that they are **Best Viewed Through Netscape Navigator** or are **Designed For Internet Explorer**. On top of all this, we now expect to be able to produce web pages that resemble documents created on the most sophisticated Desktop Publishing systems.

Meanwhile the browser's potential as a new application platform was quickly recognized, and web developers started creating distributed applications for businesses, using the Internet as a medium for information and financial transactions.

Drawbacks of HTML

While the widespread adoption of HTML propelled the rise in the number of people on the web, users wanted to do an ever-increasing variety of new and more complex things, and weaknesses with HTML became apparent:

❑ **HTML has a fixed tag set.** You cannot create your own tags that can be interpreted by others.

❑ **HTML is a presentation technology.** It doesn't carry information about the **meaning** of the content held within its tags

❑ **HTML is "flat".** You cannot specify the **importance** of tags, so a hierarchy of data cannot be represented.

❑ **Browsers are being used as an application platform.** HTML does not provide the power needed to create advanced web applications, at least not at the level at which developers are currently aiming. For example, it does not readily offer the ability for advanced retrieval of information from documents marked up in HTML and it is not easy to process the data within the document, because the text is only marked up for display.

❑ **High traffic volumes.** HTML documents that are used as applications clog up the Internet with high volumes of client-server traffic. For example, sending large general sets of data across a network when only small amounts are required.

While HTML has proven a very useful way of marking up documents for display in a web browser, a document marked up in HTML tells us very little about its actual content. For most documents to be useful in a business environment, there is a need to know about the document's content. When a document contains content details, then it is possible to perform generalized processing and retrieval on that file. This means that it is no longer suitable for just one purpose – rather than just being used for display on the web, it can also be used as part of an application. Marking up data in a way that tells us about its content makes it **self-describing**. This means that the data can be re-used in different situations. SGML made this possible, but it is now also possible with XML – which is far simpler and rapidly gaining in popularity.

How XML Came About

The major players in the browser market made it clear that they had no intention of fully supporting SGML. Furthermore, its complexity prevented many people from learning it. So, moves were made to create a simplified version for use on the web, signaling a return to documents being marked up according to their content. In the same way that HTML was designed for technical papers, with tags such as the heading and paragraph tags, there was a move to allow people greater flexibility. They wanted to create their own tags and markup languages so that they could markup whatever they wanted, however they wanted, with the intention of making it self-describing.

The W3C saw the worth of creating a simplified version of SGML for use on the Web, and agreed to sponsor the project. When SGML was put under the knife, several of the non-essential parts were cut, thus molding it into a new language called XML. This lean alternative is far more accessible, its specification running to around a fifth of the size of the specification that defined SGML.

What is XML?

XML got the name **Extensible Markup Language** because it is not a fixed format like HTML. While HTML has a fixed set of tags that the author can use, XML users can create their own tags (or use those created by others, if applicable) so that they actually describe the content of the element. So, let's dive straight in and look at an example.

At its simplest level XML is just a way of marking up data so that it is self-describing. What do we mean by this? Well, as a publisher Wrox makes details about their books available in HTML over the web. For example, in HTML we might display details about this book like so:

```
<DOCTYPE HTML PUBLIC "-//W3C//DTD HTML 4.0 //EN">
<HTML>
<HEAD>
   <TITLE>Beginning ASP 3.0</TITLE>
</HEAD>

<BODY>
<H1>Beginning ASP 3.0</H1>
   <H3>ISBN 1-861003-38-2</H3>
```

```
<H4>Authors</H4><H4>Brian Francis, Chris Ullman, Dave Sussman, John Kauffman, Jon
Duckett, Juan Llibre</H4>

<P>US $49.99<BR>

<P>ASP is a powerful technology for dynamically creating web site content. Learn how
to create exciting pages that are tailored to your audience. Enhance your web/intranet
presence with powerful web applications.</P>

</BODY>
</HTML>
```

That's all you need to do if you want to put information about a book on a Web page. It will look something like this:

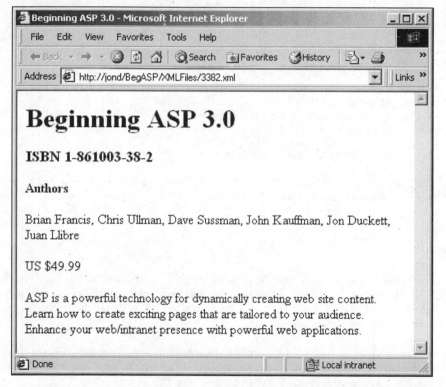

So, when we are building our web pages we have a lot of this data in HTML. As an up and coming ASP developer you are probably using script and generating content dynamically now, however you still have a lot of information marked up just for display on the web.

But the tags (or markup) don't give you any information about what you are displaying. There is no way that you can tell, from the tags, that you are displaying information about a book. With XML, however, you can create your own tags; they can actually describe whatever content you are marking up and hence the term 'self-describing data'.

So, how could we mark up the information in a more logical way, using XML, so that we know what we have in the file? In the following Try It Out, we will create our first XML document that mimics the data held in the above HTML example.

Try It Out – My First XML Document

All you need to create an XML document is a simple text editor; something like Notepad will do just fine for our first example.

1. Fire up your text browser and type in the following, which we will call books.xml. Make sure you type it in exactly as shown, since XML is case sensitive and spaces must be in the correct positions:

```xml
<?xml version="1.0"?>
<books>
<book>
    <title>Beginning ASP 3.0</title>
    <ISBN>1-861003-38-2</ISBN>
    <authors>
        <author_name>Brian Francis</author_name>
        <author_name>Chris Ullman</author_name>
        <author_name>Dave Sussman</author_name>
        <author_name>John Kauffman</author_name>
        <author_name>Jon Duckett</author_name>
        <author_name>Juan Llibre</author_name>
    </authors>
    <description> ASP is a powerful technology for dynamically creating web site
content. Learn how to create exciting pages that are tailored to your audience.
Enhance your web/intranet presence with powerful web applications.</description>
    <price US="$49.99"/>
</book>
</books>
```

2. Save our file as books.xml to any folder you want on your hard drive. It could be with the other directories on your web server, or it could be completely separate. I have placed all my XML files in a folder called XMLfiles as a subfolder to our BegASPFiles directory.

3. To open your XML file in Internet Explorer just use select Open from the file menu and browse to it. Or you can type in the URL. Here is how our XML version of the book details is displayed when we open it in IE5.

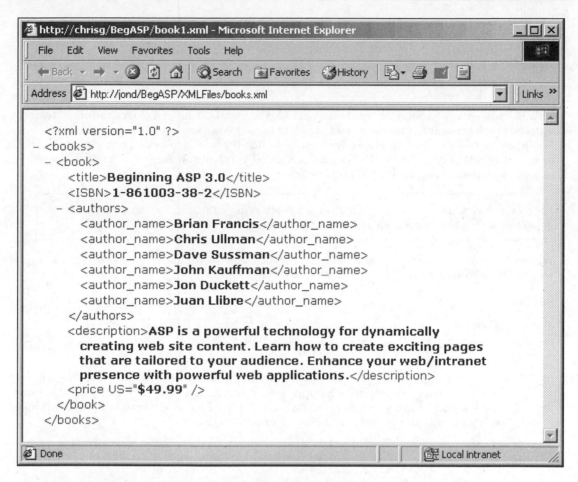

If you do not have a copy of IE5, you can download it for free from the Microsoft web site http://www.microsoft.com/ although it comes as standard with any Windows 2000 installation (but it doesn't require Windows 2000 to run – you could use it on Windows 98, for example).

How It Works

Let's go through our code step-by-step and take a look at exactly what is happening:

```
<?xml version="1.0"?>
```

This is the **XML prolog**. It tells the receiving application that they are getting an XML document compatible with version one of the XML specification. Note that the xml is in lowercase and that there are no white spaces between the question mark and the opening xml.

All XML documents must have a unique opening and closing tag; `<books>` is ours, as we have a file containing data about books:

```
<books>
  ...
</books>
```

This is known as the **root** element. Nearly all XML tags MUST have a corresponding closing tag; unlike HTML you cannot miss out end tags and expect your application to accept it. The only exception to this is called an **empty** element, in which there is no element content. An example of this in HTML would be an <IMG> tag. In XML, if you have an empty element you must add a slash before the closing delimiter, such as `<tag attribute="value" />`.

> Note that XML, unlike HTML, is case sensitive, so `<BOOK>`, `<Book>` and `<book>` would be treated as three different tags.

Within this we are describing data about a specific book, so we use an opening tag that explains what will be contained by the tag. Here we are using `<book>`.

```
<books>
<book>
  ...
</book>
</books>
```

In the same way that we made sensible opening and closing tags for the document using the `<books>` element, we use similarly descriptive tags to mark up some more details, this time the title of the book and its ISBN number (the one that is just above the bar code on the back of the book). These go inside the opening and closing `<book>` tags.

```
<title>Beginning ASP 3.0</title>
<ISBN>1-861003-38-2</ISBN>
```

As there are several authors on this book we put the list of authors in **nested** elements. We start with an opening `<authors>` tag and then nest inside this an `<author_name>` tag for each author. Again these go between the opening and closing `<book>` tags. In this example we put them under the ISBN.

```
<authors>
    <author_name>Brian Francis</author_name>
    <author_name>Chris Ullman</author_name>
    <author_name>Dave Sussman</author_name>
    <author_name>John Kauffman</author_name>
    <author_name>Jon Duckett</author_name>
    <author_name>Juan Llibre</author_name>
</authors>
```

This is a very important aspect of XML as data, because it allows us to create **hierarchical** data records. This structure would not fit easily into the row and table model of relational databases (without the use of linked tables), whereas it fits fine in our text file.

Next, we added the description of the book. Here we are using an element called `<description>`, although it could equally be something like `<precis>`, `<details>` or `<synopsis>`.

```
<description> ASP is a powerful technology for dynamically creating web site
content. Learn how to create exciting pages that are tailored to your audience.
Enhance your web/intranet presence with powerful web applications.</description>
```

We then added the price of the book to the document. Here you can see that we are using an empty element tag, with the closing slash in the tag. The currency and amount are actually held within the US attribute:

```
<price US="$49.99"/>
</book>
```

> Note that, in XML, all attribute values must be contained in quotes.

And that's all there is to it. You have just created your first XML document. It is plain text, its tags describe their content, and it is easily human-readable.

From this alone, you can tell that we are now talking about a book. The tags that meant little in our HTML version, such as `<H3>` and `<P>` are gone. In our HTML example, the ISBN number of the book was held in `<H3>` tags. When we markup the data about a book using XML, the ISBN number is in tags that are called `<ISBN>`. Now, this seems a lot more logical and it is simple to see what we are talking about.

But what about how it looks in a web browser? Browsers understand tags such as <H3>, referring to a category 3 heading, but we cannot expect a browser to understand tags that we are making ourselves. As XML is such a new technology, browsers are only just starting to support it; Internet Explorer 5 was the first browser to offer full support for the XML specification. For this reason, we will use Internet Explorer 5 for the examples in this chapter.

As it is, our XML version is not as attractive to look at as the HTML version but, as we said, HTML is language specifically for displaying data on the web. XML is just a way of marking up your data. It is still possible to make our XML documents more attractive using a style sheet. In fact there are several reasons why you might want to keep your data separate from styling rules. We shall look at these in a moment.

Technologies surrounding XML

As you might have guessed by now, if XML is just a way of describing your data, then there are several other things that you need to learn in order to use XML in the same way that we use HTML. These include:

❑ **Schemas** to define what these tags we are making up mean

❑ **Style sheets** for presenting the XML in an attractive way

❑ **Linking rules**, since XML has no built in hyper linking mechanism

But don't let this put you off. The advantages of using XML in certain situations easily outweigh the disadvantages of having to learn these new specifications. Before we learn some of the rules for writing XML and using the associated technologies, let's consider why it is so important.

The Data Revolution

As computers have found their way into more areas of our work and home life, we are storing ever-increasing amounts of information electronically. The tendency is to think of our business data mainly residing in relational databases, such as SQL Server, Oracle or DB2. The reality, however, is that we probably have more data in other formats:

- ❏ Quotes and reports in word processor formats, such as Word or Word Perfect
- ❏ Web pages in HTML
- ❏ Presentations in PowerPoint
- ❏ Mail and memos in mail servers such as Exchange and Notes

Some of this data is replicated and some of it is as good as lost, because not everyone knows how to access it. In addition, the ubiquity of the Internet has meant that we are trying to share more and more data with people in other physical places.

But what has all this got to do with XML? Going back to our book example, Wrox uses the type of book information we have just seen for many purposes: for web pages, trade catalogs, public catalogs, information for retail purchasers (bookshops) and so on. Many of these require the information in different formats so we need to be able to use the information in different ways.

The great news is that if we can mark up our book details just once in XML, and then we can re-purpose it. So, if we were to create an XML file containing all of our book catalog we would *not* need to put it in HTML for the web, and then individually mail the retailers with new book details, and so on. As we will see later in the chapter, we can just re-format the one XML source to suit each purpose.

Furthermore, if people want to find out about specific books, they could just collect information about those that they are interested in, rather than wasting bandwidth having to download a large file with a lot of irrelevant data. This is because we can easily offer a search facility that goes through `<title>` elements looking for the title they want.

Breaking Beyond Data Display

Up to now, it may seem as though we have been concentrating on how XML can be an alternative to HTML. Let's quickly expand this view a little and see the other effects of marking up our data as XML. We will then take a look at some of the associated specifications and techniques that you need to learn.

As XML is just stored and transferred as plain text it has strong advantages over most other data formats. For example, because it is pure text it is not a proprietary format that can only be used on certain platforms or with limited applications – **any** application could be written to accept pure text. Also, the data is easy to validate. You may recall that we said SGML uses a DTD to define the rules of any markup language written in SGML. Well, so does XML. This means that applications can verify the structure and content of an XML file.

This universality is one of the main reasons why XML is an ideal subject for applications, as well as displaying data on the web. It can transcend different operating systems and is ideal for distributed computing environments.

So, not only are we seeing XML being used as a way of presenting data that is marked up as HTML, it is also being used for many other purposes, including:

❑ Data transfer, from the book details we could send details of orders and financial transactions, in XML, that will be able to be understood by any platform

❑ Re-usable data storage in plain text files rather than pre-purposed formats, such as HTML and proprietary word processor files

❑ Interface descriptors for components, as you have seen with Windows Script Components

Of course, we cannot cover all of the reasons in this chapter. But what we will do is teach you enough to get you using XML. From this point you will be able to see how it can help you in your programming activities.

> *Perhaps you've already decided that XML is something you definitely need to find out more about. In which case you might want to refer to two other books published by Wrox Press: XML IE5 Programmer's Reference (ISBN 1-861001-57-6) and Professional XML (1-8610013-11-0).*

A Closer Look at Creating XML Documents

The XML 1.0 specification lays out two types of XML document, either **well-formed** or **valid**. The distinction between the two is simple:

❑ Well-formed documents comply with the rules of XML syntax. For example, all elements must have a corresponding end tag, or else have a closing slash in the empty elements; every document must have a unique opening and closing tag, etc.

❑ Valid documents are not only well-formed, they also comply with a DTD.

Well-Formed Documents

The XML 1.0 specification defines the syntax for XML. If you understand the specification properly, you can construct a program that will be able to 'look' at a document that is supposed to be XML. If the document conforms to the specification for XML, then the program can do further processing on it. The idea underlying the XML specification is, therefore, that XML documents should be intelligible as such, either to humans or processing applications.

Being well-formed is the minimum set of requirements (defined in the specification) that a document needs to satisfy in order for it to be considered an XML document. Here, requirements are a mixture of ensuring that the correct language terms are employed and that the document is logically coherent in the manner defined by the specification (in other words that the terms of the language are used in the right way). You can see the XML specification at http://www.w3.org/tr/xml/. There is also a helpful annotated version of the specification available at http://www.xml.com/axml/testaxml.htm.

So, what are these rules? You'll be pleased to hear that nearly everything we need to know about well-formed documents can be summed up in three rules:

- ❏ The document must contain one or more elements
- ❏ It must contain a uniquely named element, no part of which appears in the content of any other element. This is known as the root element
- ❏ All other elements must be kept within the root element and must be nested correctly

So, let's look at how we construct a well-formed document.

The XML Declaration

This is actually optional, although you are strongly advised to use it so that the receiving application knows that it is an XML document and also the version used (at the time of writing this was the only version).

```
<?xml version="1.0"?>
```

Note that the xml should be in lowercase. Note also that the XML declaration, when present, must not be preceded by any other characters (not even white space). As we saw previously, this declaration is also referred to as the XML prolog.

In this declaration, you can also define the language in which you have written your XML data. This is particularly important if your data contains characters that aren't part of the English ASCII character set. You can specify the language encoding using the optional encoding attribute:

```
<?xml version="1.0" encoding="iso-8859-1" ?>
```

The most common ones are shown in the following table:

Language	Character set
Unicode (8 bit)	UTF-8
Latin 1 (Western Europe, Latin America)	ISO-8859-1
Latin 2 (Central/Eastern Europe)	ISO-8859-2
Latin 3 (SE Europe)	ISO-8859-3
Latin 4 (Scandinavia/Baltic)	ISO-8859-4
Latin/Cyrillic	ISO-8859-5
Latin/Arabic	ISO-8859-6
Latin/Greek	ISO-8859-7
Latin/Hebrew	ISO-8859-8
Latin/Turkish	ISO-8859-9
Latin/Lappish/Nordic/Eskimo	ISO-8859-10
Japanese	EUC-JP or Shift_JIS

If you want to read more about internationalization, check out the W3Cs page on this topic at http://www.w3.org/International/.

Elements

As we have already seen, the XML document essentially consists of data marked up using tags. Each start-tag/end-tag pair, with the data that lies between them, is an element:

```
<mytag>Here we have some data</mytag>
```

The start and end tags must be exactly the same, except for the closing slash in the end-tag. Remember that they must be in the same case: <mytag> and <MyTag> would be considered as different tags.

The section between the tags that says, "Here we have some data", is called **character data**, while the tags either side are the **markup**. The character data can consist of any sequence of legal characters (conforming to the Unicode standard), except the start element character <. This is not allowed in case a processing application treats it as the start of a new tag. If you do need to include them you can represent them using the numeric character references in ASP; < for < and > for >.

The tags can start with a letter, an underscore (_), or a colon character (:), followed by any combination of letter, digits, hyphens, underscores, colons, or periods. The only exception is that you cannot start a tag with the letters XML in any combination of upper or lowercase letters. You are also advised not to start a tag with a colon, in case it gets treated as a namespace (something we shall meet later on).

Here is another example, marking up some details for a hardware store:

```
<inventory>
   <buckets>
      <bucket>
         <make>Addis</make>
         <capacity>3 litres</capacity>
      </bucket>
      <bucket>
         <make>Metro</make>
         <capacity>2.5 litres</capacity>
      </bucket>
   </buckets>
</inventory>
```

If you remember back to the three rules at the beginning of this section, you will be able to work out that this is a well-formed XML document. We have more than our one required element. We have a unique opening and closing tag: `<inventory>`, which is the root element. The elements are nested properly inside the root element.

Let's have a look at some more examples to help us get the idea how a well-formed XML document should be constructed.

At the simplest level we could have either:

```
<my_document></my_document>
```

or even

```
<my_document/>
```

To make sure that tags nest properly, there must be no overlap. So this is correct:

```
<parent>
   <child>Some character data</child>
</parent>
```

while this would be incorrect:

```
<bad_parent>
      <naughty_child>
            Some character data
</bad_parent>
      </naughty child>
```

This is because the closing `</naughty_child>` element is after the closing `</bad_parent>` element.

Attributes

Elements can have attributes. These are values that are passed to the application, but do not constitute part of the content of the element. Attributes are included as part of the element's opening tag, as in HTML. In XML all attributes must be enclosed in quote marks. For example:

```
<food healthy="yes">spinach</food>
```

Elements can have as many attributes as you want. So you could have:

```
<food healthy="no" tasty="yes" high_in_cholesterol="no">fries</food>
```

For well-formedness, however, you cannot repeat the attribute within an instance of the element. So you could not have:

```
<food tasty="yes" tasty="no">spinach</food>
```

Also, the string values between the quote marks can not contain the characters <, &, ' or ".

Other Features

There are also a number of other features of the XML specification that you need to learn if you progress to using XML frequently. Unfortunately there is not space to cover them all here. We will, however, briefly describe a few of them.

Entities

There are two categories of entity: **general entities** and **parameter entities**. Entities are usually used within a document as a way of avoiding having to type out long pieces of text several times within that document. They provide a way of associating a name with the long piece of text so that wherever you need to mention the text you just mention the name instead. As a result, if you have to modify the text, you only have to do it once (rather like the benefits offered by server-side includes).

CDATA Sections

CDATA sections can be used wherever character data can appear within a document. They are used to escape (or delimit) blocks of text that would otherwise be considered as markup. So if we wanted to include the whole of the following line, including the tags:

```
<to_be_seen>Always wear light clothing when walking in the dark</to_be_seen>
```

we could use a CDATA section like so:

```
<element>
<! [CDATA[ <to_be_seen>Always wear light clothing when walking in the
dark</to_be_seen> ]]>
</element>
```

And the whole line, including the opening and closing `<to_be_seen>` tags, would not be processed or treated as tags by the receiving application.

Comments

It is always good programming practice to comment your code – it so much easier to read if it is commented in a manner that helps explain, reminds you about, or simply points out salient sections of code. It is surprising how code that seemed perfectly clear when you wrote it can soon become a jumble when you come back to it. While the descriptive XML tags often help you understand your own markup, there are times when the tags alone are not enough.

The good news is that comments in XML use exactly the same syntax as those in HTML:

```
<!--I really should add a comment here to remind me about xxxxx -->
```

In order to avoid confusing the receiving application, you should not include either the - or -- character in your comment text.

Processing Instructions

These allow documents to contain instructions for applications using the XML data. They take the form:

```
<?NameOfTargetApplication      Instructions for Application?>
```

The target name cannot contain the letters xml in any combination of upper or lower case. Otherwise, you can create your own to work with the processing application (unless there are any predefined by the application at which you are targeting your XML).

In our next Try It Out, we will be looking at badly formed XML. We can tell a lot about whether our XML is well-formed by simply loading it into Internet Explorer 5. It has the ability to tell us about all sorts of errors (though it does let some slip). When you are first writing XML, it is very helpful to do this quick check so that you know your XML is well-formed.

Try It Out – Badly formed XML

1. Open up your `books.xml` file.

2. Remove the opening `<book>` tag

3. Save the file as `bad_book.xml`

4. Load it into Internet Explorer 5

Here is the result:

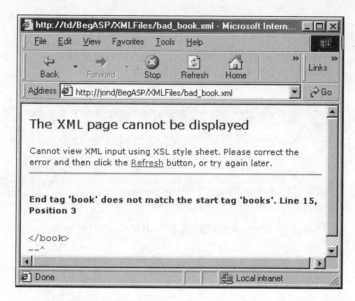

As you can see, the error message is pretty accurate. It more or less explicitly tells you that it was expecting an opening <book> tag. It certainly wouldn't take you long to find out what was wrong.

5. Put the opening book tag in again and change the line:

```
<title>Beginning ASP 3.0</title>
```

to

```
<title>Beginning ASP 3.0<title>
```

removing the closing slash.

6. Save the file again, and open it up in IE5 (or simply click the **Refresh** button, if you have it open already). You should get a result like this:

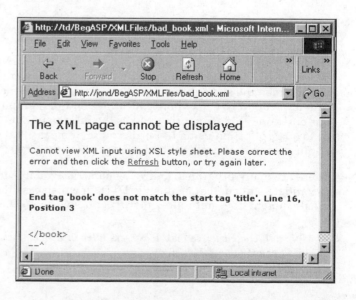

Again, we are not given the exact error, but IE was expecting a closing `<title>` tag, which it did not receive.

7. Finally, correct the closing `<title>` tag, and remove the opening quote form the US price attribute. Save the file and refresh your browser. This time you get the exact error:

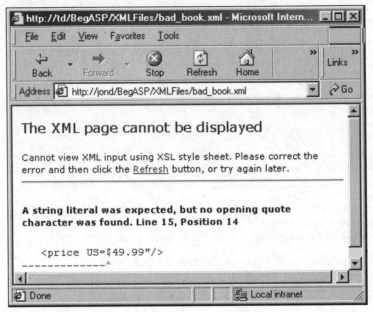

While it is not the most elegant way to test code, it certainly does help find errors quickly. If you have made more than one error, just correct your mistakes one at a time and watch the error messages change.

Valid Documents

As we mentioned earlier, valid documents are well-formed documents that conform to a DTD. When we read a book, manual or magazine article we rarely notice its structure; if it is well written then the structure will be transparent. Yet, without structure there would be no communication. We may notice headings and paragraphs, but many other aspects pass us by. For one thing this structuring makes the information in the document intelligible, either by us or to an application using it. Furthermore, it means that when a document is parsed, by an application for example, it can be checked for the presence of required portions.

There are many programs, known as **parsers**, available for XML. Some of these parsers are able to validate a document against its DTD, in which case they are known as **validating parsers**. If the document does not follow the structure of the DTD the parser will raise an error.

> *We will come back to look at parsers later in the chapter, when we talk about the Document Object Model.*

Assuming that, in the first instance, we have an appropriate and well-planned structure for a type of document, then the resulting document instances should be logically complete with respect to its predefined structure. So, in our book example earlier we had:

❑ The unique opening and closing tags of `<books>`

❑ A `<book>` element, which encapsulates all information on a specific book

❑ Followed by a title, in a `<title>` element

❑ Then the ISBN in the `<ISBN>` tags

❑ Followed by the author, description, and price elements

If we had to exchange a lot of information about books in this format, with different people, then there would be many advantages to writing a DTD (or document type definition). Such a book DTD would lay out the structure of how we expect books following the book DTD to be marked up. While we do not need one to write an XML document, it would mean that anyone following the DTD would be able to write an XML file about books that would be valid according to our DTD. In this manner, we could guarantee that any application using the book information, marked up according to our DTD, could understand the document; it could even check that the document followed the DTD in order to prevent the application showing errors if we passed in the wrong data. You could think of this as being similar to form validation for incoming and outgoing data, to make sure that it conforms to the DTD without the need for writing complex script to check the document.

So, if we had written any applications to process an XML file, created according to our book DTD then, in fact, we would be able to process *any* files that were valid according to the book DTD. In which case, if Wrox had different members of staff all writing XML documents about the books they could all follow the DTD to make sure that they were valid. Then, should other publishers adopt the same DTD, the bookstores who might make use of our XML files would be able to use the same applications to process the files sent from several different publishers.

Writing DTDs

Document Type Definitions are part of the original core XML 1.0 specification. In order to learn about DTDs we will develop one for our sample `books.xml` file. They are written in a language called **Extended Backus-Naur Form**, or EBNF for short. The DTD needs to declare the rules of the markup language, which we said at the beginning of this chapter:

❑ Declare what exactly constitutes markup

❑ Declare exactly what our markup means

Practically speaking, this means that we have to give details of each of the elements, their order, and say what attributes (and other types of markup) they can take.

> *They are an example of what is known as a **schema**, but this should not be confused with XML Schemas, which offer similar extended functionality above DTDs but are written in XML syntax.*

The DTD can be declared internally (actually in the XML document) within a **Document Type Declaration** (note that, to avoid total confusion, we **do not** shorten this term to DTD!). Nevertheless, this *is* where the terminology starts to get confusing! The document type declaration is used in the XML file, which is written according to a document type definition, so that a processing application knows that the XML file has been written according to a document type definition. The DTD can, alternatively, be an external file. In this case, a document type declaration within the XML document will 'point' to this external DTD.

Referencing a DTD From an XML Document

In order that many XML documents can be written according to a single DTD, the DTD for our books example would be external. So, we need to add a document type declaration to the `books.xml` example, so that a processing application knows that it has been written according to the books document type definition:

```
<!DOCTYPE books SYSTEM "books.dtd">
```

Here, `books` is the name of the root element and the name of the document type definition. In this case we have followed it with the keyword `SYSTEM` and the URI of the DTD, a value that a processing application could use to validate the document against the DTD. This, of course, means that there must be an instance of it available from that location.

> *A URI is a Unique Resource Identifier. This could be a URL, but it doesn't have to be –
> as long as the location it provides is unique and it allows the processing application to
> locate the resource.*

As we are just trying this out as a test we could just keep the DTD in the same folder as the XML document. However, if we were to make it available to all we would have to give a location for it that would be available to any application. So we might choose:

```
<!DOCTYPE books SYSTEM "http://www.wrox.com/DTDlibrary/books.dtd">
```

As we discussed earlier, it is possible to include the DTD within the document type declaration (in the XML document). In other words, the rules in the DTD could be placed within this declaration, rather than in a separate file. However, in most cases you will want to reference an external file, so we will only look at this. After all, there is no point copying the DTD into several files, if you can just have it in one place.

To do this we also add the `standalone` attribute to the XML declaration of the XML document (which comes directly before the document type declaration – remember that nothing is allowed to come before the XML declaration, not even white space).

```
<?xml version="1.0" standalone="no" ?>
<!DOCTYPE books SYSTEM "books.dtd">
```

If the value of the `standalone` attribute is `no`, this indicates that there may be an external DTD (or internally declared external parameter entities – but do not worry about this second option until you get more involved in creating complex XML documents). If the value is `yes`, then there are no other dependencies and the file can truly stand on its own.

> It is very easy to get confused between Document Type Definitions and Document Type Declarations... To clarify, just remember that a document type declaration either refers to an external document type definition, as in the example we are about to see, or else it actually contains one in the form of markup declarations.

Writing a DTD for the Books Example

Creating your own markup language using a DTD need not be excessively complicated. Here is the external DTD for our books example. As you can see, it is very simple.

```
<!ELEMENT books (book+)>
<!ELEMENT book (title, ISBN, authors, description?, price+)>
<!ELEMENT title (#PCDATA)>
<!ELEMENT authors (author+)>
<!ELEMENT author (#PCDATA)>
<!ELEMENT description (#PCDATA)>
<!ELEMENT price EMPTY>
<!ATTLIST price
          US        CDATA        #REQUIRED
>
```

You can write it in a simple text editor, just as we did with the XML document. Alternatively, there are pieces of software that will help you to create them (for more details on these check out http://www.schema.net/). Let's take a closer look at this. Here is the opening line:

```
<!DOCTYPE books [
```

This gives the same name as the root element of the document. While <!Element is used to declare elements, in the format:

```
<! ELEMENT name (contents)>
```

Where name gives the name of the element, and contents describes what type of data can be included and which elements can be nested inside that element. The books element must include the element book at least once, denoted by the use of the + symbol (which indicates one or more instances).

```
<!ELEMENT books (book+)>
```

The book element, declared in this line:

```
<! ELEMENT book (title, ISBN, authors, description?, price+)>
```

must include exactly one instance of each of the `title`, `ISBN` and `authors` elements, and at least one `price` element, in that particular order. The question mark after the `description` element means that this element is optional. We then have to define each of these elements individually. Here is a brief summary of the operators we can use to describe element content:

Symbol	Usage
,	Strict ordering
|	Selection, in any order (can be used in conjunction with +, * and ?.
+	Repetition (minimum of 1)
*	Repetition
?	Optional
()	Grouping

Next we see the line:

```
<!ELEMENT title (#PCDATA)>
```

This indicates that the title element can contain **character data**, indicated by #PCDATA. The # symbol prevents PCDATA from being interpreted as an element name. While the authors element can contain one or more author elements:

```
<!ELEMENT authors (author+)>
```

The author elements contain character data, as does the description element.

When we came to the price element in our books.xml file, there were no closing tags; the element was an **empty** element. It did, however, have an attribute to indicate its currency. This was how it looked in our books.xml example:

```
<price US="$49.99"/>
```

So we need to declare the element as being empty, and also declare the attribute that it can take. First we will use this line:

```
<!ELEMENT price EMPTY>
```

to indicate that the elements name is price, but that it is an empty element. Then we have to declare the attribute using the `<!ATTLIST...` instruction, the data types or possible values and the default values for the attributes:

```
<!ATTLIST price
         US       CDATA      #REQUIRED
>
```

Each attribute has three components: a name (e.g. US), the type of information to be passed (in this case character data, CDATA), and the default value (in this case there is not one, but we are required to provide a value).

Then we just have to close the opening DOCTYPE declaration:

```
]>
```

That covers the example book DTD, book.dtd, for the books.xml example. You will find it with the rest of the code for this chapter at http://www.wrox.com/. If you want to create one yourself, you can simply use a text editor, such as Notepad, just save the file (which will have the same name as your root element) as "books.dtd".

Obviously, if you have a well-formed instance of an element in a document, but do not declare it in the DTD, then it cannot be validated. An element is only valid if:

❑ There is a declaration for the element type in the DTD which has a name matching that of the element itself

❑ There are declarations for all of the element types, attributes and their value types in the DTD

❑ The data type of the content matches that of the content schema defined in the declaration (e.g. PCDATA)

We have just created our own XML application, containing our own markup language for exchanging data about books. However, it is worth noting that there are other types of schema on the horizon. The W3C is working on a version of schemas written in XML rather than Extended Backus-Naur Form, to be called XML Schemas.

XML Schemas

XML Schemas have several advantages over their DTD counterparts. The group working on the specification has looked at several proposals, which you can see if you want to get an idea of what XML Schemas are going to be like. The main ones are XML-Data and Document Content Description. Links to both can be found, with all of the submissions and specifications in progress, on the W3C site at http://www.w3.org/tr/.

There are number of reasons why these XML Schemas will be an advantage over DTDs. Firstly, they use XML syntax rather than Extended Backus-Naur Form, which many people find difficult to learn. Secondly, if you needed to parse the schema (we will look at parsers shortly), it will be possible to do so using an existing XML parser, rather than having to use a special parser. Another strong advantage is the ability to specify data types in XML Schemas, for the content of elements and attributes. This means that applications using the content will not have to convert it into the appropriate data type from a string. Think about an application that has to add two numbers together, or perform a calculation on a date – it would not have to convert this data to the appropriate type, from a string, before it could perform the calculation. There will be other advantages too, such as support for namespaces, which we meet shortly. Also, XML Schemas can be extended, whereas DTDs cannot simply be extended once written.

Even HTML Has Schemas

Being an SGML application, HTML has several SGML DTDs (at least a strict and loose one for each version), and the coming XHTML specification has an XML DTD (as opposed to an SGML DTD). XHTML is a new version of HTML that is designed as an XML application, as opposed to an SGML application. This means that you will be able to parse XHTML documents using an XML parser. You can view an HTML DTD at http://www.w3.org/TR/REC-html40/loose.dtd. According to the HTML standard you should include the following line:

```
<DOCTYPE HTML PUBLIC "-//W3C//DTD HTML 4.0 //EN">
```

It tells the user agent the location of HTML's DTD. However, it is often left out because, practically speaking, it is not necessary and if you are using browser specific tags, which deviate from the specification, it may cause unpredictable results.

Styling XML

So far we have created our first application of XML, a language for exchanging data about books, and we have created an XML document in our `books.xml` file. This is great for defining data, as our tags clearly explain their content and it is written in plain text, which is easy to transfer. However, if we are putting things up on the Web we want our pages to look good. As our earlier example showed, even in an XML-aware browser, such as IE5, a plain XML file did not look that impressive:

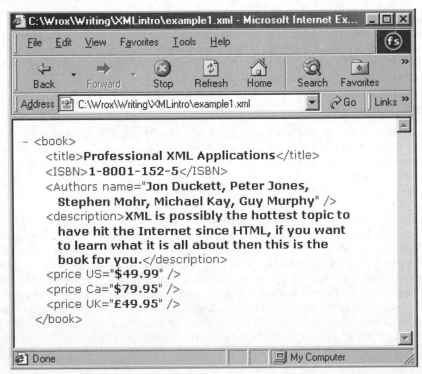

This is because the tags that we have proposed for our book example don't say anything about how the tags should appear on the page, whereas HTML tells the browser how the data should look.

So, to make it look attractive we must supply another file, a style sheet. In case having to write a style sheet as well sounds like a lot of extra effort, let's just have a look at what it means for us.

Why Use Style Sheets?

Unfortunately, using style sheets means that we have to use a completely separate language, in a separate file, to declare how we want our document to be presented.

We can, however, use our good friend Cascading Style Sheets (CSS) to do this (and if you don't know CSS, don't worry; it's very similar to HTML styling directives). In any case HTML 4.0 deprecated many of the style elements in HTML in favor of using CSS. So what are the real advantages of using style sheets?

- ❑ Improved clarity of the document
- ❑ Can help reduce download time, network traffic and server load
- ❑ Allow you to change the presentation of several files, just by altering one style sheet
- ❑ Allow you to present the same data in different ways for different purposes

If we do not have to have a lot of rules, telling us how we should display our document, included in with the data then the core content of the file will be easier to read. It is not cluttered up with styling directives like `<font>` tags, which are not important to the actual content of, say, our books file.

With a style sheet, all of the style rules are kept in one file and the source document simply links to this file. This means that if several pages use the same type of display, which is often the case as we display an ever-increasing amount of data on web pages, we do not need to repeat the style rules in each page. The browser can download the style sheet and cache it on the client. All other pages can then use the same styling rules. This also means that should you need to change the style of your site – perhaps your company changes its corporate colors – then you do not need to laboriously change every file individually by hand, you just change one style sheet and the changes are propagated across the pages. Indeed, on the other hand, it also means that you can use the same data, and display it in different ways for different purposes by applying different style sheets.

Cascading Style Sheets

The Cascading Style Sheets Level 1 specification was released by the W3C in late 1996. It was supported to a large degree in both Netscape Communicator 4 and Internet Explorer 4. Since then a Level 2 specification has been released (May 1998), some of which has been incorporated into Internet Explorer 5. In addition, at the time of writing, a third level is in progress.

Cascading Style sheets are already popular with HTML developers for the same reasons that we have just expanded upon here.

How CSS Works

CSS is a rule-based language comprising of two sections:

❑ A **pattern matching** section, which expresses the association between an element and some action

❑ An **action section**, which specifies the action to be taken upon the specified section

For CSS, this means that we have to specify an element and then specify how it has to be displayed. So, if we were to develop a cascading style sheet for our books.xml file, we would have to specify a style for each of the elements that contain markup that we want to display.

CSS splits up the browser screen into areas that take a tree-like form, as shown in the following diagram. You can think of this much like the tree that Windows Explorer exposes:

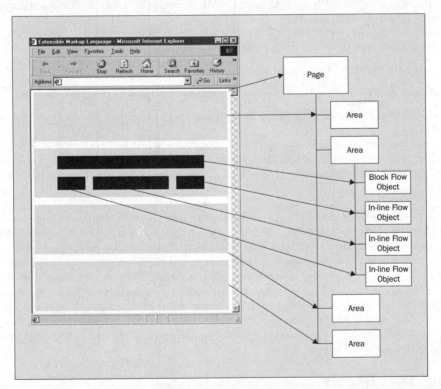

Here we have a page, with several **areas**. Inside the second area are a **block flow object** and a number of **in-line flow objects**. So, using CSS we can specify a style for each of these objects, page, area and flow. Note that the block flow object is taking up the whole line, while the others are on the same line. The one that is taking up the whole line need not contain text or an image that will take up the whole line, it may just be a short title that needs to be displayed in a line of its own.

It is important to decide whether the values are to be displayed in-line or as a block. The difference being that, if they are in-line the next element will be displayed as if it were on the same line as the previous one, whereas if it is displayed as a block, each will be treated separately. We need to make this decision for each object in CSS.

While we cannot cover a full reference to CSS here you should find it fairly easy to catch on and, if you need to find out a special implementation, you can always check the specification at http://www.w3.org/style/css/.

Let's try it out and write a style sheet for our books.xml file.

Try it Out – Displaying XML with CSS

1. We start by opening up our favorite text editor again we will be saving this file as books.css. Type in the following code:

```css
title {
    display:block;
    font-family: Arial, Helvetica;
    font-weight: bold;
    font-size: 20pt;
    color: #9370db;
    text-align: center;
}
ISBN {
    display:block;
    font-family: Arial, Helvetica;
    font-weight: bold;
    font-size: 12pt;
    color: #c71585;
    text-align: left;
}

authors {
    display:inline;
    font-family: Arial, Helvetica;
    font-style: italic;
    font-size: 10pt;
    color: #9370db;
    text-align: left;
}

description {
    display:block;
    font-family: Arial, Helvetica;
    font-size: 12pt;
    color: #ff1010;
    text-align: left;
}
```

2. Save the file as `books.css`. We have now finished creating our first style sheet for XML. The only problem is that our `books.xml` file has no way of telling how it should be associated with this style sheet. So we will have to add a link to this style sheet into our original XML file.

3. To add the link to the style sheet, open up your `books.xml` file again, and add the following line between the XML prolog and the opening `<books>` element.

```
<?xml version="1.0"?>
<?xml:stylesheet href="books.css" type="text/css" ?>
<books>
```

4. Open `books.xml` in your browser and you should see something like this:

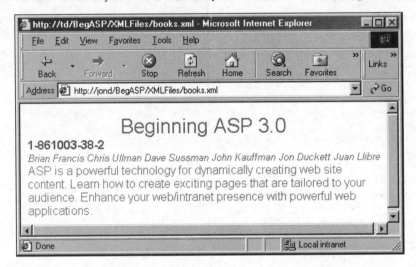

How It Works

CSS files do not need a special header, so we went straight on and declared which elements we needed to display. In this case we are just adding styling for the `<title>`, `<ISBN>`, `<authors>`, and `<description>` elements. So we can add them to the file like so:

```
title {

    }
ISBN {

    }

authors {

    }

description {

    }
```

This specifies the pattern matching section.

Having declared the elements that we want to display, we must associate some action with it. So, let's see how to display the content of the <title> element. We want it to be displayed as a block, so within the curly brackets {} we add the directive to display the element as a block:

```
title {
    display:block;
    }
```

This simply specifies that we want to make the title a block level element. We still need to specify the style the title should be displayed in.

> **All properties are specified with a colon delimiting the attribute and values and have a semi-colon after them.**

So, we added a font to display the content of the <title> element. In the screen shot you have just seen the browser is using the Arial font. However, in case the machine using the file does not have Arial, we have allowed it to use Helvetica instead. In addition, we want it to appear in the center of the screen, in a size 20pt, bold font, and in a lilac color. So, we add some more action rules, or style elements. As you can see, these are very similar to those used for HTML.

```
title {
    display:block;
    font-family: Arial, Helvetica;
    font-weight: bold;
    font-size: 20pt;
    color: #9370db;
    text-align: center;
    }
```

We can then add some similar rules for the other element content we want to display, for example:

```
authors {
    display:inline;
    font-family: Arial, Helvetica;
    font-style: italic;
    font-size: 10pt;
    color: #9370db;
    text-align: left;
    }
```

You can see from the screen shot that the authors, despite being in separate elements in the books.xml file are displayed on the same line.

Finally, we included an extra line in our books.xml file to tell it to use the correct CSS file:

```
<?xml version="1.0"?>
<?xml:stylesheet href="books.css" type="text/css" ?>
<books>
```

The href attribute acts just like it would in HTML, while the type attribute specifies the type of style sheet that is being attached. This is an example of a processing instruction, which you may remember us talking about them earlier in the chapter when we were discussing XML syntax.

> **Remember that, because the style sheet link is still in the XML file, the values of the attributes still need to be kept in quotation marks for the XML to be well-formed.**

Obviously, there is a lot more to CSS than we can describe here, such as all of the appropriate styling tags. To find our more, check out the specification at http://www.w3.org/style/css/ or pick up a copy of a dedicated book, such as *Professional Style Sheets for HTML and XML published by Wrox Press (ISBN 1-861001-65-7)* – although the XSL section of this book is somewhat out-of-date. However, you are about to hear of some of the latest developments.

XSL

Having seen how easy it is to create a style sheet for our XML using CSS, we should briefly introduce the Extensible Style sheet Language, or XSL. XSL is far more powerful than CSS, *but*, if you are only interested in displaying the XML *as it is* for display on the Web, then CSS is a far simpler option.

There are two key parts to XSL. The first covers its transformation abilities: it can actually be used to transform XML into HTML, or a number of other languages. At the time of writing, this section, known as **XSLT**, was still a working draft although it was near completion. It is ideal for transforming data into another form for use on the Web.

In addition, there is another area in development to specify formatting semantics. This is particularly useful for creating print versions of documents, such as PDF or TeX documents.

Undoubtedly one of the prime uses of XSLT at the moment is to transform XML into HTML for display in browsers that do not support XML, and to transform one XML vocabulary into another. XSLT is far too big a subject to go into in depth in this book. All we can really do is to point out what you can do with it, to help you decide if you need to look into it more.

If you want more information you might try http://www.w3.org/tr/xslt.

XML as Data

You may still be thinking that this is a lot to learn, just to have data in a self-describing format that you, as a programmer, can read a bit more clearly. After all, we are still getting similar results to what we can already achieve with HTML. Well, let's stop looking at our XML file as just being used for display on the Web, and let's take a look at the different ways that we might want to use the same data (that is currently used in HTML-based applications).

If we are keeping our data separate from the rules in which it can be displayed then we can easily use it in other applications. There are two reasons for this:

❑   It is not cluttered with style rules

❑   The tags are describing their content

Taking our book example further, imagine we own a bookstore. As we are interested in computers, our small bookstore does more than display details of books on the Web. We use it for the following:

❑   A browser-based application for staff to monitor stock

❑   To send out to collectors details of our catalog of books in stock

Rather than keeping several versions of the same information in different places, we decided to re-use the same data in different ways. In order to do this, we can add a quantity tag to our XML document to show the numbers of each book we have in stock.

```
<books>
<book>
   <title>Beginning ASP 3.0</title>
   <quantity>20</quantity>
   <ISBN>1-861002-11-0</ISBN>
...
```

You may be wondering how a text file like this could actually be used in a practical situation. There are, in fact, a number of ways:

❑   To expose the elements and their values using the W3C Document Object Model

❑   To write a specialized component, that can read XML data, and use it to interact with the application or data store directly

❑   Using text string manipulation techniques, which look for matching text in the tags and then retrieves their values

❑   Data Binding in IE4/5

In the remainder of this chapter we will show you some ways in which you can access and create data in XML documents using the Document Object Model.

XML Parsers

For a system to use XML, it requires two components:

❑ The XML processor

❑ The application

The first part, known as the XML processor, has the job of checking that the XML file follows the specification. Then, so that the computer can interpret the file, the XML processor creates a document tree (which we shall see in a moment). It is the parser that takes up the role of the XML processor. The application is the part that then uses the data in the tree.

As we mentioned earlier, validating parsers can also check that the syntax of your document instance, such as the books.xml file, is written in accordance with the markup language that defined it, which would be specified in the DTD, such as our books.dtd schema (or a different type of schema).

Parsers expose the document as a tree – essentially a structured set of objects and properties that implement the methods that allow you to work with them. Several do this in accordance with the Document Object Model specification from the W3C, which we shall meet in a moment.

This is, in fact, what happens when Internet Explorer 5 opens an XML document, it loads it using a parser called **MSXML**, which is a COM component housed in msxml.dll. It can be used like any other COM component in both client and server applications and web pages.

There are many implementations of parsers available, written in a number of languages and for different uses. MSXML is also available as a standalone parser for those who need to re-distribute it, and for use on servers that do not have IE5 installed. As this book is about ASP 3.0 (which comes with Windows 2000 which, in turn, includes IE5) you should have this installed on your machine. If not, you can download the standalone component from Microsoft at http://msdn.microsoft.com/xml/. You just register it like any other COM component. Go to the Start menu, and choose Run. Then type:

```
Regsvr32 c:\folder_name\msxml.dll
```

To use the MSXML parser on the client, the client machine must have IE5 installed, or have the standalone component registered. Then we can create an instance of it, as we do any other client side component, using:

```
CreateObject("microsoft.xmldom")
```

On the server, in our ASP pages, we use:

```
Server.CreateObject("microsoft.xmldom")
```

In order to manipulate the XML document, MSXML implements the W3C XML Document Object Model, so let's turn our attention to that for a moment.

The W3C Document Object Model

The W3C Document Object Model is a set of object-oriented Application Programming Interfaces (API's) for HTML and XML documents. These define how our documents are structured, setting out objects, properties and methods that allow us to access parts of any XML document (such as their elements, attributes, and their values) and to manipulate their structure with programming languages (such as adding elements and attributes and changing their values and order).

> *Note that Document Object Model is a term that has been applied to browsers for some time, with intrinsic objects such as* window, document *and* history, *being considered part of the browser object model. The W3C DOM is an attempt to standardize the different implementations of browsers.*

Here we are not particularly interested in the part of the model that holds information about the browser environment or the HTML pages that it loads. Rather we are interested in the area that contains information about an XML document that a browsers hosts. The browser may load the document directly, but it is often likely to expose it using the <XML> element in IE5, which we shall meet later.

The part of the model that deals with our XML document is known as the DOM Level 1 and can be seen at http://www.w3.org/tr/rec-dom-level1/. At the time of writing, this was at version 1.0. The W3C recommendation does not actually use the term objects; it uses the term **interfaces** instead, although objects can be an easier way of thinking about them for ASP developers.

If we look at our books.xml file, we can see that its structure is hierarchical. As we have already seen, we have a **root** element, which is <books>, under which there are a number of other elements, known as **child** elements.

```
<books>
  <book>
   <title>Beginning ASP 3.0</title>
   <quantity>20</quantity>
   <ISBN>1-861002-11-0</ISBN>
   <authors>
      <author_name>Brian Francis</author_name>
      <author_name>Chris Ullman</author_name>
      <author_name>Dave Sussman</author_name>
      <author_name>John Kauffman</author_name>
      <author_name>Jon Duckett</author_name>
      <author_name>Juan Llibre</author_name>
   </authors>
   <description> ASP is a powerful technology for dynamically creating web site
content. Learn how to create exciting pages that are tailored to your audience.
Enhance your web/intranet presence with powerful web applications.</description>
   <price US="$49.99"/>
  </book>
</books>
```

We could actually show this in terms of a diagram, like so:

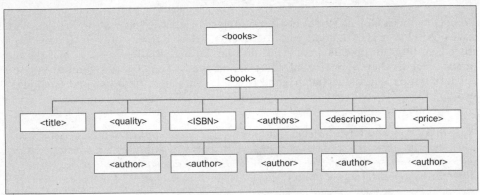

You can think of this as a tree, similar to a family tree in the way that it can be represented. You can see that the root of the tree grows from the `<books>` element, which then branches out with child elements. The more child elements there are, the more the tree would branch out. If there were more `<book>` elements, the tree would get wider, and if there were more elements under each `<title>` or `<authors>` element the tree would become deeper.

Each of the elements is referred to as a **node** in the W3C XML DOM, and there is an important reason for this. The DOM for HTML is actually quite different from the XML DOM. This is mainly because we are using XML to create our own languages, whose structure is unknown. In contrast, HTML is a fixed language. In HTML you always have an `images` collection, whether or not your HTML page includes images. In addition, in HTML you always have one `forms` collection, no matter how many `form` elements there may be in an HTML document instance. Each form is accessed using the `document.forms` collection, with its own `elements` collection. However, when we are creating our own markup languages, we do not have this previous knowledge. We can be certain that there is a root element, but we cannot be sure of what is underneath it, and we do not know what name it is.

To counter this problem each item within the tree is referred to as a generic **node**. Earlier we said that you could think of the tree in terms of a family tree. If a node has a node underneath it, the node underneath is called a **child**, and the node that sprouts the child is known as a **parent**. So, book is a parent of title, quantity, ISBN etc. and they are children of book. If a child has no other children, then it is known as a **leaf** node.

In this section, we will see how we can use the DOM to retrieve elements from the DOM tree, and how to add elements to the tree. Thus we will see how we can use the data in our XML files. But, before we can look at how to retrieve them, we should have a look at the Node object and its properties that make nodes available.

The Base Object

As we have said, the DOM provides a set of objects, methods and properties, that allow us to access and manipulate the DOM, and which represent the hierarchical nature of the tree. We will not be covering all of the DOM objects here – however, since we have been referring to Nodes, we should look at the base objects:

Object	Description
Node	A single node in the hierarchy.
NodeList	A collection of nodes.
NamedNodeMap	A collection of nodes allowing access by name as well as index.

There are a number of properties that allow us to navigate through the tree with the nodes:

Property	Description
ChildNodes	Returns a NodeList containing the children of the node.
FirstChild	Returns a Node that is a reference to the first child.
LastChild	Returns a Node that is a reference to the last child.
ParentNode	Returns a Node that is a reference to the parent node.
PreviousSibling	Returns a Node that is a reference to the previous sibling, i.e., the previous node at the same level in the hierarchy.
NextSibling	Returns a Node that is a reference to the next sibling, i.e., the next node at the same level in the hierarchy.
NodeName	The name of the node.
NodeValue	The value of the node.

This isn't a complete list, but it gives you an idea of what's possible. If we refer back to our diagram, and then add in some of the relationships, we will be able to see how these work:

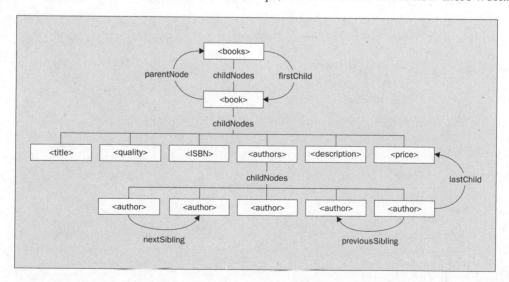

Specific DOM Objects

Because XML is designed to be extensible, in contrast to the fixed structure of HTML, there are also specific objects for different types of node. Most inherit the properties and methods of the Node object, as well as adding specific methods and properties relevant to the particular node type.

Object	Description
Document	The root object for an XML document
Element	An XML element.
Attr	An XML attribute.
CharacterData	The base object for text information in a document.
CDATASection	Unparsed character data. Equivalent to !CDATA.
Text	The text contents of an element or attribute node.
Comment	An XML comment element.
ProcessingInstruction	A processing instruction, as held in the <? ?> section.

So, having seen some of the objects and properties of the DOM, let's use them to discover values of an XML document programmatically.

To do this we will use the MSXML parser (provided by Microsoft) that, as we said, exposes the W3C XML DOM.

Retrieving Values from an XML Document

Having said that MSXML exposes the W3C DOM, let's see how our tree would look in terms of nodes in the parser. MSXML adds an error object of the document object model to help us troubleshoot any problems in our application.

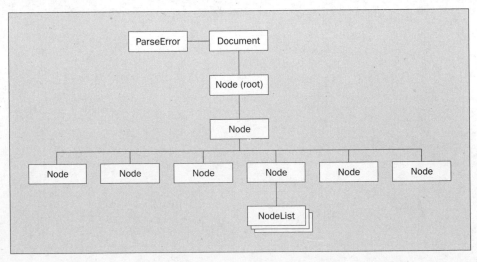

So, the root node represents the `<books>` element, and its child node the `<book>` element. Underneath that we have the elements `<title>`, `<quantity>`, `<ISBN>`, `<author>`, `<description>` and `<price>`. The `<authors>` element also exposes a set of `<author>` nodes, which can be referred to as a `NodeList`.

The error object that MSXML exposes is called `ParseError`, which contains information about the last parsing error. The `ParseError` object exposes a lot of useful information for debugging and error handling within ASP pages. It exposes the following information:

Property	Description
errorCode	The error code
filepos	The absolute position of the error in the XML document
line	The line number of the line that caused the error
linepos	The character position of the line containing the error
reason	The cause of the error
srcText	The data where the error occurred
url	The URL of the XML document containing the error

This is where the information came from when we loaded our badly formed XML example earlier.

Using the MSXML parser, we can get to the values of any of these nodes, navigating the tree using the DOM. We shall now do precisely this. However, as this is an ASP book, we shall use the parser on the server in an ASP page, and write the values of the `title`, `ISBN` and `description` to the client.

Try It Out – Walking the DOM

1. Fire up your favorite text editor and type in the following file. We will save this file as `DomExample1.asp`

```
<%
'create an instance of MSXML to retreive the book details
set objXML = Server.CreateObject("microsoft.XMLDOM")

'load the XML document that we want to add to the database
objXML.load("C:\Inetpub\wwwroot\BegASPFiles\XMLFiles\books.xml")

'see if it loaded OK, i.e. is a well-formed XML file
If objXML.parseError.errorCode = 0 Then

  strTitle = objXML.documentElement.firstChild.firstChild.text
  strISBN = objXML.documentElement.firstChild.childNodes(1).text
  strDescription = objXML.documentElement.firstChild.childNodes(3).text
```

```
  Response.Write (strTitle & "<BR>")
  Response.Write (strISBN & "<BR>")
  Response.Write (strDescription & "<BR>")

'write out if an error occured
Else

  Response.Write ("Sorry, an error occurred retreiving information.")

End If

Set objXML = nothing
%>
```

2. Save the file with the name DomExample1.asp

3. When the results are written to the screen they should look like this, displaying the title, ISBN and the description:

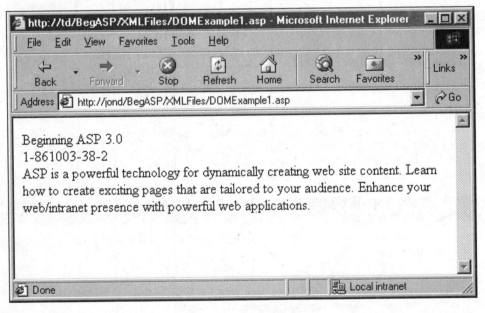

How It Works

Firstly, we will create an instance of the MSXML parser when the page is executed. We set it to the value of a variable called objXML.

```
<%
'create an instance of MSXML to retrieve the book details
set objXML = Server.CreateObject("microsoft.XMLDOM")
```

Next we have to load the XML file into the DOM, so we use the load method of MSXML. We reference the object and the load method using the traditional dot notation, as with any other component. The value of the load method is the URL of the file that is holding the XML.

```
'load the XML document that we want to add to the database
objXML.load("C:\Inetpub\wwwroot\BegASPFiles\XMLFiles\books.xml")
```

Next we use MSXML's special `parseError` object to check that the file loaded properly. We do this by checking whether the error code of the `parseError` object is 0. If it is, this indicates that there is no reported error. Using an `If...Then` statement, providing everything went well, we continue processing (if not we will raise an error, as you will see soon):

```
'see if it loaded OK, i.e. is a well-formed XML file
If objXML.parseError.errorCode = 0 Then
```

Provided no error occurs, we set a variable `strTitle` to the value of the child node of the book element exposed by the `text` property of the node:

```
strTitle = objXML.documentElement.firstChild.firstChild.text
```

This string will now be holding the value `Beginning ASP 3.0`, since this is the title.

We then use the `nodeList` object, which exposes collections of nodes, to obtain the ISBN and the description, into strings. Note that this is a zero-based index, so the `<title>` would be 0. We, however, want the `<ISBN>`, and then the `<description>` elements, which are 1 and 3 respectively in the index:

```
strISBN = objXML.documentElement.firstChild.childNodes(1).text
strDescription = objXML.documentElement.firstChild.childNodes(3).text
```

Next we use a simple `Response.Write` to write out the value of the strings:

```
Response.Write (strTitle & "<BR>")
Response.Write (strISBN & "<BR>")
Response.Write (strDescription & "<BR>")
```

To cover ourselves in case an error occurred, we have to finish our `If...Then` statement with an `Else`. If it fails we will write a simple message back to the client.

```
'write out if an error occured
Else
  Response.Write ("Sorry, an error occurred retreiving information.")
End If
```

Finally we clean up our resources by setting our XML parser to `nothing`.

```
Set objXML = nothing
%>
```

This example relies on you knowing the structure of the document so that you can navigate the document. However, if you know an element's name, but not necessarily its position, you can also use the `getElementsByTagName()` method. It can be run against any node, and is used to find children of the current node you are working with (it can be used with the root node or a more specific collection, where the element you are looking for is the child). It returns a `NodeList` object, which is an unordered collection of nodes that match the query.

OK, what we have done here is fine for displaying selected nodes of an XML document. However, in order for it to be truly useful programmatically, we not only need to retrieve nodes, we also need to change the structure of a document. This is done using the Node objects methods.

Node Object Methods

In order to change the content of a loaded XML document, using the XML DOM, we use the read/write methods exposed by the Node object. The Node object offers us a set of methods for use when editing an XML document.

For example, the cloneNode() method copies an existing node and creates a new Node object to hold it. You can also set a value to copy all of its descendant nodes as well:

Method	Description
cloneNode(recurse_children)	Creates a new Node object that is an exact clone of this node. If you include the Boolean parameter recurse_children, it will copy all child objects.

There are also four methods that allow us to add, replace, insert or remove existing nodes:

Method	Description
appendChild(new_node)	Appends a new object new_node to the end of the list of child nodes for this node
replaceChild(new_node, old_node)	Replaces the child node old_node with the new child node new_child, and returns the old child node
insertBefore(new_node, this_node)	Inserts a new Node object new_node into the list of child nodes for this node, before this_node or at the end of the list if no this_node is specified
RemoveChild(this_node)	Removes the child node this_node from the list of child nodes for this node, and returns it

Don't let the use of child nodes confuse you – it is not a limitation, as it is expected that you would not need to alter a root element.

We can also check to see if the current node has any child nodes by calling the hasChildNodes() method, which returns True if the selected node has any nodes.

In the following Try It Out we will be using the DOM methods to create the following XML document:

```xml
<?xml version="1.0"?>
<books>
<book>
<title>Professional XML</title>
<quantity>30</quantity>
<ISBN>1-861003-11-0</ISBN>
</book>
</books>
```

Try It Out – Creating an XML Document on the Server

1. Open your text editor and type in the following code.

```asp
<%@LANGUAGE="VBScript"%>
<%
  Response.Buffer = False
  Response.ContentType = "text/xml"
%>
<?xml version="1.0"?>

<%
  Response.Write makeXML()

  Function makeXML()
    Dim objParser
    Dim book

    Set objParser = Server.CreateObject("Microsoft.XMLDOM")

    ' Build an XML document using the DOM.
    ' Create the root node
    Set objParser.documentElement = objParser.createElement("books")

    ' Create the book element and child elements
    Set book = objParser.createElement("book")
    book.appendChild objParser.createElement("title")
    book.appendChild objParser.createElement("quantity")
    book.appendChild objParser.createElement("ISBN")

    ' Set the PCDATA values
    book.childNodes(0).text = "Professional XML"
    book.childNodes(1).text = "30"
    book.childNodes(2).text = "1-861003-11-0"

    ' Append a clone to the document
    objParser.documentElement.appendChild book.cloneNode(true)

    makeXML = objParser.xml
  End Function
%>
```

2. Save the file as `CreateXML.asp` and view it in your web browser.

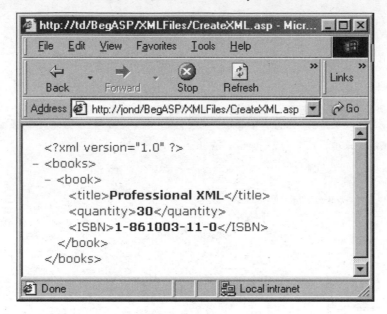

How It Works

We create an ASP page called `CreateXML.asp` and set the language to VBScript:

```
<%@LANGUAGE="VBScript"%>
```

We will be sending the resulting XML document that we create in this example back to the client, so we set the `ContentType` property of the `Response` object to `"text/xml"` to ensure that the proper HTTP headers are sent back to the client:

```
<%
  Response.Buffer = False
  Response.ContentType = "text/xml"
%>
```

As our browser knows that we are sending it back XML, we can just write in the XML prolog. We do this outside of the ASP delimiters, because we do not want it processed on the server, we want it sent back to the client:

```
<?xml version="1.0"?>
```

We then set the `Response` object to send back the value of the function `makeXML()` to the browser:

```
<%
  Response.Write makeXML()
```

All of the functionality required to create the XML is held in the function `makeXML()`. We start by declaring a couple of variables, `objParser` and `book`. We set a variable called `objparser` to an instance of the DOM, as implemented by MSXML:

```
Function makeXML()
  Dim objParser
  Dim book

  Set objParser = Server.CreateObject("Microsoft.XMLDOM")
```

We start building up the document by creating a root element in the DOM exposed by the parser, which is held by the variable objParser, using the createElement method. We call it books to form the root tag <books>:

```
' Build an XML document using the DOM.
' Create the root node
Set objParser.documentElement = objParser.createElement("books")
```

We can now continue to build up the document. We set the book variable we declared earlier to the value of objParser and use the createElement() method to add a <book> element, which holds the details about this book. After this we can just append the three child nodes to the book element using the appendChild() method:

```
' Create the book element and child elements
Set book = objParser.createElement("book")
book.appendChild objParser.createElement("title")
book.appendChild objParser.createElement("quantity")
book.appendChild objParser.createElement("ISBN")
```

So, book is now holding the empty elements to which we need to add values.

We add the values to the <title>, <quantity> and <ISBN> elements:

```
' Set the PCDATA values
book.childNodes(0).text = "Professional XML"
book.childNodes(1).text = "30"
book.childNodes(2).text = "1-861003-11-0"
```

Having set the values, we add the <book> element (and its newly created children) to the <books> element held in the objParser variable, using the appendChild() method:

```
' Append a clone to the document
objParser.documentElement.appendChild book.cloneNode(true)
```

Finally we send the newly created document using the xml method of the parser, which is held by objParser:

```
    makeXML = objParser.xml
  End Function
%>
```

As you can see from the result on your browser, we have created a proper XML document on the server.

Having looked at how to create an XML document using the DOM, let's now see how we can provide an interface for users to create XML documents over the web.

Creating XML Documents from a Web Page

Up to now, we have only seen how to create XML documents in a text editor. This requires the author of the files to understand the way in which we are marking up our data. However, there are going to be situations where we need to allow people to create XML files without understanding our markup, let alone understanding how to read our DTD.

ASP enables us to provide a mechanism, whereby we can allow users of a web page to create XML documents without the need to understand what format they are being stored in, let alone how to write them. In this section, we will look at a way in which we can allow people to visit a page on our site and create an XML file. One easy way to do this is by providing users with a form.

Creating XML Documents from a Form

So that users who do not understand how to mark up data can still create XML files, we provide them with a form. What they enter into the form will be written to an XML file on the server when they click the Submit button.

The screen shot opposite shows the form that we will be using in our example. Here we are allowing users to file a report using the simple form, the contents of the report will then be created in an XML file:

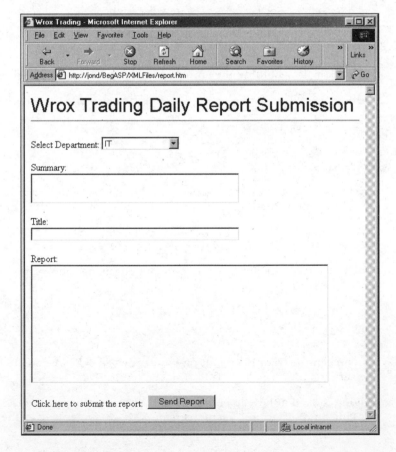

As you can see, we have a drop down list box for the users to provide a department name, along with input boxes for a summary, a title and the body of the report. When the user clicks on **Send Report**, the contents of the form are POSTed to the server. When the server receives the information from the POST operation on the client, we need to construct an XML document from it. We could do this using a similar technique to that we used in the example of creating an XML document using the DOM and JavaScript earlier in the chapter. However, it would be easier to do some simple string manipulation. Once we have created the XML document we just need to write this to the server as a text-based file. We will do this using the FileSystemObject.

OK, let's see how all this works.

Try It Out – Building an XML Document from Form Data

1. Let's start with the user form, which will be used to create our XML file. Open up your favorite text editor and enter the following code:

```html
<HTML>
<HEAD>
<TITLE>Wrox Trading</TITLE>
</HEAD>
<BODY>

<FONT FACE="Arial" SIZE="6">Wrox Trading Daily Report Submission</FONT><HR>

<FORM ACTION="makeReport.asp" METHOD="post">

<P>Select Department: <SELECT id="Dept" name="Dept" style="HEIGHT: 22px; WIDTH:
131px">
<OPTION selected value="IT" name="Dept">IT</OPTION>
<OPTION value="Pharm" name="Pharm"> Pharmaceuticals</OPTION>
<OPTION value="Petro" name="Petro">Petrochemicals</OPTION>
</SELECT>
</P>

<P>Summary:<BR>
<INPUT id="KeyInfo" name="KeyInfo" style="Width:350px; Height:50px"></P>

<P>Title:<BR>
<INPUT id="Title" name="Title" style="Width:350px"></P>

<P>Report:<BR>
<INPUT id="Report" name="Report" style="Width: 500px; Height: 200px;"></P>

<P>Click here to submit the report: 
<INPUT type="submit" value="Send Report">
</P>

</FORM>
</BODY>
</IITML>
```

865

2. Save the file as `report.htm` in your **XMLFiles** directory. We now need to create an ASP page that will allow us to retrieve the form information, make the XML and save it to disk. Open a new file in your favorite editor and enter the following code:

```asp
<%@LANGUAGE="VBScript"%>
<HTML>
<BODY>
<FONT FACE="arial" SIZE="6">Creating Daily Report XML File</FONT><HR>
<P>
<%
  'set variables collected from the form
  'used to write to the XML file and populate session object for re-use
  strDept = Request.Form("Dept")
  strKeyInfo = Request.Form("KeyInfo")
  strTitle = Request.Form("Title")
  strReport = Request.Form("Report")

  strDate = Year(Now) & "-" & Right("00" & Month(Now), 2) & "-" & _
            Right("00" & Day(Now), 2)

  'directory with full permissions set on Web server, where file will be created
  strFileName = "c:\InetPub\wwwroot\BegASPFiles\XMLFiles\" & strDate & strDept & ".xml"
  QUOT = Chr(34)
  CRLF = VbCrLf

  'create new file, overwriting any existing one

  Set objFSO = Server.CreateObject("Scripting.FileSystemObject")
  Set objFile = objFSO.CreateTextFile(strFileName, True)

  'write XML page headings to file
  strLine = "<?xml version=" & QUOT & "1.0" & QUOT & " ?>"
  objFile.WriteLine strLine & CRLF

  strLine = "<dailyReport dateCreated=" & QUOT & strDate & QUOT & " dept=" & _
            QUOT & strDept & Quot & ">"
  objFile.WriteLine strLine & CRLF

  strLine = " <keyInfo>" & strKeyInfo & "</keyInfo>"
  objFile.WriteLine strLine & CRLF

  strLine = " <title>" & strTitle & "</title>"
  objFile.WriteLine strLine & CRLF

  strLine = " <report>" & strReport & "</report>"
  objFile.WriteLine strLine & CRLF

  strLine = "</dailyReport>"
  objFile.WriteLine strLine

  objFile.Close
  Set objjFile = Nothing
  Set objFSO = Nothing
```

```
Response.Write("You have created the report for the " & strDept & _
               " department, for the " & strDate & ".<BR>")

   Response.Write("<HR>")
   Response.Write (strReport)
   Response.Write("<HR>")

%>

</BODY>
</HTML>
```

3. Save the file as makeReport.asp in the XMLFiles folder.

4. Open up report.htm and enter some values. Then click on the Submit button. You should end up with a screen that looks something like this, telling you the department and the report information:

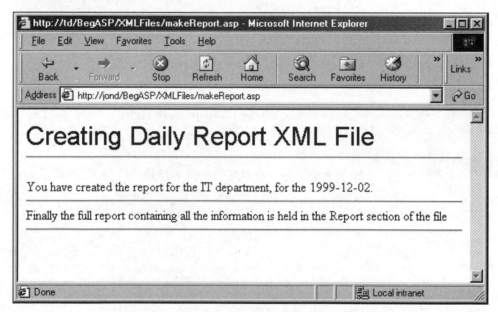

5. Open up Windows Explorer and go to the folder that is holding your files. You should find that a new XML file has been created. Its name is constructed from the curent date and the name of the department you selected from the drop down list (for example, 1999-12-02IT.xml).Open up the XML file in a text editor. You should see something like this, with whatever you entered in the form between the tags:

```
<?xml version="1.0" ?>

<dailyReport dateCreated="1999-11-30" dept="IT">

 <keyInfo>The summary information for the IT department goes here</keyInfo>
```

```
<title>The title of the report is held in the title</title>

<report>Finally the full report containing all the information is held in the Report
section of the file</report>

</dailyReport>
```

How It Works

Let's start with our web page, report.htm. The details are added in HTML <FORM> elements, which will be sent to makeReport.asp on the server:

```
<FORM ACTION="makeReport.asp" METHOD="post">
```

We then have the drop down list box that allows the user to select for which department they are filing the report. The important bit of this is the value attribute, whose value will be sent to the server as the value of Dept, which is the name of the select list:

```
<SELECT id="Dept" name="Dept" style="HEIGHT: 22px;
                        WIDTH: 131px">
   <OPTION selected value="IT" name="Dept">IT</OPTION>
   <OPTION value="Pharm" name="Pharm">Pharmaceuticals</OPTION>
   <OPTION value="Petro" name="Petro">Petrochemicals</OPTION>
</SELECT>
```

We then have three simple input boxes, whose id attributes will be used in the forms collection on the server to retrieve the important information.

```
<P>Summary:<BR>
<INPUT id="KeyInfo" type="text" name="KeyInfo" style="Width:350px; Height:50px"></P>

<P>Title:<BR>
<INPUT id="Title" type="text" name="Title" style="Width:350px"></P>

<P>Report:<BR>
<INPUT id="Report" type="text" name="Report" style="Width: 500px; Height: 200px;">
</P>
```

So, when the user clicks on the **Send Report** button, the form details are sent to makeReport.asp, which we shall look at next.

```
<P>Click here to submit the report: 
<INPUT type="submit" value="Send Report">
</P>
</FORM>
```

Creating XML from the Form Data and Writing it to Disk

The file we used to do all the work was called makeReport.asp, so, let's see how this achieved its task.

We start with the familiar language statement, and write out some opening HTML:

```
<% LANGUAGE="VBScript"%>
<HTML>
<BODY>
<FONT FACE="arial" SIZE="6">Creating Daily Report XML File</FONT><HR>
<P>
```

The first real bit of work involves retrieving the data from the Forms collection of the ASP Request object. You will have seen this technique already in Chapter 7. We set the values of the form data to variables that we can then use when it comes to creating the XML, and displaying the entry for the user to check.

```
<%
'set variables collected from the form
strDept = Request.Form("Dept")
strKeyInfo = Request.Form("KeyInfo")
strTitle = Request.Form("Title")
strReport = Request.Form("Report")
```

The variable strDept will hold the name of the department, strKeyInfo will hold the summary of the report, strTitle holds the title and strReport holds the full report.

We also need to use VBScript functions to create today's date in the format *YYYY-MM-DD*.

```
strDate = Year(Now) & "-" & Right("00" & Month(Now), 2) & "-" & _
          Right("00" & Day(Now), 2)
```

Next we have to create the pathname and file for the XML document that we are going to create and store, in a variable called strFileName. We start by choosing the directory in which our XML files will be stored.

Our reports' filenames will be created from the date for the report, and a string representing the department:

- ❑ IT for the IT department
- ❑ Pharm for the pharmaceutical department
- ❑ Petro for the petrochemical department

So, onto this path we add the date, using the strDate variable, and the department that the report is for (remember that we collected this from the forms collection and set it to a variable strDept). Of course, as this is an XML file we need to append the .xml file extension to the end of this string.

```
'directory with full permissions set on Web server, where file will be created
strFileName = "c:\InetPub\wwwroot\BegASPFiles\XMLFiles\" & strDate & strDept & _
              ".xml"
QUOT = Chr(34)
CRLF = VbCrLf
```

So, the IT department's report for the 21st January 2002 would be 2002-01-21IT.xml.

> *Note that the folder in which you are storing your reports must already exist, before you can run the page successfully.*

Having done the preparatory work, we can create a text file on the server, in which we will store our report as XML. We do this using the FileSystemObject, as you will have seen in Chapter 10. As you can see, this is where we need the file name and path that we just created in strFileName:

```
'create new file, overwriting any existing one
Set objFSO = CreateObject("Scripting.FileSystemObject")
Set objFile = objFSO.CreateTextFile(strFileName, True)
```

That has created the text file, so now we need to generate the XML to store in the file. The reports will be stored in the following format:

```
<?xml version="1.0" ?>
<dailyReport dateCreated="yyyy-mm-dd">
    <keyInfo></keyInfo>
    <title></title>
    <report></report>
</dailyReport>
```

We can now start writing the XML to the file we have just created.

The creation of the file uses a string manipulation technique. We add the XML line-by-line, setting a variable to the line we want to create, and then writing it to the text file we have created. Let's look at the first line we are writing.

```
'write XML page headings to file
strLine = "<?xml version=" & QUOT & "1.0" & QUOT & " ?>"
objFile.WriteLine strLine & CRLF
```

As you can probably see, this will create the XML prolog. As with any ASP code, we have to watch for certain characters and here we add the quotation marks in a second string. This single line is then written to the file using the WriteLine method of the instance of the FileSystemObject that is held in the objFile.

Now we can start writing out the content of the XML file. Of course, this begins with the root node `<dailyReport>`, which has the date as an attribute.

```
strLine = "<dailyReport dateCreated=" & QUOT & strDate & QUOT & " dept=" _
                    & QUOT & strDept & Quot & ">"
objFile.WriteLine strLine & CRLF
```

Now we are ready to write the actual contents of the report to the file. Each of the element's contents is collected from the variable that we set earlier.

```
strLine = " <keyInfo>" & strKeyInfo & "</keyInfo>"
objFile.WriteLine strLine & CRLF
strLine = " <title>" & strTitle & "</title>"
objFile.WriteLine strLine & CRLF
strLine = " <report>" & strReport & "</report>"
objFile.WriteLine strLine & CRLF
```

Having written out the report, we add a closing root tag, and close the file that we have created.

```
strLine = "</dailyReport>"
  objFile.WriteLine strLine
  objFile.Close
  Set objFile = Nothing
  Set objFSO = Nothing
```

We also clean up our resources. The XML file will now be residing on the server in the directory that you specified.

We then let the user know that they have created the report, remind them of the date and department that it is for:

```
Response.Write ("You have created the report for the " & strDept & _
                    " department, for the " & strDate & ".<BR>")
```

Finally, we write out the report again, using the variable from the top of the page that collected the report from the form.

```
Response.Write (strReport)
Response.Write("<HR>")
%>

</BODY>
</HTML>
```

OK, we've covered how to create an XML document on the server using the DOM and how to create XML from a web page. Consider now that we already have a large amount of data stored in relational databases, so wouldn't it be helpful to expose this content as XML as well...?

Creating XML from a Relational Database

So far, we have been talking about XML documents that reside in files on the server, rather like our HTML or ASP files. However, there are many situations where these are not going to be the ideal storage format for our data. For example:

❑ **Size**: We have been dealing with fairly small documents, with a limited number of records. However, if you had several hundred or thousands of records in an XML document, you would end up with a very large document to navigate or pass around the network. Databases are better suited to some kinds of information storage, especially large quantities of data that are not all required at the same time.

❑ **Concurrency**: If we are working with an XML document on a file system, it is very difficult to control who can edit the document. For example, you may only allow one person to view and edit the file at a time, or you may end up with two people editing the file, and only one person's changes taking effect.

❑ **Security**: It is hard to control what parts of a document different people can see or modify.

Relational databases can handle these problems a lot easier than we can with XML files. So, we should have a look at creating some XML data from a database.

Indeed, whether there are advantages or not, many businesses already have a lot of information held in relational databases anyway. If we are either writing systems that are based on XML, or want to take advantage of the ability to pass data around as XML we need a way of generating XML from the data stored in relational databases. Luckily we can do this quite easily with ASP.

There are different ways we could approach this problem:

❑ Using ASP and string manipulation

❑ Using ASP and the DOM

❑ Using ADO 2.5 to create the XML

Let's look at using string manipulation first, as it is the easiest way.

> We have provided a sample Access database with the downloads for this chapter so that you can get started without having to create your own table. It is called `Reports.mdb`

Collecting Table of Reports

The database is holding details of old reports, of the type we created in the previous section. They are stored in full as text-based XML files. Here, we have the `dailyReports` table, from the `Reports` database. We are holding a unique ID for each file, the short name for the department in the **Dept** column, the date of the report in the **Date** column, the main body of the report in the **FullReport** column and some summary information about the report in the **KeyInfo** column:

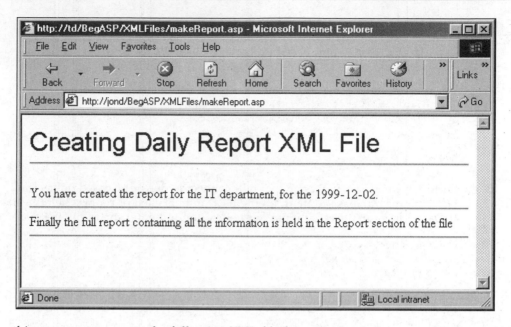

From this, we want to create the following XML file from the database:

```xml
<?xml version="1.0" ?>
<dailyReports dateCreated="yyyy-mm-dd">
  <intro> This is a list of reports on the Wrox Finance site using ASP to create XML
from database content </intro>

    <report>
      <date>date</date>
      <dept>dept</dept>
      <keyInfo>Summary</keyInfo>
    </report>

</dailyReports>
```

So, let's see how we create the XML using ASP.

Try It Out – Creating XML from a Database

1. In order to connect to the database we are going to use our trusty datastore.asp
file, that we created in Chapter 12. You should find it in your BegASPFiles directory.
Create a copy of this file in your XMLFiles folder then open up this copy and make
sure it looks something like this:

```asp
<%
  Dim strDatabaseType

  'Choose one of the following two lines, and comment out the other
  strDatabaseType = "Access"
  'strDatabaseType = "SQLServer"

  'Now we use this selection to specify the connection string
```

```
   If strDatabaseType = "Access" Then
     strConnect = "Provider=Microsoft.Jet.OLEDB.4.0;" & _
                  "Data Source=C:\datastores\reports.mdb;" & _
                  "Persist Security Info=False"
   Else
     strConnect =      "Provider= SQLOLEDB;Persist Security Info=False;" & _
     "User ID=sa;Initial Catalog=Movie2000;" & _
     "Initial File Name=C:\MSSQL7\Data\Movies2000.mdf"

   End If
%>
```

2. Basically we need an ASP page that will connect to our reports database and create XML from the database content, giving us a summary list of reports held in the database. Open up a fresh file in your text editor and enter the following code:

```
<%@LANGUAGE="VBScript"%>
<!-- #include file="datastore.asp" -->
<% Response.ContentType = "text/xml" %>

<% strDate = Year(Now) & "-" & Right("00" & Month(Now), 2) & "-" &_
                             Right("00" & Day(Now), 2) %>
<?xml version="1.0" ?>
<dailyReports dateCreated="<% = strDate %>">
  <intro>This is a list of reports on the Wrox Finance site using ASP to create XML
from database content</intro>
<% '-- select all the report details --
  QUOT = Chr(34)
  On Error Resume Next
  Set oConn = Server.CreateObject("ADODB.Connection")
  oConn.Open strConnect
  strSQL="SELECT * FROM dailyReports ORDER BY Dept"
  Set oRs = oConn.Execute(strSQL)
  Do While Not oRs.EOF
    strDate = oRs("Date")
    strDept = oRs("Dept")
    strKeyInfo = oRs("KeyInfo")
%>
    <report>
      <date><% = strDate %></date>
      <dept><% = strDept %></dept>
      <keyInfo><% = strKeyInfo %></keyInfo>
    </report>
<%
    oRs.MoveNext
  Loop
  oRs.Close
  oConn.Close
  Set oConn = Nothing
  Set oRs = Nothing
%>
</dailyReports>
```

3. Save the file as `makeList.asp`, and save it in the file with the other samples.

4. Open up your browser, and choose the file. You should get something like this.

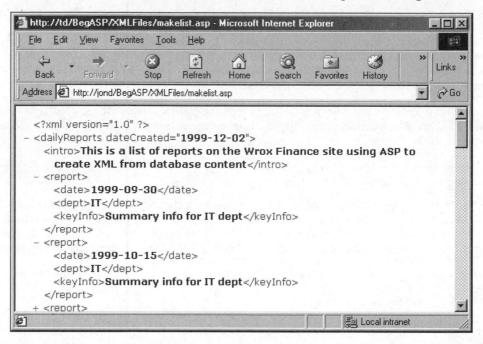

How It Works

Our `makeXML.asp` page starts by setting the language that we are using. Then we have our include command that inserts the connection string definition from datastore.asp. We then set the `ContentType` property of the `Response` object to ensure that we have the correct headers written back to the client. As we will be sending back XML, the value is `"text/xml"`. This allows us to write XML back to the client rather than HTML outside of the ASP delimiters:

```
<%@LANGUAGE="VBScript"%>
<!-- #include file="datastore.asp" -->
<% Response.ContentType = "text/xml" %>
```

We then build up the current date using VBScript functions, and set them to a variable `strDate` (this will allow us to write the date to the `dateCreated` attribute of the root `<dailyReports>` tag):

```
<% strDate = Year(Now) & "-" & Right("00" & Month(Now), 2) & "-" & _
        Right("00" & Day(Now), 2) %>
```

Next, we write the XML prolog back to the client, and the root `<dailyReports>` tag. The root tag has a `dateCreated` attribute, which takes the value of the date created in the last section:

```
<?xml version="1.0" ?>
<dailyReports dateCreated="<% = strDate %>">
```

The result of the second line will be an XML tag with the current date in it:

```
<dailyReports dateCreated="yyyy-mm-dd">
```

This shows you how we can mix the XML tags with ASP. This is exactly the same as the way that we write HTML tags to the client page when using ASP. Since we have set the ContentType property of the Response object to "text/xml", the receiving application knows that we are sending it as XML rather than HTML. Therefore, when we have the strDate variable in between the ASP delimiters, we will just be writing back the value of the strDate variable to the client as the content of the tags.

We also have an <intro> tag, which holds some text, which we will use to display on the browser, as an introduction to the information we are displaying for the list that we are creating:

```
<intro>This is a list of reports on the Wrox Finance site using ASP to create XML
from database content</intro>
```

We then have to establish a connection to the database that holds the data we want to transform into XML, in this case the Reports database. It should come as no surprise that the first thing we do is to create an ADO Connection object. We store this in the variable oConn. And then we open the Connection object held in this variable, passing in the appropriate connection details:

```
<% '-- select all the report details --
  QUOT = Chr(34)
  On Error Resume Next
  Set oConn = Server.CreateObject("ADODB.Connection")
  oConn.Open strConnect
```

We want to retrieve information from the dailyReports table in the database. To do this we need to compose a SQL query:

```
strSQL="SELECT * FROM dailyReport ORDER BY File"
```

The variable strSQL is set to hold the query that retrieves all of the information from the dailyReport table.

Next, we implicitly create a Recordset object in which to place all of the table's information. We execute the SQL query held in the strSQL variable SQL using the Execute method of our Connection object. We assign the results to our oRs variable:

```
Set oRs = oConn.Execute(strSQL)
```

We then navigate through each record and, as we go, we set four variables to hold the date, department, summary, and file name:

```
Do While Not oRs.EOF
   strDate = oRs("Date")
   strDept = oRs("Dept")
   strKeyInfo = oRs("KeyInfo")
   strFile = oRs("File")
%>
```

The query will go through the records until the end of the table is found, using the end of file method EOF. This is because we have started a Do...While function, which allows us to loop through the following procedure for each record in the database. The Loop command comes later, after we have written the XML for the current entry.

To create the XML from the database we use the same technique as that used to insert the date in the dateCreated attribute of the dailyReports root element. First we write the opening <report> tag back to the client, followed by the opening <date> tag. Then we write the value of the strDate variable that holds the date for the current record back to the client as the content of the <date> element. We do the same for the <dept> and <keyInfo> elements. After retrieving the information, we just write in the closing </report> tag:

```
<report>
  <date><% = strDate %></date>
  <dept><% = strDept %></dept>
  <keyInfo><% = strKeyInfo %></keyInfo>
</report>
```

So far, this will write one record of XML back to the client. We now have to loop through the remaining records, until the end of the file is found, and write a record for each of them. We then close the recordset and the database connection and clean up after ourselves, to save system resources.

```
<%
'loop through the records creating XML
   oRs.MoveNext
  Loop
  oRs.Close
  oConn.Close
  Set oConn = Nothing
  Set oRs = Nothing
%>
```

Finally we write out the closing </dailyReport> root element tag.

```
</dailyReports>
```

Let's now have a brief look at how we could achieve the same thing using ADO 2.5 to create the XML.

Using ADO 2.5 to Create XML from Databases

With ADO 2.5 Microsoft allows us to create XML from database content and save it to a file or return it as a stream (a stream being a block of data in memory that is not processed), see Chapter 14. However, at the time of writing, ADO would only create XML as element content. For example:

```
<z:row id="1" dept="Pharm" date="1999-10-11"
      Full_Report="Full Pharm Report is here… "
      KeyInfo="Summary info for Pharm dept" />
<z:row id="2" dept="Petro" date="1999-10-11"
      Full_Report="Full Petro Report is here… "
      KeyInfo="Summary info for Petro dept" />
```

There is no reason why you should not use this format. Indeed, it can be considered beneficial as the network traffic is less. However, at the time of writing, it allowed no flexibility in the format in which it creates this output. So, it depends upon the way in which you want to structure your data, and on the DTD you are using, as to whether this format is suitable to you. If this will suffice you can learn how to use it from either Professional ADO 2.5 *(ISBN 1-861002-75-0, due out in January)* or Professional ASP 3.0 *(1-861002-61-0)* – both published by Wrox Press. Information is also available at the Microsoft web site: http://msdn.Microsoft.com.

So far in this chapter we have seen several ways of creating XML and we have seen how to display it using CSS. IE5 also provides a helpful way of displaying and navigating through our XML documents, using databinding in a standard HTML page.

Databinding

Another way of exposing XML in web pages is using an **XML Data Island**. They were introduced in IE5 and use the **XML Data Source Object** (DSO), which is made available to IE5 using the `<XML>` tag. Using the XML DSO we can bind HTML elements to an XML data set, so we can use a table to display the data and move between the records in the XML file.

Embedding an XML data island into an HTML page is easy, we just add an `<XML>` tag and give a name for our data island using the `id` attribute, like so:

```
<XML id="xmldata"></XML>
```

This creates a data island we can refer to through the name `xmldata`. It is actually a COM object, but we do not need to use the `CreateObject` method, because of this new `<XML>` tag.

> *Note that this is an HTML element and not an XML element, so it must have a separate closing tag-you can't use `<XML ID="XMLData" />`.*

So, we now have our data island — which exposes the DSO — but, as yet, it has no content. There are two ways of providing this content. The first and simplest is to simply place the XML content within the boundaries of the `<XML>` tag:

```
<XML id="XMLdata">
<books>
   <book>
      <title>XML Applications</title>
      <quantity>23</quantity>
      <ISBN>1-861001-52-5</ISBN>
   </book>
   <book>
      <title>IE5 XML Programmer's Reference</title>
      <quantity>37</quantity>
      <ISBN>1-861001-57-6</ISBN>
   </book>
<books>
</XML>
```

Note that the top-level tag `<books>` is analogous to a recordset. It contains, in this example, two 'rows', named `book`, and each of these 'rows' contains three columns, named `title`, `quantity` and `ISBN` respectively. Directly listing XML content in a data island is a simple yet effective approach for small quantities of data.

The other technique for populating the data island with XML, which we will use shortly, is to specify an external source for the content through the src attribute of the <XML> tag. This external source need not necessarily be an XML file, it just needs to be a file that will provide the data island with XML (we could, for example, use an ASP page that creates XML).

Before we get down to using a data island, we need to discuss the XML Data Source Object in a little more detail.

The XML Data Source Object

Microsoft Data Access Components (also referred to as Universal Data Access) are a set of COM interfaces, designed to replace ODBC. Rather than merely putting a component wrapper around relational data access, a new layer of abstraction was introduced. Their aim is to provide one single approach to accessing any body of persistent data that can be expressed in terms of rows and columns (comma delimited text, XML, Excel Spreadsheets, relational databases, etc.). This family of interfaces collectively take the name Microsoft Data Access Components (MDAC), providing robust data access services to COM-aware applications.

Although comparatively new, MDAC are the designated successor to ODBC. Although MDAC provides a driver for ODBC sources, database vendors are beginning to provide native OLE-DB drivers in order to support MDAC. We have already met ADO (ActiveX Data Objects) earlier in the book. They provide the client side of MDAC. Data binding, which has been used in Microsoft Foundation Classes for a long time, and more recently a feature of Microsoft's implementation of Dynamic HTML (or DHTML), is a popular technique now built on top of MDAC.

One of the key ideas behind Microsoft's Universal Data Access strategy is the ability to provide access to data without respect to their underlying native storage format. The XML Data Source Object is an ideal demonstration of this. In the earliest implementation of XML support in Windows, XML DSO was a Java applet. In the latest version, however, the DSO is a COM object closely integrated with Internet Explorer. The DSO exposes XML-encoded text as both data rowsets (as if they were from a relational database), and also as XML DOM parse trees. The choice of which to use is ours; we are able to use whichever model best suits our programming needs. We shall start off by embedding an XML data island into our page, because XML data islands actually expose the XML DSO.

OK, let's use the XML DSO to create a table that allows users to scroll through books, their ISBNs and the quantity available.

These are the steps we shall take:

- ❑ Create an XML data source
- ❑ Embed a data island into an HTML page
- ❑ Link the data island our XML data source
- ❑ Link HTML < INPUT> tags into the DSO
- ❑ Provide buttons for navigating through the XML

1. Fire up your favourite text editor; the first thing we are going to do is create our XML document. Type in the following code:

```
<books>
   <book>
      <title>XML Applications</title>
      <quantity>23</quantity>
      <ISBN>1-861001-52-5</ISBN>
   </book>
   <book>
      <title>IE5 XML Programmer's Reference</title>
      <quantity>37</quantity>
      <ISBN>1-861001-57-6</ISBN>
   </book>
   <book>
      <title>Designing Distributed Applications</title>
      <quantity>15</quantity>
      <ISBN>1-861002-27-0</ISBN>
   </book>
   <book>
      <title>XML Design and Implementation</title>
      <quantity>12</quantity>
      <ISBN>1-861002-28-9</ISBN>
   </book>
</books>
```

2. Save the file with the name booklist.xml, in your XMLFiles folder. We have now created our XML source file. We now want to populate a data island with XML from this source.

3. We need to create an HTML page that incorporates a data island, using the HTML `<XML>` tag. In your text editor, create a new file called databinding.html (again, save it in the XMLFiles folder). Type in the following code:

```
<HTML>
<HEAD>
<TITLE>Data Binding Sample 1</TITLE>
</HEAD>
<BODY>
<XML id=xmlData src = "booklist.xml"></XML>
```

We have now created our data island, which exposes the DSO. We access our XML source file via the DSO interfaces, using `<input>` tags in our HTML page.

4. At the bottom of your `databinding.html` file, add the following:

```html
<h1>Navigating the BookList XML file</h1>
<TABLE border="1" borderColor="maroon" cellPadding="1" cellSpacing="1" width="75%">
  <TR bgColor="#999999">
    <TD><FONT color="maroon" size="2">Title</FONT></TD>
    <TD>
      <INPUT dataFld="title" dataSrc="#xmlData" style="HEIGHT: 22px; WIDTH:
                286px">
    </TD>
  </TR>
  <TR bgColor="#999999">
    <TD><FONT color="darkred" size="2">Quantity</FONT></TD>
    <TD>
      <INPUT dataFld="quantity" dataSrc="#xmlData" style="HEIGHT: 22px; WIDTH:
                286px">
    </TD>
  </TR>
  <TR bgColor="#999999">
    <TD><FONT color="maroon" size="2">ISBN</FONT></TD>
    <TD>
      <INPUT dataFld="ISBN" dataSrc="#xmlData"
          style="HEIGHT: 22px; WIDTH: 286px">
    </TD>
  </TR>
</TABLE>
```

5. Our last task is to add some buttons to our page to navigate through the data island (and thus the data in our XML page). Add the following HTML to the bottom of the `databinding.html` page:

```html
<INPUT id="button1" name="button1" onclick="xmlData.recordset.moveFirst()"
                type="button" value="First">
<INPUT id="button2" name="button2" type="button" value="<" onClick="if
                              (xmlData.recordset.absoluteposition > 1)
                                  xmlData.recordset.movePrevious()">
<INPUT id="button3" name="button3" type="button" value=">" onClick="if
                          (xmlData.recordset.absoluteposition <
                                    xmlData.recordset.recordcount)
                                  xmlData.recordset.moveNext()">
<INPUT id="button4" name="button4" type="button" value="Last"
                      onClick="xmlData.recordset.moveLast()">
</BODY>
</HTML>
```

6. Save your `databinding.html` file, open up your browser and navigate it. You should be able to scroll through the records, checking the stock levels of the books, just as if the data were coming from a relational database:

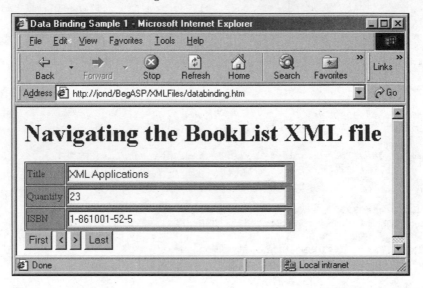

How It Works

The first thing we did was to create the XML file, `booklist.xml`, which will be our data source:

```
<books>
   <book>
      <title>XML Applications</title>
      <quantity>23</quantity>
      <ISBN>1-861001-52-5</ISBN>
   </book>
   ...
```

The top-level tag `<books>` is analogous to a recordset. Underneath it is the first 'row', identified by the `<book>` tag. This 'row' contains three columns, named `title`, `quantity` and `ISBN` respectively. The `books` 'recordset' contains three other `book` rows, each containing three columns that describe a particular book. This is the source file that will feed our data island.

Creating the Data Island

The next thing we did was to start to construct an HTML page that incorporated a data island, using the `<XML>` tag:

```
<HTML>
<HEAD>
<TITLE>Data Binding Sample 1</TITLE>
</HEAD>
<BODY>
<XML id=xmlData src = "booklist.xml"></XML>
```

Thus we have created a data island called `xmlData` and thus have exposed the DSO. We used the `src` attribute of the `<XML>` tag to define our booklist.xml file as the data source.

When the page is loaded, Internet Explorer will read the data from `booklist.xml` file. When a data island is loaded with a page, Internet Explorer transparently loads the data into a parse tree and offers several COM interfaces (exposing methods and properties) for our use. The standard DSO interfaces allow XML elements to participate in data binding as if the data were coming from a database. In addition, the familiar XML DOM interfaces are available as well. This is not surprising, as MSXML is the component that implements the XML DSO. The DSO parses the XML content and keeps bound elements synchronized with the content. As the user navigates through the rowset, the DSO will navigate through the parse tree, exposing each top-level child in turn as a 'row' of data.

We already have our XML data island, which exposes the XML DSO. Once the page is loaded we can either access the XML file through the standard DOM interfaces or through the COM interfaces supplied by the XML DSO (whichever you prefer to program in).

Displaying the Data

We display our book data by binding the XML DSO to HTML `<INPUT>` elements, allowing us to navigate the data as if it were coming from a relational database.

We simply link the `<INPUT>` elements in our page to the XML DSO by adding two attributes:

- ❏ `dataSrc`
- ❏ `dataFld`

The `dataSrc` attribute value is the name of the DSO with the prefix #. Remember, in this example, we called our data island `xmlData`, so we use `dataSrc="#xmlData"`.

The `dataFld` attribute specifies which column of the rowset provided by the DSO should be bound to the page element. So, in this example, our first `<INPUT>` element displays the title of the book, so we need to link to the `<title>` element of our XML file.

```
<h1>Navigating the BookList XML file</h1>
<TABLE border="1" borderColor="maroon" cellPadding="1" cellSpacing="1" width="75%">
  <TR bgColor="#999999">
    <TD><FONT color="maroon" size="2">Title</FONT></TD>
    <TD>
      <INPUT dataFld="title" dataSrc="#xmlData" style="HEIGHT: 22px; WIDTH:
                286px">
    </TD>
  </TR>
```

We specify `dataFld` and `dataSrc` attributes for each of the other INPUT elements in the same manner:

```
<TR bgColor="#999999">
  <TD><FONT color="darkred" size="2">Quantity</FONT></TD>
  <TD>
    <INPUT dataFld="quantity" dataSrc="#xmlData" style="HEIGHT: 22px; WIDTH:
              286px">
```

```
      </TD>
    </TR>
    <TR bgColor="#999999">
      <TD><FONT color="maroon" size="2">ISBN</FONT></TD>
      <TD>
        <INPUT dataFld="ISBN" dataSrc="#xmlData"
               style="HEIGHT: 22px; WIDTH: 286px">
      </TD>
    </TR>
  </TABLE>
```

That will bind the user interface elements to the XML data. But, when we first view the page it will display the first `<title>` element from our XML file - which was XML Applications. So, we need to give the users some way of looking at the details of the other books.

Navigating through the Data Island

There are a number of ways we could move between the data in the XML file. In this example we use a recordset property. All the properties and methods of an ADO recordset are accessible through the data island's recordset property. In our example, we would move the internal cursor of the DSO to the next row of the recordset like so:

```
XMLdata.Recordset.MoveNext()
```

This is what we use to allow the users to move between the books in stock on our page. This is just how we can manipulate data from a database using the ADO recordset property.

```
<INPUT id="button1" name="button1" onclick="xmlData.recordset.moveFirst()"
                 type="button" value="First">
<INPUT id="button2" name="button2" type="button" value="<" onClick="if
                                    (xmlData.recordset.absoluteposition > 1)
                                        xmlData.recordset.movePrevious()">
<INPUT id="button3" name="button3" type="button" value=">" onClick="if
                            (xmlData.recordset.absoluteposition <
                                    xmlData.recordset.recordcount)
                                    xmlData.recordset.moveNext()">
<INPUT id="button4" name="button4" type="button" value="Last"
                        onClick="xmlData.recordset.moveLast()">
```

The key is in the inline fragments we provide to handle the `onClick` event. For example, look at the handler for moving ahead one row:

```
If (xmlData.recordset.absoluteposition < xmlData.recordset.recordcount)
                                    xmlData.recordset.moveNext()
```

The ADO recordset object is a child of the data island, and the `absoluteposition` property tells us what row the cursor is on. In this handler, if the cursor isn't on the last row of the recordset, we tell it to advance to the next row. When this happens, the DSO keeps the `<INPUT>` elements synchronized with the recordset, and the user sees the values for the next `<book>` element. Then simply add the following to end the page.

```
</BODY>
</HTML>
```

That's it! We can now scroll through the records, checking the stock levels of books. It's as simple as that, we don't need manipulation scripts since we have the data exposed by the XML DSO as if it were coming from a relational database.

Summary

In this chapter we have looked at XML, and some of the technologies surrounding this new buzzword. We have seen the syntax we use to write XML documents, and how to define our own markup languages using DTDs. This gives us the core skills for writing XML. The ability to read DTDs will also allow you to read other markup languages created in XML. We then went on to see how to make our XML attractive when displayed on the Web using Cascading Style Sheets.

We then went on to see how we might use XML in our applications. We have seen how we can use the DOM to navigate around a tree that can be exposed by a parser. We created XML from a web page and from a relational database. We also saw how we can bind an XML Data Island to an XML source. Hopefully this will have whetted your appetite to see some more advanced things we can do with XML.

Hopefully, this book will only be the beginning of your programming challenges with ASP. You'll have seen that ASP can be used for simple dynamic, customized pages or for creating large web applications that rely on data stores, so what next? Even in the last few months the number of major companies that have used ASP to help power their web sites has increased dramatically. There are plenty of subject areas that you can choose to follow and learn more about. If you want to know more about ASP then we suggest that you progress straight to *Professional Active Server Pages – ISBN-1-861002-61-0*. If you are more interested in setting up an application that utilizes ASP and databases then, you should take a look *at Beginning ASP Databases ISBN 1-861002-72-6*, by one of the authors of this book, John Kauffman. If you're looking to apply some of these techniques presented here to start building your own commercial site, then try *Beginning E-Commerce 1-861003-986* for an overview of the problems involved. If you're interesting in building an application from the ground up with your own customized components, then *Beginning Components with ASP ISBN 1-861002-882* is a great place to start. Finally, if you're interested in how the potentially groundbreaking technology of XML will next evolve, and where it fits in with ASP then try *Professional XML ISBN 1-861003-11-0*.

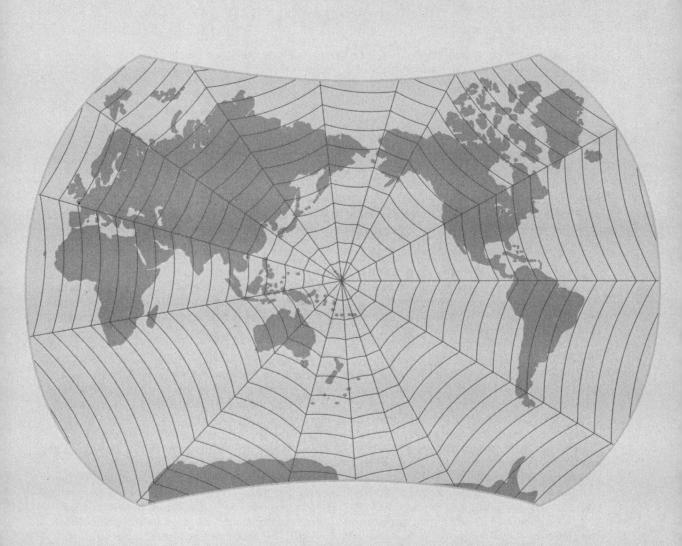

The ASP 3.0 Object Model

The ASP object model is made up of six objects. The following diagram shows conceptually how these objects relate to the client and the server, the requests made by the client and the responses sent back to them from the server:

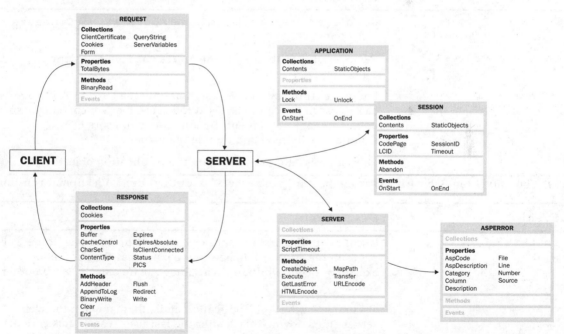

The Application Object

The Application object is created when the ASP DLL is loaded in response to the first request for an ASP page. It provides a repository for storing variables and object references that are available to all the pages that all visitors open.

Collection	Description
Contents	A collection of all of the variables and their values that are stored in the Application object, and are not defined using an `<OBJECT>` element. This includes Variant arrays and Variant-type object instance references.
StaticObjects	A collection of all of the variables that are stored in the Application object by using an `<OBJECT>` element.

Method	Description
Contents.Remove ("*variable_name*")	Removes a named variable from the `Application.Contents` collection.
Contents.RemoveAll()	Removes all variables from the `Application.Contents` collection.
Lock()	Locks the Application object so that only the current ASP page has access to the contents. Used to ensure that concurrency issues do not corrupt the contents by allowing two users to simultaneously read and update the values.
Unlock()	Releases this ASP page's lock on the Application object.

* You *cannot* remove variables from the `Application.StaticObjects` collection at run-time.

Event	Description
onStart	Occurs with the first instance of a user requesting one of the web pages in the application, before the page that the user requests is executed. Used to initialize variables, create objects, or run other code.
onEnd	Occurs when the ASP application ends, that is, when the web server shuts down. This is after the last user session has ended, and after any code in the onEnd event for that session has executed. All variables existing in the application are destroyed when it ends.

The ASPError Object

The ASPError object is a new object in ASP 3.0, and is available through the `GetLastError` method of the Server object. It provides a range of detailed information about the last error that occurred in ASP.

Property	Description
ASPCode	*Integer.* The error number generated by IIS.
ASPDescription	*Integer.* A detailed description of the error if it is ASP-related.
Category	*String.* Indicates the source of the error: e.g. ASP itself, the scripting language, or an object.
Column	*Integer.* The character position within the file that generated the error.
Description	*String.* A short description of the error.
File	*String.* The name of the file that was being processed when the error occurred.
Line	*Integer.* The number of the line within the file that generated the error.
Number	*Integer.* A standard COM error code.
Source	*String.* The actual code, where available, of the line that caused the error.

The Request Object

The Request object makes available to the script all the information that the client provides when requesting a page or submitting a form. This includes the HTTP server variables that identify the browser and the user, cookies that are stored on the browser for this domain, and any values appended to the URL as a query string or in HTML controls in a <FORM> section of the page. It also provides access to any certificate that they may be using through **Secure Sockets Layer** (SSL) or other encrypted communication protocol, and properties that help to manage the connection.

Collection	Description
ClientCertificate	A collection of the values of all the fields or entries in the client certificate that the user presented to our server when accessing a page or resource. Each member is read-only.
Cookies	A collection of the values of all the cookies sent from the user's system along with their request. Only cookies valid for the domain containing the resource are sent to the server.
Form	A collection of the values of all the HTML control elements in the <FORM> section that was submitted as the request, where the value of the METHOD attribute is POST. Each member is read-only.

Table Continued on Following Page

Collection	Description
QueryString	A collection of all the name/value pairs appended to the URL in the user's request, or the values of all the HTML control elements in the <FORM> section that was submitted as the request, where the value of the METHOD attribute is GET or the attribute is omitted. Each member is read-only.
ServerVariables	A collection of all the HTTP header values sent from the client with their request, plus the values of several environment variables for the web server. Each member is read-only.

Property	Description
TotalBytes	*Integer*. Read-only value holding the total number of bytes in the body of the request sent by the client.

Method	Description
BinaryRead(*count*)	Retrieves *count* bytes of data from the client's request when the data is sent to the server as part of a POST request. It returns as a Variant array (or SafeArray). This method *cannot* be used successfully if the ASP code has already referenced the Request.Form collection. Likewise, the Request.Form collection *cannot* be successfully accessed if you have used the BinaryRead method.

The Response Object

The Response object is used to access the response that is being created to send back to the client. It makes available the HTTP variables that identify the server and its capabilities, information about the content being sent to the browser, and any new cookies that will be stored on the browser for this domain. It also provides a series of methods that are used to create the returned page.

Collection	Description
Cookies	A collection containing the values of all the cookies that will be sent back to the client in the current response. Each member is write-only.

The Response object provides a range of properties that can be read (in most cases) and modified to tailor the response:

Property	Description
Buffer = True|False	*Boolean*. Read/write. Specifies if the output created by an ASP page will be held in the IIS buffer until all of the server scripts in the current page have been processed, or until the Flush or End method is called. It must be set before any output is sent to IIS, including HTTP header information, so it should be the first line of the .asp file after the <%@LANGUAGE=..%> statement. Buffering is on (True) by default in ASP 3.0, whereas it was off (False) by default in earlier versions.
CacheControl "*setting*"	*String*. Read/write. Set this property to "Public" to allow proxy servers to cache the page, or "Private" to prevent proxy caching taking place.
Charset = "*value*"	*String*. Read/write. Appends the name of the character set (for example, ISO-LATIN-7) to the HTTP Content-Type header created by the server for each response.
ContentType "*MIME-type*"	*String*. Read/write. Specifies the HTTP content type for the response, as a standard MIME-type (such as "text/xml" or "image/gif"). If omitted the MIME-type "text/html" is used. The content type tells the browser what type of content to expect.
Expires *minutes*	*Number*. Read/write. Specifies the length of time in minutes that a page is valid for. If the user returns to the same page before it expires, the cached version is displayed. After that period it expires, and should not be held in a private (user) or public (proxy) cache.
ExpiresAbsolute #*date[time]*#	*Date/Time*. Read/write. Specifies the absolute date and time when a page will expire and no longer be valid. If the user returns to the same page before it expires, the cached version is displayed. After that time it expires, and should not be held in a private (user) or public (proxy) cache.
IsClientConnected	*Boolean*. Read-only. Returns an indication of whether the client is still connected to and loading the page from the server. Can be used to end processing (with the Response.End method) if a client moves to another page before the current one has finished executing.
PICS ("*PICS-label-string*")	*String*. Write-only. Creates a PICS header and adds it to the HTTP headers in the response. PICS headers define the content of the page in terms of violence, sex, bad language, etc.
Status = "*code message*"	*String*. Read/write. Specifies the status value and message that will be sent to the client in the HTTP headers of the response to indicate an error or successful processing of the page. Examples are "200 OK" and "404 Not Found".

Method	Description
AddHeader ("*name*", "*content*")	Creates a custom HTTP header using the *name* and *content* values and adds it to the response. Will *not* replace an existing header of the same name. Once a header has been added, it cannot be removed. Must be used before any page content (i.e. text and HTML) is sent to the client.
AppendToLog ("*string*")	Adds a string to the end of the web server log entry for this request when **W3C Extended Log File Format** is in use. Requires at least the **URI Stem** value to be selected in the **Extended Properties** page for the site containing the page.
BinaryWrite (*SafeArray*)	Writes the content of a Variant-type *SafeArray* to the current HTTP output stream without any character conversion. Useful for writing non-string information, such as binary data required by a custom application, or the bytes to make up an image file.
Clear()	Erases any existing buffered page content from the IIS response buffer when Response.Buffer is True. Does *not* erase HTTP response headers. Can be used to abort a partly completed page.
End()	Stops ASP from processing the page script and returns the currently created content, then aborts any further processing of this page.
Flush()	Sends all currently buffered page content in the IIS buffer to the client when Response.Buffer is True. Can be used to send parts of a long page to the client individually.
Redirect ("*url*")	Instructs the browser to load the page in the string *url* parameter by sending a "302 Object Moved" HTTP header in the response.
Write ("*string*")	Writes the specified *string* to the current HTTP response stream and IIS buffer so that it becomes part of the returned page.

The Server Object

The Server object provides a series of methods and properties that are useful in scripting with ASP. The most obvious is the Server.CreateObject method, which properly instantiates other COM objects within the context of the current page or session. There are also methods to translate strings into the correct format for use in URLs and in HTML, by converting non-legal characters to the correct legal equivalent.

Property	Description
ScriptTimeout	*Integer*. Has the default value 90. Sets or returns the number of seconds that script in the page can execute for before the server aborts page execution and reports an error. This automatically halts and removes from memory pages that contain errors that may lock execution into a loop, or those that stall while waiting for a resource to become available. This prevents the server becoming overloaded with badly behaved pages. You may need to increase this value if your pages take a long time to run.

Method	Description
CreateObject ("*identifier*")	Creates an instance of the object (a component, application or scripting object) that is identified by "*identifier*", and returns a reference to it that can be used in our code. Can be used in the global.asa page of a virtual application to create objects with session-level or application-level scope. The object can be identified by its ClassID (i.e. "{CLSID:FDC8-...-37A9}") value, or by a ProgID string such as "ADODB.Connection".
Execute ("*url*")	Stops execution of the current page and transfers control to the page specified in "*url*". The user's current environment (i.e. session state and any current transaction state) is carried over to the new page. After that page has finished execution, control passes back to the original page and execution resumes at the statement after the Execute method call.
GetLastError()	Returns a reference to an ASPError object that holds details of the last error that occurred within the ASP processing, i.e. within asp.dll. The information exposed by the ASPError object includes the file name, line number, error code, etc.
HTMLEncode ("*string*")	Returns a string that is a copy of the input value "*string*" but with all non-legal HTML characters, such as '<', '>', '&' and double quotes, converted into the equivalent HTML entity – i.e. <, >, &, ", etc.
MapPath ("*url*")	Returns the full physical path and filename of the file or resource specified in "*url*".
Transfer ("*url*")	Stops execution of the current page and transfers control to the page specified in "*url*". The user's current environment (i.e. session state and any current transaction state) is carried over to the new page. Unlike the Execute method, execution *does not* resume in the original page, but ends when the new page has completed executing.
URLEncode ("*string*")	Returns a string that is a copy of the input value "*string*" but with all characters that are not valid in a URL, such as '?', '&' and spaces, converted into the equivalent URL entity – i.e. '%3F', '%26', and '+'.

The Session Object

The Session object is created for each visitor when they first request an ASP page from the site, and remains available until the default timeout period (or the timeout period determined by the script) expires. It provides a repository for storing variables and object references that are available just to the pages that this visitor opens during the lifetime of this session.

Collection	Description
Contents	A collection of all the variables and their values that are stored in this particular Session object, and are *not* defined using an <OBJECT> element. This includes Variant arrays and Variant-type object instance references.
StaticObjects	A collection of all of the variables that are stored in this particular Session object by using an <OBJECT> element.

Property	Description
CodePage	*Integer*. Read/write. Defines the code page that will be used to display the page content in the browser. The code page is the numeric value of the character set, and different languages and locales may use different code pages. For example, ANSI code page 1252 is used for American English and most European languages. Code page 932 is used for Japanese Kanji.
LCID	*Integer*. Read/write. Defines the locale identifier (LCID) of the page that is sent to the browser. The LCID is a standard international abbreviation that uniquely identifies the locale; for instance 2057 defines a locale where the currency symbol used is '£'. This LCID can also be used in statements such as FormatCurrency, where there is an optional LCID argument. The LCID for a page can also be set in the opening <%@...%> ASP processing directive, and overrides the setting in the LCID property of the session.
SessionID	*Long*. Read-only. Returns the session identifier for this session, which is generated by the server when the session is created. Unique only for the duration of the parent Application object, and so may be re-used when a new application is started.
Timeout	*Integer*. Read/write. Defines the timeout period in minutes for this Session object. If the user does not refresh or request a page within the timeout period, the session ends. Can be changed in individual pages as required. The default is 20 minutes, and shorter timeouts may be preferred on a high-usage site.

Method	Description
Contents.Remove ("*variable_name*")	Removes a named variable from the Session.Contents collection.
Contents.RemoveAll()	Removes all variables from the Session.Contents collection.
Abandon()	Ends the current user session and destroys the current Session object once execution of this page is complete. You can still access the current session's variables in this page, even after calling the Abandon method. However the next ASP page that is requested by this user will start a new session, and create a new Session object with only the default values defined in global.asa (if any exist).

* You *cannot* remove variables from the Session.StaticObjects collection at run-time.

Event	Description
onStart	Occurs when an ASP user session starts, before the first page that the user requests is executed. Used to initialize variables, create objects, or run other code.
onEnd	Occurs when an ASP user session ends. This is when the predetermined session timeout period has elapsed since that user's last page request from the application. All variables existing in the session are destroyed when it ends. It is also possible to end ASP user sessions explicitly in code, and this event occurs when that happens.

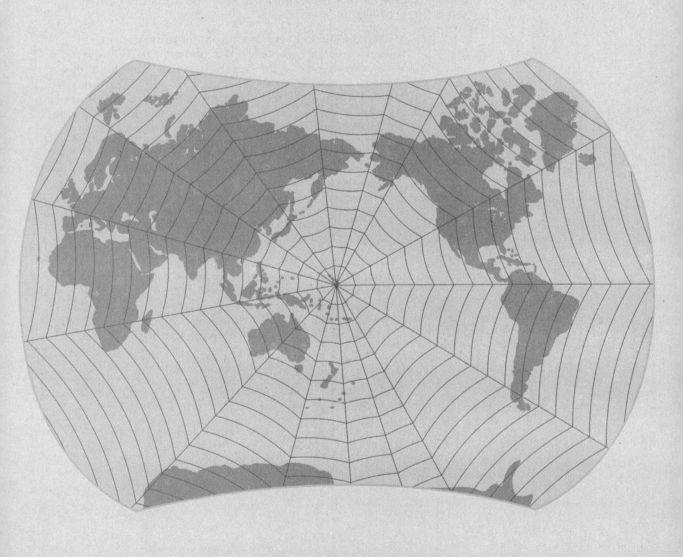

The Scripting Run-Time Library Objects

The default scripting languages installed with Windows 2000 and ASP 3.0 provide a scripting run-time library in the file scrrun.dll, which implements a series of objects that can be used in ASP on the server and in client-side code running on the client.

The Scripting.Dictionary Object

The Dictionary object provides a useful storage object that we can use to store values accessed and referenced by their name, rather than by index as would be the case in a normal array. The properties and methods exposed by the Dictionary object are:

Property	Description
CompareMode	(*VBScript only*). Sets or returns the string comparison mode for the keys.
Count	Read-only. Returns the number of key/item pairs in the Dictionary.
Item(*key*)	Sets or returns the value of the item for the specified *key*.
Key(*key*)	Sets or returns the value of a key.

Method	Description
Add (*key, item*)	Adds the *key/item* pair to the Dictionary.
Exists (*key*)	Returns True if the specified *key* exists or False if not.
Items ()	Returns an array containing all the items in a Dictionary object.
Keys ()	Returns an array containing all the keys in a Dictionary object.
Remove (*key*)	Removes a single key/item pair specified by *key*.
RemoveAll ()	Removes all the key/item pairs.

* An error will occur if we try to add a key/item pair when that key already exists, remove a key/item pair that doesn't exist, or change the CompareMode of a Dictionary object that already contains data.

The Scripting.FileSystemObject Object

The FileSystemObject object provides us with access to the underlying file system on the server (or on the client in IE5 when used in conjunction with a special type of page named a **Hypertext Application** or **HTA**). The FileSystemObject object exposes a series of properties and methods of its own, some of which return other objects that are specific to objects within the file system. These subsidiary objects are:

❑ The Drive object, which provides access to all the drives available on the machine

❑ The Folder object, which provides access to the folders on a drive

❑ The File object, which provides access to the files within each folder

While these three objects form a neat hierarchy, the FileSystemObject object also provides methods that can bridge the hierarchy by creating instances of the subsidiary objects directly. The diagram below shows the way that you can navigate the file system of the machine using the various objects:

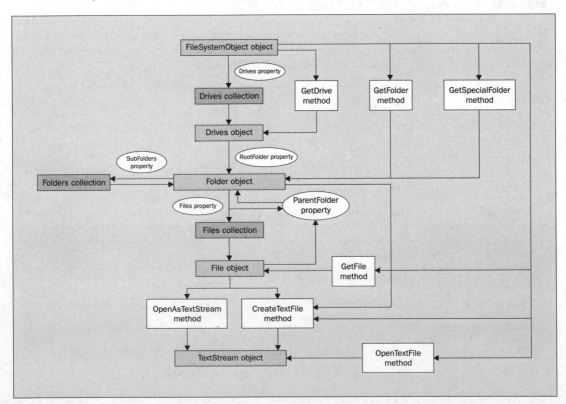

Property	Description
Drives	Returns a collection of Drive objects that are available from the local machine. This includes network drives that are mapped from this machine.

Method	Description
BuildPath (*path*, *name*)	Adds the file or folder specified in *name* to the existing *path*, adding a path separator character ('\') if required.
CopyFile (*source*, *destination*, *overwrite*)	Copies the file or files specified in *source* (wildcards can be included) to the folder specified in *destination*. If *source* contains wildcards or *destination* ends with a path separator character ('\') then *destination* is assumed to be a folder, otherwise it is assumed to be a full path and name for the new file. An error will occur if the *destination* file already exists and the optional *overwrite* parameter is set to False. The default for *overwrite* is True.
CopyFolder (*source*, *destination*, *overwrite*)	Copies the folder or folders specified in *source* (wildcards can be included) to the folder specified in *destination*, including all the files contained in the *source* folder(s). If *source* contains wildcards or *destination* ends with a path separator character ('\') then *destination* is assumed to be a folder into which the copied folder(s) will be placed, otherwise it is assumed to be a full path and name for a new folder to be created. An error will occur if the *destination* folder already exists and the optional *overwrite* parameter is set to False. The default for *overwrite* is True.
CreateFolder (*foldername*)	Creates a new folder that has the path and name specified in *foldername*. An error occurs if the specified folder already exists.
CreateTextFile (*filename*, *overwrite*, *unicode*)	Creates a new text file on disk with the specified *filename* and returns a TextStream object that refers to it. If the optional *overwrite* parameter is set to True, any existing file with the same path and name will be overwritten. The default for *overwrite* is False. If the optional *unicode* parameter is set to True, the content of the file will be stored as Unicoded text. The default for *unicode* is False.
DeleteFile (*filespec*, *force*)	Deletes the file or files specified in *filespec* (wildcards can be included). If the optional *force* parameter is set to True the file(s) will be deleted even if the Read-only attribute is set. The default for *force* is False.

Method	Description
DeleteFolder (*folderspec*, *force*)	Deletes the folder or folders specified in *folderspec* (wildcards can be included in the final component of the path) together with all their contents. If the optional *force* parameter is set to True, the folders will be deleted even if their, or any contained files', Read-only attribute is set. The default for *force* is False.
DriveExists (*drivespec*)	Returns True if the drive specified in *drivespec* exists, or False if not. The *drivespec* parameter can be a drive letter as a string, or a full absolute path for a folder or file.
FileExists (*filespec*)	Returns True if the file specified in *filespec* exists, or False if not. The *filespec* parameter can contain an absolute or relative path for the file, or just the file name to look in the current folder.
FolderExists (*folderspec*)	Returns True if the folder specified in *folderspec* exists, or False if not. The *folderspec* parameter can contain an absolute or relative path for the folder, or just the folder name to look in the current folder.
GetAbsolutePathName (*pathspec*)	Takes a *path* that unambiguously identifies a folder and, taking into account the current folder's path, returns a full path specification for the *pathspec* folder. For example, if the current folder is "c:\docs\sales\" and *pathspec* is "jan", the returned value is "c:\docs\sales\jan". Wildcards and the ".." and "\\" path operators are accepted.
GetBaseName (*filespec*)	Returns just the name of the file specified in *filespec*, i.e. with the path and file extension removed.
GetDrive (*drivespec*)	Returns a Drive object corresponding to the drive specified in *drivespec*. The format for *drivespec* can include the colon, path separator or be a network share, i.e. "c", "c:", "c:\" or "\\machine\sharename".
GetDriveName (*drivespec*)	Returns the name of the drive specified in *drivespec* as a string. The *drivespec* parameter must be an absolute path to a file or folder, or just the drive letter such as "c:" or "c".
GetExtensionName (*filespec*)	Returns just the file extension of a file specified in *filespec*, i.e. with the path and file name removed.
GetFile (*filespec*)	Returns a File object corresponding to the file specified in *filespec*. This can be a relative or absolute path to the required file.
GetFileName (*pathspec*)	Returns the name part of the path and filename specified in *pathspec*, or the last folder name if there is no file name. Does not check for the existence of the file or folder.

Method	Description
GetFolder (*folderspec*)	Returns a Folder object corresponding to the folder specified in *folderspec*. This can be a relative or absolute path to the required folder.
GetParentFolderName (*pathspec*)	Returns the name of the parent folder of the file or folder specified in *pathspec*. Does not check for the existence of the folder.
GetSpecialFolder (*folderspec*)	Returns a Folder object corresponding to one of the special Windows folders. The permissible values for *folderspec* are WindowsFolder (0), SystemFolder (1) and TemporaryFolder (2).
GetTempName ()	Returns a randomly generated file name that can be used for performing operations that require a temporary file or folder.
MoveFile (*source*, *destination*)	Moves the file or files specified in *source* to the folder specified in *destination*. Wildcards can be included in *source* but not in *destination*. If *source* contains wildcards or *destination* ends with a path separator character ('\') then *destination* is assumed to be a folder, otherwise it is assumed to be a full path and name for the new file. An error will occur if the *destination* file already exists.
MoveFolder (*source*, *destination*)	Moves the folder or folders specified in *source* to the folder specified in *destination*. Wildcards can be included in *source* but not in *destination*. If *source* contains wildcards or *destination* ends with a path separator character ('\') then *destination* is assumed to be the folder in which to place the moved folders, otherwise it is assumed to be a full path and name for a new folder. An error will occur if the *destination* folder already exists.
OpenTextFile (*filename*, *iomode*, *create*, *format*)	Creates a file named *filename*, or opens an existing file named *filename*, and returns a TextStream object that refers to it. The *filename* parameter can contain an absolute or relative path. The *iomode* parameter specifies the type of access required. The permissible values are ForReading (1 – the default), ForWriting (2), and ForAppending (8). If the *create* parameter is set to True when writing or appending to a file that does not exist, a new file will be created. The default for *create* is False. The *format* parameter specifies the format of the data to be read from or written to the file. Permissible values are TristateFalse (0 – the default) to open it as ASCII, TristateTrue (-1) to open it as Unicode, and TristateUseDefault (-2) to open it using the system default format.

The Drive Object

The Drive object provides access to all the drives available on the machine.

Property	Description
AvailableSpace	Returns the amount of space available to this user on the drive, taking into account quotas and/or other restrictions.
DriveLetter	Returns the drive letter of the drive.
DriveType	Returns the type of the drive. The values are: Unknown (0), Removable (1), Fixed (2), Remote (3), CDRom (4), and RamDisk (5). However, note that the current version of scrrun.dll does not include the pre-defined constant for Network, so you must use the decimal value 3 instead.
FileSystem	Returns the type of file system for the drive. The values include "FAT", "NTFS" and "CDFS".
FreeSpace	Returns the actual amount of free space available on the drive.
IsReady	Returns a Boolean value indicating if drive is ready (True) or not (False).
Path	Returns the path for the drive as a drive letter and colon, i.e. "C:".
RootFolder	Returns a Folder object representing the root folder of the drive.
SerialNumber	Returns a decimal serial number used to uniquely identify a disk volume.
ShareName	Returns the network share name for the drive if it is a networked drive.
TotalSize	Returns the total size (in bytes) of the drive.
VolumeName	Sets or returns the volume name of the drive if it is a local drive.

The Folder Object

The Folder object provides access to the folders on a drive.

Property	Description
Attributes	Returns the attributes of the folder. Can be a combination of any of the values: Normal (0), ReadOnly (1), Hidden (2), System (4), Volume (name) (8), Directory (folder) (16), Archive (32), Compressed (128) and Alias (1024).

Property	Description
DateCreated	Returns the date and time that the folder was created.
DateLastAccessed	Returns the date and time that the folder was last accessed.
DateLastModified	Returns the date and time that the folder was last modified.
Drive	Returns the drive letter of the drive on which the folder resides.
Files	Returns a Files collection containing File objects representing all the files within this folder.
IsRootFolder	Returns a Boolean value indicating if the folder is the root folder of the current drive.
Name	Sets or returns the name of the folder.
ParentFolder	Returns the Folder object for the parent folder of this folder.
Path	Returns the absolute path of the folder, using long file names where appropriate.
ShortName	Returns the DOS-style 8.3 version of the folder name.
ShortPath	Returns the DOS-style 8.3 version of the absolute path of this folder.
Size	Returns the size of all files and subfolders contained in the folder.
SubFolders	Returns a Folders collection consisting of all folders contained in the folder, including hidden and system folders.
Type	Returns a string that is a description of the folder type (such as "Recycle Bin") if available.

Method	Description
Copy(*destination*, *overwrite*)	Copies this folder and all its contents to the folder specified in *destination,* including all the files contained in this folder. If *destination* ends with a path separator character ('\') then *destination* is assumed to be a folder into which the copied folder will be placed, otherwise it is assumed to be a full path and name for a new folder to be created. An error will occur if the destination folder already exists and the optional *overwrite* parameter is set to False. The default for *overwrite* is True.

Method	Description
CreateTextFile (*filename*, *overwrite*, *unicode*)	Creates a new text file within this folder with the specified *filename*, and returns a TextStream object that refers to it. If the optional *overwrite* parameter is set to True, any existing file with the same name will be overwritten. The default for *overwrite* is False. If the optional *unicode* parameter is set to True, the content of the file will be stored as Unicoded text. The default for *unicode* is False.
Delete(*force*)	Deletes this folder and all its contents. If the optional *force* parameter is set to True the folder will be deleted even if the Read-only attribute is set on it or on any contained files. The default for *force* is False.
Move (*destination*)	Moves this folder and all its contents to the folder specified in *destination*. If *destination* ends with a path separator character ('\') then *destination* is assumed to be the folder in which to place the moved folder, otherwise it is assumed to be a full path and name for a new folder. An error will occur if the destination folder already exists.

The File Object

The File object provides access to the files within each folder.

Property	Description
Attributes	Returns the attributes of the file. Can be a combination of any of the values: Normal (0), ReadOnly (1), Hidden (2), System (4), Volume (name) (8), Directory (folder) (16), Archive (32), Compressed (128) and Alias (1024).
DateCreated	Returns the date and time that the file was created.
DateLastAccessed	Returns the date and time that the file was last accessed.
DateLastModified	Returns the date and time that the file was last modified.
Drive	Returns the drive letter of the drive on which the file resides.
Name	Sets or returns the name of the file.
ParentFolder	Returns the Folder object for the parent folder of this file.
Path	Returns the absolute path of the file using long file names where appropriate.
ShortName	Returns the DOS-style 8.3 version of the file name.
ShortPath	Returns the DOS-style 8.3 version of the absolute path of this file.

Property	Description
Size	Returns the size of the file in bytes.
Type	Returns a string that is a description of the file type (such as "Text Document" for a .txt file) if available.

Method	Description
Copy (*destination*, *overwrite*)	Copies this file to the folder specified in *destination*. If *destination* ends with a path separator character ('\') then *destination* is assumed to be a folder into which the copied file will be placed, otherwise it is assumed to be a full path and name for a new file to be created. An error will occur if the destination file already exists and the optional *overwrite* parameter is set to False. The default for *overwrite* is True.
CreateTextFile (*filename*, *overwrite*, *unicode*)	Creates a new text file on disk with the specified *filename*, and returns a TextStream object that refers to it. If the optional *overwrite* parameter is set to True, any existing file with the same path and name will be overwritten. The default for *overwrite* is False. If the optional *unicode* parameter is set to True, the content of the file will be stored as Unicoded text. The default for *unicode* is False.
Delete(*force*)	Deletes this file. If the optional *force* parameter is set to True the file will be deleted even if the Read-only attribute is set. The default for *force* is False.
Move (*destination*)	Moves this file to the folder specified in *destination*. If *destination* ends with a path separator character ('\') then *destination* is assumed to be the folder in which to place the moved file, otherwise it is assumed to be a full path and name for a new file. An error will occur if the destination file already exists.
OpenAsTextStream (*iomode*, *format*)	Opens a specified file, and returns a TextStream object that can be used to read from, write to, or append to the file. The *iomode* parameter specifies the type of access required. The permissible values are ForReading (1 – the default), ForWriting (2), and ForAppending (8). The *format* parameter specifies the format of the data to be read from or written to the file. Permissible values are TristateFalse (0 – default) to open it as ASCII, TristateTrue (-1) to open it as Unicode, and TristateUseDefault (-2) to open it using the system default format.

The Scripting.TextStream Object

The TextStream object provides access to files stored on disk, and is used in conjunction with the FileSystemObject object.

Property	Description
AtEndOfLine	Returns True if the file pointer is at the end of a line in the file.
AtEndOfStream	Returns True if the file pointer is at the end of the file.
Column	Returns the column number of the current character in the file, starting from 1.
Line	Returns the current line number in the file, starting from 1.

The AtEndOfLine and AtEndOfStream properties are only available for a file that is opened with iomode of ForReading. Referring to them otherwise causes an error.

Method	Description
Close()	Closes an open file.
Read(*numchars*)	Reads *numchars* characters from the file.
ReadAll()	Reads the entire file as a single string.
ReadLine()	Reads a line from the file as a string.
Skip(*numchars*)	Skips and discards *numchars* characters when reading from the file.
SkipLine()	Skips and discards the next line when reading from the file.
Write(*string*)	Writes *string* to the file.
WriteLine(*string*)	Writes *string* (optional) and a newline character to the file.
WriteBlankLines(*n*)	Writes *n* newline characters to the file.

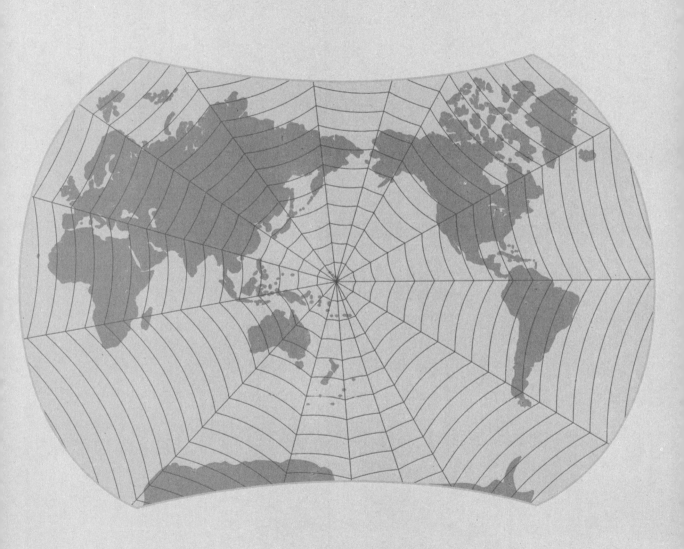

The ADO 2.5 Object Model

Properties or methods new to version 2.5 are shown *italicized*.

All properties are read/write unless otherwise stated.

The ADO Objects

Name	Description
Command	The Command object is a definition of a specific command that you intend to execute against a data source.
Connection	The Connection object represents an open connection to a data store.
Error	The Error object contains the details about data access errors pertaining to a single operation involving the provider.
Errors	The Errors collection contains all of the Error objects created in response to a single failure involving the provider.
Field	The Field object represents a column of data within a common data type.
Fields	The Fields collection contains all of the Field objects of a Recordset object.
Parameter	The Parameter object represents a parameter or argument associated with a Command object, based on a parameterized query or stored procedure.
Parameters	The Parameters collection contains all the Parameter objects of a Command object.
Properties	The Properties collection contains all the Property objects for a specific instance of an object.
Property	The Property object represents a dynamic characteristic of an ADO object that is defined by the provider.
Record	The Record object represents a row in a recordset, or a file or directory in a file system or web resource.
Recordset	The Recordset object represents the entire set of records from a base table or the results of an executed command. At any time, the Recordset object only refers to a single record within the set as the current record.
Stream	The Stream object represents a stream of text or binary data.

The Command Object

Methods

Name	Returns	Description
Cancel		Cancels execution of a pending Execute or Open call.
CreateParameter	Parameter	Creates a new Parameter object.
Execute	Recordset	Executes the query, SQL statement or stored procedure specified in the CommandText property.

Properties

Name	Returns	Description
ActiveConnection	Variant	Indicates to which Connection object the command currently belongs.
CommandText	String	Contains the text of a command to be issued against a data provider.
CommandTimeout	Long	Indicates how long to wait, in seconds, while executing a command before terminating the command and generating an error. Default is 30.
CommandType	CommandType Enum	Indicates the type of Command object.
Name	String	Indicates the name of the Command object.
Parameters	Parameters	Contains all of the Parameter objects for a Command object.
Prepared	Boolean	Indicates whether or not to save a compiled version of a command before execution.
Properties	Properties	Contains all of the Property objects for a Command object.
State	Long	Describes whether the Command object is open or closed. Read-only.

The Connection Object

Methods

Name	Returns	Description
BeginTrans	Integer	Begins a new transaction.
Cancel		Cancels the execution of a pending, asynchronous Execute or Open operation.
Close		Closes an open connection and any dependent objects.
CommitTrans		Saves any changes and ends the current transaction.
Execute	Recordset	Executes the query, SQL statement, stored procedure, or provider specific text.
Open		Opens a connection to a data source, so that commands can be executed against it.
OpenSchema	Recordset	Obtains database schema information from the provider.
RollbackTrans		Cancels any changes made during the current transaction and ends the transaction.

Properties

Name	Returns	Description
Attributes	Long	Indicates one or more characteristics of a Connection object. Default is 0.
CommandTimeout	Long	Indicates how long, in seconds, to wait while executing a command before terminating the command and generating an error. The default is 30.
ConnectionString	String	Contains the information used to establish a connection to a data source.
ConnectionTimeout	Long	Indicates how long, in seconds, to wait while establishing a connection before terminating the attempt and generating an error. Default is 15.
CursorLocation	CursorLocation Enum	Sets or returns the location of the cursor engine.

Name	Returns	Description
DefaultDatabase	String	Indicates the default database for a Connection object.
Errors	Errors	Contains all of the Error objects created in response to a single failure involving the provider.
IsolationLevel	IsolationLevel Enum	Indicates the level of transaction isolation for a Connection object. Write-only.
Mode	ConnectMode Enum	Indicates the available permissions for modifying data in a Connection.
Properties	Properties	Contains all of the Property objects for a Connection object.
Provider	String	Indicates the name of the provider for a Connection object.
State	Long	Describes whether the Connection object is open or closed. Read-only.
Version	String	Indicates the ADO version number. Read-only.

Events

Name	Description
BeginTransComplete	Fired after a BeginTrans operation finishes executing.
CommitTransComplete	Fired after a CommitTrans operation finishes executing.
ConnectComplete	Fired after a connection starts.
Disconnect	Fired after a connection ends.
ExecuteComplete	Fired after a command has finished executing.
InfoMessage	Fired whenever a ConnectionEvent operation completes successfully and additional information is returned by the provider.
RollbackTransComplete	Fired after a RollbackTrans operation has finished executing.
WillConnect	Fired before a connection starts.
WillExecute	Fired before a pending command executes on the connection.

The Error Object

Properties

Name	Returns	Description
Description	String	A description string associated with the error. Read-only.
HelpContext	Integer	Indicates the `ContextID` in the help file for the associated error. Read-only.
HelpFile	String	Indicates the name of the help file. Read-only.
NativeError	Long	Indicates the provider-specific error code for the associated error. Read-only.
Number	Long	Indicates the number that uniquely identifies an `Error` object. Read-only.
Source	String	Indicates the name of the object or application that originally generated the error. Read-only.
SQLState	String	Indicates the SQL state for a given `Error` object. It is a five-character string that follows the ANSI SQL standard. Read-only.

The Errors Collection

Methods

Name	Returns	Description
Clear		Removes all of the `Error` objects from the `Errors` collection.
Refresh		Updates the `Error` objects with information from the provider.

Properties

Name	Returns	Description
Count	Long	Indicates the number of `Error` objects in the `Errors` collection. Read-only.
Item	Error	Allows indexing into the `Errors` collection to reference a specific `Error` object. Read-only.

Field Object

Methods

Name	Returns	Description
AppendChunk		Appends data to a large or binary Field object.
GetChunk	Variant	Returns all or a portion of the contents of a large or binary Field object.

Properties

Name	Returns	Description
ActualSize	Long	Indicates the actual length of a field's value. Read-only.
Attributes	Long	Indicates one or more characteristics of a Field object.
DataFormat	Variant	Identifies the format that the data should be display in.
DefinedSize	Long	Indicates the defined size of the Field object. Write-only.
Name	String	Indicates the name of the Field object.
NumericScale	Byte	Indicates the scale of numeric values for the Field object. Write-only.
OriginalValue	Variant	Indicates the value of a Field object that existed in the record before any changes were made. Read-only.
Precision	Byte	Indicates the degree of precision for numeric values in the Field object. Read-only.
Properties	Properties	Contains all of the Property objects for a Field object.
Type	DataType Enum	Indicates the data type of the Field object.
UnderlyingValue	Variant	Indicates a Field object's current value in the database. Read-only.
Value	Variant	Indicates the value assigned to the Field object.

The Fields Collection

Methods

Name	Returns	Description
Append		Appends a `Field` object to the `Fields` collection.
CancelUpdate		Cancels any changes made to the `Fields` collection.
Delete		Deletes a Field object from the `Fields` collection.
Refresh		Updates the `Field` objects in the `Fields` collection.
Resync		Resynchronizes the data in the `Field` objects.
Update		Saves any changes made to the `Fields` collection.

Properties

Name	Returns	Description
Count	Long	Indicates the number of `Field` objects in the `Fields` collection. Read-only.
Item	Field	Allows indexing into the `Fields` collection to reference a specific `Field` object. Read-only.

The Parameter Object

Methods

Name	Returns	Description
AppendChunk		Appends data to a large or binary `Parameter` object.

Properties

Name	Returns	Description
Attributes	Long	Indicates one or more characteristics of a `Parameter` object.
Direction	ParameterDirection Enum	Indicates whether the `Parameter` object represents an input parameter, an output parameter, or both, or if the parameter is a return value from a stored procedure.
Name	String	Indicates the name of the `Parameter` object.
NumericScale	Byte	Indicates the scale of numeric values for the `Parameter` object.
Precision	Byte	Indicates the degree of precision for numeric values in the `Parameter` object.
Properties	Properties	Contains all of the `Property` objects for a `Parameter` object.
Size	Long	Indicates the maximum size, in bytes or characters, of a `Parameter` object.
Type	DataTypeEnum	Indicates the data type of the `Parameter` object.
Value	Variant	Indicates the value assigned to the `Parameter` object.

The Parameters Collection

Methods

Name	Returns	Description
Append		Appends a `Parameter` object to the `Parameters` collection.
Delete		Deletes a `Parameter` object from the `Parameters` collection.
Refresh		Updates the `Parameter` objects in the `Parameters` collection.

Properties

Name	Returns	Description
Count	Long	Indicates the number of `Parameter` objects in the `Parameters` collection. Read-only.
Item	Parameter	Allows indexing into the `Parameters` collection to reference a specific `Parameter` object. Read-only.

The Properties Collection

Methods

Name	Returns	Description
Refresh		Updates the `Property` objects in the `Properties` collection with the details from the provider.

Properties

Name	Returns	Description
Count	Long	Indicates the number of `Property` objects in the `Properties` collection. Read-only.
Item	Property	Allows indexing into the `Properties` collection to reference a specific `Property` object. Read-only.

The Property Object

Properties

Name	Returns	Description
Attributes	Long	Indicates one or more characteristics of a `Property` object.
Name	String	Indicates the name of the `Property` object. Read-only.
Type	DataType Enum	Indicates the data type of the `Property` object.
Value	Variant	Indicates the value assigned to the `Property` object.

The Record Object

Methods

Name	Returns	Description
Cancel		Cancels the execution of an asynchronous Execute or Open.
Close		Closes the open record.
CopyRecord	String	Copies the object the record represents, or a file or directory, from one location to another.
DeleteRecord		Deletes the object the record represents, or a file or directory.
GetChildren	Recordset	Returns a Recordset containing the files and folders in the directory that the record represents.
MoveRecord	String	Moves the object the record represents, or a file or directory, from one location to another.
Open		Opens, or creates a new, existing file or directory.

Properties

Name	Returns	Description
ActiveConnection	Variant	Indicates to which Connection object the specified Recordset object currently belongs.
Fields	Fields	Contains all of the Field objects for the current Recordset object. Read-only
Mode	ConnectMode Enum	Indicates the available permissions for modifying data in a Connection.
ParentURL	String	Indicates the absolute URL of the parent record of the current record. Read-only
Properties	Properties	Contains all of the Property objects for the current Recordset object. Read-only
RecordType	RecordType Enum	Indicates whether the record is a simple record, a structured document, or a collection. Read-only
Source	Variant	Indicates what the record represents – a URL or a reference to an open Recordset.
State	ObjectState Enum	Indicates whether the record is open or closed, and if open, the state of asynchronous actions. Read-only

The Recordset Object

Methods

Name	Returns	Description
AddNew		Creates a new record for an updateable Recordset object.
Cancel		Cancels execution of a pending asynchronous Open operation.
CancelBatch		Cancels a pending batch update.
CancelUpdate		Cancels any changes made to the current record, or to a new record prior to calling the Update method.
Clone	Recordset	Creates a duplicate Recordset object from an existing Recordset object.
Close		Closes the Recordset object and any dependent objects.
CompareBookmarks	Compare Enum	Compares two bookmarks and returns an indication of the relative values.
Delete		Deletes the current record or group of records.
Find		Searches the recordset for a record that matches the specified criteria.
GetRows	Variant	Retrieves multiple records of a Recordset object into an array.
GetString	String	Returns a recordset as a string.
Move		Moves the position of the current record in a recordset.
MoveFirst		Moves the position of the current record to the first record in the recordset.
MoveLast		Moves the position of the current record to the last record in the recordset.
MoveNext		Moves the position of the current record to the next record in the recordset.
MovePrevious		Moves the position of the current record to the previous record in the recordset.

Name	Returns	Description
NextRecordset	Recordset	Clears the current Recordset object and returns the next recordset by advancing through a series of commands.
Open		Opens a recordset.
Requery		Updates the data in a Recordset object by re-executing the query on which the object is based.
Resync		Refreshes the data in the current Recordset object from the underlying database.
Save		Saves the recordset to a file.
Seek		Searches the recordset index to locate a value
Supports	Boolean	Determines whether a specified Recordset object supports particular functionality.
Update		Saves any changes made to the current Recordset object.
UpdateBatch		Writes all pending batch updates to disk.

Properties

Name	Returns	Description
AbsolutePage	PositionEnum	Specifies in which page the current record resides.
AbsolutePosition	PositionEnum	Specifies the ordinal position of a Recordset object's current record.
ActiveCommand	Object	Indicates the Command object that created the associated Recordset object. Read-only.
ActiveConnection	Variant	Indicates to which Connection object the specified Recordset object currently belongs.
BOF	Boolean	Indicates whether the current record is before the first record in a Recordset object. Read-only.
Bookmark	Variant	Returns a bookmark that uniquely identifies the current record in a Recordset object, or sets the current record to the record identified by a valid bookmark.

Name	Returns	Description
CacheSize	Long	Indicates the number of records from a Recordset object that are cached locally in memory.
CursorLocation	CursorLocation Enum	Sets or returns the location of the cursor engine.
CursorType	CursorType Enum	Indicates the type of cursor used in a Recordset object.
DataMember	String	Specifies the name of the data member to retrieve from the object referenced by the DataSource property. Write-only.
DataSource	Object	Specifies an object containing data to be represented as a Recordset object. Write-only.
EditMode	EditModeEnum	Indicates the editing status of the current record. Read-only.
EOF	Boolean	Indicates whether the current record is after the last record in a Recordset object. Read-only.
Fields	Fields	Contains all of the Field objects for the current Recordset object.
Filter	Variant	Indicates a filter for data in the Recordset.
Index	String	Identifies the name of the index currently being used.
LockType	LockTypeEnum	Indicates the type of locks placed on records during editing.
MarshalOptions	MarshalOptions Enum	Indicates which records are to be marshaled back to the server.
MaxRecords	Long	Indicates the maximum number of records to return to a Recordset object from a query. Default is zero (no limit).
PageCount	Long	Indicates how many pages of data the Recordset object contains. Read-only.
PageSize	Long	Indicates how many records constitute one page in the recordset.
Properties	Properties	Contains all of the Property objects for the current Recordset object.

Name	Returns	Description
RecordCount	Long	Indicates the current number of records in the Recordset object. Read-only.
Sort	String	Specifies one or more field names the recordset is sorted on, and the direction of the sort.
Source	String	Indicates the source for the data in a Recordset object.
State	Long	Indicates whether the recordset is open, closed, or whether it is executing an asynchronous operation. Read-only.
Status	Integer	Indicates the status of the current record with respect to match updates or other bulk operations. Read-only.
StayInSync	Boolean	Indicates, in a hierarchical Recordset object, whether the parent row should change when the set of underlying child records changes. Read-only.

Events

Name	Description
EndOfRecordset	Fired when there is an attempt to move to a row past the end of the recordset.
FetchComplete	Fired after all the records in an asynchronous operation have been retrieved into the recordset.
FetchProgress	Fired periodically during a length asynchronous operation, to report how many rows have currently been retrieved.
FieldChangeComplete	Fired after the values of one or more Field objects have been changed.
MoveComplete	Fired after the current position in the recordset changes.
RecordChangeComplete	Fired after one or more records change.
RecordsetChangeComplete	Fired after the recordset has changed.
WillChangeField	Fired before a pending operation changes the value of one or more Field objects.
WillChangeRecord	Fired before one or more rows in the recordset change.

Name	Description
WillChangeRecordset	Fired before a pending operation changes the recordset.
WillMove	Fired before a pending operation changes the current position in the recordset.

The Stream Object

Methods

Name	Returns	Description
Cancel		Cancels execution of a pending asynchronous open operation.
Close		Closes an open stream.
CopyTo		Copies characters or bytes from one stream to another.
Flush		Flushes the contents of the stream to the underlying object.
LoadFromFile		Loads a stream from a file.
Open		Opens a stream object from a URL or an existing record, or creates a blank stream.
Read	Variant	Reads a number of bytes from the stream.
ReadText	String	Reads a number of characters from a text stream.
SaveToFile		Saves an open stream to a file.
SetEOS		Sets the current position to be the end of the stream.
SkipLine		Skips a line when reading from a text stream.
Write		Writes binary data to a stream.
WriteText		Writes text data to a stream.

Properties

Name	Returns	Description
Charset	String	Identifies the character set used by the stream.
EOS	Boolean	Is set to True if the current position is the end of the stream. Read-only

Name	Returns	Description
LineSeparator	LineSeparator Enum	Indicates the character used to separate lines in a text stream. The default is vbCrLf.
Mode	ConnectMode Enum	Indicates the available permissions for modifying data in a Connection.
Position	Long	Specifies the current position in the stream.
Size	Long	Indicates the length, in bytes, of the stream. Read-only
State	ObjectState Enum	Indicates whether the stream is open or closed, and if open, the state of asynchronous actions. Read-only
Type	StreamType Enum	Indicates whether the stream contains text or binary data.

Method Calls – Syntax

Command

```
Command.Cancel
Parameter = Command.CreateParameter([Name As String], [Type As DataTypeEnum], _
                                    [Direction As ParameterDirectionEnum], _
                                    [Size As Long], [Value As Variant])
Recordset = Command.Execute([RecordsAffected As Variant], [Parameters As Variant], _
                            [Options As Long])
```

Connection

```
Long = Connection.BeginTrans
Connection.Cancel
Connection.Close
Connection.CommitTrans
Recordset = Connection.Execute(CommandText As String, _
                              [RecordsAffected As Variant], _
                              [Options As Long])
Connection.Open([ConnectionString As String], [UserID As String], _
                [Password As String], [Options As Long])
Recordset = Connection.OpenSchema(Schema As SchemaEnum, _
                                  [Restrictions As Variant], _
                                  [SchemaID As Variant])
Connection.RollbackTrans
```

Errors

Errors.Clear
Errors.Refresh

Field

Field.AppendChunk(*Data As Variant*)
Variant = *Field*.GetChunk(*Length As Long*)

Fields

Fields.Append(*Name As String*, *Type As DataTypeEnum*, [*DefinedSize As Long*], _
          [*Attrib As FieldAttributeEnum*], [*FieldValue As Variant*])
Fields.CancelUpdate
Fields.Delete(*Index As Variant*)
Fields.Refresh
Fields.Resync(*ResyncValues As ResyncEnum*)
Fields.Update

Parameter

Parameter.AppendChunk(*Val As Variant*)

Parameters

Parameters.Append(*Object As Object*)
Parameters.Delete(*Index As Variant*)
Parameters.Refresh

Properties

Properties.Refresh

Record

Record.Cancel
Record.Close
String = *Record*.CopyRecord([*Source As String*], *Destination As String*, _
                     [*UserName As String*], [*Password As String*], _
                     [*Options As CopyRecordOptionsEnum*], _
                     [*Async As Boolean*])
Record.DeleteRecord(*Source As String*, *Async As Boolean*)
Recordset = *Record*.GetChildren
String = *Record*.MoveRecord([*Source As String*], *Destination As String*, _
                     [*UserName As String*], [*Password As String*], _
                     [*Options As MoveRecordOptionsEnum*], _
                     [*Async As Boolean*])

```
Record.Open([Source As Variant], [ActiveConnection As Variant],_
            [Mode As ConnectModeEnum], [CreateOptions As RecordCreateOptionsEnum],_
            [Options As RecordOpenOptionsEnum], [UserName As String],_
            [Password As String])
```

Recordset

```
Recordset.AddNew([FieldList As Variant], [Values As Variant])
Recordset.Cancel
Recordset.CancelBatch([AffectRecords As AffectEnum])
Recordset.CancelUpdate
Recordset = Recordset.Clone([LockType As LockTypeEnum])
Recordset.Close
CompareEnum = Recordset.CompareBookmarks(Bookmark1 As Variant,_
                                          Bookmark2 As Variant)
Recordset.Delete(AffectRecords As AffectEnum)
Recordset.Find(Criteria As String, [SkipRecords As Long],_
               [SearchDirection As SearchDirectionEnum], [Start As Variant])
Variant = Recordset.GetRows(Rows As Long, [Start As Variant], [Fields As Variant])
String = Recordset.GetString(StringFormat As StringFormatEnum, [NumRows As Long],_
                             [ColumnDelimeter As String], [RowDelimeter As String],_
                             [NullExpr As String])
Recordset.Move(NumRecords As Long, [Start As Variant])
Recordset.MoveFirst
Recordset.MoveLast
Recordset.MoveNext
Recordset.MovePrevious
Recordset = Recordset.NextRecordset([RecordsAffected As Variant])
Recordset.Open([Source As Variant], [ActiveConnection As Variant],_
               [CursorType As CursorTypeEnum], [LockType As LockTypeEnum],_
               [Options As Long])
Recordset.Requery([Options As Long])
Recordset.Resync([AffectRecords As AffectEnum], [ResyncValues As ResyncEnum])
Recordset.Save([Destination As Variant], [PersistFormat As PersistFormatEnum])
Recordset.Seek(KeyValues As Variant, SeekOption As SeekEnum)
Boolean = Recordset.Supports(CursorOptions As CursorOptionEnum)
Recordset.Update([Fields As Variant], [Values As Variant])
Recordset.UpdateBatch([AffectRecords As AffectEnum])
```

Stream

```
Stream.Cancel
Stream.Close
Stream.CopyTo(DestStream As Stream, [CharNumber As Long])
Stream.Flush
Stream.LoadFromFile(FileName As String)
Stream.Open([Source As Variant], [Mode As ConnectModeEnum], _
        [Options As StreamOpenOptionsEnum], [UserName As String], _
        [Password As String])
Variant = Stream.Read([NumBytes As Long])
String = Stream.ReadText([NumChars As Long])
Stream.SaveToFile(FileName As String, Options As SaveOptionsEnum)
Stream.SetEOS
Stream.SkipLine
Stream.Write(Buffer As Variant)
Stream.WriteText(Data As String, [Options As StreamWriteEnum])
```

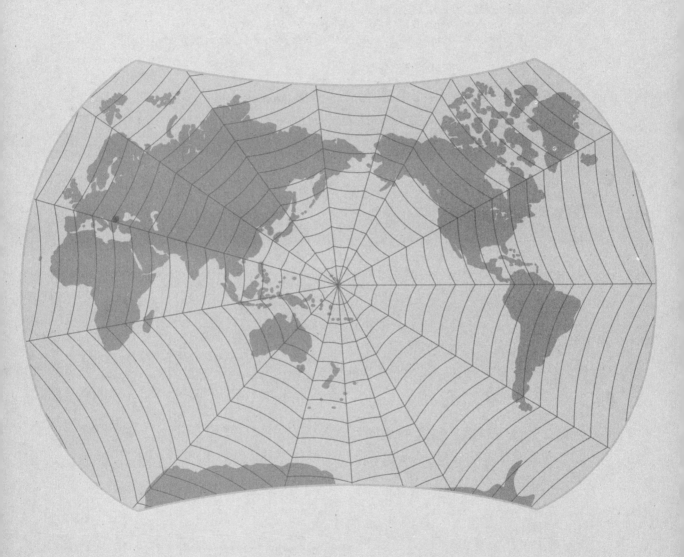

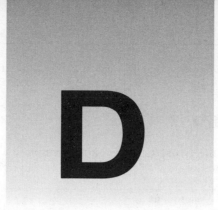

VB Script Reference

Overview

This Appendix contains a complete reference of functions and keywords in VBScript 5. You will also find a list of the VB/VBA functions and keywords that are not supported in VBScript. Where appropriate an alternative to an unsupported function or keyword is shown.

The function and keyword references are grouped in categories and they include the full syntax, an explanation, notes, sample code, and a "See also" list. The function references also include a list of named constants and their values.

Please note that there are a number of VB constructs that are not supported in VBScript. This includes File I/O (for security reasons), the Debug and Collection objects, some conversion functions, and the complete set of financial functions. For a complete list, see "Differences Between VB/VBA and VBScript" in Appendix B.

Operators

An operator acts on one or more operands when comparing, assigning, concatenating, calculating, and performing logical operations.

Say you want to calculate the difference between two variables A and B and save the result in variable C. These variables are the operands and to find the difference you use the subtraction operator like this:

```
C = A - B
```

Here we used the assignment operator (=) to assign the difference between A and B, which was found by using the subtraction operator (-). Operators are one of the single-most important parts of any programming language. Without them, you would not be able to assign values to variables or perform calculations and comparisons! It would be a bit like a bicycle without pedals...

There are different types of operators and they each serve a specific purpose, as you will see from the following.

Assignment Operator

The assignment operator is simply used for assigning a value to a variable or property. See the **Set** keyword for an explanation of how to reference and assign objects.

=	Name	**Assignment**
	Description	Assigns the result of an expression, the value of a constant, or the value of another variable to a variable or property.
	Syntax	`Variable = value`

Arithmetic Operators

The arithmetic operators are all used to calculate a numeric value, and are normally used in conjunction with the *Assignment Operator* and/or one of the *Comparison Operators*; they are listed in order of *Operator Precedence*.

^	Name	**Exponentiation**
	Description	Raises a number to the power of an exponent.
	Syntax	`Result = number ^ exponent`
		number and *exponent* is any valid numeric expression.
	Example	`MsgBox 5 ^ 5`
		MsgBox displays *3125*, which is the result of raising the number 5 to the exponent 5.

*	Name	**Multiplication**
	Description	Multiplies two numbers.
	Syntax	`Result = number1 * number2`
		number1 and *number2* is any valid numeric expression.
	Example	`MsgBox 5 * 5`
		MsgBox displays *25*, which is the result of multiplying the number 5 by 5.

/	Name	**Floating Point Division**
	Description	Returns a floating point result when dividing two numbers.
	Syntax	**Result = number1 / number2**
		number1 and *number2* is any valid numeric expression.
	Example	``` MsgBox 5 / 4 ```
		MsgBox displays *1.25*, which is the result of dividing the number 5 by 4.

\	Name	**Integer Division**
	Description	Returns the integer part of the result when dividing two numbers.
	Syntax	**Result = number1 \ number2**
		number1 and *number2* is any valid numeric expression.
	Example	``` MsgBox 5 \ 4 ```
		MsgBox displays *1*, which is the integer part of the result, when dividing the number 5 with 4.
	Note	The numeric expressions are rounded to `Byte`, `Integer`, or `Long` subtype expressions, before the integer division is performed. They are rounded to the smallest possible subtype, i.e. a value of 255 will be rounded to a `Byte`, and 256 will be rounded to an `Integer` and so on.

Mod	Name	**Modulus Division**
	Description	Returns the remainder when dividing two numbers.
	Syntax	**Result = number1 Mod number2**
		number1 and *number2* is any valid numeric expression.
	Example	``` MsgBox 5 Mod 4 ```
		MsgBox displays *1*, which is the remainder part of the result, when dividing the number 5 with 4.

Table Continued on Following Page

Note	The numeric expressions are rounded to `Byte`, `Integer`, or `Long` subtype expressions, before the modulus division is performed. They are rounded to the smallest possible subtype, i.e. a value of 255 will be rounded to a `Byte`, and 256 will be rounded to an `Integer` and so on.

+	Name	**Addition**
	Description	Sums two expressions.
	Syntax	**`Result = expression1 + expression2`**
		expression1 and *expression2* is any valid numeric expression.
	Example	`MsgBox 5 + 5`
		MsgBox displays *10*, which is the result of adding the expression 5 to 5.
	Note	If one or both expressions are numeric, the expressions will be summed, but if both expressions are strings, they will be concatenated. This is important to understand, especially if you have a Java background, in order to avoid runtime errors. In general use the **&**operator (*see under **Concatenation Operators***), when concatenating and the **+** operator when dealing with numbers.

-	Name	**Subtraction**
	Description	Subtracts one number from another or indicates the negative value of an expression.
	Syntax (1)	**`Result = number1 - number2`**
		number1 and *number2* is any valid numeric expression.
	Example (1)	`MsgBox 5 - 4`
		MsgBox displays *1*, which is the result of subtracting the number 4 from 5.
	Syntax (2)	**`-number`**
		number is any valid numeric expression.
	Example (2)	`MsgBox -(5 - 4)`
		MsgBox displays *-1*, which is the result of subtracting the number 4 from 5 and using the unary negation operator (-) to indicate a negative value.

Concatenation Operators

Concatenation operators are used for concatenating expressions; they are listed in order of *Operator Precedence*.

&	Name	**Ampersand**
	Description	Concatenates two expressions.
	Syntax	Returns the concatenated expressions:
		`Result = expression1 & expression2`
	Example	If *expression1* is "WROX " and *expression2* is " Press" then the result is "WROX Press".
	Note	The expressions are converted to a String subtype, if they are not already of this subtype.

+	Name	**+ Operator**
	Description	Does the same as the **&** operator if both expressions are strings.
	Syntax	Returns the concatenated or summed expressions:
		`Result = expression1 + expression2`
	Example	1 + "1" = 2 "1" + "1" = "11"
	Note	If one or both expressions are numeric, the + operator will work as an arithmetic + operator and sum the expressions. A runtime error occurs if one expression is numeric and the other a string containing no numbers. It is recommended that + should only be used for numeric addition and never for concatenation purposes (use **&** instead).

Comparison Operators

The comparison operators are used for comparing variables and expressions against other variables, constants or expressions; they are listed in order of *Operator Precedence*.

One important thing to remember when comparing strings is case sensitivity. You can use the *UCase* and *LCase* functions to make sure that the strings you compare are the same case; the *StrComp* function offers another way of dealing with case sensitivity (*see under String Functions*). In VB/VBA you have the Option Compare statement, but this is not supported in VBScript. So keep in mind, when using the operators listed below, that if you compare strings (when both expressions are strings), a binary comparison is performed on the sequences of characters. A binary comparison is always case sensitive. If only one of the expressions is a string and the other is numeric, the numeric expression is always less than the string expression.

Null is returned if either expression is Null. If either expression is Empty, it is converted to the value 0 if the other expression is numeric, and to an empty string ("") if the other expression is a string. In the case where both expressions are Empty, they are obviously equal.

The **Is** operator is for dealing with objects and Variants.

=	Name	**Equal to**
	Description	Returns true if *expression1* is equal to *expression2*; false otherwise.
	Syntax	`Result = expression1 = expression2`

<>	Name	**Not equal to (different from)**
	Description	Returns true if *expression1* is not equal to *expression2*; false otherwise.
	Syntax	`Result = expression1 <> expression2`

<	Name	**Less than**
	Description	Returns true if *expression1* is less than *expression2*; false otherwise.
	Syntax	`Result = expression1 < expression2`

>	Name	**Greater than**
	Description	Returns true if *expression1* is greater than *expression2*; false otherwise.
	Syntax	`Result = expression1 > expression2`

<=	Name	**Less than or equal to**
	Description	Returns true if *expression1* is less than or equal to *expression2*; false otherwise.
	Syntax	`Result = expression1 <= expression2`

>=	Name	**Greater than or equal to**
	Description	Returns true if *expression1* is greater than or equal to *expression2*; false otherwise.
	Syntax	`Result = expression1 >= expression2`

Is	Name	**Compare objects**
	Description	Returns true if *object1* and *object2* refers to the same memory location (if they are in fact the same object).
	Syntax	`Result = object1 Is object2`
	Note	Use the **Not** operator (*see under Logical Operators*) with the **Is** operator to get the opposite effect:
		`Result = object1 Not Is object2`
		Use the **Nothing** keyword with the **Is** operator to check if an object reference is valid. Returns true if object has been destroyed (`Set object = Nothing`):
		`Result = object Is Nothing`
		Be careful, **Nothing** is NOT the same as **Empty**. **Nothing** references an invalid object reference, whereas **Empty** is used for any variable, which has been assigned the value of Empty, or has not yet been assigned a value.

Logical Operators

The logical operators are used for performing logical operations on expressions; they are listed in order of *Operator Precedence*. All logical operators can also be used as bitwise operators (*see under Bitwise Operators*).

Not	Used to	Negate the expression.
	Returns	Returns the logical negation of an expression.
	Syntax	`Result = Not expression`
	Note	Result will be true if *expression* is false; and false if *expression* is true. `Null` will be returned if expression is `Null`.

And	Used to	Check if both expressions are true.
	Returns	Returns true if both expressions evaluate to true; otherwise, false is returned.
	Syntax	`Result = expression1 And expression2`

Or	Used to	Check if one or both expressions are true.
	Returns	Returns true if one or both expressions evaluate to true; otherwise, false is returned.
	Syntax	`Result = expression1 Or expression2`

Xor	Used to	Check if one and only one expression is true.
	Returns	Null will be returned if either expression is Null.
	Syntax	**Result = expression1 Xor expression2**
	Note	Returns true if only one of the expressions evaluates to true; otherwise, false is returned.

Eqv	Used to	Check if both expressions evaluate to the same value.
	Returns	Returns true if both expressions evaluate to the same value (true or false).
	Syntax	**Result = expression1 Eqv expression2**
	Note	Null will be returned if either expression is Null.

Imp	Used to	Perform a logical implication.

	Returns	Returns these values:
		
		`true Imp true = true`
		`false Imp true = true`
		`false Imp false = true`
		`false Imp Null = true`
		`Null Imp true = true`
		`true Imp false = false`
		`true Imp Null = Null`
		`Null Imp false = Null`
		`Null Imp Null = Null`

	Syntax	**Result = expression1 Imp expression2**

Bitwise Operators

Bitwise operators are used for comparing binary values bit-by-bit; they are listed in order of *Operator Precedence*. All bitwise operators can also be used as logical operators (*see under* **Logical Operators**).

Not	Used to	Invert the bit values.
	Returns	Returns 1 if bit is 0 and vice versa.
	Syntax	**Result = Not expression**
		If *expression* is 101 then *result* is 010.

And	Used to	Check if both bits are set to 1.
	Returns	Returns 1 if both bits are 1; otherwise, 0 is returned.
	Syntax	`Result = expression1 And expression2`
		If *expression1* is 101 and *expression2* is 100 then *result* is 100.

Or	Used to	Check if one of the bits is set to 1.
	Returns	Returns 1 if one or both bits are 1; otherwise, 0 is returned.
	Syntax	
		`Result = expression1 Or expression2`
		If *expression1* is 101 and *expression2* is 100 then *result* is 101.

Xor	Used to	Checks if one and only one of the bits are set to 1.
	Returns	Returns 1 if only one bit is 1; otherwise, 0 is returned.
	Syntax	`Result = expression1 Xor expression2`
		If *expression1* is 101 and *expression2* is 100 then *result* is 001.

Eqv	Used to	Checks if both bits evaluate to the same value.
	Returns	Returns 1 if both bits have the same value (0 or 1).
	Syntax	`Result = expression1 Eqv expression2`
		If *expression1* is 101 and *expression2* is 100 then *result* is 110.

Imp	Used to	Performs a logical implication on two bits.
	Returns	Returns these values:
		0 Imp 0 = 1
		0 Imp 1 = 1
		1 Imp 1 = 1
		1 Imp 0 = 0
	Syntax	`Result = expression1 Imp expression2`
		If *expression1* is 101 and *expression2* is 100 then *result* is 110.

Operator Precedence

When more than one operation occurs in an expression they are normally performed from left to right. However, there are several rules.

Operators from the arithmetic group are evaluated first, then concatenation, comparison and logical operators.

This is the complete order in which operations occur (operators in brackets have the same precedence):

^, -, (*, /), \, Mod, (+, -),
&,
=, <>, <, >, <=, >=, Is,
Not, And, Or, Xor, Eqv, Imp

This order can be overridden by using parentheses. Operations in parentheses are evaluated before operations outside the parentheses, but inside the parentheses, the normal precedence rules apply.

Unsupported Operators

The following VB/VBA operator is not supported in VBScript:

Like

Math Functions

Every now and then, depending on what kind of applications you design, you will need to do some math calculations and VBScript goes a long way towards helping you here. There are a number of intrinsic functions, but it is also possible to derive many other math functions from the intrinsic ones. Math functions are especially helpful when you need to display graphics, charts etc; the listing is in alphabetical order.

Abs	Returns the absolute value of a number, i.e. its unsigned magnitude.
Syntax	`Abs(number)`
	number is any valid numeric expression.
Note	`Null` will be returned if *number* contains `Null`.
Example	`Abs(-50)  ' 50` `Abs(50)   ' 50`
See Also	*Sgn*

Atn	Returns the arctangent of a number as Variant subtype `Double` (5).
Syntax	`Atn(number)`
	number is any valid numeric expression.
Note	This function takes the ratio of two sides of a right-angled triangle (*number*) and returns the corresponding angle in radians. The ratio is the length of the side opposite the angle divided by the length of the side adjacent to the angle. The range of the result is -pi/2 to pi/2 radians.
Example	

```
Dim dblPi


        ' Calculate the
        ' value of Pi
        dblPi = 4 * Atn(1)
```

See Also	*Cos*, *Sin* and *Tan*

Cos	Returns the cosine of an angle as Variant subtype `Double` (5).
Syntax	`Cos(number)`
	number is any valid numeric expression that expresses an angle in radians.
Note	This function takes an angle and returns the ratio of two sides of a right-angled triangle. The ratio is the length of the side adjacent to the angle divided by the length of the hypotenuse (`dblSecant`). The result is within the range -1 to 1, both inclusive.
Example	

```
Dim dblAngle, dblSecant
Dim dblLength

    dblLength = 10
            ' Convert 30° to radians
    dblAngle = (30 * 3.14 / 180)
    dblSecant = dblLength / Cos(dblAngle)
```

Here the **Cos** function is used to return the cosine of an angle.

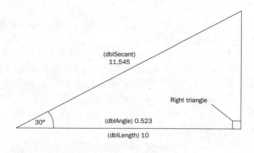

See Also	*Atn*, *Sin* and *Tan*

Exp	Returns a Variant subtype Double (5) specifying *e* (the base of natural logarithms) raised to a power.
Syntax	`Exp(number)`
	number is any valid numeric expression.
Note	A runtime error occurs if *number* is larger than 709.782712893. *e* is approximately 2.718282.
	Sometimes this function is referred to as the *antilogarithm*, and complements the action of the ***Log*** function.
| Example | ```
Dim dblAngle, dblHSin

    dblAngle = 1.3
    dblHSin = (Exp( dblAngle) - Exp( -1 * dblAngle)) / 2
``` |
| | Here the ***Exp*** function is used to return *e* raised to a power. |
| See Also | ***Log*** |

Fix	Returns the integer part of a number.
Syntax	`Fix(number)`
Note	***Fix*** is internationally aware, which means that the return value is based on the locale settings on the machine.
	`Null` is returned if *number* contains `Null`. The data type returned will be decided from the size of the integer part. Possible return data types in ascending order: `Integer`, `Long`, and `Double`.
	If *number* is negative, the first negative integer equal to or greater than *number* is returned.
| Example | ```
Dim vntPosValue
Dim vntNegValue

    vntPosValue = Fix(5579.56)
    vntNegValue = Fix(-5579.56)
``` |
	`vntPosValue` now holds the value 5579, and `vntNegValue` the value -5579.
	Fix is the equivalent of ***Int*** when dealing with non-negative numbers. When you handle negative numbers, ***Fix*** returns the first negative integer, greater than, or equal to the number supplied.
See Also	***Int***, ***Round*** and the ***Conversion Functions CInt*** and ***CLng***

Int	Returns the integer part of a number.
Syntax	`Int(number)`
	number is any valid numeric expression.
Note	*Int* is internationally aware, which means that the return value is based on the locale settings on the machine.
	`Null` is returned if *number* contains `Null`. The data type returned will be decided from the size of the integer part. Possible return data types in ascending order: `Integer`, `Long`, and `Double`.
	If *number* is negative, the first negative integer equal to or less than *number* is returned.
Example	```Dim vntPosValue Dim vntNegValue vntPosValue = Int(5579.56) vntNegValue = Int(-5579.56)```
	`vntPosValue` now holds the value 5579, and `vntNegValue` the value -5580.
	Int is the equivalent of *Fix* when dealing with non-negative numbers. When you handle negative numbers, Int returns the first negative integer, less than, or equal to the number supplied.
See Also	*Fix*, *Round* and the *Conversion Functions CInt* and *CLng*

Log	Returns the natural logarithm of a number.
Syntax	`Log(number)`
	number is any valid numeric expression greater than zero.
Example	```Dim vntValueBase10 vntValueBase10 = Log(5) / Log(10)```
	The above sample code calculates the base-10 logarithm of the number 5, which is *0.698970004336019*.
See Also	*Exp*

Randomize	Initializes the random number generator, by giving it a new seed-value. A seed-value is an initial value used for generating random numbers.
Syntax	`Randomize [number]` *number* is any valid numeric expression.
Note	You can repeat a sequence of random numbers, by calling the *Rnd* function with a negative *number*, before using the *Randomize* statement with a numeric argument.
Example	

```
Const LNG_UPPER_BOUND = 20
Const LNG_LOWER_BOUND = 1

Dim intValue
Dim lngCounterIn
Dim lngCounterOut

   For lngCounterOut = 1 To 3
      Rnd -1
      Randomize 3

      For lngCounterIn = 1 To 3
         intValue = Int((LNG_UPPER_BOUND - LNG_LOWER_BOUND + 1) * _
         Rnd + LNG_LOWER_BOUND)
         MsgBox intValue
      Next
   Next
```

The above sample has an inner loop that generates three random numbers and an outer loop that calls the *Rnd* function with a negative number, immediately before calling *Randomize* with an argument. This makes sure that the random numbers generated in the inner loop will be the same for every loop the outer loop performs.

See Also	*Rnd*

Rnd	Returns a random number, less than 1 but greater than or equal to 0.
Syntax	`Rnd[(number)]` *number* (Optional) is any valid numeric expression that determines how the random number is generated; if *number* is: **< 0** – uses same number every time, **> 0 or missing** – uses next random number in sequence, **= 0** – uses most recently generated number.

Note	Use the *Randomize* statement, with no argument, to initialize the random-number generator with a seed based on the system timer, before calling *Rnd*.
	The same number sequence is generated for any given initial seed, because each successive call to *Rnd* uses the previous number as the seed for the next number in the sequence.
	Call *Rnd* with a negative argument immediately before using *Randomize* with a numeric argument, in order to repeat sequences of random numbers.
| Example | ```
Const LNG_UPPER_BOUND = 20
Const LNG_LOWER_BOUND = 1

Dim intValue
Dim lngCounter

   For lngCounter = 1 To 10
      intValue = Int( _
                  (LNG_UPPER_BOUND - _
                  LNG_LOWER_BOUND + 1) * _
                  Rnd + LNG_LOWER_BOUND)

      MsgBox intValue
   Next
``` |
| | This produces 10 random integers in the range 1-20. |
| See Also | *Randomize* |

Round	Returns a number rounded to a specified number of decimal places as a Variant subtype `Double` (5).
Syntax	**Round(number, [numdecimalplaces])**
	number is any valid numeric expression.
	numdecimalplaces, (Optional) indicates how many places to the right of the decimal separator should be included in the rounding.
Note	An integer is returned if *numdecimalplaces* is missing.
| Example | ```
Round(10.4)        ' Returns 10
Round(10.456)      ' Returns 10
Round(-10.456)     ' Returns -10
Round(10.4, 1)     ' Returns 10.4
Round(10.456, 2)   ' Returns 10.46
Round(-10.456, 2)  ' Returns -10.46
``` |
| See Also | *Int* and *Fix* |

Sgn	Returns an integer indicating the sign of a number.
Syntax	`Sgn(number)`
	number is any valid numeric expression.
Note	*Sgn* returns the following when number is:
	< 0 – -1 **= 0 – 0** **> 0 – 1**
| Example | ```
Sgn(10.4) ' Returns 1
Sgn(0)    ' Returns 0
Sgn(-2)   ' Returns -1
``` |
| See Also | *Abs* |

Sin	Returns a Variant subtype `Double` (5) specifying the sine of an angle.
Syntax	`Sin(number)`
	number is any valid numeric expression that expresses an angle in radians.
Note	This function takes an angle and returns the ratio of two sides of a right-angled triangle. The ratio is the length of the side opposite the angle (`dblCosecant`) divided by the length of the hypotenuse (`dblSecant`). The result is within the range -1 to 1, both inclusive.
| Example | ```
Dim dblAngle, dblCosecant
Dim dblSecant
    dblSecant = 11.545
           ' Convert 30° to radians
    dblAngle = (30 * 3.14 / 180)
    dblCosecant = dblSecant * Sin(dblAngle)
``` |

Here the *Sin* function is used to return the sine of an angle.

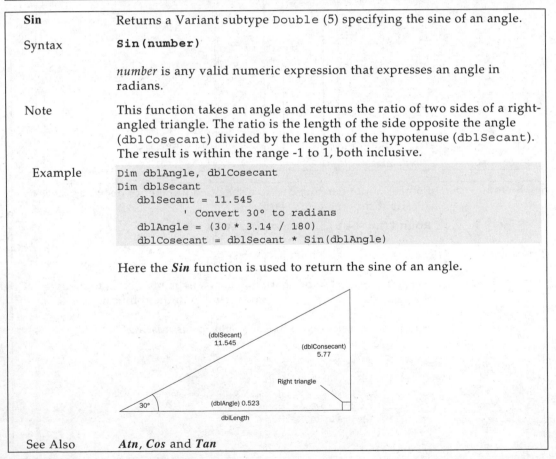

See Also	*Atn*, *Cos* and *Tan*

Sqr	Returns the square root of a number.
Syntax	`Sqr(number)` *number* is any valid numeric expression greater than or equal to zero.
Example	`Sqr(16) ' Returns 4`

Tan	Returns a Variant subtype `Double` (5) specifying the tangent of an angle.
Syntax	`Tan(number)` *number* is any valid numeric expression that expresses an angle in radians.
Note	This function takes an angle and returns the ratio of two sides of a right-angled triangle. The ratio is the length of the side opposite the angle (`dblCosecant`) divided by the length of the side adjacent to the angle (`dblLength`), - see diagram of Sin function. The result is within the range -1 to 1, both inclusive.

Example	`Tan(10.4) ' Returns 1.47566791425166`
	`Tan(0)    ' Returns 0`
	`Tan(-2)   ' Returns 2.18503986326152`

See Also	*Atn*, *Cos* and *Sin*

Date and Time Functions and Statements

There are a number of ways to display and represent dates and times. This includes date literals, which are valid date expression, enclosed in number signs (#). You need to be careful when using date literals because VBScript only lets you use the US-English date format, mm/dd/yyyy. This is true even if a different locale is being used on the machine. This might lead to problems when trying to use date literals in other formats, because in most cases the date will be accepted although converted to a different date. #10/12/1997# will be interpreted as October 12, 1997, but you might in fact want December 10, 1997, because your locale settings interprets dates as dd/mm/yyyy. `Date` literals only accept the forward slash (/) as the date separator.

The data range for a date is January 1, 100 to December 31, 9999, both inclusive. Internally, dates are stored as part of real numbers or to be more specific as a Variant subtype `Double` (5). The digits to the left of the decimal separator represent the date and the digits to the right of the decimal separator represent the time. Negative numbers are used internally for representing dates prior to December 30, 1899.

Below is a list of functions used for converting and formatting dates and times.

CDate	Returns an expression converted to Variant subtype `Date` (7).
Syntax	`CDate(date)`
	date is any valid `Date` expression.
Note	*CDate* is internationally aware, which means that the return value is based on the locale settings on the machine. Dates and times will be formatted with the appropriate time and date separators, and for dates the correct order of year, month and day are applied. Date and time literals are recognized.
| Example | ```
Dim dtmValue

    dtmValue = CDate( #12/10/1997#)
``` |
| | dtmValue now holds the value "10-12-97", if your locale settings use the dash (–) as the date separator and the short date format is dd/mm/yy. |
| See Also | *IsDate* |

Date	Returns a Variant subtype `Date` (7) indicating the current system date.
Syntax	`Date`
Example	`MsgBox Date`
	Assuming that today is July 29 1999, the `MsgBox` now displays **29-07-99**, if your locale settings use the dash (–) as the date separator and the short date format is dd/mm/yy.
See Also	*Now* and *Time*

DateAdd	Adds or subtracts a time interval to a specified date and returns the new date.
Syntax	`DateAdd(interval, number, date)`
	interval can have these values:

d	Day
h	Hour
m	Month
n	Minute
q	Quarter
s	Second
```

	w	Weekday
	ww	Week of year
	y	Day of year
	yyyy	Year

number is a numeric expression that must be positive if you want to add or negative if you want to subtract.

number is rounded to the nearest whole number if it's not a `Long` value.

Note

date must be a Variant or `Date` literal to which *interval* is added. **DateAdd** is internationally aware, which means that the return value is based on the locale settings on the machine. Dates and times will be formatted with the appropriate time and date separators and for dates the correct order of year, month and day are applied. An error occurs if the date returned precedes the year 100.

Example

```
MsgBox DateAdd("m", 3, "1-Jan-99")
```

This will add 3 months to January 1, 1999 and the `MsgBox` now displays **01-04-99**, if your locale settings use the dash (–) as the date separator and the short date format is dd/mm/yy.

See Also   **DateDiff, DatePart**

DateDiff   Returns the interval between two dates.

Syntax

```
DateDiff(interval, date1, date2, [firstdayofweek],
[firstweekofyear])
```

interval can have these values:

	d	Day
	h	Hour
	m	Month
	n	Minute
	q	Quarter
	s	Second
	w	Weekday
	ww	Week of year
	y	Day of year
	yyyy	Year

date1 and *date2* are date expressions.

firstdayofweek (Optional) specifies the first day of the week. Use one of the following constants:

Table Continued on Following Page

vbUseSystemDayOfWeek   **0**   (National Language Support (NLS) API setting. NLS functions help Win32-based applications support the differing language- and location-specific needs of users around the world.)

vbSunday	**1** (default)
vbMonday	**2**
vbTuesday	**3**
vbWednesday	**4**
vbThursday	**5**
vbFriday	**6**
vbSaturday	**7**

firstweekofyear (Optional) specifies the first week of the year. Use one of the following constants:

vbUseSystem	**0** (Use NLS API setting)
vbFirstJan1	**1** (default) Week in which January 1 occurs.
vbFirstFourDays	**2** First week in the new year with at least four days.
vbFirstFullWeek	**3** First full week of the new year.

Note   A negative number is returned if *date1* is later in time than *date2*.

Example   `MsgBox DateDiff("yyyy", #11-22-1967#, Now)`

This will calculate the number of years between 11/22/1967 and now. In 1999, the `MsgBox` will display 32.

See Also   ***DateAdd, DatePart***

DatePart   Returns a specified part of a date.

Syntax   `DatePart(interval, date, [firstdayofweek],`
              `[firstweekofyear])`

interval can have these values:

d	Day
h	Hour
m	Month
n	Minute
q	Quarter
s	Second
w	Weekday
ww	Week of year
y	Day of year
yyyy	Year

date is a date expression.

firstdayofweek (Optional) specifies the first day of the week. Use one of the following constants:

vbUseSystemDayOfWeek	**0** (NLS API setting)
vbSunday	**1** (default)
vbMonday	**2**
vbTuesday	**3**
vbWednesday	**4**
vbThursday	**5**
vbFriday	**6**
vbSaturday	**7**

firstweekofyear (Optional) specifies the first week of the year. Use one of the following constants:

vbUseSystem	**0** (Use NLS API setting)
vbFirstJan1	**1** (default) Week in which January 1 occurs.
vbFirstFourDays	**2** First week in the new year with at least four days.
vbFirstFullWeek	**3** First full week of the new year.

Example

```
MsgBox DatePart("ww", Now, vbMonday, vbFirstFourDays)
```

This will extract the week number from the current system date. On July 29, 1999 the `MsgBox` will display **30**.

See Also   ***DateAdd, DateDiff***

DateSerial   Returns a Variant subtype `Date` (7) for the specified year, month and day.

Syntax   **`DateSerial(year, month, day)`**

year is an expression that evaluates to a number between 0 and 9999. Values between 0 and 99, both inclusive, are interpreted as the years 1900 – 1999.

month is an expression that must evaluate to a number between 1 and 12.

day is an expression that must evaluate to a number between 1 and 31.

Note   If an argument is outside the acceptable range for that argument, it increments the next larger unit. Specifying 13 as the month will automatically increment year by one and subtract 12 from month leaving a value of 1. The same is true for negative values and a value of 0. However, instead of incrementing, the next larger unit is decremented.

Table Continued on Following Page

An error occurs if any of the arguments is outside the Variant subtype `Integer` range, which is -32768 – +32767. The same is true if the result is later than December 31, 9999. If you specify the year as 0, and the month and day as 0 or a negative value, the function wrongly assumes that the year is 100 and decrements this value.
So `DateSerial(0, 0, 0)` returns 11/30/99.

Example

```
MsgBox DateSerial( 1999, 07, 29)
```

The `MsgBox` will display 29-07-99, if your locale settings use the dash (–) as the date separator and the short date format is dd/mm/yy.

See Also *Date*, *DateValue*, *Day*, *Month*, *Now*, *TimeSerial*, *TimeValue*, *Weekday* and *Year*

DateValue Returns a Variant subtype `Date` (7).

Syntax

```
DateValue(date)
```

date is an expression representing a date, a time, or both, in the range January 1, 100 – December 31, 9999.

Note Time information in *date* is not returned, but invalid time information will result in a runtime error. *DateValue* is internationally aware and uses the locale settings on the machine, when recognizing the order of a date with only numbers and separators. If the year is omitted from *date*, it is obtained from the current system date.

Example

```
DateValue("07/29/1999")
DateValue("July 29, 1999")
DateValue("Jul 29, 1999")
DateValue("Jul 29")
```

All of the above will return the same valid date of 07/29/99.

See Also *Date*, *DateSerial*, *Day*, *Month*, *Now*, *TimeSerial*, *TimeValue*, *Weekday* and *Year*

Day Returns a number between 1 and 31 representing the day of the month.

Syntax

```
Day(date)
```

date is any valid date expression.

Note A runtime error occurs if *date* is not a valid date expression. `Null` will be returned if *date* contains `Null`.

Example

```
MsgBox Day("July 29, 1999")
```

The `MsgBox` will display 29.

See Also *Date*, *Hour*, *Minute*, *Month*, *Now*, *Second*, *Weekday* and *Year*

FormatDateTime	*See under* ***String Functions***

Hour   Returns an integer between 0 and 23, representing the hour of the day.

Syntax   **Hour(time)**

time is any valid time expression.

Note   A runtime error occurs if *time* is not a valid time expression. `Null` will be returned if *time* contains `Null`.

Example
```
MsgBox Hour("12:05:12")
```

The `MsgBox` will display 12.

See Also   ***Date, Day, Minute, Month, Now, Second, Weekday*** and ***Year***

IsDate   Returns a Variant subtype `Boolean` (11) indicating whether an expression can be converted to a valid date.

Syntax   **IsDate(expression)**

expression is any expression you want to evaluate as a date or time.

Example
```
MsgBox IsDate(Now)        ' true
MsgBox IsDate("")         ' false
MsgBox IsDate(#7/29/1999#) ' true
```

See Also   ***CDate, IsArray, IsEmpty, IsNull, IsNumeric, IsObject*** and ***VarType***

Minute   Returns a number between 0 and 59, both inclusive, indicating the minute of the hour.

Syntax   **Minute(time)**

time is any valid time expression.

Note   A runtime error occurs if *time* is not a valid time expression. `Null` will be returned if *time* contains `Null`.

Example
```
MsgBox Minute("12:45")
```

The `MsgBox` will display 45.

See Also   ***Date, Day, Hour, Month, Now, Second, Weekday*** and ***Year***

Month	Returns a number between 1 and 12, both inclusive, indicating the month of the year.
Syntax	`Month(date)`
	date is any valid date expression.
Note	A runtime error occurs if *date* is not a valid date expression. `Null` will be returned if *date* contains `Null`.
Example	`MsgBox Month(#7/29/1999#)`
	The `MsgBox` will display 7.
See Also	*Date*, *Day*, *Hour*, *Minute*, *Now*, *Second*, *Weekday* and *Year*

MonthName	Returns a Variant subtype `String` (8) for the specified month.
Syntax	`MonthName(month, [abbreviate])`
	month is a number between 1 and 12 for each month of the year beginning with January.
	abbreviate (Optional) is a boolean value indicating if the month name should be abbreviated or spelled out (default)
Note	A runtime error occurs if *month* is outside the valid range (1-12). *MonthName* is internationally aware, which means that the returned strings are localized into the language specified as part of your locale settings.
Example	`MsgBox MonthName(2)          ' February` `MsgBox MonthName(2, true) ' Feb`
See Also	*WeekdayName*

Now	Returns the system's current date and time.
Syntax	`Now`
Example	`Dim dtmValue` `        dtmValue = Now`
	`dtmValue` now holds the current system date and time.
See Also	*Date*, *Day*, *Hour*, *Month*, *Minute*, *Second*, *Weekday* and *Year*

Second	Returns a Variant subtype `Date` (7) indicating the number of seconds (0-59) in the specified time.
Syntax	`Second(time)`
	time is any valid time expression.
Note	A runtime error occurs if *time* is not a valid time expression. `Null` will be returned if *time* contains `Null`.
Example	`MsgBox Second("12:45:56")`
	The `MsgBox` will display **56**.
See Also	*Date*, *Day*, *Hour*, *Minute*, *Month*, *Now*, *Weekday* and *Year*

Time	Returns a Variant subtype `Date` (7) indicating the current system time.
Syntax	`Time`
Example	`Dim dtmValue` `        dtmValue = Time`
	`dtmValue` now holds the current system time.
See Also	*Date*, *Now*

Timer	Returns a Variant subtype `Single` (5) indicating the number of seconds that have elapsed since midnight. This means that it is "reset" every 24 hours.
Syntax	`Timer`

Example	`Dim dtmStart, dtmStop`
	
	`        dtmStart = Timer`
	`        ' Do processing here`
	`        dtmStop = Timer`
	`        ' Display how many`
	`        ' seconds the operation`
	`        ' took`
	`        MsgBox dtmStop - dtmStart`

TimeSerial	Returns a Variant subtype `Date` (7) for the specified hour, minute and second.

Table Continued on Following Page

953

Syntax	**TimeSerial(hour, minute, second)**
	hour is an expression that evaluates to a number between 0 and 23.
	minute is an expression that must evaluate to a number between 0 and 59.
	second is an expression that must evaluate to a number between 0 and 59.
Note	If an argument is outside the acceptable range for that argument, it increments the next larger unit. Specifying 61 as *minute* will automatically increment *hour* by one and subtract 60 from *minute* leaving a value of 1. The same is true for negative values and a value of 0. However, instead of incrementing, the next larger unit is decremented.
	An error occurs if any of the arguments is outside the Variant subtype `Integer` range, which is -32768 – +32767.
Example	`MsgBox TimeSerial(23, 07, 29)`
	The `MsgBox` will display 23:07:29.
See Also	*Date*, *DateSerial*, *DateValue*, *Day*, *Month*, *Now*, *TimeValue*, *Weekday* and *Year*

TimeValue	Returns a Variant subtype `Date` (7) containing the time.
Syntax	**TimeValue(time)**
	time is an expression in the range 0:00:00 – 23:59:59.
Note	Date information in *time* is not returned, but invalid date information will result in a runtime error. `Null` is returned if *time* contains `Null`. You can use both 24 and 12-hour representations for the *time* argument.
Example	`TimeValue("23:59")` `TimeValue("11:59 PM")`
	Both will return the same valid time.
See Also	*Date*, *DateSerial*, *DateValue*, *Day*, *Month*, *Now*, *TimeSerial*, *Weekday* and *Year*

Weekday	Returns a number indicating the day of the week.
Syntax	**Weekday(date, [firstdayofweek])**
	date is any valid date expression.
	firstdayofweek (Optional) specifies the first day of the week. Use one of the following constants:

vbUseSystemDayOfWeek	**0**	(Use NLS API setting)
vbSunday	**1**	(Default)
vbMonday	**2**	
vbTuesday	**3**	
vbWednesday	**4**	
vbThursday	**5**	
vbFriday	**6**	
vbSaturday	**7**	

Note	Null is returned if *date* contains Null. A runtime occurs if *date* is invalid. Possible return values are:

vbSunday	**1**
vbMonday	**2**
vbTuesday	**3**
vbWednesday	**4**
vbThursday	**5**
vbFriday	**6**
vbSaturday	**7**

Example	`Weekday(#July 29, 1999#)`
	Returns **5** for Thursday.
See Also	***Date*, *Day*, *Month*, *Now* and *Year***

WeekdayName	Returns a Variant subtype String (8) for the specified weekday.
Syntax	**WeekdayName(weekday, [abbreviate], [firstdayofweek])**
	weekday is a number between 1 and 7 for each day of the week. This value depends on the *firstdayofweek* setting.
	abbreviate (Optional) is a boolean value indicating if the weekday name should be abbreviated or spelled out (default)
	firstdayofweek (Optional) is a numeric value indicating the first day of the week. Use one of the following constants:

Table Continued on Following Page

	vbUseSystemDayOfWeek	**0** (Use NLS API setting)
	vbSunday	**1** (Default)
	vbMonday	**2**
	vbTuesday	**3**
	vbWednesday	**4**
	vbThursday	**5**
	vbFriday	**6**
	vbSaturday	**7**

Note   A runtime error occurs if *weekday* is outside the valid range (1-7). *WeekdayName* is internationally aware, which means that the returned strings are localized into the language specified as part of your locale settings.

Example

```
WeekdayName(2, , vbSunday) ' Monday
WeekdayName(1, , vbMonday) ' Monday
```

See Also   *MonthName*

Year   Returns a number indicating the year.

Syntax   `Year(date)`

date is any valid date expression.

Note   A runtime error occurs if *date* is not a valid date expression. `Null` will be returned if *date* contains `Null`.

Example

```
MsgBox Year(#7/29/1999#)
```

The `MsgBox` will display **1999**.

See Also   *Date, Day, Month, Now* and *Weekday*

Unsupported Date Functions and Statements

The following VB/VBA statements are not supported in VBScript:

Function/Statement Name	Alternative
Date statement	Sets the system date, which is not possible in VBScript.
Time statement	Sets the system time, which is not possible in VBScript.

Array Functions and Statements

One major difference between VB/VBA and VBScript is the way you can declare your arrays. VBScript does not support the `Option Base` statement and you cannot declare arrays that are not zero-based. Below is a list of functions and statements that you can use for array manipulation in VBScript.

Array	Returns a comma-delimited list of values as a Variant subtype Array (8192).
Syntax	`Array(arglist)`
	arglist is a comma-delimited list of values that is inserted into the one dimensional array in the order they appear in the list
Note	An array of zero length is created if arglist contains no arguments.
	All arrays in VBScript are zero-based, which means that the first element in the list will be element 0 in the returned array.
Example	Dim `arrstrTest`
	' Create an array with three elements
	arrstrTest = Array(_
	"Element0", "Element1", "Element2")
	' Show the first list element
	' now in the array
	MsgBox arrstrTest(0)
	`MsgBox` displays Element0
See Also	**Dim**

Erase	Reinitializes the elements if it is a fixed-size array and de-allocates the memory used if it is a dynamic array.
Syntax	**`Erase array`**
	array is the array to be reinitialized or erased.
Note	You must know if you are using a fixed-size or a dynamic array, because this statement behaves differently depending on the array type.
	Because the memory is de-allocated when using *Erase* with dynamic arrays, you must re-declare the array structure with the *ReDim* statement, before you use it again.
	Fixed-size arrays are reinitialized differently depending on the contents of the elements:
	Numeric Set to 0.
	Strings Set to ""
	Objects Set to `Nothing`.

Table Continued on Following Page

957

| Example | ```
Dim arrstrDynamic()
Dim arrstrFixed(3)

        ' Allocate space for the
        ' dynamic array
        ReDim arrstrDynamic(3)
        ' Free the memory used by
        ' the dynamic array
        Erase arrstrDynamic
        ' Reinitialize the elements
        ' in the fixed-size array
        Erase arrstrFixed
``` |
| See Also | **Dim** and **ReDim** |

For Each	Performs a group of statements repeatedly for each element in a collection or an array.
Syntax	```
For Each element In group
    [statements]
    [Exit For]
Next [element]
```
*element* is a variable used for iterating through the elements in a collection or an array.

*group* is the name of the object or array.

*statements* is one or more statements you want to execute on each item in the group. |
| Note | The **For Each** loop is only entered if there is at least one element in the collection or array. All the statements in the loop are executed for all the elements in the group. You can control this by executing the Exit For statement if a certain condition is met. This will exit the loop and start executing on the first line after the Next statement.

The **For Each** loops can be nested, but you must make sure that each loop element is unique. |
| Example | ```
Dim arrstrLoop
Dim strElement

        ' Create the array
        arrstrLoop = Array( "Element0", "Element1",
"Element2")
        ' Loop through the array
        For Each strElement In arrstrLoop
                ' Display the element content
                MsgBox strElement
        Next
``` |
```

IsArray	Returns a Variant subtype `Boolean` (11) indicating if a variable is an array.
Syntax	`IsArray(varname)` *varname* is a variable you want to check is an array.
Note	Only returns true if *varname* is an array.

Example	```Dim strName
	Dim arrstrFixed(3)
	
	        strName = "WROX rocks!"
	        MsgBox IsArray(strName) ' false
	        MsgBox IsArray(arrstrFixed) ' true```

See Also	*IsDate, IsEmpty, IsNull, IsNumeric, IsObject* and *VarType*

LBound	Returns the smallest possible subscript for the dimension indicated.
Syntax	`LBound(arrayname[, dimension])` *arrayname* is the name of the array variable. *dimension* is an integer indicating the dimension you want to know the smallest possible subscript for. The dimension starts with 1, which is also the default that will be used if this argument is omitted.
Note	The smallest possible subscript for any array is always 0 in VBScript. *LBound* will raise a runtime error if the array has not been initialized.
Example	```Dim arrstrFixed(3) MsgBox LBound(arrstrFixed)``` MsgBox displays 0.
See Also	*Dim, ReDim* and *UBound*

ReDim	This statement is used to size or resize a dynamic array.
Syntax	`ReDim [Preserve] varname(subscripts[,` `varname(subscripts)]...)`

Preserve (Optional) is used to preserve the data in an existing array, when you resize it. The overhead of using this functionality is quite high and should only be used when necessary.

varname is the name of the array variable.

subscripts is the dimension of the array variable *varname*. You can declare up to 60 multiple dimensions. The syntax is:

`upper[, upper]...`

where you indicate the upper bounds of the subscript. The lower bound is always zero.

Note   A dynamic array must already have been declared without dimension subscripts, when you size or resize it. If you use the `Preserve` keyword, only the last array dimension can be resized and the number of dimensions will remain unchanged.

Since an array can be made smaller when resizing, you should take care that you don't lose any data already in the array.

Example

```
Dim arrstrDynamic()

        ' Size the dimension to
        ' contain one dimension
        ' with 3 elements
        ReDim arrstrDynamic(3)
        ' Put data in the array
        arrstrDynamic(0) = "1"
        arrstrDynamic(1) = "2"
        arrstrDynamic(2) = "3"
        ' Resize the array, but
        ' keep the existing data
        ReDim Preserve arrstrDynamic(5)
        ' Display the 3rd element
        MsgBox arrstrDynamic(2)
```

`MsgBox` displays **3**.

See Also   *Dim* and *Set*

UBound	Returns the largest possible subscript for the dimension indicated
Syntax	`UBound(arrayname[, dimension])`
	arrayname is the name of the array variable.
	dimension is an integer indicating the dimension you want to know the largest possible subscript for. The dimension starts with 1, which is also the default that will be used if this argument is omitted.
Note	*UBound* will raise a runtime error if the array has not been initialized. If the array is empty, -1 is returned.

Example	`Dim arrstrFixed(3)`
	
	    `MsgBox UBound(arrstrFixed)`
	
	MsgBox displays 3.

See Also	*Dim* statement, *UBound* and *ReDim* statement

Unsupported Array Functions and Statements

The following VB/VBA constructs are not supported in VBScript:

Option Base

String Functions and Statements

Whatever your application does, you are likely to use string manipulation. By string manipulation we mean things like extracting a name from a string, checking if a particular string is part of another string, formatting numbers as strings with delimiters, and so on. Below is a list of the various string functions in VBScript.

Some functionality is not exposed as functions, but as methods of objects. For Example, the RegExp object exposes regular expression support. *See Chapter 10 **The Scripting Objects**.*

Format Currency	Formats an expression as a currency value with the current currency symbol. The currency symbol is defined in Regional Settings in the Control Panel
Syntax	`FormatCurrency(expression [,numdigitsafterdecimal [,includeleadingdigit [,useparensfornegativenumbers [,groupdigits]]]])` *expression* is the expression that you want formatted. *numdigitsafterdecimal* (Optional) is a numeric value that indicates how many places to the right of the decimal separator should be displayed. If you omit this argument, the default value (-1) will be assumed and the settings from Control Panel will be used. *includeleadingdigit* (Optional) indicates if a leading zero is displayed for fractional values. Use one of the following constants:

vbUseDefault	2 (Uses the settings from the Number tab in Control Panel)
vbtrue	-1
vbfalse	0

useparensfornegativenumbers (Optional) indicates if negative numbers are enclosed in parentheses. Use one of the following constants:

vbUseDefault	2 (Uses the settings from the Regional Settings tab in Control Panel)
vbTrue	-1
vbFalse	0

groupdigits (Optional) indicates if numbers are grouped using the thousand separator specified in Control Panel. Use one of the following constants:

vbUseDefault	2 (Uses the settings from the Regional Settings tab in Control Panel)
vbtrue	-1
vbfalse	0

Note	The way the currency symbol is placed in relation to the currency value is determined by the settings in the Regional Settings tab in Control Panel. (Is the currency symbol placed before the number, after the number, is there a space between the symbol and the number and so on.)

Example	```MsgBox FormatCurrency(7500)```
	```MsgBox FormatCurrency(7500, , vbtrue)```
	```MsgBox FormatCurrency(7500, 2, vbtrue)```
	
	If the currency symbol is a pound sign (£), the thousand separator a comma (,), and the currency symbol placed in front of the number with no spaces between, then `MsgBox` will display £7,500.00 in all of the above statements.

See Also	*FormatDateTime*, *FormatNumber* and *FormatPercent*

FormatDateTime	Returns a string formatted as a date and/or time.
Syntax	`FormatDateTime(date, [namedformat])`
	date is any valid date expression.
	namedformat (Optional) is a numeric value that indicates the date/time format used. Use one of the following constants:

vbGeneralDate	0	Format date (if present) and time (if present) using the short date and long time format from the machine's locale settings.
vbLongDate	1	Format date using the long date format from the machine's locale settings.
vbShortDate	2	Format date using the short date format from the machine's locale settings.
vbLongTime	3	Format time using the long time format from the machine's locale settings.
vbShortTime	4	Format time using the short time format from the machine's locale settings.

Note	A runtime error occurs if *date* is not a valid date expression. `Null` will be returned if *date* contains `Null`.
Example	`MsgBox FormatDateTime(Now, vbShortDate)`
	On July 29, 1999 the `MsgBox` will display **07/29/99**, if the locale settings use mm/dd/yy as the short date order and the forward slash (/) as the date separator.
See Also	*FormatCurrency*, *FormatNumber*, and *FormatPercent*

FormatNumber	Returns a string formatted as a number.

Syntax	`FormatNumber (expression,`
	`[, numdigitsafterdecimal`
	`[, includeleadingdigit`
	`[, useparensfornegativenumbers [, groupDigits]]]])`

	expression is the expression that you want formatted.
	numdigitsafterdecimal (Optional) is a numeric value that indicates how many places to the right of the decimal separator should be displayed. If you omit this argument, the default value (-1) will be assumed and the settings from Control Panel will be used.

Table Continued on Following Page

includeleadingdigit (Optional) indicates if a leading zero is displayed for fractional values. Use one of the following constants:

vbUseDefault	2 (Uses the settings from the **Number** tab in **Control Panel**)
vbtrue	-1
vbfalse	0

useparensfornegativenumbers (Optional) indicates if negative numbers are enclosed in parentheses. Use one of the following constants:

vbUseDefault	2 (Uses the settings from the **Regional Settings** tab in **Control Panel**)
vbtrue	-1
vbfalse	0

groupdigits (Optional) indicates if numbers are grouped using the thousand separator specified in **Control Panel**. Use one of the following constants:

vbUseDefault	2 (Uses the settings from the **Regional Settings** tab in **Control Panel**)
vbtrue	-1
vbfalse	0

Note The **Number** tab in **Regional Settings** in **Control Panel** supplies all the information used for formatting.

Example
```
MsgBox FormatNumber("50000", 2, vbtrue, vbfalse, vbtrue)
MsgBox FormatNumber("50000")
```

The `MsgBox` will display **50,000.00**, if the locale settings use a comma (,) as the thousand separator and a period (.) as the decimal separator.

See Also *FormatCurrency*, *FormatDateTime*, and *FormatPercent*

FormatPercent Returns a string formatted as a percentage, like 50%.

Syntax
```
FormatPercent(expression,
[, numdigitsafterdecimal
[, includeleadingdigit
[, useparensfornegativenumbers [,groupDigits]]]])
```

expression is any valid expression that you want formatted.

numdigitsafterdecimal (Optional) is a numeric value that indicates how many places to the right of the decimal separator should be displayed. If you omit this argument, the default value (-1) will be assumed and the settings from **Control Panel** will be used.

includeleadingdigit (Optional) indicates if a leading zero is displayed for fractional values. Use one of the following constants:

vbUseDefault	2 (Uses the settings from the **Number** tab in **Control Panel**)
vbtrue	-1
vbfalse	0

useparensfornegativenumbers (Optional) indicates if negative numbers are enclosed in parentheses. Use one of the following constants:

vbUseDefault	2 (Uses the settings from the **Regional Settings** tab in **Control Panel**)
vbtrue	-1
vbfalse	0

groupdigits (Optional) indicates if numbers are grouped using the thousand separator specified in **Control Panel**. Use one of the following constants:

vbUseDefault	2 (Uses the settings from the **Regional Settings** tab in **Control Panel**)
vbtrue	-1
vbfalse	0

Note	The **Number** tab in **Regional Settings** in **Control Panel** supplies all the information used for formatting.
Example	`MsgBox FormatPercent(4 / 45)` `MsgBox FormatPercent(4 / 45, 2, vbtrue, vbtrue, vbtrue)`

The `MsgBox` will display 8.89%, if the locale settings use a period (.) as the decimal separator.

See Also	*FormatCurrency*, *FormatDateTime*, and *FormatNumber*

InStr	Returns an integer indicating the position for the first occurrence of a sub string within a string.
Syntax	`InStr([start,] string1, string2[, compare])`

start (Optional) is any valid non-negative expression indicating the starting position for the search within *string1*. Non-integer values are rounded. This argument is required if the compare argument is specified.

string1 is the string you want to search within.

string2 is the sub string you want to search for.

compare (Optional) indicates the comparison method used when evaluating. Use one of the following constants:

| Syntax | **vbBinaryCompare** | 0 (Default) Performs a binary comparison, i.e. a case sensitive comparison. |
| | **vbTextCompare** | 1 Performs a textual comparison, i.e. a non-case sensitive comparison. |

Note

A runtime error will occur, if *start* contains Null. If *start* is larger than the length of string2 (> Len(*string2*)) 0 will be returned.

Possible return values for different *stringx* settings:

string1	zero-length	**0**
string1	Null	**Null**
string2	zero-length	*start*
string2	Null	**Null**
string2	not found	**0**
string2	found	**Position**

Example

```
Dim lngStartPos
Dim lngFoundPos
Dim strSearchWithin
Dim strSearchFor


   ' Set the start pos
   lngStartPos = 1
   ' Initialize the strings
   strSearchWithin = "This is a test string"
   strSearchFor = "t"
   ' Find the first occurrence
   lngFoundPos = InStr( lngStartPos, strSearchWithin, strSearchFor)
   ' Loop through the string
   Do While lngFoundPos > 0
      ' Display the found position
      MsgBox lngFoundPos
      ' Set the new start pos to
               ' the char after the found position
      lngStartPos = lngFoundPos + 1
      ' Find the next occurrence
      lngFoundPos = InStr( lngStartPos, strSearchWithin,
strSearchFor)
   Loop
```

The above code finds all occurrences of the letter t in *string1*, at position 11, 14 and 17. Please note that we use binary comparison here, which means that the uppercase T will not be "found". If you want to perform a case-insensitive search, you will need to specify the *compare* argument as **vbTextCompare**.

See Also

InStrB, InStrRev

InStrB	Returns an integer indicating the byte position for the first occurrence of a sub string within a string containing byte data.
Syntax	`InStrB([start,] string1, string2[, compare])`

start (Optional) is any valid non-negative expression indicating the starting position for the search within *string1*. Non-integer values are rounded. This argument is required, if the compare argument is specified.

string1 is the string containing byte data you want to search within.

string2 is the sub string you want to search for.

compare (Optional) indicates the comparison method used when evaluating. Use one of the following constants:

vbBinaryCompare – 0 (Default) Performs a binary comparison, i.e. a case sensitive comparison.

vbTextCompare – 1 Performs a textual comparison, i.e. a non-case sensitive comparison.

Note	A runtime error will occur, if *start* contains `Null`. If *start* is larger than the length of string2 (`> Len(string2)`) 0 will be returned.

Possible return values for different *stringx* settings:

string1	zero-length	**0**
string1	Null	**Null**
string2	zero-length	***start***
string2	Null	**Null**
string2	not found	**0**
string2	found	**Position**

Example	

```
Dim lngStartPos
Dim lngFoundPos
Dim strSearchWithin
Dim strSearchFor

    ' Set the start pos
    lngStartPos = 1
    ' Initialize the strings
    strSearchWithin = "This is a test string"
    strSearchFor = ChrB(0)

    ' Find the first occurrence
    lngFoundPos = InStrB( lngStartPos, strSearchWithin, strSearchFor)
    ' Loop through the string
    Do While lngFoundPos > 0
       ' Display the found position
       MsgBox lngFoundPos
       ' Set the new start pos to
          ' the char after the found position
       lngStartPos = lngFoundPos + 1
       ' Find the next occurrence
       lngFoundPos = InStrB( lngStartPos, strSearchWithin, strSearchFor)
    Loop
```

The above code finds all occurrences of the byte value 0 in *string1*, at position 2, 4, 6, ...40 and 42. This is because only the first byte of the Unicode character is used for the character. If you use a double-byte character set like the Japanese, the second byte will also contain a non-zero value.

See Also	***InStr, InStrRev***

InStrRev	Returns an integer indicating the position of the first occurrence of a sub string within a string starting from the end of the string. This is the reverse functionality of *InStr*.
Syntax	`InStrRev(string1, string2[, start[, compare]])`

string1 is the string you want to search within.

string2 is the sub string you want to search for.

start (Optional) is any valid non-negative expression indicating the starting position for the search within *string1*; –1 is the default and it will be used if this argument is omitted.

compare (Optional) indicates the comparison method used when evaluating. Use one of the following constants:

vbBinaryCompare – 0 (Default) Performs a binary comparison, i.e. a case sensitive comparison.
vbTextCompare – 1 Performs a textual comparison, i.e. a non-case sensitive comparison.

Note	A runtime error will occur, if *start* contains `Null`. If *start* is larger than the length if string2 (`> Len(string2)`) 0 will be returned.

Possible return values for different *stringx* settings:

string1	zero-length	**0**
string1	Null	**Null**
string2	zero-length	***start***
string2	Null	**Null**
string2	not found	**0**
string2	found	**Position**

`InStrRev` and `InStr` do not have same syntax!

| Example | ```
Dim lngStartPos
Dim lngFoundPos
Dim strSearchWithin
Dim strSearchFor

    ' Set the start pos
    lngStartPos = -1
    ' Initialize the strings
    strSearchWithin = "This is a test string"
    strSearchFor = "t"

    ' Find the first occurrence
    lngFoundPos = InStrRev( strSearchWithin, strSearchFor, lngStartPos)
    ' Loop through the string
    Do While lngFoundPos > 0
        ' Display the found
            ' position
        MsgBox lngFoundPos
        ' Set the new start pos to
            ' the char before the found position
        lngStartPos = lngFoundPos - 1
        ' Find the next occurrence
        lngFoundPos = InStrRev( strSearchWithin, strSearchFor,-
                            lngStartPos)
    Loop
``` |
```

	The above code finds all occurrences of the letter t in *string1*, at position 17, 14 and 11. Please note that we use binary comparison here, which means that the uppercase T will not be "found". If you want to perform a case-insensitive search, you will need to specify the *compare* argument as **vbTextCompare**.
See Also	***InStr, InStrB***

Join	Joins a number of substrings in an array to form the returned string.
Syntax	`Join(list[, delimiter])`
	list is a one dimensional array that contains all the substrings that you want to join.
	delimiter (Optional) is the character(s) used to separate the substrings. A space character " " is used as the delimiter if this argument is omitted.
Note	All the substrings are concatenated with no delimiter if a zero-length string is used as *delimiter*. If any element in the array is empty, a zero-length string will be used as the value.
| Example | ```
Dim strLights
Dim arrstrColors(3)

    ' Fill the array
    arrstrColors(0) = "Red"
    arrstrColors(1) = "Yellow"
    arrstrColors(2) = "Green"

    ' Join the array into a string
    strLights = Join( arrstrColors, ",")
``` |
| | `strLights` contains "Red,Yellow,Green". |
| See Also | ***Split*** |

LCase	Converts all alpha characters in a string to lowercase.
Syntax	`LCase(string)`
	string is the string you want converted to lowercase.
Note	`Null` is returned if *string* contains `Null`. Only uppercase letters are converted.
Example	`MsgBox LCase("ThisIsLowerCase")`
	`MsgBox` displays thisislowercase
See Also	***UCase***

Left	Returns *length* number of leftmost characters from *string*.
Syntax	`Left(string, length)`
	string is the string you want to extract a number of characters from.
	length is the number of characters you want to extract starting from the left. The entire *string* will be returned if *length* is equal to or greater than the total number of characters in *string*.

Table Continued on Following Page
```

Note	Null is returned if *string* contains Null.

Example	

```
Dim strExtract

        strExtract = "LeftRight"
        MsgBox Left(strExtract, 4)
```

MsgBox displays Left.

See Also	*Len*, *LenB*, *Mid*, *MidB* and *Right*

Len Returns the number of characters in a string.

Syntax **Len(string)**

string is any valid string expression you want the length of.

Note Null is returned if *string* contains Null.

Example

```
Dim strLength

        strLength = "1 2 3 4 5 6 7 8 9"
        MsgBox Len(strLength)
```

MsgBox displays 17.

See Also *Left*, *LenB*, *Mid*, *MidB* and *Right*

LenB Returns the number of bytes used to represent a string.

Syntax **LenB(string)**

string is any valid string expression you want the number of bytes for.

Note Null is returned if *string* contains Null.

Example

```
Dim strLength

        strLength = "123456789"
        MsgBox LenB(strLength)
```

MsgBox displays 18.

See Also *Left*, *Len*, *Mid*, *MidB* and *Right*

LTrim	Trims a string of leading spaces; " " or `Chr(32)`.
Syntax	**LTrim(string)**
	string is any valid string expression you want to trim leading (leftmost) spaces from.
Note	`Null` is returned if *string* contains `Null`.
| Example | ```
Dim strSpaces

        strSpaces = " Hello again *"
        MsgBox LTrim(strSpaces)
``` |
| | MsgBox displays Hello again * |
| See Also | *Left*, *Mid*, *Right*, *RTrim* and *Trim* |

Mid	Returns a specified number of characters from any position in a string.
Syntax	**Mid(string, start[, length])**
	string is any valid string expression you want to extract characters from.
	start is the starting position for extracting the characters. A zero-length string is returned if it is greater than the number of characters in *string*.
	length (Optional) is the number of characters you want to extract. All characters from *start* to the end of the string are returned if this argument is omitted or if *length* is greater than the number of characters counting from *start*.
Note	`Null` is returned if *string* contains `Null`.
| Example | ```
Dim strExtract

        strExtract = "Find ME in here"
        MsgBox Mid(strExtract, 6, 2)
``` |
| | MsgBox displays ME |
| See Also | *Left*, *Len*, *LenB*, *LTrim*, *MidB*, *Right*, *RTrim* and *Trim* |

MidB   Returns a specified number of bytes from any position in a string containing byte data.

Syntax   `MidB(string, start[, length])`

string is a string expression containing byte data you want to extract characters from.

start is the starting position for extracting the bytes. A zero-length string is returned if it is greater than the number of bytes in *string*.

length (Optional) is the number of bytes you want to extract. All bytes from *start* to the end of the string are returned if this argument is omitted or if *length* is greater than the number of bytes counting from *start*.

Note   `Null` is returned if *string* contains `Null`.

Example

```
Dim strExtract

        strExtract = "Find ME in here"
        MsgBox MidB(strExtract, 11, 4)
```

`MsgBox` displays **ME** , because VBScript uses 2 bytes to represent a character. The first byte contains the ANSI character code when dealing with 'normal' ANSI characters like M, and the next byte is 0. So byte 11 in the string is the first byte for the letter M and then we extract 4 bytes/2 characters.

See Also   *Left*, *Len*, *LTrim*, *Mid*, *Right*, *RTrim* and *Trim*

Replace   Replaces a substring within a string with another substring a specified number of times.

Syntax   `Replace(expression, find, replacewith[, start[, count[, compare]]])`

expression is a string expression that contains the substring you want to replace.

find is the substring you want to replace.

replacewith is the substring you want to replace with.

start (Optional) is the starting position within *expression* for replacing the substring. 1 (default), the first position, will be used if this argument is omitted. You must also specify the *count* argument if you want to use *start*.

count (Optional) is the number of times you want to replace *find*. -1 (default) will be used if this argument is omitted, which means all *find* in the expression. You must also specify the *start* argument if you want to use *count*.

compare (Optional) indicates the comparison method used when evaluating. Use one of the following constants:

vbBinaryCompare – 0 (Default) Performs a binary comparison, i.e. a case sensitive comparison.
vbTextCompare – 1 Performs a textual comparison, i.e. a non-case sensitive comparison.

| Note | If *start* and *count* are specified, the return value will be the original expression, with *find* replaced *count* times with *replacewith*, from *start* to the end of the expression, and not the complete string. A zero-length string is returned if *start* is greater than the length of *expression* (`start > Len(expression)`). All occurrences of *find* will be removed if *replacewith* is a zero-length string ("")

Possible return values for different argument settings:

expression	zero-length	**zero-length**
expression	Null	**Error**
find	zero-length	*expression*
count	0	*expression*

| Example |
```
Dim strReplace

        strReplace = Replace( "****I use binary", "I", "You", 5, _
                              1, vbBinaryCompare) ' You use binary
        strReplace = Replace( "****I use text", "i", "You", , , _
                              vbTextCompare)       ' ****You use text
```

| See Also | *Left*, *Len*, *LTrim*, *Mid*, *Right*, *RTrim* and *Trim* |

| **Right** | Returns *length* number of rightmost characters from *string* |

| Syntax | **Right(string, length)**

string is the string you want to extract a number of characters from.

length is the number of characters you want to extract starting from the right. The entire *string* will be returned if *length* is equal to or greater than the total number of characters in *string*.

| Note | Null is returned if *string* contains Null. |

Table Continued on Following Page

| Example | ```
Dim strExtract

        strExtract = "LeftRight"
        MsgBox Right(strExtract, 5)
``` |
| --- | --- |
| | MsgBox displays Right |
| See Also | *Left*, *Len*, *LenB*, *Mid* and *MidB* |

RTrim	Trims a string of trailing spaces; " " or `Chr(32)`.
Syntax	**RTrim(string)**
	string is any valid string expression you want to trim trailing (rightmost) spaces from.
Note	`Null` is returned if *string* contains `Null`.
| Example | ```
Dim strSpaces

        strSpaces = "* Hello again     "
        MsgBox RTrim(strSpaces)
``` |
| | MsgBox displays * Hello again |
| See Also | *Left*, *LTrim*, *Mid*, *Right* and *Trim* |

Space	Returns a string made up of a specified number of spaces (" ").
Syntax	**Space(number)**
	number is the number of spaces you want returned.
| Example | ```
Dim strSpaces

        strSpaces = "Hello again"
        MsgBox "*" & Space(5) & strSpaces
``` |
| | MsgBox displays *   Hello again |
| See Also | *String* |

Split	Returns a zero-based one-dimensional array "extracted" from the supplied string expression.
```

Syntax	**Split(expression[, delimiter[, count[, compare]]]))**

expression is the string containing substrings and delimiters that you want to split up and put into a zero-based one-dimensional array.

delimiter (Optional) is the character that separates the substrings. A space character will be used if this argument is omitted.

count (Optional) indicates the number of substrings to return. -1 (default) means all substrings will be returned.

compare (Optional) indicates the comparison method used when evaluating. Use one of the following constants:

vbBinaryCompare – 0 (Default) Performs a binary comparison, i.e. a case sensitive comparison.

vbTextCompare – 1 Performs a textual comparison, i.e. a non-case sensitive comparison.

Note	An empty array will be returned if *expression* is a zero-length string. The result of the Split function cannot be assigned to a variable of Variant subtype Array (8192). A runtime error occurs if you try to do so.
Example	

```
Dim arrstrSplit
Dim strSplit

        ' Initialize the string
    strSplit = "1,2,3,4,5,6,7,8,9,0"
        ' Split the string using comma as the delimiter
    arrstrSplit = Split(strSplit,  ",")
```

The array arrstrSplit now holds 10 elements, 0,1,2...0.

See Also	*Join*

StrComp	Performs a string comparison and returns the result.
Syntax	**StrComp(string1, string2[, compare])**

string1 is a valid string expression.

string2 is a valid string expression.

compare (Optional) indicates the comparison method used when evaluating. Use one of the following constants:

vbBinaryCompare – 0 (Default) Performs a binary comparison, i.e. a case sensitive comparison.

vbTextCompare – 1 Performs a textual comparison, i.e. a non-case sensitive comparison.

Table Continued on Following Page

Note	Possible return values for different *stringx* settings: *string1 < string2* **-1** *string1 = string2* **0** *string1 > string2* **1** Null is returned if *string1* or *string2* is Null.
Example	```Dim intResult

        intResult = StrComp("abc", "ABC", vbTextCompare)   ' 0
        intResult = StrComp("ABC", "abc", vbBinaryCompare) ' -1
        intResult = StrComp("abc", "ABC")   ' 1``` |
| See Also | ***String*** |

String	Returns a string with a substring repeated a specified number of times.
Syntax	**String(number, character)** *number* indicates the length of the returned string. *character* is the character code or string expression for the character used to build the returned string. Only the first character of a string expression is used.
Note	Null is returned if *number* or *character* contains Null. The character code will automatically be converted to a valid character code if it is greater than 255. The formula is: *character* Mod 256.
Example	```Dim strChars

        strChars = "Hello again"
        MsgBox String(5, "*") & strChars```

MsgBox displays *****Hello again |
| See Also | ***Space*** |

StrReverse	Returns a string with the character order reversed.
Syntax	**StrReverse(string)** *string* is the string expression you want reversed.
Note	A runtime error occurs if *string* is Null. If *string* is a zero-length string, a zero-length string will be returned. The case of the characters is not changed.
Example	``` MsgBox StrReverse("Hello again")``` MsgBox displays niaga olleH

Trim	Trims a string of leading and trailing spaces; " " or Chr(20).
Syntax	**Trim(string)**
	string is any valid string expression you want to trim leading (leftmost) and trailing (rightmost) spaces from.
Note	Null is returned if *string* contains Null.
| Example | ```
Dim strSpaces

        strSpaces = " *Hello again* "
        MsgBox Trim(strSpaces)
``` |
| | MsgBox displays *Hello again* |
| See Also | *Left*, *LTrim*, *Mid*, *Right* and *RTrim* |

UCase	Converts all alpha characters in a string to uppercase and returns the result.
Syntax	**UCase(string)**
	string is the string you want converted to uppercase.
Note	Null is returned if *string* contains Null. Only lowercase letters are converted.
| Example | ```
            MsgBox UCase("ThisIsUpperCase")
``` |
| | MsgBox displays THISISUPPERCASE |
| See Also | *LCase* |

Unsupported String Functions, Statements and Constructs

The following VB/VBA string functions/statements and constructs are not supported in VBScript:

Function Statement Name	Alternative
Format	*FormatCurrency*, *FormatDateTime*, *FormatNumber*, *FormatPercent*
LSet	*Left*, *Len* and *Space* functions in conjunction:

```
Dim strTest
Dim strNewText
            ' strTest is now 5 chars wide
    strTest = "01234"
            ' Assign the text to left align
    strNewText = "<-Test"
            ' Use the VB/VBA LSet (Unsupported)
    LSet strTest = strNewText

            ' Check if the New Text is wider than
            ' the variable we will align it in
    If Len(strNewText) <= Len(strTest) Then
                    ' Copy the text across and pad the
                    ' rest with spaces
        strTest = strNewText & Space(Len(strTest) - Len(strNewText))
    Else
                    ' Copy as many chars from the new
                    ' text as strTest is wide
        strTest = Left(strNewText, Len(strTest))
    End If
```

In both cases `strTest` will hold the value "<-Tes", because the original string `strTest` is only 5 characters wide and thus cannot hold all of `strNewText`. Had `strTest` been larger, the remaining places would have been filled with spaces.

Mid (statement) — *Left*, *Mid* and *InStr* functions, or the *Replace* function:

Here is how to replace a substring identified by characters using the *Replace* function:

```
Dim strText
Dim strFind
Dim strSubstitute
    strText = "This is the text I want to replace a substring in"
    strFind = "want to replace"
    strSubstitute = "have replaced"
    strText = Replace(strText, strFind, strSubstitute)
```

`strText` now holds This is the text I have replaced a substring in

Here is how to replace a substring identified by position and length using the *InStr*, *Left* and *Mid* functions:

```
Dim strText
Dim strSubstitute
   strText = "This is the text I want to replace a substring in"
   strSubstitute = "have replaced"
   strText = Left$(strText, 19) & strSubstitute & Mid$(strText, _
           35, Len(strText) - 34)
```

`strText` now holds This is the text I have replaced a substring in

RSet

Left, *Len* and *Space* functions in conjunction:

```
Dim strTest
Dim strNewText
        ' strTest is now 5 chars wide
   strTest = "01234"
        ' Assign the text to right align
   strNewText = "Test->"
        ' Use the VB/VBA RSet (Unsupported)
   RSet strTest = strNewText

        ' Check if the New Text is wider than
        ' the variable we will assign it in
   If Len(strNewText) <= Len(strTest) Then
                 ' Pad with spaces and copy the
                 ' text across
      strTest = Space(Len(strTest) - Len(strNewText)) &
strNewText
   Else
                 ' Copy as many chars from the new
                 ' text as strTest is wide
      strTest = Left(strNewText, Len(strTest))
   End If
```

In both cases `strTest` will hold the value "Test-", because the original string `strTest` is only 5 characters wide and thus cannot hold all of `strNewText`. Had `strTest` been larger, the remaining places would have been filled with spaces.

StrConv

Very unlikely that this will be needed as all variables are Variant and this will be done implicitly.

Fixed length strings (`Dim strMessage As String * 50`) are not supported.

String Constants

Constant	Value	Description
vbCr	Chr(13)	Carriage Return.
vbCrLf	Chr(13) & Chr(10)	A combination of Carriage Return and linefeed.
vbFormFeed	Chr(12)	Form Feed*
vbLf	Chr(10)	Line Feed
vbNewLine	Chr(13) & Chr(10) or Chr(10)	New line character. This is platform-specific, meaning whatever is appropriate for the current platform.
vbNullChar	Chr(0)	Character with the value of 0.
vbNullString	String with the value of 0	This is not the same as a zero-length string (""). Mainly used for calling external procedures.
vbTab	Chr(9)	Tab (horizontal)
vbVerticalTab	Chr(11)	Tab (vertical)*

* = Not useful in Microsoft Windows.

Conversion Functions

Normally you don't need to convert values in VBScript, because there is only one data type, the Variant.

Implicit conversion is generally applied when needed, but when you pass a value to a non-variant procedure in a COM object that needs the value passed ByRef, you will have to pass the value with the precise data subtype. This can be done by placing the argument in it's own set of parentheses, which forces a temporary evaluation of the argument as an expression:

```
Dim objByRefSample
Dim intTest
   ' Initialize the variable
   intTest = "5"
   ' Create the object
   Set objByRefSample = CreateObject ("MyObject.ByRefSample")
   ' Call the method
   objByRefSample.PassIntegerByReference (intTest)
   ' Destroy the object
   Set objByRefSample = Nothing
```

The `PassIntegerByReference` method is a VB sub-procedure with just one argument of type integer that is passed `ByRef`.

What happens is that the value 5 stored in the `intTest` variable is actually explicitly coerced into a variable of subtype Integer, so that it conforms to the methods argument type. If you remove the parentheses, you will get a runtime error, because the implicit coercion will treat the string value as a double.

This is just one way of solving the problem. Another way is to use the **CInt** conversion function (listed below) when calling the method.

At some point however, you might need to convert a value of one data subtype to another data subtype. This can be necessary for various reasons:

❑ You need to present a number in hexadecimal notation instead of decimal

❑ You need the corresponding character code for a character or vice versa

❑ You need to pass values to a non-variant property procedure or as a function parameter in a COM object

❑ You need to save data in a database

*See Chapter 2 **Variables and Data Types** for an explanation of the different data types.*

Asc	Returns the ANSI character code for the first character in a string.
Syntax	**Asc(string)**
	string is any valid string expression.
Note	A runtime error occurs if *string* doesn't contain any characters. *string* is converted to a `String` subtype if it's a numeric subtype.

Table Continued on Following Page

Example	`intCharCode = Asc("WROX")`
	intCharCode now holds the value 87, which is the ANSI character code for "W".
See Also	*AscB*, *AscW*, *Chr*, *ChrB* and *ChrW*

AscB	Returns the ANSI character code for the first byte in a string containing byte data.
Syntax	**AscB(string)**
	string is any valid string expression.
Note	A runtime error occurs if *string* doesn't contain any characters. For normal ANSI strings this function will return the same as the *Asc* function. Only if the string is in Unicode format will it be different from *Asc*. Unicode characters are represented by two bytes as opposed to ANSI characters that only need one.
Example	`intCharCode = AscB("WROX")`
	intCharCode now holds the value 87, which is the ANSI character code for "W".
See Also	*Asc*, *AscW*, *Chr*, *ChrB* and *ChrW*

AscW	Returns the Unicode character code for the first character in a string.
Syntax	**AscW(string)**
	string is any valid string expression.
Note	A runtime error occurs if *string* doesn't contain any characters. *string* is converted to a String subtype if it's a numeric subtype. For use on 32-bit Unicode enabled platforms only, to avoid conversion from Unicode to ANSI.
Example	`intCharCode = AscW("WROX")`
	intCharCode now holds the value 87, which is the Unicode character code for "W".
See Also	*Asc*, *AscB*, *Chr*, *ChrB* and *ChrW*

CBool	Returns a `Boolean` value (Variant subtype 11) corresponding to the value of an expression.
Syntax	`CBool(expression)`
	expression is any valid expression.
Note	A runtime error occurs if *expression* can't be evaluated to a numeric value.
	If *expression* evaluates to zero then false is returned; otherwise, true is returned.
| Example | ```
Dim intCounter, blnValue
        intCounter = 5
        blnValue = CBool(intCounter)
``` |
| | `blnValue` now holds the value true, because `intCounter` holds a non-zero value. |
| See Also | ***CByte*, *CCur*, *CDbl*, *CInt*, *CLng*, *CSng* and *CStr*** |

CByte	Returns an expression converted to Variant subtype `Byte` (17).
Syntax	`CByte(expression)`
	expression is any valid numeric expression.
Note	A runtime error occurs if *expression* can't be evaluated to a numeric value or if *expression* evaluates to a value outside the acceptable range for a `Byte` (0-255). Fractional values are rounded.
| Example | ```
Dim dblValue, bytValue
        dblValue = 5.456
        bytValue = CByte(dblValue)
``` |
| | `bytValue` now holds the value 5, because `dblValue` is rounded. |
| See Also | ***CBool*, *CCur*, *CDbl*, *CInt*, *CLng*, *CSng* and *CStr*** |

CCur	Returns an expression converted to Variant subtype Currency (6).
Syntax	`CCur(expression)` *expression* is any valid expression.
Note	CCur is internationally aware, which means that the return value is based on the locale settings on the machine. Numbers will be formatted with the appropriate decimal separator and the fourth digit to the right of the separator is rounded up if the fifth digit is 5 or higher.

Example	```Dim dblValue, curValue```
	``` dblValue = 724.555789```
	``` curValue = CCur(dblValue)```
	
	curValue now holds the value 724.5558 or 724,5558, depending on the separator.

See Also	*CBool*, *CByte*, *CDbl*, *CInt*, *CLng*, *CSng* and *CStr*

CDate	*See under **Date & Time Functions***

CDbl	Returns an expression converted to Variant subtype Double (5).
Syntax	`CDbl(expression)` *expression* is any valid expression.
Note	*CDbl* is internationally aware, which means that the return value is based on the locale settings on the machine. Numbers will be formatted with the appropriate decimal separator. A runtime error occurs if *expression* lies outside the range (-1.79769313486232E308 to -4.94065645841247E-324 for negative values, and 4.94065645841247E-324 to 1.79769313486232E308 for positive values) applicable to a Double.

Example	```Dim dblValue```
	``` dblValue = CDbl("5,579.56")```
	
	dblValue now holds the value 5579.56 or 5,57956, depending on the thousand and decimal separators in use.

See Also	*CBool*, *CByte*, *CCur*, *CInt*, *CLng*, *CSng* and *CStr*

Chr	Returns the ANSI character corresponding to *charactercode*.
Syntax	**Chr(charactercode)** *charactercode* is a numeric value that indicates the character you want.
Note	Supplying a *charactercode* from 0 to 31 will return a standard non-printable ASCII character.
| Example | ```
Dim strChar
        strChar = Chr(89)
```<br><br>strChar now holds the character Y which is number 89 in the ANSI character table. |
| See Also | *Asc, AscB, AscW, ChrB* and *ChrW* |

ChrB	Returns the ANSI character corresponding to *charactercode*.
Syntax	**ChrB(charactercode)** *charactercode* is a numeric value that indicates the character you want.
Note	Supplying a *charactercode* from 0 to 31 will return a standard non-printable ASCII character. This function is used instead of the **Chr** (returns a two-byte character) function when you only want the first byte of the character returned.
| Example | ```
Dim strChar
        strChar = ChrB(89)
```<br><br>strChar now holds the character Y which is number 89 in the ANSI character table. |
| See Also | *Asc, AscB, AscW, Chr* and *ChrW* |

ChrW	Returns the Unicode character corresponding to *charactercode*.
Syntax	**ChrW(charactercode)** *charactercode* is a numeric value that indicates the character you want.
Note	Supplying a *charactercode* from 0 to 31 will return a standard non-printable ASCII character. This function is used instead of the ***Chr*** function when you want to return a double byte character. For use on 32-bit Unicode enabled platforms only, to avoid conversion from Unicode to ANSI.
Example	``` Dim strChar strChar = ChrW(89) ``` strChar now holds the character Y which is number 89 in the Unicode character table.
See Also	***Asc*, *AscB*, *AscW*, *Chr* and *ChrB***

CInt	Returns an expression converted to Variant subtype Integer (2).
Syntax	**CInt(expression)** *expression* is any valid expression.
Note	***CInt*** is internationally aware, which means that the return value is based on the locale settings on the machine. Please note that decimal values are rounded, before the fractional part is discarded. A runtime error occurs if *expression* lies outside the range (-32,768 to 32,767) applicable to an Integer.
Example	``` Dim intValue intValue = CInt("5,579.56") ``` intValue now holds the value 5580 or 6, depending on the thousand and decimal separators in use.
See Also	***CBool*, *CByte*, *CCur*, *CDbl*, *CLng*, *CSng*, *CStr*** and the ***Math Functions Fix*** and ***Int***

CLng	Returns an expression converted to Variant subtype Long (3).

Syntax

`CLng(expression)`

expression is any valid expression.

Note

CLng is internationally aware, which means that the return value is based on the locale settings on the machine. Please note that decimal values are rounded, before the fractional part is discarded. A runtime error occurs if *expression* lies outside the range (-2,147,483,648 to 2,147,483,647) applicable to a Long.

Example

```
Dim lngValue
        lngValue = CLng("5,579.56")
```

lngValue now holds the value 5580 or 6, depending on the thousand and decimal separators in use.

See Also

CBool, CByte, CCur, CDbl, CInt, CSng, CStr, and the *Math Functions Fix* and *Int*

CSng	Returns an expression converted to Variant subtype Single (4).

Syntax

`CSng(expression)`

expression is any valid expression.

Note

CSng is internationally aware, which means that the return value is based on the locale settings on the machine. A runtime error occurs if *expression* lies outside the range (-3.402823E38 to -1.401298E-45 for negative values, and 1.401298E-45 to 3.402823E38 for positive values) applicable to a Single.

Example

```
Dim sngValue
        sngValue = CSng("5,579.56")
```

sngValue now holds the value 5579.56 or 5,57956, depending on the thousand and decimal separators in use.

See Also

CBool, CByte, CCur, CDbl, CInt, CLng, CStr and the *Math Functions Fix* and *Int*

CStr	Returns an expression converted to Variant subtype String (8).
Syntax	`CStr(expression)` *expression* is any valid expression.
Note	*CStr* is internationally aware, which means that the return value is based on the locale settings on the machine. A runtime error occurs if *expression* is Null. Numeric and Err values are returned as numbers, Boolean values as true or false, and Date values as a short date.

Example	```Dim strValue```
	``` strValue = CStr("5,579.56")```
	
	strValue now holds the value 5,579.56.

See Also	*CBool*, *CByte*, *CCur*, *CDbl*, *CInt*, *CLng*, *CSng* and the *Math Functions Fix* and *Int*

Fix	*See under **Math Functions***

Hex	Returns the hexadecimal representation (up to 8 characters) of a number as a Variant subtype String (8).
Syntax	`Hex(number)` *number* is any valid expression.
Note	*number* is rounded to nearest even number before it is evaluated. Null will be returned if *number* is Null.

Example	```Dim strValue```
	``` strValue = Hex(5579.56)```
	
	strValue now holds the value 15CC.

See Also	*Oct*

Int	*See under **Math Functions***

Oct	Returns the octal representation (up to 11 characters) of a number as a Variant subtype `String` (8).
Syntax	`Oct(number)`
	expression is any valid expression.
Note	*number* is rounded to nearest whole number before it is evaluated. `Null` will be returned if *number* is `Null`.
| Example | ```
Dim strValue
        strValue = Oct(5579.56)
``` |
| | `strValue` now holds the value 12714. |
| See Also | *Hex* |

Unsupported conversion functions

The following VB/VBA conversion functions are not supported in VBScript:

Function Name	Alternative
CVar	Not needed since conversion to a Variant is implicit.
CVDate	*CDate*, *Date*
Str	*CStr*
Val	*CDbl*, *CInt*, *CLng* and *CSng*

Miscellaneous Functions, Statements and Keywords

Some functionality does not fit under any of the other categories, and so they have been gathered here. Below you will find descriptions of various functions for handling objects, user input, variable checks, output on screen, etc.
```

Create Object	Returns a reference to an Automation/COM/ActiveX object. The object is created using COM object creation services.
Syntax	`CreateObject(servername.typename[, location])`
	servername is the name of the application that provides the object.
	typename is the object's type or class that you want to create.
	location (Optional) is the name of the network server you want the object created on. If missing the object is created on the local machine.
Note	An Automation/COM/ActiveX object always contains at least one type or class, but usually several types or classes are contained within. *servername* and *typename* are often referred to as progid. Please note that a progid is not always a two part one, like `servername.typename`. It can have several parts, like `servername.typename.version`.
| Example | ```
Dim objRemote
Dim objLocal

        ' Create an object from class
        ' MyClass contained in the
        ' COM object MyApp on a
        ' remote server named FileSrv
        Set objRemote = CreateObject( "MyApp.MyClass", "FileSrv")

        ' Create an object from class
        ' LocalClass contained in the
        ' COM object LocalApp on the
        ' local macine
        Set objLocal = CreateObject( "LocalApp.LocalClass)
``` |
| See Also | *GetObject* |

Dim	Declares a variable of type Variant and allocates storage space.
Syntax	`Dim varname[([subscripts])] [, varname[([subscripts])]]...`
	varname is the name of the variable
	subscripts (Optional) indicates the dimensions when you declare an array variable. You can declare up to 60 multiple dimensions using the following syntax:
	upperbound[, *upperbound*]...
	upperbound specifies the upper bounds of the array. Since the lower bound of an array in VBScript is always zero, *upperbound* is one less than the number of elements in the array.
	If you declare an array with empty subscripts, you can later resize it with `ReDim`; this is called a dynamic array.
```

Note	This statement is scope specific, i.e. you need to consider when and where you want to declare your variables. Variables that are only used in a specific procedure should be declared in this procedure. This will make the variable invisible and inaccessible outside the procedure. You can also declare your variables with script scope. This means that the variables will be accessible to all procedures within the script. This is one way of sharing data between different procedures. Dim statements should be put at the top of a procedure to make the procedure easier to read.

Example
```
' Declare a dynamic array
Dim arrstrDynamic()
' Declare a fixed size array
' with 5 elements
Dim arrstrFixed(4)
' Declare a non-array variable
Dim vntTest
```

See Also **_ReDim_** and **_Set_**

Eval   Evaluates and returns the result of an expression.

Syntax   **result = Eval(expression)**

result (Optional) is the variable you want to assign the result of the evaluation to. Although _result_ is optional, you should consider using the **_Execute_** statement, if you don't want to specify it.

expression is a string containing a valid VBScript expression.

Note   Because the assignment operator and the comparison operator is the same in VBScript, you need to be careful when using them with **_Eval_**. **_Eval_** always uses the equal sign (=) as a comparison operator, so if you need to use it as an assignment operator, you should use the **_Execute_** statement instead.

Example
```
Dim blnResult
Dim lngX, lngY

        ' Initialize the variables
        lngX = 15: lngY = 10
        ' Evaluate the expression
        blnResult = Eval( "lngX = lngY")
```

blnResult holds the value false, because 15 is not equal to 10.

See Also   **_Execute_** statement

Execute	Executes one or more statements in the local namespace.
Syntax	`Execute statement`
	statement is a string containing the statement(s) you want executed. If you include more than one statement, you must separate them using colons or embedded line breaks.
Note	Because the assignment operator and the comparison operator is the same in VBScript, you need to be careful when using them with *Execute*. *Execute* always uses the equal sign (=) as an assignment operator, so if you need to use it as a comparison operator, you should use the *Eval* function instead.
	All in-scope variables and objects are available to the statement(s) being executed, but you need to be aware of the special case when your statements create a procedure:
	`Execute "Sub ExecProc: MsgBox ""In here"": End Sub"`
	The `ExecProc`'s scope is global and thus everything from the global scope is inherited. The context of the procedure itself is only available within the scope it is created. This means that if you execute the above shown *Execute* statement in a procedure, the `ExecProc` procedure will only be accessible within the procedure where the *Execute* statement is called. You can get around this by simply moving the `Execute` statement to the script level or using the `ExecuteGlobal` statement.
| Example | ```
Dim lngResult
Dim lngX, lngY

        ' Initialize the variables
        lngX = 15: lngY = 10
        ' Execute the statement
        Execute( "lngResult = lngX + lngY")
``` |
| | `lngResult` holds the value 25. |
| See Also | *Eval* and *ExecuteGlobal statement* |

ExecuteGlobal	Executes one or more statements in the global namespace.
Syntax	`ExecuteGlobal statement`
	statement is a string containing the statement(s) you want executed. If you include more than one statement, you must separate them using colons or embedded line breaks.
```

Note	Because the assignment operator and the comparison operator is the same in VBScript, you need to be careful when using them with *ExecuteGlobal*. *ExecuteGlobal* always uses the equal sign (=) as an assignment operator, so if you need to use it as a comparison operator, you should use the *Eval* function instead.
	All variables and objects are available to the statement(s) being executed.
| Example | ```
Dim lngResult
Dim lngX, lngY

        ' Initialize the variables
        lngX = 15: lngY = 10
        ' Execute the statement
        ExecuteGlobal( "lngResult = lngX + lngY")
``` |
| | `lngResult` holds the value 25. |
| See Also | *Eval* and *Execute* |

Filter	Returns an array that contains a subset of an array of strings. The array is zero-based as are all arrays in VBScript and it holds as many elements as are found in the filtering process The subset is determined by specifying a criteria.
Syntax	`Filter(inputstrings, value[, include[, compare]])`
	inputstrings is a one dimensional string array that you want to search.
	value is the string you want to search for.
	include (Optional) is a `Boolean` value indicating if you want to include (true) or exclude (false) elements in *inputstrings* that contains *value*.
	compare (Optional) indicates the comparison method used when evaluating. Use one of the following constants:
	vbBinaryCompare – 0 (Default) Performs a binary comparison, i.e. a case sensitive comparison.
	vbTextCompare – 1 Performs a textual comparison, i.e. a non-case sensitive comparison.
Note	An empty array is returned if no matches are found. A runtime error occurs if *inputstrings* is not a one-dimensional array or if it is `Null`.

Table Continued on Following Page
```

| Example | ```
Dim arrstrColors(3)
Dim arrstrFilteredColors

        ' Fill the array
        arrstrColors(0) = "Red"
        arrstrColors(1) = "Green"
        arrstrColors(2) = "Blue"

        ' Filter the array
        arrstrFilteredColors = Filter(arrstrColors, "Red")
``` |
|---|---|
| | arrstrFilteredColors now holds one element (0) which has the value Red. |
| See Also | *See the **String Function Replace*** |

GetObject	Returns a reference to an Automation object.
Syntax	**GetObject([pathname] [, class]])**

pathname (Optional) is a string specifying the full path and name of the file that contains the object you want to retrieve. You need to specify *class* if you omit this argument.

class (Optional) is a string that indicates the class of the object. You need to specify *pathname* if you omit this argument. The following syntax is used for *class*:

    appname.objecttype

appname is a string indicating the application that provides the object.

objecttype is a string specifying the object's type or class that you want created.

Note	You can use this function to start the application associated with ***pathname*** and activate/return the object specified in the *pathname*. A new object is returned if ***pathname*** is a zero-length string ("") and the currently active object of the specified type is returned if ***pathname*** is omitted. Please note, that if the object you want returned has been compiled with Visual Basic, you cannot obtain a reference to an existing object by omitting the ***pathname*** argument. A new object will be returned instead. The opposite is true for objects that are registered as single-instance objects; the same instance will always be returned. However, you should note the above-mentioned problems with ActiveX DLL's compiled using Visual Basic.
	Some applications allow you to activate part of a file and you can do this by suffixing pathname with an exclamation mark (!) and a string that identifies the part of the object you want.
	You should only use this function when there is a current instance of the object you want to create, or when you want the object to open up a specific document. Use **CreateObject** to create a new instance of an object.
```

| Example | ```
Dim objAutomation

        ' Create a reference to an
        ' existing instance of an
        ' Excel application (this
        ' call will raise an error
        ' if no Excel.Application
        ' objects already exists)
        Set objAutomation = GetObject(, "Excel.Application")

        ' Create a reference to a
        ' specific workbook in a new
        ' instance of an Excel
        ' application
        Set objAutomation = GetObject( "C:\Test.xls ")
``` |
|---|---|
| See Also | *CreateObject* |

GetRef	Returns a reference to a procedure. This reference can be bound to an object event. This will let you bind a VBScript procedure to a DHTML event.
Syntax	**Set object.eventname = GetRef(procname)**

object is the name of the object in which *eventname* is placed.

eventname is the name of the event to which the procedure is to be bound.

procname is the name of the procedure you want to bind to *eventname*. |
| Example | ```
Sub NewOnFocus()
        ' Do your stuff here
End Sub

        ' Bind the NewOnFocus
        ' procedure to the
        ' Window. OnFocus event
        Set Window.OnFocus = GetRef("NewOnFocus ")
``` |

InputBox	Displays a dialog box with a custom prompt and a text box. The content of the text box is returned when the user clicks OK.
Syntax	`InputBox(prompt[, title][, default][, xpos][, ypos][, helpfile, context])`

prompt is the message you want displayed in the dialog box. The string can contain up to 1024 characters, depending on the width of the characters you use. You can separate the lines using one of these VBScript constants:

> `vbCr, vbCrLf, vbLf or vbNewLine`

title (Optional) is the text you want displayed in the dialog box title bar. The application name will be displayed, if this argument is omitted.

default is the default text that will be returned, if the user doesn't type in any data. The text box will be empty if you omit this argument.

xpos (Optional) is a numeric expression that indicates the horizontal distance of the left edge of the dialog box measured in twips (1/20 of a printer's point, which is 1/72 of an inch) from the left edge of the screen. The dialog box will be horizontally centered if you omit this argument.

ypos (Optional) is a numeric expression that indicates the vertical distance of the upper edge of the dialog box measured in twips from the upper edge of the screen. The dialog box will be vertically positioned approximately one-third of the way down the screen, if you omit this argument.

helpfile (Optional) is a string expression that indicates the help file to use when providing context-sensitive help for the dialog box. This argument must be used in conjunction with *context*. This is not available on 16-bit platforms.

context (Optional) is a numeric expression that indicates the help context number that makes sure that the right help topic is displayed. This argument must be used in conjunction with *helpfile*. This is not available on 16-bit platforms.

Note	A zero-length string will be returned if the user clicks **Cancel** or presses *ESC*.
Example	```

```
Dim strInput
    strInput = InputBox( "Enter User Name:", "Test")
    MsgBox strInput
```

The `MsgBox` will display either an empty string or whatever the user entered into the text box.

See Also	*MsgBox*

IsEmpty	Returns a `Boolean` value indicating if a variable has been initialized.
Syntax	`IsEmpty(expression)` *expression* is the variable you want to check has been initialized.
Note	You can use more than one variable as *expression*. If for Example, you concatenate two Variants and one of them is empty, the ***IsEmpty*** function will return false, because the expression is not empty.
| Example | ```
Dim strTest
Dim strInput
    strInput = "Test"
    MsgBox IsEmpty(strTest)           ' true
    MsgBox IsEmpty(strInput & strTest) ' false
``` |
| See Also | ***IsArray, IsDate, IsNull, IsNumeric, IsObject*** and ***VarType*** |

IsNull	Returns a `Boolean` value indicating if a variable contains `Null` or valid data.
	`IsNull(expression)` *expression* is any expression.
Syntax	This function returns true if the whole of *expression* evaluates to `Null`. If you have more than one variable in *expression*, all of them must be `Null` for the function to return true. Please be aware that `Null` is not the same as `Empty` (a variable that hasn't been initialized) or a zero-length string (""). `Null` means no valid value! You should always use the ***IsNull*** function when checking for `Null` values, because using the normal operators will return false even if one variable is `Null`.
| Example | ```
Dim strInput
    strInput = "Test"
    MsgBox IsNull( strInput & Null) ' false
    MsgBox IsNull(Null)             ' true
``` |
| See Also | ***IsArray, IsDate, IsEmpty, IsNumeric, IsObject*** and ***VarType*** |

IsNumeric	Returns a `Boolean` value indicating if an expression can be evaluated as a number.
Syntax	`IsNumeric(expression)`
	expression is any expression.
Note	This function returns true if the whole expression evaluates to a number. A `Date` expression is not considered a numeric expression.
Example	

```
MsgBox IsNumeric(55.55)              ' true
MsgBox IsNumeric("55.55")            ' true
MsgBox IsNumeric("55.55aaa")         ' false
MsgBox IsNumeric( "March 1, 1999")   ' false
MsgBox IsNumeric(vbNullChar)         ' false
```

See Also	*IsArray*, *IsDate*, *IsEmpty*, *IsNull*, *IsObject* and *VarType*

IsObject	Returns a `Boolean` value indicating if an expression is a reference to a valid Automation object.
Syntax	`IsObject(expression)`
	expression is any expression.
Note	This function returns true only if *expression* is in fact a variable of Variant subtype `Object` (9) or a user-defined object.
Example	

```
Dim objTest

        MsgBox IsObject(objTest)                          '
false
        Set objTest = CreateObject( "Excel.Application")
        MsgBox IsObject(objTest)                          '
true
```

See Also	*IsArray*, *IsDate*, *IsEmpty*, *IsNull*, *IsNumeric*, *Set* and *VarType*

LoadPicture	Returns a picture object.
Syntax	`LoadPicture(picturename)`
	picturename is a string expression that indicates the file name of the picture you want loaded.

Note	This function is only available on 32-bit platforms. The following graphic formats are supported:

Bitmap	.bmp
Icon	.ico
Run-length encoded	.rle
Windows metafile	.wmf
Enhanced metafile	.emf
GIF	.gif
JPEG	.jpg

A runtime error occurs if *picturename* doesn't exist or if it is not a valid picture file. Use *LoadPicture("")* to return an "empty" picture object in order to clear a particular picture.

Example

```
Dim objPicture

    ' Load a picture into objPicture
    objPicture = LoadPicture( "C:\Test.bmp")
    ' Clear objPicture
    objPicture = LoadPicture( "")
```

MsgBox

Displays a dialog box with a custom message and a custom set of command buttons. The value of the button the user clicks is returned as the result of this function.

Syntax

```
MsgBox(prompt[, buttons][, title [, helpfile,
context])
```

prompt is the message you want displayed in the dialog box. The string can contain up to 1024 characters, depending on the width of the characters you use. You can separate the lines using one of these VBScript constants:

vbCr, vbCrLf, vbLf or vbNewLine

buttons (Optional) is the sum of values indicating the number and type of button(s) to display, which icon style to use, which button is the default and if the *MsgBox* is modal. The settings for this argument are:

vbOKOnly	0	Displays OK button.
vbOKCancel	1	Displays OK and Cancel buttons.
vbAbortRetryIgnore	2	Displays Abort, Retry, and Ignore buttons.
vbYesNoCancel	3	Displays Yes, No, and Cancel buttons.

Table Continued on Following Page

vbYesNo	4	Displays Yes and No buttons.
vbRetryCancel	5	Displays Retry and Cancel buttons.
vbCritical	16	Displays critical icon.
vbQuestion	32	Displays query icon.
vbExclamation	48	Displays warning icon.
vbInformation	64	Displays information icon.
vbDefaultButton1	0	Makes the first button the default one.
vbDefaultButton2	256	Makes the second button the default one.
vbDefaultButton3	512	Makes the third button the default one.
vbDefaultButton4	768	Makes the fourth button the default one
vbApplicationModal	0	When the MsgBox is application modal, the user must respond to the message box, before he/she can continue.
vbSystemModal	4096	The same effect as vbApplicationModal. Presumably this is a "left-over" from the good old 16-bit Windows days. The dialog box will stay on top of other windows though.

Please note how the values are grouped:

Buttons (values 0-5)

Icon (values 16, 32, 48 and 64)

Default button (values 0, 256, 512 and 768)

Modal (values 0 and 4096)

You should only pick one value from each group when creating your *MsgBox*.

title (Optional) is the text you want displayed in the dialog box title bar. The application name will be displayed if this argument is omitted.

helpfile (Optional) is a string expression that indicates the help file to use when providing context-sensitive help for the dialog box. This argument must be used in conjunction with *context*. This is not available on 16-bit platforms.

context (Optional) is a numeric expression that indicates the help context number that makes sure that the right help topic is displayed. This argument must be used in conjunction with *helpfile*.

Note   The following values can be returned:

vbOK (1)
vbCancel(2)
vbAbort (3)
vbRetry (4)
vbIgnore (5)
vbYes (6)
vbNo (7)

The *ESC* key has the same effect as the Cancel button. Clicking the Help or pressing *F1* will not close the *MsgBox*.

Example

```
Dim intReturn

    intReturn = MsgBox( "Exit the application?", vbYesNoCancel + _
                vbQuestion)
```

The *MsgBox* will display the message "Exit the application?", the buttons Yes, No and Cancel, and the question mark icon. This *MsgBox* will be application modal.

See Also   **InputBox**

RGB   Returns an integer that represents an *RGB* color value. The *RGB* color value specifies the relative intensity of red, green, and blue to cause a specific color to be displayed.

Syntax   **RGB(red, green, blue)**

red is the red part of the color. Must be in the range 0-255.

green is the green part of the color. Must be in the range 0-255.

blue is the blue part of the color. Must be in the range 0-255.

Table Continued on Following Page

Note	255 will be used, if the value for any of the arguments is larger than 255. A runtime error occurs if any of the arguments cannot be evaluated to a numeric value.
Example	```' Returns the RGB number for white``` ```RGB(255, 255, 255)```

ScriptEngine	Returns a string indicating the scripting language being used.
Syntax	```ScriptEngine```
Note	The following scripting engine values can be returned:

VBScript	MS VBScript
JScript	MS JScript
VBA	MS Visual Basic for Applications

	Other third-party ActiveX Scripting Engines can also be returned, if you have installed one.
See Also	*ScriptEngineBuildVersion*, *ScriptEngineMajorVersion* and *ScriptEngineMinorVersion*

ScriptEngineBuildVersion	Returns the build version of the script engine being used.
Syntax	```ScriptEngineBuildVersion```
Note	This function gets the information from the DLL for the current scripting language.
See Also	*ScriptEngine*, *ScriptEngineMajorVersion* and *ScriptEngineMinorVersion*

ScriptEngineMajorVersion	Returns the major version number of the script engine being used. The major version number is the part before the decimal separator, e.g. 5 if the version is 5.1.
Syntax	```ScriptEngineMajorVersion```
Note	This function gets the information from the DLL for the current scripting language.
See Also	*ScriptEngine*, *ScriptEngineBuildVersion* and *ScriptEngineMinorVersion*

ScriptEngineMajorVersion	Returns the minor version number of the script engine being used. The minor version number is the part after the decimal separator, e.g. 1 if the version is 5.1.

Syntax	`ScriptEngineMinorVersion`
Note	This function gets the information from the DLL for the current scripting language.
See Also	*ScriptEngine*, *ScriptEngineBuildVersion* and *ScriptEngineMajorVersion*

Set	Returns an object reference, which must be assigned to a variable or property, or returns a procedure reference that must be associated with an event.
Syntax	`Set objectvar = {objectexpression	New classname	Nothing}`
	objectvar is the name of a variable or property.
	objectexpression (Optional) is the name of an existing object or another variable of the same object type. It can also be a method or function that returns either.
	classname (Optional) is the name of the class you want to create.
	`Set object.eventname = GetRef(procname)`
	object is the name of the object that *eventname* is associated with.
	eventname is the name of the event you want to bind *procname* to.
	procname is the name of the procedure you want to associate with *eventname*.
Note	*objectvar* must be an empty variable or an object type consistent with *objectexpression* being assigned.
	Set is used to create a reference to an object and not a copy of it. This means that if you use the *Set* statement more than once on the same object, you will have more than one reference to the same object. Any changes made to the object will be "visible" to all references.
	New, is only used in conjunction with *classname*, when you want to create a new instance of a class.
	If you use the *Nothing* keyword, you release the reference to an object, but if you have more than one reference to an object, the system resources are only released when all references have been destroyed (by setting them to *Nothing*) or they go out of scope.

| Example | ```
Dim objTest1
Dim objTest2
Dim objNewClass

    ' Create a new dictionary object
    Set objTest1 = CreateObject( "Scripting.Dictionary")
    ' Create a reference to the
    ' newly created dictionary object
    Set objTest2 = objTest1

    ' Destroy the object reference
    Set objTest1 = Nothing
    ' Although objTest2 was set
    ' to refer to objTest1, you can
    ' still refer to objTest2,
    ' because the system resources
    ' will not be released before
    ' all references have been
    ' destroyed. So let's add a key
    ' and an item
    objTest2.Add "TestKey", "Test"
    ' Destroy the object reference
    Set objTest2 = Nothing

    ' Create an instance of the
    ' class clsTest (created with
    ' the Class keyword)
    Set objNewClass = New clsTest
    ' ...
    ' Destroy the class instance
    Set objNewClass = Nothing
``` |
| See Also | *Class* (Chapter 8: Classes in VBScript) and *GetRef* |

| **TypeName** | Returns the Variant subtype information for an expression as a Variant subtype `String` (8). |
| Syntax | **TypeName(expression)**

expression is the variable or constant you want subtype information for. |
```

Note	This function has the following return values (strings):

Byte	Byte
Integer	Integer
Long	Long integer
Single	Single-precision floating-point
Double	Double-precision floating-point
Currency	Currency
Decimal	Decimal
Date	Date and/or time
String	Character string
Boolean	true or false
Empty	Unitialized
Null	No valid data
<object type>	Actual type name of an object
Object	Generic object
Unknown	Unknown object type
Nothing instance	Object variable that doesn't refer to an object
Error	Error

| Example | ```
Dim arrstrTest(10)

    MsgBox TypeName(10)          ' Integer
    MsgBox TypeName("Test")      ' String
    MsgBox TypeName(arrstrTest)  ' Variant()
    MsgBox TypeName(Null)        ' Null
``` |
| See Also | *IsArray, IsDate, IsEmpty, IsNull, IsNumeric, IsObject* and *VarType* |

VarType	Returns an integer indicating the subtype of a variable or constant.
Syntax	**VarType(expression)**
	expression is the variable or constant you want subtype information for.
```

Note	This function has the following return values:		
	vbEmpty	0	uninitialized
	vbNull	1	no valid data
	vbInteger	2	Integer
	vbLong	3	Long integer
	vbSingle	4	Single-precision floating-point number
	vbDouble	5	Double-precision floating-point number
	vbCurrency	6	Currency
	vbDate	7	Date
	vbString	8	String
	vbObject	9	Automation object
	vbError	10	Error
	vbBoolean	11	Boolean
	vbVariant	12	Variant (only used only with arrays of Variants)
	vbDataObject	13	A data-access object
	vbByte	17	Byte
	vbArray	8192	Array

Example

```
Dim arrstrTest(10)

    MsgBox VarType(10)          ' 2
    MsgBox VarType("Test")      ' 8
    MsgBox VarType(arrstrTest)  ' 8204
    MsgBox VarType(Null)        ' 1
```

See Also   *IsArray, IsDate, IsEmpty, IsNull, IsNumeric, IsObject* and *TypeName*

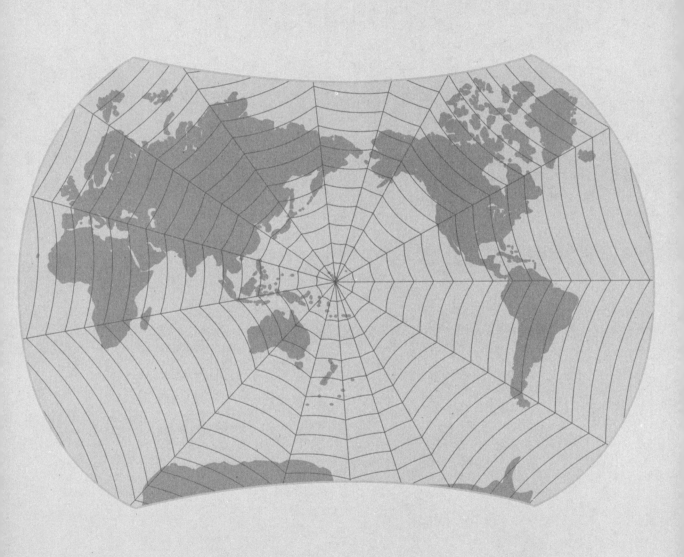

John Kauffman's tips for Installing Personal Web Server on Win 9x

The main strength of PWS is that it provides a convenient and inexpensive development environment for pre-Windows 2000 machines, without the need for powerful hardware. A copy of your web site can be made to a local machine and then worked upon without the possibility of damaging the real site during development. Saving and viewing sites on a local drive enables the developer to review progress without having to repeatedly transfer files. At the end of development all the code must be transferred by FTP or HTTP, but that one-time transfer is less expensive in terms of time and resources than repeated transfers.

One of the main drawbacks of PWS is that it can be awkward to install and get up and running correctly. I have tried to summarize in this section all of the main problems that I have encountered, and that my students have encountered, to ease what can prove to be a tricky process sometimes. Indeed even the first question can prove an obstacle: where should I get it from?

Sources of PWS

The version of PWS, you need to install is version 4.0, which was first released in NT4 Option Pack of Dec 1997 as part of IIS 4.0. It is available from several sources, as follows.

VID

Microsoft's Visual InterDev version 6.0 includes PWS. It can be installed at the time VID is set up or can be installed afterwards as an option from a custom set-up.

Win98

The Win98 CD contains a folder named **Add-Ons/PWS**. Within that folder is a `Setup.exe` for PWS. My students who have installed PWS from the Win98 CD onto a Win98 OS seem to have less problems then students who use other sources.

FP

Front Page, Front Page97 and FrontPage98 included PWS, however in different flavors.

The early releases of Front Page had a program named HTTPD which was sold as Front Page Server. The function was the same as PWS, but it was an entirely different set of code and did not run ASP.

FP 97 contained PWS 1.0, and FP 98 contains PWS 4.0, the current incarnation of PWS.

Download

Microsoft offers PWS as a download, but with a strange nomenclature. When you go to http://www.microsoft.com/windows/ie/pws you will see that there is the WinNT option pack for NT and a WinNT option pack for Win95. If you run the Windows NT Option Pack on a Windows9x machine, the option pack will recognize that this is not an NT OS and will install PWS instead of IIS.

"Wait A Minute! Run the Windows NT Option Pack on Windows9x?" Many students have a hard time believing that one possible technique to install PWS was to run the NT Option Pack on their Windows 9x machines. But it does work and is the recommended method.

Which Source to Use?

I have found that students have the fewest problems when installing PWS on Win98 from the Win98 CD. The second least-problematic source seems to be the NT download which is good for Win95 as well as Win98. Another strategy with minimum complaints has been the installation from NT 4 Option pack onto NT workstation. Folks that are installing from VID and FrontPage CD-ROMs seem to have the most problems. I also suggest that if students are considering moving from Win95 to Win98 or WinNT, they do so prior to attempting to install PWS.

Install Steps for PWS From Win98CD to Windows98

This is the safest option for installing PWS, in my experience, but is only possible if using Win98. The steps are as follows:

1. Ensure that the Windows 98 CD is in the drive.

2. Go to Start | Run...

3. Type x:\add-ons\pws\setup.exe where x: is the letter of your CD-ROM drive.

4. You will be greeted with a splash screen similar to this:

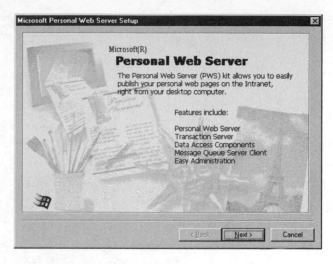

5. For most users, the typical install will work fine. If you choose to do a custom install, then ensure that the following components are selected:

Common Program Files
MDAC 1.5
Personal Web Server
Transaction Server

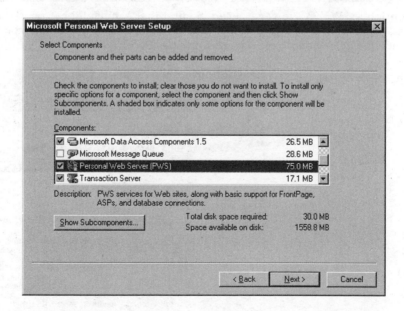

6. You will then be prompted for your default web publishing home directory.

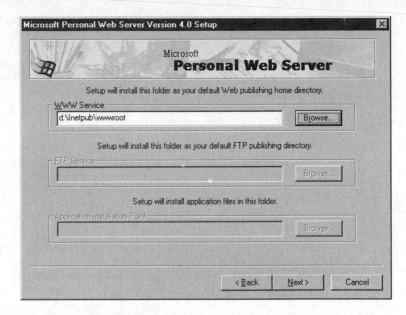

7. Leave the default install folder as it is for Transaction Server. The installation program will install the required files. Reboot your computer and it's all done.

Install Steps Using Downloaded NT Option Pack onto Win95

This is the best option for Win95. However, keep in mind that a much higher percentage of my students have had problems with PWS on Win95 then PWS on Win98. IF you are considering upgrading to Win98 I suggest you do it prior to installing PWS.

1. Close all applications.

2. Download WinNT Option Pack for Win95 from http://www.microsoft .com/windows/ie/pws using the link at the bottom of the page.

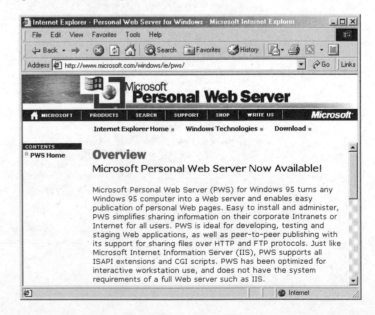

3. Select Option 1 of the the Download options, and then on the next page select the operating system you are running on. On the next page click on download.exe for the site nearest to you.

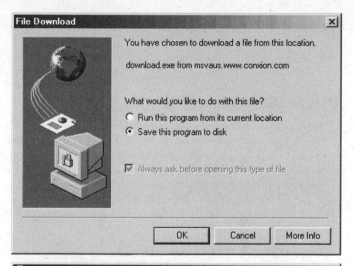

4. Save the program to disk.

5. Select Start | Run on download.exe and the wizard will first ask you to agree to the licensing terms, and then present you with the following screen:

6. Choose to download only, as, if the install option quits halfway through, it can possibly mess up your machine's configuration.

7. Click Next and choose x86: Windows 95 for the operating system and click Next.

8. Choose the Typical Installation and click Next.

9. Choose a location on your hard drive of where to download the pack to, and click Next.

10. Choose a location from where to download the pack.

11. Accept the verification certificate that appears and then the option pack will download.

12. Finally Start | Run the newly downloaded setup.exe and the setup is then same as the previous install from step 4.

Typical Problems of PWS on Win9x

Over the years I have helped many students to get PWS running. In turn, many experts have passed their knowledge on to me. Here are our solutions to the most common problems.

First, Be Sure You are Testing Correctly

Many times I have been asked to give a hand troubleshooting an ASP install. It appears that ASP is not working correctly, but I find that the problem is in the test page. I suggest that you test with a page from the ASP RoadMap (more later) or else the simple test file we'll look at a little further on in this chapter. If you are using your own test page and have problems, then check for the following common errors:

- ❑ File name does not end in .asp or the test page is misspelled in the browser address.
- ❑ Incorrect path for the page.
- ❑ VBScript is missing the delimiters <%%> or <SCRIPT> tags.
- ❑ VBScript has errors in syntax
- ❑ Check that PWS is running by either looking for its symbol in the tray or by Start | Programs | Microsoft Personal Web Server | Personal Web Manager and seeing the Stop button displayed.
- ❑ Also, on a few occasions when I created a page after PWS was running, I needed to stop and restart before PWS could find the page.

Opening an ASP Page Launches Visual Interdev, FrontPage or PhotoShop

When trying to load a local (127.0.0.1) ASP page, Windows opens up Adobe Photoshop or VID instead. Regular .htm or .html pages view fine in the browser. In other cases the browser will load the ASP page, but also start Photoshop. This usually does not happen when viewing .asp pages sitting on a non-local host.

Solution

The problem here is that there is a support file for Photoshop that has the .asp extension. We want to change the association for .asp to our editor. You can change the association by starting Windows Explorer then clicking on the menu View | Options | Win95-FileTypes | Win98-FileOptions. Click on ActiveServerDocument | Edit | Actions-Edit and set this to the same as the file type of Internet Document Set.

If there is no Active Server Document file type listed, then you need to find what file type is currently assigned to .asp and change it to be associated with your browser. Unfortunately Windows does not offer an alphabetical list of extensions, so do this:

1. Add a New Type.

2. Give it Description=test and Associated Extension = .ASP and click OK to save.

3. Windows will respond that .ASP is already taken by *xxx*. Make a note of the *xxx* file type and click OK to exit the error message.

4. Click Cancel to exit the Add New File Type dialog box.

5. Find and select the *xxx* file type in the list of files types.

6. Click Edit and change as follows:

> Description of Type = Active Server Document
>
> Content Type = text/asp
>
> Default Extension for Current Type = .asp

7. Under Actions = Edit:

> Enter your location of IE software, for example "C:\PROGRA~1\INTERN~1\iexplore.exe".
>
> Click the icon for `.asp` files in a `Photoshop.sep` table.

In some cases the above will not work because Windows does not let you create the new file type. You will have to first delete the old association by hand in the registry as follows.

1. Start | Run | Regedit

2. Select HKEY_CLASSES_ROOT

3. Select the `.asp` folder

4. Find the key that has the PhotoShop.SepTablesFile value in it

5. Delete the data (not the key itself, just the text in it)

6. Now you can create the file type as described above

IE Connects to Internet Even When Page is Local on PWS

After some installs, IE4 wants to connect to the Internet even when the page is sitting locally on PWS. This defeats one of the main advantages of PWS – the ability to work off-line. I observe this problem only in IE, not Netscape, and more frequently from students that install PWS from VID 6 CDs.

Solution 1

You can control how IE looks for pages. For IE 3 go to View | Internet Options | Connection. The choices are Connect to the Internet using a modem and Connect to the Internet using Local Area Network. Once the LAN option is selected IE will no longer dial-up to find a page. However, whenever you do want to access a page by dial-up, you will have to do so by connecting before requesting the page. IE 4 and 5 have the same feature under Tools | Connections – select the option for Never dial a connection.

Solution 2 (a variant of solution 1)

Install a network card as well as the modem. The NIC can just have a BNC terminator on it; it does not have to be physically attached to anything. Bind TCP/IP to the NIC card. Then set IE to connect by LAN. However, like solution 3, you still have to dial manually when you want the Internet.

Solution 3

Use the URL http://localhost/MySite/MyPage.ASP. If you just use MySite/MyPage.asp or MyPage.asp, IE connects to the Internet just in case the page is not found locally.

Solution 4

When IE displays the dial-up connection screen, don't click Cancel or close the window. Just press *Alt+Tab* or click on the IE window to change the focus back to IE.

Loss of FTP Message

If PWS version 1 is installed and then you install PWS version 4, you get a message "The Microsoft FTP service is no longer supported. If you click OK to continue the installation, FTP will be removed. Otherwise click Cancel to exit setup." This means you will lose the server-side FTP capability which was part of PWS 1 but not PWS 4. This is not a problem since you can still transfer files by using FrontPage with File | Publish, or you can install FTP software such as WS_FTP from www.Ipswitch.com.

NotePad Adds a .txt Extension

Notepad may add .txt to the end of each page so you get, for example, MyPage.asp.txt. Then VBScript does not execute since PWS or IIS is looking at an extension of .txt instead of .asp.

Solution 1

When naming your file select File Type *.* All Files. Name your file with its name and extension, for example MyPage.asp. Notepad will not add a .txt extension.

Solution 2

Rename your file using Windows Explorer after saving it. If you are FTPing your files up to a server, do the rename before the FTP operation.

Solution 3

When typing in the name of a file put double quotes around it. Then Notepad will save it exactly as typed.

Solution 4

Change the way Notepad saves names on files. There are two ways of doing this:

1. Open Windows Explorer and click on View | Options. Uncheck Hide File Extensions for registered types.

2. On the desktop open My Computer, and click on View | Folder Options. Choose the View tab and uncheck Hide file extensions for known file types.

IE Erroneously Changes the URL type

In some set-ups of IE, when you type http://MyComputer/MySite/MyPage.asp IE automatically adds .com. So, it becomes http://www.MyComputer.com/MySite/Mypage.asp, which causes a "file not found" message.

Solution

Open IE and select View | Internet Options | Advanced | Browsing. Uncheck Use Autocomplete.

In Internet Explorer 5 you can find the same information under a different path: click Tools | Internet Options and select the Advanced tab. You will need to uncheck Use inline AutoComplete for Web addresses.

Installation Error Message: Requires 32 bit TCP/IP Networking or Missing WinSock

When running the Personal Web Server setup.exe file on Win9x, you may get a message WinSock 2 is required to run this setup utility. Please click OK. Alternatively, you may find that on first running Front Page after installing PWS you get an error message along the lines of FrontPage requires 32 bit TCP/IP networking... not installed. These are both caused by PWS not being able to see a Dynamic Host Configuration Protocol.

Solution 1

Both of these problems can be solved by Start | Settings | Control Panel | Network | Add | Protocol. Add the Microsoft TCP/IP protocol & bind to a dial-up networking adapter. Save and reboot. Adding the TCP stack will provide not only TCP/IP but also the WinSock.

Solution 2

Sometimes the version of Winsock causes this problem. You must revert to WinSock version 1.1, then run the Windows Sockets 2 update.

1. Restore Windows Sockets 1.1 with Start | Run
   `C:\YourWindowsDirectory\ws2bakup\ws2bakup.bat`. If you get a sharing violation message, strike a key to abort. Repeat this step until the batch file has finished running.

2. Restart the computer in MS-DOS mode.

3. Enter `c:\YourWindowsDirectory\ws2bakup\ws2bakup.bat` and ignore the any errors about updating the registry.

4. Enter `exit` to leave DOS mode and restart Windows.

5. Download the `W95ws2Setup.exe` file from the following Microsoft URL and save it in your *Temp* folder: `http://www.microsoft.com/windows/downloads`.

6. Click Start | Run and execute `c:\Temp\W95ws2Setup.exe`.

7. When the Windows Sockets 2 Setup program has finished running, restart the computer. You will now have Windows Sockets 2 installed.

PWS Install Can't see IE 4.01

Install of PWS requires IE4.01 or higher. In some cases, particularly with the FrontPage 98 PWS and Windows 95, there is an error message that setup cannot continue because setup requires IE4.01, even though IE4.01 is installed and working.

Solution

There are multiple problems with installing the NT4 download version over the FP98 version with Win 95. The first option would be to upgrade the OS to Win98 and use the PWS on the Win98 CD. In addition this problem is usually solved if you have run the IE4.01 Service Pack 1 or upgrade to IE5.

Synchronizing Default Pages

Every site must have a page set as the default page. FrontPage uses `Default` (`.htm`, `.html` or `.asp` all work the same). Other web servers (perhaps the one on your host) use `Index.xxx`. When you create a site using FrontPage you may get a default page that is not recognized by your host.

Temporary Solution

Change the name of your file before uploading to your ISP. When using PWS on your local machine, your home page is `default.htm`. Before FTPing the site to your ISP, change the filename or make a copy of it with the correct default name for your host such as `Index.html`.

Solution 1

Change the name of your PWS default file name to match your host's default file name:

1. Start PWS (if it doesn't start automatically)

2. Right mouse click on the PWS icon in the Windows tray

3. Select Administer

4. Select WWW Administration

5. Click the Directories tab, then scroll to the very bottom of the page

6. Enable Default Document should be checked on

7. Change the Default Document to the name specified by your host

8. Close the Internet Services Administrator

With NT4 Service Pack 4, Option Pack 4, PWS, double click on the PWS icon on the taskbar. In the left pane select Advanced, then pick up with step 6 above.

If PWS is running when you make the change you may have to stop and restart PWS for the change to take effect. Assuming that PWS is running:

1. Right mouse click on the PWS icon in the Windows tray

2. Select Properties

3. Click on the Startup tab

4. Click on STOP, wait for the message to change to "The server is stopped"

5. Click on Start, wait for the message to change to "The server is running"

6. Close the Personal Web Server Properties dialog box

Solution 2

If replacing the name of the home page doesn't work, try adding it. You can set "Default Document" = Default.asp, Index.asp. Note that multiple names are separated by a comma.

Solution 3

You can create a file that is named according to your host's requirements but that redirects visitors to your actual home page. This may be your best bet if you don't have control of the server.

The following code is put in a small file named `Default.htm`:

```
<HTML><HEAD>
<TITLE>Redirect Default.htm to Index.asp</TITLE>
<META HTTP-EQUIV="REFRESH" CONTENT="0; URL=index.asp">
<BODY></BODY></HTML>
```

In this case the file is named according to the host requirement `Default.htm` and redirects to your home, named `Index.asp`. Note that this will have to go in every directory where your host expects to see `Default.htm`. There is a performance hit for this solution as the server must open two files instead of one.

Of the above solutions, I recommend modifying your PWS to accept the default file accepted by your host. This only has to be done once and you will not suffer a performance penalty.

MTS registry not installed

At the end of some installations there is a message that the Microsoft Transaction Server was not installed. Although MTS is required with IIS it is not required for PWS. This message can be ignored and PWS will run ASP fine.

More Troubles and Troubleshooting

If you encounter other problems, there are newsgroups that discuss PWS install issues. Several can be found at `http://www.dejanews.com/`, or by performing a search for "PWS".

Installation Completed

Once PWS is installed you will have two new addressing techniques to understand.

- ❏ First is that your personal web server will be at the TCP/IP address 127.0.0.1. Sites you develop can be accessed from your browser by providing the URL of `127.0.0.1/MySiteName/MyPageName.asp`.

- ❏ The second location is of the physical file. Whereas on NT/IIS your files are in the folder named `InetPub`, in PWS they are in `C:\WebShare\WWWRoot\MySiteName\MyPages`.

The files for pages can be seen using Windows Explorer, as well as copied or renamed. Keep in mind that manipulations of page files can cause a site to become out of synchrony with some editors or site management software. It is safer to perform file management tasks for a site using the explorer features of your page editing software, such as VID or FrontPage.

Installing ADO on Win9x/PWS

I have talked at length about installing ASP, but the version of ADO that comes with this older ASP is out of date and will need updating. ADO is a part of **MDAC (Microsoft Data Access Components)**. There have been several different versions of ADO to date, and it's important that you have an up to date one. The version numbering of MDAC reflects the version numbering of ADO, so MDAC 2.0 contains ADO 2.0 etc. The examples in this book require you to have ADO 2.5 for all the examples to work, but to get through most of them you will need *at least* ADO 2.0 or a more recent version. Now PWS 4.0 (aka the NT Option Pack 4.0) and Windows 98 only come with ADO 1.5. You can get more updated versions from Office 2000, IE5 or Visual Studio 6.0, but if you don't have one of these, and haven't downloaded the MDAC separately, then you will need to do so.

The MDAC service packs are available at
http://www.microsoft.com/data/download.htm.

Installing ADO

1. Go to http://www.microsoft.com/data/download.htm and then download the most recent version of MDAC.

2. Run the mdac_typ.exe and after it has installed a few bits and pieces you will get to the following screen to begin setup:

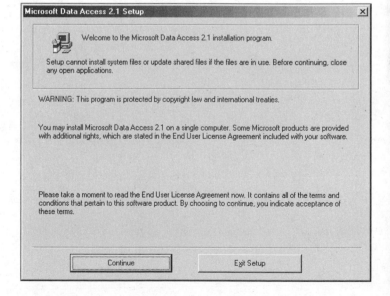

3. Press Continue and you get to the following screen:

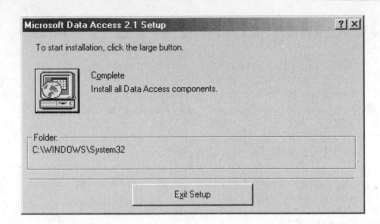

4. Click the large button to finish ADO's installation.

That's all there is to it.

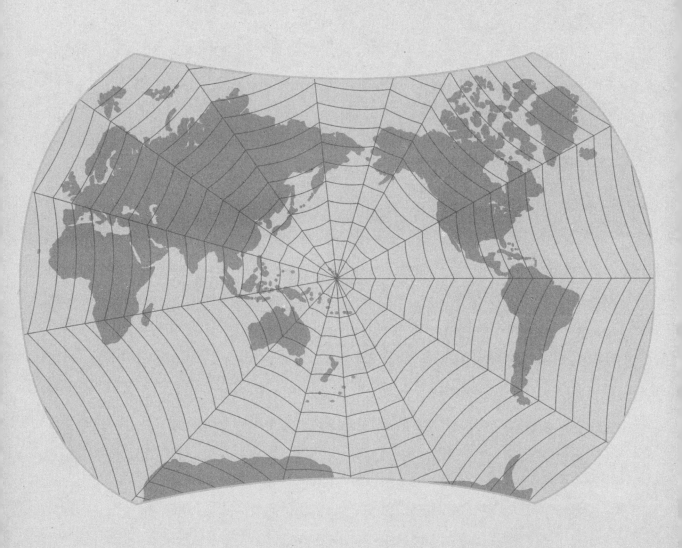

Forms and ASP

One of the fundamental tasks for most site designers is to gather information from the user. This information may be as simple as a zip code, or as complex as credit card numbers, shipping addresses and choices of delivery method. The gathering of information generally uses two pages of code:

❑ A Form page which uses HTML to ask for the information

❑ A Response page written in ASP, which accepts and processes the information

Many HTML books discuss the form side but leave out the response side, since it's server-specific. Many ASP books discuss the response side but assume that you're familiar with the form side, since it is HTML specific. So beginners are frequently left without an integrated form- and response- side manual. This appendix aims to be your one-stop source for cut and paste code to handle both sides of the coin.

> *Please note that this appendix does not cover the aesthetic attributes of forms, such as ALIGN or SIZE, which don't affect the interaction of ASP and forms. These topics are covered in any HTML book, including Instant HTML Programmer's Reference by Steve Wright, Alex Homer and Chris Ullman from Wrox Press, ISBN 1861001568. They are important for good user interface design, but we'll leave them out here in order to compact the code and focus our attention on the structural aspects of the examples.*

We will cover:

❑ General procedures of forms and response pages

❑ RequestSniffer, a tool to learn about forms and ASP

❑ Text Boxes

❑ Checkboxes

❑ Option buttons

❑ Multiple submit buttons on one form

- ❑ Lists and their variations

- ❑ Hidden fields

- ❑ Passwords

- ❑ Text Area

- ❑ Multiple forms on one page

- ❑ Images and Hotspots

- ❑ File Selector

- ❑ HotKeys (shortcut keys) and Tab Order

Remember that all of the code samples from this appendix can be downloaded from our web site at http://www.wrox.com.

Basic Procedure of a Form and Response

The simplest technique used to gather data from a user deploys two pages, generally called the **form** and **response** pages. These pages are used as follows:

- ❑ The form page holds a complex of HTML <FORM> tags asking the user for information.

- ❑ The user fills in the form fields then clicks the submit button. Acting on that click, the browser sends the data to the server along with an URL to a response page.

- ❑ The server does two things:

  - ❑ Opens the response page and sends the page (including its scripts) to ASP

  - ❑ Fills the ASP Request object with all of the data the user entered in the form

- ❑ The ASP script interpreter runs the scripts, which extract and use the data from the ASP Request object to build the response page.

- ❑ ASP sends the response page it has built back to the user, generally containing information germane to the user's choices.

ASP vs HTML Pages

You may have noticed that there is no scripting required on simple HTML form pages – browsers are able to display the fields with no more instruction than the proper use of the HTML tags. In contrast, the response page requires the use of some type of scripting (in this book we use VBScript within ASP). Therefore the form page can be a .htm file, but the response page must be a .asp.

However, in the real world it's difficult to find bosses or clients who will accept minimal pages. You'll probably want to include a standard header and footer file on each page, which will utilize some scripting. Furthermore, you may want to build the form HTML using ASP, for example, if you want to look up list box choices from a data store. So although the form itself doesn't require scripting, other elements of the page probably will, and thus programmers usually name form pages, as well as Response pages, .asp.

The Form Tag

Forms are built by a browser when it reads the <FORM> tag. Within that tag are two important attributes: ACTION and METHOD.

Between the <FORM> and </FORM> tags are the <INPUT> tags, the main topic of this appendix.

ACTION

The ACTION attribute causes the most errors among beginning students of forms and ASP. It must exactly match the URL of the page that is to be called when the Submit button is clicked. Normally this would be in the same folder and thus there is no need to include a path. ACTION value is simply the page name and extension, as follows:

```
<FORM ACTION="MyResponse.asp">
```

If the response page is located in another folder you must reference the entire path (the virtual directory).

METHOD

Using the METHOD attribute, there are two HTML techniques by which a browser can send form information back to the server: POST and GET. By default, the data will be sent to the server with the GET method.

When information is sent via a form, GET adds the data to the end of the returned URL. Once the URL/data arrives at the server, ASP strips off the data and puts it in the Request object's QueryString collection.

The problem with GET is the visibility of the data. It's easy to read the information on the address line when the browser displays the response page, and it's more visible to nefarious individuals who may be sniffing the connection or examining the server logs. Furthermore, there are limits to the length of a URL +Data string (about 2K or 2047 characters to be precise), so large forms may be unable to send all of the data gathered. On the other hand, GET is useful for beginners, since it lets us see exactly what was sent by the form and gives us a feel for how forms actually return data. Although GET is rarely used in the real world, we'll use it in this appendix for learning purposes.

The preferred method is POST, which puts the information into a data stream that is sent to the server and then routed directly into the ASP Request.Form collection. By using a separate stream, the data is no longer easily visible and is not affected by the URL length limits. The biggest disadvantage to POST is that some firewalls watch for and delete these separate data streams.

For students, the most frequent problems result from disagreement in the METHOD between the form and request pages. There is no specific statement of the METHOD in the response page: the data is sitting in either the Request.QueryString or the Request.Form collection, depending on whether the METHOD used by the form is GET or POST. If you try to gather data from the wrong place you'll get nothing.

The following table summarizes the differences:

	GET	POST
How sent	Appends to URL request	Sent inside HTTP Request body
Hidden?	No	Yes
Advantages	Students can see form results	More hidden
	Not stopped by Firewalls	No length restrictions
Disadvantages	More visible	Stopped by some firewalls
	Length restrictions	
Obtain data using Request.	Request.QueryString	Request.Form
Use	Teaching	Most applications
	If Firewalls destroy datastreams	

General Information on Data Returned from Forms

Before we begin to work with more complicated forms, it's important to understand the syntax that forms use to return data to the server.

The data starts with the URL of the page to which the data is sent. Following that is a question mark, which separates the URL from the data. The data from the form is then presented as the DataName followed by an equal sign and then the DataValue. If there is more than one piece of data, there will be an & separating each DataName= DataValue.

For example, if we send two values to page MyResponse.asp via the GET method, we'll see the following in the QueryString:

MyResponse.asp?DataName1=DataValue1&DataName2=DataValue2

Harvesting Data for Use in the Response Page

When the server receives the URL+data (from GET method) or the URL and separate data (from the POST method), ASP grabs the data, parses it, and stores it in a collection of the Request object. In the case of POST, it goes into the Forms collection, and in the case of GET, into the QueryString collection. You can extract the information one of two ways:

- ❑ Parse the information out of the entire string by hand
- ❑ Read the data as members of a Request object collection

In most cases you'll do the latter, but we'll also demonstrate the former for use with text areas.

As we've seen, data is returned from the GET method in several parts. The first is the URL for the response page itself, which is no different to a URL sent by a non-form hyperlink. Next is the question mark that separates the URL from the Data. The data then appears in a pattern of name=value pairs, separated by an ampersand (&). The name will be the string given in the NAME value of the INPUT tag (see details specific to each type below). The value will be what the user typed or selected in the field.

Although this sounds like a lot of characters to remember, keep in mind that you will rarely have to deal with them directly, since ASP takes care of parsing the information into its Request collections. Furthermore, once you use the RequestSniffer (below) on a few forms, you will have a good feel for what these strings look like.

The use of characters such as the ampersand and question mark create the problem of how to handle those characters if they are part of the data. HTTP converts most non-alphanumeric characters into code (their decimal equivalents delimited by a % character: this is known as character escaping). The most common codes are introduced in the section below on text area fields. The most important exception is a space, which is converted to the plus sign.

Data is returned from the POST method differently, since it is hidden in a separate data stream. The URL will appear the same as that from a non-form hyperlink, and there are no issues of data separation because the data goes directly into the ASP Request.Form collection.

The syntax to read information from a collection is not difficult:

```
varMyVariable = Request.Querystring("NameOfFormElement")
```

We discussed this in depth in the chapter on the Request object. For this appendix, we want to move right on to handling the scores of permutations of data from forms.

Common Errors in the Use of Forms

- ❑ Wrong name or extension for the response page
- ❑ Wrong path for the response page
- ❑ ACTION specifies a response page that doesn't exist
- ❑ Forgetting to include a submit button (or some form of submit method)
- ❑ Leaving out the </FORM> closing tag
- ❑ Writing the wrong code on the wrong page: the first page must have the Form and the response page picks up the user's data and works with it
- ❑ Using POST and looking for data in Request.QueryString (POST data goes into the Forms collection)
- ❑ Using GET and look for the data in the Request.Form collection (GET data goes into the QueryString collections)
- ❑ Directing the visitor to the response page prior to the form page
- ❑ Leaving the .asp extension off of the response page
- ❑ Including some server-side scripting in the form page (for features outside the form) and not adding the .asp extension
- ❑ Using an include in the form which has script but the form itself lacks the .asp ending

RequestSniffer.asp

An important lesson to understand about forms is what data looks like as returned from a browser. Once you understand that, it's possible to write script control structures that can react to the user's input. The following code is a "RequestSniffer", which can be used during development to display information about the nature and syntax of the data that ASP receives from a form.

> *Our sample RequestSniffer is listed below, or it can be downloaded from the Wrox Press website at http://www.wrox.com.*

```
<%@ Language=VBScript %>
<HTML><HEAD>
</HEAD>

<BODY>

<H3>Request Sniffer</H3><hr>
```

```
<%
' /////// Decide whether to reap data from QueryString or Form collection
If Request.QueryString <> "" Then
  call ShowQueryString
ElseIf Request.Form <> "" then
  Call ShowForm
Else
  Response.Write "Both the QueryString and Forms collection are empty"
End If


' //////// Call this if data is in Form collection

Sub ShowForm

Response.write "From Form collection - POST<BR>"
Response.Write "Total # of values = "
Response.Write Request.Form.Count & "<BR>"
Response.Write "Entire Form Collection as String: <BR>"
Response.Write Request.Form & "<BR><BR>"
Response.Write "<TABLE BORDER=1><TR>"

For Each MyItem in Request.Form
  Response.Write "<TR><TD>"
  Response.Write MyItem & "</TD><TD>"
  Response.Write Request.Form(MyItem).Item
  Response.Write "</TD></TR>"
Next

Response.Write "</TABLE>"

End Sub


' /////// Call this if data is in QueryString collection

Sub ShowQueryString

Response.Write "From QueryString collection - GET<BR>"
Response.Write "Total # of values = "
Response.Write Request.QueryString.Count & "<BR>"
Response.Write "Entire QueryString Collection as String: <BR>"
Response.Write Request.QueryString & "<BR><BR>"
Response.Write "<TABLE BORDER=1><TR>"

For Each MyItem in Request.QueryString
  Response.Write "<TR><TD>"
  Response.Write MyItem & "</TD><TD>"
  Response.Write Request.QueryString(MyItem).Item
  Response.Write "</TD></TR>"
Next
```

```
Response.Write "</TABLE>"

End sub
%>

</BODY>
</HTML>
```

This works quite simply. There are three sections, separated by the rows of slashes. The first looks at the QueryString. If it holds anything then we call the procedure called ShowQueryString. If not, then we call the procedure called ShowForm. In this way, the RequestSniffer works equally well for forms that use GET, POST or have no data fields at all.

Within the ShowQueryString or ShowForm subs (they take the same approach), the first line notes which collection is being read. Then the number of items in the collection is printed using the Count property, and the entire QueryString is printed to the page. A table is created, where column one is the data name and column two the data value, with each row being another result from a form field. We build the table with a For Each... loop, which is specifically used for collections; it iterates one loop for each item in the collection without the programmer having to perform tests (like for example a Do...While loop) or know the number of items in the collection (like a simple FOR...NEXT loop).

Using RequestSniffer

To use this tool you copy or create the RequestSniffer.asp page in an appropriate folder on your site (probably the root folder). Then create any form that you want to test. This form can send data by either the POST or GET method, and with any number or combination of field types. Set the form's ACTION=RequestSniffer.asp. Save and then open the form in your browser. When you click submit you'll get the RequestSniffer, which shows you what names and values are being returned from the form. With that knowledge you can then write your real response page, and change the ACTION of your form from RequestSniffer to the response page.

For a demonstration of the RequestSniffer, let's look at some differences between the GET and POST methods. Remember that we are using the RequestSniffer in every case, so there is no other response page. Also note that even though the code changes slightly in these three demo pages the appearance on the screen is the same, so I won't show the form screen shot again and again.

Sample Sniffer 01 – Using GET

We'll start with a form that uses GET to send one data value – this is the page Sniffer01Form.htm:

```
<HTML>
<HEAD>
<META NAME="GENERATOR" Content="Microsoft Visual Studio 6.0">
<TITLE>Sniffer_01_Form</TITLE>
</HEAD>
```

```
<BODY>
<H3>Sniffer 01 Form Using Get</H3>
<FORM ACTION="RequestSniffer.asp" METHOD=GET NAME="Form1">
<INPUT NAME="NameFirst" VALUE="Type Your Name Here"><BR>
<INPUT TYPE="SUBMIT" VALUE="Submit Query">
</FORM>
</BODY>
</HTML>
```

When you run this page in a browser, enter a name and click Submit Query , you should see something like the following. Note that when using GET the data from the form is held in the QueryString collection of the Request object. Also note that the data is appended to the URL, and is thus visible on the address line:

Sample Sniffer 02 – Using POST

We can also send the same information using the POST method – this is the page Sniffer02:

```
...
<TITLE>Sniffer_02_Form</TITLE>
</HEAD>
<BODY>
<H3>Sniffer 02 Form Using POST</H3>
<FORM ACTION="RequestSniffer.asp" METHOD=POST NAME="Form1">
<INPUT NAME="NameFirst" VALUE="Type Your Name Here"><BR>
<INPUT TYPE="SUBMIT" VALUE="Submit Query">
</FORM>
</BODY>
...
```

This time, the data from the form is held in the Form collection of the Request Object. With POST the data is not visible with the URL, and is thus protected from the casual observer:

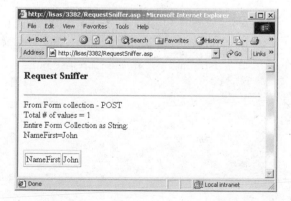

1033

Sample Sniffer 03 – Using Default

Finally, try running the last .htm with the METHOD attribute omitted: the result will be identical to the first screenshot, equivalent to using a GET.

Text Fields

Name & Value

The NAME of the element will be the identifier for this piece of data when it is sent back to the server. Each text field should have its own unique name.

The VALUE will be the default text that will appear in the element. This value will always be treated as a string (text), even if it appears to the user as a date or number. The string can be hard coded, or be from a variable, data store or even returned from a previous form. Note that default values are passed back to the server, so if you use VALUEs you can not check for an empty string to determine if the user has entered data. You must check if the contents equal the VALUE string or have been changed.

Multiple Text Fields

Multiple text fields pose no problem as long as each has its own name. If by mistake you name more then one text field with the same name, your browser will concatenate the text from all the fields. The data is with returned with a concatenation indicator (&), for example:

```
NameFirst= Name1&NameFirst= Name2
```

This shows that more than one field had the same name (NameFirst), with the first rendered field being first in the string.

Common Errors for Text Type Fields

❑ Leaving out the NAME attribute

❑ Inadvertently having more then one text field with the same NAME

❑ Using a NAME in the response page which differs from the form page

Sample Text Fields

The following code, `Text01Form.htm`, demonstrates the use of text fields:

```
<TITLE>Text_01_Form</TITLE>
</HEAD>
<BODY>
<H3>Text 01 Form</H3>
<FORM ACTION="Text01Response.asp" METHOD=GET>
Please type your First Name
<INPUT TYPE=TEXT NAME="NameFirst" VALUE="First Name"><BR>
Please type your Middle Name
<INPUT TYPE=TEXT NAME="NameMiddle" VALUE="Middle Name"><BR>
Please type your Last Name
<INPUT TYPE=TEXT NAME="NameLast" VALUE="Last Name"><BR>
<INPUT TYPE=SUBMIT>
</FORM>
</BODY>
```

This gives us the following screen:

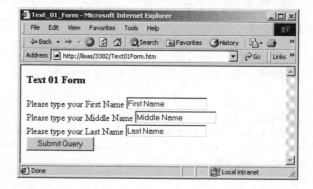

The response page is `Text01Response.asp`:

```
...
<TITLE>Text_01_Response</TITLE>
</HEAD>
<BODY>
<H3>Text 01 Response</H3>
<%
Response.Write "We have received your name as "
Response.Write Request.QueryString("NameFirst") & " "
Response.Write Request.QueryString("NameMiddle") & " "
Response.Write Request.QueryString("NameLast") & "."
...%>
```

And the result is:

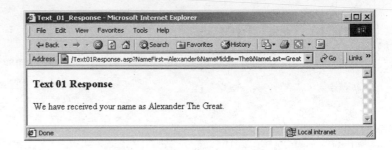

Check Boxes

Names and Values

In the most common case each check box concerns an independent issue. For example, you can ask customers to check one box if they want a fax confirmation of an order, and to check another box if they want gift wrapping. In these cases, each check box will have its own name, and you won't use the VALUE attribute. Whether data is sent to the server depends on whether the box is checked: if it is checked, the browser will send NAME="on", and if it's not checked nothing will be sent. If you have used the VALUE attribute, then the browser will send Name=Value. Boxes by default are unchecked, but you can change that by adding the CHECKED attribute to the tag.

However, you may want the visitor to be able to choose several options from a group of checkboxes. For example, you may be offering to include some of your free catalogs in a shipment of an order of clothing. You could have checkboxes for Hat Catalog, Shoe Catalog, Western Wear Catalog, etc. In the case of allowing multiple selections you make all of the names the same and the values different. The data value sent to the server will consist of the concatenation of all of the values that were checked.

In summary, try to remember that for:

- ❑ Independent check boxes:
  - ❑ Each NAME is different
  - ❑ Don't use VALUE
  - ❑ Test for NAME="on"

- ❑ Grouped check boxes:
  - ❑ All NAMES are the same
  - ❑ Each box gets its own VALUE
  - ❑ Results will be NAME=value1&NAME=value2&NAME=value3
  - ❑ Results are also available in a collection Request.QueryString("name")(i)

Common Errors with Check Boxes

- ❏ The `TYPE` syntax is `Checkbox`, not `Check`
- ❏ Test for `="on"` is case sensitive
- ❏ Test for `NAME="off"` if the box is not checked (nothing will be sent to the server)

Sample Check 01 – Single Check Box

The sample `Check01Form.htm` uses a single check box:

```
...
<BODY>
<H3>Check 01 Form</H3>
<FORM ACTION="Check01Response.asp" METHOD=GET>
  <INPUT TYPE=CHECKBOX NAME="Swahili">Please show page in Swahili Language<BR>
  <INPUT TYPE=SUBMIT>
</FORM></BODY>
...
```

The result is as follows:

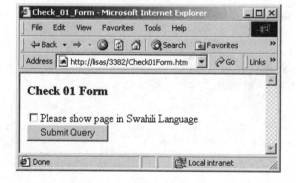

Our response page is `Check01Response.asp`:

```
...
<BODY>
<H3>Check 01 Response</H3>
<%
If Request.QueryString("Swahili")="on" Then
  Response.Write "Karibu"
Else
  Response.write "Welcome"
End If
%></BODY>
...
```

And the result of checking the box and submitting the form is:

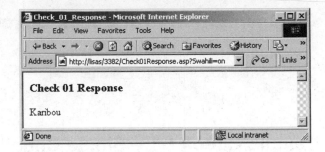

Sample Check 02 – Multiple Independent Check Boxes

We can extend the previous sample to use multiple independent check boxes:

```
...
<BODY>
<H3>Check 02 Form</H3>
<FORM ACTION="Check02Response.asp" METHOD=GET>
   <INPUT TYPE=CHECKBOX NAME="Swahili">Please show page in Swahili Language<BR>
   <INPUT TYPE=CHECKBOX NAME="LargePrint" CHECKED>Please show greeting in Large
Type<BR>
   <INPUT TYPE=SUBMIT>
</FORM></BODY>
...
```

Note that the box named `LargePrint` is checked when the page loads. The response page is `Check02Response.asp`:

```
...
<BODY>
<H3>Check 02 Response</H3>
<%
If Request.QueryString("LargePrint")="on" Then
  Response.Write "<H2>"
End If
If Request.QueryString("Swahili")="on" Then
  Response.Write "Karibou"
Else
  Response.write "Welcome"
End If
If Request.QueryString("LargePrint")="on" Then
  Response.Write "</H2>"
End If
%></BODY>
...
```

And if we submit the form without changing anything we get something like this:

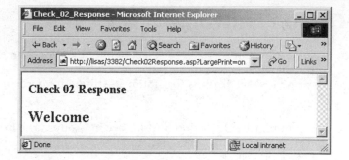

Sample Check 03 – Groups of Check Boxes

Check03Form.htm uses multiple choice checkboxes:

```
...
<BODY>
<H3>Check 03 Form</H3>
Please Czech the cities you would like to visit
<FORM ACTION="Check03Response.asp" METHOD=get>
  <INPUT TYPE=Checkbox NAME="Cities" VALUE="Prague">Prague<BR>
  <INPUT TYPE=Checkbox NAME="Cities" VALUE="Cheb" Checked>Cheb<BR>
  <INPUT TYPE=Checkbox NAME="Cities" VALUE="Kladno">Kladno<BR>
  <INPUT TYPE=Checkbox NAME="Cities" VALUE="Mlada">Mlada<BR>
  <INPUT TYPE="SUBMIT">
</FORM></BODY>
...
```

And the response page is Check03Response.asp:

```
...
<BODY>
<H3>Check 03 Response</H3>
We will schedule your itinerary for:<BR>
<%
For iCityCount=1 to Request.QueryString("Cities").COUNT
  Response.Write Request.QueryString("Cities")(iCityCount)
  Response.Write " "
Next
%></BODY>
...
```

This gives the following result if the first, third and fourth cities are checked (and the second is unchecked):

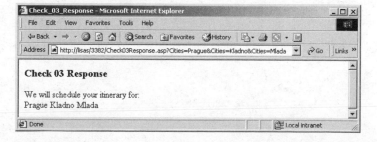

Option Buttons

When you want the user to select only one option from several, you use Option buttons. These input types are commonly called Radio buttons, as they're similar to a car radio that allows you to press pre-set buttons for stations. Although Microsoft clings to the term Option buttons, the W3C uses Radio.

Keep in mind that Option buttons are in groups. The browser ensures that only a single button in the group can be selected at any one time, so the server-side programmer doesn't need to address this issue.

Name and Value

The NAME attribute identifies the group to which the button belongs. The results available to the response page will be identified by the NAME. The browser will make buttons with the same NAME mutually exclusive, and the name must be exactly the same for all of the options in a group. If your form page does not deselect the first choice when a second choice is selected, you've probably assigned, erroneously, different names within a group.

The VALUE attribute will be the text sent to identify which choice was made by the user. Each button within a group should have a unique value. Note that the VALUE is not visible to the user in the browser: the text that will be visible is outside the < INPUT... > tag.

Remember:

❑ NAME: same for all buttons in the group

❑ VALUE: different for each button in the group

❑ CHECKED: one button only in the group

❑ The QueryString will hold NAME=VALUE

Common Errors

❑ Spelling the name differently in the form and response pages

❑ Making two or more values the same within a group; it's good to cut/paste, but don't forget to change the values after pasting

❑ Using different names for buttons that are within one group

Sample Option 01 – One Group

The sample `Option01Form.htm` uses just one group with three buttons, where the first is checked by default:

```
...
<BODY>
<H3>Option 01 Form - One Group</H3>
<FORM ACTION="Option01Response.asp" METHOD=GET>
  <INPUT TYPE="RADIO" NAME=Member VALUE="pro" CHECKED>Professional<BR>
  <INPUT TYPE="RADIO" NAME=Member VALUE="stud">Student<BR>
  <INPUT TYPE="RADIO" NAME=Member VALUE="emir">Emiritus<BR>
  <INPUT TYPE="SUBMIT" VALUE="Submit">
  <INPUT TYPE="RESET" VALUE="Reset">
</FORM></BODY>
...
```

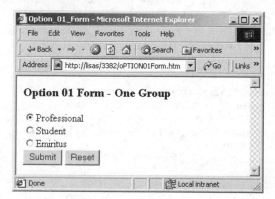

The response page is `Option01Response.asp`:

```
...
<BODY>
<H3>Option 01 Response - One Group</H3>
<%
Response.Write "We have received your preference to register as a "
Select Case Request.QueryString("Member")
  Case "pro"
    Response.Write "Professional Member"
  Case "emir"
    Response.Write "Member Emiritus"
  Case "stud"
    Response.Write "Student Member"
  Case Else
    Response.Write "Please contact the webMaster"
End Select
%></BODY>
...
```

And the result of submitting the previous screenshot without making any changes is:

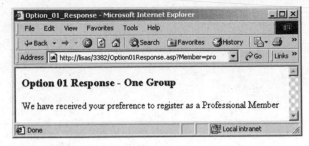

Sample Option 02 – Multiple Groups

We may want to present the user with more than one set of choices, for example first pick a shipping company, and then pick a level of service. All of the buttons in the first group should have the same name, and all of the options in the second group should have the same but different name. Then, within each group, the values of the buttons should be different. The request will hold one value equal to the first name and one value equal to the second name. The following code is from `Option02Form.htm`:

```
...
<BODY>
<H3>Option 02 Form - Multiple Groups</H3>
Please ship by:
<FORM ACTION="Option02Response.asp" METHOD=GET><HR>
<INPUT TYPE="RADIO" NAME=ShipComp VALUE="FedEx" CHECKED>
  Federal Express<BR>
<INPUT TYPE="RADIO" NAME=ShipComp VALUE="UPS">
  United Parcel Service - UPS<BR><HR>
<INPUT TYPE="RADIO" NAME=ShipSpeed VALUE="1" checked>
  Overnight<BR>
<INPUT TYPE="RADIO" NAME=ShipSpeed VALUE="2">
  Second Day<BR><HR>
<INPUT TYPE="SUBMIT" VALUE="Send My Data">
<INPUT TYPE="RESET" VALUE="Start Over">
</FORM></BODY>
...
```

And the result is:

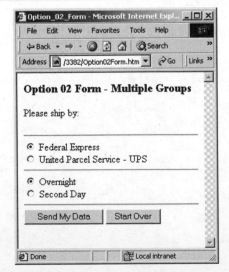

The response page is `Option02Response.asp`:

```
...
<BODY>
<H3>Option 02 Response - Multiple Groups</H3>
<%
Response.Write "We will ship using the "
Select Case Request.QueryString("ShipComp")
  Case "FedEx"
    Response.Write "Federal Express"
  Case "UPS"
    Response.Write "United Parcel Service"
  Case Else
    Response.Write "Please contact the webMaster"
End Select

Response.Write " company with "
Select Case Request.QueryString("ShipSpeed")
  Case "1"
    Response.Write "Overnight service."
  Case "2"
    Response.Write "Second day Service."
  Case Else
    Response.Write "Please contact the webMaster"
End Select
%>
</BODY>
...
```

If the previous screen is submitted, the result is:

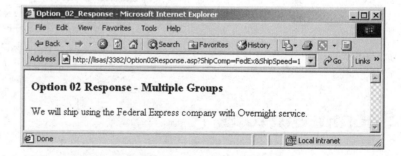

Sample Option 03 – Arranging Multiple Groups

The buttons of multiple groups can be intermingled in the layout of the page, as long as all the members of a group have the same name. `Option02Form.htm` and `Option03Form.htm` have different appearances, but the responses are identical:

```
...
<BODY>
<H3>Option 03 Form - Arranging Multiple Option Groups</H3>
Please Select Your Preferred Shipping Options<BR>
<FORM ACTION="Option03Response.asp" METHOD=GET>
<TABLE border=1>
  <TR>
```

```
    <TD>Shipper</TD>
    <TD>Speed</TD></TR>
  <TR>
    <TD><INPUT TYPE=RADIO NAME=ShipComp VALUE="FedEx">Federal Express </TD>
    <TD><INPUT TYPE=RADIO NAME=ShipSpeed VALUE="1">Overnight</TD></TR>
  <TR>
    <TD><INPUT TYPE=RADIO NAME=ShipComp VALUE="UPS">UPS</TD>
    <TD><INPUT TYPE=RADIO NAME=ShipSpeed VALUE="2">Second Day</TD></TR>
</TABLE>
<INPUT TYPE="SUBMIT" VALUE="Submit"> 
<INPUT TYPE="RESET" VALUE="Reset">
</FORM></BODY>
...
```

The form will look like this:

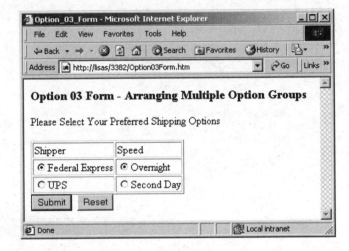

The response code and screen would be the same as for the previous example, since the same data comes from both.

Submit Buttons

Name and Value

The name of the submit button is not important if there is one button only. In that case, there's no DataName=DataValue returned. The more interesting case is when there are two or more submit type buttons, like in the sample below. With more then one submit type button you use a NAME attribute for each and the VALUE will be the data returned. Note, then, that VALUE does double duty for submit buttons:

❑ The source of the string for the caption that appears on the button

❑ The string that will be sent to the server

Common Errors

❑   Expecting data for the submit button when it is not named

Using two submit buttons with the same name.

Sample Multiple Submit Buttons

The page `Submit01Form.htm` has two submit buttons:

```
...
<BODY>
<H3>Submit 01 Form</H3>
<FORM ACTION="Submit01Response.asp" METHOD=GET NAME="Form1">
Name of Item   
<INPUT NAME="Item"  VALUE="Type name of item here" SIZE=30>
<DR>
<INPUT TYPE="SUBMIT" value="Place Order Now" NAME=SubOrderNow>
<INPUT TYPE="SUBMIT" value="Quote Price, no order yet" NAME=SubQuoteOnly>
</FORM>
...
```

The result of this code is:

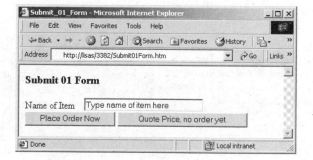

Our response page would be something like `Submit01Response.asp`:

```
...
<BODY>
<H3>Submit 01 Response</H3>

<%
If Request.QueryString("SubOrderNow")="Place Order Now" Then
  Response.Write "Code to process the order"
Else
  Response.Write "Code to generate a quote"
End If
Response.Write " for a " & Request.QueryString("Item")
%>
</BODY></HTML>
...
```

List Boxes

Name and Value

A list box is assigned just one name. Within that list box are options that are not named: they are only known by the string shown to the visitor. The browser will return the list box name equal to the string within the option which was clicked by the user.

Common Errors

❑   Forgetting that the browser returns an & between items in a multiple-selected list

❑   Trying to assign NAMEs or VALUEs for each SELECTion in a list

Sample List 01 – Simple List Box

List01Form.htm contains a simple list box:

```
...
<BODY>
<H3>List 01 Form</H3>
Please click on one selection of music from the Liszt:
<FORM ACTION="List01Response.asp" METHOD=GET>
<SELECT NAME="MusicTitle">
  <OPTION>Hunnenschlacht</OPTION>
  <OPTION>Malediction</OPTION>
  <OPTION>Tannhauser</OPTION>
</SELECT>
<INPUT TYPE="SUBMIT">
</FORM></BODY>
...
```

The result is:

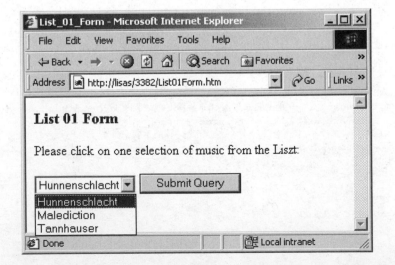

The response page is `List01Response.asp`:

```
...
<BODY>
<H3>List 01 Response</H3>
We will set your background music to
<%
Response.Write Request.QueryString("MusicTitle")
%>
 as requested
</BODY>
...
```

Selecting the option shown in the previous screen shot results in the message:

We will set your background music to Hunnenschlacht as requested

Sample List 02 – Multiple Lists

We can extend the previous example as in `List02Form.htm`, which contains two separate lists named `MusicTitle` and `MusicDynamic`:

```
...
<BODY>
<H3>List 02 Form - Multiple Lists</H3>
Please click on one selection of music from the Liszt:
<FORM ACTION="List02Response.asp" METHOD=GET>
<SELECT SIZE=3 NAME="MusicTitle">
  <OPTION>Hunnenschlacht</OPTION>
  <OPTION>Malediction</OPTION>
  <OPTION>Tannhauser</OPTION>
  <OPTION>Hexamaron</OPTION>
  <OPTION SELECTED>Lohengrin</OPTION>
  <OPTION>Christus</OPTION>
</SELECT>
<SELECT SIZE=1 NAME="MusicDynamic">
  <OPTION SELECTED>Pianissimo</OPTION>
  <OPTION>Mezzo</OPTION>
  <OPTION>Forte</OPTION>
</SELECT>
<INPUT TYPE="SUBMIT">
</FORM></BODY>
...
```

Note how we specify which option we want to be `SELECTED`, and how we can control how much of the list is displayed using the `SIZE` attribute:

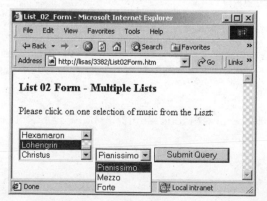

The response page is `List02Response.asp`:

```
...
<BODY>
<H3>List 02 Response</H3>
We will set your background music to
<%=Request.QueryString("MusicTitle")%>
 performed at
<%=Request.QueryString("MusicDynamic")%>
 as requested.
</BODY>
...
```

And the output is as follows (note how values are concatenated in the QueryString):

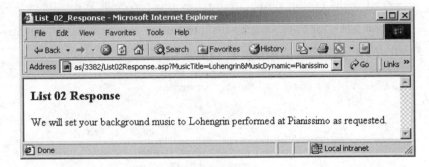

Sample List 03 – Multiple Selections, Simple Result

You can enable the user to make multiple selections from a list by including the attribute MULTIPLE in the SELECT tag. The resulting data stream will then consist of all of the choices made concatenated into one data value and separated by &s. This data stream can be used directly, as in the form `List03Form.htm`:

```
...
<BODY>
<H3>List 03 Form</H3>
Please select one or more pieces of music from the Liszt:
<FORM ACTION="List03Response.asp" METHOD=GET>
<SELECT SIZE=3 NAME="MusicTitle" MULTIPLE>
  <OPTION SELECTED>Hunnenschlacht</OPTION>
  <OPTION>Malediction</OPTION>
  <OPTION SELECTED >Tannhauser</OPTION>
  <OPTION>Hexamaron</OPTION>
  <OPTION>Lohengrin</OPTION>
  <OPTION>Christus</OPTION>
</SELECT>
<INPUT TYPE="SUBMIT">
</FORM></BODY>
...
```

The form will look similar to `List02Form.htm`.

Note that you can highlight multiple choices in the list box by holding down the Ctrl key.

The response page `List03Response.asp` looks like this:

```
...
<BODY>
<H3>List 03 Response</H3>
We will set your background
<%
If Request.QueryString("MusicTitle").Count=0 then
  Response.Write " to be silent "
ElseIf Request.QueryString("MusicTitle").Count=1 then
  Response.Write " music to be "
  Response.Write Request.QueryString("MusicTitle")
Else
  Response.Write " music to rotate among "
  Response.Write Request.QueryString("MusicTitle")
End If
%>
 as requested.
</BODY>
...
```

If multiple values are selected, the contents of MusicTitle are written directly from the QueryString:

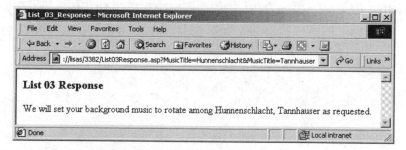

Sample List 04 – Multiple Selections, Looping the Result

`List03Form`, `List04Form` and `List05Form` use identical forms but different code in response. In `List04Response.asp` we parse the values from the QueryString and write them individually:

```
...
<BODY>
<H3>List 04 Response</H3>
We will set your background
<%
If Request.QueryString("MusicTitle").Count=0 then
  Response.Write " to be silent "
ElseIf Request.QueryString("MusicTitle").Count=1 Then
  Response.Write " music to be "
  Response.Write Request.QueryString("MusicTitle")
Else
  Response.Write " music to rotate among <BR><BR>"
  For iTitleCount=1 to Request.QueryString("MusicTitle").Count
    Response.Write Request.QueryString("MusicTitle")(iTitleCOunt)
    Response.Write "<BR>"
  Next
```

```
End If
%>
<BR>as requested.
</BODY>
...
```

So the result is:

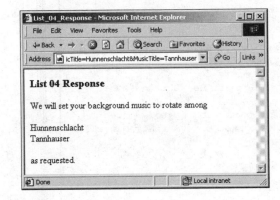

Sample List 05 – Multiple Selections, Looping With Correct Grammar

Again, we'll use the same form code as for the `List03Form.htm` page (except for the `ACTION`). This time, we'll be more careful with the grammar:

```
...
<BODY>
<H3>List 05 Response</H3>
We will set your background
<%
If Request.QueryString("MusicTitle").Count=0 Then
  Response.Write " to be silent "
ElseIf Request.QueryString("MusicTitle").Count=1 Then
    Response.Write " music to be "
    Response.Write Request.QueryString("MusicTitle")
Else
  Response.Write " music to rotate among "
  For iTitleCount=1 To (Request.QueryString("MusicTitle").Count-2)
    Response.Write Request.QueryString("MusicTitle")(iTitleCount)
    Response.Write ", "
  Next
  Response.Write Request.QueryString("MusicTitle")_
                (Request.QueryString("MusicTitle").Count-1)
  Response.Write " and "
  Response.Write Request.QueryString("MusicTitle")_
                (Request.QueryString("MusicTitle").Count)
End If
%>
as requested.
</BODY>
...
```

So if we select Tannhauser, Lohengrin and Christus in the form, we get the message:

We will set your background music to rotate among Tannhauser, Lohengrin and Christus as requested.

Sample List 06 – Parsing From Complex Choices

One frequently asked question is how to use only part of the data that is shown in a list box: for example, you could show information in a list box such as first and last name, telephone extensions and department, but only want to use part of that data, say the telephone number. In a browser this is not as easy to do as in, for example, Access, where multiple columns are allowed in list boxes. However you can build complex choices and then parse out the data of interest, as demonstrated in this example, and using techniques from the chapter on VBScript techniques.

Our form, `List06Form.htm`, has options containing several pieces of information:

```
...
<BODY>
<H3>List 06 Form</H3>
Please click on one selection of music from the Liszt:
<FORM ACTION="List06Response.asp" METHOD=GET>
<SELECT NAME="MusicTitle">
   <OPTION>Hunnenschlacht - 1856 - Symphonic poem</OPTION>
   <OPTION>Malediction - 1842 - Piano & Orch.</OPTION>
   <OPTION>Tannhauser - 1864 - Piano Transcription</OPTION>
</SELECT>
<INPUT TYPE="SUBMIT">
</FORM></BODY>
...
```

The file `List06Response.asp` parses this information and prints it in a readable form:

```
...
<BODY>
<H3>List 06 Response</H3>
We will set your background music to
<%
varRaw = Request.QueryString("MusicTitle")
varLocDashOne = instr(varRaw,"-")
varLocDashTwo = instr(varLocDashOne+1,varRaw,"-")
varTitle = left(varRaw,varLocDashOne-1)
Response.Write varTitle
%>
<BR>A piece from
<%
varDate = mid(varRaw,varLocDashOne+2,4)
Response.Write varDate
%>
<BR>Written by Liszt as a
<%
varGenre = mid(varRaw,varLocDashTwo+2)
Response.Write varGenre
%>
</BODY>
...
```

Note how the white space appears in the QueryString:

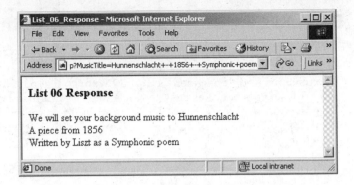

Password Fields

The password type of field displays the same behavior as the Text type field, but as the user types the text is not shown on the screen (it appears as asterisks (*)). The collection will hold the name of the field equal to the value typed by the user.

There is one very important point to understand. The password type performs absolutely no further hiding, encryption or any other security function, other then replacing the typed keys with asterisks on the display. In fact, if you use the GET method, as demonstrated below, the user's password will appear in the address line when the response page is displayed.

Sample Password Field

Our example Password01Form.htm simply requests you to enter a password:

```
...
<BODY>
<H3>Password 01 Form</H3>
<FORM ACTION="Password01Response.asp" METHOD=GET>
  <INPUT TYPE="PASSWORD" NAME="SecretWord">
  <INPUT TYPE="SUBMIT" VALUE="Submit">
</FORM>
<H6>clue: Joseph Anthony Passalaqua</H6>
</BODY>
...
```

The response page Password01Response.asp then attempts to verify this:

```
...
<BODY>
<H3>Password 01 Response</H3>
<%
Select Case Request.QueryString("SecretWord")
Case "Peterson&Pass"
  Response.Write "You are in"
```

```
Case "JoePassAtTheMontreux"
  Response.Write "You are in"
Case Else
  Response.Write "Sorry, wrong PASSword"
End Select
%>
</BODY>
...
```

The following is the result of entering `Peterson&Pass` on the form page. Note that the password is not encrypted as it is sent across the Internet: in fact you can read it in the URL. However, the browser did not echo the typing on the form page. Also note how the & is treated in the address bar:

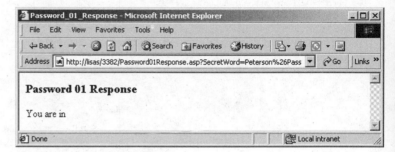

Hidden Fields and Returning Data

Sometimes we want to send data from the server to the user. Note that this is different than just sending out unorganized information as HTML text. Hidden fields allow us to send data that is named and available for use in programming.

For example, we may have a form that stretches over three pages. We want to have the user submit the first page, then have that information travel back to the browser so the second page data can be added. Next the data of the first and second pages goes back, and is the base for adding the third page. After all three pages are built up we will make one database write. A two-page version of this is demonstrated in Sample 2 below.

Another use of hidden fields (as shown in Sample 1 below) is to send some information out with the form, for example a time stamp.

Name and Value

Hidden fields are very similar to text fields. They have a NAME attribute which identifies the data and a VALUE attribute which holds the actual data. Note that hidden fields can easily be read from the source code. Don't be fooled by the term "hidden": there is no more than the most meager level of privacy.

Common Errors

❑ Trying to hide confidential information in a hidden field

❑ Using inconsistent names for the field in the form and the response pages

Sample Hidden Fields 01 – Simple Example

This example uses hidden fields to determine the length of time a visitor takes to fill in the form. The page `Hidden01Form.asp` simply asks the user to enter a value:

```
...
<BODY>
<H3>Hidden 01 Form</H3>
Calculate then type the square root of three<BR>
<FORM ACTION="hidden01Response.asp" METHOD=GET NAME="Form1">
  <INPUT TYPE=HIDDEN NAME="TimeSent" VALUE="<%=time()%>">
  <INPUT NAME="NameFirst"><BR>
  <INPUT TYPE="SUBMIT" VALUE="Submit Query">
</FORM>
</BODY>
...
```

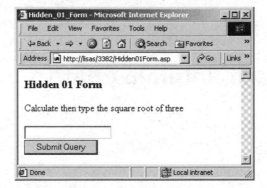

Both the value entered and the `TimeSent` are sent to the response page
`Hidden01Response.asp`:

```
...
<BODY>
<H3>Hidden 01 Response</H3>
Code demonstrating use of hidden fields<BR>
Objective: determine the length of time<BR>
a visitor takes to fill in the form
<HR>
<%
'Visitor never knows about this
'Response.write lines below are for proof of concept
varTimeSent = (Request.QueryString("TimeSent"))
Response.Write "sent  = " & varTimeSent & "<BR>"
varTImeBack = time()
Response.Write "back  = " & varTimeBack & "<BR>"
varTimeToFill = cDate(varTimeBack) - cDate(varTimeSent)
```

```
Response.Write "Time to Fill in Form =  " & DateDiff("s",varTimeSent,varTimeBack) & "
seconds"
'code that uses time measurement
%>
<BR><BR><HR>
Compact Version:<BR>
<%
'Above code can be compacted to:
varTimeFill = DateDiff("s",Request.QueryString("TimeSent"),time())
Response.Write varTimeFill
%>
</BODY>
...
```

And the time difference is estimated:

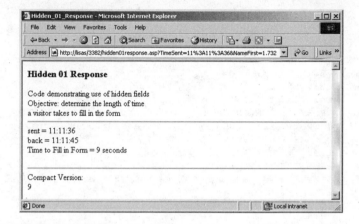

Sample Hidden 02 – Two Page Questionaire

Hidden02Form.htm is the first page in a two page form:

```
...
<BODY>
<H3>Hidden 02 A Form</H3>
This is page one of a two-page form.<BR>
<FORM ACTION="Hidden02-A-Response.asp" METHOD=GET NAME="Form1">
FirstName<INPUT NAME="NameFirst"><BR>
<INPUT TYPE="SUBMIT" VALUE="Submit Query">
</FORM></BODY>
...
```

The form requests the value `FirstName`:

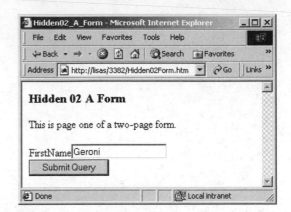

This value is submitted to the second page of the form, `Hidden02-A-Response.asp`:

```
...
<BODY>
<H3>Hidden 02 Response A</H3>
This is page two of a two-page form.<BR>
<FORM ACTION="hidden02-B-Response.asp" METHOD=GET>
<INPUT TYPE=HIDDEN VALUE="<%=Request.QueryString("NameFirst")%>"
  NAME=NameFirst>
LastName
<INPUT TYPE=TEXT NAME="NameLast"><BR>
<INPUT TYPE="SUBMIT" VALUE="Submit Query">
</FORM></BODY>
...
```

The second form requests the value `LastName`:

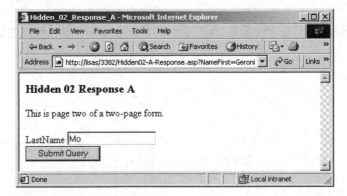

And this is sent to `Hidden02-B-Response.asp`:

```
...
<BODY>
<H3>Hidden 02 Response B</H3>
We have you registered as 
<%=Request.QueryString("NameFirst")%>
 <%=Request.QueryString("NameLast")%>
</BODY>
...
```

along with FirstName as hidden text:

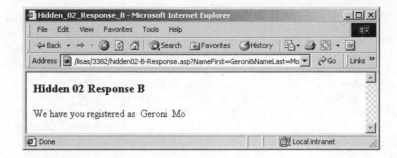

Sample 03 – Looping Data by Appending the URL

`LoopingData01Form.asp` uses a related technique to actually append the data to the URL in the same manner that the form sends data to the server. In this case we must make the form an ASP page, so that it can extract the data from the Request object:

```
...
<BODY>
<H3>LoopingData 01 Form</H3>
<FORM ACTION="LoopingData01Response.asp" METHOD=GET NAME="Form1">
  Kids Page - Ages 12 and under only<BR>
  *You must provide your date of birth and nickname*
  <BR>Please type your Last name
  <INPUT NAME="NameLast" VALUE=<%=Request.QueryString("NameLast")%>><BR>
  Please type your Nick name
  <INPUT NAME="NameNick" VALUE=<%=Request.QueryString("NameNick")%>><BR>
  Please type your Birthdate
  <INPUT NAME="DOB"><BR>
  <INPUT TYPE="SUBMIT" VALUE="Submit Query">
</FORM></BODY>
...
```

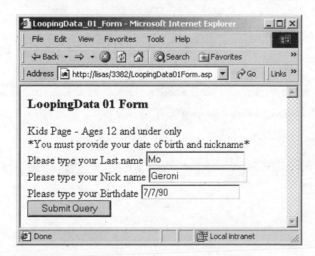

The response page is `LoopingData01Response.asp`:

```
...
<BODY>
<H3>LoopingData 01 Response</H3>
<%varNameLast = Request.QueryString("NameLast")
varNameNick = Request.QueryString("NameNick")
varDOB = Request.QueryString("DOB")

If varNameNick="" Then
  varBack = "LoopingData01Form.asp"
  varBack = varBack & "?NameLast=" & varNameLast
  Response.Redirect(varBack)
End If

If Not isdate(varDOB) Then
  varBack = "LoopingData01Form.asp"
  varBack = varBack & "?NameLast=" & varNameLast
  varBack = varBack & "&NameNick=" & varNameNick
  Response.Redirect(varBack)
Else
  If DateDiff("yyyy",varDOB,Date())>=13 Then
    varBack = "LoopingData01Form.asp"
    varBack = varBack & "?NameLast=" & varNameLast
    varBack = varBack & "&NameNick=" & varNameNick
    Response.Redirect(varBack)
  Else
    Response.Write "We have received your name as "
    Response.Write varnameNick & " " & varNameLast
    Response.Write " born on " & varDOB
  End If
End If
%>
</BODY>
...
```

And the result is:

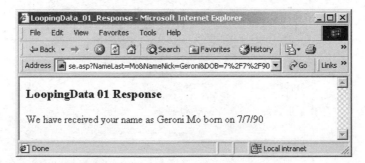

Text Areas

Most data can be obtained in fields which hold defined kinds of data. This fits in well with our programming concepts of normalized data. However, not every bit of information from the user will fit neatly into one of your fields. For many forms we need to also allow the visitor to enter information with less constraints, like miscellaneous information about shipping or suggestions on how to improve the site. HTML supports <TextArea> tags to allow just this type of field. Although you could gather some limited comments in a large text field, the <TextArea> provides a space with multiple lines and word wrap.

In fact, gathering free-form user comments is a great way to discover what needs to be changed about your form. If visitors perceive a problem you'll hear heaps about it in no time if you include a TextArea field for feedback. Not only can the feedback be stored with the user's record, but a separate table can hold just feedback, for the Webmaster to review where on the site visitors are frustrated.

Name and Values

First, note that <TextArea> is its own tag within a form: it's not a TYPE attribute of the INPUT tag. Second, the objective of a text area is to allow multi-line data, such as an address or comments. Thus, we must deal with identifying where the user typed a return (enter key).

The confusion comes in that HTML handles this one way and the ASP Request QueryString and Form collections handle it another. HTML will put codes %0D%0A in place of each return, so that's what you see if you look at the entire QueryString (for example the "Entire collection as string" line of RequestSniffer). But ASP will put a space in place of the return when it parses a single field from the entire collection.

Therefore, your only option when trying to make sense of data from a text area is to parse it from the entire QueryString rather than from the collection (as demonstrated in the sample below). Because this technique is complicated, it's easier to use separate fields whenever possible for the five or so data items that make up an address. However, in a field to gather comments or shipping instructions you may be stuck using a TextArea, and parsing to get human-readable useable data.

Common Errors

❑ Note that the replaced code characters contain a zero, not the uppercase letter O

❑ Write parsing to apply only to TextArea data and not the whole QueryString; you don't need to parse the other fields

❑ If possible use multiple fields rather then TextArea: addresses should be requested using several text fields, not a text area

Sample TextArea Parsing

In this example, `TextArea01Form.htm`, we ask for some comments on an order.

```
...
<BODY>
<H3>TextArea 01 Form</H3>
<FORM ACTION="TextArea01Response.asp" METHOD=GET>
(Dummy data to make parsing example more illustrative)<BR>
Please enter your name<INPUT NAME=NameUser><BR><BR>
Please enter your comments in this Text Area:<BR>
<TextArea NAME="ta" COLS=30 ROWS = 4></TextArea><BR><BR>
(Dummy data to make parsing example more illustrative)<BR>
Please enter your Start Date<INPUT NAME=DateStart>
<BR><INPUT TYPE="SUBMIT" VALUE="Submit Query">
</FORM></BODY>
...
```

The comments will be read by a shipping clerk, so we want them to be formatted with line breaks as created when the visitor struck the *Enter* key when filling in the form.

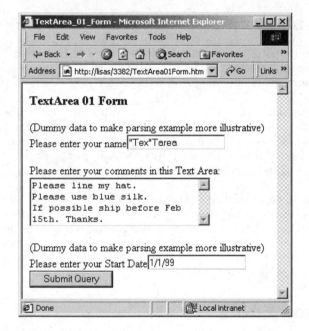

The code `TextArea01Response.asp` uses the following variables:

varStringEntire	String	Includes all the data from all the fields
varStart	Number	Location of the first character of the text area field
varEnd	Number	Location of first ampersand after the text area field
varTA	String	Includes only data from the text area field
iCharCounter	Number	As the loop steps through each character, this variable keeps track of the number of the character we are now examining
varTAFormatted	String	Same as varTA but with spaces instead of plus signs and tags instead of %0D%0A codes

For help in your understanding of the code, we've included (but changed to remarks) two lines which write intermediate constructions to the page.

```
...
<BODY>
<H3>TextArea 01 Response</H3>
<HR>Here is the data as one item from the collection:<BR>
<%=Request.QueryString("ta")%>

<HR>Here is the data parsed by hand from the entire string<BR>
<%
varStringEntire = Request.QueryString
'Response.Write "varStringEntire = " & varStringEntire & "<BR><BR>"
varStart = instr(varStringEntire,"ta=") + 3
varEnd = instr(varStart,varStringEntire,"&")-1

varTA = mid(varStringEntire,varstart,varEnd-VarStart+1)
'Response.Write "varTA = " & varTA & "<BR><BR>"

Dim varTAFormatted
iCharCounter = 1
Do While iCharCounter<=Len(varTA)
  If mid(varTA,iCharCounter,6) = "%0D%0A" Then
    varTAFormatted = varTAFormatted & "<br>"
    iCharCounter = iCharCounter + 6
```

```
  ElseIf mid(varTA,iCharCounter,1) = "+" then
    varTAFormatted = varTAFormatted & " "
    iCharCounter = iCharCounter + 1
  Else
    varTAFormatted = varTAFormatted & mid(varTA,iCharCounter,1)
    iCharCounter = iCharCounter + 1
  End If
Loop
Response.Write varTAFormatted
%>
</BODY>
...
```

Note how in the entire QueryString:

❑ Words are separated by plus signs

❑ Lines are separated by %0D%0A (escape character) codes

However in the parsed data values of the collection:

❑ Words are separated by spaces

❑ Lines are also separated by spaces

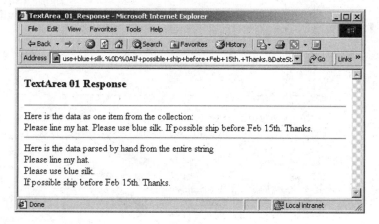

Multiple Forms on One Page

HTML allows the use of multiple forms on one page. Many times we want to direct the user to one of several pages depending on their data. We know how to handle that on the response page by using Server.Execute (or the older Response.Redirect), but that requires a round trip to the server, which is slow. However, a form can only have one ACTION, so we can't have multiple sections of a form, each with their own ACTION.

Instead we have multiple forms on one page, each with an ACTION to its appropriate response page. The benefit is that when the user clicks a submit, the appropriate page is called directly, rather than going to an intermediate page which .Executes or .Redirects to the appropriate page.

Many students get hung up on identifying which form was used, because even though you can use a NAME attribute in each FORM tag, that name is not passed to the server in a useful way (try it with the RequestSniffer). But this is not an issue: each form would have its own ACTION response page, so the fact that a given page is called defines which form's submit button the user clicked.

Sample Page with Multiple Forms

The page MultiForms01Form.htm contains two separate forms for members and non-members of an organization:

```
...
<BODY>
<H3>MultiForms 01 Form</H3>

<FORM ACTION="MultiForms01-A-Response.asp" METHOD=GET>
Members:<BR>
Please type your membership number: <INPUT NAME="MemNumber"><BR>
<INPUT TYPE="SUBMIT">
</FORM>

<FORM ACTION="MultiForms01-B-Response.asp" METHOD=GET>
  NON members: please fill in the information below<BR>
  Your First Name: <INPUT NAME="NameFirst"><BR>
  Your Last Name: <INPUT NAME="NameLast"><BR>
  Your Postal Code: <INPUT NAME="PostalCode"><BR>
  <INPUT TYPE="SUBMIT">
</FORM></BODY>
...
```

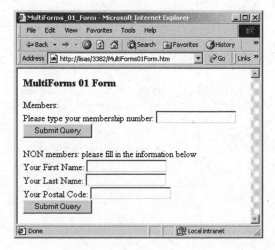

If a member fills in the first form, they are redirected to the member's page, `MultiForms01-A-Response.asp`:

```
...
<BODY>
<H3>MultiForms 01 A Response</H3>
<%
varMemNumber = Request.QueryString("MemNumber")
' Code to look up member and get name, preferences
' use member data to personalize page, for example:
Response.Write "Greetings to Member # " & varMemNumber
%>
<BR>Calendar of events for Members goes here...
</BODY>
...
```

And non-members submitting the second form are redirected to `Multiform01-B-Response.asp`, the non-member's page:

```
<TITLE>MultiForms_01-A_Response</TITLE></HEAD><BODY>
<H3>MultiForms 01-A Response</H3>
<%
' code that logs person's name for future reference
' code that logs postal code for marketing statistics%>
Welcome, <%=Request.QueryString("NameFirst")%>.
Please consider joining our society.<BR><BR>
Calendar of events open to non-members:
</BODY></HTML>
```

Images

HTML forms support an INPUT type of image that functions like a submit button. When clicked, the data of all fields is submitted to the action URL of the FORM tag.

Three pieces of information are sent from the image field: first the name of the image, but more usefully the x and y coordinates of the point on which the picture was clicked. With the "point of click" data, you can customize the return to be specific to just one portion of the picture. These areas are referred to as **hotspots**. There are automated ways to divide up the hotspots on a picture, but to do it yourself you have to do some experimenting with the RequestSniffer, to feel out the boundaries of the hotspots.

Note that you will get new x and y coordinates if you make any changes to an image, including:

❑ Resizing

❑ Changes made to the graphic itself in the graphic editor

❑ Recropping

However, you can move the image to a new location on the page without affecting the hotspots. And, to answer a frequent question, you don't *have* to use the hotspots to subdivide an image. If the user clicks an image on the form you can just use the name of the image in your response, without using the point of click data.

Sample Image Hotspots

The page Image01Form.htm contains our image:

```
...
<BODY>
<H3>Image 01 Form</H3>
Click on the arms or legs of this pitcher.
<FORM ACTION="Image01Response.asp" METHOD="GET"><BR>
<INPUT TYPE="IMAGE" SRC="AG00414_.GIF" NAME="pitcher" WIDTH="175" HEIGHT="113">
<INPUT TYPE="SUBMIT" VALUE="Submit Query">
</FORM></BODY>
...
```

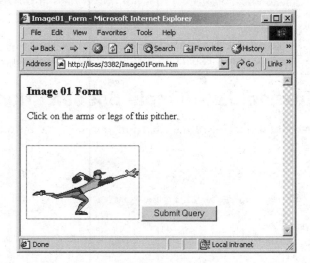

When the image is clicked, the response page Image01Response.asp displays a message telling us exactly where it was clicked:

```
...
<BODY>
<H3>Image 01 Response</H3>
<%
Dim varLocation
If Request.QueryString("pitcher.x")<50 Then
  varLocation = "right "
  If Request.QueryString("pitcher.y")<50 Then
    varLocation = varLocation & "arm."
  Else              'y point <=50 so ball player's legs
    varLocation = varLocation & "leg."
  End If
```

```
Else                    'x point is >=50, ball player's left side
  varLocation = "left "
  If request.QueryString("pitcher.y")<50 Then
    varLocation = varLocation & "arm."
  Else
    varLocation = varLocation & "leg."
  End If
End If
Response.Write "You clicked on the ball player's " & varLocation
%>
</BODY>
...
```

File Selector

HTML forms support input tags that allow the visitor to browse his or her own computer and select a file. The input field appears on screen with a space to type text and a browse button. The drive, path, name and extension of the selected file (but not the actual file contents) are sent to the server.

The entire file specification will be available in normal characters from the QueryString or Form collection. You can also parse the file name, extension, drive or path, as in sample 2 below.

Sample File Specification 01 – Simple Specification

The page File01Form.htm contains just a Browse... button and a Submit button:

```
...
<BODY>
<H3>File 01 Form</H3>
<FORM ACTION="File01Response.asp" METHOD=GET NAME="Form1">
<INPUT TYPE="FILE" value="" NAME="FilePicked">
<INPUT TYPE="SUBMIT" VALUE="Submit">
</FORM></BODY>
...
```

Clicking Browse... brings up a window allowing you to browse the files on your computer:

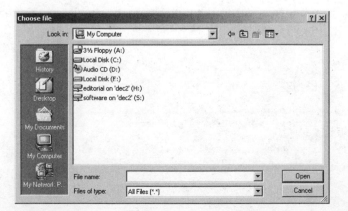

The response page simply confirms your selection:

```
...
<BODY>
<H3>File 01 Response</H3>
We have received your file selection as <BR>
<%=Request.QueryString("FilePicked")%>
</BODY>
...
```

Note that the file data is not actually received at the server. Only specific file elements available in the QueryString collection can be accessed.

Sample File Specification 02 – Parsing Data

This example uses the same form code as `File01Form.htm`, with the `ACTION` changed to the response page `Form02Response.asp`. However, this time we will parse the data to retrieve information such as the drive or extension of the file.

In a simple case of a file like a `.doc` we could just take the right 3 characters as the extension, but the code must handle cases where extensions are 1 or 2 characters. In addition, with current versions of Windows, periods can be used within a file name, which means we can't just search for periods – we must find a period which is in the last four characters.

The following code uses these variables:

varFileSpec	String	Whole string returned from form
varDrive	String	Characters to the left of the first colon
varExtArea	String	Area where the file extension would be located, if it exists: Last four characters of the whole string
varLen	integer	Number of characters in the whole string, i.e. the varFileSpec.
varLocExtDot	Integer	Location of period in varExtArea, counting from the left
varRLocExtDot	Integer	Location of period in varExtArea, counting from the right
varExt	String	The file extension

```
...
<BODY>
<H3>File 02 Response</H3>

Full File Spec =
<%varFileSpec = Request.QueryString("FilePicked")
Response.Write varFileSpec%><BR><BR>

Drive = <%varDrive = left(varFileSpec,instr(varFileSpec,":"))
Response.Write varDrive%><BR><BR>

Extension =
<%
varExtArea = right(varFileSpec,4)
  varLocExtDot = instr(varExtArea,".")
  If  varLocExtDot<>0 then
    varLocExtDot = instr(varExtArea,".")
    varRLocExtDot = len(varExtArea)-instr(varExtArea,".")+1
    varExt = right(varExtArea,varRLocExtDot)
    Response.Write varExt
  Else
    Response.write "There is no discernable extension"
  End If%><BR><BR>

Path =
<%varLen = len(varFileSpec)
varLocColon = instr(varFileSpec,":")
For CharCount=1 To varLen
  If mid(varFileSpec,CharCount,1)="\" Then
    varLocLastSlash=CharCount
  End If
Next
varDriveAndPath = left(varFiLeSpec,varLocLastSlash-1)
varPath = mid(varDriveAndPath,varLocColon+1)
Response.Write varPath
%></BODY>
...
```

The result will look something like this:

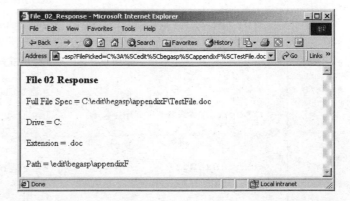

1068

Two Frequently Asked Questions about Forms

This has nothing to do with ASP, only HTML Forms, but I get so many questions that I wanted to get it into this edition of the book.

How Do I Create Hotkeys (Keyboard Shortcuts) for My Form Fields?

Starting with HTML 4, you can use an ACCESSKEY attribute with any INPUT tag. The use of ACCESSKEY attributes has no effect on the data sent back to the server

```
...
<BODY>
<H3>HotKey 01 Form</H3>
<H3>ASPalliance01 Form</H3>
<FORM ACTION="RequestSniffer.asp" METHOD=GET NAME="Form1">
<U>F</U>irst Name <INPUT NAME="NameFirst"  ACCESSKEY="f" VALUE="aaa"><BR>
<U>L</U>ast Name <INPUT NAME="NameLast"   ACCESSKEY="l" VALUE="bbb"><BR>
<INPUT TYPE="SUBMIT" VALUE="Submit Query">
</FORM>
</BODY>
...
```

How Can I Change the Tab Order for My Form Fields?

Also starting with HTML 4 you can add a TabIndex attribute to each INPUT field.

```
...
<BODY>
<H3>Tab Index 01 Form</H3>
<FORM ACTION="RequestSniffer.asp" METHOD=GET NAME="Form1">
First Name <INPUT NAME="NameFirst"  VALUE="Tab"
   TabIndex=2><BR>
Middle Name <INPUT NAME="NameMiddle"  VALUE="Eton"
   TabIndex=1><BR>
Last Name <INPUT NAME="NameLast" VALUE="Monk"
   TabIndex=3><BR>
<INPUT TYPE="SUBMIT" VALUE="Submit Query" TabIndex=4>
</FORM>
</BODY>
...
```

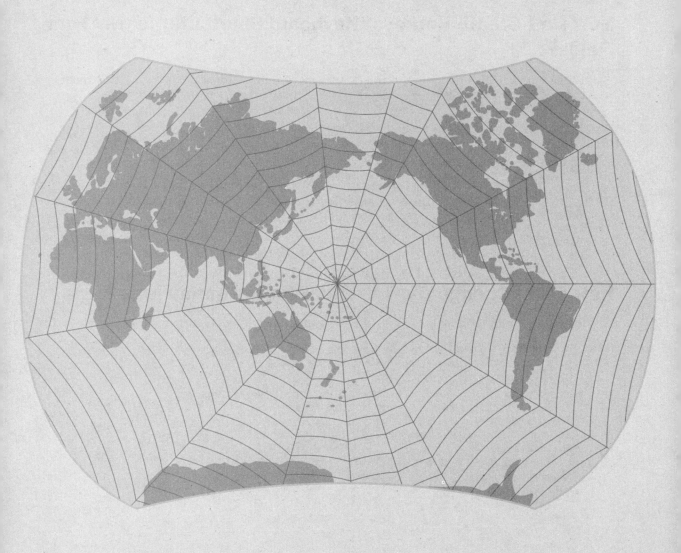

G

Error Codes

VBScript Error Codes

Syntax Errors

Syntax errors occur wherever your script contains statements that do not follow the pre-defined rules for that language. Note that this type of error should be caught during development. VBScript contains 53 syntax errors, listed below:

Decimal	Hexadecimal	Description
1001	800A03E9	Out of memory
1002	800A03EA	Syntax error
1003	800A03EB	Expected ':'
1005	800A03ED	Expected '('
1006	800A03EE	Expected ')'
1007	800A03EF	Expected ']'
1010	800A03F2	Expected identifier
1011	800A03F3	Expected '='
1012	800A03F4	Expected 'If'
1013	800A03F5	Expected 'To'
1014	800A03F6	Expected 'End'
1015	800A03F7	Expected 'Function'
1016	800A03F8	Expected 'Sub'
1017	800A03F9	Expected 'Then'
1018	800A03FA	Expected 'Wend'

Decimal	Hexadecimal	Description
1019	800A03FB	Expected 'Loop'
1020	800A03FC	Expected 'Next'
1021	800A03FD	Expected 'Case'
1022	800A03FE	Expected 'Select'
1023	800A03FF	Expected expression
1024	800A0400	Expected statement
1025	800A0401	Expected end of statement
1026	800A0402	Expected integer constant
1027	800A0403	Expected 'While' or 'Until'
1028	800A0404	Expected 'While', 'Until' or end of statement
1029	800A0405	Expected 'With'
1030	800A0406	Identifier too long
1031	800A0407	Invalid number
1032	800A0408	Invalid character
1033	800A0409	Unterminated string constant
1034	800A040A	Unterminated comment
1037	800A040D	Invalid use of 'Me' keyword
1038	800A040E	'loop' without 'do'
1039	800A040F	Invalid 'exit' statement
1040	800A0410	Invalid 'for' loop control variable
1041	800A0411	Name redefined
1042	800A0412	Must be first statement on the line
1043	800A0413	Cannot assign to non-ByVal argument
1044	800A0414	Cannot use parentheses when calling a Sub
1045	800A0415	Expected literal constant
1046	800A0416	Expected 'In'
1047	800A0417	Expected 'Class'
1048	800A0418	Must be defined inside a Class

Decimal	Hexadecimal	Description
1049	800A0419	Expected Let or Set or Get in property declaration
1050	800A041A	Expected 'Property'
1051	800A041B	Number of arguments must be consistent across properties specification
1052	800A041C	Cannot have multiple default property/method in a Class
1053	800A041D	Class initialize or terminate do not have arguments
1054	800A041E	Property set or let must have at least one argument
1055	800A041F	Unexpected 'Next'
1056	800A0420	'Default' can be specified only on 'Property' or 'Function' or 'Sub'
1057	800A0421	'Default' specification must also specify 'Public'
1058	800A0422	'Default' specification can only be on Property Get

Runtime Errors

Runtime errors occur wherever your script attempts to perform an invalid action. Note that the vast majority of these errors should be caught during the debugging and testing stage. VBScript contains 65 runtime errors, listed below:

Decimal	Hexadecimal	Description
5	800A0005	Invalid procedure call or argument
6	800A0006	Overflow
7	800A0007	Out of memory
9	800A0009	Subscript out of range
10	800A000A	This array is fixed or temporarily locked
11	800A000B	Division by zero
13	800A000D	Type mismatch
14	800A000E	Out of string space

Decimal	Hexadecimal	Description
17	800A0011	Can't perform requested operation
28	800A001C	Out of stack space
35	800A0023	Sub or Function not defined
48	800A0030	Error in loading DLL
51	800A0033	Internal error
52	800A0034	Bad file name or number
53	800A0035	File not found
54	800A0036	Bad file mode
55	800A0037	File already open
57	800A0039	Device I/O error
58	800A003A	File already exists
61	800A003D	Disk full
62	800A003E	Input past end of file
67	800A0043	Too many files
68	800A0044	Device unavailable
70	800A0046	Permission denied
71	800A0047	Disk not ready
74	800A004A	Can't rename with different drive
75	800A004B	Path/File access error
76	800A004C	Path not found
91	800A005B	Object variable not set
92	800A005C	For loop not initialized
94	800A005E	Invalid use of Null
322	800A0142	Can't create necessary temporary file
424	800A01A8	Object required
429	800A01AD	ActiveX component can't create object
430	800A01AE	Class doesn't support Automation
432	800A01B0	File name or class name not found during Automation operation

Decimal	Hexadecimal	Description
438	800A01B6	Object doesn't support this property or method
440	800A01B8	Automation error
445	800A01BD	Object doesn't support this action
446	800A01BE	Object doesn't support named arguments
447	800A01BF	Object doesn't support current locale setting
448	800A01C0	Named argument not found
449	800A01C1	Argument not optional
450	800A01C2	Wrong number of arguments or invalid property assignment
451	800A01C3	Object not a collection
453	800A01C5	Specified DLL function not found
455	800A01C7	Code resource lock error
457	800A01C9	This key is already associated with an element of this collection
458	800A01CA	Variable uses an Automation type not supported in VBScript
462	800A01CE	The remote server machine does not exist or is unavailable
481	800A01E1	Invalid picture
500	800A01F4	Variable is undefined
501	800A01F5	Illegal assignment
502	800A01F6	Object not safe for scripting
503	800A01F7	Object not safe for initializing
504	800A01F8	Object not safe for creating
505	800A01F9	Invalid or unqualified reference
506	800A01FA	Class not defined
5016	800A1398	Regular Expression object expected
5017	800A1399	Syntax error in regular expression
5018	800A139A	Unexpected quantifier

Decimal	Hexadecimal	Description
5019	800A139B	Expected ']' in regular expression
5020	800A139C	Expected ')' in regular expression
5021	800A139D	Invalid range in character set
32811	800A802B	Element not found

JScript Error Codes

Syntax Errors

Syntax errors occur wherever your script contains statements that do not follow the pre-defined rules for that language. Note that this type of error should be caught during development. JScript contains 32 syntax errors, listed below:

Number	Hexadecimal	Description
1001	800A03E9	Out of memory
1002	800A03EA	Syntax error
1003	800A03EB	Expected ':'
1004	800A03EC	Expected ';'
1005	800A03ED	Expected '('
1006	800A03EE	Expected ')'
1007	800A03EF	Expected ']'
1008	800A03F0	Expected '{'
1009	800A03F1	Expected '}'
1010	800A03F2	Expected identifier
1011	800A03F3	Expected '='
1012	800A03F4	Expected '/'
1013	800A03F5	Invalid number
1014	800A03F6	Invalid character
1015	800A03F7	Unterminated string constant
1016	800A03F8	Unterminated comment

Number	Hexadecimal	Description
1018	800A03FA	'return' statement outside of function
1019	800A03FB	Can't have 'break' outside of loop
1020	800A03FC	Can't have 'continue' outside of loop
1023	800A03FF	Expected hexadecimal digit
1024	800A0400	Expected 'while'
1025	800A0401	Label redefined
1026	800A0402	Label not found
1027	800A0403	'default' can only appear once in a 'switch' statement
1028	800A0404	Expected identifier or string
1029	800A0405	Expected '@end'
1030	800A0406	Conditional compilation is turned off
1031	800A0407	Expected constant
1032	800A0408	Expected '@'
1033	800A0409	Expected 'catch'
1034	800A040A	Expected 'var'
1035	800A040B	throw must be followed by an expression on the same source line

Runtime Errors

Runtime errors occur wherever your script attempts to perform an invalid action. Note that the vast majority of these errors should be caught during the debugging and testing stage. JScript contains 76 runtime errors, listed below:

Number	Hexadecimal	Description
5	800A0005	Invalid procedure call or argument
6	800A0006	Overflow
7	800A0007	Out of memory
9	800A0009	Subscript out of range

Number	Hexadecimal	Description
10	800A000A	This array is fixed or temporarily locked
11	800A000B	Division by zero
13	800A000D	Type mismatch
14	800A000E	Out of string space
17	800A0011	Can't perform requested operation
28	800A001C	Out of stack space
35	800A0023	Sub or Function not defined
48	800A0030	Error in loading DLL
51	800A0033	Internal error
52	800A0034	Bad file name or number
53	800A0035	File not found
54	800A0036	Bad file mode
55	800A0037	File already open
57	800A0039	Device I/O error
58	800A003A	File already exists
61	800A003D	Disk full
62	800A003E	Input past end of file
67	800A0043	Too many files
68	800A0044	Device unavailable
70	800A0046	Permission denied
71	800A0047	Disk not ready
74	800A004A	Can't rename with different drive
75	800A004B	Path/File access error
76	800A004C	Path not found
91	800A005B	Object variable or With block variable not set
92	800A005C	For loop not initialized
94	800A005E	Invalid use of Null
322	800A0142	Can't create necessary temporary file

Number	Hexadecimal	Description
424	800A01A8	Object required
429	800A01AD	Automation server can't create object
430	800A01AE	Class doesn't support Automation
432	800A01B0	File name or class name not found during Automation operation
438	800A01B6	Object doesn't support this property or method
440	800A01B8	Automation error
445	800A01BD	Object doesn't support this action
446	800A01BE	Object doesn't support named arguments
447	800A01BF	Object doesn't support current locale setting
448	800A01C0	Named argument not found
449	800A01C1	Argument not optional
450	800A01C2	Wrong number of arguments or invalid property assignment
451	800A01C3	Object not a collection
453	800A01C5	Specified DLL function not found
458	800A01CA	Variable uses an Automation type not supported in JScript
462	800A01CE	The remote server machine does not exist or is unavailable
501	800A01F5	Cannot assign to variable
502	800A01F6	Object not safe for scripting
503	800A01F7	Object not safe for initializing
504	800A01F8	Object not safe for creating
5000	800A1388	Cannot assign to 'this'
5001	800A1389	Number expected
5002	800A138A	Function expected
5003	800A138B	Cannot assign to a function result
5004	800A138C	Cannot index object

Number	Hexadecimal	Description
5005	800A138D	String expected
5006	800A138E	Date object expected
5007	800A138F	Object expected
5008	800A1390	Illegal assignment
5009	800A1391	Undefined identifier
5010	800A1392	Boolean expected
5011	800A1393	Can't execute code from a freed script
5012	800A1394	Object member expected
5013	800A1395	VBArray expected
5014	800A1396	JScript object expected
5015	800A1397	Enumerator object expected
5016	800A1398	Regular Expression object expected
5017	800A1399	Syntax error in regular expression
5018	800A139A	Unexpected quantifier
5019	800A139B	Expected ']' in regular expression
5020	800A139C	Expected ')' in regular expression
5021	800A139D	Invalid range in character set
5022	800A139E	Exception thrown and not caught
5023	800A139F	Function does not have a valid prototype object

ASP Error Codes Summary

For errors that involve a failure within the ASP DLL, the following are the common error codes that are returned. These are the codes you'll find in the `ASPCode` property of the ASPError object when an error of this type occurs:

Error Code	Error Message and Extended Information
ASP 0100	Out of memory. (Unable to allocate the required memory.)
ASP 0101	Unexpected error. (The function returned *exception_name*.)

Error Code	Error Message and Extended Information
ASP 0102	Expecting string input.
ASP 0103	Expecting numeric input.
ASP 0104	Operation not allowed.
ASP 0105	Index out of range. (An array index is out of range.)
ASP 0106	Type Mismatch. (A data type was encountered that cannot be handled.)
ASP 0107	Stack Overflow. (The quantity of data being processed is above the permitted limit.)
ASP 0115	Unexpected error. (A trappable error *exception_name* occurred in an external object. The script cannot continue running.)
ASP 0177	Server.CreateObject Failed. (Invalid ProgID.)
ASP 0190	Unexpected error. (A trappable error occurred while releasing an external object.)
ASP 0191	Unexpected error. (A trappable error occurred in the OnStartPage method of an external object.)
ASP 0192	Unexpected error. (A trappable error occurred in the OnEndPage method of an external object.)
ASP 0193	OnStartPage Failed. (An error occurred in the OnStartPage method of an external object.)
ASP 0194	OnEndPage Failed. (An error occurred in the OnEndPage method of an external object.)
ASP 0240	Script Engine Exception. (A script engine threw exception *exception_name* in *object_name* from *object_name*.
ASP 0241	CreateObject Exception. (The CreateObject of *object_name* caused exception *exception_name*.)
ASP 0242	Query OnStartPage Interface Exception. (The querying object *object_name*'s OnStartPage or OnEndPage method caused exception *exception_name*.

HTTP 1.1 Header Codes

Code	Reason Phrase
Group 1: Information	
100	Continue
101	Switching Protocols
Group 2: Success	
200	OK
201	Created
202	Accepted
203	Non-Authoritative Information
204	No Content
205	Reset Content
206	Partial Content
Group 3: Redirection	
300	Multiple Choices
301	Moved Permanently
302	Moved Temporarily
303	See Other
304	Not Modified
305	Use Proxy

Code	Reason Phrase
Group 4: Client Error	
400	Bad Request
401	Unauthorized
402	Payment Required
403	Forbidden
404	Not Found
405	Method Not Allowed
406	Not Acceptable
407	Proxy Authentication Required
408	Request Time-out
409	Conflict
410	Gone
411	Length Required
412	Precondition Failed
413	Request Entity Too Large
414	Request-URI Too Large
415	Unsupported Media Type
Group 5: Server Error	
500	Internal Server Error
501	Not Implemented
502	Bad Gateway
503	Service Unavailable
504	Gateway Time-out
505	HTTP Version not supported

Client error and server error codes – with default explanations as provided by Microsoft Internet Information Server – are listed below:

Error Code	Short Text	Explanation
400	Bad Request	Due to malformed syntax, the request could not be understood by the server. The client should not repeat the request without modifications.
401.1	Unauthorized. Logon Failed	This error indicates that the credentials passed to the server do not match the credentials required to log on to the server. Please contact the web server's administrator to verify that you have permission to access the requested resource.
401.2	Unauthorized: Logon Failed due to server configuration	This error indicates that the credentials passed to the server do not match the credentials required to log on to the server. This is usually caused by not sending the proper WWW-Authenticate header field. Please contact the web server's administrator to verify that you have permission to access to requested resource.
401.3	Unauthorized: Unauthorized due to ACL on resource	This error indicates that the credentials passed by the client do not have access to the particular resource on the server. This resource could be either the page or file listed in the address line of the client, or it could be another file on the server that is needed to process the file listed on the address line of the client. Please make a note of the entire address you were trying to access and then contact the web server's administrator to verify that you have permission to access the requested resource.
401.4	Unauthorized: Authorization failed by filter	This error indicates that the web server has a filter program installed to verify users connecting to the server. The authentication used to connect to the server was denied access by this filter program. Please make a note of the entire address you were trying to access and then contact the web server's administrator to verify that you have permission to access the requested resource.

Error Code	Short Text	Explanation
401.5	Unauthorized: Authorization failed by ISAPI/CGI app	This error indicates that the address on the web server you attempted to use has an ISAPI or CGI program installed that verifies user credentials before proceeding. The authentication used to connect to the server was denied access by this program. Please make a note of the entire address you were trying to access and then contact the web server's administrator to verify that you have permission to access the requested resource.
403.1	Forbidden: Execute Access Forbidden	This error can be caused if you try to execute a CGI, ISAPI, or other executable program from a directory that does not allow programs to be executed. Please contact the web server's administrator if the problem persists.
403.2	Forbidden: Read Access Forbidden	This error can be caused if there is no default page available and directory browsing has not been enabled for the directory, or if you are trying to display an HTML page that resides in a directory marked for Execute or Script permissions only. Please contact the web server's administrator if the problem persists.
403.3	Forbidden: Write Access Forbidden	This error can be caused if you attempt to upload to, or modify a file in, a directory that does not allow Write access. Please contact the web server's administrator if the problem persists.
403.4	Forbidden: SSL required	This error indicates that the page you are trying to access is secured with Secure Sockets Layer (SSL). In order to view it, you need to enable SSL by typing "https://" at the beginning of the address you are attempting to reach. Please contact the web server's administrator if the problem persists.
403.5	Forbidden: SSL 128 required	This error message indicates that the resource you are trying to access is secured with a 128-bit version of Secure Sockets Layer (SSL). In order to view this resource, you need a browser that supports this level of SSL. Please confirm that your browser supports 128-bit SSL security. If it does, then contact the web server's administrator and report the problem.
403.6	Forbidden: IP address rejected	This error is caused when the server has a list of IP addresses that are not allowed to access the site, and the IP address you are using is in this list. Please contact the web server's administrator if the problem persists.

Error Code	Short Text	Explanation
403.7	Forbidden: Client certificate required	This error occurs when the resource you are attempting to access requires your browser to have a client Secure Sockets Layer (SSL) certificate that the server recognizes. This is used for authenticating you as a valid user of the resource. Please contact the web server's administrator to obtain a valid client certificate.
403.8	Forbidden: Site access denied	This error can be caused if the web server is not servicing requests, or if you do not have permission to connect to the site. Please contact the web server's administrator.
403.9	Access Forbidden: Too many users are connected	This error can be caused if the web server is busy and cannot process your request due to heavy traffic. Please try to connect again later. Please contact the web server's administrator if the problem persists.
403.10	Access Forbidden: Invalid Configuration	There is a configuration problem on the web server at this time. Please contact the web server's administrator if the problem persists.
403.11	Access Forbidden: Password Change	This error can be caused if the user has entered the wrong password during authentication. Please refresh the page and try again. Please contact the web server's administrator if the problem persists.
403.12	Access Forbidden: Mapper Denied Access	Your client certificate map has been denied access to this web site. Please contact the site administrator to establish client certificate permissions. You can also change your client certificate and retry, if appropriate.
404	Not Found	The web server cannot find the file or script you asked for. Please check the URL to ensure that the path is correct. Please contact the server's administrator if this problem persists.
405	Method Not Allowed	The method specified in the Request Line is not allowed for the resource identified by the request. Please ensure that you have the proper MIME type set up for the resource you are requesting. Please contact the server's administrator if this problem persists.

Error Code	Short Text	Explanation
406	Not Acceptable	The resource identified by the request can only generate response entities that have content characteristics that are "not acceptable" according to the Accept headers sent in the request. Please contact the server's administrator if this problem persists.
407	Proxy Authentication Required	You must authenticate with a proxy server before this request can be serviced. Please log on to your proxy server, and then try again. Please contact the web server's administrator if this problem persists.
412	Precondition Failed	The precondition given in one or more of the Request-header fields evaluated to FALSE when it was tested on the server. The client placed preconditions on the current resource meta-information (header field data) to prevent the requested method from being applied to a resource other than the one intended. Please contact the web server's administrator if the problem persists.
414	Request-URI Too Long	The server is refusing to service the request because the Request-URI is too long. This rare condition is likely to occur only in the following situations: ❑ A client has improperly converted a POST request to a GET request with long query information. ❑ A client has encountered a redirection problem (for example, a redirected URL prefix that points to a suffix of itself). ❑ The server is under attack by a client attempting to exploit security holes present in some servers using fixed-length buffers for reading or manipulating the Request-URI. Please contact the web server's administrator if this problem persists.
500	Internal Server Error	The web server is incapable of performing the request. Please try your request again later. Please contact the web server's administrator if this problem persists.

Error Code	Short Text	Explanation
501	Not Implemented	The web server does not support the functionality required to fulfill the request. Please check your URL for errors, and contact the web server's administrator if the problem persists.
502	Bad Gateway	The server, while acting as a gateway or proxy, received an invalid response from the upstream server it accessed in attempting to fulfill the request. Please contact the web server's administrator if the problem persists.

> Note that Server error message files are placed in HELP\COMMON folder of Windows or Windows NT.

ADO Error Codes

The following table lists the standard errors than might get returned from ADO operations.

Constant Name	Number	Description
adErrBoundToCommand	3707	The application cannot change the ActiveConnection property of a Recordset object with a Command object as its source.
adErrCannotComplete	3732	The action could not be completed.
adErrCantChangeConnection	3748	The connection cannot be changed.
adErrCantChangeProvider	3220	The provider cannot be changed.
adErrCantConvertvalue	3724	The value cannot be converted.
adErrCantCreate	3725	The resource cannot be created.
adErrCatalogNotSet	3747	The action could not be completed because the catalog is not set.
adErrColumnNotOnThisRow	3726	The specified column doesn't exist on this row.
adErrDataConversion	3421	The application is using a value of the wrong type for the current application.
adErrDataOverflow	3721	The data was too large for the supplied data type.

Constant Name	Number	Description
adErrDelResOutOfScope	3738	The resource cannot be deleted because it is out of the allowed scope.
adErrDenyNotSupported	3750	You cannot set Deny permissions because the provider does not support them.
adErrDenyTypeNotSupported	3751	The provider does not support the type of Deny requested.
adErrFeatureNotAvailable	3251	The provider does not support the operation requested by the application.
adErrFieldsUpdateFailed	3749	The Update method of the Fields collection failed.
adErrIllegalOperation	3219	The operation requested by the application is not allowed in this context.
adErrIntegrityViolation	3719	The action failed due to a violation of data integrity.
adErrInTransaction	3246	The application cannot explicitly close a Connection object while in the middle of a transaction.
adErrInvalidArgument	3001	The application is using arguments that are the wrong type, are out of the acceptable range, or are in conflict with one another.
adErrInvalidConnection	3709	The application requested an operation on an object with a reference to a closed or invalid Connection object.
adErrInvalidParamInfo	3708	The application has improperly defined a Parameter object.
adErrInvalidTransaction	3714	The transaction is invalid.
adErrInvalidURL	3729	The supplied URL is invalid.
adErrItemNotFound	3265	ADO could not find the object in the collection.
adErrNoCurrentRecord	3021	Either BOF or EOF is True, or the current record has been deleted. The operation requested by the application requires a current record.
adErrNotExecuting	3715	The operation is not executing.

Constant Name	Number	Description
adErrNotReentrant	3710	The operation is not reentrant.
adErrObjectClosed	3704	The operation requested by the application is not allowed if the object is closed.
adErrObjectInCollection	3367	Can't append. Object already in collection.
adErrObjectNotSet	3420	The object referenced by the application no longer points to a valid object.
adErrObjectOpen	3705	The operation requested by the application is not allowed if the object is open.
adErrOpeningFile	3002	An error occurred whilst opening the requested file.
adErrOperationCancelled	3712	The operation was cancelled.
adErrOutOfSpace	3734	The operation failed because the server could not obtain enough space to complete the operation.
adErrPermissionDenied	3720	The action failed because you do not have sufficient permission to complete the operation.
adErrPropConflicting	3742	Setting this property caused a conflict with other properties.
adErrPropInvalidColumn	3739	This property is invalid for the selected column.
adErrPropInvalidOption	3740	You have supplied an invalid option for this property.
adErrPropInvalidValue	3741	You have supplied an invalid value for this property.
adErrPropNotAllSettable	3743	Not all properties can be set.
adErrPropNotSet	3744	The property was not set.
adErrPropNotSettable	3745	The property cannot be set.
adErrPropNotSupported	3746	The property is not supported.
adErrProviderFailed	3000	The provider failed to complete the requested action.
adErrProviderNotFound	3706	ADO could not find the specified provider.

Constant Name	Number	Description
adErrReadFile	3003	There was an error reading from the specified file.
adErrResourceExists	3731	The resource already exists.
adErrResourceLocked	3730	The resource is locked.
adErrResourceOutOfScope	3735	The resource is out of scope.
adErrSchemaViolation	3722	The action caused a violation of the schema.
adErrSignMismatch	3723	The expression contained mismatched signs.
adErrStillConnecting	3713	The operation is still connecting.
adErrStillExecuting	3711	The operation is still executing.
adErrTreePermissionDenied	3728	You do not have permission to view the directory tree.
adErrUnavailable	3736	The command is unavailable.
adErrUnsafeOperation	3716	The operation is unsafe under these circumstances.
adErrURLDoesNotExist	3727	The URL does not exist.
adErrURLNamedRowDoes NotExist	3737	The URL in the named row does not exist.
adErrVolumeNotFound	3733	The file volume was not found.
adErrWriteFile	3004	There was an error whilst writing to the file.
adwrnSecurityDialog	3717	The operation caused a security dialog to appear.
adwrnSecurityDialogHeader	3718	The operation caused a security dialog header to appear.

The following lists the extended ADO errors and their descriptions:

Error Number	Description
-2147483647	Not implemented.
-2147483646	Ran out of memory.
-2147483645	One or more arguments are invalid.
-2147483644	No such interface supported.
-2147483643	Invalid pointer.
-2147483642	Invalid handle.
-2147483641	Operation aborted.
-2147483640	Unspecified error.
-2147483639	General access denied error.
-2147483638	The data necessary to complete this operation is not yet available.
-2147467263	Not implemented.
-2147467262	No such interface supported.
-2147467261	Invalid pointer.
-2147467260	Operation aborted.
-2147467259	Unspecified error.
-2147467258	Thread local storage failure.
-2147467257	Get shared memory allocator failure.
-2147467256	Get memory allocator failure.
-2147467255	Unable to initialize class cache.
-2147467254	Unable to initialize RPC services.
-2147467253	Cannot set thread local storage channel control.
-2147467252	Could not allocate thread local storage channel control.
-2147467251	The user supplied memory allocator is unacceptable.
-2147467250	The OLE service mutex already exists.
-2147467249	The OLE service file mapping already exists.
-2147467248	Unable to map view of file for OLE service.
-2147467247	Failure attempting to launch OLE service.

Error Number	Description
-2147467246	There was an attempt to call `CoInitialize` a second time while single threaded.
-2147467245	A Remote activation was necessary but was not allowed.
-2147467244	A Remote activation was necessary but the server name provided was invalid.
-2147467243	The class is configured to run as a security id different from the caller.
-2147467242	Use of OLE1 services requiring DDE windows is disabled.
-2147467241	A `RunAs` specification must be <domain name>\<user name> or simply <user name>.
-2147467240	The server process could not be started. The pathname may be incorrect.
-2147467239	The server process could not be started as the configured identity. The pathname may be incorrect or unavailable.
-2147467238	The server process could not be started because the configured identity is incorrect. Check the username and password.
-2147467237	The client is not allowed to launch this server.
-2147467236	The service providing this server could not be started.
-2147467235	This computer was unable to communicate with the computer providing the server.
-2147467234	The server did not respond after being launched.
-2147467233	The registration information for this server is inconsistent or incomplete.
-2147467232	The registration information for this interface is inconsistent or incomplete.
-2147467231	The operation attempted is not supported.
-2147418113	Catastrophic failure.
-2147024891	General access denied error.
-2147024890	Invalid handle.
-2147024882	Ran out of memory.
-2147024809	One or more arguments are invalid.

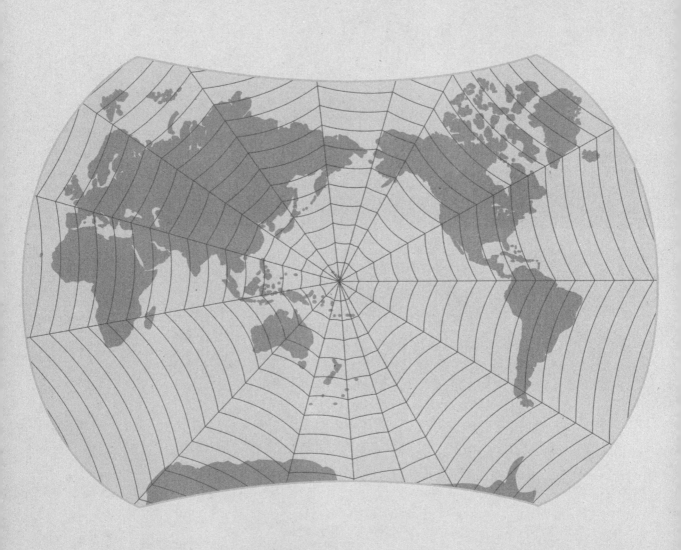

Colors Codes and Special Characters in HTML

Colour Names and Values

Colors Sorted by Name

Color Name	Value	IE4 Color Constant
aliceblue	F0F8FF	htmlAliceBlue
antiquewhite	FAEBD7	htmlAntiqueWhite
aqua	00FFFF	htmlAqua
aquamarine	7FFFD4	htmlAquamarine
azure	F0FFFF	htmlAzure
beige	F5F5DC	htmlBeige
bisque	FFE4C4	htmlBisque
black	000000	htmlBlack
blanchedalmond	FFEBCD	htmlBlanchedAlmond
blue	0000FF	htmlBlue
blueviolet	8A2BE2	htmlBlueViolet
brown	A52A2A	htmlBrown
burlywood	DEB887	htmlBurlywood
cadetblue	5F9EA0	htmlCadetBlue
chartreuse	7FFF00	htmlChartreuse
chocolate	D2691E	htmlChocolate
coral	FF7F50	htmlCoral
cornflowerblue	6495ED	htmlCornflowerBlue

Color Name	Value	IE4 Color Constant
cornsilk	FFF8DC	htmlCornsilk
crimson	DC143C	htmlCrimson
cyan	00FFFF	htmlCyan
darkblue	00008B	htmlDarkBlue
darkcyan	008B8B	htmlDarkCyan
darkgoldenrod	B8860B	htmlDarkGoldenRod
darkgray	A9A9A9	htmlDarkGray
darkgreen	006400	htmlDarkGreen
darkkhaki	BDB76B	htmlDarkKhaki
darkmagenta	8B008B	htmlDarkMagenta
darkolivegreen	556B2F	htmlDarkOliveGreen
darkorange	FF8C00	htmlDarkOrange
darkorchid	9932CC	htmlDarkOrchid
darkred	8B0000	htmlDarkRed
darksalmon	E9967A	htmlDarkSalmon
darkseagreen	8FBC8F	htmlDarkSeaGreen
darkslateblue	483D8B	htmlDarkSlateBlue
darkslategray	2F4F4F	htmlDarkSlateGray
darkturquoise	00CED1	htmlDarkTurquoise
darkviolet	9400D3	htmlDarkViolet
deeppink	FF1493	htmlDeepPink
deepskyblue	00BFFF	htmlDeepSkyBlue
dimgray	696969	htmlDimGray
dodgerblue	1E90FF	htmlDodgerBlue
firebrick	B22222	htmlFirebrick
floralwhite	FFFAF0	htmlFloralWhite
forestgreen	228B22	htmlForestGreen
fuchsia	FF00FF	htmlFuchsia
gainsboro	DCDCDC	htmlGainsboro
ghostwhite	F8F8FF	htmlGhostWhite
gold	FFD700	htmlGold
goldenrod	DAA520	htmlGoldenRod
gray	808080	htmlGray

Color Name	Value	IE4 Color Constant
green	008000	htmlGreen
greenyellow	ADFF2F	htmlGreenYellow
honeydew	F0FFF0	htmlHoneydew
hotpink	FF69B4	htmlHotPink
indianred	CD5C5C	htmlIndianRed
indigo	4B0082	htmlIndigo
ivory	FFFFF0	htmlIvory
khaki	F0E68C	htmlKhaki
lavender	E6E6FA	htmlLavender
lavenderblush	FFF0F5	htmlLavenderBlush
lawngreen	7CFC00	htmlLawnGreen
lemonchiffon	FFFACD	htmlLemonChiffon
lightblue	ADD8E6	htmlLightBlue
lightcoral	F08080	htmlLightCoral
lightcyan	E0FFFF	htmlLightCyan
lightgray	D3D3D3	htmlLightGray
lightgreen	90EE90	htmlLightGreen
lightpink	FFB6C1	htmlLightPink
lightsalmon	FFA07A	htmlLightSalmon
lightseagreen	20B2AA	htmlLightSeaGreen
lightskyblue	87CEFA	htmlLightSkyBlue
lightslategray	778899	htmlLightSlateGray
lightsteelblue	B0C4DE	htmlLightSteelBlue
lightyellow	FFFFE0	htmlLightYellow
lime	00FF00	htmlLime
limegreen	32CD32	htmlLimeGreen
linen	FAF0E6	htmlLinen
magenta	FF00FF	htmlMagenta
maroon	800000	htmlMaroon
mediumaquamarine	66CDAA	htmlMediumAquamarine
mediumblue	0000CD	htmlMediumBlue
mediumorchid	BA55D3	htmlMediumOrchid
mediumpurple	9370DB	htmlMediumPurple

Color Name	Value	IE4 Color Constant
mediumseagreen	3CB371	htmlMediumSeaGreen
mediumslateblue	7B68EE	htmlMediumSlateBlue
mediumspringgreen	00FA9A	htmlMediumSpringGreen
mediumturquoise	48D1CC	htmlMediumTurquoise
mediumvioletred	C71585	htmlMediumVioletRed
midnightblue	191970	htmlMidnightBlue
mintcream	F5FFFA	htmlMintCream
mistyrose	FFE4E1	htmlMistyRose
moccasin	FFE4B5	htmlMoccasin
navajowhite	FFDEAD	htmlNavajoWhite
navy	000080	htmlNavy
oldlace	FDF5E6	htmlOldLace
olive	808000	htmlOlive
olivedrab	6B8E23	htmlOliveDrab
orange	FFA500	htmlOrange
orangered	FF4500	htmlOrangeRed
orchid	DA70D6	htmlOrchid
palegoldenrod	EEE8AA	htmlPaleGoldenRod
palegreen	98FB98	htmlPaleGreen
paleturquoise	AFEEEE	htmlPaleTurquoise
palevioletred	DB7093	htmlPaleVioletRed
papayawhip	FFEFD5	htmlPapayaWhip
peachpuff	FFDAB9	htmlPeachPuff
peru	CD853F	htmlPeru
pink	FFC0CB	htmlPink
plum	DDA0DD	htmlPlum
powderblue	B0E0E6	htmlPowderBlue
purple	800080	htmlPurple
red	FF0000	htmlRed
rosybrown	BC8F8F	htmlRosyBrown
royalblue	4169E1	htmlRoyalBlue
saddlebrown	8B4513	htmlSaddleBrown
salmon	FA8072	htmlSalmon

Color Name	Value	IE4 Color Constant
sandybrown	F4A460	htmlSandyBrown
seagreen	2E8B57	htmlSeaGreen
seashell	FFF5EE	htmlSeashell
sienna	A0522D	htmlSienna
silver	C0C0C0	htmlSilver
skyblue	87CEEB	htmlSkyBlue
slateblue	6A5ACD	htmlSlateBlue
slategray	708090	htmlSlateGray
snow	FFFAFA	htmlSnow
springgreen	00FF7F	htmlSpringGreen
steelblue	4682B4	htmlSteelBlue
tan	D2B48C	htmlTan
teal	008080	htmlTeal
thistle	D8BFD8	htmlThistle
tomato	FF6347	htmlTomato
turquoise	40E0D0	htmlTurquoise
violet	EE82EE	htmlViolet
wheat	F5DEB3	htmlWheat
white	FFFFFF	htmlWhite
whitesmoke	F5F5F5	htmlWhiteSmoke
yellow	FFFF00	htmlYellow
yellowgreen	9ACD32	htmlYellowGreen

Colors Sorted by Group

Color Name	Value	IE4 Color Constant
Blues		
azure	F0FFFF	htmlAzure
aliceblue	F0F8FF	htmlAliceBlue
lavender	E6E6FA	htmlLavender
lightcyan	E0FFFF	htmlLightCyan
powderblue	B0E0E6	htmlPowderBlue
lightsteelblue	B0C4DE	htmlLightSteelBlue

Color Name	Value	IE4 Color Constant
paleturquoise	AFEEEE	htmlPaleTurquoise
lightblue	ADD8E6	htmlLightBlue
blueviolet	8A2BE2	htmlBlueViolet
lightskyblue	87CEFA	htmlLightSkyBlue
skyblue	87CEEB	htmlSkyBlue
mediumslateblue	7B68EE	htmlMediumSlateBlue
slateblue	6A5ACD	htmlSlateBlue
cornflowerblue	6495ED	htmlCornflowerBlue
cadetblue	5F9EA0	htmlCadetBlue
indigo	4B0082	htmlIndigo
mediumturquoise	48D1CC	htmlMediumTurquoise
darkslateblue	483D8B	htmlDarkSlateBlue
steelblue	4682B4	htmlSteelBlue
royalblue	4169E1	htmlRoyalBlue
turquoise	40E0D0	htmlTurquoise
dodgerblue	1E90FF	htmlDodgerBlue
midnightblue	191970	htmlMidnightBlue
aqua	00FFFF	htmlAqua
cyan	00FFFF	htmlCyan
darkturquoise	00CED1	htmlDarkTurquoise
deepskyblue	00BFFF	htmlDeepSkyBlue
darkcyan	008B8B	htmlDarkCyan
blue	0000FF	htmlBlue
mediumblue	0000CD	htmlMediumBlue
darkblue	00008B	htmlDarkBlue
navy	000080	htmlNavy
Greens		
mintcream	F5FFFA	htmlMintCream
honeydew	F0FFF0	htmlHoneydew
greenyellow	ADFF2F	htmlGreenYellow
yellowgreen	9ACD32	htmlYellowGreen
palegreen	98FB98	htmlPaleGreen

Color Name	Value	IE4 Color Constant
lightgreen	90EE90	htmlLightGreen
darkseagreen	8FBC8F	htmlDarkSeaGreen
olive	808000	htmlOlive
aquamarine	7FFFD4	htmlAquamarine
chartreuse	7FFF00	htmlChartreuse
lawngreen	7CFC00	htmlLawnGreen
olivedrab	6B8E23	htmlOliveDrab
mediumaquamarine	66CDAA	htmlMediumAquamarine
darkolivegreen	556B2F	htmlDarkOliveGreen
mediumseagreen	3CB371	htmlMediumSeaGreen
limegreen	32CD32	htmlLimeGreen
seagreen	2E8B57	htmlSeaGreen
forestgreen	228B22	htmlForestGreen
lightseagreen	20B2AA	htmlLightSeaGreen
springgreen	00FF7F	htmlSpringGreen
lime	00FF00	htmlLime
mediumspringgreen	00FA9A	htmlMediumSpringGreen
teal	008080	htmlTeal
green	008000	htmlGreen
darkgreen	006400	htmlDarkGreen

Pinks and Reds

Color Name	Value	IE4 Color Constant
lavenderblush	FFF0F5	htmlLavenderBlush
mistyrose	FFE4E1	htmlMistyRose
pink	FFC0CB	htmlPink
lightpink	FFB6C1	htmlLightPink
orange	FFA500	htmlOrange
lightsalmon	FFA07A	htmlLightSalmon
darkorange	FF8C00	htmlDarkOrange
coral	FF7F50	htmlCoral
hotpink	FF69B4	htmlHotPink
tomato	FF6347	htmlTomato
orangered	FF4500	htmlOrangeRed

Color Name	Value	IE4 Color Constant
deeppink	FF1493	htmlDeepPink
fuchsia	FF00FF	htmlFuchsia
magenta	FF00FF	htmlMagenta
red	FF0000	htmlRed
salmon	FA8072	htmlSalmon
lightcoral	F08080	htmlLightCoral
violet	EE82EE	htmlViolet
darksalmon	E9967A	htmlDarkSalmon
plum	DDA0DD	htmlPlum
crimson	DC143C	htmlCrimson
palevioletred	DB7093	htmlPaleVioletRed
orchid	DA70D6	htmlOrchid
thistle	D8BFD8	htmlThistle
indianred	CD5C5C	htmlIndianRed
mediumvioletred	C71585	htmlMediumVioletRed
mediumorchid	BA55D3	htmlMediumOrchid
firebrick	B22222	htmlFirebrick
darkorchid	9932CC	htmlDarkOrchid
darkviolet	9400D3	htmlDarkViolet
mediumpurple	9370DB	htmlMediumPurple
darkmagenta	8B008B	htmlDarkMagenta
darkred	8B0000	htmlDarkRed
purple	800080	htmlPurple
maroon	800000	htmlMaroon

Yellows

ivory	FFFFF0	htmlIvory
lightyellow	FFFFE0	htmlLightYellow
yellow	FFFF00	htmlYellow
floralwhite	FFFAF0	htmlFloralWhite
lemonchiffon	FFFACD	htmlLemonChiffon
cornsilk	FFF8DC	htmlCornsilk
gold	FFD700	htmlGold

Color Name	Value	IE4 Color Constant
khaki	F0E68C	htmlKhaki
darkkhaki	BDB76B	htmlDarkKhaki
Beiges and Browns		
snow	FFFAFA	htmlSnow
seashell	FFF5EE	htmlSeashell
papayawhite	FFEFD5	htmlPapayaWhite
blanchedalmond	FFEBCD	htmlBlanchedAlmond
bisque	FFE4C4	htmlBisque
moccasin	FFE4B5	htmlMoccasin
navajowhite	FFDEAD	htmlNavajoWhite
peachpuff	FFDAB9	htmlPeachPuff
oldlace	FDF5E6	htmlOldLace
linen	FAF0E6	htmlLinen
antiquewhite	FAEBD7	htmlAntiqueWhite
beige	F5F5DC	htmlBeige
wheat	F5DEB3	htmlWheat
sandybrown	F4A460	htmlSandyBrown
palegoldenrod	EEE8AA	htmlPaleGoldenRod
burlywood	DEB887	htmlBurlywood
goldenrod	DAA520	htmlGoldenRod
tan	D2B48C	htmlTan
chocolate	D2691E	htmlChocolate
peru	CD853F	htmlPeru
rosybrown	BC8F8F	htmlRosyBrown
darkgoldenrod	B8860B	htmlDarkGoldenRod
brown	A52A2A	htmlBrown
sienna	A0522D	htmlSienna
saddlebrown	8B4513	htmlSaddleBrown
Whites and Grays		
white	FFFFFF	htmlWhite
ghostwhite	F8F8FF	htmlGhostWhite
whitesmoke	F5F5F5	htmlWhiteSmoke

Color Name	Value	IE4 Color Constant
gainsboro	DCDCDC	htmlGainsboro
lightgray	D3D3D3	htmlLightGray
silver	C0C0C0	htmlSilver
darkgray	A9A9A9	htmlDarkGray
gray	808080	htmlGray
lightslategray	778899	htmlLightSlateGray
slategray	708090	htmlSlateGray
dimgray	696969	htmlDimGray
darkslategray	2F4F4F	htmlDarkSlateGray
black	000000	htmlBlack

Colors Sorted by Depth

Color Name	Value	IE4 Color Constant
white	FFFFFF	htmlWhite
ivory	FFFFF0	htmlIvory
lightyellow	FFFFE0	htmlLightYellow
yellow	FFFF00	htmlYellow
snow	FFFAFA	htmlSnow
floralwhite	FFFAF0	htmlFloralWhite
lemonchiffon	FFFACD	htmlLemonChiffon
cornsilk	FFF8DC	htmlCornsilk
seashell	FFF5EE	htmlSeashell
lavenderblush	FFF0F5	htmlLavenderBlush
papayawhip	FFEFD5	htmlPapayaWhip
blanchedalmond	FFEBCD	htmlBlanchedAlmond
mistyrose	FFE4E1	htmlMistyRose
bisque	FFE4C4	htmlBisque
moccasin	FFE4B5	htmlMoccasin
navajowhite	FFDEAD	htmlNavajoWhite
peachpuff	FFDAB9	htmlPeachPuff
gold	FFD700	htmlGold
pink	FFC0CB	htmlPink

Color Name	Value	IE4 Color Constant
lightpink	FFB6C1	htmlLightPink
orange	FFA500	htmlOrange
lightsalmon	FFA07A	htmlLightSalmon
darkorange	FF8C00	htmlDarkOrange
coral	FF7F50	htmlCoral
hotpink	FF69B4	htmlHotPink
tomato	FF6347	htmlTomato
orangered	FF4500	htmlOrangeRed
deeppink	FF1493	htmlDeepPink
fuchsia	FF00FF	htmlFuchsia
magenta	FF00FF	htmlMagenta
red	FF0000	htmlRed
oldlace	FDF5E6	htmlOldLace
linen	FAF0E6	htmlLinen
antiquewhite	FAEBD7	htmlAntiqueWhite
salmon	FA8072	htmlSalmon
ghostwhite	F8F8FF	htmlGhostWhite
mintcream	F5FFFA	htmlMintCream
whitesmoke	F5F5F5	htmlWhiteSmoke
beige	F5F5DC	htmlBeige
wheat	F5DEB3	htmlWheat
sandybrown	F4A460	htmlSandyBrown
azure	F0FFFF	htmlAzure
honeydew	F0FFF0	htmlHoneydew
aliceblue	F0F8FF	htmlAliceBlue
khaki	F0E68C	htmlKhaki
lightcoral	F08080	htmlLightCoral
palegoldenrod	EEE8AA	htmlPaleGoldenRod
violet	EE82EE	htmlViolet
darksalmon	E9967A	htmlDarkSalmon
lavender	E6E6FA	htmlLavender
lightcyan	E0FFFF	htmlLightCyan
burlywood	DEB887	htmlBurlywood

Color Name	Value	IE4 Color Constant
plum	DDA0DD	htmlPlum
gainsboro	DCDCDC	htmlGainsboro
crimson	DC143C	htmlCrimson
palevioletred	DB7093	htmlPaleVioletRed
goldenrod	DAA520	htmlGoldenRod
orchid	DA70D6	htmlOrchid
thistle	D8BFD8	htmlThistle
lightgray	D3D3D3	htmlLightGray
tan	D2B48C	htmlTan
chocolate	D2691E	htmlChocolate
peru	CD853F	htmlPeru
indianred	CD5C5C	htmlIndianRed
mediumvioletred	C71585	htmlMediumVioletRed
silver	C0C0C0	htmlSilver
darkkhaki	BDB76B	htmlDarkKhaki
rosybrown	BC8F8F	htmlRosyBrown
mediumorchid	BA55D3	htmlMediumOrchid
darkgoldenrod	B8860B	htmlDarkGoldenRod
firebrick	B22222	htmlFirebrick
powderblue	B0E0E6	htmlPowderBlue
lightsteelblue	B0C4DE	htmlLightSteelBlue
paleturquoise	AFEEEE	htmlPaleTurquoise
greenyellow	ADFF2F	htmlGreenYellow
lightblue	ADD8E6	htmlLightBlue
darkgray	A9A9A9	htmlDarkGray
brown	A52A2A	htmlBrown
sienna	A0522D	htmlSienna
yellowgreen	9ACD32	htmlYellowGreen
darkorchid	9932CC	htmlDarkOrchid
palegreen	98FB98	htmlPaleGreen
darkviolet	9400D3	htmlDarkViolet
mediumpurple	9370DB	htmlMediumPurple
lightgreen	90EE90	htmlLightGreen

Color Name	Value	IE4 Color Constant
darkseagreen	8FBC8F	htmlDarkSeaGreen
saddlebrown	8B4513	htmlSaddleBrown
darkmagenta	8B008B	htmlDarkMagenta
darkred	8B0000	htmlDarkRed
blueviolet	8A2BE2	htmlBlueViolet
lightskyblue	87CEFA	htmlLightSkyBlue
skyblue	87CEEB	htmlSkyBlue
gray	808080	htmlGray
olive	808000	htmlOlive
purple	800080	htmlPurple
maroon	800000	htmlMaroon
aquamarine	7FFFD4	htmlAquamarine
chartreuse	7FFF00	htmlChartreuse
lawngreen	7CFC00	htmlLawnGreen
mediumslateblue	7B68EE	htmlMediumSlateBlue
lightslategray	778899	htmlLightSlateGray
slategray	708090	htmlSlateGray
olivedrab	6B8E23	htmlOliveDrab
slateblue	6A5ACD	htmlSlateBlue
dimgray	696969	htmlDimGray
mediumaquamarine	66CDAA	htmlMediumAquamarine
cornflowerblue	6495ED	htmlCornflowerBlue
cadetblue	5F9EA0	htmlCadetBlue
darkolivegreen	556B2F	htmlDarkOliveGreen
indigo	4B0082	htmlIndigo
mediumturquoise	48D1CC	htmlMediumTurquoise
darkslateblue	483D8B	htmlDarkSlateBlue
steelblue	4682B4	htmlSteelBlue
royalblue	4169E1	htmlRoyalBlue
turquoise	40E0D0	htmlTurquoise
mediumseagreen	3CB371	htmlMediumSeaGreen
limegreen	32CD32	htmlLimeGreen
darkslategray	2F4F4F	htmlDarkSlateGray

Color Name	Value	IE4 Color Constant
seagreen	2E8B57	htmlSeaGreen
forestgreen	228B22	htmlForestGreen
lightseagreen	20B2AA	htmlLightSeaGreen
dodgerblue	1E90FF	htmlDodgerBlue
midnightblue	191970	htmlMidnightBlue
aqua	00FFFF	htmlAqua
cyan	00FFFF	htmlCyan
springgreen	00FF7F	htmlSpringGreen
lime	00FF00	htmlLime
mediumspringgreen	00FA9A	htmlMediumSpringGreen
darkturquoise	00CED1	htmlDarkTurquoise
deepskyblue	00BFFF	htmlDeepSkyBlue
darkcyan	008B8B	htmlDarkCyan
teal	008080	htmlTeal
green	008000	htmlGreen
darkgreen	006400	htmlDarkGreen
blue	0000FF	htmlBlue
mediumblue	0000CD	htmlMediumBlue
darkblue	00008B	htmlDarkBlue
navy	000080	htmlNavy
black	000000	htmlBlack

Special Characters in HTML

The following table gives you the codes you need to insert special characters into your documents. Some characters have their own mnemonic names – for example, the registered trademark character can be written in HTML as &reg. Where there is no mnemonic name, you can insert the character simply by including its decimal code.

Character	Decimal Code	HTML	Description
"	&#34;	&quot;	Quotation mark
&	&#38;	&amp;	Ampersand
<	&#60;	&lt;	Less than
>	&#62;	&gt;	Greater than

Character	Decimal Code	HTML	Description
			Non-breaking space
¡	&#161;	&iexcl;	Inverted exclamation
¢	&#162;	&cent;	Cent sign
£	&#163;	&pound;	Pound sterling
¤	&#164;	&curren;	General currency sign
¥	&#165;	&yen;	Yen sign
¦	&#166;	&brvbar;	Broken vertical bar
§	&#167;	&sect;	Section sign
¨	&#168;	&uml;	Diæresis/umlaut
©	&#169;	&copy;	Copyright
ª	&#170;	&ordf;	Feminine ordinal
«	&#171;	&laquo;	Left angle quote,
¬	&#172;	&not;	Not sign
	&#173;	&shy;	Soft hyphen
®	&#174;	&reg;	Registered trademark
¯	&#175;	&macr;	Macron accent
°	&#176;	&deg;	Degree sign
±	&#177;	&plusmn;	Plus or minus
²	&#178;	&sup2;	Superscript two
³	&#179;	&sup3;	Superscript three
´	&#180;	&acute;	Acute accent
µ	&#181;	&micro;	Micro sign
¶	&#182;	&para;	Paragraph sign
·	&#183;	&middot;	Middle dot
¸	&#184;	&cedil;	Cedilla
¹	&#185;	&sup1;	Superscript one
º	&#186;	&ordm;	Masculine ordinal
»	&#187;	&raquo;	Right angle quote
¼	&#188;	&frac14;	Fraction one quarter

Character	Decimal Code	HTML	Description
½	&#189;	&frac12;	Fraction one half
¾	&#190;	&frac34;	Fraction three-quarters
¿	&#191;	&iquest;	Inverted question mark
À	&#192;	&Agrave;	Capital A, grave accent
Á	&#193;	&Aacute;	Capital A, acute accent
Â	&#194;	&Acirc;	Capital A, circumflex
Ã	&#195;	&Atilde;	Capital A, tilde
Ä	&#196;	&Auml;	Capital A, diæresis / umlaut
Å	&#197;	&Aring;	Capital A, ring
Æ	&#198;	&AElig;	Capital AE, ligature
Ç	&#199;	&Ccedil;	Capital C, cedilla
È	&#200;	&Egrave;	Capital E, grave accent
É	&#201;	&Eacute;	Capital E, acute accent
Ê	&#202;	&Ecirc;	Capital E, circumflex
Ë	&#203;	&Euml;	Capital E, diæresis / umlaut
Ì	&#204;	&Igrave;	Capital I, grave accent
Í	&#205;	&Iacute;	Capital I, acute accent
Î	&#206;	&Icirc;	Capital I, circumflex
Ï	&#207;	&Iuml;	Capital I, diæresis /umlaut
Ð	&#208;	&ETH;	Capital Eth, Icelandic
Ñ	&#209;	&Ntilde;	Capital N, tilde
Ò	&#210;	&Ograve;	Capital O, grave accent
Ó	&#211;	&Oacute;	Capital O, acute accent
Ô	&#212;	&Ocirc;	Capital O, circumflex
Õ	&#213;	&Otilde;	Capital O, tilde
Ö	&#214;	&Ouml;	Capital O, diæresis / umlaut
×	&#215;	&times;	Multiplication sign
Ø	&#216;	&Oslash;	Capital O, slash
Ù	&#217;	&Ugrave;	Capital U, grave accent

Character	Decimal Code	HTML	Description
Ú	&#218;	&Uacute;	Capital U, acute accent
Û	&#219;	&Ucirc;	Capital U, circumflex
Ü	&#220;	&Uuml;	Capital U, diæresis / umlaut
Ý	&#221;	&Yacute;	Capital Y, acute accent
Þ	&#222;	&THORN;	Capital Thorn, Icelandic
ß	&#223;	&szlig;	German sz
à	&#224;	&agrave;	Small a, grave accent
á	&#225;	&aacute;	Small a, acute accent
â	&#226;	&acirc;	Small a, circumflex
ã	&#227;	&atilde;	Small a, tilde
ä	&#228;	&auml;	Small a, diæresis / umlaut
å	&#229;	&aring;	Small a, ring
æ	&#230;	&aelig;	Small ae ligature
ç	&#231;	&ccedil;	Small c, cedilla
è	&#232;	&egrave;	Small e, grave accent
é	&#233;	&eacute;	Small e, acute accent
ê	&#234;	&ecirc;	Small e, circumflex
ë	&#235;	&euml;	Small e, diæresis / umlaut
ì	&#236;	&igrave;	Small i, grave accent
í	&#237;	&iacute;	Small i, acute accent
î	&#238;	&icirc;	Small i, circumflex
ï	&#239;	&iuml;	Small i, diæresis / umlaut
ð	&#240;	&eth;	Small eth, Icelandic
ñ	&#241;	&ntilde;	Small n, tilde
ò	&#242;	&ograve;	Small o, grave accent
ó	&#243;	&oacute;	Small o, acute accent
ô	&#244;	&ocirc;	Small o, circumflex
õ	&#245;	&otilde;	Small o, tilde
ö	&#246;	&ouml;	Small o, diæresis / umlaut

Character	Decimal Code	HTML	Description
÷	&#247;	&divide;	Division sign
ø	&#248;	&oslash;	Small o, slash
ù	&#249;	&ugrave;	Small u, grave accent
ú	&#250;	&uacute;	Small u, acute accent
û	&#251;	&ucirc;	Small u, circumflex
ü	&#252;	&uuml;	Small u, diæresis / umlaut
ý	&#253;	&yacute;	Small y, acute accent
þ	&#254;	&thorn;	Small thorn, Icelandic
ÿ	&#255;	&yuml;	Small y, diæresis / umlaut

Remember, if you want to show HTML code in a browser, you have to use the special character codes for the angled brackets in order to avoid the browser interpreting them as start and end of tags.

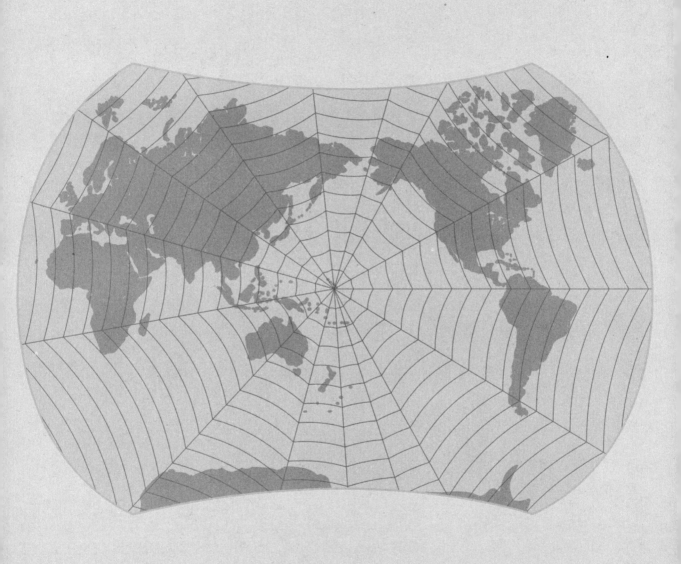

Useful Information

HTTP Server Variables

Variable	Meaning
ALL_HTTP	Complete set of HTTP Headers. In this variable, the headers have been capitalized and prefixed with HTTP_.
ALL_RAW	Complete set of HTTP Headers. Similar to ALL_HTTP, but the header names are left unchanged.
APPL_MD_PATH	Path in the Metabase for the web application (the Metabase contains the IIS4 configuration).
APPL_PHYSICAL_PATH	Physical path of the web application, i.e. the location on disk.
AUTH_PASSWORD	User's password, if the user has been authenticated using Basic Authentication.
AUTH_TYPE	Authentication type, if the user has been authenticated. Set to Basic for Basic Authentication or NTLM for Windows NT Challenge/Response Authentication.
AUTH_USER	User's name, if the user has been authenticated.
CERT_COOKIE	Unique identifier for client certificate.
CERT_FLAGS	Flags: bit 0 is set if client certificate is present; bit 1 is set if the certificate authority that issued the certificate is not recognized.
CERT_ISSUER	Certificate issuer, from the Issuer field in the client certificate.
CERT_KEYSIZE	Number of bits used to encrypt the secure channel session.
CERT_SECRETKEYSIZE	Number of bits in the server certificate's private key.

Table Continued on Following Page

Variable	Meaning
CERT_SERIALNUMBER	Serial number of certificate allocated by issuer.
CERT_SERVER_ISSUER	Certificate issuer, from the Issuer field in the server certificate.
CERT_SERVER_SUBJECT	Certificate owner, from the Subject field in the server certificate.
CERT_SUBJECT	Certificate owner, from the Subject field in the client certificate.
CONTENT_LENGTH	Number of bytes sent by the client.
CONTENT_TYPE	Type of data in HTTP Request.
GATEWAY_INTERFACE	Version of the CGI gateway specification implemented.
HTTP_*headername*	See "HTTP Headers" below
HTTPS	ON if a secure channel is used; OFF otherwise
HTTPS_KEYSIZE	Number of bits used to encrypt the secure channel session.
HTTPS_SECRETKEYSIZE	Number of bits in the server certificate's private key.
HTTPS_SERVER_ISSUER	Certificate issuer, from the Issuer field in the server certificate.
HTTPS_SERVER_SUBJECT	Certificate owner, from the Subject field in the server certificate.
INSTANCE_ID	Identifies the instance of the web server in the Metabase.
INSTANCE_META_PATH	Path in the Metabase for the IIS instance.
LOCAL_ADDR	IP address on the server that received the HTTP request.
LOGON_USER	User's Windows NT account name, if the user has been authenticated.
PATH_INFO	The part of the URL after the server name but before any query string.
PATH_TRANSLATED	Value of PATH_INFO with any virtual path converted to a physical directory name.
QUERY_STRING	Information following the question mark (?) in the URL string.
REMOTE_ADDR	IP address of the client that issued the HTTP request.
REMOTE_HOST	Hostname (if known) of the client that issued the HTTP request.

Variable	Meaning
REMOTE_USER	User's name, if the user has been authenticated. This will be the name released from the client and will not be affected by any ISAPI authentication filters.
REQUEST_METHOD	Type of HTTP Request, defines how the payload is carried, i.e. GET, POST or PUT
SCRIPT_NAME	Virtual pathname to the script or application being executed.
SERVER_NAME	Hostname or IP address of server.
SERVER_PORT	TCP/IP port number on the server that received the HTTP request.
SERVER_PORT_SECURE	Set to 1 if the HTTP Request is on an encrypted port; otherwise set to 0.
SERVER_PROTOCOL	Protocol name and version (usually HTTP/1.1) that the software on the server and the client are using to satisfy the information request.
SERVER_SOFTWARE	Name and version of the server software that is handling the information request.
URL	The part of the URL after the server name but before any query string.

HTTP Headers

The HTTP Request includes a number of items on information about the request and the capabilities of the client; these items are name / value pairs and are known as HTTP Headers. Any of the HTTP Headers that are not parsed into one of the variables listed above can be obtained using the server variable name HTTP_*headername*, where *headername* is the name of the header item. Commonly used examples are:

Variable	Meaning
HTTP_ACCEPT	List of the MIME data types that the client can accept.
HTTP_ACCEPT_ENCODING	List of encoding types that the by client can accept.
HTTP_ACCEPT_LANGUAGE	List of the human languages that the client prefers
HTTP_CONNECTION	Type of connection
HTTP_USER_AGENT	Client software information, usually consisting of the browser version, plus the operating system, plus the browser type
HTTP_REFERER	URL of the page containing the link used to get to this page
HTTP_COOKIE	Cookies sent from the client's browser

Language Codes Supported by Microsoft Internet Explorer 4/5

Language	Code
Afrikaans	af
Albanian	sq
Arabic	ar
Arabic (Algeria)	ar-dz
Arabic (Bahrain)	ar-bh
Arabic (Egypt)	ar-eg
Arabic (Iraq)	ar-iq
Arabic (Jordan)	ar-jo
Arabic (Kuwait)	ar-kw
Arabic (Lebanon)	ar-lb
Arabic (Libya)	ar-ly
Arabic (Morocco)	ar-ma
Arabic (Oman)	ar-om
Arabic (Qatar)	ar-qa
Arabic (Saudi Arabia)	ar-sa
Arabic (Syria)	ar-sy
Arabic (Tunisia)	ar-tn
Arabic (U.A.E.)	ar-ae
Arabic (Yemen)	ar-ye
Basque	eu
Belarusian	be
Bulgarian	bg
Catalan	ca
Chinese	zh
Chinese (Hong Kong)	zh-hk

Language	Code
Chinese (PRC)	zh-cn
Chinese (Singapore)	zh-sg
Chinese (Taiwan)	zh-tw
Croatian	hr
Czech	cs
Danish	da
Dutch (Belgian)	nl-be
Dutch (Standard)	nl
English	en
English (Australian)	en-au
English (Belize)	en-bz
English (British)	en-gb
English (Canadian)	en-ca
English (Ireland)	en-ie
English (Jamaica)	en-jm
English (New Zealand)	en-nz
English (South Africa)	en-za
English (Trinidad)	en-tt
English (United States)	en-us
Estonian	et
Faeroese	fo
Farsi	fa
Finnish	fi
French (Belgian)	fr-be
French (Canadian)	fr-ca

Language	Code	Language	Code
French (Luxembourg)	fr-lu	Norwegian (Nynorsk)	no
French (Standard)	fr	Polish	pl
French (Swiss)	fr-ch	Portuguese (Brazilian)	pt-br
Gaelic	gd	Portuguese (Standard)	pt
German (Austrian)	de-at	Rhaeto-Romanic	rm
German (Liechtenstein)	de-li	Romanian	ro
German (Luxembourg)	de-lu	Romanian (Moldavia)	ro-mo
German (Standard)	de	Russian	ru
German (Swiss)	de-ch	Russian (Moldavia)	ru-mo
Greek	el	Serbian (Cyrillic)	sr
Hebrew	he	Spanish (Uruguay)	es-uy
Hindi	hi	Spanish (Venezuela)	es-ve
Hungarian	hu	Serbian (Latin)	sr
Icelandic	is	Slovak	sk
Indonesian	in	Slovenian	sl
Italian (Standard)	it	Sorbian	sb
Italian (Swiss)	it-ch	Spanish	es
Japanese	ja	Spanish	es-do
Korean	ko	Spanish	es
Latvian	lv	Spanish (Argentina)	es-ar
Lithuanian	lt	Spanish (Bolivia)	es-bo
Macedonian	mk	Spanish (Chile)	es-cl
Malaysian	ms	Spanish (Colombia)	es-co
Maltese	mt	Spanish (Costa Rica)	es-cr
Norwegian (Bokmal)	no	Spanish (Ecuador)	es-ec

Table Continued on Following Page

Language	Code
Spanish (El Salvador)	es-sv
Spanish (Guatemala)	es-gt
Spanish (Honduras)	es-hn
Spanish (Mexican)	es-mx
Spanish (Nicaragua)	es-ni
Spanish (Panama)	es-pa
Spanish (Paraguay)	es-py
Spanish (Peru)	es-pe
Spanish (Puerto Rico)	es-pr
Sutu	sx
Swedish	sv

Language	Code
Swedish (Finland)	sv-fi
Thai	th
Tsonga	ts
Tswana	tn
Turkish	tr
Ukrainian	uk
Urdu	ur
Vietnamese	vi
Xhosa	xh
Yiddish	ji
Zulu	zu

Common Codepages

Codepage	Name	Alias
1200	Universal Alphabet	unicode
1201	Universal Alphabet (Big-Endian)	unicodeFEFF
1250	Central European Alphabet (Windows)	windows-1250
1251	Cyrillic Alphabet (Windows)	windows-1251
1252	Western Alphabet	iso-8859-1
1253	Greek Alphabet (Windows)	windows-1253
1254	Turkish Alphabet	iso-8859-9
1255	Hebrew Alphabet (Windows)	iso-8859-8
1256	Arabic Alphabet (Windows)	windows-1256
1257	Baltic Alphabet (Windows)	windows-1257
1258	Vietnamese Alphabet (Windows)	windows-1258
20866	Cyrillic Alphabet (KOI8-R)	koi8-r
21866	Ukrainian Alphabet (KOI8-RU)	koi8-ru

Codepage	Name	Alias
28592	Central European Alphabet (ISO)	iso-8859-2
28593	Latin 3 Alphabet (ISO)	iso-8859-3
28594	Baltic Alphabet (ISO)	iso-8859-4
28595	Cyrillic Alphabet (ISO)	iso-8859-5
28596	Arabic Alphabet (ISO)	iso-8859-6
28597	Greek Alphabet (ISO)	iso-8859-7
50220	Japanese (JIS)	iso-2022-jp
50221	Japanese (JIS-Allow 1 byte Kana)	csISO2022JP
50222	Japanese (JIS-Allow 1 byte Kana)	iso-2022-jp
50225	Korean (ISO)	iso-2022-kr
50932	Japanese (Auto Select)	none
50949	Korean (Auto Select)	none
51932	Japanese (EUC)	euc-jp
51949	Korean (EUC)	euc-kr
52936	Chinese Simplified (HZ)	hz-gb-2312
65000	Universal Alphabet (UTF-7)	utf-7
65001	Universal Alphabet (UTF-8)	utf-8
852	Central European (DOS)	ibm852
866	Cyrillic Alphabet (DOS)	cp866
874	Thai (Windows)	windows-874
932	Japanese (Shift-JIS)	shift_jis
936	Chinese Simplified (GB2312)	gb2312
949	Korean	ks_c_5601-1987
950	Chinese Traditional (Big5)	big5

Locale IDs (LCIDs)

Country/Region	Language	LCID (Hex)
Albania	Albanian	041c
Algeria	Arabic	1401
Argentina	Spanish	2c0a
Australia	English	0c09
Austria	German	0c07
Bahrain	Arabic	3c01
Belarus	Belarusian	0423
Belgium	French	0813
Belize	English	2809
Bolivia	Spanish	400a
Brazil	Portuguese	0416
Brunei Darussalam	Malay	083e
Bulgaria	Bulgarian	0402
Canada	English	1009
Canada	French	0c0c
Caribbean	English	2409
Chile	Spanish	340a
Colombia	Spanish	240a
Costa Rica	Spanish	140a
Croatia	Croatian	041a
Czech Republic	Czech	0405
Denmark	Danish	0406
Dominican Republic	Spanish	1c0a

Country/Region	Language	LCID (Hex)
Ecuador	Spanish	300a
Egypt	Arabic	0c01
El Salvador	Spanish	440a
Estonia	Estonian	0425
Faeroe Islands	Faeroese	0438
Finland	Finnish	040b
France	French	040c
Germany	German	0407
Greece	Greek	0408
Guatemala	Spanish	100a
Honduras	Spanish	480a
Hong Kong	Chinese	0c04
Hungary	Hungarian	040e
Iceland	Icelandic	040f
India	Hindi	0439
Indonesia	Indonesian	0421
Iran	Farsi	0429
Iraq	Arabic	0801
Ireland	English	1809
Israel	Hebrew	040d
Italy	Italian	0410
Jamaica	English	2009
Japan	Japanese	0411

Country/ Region	Language	LCID (Hex)
Jordan	Arabic	2c01
Kenya	Swahili	0441
Korea	Korean (Ext. Wansung)	0412
Korea	Korean (Johab)	0812
Kuwait	Arabic	3401
Latvia	Latvian	0426
Lebanon	Arabic	3401
Libya	Arabic	3001
Liechtenstein	German	1407
Lithuania	Classic Lithuanian	0827
Lithuania	Lithuanian	0427
Luxembourg	French	140c
Luxembourg	German	1007
Macau	Chinese	1404
Macedonia	Macedonian	042f
Malaysia	Malay	043e
Mexico	Spanish	080a
Monaco	French	180c
Morocco	Arabic	1801
Netherlands	Dutch	0413
New Zealand	English	1409
Nicaragua	Spanish	4c0a

Country/ Region	Language	LCID (Hex)
Norway (Bokmal)	Norwegian	0414
Norway (Nynorsk)	Norwegian	0814
Oman	Arabic	2001
Pakistan	Urdu	0420
Panama	Spanish	180a
Paraguay	Spanish	280a
Peru	Spanish	280a
Philippines	English	3409
Poland	Polish	0415
Portugal	Portuguese	0816
PRC	Chinese	0804
Puerto Rico	Spanish	500a
Qatar	Arabic	4001
Romania	Romanian	0418
Russia	Russian	0419
Saudi Arabia	Arabic	0401
Serbia (Cyrillic)	Serbian	0c1a
Serbia (Latin)	Serbian	081a
Singapore	Chinese	1004
Slovakia	Slovak	041b
Slovenia	Slovene	0424
South Africa	English	1c09

Tables Continued on Following Page

1123

Country/ Region	Language	LCID (Hex)	Country/ Region	Language	LCID (Hex)
South Africa	Afrikaans	0436	Trinidad	English	2c09
Spain	Basque	042d	Tunisia	Arabic	1c01
Spain	Catalan	0403	Turkey	Turkish	041f
Spain (Mod. Sort)	Spanish	0c0a	U.A.E.	Arabic	3801
Spain (Trad. Sort)	Spanish	040a	Ukraine	Ukrainian	0422
Sweden	Swedish	041d	United Kingdom	English	0809
Switzerland	French	100c	United States	English	0409
Switzerland	German	0807	Uruguay	Spanish	380a
Switzerland	Italian	0810	Venezuela	Spanish	200a
Syria	Arabic	2801	Vietnam	Vietnamese	042a
Taiwan	Chinese	0404	Yemen	Arabic	2401
Thailand	Thai	041e	Zimbabwe	English	3009

Server-Side Include Directives and Utilities

This section describes the syntax and parameter values of the Internet Information Server 5.0 **Server Side-Include** directives. It also describes the syntax and use of the IISRESTART utility, which can be used to manage the web services remotely from another computer, from the command line, or from within an SSI directive.

SSI Directives, Attributes and Tokens

Directive	Description
#include	Inserts the contents of a specified file into the response stream being sent to the client, replacing the directive. For example: `<!-- #include FILE="usefulbits.inc" -->` See below for a list of the attributes and tokens that can be used in this directive.

Directive	Description

#config	Specifies the format that will be used for dates, times and file sizes, and the text of the generic SSI error message that is returned to the client. For example:
	
	`<!-- #config ERRMSG="SSI Processing Error" -->`
	
	`<!-- #config TIMEFMT ="%A, %B %d %Y %H:%M:%S" -->`
	
	`<!-- #config SIZEFMT ="BYTES" -->`
	
	See below for a list of the attributes and tokens that can be used in this directive.

#echo	Inserts the value of an HTTP environment variable into the response stream being sent to the client, replacing the directive. For example: `<!-- #echo VAR="SERVER_NAME" -->` See below for a list of the attributes and tokens that can be used in this directive.

#exec	Executes a program or a shell command on the server. For example:
	
	`<!-- #exec CGI="/scripts/myapp.exe?value1=this&value2=that" -->`
	
	`<!-- #exec CMD="cmd.exe /C iisrestart /stop" -->`
	
	`<!-- #exec CMD="cmd.exe /C net start cisvc" -->`
	
	See below for a list of the attributes and tokens that can be used in this directive.
	
	You must add the following entry to the Windows Registry to be able to use the CMD attribute:
	
	HKEY_LOCAL_MACHINE
	　\SYSTEM
	　　\CurrentControlSet
	　　　\Services
	　　　\W3SVC
	　　　　\Parameters
	　　　　\SSIEnableCmdDirective
	
	Set the value to 1 to and restart the **WWW** service allow the CMD attribute to be used in the #exec directive. Set it to 0 to disable it and prevent unauthorized use, which could otherwise damage the server installation.

Table Continued on Following Page

Directive	Description
#flastmod	Inserts the date and time that a specified file was last modified into the response stream being sent to the client, replacing the directive. For example: `<!-- #flastmod FILE="Default.asp" -->` See below for a list of the attributes and tokens that can be used in this directive.
#fsize	Inserts the size of a specified file into the response stream being sent to the client, replacing the directive. For example: `<!-- #fsize FILE="Default.asp" -->` See below for a list of the attributes and tokens that can be used in this directive.

Command Type Attributes for the #exec Directive

Attribute	Description
CGI	Executes the specified application in the context of the Web server (i.e. with access to the request and response via the ISAPI) and passes the value of any query string to the application. The application runs in a separate memory space from the Web server.
CMD	Starts an instance of the specified operating system command interpreter and executes the specified command.

Path Type Attributes for #include, #flastmod and #fsize

Attribute	Description
FILE	The value of the attribute is a complete or relative physical path plus the name of the file, as would be used at the DOS command prompt, i.e. `"\files\web\myfile.txt"`.
VIRTUAL	The value of the attribute is a complete or relative virtual path plus the name of the file, in relation to the root folder of the current Web site. `"/files/web/myfile.txt"`.

SIZEFMT Tokens for the #config Directive

Token	Description
BYTES	The size of the file will be returned in bytes.
ABBREV	The size of the file will be calculated and returned as the nearest number of kilobytes (KB).

TIMEFMT Tokens for the #config Directive

Token	Description
%a	The day of the week as 'Mon', 'Tue', etc.
%A	The day of the week as 'Monday', Tuesday', etc.
%b	The name of the month as 'Jan', Feb', etc.
%B	The name of the month as 'January', February', etc.
%c	The current date and time formatted appropriately for the server's locale (i.e. 11/06/99 12:51:32).
%d	The day of the month as a number (01 to 31).
%H	The current hour in 24-hour format (00 to 23).
%I	The current hour in 12-hour format (01 to 12).
%j	The day of the year as a number (001 to 366).
%m	The month as a number (01 to 12).
%M	The current minute as a number (00 to 59).
%p	The appropriate 'morning' or 'afternoon' string for the server's locale (i.e. AM or PM).
%S	The current second as a decimal number (00 to 59).
%U	The week of the year as a number with Sunday as the first day of the week (00 to 51).
%w	The day of the week as a number with Sunday as the first day of the week (0 to 6).
%W	The week of the year as a number with Monday as the first day of the week (00 to 51).
%x	The current date formatted appropriately for the server's locale (i.e. 11/06/99).

Table Continued on Following Page

Token	Description
%X	The current time formatted appropriately for the server's locale (i.e. 12:51:32).
%y	The year number without the century (i.e. 01).
%Y	The year number with the century (i.e. 2001).
%z, %Z	The name or an abbreviation for the server's time zone if known.
%%	A 'percent' character.

VAR Tokens for the #echo Directive

Token	Description
AUTH_TYPE	The type of authentication that the client and server used if this page denied anonymous access, for example 'Basic' or 'NTLM' (i.e. Challenge/Response).
AUTH_PASSWORD	The password provided by the user to the server if this page denied anonymous access and the client authenticated using the Basic method.
AUTH_USER	The username provided by the user to the server if this page denied anonymous access, under both NTLM and Basic (or other) methods.
CONTENT_LENGTH	The number of bytes sent in the body of the request, i.e. the number of bytes sent as a POST to the server.
CONTENT_TYPE	The MIME type of the data sent as a POST in the body of the request.
DOCUMENT_NAME	The full physical path and filename of the document requested by the client.
DOCUMENT_URI	The full virtual path and filename of the document requested by the client, in relation to the root folder of this Web site.
DATE_GMT	The date and time set in the server's operating system, without any adjustment from Greenwich Mean Time.
DATE_LOCAL	The date and time set in the server's operating system after adjustment from Greenwich Mean Time.
GATEWAY_INTERFACE	The type of interface used to handle the request, for example 'CGI/1.1'.

Token	Description
HTTP_ACCEPT	A comma-delimited list of MIME types that the client application has notified the server that it can accept.
LAST_MODIFIED	The date and time when the file or resource requested by the client was last changed.
PATH_INFO	The full virtual path and filename of the document requested by the client, in relation to the root folder of this Web site.
PATH_TRANSLATED	The full physical path and filename of the document requested by the client.
QUERY_STRING	The value of any query string that was appended to the URL of the document or resource the client requested, after translation from the URL-encoded format.
QUERY_STRING_ UNESCAPED	The value of any query string that was appended to the URL of the document or resource the client requested, before translation from the URL-encoded format.
REMOTE_ADDR	The IP address of the client machine that requested the page.
REMOTE_HOST	The host name or IP address of the network from which the client requested the page.
REMOTE_USER	The name (if available) of the client machine that requested the page.
REQUEST_METHOD	The method used when requesting the page, either 'GET' or 'POST'.
SCRIPT_NAME	The full virtual path and filename of the document requested by the client, in relation to the root folder of the Web site.
SERVER_NAME	The network name or URL host name of the server that received the request.
SERVER_PORT	The number of the port on which the request was received, i.e. '80' for normal page requests and '443' for SSL secure requests.
SERVER_PORT_ SECURE	The port number if this request was over a secure protocol.
SERVER_PROTOCOL	The HTTP protocol that the request was passed under, i.e. 'HTTP/1.1'.
SERVER_SOFTWARE	The name/version string of the Web server, i.e. 'Microsoft-IIS/5.0'.
URL	The complete URL that the user specified when requesting the document or resource.
ALL_HTTP	All the name/value pairs for HTTP environment variables that are not included in the list above, for example HTTP_COOKIE and HTTP_ACCEPT_LANGUAGE.

The IISRESET Utility and Switches

The iisreset.exe utility can be used to manage the Web services running on any server providing that you have the relevant permissions. It should be used in preference to the NET STOP and NET START commands, as it stops and starts the various integrated services in the correct sequence.

The syntax is iisreset [*computer_name*] /*switch* [/*switch* ...]

Where the available *switch* values are:

Switch	Meaning
RESTART	Stop and then restart all Internet services running on the specified computer.
START	Start all Internet services running on the specified computer.
STOP	Stop all Internet services running on the specified computer.
REBOOT	Reboot the specified computer.
REBOOTONERROR	Reboot the specified computer if an error occurs when starting, stopping, or restarting Internet services.
NOFORCE	Do not force Internet services to terminate if attempting to stop them gracefully fails.
TIMEOUT:*val*	Set the timeout value in seconds for all the Internet services to stop. Default is 20 for RESTART, 60 for STOP, and zero for REBOOT. If the REBOOTONERROR switch is also specified the computer will reboot if the timeout period is exceeded.
STATUS	Displays the status of all Internet services.
ENABLE	Enables restarting of Internet Services on the local system.
DISABLE	Disables restarting of Internet Services on the local system.

This utility can be used in an CMD-type #echo SSI directive, providing that the page has anonymous access removed and the user supplies details of a valid account that has **Administrator** privileges on the target server. However, in this situation the REBOOT, START and RESTART options will not function correctly.

The NET STOP and NET START Commands

The net.exe utility can be used to manage the any services running on a server, either locally or from another machine, providing that you have the relevant permissions. Although not recommended for use with Internet services such as the WWW or FTP service, it is useful for stopping and starting other services (in fact, the NET command can be used to issue a whole range of other network-related commands as well).

The syntax is net [start | stop] *service_name*

So, for example, we can use it to stop and start the Microsoft Indexing Service with the commands:
net stop cisvc and net start cisvc. It can be used in a CMD-type #echo SSI directive providing that the page has anonymous access removed and the user supplies details of a valid account that has Administrator privileges on the target server.

> *A full list of all the options and switches for the NET command can be found in the Windows 2000 Help files. Select Help from the Start menu, and in the Index page of the Help window look for 'net commands'.*

Third Party Server Components

The following are a list of useful third party server components.

Data Access and Conversion Components

ActiveDOM – Enables XML and XHTML files to be loaded, created and manipulated from just about any product or programming language that supports Microsoft COM. Implements the W3C DOM 1.0 Level 1 interfaces and is designed to be fully compatible with MSXML.
See: http://www.vivid-creations.com/dom/index.htm

ActiveSAX – Enables XML files of any size to be parsed from just about any product or programming language that supports Microsoft COM.
See: http://www.vivid-creations.com/sax/index.htm

ASP2XML – Creates XML documents from any OLE-DB or ODBC enabled data source, and can update the original data as well.
See: http://www.stonebroom.com/swindex.htm

Data Validation – Validates a wide variety of data through a series of functions and methods.
See: http://www.a-href.com/products/ahrefdvc.html

DB2XML – A tool for transforming relational databases into XML documents
See: http://www.informatik.fh-wiesbaden.de/~turau/DB2XML/index.html

RSConvert – A control for converting DAO or ADO recordsets to MDB or DBF files. It allows direct output of MDB or DBF files from ASP pages.
See: `http://www.pstruh.cz/help/RSConv/library.htm`

SaveForm – Automatically persists form data in an ASP Session, and to a database or text file between sessions. Can also send it as an email message via CDONTS.
See: `http://www.stonebroom.com/swindex.htm`

XML-DBMS – Java Packages for Transferring Data between XML Documents and Relational Databases
See: `http://www.informatik.tu-darmstadt.de/DVS1/staff/bourret/`
`            xmldbms/readme.html`

XMLServlet - A Java Servlet that uses XML instructions to combine XML or HTML templates with one another and with live database values.
See: `http://www.beyond.com/PKSN102998/prod.htm`

E-Mail ASP Components

AspMail – Allows you to send SMTP mail directly from an ASP page, and provides almost all the email message features you might want.
See: `http://www.serverobjects.com/products.htm`

AspQMail – Works just like AspMail except that messages are queued for delivery. A companion NT service is notified when messages are added to the queue, and attempts delivery while your ASP script is free to continue.
See: `http://www.serverobjects.com/products.htm`

JMail – Free, very capable e-mail component.
See: `http://www.dimac.net/`

OCX Mail/ASP – Can be used to read SMTP mail that contains attachments.
See: `http://www.flicks.com/ASPMail`

Web Essentials Listcaster – A mailing list server and SMTP/POP3 server, with ASP-based setup and administration.
See: `http://www.download.com/pc/software/0,332,0-57624-s,1000.html`

File Management Components

AspUpload – Enables an ASP application to accept, save and manipulate files uploaded from a browser through one or more `<INPUT TYPE=FILE>` elements.
See: `http://www.aspupload.com/`

File I/O – Lets you perform disk directory scans, read and write INI files, create and delete files and directories, read the `<TITLE>` from Web documents, etc.
See: `http://www.tarsus.com/asp/io2/`

LastMod – Gets a file's last modified date/time from within an ASP page.
See: http://www.serverobjects.com/products.htm

ScriptUtilities – Lets you work with safe array binary data. It enables binary file upload to ASP and multiple files/folders download from ASP, with on-the-fly compression or generation of binary data.
See: http://www.pstruh.cz/help/ScptUtl/library.htm

ServerZip – Performs on-demand compression of user-selected files into ZIP files on the server ready for downloading.
See: http://www.stonebroom.com/swindex.htm

Networking Components

AspDNS – Does forward and reverse DNS lookups, returning either the IP address or the host name.
See: http://www.serverobjects.com/products.htm

AspHTTP – Allows you to GET/POST/HEAD documents via the HTTP protocol. Exposes HTTP response headers, supports transferring requests to a file (including binary transfers), password authentication support and more.
See: http://www.serverobjects.com/products.htm

AspInet – Allows you to remotely GET and PUT files via FTP from Active Server Pages.
See: http://www.serverobjects.com/products.htm

ASPLogin – Provides basic security for any Web page or collection of pages without using Windows own security system and risking compromising system passwords over the 'Net.
See: http://www.oceantek.com/

AspPing – Allows you to check the connection with any URL through the echo protocol from within ASP.
See: http://www.serverobjects.com/products.htm

FTP/X – Provides easy, high-level access to the complete FTP client protocol (RFC 959). Can make the results available as an ADO Recordset, and has built-in features to support debugging and non-standard servers using the Quote method.
See: http://www.mabry.com/ftpx/index.htm

RAS/X – A RAS Dialer. Remote Access Services allows a computer to connect to an Internet server as though it were on a LAN.
See: http://www.mabry.com/rasx/index.htm

SOCKET/X – A WinSock ActiveX Control that provides full access to Windows 'Sockets', making it easy to write TCP/IP or UDP client and server software.
See: http://www.mabry.com/socketx/index.htm

TraceRoute – allows the route followed by a TCP/IP packet to be examined.
See: http://www.pstruh.cz/help/tcpip/library.htm

URL Replacer – An ISAPI filter that replaces specific parts of the URL sent from the browser, allowing ASP to specify different static resources for the same request.
See: `http://www.pstruh.cz/help/urlrepl/library.htm`

UserManager – Contains simple objects for creating, deleting, managing and enumerating user accounts and groups. Allows removal and addition of users to groups.
See: `http://www.pstruh.cz/help/usrmgr/library.htm`

WHOIS/X – Follows the WhoIs/NICNAME protocol, and allows queries of InterNIC or other RFC 954 servers to obtain information about a user, domain or host.
See: `http://www.mabry.com/whoisx/index.htm`

Content Creation Components

AspBible – Allows you to dynamically generate texts from the Bible.
See: `http://www.serverobjects.com/products.htm`

ASPointer – Extracts content from XML documents, HTML and ASP pages using a syntax that is based on XPointer, and can optionally insert new content into the document.
See: `http://www.stonebroom.com/swindex.htm`

Content Link Generator – Generates content links across subdirectories.
See: `http://www.serverobjects.com/products.htm`

ListView – Creates 4 different list views. Comes with an interactive designer and HTML source generator. The output is pure HTML.
See: `http://www.visualasp.com/Components.asp?ProductID=3`

Strings – Contains everything you need to manipulate strings in ASP code. Can also filter out HTML tags and other content (like profanities), and format strings in different ways.
See: `http://www.tarsus.com/asp/ts/`

Text2HTML – Converts URL and e-mail addresses that are plain text to HTML anchors. It also properly formats Access memo fields for output to an HTML page.
See: `http://members.home.net/pjsteele/asp/`

TreeView – Creates dynamically expandable and collapsible tree nodes in 8 different styles. Comes with an interactive designer and HTML source generator. The output is pure HTML.
See: `http://www.visualasp.com/Components.asp?ProductID=2`

Miscellaneous Components

10 components in one pack – Calendar, Contact Form, FAQ, Help System, Home Page, Links, Message Board, Scrapbook, User Administration and Whats New components.
See: `http://www.compo.net/products/`

AspExec – Allows you to execute DOS and Windows apps from within ASP.
See: `http://www.serverobjects.com/products.htm`

AspProc – Allows you to get a variant array of process IDs and process names, and to terminate a particular process by process ID. Does not work on WinNT 3.5x and Win95 systems.
See: `http://www.serverobjects.com/products.htm`

AspCrypt – Duplicates the one-way algorithm used by Crypt on Unix.
See: `http://www.serverobjects.com/products.htm`

EnhancedLog – An IIS ISAPI add-in that allows redirection and customized error messages for each file/directory, extended logging, RAW data logging, POST data logging, and unique cookies.
See: `http://www.pstruh.cz/el/enhlog.asp`

GUIDMaker – Creates globally unique identifiers (GUIDs) from within ASP.
See: `http://www.serverobjects.com/products.htm`

RegEx – Provides full access to the system Registry, including extended keys.
See: `http://www.stonebroom.com/swindex.htm`

WaitFor – Allows you to pause your ASP pages for a specified time, wait until a file exists, or wait until the component can get exclusive read/write permissions to a file.
See: `http://www.serverobjects.com/products.htm`

Sites that List ASP Components

Many ASP-oriented Web sites provide lists of ASP components that are available, and often provide downloads as well. Some of the better-known sites are:

15 Seconds Free Resources Center at `http://www.15seconds.com/`

Active Server Pages Resources Site at `http://www.activeserverpages.com/`

ASP 101 Resources Site at `http://www.asp101.com/`

ASP Hole IIS and ASP Guide at `http://www.asphole.com/`

ASP Toolbox at `http://www.tcp-ip.com/`

ComponentSource at `http://www.componentsource.com/`

Microsoft ASP Component Catalog at
`http://msdn.microsoft.com/workshop/server/components/catalog.asp`

ServerObjects at `http://www.serverobjects.com/`

The ASP Resource Index at `http://www.aspin.com/`

Ultimate ASP at `http://www.ultimateasp.com/`

Wynkoop BackOffice Pages at `http://www.swynk.com/`

Our thanks to the following readers who helped to compile these lists: Aaron Bertrand, Adam Wilson, Mikhail Tchikalov, Antonin Foller, Bruce Knapton, Richard Anderson, Andrew White, Jay McVinney and Neil Holmes.

Other Useful Information

Wrox Press provides two sites that contain useful information for ASP and Web developers in general:

❑ **The Wrox Web Developer Site** (`http://webdev.wrox.co.uk/`)
The main site for sample code for all the Web-developer books we publish. Run the samples on-line or download code to run on your own server. Also contains chapters and extracts from our books, industry news, and a series of useful reference tools and other resources.

❑ **ASPToday** (`http://www.asptoday.com/`)
Read focused and useful articles on ASP and other Web programming techniques from a range of experts and industry gurus. A new article is available every day of the week, and you can search the archives for previous ones.

Finding ASP-friendly ISPs

ASP runs on Microsoft Windows servers, while the majority of ISPs still use Unix-based systems or an equivalent. While there are ASP clones that run on Unix or Linux, many people want to use the full spectrum of ASP functions (such as COM components and Windows services) on their sites. This tends to rule out many traditional ISPs.

Two or three years ago, it was very difficult to find an ISP that used Windows NT servers, and would allow you to install your own components or make use of Windows services in your Web applications. Thankfully, the situation is changing fast, and there are now hundreds of ISPs that do support ASP in full on Windows NT servers (predominantly Windows NT 4 at the time of writing, but no doubt this will change fairly quickly as Windows 2000 proves itself) – just check that they allow you to install your *own* components before you sign up.

A search on **InfoSeek** (`http://www.infoseek.com/`) for ASP-enabled Windows NT based ISPs (using the criteria '+asp +Web +hosting') returned 390 matches. Many of these offer ASP on Windows NT Server, plus support for applications such as SQL Server and others. Some of the sites found (at the time of writing) were:

Active Server (http://www.active-server.com/)
DataReturn (http://www.datareturn.com/)
IMC Online (http://www.imconline.net/)
SiteCrafters Internet Services (http://www.sitecrafters.com/)
Softcom (http://www.softcomca.com)
Technocom plc (http://www.technocom.net/)
Virtualscape (http://www.virtualscape.com/)

There are also sites that allow you to search for ISPs based of a whole range of criteria, such as **Action Jackson** (http://www.actionjackson.com/hosts) and **Top Hosts** (http://www.tophosts.com).

Other ASP Web Sites

There are also many other sites that provide ASP, or general Web-oriented information, for developers. This is just a selection of those we know of and recommend:

15 Seconds Free Resources Center (http://www.15seconds.com/)
Free resource for developers working with Microsoft Internet Solutions. 15 Seconds proclaims to be the biggest IIS and ASP development resource in the world, with over 2300 pages.

ActionJackson Web Developer Central (http://www.actionjackson.com)
A comprehensive resource of news, articles, books and links, including discussion forums, components, IIS hosts, jobs and much more.

Active Server Pages Resources Site (http://www.activeserverpages.com/)
This site specializes in Active Server Pages programming issues. Maintained by Charles Carroll, it contains online programming tutorials, references, and links to a wide range of resources and articles.

ASP 101 Resources Site (http://www.asp101.com/)
The purpose of this site is to provide both expert and novice developers with useful and timely information on the emerging technology of Active Server Pages.

ASP Forums (http://www.aspforums.com/)
This site provides a range of forums and discussion groups for ASP related topics, plus lists of related companies and their software designed for use with ASP.

ASP Hole IIS and ASP Guide (http://www.asphole.com/)
Intended to help the Active Server Pages professional locate ASP-related and IIS-related resources quickly and efficiently. A huge range of various resources is available.

ASP Toolbox (http://www.tcp-ip.com/)
Here you'll find a range of tutorials and other ASP-related information to help in developing your dynamic Web sites.

The ASP Resource Index (http://www.aspin.com/)
Find all the Active Server Pages (ASP) Resources you need in one place. Contains a comprehensive list of ASP components, applications, code snippets, references, and books.

ASPWatch (http://www.aspwatch.com/)
Provides real world Active Server Pages solutions and resources. This includes articles, discussions and book lists.

Hangeng (http://www.haneng.com/)
Provides content that is free to be used commercially and non-commercially. Dedicated to ASP technology and created and maintained by Alexander Haneng on a hobby basis.

JavaScript Source (http://javascript.internet.com/)
An excellent JavaScript resource with tons of cut & paste JavaScript examples for your Web pages. All for free!

Microsoft's NT Server and BackOffice Site (http://www.microsoft.com/backoffice/)
This site is the main page for the Microsoft BackOffice products, including NT Server, SQL Server, Exchange, and other components.

PowerASP Active Server Pages (http://powerasp.com/)
This site offers code snippets, hints & tips, a discussion board, a chat room and newsletters—all related to ASP and general Web development topics.

Ultimate ASP (http://www.ultimateasp.com/)
An ever-expanding wealth of information for building dynamic web pages, including help for beginners.

Website Abstraction (http://www.wsabstract.com/)
This site is a webmaster's learning center featuring tutorials on all aspects of JavaScript and Web site construction. It has been featured in many prestigious sources such as the LA Times and Vancouver Province newspapers.

World Wide Web Consortium (http://www.w3.org/)
The home of the Web. W3C is the main body that sets and agrees the standards for HTML and Web-related technologies.

Wynkoop BackOffice Pages (http://www.swynk.com/)
Maintained by Steve Wynkoop, this site covers all Microsoft BackOffice technologies. Ideal for those who want to combine ASP and corporate databases.

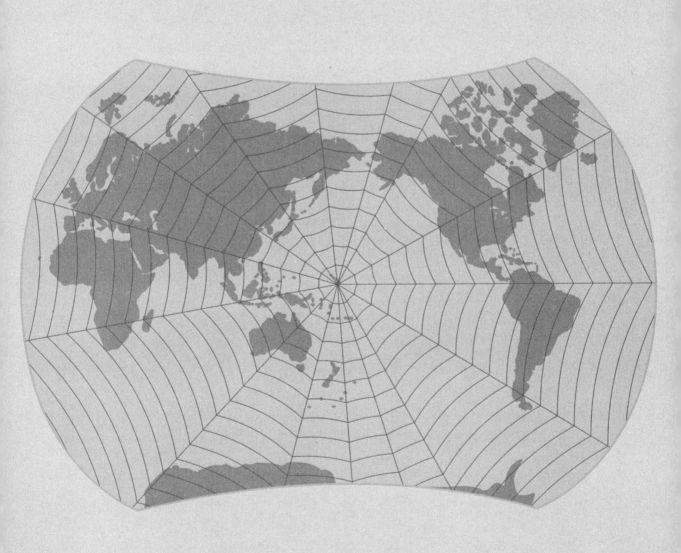

HTTP 1.1 Error Codes

This appendix lists the client and server error codes with default explanations, provided by Microsoft Internet Information Server; they are included in case you run into errors as you experiment with ASP.

Error Code	Short Text	Explanation
400	Bad Request	Due to malformed syntax, the request could not be understood by the server. The client should not repeat the request without modifications.
401.1	Unauthorized: Logon Failed	This error indicates that the credentials passed to the server do not match the credentials required to log on to the server. Please contact the Web server's administrator to verify that you have permission to access the requested resource.
401.2	Unauthorized: Logon Failed due to server configuration	This error indicates that the credentials passed to the server do not match the credentials required to log on to the server. This is usually caused by not sending the proper WWW-Authenticate header field. Please contact the Web server's administrator to verify that you have permission to access to requested resource.
401.3	Unauthorized: Unauthorized due to ACL on resource	This error indicates that the credentials passed by the client do not have access to the particular resource on the server. This resource could be either the page or file listed in the address line of the client, or it could be another file on the server that is needed to process the file listed on the address line of the client. Please make a note of the entire address you were trying to access and then contact the Web server's administrator to verify that you have permission to access the requested resource.

Table Continued on Following Page

Error Code	Short Text	Explanation
401.4	Unauthorized: Authorization failed by filter	This error indicates that the Web server has a filter program installed to verify users connecting to the server. The authentication used to connect to the server was denied access by this filter program. Please make a note of the entire address you were trying to access and then contact the Web server's administrator to verify that you have permission to access the requested resource.
401.5	Unauthorized: Authorization failed by ISAPI/CGI app	This error indicates that the address on the Web server you attempted to use has an ISAPI or CGI program installed that verifies user credentials before proceeding. The authentication used to connect to the server was denied access by this program. Please make a note of the entire address you were trying to access and then contact the Web server's administrator to verify that you have permission to access the requested resource.
403.1	Forbidden: Execute Access Forbidden	This error can be caused if you try to execute a CGI, ISAPI, or other executable program from a directory that does not allow programs to be executed. Please contact the Web server's administrator if the problem persists.
403.2	Forbidden: Read Access Forbidden	This error can be caused if there is no default page available and directory browsing has not been enabled for the directory, or if you are trying to display an HTML page that resides in a directory marked for Execute or Script permissions only. Please contact the Web server's administrator if the problem persists.
403.3	Forbidden: Write Access Forbidden	This error can be caused if you attempt to upload to, or modify a file in, a directory that does not allow Write access. Please contact the Web server's administrator if the problem persists.
403.4	Forbidden: SSL required	This error indicates that the page you are trying to access is secured with Secure Sockets Layer (SSL). In order to view it, you need to enable SSL by typing "https://" at the beginning of the address you are attempting to reach. Please contact the Web server's administrator if the problem persists.
403.5	Forbidden: SSL 128 required	This error message indicates that the resource you are trying to access is secured with a 128-bit version of Secure Sockets Layer (SSL). In order to view this resource, you need a browser that supports this level of SSL. Please confirm that your browser supports 128-bit SSL security. If it does, then contact the Web server's administrator and report the problem.

Error Code	Short Text	Explanation
403.6	Forbidden: IP address rejected	This error is caused when the server has a list of IP addresses that are not allowed to access the site, and the IP address you are using is in this list. Please contact the Web server's administrator if the problem persists.
403.7	Forbidden: Client certificate required	This error occurs when the resource you are attempting to access requires your browser to have a client Secure Sockets Layer (SSL) certificate that the server recognizes. This is used for authenticating you as a valid user of the resource. Please contact the Web server's administrator to obtain a valid client certificate.
403.8	Forbidden: Site access denied	This error can be caused if the Web server is not servicing requests, or if you do not have permission to connect to the site. Please contact the Web server's administrator.
403.9	Access Forbidden: Too many users are connected	This error can be caused if the Web server is busy and cannot process your request due to heavy traffic. Please try to connect again later. Please contact the Web server's administrator if the problem persists.
403.10	Access Forbidden: Invalid Configuration	There is a configuration problem on the Web server at this time. Please contact the Web server's administrator if the problem persists.
403.11	Access Forbidden: Password Change	This error can be caused if the user has entered the wrong password during authentication. Please refresh the page and try again. Please contact the Web server's administrator if the problem persists.
403.12	Access Forbidden: Mapper Denied Access	Your client certificate map has been denied access to this Web site. Please contact the site administrator to establish client certificate permissions. You can also change your client certificate and retry, if appropriate.
404	Not Found	The Web server cannot find the file or script you asked for. Please check the URL to ensure that the path is correct. Please contact the server's administrator if this problem persists.
405	Method Not Allowed	The method specified in the Request Line is not allowed for the resource identified by the request. Please ensure that you have the proper MIME type set up for the resource you are requesting. Please contact the server's administrator if this problem persists.

Table Continued on Following Page

Error Code	Short Text	Explanation
406	Not Acceptable	The resource identified by the request can only generate response entities that have content characteristics that are "not acceptable" according to the Accept headers sent in the request. Please contact the server's administrator if this problem persists.
407	Proxy Authentication Required	You must authenticate with a proxy server before this request can be serviced. Please log on to your proxy server, and then try again. Please contact the Web server's administrator if this problem persists.
412	Precondition Failed	The precondition given in one or more of the Request-header fields evaluated to FALSE when it was tested on the server. The client placed preconditions on the current resource meta-information (header field data) to prevent the requested method from being applied to a resource other than the one intended. Please contact the Web server's administrator if the problem persists.
414	Request-URI Too Long	The server is refusing to service the request because the Request-URI is too long. This rare condition is likely to occur only in the following situations: A client has improperly converted a POST request to a GET request with long query information. A client has encountered a redirection problem (for example, a redirected URL prefix that points to a suffix of itself). The server is under attack by a client attempting to exploit security holes present in some servers using fixed-length buffers for reading or manipulating the Request-URI. Please contact the Web server's administrator if this problem persists.
500	Internal Server Error	The Web server is incapable of performing the request. Please try your request again later. Please contact the Web server's administrator if this problem persists.

Error Code	Short Text	Explanation
501	Not Implemented	The Web server does not support the functionality required to fulfill the request. Please check your URL for errors, and contact the Web server's administrator if the problem persists.
502	Bad Gateway	The server, while acting as a gateway or proxy, received an invalid response from the upstream server it accessed in attempting to fulfill the request. Please contact the Web server's administrator if the problem persists.

Please note that Server error message files are placed in WinNT\Help\iisHelp\Common.

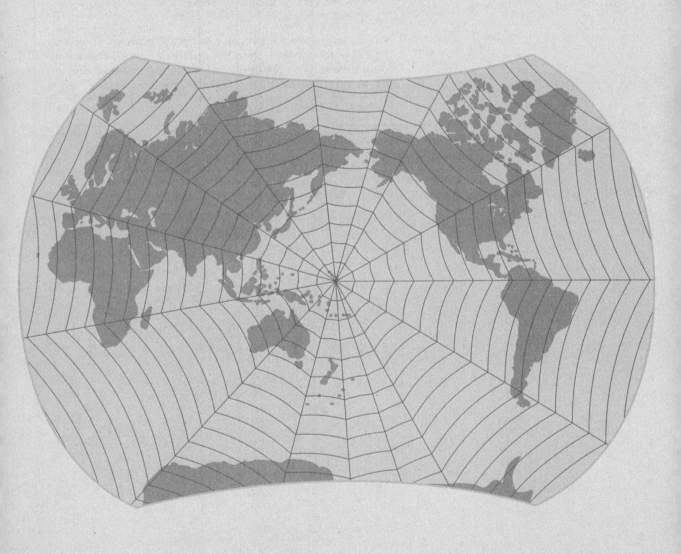

Glossary of Terms and Acronyms

As you're no doubt aware, the number of acronyms in current use increases at an astonishing rate. This is by no means a complete glossary; simply an attempt to provide translations for the most widely used acronyms. A full and up-to-date glossary is available from the Wrox Web Developer site:

http://webdev.wrox.co.uk/reference/glossary/select.asp

A

ACID   **Data transaction properties**. For a transaction to be considered valid, it must be Atomic, Consistent, Isolated and Durable - hence the acronym.

ACL   **Access Control List**. Internal object used by Windows NT to store user permissions for an individual resource, such as a disk file or directory.

ADC   **Advanced Data Connector**. An Active Server Component usually referred to as the Data Access Component, which can provide the interface between a script and a data source.

ADO   **ActiveX Data Objects**. A Microsoft data access technology that is the preferred way to provide data access capabilities to any kind of data store, such as relational databases, message stores, etc. (through an OLEDB provider

ADS   **Active Directory Services**. A network-centric repository for all kinds of information about all the resources on the network and connected networks. New in Windows NT5.

ADSI   **Active Directory Service Interface**. The **API** for the Microsoft Active Directory Service. Allows programmers to read and manipulate the contents of the directory in code.

ANSI   **American National Standards Institute**. A standards body that provides definitions on computing topics such as programming languages and character sets.

API   **Application Programming Interface**. A series of functions exposed by an application or operating system that allow programmers to access and use the services it provides.

ARP   **Address Resolution Protocol**. A high-level network protocol running over **TCP/IP** that identifies network hardware addresses on a **LAN** given an **IP** address.

ASCII   **American Standard Code for Information Interchange**. A standard definition for character sets. Limited to 255 characters and slowly being superseded by Unicode, which uses 2 bytes per character and can store all types of foreign characters.

ASP	**Active Server Pages**. A Microsoft server-based scripting language that combines **HTML** and script code into a single file. Can be used create all kinds of dynamic pages.
ATM	**Asynchronous Transfer Mode**. A communication protocol designed to offer much higher data transmission speeds over existing networks than traditional methods such as Ethernet.

B

BDC	**Backup Domain Controller**. A Windows NT Server installation that holds a read-only backup copy of security and other information for a network domain. Can authenticate users, and be promoted to a **PDC** in case of failure of the primary machine.
BSC	**Backup Site Controller**. A server within a Microsoft Message Queue Server site. It stores a backup copy of the part of the **MSMQ** Information Store database that applies to the site in case the **PSC** should fail.

C

CA	**Certificate Authority**. A (usually) well known and trusted third party that issues certificates for encryption and verification use. Examples are Verisign and Thawte Consulting.
CDF	**Channel Definition Format**. A Microsoft specialized implementation of **XML**, used to define Channels in Internet Explorer 4+ and Windows 98.
CDO	**Collaboration Data Objects**. The object programming interface for Microsoft Exchange Server 5.5, which allows other applications to access the mail features of Exchange Server.
Certificate	**A form of identification for secure communication**. Certificates are used to pass public encryption keys between applications, and to verify the certificate holder. Used for secure communication with **HTTPS** and by **MSMQ**.
CGI	**Common Gateway Interface**. A standardized interface exposed by most Web servers. Allows script and executable programs to access the user requests and server responses in order to create dynamic pages.
CIFS	**Common Internet File System**. An open and cross-platform mechanism for clients to request files over a network. Based on the **SMB** protocol widely used by PCs and workstations on a variety of operating systems.
COM	**Component Object Model**. The Microsoft open standard that defines how components communicate. Extended as COM+, which adds extra features that make building component interfaces easier.
CORBA	**Common Object Request Broker Architecture**. A standard for integration and communication between components. Generally UNIX-based, and supported by Sun, Netscape, IBM, etc.
Corpus	**Index Server document collection**. The set of documents, files and other resources that are indexed by Microsoft Index Server or other indexing service.
CRL	**Certificate Revocation List**. A list of certificates that are no longer valid. Maintained and published by the **CA** that originally issued these certificates.
Crossware	**Netscape development environment**. A design methodology that defines how applications can be built so that they can run both over an internal network, and out to external partners over the Internet.

CryptoAPI	**Cryptographic Application Programming Interface**. A Microsoft **API** that provides services for authentication, encoding and encryption in Windows 32-bit applications.
CSP	**Cryptographic Service Provider**. A code module that integrates with the **CryptoAPI** to perform the authentication, encoding and encryption. Often created by **ISVs**.
CSS1	**Cascading Style Sheets (Level 1)**. The W3C-approved way to specify text formatting and layout in a Web page. Currently being expanded to **CSS2**. Several style sheets can be linked to a Web page, or the style information embedded within the page.

D

Daemon	**Background network program**. A software application or service that runs continually within a network node to handle any of a range of tasks such as directing mail or routing data.
DAO	**Data Access Objects**. A Microsoft data access technology with a complex multi-level object model, introduced for use with MS Access and Office. Now superseded by **ADO**.
DBMS	**Database Management System**. A program or environment that stores, manages and retrieves data, for example SQL Server, Oracle, DB2, etc. Usually a relational database system.
DCOM	**Distributed Component Object Model**. The implementation of **COM** that allows components to communicate over a network connection, rather than being limited to the same machine.
DES	**Data Encryption Standard**. A standard that protects passwords from being read and then used again on the same a network to obtain unofficial access.
DHCP	**Dynamic Host Configuration Protocol**. A protocol under which a client can contact a server to obtain a valid IP network address for its own use, rather than using one hard-wired into the client. Useful on large networks to prevent **IP** address conflicts.
DHTML	**Dynamic HTML**. The overall moniker for the ability of the latest generation of browsers to change the contents of a Web page using script code, while it is loaded.
DLL	**Dynamic Link Library**. A software component or library of functions stored as a disk file in a special format. Used by other applications that require these functions.
DNA	**Distributed interNet Applications** Architecture. A methodology for three-tier application design using components that communicate via **COM** and **DCOM**. Also a broad marketing term for the combination of the different services offered by Windows NT.
DNS	**Domain Name System**. Also refers to a Domain Name Server. Translates a text **URL** (such as `http://webdev.wrox.co.uk`) into the equivalent **IP** address.
DOM	**Document Object Model**. A standard definition of the structure and content of a Web page when displayed in a browser or other user agent. Used in scripting to manipulate the contents of the document.
DRP	**Distribution and Replication Protocol**. An index-based protocol proposal designed to improve the efficiency and reliability of data distribution over HTTP. Based on XML and RDF, and provides content identifiers, an index format, and new HTTP header fields.

DSN	**Data Source Name**. A specification of all the information required to connect to and access a data store. Used with **ODBC**, and can also be stored a file on disk (File **DSN**) or with system-wide access (System **DSN**).
DSO	**Data Source Object**. A control embedded into a Web page that provides an OLE-DB interface allowing ADO to connect to a remote data store. Used in databinding.
DTC	**Distributed Transaction Coordinator**. A software component that manages changes to a data source under control of a transaction manager. Allows updates to be rolled back if the transaction needs to be aborted, leaving the data store unchanged.
DTD	**Document Type Definition**. A set of rules that define how the rules of **SGML** are applied to a particular markup language.

E

ECMA	**European Computer Manufacturers Association**. A standards body that manages and ratifies proposals for computer technologies. Issues the open standard for the scripting language ECMAScript, which is based on JavaScript and JScript.

F

FAT	**File Allocation Table**. The original MS-DOS format for disks. Has no built-in security, and imposes restrictions on the way files are physically stored. The limited number of allocation units it supports means that it is inefficient on large disks.
FAT32	**32-bit File Allocation Table**. An upgraded version of **FAT** introduced with the Windows 95 OSR2 update. Can handle more allocation units on large disks, with corresponding reduction in cluster size, to provide more efficient file storage.
Firewall	**Network security component**. A software component that acts as a filter restricting specific types of network packets from passing from one network to another. Often used between a **LAN** and the Internet.
FTP	**File Transfer Protocol**. A standard Internet protocol for transferring files between machines. Generally faster and more efficient than email or **HTTP**.

G

GIF	**Graphics Interchange Format**. A format for graphics and images that compresses the content to provide efficient transmission over a network. Developed by CompuServe and now in common use on the Internet.
GINA	**Password filter component**. A software component that can be added to Windows NT to perform extra checking on user passwords as they are changed, ensuring they are strong enough to meet security requirements.
Gopher	**Internet search and retrieve protocol**. A protocol designed to allow clients to search for, retrieve and display documents over the Internet. Generally superseded by the Web, and no longer in common use.
GUID	**Globally Unique Identifier**. A 128-bit number that is generated automatically and used to refer to a resource, component, directory entry or any other type of object. Guaranteed to be unique.

H

HTML   **Hypertext Markup Language**. The language of the Web. A way of inserting tags (elements and attributes) into a text page to add formatting, rich content, and other information.

HTTP   **Hypertext Transfer Protocol**. A protocol running over **IP** and designed for the World Wide Web. Provides packaging of information that can contain instruction headers and other data about the content.

HTTPS   **Hypertext Transfer Protocol Secure**. The secure version of **HTTP** using certificates that can uniquely identify the server and client, and encrypt all communication between them.

I

ICMP   **Internet Control Message Protocol**. An extension to **IP** that permits extra control, test and error messages to be incorporated into the packet stream.

IDC   **Internet Database Connector**. A Microsoft server-based scripting language for linking **ODBC** data sources to a Web server, so as to create dynamic pages based on a database.

IE   **Internet Explorer**. Microsoft's Web browser. What more can you say?

IETF   **Internet Engineering Task Force**. A large multi-vendor international group of engineers, operators, vendors and researchers that defines, proposes and ratifies technical standards for the Internet.

IIOP   **Internet Inter-Orb Protocol**. A standard, like **CORBA**, for communication between Java-based components such as JavaBeans. Allows components to communicate over the Internet in a Crossware application.

IIS   **Internet Information Server**. The Web server software included with Microsoft Windows NT. Supports applications that use **CGI**, **ASP**, **IDC** and **ISAPI**; and interfaces with Windows NT and other services running on the server machine.

IP   **Internet Protocol**. The low-level part of the **TCP/IP** protocol. **IP** assembles the **TCP** packets, adds address information, and dispatches them over the network.

IPX/SPX   **Novell NetWare network protocol**. A network protocol developed by Novell to allow servers to provide an easily navigable network structure, and to share network resources.

ISAPI   **Internet Server Application Programming Interface**. A broadly standardized interface that allows server-side programs to create dynamic Web pages, in a similar way to **CGI**.

ISDN   **Integrated Services Digital Network**. A technology for combining voice and data in separate streams over a standard PSTN phone line to provide higher speeds, increased capacity and multiple channels.

ISO   **International Standards Organization**. A world-wide group of standards bodies that create international standards, including information technology related areas.

ISP   **Internet Service Provider**. An agency or company that provides a connection to the Internet, usually as a leased line or a dial-up link.

ISV   **Independent Software Vendor**. Term used to describe companies that produce software or components for use with other companies operating systems or technologies.

ITU   **International Telecommunications Union**. An international body that defines the standards for modems and low-level transmission of data, typically over public networks like the PSTN.

J

JavaBean	**Java software component**. A software component, built in Java, that implements a control or provides a series of functions for use within another application.
JDBC	**Java Database Connectivity**. A software interface layer that allows Java applications and components to access data stores via **ODBC**.
JDK	**Java Development Kit**. A set of documentation, samples and tools that provide programmers with the information required when creating Java applications and components.
JIT	**Just In Time**. An acronym applied to several technologies to indicate that a process, such as compilation of byte code, is carried out just before it is required by an application.
JPEG	**Joint Photographic Experts Group**. A body that designed and promotes the **JPEG** (**JPG**) graphics format, which combines high color depth with small file size for photographic still images by using a lossy compression scheme.
JSP	**Java Server Pages** Server-side programming language combining HTML and Java code to generate custom servlets for dynamic web pages.

K

Kerberos	**Network security protocol**. A security technology that has been under development in academic institutes for some time. Windows NT 5 uses this, replacing the existing **LAN** Manager based security methods in NT 3.5 and NT 4.

L

LAN	**Local Area Network**. A series of machines in close proximity, usually in the same building, connected together. Uses any of a range of common network protocols, often referred to as Ethernet.
LDAP	**Lightweight Directory Access Protocol**. An Internet standard used to access directory information on remote servers. Uses less resources than the traditional **X.500** protocol.
Linux	**Operating system**. Open-source UNIX-clone operating system first built by Linus Torvalds and developed by a distributed community over the Internet. In large part responsible for giving free software a good name in enterprise due to its reliability and performance.
Locale	**Language and locality information**. A text string such as "en-us" that accurately identifies a language and locality to allow programs to use language-specific formatting and processes. Can also be identified by a number called the `LocaleID`.

M

MAPI	**Mail (or Message) Application Programming Interface**. The Microsoft standard application programming interface for email software. Allows programs to read, create, send and manipulate stored messages.
MDA	**Message Digest Algorithm**. A software algorithm that creates a digest for a message or other stream of data. The digest is unique, and the original data cannot be recreated from it. Generally specified as MD2, MD4, MD5, etc.

MDAC	**Microsoft Data Access Components**. A series of component objects that provide data access services such as **ADO** to Windows applications.
MIME	**Multipurpose (or Multimedia) Internet Mail Extension**. Defines the content type of a document, file or message attachment, for example "image/mpeg" or "text/plain".
MPEG	**Motion Pictures Expert Group**. A body that designed and promotes the **MPEG** (**MPG**) moving graphics format, which combines high color depth with small file size for photographic moving images by using a lossy compression scheme.
MQIS	**Message Queue Information Store**. The central repository of information about an **MSMQ** enterprise, stored on the **PEC** and distributed to each site via the **PSC**s and **BSC**s.
MSMQ	**Microsoft Message Queue Server**. A Windows NT service that provides robust and secure transmission of messages between servers, which can be on different connected networks.
MTS	**Microsoft Transaction Server**. A Windows NT service that acts as both an object broker for components and as a distributed transaction manager. The basis for most **DNA** applications that require data access.

N

Namespace	**A name resolution area**. The bounded area within which a named object can be resolved. Examples are a subtree in a directory service, or a class within a component.
NDS	**Novell Directory Service**. Novell's implementation of a network-centric directory service. Has been available for some time, and is in common use on large NetWare networks. Supported by Windows NT.
NetBEUI	**Networking protocol**. The native protocol that forms the basis for Microsoft Networking in Windows environments.
NetBIOS	**Networking protocol**. A widely accepted and implemented standard for networking in a **LAN** environment.
NIC	**Network Interface Card**. The hardware providing the connection between a computer or peripheral and the network. Usually a plug-in card with sockets for a range of cable connector types.
NNTP	**Network News Transfer Protocol**. A protocol that transports news messages to special servers and client software over the Internet. Provides cross referencing, expiration, and search and retrieval facilities.
NOS	**Network Operating System**. A generic term for the protocol and software that provides communication services over a network. Examples are **NetBIOS**, **TCP/IP**, etc.
NTFS	**NT File System**. The Windows NT native disk format. Provides an efficient data storage format, and allows a range of security settings to be applied to individual files and directories.
NTLM	**NT LAN Manager authentication**. The protocol normally referred to as Challenge/Response that Windows NT uses to pass authentication information between the client and server when logging on.

O

OCX	**OLE Control Extension**. A software component stored as a disk file in a special format for use by other applications. Similar to a **DLL**, but generally offers a single function to create an object or control.
ODBC	**Open Database Connectivity**. An open standard originally developed by Microsoft to allow transparent data access to all kinds of data stores such as relational databases. Drivers are manufactured by third parties to suit their own data store.
ODSI	**Open Directory Services Interface**. A set of industry-standard functions that can be implemented by a directory service, such as **LDAP** and **ADS**, to allow other applications to access the directory content.
OLAP	**On-line Analytical Processing**. A data store (or data warehouse) holding data in a multi-dimensional fashion. Often used for decision support and other commercial enquiry systems.
OLE	**Object Linking and Embedding**. The fore-runner to ActiveX. Uses COM to let components communicate, and allows applications to use the services of other applications as though they were just components.
OLE DB	**Object Linking and Embedding Database**. The new standard data access programming interface from Microsoft that is designed to replace **ODBC**, and provide wider coverage of different types of data stores.
OLTP	**On-line Transaction Processing**. The technique of performing order or information processing in real time, rather than storing the transactions for execution as a batch at a later time.
OMG	**Object Management Group**. An alliance of vendors formed to define and promote the **CORBA** object specification. Prominent members are Sun, Netscape and IBM.
ONE	**Open Network Environment**. A Netscape development environment based on open standards that makes it easy to build, deploy and run applications over the Internet. See also **Crossware**.
Open Source	**Availability of software in source code form**. Movement and practice dedicated to providing software (whether free or paid for) in both binary and source code form, enabling end-users to adapt the software to suit their own needs.
OSF	**Open Software Federation**. A multi-vendor body that defines and promotes open standards for Unix-based operating systems and software.

P

Package	**Group of MTS components**. A set of related components installed into **MTS** that are defined and used together in an application. The package defines the security trust boundary for the component group.
PASSFILT	**Password filter component.** An interchangeable software component within Windows NT that performs checking on user passwords as they are entered, ensuring they are strong enough to meet security requirements.
PDA	**Personal Digital Assistant**. A small, usually hand-held device for personal portable data storage and management. Examples are the 3COM Palm Pilot and Psion Organizer. Often regarded as small electronic Filofaxes.
PDC	**Primary Domain Controller**. The Windows NT server installation that holds the central security and other information for the entire network domain.

PEC	**Primary Enterprise Controller**. The server that is at the root of Microsoft Message Queue Server enterprise. It stores the complete **MSMQ** Information Store database.
Perl	**Practical Extraction and Reporting Language**. A scripting language used with the first Web applications. Runs on the server and can create dynamic pages via the **CGI**.
PFX	**Personal Information Exchange**. A protocol that can safely and securely transfer the contents of a **PStore** from one location to another.
PGP	**Pretty Good Privacy**. An independently developed encryption application that uses public keys to allow secure transmission of messages.
PHP	**Personal Home Pages**. A server-side, cross-platform, HTML embedded scripting language with dedicated database abstraction layer. It is also opensource, therefore "You can give it to your friends, print it out and hang it on your wall, or eat it for lunch".
PING	**Packet Internet Grouper**. A diagnostic utility program that uses **ICMP** to request messages from a remote server to check that it is available and can respond.
PKCS	**Public Key Cryptography Standard**. A generic term used to describe the various available types of public key encryption standards such as **DES**, **RSA**, etc.
PNG	**Portable Network Graphics**. A format for graphics and images that compresses the content to provide efficient transmission over a network. Developed by W3C, but not yet in commmon use.
POP3	**Post Office Protocol**. An Internet protocol designed to transmit email messages and attachments between mail servers. Offers extra features over the earlier **SMTP** protocol.
PPP	**Point-to-Point Protocol**. An industry-wide standard protocol that defines how packets are exchanged over the Internet, particularly via a modem.
PPTP	**Point-To-Point Tunneling Protocol**. A protocol that allows native network services such as **NetBEUI** and **IPX** to be used to create a secure and reliable connection over the Internet.
Proxy	**Software connection component**. A software program or service (as in proxy server) that acts as an intermediate gateway and connects two processes or users. In the case of a proxy server, it can also filter the network packets.
PSC	**Primary Site Controller**. A server that is at the root of Microsoft Message Queue Server site. It stores a copy of the part of an **MSMQ** Information Store database that applies to the site.
PStore	**Protected Information Store**. A Windows NT technology that provide a secure store for personal and security information about the network users. Can contain certificates, credit card details, personal information, etc.

R

RAS	**Remote Access Service**. A Windows technology that allows dial-up users to connect to a network (over a phone line or the Internet, for example) and access the resources on the network as though they were a local user.
RDF	**Resource Description Framework**. An XML-based specification being developed under the authority of the W3C, which governs the interoperability of applications in terms of metadata property sets. Formerly called the Meta Content Framework
RDO	**Remote Data Objects**. A Microsoft remote data access technology with a complex multi-level object model, introduced for use with programming languages like Visual Basic. Now superseded by **ADO**.

RDS	**Remote Data Service**. A Microsoft technology that provides a persistent and automatic method for caching data from a server-side data source on the client, for use in a Web page or other application.
RIP	**Routing Information Protocol**. A network routing protocol for IP that allows routers to pass network and routing information between themselves as the topology of a network changes
Role	**Transaction Server security context**. Roles are used to define the user accounts that can execute a component running under **MTS**. They simplify security management in **DNA**-based applications.
RPC	**Remote Procedure Call**. A standard defined by the Open Software Foundation that allows one process to execute methods defined by another process, either on the same machine or across a network.
RSA	**Public key cryptography method**. A standard type of encryption technique designed by Rivest, Shamir and Adleman for securing data passing over a network or between components.
RSVP	**Resource Reservation Protocol**. A protocol that is used to allocate bandwidth for particular applications over a network

S

S/MIME	**Secure Multipurpose Internet Mail Extension**. A version of **MIME** that allows the contents of the message and attachments to be digitally signed and encrypted, using standard public key ciphers, hash functions and certificates.
SChannel	**Secure Channel**. A security service provider module that sits on top of the Microsoft **CryptoAPI**, and implements the public key encryption between a client and the server.
SDK	**Software Development Kit**. A set of documentation, samples and tools that provide programmers with the information required to work with a technology - for example the **IE4 SDK** for Internet Explorer 4.
Servlet	**Java server-based executable**. An executable program written in Java that runs on a Web server in response to a request. Can be a simple replacement for a Perl script, or as complex as a business object or other component.
SET	**Secure Electronic Transaction**. A protocol for implementing secure electronic transactions over the Internet. Particularly aimed at financial institutions for handling credit card and related information.
SGML	**Standard Generalized Markup Language**. A root language for the formal definition of other markup languages, and not directly used for programming. Designed to provide portability and flexibility between markup languages based on it.
SHA	**Secure Hash Algorithm**. A software algorithm that creates a digest for a message or other stream of data. The digest is unique, and the original data cannot be recreated from it.
SID	**Security Identifier**. A non-volatile hidden **GUID** that identifies a user account in Windows NT. When accounts are deleted and recreated, a new **SID** is applied to them. The **SID** is passed between applications running under NT, instead of the username.
SMB	**Server Message Block**. A protocol used in Windows Networking to provide network-wide access to files and printers.
SMTP	**Simple Mail Transfer Protocol**. The first email transfer protocol for the Internet. Still used to transmit simple mail messages, but slowly being replaced by **POP3**.

SNA	**System Network Architecture**. A standard communication framework developed by IBM to allow communication between different models of computer, including minicomputers and mainframes.
SNMP	**Simple Network Management Protocol**. A standard for remote management of devices such as routers and other services over a **TCP/IP** network. Also provides monitoring services for a network.
SQL	**Structured Query Language**. A standard language for accessing data in relational databases. **ANSI** provide a base definition but many vendors have added extra proprietary features and extensions.
SSI	**Server-side Include**. An instruction within a Web page or script that causes the Web server to execute a program, or insert a file or other information into the **HTML** stream sent to the client.
SSL	**Secure Sockets Layer**. A technology originally developed by Netscape to provide client and server verification, and secure communication between a Web browser and server. Uses public key and secret key encryption.
SSP	**Security Support Provider**. A software library that manages a set of security functions. Multiple **SSP**s can be installed, each from a different vendor if required. See **SSPI**.
SSPI	**Security Service Provider Interface**. A standard programming interface specification that allows applications to query any SSP and use its services. Example **SSP**s are **Kerberos**, **NTLM**, and **SSL**.
Stub	**Software connection component**. A software component within an application that links to a corresponding proxy elsewhere, and handles the communication of data between them. May be running in a separate environment from the proxy, or just on a different execution thread.

T

TAPI	**Telecommunications Application Programming Interface**. A set of standard programming functions that can be implemented by applications that interface with telecommunications equipment, i.e. telephones, exchanges, fax machines, voice mail, etc.
TCO	**Total Cost of Ownership**. The cost, generally far exceeding original purchase price, of a computer system. Includes such things as training, maintenance, support, consumables, etc.
TCP	**Transport Control Protocol**. The high-level part of the **TCP/IP** protocol. **TCP** creates the data packets and passes them to **IP** for transmission over the network. It is also responsible for marshalling and sorting received packets, and basic packet error detection.
TCP/IP	**Transport Control Protocol/Internet Protocol**. The base protocol of the Internet, also used on internal networks and Intranets. Passes data in routable packets between servers, and supports high-level protocols like **HTTP**, **FTP**, etc.
TDC	**Tabular Data Control**. An ActiveX control, part of the **MDAC** Universal Data Access components package, that provides client-side access and caching over **HTTP** for data stored in text format.
TLA	**Three Letter Acronym**. A recursive definition designed to make fun of the way the industry tends to name its products and services.
TRID	**OLE Transaction Identifier**. A unique identifier (**GUID**) for a transaction process that is executing against an **OLE** Transactions resource manager.

TSAPI   **Telephony Services Application Programming Interface**. A standard developed by Novell for Netware-based applications that interface with telephones and associated equipment.

TSQL   **Transact SQL**. A set of extensions to **SQL** implemented in MS SQL Server, which allow (amongst other things) more complex queries to be created and compiled as stored procedures within the database.

U

UDA   **Universal Data Access**. Microsoft term describing a concept of using one data access technology with all enterprise data sources. Based on **ADO** and **OLE DB**. See also **MDAC**.

UHTTP   **Unidirectional Hypertext Transfer protocol**. A protocol designed to allow the multicasting of IP packets over the Internet or other network, in order to provide a combination of Internet content and ordinary broadcast television.

UML   **Unified Modeling Language**. A specification from the Object Management Group aimed at providing a common language for specifying, visualizing, constructing, and documenting distributed objects and business models for application developers.

UNC   **Uniform Naming Convention.** A combination of server name and resource path and name which identifies a resource on a local or wide-area network. Common **UNC**s start with the double-backslash, such as

`\\sunspot\C\documents\myfile.doc`.

URL   **Universal Resource Locator**. A combination of a protocol, host name, (optional) port, path and resource name. Uniquely identifies a resource on the Internet. For example *http://webdev.wrox.co.uk/reference/glossary/select.asp*

V

VB   **Visual Basic**. Microsoft's entry-level programming language and environment for Windows programming, including building components and specialist applications.

VBA   **Visual Basic for Applications**. Microsoft's version of Visual Basic that is designed to be used as a replacement and extension of macros in applications, rather than as a stand-alone programming language.

VJS   **Visual JavaScript**. A Netscape tool for rapid crossware development, providing an array of components and services together with an **HTML** page designer.

VPN   **Virtual Private Network**. The use of special encryption and protocol management software at each end of a network connection that allows a private virtual connection to exist. Useful on unsecured networks such as the Internet.

VRML   **Virtual Reality Modelling Language**. A strandardized programming language that allows moving 3D-style effects to be created within **HTML** applications.

W

W3C   **World Wide Web Consortium**. The main body responsible for managing and ratifying standards for the Internet, especially the World Wide Web (WWW).

WAM   **Web Application Manager**. A sub-system component of **IIS** that is used to control applications that run in a separate area of memory (i.e. out of process) from the Web server.

WAN   **Wide Area Network**. A series of machines or networks that are outside the limits of normal network cable length limits. Usually connection is via phone lines or fibre optic cables, radio or satellite links, or the Internet.

WAP   **Wireless Access Protocol**. An industry-wide protocol for use over wireless communication networks. Supported by most major mobile equipment manufacturers and many software companies including Microsoft.

WIDL   **Web Interface Definition Language**. A proposal for a set HTML extentions designed to allow interactions with Web servers to be defined as functional interfaces that can be accessed by remote systems over standard Web protocols, using Java, C/C++, COBOL, and Visual Basic.

WINS   **Windows Internet Name Service**. A protocol and corresponding service that maps textual addresses to the equivalent **IP** address in Windows-based networks. See also **DNS**.

WinSock   **Windows Sockets**. The software component that forms the connection to an **IP**-based network, and handles the transfer of data from the machine onto and off the network at the lowest level.

WML   **Wireless Markup Language**. An industry-wide language for applications using wireless communication networks. Based on XML, and intended for devices with small displays, limited user input facilities, narrow-band network connections, and limited memory or computational resources.

WOSA   **Windows Open System Architecture**. A range of **API**s that allow programmers to access various Windows technologies in a uniform and standard way. Includes specifications for **ODBC**, **MAPI**, and **TAPI**.

WSH   **Windows Scripting Host**. A server-based script interpreter that allows automation of common administration tasks using scripting languages such as VBScript and JScript

X

X.500   **Directory access protocol**. The high-level specification and interface definition for directory access. Generally used in commercial mainframe environments.

X.509   **Certificate format standard.** The principal standard format definition for certificates that are used to provide encryption and authentication.

XA   **X/Open transaction interface**. The X/Open organization defined standard for communication between transaction managers and resource managers in a two-phase commit distributed transaction system.

XATM   **XA Transaction Manager**. A component included in **MTS** that allows transactions against data stores which use the **XA** interface to be integrated into **MTS** transactions.

XID   **XA Transaction Identifier**. A unique identifier for a transaction process that is executing against an **XA** resource manager.

XLL/Xlink **Extensible Linking Language**. A set of constructs for use in XML documents to describe links between it and other resources. Uses XML syntax to create structures that can describe both simple unidirectional hyperlinks and more sophisticated multi-ended and typed links.

XMI **XML Metadata Interchange Format**. A project designed to unifying XML and related W3C specifications with several object/component modeling standards to assist in defining, validating, and sharing document formats over the Web

XML **Extensible Markup Language**. A new markup language based on **SGML**, and designed to remove the limitation imposed by **HTML**. Allows a page to contain a definition and execution plan for the elements, and well as their content.

XSL **Extensible Stylesheet Language**. A specialist development of **XML** designed to provide flexible ways of adding style, display and layout information to a document.

Z

ZAW **Zero Administration for Windows**. A Microsoft initiative incorporated into NT5 which provides ways to reduce the Total Cost of Ownership in networked environments by providing automatic software installation and fixes, and other features.

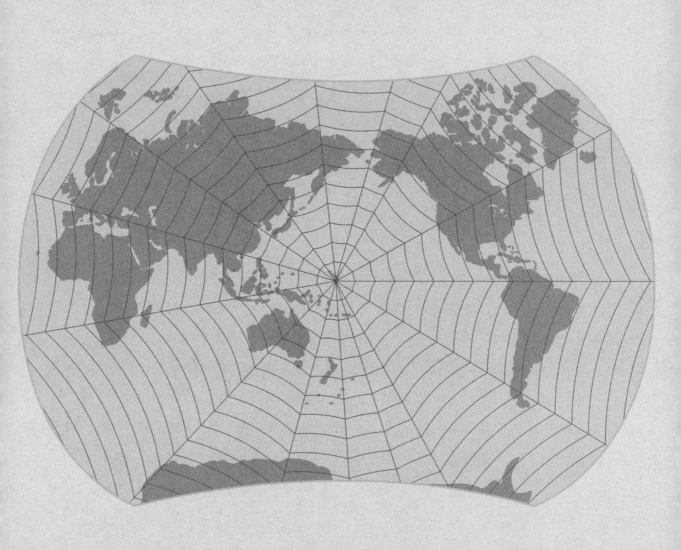

Creating an Access 2000 Project

Although SQL Server 7.0 is a great database, in it's MSDE form you don't get any good administration or query tools. This can seriously hinder development time, and it especially makes it hard to manipulate the database. Luckily, Access 2000 allows you to create an Access project that links into an MSDE (or SQL Server) database.

This works by having a normal Access database, with Forms, Tables, and so on, where the tables are actually links to the MSDE data. The data doesn't exist inside Access, so if you modify it, you're actually modifying the MSDE data. The great thing about this is that you get all of the Access table editing facilities.

Here's what you need to do to get this working:

1. Start Access 2000. From the main dialog select the second option, titled **Access database wizards, pages, and projects**, and press the **OK** button.

2. In the next dialog, make sure you have the **General** tab selected, click on the **Project (Existing Database)** option, and then click the **OK** button:

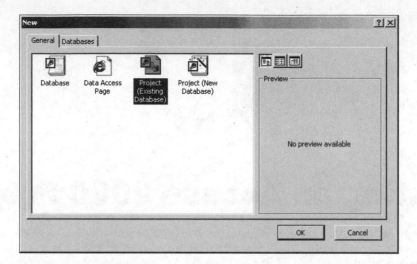

3. The next dialog is the **File New Database** dialog, where you enter the name and location of the Access part of the database. This is stored as a file with a `.adp` extension.

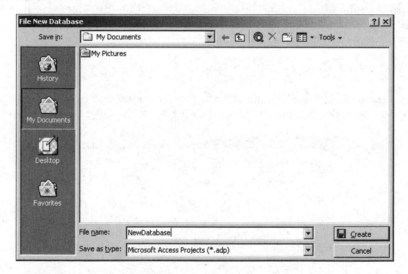

Next you're shown the **Data Link Properties** dialog, allowing you to select the source of the data.

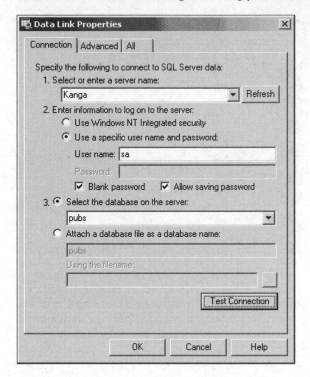

The **server name** (under section 1) should be the name of the machine where the MSDE or SQL Server is located. This will probably be the name of your local machine.

If you're using Integrated Security with your SQL Server, then you can select the appropriate option under section 2. For a local machine you can use the user name **sa**, with a blank password.

Finally, for section 3 you can select either the name of a database on the server, or you can attach a SQL data file (this is the MDF file, available from the Wrox Web site). Once you've entered the details you can press the **OK** button

4. Access will now link all of the tables and queries from the database into the ADP file.

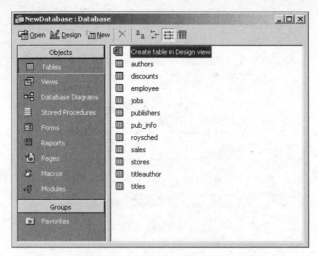

At this stage you have a fully functional Access database, with data coming from the MSDE or SQL Server. The only thing that's different is that instead of having a Queries Object, you have Views, Database Diagrams and Stored Procedures. This should make it clear that you're really not working with an Access database, but with SQL Server, since these are SQL Server items.

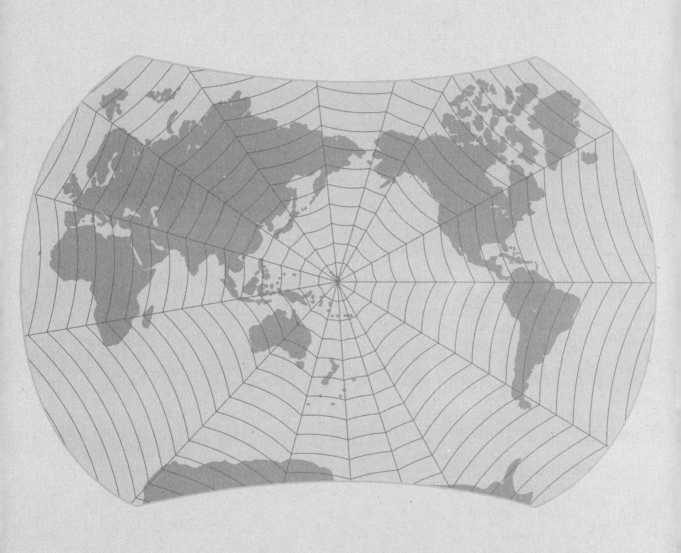

P2P.WROX.COM

Join the Pro ASP 3 mailing lists for author and peer support. Our unique system provides **programmer to programmer™** support on mailing lists, forums and newsgroups all in addition to our one-to-one email system. Be confident that your query is not just being examined by a support professional, but by the many Wrox authors and other industry experts present on our mailing lists.

We've extended our commitment to support beyond just while you read the book, to when you start developing applications as well. We'll be there on this crucial second step of your learning. You have the choice of how to receive this information, you can either enroll onto one of several mailing lists, or you can just browse the online forums and newsgroups for an answer. Go to p2p.wrox.com. You'll find three different lists, each tailored to a specific support issue:

- ❑ **BegASP_Errata**
  You find something wrong with the book, or you just think something has been badly or misleading explained then leave your message here. You'll still receive our customary quick reply, but you'll also have the advantage that every author will be able to see your problem at once and help deal with it.

- ❑ **Code Clinic**
  You've read the book, and you're sat at home or work developing your own application, it doesn't work in the way you think it should. Post your code here for advice and supports from our authors and from people in the same position as yourself.

- ❑ **How to?**
  Something you think the book should have talked about, something you'd just like to know more about, a completely baffling problem with no solution, then this is your forum. If you're developing an application at work then chances are there's someone out there who's already done the same as you, and has a solution to your problem here.

How To Enroll For Support

Just follow this four-step system:

1. Go to p2p.wrox.com

2. Click on the Beginning ASP 3.0 cover graphic

3. Click on the type of mailing list you wish to join

4. Fill in your email address and password (of at least 4 digits) and email it to us

Index

L

M

P

Q

R